W9-BYY-399

SHELTON STATE COMMUNITY
COLLEGE
JUNIOR COLLEGE DIVISION
LIBRARY
DISCARDED

W · W · NORTON & COMPANY · INC ·  NEW YORK

ECONOMICS

PRINCIPLES, PROBLEMS, DECISIONS

EDWIN MANSFIELD
WHARTON SCHOOL / UNIVERSITY OF PENNSYLVANIA

To Edward Deering Mansfield (1801-1880)
and his brother-in-law Charles Davies (1798-1876),
neither of whom should be held responsible
for the views expressed here.

First Edition

Library of Congress Cataloging in Publication Data

Mansfield, Edwin.
Economics: principles, problems, decisions.

1. Economics. I. Title.
HB171.5.M266   330   74-1216
ISBN 0-393-09314-X

Published simultaneously in Canada by George J. McLeod Limited, Toronto

Printed in the United States of America

1 2 3 4 5 6 7 8 9 0

Permission from the following sources to reprint photographs is hereby gratefully acknowledged:
Mansell Collection (pp. 17, 332); Time-LIFE Picture Agency (p. 25, photograph by Stephen Northrup; p. 363, photograph by Walter Sanders; p. 553, photograph by Hank Walker); The Department of the Treasury (p. 106); United Press International (p. 195); Board of Governors of the Federal Reserve System (p. 287); Ford Archives (p. 412); German Information Center (pp. 632, 699); Swiss Bank Corporation (p. 655).

CONTENTS

Preface XVII

Suggested Outlines XIX

PART ONE
INTRODUCTION TO ECONOMICS

1 • Economic Problems, Policies, and Decisions 1

Unemployment and Inflation 2 Government Regulation of Business 3 The Elimination of Poverty 4 Environmental Pollution 5 The Planned Economies 7 Rational Decision Making 7 The Energy Crisis 8 Economic Problems: Some Common Threads 8 The Role of Economics in Public Policy 9 The Role of Economics in Private Decision Making 11 Economics: A Social Science 12 *Summary* 13 *Concepts for Review* 13 *Questions for Discussion and Review* 14

2 • Economic Analysis: Models and Measurement 15

Adam Smith, Father of Modern Economics 16 *Adam Smith on the "Invisible Hand" and Specialization* 17 How Successful Are Economics and Economists? 18 Model Building and the Methodology of Economics 19 Economic Measurement 20 Simple Economic Models: A Case Study 22 The Use of Economic Models: Another Case Study 24 Values and Decisions 24 *Arthur Okun and George Shultz* 25 Methodological Hazards in Economics 26 *Summary* 27 *Concepts for Review* 28 *Questions for Discussion and Review* 28

PART TWO

THE PRIVATE SECTOR AND THE PUBLIC SECTOR: AN OVERVIEW

3 • The American Economy: Our Mixed Capitalist System **31**

The American Economy: Some Salient Facts 32 The Tasks of an Economic System 34 The Product Transformation Curve and the Determination of What Is Produced 36 The Product Transformation Curve and the Determination of How Goods Are Produced 38 The Product Transformation Curve, Income Distribution, and Growth 39 What Is Capitalism? 40 How Does Capitalism Perform the Four Basic Economic Tasks? 43 Our Mixed Capitalist System and the Role of Government 44 Capital, Specialization, and Money: Other Characteristics of the American Economy 45 *Summary* 46 *Concepts for Review* 47 *Questions for Discussion and Review* 47

4 • The Price System: Consumers, Firms, and Markets **48**

Consumers 49 Firms 49 Markets 50 The Demand Side of a Market 50 The Supply Side of a Market 52 The Equilibrium Price 55 Actual Price versus Equilibrium Price 56 Changes in the Demand and Supply Curves 57 The Price System and the Determination of What Is Produced 59 The Price System and the Determination of How Goods Are Produced 60 The Price System and the Determination of Who Gets What 61 The Price System and Economic Growth 61 The Price System in Action behind Enemy Lines 62 The Price System in Action on the Great White Way 64 Rationing, Coupons, and All That 65 The Circular Flows of Money and Products 65 *Summary* 66 *Concepts for Review* 67 *Questions for Discussion and Review* 68

5 • The Economic Role of the Government **69**

Limitations of the Price System 70 What Functions Should the Government Perform? 71 A Legal, Social, and Competitive Framework 72 Redistribution of Income 73 Economic Stabilization 74 Public Goods and Externalities 74 Government Production and "Creeping Socialism" 75 How Big Is the Government? 76 What the Federal, State, and Local Governments Spend Money On 78 Changes in Views of Government Responsibilities 79 What the Federal, State, and Local Governments Receive in Taxes 80 The Role of Government in American Agriculture: A Case Study 81 Causes of the Farm Problem 82 Government Aid to Agriculture 84 Price Supports and Surplus Controls 85 The 1973 Changes in the Farm Program 87 The Wheat Program: A Case Study 88 Evaluation of Government Farm Programs 89 *Summary* 90 *Concepts for Review* 91 *Questions for Discussion and Review* 91

6 • Government Expenditures, Taxation, and the Public Debt **92**

The Federal Budgetary Process 93 Benefit-Cost Analysis and Program Budgeting 93 Benefit-Cost Analysis: A Case Study 94 Government Expenditures and the Problem of Social Balance 95 Military Spending and the Military-Industrial Complex 97 The Office of Coal Research: Another Case Study 98 The Federal Tax Legislative Process 99 Principles of Taxation 100 The Personal and Corporate Income Taxes 100 The Property Tax and the Sales Tax 102 Tax Reform 103 State and Local Finance and Revenue Sharing 104 The National Debt: Size and Growth 105 *The Department of the Treasury and the National Debt* 106 Burdens and Advantages of the National Debt 108 *Summary* 108 *Concepts for Review* 109 *Questions for Discussion and Review* 110

7 • The Business Firm: Organization, Motivation, and Technology **111**

General Motors: A Case Study 112 Characteristics of American Firms: Some Salient Facts 113 Proprietorships 114 Partnerships 115 Corporations 115 Corporate Securities 116 The Stock Market 117 The Giant Corporation 118 The New Industrial State 119 Profit Maximization 120 Technology and Inputs 121 The Short Run and the Long Run 121 The Production Function 122 Elements of Accounting: The Firm's Balance Sheet 123 The Firm's Profit and Loss Statement 125 Relationship between Balance Sheet and Profit and Loss Statement 126 Economic versus Accounting Profits 127 The Financial Statements of General Motors: A Case Study 128 *Summary* 129 *Concepts for Review* 130 *Questions for Discussion and Review* 130

PART THREE

NATIONAL OUTPUT, INCOME, AND EMPLOYMENT

8 • Unemployment, Inflation, and National Output **133**

Unemployment 134 How Much Unemployment Is There? 133 Unemployment: A Case Study 136 Inflation 137 The Relationship between Inflation and Unemployment 138 The Menu of Policy Choices 140 Estimates of Gross National Product: Uses and History 141 Measuring Gross National Product 142 Gross National Product: Adjusting for Price Changes 143 Intermediate Goods, Value-Added, and Net National Product 145 The Limitations of Gross National Product and Net National Product 146 Gross National Income 148 National Income, Personal Income, and Disposable Income 150 Consumption, Investment, and Government Expenditure 151 Three Basic Facts 152 The Gap between Actual and Potential Output 154 *Summary* 155 *Concepts for Review* 157 *Questions for Discussion and Review* 157

9 • The Determination of National Output **158**

The Classical View of Unemployment 159 The Views of Karl Marx 160 John Maynard Keynes and the Great Depression 161 Flaws in the Classical View 161 The Modern Theory: The Consumption Function 163 The Marginal Propensity to Consume 164 The Saving Function and the Marginal Propensity to Save 166 Determinants of Investment 167 The Determination of the Equilibrium Level of National Output 168 The Process Leading toward Equilibrium: A Tabular Analysis 169 A Graphical Analysis 170 Saving and Investment: Desired and Actual 172 The Multiplier: A Geometric Formulation 174 The Multiplier: An Algebraic Interpretation 175 The Multiplier and the Spending Process 177 Application of the Mutiplier: A Case Study 178 Multiplier Effects of Shifts in the Consumption Function 179 The Accuracy of the Postwar Forecasts 180 Induced Investment 181 *Summary* 182 *Concepts for Review* 183 *Questions for Discussion and Review* 183

10 • Fiscal Policy and National Output **185**

Government Expenditures and Net National Product 186 Taxation and Net National Product 189 The Nature and Objectives of Fiscal Policy 192 Makers of Fiscal Policy 194 *The Council of Economic Advisers* 195 Automatic Stabilizers 196 The Tools of Discretionary Fiscal Policy 197 The Tax Cut of 1964: An Application of Modern Economic Analysis 198 The Impact of Vietnam: Another Case Study 198 Deficit and Surplus Financing 199 Deficit Spending in the 1930s: A Case Study 200 Alternative Budget Policies 201 The Full-Employment Budget 202 Recent American Experience with Fiscal Policy 203 Improving the Workings of Fiscal Policy 205 *Summary* 206 *Concepts for Review* 207 *Questions for Discussion and Review* 207

11 • Business Fluctuations and Economic Forecasting **208**

Business Fluctuations 209 Government Spending and Expectations 211 The Acceleration Principle 211 The Interaction between the Acceleration Principle and the Multiplier 213 Inventory Cycles 214 Innovations and Random External Events 215 Monetary Factors 216 Can Business Fluctuations Be Avoided? 216 Can Business Fluctuations Be Forecasted? 217 Leading Indicators 218 Simple Keynesian Models 218 Econometric Models 220 A Small Econometric Model 221 Econometric Models, Big and Bigger 224 Econometric Forecasts: The Track Record 225 The Economic Forecasts for 1972: A Case Study 226 *Summary* 228 *Concepts for Review* 229 *Questions for Discussion and Review* 229

PART FOUR
MONEY, BANKING, AND STABILIZATION POLICY

12 • The Role and Importance of Money **233**

What Is Money? 234 Three Kinds of Money 235 Near-Monies 236 The Value of Money 237 Runaway Inflation and the Value of Money 238 Creeping Inflation and the Value of Money 239 Unemployment and the Quantity of Money 240 Determinants of the Quantity of Money 240 The Federal Reserve System 241 Commercial Banks in the United States 243 The Demand for Money 244 The Role of Money in the Keynesian Model 245 Money Makes a Comeback 247 The Velocity of Money and the Equation of Exchange 248 The Crude Quantity Theory of Money and Prices 249 A More Sophisticated Version of the Quantity Theory 250 Two Alternative Models 252 *Summary* 253 *Concepts for Review* 254 *Questions for Discussion and Review* 254

13 • The Banking System and the Quantity of Money **255**

The Bank of America: A Case Study 256 How Banks Operate 257 The Balance Sheet of an Individual Bank 257 Fractional-Reserve Banking 258 Legal Reserve Requirements 260 The Safety of the Banks 261 The Lending Decision: A Case Study 261 Two Ways Banks Cannot Create Money 262 How Banks Can Create Money 265 Impact on Other Banks 266 The Total Effect of the Original $10,000 Deposit 270 The Effect of a Decrease in Reserves 272 Currency Withdrawals and Excess Reserves 274 *Summary* 275 *Concepts for Review* 276 *Questions for Discussion and Review* 276

14 • Monetary Policy **277**

The Aims and Role of Monetary Policy 278 Makers of Monetary Policy 279 Tools of Monetary Policy: Open Market Operations 279 Changes in Legal Reserve Requirements 282 Changes in the Discount Rate 282 Other Tools of Monetary Policy 283 When Is Monetary Policy Tight or Easy? 284 Decision Making at the Fed: A Case Study 285 Monetary Policy in the 1950s and 1960s 286 *William McChesney Martin and Arthur F. Burns* 287 Monetary Policy under the Nixon Administration 288 Problems in Formulating Monetary Policy 289 The Fed's Relations with the Treasury 290 How Well Has the Fed Performed? 291 *Is There an Independent Federal Reserve? Should There Be?* 292 Should the Fed Be Governed by a Rule? 293 Monetary Policy: Advantages and Disadvantages 294 Monetary Policy and Private Decision Making 295 *Summary* 295 *Concepts for Review* 297 *Questions for Discussion and Review* 297

15 • **Problems of Economic Stabilization Policy** **298**

The General Problem of Achieving Economic Stability 299 Monetarists versus Keynesians 300 The Monetarist View of the Role of Money 300 The Debate over Stabilization Policy 302 *Milton Friedman versus Walter Heller* 303 Elements of a New Synthesis 304 The IS and LM Curves 305 Demand-Pull and Cost-Push Inflation 308 The Phillips Curve 309 Shifts in the Phillips Curve 311 The Phillips Curve: Short versus Long Run 313 Price Controls and the Reduction of Market Power: Two Suggested Remedies 314 Peacetime Wage and Price Controls under the Nixon Administration 315 Incomes Policies 316 The Steel Price Increase of 1962: A Case Study 317 The Kennedy-Johnson Guidelines: Criticism and Experience 318 Economic Stabilization: Where We Stand 319 *Summary* 320 *Concepts for Review* 321 *Questions for Discussion and Review* 321

PART FIVE

ECONOMIC GROWTH AND THE ENVIRONMENT

16 • **Economic Growth** **325**

What Is Economic Growth? 326 Economic Growth as a Policy Objective 326 Economic Growth, the Product Transformation Curve, and the Aggregate Production Function 328 The Law of Diminishing Marginal Returns 329 Thomas Malthus and Population Growth 331 *Thomas Malthus on Population* 332 Effects of Population Growth 333 David Ricardo: Trade and Economic Growth 335 Ricardo's View of Capital Formation 335 Effects of Capital Formation 337 The Role of Human Capital 339 The Role of Technological Change 339 The Electronic Computer: A Case Study 340 Technological Change: Determinants and Measurement 341 Entrepreneurship and the Social Environment 343 The Gap between Actual and Potential Output 343 Japan: A Case Study of Rapid Economic Growth 344 *Summary* 345 *Concepts for Review* 346 *Questions for Discussion and Review* 346

17 • **American Economic Growth: History, Policies, Problems, and Prospects** **347**

Economic Growth in the United States 348 Population and Human Resources 349 Technological Change 350 Capital Formation and Natural Resources 352 The Social and Entrepreneurial Environment, the GNP Gap, and Allocative Efficiency 352 Past and Present Views of Economic Growth 353 The Case for Economic Growth 354 The Case against Economic Growth 355 Public Policies to Stimulate Economic Growth 356 Policies for Economic Growth in the Early 1960s: A Case Study 357 Technological Unemployment 358 Structural Unemployment

360 Labor Displacement 361 Manpower and Training Policies 362 Visions of the Economic Future 362 *John Maynard Keynes on "Economic Possibilities for Our Grandchildren"* 363 *Summary* 364 *Concepts for Review* 365 *Questions for Discussion and Review* 365

18 • Environmental Pollution **366**

The Nature and Extent of Environmental Pollution 367 The Important Role of External Diseconomies 370 The Polluted Hudson and the Tin Can: Two Case Studies 371 Economic Growth and Environmental Pollution 373 Public Policy toward Pollution 374 Direct Regulation 374 Effluent Fees 375 The Ruhr: A Case Study 376 Tax Credits for Pollution-Control Equipment 377 Pollution-Control Programs in the United States 377 Cost of Cleaning Up the Environment 379 How Should We Dispose of Materials? 382 *Summary* 382 *Concepts for Review* 383 *Questions for Discussion and Review* 383

PART SIX

CONSUMER BEHAVIOR AND BUSINESS DECISION MAKING

19 • Consumer Behavior and Rational Choice **387**

Consumer Expenditures: The Walters of San Diego 388 Consumer Expenditures: Aggregate Data for the United States 389 A Model of Consumer Behavior 390 Indifference Curves and Utility 391 The Consumer as a Rational Decision Maker 393 An Overview of the Model and Its Uses 396 Purchasing a Sprinkler System: A Case Study 397 The Optimal Budget Allocation 398 Allocating Government Expenditures: Another Case Study 399 Protecting the Consumer 401 *Summary* 402 *Concepts for Review* 403 *Questions for Discussion and Review* 403

20 • Market Demand **404**

Market Demand Curves: Role and Importance 405 Measuring Market Demand Curves 406 Railroad Transportation in Metropolitan Boston: A Case Study 407 The Price Elasticity of Demand 408 Calculating the Price Elasticity of Demand 409 Determinants of the Price Elasticity of Demand 410 Price Elasticity and Total Money Expenditure 411 *Henry Ford and the Price Elasticity of Demand for Autos* 412 The Farm Problem and the Price Elasticity of Demand 413 Derivation of the Consumer's Demand Curve 415 Transition to the Market Demand Curve 417 The Demand Curve for Automobiles: A Case Study 418 Industry and Firm Demand Curves 419 Income Elasticity of Demand 420 Cross Elasticity of Demand 421 Criticisms and Extensions of the Model 422 *Summary* 423 *Concepts for Review* 424 *Questions for Discussion and Review* 424

21 • **Optimal Input Decisions and Cost Analysis** **425**

Average and Marginal Products 426 The Law of Diminishing Marginal Returns 427 Isoquants 429 The Optimal Input Decision 431 Isocost Curves and Isoquants 432 Determining the Optimal Input Combination: A Case Study 434 What Are Costs? 435 Total Costs in the Short Run 436 Average Costs in the Short Run 438 Marginal Cost in the Short Run 441 The Short-Run Cost Functions of a Crude Oil Pipeline: A Case Study 443 The Long-Run Average Cost Function 444 Returns to Scale 446 Measurement of Cost Functions and Break-Even Charts 447 *Summary* 450 *Concepts for Review* 451 *Questions for Discussion and Review* 451

22 • **Optimal Output Decisions and Linear Programming** **452**

The Output of the Firm 453 The Golden Rule of Output Determination 455 Does It Pay to Be a Dropout? 456 Decision Making at Continental Air Lines: A Case Study 457 The Firm's Supply Curve and the Market Supply Curve 458 Measurement of Market Supply Curves and the Price Elasticity of Supply 460 Linear Programming 462 The Linear-Programming View of the Firm 462 Removing Defects from Sheet Metal: A Case Study 463 Solving the Problem: No Constraints on Inputs 465 Solving the Problem: Constraint on Machine Time 467 Applications of Linear Programming and Management Science 468 *Summary* 469 *Concepts for Review* 470 *Questions for Discussion and Review* 471

PART SEVEN

MARKET STRUCTURE AND ANTITRUST POLICY

23 • **Perfect Competition and Monopoly** **475**

Market Structure and Economic Performance 476 Perfect Competition 476 Price and Output under Perfect Competition: The Market Period and the Short Run 477 Price and Output under Perfect Competition: The Long Run 478 Constant, Increasing, and Decreasing Cost Industries 480 The Allocation of Resources under Perfect Competition: A More Detailed View 482 Bituminous Coal: A Case Study 483 Monopoly 483 Causes of Monopoly 484 Demand Curve and Marginal Revenue under Monopoly 485 Price and Output under Monopoly: The Short Run 486 Price and Output under Monopoly: The Long Run 490 Perfect Competition and Monopoly: A Comparison 490 Public Regulation of Monopoly 492 Natural Gas: A Case Study 494 *Summary* 494 *Concepts for Review* 496 *Questions for Discussion and Review* 496

24 • **Monopolistic Competition and Oligopoly** **497**

Monopolistic Competition and Oligopoly: Their Major Characteristics 498 Monopolistic Competition 499 Price and Output under Monopolistic Competition 499 Comparisons with Perfect Competition and Monopoly 501 Retailing: A Case Study 502 Oligopoly 503 Mergers and Oligopoly 504 Oligopoly Behavior and the Stability of Prices 505 The Theory of Games 506 Collusion and Cartels 507 Barriers to Collusion 509 Price Leadership 510 Cost-Plus Pricing 511 Nonprice Competition 511 The Automobile Industry: A Case Study 512 Comparison of Oligopoly with Perfect Competition 513 *Summary* 514 *Concepts for Review* 515 *Questions for Discussion and Review* 516

25 • **Industrial Organization and Antitrust Policy** **517**

Monopoly and the Misallocation of Resources 518 Income Distribution and Efficiency 519 The Case against Oligopoly and Monopolistic Competition 519 The Defense of Monopoly Power 520 Monopoly Power, Big Business, and Technological Change 521 Monopoly, Big Business, and Economic Power 522 Industrial Concentration in the United States 523 The Antitrust Laws 524 The Courts and the Justice Department 525 Post-World War II Developments 526 Standards for Antitrust Policy 527 The Effectiveness of Antitrust Policy 528 The Pabst Case: Antitrust in Action 529 The Patent System 530 Other Policies Designed to Restrict Competition 531 *Summary* 532 *Concepts for Review* 533 *Questions for Discussion and Review* 534

PART EIGHT

DISTRIBUTION OF INCOME AND GENERAL EQUILIBRIUM

26 • **Determinants of Wages** **537**

The Labor Force 538 Labor Utilization by the Perfectly Competitive Firm 538 The Firm's Demand Curve for Labor 539 The Market Demand and Supply Curves for Labor 540 Equilibrium Price and Quantity of Labor 542 Wage Differentials 544 The All-Volunteer Army: A Case Study 545 Monopsony 546 Labor Unions 547 Early History of the American Labor Movement 548 The New Deal and World War II 549 The United Automobile Workers: A Case Study 550 Creation and Structure of the AFL-CIO 551 Internal Problems in Labor Unions 552 Postwar Labor Legislation 552 *James Hoffa: A Man Who Understands the Economics of Trucking* 553 Recent Trends in Union Membership 554 How Unions Increase Wages 555 Collective Bargaining 556 Strikes and Pattern Bargaining 557 The Pros and Cons of Big Unions 558 *Summary* 559 *Concepts for Review* 560 *Questions for Discussion and Review* 561

27 • Interest, Rent, and Profits **562**

What Determines the Interest Rate? 563 Functions of the Interest Rate 565 Capital and Roundabout Methods of Production 565 Capitalization of Assets 566 Capital Budgeting 567 Rates of Return from Investing in Human Capital 568 Rent: Nature and Significance 569 Profits: Definition and Statistics 571 Innovation, Uncertainty, and Monopoly Power 572 The Functions of Profits 572 *Summary* 573 *Concepts for Review* 574 *Questions for Discussion and Review* 574

28 • Income Inequality, Poverty, and Discrimination **575**

Inequality of Income 576 A Measure of Income Inequality 577 Trends in Income Inequality 579 Effects of the Tax Structure on Income Inequality 580 Income Inequality: The Pros and Cons 582 What Is Poverty? 583 The Characteristics of the Poor 585 Social Insurance 586 Antipoverty Programs 586 The Negative Income Tax 587 The Rise and Fall of "Workfare" 588 Racial Discrimination in the United States 589 Discrimination against Women 591 *Summary* 592 *Concepts for Review* 594 *Questions for Discussion and Review* 594

29 • General Equilibrium and Welfare Economics **595**

Partial Equilibrium versus General Equilibrium Analysis 596 The Nature and Existence of General Equilibrium 597 Input-Output Analysis 597 Applicability of Input-Output Analysis 599 The Nature of Welfare Economics 600 Conditions for Optimal Resource Allocation 601 Perfect Competition and Welfare Maximization 603 Marginal Cost Pricing 604 External Economies and Diseconomies 605 The Planning of Urban Land Use 607 *Summary* 608 *Concepts for Review* 610 *Questions for Discussion and Review* 610

PART NINE

INTERNATIONAL ECONOMICS

30 • International Trade **613**

America's Foreign Trade 614 Specialization and Trade 614 Absolute Advantage 616 Comparative Advantage 617 Comparative Advantage: A Geometric Representation 618 Comparative Advantage and Actual Trade Patterns: A Case Study 620 International Trade and Individual Markets 621 Economies of Scale, Learning, and Technological Change 623 Multinational Firms 624 The Social Costs of Tariffs 625 The Social Costs of Quotas 627 Considerations of National

Defense 628 Oil Import Quotas: A Case Study 628 Other Arguments for Tariffs 629 Frequently Encountered Fallacies 630 Tariffs in the United States 631 *The European Economic Community* 632 *Summary* 634 *Concepts for Review* 635 *Questions for Discussion and Review* 635

31 • Exchange Rates and the Balance of Payments **636**

International Transactions and Exchange Rates 637 Exchange Rates under the Gold Standard 637 Flexible Exchange Rates 638 Fixed Exchange Rates 640 Fixed versus Flexible Exchange Rates 642 Experience with the Gold Standard and Gold Exchange Standard 643 The Fight to Save the Pound: A Case Study 644 The Balance of Payments 645 Goods and Services 646 Transfers, Capital Movements, and Reserve Assets 647 Financing the Deficit 649 U.S. Balance of Payments Deficits, 1950–72 650 Autonomous and Accommodating Transactions 651 Ways to Restore Equilibrium 652 Britain's Balance of Payments: A Case Study 654 *The International Money Game* 655 International Lending 656 America's Role as International Lender 656 *Summary* 657 *Concepts for Review* 658 *Questions for Discussion and Review* 659

32 • International Finance: History, Problems, and Policies **660**

Pre-World War II Days 661 The Effects of Foreign Trade on Net National Product 661 World War II 663 The Dollar Shortage 663 Postwar Aid Programs 664 The World Bank 666 The International Monetary Fund 666 The IMF in Action: A Case Study 667 The Dollar Glut 668 Alchemy in the Nuclear Age 669 Problems of International Adjustment 670 The Relation between International and Domestic Economic Policies 671 The Liquidity Shortage 671 Flexible Exchange Rates: A Suggested Remedy 672 The Formation of Recent American Policy 673 *Summary* 674 *Concepts for Review* 675 *Questions for Discussion and Review* 675

33 • The Less Developed Countries **676**

What Is a "Less Developed Country"? 677 A Closer Look at the LDCs 679 Barriers to Development and the Need for Capital Formation 679 The Population Explosion 681 Technology: A Crucial Factor 683 Entrepreneurship, Social Institutions, and Natural Resources 684 The Role of Government 686 Balanced Growth 686 Development Planning in Less Developed Countries 688 Planning in Action: The Case of India 688 Choosing Investment Projects in Less Developed Countries 689 American Foreign Aid 690 The World Bank and Other Aid Programs 693 *Summary* 694 *Concepts for Review* 696 *Questions for Discussions and Review* 696

34 • **The Communist Countries, Marxism, and Radical Economics** **697**

Karl Marx and the Class Struggle 698 *Karl Marx on Capitalism* 699 Marx's Vision of the Future 700 Communism in the USSR 701 Soviet Economic Planning: Problems and Controls 703 Prices in the USSR 705 The Distribution of Income 705 Economic Growth 706 The Performance of the Soviet Economy 707 Changes in the Soviet Economy 708 Communism in China 709 Economic Life in China 710 Communism in Yugoslavia 711 Democratic Socialism 712 Radical Economics and the New Left 712 Response to Radical Economics 713 *Summary* 714 *Concepts for Review* 716 *Questions for Discussion and Review* 716

Index **717**

PREFACE

As economists extend the reach of their discipline into more and more areas of practical concern, opportunities multiply to shape economics courses along new lines. And yet, many introductory texts continue to protect much of economics from contamination by actual events. I think that this is a mistake. Economics has its share of elegant theories; but their elegance is enhanced, not diminished, by application to real problems of the economy.

This text, like my intermediate text *(Microeconomics: Theory and Applications)* blends theory with case studies and relevant empirical matter. It draws heavily on my experience in teaching the principles course over the past decade. Along with many of my colleagues at a wide variety of colleges and universities, I have found student interest invariably heightened when time is taken to demonstrate how the principles of economics can be, and have been, used by decision makers, both in the public and private sectors.

In keeping with this emphasis on the real world, primary attention in this book is focused on social issues. The problems of unemployment, inflation, poverty, economic growth, environmental pollution, monopoly, the less developed countries, and international trade and finance are what make economics so fascinating. While most discussions are well within the mainstream of economic thought, consideration is also given to present-day Marxist, radical, and conservative thought—not because anyone wants to indoctrinate the student one way or another, but because a subject retains its vitality by allowing and responding to criticism, dissent, and change.

In most elementary texts the decisions of firms and consumers seem to be regarded as problems almost too trivial for analysis. In contrast, I try to inject at numerous points some idea of how economics can improve private decision making, for what may appear to be low-level problems actually are of great importance to society.

Similarly, more attention is devoted here to modern tools of economic analysis, such as linear programming, input-output analysis, game theory, and econometric forecasting models. To ignore these techniques or to confine them to cryptic appendices is to give the student an incomplete and somewhat distorted idea of current economic practice. Unusually complete descriptions of these techniques are provided, but at a level that requires no mathematics beyond high-school algebra. Indeed, the very few sections requiring any high-school mathematics at all are written so that they can be skipped; these are identified by footnotes.

There are other departures. An entire chapter is devoted to modern welfare economics, general equilibrium analysis, and their applications. Extensive treatment is given to the theory of rational choice, the nature of the decision-making process in government and business, and the role and importance of incomes policy in the modern economy. Further, the energy crisis, so much in the news, figures in several chapters. And an entire chapter is devoted to the economics of environmental pollution. These topics ordinarily are slighted or omitted in elementary texts. In view of their importance, I believe that they deserve a better fate.

When I began this book, I hoped to present the relevant material in briefer compass than in fact turned out to be the case. I have, however, constantly kept in mind that this is a book intended for students taking their first course in economics, and for them alone. This means that much complicated detail has been eliminated. I have tried to stress clarity and the essentials, and to shun all forms of unnecessary complexity.

Since instructors differ considerably in their choice and ordering of topics, this book is organized for maximum flexibility. Many instructors take up microeconomics before macroeconomics. I have gone to considerable pains to make sure that this book will work just as well for these instructors as for those who prefer to present macroeconomics first. (A suggested ordering of chapters is presented for them on p. XIX.) As an alternative to reversing the chapter sequence in the one-volume editions, some instructors may want to consider the two-volume paperbound version, *Principles of Microeconomics* and *Principles of Macroeconomics.*

This book can also be adapted for use in one-semester courses. Pages XX–XXI present outlines for a one-semester course stressing microeconomics, a one-semester course stressing macroeconomics, and a one-semester course covering both.

As supplements to this text, I have prepared both a book of readings and a workbook containing problems and exercises. *Economics: Readings, Issues, and Cases* is designed to acquaint the student with a wide range of economic analysis, spanning the spectrum from the classics to the present-day radicals. The emphasis, as in the text, is on integrating theory, measurement, and applications. *Economic Problems* contains problems, concepts, cases, and tests, as well as brief answers to practically all of them. This volume should be helpful to the student as a device for self-evaluation and practice. It also provides the instructor with material for quizzes and for other uses.

Finally, it is a pleasure to acknowledge the debts that I owe to the many teachers at various colleges and universities who have commented in detail on various parts of the manuscript. Without question, this book has benefited greatly from the advice I received from the following distinguished economists, none of whom is responsible, of course, for the outcome: Bela Balassa, Johns Hopkins; Robert Baldwin, University of Wisconsin (Madison); Arthur Benavie, North Carolina; William Branson, Princeton; Martin Bronfenbrenner, Duke; Edward Budd, Penn State; Richard Cooper, Yale; F. Trenery Dolbear, Brandeis; Robert Dorfman, Harvard; James Duesenberry, Harvard; David Fand, Wayne State; Robert Gordon, Northwestern; Herschel Grossman, Brown; Albert Hirschman, Harvard; Ronald Jones, Rochester; John Kareken, Minnesota; Ann Krueger, Minnesota; Robert Kuenne, Princeton; Simon Kuznets, Harvard; Raymond Lubitz, Columbia and the Federal Reserve; Sherman Maisel, University of California

(Berkeley); Thomas Mayer, University of California (Davis); Arthur Okun, Brookings Institution; Lloyd Orr, Indiana; Roger Ransom, University of California (Berkeley); Albert Rees, Princeton; Vernon Ruttan, Minnesota; David Schulze, Florida; Nicolas Spulber, Indiana; Michael Taussig, Rutgers; and Fred Westfield, Vanderbilt.

I would like to thank Elisabeth Allison of Harvard University for contributing the inserts that appear (over her initials) in various chapters, and Donald S. Lamm of W. W. Norton for his efficient handling of the editorial and publishing end of the work. Above all, my wife, Lucile, has contributed an enormous amount to the completion of this book. She encouraged and helped and even read the book—which, for a clinical psychologist, means paying the ultimate price.

Philadelphia, 1974 E. M.

Outline of a One-Year Course with Macroeconomics Following Microeconomics.

1 Economic Problems, Policies, and Decisions
2 Economic Analysis: Models and Measurement
3 The American Economy: Our Mixed Capitalist System
4 The Price System: Consumers, Firms, and Markets
5 The Economic Role of the Government
6 Government Expenditures, Taxation, and the Public Debt
7 The Business Firm: Organization, Motivation, and Technology
19 Consumer Behavior and Rational Choice
20 Market Demand
21 Optimal Input Decisions and Cost Analysis
22 Optimal Output Decisions and Linear Programming
23 Perfect Competition and Monopoly
24 Monopolistic Competition and Oligopoly
25 Industrial Organization and Antitrust Policy
26 Determinants of Wages
27 Interest, Rent, and Profits
28 Income Inequality, Poverty, and Discrimination
29 General Equilibrium and Welfare Economics
8 Unemployment, Inflation, and National Output
9 The Determination of National Output
10 Fiscal Policy and National Output
11 Business Fluctuations and Economic Forecasting
12 The Role and Importance of Money
13 The Banking System and the Quantity of Money
14 Monetary Policy
15 Problems of Economic Stabilization Policy
16 Economic Growth
17 American Economic Growth: History, Policies, and Problems
18 Environmental Pollution
30 International Trade
31 Exchange Rates and the Balance of Payments
32 International Finance: History, Problems, and Policies
33 The Less Developed Countries
34 The Communist Countries, Marxism, and Radical Economics

Outline of a One-Semester Course Emphasizing Microeconomics.

1 Economic Problems, Policies, and Decisions
2 Economic Analysis: Models and Measurements
3 The American Economy: Our Mixed Capitalist System
4 The Price System: Consumers, Firms, and Markets
5 The Economic Role of the Government
7 The Business Firm: Organization, Motivation, and Technology
19 Consumer Behavior and Rational Choice
20 Market Demand
21 Optimal Input Decisions and Cost Analysis
22 Optimal Output Decisions and Linear Programming
23 Perfect Competition and Monopoly
24 Monopolistic Competition and Oligopoly
25 Industrial Organization and Antitrust Policy
28 Income Inequality, Poverty, and Discrimination [optional]
8 Unemployment, Inflation, and National Output
9 The Determination of National Output
10 Fiscal Policy and National Output
12 The Role and Importance of Money[1]
13 The Banking System and the Quantity of Money
14 Monetary Policy

[1]Also, assign the beginning sections of Chapter 11.

Outline of a One-Semester Course Emphasizing Macroeconomics.

1 Economic Problems, Policies, and Decisions
2 Economic Analysis: Models and Measurement
3 The American Economy: Our Mixed Capitalist System
4 The Price System: Consumers, Firms, and Markets
5 The Economic Role of the Government
6 Government Expenditures, Taxation, and the Public Debt
7 The Business Firm: Organization, Motivation, and Technology
8 Unemployment, Inflation, and National Output
9 The Determination of National Output
10 Fiscal Policy and National Output
11 Business Fluctuations and Economic Forecasting
12 The Role and Importance of Money
13 The Banking System and the Quantity of Money
14 Monetary Policy
15 Problems of Economic Stabilization Policy
16 Economic Growth
17 American Economic Growth: History, Policies, and Problems
30 International Trade
31 Exchange Rates and the Balance of Payments
33 The Less Developed Countries

Outline of a One-Semester Course Emphasizing Both Macroeconomics and Microeconomics.

1 Economic Problems, Policies, and Decisions
2 Economic Analysis: Models and Measurement
3 The American Economy: Our Mixed Capitalist System
4 The Price System: Consumers, Firms, and Markets
5 The Economic Role of the Government
6 Government Expenditures, Taxation, and the Public Debt
7 The Business Firm: Organization, Motivation, and Technology
8 Unemployment, Inflation, and National Output
9 The Determination of National Output
10 Fiscal Policy and National Output
11 Business Fluctuations and Economic Forecasting
12 The Role and Importance of Money
13 The Banking System and the Quantity of Money
14 Monetary Policy
15 Problems of Economic Stabilization Policy
19 Consumer Behavior and Rational Choice
20 Market Demand
21 Optimal Input Decisions and Cost Analysis
22 Optional Output Decisions and Linear Programming
28 Income Inequality, Poverty, and Discrimination

PART ONE

Introduction to Economics

CHAPTER 1

Economic Problems, Policies, and Decisions

John Ruskin, the famous nineteenth-century English author and critic, had a point when he said, "Life being short, and the quiet hours of it few, we ought to waste none of them in reading valueless books." You have a right to expect some convincing evidence that economics is important enough to warrant your spending the time to master the material in this book. This is doubly true when you recognize that economics is a fairly technical subject and that, although it hurts to say so, no introductory economics text, including this one, can hold a candle to a Hemingway or Dostoevski novel as sheer entertainment.

Introductory texts often begin by defining economics, and one standard definition is this one: *economics is concerned with the way resources are allocated among alternative uses to satisfy human wants.* Such definitions may help get you oriented, but being chock-full of vague words like "resources" and "human wants," they communicate little of the power and usefulness of economics. Really, the only way you can get an idea of what economics is all about is by looking at some of the problems it can help you solve. This introductory chapter will describe seven fairly typical problems economics can help with. Although this is only a small sample of the problems where economics is useful, it gives you a reasonable first impression of the nature of economics and its relevance to the real world. After considering this sample, you will be better able to judge for yourself whether this is one of those "valueless books" Ruskin warned against.

Unemployment and Inflation

The history of the American economy is for the most part a story of growth. Our output—the amount of goods and services we produce annually—has grown rapidly over the years, giving us a standard of living that could not have been imagined a century ago. For example, output per person in the United States was about $6,000 in 1973; in 1909 it was about $1,840. Nonetheless, the growth of output has not been steady or uninterrupted; instead, our output has tended to fluctuate—and so has unemployment. In periods when output has fallen, thousands, even millions, of people have been thrown out of work. In the Great Depression of the 1930s, for example, over 20 percent of the labor force was unemployed (see Figure 1.1). Unemployment on this scale results in enormous economic waste and social misery.

The first of our sample of economic problems is: *what determines the extent of unemployment in the American economy, and what can be done to reduce it?* This problem is complicated by a related phenomenon: the level of prices tends to rise when we reduce the level of unemployment. In other words, inflation occurs. Thus, the problem is not only to curb unemployment, but to do this without producing an inflation so ruinous to the nation's economic health that the cure proves more dangerous than the ailment. As Figure 1.2 shows, we have experienced considerable inflation between 1929 and 1972. The dollar has lost about ⅔ of its purchasing power during this period.

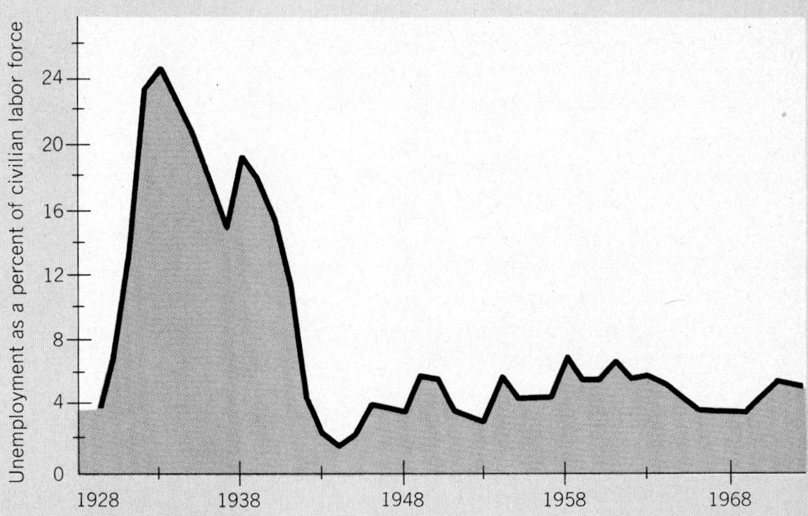

Figure 1.1
Unemployment Rates, United States, 1929–72

The unemployment rate has varied substantially from year to year. In the Great Depression, it reached a high of about 25 percent.

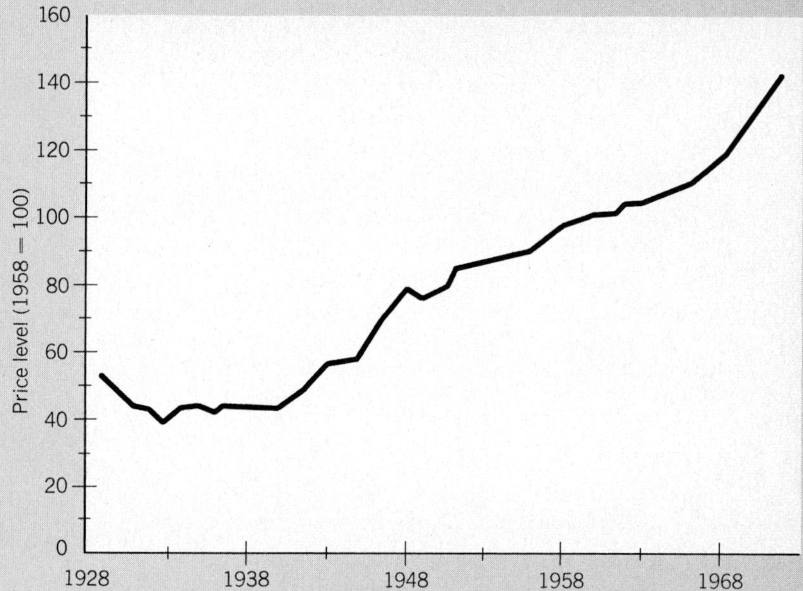

Figure 1.2
Changes in Price Level, United States, 1929–72

The price level has increased steadily since the 1930s, and is now over 3 times as high as it was in 1935.

During the past 50 years, economists have learned a great deal about the factors that determine the extent of unemployment. Since, contrary to earlier opinion, our economy has no automatic regulator that keeps it moving quickly and dependably toward minimal unemployment with stable prices, the American people, as well as people in other lands, have given their government the responsibility of promoting full employment[1] without serious inflation. Economists have developed useful techniques to help the government do this job. In particular, they have shown how government can use its control over the money supply and interest rates, as well as its power to spend and tax, to promote full employment with reasonably stable prices. As a responsible citizen, you must be interested in this matter. To judge how well Congress and the president are doing their jobs, and to determine how you should vote, you must know what the government can do to reduce unemployment and how much it is doing.

[1] By full employment, we mean a minimal level of unemployment, recognizing that there will always be some frictional and structural unemployment of the sort described in Chapter 8.

In recent years, the United States has experienced very substantial inflation. In 1971 and again in 1973, President Nixon imposed price controls in an attempt to stem the rapid rate of inflation. The federal government has established one anti-inflation program after another, the newest program in 1973 being designated Phase IV. Yet the price level has continued to rise. For example, food prices jumped by about 25 percent during a single year, 1973. To understand the reasons for this inflation, and the ways that the government can reduce the rate of inflation, you must understand some economics.

Government Regulation of Business

The 100 largest manufacturing firms control about

½ of all manufacturing assets in the United States (and their share of total assets seems to have increased since World War II). In certain industries, like automobiles and aluminum, the four largest firms account for over 90 percent of the market (see Table 1.1). Nonetheless, although the large corporations obviously wield considerable power in their markets, the American economic system is built on the idea that firms should compete with one another. In particular, the producers of steel, automobiles, oil, toothpicks, and other goods are expected to set their prices independently and not to collude. Certain acts of Congress, often referred to as the antitrust laws, make it illegal for firms to get together and set the price of a product.

Table 1.1

Market Share of 4 Largest Firms, Selected Manufacturing Product Markets, United States

Industry	Market share of 4 largest firms (percent)
Automobiles	99
Aluminum	96
Cigarettes	80
Soap	72
Tires	70
Aircraft	59
Blast furnaces and steel plants	50

Source: Concentration Ratios in Manufacturing Industry, Senate Judiciary Committee, 1967.

Our second example of an economic problem is: *why is competition of this sort socially desirable?* More specifically, why should we be in favor of the antitrust laws? What reasons are there to believe that such laws will result in a more efficient economic system? (And what do we mean by "efficient"?) To a business executive, lawyer, government official, or judge, these questions are very important, since it is likely that at one time or another these people will be concerned with an antitrust case. But these issues matter to every citizen, because they deal with the basic rules of the game for firms in our economy. Of course, one reason why Americans have traditionally favored competition over collusion, and relatively small firms over giant ones, is that they have mistrusted the concentration of economic power, and obviously, this mistrust was based on both political and economic considerations. But beyond this, you should know when competition generally benefits society, and when it does not.

One way that society has attempted to control the economic power of corporations that dominate an entire industry is through public regulation. Take the case of radio and TV. The Federal Communications Commission, a government agency, monitors the activities of broadcasting stations and networks to prevent misuse of the airwaves. Other regulatory commissions supervise the activities of the power companies, the airlines, the railroads, and other industries where it is felt that competition cannot be relied on to produce socially desirable results.

The regulatory commissions and the principles they use are currently a subject of tremendous controversy: Many observers feel that they tend to be lax, or, worse still, to be captured by the industries they are supposed to regulate. Since these regulated industries produce about 8 percent of national income, we all have a big stake in understanding how they operate and whether they are being regulated properly. This is another aspect of the same general problem of how industries should be organized.

The Elimination of Poverty

As pointed out by Philip Wicksteed, a prominent twentieth-century British economist, "A man can be neither a saint, nor a lover, nor a poet, unless he has comparatively recently had something to eat." Although relatively few people in the United States lack food desperately, over 24 million American people, about 12 percent of the population of the United States, live in what is officially designated as poverty. These people have frequently been called invisible in a nation where the average yearly income per person is about $6,000; but the poor are invisible only to those who shut their eyes, since they exist in ghettos in the wealthiest American cities, like New York, Chicago, and Los Angeles, as well as near Main Street in thousands of small towns. They can also be found in areas where industry has come and gone, as in the former coal-mining towns of Pennsylvania and West Virginia, and in areas where decades of farming have depleted the soil.

Table 1.2 shows the distribution of income in the United States in 1972. Clearly, there are very substantial differences among families in income level. Indeed, the cats and dogs of the very rich eat better than some human beings. You as a citizen and a human being need to understand the social mechanisms underlying the distribution of income, both in the United States and in other countries, and how reasonable and just they are. Our third economic problem is: *why does poverty exist in the world today, and what can be done to abolish it?* To help the poor effectively, we must understand the causes of poverty. Does it make sense, for example, to pour billions of dollars into programs often denounced by politicians and even the recipients themselves as a "welfare mess"?

Table 1.2

Percentage Distribution of Families, by Income, United States, 1972

Money income	Percent of all families
Under $2,000	4
2,000– 3,999	8
4,000– 5,999	10
6,000– 7,999	11
8,000– 9,999	11
10,000–14,999	26
15,000–24,999	23
25,000 and over	7
Total	100

Source: Department of Commerce.

Since poverty is intimately bound up with our racial problems and the decay of our cities, the success or failure of measures designed to eradicate poverty may also help us determine whether we can achieve a society where equality of opportunity is more than a slogan and where people do not have to escape to the suburbs to enjoy green space and fresh air. Nor does the economist's concern with poverty stop at our shoreline. One of the biggest problems of the world today is the plight of the poor countries of Asia, Africa and Latin America—the so-called "less developed countries." The industrialized countries of the world, like the United States, Western Europe, Japan, and the Soviet Union, are really just rich little islands surrounded by seas of poverty. Over 2 billion people live in countries where income per person is less than $500 per year. These countries lack equipment, technology, and education; sometimes (but by no means always) they also suffer from overpopulation. Economists have devoted considerable attention to the problems of the less developed countries, and to developing techniques to assist them.

Environmental Pollution

The poor seem always to be with us; and in our industrialized world, so too is pollution. For many years, people in the United States paid relatively little attention to the environment and what they were doing to it, but this attitude has changed markedly in the past decade. Now the public is really concerned about environmental pollution.

Table 1.3

Water Pollution for Major Drainage Areas, United States, 1970 and 1971

Major watershed	Stream miles	Polluted miles 1970	Polluted miles 1971	Change
Ohio	28,992	9,869	24,031	+14,162
Southeast	11,726	3,109	4,490	+ 1,381
Great Lakes	21,374	6,580	8,771	+ 2,191
Northeast	32,431	11,895	5,823	− 6,072
Middle Atlantic	31,914	4,620	5,627	+ 1,007
California	28,277	5,359	8,429	+ 3,070
Gulf	64,719	16,605	11,604	− 5,001
Missouri	10,448	4,259	1,839	− 2,420
Columbia	30,443	7,443	5,685	− 1,758
United States	260,324	69,739	76,299	+ 6,560

Source: Council on Environmental Quality, *Third Annual Report*, August 1972.

You may have seen the considerable air pollution in Los Angeles, New York, or many other cities. Chances are that a river near you is no longer fit for swimming or an abundant fish life, even if it is not as badly polluted as Cleveland's Cuyahoga, which was so full of wastes that it literally caught fire in 1969. You can get an idea of the scope of the water pollution problem from Table 1.3. In response to the pollution problem, the government and interested groups of private citizens are trying to control pollution, whether from auto exhausts, combustion of fossil fuels, solid waste disposal, or the noise of sirens and jackhammers. But this is a difficult task, not unlike the job performed by Hercules in the Augean stables.

Our fourth example of an economic problem is: *what causes environmental pollution, and how can we reduce it to the proper levels?* Consider as an example, Richmond, a village south of Albany, New York, on the Hudson River.[2] It is situated at a place where the river is polluted very badly: the water is brown with the human and industrial wastes of Albany, Troy, and other cities upstream, as well as with the wastes dumped into the river locally. In the area immediately around Richmond, two of the principal polluters are the village of Richmond itself and the Smith Paper Company. The village's sewer mains dump their contents into the river, and the Smith Paper Company discharges its untreated wastes into a creek that flows into the river. The people of Richmond have dragged their heels about building a sewage treatment system, feeling that unless the towns upstream took action their own efforts would be fruitless. The Smith Paper Company, for other reasons, has also been slow to do anything about water pollution.

In a situation of this sort, what should be done? For example, should the village of Richmond and the Smith Paper Company be required by the federal government to treat their wastes in certain ways? If so, how pure should the water be, and who should pay for the treatment costs—the village and the Smith Paper Company, or the general public? Or, instead of imposing such standards, should the government charge a fee for pollution,

[2] The names Richmond and Smith are fictitious; otherwise, this is a factual account.

and if so, how high should it be? Economists have devoted substantial attention to questions like this in recent years. To a considerable extent, the problem of environmental pollution is an economic problem—and economics must play an important role in any attempted solution.

The Planned Economies

Roughly ⅓ of the world's people live and work under a set of economic rules quite different from ours. The object of the game—achieving material prosperity and living the good life—may be broadly similar, but differences in how it is played account for a distinct cleavage between Communist and capitalist countries. Some of these differences can be spotted at once. For example, the steel mills of the Soviet Union are owned and operated by the government, whereas the steel mills of Gary, Indiana, or Pittsburgh belong to private corporations that compete against each other for sales, striving to make the profits that will fuel their further growth and insure a favorable return to their owners—the hundreds of thousands of people who have invested in their stocks. The Communist nations believe that factories, mines, and other such productive units should be owned by the state; most Americans believe that they should be owned by individuals.

Under the Communist system, the productive activities of a country are planned by a small group of bureaucrats in government ministries. In the capitalist world, industrial decision making is dispersed among many firms, each sizing up the demand for its products and choosing its own methods of production. Much is made of these contrasts in the economic life of the Communist and the capitalist nations, and rightly so. But it is important to recognize that neither the Communist nor the capitalist system is quite as pristine pure as its more zealous admirers would have us believe. For example, when the American government provides huge loans to a giant defense contractor faced with bankruptcy, this can hardly be regarded as a triumph of pure capitalism. And when the Soviet planners adopt various capitalist techniques, some people do not regard it as a triumph of pure communism.

Our fifth example of an economic problem is: *How do the economic systems of the Communist countries work? In what respects are their systems like ours, and in what respects do they differ? How well have their economic systems been performing?* Economics helps you understand the differences between communism and capitalism. Of course there are political, social, and cultural differences as well, but a major part of the differences is economic—and economists, here and in the Communist countries, have devoted considerable time and effort to studying each other's economic systems, in the process laying to rest many pernicious myths. This is all to the good, because sensible dealings with other nations must rest on fact, not myth. It will be a long time before the tensions between the Communist and capitalist blocs are eliminated, but a realistic understanding of the Communist systems is bound to promote the chances of harmonious international relations.

Rational Decision Making

The problems discussed in previous sections are problems that concern our entire society. Obviously, they merit study by economists. But much of economics deals with narrower problems, such as the operations of the business firm. Consider for example, the cost calculations that must be made by the management of Continental Air Lines, to determine how many flights to run between Houston and Los Angeles. Or take the case of the International Business Machines Corporation (IBM), which must decide how to make, market, and price its next generation of electronic computers. These firms face very difficult problems, often involving millions of dollars. It is important, both to the firms themselves and to society at large, that they make the best decisions possible.

This is our sixth example of an economic problem: *how should a firm decide what to produce, how much to produce, and how to produce it?* Suppose that a metalworking firm has signed a contract to remove impurities from 100 square feet of sheet metal per week, at a price of $10 per square foot. There are three processes the firm can use. Process A requires 2 manhours of labor and 1 hour of machine time to remove the defects from 1 square foot of sheet metal, Process B requires 1.5 manhours of labor and 1.5 hours of machine time for the same job, and Process C can do it with 1.1 manhours of labor and 2.2 hours of machine time. The same kind of machine is used for each process. The firm must pay $3 per manhour for labor and $2 for an hour of machine time.

Given these circumstances, what process should the firm use to satisfy its contract? Should it use one process for all 100 square feet of sheet metal per week? Or should it use Process A to remove the defects from 50 square feet and Process B for the other 50 square feet? Or some other combination of processes? Which of the myriad possibilities will yield the firm the highest profits? You may not care much about sheet metal, but if you are interested in managing or working for a business firm, you should want to know how to solve this type of problem, for of course the same principles apply to many other fields. (Answer: Process B used for all 100 square feet will return the highest profits. You will find out why in Chapter 22.)

Economics can give you tools that will help you solve managerial problems, whatever sort of career you choose. For example, one large newsprint company with 6 mills in Canada and 200 customers in various parts of the United States had to decide how much newsprint to ship from each mill to each customer. The sorts of economic techniques described in subsequent chapters enabled it to find the optimal solution. Moreover, many of these principles and tools are just as applicable in government as in business. For example, they have been used to determine whether programs designed to reduce the dropout rates in high schools are worth the amounts spent on them.

The Energy Crisis

Since World War II, Americans have had relatively little experience with shortages—situations where, at the going price, the quantity demanded of particular commodities exceeds the quantity supplied. In 1973, our affluent society was jolted by shortages in a number of areas, particularly in the production and distribution of fossil fuels like oil. The "energy crisis" hit the headlines, and stayed there for some time. Responding to apparently serious fuel shortages, the United States set out to expand domestic supplies of energy.

Our seventh example of an economic problem is: *what factors are responsible for our energy problems, and how can these problems be solved?* In later chapters, we shall examine how shortages of this sort can occur, and discuss a variety of issues pertaining to our energy problems. Among other things, we shall look at the shortage of natural gas, the behavior of our oil imports, the economics of coal research and development, and the nature of some rationing schemes considered in 1973. To comprehend our energy problems, one must understand these matters.

Economic Problems: Some Common Threads

Even this brief sample of economic problems shows certain important characteristics they tend to have in common. First, economic problems generally involve *choice*. There are often a number of alternative ways to handle a problem, and the question is which is best. What is the best way to reduce unemployment without causing inflation? Or the best way to deal with poverty in the United States? To throw light on such questions, one must examine the costs and benefits associated with each alternative feasible solution, and choose the solution whose benefits are greatest relative to its costs. This is often a complicated and subtle business, since neither the costs nor the benefits may be easy to conceptualize and measure. Economists have spent a great deal of time and energy developing sophisticated ways to help solve such problems of choice.

To illustrate problems of choice, let's return to our earlier example of the metalworking firm that has to decide which process to use to remove impurities from a certain quantity of sheet metal per week. To solve this problem, the firm must consider the costs and benefits of each alternative process. This sounds easy, but there are many pitfalls, since costs and benefits often are overlooked, misinterpreted, or miscalculated. Any economist worth his salt can entertain you with horror stories of major corporations that have gone astray in estimating the costs of alternative manufacturing processes. This is quite understandable, because unlike the simple problem confronting the metalworking firm, many of the problems faced by these corporations are very complicated indeed. Nonetheless, the basic principles of economics can be surprisingly effective in guiding you to a solution.

A second characteristic of many economic problems is that, to choose among a number of feasible solutions, one must *forecast what will occur* if each solution is adopted. This emphasis on the future necessarily entails some uncertainty. For example, in a period of substantial unemployment, the government can reduce the extent of unemployment in a variety of ways: it can reduce taxes, increase its expenditures, or increase the amount of money in circulation, among other methods. Which measure is best depends on the magnitude and nature of the effects of each one, which must be forecasted. Unfortunately, economic forecasting is by no means an exact science, but there is no way to avoid making such forecasts. One way or another, a choice will be made, and any choice involves a forecast, explicit or implicit. Each year, thousands of studies are carried out by economists in an effort to improve their ability to forecast various phenomena. Judging by the available evidence, these efforts have been paying off, and economic forecasting has become increasingly reliable.

A third characteristic of many economic problems is that they involve choices concerning *the role of government* in economic affairs. Consider the problem of stemming inflation. Should the government impose wage and price controls, or should the government leave prices and wages to private bargaining and markets? Or how much government intervention to reduce pollution should be accepted? Should the Environmental Protection Agency be given the power to impose regulations of various kinds on the extent to which any firm or individual can pollute the environment, or should we allow firms and individuals to make these decisions themselves?

Turn to a different area: the antitrust laws, which are designed to stimulate and preserve competition and to discourage monopoly. In the Von's Grocery case of 1965, the Supreme Court disallowed a merger between two supermarkets that together had less than 8 percent of the Los Angeles market. Is this carrying government intervention too far? Or consider the regulation of natural gas prices by the Federal Power Commission. When it instructed the Commission to regulate these prices, the Supreme Court said that the producers of natural gas had appreciable power over the market; but there are thousands of natural gas producers, and many observers believe that the industry is highly competitive. Is governmental regulation of this sort justified?

A fourth noteworthy characteristic of many economic problems is their *interdependence*. Often they cannot be considered in isolation, because attempts to solve one problem may worsen another problem. For example, measures designed to reduce the rate of inflation may increase unemployment, unless the government is very careful. Similarly, stepping up the rate of increase of national output may also increase environmental pollution, and attempts to reduce pollution may worsen the poverty problem, because the antipollution programs may hurt the poor more than the rich.

Needless to say, an attempt to solve a particular problem does not always aggravate another problem. However, since it *may* make another problem worse, we must determine its side effects before we act.

The Role of Economics in Public Policy

The problems we have touched on are only a sample of the ways economics affects your life as a citizen, administrator, worker, investor, or consumer. But even this small sample makes it clear that some economic problems are problems facing our entire society. For example, avoiding excessive unemployment is not a task that can be assigned to a particular individual, family, or firm. It requires the concerted effort of our entire society. In other words, it is a problem of public policy—a problem that is considered and debated in the political arena. As citizens, we are all entitled to take part in making public policy—and we are all affected by the policies adopted.

Economics, and economists, play an extremely important role in the formulation of public policy. Skim through the articles in a daily newspaper. Chances are that you will find a report of an economist testifying before Congress, perhaps on the costs and benefits of a program to reduce unemployment among black teenagers in the Bedford-Stuyvesant area of New York City, or on the steps that can be taken to make American goods more competitive with those produced by Japan or West Germany. In the financial pages, you may read about an economist who has explained to a group of bankers why higher interest rates may be necessary to curb inflation. Still another economist may crop up on the sports page, arguing that professional athletes should be allowed to sell their talents to any team, not merely the team that has acquired the right to negotiate with them through a players' draft.

Economics and economists play a key role at the highest levels of our government. Consider the package of proposals concerning trade agreements with foreign countries that President Nixon submitted to Congress in April 1973. This package was devised in large part by economists, inside and outside the government, and the work was coordinated by George P. Shultz, Secretary of the Treasury and chairman of the President's Council on Economic Policy, a distinguished economist who was formerly professor of economics at M.I.T. and the University of Chicago. Some idea of the range of issues economists deal with is suggested by the fact that, in early April, Shultz "negotiated with European finance ministers, with Soviet leaders, with key Republican and Democratic lawmakers, and with AFL-CIO President George Meany on such diverse subjects as [the preceding] February's dollar devaluation; the Soviet exit fees on Jewish emigrants, the legislation to extend Nixon's authority [to impose wage and price controls], and, of course, the trade package." [3]

In addition, economics plays a very important role in the decisions made by individual government agencies. For example, in April 1973 the Environmental Protection Agency decided to allow automobile manufacturers a one-year extension in meeting the 1975 emission standards for pollutants, but to establish relatively stringent interim standards for 1975. This decision required the auto makers, like General Motors, Ford, and Chrysler, to use catalyst systems, mufflerlike devices in the exhaust system that convert polluting gases into less harmful vapors. The car makers argued that such major changes in engine design would be very costly and risky, and have tried to show that less stringent standards should be imposed. Both the Environmental Protection Agency and the auto companies relied on economic evidence and opinion in arguing their sides of this important question.

In the Congress, too, economics plays a major role. Economists are frequent witnesses before congressional committees, staff members for the committees, and advisers to individual congressmen and senators. Many congressional committees focus

[3] *Business Week*, April 14, 1973, p. 26.

largely on economic matters. For example, some, including the powerful Ways and Means Committee of the House of Representatives, deal with taxes. In recent years, tax reform has been a hot subject, as the public has clamored for the reduction of various loopholes in the tax laws, such as the oil depletion allowance, a boon to the petroleum industry. These loopholes frequently favor the rich at the expense of the poor. The Congress also decides how much the government will spend each year on various programs. There is frequently considerable politicking over the size and distribution of government expenditures. For example, in 1973 many congressmen fought hard against President Nixon's attempt to keep a tight lid on government spending, and there was considerable debate over the adequacy of the amounts allotted for antipoverty, health, and educational programs.

Finally, perhaps the most dramatic evidence of the importance of economics in the formulation of public policy is provided during presidential elections, when each candidate—with his or her own cadre of economic advisers supplying ideas and reports—stakes out a position on the major economic issues of the day. This position can be of crucial importance in determining victory or defeat, and you, the citizen, must know some economics to understand whether a candidate is talking sense or nonsense (or merely evading an issue). For example, if a candidate promises to increase government expenditures, lower taxes, and reduce the federal deficit, you can be pretty certain that he is talking through his hat. This may not be obvious now, but it should be later on.

The Role of Economics in Private Decision Making

Not all economic problems affect all, or a major part, of our society: some affect a particular individual, household, or firm, and are largely a matter of private decision making. Because these problems tend to be narrow and localized, they are sometimes viewed as less important or interesting than those involving public policy. But this is not the case. If individuals, households, and firms do a reasonably good job of solving their own problems, many social problems are solved automatically. Moreover, most of us spend most of our lives wrestling with these narrower questions. Thus, we all have an interest in learning how to cope better with them.

Economics and economists play an extremely important role in private decision making. Their role in the decision-making process in business firms is particularly great, since many of the nation's business executives have studied economics in college or in postgraduate programs, and many of the nation's larger corporations hire professional economists to forecast their sales, reduce their costs, increase their efficiency, negotiate with labor and government, and carry out a host of other tasks. Judging from the fancy salaries business economists are paid, the firms seem to think they can deliver the goods; and in fact the available evidence seems to indicate that they do provide important guidance to firms in many areas of their operations.

As an illustration, consider the Magnavox Company, a major manufacturer of television sets. In 1971, Magnavox's president, Robert Platt, decided to move slowly in converting Magnavox's TV sets from electron tubes to all solid-state sets, because he did not believe that the solid-state sets would catch on quickly with the public, and because he wanted to wait until an improved picture tube was available in 1973 before making the transition. This was a mistake. Consumers rushed to buy the solid-state sets, and Magnavox's sales fell to $226 million in 1972, down 36 percent from their peak in 1968. Economics is concerned with decisions of this sort, and although it cannot insure success or prevent mistakes, it can shed important light on the way such decisions should be made.

In addition, economics is essential to firms in their dealings with the government. For example, IBM, the huge producer of electronic computers and other business machines, has been charged with violation of the antitrust laws. In 1972 the

Justice Department accused IBM of monopolizing the market for general-purpose electronic computers and employing its "market power" to maintain its dominance. The outcome of the case will determine the shape of the computer industry for years to come, as well as the health and vitality of IBM. IBM's economists have been trying to punch holes in the government's case, just as the government's economists have been trying to strengthen it. To understand what this and similar cases are all about, and to argue the pros and cons, economics is essential.

Finally, economics and economists influence the decision making of households as well as firms. Few households—other, perhaps, than the Rockefellers and the Gettys—can afford to hire their own professional economist, but this does not mean that many households do not receive and use a considerable amount of economic advice. On the contrary, most households take magazines and newspapers that contain a great deal of economic information. *The Wall Street Journal* is packed with it; so are the financial pages of the *New York Times* and other leading newspapers. Even a general news magazine like *Time* now has a board of economic advisers—and puts an economist on its cover from time to time. Based on information provided in such publications, households can make more informed decisions on their investments and expenditures. Through this channel, among others, economics can play a major role in their decision making.

Economics: A Social Science

In previous sections, we have tried to indicate the practical importance of economics. But economics is much more than a bag of techniques for solving practical problems. *Like any other natural or social science, it is concerned with explaining and predicting observed phenomena, whether or not these explanations and predictions have any immediate practical application.* One need only look at some of the books economists write for each other—books bristling with complicated mathematical formulas and highly theoretical arguments—to realize that not all economics is a search for immediate answers to the world's ailments. Instead, many fields of economics pursue abstract truth, immediately useful or not.

Thus much economic research is directed at questions like these: what determines the level of national output? (Why did the total amount of goods and services produced in the United States plummet by about 30 percent between 1929 and 1933?) What determines the price of various commodities? (Why are lamb chops more expensive than hot dogs?) What determines the overall price level? (Why is the average level of prices so much higher now than it was 40 years ago?) What determines how much a worker makes? (Why are brain surgeons paid more than pipefitters?) What determines the rate of increase of per capita output? (Why has Japan's per capita output increased so much more rapidly than other industrialized countries' in recent years?) What determines how a consumer allocates his or her income among various commodities? (How will an increase in the price of honeydew melons influence the quantity you buy?) What determines the goods a country exports and those it imports? (Why do we export electronic computers and import transistor radios?) What determines the value of foreign money? (Why was a British pound worth about $2.50 in 1973?)

As these questions and their parenthetical accompaniments stand, they are not in the form of practical problems. Yet a knowledge of the answers to these questions is obviously of interest and of value. In this respect, many branches of economics recall mathematics. Pure mathematics is not concerned with day-to-day affairs, but various branches of mathematics are very valuable in solving practical problems, and some knowledge of mathematics is indispensable for understanding the world around us and for professional and technical training. Or think of physics. Although many of its branches are rather far removed from practical application, a general knowledge of physics has proved necessary to solve many types of practical problems; and certain branches, like solid-state physics, have had enormous practical impact on technology and industry.

The crucial consideration is that *economics is a science*. Like other sciences, it formulates and tests basic propositions that can be used to predict and explain the phenomena we observe in the world around us. This does not mean it cannot be useful; but because it is a science—a social science—economics goes beyond problem-solving *to deal with the basic principles and mechanisms that make economic systems work as they do.*

Finally, it is important to recognize that economics, although probably the most highly developed of the social sciences, is still far from being able to solve many of the pressing social issues we face. Nor will a knowledge of economics insure that your bank balance will soar. Economics can help solve important social problems, and it can help you come to better decisions, but it is no panacea. As you will see in subsequent chapters, there are many economic questions that are unsettled and debated by the experts. Consequently, one should not expect too much. But even Ruskin would probably admit that, to be valuable, a book need not provide reliable answers to all interesting questions.

Summary

Economics helps you to understand the nature and organization of our society (and other societies), the arguments underlying many of the great public issues of the day, and the operation and behavior of business firms and other economic decision-making units. It is no exaggeration to say that everyone must know something about economics to function responsibly and effectively as a citizen, administrator, worker, or consumer. According to one standard definition, economics is concerned with the way resources are allocated among alternative uses to satisfy human wants. Perhaps the best way to become acquainted with what economics is all about is to look at some of the problems it can help solve. Some of these are matters of public policy, whereas others concern private decisions.

Seven representative problems that economics deals with are: (1) What determines the extent of unemployment, and what can be done to reduce it? (2) Why should we expect competition among firms to produce socially desirable effects? (3) Why does poverty exist, and what can be done to abolish it? (4) What causes environmental pollution, and how can we reduce it to the proper levels? (5) How do the economic systems of the Communist nations work, and how does their economic performance stack up against ours? (6) How should a firm decide what to produce, how much to produce, and how to produce it? (7) What factors are responsible for our energy problems, and how can these problems be solved? This is only a sample—and a very small sample at that—of the questions to which economics relates. Many more will be discussed in subsequent chapters.

Although economics plays an important role in helping to solve basic social and private problems, you should not jump to the conclusion that economics is wholly a bag of techniques designed to solve practical problems; this is far from the case. Economics—like any natural or social science—is concerned with explaining and predicting observed phenomena, whether or not these explanations or predictions have any immediate application to practical problems. Also, it is important to recognize that, although economics can help solve social and private problems, it is no panacea. Nor is economics able to answer every important question about the workings of the economic system. As we shall see, our understanding of some questions is far from adequate. Nonetheless, a knowledge of economics is very useful and important in understanding the world around us.

CONCEPTS FOR REVIEW

Economics
Unemployment
Inflation
Forecasting
Choice
Government regulation
Poverty
Pollution
Planned economy
Interdependence

QUESTIONS FOR DISCUSSION AND REVIEW

1. According to Charles Schultze, "Modern economics can and has successfully prescribed the means of preventing large-scale unemployment without bringing on major inflation." What does this statement mean? Is it a matter worth worrying about?

2. According to Robert Heilbroner, "Relevance is a word that makes professors of economics wince these days." Is economics relevant to the major social issues and private problems of the day? Why or why not?

3. In Communist nations, about all of the factories, mines, and equipment are publicly owned. True or False?

4. At present, yearly income per capita in the United States is about:
   a. $2,000. b. $4,000. c. $6,000. d. $10,000.

CHAPTER 2

Economic Analysis: Models and Measurement

As a formal field of study, economics is a Johnny-come-lately. Copernicus paved the way for modern astronomy 400 years ago, and Newton started his revolution in physics in the seventeenth century. By contrast, modern economics is generally said to have begun in 1776, the same year as the American Revolution, with the publication of Adam Smith's *The Wealth of Nations,* and to have developed into a science only a century or so ago. But despite its relative youth, economics has influenced generations of statesmen, philosophers, and ordinary citizens, and played a significant role in shaping our society today. To understand the great ideas that underlie important parts of our civilization and to appreciate great segments of our intellectual heritage, you must understand some economics.

Apart from its value as an intellectual discipline, economics provides keys that help to interpret the broad sweep of the world's history. Economic forces have strongly influenced the course of human events. It would be a gross oversimplification to argue that taxes levied by the British on the American colonies were the sole cause of the American Revolution; yet the movement for independence cannot be understood without some knowledge of the economic ties of the colonies to the mother country. Few historians would call the triumph of Nazism in the 1930s solely a consequence of raging inflation; yet Hitler used the economic plight of Germany as a lever in his rise to power.

In 1960, John F. Kennedy's pledge "to get the economy moving ahead" scored effectively at the political box office. In 1972, Richard Nixon's campaign appealed to the majority of voters who, rightly or wrongly, seemed to mistrust the economic proposals of his opponent, Senator George McGovern. It is safe to say that many elections have turned on economic issues, that many wars have resulted from economic causes, and that many revolutions have occurred because of economic discontent. Of course, economics is only one key to history; political, social, religious, and cultural factors are extremely important too. But to understand much about history—either the history of ideas or the history of events—you need to know something about economics.

Since economic factors are closely intertwined with social, psychological, and political factors, it is worth pointing out that there is no well-defined border between economics and the other social sciences—sociology, anthropology, psychology, and political science. To understand many problems in society, one must consider the sociological and political, as well as economic angles. For example, noneconomic factors are important in explaining why some countries are richer than others. Even in solving narrower problems, such as why consumers buy a particular product, psychological as well as economic factors must be considered. Thus, the economist must continually keep abreast of the advances made in other fields, since they can help him solve his own problems. Conversely, political scientists, psychologists, and other social scientists can often use economic techniques in their work. Just as such cross-fertilization of disciplines is mutually helpful to professionals, so you too should relate what you learn in economics to your knowledge of these other fields.

Adam Smith, Father of Modern Economics

As pointed out in the previous section, Adam Smith (1723–90) is often called the father of modern economics. Smith, who was one of the first scholars to understand many of the central mechanisms of a free, or unplanned, economy, lived in Great Britain at the time when our forefathers were fighting for their independence. They were tough days, in Great Britain and elsewhere. Of course, a small segment of society led rich lives in city drawing rooms or on country estates, but the great bulk of the population lived in abject poverty. To take one small example, in some coal mines, both men and women worked, often half-naked, for long hours; children worked in the mines too—and some seldom saw daylight for months. In the factory towns, as in the mines, the hours were long, and children often spent their early years at work. Shifts of 10 to 12 hours a day were not uncommon, and wages were very low.

Smith spent much of his life as professor of moral philosophy at the University of Glasgow in Scotland. He was a popular lecturer and a very distinguished author—as well as one of the most absent-minded men of his (or any other) day. In 1759, he published *The Theory of Moral Sentiments,* which established him as one of Britain's foremost philosophers, but this was not the book for which he is famous today. His masterpiece, published in 1776 (while the American colonists were brewing rebellion), was *The Wealth of Nations,*[1] a long, encyclopedic book 12 years in the writing. It was not an instant success, but the laurels it eventually won undoubtedly compensated for its early neglect. It is unquestionably one of the most influential books ever written.

[1] Adam Smith, *The Wealth of Nations,* New York: Modern Library, 1937.

Adam Smith
on the "Invisible Hand" and Specialization

It is only for the sake of profit that any man employs [his] capital in the support of industry, and he will always, therefore, endeavor to employ it in the support of that industry of which the produce is likely to be of the greatest value, or to exchange for the greatest quantity either of money or of other goods. But the annual revenue of every society is always precisely equal to the exchangeable value of the whole annual produce of its industry, or rather is precisely the same thing with that exchangeable value. As every individual, therefore, endeavors as much as he can both to employ his capital in the support of domestic industry, and so to direct that industry that its produce may be of the greatest value, every individual necessarily labors to render the annual revenue of the society as great as he can: He generally, indeed, neither intends to promote the public interest, nor knows how much he is promoting it.... He intends only his own security; and by directing that industry in such a manner as its produce may be of the greatest value, he intends only his own gain, and *he is in this, as in many other cases, led by an invisible hand to promote an end which was no part of his intention.* Nor is it always the worse for the society that it was no part of it. *By pursuing his own interest he frequently promotes that of the society more effectually than when he really intends to promote it.* I have never known much good done by those who affected to trade for the public good. It is an affectation, indeed, not very common among merchants, and very few words need be employed in dissuading them from it...

It is the maxim of every prudent master of a family, never to attempt to make at home what it will cost him more to make than to buy. The tailor does not attempt to make his own shoes, but buys them of the shoemaker. The shoemaker does not attempt to make his own clothes, but employs a tailor. The farmer attempts to make neither the one nor the other, but employs those different artificers. All of them find it for their interest to employ their whole industry in a way in which they have some advantage over their neighbors, and to purchase with a part of its produce, or with the price of a part of it, whatever else they have occasion for.

Adam Smith, *The Wealth of Nations,* London: George Routledge, 1900, p. 345. Originally published in 1776. (Italics added.)

Much of *The Wealth of Nations* seems trite today, because it has been absorbed so thoroughly into modern thought, but it was not trite when it was written. On the contrary, Smith's ideas were revolutionary. *He was among the first to describe how a free, competitive economy can function—without central planning or government interference—to allocate resources efficiently. He recognized the virtues of the "invisible hand" that leads the private interests of firms and individuals toward socially desirable ends, and he was properly suspicious of firms that are sheltered from competition, since he recognized the potentially undesirable effects on resource allocation.*

In addition, Smith—with the dire poverty of his times staring him in the face—was interested in the forces that determined the evolution of the economy—that is, the forces determining the rate of growth of average income per person. Although Smith did not approve of avarice, he felt that saving was good because it enabled society to invest in machinery and other forms of capital. Accumulating more and more capital would, according to Smith, allow output to grow. In addition, he emphasized the importance of increased specialization and division of labor in bringing about economic progress. Moreover, he recognized that the rate of population increase was an important determinant of a country's economic development.

All in all, Smith's views were relatively optimistic, in keeping with the intellectual climate of his time—the era of Voltaire, Diderot, Franklin, and Jefferson, the age of the Enlightenment, when men believed in rationality. Leave markets alone, said Smith, and beware of firms with too much economic power and government meddling. If this is done, there is no reason why considerable economic progress cannot be achieved.

How Successful Are Economics and Economists?

Economics has come a long way since Adam Smith. Due to the efforts of such great figures as David Ricardo, Thomas Malthus, John Stuart Mill, Alfred Marshall, and John Maynard Keynes, as well as the work of countless other talented people, our understanding of the workings of the economic system has improved continually and significantly. But you may still have some doubts about how much of a science economics is, and whether it will give you valid, useful answers, or just ivory-tower concoctions with little or no applicability to the real world. These questions deserve an answer, although finding a concise one is not easy. One reason for the difficulty is that some aspects of economics are not as well understood as others, in part because less research has been done on them. Any discipline—physics, chemistry, or biology, for example—has such areas. Another reason is that all scientific predictions contain some error. Thus, the real question isn't whether economic predictions and propositions are accurate, but how accurate they are.

Even in this more meaningful form, the question is not easy to answer, however, since, as noted above, some economic predictions and propositions are much more accurate than others. For example, advances in economics and related disciplines in the postwar period have allowed economists to figure out more efficient ways for firms to run many aspects of their operations. Linear programming and related economic techniques have been applied to petroleum refineries, for example, to determine the minimum-cost blend of gasoline stocks and the most profitable outputs of regular and premium gasoline, enabling firms to increase their profits substantially. Short-range forecasting of changes in business conditions is another area where economics has proved very useful. Such forecasts are used by the government, as well as a host of business firms, to guide major decisions involving billions of dollars.

On the other hand, economic knowledge in other areas is very limited. For example, economists are still uncertain about many effects of the government's monetary and fiscal policies. Most economists believe that both *monetary policy* (the government's policy concerning the money supply and interest rates) and *fiscal policy* (the government's policy concerning spending and taxes) play an important role in determining the size of national output, the extent of unemployment, and the rate of inflation. But an influential minority of the economics profession believes monetary policy to be far more important than fiscal policy, and the available evidence is too weak to show conclusively whether they are right or wrong. Our knowledge of the modern process of inflation is also limited. This the Nixon administration found out in the late 1960s when it tried to control the inflation occurring then. The standard remedies it applied did not work as many distinguished economists predicted they would.

However, even though economic knowledge in some areas is much more limited than we would like, you should recognize this important fact: *judging from all available evidence, a knowledge of economics will enable you to solve economic problems better than you would without it. Even though economic predictions and propositions are not always very precise, they tend to work better than predictions and propositions not based on economics.* And this is really the crucial consideration.

One important signal that economics has become a full-fledged science is the establishment in 1969 of a Nobel Prize in economics. The beginning of these awards was an indication that economics was the first of the social sciences to "arrive." The first Nobel Prizes went to Professors Ragnar Frisch of Norway and Jan Tinbergen of Holland. Paul Samuelson, Simon Kuznets, Kenneth Arrow, and Wassily Leontief of the United States, as well as England's Sir John Hicks, received subsequent prizes. All these scholars have contributed greatly to economics, but each in a quite different way: Samuelson, Arrow, and Hicks have been responsible primarily for theoretical advances, while Kuznets has done basic empirical work, and Frisch, Tinbergen, and Leontief have pioneered in the blending of theoretical and statistical techniques. Like any science, economics requires advances of many types —theoretical, empirical, statistical—to develop and flourish.

Another clear signal that economics has become a useful science is the very high salaries economists pull down in industry and government. Years ago, the taunt may have been: "If you're so smart, why aren't you rich?" Today the reply could be: "Those economists who are interested in making money seem to be doing very well indeed!" For example, Pierre Rinfret, an economic consultant and adviser to President Nixon, has an income in excess of $150,000 per year; and Arthur Okun, chairman of President Johnson's Council of Economic Advisers, reportedly said that it would not be difficult for him to make twice as much. Of course, this does not mean that most economists in universities are making loads of money. Like other academic scientists, they are willing to earn less than they could in industry or government in order to enjoy the freedom to do research and teach. But if an economist wants to make lots of money, he certainly has the opportunity.

Model Building and the Methodology of Economics

By now, you may think it worthwhile to devote a little time to economics, but you still don't know anything about how economists approach their subject or the methods they use. To complete this chapter, we will provide a general description of the methodology of economics. Like other types of scientific analysis, economics is based on the formulation of ***models.*** *A model is a theory. It is composed of a number of assumptions from which conclusions—or predictions—are deduced.* If an astronomer wants to formulate a model of the solar system, he might represent each planet by a point in space and assume that each would change position in accord with certain mathematical equations. Based on this model, he might predict when an eclipse would occur, or estimate the probability of a planetary collision. The economist proceeds along similar lines when he sets forth a model of economic behavior.

There are several important aspects of models. First, *to be useful, a model must in general simplify and abstract from the real situation.* The assumptions made by a model need not be exact replicas of reality. If they were, the model would be too complicated to use. The basic reason for using a model is that the real world is so complex that masses of detail often obscure underlying patterns. The economist faces the familiar problem of seeing the forest, as distinct from just the trees. Other scientists must do the same; physicists work with simplified models of atoms, just as economists work with simplified models of markets. However, this does not mean that *all* models are good or useful. A model may be so oversimplified and distorted that it is utterly useless. The trick is to construct a model so that irrelevant and unimportant considerations and variables are neglected, but the major factors —those that seriously affect the phenomena the model is designed to predict—are included.

Second, the purpose of a model is to make predictions about the real world, and in many respects the most important test of a model is how well it predicts. In this sense, a model that predicts the price of copper within plus or minus $.01 a pound is better than a model that predicts it within plus or minus $.02 a pound. Of course, this does not mean that a model is useless if it cannot predict very accurately. We do not always need a very accurate prediction. For example, a road map is a model that can be used to make predictions about the route a driver should take to get to a particular destination. Sometimes, a very crude map is good enough to get you where you want to go, but such a map would not, for instance, serve the hiker who needs to know the characteristics of the terrain through which he plans to walk. How detailed a map you need depends on where you are going and how you want to get there.

Third, *if one wants to predict the outcome of a particular event, he will be forced to use the model that predicts best, even if this model does not predict very well.* The choice is not between a model and no model; it is between one model and another. After all, if one must make a forecast, he will use the most accurate device available—and any such device is a model of some sort. Consequently, when economists make simplifying assumptions and derive conclusions that are only approximately true, it is somewhat beside the point to complain that the assumptions are simpler than reality or that the predictions are not always accurate. This may be true, but if the predictions based on the economists' model are better than those obtained on the basis of other models, their model must, and will, be used until something better comes along. Thus, if a model can predict the price of copper to within plus or minus $.01 per pound, and no other model can do better, this model will be used even if those interested in the predictions bewail the model's limitations and wish it could be improved.

Economic Measurement

To utilize and test economic models, economists need facts of many kinds. As Lord William Beveridge said almost 40 years ago, "There can be no science of society until the facts about society are available . . . It matters little how wrong we are with our existing theories, if we are honest and careful with our observations." As economics has become more of a science, more and more economists have spent more and more time digging out the facts and seeing what their implications are. Each economic model yields predictions, and to determine whether these predictions are accurate enough to be worth anything, economists must continually collect data to see how accurate the predictions are. For example, if a model predicts that the price of copper should be $.03 a pound higher in 1974 than in 1973, it is important to determine what price change really occurred, and how close the model's predictions were to reality.

At the outset, note that, to a very large extent, economics is not an experimental, or laboratory, science. In other words, economists, unlike physicists, chemists, or biologists, cannot generally carry out experiments under carefully controlled conditions. Consequently, they usually cannot study the effects of varying one factor, while holding constant other factors that may influence the outcome. Such controlled experiments are common in the natural sciences and in technology. For example, a controlled experiment might be performed in agriculture to learn the effect of various amounts of fertilizer on the amount of wheat produced on an acre of land. A sample of plots of ground might be planted with wheat, the amount of fertilizer varying from plot to plot. Then the yield obtained from each plot might be related to the amount of fertilizer used on that plot.

Since controlled experimentation of this sort is often, but not always, impossible in economics, economists must rely on data generated by the economic system. To test a certain model of consumer behavior, an economist may set out to estimate the effect of a household's income on the amount of money it spends per year on clothing. To make such an estimate, the economist cannot perform an experiment in which he varies the income of a household and sees the effect on its clothing expenditures. Instead, he must gather data concerning the incomes and clothing expenditures of a large number of households, and study the relationship between them. The relationship he finds may, for example, resemble that shown in Figure 2.1: The line *AA′* represents an average relationship between household income and household clothing expenditure. Each family is represented by a dot. Clearly, the relationship, *AA′* does not fit all families exactly, since all the points do not fall on the line. *AA′* does, however, give the average clothing expenditure for each level of income: it is an average relationship. Most economic relationships are like *AA′* in the sense that they are relationships that hold on the average, but that do not fit every case exactly.

Based on the study of relationships of this sort, economists determine how well various models fit

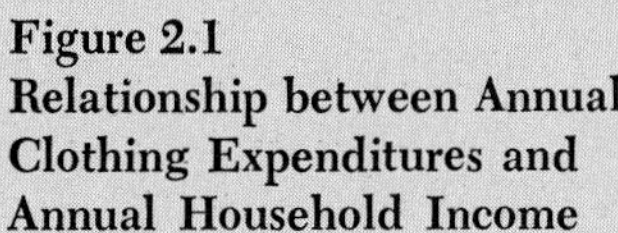

Figure 2.1
Relationship between Annual Clothing Expenditures and Annual Household Income

The line *AA′* represents an average relationship. Each family is a dot. Clearly, *AA′* does not fit all families exactly, since all the points do not fall on the line. *AA′* does give average clothing expenditure for each income level.

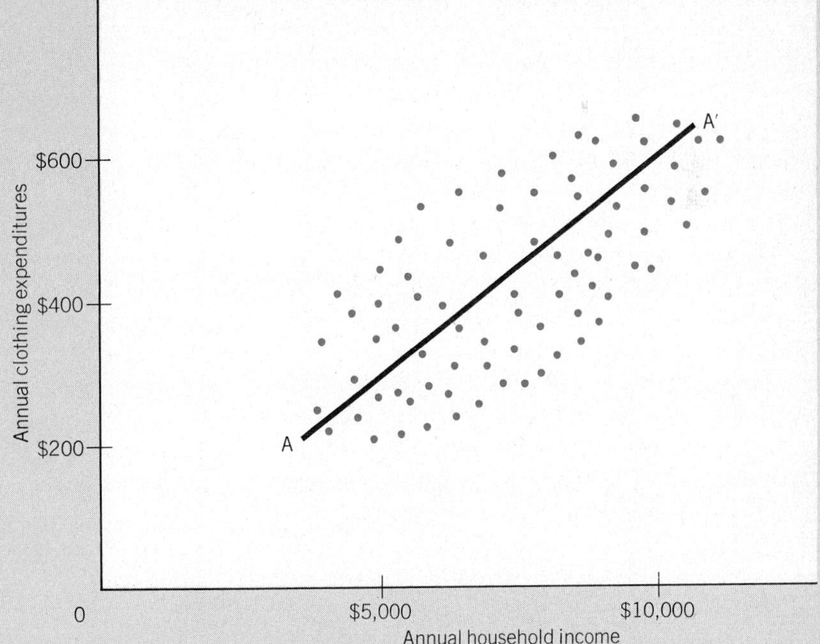

reality. In other words, they perform statistical tests to see whether a particular model is satisfactory. Two types of error can be made: they can reject a satisfactory model, or they can accept an unsatisfactory one. Which of these errors is more important will depend, of course, on the costs involved. For example, if the cost of accepting an unsatisfactory model is low, while the cost of rejecting a satisfactory model is high, then one should worry more about the latter type of error than the former. Using standard statistical methods, economists formulate their tests so that the probability that they will commit each type of error is roughly commensurate with the costs. Generally, it is impossible to eliminate completely the probability of error; the costs of doing so would be prohibitive.

Measurements like those in Figure 2.1 enable economists to ***quantify*** their models: in other words, they enable them to construct models that predict *how much* effect one variable has on another. For example, economists could be content with a model that predicts that higher household income results in higher household clothing expenditures; but this model would not be interesting or useful, since you don't need an economist to tell you that. A more valuable model is one that is quantitative, that predicts *how much* clothing expenditure will increase if household income increases by a certain amount. A model of this sort might predict that clothing expenditures tend to increase by $60 when income increases by $1,000. Judging by Figure 2.1, such a model would be reasonably accurate, at least for households with incomes between $5,000 and $10,000 per year. Such quantitative models, tested against data like those in Figure 2.1, can be extremely valuable to firms that sell clothing and related products, to government agencies concerned with consumer expenditures, and to economists and other social scientists interested in consumer behavior.[2]

[2] It is worth noting that, although it is useful to see how well a model would have fit the historical facts, this is no substitute for seeing how well it will predict the future. As a distinguished mentor of mine once observed, "It's a darned poor person who can't predict the past."

Simple Economic Models: A Case Study

To illustrate the nature and practical importance of economic models, consider the situation faced by the Boston and Maine Railroad in the early 1960s. The Boston and Maine wanted to discontinue its unprofitable railroad passenger commuter service into Boston. According to the railroad, the revenues it obtained from its commuter operations did not and could not meet the costs of providing the service. However, the Mass Transportation Commission of Massachusetts was not at all sure that such service had to be unprofitable for the Boston and Maine. The commission thought that lowering the price of commuter tickets might increase the service's profitability. This issue was of considerable importance both to the railroad and to Boston commuters.

To understand the Commission's view, we need the concept of a demand curve. Assuming that the incomes and tastes of the Boston commuting public, as well as the cost of commuting by alternative means of transportation, remain constant, it is extremely likely that the number of commuter tickets sold by the Boston and Maine will be inversely related to the price it charges for a ticket. In other words, holding constant these other factors, the lower the price, the greater the quantity of tickets sold. *This relationship between price and quantity of tickets sold can be represented graphically by a* ***demand curve,*** *which shows the number of tickets that will be sold at each price.*

The Commission suspected that the demand curve might be shaped like *BB′* in Figure 2.2, in which case the quantity of tickets sold would increase very substantially in response to a price cut. If *BB′* is the demand curve, and if the price of a ticket is reduced from $1 to $.75, the quantity of tickets sold per day increases from 1 million to 2 million, with the result that the railroad's total revenue from suburban passenger service increases from $1 million per day (if the ticket price is $1)

Figure 2.2
Demand Curve for Commuter Tickets, the Commission's View and the Skeptics' View

The commission suspected the demand curve might be *BB'*; the skeptics thought it might be *AA'*.

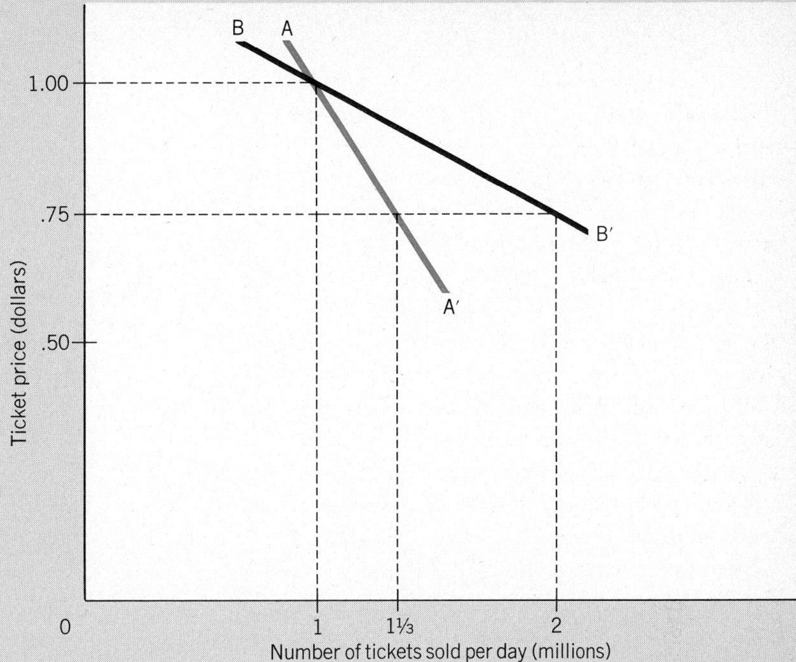

to $1.5 million per day (if the ticket price is $.75).[3] Since the extra $500,000 per day in revenue is greater than the extra cost of carrying the extra million passengers per day, such a price reduction would increase the railroad's profits. Indeed, according to the Commission, it might increase the Boston and Maine's profits enough to push its suburban passenger service into the black.

On the other hand, skeptics had a different model of the situation. According to their model, the demand curve was shaped like *AA'* in Figure 2.2, in which case the quantity of tickets sold does not increase very much in response to price cuts. For example, if the price of a ticket is reduced from $1 to $.75, the quantity of tickets sold per day increases only from 1 million to 1⅓ million, with the result that the total revenues of the railroad remain constant at $1 million per day. Since it will cost the railroad more to transport 1⅓ million people than 1 million people per day, it follows that the railroad will make less money by reducing the price of a ticket. Thus, according to the skeptics, a price cut of this sort would not make the Boston and Maine's suburban passenger service profitable. On the contrary, it would make it more unprofitable.

Which model was correct, the Commission's or the skeptics'? As in any science, a question of this sort must be answered by an appeal to facts. Measurements must be made, and data gathered to shed light on the shape of this demand curve. Once such data are in hand, statistical tests can be carried out to see which model is closer to reality. The Commission asked the Boston and Maine to experiment with a reduction in ticket prices to see its effect on the quantity of tickets sold. This experiment, made in 1963, indicated

[3] The total revenue equals 1 million tickets times $1 when the price is $1, and 2 million tickets times 75 cents when the price is 75 cents. Thus, it is $1 million in the former case and $1.5 million in the latter. Of course, the demand curves in Figure 2.2 (and the other numbers in this example) are hypothetical, but they illustrate the essential point.

that the skeptics' model was more nearly correct than the Commission's, and the railroad continued with its petition to terminate commuter passenger service when the experiment ended. However, public subsidies eventually were instituted to keep the service from terminating.

The models used in the Boston and Maine case were very simple, relative to most others employed by economists. All economic models are not this straightforward. Moreover, in this brief sketch we cannot do justice to all the subtleties and nuances involved in interpreting and testing these models: there are lots of problems and pitfalls. Yet, even so, this case study is a useful introduction to the construction and use of economic models.

The Use of Economic Models: Another Case Study

Turning to more complicated economic models, let's look at how such models were used by the Kennedy administration in the early 1960s to reduce unemployment and stimulate economic growth. When the Kennedy administration took office in 1961, it was confronted with a relatively high unemployment rate (about 7 percent of the labor force was unemployed in mid-1961), and a widespread feeling that the United States was not increasing its average income per person as fast as it should. These two problems—unemployment and inadequate economic growth—were regarded as among the most important ones facing the new administration.

Decades of research by many economists all over the world had produced models that indicated the factors influencing the unemployment rate, as well as the factors influencing the rate of growth of average income per person. Thus, when the Kennedy administration took office, it could draw on some reasonably well-formulated economic models to help in the framing of its policies. The economists advising the president and the Congress did not have to make up entirely new models to describe the phenomena they were interested in. Models already existed. These models indicated a number of ways in which the government could reduce the unemployment rate and increase the rate of growth of per capita income. One such way was to reduce taxes. Having made its own evaluation of the advantages and disadvantages of each approach, the Kennedy administration decided to press for the tax cut. It also proposed a variety of policies to increase the nation's investment in research and development, education, and plant and equipment, policies which, according to these models, would increase the rate of growth of per capita income.

Led by economists like Walter W. Heller, Chairman of President Kennedy's Council of Economic Advisers, the administration argued strongly for the adoption of the tax cut and other policies; and in 1964, the tax cut was passed by Congress. Without question, modern economics—and the reasonably sophisticated models at hand—played an important role in the formulation and passage of these measures. And most important of all, the measures seemed to work. As the models predicted, unemployment fell and the rate of growth of per capita income increased. Of course, the models used by Heller and his colleagues may have been wrong; perhaps unemployment fell and the growth rate increased for reasons other than the measures adopted by the government. One cannot rule out this possibility, but it seems unlikely.[4]

Values and Decisions

Economists make an important distinction between positive economics and normative economics. ***Positive economics*** *contains descriptive statements, propositions, and predictions about the world.* For

[4] However, it should be noted that some prominent economists—the monetarists—feel that the models used by Heller and his colleagues were wrong, at least in part. To understand this issue, you need to know more about fiscal and monetary policy, discussed in Chapters 10 and 14.

Arthur Okun and George Shultz

As any baseball player who ever took a third strike knows, many distinctions are clearer in theory than they appear in practice. The distinction between positive and normative economics is no exception.

The first Nixon victory in 1968 formally ended the reign of the liberal economists in Washington. Arthur Okun, chairman of the Council of Economic Advisers and a former Yale professor, prepared a final Economic Report for Lyndon Johnson and packed his bags. His final year had been brightened by passage of a tax surcharge, a measure designed to give the economy a strong dose of anti-inflationary medicine; yet the inflationary fever persisted.

ARTHUR OKUN

GEORGE SHULTZ

Among the economists who came to Washington with the Nixon administration was George Shultz, former dean of the Business School of the University of Chicago and the new Secretary of Labor. A staunch advocate of government restraint in economic policy making, Shultz ultimately was to become Secretary of the Treasury and head of the Office of Management and the Budget. From the start, he was a chief administration spokesman on economic affairs.

Within a year, Okun and Shultz locked verbal horns over the proper course of national economic policy: Okun became an avid advocate of wage and price policies for curbing the post-Vietnam inflation; Shultz the public defender of the original administration policy of keeping the government's hands off prices and wages. Why this disagreement between two distinguished economists? In part, the disagreement was one over values. Okun, one of the most steadfastly liberal Keynesians, regarded unemployment of 6 percent falling upon the minorities and the young as a very heavy burden. He had no reservations about a massive government presence in the economy. Indeed, he worried that "the most serious consequence of the 1968–69 disappointment is that it [may] make economists lose their nerve." Shultz was more inclined to count the costs of inflation. He had declared himself skeptical of the federal government's ability to manage affairs better than private citizens and private business.

But it is worth noting that this disagreement on values was in part predicated on a disagreement as to facts. The two economists disagreed as to the nature of the markets to be controlled. Shultz looked at the American economy and tended to see thousands of competitive markets. Okun looked at the same economy and saw it in the grip of big business, like General Motors, on one side of the bargaining table, and big labor, like the Auto Workers and the Electrical Workers, on the other. Although there is considerable agreement among economists about most aspects of positive economics, there is by no means complete agreement. In part, the differences between these two distinguished economists stemmed from their different views of the way the economy works, interacting with their values, to produce different policy conclusions.

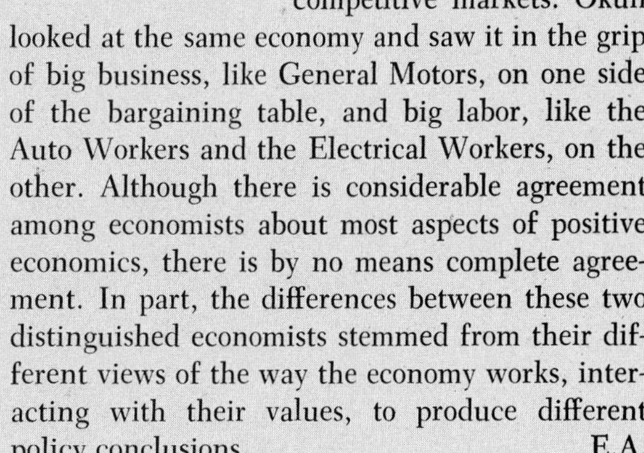

E.A.

instance, an economic model may predict that the price of copper will increase by a penny a pound if income per person in the United States rises by 10 percent; this is positive economics. Positive economics tells us only what will happen under certain circumstances. It says nothing about whether the results are good or bad—or about what we should do. ***Normative economics,*** *on the other hand, makes statements about what ought to be, or about what a person, organization, or nation ought to do.* For instance, a model might say that Chile should nationalize its copper industry and use the profits to reduce poverty; this is normative economics.

Clearly positive economics and normative economics must be treated differently. Positive economics is science in the ordinary sense of the word. Propositions in positive economics can be tested by an appeal to the facts. Needless to say, in a nonexperimental science like economics, it is sometimes difficult to get the facts you need to test particular propositions. For example, if income per person in the United States does not rise by 10 percent, it may be difficult to tell what the effect of such an increase would be on the price of copper. Moreover, even if per capita income does increase by this amount, it may be difficult to separate the effect of the increase in income per person on the price of copper from the effect of other factors. But nonetheless, we can, in principle, test propositions in positive economics by an appeal to the facts.

In normative economics, however, this is not the case. *In normative economics, the results you get depend on your values or preferences.* For example, if you believe that reducing unemployment is more important than maintaining the purchasing power of the dollar, you will get one answer to certain questions; whereas if you believe that maintaining the purchasing power of the dollar is more important than reducing unemployment, you are likely to get a different answer to the same questions. This is not at all strange. After all, if people desire different things (which is another way of saying that they have different values), they may well make different decisions and advocate different policies. It would be strange if they did not.

People sometimes make fun of economists because they disagree, and their differences are sometimes held up as evidence that economics is really not a science at all. In truth, of course, they prove nothing of the kind. *Because economists—like physicists, mathematicians, lawyers, and plumbers—differ in their preferences and values, they come to different conclusions when they enter the realm of normative economics.* Thus, liberal economists often differ from conservative economists in their conclusions on public policy, and the disagreements can be over means as well as ends. *However, there is very substantial agreement on most of the propositions of positive economics.* Of course, this does not mean that everything is settled, but the areas of disagreement are generally relatively narrow. And this, it should be noted, is the important thing, since the pure science of economics is positive economics.

This book will spend a lot of time on the principles of positive economics—the principles and propositions concerning the workings of the economic system about which practically all economists tend to agree. Also, normative economics will be treated as well, since we must discuss questions of policy—and all policy discussions involve individual preferences, not solely hard facts. In these discussions, we shall try to indicate how the conclusions depend on one's values. Then you can let your own values be your guide. The purpose of this book is not to convert you to a particular set of values. It is to teach you how to obtain better solutions to economic problems, whatever set of values you may have.

Methodological Hazards in Economics

There are lots of impediments to straight thinking in economics that are not present in other disciplines like chemistry or biology. To begin with, people have preconceptions about economic matters that they don't have about chemical or biological matters. Few people have a long-standing bias against two hydrogen atoms combining with an oxygen atom to form water, but some people grow up with the idea that profits are a bad thing or that unions are a social evil. These biases get in the way of objective analysis, because people tend to believe what they want to believe. If you want to learn any economics, you must respect facts, unpleasant though they may be at times.

Another hazard in economics is the use of loaded, emotional words. Unless you school yourself to look carefully at what words mean—and don't mean—you can be gulled by misleading terminology. For example, Marxists often refer to the exploitation of labor by capitalists, which sounds bad, since no one can be in favor of exploitation. But you must remember that labels can be misleading. What the Marxists call exploitation, most Western economists do not regard as exploitation at all.

Social scientists are often and justly accused of using unfamiliar words, or jargon, to describe common phenomena. Economists do not escape this charge. You would probably not refer to your checking account in a bank as a demand deposit: economists do. What is more, economists define some terms in a different way from the man on the street. You will find out that rent to the economist is not an amount paid each month for an apartment, but a payment for a resource that is fixed in supply. Of course, economists have a right to define terms as they please, but you can be confused if you assume that seemingly familiar terms mean what you think they mean.

Still another pitfall is to assume that, because one event follows another, the former event is caused by the latter. The Romans had a phrase for this kind of reasoning: *post hoc ergo propter hoc* (after this, therefore because of this). This fallacy occurs all the time. Consider the people who attributed a spell of bad weather that occurred after the first moon landing to the astronauts' trip to the moon. The bad weather followed the lunar trip—therefore it must have been caused by it. Needless to say, this sort of reasoning is treacherous indeed, since many events occur on the heels of other events without being caused by them. To jump to the conclusion that an event following another event is caused by the earlier event is clearly to court disaster.

Still another common pitfall to sound economic reasoning is the fallacy of composition. Some people assume that what is true of part of a system must be true for the whole system. This can be quite wrong. For example, it may be true that a farmer will gain from producing a larger crop. But it may not be true that farmers as a whole will gain if all produce a larger crop. Or consider another case: a business firm will go bankrupt by continuing to spend more than it takes in, but it does not follow that an entire nation will go bankrupt if its government spends more than it takes in. The fallacy of composition—that what is true of the part must be true of the whole—lies in wait for the unwary student of economics, and for the experienced economist too. Grievous errors can be avoided by keeping clear of this fallacy's clutches.

Summary

Economics—and economists—have played a significant role in shaping the present nature of society. A knowledge of economics is necessary to understand the history of human events, and the masterpieces of economics produced in the past are important segments of our intellectual heritage. The methodology used by economists is much the same as that used in any other kind of scientific analysis. The basic procedure is the formulation and testing of models. A model must in general simplify and abstract from the real world. Its purpose is to make predictions concerning phenomena in the real world, and in many respects the most important test of a model is how well it predicts these phenomena. One illustration of the construction and use of an economic model was the discussion concerning the Boston and Maine's decision to discontinue suburban passenger service. Another example of the use of economic models was the decision made by the Kennedy administration to press for a tax cut to reduce unemployment.

To test and quantify their models, economists gather data and utilize various statistical techniques. Economists often distinguish between positive economics and normative economics. Positive economics contains descriptive statements, propositions, and predictions about the world, whereas normative economics contains statements about what ought to be, or about what a person, organization, or nation ought to do. In normative economics, the results you get depend on your basic values and preferences; in positive economics, the results are testable, at least in principle, by an appeal to the facts.

CONCEPTS FOR REVIEW

Model
Measurement
Demand curve
Positive economics
Normative economics
Fallacy of composition

QUESTIONS FOR DISCUSSION AND REVIEW

1. Suppose that you wanted to construct a model to explain and predict the breakfast cereal that your father will choose tomorrow. What factors would you include? How well do you think you could predict?

2. Suppose that you were given the job of estimating the demand curve for commuter tickets in metropolitan Boston. How would you proceed? What sorts of difficulties would you anticipate?

3. There is almost complete agreement with regard to most of the propositions of normative economics. True or False?

4. To be useful a model must
   a. have assumptions that are close to exact replicas of reality.
   b. predict better than any other that is available.
   c. predict very accurately or it is useless.
   d. have few assumptions and be as simple as possible.

PART TWO

The Private Sector and the Public Sector: An Overview

CHAPTER 3

The American Economy: Our Mixed Capitalist System

The economy of the United States is the richest in the world. The typical American family has plenty of food, clothing, housing, appliances, and luxuries of many kinds, and the typical American worker is well-educated and well-trained. American agriculture is enormously efficient and productive, American industry is known the world over for its productivity, and American engineers and scientists are in the forefront of science and technology. Yet, despite these successes, the American economy faces serious problems. A substantial minority of our citizens live in what most Americans would regard as poverty. There are obvious and far-reaching problems of discrimination and urban decay. Industrial pollution literally brings tears to the eyes of some city dwellers, and a weekend exodus to the country may involve battling traffic bottlenecks only to reach lakes and ocean beaches contaminated by agricultural and industrial wastes. In the early 1970s, a rash of shortages broke out in several industries, including oil, paper, and lumber.

And in world markets, American firms were facing stiff competition from foreign producers.

As a first step toward understanding why we are so well off in some respects and so lacking in others, we need to understand how our economy works. Of course, this is a big task. Indeed, you could say that this whole book is devoted to discussing this subject. So we will not try to present a detailed picture of the operation of the American economy at this point. All we shall do now is give a preliminary sketch, a basic blueprint of some of the highlights. The details will be provided later, as they are needed.

The American Economy: Some Salient Facts

A good way to begin studying practically any subject is to get a few facts about it. The difference between wise men and fools is that the former respect and heed the facts whereas the latter reject or ignore them. Here are some salient facts about the American economy. First, it is huge. The United States contains over 200 million people, about 90 million of whom are in the labor force. Table 3.1 shows how large our population is, relative to other major industrialized nations. In addition, the American economy contains over 10 million business firms, and thousands of local and state governments, as well as the enormous federal government with its many departments and agencies. By practically any standard, ours is the biggest economic show on earth.

Table 3.1

Population, 1970, Selected Countries

Country	Population (millions of people)
United States	205
Soviet Union	243
Japan	103
France	51
United Kingdom	56
Italy	54
Sweden	8

Source: United Nations.

Second, the American economy is very rich and productive. In 1973, our income per capita was about $6,000 per year. In other words, if you take the total amount of income that Americans made that year and divide by the number of Americans in existence (including all ages), the result equals about $6,000. As shown in Table 3.2, this figure is higher than for any other country. Moreover, the United States produces an enormous amount of such basic products as steel, petroleum, chemicals, electric power, automobiles, electronic computers, and a myriad of other goods. For example, Tables 3.3–3.5 show that we lead the world in steel production, electric energy production, and computer production, three basic indices of industrial might.

Third, the American economy is based on freedom of choice. Consumers can buy what they like, and reject what they do not like; workers can take jobs when and where they please, and quit if they please; firms can produce whatever products they want to produce, and use whatever techniques they want to use. Of course, this freedom is not unlimited. For example, there are laws to prevent people and firms from engaging in antisocial dealings. Moreover, this freedom is not all it might be. For example, it is sometimes difficult for a firm to enter a market, or for a person to get a particular type of job. Yet relative to other countries, our economy is very free.

Fourth, the American economy is organized for the basic purpose of satisfying human wants. Human wants are the goods, services, and circumstances people desire. Wants vary greatly among individuals, and, for a given individual, they vary greatly over time. Some people like to ride horseback, others like to read. Some want to carouse

Table 3.2

Income Per Capita, 1973, Selected Countries

Country	Income per capita (dollars)
United States	6,000
Canada	4,900
Sweden	4,900
Germany	3,800
France	3,700
United Kingdom	2,700
Japan	2,600
Italy	2,100
Soviet Union	1,800
Brazil	500
India	100
China	100

These estimates are rough, because of problems in converting other currencies into dollars, and for other reasons. Nonetheless, they should provide reasonable indications of relative orders of magnitude.

Table 3.4

Electric Energy Production, Selected Countries, 1969

Country	Electric energy production (millions of kilowatt hours)
United States	1,553
Soviet Union	659
United Kingdom	222
Japan	306
Germany	211
Canada	190
France	132
Italy	106
China	50
India	55

Source: World Almanac.

Table 3.3

Steel Production, Selected Countries, 1970

Country	Steel production (million short tons)
United States	131
Belgium	14
Canada	12
China	19
France	26
Germany	50
Italy	19
Japan	103
Soviet Union	128
United Kingdom	31

Source: Statistical Abstract of the United States.

Table 3.5

Production of Electronic Computers, Selected Countries, 1965

Country	Production of computers ($ millions)
United States	3,200
France	240
Germany	200
United Kingdom	190
Italy	135
Sweden	8
Denmark	5

Source: Organization for Economic Cooperation and Development, 1969.

until 3 A.M., others follow Ben Franklin's maxim of early to bed, early to rise. An individual's desire for a particular good during a particular period of time is not infinite, but in the aggregate human wants seem to be insatiable. Besides the basic desires for food, shelter, and clothing, which must be fulfilled to some extent if the human organism is to maintain its existence, wants arise from cultural factors. To some extent, wants are encouraged and manufactured by advertising, social pressures, education, and emulation of other people.

Fifth, the American economy is rich in resources. Resources are the materials and services used to produce goods that can be used to satisfy wants. ***Economic resources*** are scarce, while ***free resources,*** such as air, are so abundant that they can be obtained without charge. The test of whether a resource is an economic resource or a free resource is price: economic resources command a nonzero price but free resources do not. Economists often classify economic resources into three categories: land, labor and capital. ***Land*** is a shorthand expression for natural resources. ***Labor*** is human effort, both physical and mental. ***Capital*** includes equipment, buildings, inventories, raw materials, and other nonhuman producible resources that contribute to the production, marketing, and distribution of goods and services. Relative to other countries, the United States is rich in all three of these types of resources.

Finally, the American economy is noted for its sophisticated and advanced technology. ***Technology*** is society's pool of knowledge concerning the industrial arts. It includes knowledge, needed in industry, of the principles of social and physical phenomena (such as the laws of motion and the properties of fluids); knowledge regarding the application of these principles to production (such as applying various aspects of genetic theory to the breeding of new plants); and knowledge regarding the day-to-day operation of productive processes (such as the rules of thumb of the skilled craftsman). Note that technology is different from the techniques in use, since not all that is known is likely to be in use. Also, technology is different from pure science, although the distinction is not very precise. Pure science is directed toward understanding, whereas technology is directed toward use. Table 3.6 shows that, according to data collected by the Organization for Economic Cooperation and Development, the United States has been responsible for a very large share of the major new processes and products introduced since World War II.

The Tasks of an Economic System

The statistics concerning the American economy make an impressive score card, but we cannot evaluate how well an economic system (or any system) is working unless we know what it is meant to do. Basically, there are four things that any economic system—*ours or any other*—must do. *First, it must determine the level and composition of society's output.* It must answer questions such as these: To what extent should society's resources be used to produce new destroyers and missiles? To what extent should they be used to produce sewage plants to reduce water pollution? To what extent should they be used to produce swimming pools for the rich? To what extent should they be used to produce low-cost housing for the poor? Pause for a moment to think about how important—and how vast—this function is. Most people simply take for granted that somehow it is decided what we as a society are going to produce, and far too few people really think about the social mechanisms that determine the answers to such questions.

Second, *an economic system must determine how each good and service is to be produced.* Given existing technology, a society's resources can be used in various ways. Should the skilled labor in Birmingham, Alabama be used to produce cotton or steel? Should a particular machine tool be used to produce aircraft or automobiles? The way questions of this sort are answered will determine the way each good and service is produced. In other words, it will determine which resources are used to produce which goods and services. If this func-

Table 3.6

Location of First Commercial Exploitation of 110 Significant Technological Innovations (New Products and Processes) Occurring since 1945

	Industry									
Country	Plastics	Metal working	Non-ferrous metals	Electric power	Computers	Instruments	Semi-conductors	Electronic consumer goods	Other	Total
United States	15	4	5	2	10	10	16	—	11	74
Belgium	—	1	—	—	—	—	—	—	—	1
France	—	1	—	—	1	—	—	—	—	2
Germany	3	3	1	—	1	3	—	—	3	14
Italy	2	—	1	—	—	—	—	—	—	3
Netherlands	—	—	—	—	—	—	—	—	—	—
Sweden	—	1	—	2	—	—	—	—	1	4
Switzerland	1	1	—	2	—	—	—	—	—	4
United Kingdom	1	4	2	1	2	2	1	—	5	18
Japan	—	—	—	—	—	1	—	2	1	4
Austria	—	1	—	—	—	—	—	—	—	1
Total[a]	17	12	9	7	14	16	17	2	16	

Source: Organization for Economic Cooperation and Development, 1970.
[a] The sum of the figures for individual countries does not necessarily equal the total number of innovations, since innovations sometimes originate in two or more countries at the same time.

tion is performed badly, society's resources are put to the wrong uses, resulting in less output than if this function is performed well.

Third, *an economic system must determine how the goods and services that are produced are to be distributed among the members of society.* In other words, how much of each type of good and service should each person receive? Should there be a considerable amount of income inequality, the rich receiving much more than the poor? Or should incomes be relatively equal? Take your own case: somehow or other, the economic system determines how much income you will receive. In our economic system, your income depends on your skills, the property you own, how hard you work, and prevailing prices, as we shall see in succeeding chapters. But in other economic systems, your income might depend on quite different factors. This function of the economic system has generated, and will continue to generate, heated controversy. Some people favor a relatively egalitarian society where the amount received by one family varies little from that received by another family of the same size. Other people favor a less egalitarian society where the amount a family or person receives varies a great deal. Few people favor a thoroughly egalitarian society, if for no other reason than that some differences in income are required to stimulate workers to do certain types of work.

Fourth, an economic system must maintain and provide for an adequate rate of growth of per capita income. The goal of economic growth is a relatively new one, there having been less emphasis on growth many years ago. Regardless of its newness, however, it has come to be regarded as an extremely important function, particularly in the less developed countries of Africa, Asia, and Latin America. There is very strong pressure in these countries for changes in technology, the adoption of superior techniques, increases in the stock of capital resources, and better and more extensive education and training of the labor force. These are viewed as some of the major ways to promote the growth of per capita income. In the industrialized nations, the goal of economic growth has become somewhat more controversial. Some observers claim that we have become rich enough, while others point out that since so many of the world 's people, here and abroad, are poor, it seems hard to believe that extra output would not be useful.

The Product Transformation Curve and the Determination of What Is Produced

In the previous chapter, we said that economists use models to throw light on economic problems. At this point, let's try our hand at constructing a simple model to illuminate the basic functions any economic system, ours included, must perform. You will recall that these functions are: (1) It must determine the level and composition of society's output. (2) It must determine how each good and service is to be produced. (3) It must determine how the goods and services that are produced are to be distributed among the members of society. (4) It must maintain and provide for an adequate rate of growth of per capita income.

To keep things simple, suppose that society produces only two goods, food and tractors. This, of course, is unrealistic, but, as we stressed in the previous chapter, a model does not have to be realistic to be useful. Here, by assuming that there are only two goods, we eliminate a lot of unnecessary complexity and lay bare the essentials. In addition, we suppose that society has at its disposal a certain amount of resources, and that this amount is fixed for the duration of the period in question. This assumption is quite realistic. So long as the period is relatively short, the amount of a society's resources is relatively fixed (except, of course, under unusual circumstances, such as if a country annexes additional land). Finally, we suppose as well that society's technology is fixed. So long as the period is relatively short, this assumption too is realistic.

Under these circumstances, it is possible to figure out the various amounts of food and tractors that society can produce. Let's begin with how many tractors society can produce if all resources are devoted to tractor production: According to Table 3.7, the answer is 15 million tractors. Next, let's consider the opposite extreme, where society devotes all its resources to food production: According to Table 3.7, it can produce 12 million tons of food in this case. Next, let's consider cases where both products are being produced: Such cases are represented by possibilities *B* to *F* in the table. Clearly the more of one good that is produced, the less of the other good can be produced. This is reasonable enough: to produce more of one good, resources must be taken away from the production of the other good,

Table 3.7

Alternative Combinations of Outputs of Food and Tractors That Can Be Produced

Possibility	Food (millions of tons)	Tractors (millions)
A	0	15
B	2	14
C	4	12
D	6	10
E	8	7
F	10	4
G	12	0

lessening the amount of the other good produced.

Figure 3.1 shows the various production possibilities society can attain. It is merely a different way of presenting the data in Table 3.7; the output of food is plotted on the horizontal axis and the output of tractors on the vertical axis. The curve in Figure 3.1, which shows the various combinations of output of food and tractors that society can produce, is called a ***product transformation curve.*** Economists are fond of inelegant labels of this sort: like Eliza Doolittle, heroine of *My Fair Lady* (and *Pygmalion,* in her earlier incarnation), economics is sometimes guilty of "cold-blooded murder of the English tongue." But so are other sciences. You just have to roll with the punches—and learn what these strange-sounding terms mean.

The product transformation curve is a useful indicator of the economic tasks facing any society. It shows the various production possibilities open to society. For example, in Figure 3.1, society can choose to produce 4 million tons of food and 12 million tractors (point *C*), or 6 million tons of food and 10 million tractors (point *D*), but it cannot choose to produce 6 million tons of food and 12 million tractors (point *H*). Point *H* is inaccessible with this society's resources and technology: Perhaps it will become accessible if the society's resources increase or if its technology improves, but for the present, point *H* is out of reach.

Since society must wind up somewhere on the product transformation curve, it is clear that *the first function of any economic system—to determine the level and composition of society's output—is really a problem of determining at what point along the product transformation curve society should be.* Should society choose point *A, B, C, D, E, F,* or *G*? In making this choice, one thing is obvious from the product transformation curve: *you cannot get more of one good without giving up some of the other good.* In other words, you cannot escape the problem of choice. So long as

Figure 3.1
Product Transformation Curve

This curve shows the various combinations of outputs that can be produced efficiently with given resources and technology. Point *H* is unattainable; point *K* is inefficient.

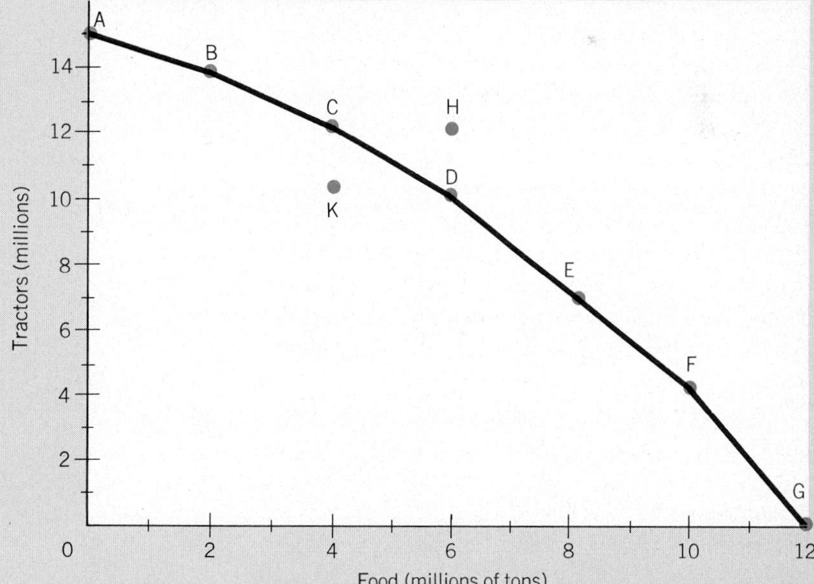

resources are limited and technology is less than magic, you must reckon with the fact that more of one thing means less of another. Once you see this, it is clear that more of anything always entails a cost—the cost being the reduction in something else. The old saw that you don't "get something for nothing" is hackneyed, but true, so long as resources are fully and efficiently utilized.

The Product Transformation Curve and the Determination of How Goods Are Produced

Let's turn now to the second basic function of any economic system: to determine how each good and service should be produced. In Table 3.7, we assumed implicitly that society's resources would be fully utilized and that the available technology would be applied in a way that would get the most out of the available resources. In other words, we assumed that the firms making food and tractors were as efficient as possible and that there was no unemployment of resources. But if there is widespread unemployment of people and machines, will society still be able to choose a point on the product transformation curve? Clearly, the answer is no. Since society is not using all of its resources, it will not be able to produce as much as if it used them all. Thus, *if there is less than full employment of resources, society will have to settle for points inside the product transformation curve.* For example, the best society may be able to do under these circumstances is to attain point K in Figure 3.1. Clearly, K is a less desirable point than C or D—but that is the price of unemployment.

Suppose, on the other hand, that there is full employment of resources but that firms are inefficient. Perhaps they promote relatives of the boss, regardless of their ability; perhaps the managers are lazy or not much interested in efficiency; or perhaps the workers like to take long coffee breaks and are unwilling to work hard. Whatever the reason, will society still be able to choose a point on the product transformation curve? Again, the answer is no. Since society is not getting as much as it could out of its resources, it will not be able to produce as much as it would if its resources were used efficiently. Thus, *if resources are used inefficiently, society will have to settle for points inside the product transformation curve.* Perhaps in these circumstances, too, the best society can do may be point K in Figure 3.1. This less desirable position is the price of inefficiency.

At this point, it should be obvious that our model at least partially answers the question of how each good and service should be produced. The answer is to *produce each good and service in such a way that you wind up on the product transformation curve, not on a point inside it.* Of course, this is easier said than done, but at least our model indicates a couple of villains to watch out for: unemployment of resources and inefficiency. When these villains are present, we can be sure that society is not on the product transformation curve. Also, the old saw is wrong and it is possible to "get something for nothing" when society is inside the product transformation curve. That is, society can increase the output of one good without reducing the output of another good in such a situation. Society need not give up anything—in the way of production of other goods—to increase the production of this good under these circumstances.

This simple model helps illuminate the sequence of events in various countries at the beginning of World War II. In certain countries, like the Soviet Union, the war effort meant a substantial decrease in the standard of living on the home front. Resources had to be diverted from the production of civilian goods to the production of military goods, and the war struck a severe blow at the living standards of the civilian population. In other countries, like the United States, it was possible to increase the production of military goods without making such a dent in the living standards of the civilian population. This happened because the United States at the beginning of World War II

Figure 3.2
Effect of Increased Production of War Goods at the Beginning of World War II

Because the United States was at a point inside its product transformation curve, we could increase our production of war goods without reducing production of civilian goods. Because the Russians were on their product transformation curve, they could increase their output of war goods only by reducing ouput of civilian goods.

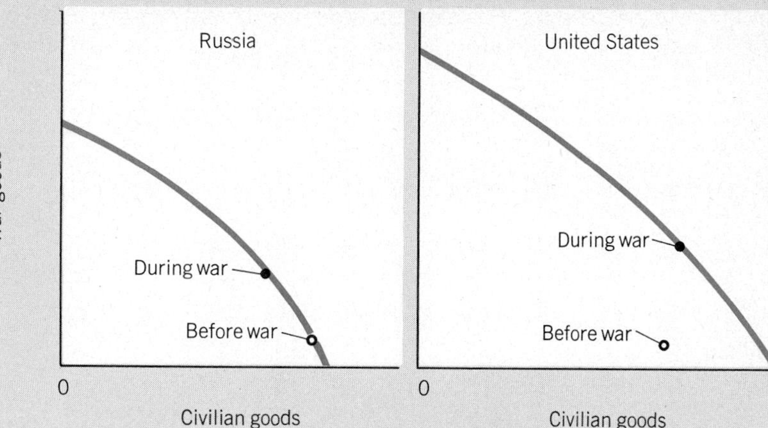

was still struggling to emerge from the Great Depression, and several million people were still unemployed. The same was not true in the Soviet Union. Thus, we could increase the production of both guns and butter, whereas they could not.

Suppose that we divide all goods into two classes: war goods and civilian goods. Then, as shown in Figure 3.2, *we were inside our product transformation curve at the beginning of the war, while the Russians were not.* Consequently, for the reasons discussed above, we could increase our production of war goods without reducing our production of civilian goods, while the Russians could not. (Note that in Figure 3.2, the two goods are war goods and civilian goods, not food and tractors.)

The Product Transformation Curve, Income Distribution, and Growth

Let's return now to the case where our economy produces food and tractors. The third basic function of any economic system is to distribute the goods and services that are produced among the members of society. Each point on the product transformation curve in Figure 3.1 represents society's total pie, but to deal with the third function, we must know how the pie is divided up among society's members. Since the product transformation curve does not tell us this, it cannot shed light on this third function.

Fortunately, the product transformation curve is of more use in analyzing the fourth basic function of any economic system: to maintain and provide for an adequate rate of growth of per capita income. Suppose that this society invests a considerable amount of its resources in developing improved processes and products. For example, it might establish agricultural experiment stations to improve farming techniques and industrial research laboratories to improve tractor designs. As shown in Figure 3.3, the product transformation curve will be pushed outward. This will be the result of improved technology, enabling more food and/or more tractors to be produced from the same amount of resources. Thus, one way for an economy to increase its output—and its per capita income—is to invest in research and development.

Another way is by devoting more of its resources to the production of capital goods rather than consumers' goods. ***Capital goods*** consist of plant and equipment that are used to make other goods; ***consumers' goods*** are items that consumers purchase

Figure 3.3
Effect of Improvement in Technology on Product Transformation Curve

An improvement in technology results in an outward shift of the product transformation curve.

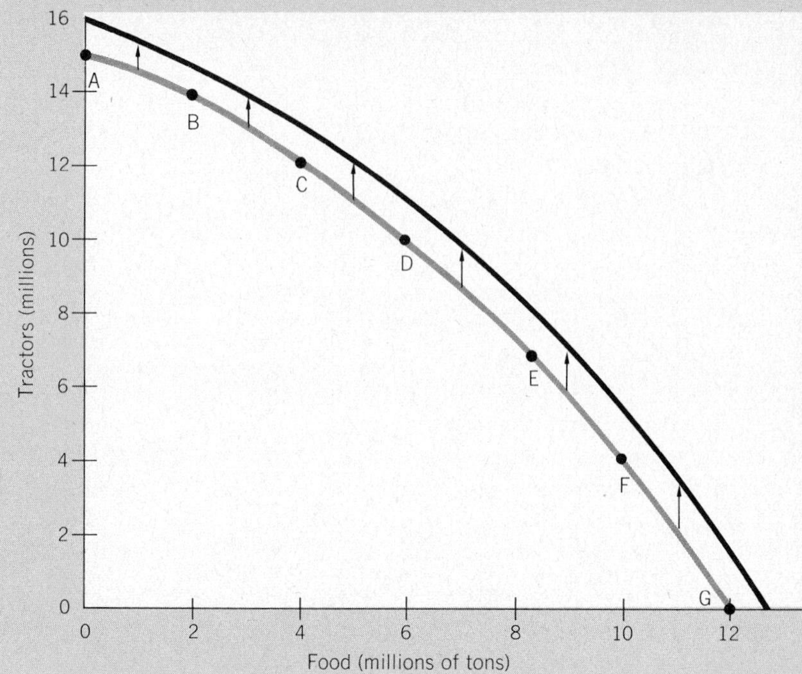

like clothing, food, and drink. Since capital goods are themselves resources, a society that chooses to produce lots of capital goods and few consumers' goods will push out its product transformation curve much farther than a society that chooses to produce lots of consumers' goods and few capital goods.

To illustrate this point, consider our simple society that produces food and tractors. The more tractors (and the less food) this society produces, the more tractors it will have in the next period; and the more tractors it has in the next period, the more of both goods—food and tractors—it will be able to produce then. Thus, the more tractors (and the less food) this society produces, the further out it will push its product transformation curve—and the greater the increase in output (and per capita income) that it will achieve in the next period. For example, if this society chooses point *F* in Figure 3.1, the effect will be entirely different than if it chooses point *C*. If it chooses point *F*, it produces 4 million tractors, which we assume to be the number of tractors worn out each year. Thus, if it chooses point *F*, it adds nothing to its stock of tractors: it merely replaces those that wear out. Since it has no more tractors in the next period than in the current period, the product transformation curve does not shift out at all if point *F* is chosen. On the other hand, if point *C* is chosen, the society produces 12 million tractors, which means that it has 8 million additional tractors at the beginning of the next period. Thus, as shown in Figure 3.4, the product transformation curve is pushed outward. By producing more capital goods (and less consumers' goods) our society has increased its production possibilities and its per capita income.

What Is Capitalism?

The particular kind of economic system the United States has adopted to carry out these four basic economic functions is ***capitalism.*** Capitalism is one of those terms that is frequently used but seldom defined, and even less frequently understood. Exactly what does it mean? Let us begin with one of its important characteristics: ***private ownership of capital.*** In other words, you or I can buy the tools of production. We can own factories, equipment, inventories, and other forms of capital. In a capitalistic system, somebody owns each piece of capital—and receives the income from it. Each piece of equipment has some sort of legal instrument indicating to whom it belongs. If it belongs to a corporation, its owners basically are the stockholders who own the corporation. Moreover, each piece of capital has a money market value. This system is in marked contrast to a Communist or socialist state where the government owns the capital. In these states, the government decides how much and what kinds of capital goods will be produced; it owns the capital goods; and it receives and distributes the income they produce. In the Soviet Union or China, no one can buy or put up a new steel plant: it simply isn't allowed.

The United States is basically a capitalistic system, but there are certain areas where the government, not individuals, owns capital, and where individual property rights are limited in various ways by the government. The government owns much of the tooling used in the defense industries; it owns dams and the Tennessee Valley Authority; and it owns research laboratories in such diverse fields as atomic energy, space exploration, and health. Further, the government determines how much of a man's assets can go to his heirs when he dies. (The rest goes to the government in the form of estate and inheritance taxes.) Also, the government can make a person sell his property to allow a road or other public project to be built. There are many such limitations on property

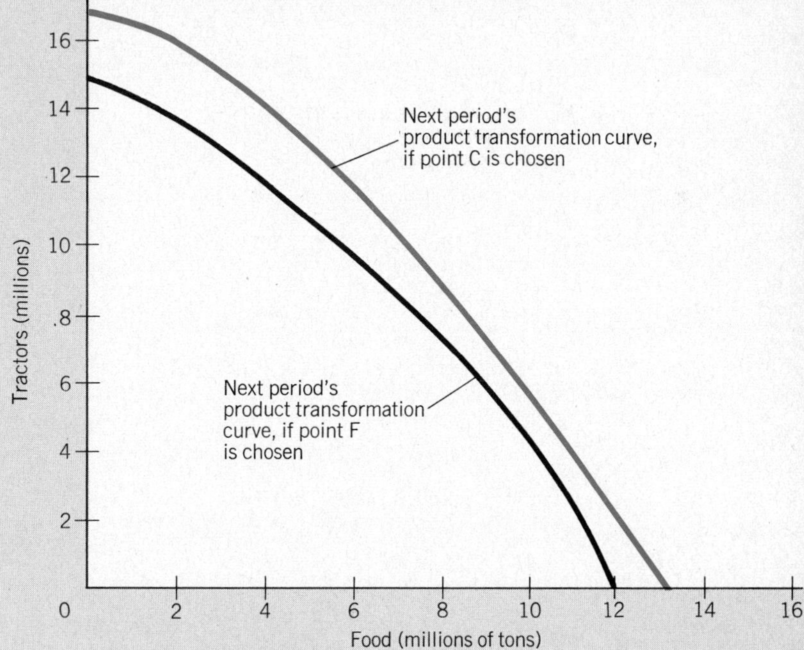

Figure 3.4
Effect of Increase in Capital Goods on Product Transformation Curve

An increase in the amount of capital goods results in an outward shift of the product transformation curve. The choice of point *C* means the production of more capital goods than the choice of point *F*.

rights. Ours is basically a capitalistic system, but it must be recognized that the government's role is important. More will be said on this score in subsequent sections.

Private ownership of capital is but one of the important characteristics of capitalism. Another is freedom of choice and freedom of enterprise. ***Freedom of choice*** means that consumers are free to buy what they please and reject what they please; that laborers are free to work where, when, and if they please; and that investors are free to invest in whatever property they please. By ***freedom of enterprise,*** we mean that firms are free to enter whatever markets they please, obtain resources in whatever ways they can, and organize their affairs as best they can. Needless to say, this does not mean that firms can run roughshod over consumers and workers. Even the strongest champions of capitalism are quick to admit that the government must set "rules of the game" to prevent firms from engaging in sharp or unfair practices. But granting such limitations, the name of the game under capitalism is economic freedom.

Freedom to do what? Under capitalism, individuals and firms are free to pursue their own self-interest. Put in today's idiom, each individual or firm can do his, her, or its own thing. However, it is important to note that this freedom is circumscribed by one's financial resources. Consumers in a capitalistic system can buy practically anything they like—if they have the money to pay for it. Similarly, workers can work wherever or whenever they please—if they don't mind the wages. And a firm can run its business as it likes—if it remains solvent. Thus, an important regulator of economic activity under capitalism is the pattern of income and prices that emerges in the marketplace.

Still another important characteristic of capitalism is ***competition.*** Firms compete with one another for sales. Under perfect competition, there are a large number of firms producing each product; indeed, there are so many that no firm controls the product's price. Because of this competition, firms are forced to jump to the tune of the consumer. If a firm doesn't produce what consumers want—at a price at least as low as other firms are charging—it will lose sales to other firms. Eventually, unless it mends its ways, such a firm will go out of business. Of course, in real-life American markets, the number of producers is not always so large that no firm has any control over price. (Much more will be said on this score below.) But in the purest form of capitalism, such imperfections do not exist. Also, lest you think that competition under capitalism is confined to producers, it must be remembered that owners of resources also compete. They are expected to offer their resources—including labor—to the buyer who gives them the best deal, and buyers of resources and products are supposed to compete openly and freely.

Finally, *still another very important characteristic of capitalism is its reliance upon markets. Under pure capitalism, the market—the free market—plays a central role. Firms and individuals buy and sell products and resources in competitive markets. Some firms and individuals make money and prosper; others lose money and fail. Each of these economic actors is allowed freedom to pursue his interests in the market place, while the government guards against shady and dishonest dealings. Such is the nature of the economic system under pure capitalism.*

Some of the major countries of the world operate with an economic system that is completely different from capitalism. In particular, the economic system in the Communist countries, such as the Soviet Union and China, is vastly different from the capitalist system. In these economies, capital is owned by the state, not by individuals or private firms. To determine what is produced, the Russian and Chinese governments formulate plans indicating what they want the people to produce. There is much less freedom for the consumer, the producer, or the resource owner (including laborers) in the Communist economies than under capitalism.

When we compare institutional characteristics and basic suppositions there is obviously a considerable gap between the Communist economies and a purely capitalistic economy. Most of the non-Communist nations of the world are somewhere between these two extremes. Even the United States, which is basically capitalistic, has adopted a mixed form of capitalism that combines the basic elements of capitalism with considerable government intervention. As will become evident, if it is not evident already, the American economy is by no means a purely capitalistic one, but it is closer to pure capitalism than many of the non-Communist nations of the world. In many of the other non-Communist nations, the economic system can be described as democratic, or liberal socialism. In such nations, there is much more government intervention than under pure capitalism, but much less than under communism; and there is much more economic freedom (and reliance on free markets) than under communism, but much less than under pure capitalism.

How Does Capitalism Perform the Four Basic Economic Tasks?

The ***price system*** lies at the heart of any capitalist economy. In a purely capitalist economy, it is used to carry out the four basic economic functions discussed above. The price system is a way to organize an economy. Under such a system, every commodity and every service, including labor, has a price. Everyone receives money for what he sells, including labor, and uses this money to buy the goods and services he wants. If more is wanted of a certain good, the price of this good tends to rise; if less is wanted, the price of the good tends to fall. Producers base their production decisions on the prices of commodities and inputs. Thus, increases in a commodity's price generally tend to increase the amount of it produced, and decreases generally tend to decrease the amount produced. In this way, firms' output decisions are brought into balance with consumers' desires.

The very important question of how the price system performs the basic economic functions we discussed above will be answered in some detail in the next chapter. All we can do here is provide a preliminary sketch of the way the price system carries out each of these four tasks. First, consider the determination of what the society will produce. In a substantially capitalistic economy, such as ours, consumers choose the amount of each good that they want, and producers act in accord with these decisions. The importance consumers attach to a good is indicated by the price they are willing to pay for it. Of course, the principle of ***consumer sovereignty***—producers dancing to the tune of consumers' tastes—should not be viewed as always and completely true, since producers do attempt to manipulate the tastes of consumers through advertising and other devices, but it is certainly a reasonable first approximation.

In its second fundamental task, the price system helps determine how each good and service will be produced by indicating the desires of workers and the relative value of various types of materials and equipment as well as the desires of consumers. For example, if plumbers are scarce relative to the demand for them, their price in the labor market —their wage—will be bid up, and they will tend to be used only in the places where they are productive enough so that their employers can afford to pay them the higher wages. The forces that push firms toward actually carrying out the proper decisions are profits and losses. Profits are the carrot and losses are the stick used to eliminate the less efficient and alert firms and to increase the more efficient and the more alert.

How does the price system accomplish its third task, of determining how much in the way of goods and services each member of the society is to receive? In general, an individual's income depends largely on the quantities of resources of various kinds that he owns and the prices he gets for them. For example, if a man both works and rents out farm land he owns, his income is the number of hours he works per year times his hourly wage rate plus the number of acres of land he owns times the annual rental per acre. Thus, the distribution of income depends on the way resource ownership—including talent, intelligence, training, work habits, and, yes, even character—is distributed among the population. Also, to be candid, it depends on just plain luck.

Finally, how does the price system provide for an adequate rate of growth of per capita income? A nation's rate of growth of per capita income depends on the rate of growth of its resources and the rate of increase of the efficiency with which they are used. In our economy, the rate at which labor and capital resources are increased is motivated, at least in part, through the price system. Higher wages for more skilled work are an incentive for an individual to undergo further education and training. Capital accumulation occurs in response to the expectation of profit. Increases in efficiency, due in considerable measure to the advance of technology, are also stimulated by the price system.

Our Mixed Capitalist System and the Role of Government

Since the days of Adam Smith, economists have been fascinated by the features of a purely capitalistic economic system—an economy that relies entirely on the price system. Smith, and many generations of economists since, have gone to great pains to explain that in such an economic system, *the price system, although it is not controlled by any person or small group, results in economic order, not chaos.* The basic economic tasks any economy must perform can, as we have said, be carried out in such an economic system by the price system. It is an effective means of coordinating economic activity through decentralized decision making based on information disseminated through prices and related data.

But does this mean that the American economy is purely capitalistic? As we have stressed repeatedly in previous sections, the answer is no. A purely capitalistic system is a useful model of reality, not a description of our economy as it exists now or in the past. It is useful because a purely capitalistic economy is, for some purposes, a reasonably close fit to our own. However, this does not mean that such a model is useful for all purposes. Many American markets are not entirely competitive and never will be; they are dominated by a few producers or buyers who can influence price and thus distort the workings of the price system. Moreover, *the American economy is a mixed capitalistic economy, an economy where both government and private decisions are important.* The role of the government in American economic activity is very large indeed. Although it is essential to understand the workings of a purely capitalistic system, any model that omits the government entirely cannot purport to be adequate for the analysis of many major present-day economic issues.

To create a more balanced picture of the workings of the American economy, we must recognize that, although the price system plays an extremely important role, it is not permitted to solve all of the basic economic problems of our society. Consumer sovereignty does not extend—and cannot realistically be extended—to all areas of society. For example, certain public services cannot be left to private enterprise. The provision of fire protection, the operation of schools, and the development of weapons systems are examples of areas where we rely on political decision making, not the price system alone. Moreover, with regard to the consumption of commodities like drugs, society imposes limits on the decisions of individuals.

In addition, certain consequences of the price system are, by general agreement, unacceptable. Reliance on the price system alone does not assure a just or equitable or optimal distribution of income. It is possible, for example, that one person will literally have money to burn while another person will live in degrading poverty. Consequently, the government modifies the distribution of income by imposing taxes that take more from the rich than the poor, and by "welfare" programs that try to keep the poor from reaching the point where they lack decent food, adequate clothing, or shelter. Besides providing public services and maintaining certain minimum income standards, the government also carries out a variety of regulatory functions. Industries do not police the actions of their constituent firms, so it falls to the government to establish laws that impose limits on the economic behavior of firms. For example, these laws say that firms must not misrepresent their products, that child labor must not be employed, and that firms must not collude and form monopolies to interfere with the proper functioning of the price system. In this way, the government tries, with varying effectiveness, to establish the "rules of the game"—the limits within which the economic behavior of firms (and consumers) should lie.

Capital, Specialization, and Money: Other Characteristics of the American Economy

Finally, we must point out three additional characteristics of the American economy: the use of a great deal of capital per worker, specialization, and the use of money. These characteristics are common to all modern, industrialized nations, not just the United States, and they are so obvious that you may take them for granted. But they are too important to be ignored.

First, consider the enormous amount of capital American labor has to work with. Think of the oil refineries in New Jersey and Philadelphia, the blast furnaces and open hearths in Pittsburgh and Cleveland, the railroad yards in Chicago and Wichita, the aircraft plants in California and Georgia, the skyscrapers in New York, and the host of additional types of capital that we have and use in this country. To understand this idea fully, stop and think about what we mean by capital. As noted earlier in this chapter, to the economist capital is not the same as money. A man with a hot-dog stand who has $100 in his pocket may say that he has $100 in capital. But his definition is different from that of the economist, who would also include in the man's capital the value of his stand, the value of his equipment, the value of his inventories of hot dogs, buns, and mustard, and the value of other nonlabor resources (other than land) that he uses.

Defining capital as economists do, it is evident that American workers have an enormous amount of capital to work with. And it is evident as well that this enormous amount of capital, together with an advanced technology and a well-trained labor force, is responsible for the tremendous amount of goods and services the American economy produces. All this capital contributes to increased production because it is often more efficient to adopt ***roundabout methods of production.*** For example, it is often more efficient to build a blast furnace and open hearth to produce steel rather than to try to produce steel directly. On the other hand, harking back to our discussion of Figure 3.4, it is also true that the production of capital goods means that less consumers' goods can be produced. In other words, although a greater amount of capital means greater production, consumers must be willing—or forced—to forgo current consumption of goods and services to produce this capital.

Next, consider the tremendous amount of specialization in the American economy. You may decide to specialize in tax law (and a particular branch of tax law at that), a classmate may specialize in brain surgery, another may specialize in repairing hi-fi sets, and another in monitoring certain types of equipment in an oil refinery. In contrast to more primitive economies, where people specialize much less, the American economy is characterized by an intricate web of specialization. What does it accomplish? As stressed by Adam Smith over two centuries ago, it results in much greater output than if people attempted to be jacks-of-all-trades. Because of this specialization, people can concentrate on the tasks they do best. For example, Bobby Fischer, the world champion chess player, can concentrate on chess and leave the hi-fi repairs to people who understand more about woofers and tweeters. However, it should be recognized that this specialization also results in great interdependence. Because each of us performs such specialized tasks, each of us depends on others for most of the things he needs. For example, unless you are much better at farming than I am, you would lose a lot of weight—and not because you wanted to—if farmers decided that they no longer wanted to provide us city folks with the fruits (and vegetables) of their labor.

Finally, the use of money is another important characteristic of all modern economies, including the American economy. Unquestionably you take the use of money as much for granted as you do the fact that the moon revolves about the earth. But money is a social invention. There is no evidence that Adam and Eve were created with the idea of money. They, or their descendants, had to think it up themselves, and this took time, as evidenced by the fact that extremely primitive cultures resorted to barter, which meant that to get a particular commodity, you had to swap a commodity that you owned for it. Since the exchange of commodities and services by barter was very difficult, the use of money has made trade and exchange much, much easier and facilitated the specialization of labor.

Summary

The American economy is the richest in the world. Based on freedom of enterprise, the American economy is rich in resources—land, labor, and capital—and American technology is among the most advanced in the world. The American economy, like any economic system, must perform four basic tasks: (1) It must determine the level and composition of society's output. (2) It must determine how each good and service is to be produced. (3) It must determine how the goods and services that are produced are to be distributed among the members of society. (4) It must maintain and provide for an adequate rate of growth of per capita income.

The product transformation curve, which shows the various production possibilities a society can attain, is useful in indicating the nature of the economic tasks any society faces. The task of determining the level and composition of society's output is really a problem of determining at what point along the product transformation curve society should be. Society, in performing this task, has to recognize that it cannot get more of one good without giving up some of another good, if resources are fully and efficiently used. However, if they are not fully and efficiently used, society will have to settle for points inside the product transformation curve—and it will be possible to obtain more of one good without giving up some of another good. Clearly, the task of determining how each good and service should be produced is, to a considerable extent, a problem of keeping society on its product transformation curve, rather than at points inside the curve. The product transformation curve does not tell us anything about the distribution of income, but it does indicate various ways that a society can promote growth in per capita income. By doing lots of research and development, or by producing lots of capital goods (rather than consumers' goods), society can push its product transformation curve outward, thus increasing per capita income.

Ours is a capitalistic economy, an economic system in which there is private ownership of capital, freedom of choice, freedom of enterprise, competition, and reliance upon markets. Many countries do not have a capitalistic economy, and even ours is not a purely capitalistic system. Under pure capitalism, the price system is used to perform the four basic economic tasks. Although it is not controlled by any person or small group, the price system results in order, not chaos. A purely capitalistic system is a useful model of reality, not a description of our economy as it exists now or in the past. The American economy is a mixed capitalistic economy, in which both government and private decisions are important. For example, certain public services, like fire protection and schools, cannot be left to private enterprise. In addition, society has said that certain consequences of the price system—like the existence of abject poverty—are unacceptable. Moreover, the government carries out a bewildering array of additional functions, many of which are described in Chapter 5.

CONCEPTS FOR REVIEW

Economic resources	Product transformation curve	Capitalism
Free resources	Capital goods	Capital
Technology	Consumers' goods	Consumer sovereignty
		Money

QUESTIONS FOR DISCUSSION AND REVIEW

1. Suppose that you were appointed to the position of philosopher-king in a small country. In what way would you dictate that each of the four tasks of the economic system be carried out? Would you rely on the price system? Why or why not? Would you permit private ownership of capital? Why or why not?

2. As philosopher-king, would you find the concept of the product transformation curve useful? If not, why not; and if so, how?

3. Suppose that a society's product transformation curve is as follows:

	Output (per year)	
Possibility	Food (millions of tons)	Tractors (millions)
A	0	30
B	4	28
C	8	24
D	12	20
E	16	14
F	20	8
G	24	0

a. Is it possible for the society to produce 30 million tons of food per year?
b. Can it produce 30 million tractors per year?
c. Suppose this society produces 20 million tons of food and 6 million tractors per year. Is it operating on the product transformation curve? If not, what factors might account for this?

4. Which of the following is *not* a characteristic of capitalism?
a. Competition
b. General denial of self-interest for the public good
c. Private ownership of capital
d. Freedom of enterprise

The Price System: Consumers, Firms, and Markets

Capitalist economies use the price system to perform the four basic tasks any economic system must carry out. Of course, as we pointed out in the previous chapter, the American economy is a mixed capitalist system, not a pure one. But this does not mean that the price system is unimportant. On the contrary, the price system plays a vital role in the American economy, and to obtain even a minimal grasp of the workings of our economic system, one must understand how the price system operates. This chapter takes up the nature and functions of the price system, as well as some applications of our theoretical results to real-life problems. For example we show how the price system determines the quantity produced of a commodity like wheat, and how the pricing policies of the Broadway theater hurt show business in a variety of ways. These applications should help illustrate the basic theory and indicate its usefulness.

Consumers

We begin by describing and discussing consumers and firms, the basic building blocks that make up the private, or nongovernmental, sector of the economy. What is a consumer? Sometimes—for example, when a man buys himself a beer on a warm day—the consumer is an individual. In other cases—for example, when a family buys a new car—the consumer may be an entire household. Consumers purchase the goods and services that are the ultimate end-products of the economic system. When a man buys tickets to a ball game, he is a consumer; when he buys himself a Coke at the game, he is a consumer; and when he buys his wife a book on baseball for their twentieth wedding anniversary, he is also a consumer.

Consumers—whether individuals or households—are an extremely varied lot. To get some idea of the variation, let's look at two families, the Onassises and the Ríoses. First, consider Aristotle Onassis, the Greek shipping and industrial magnate, and his wife, the former Mrs. John F. Kennedy. According to one reporter, Mr. and Mrs. Onassis were spending money during the first year of their marriage at the rate of $20 million per year. Mr. Onassis maintains fully staffed homes in Monte Carlo, Paris, Montevideo, Athens, New York, and the island of Skorpios, as well as hotel suites and a yacht. He has over 200 servants. Certainly Mr. Onassis is an extraordinary consumer, a man who consumes on a mammoth scale. Given his rate of expenditure, one might expect him to wind up in the poorhouse. But since he is estimated to be worth between $500 million and $1 billion, even if he put his money in a savings bank at 5 percent interest, he would have more than $20 million per year coming in. Clearly, Mr. Onassis has kept the wolf at a remarkable distance from the door!

In contrast, let's look at the Ríoses, a Puerto Rican family living in La Esmeralda, a slum section of San Juan. There are three branches of the Ríos family. One is headed by a man who works as a messenger and makes about $1,700 a year, another by a woman who works as a barmaid and makes about $1,500 a year, and another by a woman who makes about $500 a year. The Ríoses consume relatively little. They live in crowded quarters with inadequate sanitary facilities, none of them has a refrigerator, and the average number of years spent in school by the members of the family is about 4 years. Excluding clothing, the total value of the possessions of these households is $436, $149, and $120; and the total value of each household's clothing is $496, $70, and $53.[1] Clearly, the Ríos family, which is quite typical of the families in La Esmeralda, is an example of abject poverty. To compare the level of consumption of the Onassises with that of the Ríoses is to compare an ocean liner with a frail canoe: yet both are consumers.

Firms

There are over 10 million firms in the United States. About 9/10 of the goods and services produced in this country are produced by firms. (The rest are provided by government and not-for-profit institutions like universities and hospitals.) A firm is an organization that produces a good or service for sale. In contrast to not-for-profit organizations, firms attempt to make a profit. It doesn't take great analytical power to see that an economy like ours is centered around the activities of firms.

Like consumers, firms are extremely varied in size, age, power, and purpose. Consider two examples, Peter Amacher's drugstore on Chicago's South Side and the General Motors Corporation. The Amacher drugstore, started in 1922 by Mr. Amacher's father-in-law, is known in the retail drug trade as an independent, because it has no affiliation with a chain-store organization. Mr. Amacher and two other pharmacists keep the store open for business 13 hours a day, except on Sundays. The store sells about $150,000 worth

[1] Oscar Lewis, *La Vida*, New York: Random House, 1966.

of merchandise per year. Prescriptions account for about 25 percent of total sales, and cosmetics and greeting cards are the other principal sales items. Amacher's drugstore is an example of the small-business segment of the American business community.

In contrast, General Motors is one of the giants of American industry. It is the largest manufacturer of automobiles in the United States, its sales in 1971 being over $28 billion. Besides cars, it makes trucks, locomotives, aircraft engines, household appliances, and other products. Its total assets amounted to over $18 billion in 1971; and its total employment was over 700,000. General Motors, which was formed by merger, was set up as a holding company in 1908 by William C. Durant, owner of the Buick Motor Car Company. Durant acquired about 50 auto companies and parts manufacturers and put them all together as General Motors. Its present share of the market is greater than it was in 1908, when it produced about 25 percent of all cars in this country. In 1971, for example, it produced about 55 percent of all domestically produced cars.[2]

Markets

Consumers and firms come together in a market. The concept of a market is not quite as straightforward as it may seem, since most markets are not well defined geographically or physically. For example, the New York Stock Exchange is an atypical market because it is located principally in a particular building. For present purposes, *a **market** can be defined as a group of firms and individuals that are in touch with each other in order to buy or sell some good.* Of course, not every person in a market has to be in contact with every other person in the market. A person or firm is part of a market even if it is in contact with only a subset of the other persons or firms in the market.

[2] L. Weiss, *Economics and American Industry,* New York: Wiley, 1961, p. 329; and *Moody's Industrials,* annual.

Markets vary enormously in their size and procedures. For some toothpastes, most people who have their own teeth (and are interested in keeping them) are members of the same market; while for other goods like Picasso paintings, only a few dealers, collectors, and museums in certain parts of the world may be members of the market. And for still other goods, like lemonade sold by neighborhood children for a nickel a glass at a sidewalk stand, only people who walk by the stand—and are brave enough to drink the stuff—are members of the market. Basically, however, all markets consist primarily of buyers and sellers, although third parties like brokers and agents may be present as well.

Markets also vary in the extent to which they are dominated by a few large buyers or sellers. For example, in the United States, there was for many years only one producer of aluminum. Clearly this firm, the Aluminum Corporation of America, had great power in the market for aluminum. In contrast, the number of buyers and sellers in some other markets is so large that no single buyer or seller has any power over the price of the product. This is true in various agricultural markets, for example. When a market for a product contains so many buyers and sellers that none of them can influence the price, economists call the market ***perfectly competitive.*** In these introductory chapters, we make the simplifying assumption that markets are perfectly competitive. We will relax that assumption later.

The Demand Side of a Market

There are two sides of every market, just as there are of every argument. A market has a demand side and a supply side. *The **demand** side can be represented by a market demand curve, which shows the amount of the commodity buyers demand at various prices.* Consider Figure 4.1, which shows the demand curve for wheat in the American market during the early 1960s, as estimated by Iowa

Figure 4.1
Market Demand Curve for Wheat, Early 1960s

The curve shows the amount of wheat buyers would demand at various prices.

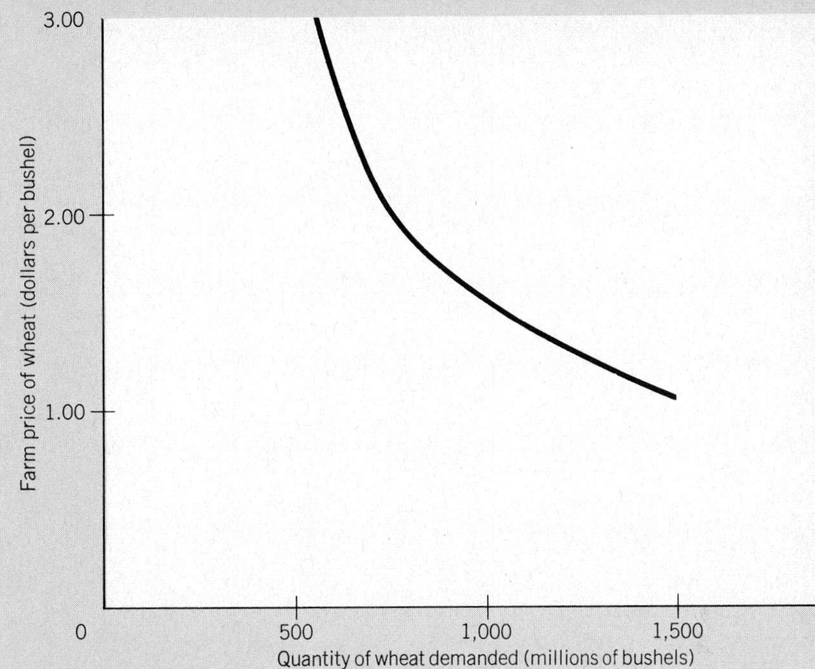

State's Karl Fox.[3] The figure shows that about 550 million bushels of wheat will be demanded annually if the farm price is $3 per bushel, about 700 million bushels will be demanded annually if the farm price is $2 per bushel, and about 1,500 million bushels will be demanded annually if the farm price is $1 per bushel. The total demand for wheat is of several types: to produce bread and other food products for domestic use, as well as for feed use, for export purposes, and for industrial uses. The demand curve in Figure 4.1 shows the total demand—including all these components—at each price. Any demand curve pertains to a particular period of time, and its shape and position depend on the length of this period.

[3] Karl Fox, "Commercial Agriculture: Perspectives and Prospects" in K. Fox, V. Ruttan, and L. Witt, *Farming, Farmers, and Markets for Farm Goods,* Committee for Economic Development, 1962. Of course, these estimates are only rough approximations, but they are good enough for present purposes.

Take a good look at the demand curve for wheat in Figure 4.1. This simple, innocent-looking curve influences a great many people's lives. After all, wheat is the principal grain used for direct human consumption in the United States. To states like Kansas, North Dakota, Oklahoma, Montana, Washington, Nebraska, Texas, Illinois, Indiana, and Ohio, wheat is a mighty important cash crop. Note that the demand curve for wheat slopes downward to the right. In other words, the quantity of wheat demanded increases as the price falls. This is true of the demand curve for most commodities: they almost always slope downward to the right. This makes sense: only the most obtuse of our citizenry would expect increases in a good's price to result in a greater quantity demanded.

What determines the position of the demand curve for a commodity? Why isn't the demand curve for wheat higher or lower, and what factors will cause it to shift? Although the position of the demand curve for a commodity depends on a host of factors, several are generally of primary importance. First, there are the tastes of consumers. If consumers show an increasing preference for a product, the demand curve will shift to the right; that is, at each price, consumers will desire to buy more than previously. On the other hand, if consumers show a decreasing preference for a product, the demand curve will shift to the left, since, at each price, consumers will desire to buy less than previously. Take wheat. If consumers become convinced that foods containing wheat prolong life and promote happiness, the demand curve may shift, as shown in Figure 4.2; and the greater the shift in preferences, the larger the shift in the demand curve.

Second, the demand curve for a commodity is affected by the income level of consumers. For some types of products, the demand curve shifts to the right if per capita income increases; whereas for other types of commodities, the demand curve shifts to the left if per capita income rises. Economists can explain why some goods fall into one category and other goods fall into the other, but, at present, this need not concern us. All that is important here is that changes in per capita income affect the demand curve, the size and direction of this effect varying from product to product. For example, in the case of wheat, a 10 percent increase in per capita income would probably have a relatively small effect on the demand curve, as shown in Figure 4.3.

Third, the demand curve for a commodity is affected by the number of consumers in the market. Compare Austria's demand for wheat with America's. Austria is a small country with a population of about 7 million; the United States is a huge country with a population of over 200 million. Clearly, at a given price of wheat, the quantity demanded by American consumers will greatly exceed the quantity demanded by Austrian consumers, as shown in Figure 4.4. Even if consumer tastes, income, and other factors were held constant, this would still be true simply because the United States has so many more consumers in the relevant market.[4]

Fourth, the demand curve for a commodity is affected by the level of other prices. For example, since wheat can be substituted to some extent for corn as livestock feed, the quantity of wheat demanded depends on the price of corn as well as on the price of wheat. If the price of corn is high, more wheat will be demanded since it will be profitable to substitute wheat for corn. If the price of corn is low, less wheat will be demanded since it will be profitable to substitute corn for wheat. Thus, as shown in Figure 4.5, increases in the price of corn will shift the demand curve for wheat to the right, and decreases in the price of corn will shift it to the left.

The Supply Side of a Market

So much for our first look at demand. What about the other side of the market: supply? *The **supply** side of a market can be represented by a market supply curve that shows the amount of the commodity sellers will supply at various prices.* Let's continue with the case of wheat. Figure 4.6 shows the supply curve for wheat in the United States in the early 1960s, based on estimates made informally by government experts.[5] According to the figure, about 1,750 million bushels of wheat would be supplied if the farm price were \$3 per bushel, about 1,400 million bushels if the farm price were \$2 per bushel, and about 750 million bushels if the farm price were \$1 per bushel.

Look carefully at the supply curve shown in Figure 4.6. Although it looks innocuous enough, it summarizes the potential behavior of thousands of American wheat farmers—and their behavior plays an important role in determining the pros-

[4] Note that no figures are given along the horizontal axis in Figure 4.4. This is because we do not have reasonably precise estimates of the demand curve in Austria. Nonetheless, the hypothetical demand curves in Figure 4.4 are close enough to the mark for present purposes.

[5] I am very much indebted to officials of the U.S. Department of Agriculture for providing me with these estimates. Of course, they are only rough approximations, but they are good enough for present purposes.

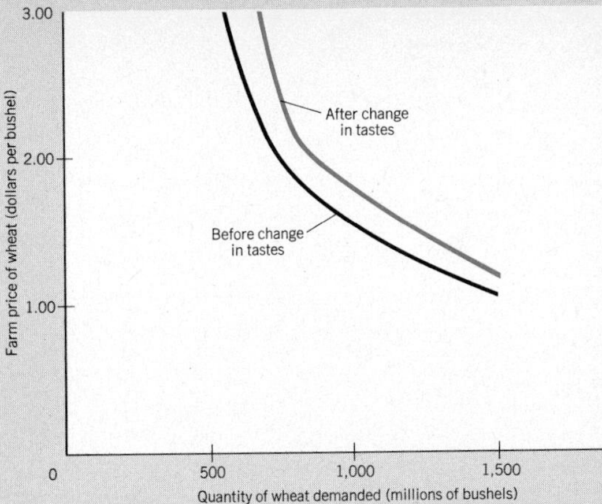

Figure 4.2
Effect of Increased Preference for Wheat on Market Demand Curve

An increased preference would shift the demand curve to the right.

Figure 4.3
Effect of Increase in Income on Market Demand Curve for Wheat

An increase in income would shift the demand curve for wheat to the right, but only slightly.

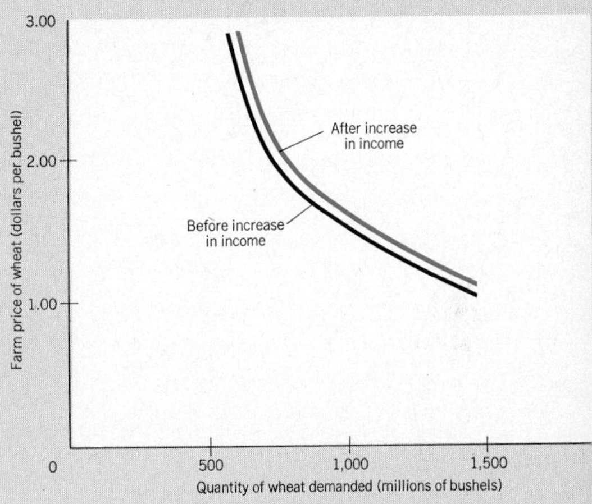

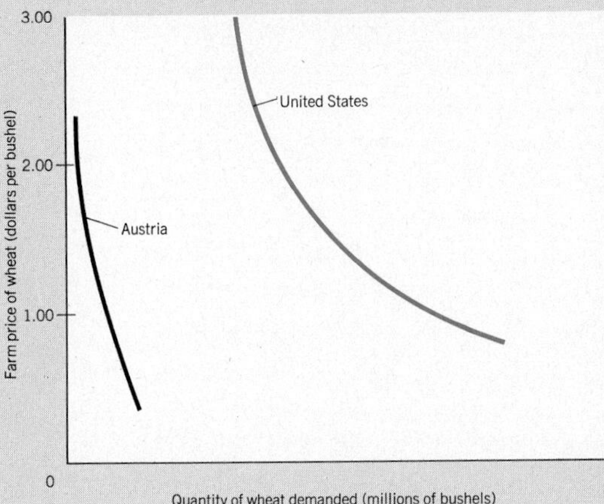

Figure 4.4
Market Demand Curves for Wheat, Austria and United States

Since the United States has far more consumers than Austria, the demand curve in the United States is far to the right of Austria's.

Figure 4.5
Effect of Price of Corn on Market Demand Curve for Wheat

Price increases for corn will shift the demand curve to the right.

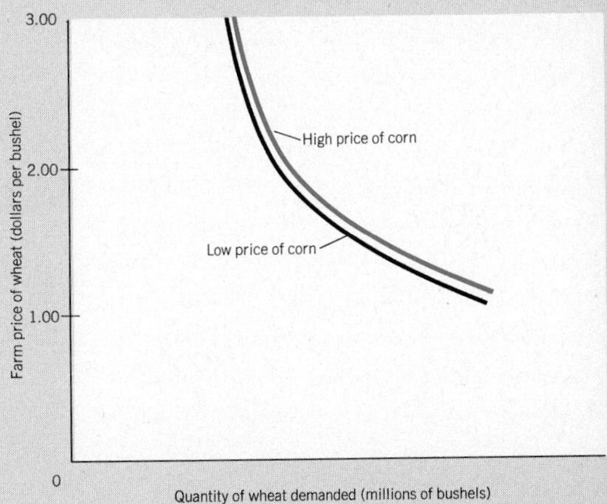

Figure 4.6
Market Supply Curve for Wheat, Early 1960s

The curve shows the amount of wheat sellers would supply at various prices.

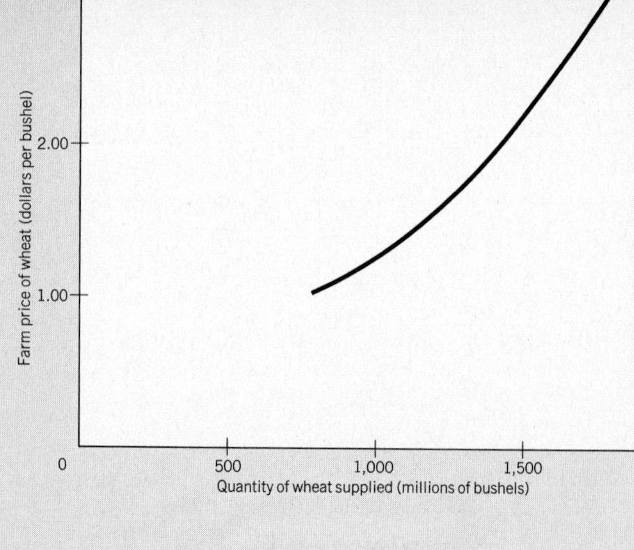

3.00
2.00
1.00
0
500
1,000
1,500
Farm price of wheat (dollars per bushel)
Quantity of wheat supplied (millions of bushels)

3.00
2.00
1.00
0
Farm price of wheat (dollars per bushel)
Before technological change
After technological change
Quantity of wheat supplied (millions of bushels)

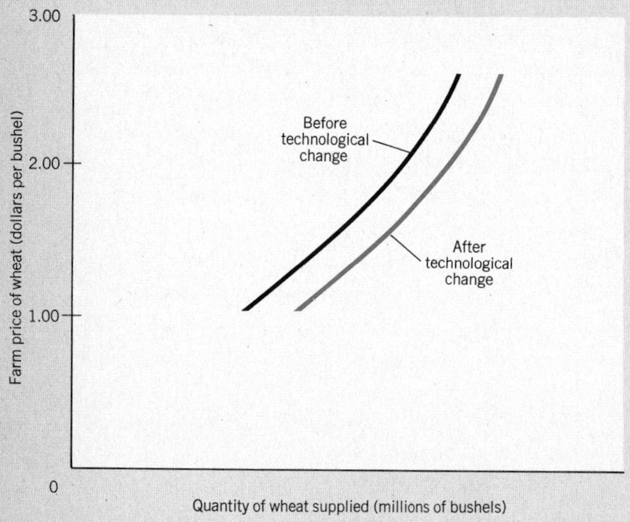

Figure 4.7
Effect of Technological Change on Market Supply Curve for Wheat

Improvements in technology often shift the supply curve to the right.

Figure 4.8
Effect of Decrease in Farm Wage Rates on Market Supply Curve for Wheat

A reduction in the wage rate might shift the supply curve to the right.

3.00
2.00
1.00
0
Farm price of wheat (dollars per bushel)
Before decrease in wage rates
After decrease in wage rates
Quantity of wheat supplied (millions of bushels)

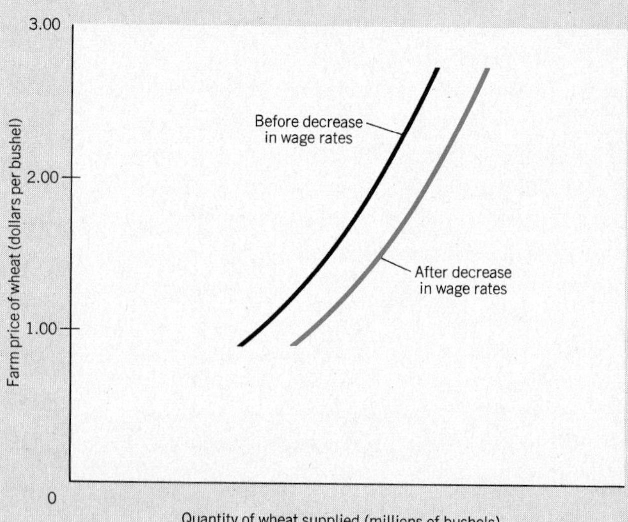

perity of many states and communities. Note that the supply curve for wheat slopes upward to the right. In other words, the quantity of wheat supplied increases as the price increases. This seems plausible, since increases in price give a greater incentive for farms to produce wheat and offer it for sale. Empirical studies indicate that the supply curves for a great many commodities share this characteristic of sloping upward to the right.

What determines the position of the supply curve for a commodity? As you might expect, it depends on a host of factors. But several stand out. First, there is the state of technology, defined in the previous chapter as society's pool of knowledge concerning the industrial arts. As technology progresses, it becomes possible to produce commodities more cheaply, so that firms often are willing to supply a given amount at a lower price than formerly. Thus, technological change often causes the supply curve to shift to the right. For example, this certainly has occurred in the case of wheat, as shown in Figure 4.7. There have been many important technological changes in wheat production, ranging from advances in tractors to the development of improved varieties like semidwarf wheats.

Second, the supply curve for a commodity is affected by the prices of the resources (labor, capital, and land) used to produce it. Decreases in the price of these inputs make it possible to produce commodities more cheaply, so that firms may be willing to supply a given amount at a lower price than they formerly would. Thus, decreases in the price of inputs may cause the supply curve to shift to the right. On the other hand, increases in the price of inputs may cause it to shift to the left. For example, if the wage rates of farm labor decrease, the supply curve for wheat may shift to the right, as shown in Figure 4.8.

The Equilibrium Price

The two sides of a market, demand and supply, interact to determine the price of a commodity. Recall from the previous chapter that prices in a capitalistic system play a central role in determining what is produced and how, who receives it, and how rapidly per capita income grows. It behooves us, therefore, to look carefully at how prices themselves are determined in a capitalist system. As a first step toward describing this process, we must define the equilibrium price of a product. At various points in this book, you will encounter the concept of an equilibrium, which is very important in economics, as in many other scientific fields.

Put briefly, an ***equilibrium*** *is a situation where there is no tendency for change:* in other words, it is a situation that can persist. Thus, *an* ***equilibrium price*** *is a price that can be maintained.* Any price that is not an equilibrium price cannot be maintained for long, since there are basic forces at work to stimulate a change in price. The best way to understand what we mean by an equilibrium price is to take a particular case, such as the wheat market. Let's put both the demand curve for wheat (in Figure 4.1) and the supply curve for wheat (in Figure 4.6) together in the same diagram. The result, shown in Figure 4.9, will help us determine the equilibrium price of wheat.

We begin by seeing what would happen if various prices were established in the market. For example, if the price were $3 per bushel, the demand curve indicates that 550 million bushels of wheat would be demanded, while the supply curve indicates that 1,750 million bushels would be supplied. Thus, if the price were $3 a bushel, there would be a mismatch between the quantity supplied and the quantity demanded per year, since the rate at which wheat is supplied would be greater than the rate at which it is demanded. Specifically, as shown in Figure 4.9, there would be an *excess supply* of 1,200 million bushels. Under these circumstances, some of the wheat supplied by farmers could not be sold, and as inventories of wheat built up, suppliers would tend to cut their prices in order to get rid of unwanted inventories. Thus, a price of $3 per bushel would not be maintained for long—and for this reason, $3 per bushel is not an equilibrium price.

Figure 4.9
Determination of the Equilibrium Price of Wheat in a Free Market, Early 1960s

The equilibrium price is $1.40 per bushel, and the equilibrium quantity is 1,100 million bushels. At a price of $3.00 per bushel, there would be an excess supply of 1,200 million bushels. At a price of $1.00 per bushel, there would be an excess demand of 750 million bushels.

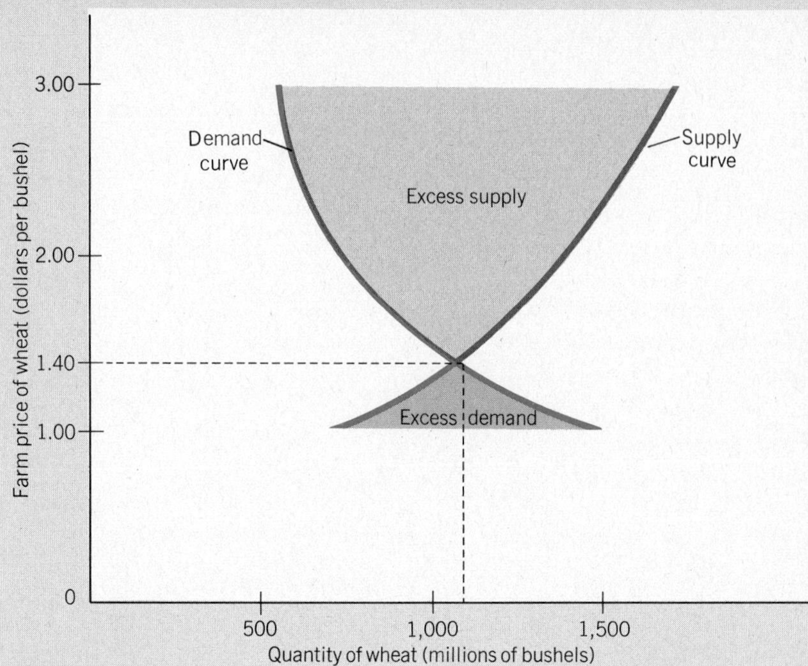

If the price were $1 per bushel, on the other hand, the demand curve indicates that 1,500 million bushels would be demanded, while the supply curve indicates that 750 million bushels would be supplied. Again we find a mismatch between the quantity supplied and the quantity demanded per year, since the rate at which wheat is supplied would be less than the rate at which it is demanded. Specifically, as shown in Figure 4.9, there would be an *excess demand* of 750 million bushels. Under these circumstances, some of the consumers who want wheat at this price would have to be turned away empty-handed. There would be a shortage. And given this shortage, suppliers would find it profitable to increase the price, and competition among buyers would bid the price up. Thus, a price of $1 per bushel could not be maintained for long—so $1 per bushel is not an equilibrium price.

Under these circumstances, the equilibrium price must be the price where the quantity demanded equals the quantity supplied. Obviously, this is the only price at which there is no mismatch between the quantity demanded and the quantity supplied; and consequently the only price that can be maintained for long. In Figure 4.9, the price at which the quantity supplied equals the quantity demanded is $1.40 per bushel, the price where the demand curve intersects the supply curve. Thus, $1.40 per bushel is the equilibrium price of wheat under the circumstances visualized in Figure 4.9, and 1,100 million bushels is the equilibrium quantity.

Actual Price versus Equilibrium Price

The price that counts in the real world, however, is the actual price, not the equilibrium price, and it is the actual price that we set out to explain. In general, economists simply assume that the actual price will approximate the equilibrium price, which seems reasonable enough, since the basic forces at work tend to push the actual price toward the equilibrium price. Thus, if conditions remain fairly stable for a time, the actual price should move toward the equilibrium price.

To see that this is the case, consider the market for wheat, as described by Figure 4.9. What if the price somehow is set at $3 per bushel? As we saw in the previous section, there is downward pressure on the price of wheat under these conditions. Suppose the price, responding to this pressure, falls to $2.50. Comparing the quantity demanded with the quantity supplied at $2.50, we find that there is still downward pressure on price, since the quantity supplied exceeds the quantity demanded at $2.50. The price, responding to this pressure, may fall to $2.00, but comparing the quantity demanded with the quantity supplied at this price, we find that there is still a downward pressure on price, since the quantity supplied exceeds the quantity demanded at $2.00.

So long as the actual price exceeds the equilibrium price, there will be downward pressure on price. Similarly, so long as the actual price is less than the equilibrium price, there will be an upward pressure on price. Thus there is always a tendency for the actual price to move toward the equilibrium price. But it should not be assumed that this movement is always rapid. Sometimes it takes a long time for the actual price to get close to the equilibrium price. Sometimes the actual price never gets to the equilibrium price because by the time it gets close, the equilibrium price changes. All that safely can be said is that the actual price will move toward the equilibrium price. But of course this information is of great value, both theoretically and practically. For many purposes, all that is needed is a correct prediction of the direction in which the price will move.

Changes in the Demand and Supply Curves

Heraclitus, the ancient Greek philosopher, said you cannot step in the same stream twice: everything changes, sooner or later. One need not be a disciple of Heraclitus to recognize that demand curves and supply curves shift. Indeed, we have already seen that demand curves shift in response to changes in tastes, income, population, and prices of other products, and that supply curves shift in response to changes in technology and input prices. Any supply-and-demand diagram like Figure 4.9 is essentially a snapshot of the situation during a particular period of time. The results in Figure 4.9 are limited to a particular period because the demand and supply curves in the figure, like any demand and supply curves, pertain only to a certain period.

What happens to the equilibrium price of a product when its demand or supply curve changes? This is an important question because it sheds a good deal of light on how the price system works. Suppose that consumer tastes shift in favor of foods containing wheat, causing the demand curve for wheat to shift to the right. This state of affairs is shown in Figure 4.10, where the demand curve shifts from DD' to D_1D_1'. It is not hard to see the effect on the equilibrium price of wheat. When DD' is the demand curve, the equilibrium price is OP. But when the demand curve shifts to D_1D_1', a shortage of (OQ_2–OQ) develops at this price: that is, the quantity demanded exceeds the quantity supplied at this price by (OQ_2–OQ). Consequently, suppliers raise their prices. After some testing of market reactions and trial-and-error adjustments, the price will tend to settle at OP_1, the new equilibrium price, and quantity will tend to settle at OQ_1. On the other hand, suppose that consumer demand for wheat products falls off, perhaps because of a great drop in the price of corn products. The demand for wheat now shifts to the left. Specifically, as shown in Figure 4.11, it shifts from DD' to D_2D_2'. What will be the effect on the equilibrium price of wheat? Clearly, the new equilibrium price will be OP_2, where the new demand curve intersects the supply curve.

In general, a shift to the right in the demand curve results in an increase in the equilibrium price, and a shift to the left in the demand curve results in a decrease in the equilibrium price. This

Figure 4.10
Effect on the Equilibrium Price of a Shift to the Right of the Market Demand Curve

A shift to the right from DD' to D_1D_1' results in an increase in the equilibrium price from OP to OP_1 and an increase in the equilibrium quantity from OQ to OQ_1.

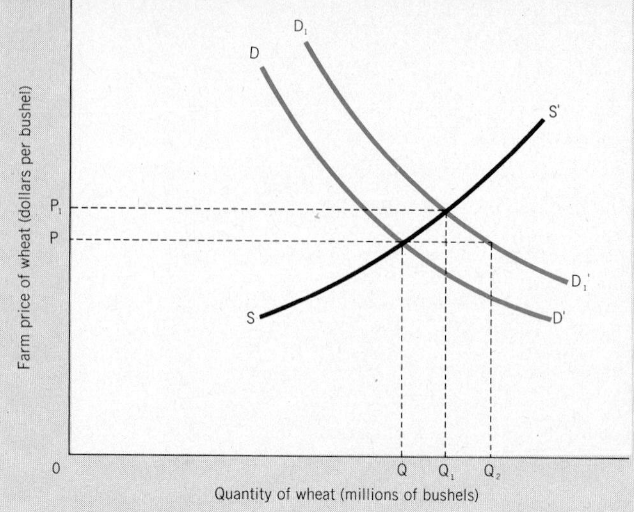

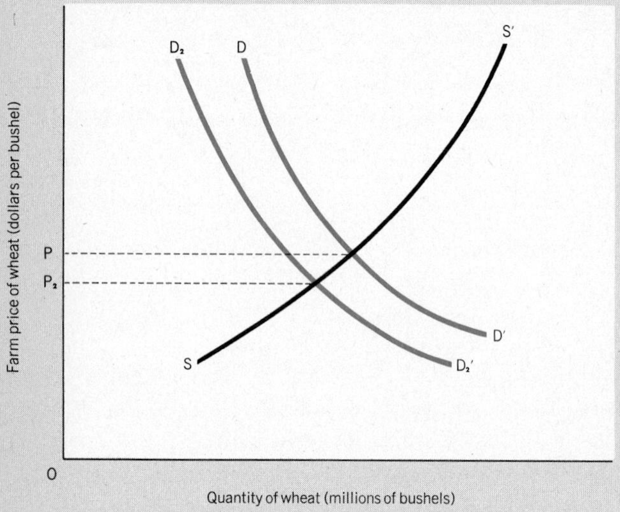

Figure 4.11
Effect on the Equilibrium Price of a Shift to the Left of the Market Demand Curve

A shift to the left from DD' to D_2D_2' results in a decrease in the equilibrium price from OP to OP_2 and a decrease in the equilibrium quantity.

Figure 4.12
Effects on the Equilibrium Price of Shifts in the Market Supply Curve

A shift to the right from SS' to S_1S_1' results in a decrease in the equilibrium price from OP to OP_3. A shift to the left from SS' to S_2S_2' increases the equilibrium price from OP to OP_4.

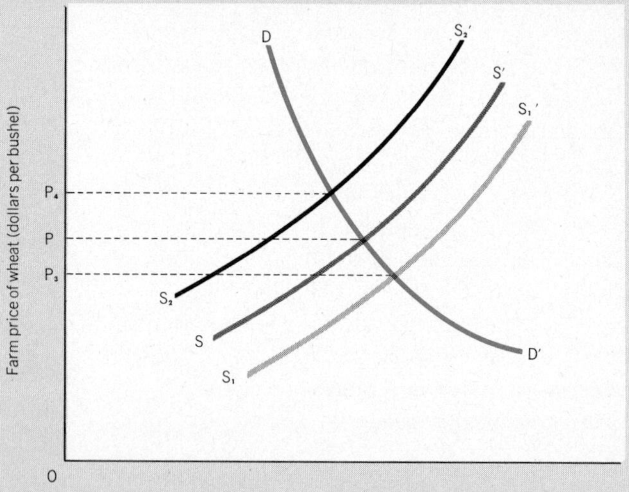

is the lesson of Figures 4.10 and 4.11. Of course, this conclusion depends on the assumption that the supply curve slopes upward to the right, but, as we noted in a previous section, this assumption is generally true.

At this point, since all of this is theory, you may be wondering how well this theory works in practice. In 1972 and 1973, there was a vivid demonstration of the accuracy of this model in various agricultural markets, including wheat. Because of poor harvests abroad and greatly increased foreign demand for American wheat, the demand curve for wheat shifted markedly to the right. What happened to the price of wheat? In accord with our model, the price increased spectacularly, from about $1.35 a bushel in the early summer of 1972 to over $4 a year later. Anyone who witnessed this phenomenon could not help but be impressed by the usefulness of this model.

Let's turn now to changes in the supply curve. Suppose that, because of technological advances in wheat production, wheat farmers are willing and able to supply more wheat at a given price than they used to. Specifically, suppose that the supply curve shifts from SS' to S_1S_1' in Figure 4.12. What will be the effect on the equilibrium price? Clearly, it will fall from OP (where the SS' supply curve intersects the demand curve) to OP_3 (where the S_1S_1' supply curve intersects the demand curve). On the other hand, suppose that the weather is poor, with the result that the supply curve shifts to the left. Specifically, suppose that the supply curve shifts from SS' to S_2S_2' in Figure 4.12. Clearly, the equilibrium price will increase from OP (where the SS' supply curve intersects the demand curve) to OP_4 (where the S_2S_2' supply curve intersects the demand curve).

In general, a shift to the right in the supply curve results in a decrease in the equilibrium price, and a shift to the left in the supply curve results in an increase in the equilibrium price. Of course, this conclusion depends on the assumption that the demand curve slopes downward to the right, but, as we noted in a previous section, this assumption is generally true.

The Price System and the Determination of What Is Produced

Having described how prices are determined in free markets, we can now describe more adequately how the price system goes about performing the four basic tasks that face any economic system. (In the previous chapter, we sketched out the functions of the price system, but in a very cursory manner.) Let's begin by considering the determination of what society will produce: how does the price system carry out this task? As pointed out in the previous chapter, consumers indicate what goods and services they want in the marketplace, and producers try to meet these wants. More specifically, the demand curve for a product shows how much of that product consumers want at various prices. If consumers don't want much of it at a certain price, its demand curve will indicate that fact by being positioned close to the vertical axis at that price. In other words, the demand curve will show that, at this price for the product, the amount consumers will buy is small. On the other hand, if consumers want lots of the product at this price, its demand curve will be far from the vertical axis.

A product's demand curve is an important determinant of how much firms will produce of the product, since it indicates the amount of the product that will be demanded at each price. From the point of view of the producers, the demand curve indicates the amount they can sell at each price. In a capitalist economy, firms are in business to make money. Thus, the manufacturers of any product will turn it out only if the amount of money they receive from consumers exceeds the cost of putting the product on the market. Acting in accord with the profit motive, firms are led to produce what the consumers desire. For example, we saw in the previous section that if consumers' tastes shift in favor of foods containing wheat, the demand curve for wheat will shift to the right, which will result in an increase in the price of wheat. This increase will stimulate farmers to produce more wheat. For example, when the demand curve shifts from *DD′ to* D_1D_1' in Figure 4.10, the equilibrium quantity produced increases from *OQ* to OQ_1. Given the shift in the demand curve, it is profitable for firms to step up their production. Acting in their own self-interest, they are led to make production decisions geared to the wants of the consumers.

Thus, the price system uses the self-interest of the producers to get them to produce what consumers want. Consumers register what they want in the marketplace by their purchasing decisions—i.e., their demand curves. Producers can make more money by responding to consumer wants than by ignoring them. Consequently, they are led to produce what consumers want—and are willing to pay enough for to cover the producers' costs. Note that costs as well as demand determine what will be produced, and that producers are not forced by anyone to do anything. They can produce air conditioners for Eskimos if they like—and if they are prepared to absorb the losses. The price system uses prices to communicate the relevant signals to producers, and metes out the penalties and rewards in the form of losses or profits.

The Price System and the Determination of How Goods Are Produced

Next, consider how society determines how each good and service is produced. How does the price system carry out this task? As pointed out in the previous chapter, the price of each resource gives producers an indication of how scarce this resource is, and how valuable in other uses. Clearly, firms should produce goods and services at minimum cost. Suppose that there are two ways of producing tables: Technique A and Technique B. Technique A requires 4 manhours of labor and $10 worth of wood per table, whereas Technique B requires 5 manhours of labor and $8 worth of wood. If the price of a manhour of labor is $4, Technique A should be used since a table costs $26 with this technique, as opposed to $28 with technique B.[6] In other words, Technique A uses fewer resources per table.

The price system nudges producers to opt for Technique A rather than Technique B through profits and losses. If each table commands a price of $35, then by using Technique A, producers make a profit of $35 – $26 = $9 per table. If they use Technique B, they make a profit of $35 – $28 = $7 per table. Thus producers, if they maximize profit, will be led to adopt Technique A. Their desire for profit leads them to adopt the techniques that will enable society to get the most out of its resources. No one commands firms to use particular techniques. Washington officials do not order steel plants to substitute the basic oxygen process for open hearths, or petroleum refineries to substitute catalytic cracking for thermal cracking. It is all done through the impersonal marketplace.

You should not, however, get the idea that the price system operates with kid gloves. Suppose all firms producing tables used Technique B until this past year, when Technique A was developed: in other words, Technique A is based on a new technology. Given this technological change, the supply curve for tables will shift to the right, as we saw in a previous section, and the price of a table will fall. Suppose it drops to $27. If some firm insists on sticking with Technique B, it will lose money at the rate of $1 a table; and as these losses mount, the firm's owners will become increasingly uncomfortable. The firm will either switch to Technique A or go bankrupt. The price system leans awfully hard on producers that try to ignore its signals.

[6] To obtain these figures, note that the cost with Technique A is 4 manhours times $4 plus $10, or $26, while the cost with Technique B is 5 manhours times $4 plus $8, or $28.

The Price System and the Determination of Who Gets What

Let's turn now to how society's output will be distributed among the people: how does the price system carry out this task? How much a person receives in goods and services depends on his money income, which in turn is determined under the price system by the amount of various resources that he owns and by the price of each resource. Thus, under the price system, each person's income is determined in the marketplace: he comes to the marketplace with certain resources to sell, and his income depends on how much he can get for them.

The question of who gets what is solved at two levels by the price system. Consider an individual product—for example, the tables discussed in the previous section. For the individual product, the question of who gets what is solved by the equality of quantity demanded and quantity supplied. If the price of these tables is at its equilibrium level, the quantity demanded will equal the quantity supplied. Consumers who are willing and able to pay the equilibrium price (or more) get the tables, while those who are unwilling or unable to pay it do not get them. It is just as simple—and as impersonal—as that. It doesn't matter whether you are a nice guy or a scoundrel, or whether you are a connoisseur of tables or someone who doesn't know good workmanship from poor: all that matters is whether you are able and willing to pay the equilibrium price.

Next, consider the question of who gets what at a somewhat more fundamental level. After all, whether a consumer is able and willing to pay the equilibrium price for a good depends on his money income. Thus, Aristotle Onassis can pay the equilibrium price for an astonishing variety of things, whereas the Ríos family can scrape up the equilibrium price for very little. As we have already seen, a consumer's money income depends on the amount of resources of various kinds that he owns and the price that he can get for them. Some people have lots of resources: they are endowed with skill and intelligence and industry, or they have lots of capital or land. Other people have little in the way of resources. Moreover, some people have resources that command a high price, while others have resources that are of little monetary value. The result is that, under the price system, some consumers, like Aristotle Onassis, get a lot more of society's output than other consumers, like the Ríos family.

The Price System and Economic Growth

Let's turn now to the task of providing for an adequate rate of growth of per capita income. How does the price system do this? As pointed out in the previous chapter, a nation's rate of increase of per capita income depends on the rate of growth of its resources and the rate of increase of the efficiency with which they are used. First, consider the rate of growth of society's resources. The price system controls the amount of new capital goods produced much as it controls the amount of consumer goods produced. Similarly, the price system influences the amount society invests in educating, training, and upgrading its labor resources. To a considerable extent, the amount invested in such resource-augmenting activities is determined by the profitability of such investments, which is determined in turn by the pattern of prices.

Next, consider the rate of increase of the efficiency with which a society's resources are used. Clearly, this factor depends heavily on the rate of technological change. If technology is advancing at a rapid rate, it should be possible to get more and more out of a society's resources. But if technology is advancing rather slowly, it is likely to be difficult to get much more out of them. The price system affects the rate of technological change in a variety of ways: it influences the profitability of investing in research and development, the profitability of introducing new processes and products into commercial practice, and the profitability of accepting technological change—as well as the losses involved in spurning it.

The price system establishes strong incentives for firms to introduce new technology. Any firm that can find a cheaper way to produce an existing product, or a way to produce a better product, will have a profitable jump on its competitors. Until its competitors can do the same thing, this firm can reap higher profits than it otherwise could. Of course, these higher profits will eventually be competed away, as other firms begin to imitate this firm's innovation. But lots of money can be made in the period during which this firm has a lead over its competitors. These profits are an important incentive for the introduction of new technology.

The Price System in Action behind Enemy Lines

Just as general discussions of tennis will take a neophyte only so far, after which he or she must watch and participate in a few matches, so a general discussion of the price system will take a student only so far. Then he should look at real-life examples of the price system at work. Our first illustration of the price system in operation is a prisoner-of-war camp in World War II. This case is not chosen because of its inherent importance, but because of its simplicity. Just as certain elementary forms of life illustrate important biological principles in a simple way, so the economic organization of a prisoner-of-war camp is an elementary form of economic system that illustrates certain important economic principles simply and well.

The prisoner-of-war camp was so elementary because no goods were produced there. All commodities were provided by the country running the camp, by the Red Cross, and by other outside donors. Each prisoner received an equal amount of food and supplies—canned milk, jam, butter, cookies, cigarettes, etc. In addition, private parcels of clothing, cigarettes, and other supplies were received, with different prisoners, of course, receiving different quantities. Because no goods were produced in the prisoner-of-war camp, the first two tasks of an economic system (What will be produced? How will it be produced?) were not relevant; neither was the fourth task (What provision is to be made for growth?).

All that did matter in this elementary economic system was the third task: to determine who would consume the various available goods. At first blush, the answer may seem obvious: each prisoner would consume the goods he received from the detaining country, the Red Cross, and private packages. But this assumes that prisoners would not trade goods back and forth ("I'll swap you a cigarette for some milk"), which is clearly unrealistic. After all, some prisoners smoked cigarettes, others did not; some liked jam and didn't like canned beef, others liked canned beef and didn't like jam. Thus, there was bound to be exchange of this sort, and the real question is in what way and on what terms such exchange took place.

How did the prisoners go about exchanging goods? According to one observer, the process developed as follows:

> Starting with simple direct barter, such as a nonsmoker giving a smoker friend his cigarette issue in exchange for a chocolate ration, more complex exchanges soon became an accepted custom . . . Within a week or two, as the volume of trade grew, rough scales of exchange values came into existence. [Some prisoners], who had at first exchanged tinned beef for practically any other foodstuff, began to insist on jam and margarine. It was realized that a tin of jam was worth one half lb. of margarine plus something else, that a cigarette issue was worth several chocolate issues, and a tin of diced carrots was worth practically nothing . . . By the end of the month, there was a lively trade in all commodities and their relative values were well known, and expressed not in terms of one another—one didn't quote [jam] in terms of sugar—but in terms of cigarettes. The cigarette became the standard of value.[7]

[7] R. A. Radford, "The Economic Organization of a Prisoner of War Camp," reprinted in E. Mansfield, *Economics: Readings, Issues, and Cases,* New York: Norton, 1974.

Thus, the prisoners used the price system to solve the problem of allocating the available supply of goods among consumers. A market developed for each good. This market had, of course, both a demand and a supply side. Each good had its price—but this price was quoted in cigarettes, not dollars and cents. These markets were not started in a self-conscious, deliberate way. No one said, "Let's adopt the price system to allocate available supplies," or "Let's vote on whether or not to adopt the price system." Instead, the system just evolved. . . and it worked.

To see how the supply of a particular good—jam, say—was allocated, look at Figure 4.13, which shows the market supply curve for jam, *SS′*. In the short run, this supply was fixed, so *SS′* is a vertical line. Figure 4.13 also provides the market demand curve for jam, *DD′*, which shows the amount of jam the prisoners wanted to consume at various prices of jam—expressed in terms of cigarettes. For example, *DD′* shows that the prisoners wanted OQ_1 tins of jam when a tin of jam cost OP_1 cigarettes, and OQ_2 tins of jam when a tin of jam cost OP_2 cigarettes. For the quantity demanded to equal the available supply, the price of a tin of jam had to be *OP* cigarettes: one tin of jam had to exchange for *OP* cigarettes. At this price, the available supply of jam was rationed, without resort to fights among prisoners or intervention by the prison authorities. Those prisoners who could and would pay the price had the jam—and there were just enough such consumers to exhaust the available supply. Moreover, this held true for each of the other goods (including cigarettes) as well.

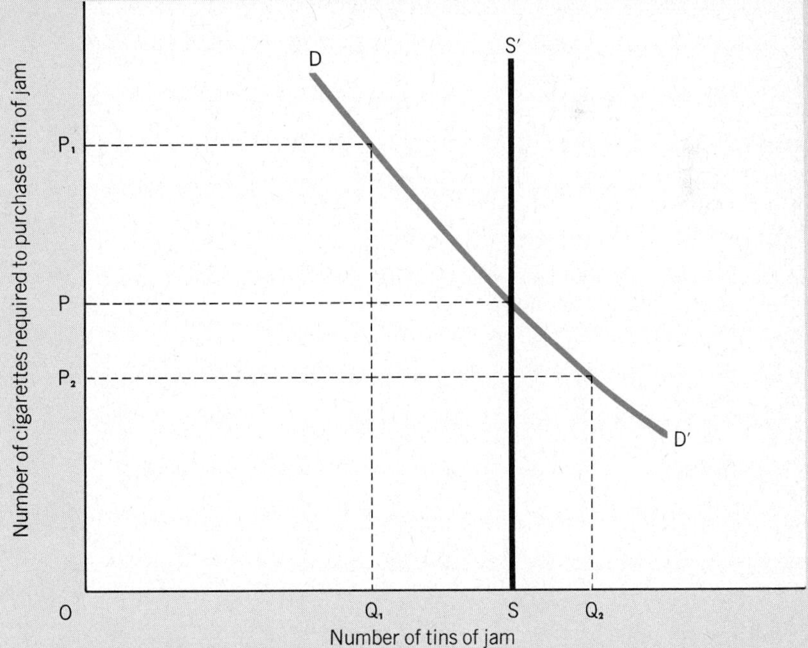

Figure 4.13
Determinants of Equilibrium Price of a Tin of Jam (in Terms of Cigarettes) in a Prisoner-of-War Camp

The market supply for jam is fixed at *OS* tins. The market demand curve is *DD′*. Thus the equilibrium price of a tin of jam is *OP* cigarettes. If the price were OP_1, OQ_1 tins would be demanded; if the price were OP_2, OQ_2 tins would be demanded.

The Price System in Action on the Great White Way

It is a long way from a prisoner-of-war camp to the Broadway theater, but economics, like any good tool of analysis, applies to a very wide variety of problems. In this section, we discuss the theater's pricing problems—and the role of the price system in helping to solve these problems. Prices for tickets to Broadway shows are established at levels that are much the same whether the show is a success or a flop. For example, an orchestra ticket to *Kelly* (which managed to hold out for one performance before closing) cost about as much as an orchestra ticket to such hits as *Hair* or *A Little Night Music*. And once a play opens, the price of a ticket remains much the same whether the play is greeted with universal praise or with discontented critics and customers.

Because of these pricing methods, the Broadway theater has been beset for many years by serious problems. Here they are described by two veteran observers of the Broadway stage:

> For centuries the sale of theater tickets has brought on corruption and confusion. When there are more buyers than sellers, a black market results. The so-called "retail" price, the price printed on the ticket, becomes meaningless. Speculation doubles, triples, or quadruples the "real" as opposed to the "legal" asking price. A smash hit on Broadway means "ice"—the difference between the real and legal prices—a well-hidden but substantial cash flow that is divided among shadowy middlemen. Ticket scandals break out in New York as regularly as the flu. The scenario is familiar. A play opens and becomes a superhit. Tickets become difficult, then impossible, to obtain. There are letters to the newspapers . . . Shocking corruption is discovered. Someone . . . is convicted of overcharging and accepting illegal gratuities. Someone may even go to jail. The black market, valiantly scotched, *never stops for a single moment.*[8]

Besides enriching crooked box-office men and managers, as well as other shadowy elements of society, the black market for theater tickets has the additional undesirable effect of excluding the authors, composers, directors, and stars of the play from participation in the premium revenue. Almost all of these people receive a percentage of the play's revenues; and if the revenues at the box office are less than the customers pay for their seats (because of "ice"), these people receive less than they would if no black market existed. The amount of "ice" can be substantial. For example, Rodgers and Hammerstein estimated that, at one performance of their play, *South Pacific,* the public probably paid about $25,000 for tickets with a face value of $7,000, the amount turned in at the box office.

To focus on the problem here, let's look at the market for tickets to a particular performance of *My Fair Lady* (one of Broadway's all-time big hits) when it was at the height of its popularity. Since the supply of tickets to a given performance is fixed, the market supply curve, SS' in Figure 4.14, is a vertical line at the quantity of tickets corresponding to the capacity of the theatre. The price set officially on the price of a ticket was $8. But because the show was enormously popular, the market demand curve was DD' in Figure 4.14, and the equilibrium price for a ticket was $50.[9]

Figure 4.14 makes the nature of the problem apparent: at the official price of $8, the quantity of tickets demanded is much greater than the quantity supplied. Supply and demand don't match. Obviously, there is an incentive for people to buy the tickets from the box office at $8 and sell them at the higher prices customers are willing to pay. There is also an incentive for box-office men to sell them surreptitiously at higher prices and turn in only $8. The price system cannot play the role it did in the prisoner-of-war camp for jam and other goods. It cannot act as an effective rationing device because, to do so, the price of tickets would have to increase to its equilibrium level, $50.

[8] S. Little and A. Cantor, *The Playmakers,* New York: Norton, 1970, p. 220.

[9] This figure is an estimate based on an article in *Variety.*

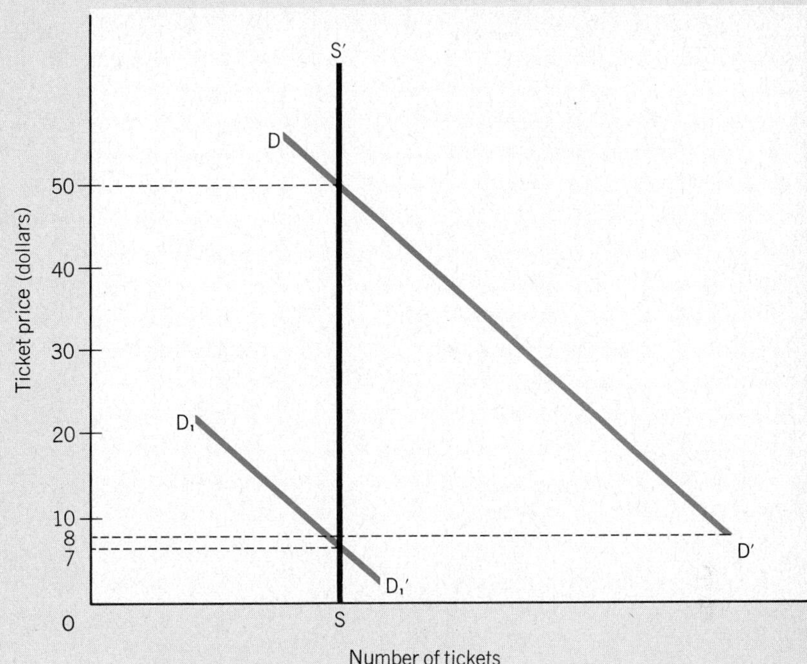

Figure 4.14
Equilibrium Price for Tickets to *My Fair Lady*

The market supply for tickets is fixed at *OS* per performance. If the demand curve is *DD′*, the equilibrium price of a ticket is \$50. (If the demand curve is D_1D_1', the equilibrium price is \$7.) If the demand curve is *DD′* and the price of a ticket is \$8, the quantity of tickets demanded will far exceed the quantity supplied.

Many theater experts believe that the solution to Broadway's pricing problems lies in allowing the price system to work more effectively by permitting ticket prices to vary depending on a show's popularity. For example, the official ticket price would be allowed to rise to \$50 for *My Fair Lady*. On the other hand, if *My Fair Lady* had been much less popular and its market demand curve had been D_1D_1' in Figure 4.14, its official ticket price would have been allowed to fall to \$7. In this way, the black market for tickets would be eliminated, since the equilibrium price—which equates supply and demand—would be the official price. "Ice" would also be eliminated, since there would be no difference between the official and the actual price paid, and the people responsible for the show would receive its full receipts, not share them with crooked box-office men and illegal operators.

Rationing, Coupons, and All That

During national emergencies, the government sometimes puts a lid on prices, not allowing them to reach their equilibrium levels. For example, during World War II, the government did not allow the prices of various foodstuffs to rise to their equilibrium levels, because it felt that this would have been inequitable (and highly unpopular). Under such circumstances, the quantity demanded of a product exceeds the quantity supplied. In other words, the situation is like that in Figure 4.14, where the quantity demanded of tickets for *My Fair Lady* exceeds the quantity supplied. There is a shortage.

Since the price system is not allowed to perform its rationing function, some formal system of rationing or allocating the available supply of the product may be required. Thus, in World War II,

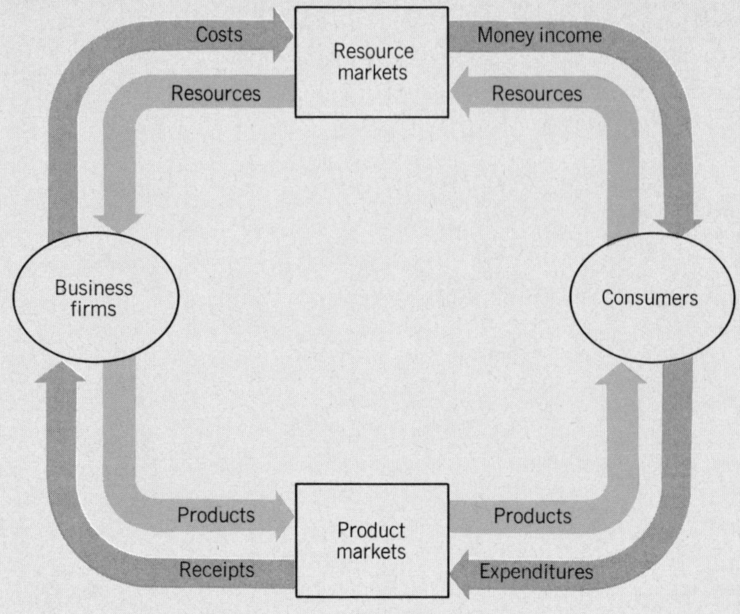

Figure 4.15
The Circular Flows of Money and Products

In product markets, consumers exchange money for products and firms exchange products for money. In resource markets, consumers exchange resources for money and firms exchange money for resources.

families were issued ration coupons which determined how much they could buy of various commodities. And in late 1973, when supplies of gasoline seemed to be cut by the curtailment of Arab exports of oil to the United States, there was serious talk that gasoline and oil might be rationed in a similar way. Such rationing schemes may be justified in emergencies (of reasonably short duration), but they can result eventually in serious distortions, since prices are not allowed to do the job normally expected of them. More will be said on this score in Chapter 15.

The Circular Flows of Money and Products

So far we have been concerned largely with the workings of a single market—the market for wheat or tables or jam or tickets to *My Fair Lady*. But how do all of the various markets fit together? This is a very important question. Perhaps the best way to begin answering it is to distinguish between product markets and resource markets. As their names indicate, ***product markets*** *are markets where products are bought and sold; and* ***resource markets*** *are markets where resources are bought and sold.* Let's first consider product markets. As shown in Figure 4.15, firms provide products to consumers in product markets, and receive money in return. The money the firms receive is their receipts; to consumers, on the other hand, it represents their expenditures.

Next, let's consider resource markets. Figure 4.15 shows that consumers provide resources—including labor—to firms in resource markets, and receive money in return. The money the consumers receive is their income; to firms, on the other hand, it represents their costs. Note that the flow of resources and products in Figure 4.15 is counterclockwise: that is, *consumers provide resources to firms which in turn provide goods and services to consumers.* On the other hand, the flow of money in Figure 4.15 is clockwise: that is, *firms pay money for resources to consumers who in turn use the money to buy goods and services from the firms.* Both flows—that of resources and products, and that of money—go on simultaneously and repeatedly.

So long as consumers spend all their income, the flow of money income from firms to consumers is exactly equal to the flow of expenditure from consumers to firms. Thus, these circular flows, like Ole Man River, just keep rolling along. As a first approximation, this is a perfectly good model. But as we pointed out in Chapter 1, capitalist economies have experienced periods of widespread unemployment and severe inflation that this model cannot explain. Also, note that our simple economy in Figure 4.15 has no government sector. In the following chapter, we shall bring the government into the picture. Under pure capitalism, the government would play a limited role in the economic system, but in the mixed capitalistic system we have in the United States, the government plays an important role indeed.

Summary

Consumers and firms are the basic units comprising the private sector of the economy. Consumers, whether individuals or households, purchase the goods and services that are the ultimate end-products of the economic system. Consumers are obviously an extremely varied lot, as a brief comparison of Aristotle Onassis and the Ríos family indicates. A firm is a unit that produces a good or service for sale. About 9/10 of the goods and services produced in the United States are produced by firms, which number in the millions. Like consumers, they are extremely varied in size, age, power, and purpose, as illustrated by a comparison of Amacher's drugstore and General Motors. A market is a group of firms and individuals that are in touch with each other in order to buy or sell some commodity or service. When a market for a homogeneous product contains so many buyers and sellers that none of them can influence the price, economists call it a perfectly competitive market.

There are two sides of every market: the demand side and the supply side. The demand side can be represented by the market demand curve, which almost always slopes downward to the right and whose location depends on consumer tastes, the number and income of consumers, and the prices of other commodities. The supply side of the market can be represented by the market supply curve, which generally slopes upward to the right and whose location depends on technology and resource prices. The equilibrium price and equilibrium quantity of the commodity are given by the intersection of the market demand and supply curves. If conditions remain reasonably stable for a time, the actual price and quantity should move close to the equilibrium price and quantity. Changes in the position and shape of the demand curve—in response to changes in consumer tastes, income, population, and prices of other commodities—result in changes in the equilibrium price and equilibrium output of a product. Similarly, changes in the position and shape of the supply curve—in response to changes in technology and resource prices, among other things—also result in changes in the equilibrium price and equilibrium output of a product.

To determine what goods and services society will produce, the price system sets up incentives for firms to produce what consumers want. To the extent that they produce what consumers want and are willing to pay for, firms reap profits; to the extent that they don't, they experience losses. Similarly, the price system sets up strong incentives for firms to produce these goods at minimum cost. These incentives take the form of profits for firms that minimize costs and losses for firms that operate with relatively high costs. To determine who gets what, the price system results in each person's receiving an income that depends on the quantity of resources he owns and the prices that they command. The price system also establishes incentives for activities that result in increases in a society's per capita income. The very simple case of a prisoner-of-war camp and the more complicated case of the Broadway theater provide real illustrations of the price system in action.

There are circular flows of money and products in a capitalist economy. In product markets, firms provide products to consumers and receive money in return. In resource markets, consumers provide resources to firms, and receive money in return. The flow of resources and products is as follows: consumers provide resources to firms which in turn provide goods and services to consumers. The flow of money is as follows: firms pay money for resources to consumers who in turn use the money to buy goods and services from firms. Both flows go on simultaneously and repeatedly.

CONCEPTS FOR REVIEW

Consumer	Supply	Equilibrium price
Firm	Perfect competition	Product market
Market	Market demand curve	Resource market
Demand	Market supply curve	Actual price

QUESTIONS FOR DISCUSSION AND REVIEW

1. According to W. Allen Wallis, "Not only do prices convey information on how an individual should act, but they provide at the same time a powerful inducement for him to do so." Do you agree? If you do, explain why it is true. If you don't, explain where it is wrong.

2. Suppose that you were appointed head of a blue-ribbon commission to recommend changes in pricing practice for the entertainment industry. Would you recommend a free market for tickets for Broadway shows? For tickets to the San Francisco Opera? For the Dallas Cowboys games? In each case, why or why not?

3. If consumers show a decreasing preference for a product, this will cause the demand curve to shift to the right. True or False?

4. The demand curve for a commodity is *not* likely to be affected by
   a. number of consumers.
   b. changes in per capita income.
   c. prices of the resources used to produce the product.
   d. prices of other commodities.

CHAPTER 5

The Economic Role of the Government

To state that the United States is a mixed capitalist system, in which both government decisions and the price system play important roles, is hardly to provoke a controversy. But going a step beyond, as we shall in this chapter, takes us into areas where viewpoints often diverge. The proper functions of government and the desirable size and nature of government expenditures and taxes are not matters on which all agree. Indeed, the question of how big government should be, and what its proper functions are, is hotly debated by conservatives and liberals throughout the land. Of course, this is only a preliminary airing of many of these issues. As the base of economic analysis is broadened in subsequent chapters, much more will be said on these matters, and you will be in a far better position to judge them for yourself.

In the latter part of this chapter, we describe the nature and causes of our farm problem, and indicate the extent to which government programs seem to have solved this problem. This is an interesting application of the supply and demand theory presented in the previous chapter, as well as an example of the economic role of the government. Whether you are from the city or the country, you should be interested in the nature and success of our farm programs—if for no other reason than that you and your tax-paying and food-consuming friends and relatives pay for them.

Limitations of the Price System

Despite its many advantages, the price system suffers from serious limitations. Critics of capitalism never tire of citing them, and of arguing that the price system should be replaced by some other mechanism for solving our society's basic economic problems. But the important limitations of the price system do not mean that it should be scrapped—and in fact we have not scrapped it. Instead, we have charged the government with the responsibility for correcting many of its shortcomings. Thus, to a considerable extent, the government's role in the economy has developed in response to the limitations of the price system.

What are these limitations? First, *there is no reason to believe that the distribution of income generated by the price system is fair or, in some sense, best.* Aristotle Onassis obviously receives much more income in a day than the Ríos family does in a year. Most people feel that the distribution of income generated by the price system should be altered to suit humanitarian needs; in particular, that help should be given to the poor. Both liberals and conservatives tend to agree on this score, although there are arguments over the extent to which the poor should be helped and the conditions under which they should be eligible for help. But the general principle that the government should step in to redistribute income in favor of the poor is generally accepted in the United States today.[1]

Second, *some goods and services cannot be provided through the price system because there is no way to exclude a citizen from consuming the good whether he pays for it or not.* For example, there is no way to prevent a citizen from benefiting from national expenditures on defense, whether he pays money toward defense or not. Consequently, the price system cannot be used to provide such goods; no one will pay for them since they will receive them whether they pay or not. Such goods are called ***public goods.*** It is generally agreed that the government must provide public goods. Such goods are consumed collectively or jointly, and are indivisible in the sense that their benefits cannot be priced in a market.

Third, *in cases where the production or consumption of a good by one firm or consumer has adverse or beneficial uncompensated effects on other firms or consumers, the price system will not operate effectively.* An **external economy** is said to occur when consumption or production by one person or firm results in uncompensated benefits to another person or firm. A good example of an external economy exists where fundamental research carried out by one firm is used by another firm. (To cite one such case, there were external economies from the Bell Telephone Laboratories' invention of the transistor.) Where external economies exist, it is generally agreed that the price system will produce too little of the good in question and that the government should supplement the amount produced by private enterprise. This is the basic rationale for much of the government's huge investment in basic science. An ***external diseconomy*** is said to occur when consumption or production by one person or firm results in uncompensated costs to another person or firm. A good example of an external diseconomy occurs when a firm dumps pollutants into a stream and makes the water unfit for use by firms and people

[1] Also, because the wealthy have more "dollar votes" than the poor, the sorts of goods and services that society produces will reflect this fact. Thus, luxuries for the rich may be produced in larger amounts and necessities for the poor may be produced in smaller amounts than some critics regard as sensible and equitable. This is another frequently encountered criticism of the price system.

downstream. Where activities result in external diseconomies, it is generally agreed that the price system will tolerate too much of the activity and that the government should curb it. For example, as we shall see in Chapter 18, the government, in keeping with this doctrine, is involving itself increasingly in environmental protection and the reduction of air and water pollution.[2]

What Functions Should the Government Perform?

There are wide differences of opinion on the proper role of government in economic affairs. Although it is generally agreed that the government should redistribute income in favor of the poor, provide public goods, and offset the effects of external economies and diseconomies, there is considerable disagreement over how far the government should go in these areas, and what additional areas the government should be responsible for. Some people feel that "Big Government" is already a problem; that government is doing too much. Others believe that the public sector of the economy is being undernourished and that government should be allowed to do more. This is a fundamental question, and one that involves a great deal more than economics.

On the one hand, conservatives, such as the University of Chicago's distinguished economist, Milton Friedman, believe that the government's role should be limited severely. They feel that economic and political freedom is likely to be undermined by excessive reliance on the state. Moreover, they tend to be skeptical about the government's ability to solve the social and economic problems at hand. They feel that the prevailing faith in the government's power to make a substantial dent in these problems is unreasonable, and they call for more and better information concerning the sorts of tasks government can reasonably be expected to do—and do well. They point to the slowness of the government bureaucracy, the difficulty in controlling huge government organizations, the inefficiencies political considerations can breed, and the difficulties in telling whether government programs are successful or not. On the basis of these considerations, they argue that the government's role should be carefully circumscribed.

The flavor of the conservative position on this question, as well as a generous helping of sarcasm and wit, is evident in the remarks of George Stigler, another distinguished economist at the University of Chicago:

> I consider myself courageous, or at least obtuse, in arguing for a reduction in governmental controls over economic life. You are surely desirous of improving this world, and it assuredly needs an immense amount of improvement. No method of displaying one's public-spiritedness is more popular than to notice a problem and pass a law. It combines ease, the warmth of benevolence, and a suitable disrespect for a less enlightened era. What I propose is, for most people, much less attractive: close study of the comparative performance of public and private economy, and the dispassionate appraisal of special remedies that is involved in compassion for the community at large.[3]

To such remarks, liberals respond with very telling salvos of their own. Just as conservatives tend to be skeptical of the government's ability to solve important social and economic problems, so liberals tend to be skeptical about the price system's ability to solve these problems. They point to the important limitations of the price system, discussed above, and they assert that the government can accomplish a great deal that will benefit the nation and the world.

[2] The effects of external economies and diseconomies can also be taken care of by legal arrangements that assign liabilities for damages and compensate for benefits. However, such arrangements often are impractical or too costly to be used.

[3] G. Stigler, "The Government of the Economy," *A Dialogue on the Proper Economic Role of the State,* University of Chicago, Graduate School of Business, Selected Paper no. 7, reprinted in E. Mansfield, *Economics: Readings, Issues, and Cases,* New York: Norton, 1974. Also, see M. Friedman, *Capitalism and Freedom,* Chicago: University of Chicago Press, 1962.

According to some distinguished liberals, like Harvard's John Kenneth Galbraith, the public sector of the economy is being starved of needed resources, while the private sector is catering to relatively unimportant wants. In his best-selling book, *The Affluent Society,* Galbraith argues that consumers are led by advertising and other promotional efforts to purchase more and more goods of marginal significance to them. On the other hand, in his opinion, the nation is suffering because too little is spent on government services like education, transportation, and urban renewal.[4] In the next chapter, we shall discuss this proposition in more detail.

Liberals tend to be less concerned than conservatives about the effects of greater governmental intervention in the economy on personal freedom. They point out that the price system also involves coercion, since the fact that the price system awards the available goods and services to those who can pay their equilibrium price can be viewed as a form of coercion. Moreover, some people are awarded only a pittance by the price system: in a real sense, they are coerced into discomfort and malnutrition.[5] The relationship between government intervention and personal freedom is a tricky and controversial one that involves a great deal more than economics. Your own feelings on this score are likely to depend on your political and ethical philosophy.

A Legal, Social, and Competitive Framework

Although there is considerable disagreement over the proper role of the government, both conservatives and liberals agree that it must do certain things. The first of these is to establish the "rules of the game"—that is, a legal, social, and competitive framework enabling the price system to function as it should. Specifically, the government must see to it that contracts are enforced, that private ownership is protected, and that fraud is prevented. Clearly, these matters must be tended to if the price system is to work properly. Also, the government must maintain order (through the establishment of police and other forces), establish a monetary system (so that money can be used to facilitate trade and exchange), and provide standards for the weight and quality of products.

As an example of this sort of government intervention, consider the Pure Food and Drug Act. This act, originally passed in 1906 and subsequently amended in various ways, protects the consumer against improper and fraudulent activities on the part of producers of foods and drugs. It prohibits the merchandising of impure or falsely labeled food or drugs, and it forces producers to specify the quantity and quality of the contents on labels. These requirements strengthen the price system. Without them, the typical consumer would be unable to tell whether food or drugs are pure or properly labeled. Unless the consumer can be sure that he is getting what he is paying for, the basic logic underlying the price system breaks down. Similar regulation and legislation have been instituted in fields other than food and drugs—and for similar reasons.

Besides establishing a legal and social framework that will enable the price system to do its job, the government must also see to it that markets remain reasonably competitive. Only if they are will prices reflect consumer desires properly. If, on the other hand, markets are dominated by a few sellers (or a few buyers), prices will be "rigged" by these sellers (or buyers) to promote their own interests. For example, if a single firm is the sole producer of aluminum, it is a safe bet that this firm will establish a higher price than if there were many aluminum producers competing among themselves. The unfortunate thing about prices determined in noncompetitive markets—rigged prices, if you will —is that they give incorrect signals concerning

[4] J. K. Galbraith, *The Affluent Society,* Boston: Houghton Mifflin, 1958.

[5] See P. Samuelson, "The Economic Role of Private Activity," *A Dialogue on the Proper Economic Role of the State,* University of Chicago, Graduate School of Business, Selected Paper no. 7, reprinted in E. Mansfield, *Economics: Readings, Issues, and Cases.*

what consumers want and how scarce resources and commodities are. Producers, responding to these incorrect signals, do not produce the right things in the right quantities. Consumers respond to these incorrect signals by not supplying the right resources in the right amounts, and by not consuming the proper amounts of the goods that are produced. Thus the price system is not permitted to solve the four basic economic problems properly in the absence of reasonable competition.

To try to encourage and preserve competition, the Congress has enacted a series of antitrust laws, such as the Sherman Antitrust Act and the Clayton Act, and has established the Federal Trade Commission. The antitrust laws make it illegal for firms to collude or to attempt to monopolize the sale of a product. Both conservative and liberal economists, with some notable exceptions, tend to favor the intent and operation of the antitrust laws. In addition, the government tries to control the activities of firms in markets where competition cannot be expected to prevail (as in the telephone industry, where efficient operations would be destroyed if more than a very few firms got in the act). In industries of this sort, the government often establishes commissions to regulate prices and standards of services. Such regulatory commissions are common in the communications, transportation, electric, and gas industries.

Redistribution of Income

We have already noted at several points the general agreement that the government should redistribute income in favor of the poor. In other words, it is usually felt that help should be given to people who are ill, handicapped, old and infirm, disabled, and unable for other reasons to provide for themselves. To some extent, the nation has decided that income—or at least a certain minimum income—should be divorced from productive services. Of course, this doesn't mean that people who are too lazy to work should be given a handout. It does mean that people who cannot provide for themselves should be helped. To implement this principle, various payments are made by the government to needy people—including the aged, the handicapped, the unemployed, pensioners, and veterans.

These welfare payments are to some extent a "depression baby," for they grew substantially during the Great Depression of the 1930s, when relief payments became a necessity. But they also represent a feeling shared by a large segment of the population that human beings should be assured that, however the Wheel of Fortune spins and whatever number comes up, they will not starve and their children will not be deprived of a healthy environment and basic schooling. Of course, someone has to pay for this. Welfare payments allow the poor to take more from the nation's output than they produce. In general, the more affluent members of society contribute some of their claims on output to pay for these programs, their contributions being in the form of taxes. By using its expenditures to help certain groups and by taxing other groups to pay for these programs, the government accomplishes each year, without revolt and without bayonets, a substantial redistribution of income. This is a crucial aspect of the government's role in our economy.

It should not be assumed, however, that all government programs transfer income from the rich to the poor. On the contrary, some programs, intentionally or unintentionally, soak the poor to give to the rich. Some government programs fatten the purses of rich farmers, some tax loopholes allow the affluent to dodge taxes through the creation of trusts and other legal devices, and some important taxes—such as sales taxes—hit the poor harder than the rich. Nonetheless, the best available evidence indicates that, when all its activities are taken into account, the government does take from the rich to give to the poor. In other words, taking account of both its expenditures and the taxes it levies, the government redistributes income in favor of the poor. Whether it goes as far as it should in this direction is a more nettlesome question, the answer to which will depend on your own ethical values.

Economic Stabilization

It is also generally agreed that the government should see to it that the economy maintains reasonably full employment with reasonably stable prices. Capitalist economies have tended to alternate between booms and depressions in the past. The Great Depression of the 1930s hit the American economy—and the world economy—a particularly devastating blow, putting millions of people out of work and in desperate shape. When World War II ended, the American people vowed that they would not let a depression of this sort occur again. The Congress passed the Employment Act of 1946, which stated that it was the responsibility of the federal government to maintain full employment in the United States. In particular, the federal government was not supposed to tolerate unemployment of the sort that materialized during severe depressions in the past.

Of course, it is one thing to charge the federal government with the responsibility for maintaining full employment and quite another thing to tell the federal government how to achieve this goal. Without a good deal of economic knowledge, this law would have been as empty as Atlantic City in December. After all, it is useless to tell the federal government to do something no one knows how to do. Fortunately, however, advances in economic knowledge during the 1930s made it much more likely that the federal government could carry out the responsibility of maintaining full employment. The man who contributed much of this new economic knowledge was John Maynard Keynes, one of the great figures of modern economics, whom we will continue to encounter in subsequent chapters.

Besides maintaining full employment, the government must also maintain a reasonably stable price level. No economy can function well if prices are gyrating wildly. Through its control of the money supply and its decisions regarding expenditures and taxation, the government has considerable impact on the price level, as well as on the level of employment.

Public Goods and Externalities

As we have indicated, most people agree that the government must provide public goods. Let's consider the nature of public goods in more detail. They often are relatively indivisible: they come in such big units that there is no way to break them into pieces that can be bought or sold in ordinary markets. Also, they are consumed by society as a whole. Once such goods are produced, there is no way to bar certain citizens from consuming them. Whether or not a citizen contributes toward their cost, he benefits from them. As pointed out in a previous section, this means that the price system cannot be used to handle the production and distribution of such goods.

An obvious example of a public good is a lighthouse. There might be general agreement that the cost of building a particular lighthouse would be more than justified by the benefits (saving of lives, fewer shipwrecks, cheaper transportation). Nonetheless, no firm or person would build and operate such a lighthouse because they could not find any way to charge the ships using the lighthouse for the service. Nor would any single user gain enough from the lighthouse to warrant constructing and operating it. Moreover, voluntary contributions are very unlikely to support such a lighthouse because each user is likely to feel that his contribution will not affect the outcome and that he will be able to use the lighthouse whether or not he contributes. Consequently, the lighthouse will be established and operated only if the government intervenes.

National defense is another example. The benefits of expenditure on national defense extend to the entire nation. There is no way of preventing a citizen from benefiting from them, whether he contributes to their cost or not. Thus, there is no way to use the price system to provide for national defense. Since it is a public good, national defense must be provided by the government. Similarly with flood control, roads, police and fire protection, public parks, and a host of other such services. In each case, although the people who benefit may not contribute to the costs of these services voluntarily, they may feel better off when the government taxes them to make such services possible.

Other services, such as education and health, can be provided by private enterprise on a fee basis, but much of the population feels that the government should intervene to see to it that everyone, regardless of income level, receives a certain minimum amount of education and health care. Free public education has, of course, been an important and conspicuous part of American society, and in recent years the government has begun to play a more significant role in the health field. Both in health and education, an important argument for government intervention has been that the social benefits of these services exceed the private benefits. However, opponents of such intervention assert that it is paternalistic and that it results in less efficiency in education and health. This is an area of controversy.

Essentially, deciding how much to produce of a public good is a political decision. The citizens of the United States elect senators and congressmen who decide how much should be spent on national defense or education, and how it should be spent. However, it is important to recognize that there are many special-interest groups that lobby hard for the production of certain public goods. For example, an alliance of military and industrial groups presses for increased defense expenditures, and other interested groups promote expenditures on highways, health, education, and other functions.

The tax system is used to pay for the production of public goods. In effect, the government says to each citizen: "Fork over a certain amount of money to pay for the expenses incurred by the government." The amount a particular citizen is assessed may depend on his income (as in the income tax), the value of all or specific types of his property (as in the property tax), the amount he spends on certain types of goods and services (as in the sales tax), or on still other criteria.

Finally, it is generally agreed that the government should encourage the production of goods and services that entail external economies and discourage the production of those that entail external diseconomies. Take the pollution of air and water. When a firm or individual dumps wastes into the water or air, other firms or individuals often must pay all or part of the cost of putting the water or air back into a usable condition. Thus the disposal of these wastes entails external diseconomies. Unless the government prohibits certain kinds of pollution, or enforces air and water quality standards, or charges polluters in accord with the amount of waste they dump into the environment, there will be socially undesirable levels of pollution. In recent years, the government has begun to do more to protect the environment in these ways.

Government Production and "Creeping Socialism"

As we pointed out in the previous section, it is generally accepted that, in the case of public goods and in situations where there are important externalities, the government should intervene to influence their production. But this does not mean that the government must actually produce the good in question. On the contrary, *the government does not produce most of the goods and services it provides.* For example, the federal government supports over ½ of the research and development carried out in the United States, but only about 20 percent of federally supported research and development is carried out in government laboratories. The rest is carried out by firms and universities working under government contracts.[6]

Some of the areas in which our government actually becomes involved in the production of goods and services are familiar. In the United States the post office, the airports, and many water, gas, and electric companies are publicly owned and operated. In these cases it would be inefficient to have many producers, and since competition is not feasible, the courts have held that such industries must be publicly owned or regulated. But there is

[6] Edwin Mansfield, *The Economics of Technological Change,* New York: Norton, 1968, Chapter 6.

no very clear line between them and other industries that have not been publicly owned. For example, many other countries have publicly owned telephone, telegraph, railroad, airline, and broadcasting industries. The reasons why these industries are not under public ownership in the United States are partly historical and cultural. Also, many people feel that public ownership tends to result in too much bureaucracy and inefficiency, and this country has been suspicious of anything smacking of "creeping socialism."

As we explained in Chapter 3, socialism means government ownership and operation of plants, farms, and mines. Clearly, *there has been little movement toward public ownership in the United States,* despite occasional cries to the contrary on the hustings and in the press. Perhaps the most important and controversial area where government ownership has been extended appreciably in the last 40 years has been in electric power. During the administration of Franklin D. Roosevelt, the Tennessee Valley Authority, Bonneville Dam, and Hoover Dam, among others, were established. But this was hardly a widespread thrust toward public ownership—and it took place several decades ago.

However, although there has been little movement toward government ownership and operation, *there has been a tendency in certain fields for the boundaries between the private sector and the public sector to become extremely blurred.* Particularly in the field of defense, it is difficult to know how to categorize some organizations. To what extent is a firm like Lockheed Aircraft Corporation really part of the private sector? Although it is privately owned, most of its output (92 percent in 1971) goes to a single customer—the government. Much of its supply of tools is provided by the government, and government officials play an important role in influencing its decisions, auditing its books, regulating its profits, and so forth. The same tendency toward blurred boundaries between the private and public sectors has occurred in atomic energy, space exploration, and other areas. To a certain extent, it appears that—in the words of Don Price, dean of Harvard's school of public administration—the government "has learned to socialize without assuming ownership."[7] This blurring of the boundaries between the private and public sectors is an important recent development, with repercussions on many aspects of our daily life.

How Big Is the Government?

Up to this point, we have been concerned primarily with the reasons why the government must intervene in our economy—and the types of role it should play—but we have made little or no attempt to describe its role in quantitative terms. It is time now to turn to some of the relevant facts. One useful measure of the extent of the government's role in the American economy is the size of government expenditures, both in absolute terms and as a percent of our nation's total output. This measure makes it clear that the government's role is large.

The sum total of government expenditures—federal, state, and local—was about $400 billion in 1973. Since our nation's total output was about $1.2 trillion, this means that government expenditures are about one-third of our total output. The ratio of government expenditures to total output in the United States has not always been this large, as Figure 5.1 shows. In 1929, the ratio was about 10 percent, as contrasted with about 30 percent in 1973. (Of course, the ratio of government spending to total output is smaller now than during World War II, but in a wartime economy, one would expect this ratio to be abnormally high.)

There are many reasons why government expenditures have grown so much faster than total output. Three of these are particularly important. First, the United States did not maintain anything like the kind of military force in pre-World War II days that it does now. In earlier days, when weapons were relatively simple and cheap, and when we viewed our military and political responsibilities much more narrowly than we do now, our

[7] Don Price, *The Scientific Estate,* Cambridge, Mass.: Belknap Press, 1965, p. 43.

Figure 5.1
Government Spending as a Percent of Total Output, United States.

Government expenditures—federal, state, and local—totaled about $400 billion in 1973. These expenditures, which include transfer payments, have grown more rapidly than total output in this period.

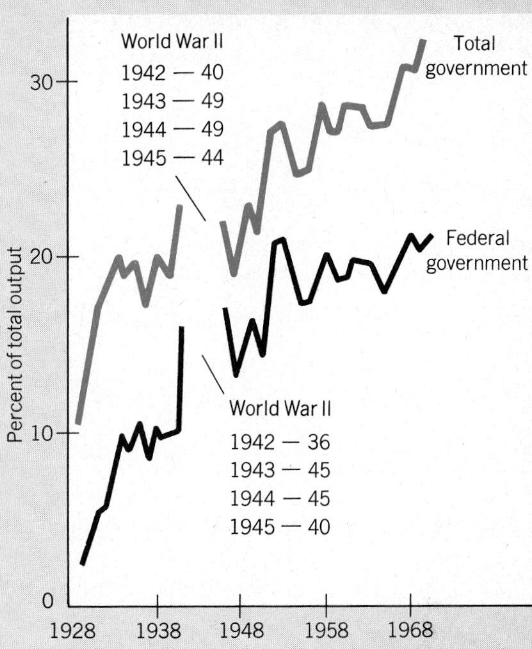

military budget was relatively small. The cost of being a superpower in the days of nuclear weaponry is high by any standards. Second, there has been a long-term increase in the demand for the services provided by government, like more and better schooling, more extensive highways, more complete police and fire protection, and so forth. As incomes rise, people want more of these services. Third, ***government transfer payments***—payments in return for no products or services—have grown substantially. For example, various types of welfare payments have increased markedly. Since transfer payments do not entail any reallocation of resources from private to public goods, but a transfer of income from one private citizen or group to another, Figure 5.1 is, in some respects, an overstatement of the role of the public sector.

When in Table 5.1 we compare the size of government spending in the United States (relative to total output) with that in other countries, we learn that the governments of Sweden, France, West Germany, and the United Kingdom spend more—as a percent of total output—than we do. In part, of course, this is because of the extensive welfare programs in Sweden and the United Kingdom. It is interesting, however, that, despite our huge military programs, we do not spend more

Table 5.1

Taxes as Percentages of Total Output, 1970

Country	Percentage
Sweden	41
France	39
West Germany	35
United Kingdom	33
Canada	29
United States	29
Japan	21
India	13
Spain	12
Mexico	10
Nigeria	9

(relative to total output) than these countries. It is also noteworthy that poor countries like Nigeria —ones with little industry and at a relatively early stage of economic development—spend the least on government services. This is understandable, since such countries must devote more of their output to the basic necessities of life. In many cases, as we saw in Chapter 1, they have a rough time merely feeding their populations.

What the Federal, State, and Local Governments Spend Money On

There are three levels of government in the United States—federal, state, and local. The state governments spend the least, while the federal government spends the most. This was not always the case. Before World War I, the local governments spent more than the federal government. In those days, the federal government did not maintain the large military establishment it does now, nor did it engage in the many programs in health, education, welfare, and other areas that it currently does. Figure 5.1 shows that federal spending is now a much larger percentage of the total than it was 40 years ago. Table 5.2 shows how the federal government spends its money. *About ⅓ of the federal expenditures goes for defense and other items connected with international relations and national security. About ⅓ goes for health, labor, and welfare. The rest goes to support farm, transportation, housing, and other such programs, as well as to run Congress, the courts, and the executive branch of the federal government.*

What about the local and state governments? On what do they spend their money? Table 5.3 shows that *the biggest expenditure of the local governments is on schools.* After the end of World War

Table 5.2

Federal Expenditures, United States, Fiscal 1973

Purpose	Amount (billions of dollars)	Percent of total
National defense	78	32
International affairs and finance	4	2
Veterans' benefits	12	5
Space research and technology	3	1
Agriculture and agricultural resources	7	3
Education	11	4
Health, labor, and welfare	88	36
Natural resources	2	1
Commerce and transportation	12	5
Housing and community development	5	2
Interest	21	9
General government and other	3	1
Total[a]	246	100

[a] Because of rounding errors, the figures may not sum to the totals.
Source: U.S. Bureau of the Budget, *The Budget in Brief.*

Table 5.3

Expenditures of State and Local Governments, United States, 1970

Type of Expenditure	State		Local	
	Amount (billions of dollars)	Percent of total	Amount (billions of dollars)	Percent of total
Education	30.9	40	39.0	47
Highways	13.5	17	5.4	7
Natural resources	2.2	3	0.6	1
Health and hospitals	5.4	7	5.0	6
Public welfare	13.2	17	6.7	8
Housing and urban renewal	0.1	[b]	2.1	2
Interest on debt	1.5	2	2.9	3
Other	10.9	14	21.5	25
Total[a]	77.6	100	83.2	100

[a] Because of rounding errors, the figures may not sum to the totals.
[b] Less than 1 percent.
Source: Statistical Abstract of the United States.

II, these expenditures increased greatly because of the "baby boom"—the increase in the number of school-age children. Traditionally, schools in the United States have been a responsibility of local governments—cities and towns. *State governments spend most of their money on highways, welfare, old age, and unemployment benefits, and providing help to localities to cover the cost of education, as well as supporting education directly.* In addition, the local and state governments support hospitals, redevelopment programs, recreation and natural resource programs, and courts, police, and fire departments.

Changes in Views of Government Responsibilities

We have already seen that government expenditures in the United States have grown considerably, both in absolute amount and as a percentage of our total output. It must be recognized that this growth in government expenditure has been part of a general trend in the United States toward a different view of the government's role. Two hundred years ago, it was not uncommon for people to believe in the slogan: "That government governs best which governs least." There was considerable suspicion of government interference and meddling, freedom was the watchword, and governments were viewed as potential tyrants. In the nineteenth century, the United States prospered mightily under this laissez-faire system, but gradually—and not without considerable protest—the nation began to interpret the role of the government more broadly.

Responding to the dangers of noncompetitive markets, states were given the power to regulate public utilities and railroads. The Interstate Commerce Commission was established in 1887 to regulate railroads operating across state lines; and the Sherman Antitrust Act was passed in 1890 to curb monopoly and promote competition. To help control recurring business fluctuations and financial panics, banking and finance were regulated. In 1913, the Federal Reserve System was established as a central bank controlling the member commercial banks. In 1933, the Federal Deposit Insurance Corporation was established to insure bank deposits. And in 1934, the Securities and Exchange Commission was established to watch over the financial markets. Responding to the "buyer-beware" attitudes of unscrupulous and careless sellers, the Pure Food and Drug Act was passed by Congress in 1906 to insure proper quality for drugs and food.

In addition, the government's role in the fields of labor and welfare expanded considerably. For example, in the 1930s, minimum wage laws were enacted, old-age pensions and unemployment insurance were established, and the government became an important force in collective bargaining and labor relations. Furthermore, the power of government has been used increasingly to insure that citizens will not fall below a certain economic level. Food-stamp programs and programs that provide aid to dependent children have been established. *In general, the broad trend in the United States in the past century has been for the government to be used to a greater and greater extent to achieve social objectives.*

Recall from your study of American history the programs of Theodore Roosevelt, Franklin D. Roosevelt, John F. Kennedy, and Lyndon B. Johnson. Although they were quite different sorts of presidents faced with quite different sorts of situations, they all had one thing in common: they promoted a broader view of government responsibilities. Theodore Roosevelt's "Square Deal," Franklin D. Roosevelt's "New Deal," John F. Kennedy's "New Frontier," and Lyndon B. Johnson's "Great Society" all extended government responsibilities. Some of these extensions were highly controversial at the time. For example, the ill-feeling generated by FDR's "wild-eyed schemes" is legendary. Yet when the Republicans took office subsequently, these schemes were not repudiated. This has been the typical pattern. Although the rate at which government involvement has grown has depended heavily on who was in power, neither political party has reversed the direction of change. As you would expect, conservatives view this trend with suspicion and alarm, while liberals view it with favor and satisfaction. Your own view will depend inevitably on your own political beliefs and preferences.

What the Federal, State, and Local Governments Receive in Taxes

To get the money to cover most of the expenditures discussed in previous sections, governments collect taxes from individuals and firms. As Table 5.4 shows, at the federal level the personal income tax is the biggest single money raiser. It brings in almost ½ of the tax revenue collected by the federal government. The next most important taxes at the federal level are the social security, payroll, and employment taxes, and the corporation income tax. Other important taxes are excise taxes—levied on the sale of tobacco, liquor, imports, and certain

Table 5.4

Federal Tax Receipts, by Tax, Fiscal 1973

Type of tax	Amount (billions of dollars	Percent of total
Personal income tax	99	44
Corporation income tax	34	15
Employment taxes	65	29
Excise taxes	16	7
Estate and gift taxes	5	2
Other revenues	7	3
Total[a]	225	100

[a] Because of rounding errors, the figures may not sum to the totals.
Source: Economic Report of the President, 1973.

Table 5.5

State and Local Tax Revenues, by Source, 1970

Source	State Revenues (billions of dollars)	State Percent of total	Local Revenues (billions of dollars)	Local Percent of total
General sales tax	14	29	2	5
Property tax	1	2	33	85
Selective excise taxes	13	27	1	3
Personal income tax	9	19	2	5
Corporate income tax	4	8	—	
Motor vehicle licenses	3	6	—	
Estate and gift taxes	1	2	—	
Other taxes	4	8	1	3
Total[a]	48	100	39	100

[a] Because of rounding errors, the figures may not sum to the totals.
Source: Statistical Abstract of the United States.

other items—and death and gift taxes. (Even when the Grim Reaper shows up, the Tax Man is not far behind.)

At the local level, on the other hand, the most important form of taxation and source of revenue is the property tax. (See Table 5.5.) This is a tax levied primarily on real estate. Other important local taxes—although dwarfed in importance by the property tax—are local sales taxes and local income taxes. Many cities—for example, New York City—levy a sales tax, equal to a certain percent—3 percent in New York City—of the value of each retail sale. The tax is simply added on to the amount charged the customer. Also, many cities—for example, Philadelphia and Pittsburgh—levy an income (or wage) tax on their residents and even on people who work in the city but live outside it. At the state level, sales (and excise) taxes are the biggest money raisers, followed by income taxes and highway user taxes. Highway user taxes include taxes on gasoline and license fees for vehicles and drivers. Often they exceed the amount spent on roads, and the balance is used for a variety of nonhighway uses.

The Role of Government in American Agriculture: A Case Study

Thus far, we have been discussing the government's role in the American economy in rather general terms. Now we need to consider in some detail a particular example of the economic programs carried out by our government. The government's farm programs are a logical choice, because they illustrate the usefulness of the supply-and-demand analysis presented in the previous chapter. It is important to recognize at the outset that these farm programs are not being held up as a representative sample of what the government does. There are a host of other government economic programs—poverty programs, urban programs, defense programs, research programs, education programs, transportation programs, fiscal programs, monetary programs, and many more. Most of these programs will be discussed at some point in this book.

Agriculture is an enormously important sector of the American economy. Even though its size is decreasing steadily—and this contraction has been going on for many decades—agriculture still employs about 4 million Americans. Its importance, moreover, cannot be measured entirely by its size. You need only think about how difficult it would be to get along without food to see the strategic role agriculture plays in our economic life. Also, when it comes to technological change, agriculture is one of the most progressive parts of the American economy. Output per manhour has grown more rapidly there than in any other major sector of the American economy, in considerable part because of government-financed agricultural research programs. The efficiency of American agriculture is admired throughout the world.

Nonetheless, it is widely acknowledged that American agriculture has had serious problems. Perhaps the clearest indication of these problems is shown by a comparison of per capita income of American farmers with per capita income among the rest of the population. It is clear that farm incomes have tended to be much lower than nonfarm incomes. For example, in 1970, per capita income on the farms was about 20 percent below that for the nonfarm population. Moreover, a large proportion of the rural population is poor. Thus, the National Advisory Commission on Rural Poverty found that "rural poverty is so widespread, and so acute, as to be a national disgrace."[8] Of course, this does not mean that all farmers are poor: on the contrary, many do very well indeed. But a large percentage of the nation's farmers are poor by any standard.

[8] National Advisory Committee on Rural Poverty, *The People Left Behind,* Washington, 1967, part of which is reprinted in E. Mansfield, *Economics: Readings, Issues, and Cases,* New York: Norton, 1974.

This farm problem is nothing new. During the first two decades of the twentieth century, farmers enjoyed relatively high prices and relatively high incomes. But in 1920, the country experienced a sharp depression that jolted agriculture as well as the rest of the economy. Whereas the Roaring Twenties saw a recovery and boom in the nonfarm sector of the economy, agriculture did not recover as completely, and the 1930s were dreadful years; the Great Depression resulted in a sickening decline in farm prices and farm incomes. World War II brought prosperity to agriculture, but in the postwar period, farm incomes continually have been well below nonfarm incomes. Thus, all in all, agriculture has been experiencing difficulties for several decades. In 1973, as we shall see, prosperity began to return to the farms. How long-lived it will be is anyone's guess.

Causes of the Farm Problem

In Chapter 1, we claimed that relatively simple economic models are of considerable use in understanding important public and private problems. To back up this claim, we will apply the simple models of market behavior presented in the previous chapter—the models involving market demand curves and market supply curves—to explain the basic causes of the problems that, until 1973, besieged agriculture. Let's start with the market demand curve for farm products. If you think about it for a moment, you will agree that this market demand curve must have two important characteristics. First, its shape must reflect the fact that food is a necessity and that the quantity demanded will not vary much with the price of food. Second, the market demand curve for food is unlikely to shift to the right very much as per capita income rises, because consumption of food per capita faces natural biological and other limitations.

Next, consider the market supply curve for farm products. Again, you should be aware of two important characteristics of this market supply curve. First, the quantity of farm products supplied tends to be relatively insensitive to price, because the farmers have only limited control over their output. (Weather, floods, insects, and other such factors are very important.) Second, because of the rapid technological change emphasized in the previous section, the market supply curve has been shifting markedly and rapidly to the right.

If you understand these simple characteristics of the market demand curve and market supply curve for farm products, it is no trick at all to understand why we had the sort of farm problem just described. Figure 5.2 shows the market demand and market supply curves for farm products at various points in time. As you would expect, the market demand curve for farm products shifts rather slowly to the right as incomes (and population) grow over time. Specifically, the market demand curve shifted from DD' in the first period to D_1D_1' in the second period to D_2D_2' in the third period. On the other hand, the market supply curve for farm products shifted rapidly to the right as technology improved over time. Specifically, it shifted from SS' in the first period to S_1S_1' in the second period to S_2S_2' in the third period.

What was the consequence of these shifts in the market demand and supply curves for food products? Clearly, *the equilibrium price of food products fell (relative to other products)*. Specifically, the equilibrium price fell from OP to OP_1 to OP_2 in Figure 5.2. This price decrease was, of course, a large part of the farm problem. If we correct for changes in the general level of prices (which have tended to rise over time), there was, until 1973, a declining trend in farm prices. That is, agricultural prices generally fell, relative to other prices, in the last 60 years. Moreover, *given this fall in*

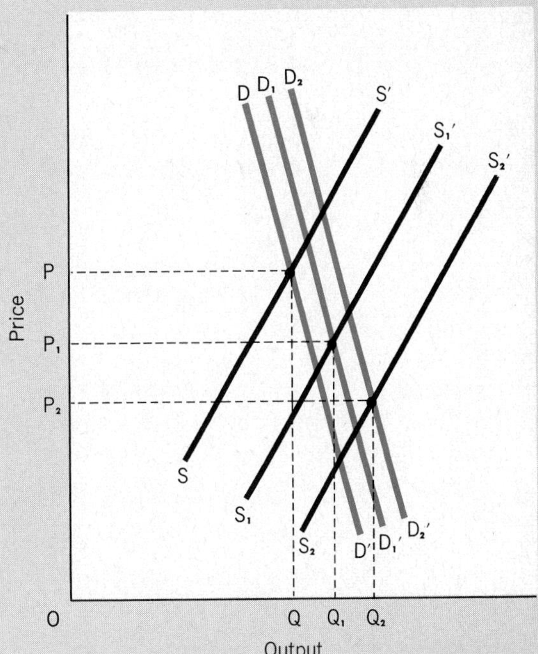

Figure 5.2
Shifts over Time in Market Demand and Supply Curves for Farm Products

The market demand curve has shifted rather slowly to the right (from DD' to D_1D_1' to D_2D_2'), whereas the market supply curve has shifted rapidly to the right (from SS' to S_1S_1' to S_2S_2'), with the result that the equilibrium price has declined (from OP to OP_1 to OP_2).

farm prices, farm incomes tended to fall, because, although lower prices were associated with greater amounts sold, the reduction in price was much greater than the increase in quantity sold, as shown in Figure 5.2.[9]

Thus the simple model of market behavior described in the previous chapter makes it possible to explain the fact that, until recently, farm prices and farm incomes have tended to fall in the United States. Certainly there is nothing mysterious about these trends. Given the nature and characteristics of the market demand curve and market supply curve for farm products, our simple model shows that these trends are as much to be expected as parades on the Fourth of July. However, one additional fact must be noted to understand the farm problem: *people and nonhuman resources have been relatively slow to move out of agriculture in response to these trends.* Recall from the previous chapter that the price system uses such trends —lower prices and lower incomes—to signal producers that they should use their resources elsewhere. Unfortunately, farmers have been loath to move out of agriculture, even though they often could make more money elsewhere. This has been a crucial cause of the farm problem. If more people and resources had left farming, agricultural prices and incomes would have risen, and ultimately farm incomes would have come closer to nonfarm incomes. Poor education and color have, of course, been significant barriers to migration.

Nonetheless, even though farmers have been slow to move out of agriculture, they have left the farm in the long run. For example, in 1930 the farm population was about 30 million, or 25 percent of the total population; in 1950, it was about 23 million, or 15 percent of the total population; and in 1970, it was about 10 million, or 5 percent of the total population. Thus, the price system has had its way. Resources have been moving out of agriculture in response to the signals and pressures of the price system. This movement of people and nonhuman resources unquestionably has contributed to greater efficiency and production for the nation as a whole. But during most of the past 40 years, we have continued to have a "surplus" of farmers—and this has been the root of the farm problem.

[9] The amount farmers receive is the amount they sell times the price. Thus, in Figure 5.2, the amount farmers receive in income is $OP \times OQ$ in the first period, $OP_1 \times OQ_1$ in the second period, and $OP_2 \times OQ_2$ in the third period. Clearly, since the price is decreasing much more rapidly than the quantity is increasing, farm incomes are falling.

Government Aid to Agriculture

Traditionally, farmers have had a disproportionately large influence in Congress; and faced with declining economic fortunes, they have appealed to the government for help. They have extolled the virtues of rural life, emphasized that agriculture is a competitive industry, and claimed that it was unfair for their prices to fall relative to the prices they have had to pay. In addition, they have pointed out that the movement of resources out of agriculture has entailed large human costs, since this movement, although beneficial to the nation as a whole, has been traumatic for the farm population. For reasons of this sort, they have argued that the government should help farmers; and in particular, that the government should act to bolster farm prices and farm incomes.

Their voices have been heard. In the Agricultural Adjustment Act of 1933, the Congress announced the concept of parity as the major objective of American farm policy. This concept has acquired great importance—and must be clearly understood. Put in its simplest terms, the concept of ***parity*** says that a farmer should be able to exchange a given quantity of his output for as much in the way of nonfarm goods and services as he could at some time in the past. For example, if a farmer could take a bushel of wheat to market in 1912 and get enough money to buy a pair of gloves, today he should be able to get enough money for a bushel of wheat to buy a pair of gloves.

To see what the concept of parity implies for

farm prices, suppose that the price of gloves triples. Obviously, if parity is to be maintained, the price of wheat must triple too. Thus, the concept of parity implies that farm prices must increase at the same rate as the prices of the goods and services farmers buy. Of course, farmers buy lots of things besides gloves, so in actual practice the parity price of wheat or other farm products is determined by the changes over time in the average price of all the goods and services farmers buy.

Several things should be noted about parity. First, to use this concept, one must agree on some base period, such as 1912 in the example above, during which the relationship of farm to nonfarm prices is regarded as equitable. Obviously, the higher farm prices were relative to nonfarm prices in the base period, the higher farm prices will be in subsequent periods if parity is maintained. It is interesting to note that 1910–14 is used as the base period (with some recent modifications). Since this was a period of relatively high farm prices and of agricultural prosperity, the farm bloc must have wielded considerable political clout on this issue. Second, note that the concept of parity is an ethical, not a scientific proposition. It states what the relative economic position of a bushel of wheat ought to be—or more precisely, it states one particular view of what the relative economic position of a bushel of wheat should be. It must also be noted that price parity is not the same thing as income parity. If price parity is maintained while productivity is increasing considerably, farm incomes will rise more rapidly than income parity would call for.

Price Supports and Surplus Controls

During the past 40 years, the concept of parity has been the cornerstone of a system of government price supports. In many cases, the government has not supported farm prices at the full 100 percent of parity. For example, Congress may have enacted a bill saying that the Secretary of Agriculture can establish a price of wheat, corn, cotton, or some other product that is between 65 and 90 percent of parity. But whatever the exact level of the price supports, the idea behind them is perfectly simple: it is to maintain farm prices above the level that would result in a free market.

Using the simple supply-and-demand model developed in the previous chapter, we can see more clearly the effects of these price supports. The situation is shown in Figure 5.3. A support price, OP', was set by the government. Since this support price was above the equilibrium price, OP, the public bought *less* of farm products (OQ_2 rather than OQ) and paid a *higher* price for them. Farmers gained from the price supports, since the amount they received for their crop under the price support was equal to $OP' \times OQ_1$, a greater amount than what they would have received in a free market, which was $OP \times OQ$.

Note, however, that since the support price exceeded the equilibrium price, the quantity supplied of the farm product, OQ_1, exceeded the quantity demanded, OQ_2. That is, *there was a surplus of the farm product in question,* which the government had to purchase, since no one else would. These surpluses were an embarrassment, both economically and politically. They showed that society's scarce resources were being utilized to produce products consumers simply did not want at existing prices. Moreover the cost of storing these surpluses was very large indeed: in some years, these storage costs alone hit the $1 billion mark.

To help reduce these surpluses, the government followed two basic strategies. First, it tried to restrict output of farm products. In particular, the government established an acreage allotment program, which said that farmers had to limit the number of acres they planted in order to get price supports on their crops. The Department of Agriculture estimated how much of each product would be demanded by buyers (other than the government) at the support price, and tried to cut back the total acreage planted with this crop to the point where the quantity supplied equaled the quantity de-

Figure 5.3
Effects of Farm Price Support Program

The support price, OP', is above the equilibrium price, OP, so the public buys OQ_2, farmers supply OQ_1 units of output, and the government buys the difference $(OQ_1 - OQ_2)$.

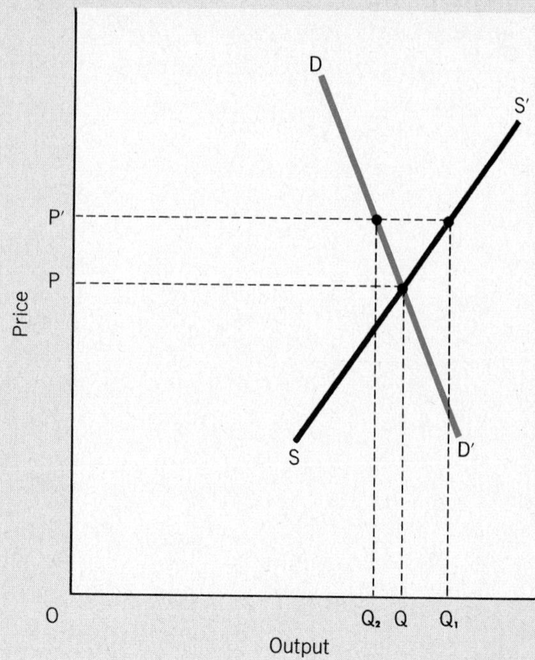

manded. These output restrictions did not eliminate the surpluses, because farmers managed to increase the yields from acreage they were allowed to plant, but undoubtedly they reduced the surpluses. With these restrictions, the situation was as shown in Figure 5.4, where OQ_3 was the total output that could be grown on the acreage that could be planted with the crop. Because of the imposition of this output control, the surplus—which the government had to purchase—was reduced from $OQ_1 - OQ_2$ to $OQ_3 - OQ_2$. Farmers continued to benefit from price supports because the amount they received for their crop—$OP' \times OQ_3$—was still greater than they would have received in a free market, because the amount demanded of farm products was not very sensitive to their price.

Second, the government tried to shift the demand curve for farm products to the right. An effort was made to find new uses for various farm products. Also, various antipoverty programs, such as the food-stamp program, used our farm surpluses to help the poor. In addition, the government tried to expand the export markets for American farm products. Western Europe and Japan have been increasing their demand for food, and the Communist countries have been purchasing our farm products to offset their own agricultural deficiencies. Moreover, the less developed countries were permitted by Public Law 480 to buy our farm products with their own currencies, rather than dollars. The result was a reduction in farm surpluses, as shown in Figure 5.5. Since the market demand curve for farm products shifted from DD' to D_1D_1', the surplus was reduced from $OQ_3 - OQ_2$ to $OQ_3 - OQ_4$. Because of these demand-augmenting and output-restricting measures, surpluses during the late 1960s and early 1970s were considerably smaller than they were during the late 1950s and early 1960s.

The 1973 Changes in the Farm Program

In 1973, farm prices increased markedly, due partly to very great increases in foreign demand for American agricultural products. This increase in foreign demand was due partly to poor harvests in the Soviet Union, Australia, Argentina, and elsewhere, as well as to devaluations of the dollar. As a result, farm incomes reached very high levels, farm surpluses disappeared, and for the first time in 30 years the government was trying to stimulate farm production rather than restrict it.

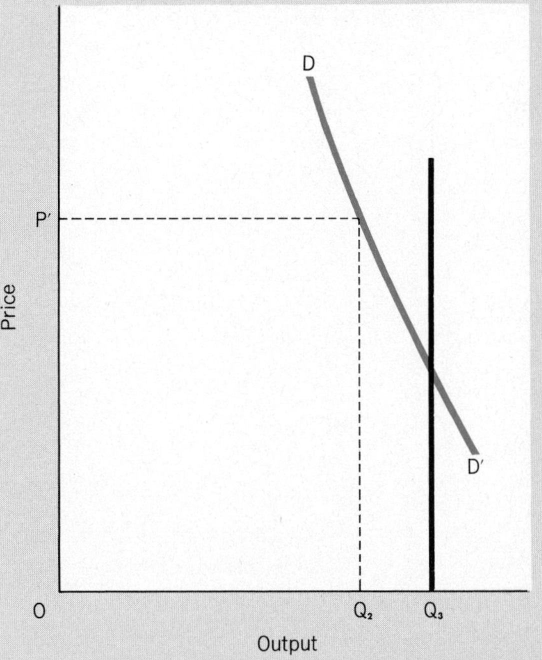

Figure 5.4
Effects of Price Supports and Output Restrictions

The government restricts output to OQ_3, with the result that it buys $(OQ_3 - OQ_2)$ units of output.

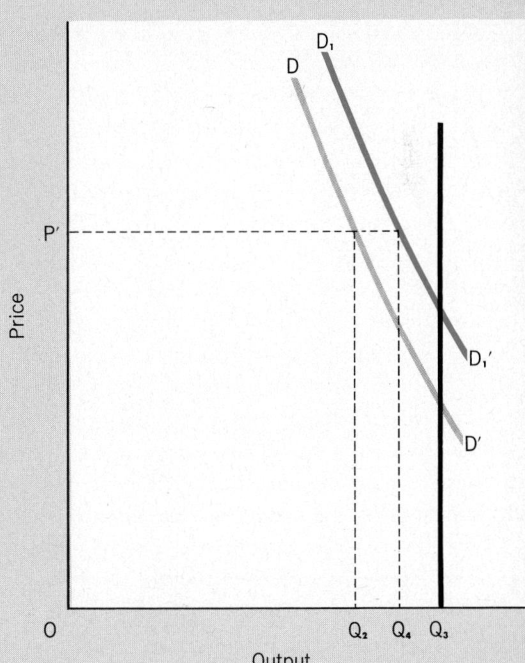

Figure 5.5
Effects of Price Supports, Output Restrictions, and a Shift to the Right in the Demand Curve for Farm Products

By shifting the demand curve from DD' to D_1D_1', the government reduces the surplus from $(OQ_3 - OQ_2)$ to $(OQ_3 - OQ_4)$ units of output.

Taking advantage of this new climate, Congress passed a new farm bill which ended price supports. Instead, agricultural prices will be allowed to fluctuate freely in accord with supply and demand. However, the government will make cash payments to farmers if prices fall below certain "target" levels established by the law. These target levels are above the prices that generally prevailed in the past, but they are far below the record prices prevailing in 1973.

A program of this kind was originally proposed in 1949 by Charles F. Brannan, who was Secretary of Agriculture under President Truman. Farm organizations and their supporters in Congress succeeded in killing the proposal. One important reason why it was passed in 1973 was that farm prices were so high. This meant that a program of this sort would cost little or nothing, so long as prices remained above the "target" levels. More will be said about the Brannan plan in Chapter 20.

The Wheat Program: A Case Study

To get a better idea of how price supports and output restrictions have worked in agriculture, we will narrow our focus to the case of wheat. In the previous chapter, we described how the price of wheat would be determined in a free market. But the market for wheat has been influenced by government programs for many decades. Let's begin our brief account of the wheat program with the situation after World War II. During the war, a rural political coalition succeeded in getting guarantees of 100 percent of parity price. After the war, there was some movement away from rigid price supports by important government officials, including President Eisenhower's Secretary of Agriculture, Ezra Taft Benson, who wanted the government to reduce its involvement in the farm economy, both because he felt that the government's programs were not succeeding and because he wanted to see a reversal of "the trend toward government invasion of farm freedoms."[10]

During Secretary Benson's eight years in office (1952–60), there was a chronic mismatch between the quantity supplied and quantity demanded of wheat. Because of rapid advances in agricultural technology, wheat farmers were able to maintain production in the face of serious droughts, production controls, and moderate reductions in wheat prices. The government was forced to buy up enormous surpluses of wheat. A big issue in the 1950s was whether price supports should remain at the high levels established during World War II. Rural interests, which included commercial wheat farmers, wanted price supports to stay high: specifically, they wanted them to be at least 90 percent of parity. Secretary Benson, on the other hand, wanted to institute flexible support levels so that they could be used to help reduce overproduction. He succeeded in reducing price support levels—as well as in alienating farmers, farm leaders, and many political liberals.

In 1960, with the election of John F. Kennedy as president, Orville Freeman became Secretary of Agriculture. In contrast to Benson, Secretary Freeman felt that the government should play a major role in American agriculture. Faced with the prospect of continuing large surpluses of wheat, he pushed for great reductions in acreage, which was held at little more than half its postwar high. Also, he urged the export of wheat to the less developed countries, both to help promote their economic growth and to stave off famine. Rather than attempt to maintain 90 percent of parity, Freeman adopted the more modest goal of maintaining 100 percent of parity prices *on the production used for domestic food* (less than half the total crop in the 1960s).

The Cotton-Wheat Act of 1964 established a voluntary wheat-marketing certificate program for 1964 and 1965, later extended with only limited changes to 1969. Under this program, farmers who complied with acreage allotments and agreed to participate in a land-diversion program received price supports, marketing certificates, and payments

[10] D. Hadwiger, *Federal Wheat Commodity Programs,* Ames: Iowa State University Press, 1970, Chapter 8.

for land diversion, but farmers who did not comply did not receive benefits. During 1964 to 1969, the price of wheat ranged from about $1.15 to $1.74 per bushel. However, the total price to farmers was more than this, because participants in the wheat program also got direct marketing certificate payments amounting to 65 cents per bushel in 1969. During the early 1970s, the wheat program remained conceptually the same, although some modifications were made.[11]

In August 1973, the wheat program, like other agricultural programs, changed drastically. Price supports were ended, and, as we know from the previous section, the government pledged to make cash payments to farmers if prices fall below certain "target" levels. (However, there is a maximum amount of $20,000 that a farmer can receive per year.) The price of wheat exceeded $4 per bushel in 1973, and was well above the "target" level. In contrast to previous years, the Secretary of Agriculture imposed no restrictions on the acreage that wheat farmers could plant in 1974. Given the enormous increase in the demand for American wheat, the emphasis was on expanding, not curtailing, production.

Evaluation of Government Farm Programs

It is obviously hard to evaluate the success of the government's farm programs. Farmers will certainly take a different view of price supports and other measures than their city cousins. Nonetheless, from the point of view of the nation as a whole, these farm programs have received considerable criticism. To understand these criticisms, we must hark back to our discussion earlier in this chapter of the proper functions of government, and ask what justification there is for the government's intervening in this way in agriculture. Perhaps the most convincing justification is that the government ought to help the rural poor. As we saw in previous sections, most people agree that the government should redistribute income in this way.

Unfortunately, however, *our farm programs have done little for the farmers most in need of help,* because the amount of money a farmer has gotten from price supports has depended on how much he produced. Thus, the big farmer has gotten the lion's share of the subsidies—and he, of course, needed help least. On the other hand, the small farmer, the farmer who is mired most deeply in poverty, has received little from these programs. Recognizing this fact, many observers have pointed out that, if these programs are really aimed at helping the rural poor, it would be more sensible to channel the money to them through direct subsidies, than to finance programs where much of the benefits go to prosperous commercial farmers.

It must also be recognized that *our farm programs have not dealt with the basic causes of the farm problem.* In the past at least, we have had too many people and resources in agriculture. This, as we stressed in previous sections, is why farmers' incomes have tended to be low. Yet the government's farm programs have been directed more toward supporting farm prices and incomes (and stabilizing a sector of the economy that historically has been unstable), rather than toward promoting the needed movement of people and resources out of agriculture. Indeed, some people would say that the government's farm programs have made it more difficult for the necessary adjustments to take place.

Given these defects, many proposals have been made to alter our farm programs. In the view of many observers, agriculture should return to something more closely approximating free markets: the price system should be allowed to work more freely. The changes that occurred in 1973 are in that direction, but it is important to note that the government is still intervening heavily in agriculture. (Moreover, if farm prices recede from their record 1973 levels, the taxpayers may have to pay very heavy subsidies to farmers, according to the

[11] See G. Shepherd and G. Futrell, *Marketing Farm Products,* Ames: Iowa State University Press, 1969, p. 417; and W. Rasmussen and G. Baker, "Programs for Agriculture, 1933–1965," *Agricultural Economics Research,* July, 1966.

new law.) Although further movements toward a free market in agriculture may not be popular among many farm groups, there are signs that such changes may occur in the years ahead.

Finally, before closing this chapter, we must point out a fundamental moral of our farm programs: *the government, like the price system, can bungle the job of organizing a nation's economic activities.* We began this chapter by stressing the fact that the price system breaks down under some circumstances, and that the government must intervene. It is also worth stressing that the government sometimes intervenes when it shouldn't—and that even when it should intervene, it sometimes does so in a way that wastes resources. This, of course, doesn't mean that the government should play no part in the American economy. On the contrary, the government must—and does—play an enormously important role. What it does mean is that, just as the price system is no all-purpose cure-all, neither is the government.

Summary

The price system, despite its many virtues, suffers from serious limitations. There is no reason to believe that the distribution of income generated by the price system is equitable or optimal. Also, there is no way for the price system to handle public goods, and because of external economies or diseconomies, the price system may result in too little or too much of certain goods being produced. To a considerable extent, the government's role in the economy has developed in response to these limitations of the price system. There is considerable agreement that government should redistribute income in favor of the poor, provide public goods, and offset the effects of external economies and diseconomies. Also, it is generally felt that the government should establish a proper legal, social, and competitive framework for the price system, and that it should see to it that the economy maintains relatively full employment with reasonably stable prices. Beyond this, however, there are wide differences of opinion on the proper role of government in economic affairs. Conservatives tend to be suspicious of "big government" while liberals are inclined to believe that the government should do more.

In the past 50 years, government spending has increased considerably, both in absolute terms and as a percent of total output. (It is now about one-third of our total output.) To a large extent, this increase has been due to our greater military responsibilities, as well as to the fact that, as their incomes have risen, our citizens have demanded more schools, highways, and other goods and services provided by government. The growth in government expenditures has also been part of a general trend in the United States whereby, more and more, the power of the government has been used to achieve social objectives. To get the money to cover most of these expenditures, governments collect taxes from individuals and firms. At the federal level, the most important is the personal income tax.

One example of the role of government in the American economy is the farm program. American agriculture has been plagued by relatively low incomes. Until 1973, the demand for farm products grew slowly, while rapid technological change meant that the people and resources currently in agriculture could supply more and more farm products. Because people and resources did not move out of agriculture as rapidly as the price system dictated, farm incomes tended to be relatively low. In response to political pressures from the farm blocs, the government set in motion a series of programs to aid farmers. A cornerstone of these programs was the concept of parity, which said that the prices farmers receive should increase at the same rate as the prices of the goods and services farmers buy. The government instituted price supports to keep farm prices above their equilibrium level. But since the support prices exceeded the equilibrium prices, there was a surplus of the commodities that the government had to purchase and store. To help reduce these surpluses, the government tried to restrict the output of farm products and expand the demand for them.

These farm programs received considerable criticism. From the point of view of income redistribution, they suffered from the fact that they did little for the farmers most in need of help. As tools of resource allocation, they suffered because they dealt more with the symptoms of the farm problem than with its basic causes. In 1973, price supports were ended, but the government pledged to make cash payments to farmers if farm prices fall below certain "target" levels. The government's farm programs illustrate the fact that government intervention, like the price system, has plenty of limitations. Neither the price system nor government intervention is an all-purpose cure-all.

CONCEPTS FOR REVIEW

Public goods	Welfare payments	Public sector
External economy	Price supports	Income tax
External diseconomy	Parity	Sales tax
Transfer payments	Depression	Property tax
Antitrust laws	Private sector	

QUESTIONS FOR DISCUSSION AND REVIEW

1. According to George Stigler, "The state never knows when to quit." What does he mean? Do you agree or disagree?

2. According to Paul Samuelson, "Libertarians fail to realize that the price system is, and ought to be, a method of coercion." What does he mean? Do you agree or disagree?

3. The distribution of income generated by the price system is not necessarily equitable or optimal. True or False?

4. Consumption or production by one firm or person resulting in uncompensated costs to another is called
   a. external economy. b. external diseconomy. c. public good. d. economic stabilization.

CHAPTER 6

Government Expenditures, Taxation, and the Public Debt

The government plays an extremely important role in the American economy. It is obvious that it influences our economic lives and fortunes in countless ways. At this point, we must look in detail at how decisions are made concerning the level and distribution of government expenditures. Also, we must discuss the principles of taxation. These topics are of central importance in understanding the public sector of our economy.

In addition, we must discuss some of the salient issues concerning the public sector, including the so-called military-industrial complex, tax reform, and revenue sharing. Further, we must describe in some detail the nature, size, and burden of the public debt, a subject that has been surrounded by as many myths as any in economics.

The Federal Budgetary Process

Determining how much the federal government should spend is a mammoth undertaking, involving literally thousands of people and hundreds of thousands of manhours. Decisions on expenditures are part of the budgetary process. The ***budget*** is a statement of the government's anticipated expenditures and revenues. The federal budget is for a fiscal year, from July 1 to June 30. Let's consider the budget for the fiscal year beginning July 1, 1973. In the summer of 1972, the various agencies of the federal government began to prepare their program proposals. By the fall they had made detailed budget requests which the president, with his Office of Management and Budget, went over from October to December 1972. Since the agencies generally wanted more than the president wanted to spend, he usually cut down their requests.

In January 1973, the president submitted his budget to Congress. Often the proposals for expenditures are first examined by the committee responsible for overseeing the particular program —for example, the Military Affairs Committee— and then by the entire Congress. The oversight committee must recommend new legislation if it is needed; it must vote authorizations for programs. Then the Appropriations Committees and the House of Representatives and Senate must vote the appropriations of money. The appropriations may be less than the authorizations, since the Appropriations Committees tend to be less generous than the oversight committees. The Congress voted these appropriations—reducing some of the president's requests, increasing others—in the spring and summer of 1973. The appropriations allowed the president to spend the allotted amounts of money, which he usually, but not always, does.

Three things should be noted about the budgetary process. First, it is a long procedure. Second, although it appears rigid, it is more flexible than it looks. If conditions change, the president usually can go to Congress for supplementary appropriations, or he can refuse to spend money already appropriated. Third, the decision-making process in Congress is fragmented. Separate committees and subcommittees of the Appropriations Committees consider various parts of the president's recommended budget, making it hard to establish any overall policy for total government expenditure. Of course, evaluation of the entire budget must be broken down into parts, since it is too big a job for any single committee, but it is also important that the total be more than the sum of largely uncoordinated parts.

Benefit-Cost Analysis and Program Budgeting

How much should the government spend on various activities and services? Basically, the answer must be provided by the nation's political processes. For example, with regard to the provision of public goods

> Voting by ballot must be resorted to in place of dollar voting . . . [D]ecision making by voting becomes a substitute for preference revelation through the market. The results will not please everybody, but they will approximate—more or less perfectly, depending on the efficiency of the voting process and the homogeneity of preferences—the community's preferences in the matter.[1]

Under certain circumstances, particular types of economic analysis can prove helpful in determining how much the government should spend on various programs. Let's begin by supposing that we can measure the benefits and costs of each such program. What is the optimal amount to spend on each one? The answer, clearly enough, is that *spending on the program should be pushed to the point where the extra benefit from an extra dollar spent is at least equal to the dollar of cost.* This would insure that the amount spent on each government program yields a benefit at least as great as the value of output forgone in the private

[1] Richard and Peggy Musgrave, *Public Finance in Theory and Practice,* New York: McGraw Hill, 1973, p. 8.

sector. This would also make sure that one government program is not being expanded at the expense of other programs that would yield greater benefits if they were expanded instead.

The principle that extra benefit should be compared with extra cost is valuable—and, as we shall see in the next section, widely applicable—but it can solve only a small part of the problem of allocating resources in the public sector. Why? Because it is impossible to measure the benefits from defense or police protection or the courts in dollars and cents. Only in certain cases can benefits be quantified at all precisely. And it is not only a question of the amount of the benefits and costs; it is also a question of who benefits and who pays. Nonetheless, it is difficult to see how rational choices can be made without paying attention to costs and benefits—even if they are measured imprecisely, and are by no means the whole story.

In recent years, there has been a noteworthy attempt to increase the use of economic analysis to help promote better decision making regarding government spending. In 1965, President Johnson established a Planning-Programming-Budgeting System throughout the federal government. This system, similar to one already established in the Department of Defense, had several objectives. It encouraged more precise identification of the goals of various programs and promoted the search for alternative means of reaching these goals, thus making it more likely that they would be fulfilled economically. It also required officials to try to obtain better measures of the true cost and output of various programs. But the PPB System encountered a number of obstacles, including the failure of agency heads to use it, lack of interest in Congress, and opposition by some private interest groups. Critics of the system have pointed to a number of failures. Its advocates, while they do not deny the problems, claim that the system has improved the decision-making process.

The PPB system has also been adopted by various state governments; the first to do so was Wisconsin in 1964. In Wisconsin, needs or goals are classified within broad functional areas, like education, commerce, environmental resources, human relations and resources, and general operations. For example, within the human relations and resources category, a specific goal may be to provide education and related training to crippled children. Then the alternative means of accomplishing this goal, such as financial aid to individuals, aid to orthopedic schools, orthopedic hospitals, or transportation aids, are considered. After their costs and effectiveness are examined, proposals are made for the techniques to use to achieve this goal. Some local governments, like New York City, have also adopted the PPB system. However, PPB is still not used in any comprehensive way by most state and local governments.[2]

Benefit-Cost Analysis: A Case Study[3]

Despite the difficulties involved, in recent years more and more benefit-cost analyses have been carried out to help guide public policy. For example, consider the following study, by the University of Wisconsin's Burton Weisbrod, of a program to reduce the dropout rate in a high school in St. Louis. In this program, potential dropouts were given counseling and help in getting part-time jobs. It cost over $500 per student. The question, of course, was whether the program did enough good to be worth the cost. To help answer this question, the experience of the students in the program was compared with the experience of a control group of comparable students who were not included in

[2] For an excellent discussion of the PPB system, see Charles Schultze, *The Politics and Economics of Public Spending,* Washington: Brookings Institution, 1968. Also, see Bernard Herber, *Modern Public Finance,* Homewood, Ill.: Irwin, 1971, pp. 389–91.

[3] This section is based on Burton Weisbrod, "Preventing High School Dropouts," in Robert Dorfman (editor), *Measuring Benefits of Government Investments,* Washington: Brookings Institution, 1965. A brief discussion of this study is also provided in Otto Eckstein, *Public Finance,* Englewood Cliffs, N.J.: Prentice-Hall, 1967.

the program. It turned out that, despite the help they received, 44 percent of the students in the program dropped out of school before graduation, while 52 percent of the students in the control group dropped out before graduation. Thus the program seemed to reduce the dropout rate by 8 percentage points.

How much was this benefit worth? Weisbrod pointed out that one principal gain was the increased income earned by students who complete high school. A high school graduate earns about $2,750 more than a dropout over a lifetime. Let us use this figure—$2,750—as a measure of the benefit of preventing a student from dropping out. Was the program worthwhile? Since the program reduced the probability of dropping out by 8 percentage points, the average benefit per student was .08 times $2,750, or $220. Since this was less than the cost per student, the program did not seem worthwhile. Of course, one can object that the measure of the benefit from preventing a student from dropping out is incomplete. It does not include the psychic and social benefits from putting people in a position to earn their own keep rather than to be prime candidates for public assistance, and even perhaps jail. Nonetheless, this study raised important questions and had significant effects.

Benefit-cost analyses have proved useful in many areas of government. In particular, they have been used for many years in the Department of Defense. Decisions to develop one weapons system rather than another, or to procure a certain amount of a given weapon, have been based in part on such studies. Other areas where benefit-cost analyses have been used extensively are water projects (irrigation, flood control, hydroelectric and other projects), transportation projects, and urban renewal, recreation, and health projects. For example, in water projects, benefit-cost analysis has frequently been used by the Corps of Engineers and others to determine whether it is worthwhile to spend additional money on flood control, and if so, how much extra expenditure is justified.

A highly simplified example of a benefit-cost analysis of the construction of a dam is shown in Table 6.1. The alternative policies are to build a low dam or a high dam. Table 6.1 shows the annual costs and benefits associated with each of these policies. Clearly, the high dam should be built because the extra cost involved ($150,000 more than for the low dam) is more than outweighed by the extra benefits received ($200,000 more than for the low dam). Note, however, that this is a very simple case. In general, data on costs and benefits are not laid out so straightforwardly. Instead, there are very wide bands of uncertainty about the relevant benefits and costs.

Table 6.1

Benefit-Cost Analysis for Constructing a Dam

Alternative policies	Annual cost	Annual benefit
Build a low dam	$100,000	$150,000
Build a high dam	$250,000	$350,000

Government Expenditures and the Problem of Social Balance

It is not easy to decide how large government expenditures should be. As we saw in Chapter 5, opinions differ widely on the proper role of government in economic affairs, and it is often impossible to measure the costs and benefits of government programs with dependable accuracy. Nonetheless, some economists—led by Harvard's John Kenneth Galbraith—believe that the public sector of the economy is being starved of needed resources, whereas the private sector is catering to relatively unimportant wants. For example, in *The Affluent Society,* Galbraith argues that consumers are led by advertising and other promotional efforts to purchase more and more goods of marginal significance to them. On the other hand, in his opinion, the nation is suffering from too little spending on government services. Thus he writes:

> In the years following World War II, the papers of any major city . . . told daily of the shortages and shortcomings in the elementary municipal and metropolitan services. The schools were old and overcrowded. The police force was understrength and underpaid. The parks and playgrounds were insufficient. Streets and empty lots were filthy, and the sanitation staff was underequipped and in need of men. Access to the city by those who work there was uncertain and painful and becoming more so. Internal transportation was overcrowded, unhealthy, and dirty. So was the air. Parking on the streets had to be prohibited, and there was no space elsewhere. These deficiencies were not in new and novel services, but in old established ones.[4]

Many economists agree with Galbraith. Particularly among liberals, there is a widespread feeling that resources are being mal-allocated, too much going for deodorants, comic books, and mouth wash, and too little going for schools and public services. But this feeling is not shared by all economists. Galbraith's critics point out that expenditures often benefit particular interest groups, which lobby hard for them in federal and state legislatures. The result is that spending programs may be carried beyond the optimal point. Further, they point out that Galbraith's assertion that private wants are becoming more and more trivial and synthetic is not scientifically verifiable and that, in any case, it ignores the large number of people living in very modest circumstances, indeed even in dire poverty.

Economic theory alone cannot settle this basic question. It is obviously a matter of politics as well as economics. However, in trying to reach an opinion, bear in mind that both sides may be partly correct. For certain types of government services, you may agree with Galbraith and his followers that too little is being spent, but for other types of government services you may agree with his critics that too much is being spent. For example, you may feel that too little is being spent on pollution control and urban problems, but that too much is being spent on agricultural subsidies (many of which go to wealthy farmers) and subsidies to the merchant marine (which are meant to keep the American shipping industry competitive with other nations).

Finally, it is important to distinguish between decisions concerning the *scope* of government activities and decisions concerning the *efficiency* of government. Thus far in this section we have been discussing the proper scope of government. Assume that we can divide all goods into public goods and private goods, and that Figure 6.1 shows the society's product transformation curve. In other words, as you recall from Chapter 3, Figure 6.1 shows the maximum amount of public goods that can be produced, given each quantity produced of private goods. Then the question that we have been discussing is: At what point along the product transformation curve should society be? For example, should society choose point A (where more public goods and less private goods are produced) or point B (where less public goods and more private goods are produced)?

But there is another important question: How can we attain a point *on* the product transformation curve, rather than one (like point C) that is *inside* it? As we know from Chapter 3, inefficiency will result in society's being on a point inside the product transformation curve. Thus, to attain a point on the product transformation curve, government officials (and others) must do their best to eliminate inefficiency. By doing so, society can get more from the available resources. For example, it can attain points A or B rather than point C. Whether society wants to use its added efficiency to attain point A or point B is then a political question. However, regardless of how this question is decided, society is better off to eliminate inefficiency.

[4] John Kenneth Galbraith, *The Affluent Society,* Boston: Houghton Mifflin, 1958, p. 252. Incidentally, Galbraith opposed the tax cut of 1964 because he felt that government spending should be increased instead.

Figure 6.1
Product Transformation Curve, Public versus Private Goods

At Point B, society produces less public goods and more private goods than at Point A. Thus, a movement from Point A to Point B reduces government expenditures by reducing the *scope* of government services. At Point C, society is producing inefficiently, and a movement from Point C to Point B or Point A can be attained by increasing the *efficiency* of government (and/or private) operations

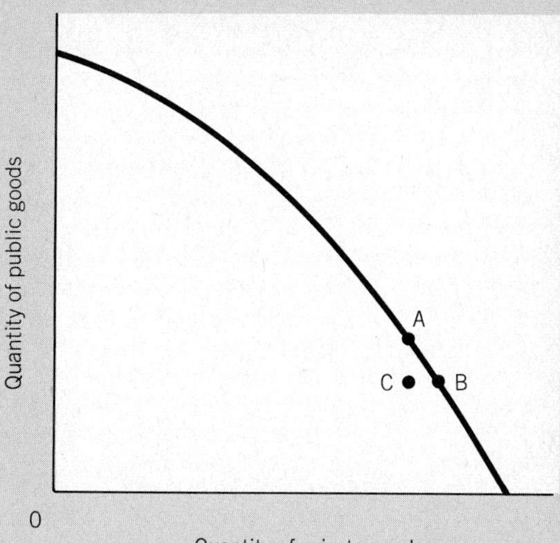

Military Spending and the Military-Industrial Complex

At this point, it is worthwhile to look briefly at two federal agencies, the Department of Defense and the Office of Coal Research. Although these two agencies cannot be held up as typical, they do represent interesting case studies. On the one hand, the Department of Defense has repeatedly been charged with overspending. But since it is hard to tell what level of defense capability is optimal, it is equally difficult to tell whether defense spending is too much or too little. However, there can be no doubt about the enormous size of our defense expenditures. In 1970, American military expenditures were more than $80 billion, which means that they constituted over 40 percent of the total federal budget and about 10 percent of national output. Moreover, this underestimates the costs of our military establishment, because it does not include defense-related expenditures by the Atomic Energy Commission and National Aeronautics and Space Administration. Some people claim that this exaggerates the cost of defense, because if defense expenditures were cut appreciably, our national output would fall. But this assumes that other forms of government spending would not be substituted for defense, or that fiscal and monetary policies could not keep the economy at a high employment level without defense spending—both very unrealistic assumptions.

However, some forms of defense and space spending, particularly on research and development, do provide important benefits to the civilian economy. The electronic computer, numerical control, integrated circuits, atomic energy, synthetic rubber, and many other significant inventions stemmed at least partly from military R and D. Moreover, there is undoubtedly considerable opportunity for such spillover from current military and space R and D. Nonetheless, there seems to be a widespread feeling that the spillover per dollar of military-space R and D is unlikely to be as great as in the past, because the capabilities that are being developed and the environment that is being probed are less intimately connected with civilian activities than formerly. For example, the devices needed to send a man to the moon may have relatively little applicability in the civilian economy because they "oversatisfy" civilian requirements and few people or firms are willing to pay for them.

There is considerable evidence that the weapons acquisition process has not been as efficient as it might have been. There have been spectacular overruns in development and production costs. For example, the cost of the Lockheed C5A transport plane increased from the $3.4 billion estimated in 1965 to $5.3 billion in 1968. To some extent, such cost increases reflect the fact that new weapons systems tend to push the state of the art, so that unexpected problems must be expected. But in addition, the firms that develop and produce these weapons systems often submit unrealistically low bids to get a contract, knowing that they are likely to get approval for cost increases later on. According to some observers, like Merton J. Peck of Yale University and F. M. Scherer of the International Institute of Management, these cost overruns have also been due to "inadequate attention to the efficient utilization of technical, production, and administrative manpower—areas in which major cost reductions are possible."[5]

In addition, some observers believe that the major defense contractors, in conjunction with the military services, apply undue political pressure in support of high defense budgets. For example, President Dwight D. Eisenhower, himself a distinguished military commander, warned of the dangers involved in this "military-industrial complex." In his last speech to the nation as president, he said, "In the councils of government, we must guard against the acquisition of unwarranted influence, whether sought or unsought, by the military-industrial complex. The potential for the disastrous rise of misplaced power exists and will persist." It seems unlikely that there is any real conspiracy, but military contractors, with their political allies, are undoubtedly a powerful lobby for defense spending.

[5] M. J. Peck and F. M. Scherer, *The Weapons Acquisition Process,* Cambridge: Harvard University Press, 1962 p. 594.

The Office of Coal Research: Another Case Study

Just as it is sometimes charged that certain agencies, like the Department of Defense, may have been spending too much, so it is sometimes charged that other agencies, like the Office of Coal Research, may have been spending too little. In recent years, there has been considerable discussion and alarm over the so-called "energy crisis," a situation where a marked shortage seems to have arisen in clean domestic fuels. One way to avoid such a crisis is to develop new technologies to convert our relatively plentiful coal supplies into a clean gas or other forms of fuel that would be less polluting than coal. The Office of Coal Research is responsible for financing research of this kind, and in accord with President Nixon's energy message of June 4, 1971, it is charged with accelerating the coal gasification program to develop a process or processes to produce clean, high-quality gas from coal on a commercial scale by 1980.

The expenditures of the Office of Coal Research (OCR) have increased very substantially in recent years. Its budget was about $52 million in 1974, about $30 million in 1972, and about $15 million in 1970. Much of this money is spent for coal gasification work; about $30 million was spent in 1973 on this program, ⅔ to be funded by OCR and about ⅓ by industry. The Office of Coal Research has helped to finance several approaches to coal gasification, including the Institute of Gas Technology's HYGAS pilot plant, the Consolidation Coal Company's CO_2 Acceptor pilot plant, FMC Corporation's COED pilot plant, and others. Each of these pilot plants costs millions of dollars. Because it is felt that the social returns from the information gained from them will exceed the private returns to the companies operating them, the government subsidizes this research and development.

Despite the increase in OCR's expenditures, many knowledgeable people feel that such work should be expanded more rapidly. For example, in 1973 Senator Henry Jackson of Washington called for a 10-year R and D program on coal gasification costing $660 million (60 percent to be paid for by government, 40 percent by industry), and a 12-year R and D program on coal liquefaction costing $750 million (75 percent to be paid for by government). Also, the Office of Science and Technology's Energy Advisory Panel called in 1972 for an expanded R and D program for coal liquefaction, as well as continued emphasis on coal gasification. In June 1973, President Nixon asked for an increase in the amount of resources devoted to such programs. It seems likely that more will be spent for these purposes.

The Federal Tax Legislative Process

It is one thing for the federal government to decide how much to spend and on what; it is another to raise the money to underwrite these programs. This section describes how the federal government decides how much to tax. Of course, this problem is not solved from scratch every year. Instead, the government takes the existing tax structure as given and changes it from time to time as seems desirable. Often the initiative leading to a change in the tax laws comes from the president, who sometimes requests tax changes in his State of the Union message, his budget message, or a special tax message. Much of the spadework underlying his proposals will have been carried out by the Treasury Department, particularly the Treasury's Office of Tax Analysis, Office of the Tax Legislative Counsel, and Internal Revenue Service.

The proposal of a major tax change generally brings about considerable public debate. Representatives of labor, industry, agriculture, and other economic and social groups present their opinions. Newspaper articles, radio shows, and television commentators analyze the issues. By the time the Congress begins to look seriously at the proposal, the battle lines between those who favor the change and those who oppose it are generally pretty clearly drawn. The tax bill incorporating the change is first considered by the Ways and Means Committee of the House of Representatives, a very powerful committee composed of 25 members drawn from both political parties. After public hearings, the committee goes into executive session and reviews each proposed change with its staff and with the Treasury staff. After careful study, the committee arrives at a bill it recommends—though this bill may or may not conform to what the president asked for. Then the bill is referred to the entire House of Representatives for approval. Only rarely is a major tax bill recommended by the committee turned down by the House.

Next, the bill is sent to the Senate. There it is referred to the Finance Committee, which is organized like the House Ways and Means Committee. The Finance Committee also holds hearings, discusses the bill at length, makes changes in it, and sends its version of the bill to the entire Senate, where there frequently is considerable debate. Ultimately, it is brought to a vote. If it does not pass, that ends the process. If it does pass (and if it differs from the House version of the bill, which is generally the case), then a conference committee must be formed to iron out the differences between the House and Senate versions. Finally, when this compromise is worked out, the result must be passed by both houses and sent to the president. The president rarely vetoes a tax bill, although it has occasionally been done.[6]

[6] For an excellent discussion of the federal tax legislative process, see J. Pechman, *Federal Tax Policy,* revised edition, New York: Norton, 1971, part of which is reprinted in E. Mansfield, *Economics: Readings, Issues, and Cases,* New York: Norton, 1974.

Principles of Taxation

According to the English political philosopher, Edmund Burke, "To tax and to please, no more than to love and to be wise, is not given to men." What constitutes a rational tax system? Are there any generally accepted principles to guide the nation in determining who should pay how much? The answer is that there are some principles most people accept, but they are so broad and general that they leave plenty of room for argument and compromise. Specifically, two general principles of taxation command widespread agreement. First, *there is the principle that people who receive more in benefits from a certain government service should pay more in taxes to support it.* Certainly few people would argue with this idea. Second, *there is the principle that people should be taxed so as to result in a socially desirable redistribution of income.* In practice, this has ordinarily meant that the wealthy have been asked to pay more than the poor. This idea, too, has generally commanded widespread assent—although this, of course, has not prevented the wealthy from trying to avoid its application to them.

It follows from these principles that if two people are in essentially the same circumstances (their income, purchases, utilization of public services are the same), then they should pay the same taxes. This is an important rule, innocuous though it may seem. It says that equals should be treated equally—*whether one is a Republican and the other is a Democrat, or whether one is a friend of the president and the other is his enemy, or whether one has purely salary income and the other has property income, they should be treated equally.* Certainly, this is a basic characteristic of an equitable tax system.

It is easy to relate most of the taxes in our tax structure to these principles. For example, the first principle—the benefit principle—is the basic rationale behind taxes on gasoline and license fees for vehicles and drivers. Those who use the roads are asked to pay for their construction and upkeep. Also, the property tax, levied primarily on real estate, is often supported on these grounds. It is argued that property owners receive important benefits—fire and police protection, for example—and that the extent of the benefits is related to the extent of their property.

The personal income tax is based squarely on the second principle—ability to pay. A person with a large income pays a higher proportion of income in personal income taxes than does a person with a smaller income. For example, in 1973, if a couple's income (after deductions but before exemptions) were $5,000, their federal income tax would be $535, whereas if their income were $20,000, their federal income tax would be $3,960. (However, the wealthy can avoid taxes in various perfectly legal ways, as we shall see in a later section.) Also, estate and inheritance taxes hit the rich much harder than the poor; but again, it is possible to take some of the sting out of them if you have a good lawyer.

The principles cited above are useful and important, but they do not take us very far toward establishing a rational tax structure. They are too vague and leave too many questions unanswered. For example, if I use about the same amount of public services as you do, but my income is twice yours, how much more should I pay in taxes? Twice as much? Three times as much? Fifty percent more? These principles throw no real light on many of the detailed questions that must be answered by a real-life tax code.

The Personal and Corporate Income Taxes

The federal personal income tax brings in almost $100 billion a year. Yet a great many people are perhaps unaware of just how much they are contributing because it is deducted from their wages each month or each week, so that they owe little extra when April 15 rolls around. (Indeed, they may even be due a refund.) This pay-as-you-go scheme reduces the pain, but, of course, it does

Table 6.2

Federal Personal Income Tax, Couple without Children, 1973

Income (after deductions but before exemptions)	Personal income tax	Average tax rate (percent)	Marginal tax rate (percent)
Below $1500	$ 0	0	0
$3000	215	7.2	15
5000	535	10.7	17
10,000	1,490	14.9	22
20,000	3,960	19.8	28
50,000	16,310	32.6	50
100,000	44,280	44.3	60
1,000,000	669,930	67.0	70

not eliminate it: taxes are never painless.

Obviously, how much a family has to pay in personal income taxes depends on the family's income. The tax schedule as of 1973, is as shown in Table 6.2. The second column shows how much a couple would have to pay if their income was the amount shown in the first column. For example, at an income of $5,000, their income tax would be $535; at an income of $20,000, their income tax would be $3,960. Clearly, the percentage of income owed in income tax increases as income increases, but this percentage does not increase indefinitely. As shown in the third column of Table 6.2, the percentage of income going for personal income taxes never exceeds 70 percent, no matter how much money the couple makes. (And on income from wages and personal effort, it never exceeds 50 percent.)

It is instructive to look further at how the "tax bite" increases with income. In particular, let's ask ourselves what proportion of an *extra* dollar of income the couple will have to pay in personal income taxes. In other words, what is the ***marginal tax rate***—the tax on an extra dollar of income? The fourth column of Table 6.2 shows that the marginal tax rate is 17 percent if the couple's income is $5,000, 28 percent if the couple's income is $20,000, 50 percent if the couple's income is $50,000, and 70 percent if the couple's income is $1 million. Thus, the greater the couple's income, the greater the proportion of an extra dollar that goes for personal income taxes.

Clearly, the personal income tax tends to reduce the inequality of after-tax income, since the rich are taxed more heavily than the poor. However, the personal income tax does not bear down as heavily on the rich as one might surmise from Table 6.2. This is because, as we shall see in a subsequent section, there are a variety of perfectly legal ways for people to avoid paying taxes on their incomes. In addition, of course, there is some illegal tax evasion, such as underreporting of income, fake expenses, and imaginary dependents. But evasion is much less important than legal tax avoidance, despite Will Rogers's quip that the income tax has made more liars among the American public than golf.

The federal government imposes a tax on the incomes of corporations as well as of people. Corporations must pay 22 percent of their first $25,000 of annual net earnings and 48 percent of the rest as corporate income tax. For example, a corporation with annual profit of $125,000 would pay $53,500 in corporate income tax—$5,500 (22 percent of the first $25,000) plus $48,000 (48 percent of the remaining $100,000). The corporate income tax involves "double taxation." The federal government taxes a corporation's earnings both through the corporate income tax (when the corporation earns the profits) and through the personal income tax (when the corporation's earnings are distributed to the stockholders as dividends).

It is generally agreed that the personal income tax is paid by the person whose income is taxed: he or she cannot shift this tax to someone else. But the incidence of the corporate income tax is not so clear. To some extent, corporations may pass along some of their income tax bill to customers in the form of higher prices or to workers in the form of lower wages. Some economists feel that a corporation shifts much of the tax burden in this way; others disagree. This is a controversial issue that has proved very difficult to resolve.

The Property Tax and the Sales Tax

The ***property tax*** is the fiscal bulwark of our local governments. The way it works is simple enough. Most towns and cities estimate the amount they will spend in the next year or two, and then determine a property tax based on the assessed property values in the town or city. For example, if there is $500 million in assessed property values in the town and the town needs to raise $5 million, the tax rate will be 1 percent of assessed property value. In other words, each property owner will have to pay 1 percent of the assessed value of his property. There are well-known problems in the administration of the property tax. First, assessed values of property often depart significantly from actual market values; the former are typically much lower than the latter. And the ratio of assessed to actual value is often lower among higher-priced pieces of property; thus wealthier people tend to

Table 6.3

State Retail Sales Tax Rates, 1970

State	Percentage	State	Percentage	State	Percentage
Alabama	4	Louisiana	2	Oklahoma	2
Arizona	3	Maine	5	Pennsylvania	6
Arkansas	3	Maryland	4	Rhode Island	5
California	4	Massachusetts	3	South Carolina	4
Colorado	3	Michigan	4	South Dakota	4
Connecticut	5	Minnesota	3	Tennessee	3
District of Columbia	4	Mississippi	5	Texas	3¼
Florida	4	Missouri	3	Utah	4
Georgia	3	Nebraska	2½	Vermont	3
Hawaii	4	Nevada	2	Virginia	3
Idaho	3	New Jersey	3	Washington	4½
Illinois	4	New Mexico	4	West Virginia	3
Indiana	2	New York	3	Wisconsin	4
Iowa	3	North Carolina	3	Wyoming	3
Kansas	3	North Dakota	4		
Kentucky	5	Ohio	4		

Source: Advisory Commission on Intergovernmental Relations.

get off easier. Second, there is widespread evasion of taxes on ***personal property***—securities, bank accounts, and so on. Many people simply do not pay up. Third, the property tax is not very flexible: assessments and rates tend to change rather slowly.

The ***sales tax,*** of course, is a bulwark of state taxation. It provides a high yield with relatively low collection costs. As Table 6.3 indicates, most of the states have some form of general sales tax, the rate being usually between 3 and 5 percent. Retailers add to the price of goods sold to consumers an amount equal to 3 to 5 percent of the consumer's bill. This extra amount is submitted to the state as the general sales tax. Some states exempt food purchases from this tax, and a few exempt medical supplies. Where they exist, these exemptions help reduce the impact of the sales tax on the poor; but in general the sales tax imposes a greater burden relative to income on the poor than on the rich, for the simple reason that the rich save a larger percentage of their income. Practically all of a poor family's income may be subject to sales taxes; a great deal of a rich family's income may not be, because it is not spent on consumer goods, but saved.

Who really pays the property tax or the sales tax? To what extent can these taxes be shifted to other people? The answer is not as straightforward as one might expect. For the property tax, the owner of unrented residential property swallows the tax, since there is no one else to shift it to. But the owner of rented property may attempt to pass along some of the tax to the tenant. In the case of the sales tax, the extent to which it can be shifted to the consumer depends on the demand and supply curves for the taxed commodity. For example, if the demand curve were a vertical line, the whole tax would be passed along to the consumer, whereas if the supply curve were a vertical line, the tax would be absorbed entirely by the producer or seller.

Tax Reform

Because the tax structure of the United States contains so many exemptions and loopholes, there is continual pressure for tax reform. Senator George McGovern, in his bid for the presidency in 1972, stressed the importance of tax reform, stating: "The tax code fills hundreds of pages. It is riddled with loopholes, special exemptions, and shelters, available to those with access to wealth and legal talent. Income which is earned on an assembly line or in an office should no longer be more heavily taxed than profits from oil or securities." In particular, there are questions about the equity of the relatively low tax rates on capital gains, the tax-free status of interest on state and local bonds, the depletion allowances, and other aspects of the tax code.

Because there are so many exemptions, exclusions, and deductions, a surprisingly small percentage of all income is subject to the federal personal income tax. In 1960, only about 3/7 of personal income in the United States was subject to the income tax. This erosion of the tax base, lamented frequently by experts on public finance, means that tax rates must be higher than they would be if the tax base were broader. In other words, if a larger proportion of all income were subject to the personal income tax, a smaller tax could be imposed on each dollar of income subject to tax. Many tax experts feel strongly that the erosion of the tax base should be stopped, and that the tax base should be broadened appreciably. But it is difficult to take away the various exemptions and deductions that have been granted in the past.

Current tax laws are favorable to homeowners, who can deduct the payment of local real estate taxes and the interest on their mortgage from their income to get the adjusted level of income on which they pay income taxes. Also, money a person makes on the stock market or from some other situation where his assets go up in value, known as a ***capital gain,*** is subject to lower personal income tax rates than other income. Interest paid by state and local governments on their bonds are not taxable at all by the federal government. Moreover, certain industries, particularly the oil industry, receive preferential tax treatment. In 1913, the

Congress, believing that the sale of minerals involves the sale of a firm's assets, allowed industries selling natural resources to deduct a small proportion of their revenues from their taxable income. This deduction is called a ***depletion allowance.*** Over the years, this proportion has been increased, until now this preferential treatment results in a tax saving of well over a billion dollars to these industries.

When the time seems ripe for a change in tax rates to stabilize the economy, there is often a tendency to try to accomplish tax reform as well. For example, if a tax cut seems advisable to reduce excessive unemployment, there may be an attempt to combine tax reform with tax reduction. Although the attempt to kill two birds—economic stabilization and tax reform—with one stone seems laudable in theory, in practice it can spell trouble. For example, here is how Thomas Dernburg of Oberlin College and Duncan McDougall of the University of Kansas describe the attempts in the early 1960s to mix tax reduction and tax reform:

> During the debate of the early 1960's, the Treasury proposed that the tax bill contain a comprehensive package of reform. Aware that congressmen cannot be interested in reforms that penalize wealthy constituents and potential campaign contributors, the Treasury attempted to tack the reform package onto the tax reduction proposed by the President. The hope was that the tasty carrot of a tax reduction might be strong enough to drag along the refractory donkey of reform. Tax reform got nowhere in Congress. Realizing that the entire bill was in jeopardy, the Administration eventually gave up on reform, and the final bill represented rate reduction and not much else. Undoubtedly, the attempt to gain reform was one factor making for delay in obtaining passage of the tax bill.[7]

State and Local Finance and Revenue Sharing

It is important to recognize that there are several levels of government in the United States—federal, state, and local—and that each level of government spends and taxes. Thus, all levels of government, not just the federal government, play a role in our economic affairs. Unfortunately, however, there has been limited coordination between the spending and tax decisions of the federal government and those of the state and local governments. From the point of view of promoting full employment without inflation, it would be desirable for the federal, state, and local governments to work in unison, or at least in the same direction, to fight excessive unemployment or inflation. But in fact they often have worked at cross purposes.

In this country the state and local governments are traditionally entrusted with the responsibility for some of the services that have had to be expanded most rapidly—education, highways, municipal facilities, and so forth. Yet the kinds of taxes the state and local governments rely on—notably sales and property taxes—do not provide a yield that increases very rapidly with increases in income. Thus a basic question arises: how can the state and local governments get the money they need to expand their services at the desired rate? Presently, the state and local governments are caught in a fiscal bind. Their expenditures are being pushed up more rapidly than their revenues. On the other hand, because the personal income tax generates a great deal of additional money as income increases, the federal government is in the fortunate position of having its revenues increase at a relatively rapid rate.

Recognizing that it has access to greater sources of revenue, the federal government has been making more and more grants to states and—on a smaller scale—to local governments. These grants have been earmarked primarily for highways, welfare, and education, the major expenditure areas for state and local governments. One effect of these grants is to offset the considerable regional differences in income. Since some states—particularly those in the South—are poor, less tax revenue is

[7] Thomas Dernburg and Duncan McDougall, *Macroeconomics,* New York: McGraw-Hill, 1972, p. 414.

generated there than in richer states even if tax rates are the same. Thus, to equalize the extent and quality of public services, the federal government in effect takes from the richer states—like New York and California—and gives to the poorer states—like Mississippi and Alabama.

In recent years, a great deal of attention has been given to ***revenue sharing***—large and unconditional grants by the federal government to the state and local governments. Initially suggested by Walter W. Heller of the University of Minnesota and Joseph Pechman of the Brookings Institution, this idea was accepted by the Nixon administration, and eventually by Congress. At first it was opposed on the grounds that those who spend money should have the responsibility of raising it, since the divorce of expenditure from financing responsibilities might lead to wasteful expenditures. Initially, other objections were raised as well. But the fiscal plight of the state and local governments is serious and undesirable: there is a mismatch between their responsibilities and their resources. Recognizing that some device must be adopted to help the local and state governments, Congress passed the first revenue sharing bill in 1972.

The National Debt: Size and Growth

No subject in economics has more confused the public than the national debt. When the federal government spends more than it receives in taxes, it borrows money to cover the difference. The national debt—composed of bonds, notes, and other government IOUs of various kinds—is the result of such borrowing. These IOUs are held by in-

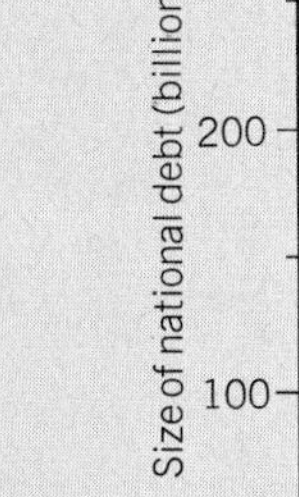

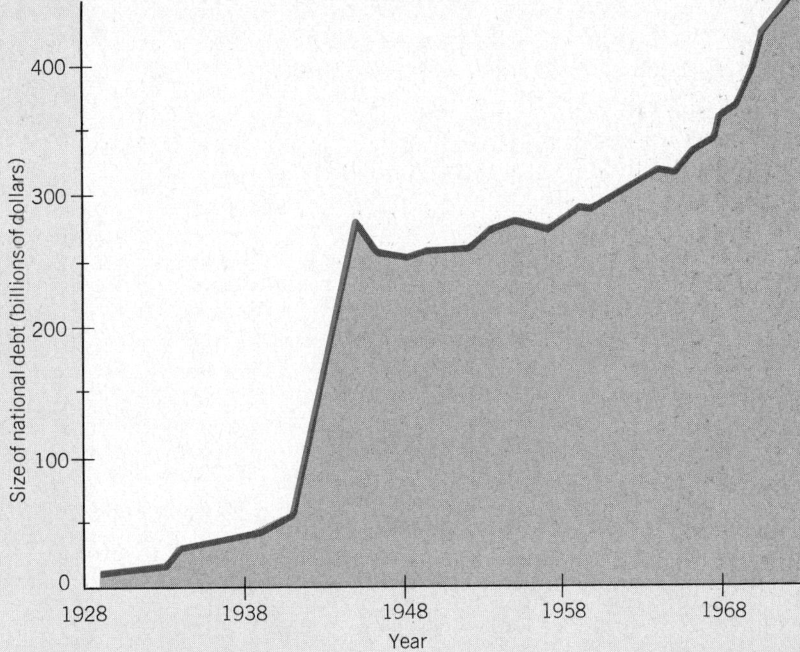

Figure 6.2
Size of the National Debt, United States, 1929–72

The national debt, currently about $450 billion, is due largely to World War II.

The Department of the Treasury and the National Debt

The average U.S. citizen has very little direct contact with the Department of the Treasury. If he works for the federal government, he receives a bimonthly check; if he is so fortunate as to have overpaid his income tax, he may receive a lovely green refund check. In fact, the processing of checks is (at least, to the nonrecipient economist) much less important than many other functions of the Treasury. Should Congress or the president wish technical advice on the effect of a new tax measure, the Treasury Department will supply the analysis. In addition, it represents American interests in negotiations over international monetary arrangements with other countries; and, through the Internal Revenue Service and the Customs Service, it collects most federal taxes.*

But from an economist's point of view, one of the most interesting tasks the Treasury performs may be the management of the national debt. Imagine yourself with a debt of over $325 billion (held by the public), with a few billion coming due each week. Obviously, much of the Treasury's time must be spent scratching for new Peters in order to pay old Pauls. This may not sound like an easy task; and, in fact, it isn't. Over the years the Treasury has developed a bewildering array of devices—refinancing Series E bonds, U.S. savings bonds, short-term bills, long-term bonds—for coaxing new lenders to release their cash, or persuading old lenders to defer collection.

The most important of these instruments is U.S. Treasury bills, which in 1973 amounted to almost $103 billion. (Should you ever have a spare $10,000, the smallest denomination in which Treasury bills are sold, their current prices can be found in the financial pages of any major newspaper.)

Almost every month the Undersecretary of the Treasury for Monetary Affairs must decide in what form the portion of the debt coming due should be refinanced. Are interest rates going up? If so, he might refinance by selling long-term bonds, locking up money at the present low rate. Will interest rates fall? If so, he might prefer the 90-day bill. Before an issue is floated, he gets a reading of market conditions from committees of the American Bankers Association and the Investment Bankers Association. But cost is not his only problem. He must also worry about the effect of Treasury operations on financial markets and must have developed future refunding policies. In any case, an elaborate financial network of banks, big insurance companies, pension funds, and investment houses is always waiting to respond to the Treasury's next offering.

E.A.

*Moreover, faithful television fans may realize that, through its Bureau of Customs, the Treasury is responsible for controlling the importation of narcotics.

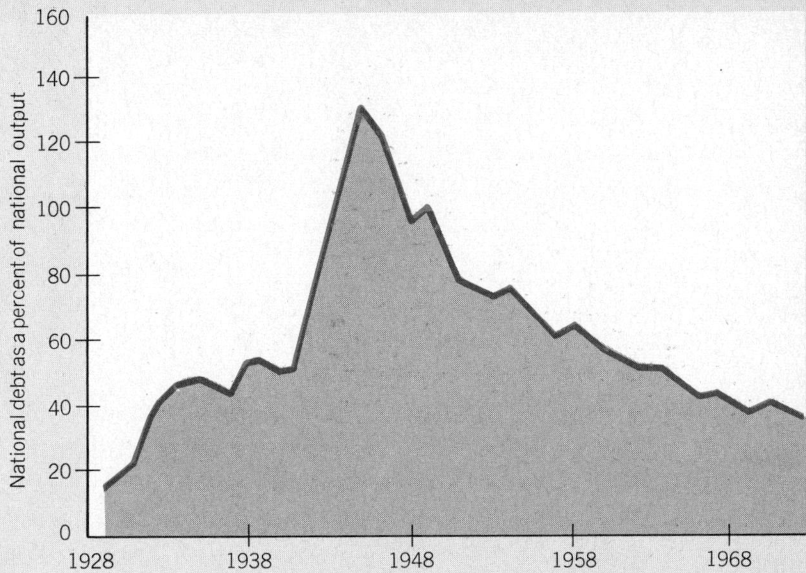

Figure 6.3
National Debt as a Percent of National Output, United States, 1929–72

As a percent of national output, the national debt has declined steadily since World War II.

dividuals, firms, banks, and public agencies. There is a large and very important market for government securities, which are relatively riskless and highly liquid. If you look at the *New York Times* or *Wall Street Journal,* for example, you can find each day the prices at which each of a large number of issues of these bonds, notes, and bills are quoted.

How large is the national debt? In 1972, as shown in Figure 6.2, it was almost $450 billion. This certainly seems to be a large amount, but it is important to relate the size of the national debt to the size of our national output. After all, a $450 billion debt means one thing if our annual output is $1 trillion, and another thing if our annual output is $100 billion. As a percent of output, the national debt is smaller now than in 1939, and no larger now than shortly after the Civil War. In 1972, the debt was about 40 percent of output; in 1939, it was about 50 percent of output; and in 1868, it was about 40 percent of output. The debt—expressed as a percentage of output—is shown in Figure 6.3. Surely the figures do not seem to provide any cause for alarm. The popular misconception that the national debt is growing at a dangerous rate seems hard to square with the facts.

It is obvious from Figure 6.2 that the size of our national debt is due largely to one thing: World War II. In 1939, the national debt was less than $50 billion; by 1945, it was close to $300 billion. This huge increase occurred to finance the war. Since 1945, the national debt has not grown fast. Indeed, as a percent of national output, it has decreased substantially since 1945. Consequently, as Richard and Peggy Musgrave point out, "The specter of an ever-rising debt to [output] ratio, which so agitated the public only a few decades ago, has become of more or less anthropological interest, a striking example of the demise of a once burning issue."[8]

[8] Richard and Peggy Musgrave, *op. cit.,* p. 587. Note too that much of the public debt is in the hands of government agencies, not held by the public. For example, in 1971 only about $325 billion was held by the public.

Burdens and Advantages of the National Debt

When I was a boy and the national debt was increasing to the "incredible" level of about $47 billion, my grandfather used to warn me repeatedly that the debt was a burden his generation was thrusting on my generation. I believed it then, but I don't believe it now. Without trying to show where my grandfather may have been led astray —after all, who needs a smart-aleck grandson!— it is worth pointing out that a public debt is not like your debt or mine, which must be paid off at a certain time in the future. In practice, new government debt is floated to pay off maturing public debt. There never comes a time when we must collectively reach into our pockets to pay off the debt. And even if we did pay it off, the same generation would collect as the one that paid.

Of course, this does not mean that the debt is of no economic consequence. On the contrary, to the extent that the debt is held by foreigners, we must send goods and services overseas to pay the interest on it. This means that less goods and services are available for our citizens. Even if the debt is internally held, there are additional effects as well. Taxes must be collected from the public at large to pay interest to the holders of government bonds, notes, and other obligations. To the extent that the bondholders receiving the interest are wealthier than the public as a whole, there is thus some redistribution of income from the poor to the rich. To the extent that the taxes needed to obtain the money to pay interest on the debt reduce incentives, the result may be a smaller national output.

Beyond this, the existence of all those government bonds, notes, and so forth in the portfolios of people and firms may make them feel richer, and this may make them spend more. Whether this is good or bad depends upon whether we are at less than full employment. If so, it is a good thing; if not, it is bad. In addition, the existence of a large, broadly marketed national debt enables the Federal Reserve System to buy and sell government securities to help stabilize the economy, as we shall see in Chapter 14. (However, problems can arise if the government forces the Federal Reserve System to keep down the interest costs on the debt—this may result in some destabilization of the economy, as in 1946–51.)

If the government's revenues fall short of its expenditures, the difference is called a ***deficit.*** Borrowing is not the only method the government can use to finance a deficit. It can also create new money to cover the difference between expenditures and revenues. In other words, rather than selling bonds and other types of IOUs to the public to obtain the amount needed to cover the deficit, the government can print new currency, or create additional money in other ways. According to many economists, a deficit will have a less expansionary effect on output and employment if it is financed by borrowing from the public than if it is financed by creating new money. Much more will be said in Chapter 12 about the effects on output and employment of changes in the quantity of money.

A final word should be added about the idea that the national debt imposes a burden on future generations. *The principal way in which one generation can impose such a burden on another is by using up some of the country's productive capacity or by failing to add a normal increment to this capacity.* This, of course, is quite different from incurring debt. For example, World War II would have imposed a burden on subsequent generations whether or not the national debt was increased. However it was financed, the war would have meant that our resources had to be used for tanks and warplanes rather than for keeping up and expanding our productive capacity during 1941–45. And this imposed a burden, a real burden, on Americans living after 1945—as well, of course, as on those living during the war!

Summary

The spending decisions of the federal government take place in the context of the budgetary process.

The president submits his budget, which is a statement of anticipated expenditures and revenues, to Congress, which votes appropriations. Basically, the amount that the government spends on various activities and services must be decided through the nation's political processes. Voting by ballots must be substituted for dollar voting. In making such decisions, it is important to distinguish between changes in government expenditure that alter the scope of government and changes in government expenditures due to changes in efficiency.

Benefit-cost analysis and program budgeting have proved useful in decision making on government expenditures. Spending on each government program should be pushed to the point where the extra benefit from an extra dollar spent is at least equal to the dollar of cost. The PPB system has encouraged more precise identification of the goals of various programs and promoted the search for alternative means of fulfilling these goals. In some areas, benefit-cost analyses have proved useful in determining which of a variety of projects can accomplish a particular goal most economically, and whether any of them is worth carrying out. However, accurate measurement of the relevant benefits and costs is frequently difficult.

The Ways and Means Committee of the House of Representatives and the Senate Finance Committee play important roles in the federal tax legislative process. It is generally agreed that people who receive more in benefits from a certain government service should pay more in taxes to support it. It is also generally agreed that people should be taxed so as to result in a socially desirable redistribution of income, and that equals should be treated equally. But these general principles, although useful, cannot throw light on many of the detailed questions a real-life tax code must answer. The personal and corporate income taxes are very important sources of federal revenue, the sales tax is an important source of state revenues, and the property tax is an important source of local revenues. In recent years, there has been continual pressure for tax reform, since the tax structure of the United States contains many exemptions and loopholes. Also, recognizing the mismatch between the responsibilities and resources of the state and local governments, the federal government has begun a program of revenue sharing.

When the government spends more than it receives in revenues, the difference is called a deficit. The national debt is the result of previous deficits, since the government borrows money to cover a deficit. It could simply print money for this purpose, but it has chosen to borrow a considerable proportion of what was needed. Despite much public worry about the size of the national debt, as a percentage of national output it has been declining over the past 25 years. There are important differences between government debt and private debt. Although the size of the debt is certainly of consequence, it is not true that it somehow transmits a serious burden to future generations or that it may lead to bankruptcy.

CONCEPTS FOR REVIEW

Planning-Programming-Budgeting system
Benefit-cost analysis
Revenue sharing
Military-industrial complex
Tax reform
Benefit principle
Personal income tax
Sales tax
Ability to pay
Marginal tax rate
Capital gains
Depletion allowance
Public debt
Tax evasion
Tax avoidance

QUESTIONS FOR DISCUSSION AND REVIEW

1. Is it possible to test Galbraith's proposition that too little is being spent on government services? What sorts of tests would you propose? In 1973, President Nixon proposed a greatly expanded program of energy research and development. What sorts of information would you look at in order to decide whether the president's proposal should be accepted or rejected?

2. Make a detailed set of recommendations concerning changes that should be made in the American tax system. With regard to every change that you propose, state your reasons for advocating the change.

3. In 1960, less than half of personal income in the United States was subject to the income tax. True or False?

4. The national debt
   a. transmits a burden to future generations.
   b. is the result of previous deficits.
   c. as a percentage of GNP, has remained relatively constant over the past 25 years.
   d. if not decreased, may lead to bankruptcy.

CHAPTER 7

The Business Firm: Organization, Motivation, and Technology

It is hard to overstate the importance of business firms in the American economy. They produce the bulk of our goods and services, hire most of the nation's workers, and issue stocks and bonds that represent a large percentage of the nation's wealth. Judged by any yardstick—even less complimentary ones like the responsibility for environmental pollution—business firms are an extremely important part of the American economy. In this chapter, we discuss the various types of business firms, such as proprietorships and corporations. Then we describe the various types of securities—common stock, bonds, and so forth—issued by firms, and discuss the workings of the stock market. Next, we take up the motivation and structure of firms, as well as their technology. Finally, we provide some essential elements of accounting. This material is a necessary introduction to the workings of the business enterprise, absolutely essential to anyone who works for, manages, or invests in a firm.

General Motors: A Case Study

In Chapter 4, when we first discussed the role of the business firm in the American economy, we cited two examples of American business firms: Peter Amacher's drugstore and the General Motors Corporation. Now that we are considering the operations of the business firm in more detail, let's look more closely at the General Motors Corporation. A description of its formation and vicissitudes should give you a better feel for what firms do and the sorts of problems they face.

General Motors was formed in 1908 by William C. Durant, an energetic and imaginative businessman who made over a million dollars in the carriage business before he was 40. Having taken over the bankrupt Buick Motor Company in 1904, Durant built it into a very successful operation. Then, in 1908, he gained control of a number of small automobile companies (including Cadillac and Olds), several truck firms, and 10 parts and accessory firms. The resulting amalgamation was General Motors.

In 1910, General Motors' sales fell below scheduled production, and Durant lacked the funds to pay his work force and suppliers. To get the

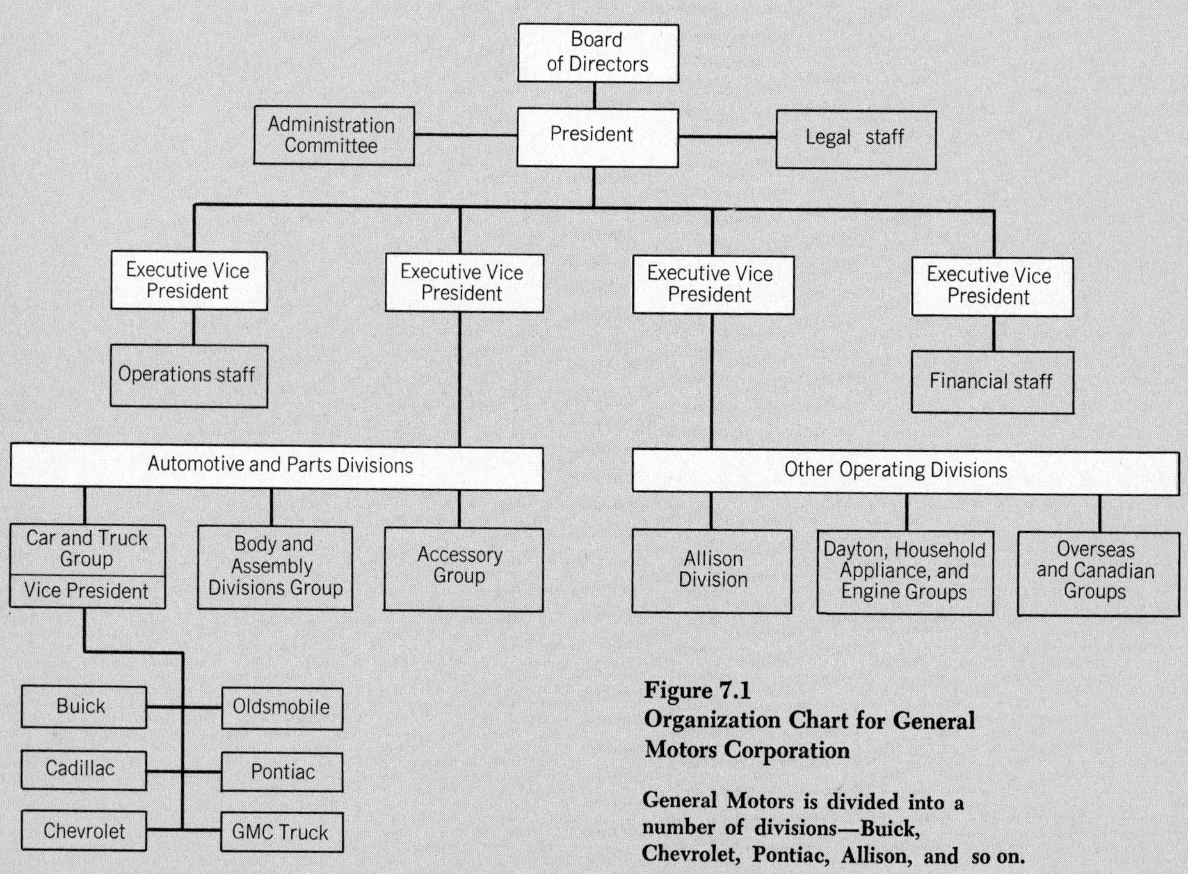

Figure 7.1
Organization Chart for General Motors Corporation

General Motors is divided into a number of divisions—Buick, Chevrolet, Pontiac, Allison, and so on.

money he needed, he went to a banking syndicate, which lent him $15 million—but required him to turn over the management of the company to them. By 1915, Durant had acquired another auto producer, Chevrolet, and had picked up formidable financial allies in the Du Ponts, the owners of the famous chemical firm. Using both these levers, Durant regained full control of General Motors in 1916; and between 1916 and 1920, he concentrated on expanding the productive capacity of the General Motors Corporation. A man of extraordinary vision, he recognized, as did few of his contemporaries, a great potential demand for moderately priced cars, and devoted his energy to putting General Motors in a position to satisfy this demand.

Although Durant was a man of great vision, he was not the sort of administrator who created a tidy organizational structure. The General Motors Corporation under Durant was a very large agglomeration of companies in a variety of product lines, with somewhat tangled lines of communication and diffuse control. When automobile sales did not come up to expectations in 1920, the firm suffered a reduction in profits. The ensuing crisis resulted in Durant's retirement as president of General Motors, and the adoption by the firm of a new organizational plan created by Alfred Sloan, a young M.I.T.-trained engineer, who soon became president. This plan divided General Motors into a number of divisions: the Buick division, the Chevrolet division, the accessory division, and so forth. Each division was given considerable freedom, but more attention was devoted to central control and coordination than under Durant's more anarchical organization. Sloan's organizational plan, an important innovation in its day, has remained in effect with little change from 1920 to the present: Figure 7.1 shows the organization of General Motors today.

During the 1920s General Motors prospered: its sales rose from $600 million in 1920 to $1,500 million in 1929, and its profits rose from about $38 million in 1920 to about $248 million in 1929. The next decade was different: the 1930s were the years of the Great Depression, when sales and profits of most firms, including General Motors, were hard hit. But during the 1940s General Motors entered another period of prosperity and growth. Its sales rose from about $1.8 billion in 1940 to about $5.7 billion in 1949, and its profits rose from about $196 million in 1940 to about $656 million in 1949. The 1950s and 1960s saw the prosperity of General Motors continue. Of course there were short intervals when sales and profits fell, but the trend was upward—in part because of population growth and because higher incomes have meant bigger sales of automobiles. The firm has experienced no prolonged period of low profits or considerable excess capacity, as was the case in the 1930s. By 1971, General Motors had sales of over $28 billion. The somewhat jumbled organization William Durant assembled in 1908 had become the biggest industrial company in the United States, a symbol of industrial might around the world.

Characteristics of American Firms: Some Salient Facts

General Motors is an economic colossus—America's biggest industrial firm. Of course it is not typical of American business firms. If we broaden our focus to take in the entire population of business firms in the United States, the first thing we note is their tremendous number; according to government statistics, there are over 10 million. The vast majority of these firms, as one would expect, are very small. There are lots of grocery stores, gas stations, auto dealers, drugstores (like Mr. Amacher's), clothing shops, restaurants, and so on. You see hundreds of them as you walk along practically any downtown city street. But these small firms, although numerous, do not control the bulk of the nation's productive capacity. The several hundred largest firms have great economic power, measured by their sales, assets, employment, or other such indexes. The small firms tend to be weak and short-lived. On the average, they tend to go out of busi-

Table 7.1

Number and Receipts of Business Firms, by Industry, United States

Industry	Number of firms (millions)	Receipts of firms (millions of dollars)
Agriculture, forestry and fisheries	3.4	52
Mining	.1	16
Construction	.8	98
Manufacturing	.4	645
Transportation, communication[a]	.4	117
Wholesale trade	.5	235
Retail trade	2.1	344
Financial	1.0	164
Services	2.8	102
Total	11.5	1,773

Source: Statistical Abstract of the United States.
[a] Includes electric and gas.

ness before they have been in existence 7 years.

The next thing to note is that most of the nation's business firms are engaged in agriculture, services, and retail trade. Table 7.1 shows that almost ¾ of the firms in the United States are in these industries, an understandable figure since these industries tend to have lots and lots of small businesses. Although manufacturing firms constitute only about 4 percent of all American firms, they account for more than ⅓ of all business receipts. On the other hand, agriculture (including forestry and fisheries) includes about 30 percent of the nation's business firms, but accounts for only 3 percent of the total receipts. Clearly, this is because manufacturing firms tend to be much bigger, in terms of receipts, employment, and assets, than agricultural firms. Think, for example, of the steel plants in Pittsburgh or Cleveland, or of the aircraft plants in California or Georgia. They dwarf the typical farm—and they are only parts of a manufacturing firm.

Finally, note that most of the nation's business firms are proprietorships: indeed, almost ⅘ fall into this category, while about 13 percent are corporations, and about 8 percent are partnerships. You often hear the terms "proprietorship," "partnership," "corporation." What do these terms mean?

Proprietorships

A proprietorship is a legal form of business organization—the most common form, as we saw in the previous section, and also the simplest. Specifically, a ***proprietorship*** is a firm owned by a single individual. A great many of the nation's small businesses are proprietorships. For example, the corner drugstore may well be one. If so, it has a single owner. He hires the people he needs to wait on customers, deliver orders, do the bookkeeping, and so forth. He borrows, if he can, whatever money he feels he needs. He reaps the profits, or incurs the losses. All his personal assets—his house, his furniture, his car—can be taken by creditors to meet the drugstore's bills: that is, he has unlimited liability for the debts of the business.

What Lincoln said about the common man applies as well to proprietorships: God must love them, or He wouldn't have created so many of them. If proprietorships didn't have advantages over other legal forms of business organization under many sorts of circumstances, there wouldn't be so many of them. What are these advantages? First, the owner of a proprietorship has complete control over the business. He doesn't have to negotiate with partners or other co-owners. He is the boss—and the only boss. Anyone who has been in a position of complete authority knows the joy it can bring: many proprietors treasure this feeling of independence. Second, a proprietorship is easy and inexpensive to establish: all you have to do is hang out your shingle and announce you are in business. This too is a great advantage.

But proprietorships have important disadvantages as well—and for this reason, they are seldom found in many important industries. One disadvantage is that it is difficult for a proprietor to put together enough financial resources to enter industries like automobiles or steel. No one in the world has enough money to establish, by himself, a firm of General Motors' present size. Another disadvantage is that the proprietor is liable for all of the debts of the firm. If his business fails, his personal assets can be taken by his creditors, and he can be completely wiped out.

Partnerships

A ***partnership*** is somewhat more complicated than a proprietorship. As its name implies, it is a form of business organization where two or more people agree to own and conduct a business. Each partner agrees to contribute some proportion of the capital and labor used by the business, and to receive some proportion of the profits or losses. There are a variety of types of partnerships. In some cases, one or more of the partners may be "silent partners," who put up some of the money, but have little or nothing to do with the operations of the firm. The partnership is a common form of business organization in some industries and professions, like the law. But as we saw in a previous section, partnerships are found less frequently than proprietorships or corporations in the United States.

A partnership has certain advantages. Like a proprietorship, it can be established without great expense or legal red tape. (However, if you ever go into partnership with someone, you would be well advised to have a good lawyer draw up a written agreement establishing such things as the salaries of each partner and how profits are to be shared.) In addition, a partnership can avoid some of the problems involved in a proprietorship. It can usually put together more financial resources and specialized know-how than a proprietorship—and this can be an important advantage.

But the partnership also has certain drawbacks. First, each partner is liable without limit for the bills of the firm. For example, even if one partner of a law firm has only a 30 percent share of the firm, he may be called upon to pay all the firm's debts if the other partners cannot do so. Second, there is some red tape in keeping a partnership in existence. Whenever a partner dies or withdraws, or whenever a new partner is admitted, a new partnership must be established. Third, like the proprietorship, the partnership is not a very effective way to obtain the large amounts of capital required for some modern industries. A modern automobile plant may cost $500 million, and not many partnerships could assemble that much capital. For these reasons, as well as others discussed in the next section, the corporation has become the dominant form of business organization.

Corporations

A far more complicated form of business organization than either the proprietorship or partnership, the ***corporation*** is a fictitious legal person, separate and distinct from its owners. A businessman forms a corporation by having his lawyer draw up the necessary papers stating (in general terms) what sorts of activities he and the other owners of the corporation intend to engage in. The owners of the corporation are the stockholders. ***Stock,*** pieces of paper signifying ownership of the corporation, is issued to the owners, generally in exchange for their cash. Ordinarily, each ***share*** of stock gives its owner one vote. The corporation's ***board of directors,*** which is responsible for setting overall policy for the firm, is elected by the stockholders. Any of the firm's owners can, if he is dissatisfied with the company's policies or thinks he has better opportunities elsewhere, sell his stock to someone else, assuming, of course, that he can find a buyer.

The corporation has many advantages over the partnership or proprietorship. In particular, each of the corporation's owners has limited, not unlimited, liability. If I decide to become one of the owners of General Motors and if a share of General Motors common stock sells for $65 a share, I can buy 10 shares of General Motors stock for $650. And I can be sure that, if General Motors falls on hard times, I cannot lose more than the $650 I paid for the stock. There is no way that I can be assessed beyond this. Moreover, the corporation, unlike the partnership or proprietorship, has unlimited life. If several stockholders want to withdraw from the firm, they simply sell their stock. The corporation goes on, although the identity of the owners changes. For these reasons, the corporation is clearly a better device for raising large sums of money than the partnership or proprietorship. This is a very important advantage of the corporation, particularly in industries like automobiles and steel, which could not otherwise finance their operations.

Without question, the corporation is a very important social invention. It permits people to assemble the large quantities of capital required for efficient production in many industries. Without limited liability and the other advantages of the corporation, it is doubtful that the opportunities and benefits of large-scale production could have been reaped. However, this does not mean that the corporate form will work for all firms. In many cases, a firm requires only a modest amount of capital, and there is no reason to go to the extra trouble and expense of establishing a corporation. Moreover, one disadvantage of the corporation is ***double taxation of income,*** since, as you will recall from Chapter 6, corporations pay income taxes —and the tax rate is often about ½ of every extra dollar earned. Thus, every dollar earned by a corporation and distributed to stockholders is taxed twice by the federal government—once when it is counted as income by the corporation, and once when the remainder is counted as income by the stockholders. This disadvantage of the corporation must be balanced against the advantage that the top tax rates for corporations are less than those that may apply to unincorporated businesses.

Corporate Securities

The corporation raises money by issuing various kinds of securities; of these, three kinds—common stock, preferred stock, and bonds—are particularly significant. Each of these types of securities is important to the workings of the corporation and to people's investment decisions. As you know from the previous section, ***common stock*** is the ordinary certificate of ownership of the corporation. A holder of common stock is an owner of the firm. He shares in the firm's profits—and in its losses as well. At frequent intervals, the board of directors of the firm may declare a dividend of so much per share for the common stockholders. For example, the common stockholders of General Motors received dividends of $3.40 per share in 1970. ***Dividends*** are thus the income the owners of common stock receive. (In addition, of course, common stockholders can make money by selling their stock for more than they paid for it; such income is called ***capital gains.***) Common stock is generally regarded as more risky than preferred stock or bonds, for reasons that will be explained.

Preferred stock is a special kind of certificate of ownership that pays at most a stated dividend. For example, owners of one type of General Motors preferred stock receive $5 a share per year, as long as the firm makes enough to pay this dividend. To protect the owners of preferred stock, it is stipulated that no dividends can be paid on the common stock unless the dividends on the preferred stock are paid in full. Since the common stockholders cannot receive their dividends unless the preferred stock's dividends have been paid, common stock is obviously more risky than preferred stock. But by the same token, the amount preferred stockholders have to gain if the company prospers is less than the amount common stockholders have to gain, since however high its profits may be, the firm will pay only the stated dividend—for example, $5 per share per year in the case of General Motors—to the owners of preferred stock.

Bonds are quite different from both common and preferred stocks. ***Bonds*** are debts of the firm; in other words, they are IOUs issued by the firm. In contrast to stockholders, the bondholders are not owners of a firm: they are its creditors, and receive interest, not dividends. Specifically, a bond is a certificate bearing the firm's promise to pay the interest every 6 months until the bond matures, at which time the firm also promises to pay the bondholder the principal (the amount he lent the firm) as well. Often, bonds are sold in $1,000 denominations. For example, one type of bond issued by General Motors is a 3¼ percent bond, due in 1979. The owner of each such bond receives $32.50 per year in interest, and General Motors promises to pay him the principal of $1,000 when the bond falls due in 1979. A firm must pay the interest on the bonds and the principal when it is due, or it can be declared bankrupt. In other words, the bondholders are legally entitled to receive what is due them before the stockholders can get anything.

Thus, from the point of view of the investor, bonds are generally considered less risky than preferred stock, and preferred stocks are considered less risky than common stock. But we have ignored another fact: inflation. The tendency for the price level in the United States to increase over time has meant that owners of common stocks have reaped substantial capital gains, while bondholders have been paid off with dollars that were worth less than those they lent. For this reason and others, many investors in recent years have tended to favor common stocks. During the 1960s and early 1970s, a "cult of equities" developed; it became fashionable to buy common stock. To understand why, it is necessary to look briefly at the workings of the stock market.

The Stock Market

In general, large corporations do not sell stock directly to the investor. Instead, the investor buys stock on the stock market. Two major stock exchanges in the United States are the New York Stock Exchange and the American Stock Exchange, both in New York City. On these and similar exchanges in other cities, the common stocks of thousands of corporations are bought and sold. The price of each common stock fluctuates from day to day, indeed from minute to minute. Basically, the factors responsible for these price fluctuations are the shifts in the demand curve and supply curve for each kind of common stock. For example, if a strike breaks out at a General Motors plant, this may cause the demand curve for General Motors stock to shift downward to the left, since the strike is liable to mean lower profits for General Motors. Because of this downward, or leftward, shift in the demand curve, the price of General Motors common stock will tend to fall.

Occasionally, the stock market gets a case of jitters over economic conditions, stock prices tumble, and old investors think back to the Great Crash of 1929. The 1920s witnessed a feverish interest in investing in the stock market. Along with raccoon coats, Stutz Bearcats, and the Charleston, common stocks were the rage. Both the professionals on Wall Street and the neophytes on Main Street bought common stocks and more common stocks. Naturally, as the demand curves for common stocks shifted upward to the right, their prices rose, thus whetting the appetites of investors for still more common stocks. This upward spiral continued until 1929, when the bubble burst. Suddenly the prices of common stocks fell precipitously—and continued to drop during the early 1930s. The most famous average of industrial stock prices, the Dow-Jones average, fell from 381 in 1929 to 41 in 1933. Many investors, large and small, were wiped out.

The Great Crash made investors wary of common stocks for many years. But by the 1960s confidence in them was fully restored, and there certainly was no tendency for investors to shy away from them. Judging from historical experience, the public's taste for common stocks seems to be justified. Studies show that, during the course of a lifetime, the typical investor would have done better to invest in common stocks than in the best-quality bonds, because stock prices have tended to rise. This tended to apply in a great many cases, even for investors who lived through the Great Crash. And it has certainly been borne out during the past 40 years. Thus, although common stocks are riskier in some respects than bonds or preferred stocks, they seem to have performed better, on the average, at least in recent times.

During periods when the average of stock prices is going up, such as the 1920s and much of the 1950s and 1960s, it is relatively easy to be a financial wizard, whether by luck or calculation. A much more exacting test of your financial acumen is how well you can pick which stocks will outperform the averages. If you can predict that increases will occur in a certain firm's profits, and if other people don't predict the same thing, you may be able to pass this test. However, the sobering truth is that "playing the stock market" is much more an art than a science. The stock market is affected by psychological as well as economic considerations. Moreover, when you try to spot stocks that will increase in price, you are pitting your knowledge and experience against those of skilled professionals with big research staffs and with friends and acquaintances working for the companies in question. And even these professionals can do surprisingly poorly at times.

Do economists have a nose for good investments? John Maynard Keynes was an extremely successful speculator who made millions of dollars. Other economists have been far less successful. Certainly, a knowledge of basic economics is not sufficient to enable you to make money on the stock market, but insofar as the market reflects economic realities, a knowledge of basic economics should be helpful.

The Giant Corporation

Much of the trading on the stock market centers around the relatively small number of giant corporations that control a very substantial percentage of the total assets and employment in the American economy. And well it might, for the largest 100 manufacturing corporations control about ½ of this country's manufacturing assets. These firms have tremendous economic and political power. They include the giant automobile manufacturers (General Motors, Ford, and Chrysler), the big oil firms (Exxon, Gulf, Standard Oil of Indiana, Mobil, Standard Oil of California, Texaco, Atlantic-Richfield), the big steel firms (U. S. Steel, Bethlehem, Jones and Laughlin, Armco), the big computer and office machinery producers (IBM and Xerox), the leading tobacco firms (American Brands, R. J. Reynolds, Philip Morris), and many others.

An interesting and important feature of the large corporation is the fact that it is owned by many, many people, practically all of whom have little or no detailed information about the firm's operations. For example, the owners of the American Telephone and Telegraph Company, the giant public utility, number several million but most of them know relatively little about what is going on in the firm. Moreover, because of the wide diffusion of ownership, working control of a large corporation can often be maintained by a group with only 1/5 or less of all the voting stock. The result is a *separation of ownership from control.* In other words, the owners control the firm in only a limited and somewhat sporadic sense.

So long as a firm's management is not obviously incompetent or corrupt, it is difficult for insurgent stockholders to remove the management from office. Most stockholders do not go to the annual meetings to vote for members of the firm's board of directors. Instead, they receive *proxies,* which, if returned, permit the management to exercise their votes. Usually enough shareholders mail in their proxies to give management the votes it needs to elect a friendly board of directors. In recent years, the Securities and Exchange Commission, which oversees and regulates the financial markets, has attempted to make the giant corporations more democratic by enabling insurgent groups to gain access to mailing lists of stockholders and so forth. But there is still a noteworthy and widespread separation of ownership from control.

The large corporation is generally organized into various operating divisions. We saw in Figure 7.1 how General Motors is divided along various product lines. An automotive division like Buick is part of the Car and Truck Group, the head of which reports to an executive vice president, who reports in turn to the president of General Motors. Usually, the president is the chief operations officer in the firm, although sometimes the chairman of the board of directors fills this role. As for the board of directors, some members are chosen for their reputations and contacts, while others are chosen for their knowledge of the firm, the industry, or some profession or specialty. Usually, the board contains at least one representative of the financial community, and a university president or former government official is often included. Members of GM's board include James Killian, Chairman of M.I.T.; John Connor, a former Secretary of Commerce; and Leon Sullivan, pastor of Zion Baptist Church of Philadelphia. The board of directors is concerned with overall policy. Since it meets only a few times a year, it seldom becomes involved in day-to-day decisions; and it usually goes along with management's policies, so long as management retains the board's confidence.

The New Industrial State

The large corporation is a subject of considerable debate among economists. Many feel that bigness can be a detriment to society, whereas others are more impressed by its virtues. One view of the large corporation that has received considerable attention in recent years can be found in John Kenneth Galbraith's *The New Industrial State.*[1] Galbraith is less concerned than most economists with the disadvantages of the large corporation; indeed, he feels that large corporations are required for much of society's business. According to Galbraith, the large corporation is free of most of the restraints imposed by the marketplace. It can, by a judicious mixture of advertising and other devices, influence the demand for its own products. Indeed, according to Galbraith, it can control its demand curve to a very considerable extent. In addition, the management of the large corporation is, in Galbraith's view, largely emancipated from the control of the stockholders, since there is a considerable separation of ownership from control. Moreover, the large corporation is free from the obligation to borrow in the capital markets, since it can reinvest its own earnings.

Under these circumstances, who runs the large corporation, and for what purpose? Galbraith's answer is that the large corporation is run by the "***technostructure***"—the professional managers, engineers, and technicians that are the corporate bureaucracy—and the large corporation's overriding goal is its own survival and autonomy. Consequently, the large corporation tries to avoid risk, and emphasizes planning and stability. It is interested in corporate growth, even if this means some sacrifice of profits. Moreover, it is often interested

[1] John Kenneth Galbraith, *The New Industrial State,* Boston: Houghton Mifflin, 1967.

in technological leadership. Galbraith does not view this situation as bad. Instead, he regards it as inevitable since, in his view, modern technology requires that huge amounts of money and huge organizations dominate the modern economy. Whether you like it or not, he says, this is the way it must be.

Although Galbraith's book has generated much useful and interesting discussion, it has not escaped criticism by the economics profession. For one thing, as Robert Solow of M.I.T. has pointed out, the large corporation does not dominate many parts of the American economy. Nor is it at all clear that modern technology requires very large firms in many industries. Nor is Galbraith's assumption that firms attempt to maximize their rate of growth of sales necessarily better than the more conventional assumption that firms maximize their profits. As we shall see, most economists seem to regard profit maximization as the more fruitful assumption.

Profit Maximization

What determines the behavior of the business firm? As a first approximation, *economists generally assume that firms attempt to maximize* **profits,** *which are defined as the difference between the firm's revenue and its costs.* In other words, economists generally assume, contrary to Galbraith, that firms try to make as much money as possible. This assumption certainly does not seem unreasonable: most businessmen appear to be interested in making money. Nonetheless, the assumption of profit maximization oversimplifies the situation. Although businessmen certainly want profits, they are interested in other things as well. For example, some firms claim that they want to promote better cultural activities or better racial relations in their community. At a less lofty level, other firms say that their aim is to increase their share of the market. Whether or not one takes these self-proclaimed goals very seriously, it is clear that firms are not interested *only* in making money—often for the same reason that Dr. Johnson gave for not becoming a philosopher: "because cheerfulness keeps breaking in."[2]

In a large corporation, there are some fairly obvious reasons why firms may not maximize profits. Various groups within such firms develop their own party lines, and intrafirm politics is an important part of the process determining firm behavior. Whereas in a small firm it may be fairly accurate to regard the goals of the firm as being the goals of the proprietor, in the large corporation the decision on the goals of the firm is a matter of politics, with various groups within the organization struggling for power. In addition, because of the separation of ownership from control, top management usually has a great deal of freedom as long as it seems to be performing reasonably well. Under these circumstances, the behavior of the firm may be dictated in part by the interests of the management group, resulting in higher salaries, more perquisites, and a bigger staff for their own benefit than would otherwise be the case.

Also, in a world of risk and uncertainty, it is difficult to know exactly what profit maximization means, since the firm cannot be sure that a certain level of profit will result from a certain action. Instead, the best the firm can do is to estimate that a certain probability distribution of profit levels will result from a certain action. Under these circumstances, the firm may choose less risky actions, even though they have a lower expectation of profit than other actions. In a world where ruin is ruinous, this may be perfectly rational policy.

Nonetheless, profit maximization remains the standard assumption in economics—in large part because it is a close enough approximation to reality for many of the economist's most important purposes. As we agreed in our discussion of model building in Chapter 2, to be useful models need

[2] This quote is taken from R. Solow, "The New Industrial State or Son of Affluence," *The Public Interest,* Fall 1967. Since footnotes are so often used to cite dreary material, it seems worthwhile to use them occasionally to cite humor as well.

not be exact replicas of reality. Economic models based on profit maximization are clearly not exact replicas of reality, but they have been very useful indeed. For one thing, they help to show how the price system functions. For another, in the real world, they suggest how a firm should operate if it wants to make as much money as possible. Even if a firm does not want to maximize profit, these theories can be utilized. For example, they can show how much the firm is losing by taking certain courses of action. In recent years, the theory of the profit-maximizing firm has been studied more and more for the sake of determining profit-maximizing rules of business behavior.

Technology and Inputs

The decisions a firm should make in order to maximize its profits are determined by the current state of technology. Technology, it will be recalled from Chapter 3, is the sum total of society's knowledge concerning the industrial arts. Just as the consumer is limited by his income, the firm is limited by the current state of technology. If the current state of technology is such that we do not know how to produce more than 40 bushels of corn per year from an acre of land and 2 manyears of labor, then this is as much as the firm can produce from this combination of land and labor. In making its decisions, the firm must take this into account.

In constructing his model of the profit-maximizing firm, the economist must somehow represent the state of technology and include it in his model. As a first step toward this end, we must define an ***input.*** Perhaps the simplest definition of an input is that it is anything the firm uses in its production process. For example, some of the inputs of a farm producing corn might be seed, land, labor, water, fertilizer, various types of machinery, as well as the time of the people managing the farm. In analyzing production processes, we suppose that all inputs can be classified into two categories: fixed and variable inputs.

A ***fixed input*** is one whose quantity cannot change during the period of time under consideration. This period will vary: it may be 6 months for one problem, 6 years for another. Among the most important inputs often included as "fixed" are the firm's plant and equipment—that is, its factory and office buildings, its machinery, its tooling, and its transportation facilities. A ***variable input*** is one whose quantity can be changed during the relevant period. For example, it is generally possible to increase or decrease the number of workers engaged in a particular activity (although this is not always the case, since they may have long-term contracts). Similarly, it frequently is possible to alter the amount of raw material that is used.

The Short Run and the Long Run

Whether an input is considered variable or fixed depends on the length of the period under consideration. The longer the period, the more inputs are variable, not fixed. Although the length of the period varies from problem to problem, economists have found it useful to focus special attention on two time periods: the short run and the long run. The ***short run*** is defined as the period of time in which some of the firm's inputs are fixed. More specifically, since the firm's plant and equipment are among the most difficult inputs to change quickly, *the short run is generally understood to mean the length of time during which the firm's plant and equipment are fixed. On the other hand, the* ***long run*** *is that period of time in which all inputs are variable.* In the long run, the firm can make a complete adjustment to any change in its environment.

To illustrate the distinction between the short run and the long run, let's return to the General Motors Corporation. Any period of time during which GM's plant and equipment cannot be altered freely is the short run. For example, a period of one year is certainly a case of the short run, because in a year GM could not vary the quantity of its plant and equipment. It takes longer than a year to construct an automotive plant, or to alter an existing plant to produce a new kind of automobile. For example, the tooling phase of the model changeover cycle currently takes about 2 years. On the other hand, any period of time during which GM can vary the quantity of all inputs is the long run: for example, a period of 50 years is certainly a case of the long run. Whether a shorter period of time—10 years, say—is a long-run situation depends on the problem at hand. If all the relevant inputs can be varied, it is a long-run situation; if not, it is a short-run situation.

The Production Function

Having defined an input and distinguished between the short and long runs, we can now describe how economists represent the state of technology. The basic concept economists use for this purpose is the production function. For any commodity, *the **production function** is the relationship between the quantities of various inputs used per period of time and the maximum quantity of the commodity that can be produced per period of time.* More specifically, the production function is a table, a graph, or an equation showing the maximum output rate that can be achieved from any specified set of usage rates of inputs. The production function summarizes the characteristics of existing technology at a given point in time. It shows the technological constraints the firm must reckon with.

To see more clearly what we mean by a production function, consider the Milwaukee Machine Company, a hypothetical machine shop that produces a simple metal part. Suppose that we are dealing with the short run. The firm's basic plant and equipment are fixed, and the only variable input is the amount of labor used by the machine shop. Suppose that the firm collects data showing the relationship between the quantity of its output and the quantity of labor it uses. This relationship, shown in Table 7.2, is the firm's production function. It shows that, when one worker is employed, 100 parts are produced per month; when 2 workers are employed, 210 parts are produced per month; and so on.

To illustrate what a production function looks like in a real case, let's consider a crude oil pipeline that transports petroleum from oilfields and storage areas over hundreds of miles to major urban and industrial centers. We begin by noting that the output of such a pipeline is the amount of oil carried per day, and that the two principal inputs are the diameter of the pipeline and the horsepower applied to the oil carried. These inputs are important. Clearly, the bigger the diameter of the pipe, the more oil the pipeline can carry, holding constant the horsepower applied. And the greater the horsepower applied, the more oil the pipeline can carry, holding constant the diameter of the pipeline.

The production function shows the maximum output rate that can be derived from each com-

Table 7.2

Production Function, Milwaukee Machine Company

Quantity of labor used per month (number of men employed)	Output per month (number of parts)
0	0
1	100
2	210
3	315
4	415
5	500

Table 7.3

Production Function, Crude Oil Pipeline[a]

Line diameter (inches)	Horsepower (thousands)				
	20	30	40	50	60
	Output rate (thousands of barrels per day)				
14	70	90	95	100	104
18	115	140	155	165	170
22	160	190	215	235	250
26	220	255	290	320	340

Source: Leslie Cookenboo, *Crude Oil Pipe Lines and Competition in the Oil Industry,* Cambridge: Harvard University Press, 1955.
[a] The output rates given in this table are only approximate, since they were read from Cookenboo's graph on p. 16.

bination of input rates. Thus, in this case, the production function shows the maximum amount of oil carried per day as a function of the pipeline's diameter and the amount of horsepower applied. On the basis of engineering estimates, one can derive the production function for crude oil pipelines. For example, Leslie Cookenboo of Standard Oil of New Jersey derived such a production function, assuming that the pipeline carries Mid-Continent crude, has ¼-inch pipe throughout the lines, has lines 1,000 miles in length with a 5 percent terrain variation, and no net gravity flow in the line.[3] Some of his results are shown in Table 7.3. For example, the production function shows that if the diameter of the pipeline is 22 inches and the horsepower is 40,000, the pipeline can carry 215,000 barrels per day. Certainly, any firm operating a pipeline or considering the construction of one is vitally interested in such information. The production function plays a strategic role in the decision making of any firm.

[3] L. Cookenboo, *Crude Oil Pipe Lines and Competition in the Oil Industry,* Cambridge: Harvard University Press, 1955.

Elements of Accounting: The Firm's Balance Sheet

In a previous section, we stated that economists generally assume that firms attempt to maximize profits. Viewed as a first approximation, this assumption does not seem too hard to swallow, but exactly what do we mean by profit? This is an important question, of interest to businessmen and investors as well as to economists. The accounting profession provides the basic figures that are reported in the newspapers and in a firm's annual reports to its stockholders. If General Motors reports that it made $1.5 billion last year, this figure is provided by GM's accountants. How do the accountants obtain this figure? What are its limitations?

Basically, accounting concepts are built around two very important statements: the balance sheet and the profit and loss statement. *A firm's* ***balance sheet*** *shows the nature of its assets, tangible and intangible, at a certain point in time.* For example, let us return to the Milwaukee Machine Company. Its balance sheet might be as shown in Table 7.4.

Table 7.4

Balance Sheet, Milwaukee Machine Company, as of December 31, 1974

Assets		Liabilities and net worth	
Current assets:		Current liabilities:	
Cash	$ 10,000	Accounts payable	$ 10,000
Inventory	60,000	Notes payable	20,000
Fixed assets:		Long-term liabilities:	
Equipment	80,000	Bonds	80,000
Buildings	90,000		
		Net worth:	
		Preferred stock	50,000
		Common stock	50,000
		Surplus	30,000
Total	$240,000	Total	$240,000

The left-hand side of the balance sheet shows the assets of the firm as of December 31, 1974. ***Current assets*** are assets that will be converted into cash relatively quickly (generally within a year), whereas ***fixed assets*** generally will not be liquidated quickly. The firm has $10,000 in cash, $60,000 in inventory, $80,000 in equipment, and $90,000 in buildings. At first glance, these figures may seem more accurate than they are likely to be. It is very difficult to know how to value various assets. For example, should they be valued at what the firm paid for them, or at what it would cost to replace them? More will be said about these problems in the next section.

The right-hand side of the firm's balance sheet shows the claims by creditors on the firm's assets and the value of the firm's ownership. For example, in Table 7.4, the Milwaukee Machine Company has total liabilities—or debts—of $110,000. There is $30,000 in ***current liabilities,*** which come due in less than a year; and $80,000 in ***long-term liabilities,*** which come due in a year or more. Specifically, there is $10,000 in ***accounts payable,*** which are bills owed for goods and services that the firm bought; $20,000 in ***notes payable,*** short-term notes owed to banks or finance companies; and $80,000 in ***bonds payable,*** or bonds outstanding.

The difference between the value of a firm's assets and the value of its liabilities is its ***net worth,*** which is the value of the firm's owners' claims against the firm's assets. In other words, the value of the firm to its owners is the total value of its assets less the value of the debts owed by the firm. Since

$$\text{total value of assets} - \text{total liabilities} = \text{net worth},$$

it follows that

$$\text{total value of assets} = \text{total liabilities} + \text{net worth}.$$

That is, the sum of the items on the left-hand side of the balance sheet must equal the sum of the items on the right-hand side. This, of course, must be true because of the way we define net worth. In the case of the Milwaukee Machine Company, the firm's net worth—the difference between its assets and its liabilities—is $130,000. Specifically, there is $50,000 worth of preferred stock and $50,000 worth of common stock; there is also $30,000 in surplus, which we shall explain below.

The Firm's Profit and Loss Statement

A firm's ***profit and loss statement*** *shows its sales during a particular period, its costs incurred in connection with these sales, and its profits during this period.* Table 7.5 shows the Milwaukee Machine Company's profit and loss statement during the period January 1, 1975 to December 31, 1975. Sales during this period were $120,000. The cost of manufacturing the items made during this period was $55,000—$15,000 for materials, $20,000 for labor, $17,000 for depreciation (discussed below), and $3,000 for miscellaneous operating expenses. However, because the firm has reduced its inventories from $60,000 to $55,000 during the period, the cost of manufacturing the items *made* during the period does not equal the cost of manufacturing the items *sold* during the period. To find the *cost of goods sold*—which is the amount that logically should be deducted from sales to get the profits made from the sale of these goods—we must add the decrease in the value of inventories to the total manufacturing cost. Or, putting it another way, we must add the beginning inventory and subtract the closing inventory, as shown in Table 7.5. The resulting figure for cost of goods sold is $60,000.

But manufacturing costs are not the only costs the firm incurs. To estimate the firm's profits, we must also deduct from sales its selling and adminis-

Table 7.5

Profit and Loss Statement, Milwaukee Machine Company, January 1, 1975 to December 31, 1975

Net sales		$120,000
Manufacturing cost of goods sold		60,000
Materials	$15,000	
Labor	20,000	
Depreciation	17,000	
Miscellaneous operating cost	3,000	
Total	$55,000	
Plus beginning inventory	60,000	
Less closing inventory	– 55,000	
Adjusted total	60,000	
Selling and administrative costs		10,000
Fixed interest charges and state and local taxes		5,000
Net earnings before income taxes		$ 45,000
Corporation income taxes		20,000
Net earnings after taxes		$ 25,000
Dividends on preferred stock		2,000
Net profits of common stockholders		$ 23,000
Dividends paid on common stock		10,000
Addition to surplus		$ 13,000

trative expenses, its interest charges and state and local taxes, as well as its federal income taxes. Table 7.5 shows that the Milwaukee Machine Company's aftertax earnings during 1975 were $25,000. This is the amount left for the owners of the business. The profit and loss statement also shows what the owners do with what is left. For example, Table 7.5 shows that the Milwaukee Machine Company used $2,000 to pay dividends to holders of preferred stock. When this was done, the holders of common stock were free to distribute some of the profits to themselves. According to Table 7.5, they distributed $10,000 to themselves in dividends on the common stock, and plowed the rest—$13,000—back into the business.

Before leaving the profit and loss statement, we should explain one element of manufacturing cost —***depreciation.*** While the other elements of manufacturing cost are self-explanatory, this one is not. The idea behind depreciation is that the buildings and equipment will not last forever; eventually will have to be replaced. Clearly, it would be foolish to charge the entire cost of replacing them to the year when they are replaced. Instead, a better picture of the firm's true profitability will be drawn if the cost of replacing them is spread gradually over the life of buildings and equipment, thus recognizing that each year's output has a hand in wearing them out. One frequently used technique is so-called ***straight-line depreciation,*** which spreads the cost of buildings and equipment (less their scrap value) evenly over their life. Thus, if the Milwaukee Machine Company buys a piece of equipment for $10,000 and if it is expected to last 10 years (its scrap value being zero), it would charge depreciation of $1,000 per year for this machine for 10 years after its purchase. The $17,000 charge for depreciation in Table 7.5 is the sum of such charges. Clearly, this is only a rough way to estimate the true depreciation charges, but it is good enough for many purposes.

Relationship between Balance Sheet and Profit and Loss Statement

The balance sheet and profit and loss statement are closely related. To see the relationship, let's com-

Table 7.6

Balance Sheet, Milwaukee Machine Company, as of December 31, 1975

Assets		Liabilities and net worth	
Currents assets:		Current liabilities:	
Cash	$ 18,000	Accounts payable	$ 5,000
Inventory	55,000	Notes payable	20,000
Fixed assets		Long-term liabilities	
Equipment	85,000	Bonds	80,000
Buildings	90,000		
		Net worth:	
		Preferred stock	50,000
		Common stock	50,000
		Surplus	43,000
Total	$248,000	Total	$248,000

pare the Milwaukee Machine Company's balance sheet at the end of the period covered by the profit and loss statement in Table 7.5 with the balance sheet at the beginning of this period. The balance sheet at the beginning of the period was shown in Table 7.4. The balance sheet at the end of the period is now given in Table 7.6. At first glance, it may not be obvious how the two balance sheets and the profit and loss statement are related; but after a little reflection, it should be clear that the firm's net worth as shown by the end-of-period balance sheet must equal the firm's net worth as shown by the beginning-of-period balance sheet plus the addition to surplus shown in the profit and loss statement.

The reason for this lies in the definition of ***addition to surplus.*** This is the amount the common stockholders plow back into the firm; in other words, the amount they add to the net worth of the firm. Since this is so, the increase (or decrease, if addition to surplus is negative) in the net worth of the firm must equal the addition to surplus (assuming, of course, that the net worth of the firm is not changed by altering the amount of stock outstanding).[4] Thus, for example, in the case of the Milwaukee Machine Company, the firm's net worth had to increase by $13,000 during 1974; and since it was $130,000 at the beginning of 1974, it must have been $143,000 at the end of 1974. Where on the balance sheet does this $13,000 show up? What part of net worth increased by $13,000? The answer is that ***surplus,*** which shows the total amount that the stockholders have plowed back into the firm in the past, went up by $13,000.

Economic versus Accounting Profits

The previous sections described the nature of profit, as defined by accountants. This is the concept on which practically all published figures in business reports are based. But economists define profits somewhat differently. In particular, the economist does not assume that the firm attempts to maximize the current, short-run profits measured by the accountant. Instead he assumes that the firm will attempt to maximize the sum of profits over a long period of time.[5] Also, when the economist speaks of profits, he means profit after taking account of the capital and labor provided by the owners. Thus, suppose that the owners of the Milwaukee Machine Company, who receive profits but no salary or wages, put in long hours for which they could receive $15,000 in 1974 if they worked for someone else. Also suppose that if they invested their capital somewhere other than in this firm, they could obtain a return of $11,000 on it in 1974. Under these circumstances, economists would say that the firm's aftertax profits in 1974 were $25,000 – $15,000 – $11,000, or – $1,000, rather than the $25,000 shown in Table 7.5. In other words, the economist's concept of profit includes only what the owners make above and beyond what their labor and capital employed in the business could have earned elsewhere. In this case, that amount is negative.

To a considerable extent, the differences between the concepts used by the accountant and the economist reflect the difference in their functions. The accountant is concerned with controlling the firm's day-to-day operations, detecting fraud or embezzlement, satisfying tax and other laws, and producing records for various interested groups. On the other hand, the economist is concerned primarily with decision making and rational choice among prospective alternatives. Although the figures published on profits almost always conform to the accountant's, not the economist's, concept, the economist's concept is the more relevant one for many kinds of decisions. (And this, of course, is recognized by sophisticated accountants.) For example, suppose the owners of the Milwaukee Machine Company are trying to decide whether they should continue

[4] This statement also makes some other assumptions—e.g., that all changes in surplus occur through changes in earned surplus. For more complete treatments, see any college accounting textbook.

[5] The profits earned at various points in time should be *discounted* before being added together, but, for simplicity's sake, we neglect this point here.

in business. If they are interested in making as much money as possible, the answer depends on the firm's profits as measured by the economist, not the accountant. If the firm's economic profits are greater than zero, the firm should continue in existence; otherwise, it should not. Thus, the Milwaukee Machine Company should not stay in existence if 1974 is a good indicator of its future profitability.

The Financial Statements of General Motors: A Case Study

To conclude this chapter, let's return once again to General Motors, and examine its financial statements—its balance sheet and profit and loss statement. These are a bit more detailed than the hypothetical statements of the Milwaukee Machine Company, but they are constructed on the same principles. Each year, General Motors issues an annual report to its stockholders, which includes these financial statements. Table 7.7 reproduces GM's balance sheet as of December 31, 1970; and Table 7.8 reproduces GM's profit and loss statement for 1970. Take a close look at these tables, and see if you understand what each item means. For example, Table 7.7 says that GM had $1,726 million in accounts receivable at the end of 1970. What are accounts receivable? (Bills its customers owe General Motors.) It also says that GM had $184 million in preferred stock at the end of 1970. What is preferred stock? (If you don't recall, turn back to the section on "Corporate Securities.") Turning to Table 7.8, GM incurred depreciation

Table 7.7

Balance Sheet, General Motors Corporation, as of December 31, 1970

Assets ($ million)		Liabilities and net worth ($ million)	
Current assets:		Current liabilities:	
Cash	323	Accounts payable	1,660
Government securities	71	Taxes owed	1,561
Accounts receivable	1,726	Other	3
Inventories	4,115		
		Long-term liabilities	
Fixed Assets:		Bonds	281
		Other[b]	815
Investments[a]	1,202		
Real estate, plant, and equipment	6,396	Net worth:	
Other	341	Preferred stock	284
		Common stock	479
		Surplus	9,091
Total	14,174	Total	14,174

[a] This is included neither as a current nor as a fixed asset, but as a separate classification in General Motors' annual report.
[b] Includes reserves.

Table 7.8

Profit and Loss Statement, General Motors Corporation, January 1, 1970 to December 31, 1970

Net sales (and other income)		18,879
Manufacturing cost of goods sold		17,094
Materials, labor, and miscellaneous operating costs	15,949	
Depreciation	1,499	
Total	17,448	
Plus beginning inventory	3,761	
Less closing inventory	−4,115	
Adjusted total	17,094	
Selling and administrative costs (and interest charges)		1,007
Net earnings before U.S. and foreign taxes		778
U.S. and foreign taxes		169
Net earnings after taxes		609
Dividends on preferred stock		13
Net profits of common stockholders		596
Dividends paid on common stock		971
Addition to surplus		−375

costs of $1,499 million in 1970. What is depreciation? (Turn back to "The Firm's Profit and Loss Statement" if you need to.) Also, GM's addition to surplus was negative in 1970. What does this mean? (See the section on "Relationship Between Balance Sheet and Profit and Loss Statement.")

Financial analysts spend an enormous amount of time poring over the financial statements of various companies to estimate whether their stock is a good or bad investment. Banks look at a firm's financial statements when they decide whether or not to grant the firm a loan. The financial pages of the major newspapers, as well as magazines specializing in financial and business news, are sprinkled liberally with summaries of these financial statements. You would do well to make sure you understand the basic definitions and principles of accounting presented in previous sections. In dealing with practical problems, this information will serve you well.

Summary

There are three principal types of business firms: proprietorships, partnerships, and corporations. The corporation has many advantages over the other two—limited liability, unlimited life, and greater ability to raise large sums of money. The corporation raises money by issuing various kinds of securities, of which three kinds—common stock, preferred stock, and bonds—are particularly important. A relatively small number of giant corporations control a very substantial proportion of the total assets and employment in the American economy. In the large corporation, ownership and control tend to be separated. So long as a firm's management is not obviously incompetent or corrupt, it is difficult for insurgent stockholders to remove the management from office.

As a first approximation, economists generally assume that firms attempt to maximize profits. In large part, this is because it is a close enough approximation to reality for many of the most important purposes of economics. Also, economists are interested in the theory of the profit-maximizing firm because it provides rules of behavior for firms that do want to maximize profits. In constructing his model of the profit-maximizing firm, the economist must somehow represent the state of technology and include it in his model. He classifies inputs used by the firm into two categories: fixed and variable. He also differentiates between the short run and the long run. Then, to summarize the characteristics of existing technology at a given point in time, he uses the concept of the production function, which shows the maximum output rate of a given commodity that can be achieved from any specified set of usage rates of inputs.

Accounting concepts are built around two very important statements: the balance sheet and the profit and loss statement. The balance sheet shows the nature of the firm's assets and liabilities at a given point in time. The difference between its assets and its liabilities is its net worth, which is the value of the firm's owners' claims against its assets. A firm's profit and loss statement shows its sales during a particular period, its costs incurred in connection with these sales, and its profits during the period. The balance sheet and the profit and loss statement are closely related. Economists define profits somewhat differently than accountants do. In particular, the economist excludes from profit the value of the capital and labor provided by the owners, and he is interested in longer periods than those to which accounting statements apply. Although the profit figures that are published almost always conform to the accountant's concept, the economist's concept is the more relevant one for many kinds of decisions.

CONCEPTS FOR REVIEW

Proprietorship	Common stock	Fixed input	Fixed assets
Partnership	Preferred stock	Variable input	Profit and loss statement
Corporation	Bond	Production function	Depreciation
Liability	Profit	Balance sheet	
Board of directors	Input	Current assets	

QUESTIONS FOR DISCUSSION AND REVIEW

1. Do you think that General Motors maximizes profits? What do you think that William C. Durant would have replied if you had asked him this question? For economic models to be useful, must firms maximize profits?

2. Suppose that a friend offered to sell you some stock in a small company. How would the firm's balance sheet and profit and loss statement be useful in evaluating how much the stock is worth?

3. In a partnership, though one partner has only a 25 percent share of the firm, he may be liable for all the firm's debts if the other partners cannot pay them. True or False?

4. A firm's assets which can be converted into cash fairly quickly are called __________ assets. a. tangible b. intangible c. current d. fixed

PART THREE

National Output, Income, and Employment

CHAPTER 8

Unemployment, Inflation, and National Output

Three of the most important indicators of the health of any nation's economy are its unemployment rate, its rate of inflation, and the size of its national output. Every government, including our own, watches these indicators with great interest. Moreover, most societies today are committed to policies designed to influence each of them, in particular to keeping unemployment and inflation to a reasonable minimum, and to promoting the growth of national output. These social goals certainly seem sensible, since high rates of unemployment can cause enormous social waste and private hardship. Also, most societies seem to believe that the benefits of greater national output outweigh the costs, and that serious inflation should not be tolerated.

In this chapter, we begin to study unemployment, inflation, and national output. Our first objective is to describe the nature of unemployment and inflation, and how the rate of inflation is related to the rate of unemployment. Then we turn to a detailed examination of how national output is measured, our purpose being to describe such concepts as gross national product and its components: consumption, investment, government spending, and net exports. Finally, we discuss how the gap between actual and potential output is related to the level of unemployment.

Unemployment

Almost a century ago, Pope Leo XIII said: "Among the purposes of a society should be to arrange for a continuous supply of work at all times and seasons."[1] The word "unemployment" is one of the most frightening in the English language—and for good reason. Unemployed people (defined by the U.S. Government as all those 16 years old or more who do not have a job and are looking for one) become demoralized, suffer loss of prestige and status, and their families tend to break apart. Sometimes they are pushed toward crime and drugs; often they feel terrible despair. Their children are innocent victims too. Indeed, perhaps the most devastating effects of unemployment are on children, whose education, health, and security may be ruined. After a few minutes' thought, most people would agree that in this or any other country every citizen who is able and willing to work should be able to get a job.

Of course we are not saying that all unemployment, whatever its cause or nature, should be eliminated. Some unemployment is ***frictional,*** which means that it is related to the entrance of new workers into the labor market and the movement of workers from one position to another. For example, Tom Smith may quit his job after the boss calls him a fathead. It may take him a month to find another job, perhaps because he is unaware of job opportunities or perhaps because the boss was right. During this month, he is numbered among the unemployed. It would not make much sense to try to eliminate all such temporary unemployment. On the contrary, a free labor market could not function without a certain amount of frictional unemployment.

[1] Pope Leo XIII, *Encyclical Letter on the Conditions of Labor,* May 15, 1891.

Another type of unemployment, called ***structural unemployment,*** exists when jobs are available for qualified workers, but the unemployed do not have the necessary qualifications. This sort of unemployment results from a mismatch between job requirements and the skills of the unemployed, as in the case of a 58-year-old cotton picker thrown out of work by the introduction of mechanical cotton pickers and lacking the skills needed to get a job in another field. To some extent, structural unemployment can be reduced by monetary and fiscal policies of the sort described in the following chapters. But in many cases, the principal way to attack it is by retraining workers whose skills are no longer in demand for jobs in other occupations, industries, or areas.

Still another type is ***cyclical unemployment,*** which is associated with business fluctuations, or the so-called business cycle. Industrialized capitalistic economies have been subject to fluctuations, with booms often succeeding busts and vice versa. Before World War II the American economy periodically went through serious depressions, during which unemployment was very high. The Great Depression of the 1930s was particularly long and severe, and when World War II ended, the American people resolved that the gigantic social costs of the enormous unemployment of the 1930s must not be repeated in the postwar period. To avoid this, Congress passed the Employment Act of 1946, which says:

> It is the continuing policy and responsibility of the Federal Government to use all practicable means . . . [to create and maintain] conditions under which there will be afforded useful employment opportunities, including self-employment, for those able, willing, and seeking to work and to promote maximum employment, production, and purchasing power.

The Employment Act of 1946 was an extremely important piece of legislation, for it committed the

Figure 8.1
Unemployment Rates, United States, 1929–72

The unemployment rate has varied substantially. Fortunately, since World War II it has not approached the very high levels of the Great Depression of the 1930s.

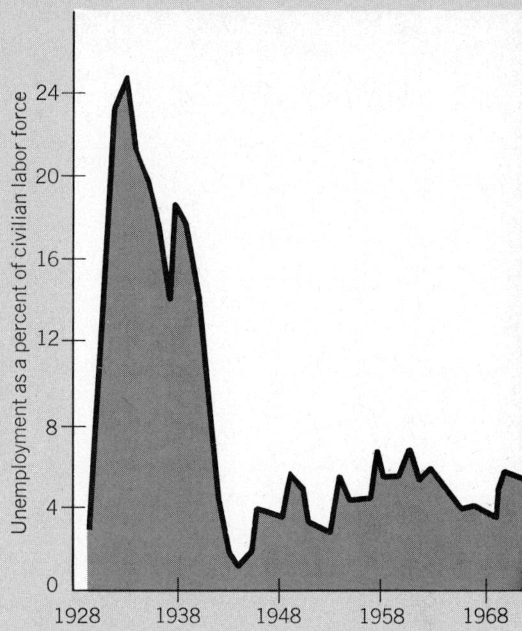

federal government to combat cyclical unemployment.

How Much Unemployment Is There?

To get some idea of the extent of unemployment, we can consult Figure 8.1, which shows the percent of the labor force unemployed during each year from 1929 to 1972. Note the wide fluctuations in the unemployment rate, and the very high unemployment rates during the 1930s. Fortunately, unemployment since World War II has never approached the tragically high levels of the Great Depression of the 1930s. In 1949 and 1950, and again in 1954, the unemployment rate pushed up toward 6 percent, but in general it remained at about 4 percent or less until 1958, when it increased to almost 7 percent. Between 1958 and 1964, it averaged about 6 percent, and then declined steadily until it fell below 4 percent in 1966–69. In 1970–72, it bounced back up to 5 or 6 percent. Although these variations in the unemployment rate may seem small, they are by no means unimportant. Any administration, Democratic or Republican, watches these figures closely, and tries to avoid significant increases in unemployment.

The importance of unemployment statistics makes it worthwhile to see how they are collected. The federal government periodically conducts a scientific survey of the American people, asking a carefully selected sample of the population whether they have a job, and, if not, whether they are looking for one. According to most expert opinion, the resulting figures are quite reliable within certain limits. One of these is that they do not indicate the extent to which people are ***underemployed.*** Some people work only part-time, or at jobs well below their level of education or skill, but the government figures count them as fully employed. Also, some people have given up looking for a job and are no longer listed among the unemployed, even though they would be glad to get work if any was offered. To count as unemployed in the government figures, one must be actively seeking employment.

In addition, aggregate figures on unemployment cover up very substantial differences among groups within a society. Unemployment rates among blacks and other minorities are much higher than among whites. Also, unemployment rates among teenagers and women tend to be very high. For example, in 1972, although the unemployment rate for all workers was 5.6 percent, it was 16.2 percent among people 16 to 19 years of age and 10.0 percent among nonwhites. Consequently, since unemployment tends to be concentrated in particular segments of the population, overall unemployment rates can be somewhat misleading.

Unemployment: A Case Study

Since general descriptions of the plight of the unemployed often have relatively little impact, a real-life case study may give you a better feel for what unemployment is like. Consider Joseph Torrio, a New Haven factory worker who was laid off after 18 years on the job. He describes in his own words how he spent several mornings:

> Up at seven, cup of coffee, and off to Sargent's. Like to be there when the gang comes to work, the lucky devils. Employment manager not in. Waited in his outer office. . . . Three others waiting, two reporting for compensation. Other one laid off two weeks ago and said he called at office every day. He inquired what I was doing and when I said "looking for work" he laughed. "You never work here? No? What chance you think you got when 400 like me who belong here out?" Employment manager showed up at 9:30. I had waited two hours. My time has no value. A pleasant fellow; told me in a kind but snappy way business was very bad. What about the future, would he take my name? Said he referred only to the present. Nothing more for me to say, so left. Two more had drifted into office. Suppose they got the same story. Must be a lot of men in New Haven that have heard it by now.
>
> [On May 21], interview with sales manager of the Real Silk Hosiery Mills. Had seen their ads for salesmen in the paper. Sales manager approached me with his hand sticking out, the first one who had offered to shake hands with me. I told him my name and inquired about the position. He took me into his private office, well furnished, and asked me if I had had any selling experience. I told him that I hadn't any but I thought I could do the work. . . . Asked me to report at 9 A.M. the next morning for further instructions. . . . [On May 22], I kept my appointment with the sales manager. Spent the morning learning about different kinds of stockings. Made another appointment for the afternoon which I did not keep because he wanted me to bring along $6 as security on a bag and some stock. I did not have the $6.[2]

No single case study can give you an adequate picture of the impact on people of being without a job. There are a wide variety of responses to unemployment. Some people weather it pretty well, others sink into despair; some people have substantial savings they can draw on, others are hard pressed; some people manage to shield their families from the blow, others allow their misfortunes to spread to the rest of the family. But despite these variations, being without work deals a heavy blow to a person's feeling of worth. It hits hard at a person's self-image, indicating that he or she is not needed, cannot support a family, is not really a full and valuable member of society. It can strike a cruel blow at men and women alike, since many women are vitally interested in achievement outside the home, sometimes because they are the family breadwinner. The impact of widespread and persistent unemployment is most clearly visible at present among the blacks and other racial minorities, where unemployment rates are much higher than among the white population. Unquestionably, the prevalence of unemployment among

[2] E. W. Bakke, *The Unemployed Worker,* Hamden, Conn.: Archon, 1969, pp. 168, 169, 174, and 175.

blacks greatly influences how the blacks view themselves, as well as the way they interact with the rest of the community.

Inflation

Almost everyone has heard the term "inflation," since it appears regularly in the press and on television. ***Inflation** is a general upward movement of the prices of both products and inputs.* In other words, inflation means that goods and services that currently cost $1 are marked up to $1.20 or $1.50, and wages and other input prices increase as well. It is essential to distinguish between the movements of individual prices and the movement of the entire price level. As we saw in Chapter 4, the price of an individual commodity can move up or down with shifts in the commodity's demand or supply curve. If the price of a particular good—corn, say—goes up, this need not be inflation, since the prices of other goods may be going down at the same time, so that the overall price level—the general average level of prices—remains much the same. Inflation occurs only if most prices for goods and services in the society move upward—that is, if the average level of prices increases.

Inflation may seem no more than a petty annoyance: after all, most people care about relative, not absolute, prices. For example, if wages (the price of labor) increase at the same rate as prices, a family may be no better or worse off under inflation than under a constant price level. But this view ignores the people—civil service employees, teachers, people living on pensions, and many others—who cannot increase their wages to compensate for price increases because they work under long-term contracts, among other reasons. These people take a considerable beating from inflation.

Also, inflation hurts lenders and benefits borrowers, since it results in the depreciation of money. A dollar is worth what it will buy, and what it will buy is determined by the price level. If the price level increases, a dollar is worth less than it was before. Consequently, if you lend Bill Jones $100 in 1972 and he pays you $100 in 1980—when a dollar will buy much less than in 1972—you are losing on the deal. In terms of what the money will buy, he is paying you less than what he borrowed. Of course, if you expect this amount of inflation, you may be able to recoup by charging him a high enough interest rate to offset the depreciation of the dollar, but it is not so easy to forecast the rate of inflation and protect yourself.

Unlike unemployment, inflation (at least in small doses) does not seem to reduce national output: in the short run, output may increase. The principal effect of inflation is on the distribution of income and wealth. Many inflations are not anticipated; and even if they are, we have just noted that many people are not knowledgeable enough to protect themselves.[3] The poor worker who has put aside some money for his old age, only to find that it will buy a fraction of what he hoped, has been victimized by inflation. Why should he bear this loss? As Arthur Okun, former chairman of President Johnson's Council of Economic Advisers, has put it, "'sharpies' . . . make sophisticated choices and often reap gains on inflation which do not seem to reflect any real contribution to economic growth. On the other hand, the unsophisticated saver who is merely preparing for the proverbial rainy day becomes a sucker."[4]

Citizens and policy makers generally agree that inflation, like unemployment, should be minimized. However, this feeling has not prevented the United States from suffering from considerable inflation. As shown in Figure 8.2, the price level has tended to increase considerably in the United States during the past 40 years. Substantial inflation followed World War II; the price level increased by about

[3] Economists often distinguish between anticipated and unanticipated inflation because if inflation is anticipated, people may be able to compensate for it by charging higher interest rates and by similar devices.

[4] Arthur Okun, "The Costs of Inflation" in his *The Battle Against Unemployment* (revised edition), New York: Norton, 1972.

Figure 8.2
The Price Level, United States, 1929–72

The price level has increased considerably in the United States during the past 40 years. In recent years, inflation has been a stubborn problem.

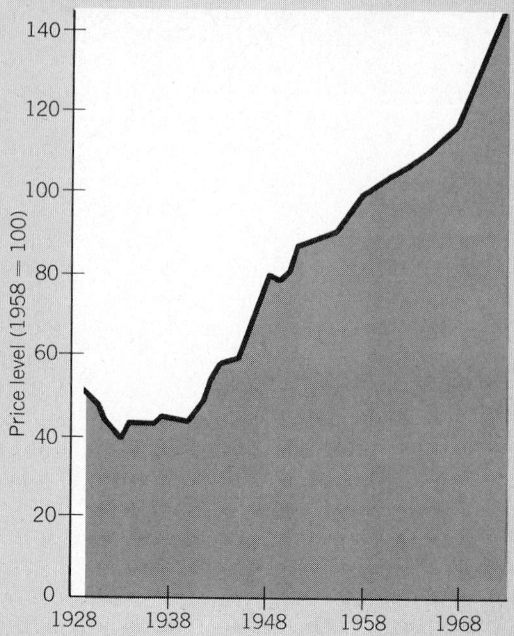

33 percent between 1945 and 1948. Bursts of inflation recurred during the Korean war and then during the Vietnam war. And in the 1960s and early 1970s, despite the government's efforts, inflation has continued. Our government's policy is to avoid both excessive unemployment and excessive inflation, but this goal, like many desirable social objectives, is by no means easy to achieve. Indeed, under certain circumstances, it may be impossible to have both stable prices and high employment, as we shall see in the next section.

The Relationship between Inflation and Unemployment

There seems to be a reasonable amount of evidence that in the short run the unemployment rate is inversely related to the rate of inflation: that is, the lower the unemployment rate, the higher the rate of inflation. This relationship is by no means fixed and immutable, and the factors underlying its shape and position are still matters of debate. But, as a first approximation, we assume that this relationship is like that shown in Figure 8.3. In Chapter 15, we shall discuss in detail why this relationship seems to exist. At this point, it is sufficient to point out that, as the unemployment rate decreases, it is easier for unions and unorganized labor to get higher wages, and for firms to pass along these wage increases to consumers in the form of price increases. As the unemployment rate decreases, demand tends to press against capacity, prompting firms and resource owners to raise prices.

Figure 8.4, which shows the aggregate supply curve for an economy, provides further insight into this relationship. Note that, up to a point (Q_1), total output increases, dollar for dollar, with total spending. But beyond that point total output does not increase by the same amount as total spending. Indeed, when output reaches Q_2, increases in total spending can tease no more production out of the

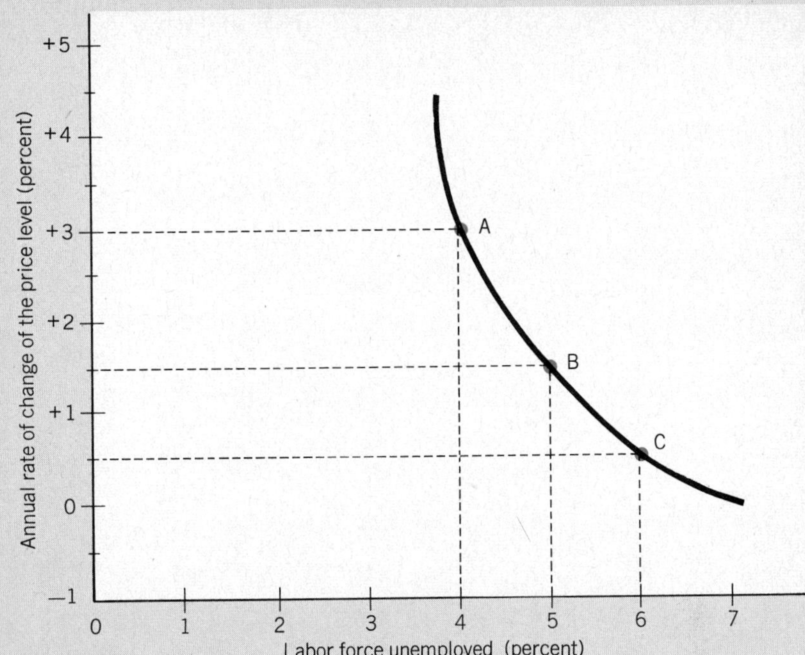

Figure 8.3
Relationship between Unemployment Rate and Rate of Inflation

There seems to be an inverse short-run relationship between the unemployment rate and the rate of inflation. If the relationship is as shown here, a 4 percent unemployment rate means a 3 percent rate of inflation, a 5 percent unemployment rate means a 1.5 percent rate of inflation, and a 6 percent unemployment rate means a 0.5 percent rate of inflation.

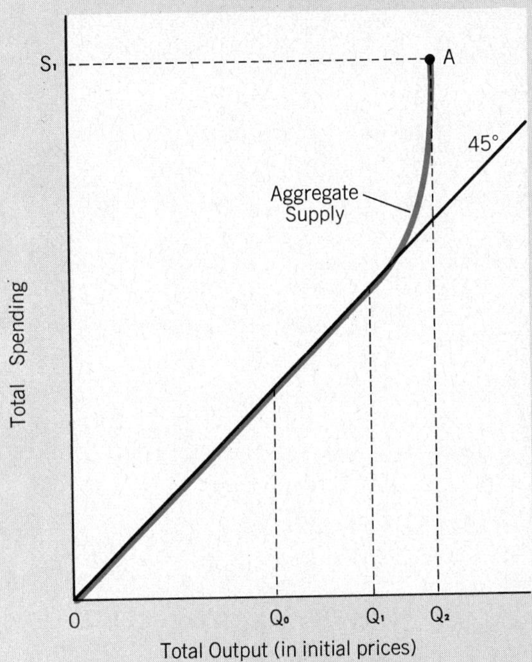

Figure 8.4
Aggregate Supply Curve

Total output increases, dollar for dollar, with total spending until it reaches Q_1, after which increases in spending do not result in equal increases in output. (The 45-degree line shows the locus of points where spending and output are equal.) If output equals Q_0, there will be considerable unemployment. As output increases, there will be less unemployment, but when output exceeds Q_1, there will be more and more inflation.

economy. This is quite reasonable, since, as you will recall from our discussion of the product transformation curve in Chapter 3, any economy can only produce so much, given its resources and the existing technology. In Figure 8.4 the maximum output level, if all the economy's resources are fully and efficiently employed, is Q_2.

On the basis of Figure 8.4, one can see why there is likely to be an inverse relationship between the unemployment rate and the rate of inflation. If actual output is much less than Q_2, say Q_0, there will be considerable unemployment, since output is much less than required to employ fully the available work force. As spending and output increase, the unemployment rate falls. Eventually, as spending and output increase further, inflation begins to occur. If output is between Q_1 and Q_2, total spending exceeds the total value of output at initial prices. In other words, as the economy approaches its maximum output, the price level begins to rise. Consumers, firms, and the government bid up the prices of goods and services. There are "too many dollars chasing too few goods." Also, as the economy approaches full employment, bottlenecks occur in some parts of the economy, and labor pushes harder for wage increases and firms are more likely to jack up prices. The result is the inverse relationship between the unemployment rate and the inflation rate shown in Figure 8.3.

The Menu of Policy Choices

The curve in Figure 8.3 is a fascinating tool. For example, suppose that you want to stabilize the price level. What level of unemployment would be required to prevent prices from rising? According to Figure 8.3, if unemployment is about 7 percent, prices will not increase. Thus 7 percent seems to be the answer. On the other hand, if you are interested in reducing unemployment to about 4 percent, what will be the effect on the rate of inflation? According to Figure 8.3, a 4 percent unemployment rate means that the price level will rise by about 3 percent per year. Of course, the curve in Figure 8.3 is an oversimplification, and it would be a mistake to assume that the relationship between unemployment and inflation is this cut and dried. But for present purposes, it is a reasonable first approximation, at least in the short run.

Suppose that the economy is faced by the kind of alternatives described by the curve in Figure 8.3: what sorts of choices are available to the government's policy makers? Obviously, the government can choose where along the curve in Figure 8.3 it wants to be. For example, it may choose point *C*, with an unemployment level of 6 percent and a rate of price increase of ½ percent. Or it may choose an unemployment level of 4 percent and a rate of price increase of 3 percent—in other words, point *A*.

Needless to say, government policy makers do not sit down and specify a point on a graph like Figure 8.3. The policy making process is neither so simple nor so neat nor so self-conscious. But policy makers do make choices—explicit or implicit—about where on such a curve they want to operate. Some administrations are more inclined than others to tolerate more unemployment in order to stem inflation. Some are more willing than others to tolerate inflation in order to reduce unemployment. Of course, in their public statements, politicians often refuse to acknowledge that any choice of this sort is required. They often claim that they will reduce *both* unemployment *and* inflation. But this can't be done, unless they shift the curve in Figure 8.3.

In fact, it is possible for the government to shift this curve, through programs to train manpower, increase labor mobility, reduce discrimination, and change people's expectations. With such programs, as well as various kinds of incomes policies, the government can push the curve downward and to the left, as shown in Figure 8.5. In this way, the government can reduce both unemployment and inflation. The curve can also shift for reasons other than government action. For expository purposes, however, it is convenient to assume temporarily that

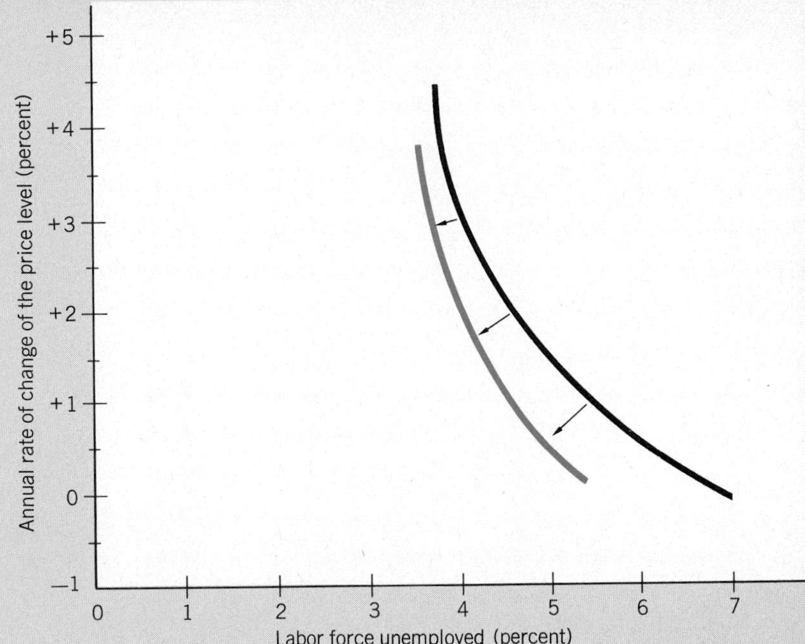

Figure 8.5
Shift in Relationship between Unemployment Rate and Rate of Inflation

The relationship between the unemployment rate and the inflation rate shifts in response to a variety of factors, including people's expectations. The government would like to push it downward and to the left, as shown here.

the curve in Figure 8.3 is fixed. In Chapter 15, when we discuss incomes policies and related matters, this assumption will be relaxed.

Given this assumption, society is faced in the short run with the menu of policy choices in Figure 8.3. Your political preferences and values determine where along the curve in Figure 8.3 you feel society should be. A commonly accepted target is point *A*, with 4 percent unemployment, but in the 1970s the Nixon administration has shown some tendency to accept point *B*, where unemployment is 5 percent, as a goal. The target one chooses depends, of course, on his evaluation of the relative social costs associated with unemployment and inflation. The more importance you give to the costs of unemployment, and the less importance to the costs of inflation, the farther up the curve you will want to be. The more importance you attach to the costs of inflation, and the less to the costs of unemployment, the farther down on the curve you will want to be.

Estimates of Gross National Product: Uses and History

Having discussed unemployment and inflation, we must turn next to national output, which is most commonly measured by the concept of gross national product. Almost everyone talks about the gross national product, and for good reason. This statistical measure tells us a great deal about how well our economy is performing, and has become a major indicator of the nation's economic condition. Put in the simplest terms, *the* ***gross national product***—or ***GNP****, as it is often called—is a measure of the total amount of goods and services produced by our economy during a particular period of time.*

Both the government and the business community watch the GNP figures like hawks. Government officials, from the president down, are interested because these figures indicate how prosperous we are, and because they are useful in forecasting the future health of the economy. Politicians are well aware that the political party in power generally gets clobbered when GNP falls substantially. Business executives are also extremely interested in the GNP figures because the sales of their firms are related to the level of GNP, and so the figures are useful in forecasting the future health of their businesses. All in all, it is no exaggeration to say that the gross national product is one of the most closely watched numbers in existence.

In view of their importance, it is noteworthy that estimates of the gross national product are of comparatively recent vintage. The Department of Commerce first made such estimates in 1932, after experiments at various universities and at the National Bureau of Economic Research. A leading pioneer in this field was Nobel Laureate Simon Kuznets, then at the University of Pennsylvania. The concepts that Kuznets and others developed are often called the ***national income accounts***, and the National Income Division of the U.S. Department of Commerce compiles these figures on a continuing basis. Just as the accounts of a firm are used to describe and analyze its financial health, so the national income accounts are used to describe and analyze the economic health of the nation as a whole.

Measuring Gross National Product

The American economy produces millions of types of goods and services. How can we add together everything from lemon meringue pie to helicopters, from books to houses? The only feasible answer is to use money as a common denominator and to make the price of a good or service—the amount the buyer is willing to pay—the measure of value. In other words, we add up the value in money terms of the total output of goods and services in the economy during a certain period, normally a year, and the result is the gross national product during that period.

At the outset, we must note several important points about the gross national product. First, it does not include the value of *all* goods and services produced: it includes only the value of *final* goods and services produced. ***Final goods and services*** are goods and services to be used by the ultimate user. For example, bread purchased by a housewife is a final good, but flour to be used in manufacturing bread is an ***intermediate good,*** not a final good. Clearly, we would be double counting if we counted both the bread and the flour used to make the bread as output. Flour bought by housewives for use in domestic cooking is, on the other hand, a final good. To avoid double counting, we include only the value of final goods and services in gross national product.

Second, some final goods and services that must be included in gross national product are not bought and sold in the marketplace, so they are valued at what they cost. For example, consider the services performed by government—police protection, fire protection, the use of the courts, defense, and so forth. Such services are not bought and sold in any market (despite the old saw about the New Jersey judge who was "the best that money could buy"). Yet they are an important part of our economy's final output. Economists and statisticians have decided to value them at what they cost the taxpayers. This is by no means ideal, but it is the best practical solution advanced to date.

Third, it is necessary for practical reasons to omit certain types of final output from gross national product. In particular, some nonmarketed goods and services, such as the services performed by housewives, are excluded from the gross national product. This is not because economists fail to appreciate these services, but because it would be extremely difficult to get reasonably reliable estimates of the money value of a housewife's services. At first glance, this may seem to be a very important weakness in our measure of total output, but so long as the value of these services does not change much (in relation to total output), the variation in gross national product will provide a reasonably accurate picture of the variation in total output—and, for many purposes, this is all that is required.

Fourth, purely financial transactions are excluded from the gross national product. Such financial transactions include government transfer payments, private transfer payments, and the sale and purchase of securities. ***Government transfer payments*** are payments made by the government to individuals who do not contribute to production in exchange for them. Payments to welfare recipients are a good example of government transfer payments. Since these payments are not for production, it would be incorrect to include them in GNP. ***Private transfer payments*** are gifts or other transfers of wealth from one person or private organization to another. Again these are not payments for production, so there is no reason to include them in GNP. The sale and purchase of securities are not payments for production, as you will recall from our discussion in Chapter 7, so they too are excluded from GNP.

Finally, the sale of secondhand goods is also excluded from the gross national product. The reason for this is clear. When a good is produced, its value is included in GNP. If its value is also included when it is sold on the secondhand market, it will be counted twice, thus leading to an overstatement of the true GNP. For example, suppose that you buy a new bicycle and resell it a year later. The value of the new bicycle is included in GNP when the bicycle is produced. But the resale value of the bicycle is not included in GNP; to do so would be double counting.

Gross National Product: Adjusting for Price Changes

In discussing inflation, we stressed that the general price level has changed over time. Since gross national product values all goods and services at their current prices, it is bound to be affected by changes in the price level as well as by changes in total output. If all prices doubled tomorrow, this would produce a doubling of gross national product. Clearly, if gross national product is to be a reliable measure of changes in total output, we must correct it somehow to eliminate the effects of changes in the price level.

Fortunately, economists have devised ways to do this—at least approximately. They choose some ***base year*** and express the value of all goods and services in terms of their prices during the base year. For example, if 1960 is taken as the base year and if the price of beef was $1 per pound in 1960, beef is valued at $1 per pound in all other years. Thus, if 200 million pounds of beef were produced in 1965, this total output is valued at $200 million even though the price of beef in 1965 was actually higher than $1 per pound. In this way, distortions caused by changes in the price level are eliminated.

It is customary to express gross national product either in current dollars or in constant dollars. Figures expressed in ***current dollars*** are actual dollar amounts, whereas those expressed in ***constant dollars*** are corrected in this way for changes in the price level. Expressed in current dollars, gross national product is affected by changes in the price level. Expressed in constant dollars, gross national product is not affected by the price level because the prices of all goods are maintained at their base-year level. In recent years, inflation has caused gross national product expressed in current dollars to increase more rapidly than gross national product in constant dollars, as shown in Figure 8.6.

It is often useful to have some measure of how much prices have changed over a certain period of time. One way to obtain such a measure is to divide the value of a set of goods and services expressed in current dollars by the value of the same set of goods and services expressed in constant (or base-year) dollars. For example, suppose that a set of goods and services costs $100 when valued at 1972 prices, but $70 when valued at 1960 prices. Apparently, prices have risen an average of 43 percent for this set of goods between 1960 and 1972. How do we get 43 percent? The ratio of the cost in 1972 prices to the cost in 1960 prices is 100 ÷

Figure 8.6
Gross National Product, Expressed in Current Prices and in 1958 Prices, United States, 1929–72

Because of inflation, GNP expressed in current dollars has increased more rapidly in recent years than GNP in constant (1958) dollars.

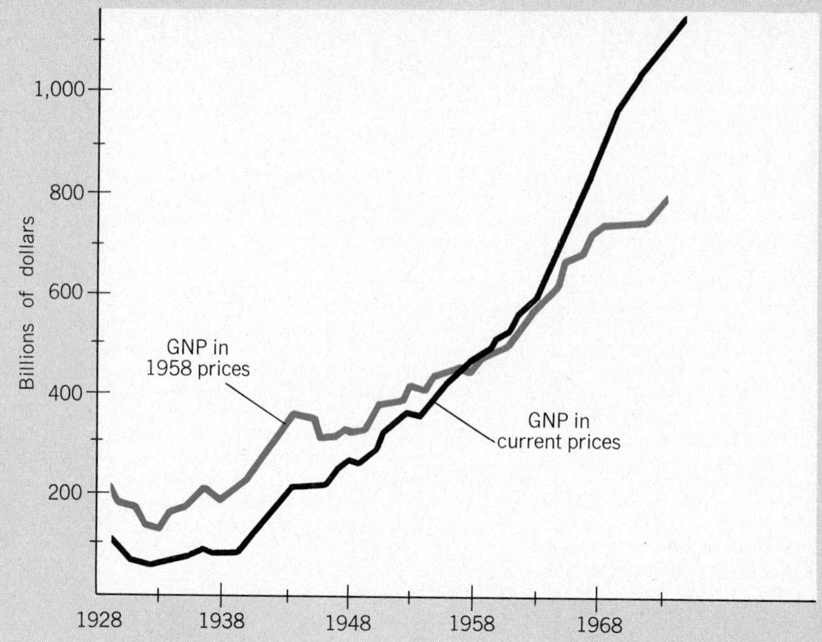

70 = 1.43; thus, prices must have risen on the average by 43 percent for this set of goods.

The ratio of the value of a set of goods and services in current dollars to the value of the same set of goods and services in constant (base-year) dollars is a ***price index.*** Thus, 1.43 is a price index in the example above. An important function of a price index is to convert values expressed in current dollars into values expressed in constant dollars. This conversion, known as ***deflating,*** can be achieved simply by dividing values expressed in current dollars by the price index. For example, in the illustration above, values expressed in 1972 dollars can be converted into constant (i.e., 1960) dollars by dividing by 1.43. This procedure is an important one, with applications in many fields other than the measurement of gross national product. For example, firms use it to compare their output in various years. To correct for price changes, they deflate their sales by a price index for their products.

To illustrate how a price index can be used to solve problems of this sort, suppose that we want to determine the extent to which the output of bread has increased in real terms between 1970 and 1974. We know that the value of output of bread in current dollars during each year was as shown in the first column of Table 8.1, and that the price of bread during each year was as shown in the second column. To determine the value of output of bread in 1970 dollars, we form a price index with 1970 as base year, as shown in the third column. Then dividing the figures in the first column by this price index, we get the value of output of bread during each year in 1970 dollars, shown in the fourth column. Thus, the fourth column shows how much the output of bread has grown in real terms. For example, the real output of bread has increased by 19 percent—(1,900 − 1,600) ÷ 1,600—between 1970 and 1974.

Table 8.1

Use of Price Index to Convert from Current to Constant Dollars

Year	(1) Output of bread in current prices	(2) Price of bread	(3) Price index (price ÷ 1970 price)	(4) Output of bread in 1970 dollars[1]
1970	$1,600 million	$0.50	1.00	$1,600 million
1971	1,768 million	$0.52	1.04	1,700 million
1972	1,980 million	$0.55	1.10	1,800 million
1973	2,090 million	$0.55	1.10	1,900 million
1974	2,204 million	$0.58	1.16	1,900 million

[1] This column was derived by dividing column 1 by column 3.

Intermediate Goods, Value-Added, and Net National Product

We have pointed out that gross national product includes the value of only the final goods and services produced. Obviously, however, the output of final goods and services is not due to the efforts of only the producers of the final goods and services. The total value of an automobile when it leaves the plant, for example, represents the work of many industries besides the automobile manufacturers. The steel, tires, glass, and many other components of the automobile were not produced by the automobile manufacturers. In reality, the automobile manufacturers only added a certain amount of value to the value of the intermediate goods—steel, tires, glass, etc.—they purchased. This point is basic to an understanding of how the gross national product is calculated.

To measure the contribution of a firm or industry to the final output, we use the concept of value-added. ***Value-added*** means just what it says: the amount of value added by a firm or industry to the total worth of the product. It is a measure in money terms of the extent of production taking place in a particular firm or industry. Suppose that $160 million of bread was produced in the United States in 1974. To produce it, farmers harvested $50 million of wheat, which was used as an intermediate product by flour mills, which turned out $80 million of flour. This flour was used as an intermediate product by the bakers who produced the $160 million of bread. What is the value-added at each stage of the process? For simplicity, assume that the farmers did not have to purchase any materials from other firms in order to produce the wheat. Then the value-added by the wheat farmers is $50 million, the value-added by the flour mills is $30 million ($80 million − $50 million); and the value-added by the bakers is $80 million ($160 million − $80 million). Of course, the total of the value-added at all stages of the process ($50 million + $30 million + $80 million) must equal the value of the output of final product ($160 million).

Table 8.2 shows the value-added by various industrial groups in the United States in 1972. Since the total of the value-added by all industries must equal the value of all final goods and sources, which, of course, is gross national product, it follows that $1,155 billion—the total of the figures in Table 8.2—must have been equal to gross national product in 1972. It is interesting to note that most of the value-added in the American economy in 1972 was not contributed by manufacturing, mining, construction, transportation, communication, or electricity or gas. Instead, most of it came from

Table 8.2

Value-added by Various Industries, United States, 1972

Industry	Value-added (billions of dollars)
Agriculture, forestry, and fisheries	37
Mining	18
Construction	56
Manufacturing	291
Transportation	46
Communication	28
Electricity, gas, and sanitation	28
Wholesale and retail trade	194
Finance, insurance, and real estate	164
Other services	133
Government[1]	153
Rest of the world	7
Gross national product	1,155

[1] Equals wages and salaries of government workers.
Source: Survey of Current Business, July 1973.

services—wholesale and retail trade, finance, insurance, real estate, government services, and other services. This is a sign of a basic change taking place in the American economy, which is turning more and more toward producing services, rather than goods.

Gross national product has one drawback as a measure that must now be faced: it does not take into account the fact that plant and equipment wear out with use. Economists have therefore developed another measure, net national product (or NNP), that allows for the fact that some of the nation's plant and equipment and structures are used up during the period. In other words, net national product recognizes what every accountant knows—the relevance of depreciation. (Recall the discussion in Chapter 7.) Specifically, ***net national product*** equals gross national product minus depreciation. To obtain net national product, government statisticians estimate the amount of depreciation—the amount of the nation's plant, equipment, and structures that are worn out during the period—and deduct it from gross national product. Net national product is a more accurate measure of the economy's output than gross national product because it takes depreciation into account, but estimates of net national product contain whatever errors are made in estimating depreciation (which is not easy to measure). As we shall see in succeeding chapters, data on gross national product are more often used, even if net national product may be a somewhat better measure. Actually, since GNP and NNP move together quite closely, which one you use doesn't matter much for most practical purposes.

The Limitations of Gross National Product and Net National Product

It is essential that the limitations of both gross national product and net national product be understood. Although they are very useful, they are by no means ideal measures of economic well-being. At least five limitations of these measures must always be borne in mind. First, GNP and NNP are not very meaningful unless one knows the size of the population of the country in question. For example, the fact that a particular nation's GNP equals $50 billion means one thing if the nation has 10 million inhabitants, and quite another thing if it has 500 million inhabitants. To correct for the size of the population, GNP per capita—GNP divided by the population—is often used as a rough measure of output per person in a particular country.

Second, GNP and NNP do not take account of one of man's most prized activities, leisure. During the past century, the average workweek in the United States has decreased substantially. It has gone from almost 70 hours in 1850 to about 40 hours today. As people have become more affluent, they have chosen to substitute leisure for increased production. Yet this increase in leisure time, which surely contributes to our well-being, does not show up in GNP or NNP. Neither does the personal satisfaction (or displeasure and alienation) people get from their jobs.

Third, GNP and NNP do not take adequate account of changes in the quality of goods. An improvement in a product is not reflected accurately in GNP and NNP unless its price reflects the improvement. For example, if a new type of drug is put on the market at the same price as an old drug, and if the output and cost of the new drug are the same as the old drug, GNP will not increase, even though the new drug is twice as effective as the old one. Because GNP and NNP do not reflect such increases in product quality, it is sometimes argued that the commonly used price indexes overestimate the amount of inflation, since, although prices may have gone up, quality may have gone up too.

Fourth, GNP and NNP say nothing about the social desirability of the composition and distribution of the nation's output. Each good and service produced is valued at its price. If the price of a Bible is $5 and the price of a pornographic novel is $5, both are valued at $5, whatever you or I may think about their respective worth. Moreover, GNP and NNP measure only the total quantity of goods and services produced. They tell us nothing about how this output is distributed among the people. If a nation's GNP is $500 billion, this is its GNP whether 90 percent of the output is consumed by a relatively few rich families or whether the output is distributed relatively equally among the citizens.

Finally, GNP and NNP do not reflect some of the social costs arising from the production of goods and services. In particular, they do not reflect the environmental damage resulting from the operation of our nation's factories, offices, and farms. It is common knowledge that the atmosphere and water supplies are being polluted in various ways by firms, consumers, and governments. Yet these costs are not deducted from GNP or NNP, even though the failure to do so results in an overestimate of our true economic welfare.

Economists are beginning to correct the GNP figures to eliminate some of these problems. For example, William Nordhaus and James Tobin at Yale University have tried to correct the GNP figures to take proper account of the value of leisure, the value of housewife's services, and the environmental costs of production, among other things.[5] They have found that, when these corrections were made, the increase in economic welfare since World War II has been much less than is indicated by the growth of uncorrected GNP per capita. Unquestionably, more work along this line is needed, and will be done. However, it is also worth noting that many of these adjustments and corrections are necessarily quite rough, since there is no accurate way to measure the relevant values and costs.

[5] W. Nordhaus and J. Tobin, "Is Growth Obsolete?", *Fiftieth Anniversary Colloquium,* National Bureau of Economic Research, 1972.

Gross National Income

We have been dealing with the measurement of national product, or output. We must also recognize *the identity between gross national product and gross national income.* ***Gross national income*** is the total annual flow of income paid out (or owed) as wages, rent, interest, and profits, plus two other items: indirect business taxes and depreciation. ***Indirect business taxes*** are sales taxes, excise taxes, and other such taxes that firms view as part of their costs. Thus, gross national income exactly equals the total claims on output—the sum total of the wages of the workers who participated in the productive efforts, the interest paid to the investors who lent money to the firms who produced the output, the profits of the owners of the firms who produced the output, and the rents paid the owners of land used to produce the output, as well as indirect business taxes and depreciation. If you think back to the circular flows of money and products described in Chapter 4, you can see why gross national income must equal gross national product.

Table 8.3

Sales, Costs, and Profit, General Electric Company, 1970

Sales ($ million)		Costs and profit ($ million)	
Sales:	$8,834	Employee compensation	$3,776
		Interest	101
		Depreciation	335
		Indirect business taxes	89
		Intermediate products bought from other firms	3,978
		Total costs	8,279
		Profits	555
Total	8,834	Total	8,834

Source: General Electric Company, 1970 Annual Report.

Table 8.4

Value-added and Claims Against Output, General Electric Company, 1970

Value-added ($ million)			Claims against output	
	Sales:	$8,834	Employee compensation	$3,776
			Interest	101
Subtract:	Intermediate products bought from other firms:	3,978	Profits	555
			Depreciation	335
			Indirect business taxes	89
	Value-added	4,856	Total	4,856

Source: General Electric Company, 1970 Annual Report.

To make sure that you understand this, let's start with a single firm, the General Electric Corporation, a huge producer of electrical equipment, appliances, and other products. By the simple rules of accounting discussed in Chapter 7,

$$\text{profit} = \text{sales} - \text{costs}. \tag{8.1}$$

Thus it follows that

$$\text{sales} = \text{costs} + \text{profit}. \tag{8.2}$$

Suppose we put the value of General Electric's output (i.e., its sales) on the left-hand side of Table 8.3 and its costs and profits on the right-hand side. Clearly, by Equation (8.2), the total of the right-hand side must equal the total of the left-hand side.

Now suppose that we deduct one element of costs, "Intermediate products bought from other firms," from both sides of Table 8.3, and present the results in Table 8.4. Since the left-hand total equals the right-hand total in Table 8.3, the same must hold in Table 8.4. The total of the left-hand side of Table 8.4 equals value-added, since General Electric's value-added equals its sales minus its expenditures on intermediate goods bought from other firms. The total of the right-hand side of Table 8.4 equals the total claims against General Electric's output, which is the total of income paid out (or owed) by the firm—wages, interest, rent, profits—plus indirect business taxes and depreciation. And, as pointed out above, the total of the left-hand side must equal the total of the right-hand side of Table 8.4.

Next, imagine constructing a table like Table 8.4 for each employer in the economy, putting sales less intermediate products bought from other firms on the left and costs plus profits less intermediate products bought from other firms on the right. For every employer, the total of the left side must equal the total of the right side. Thus, if we add up the total of the left-hand sides for all employers in the economy, the result must equal the total of the right-hand sides for all the employers in the economy. But what is the total of the left-hand sides for all employers in the economy? It is the sum of value-added for all employers, which, as we saw in a previous section, equals gross national product. And the total of the right-hand sides for all employers in the economy is the total of all income paid out (or owed) in the economy—wages, interest, rent, profits—plus indirect business taxes and depreciation. Consequently, gross national product must equal the total of all income paid out (or owed) in the economy plus indirect business taxes and depreciation.

Table 8.5 shows the total amounts of various types of income paid out (or owed) in the American economy during 1972. It also shows depreciation and indirect business taxes. You can see for yourself that the total of these items equals gross national product. Besides helping to prove the point stated at the beginning of this section, this table is an interesting description of the relative importance of various types of income. For example, it shows the great importance of wages and salaries in the total income stream in the United States. About

Table 8.5

Gross National Income, United States, 1972

Type of claim on output	Amount of claim (billions of dollars)
Employee compensation	707
Rental income	24
Net interest	45
Income of proprietors and professionals	74
Corporate profits	91
Indirect business taxes	109
Depreciation	102
Statistical discrepancy	3
Gross national income	1,155

Source: Survey of Current Business, July 1973.

60 percent of gross national income is paid out in wages and salaries, and this percentage has remained quite stable during the past 30 years.

National Income, Personal Income, and Disposable Income

There is more to gross national income than the total amount of income paid out (or owed) by employers (including government). As noted in the previous section, it also includes indirect business taxes and depreciation. We are sometimes interested only in the total amount of income paid out (or owed) by employers, an amount called ***national income.*** Clearly, it is easy to derive national income if you know gross national income. All you have to do is subtract indirect business taxes and depreciation from gross national income. Or putting it another way, all you have to do is subtract indirect business taxes from net national product, since gross national income minus depreciation equals net national product.[6] Table 8.6 shows the result for 1972.

For some purposes, we also need to know how much the people of a nation receive in income. This is ***personal income,*** and it differs from national income in two ways. First, some people who have a claim on income do not actually receive it. For example, although all a firm's profits belong to the owners, not all of its profits are paid out to them. As we saw in Chapter 7, part of the profits are plowed back into the business, and part go to the government for corporate income taxes. Also, wage earners do not actually receive the amounts they and their employers pay currently for Social Security. Second, some people receive income that is not obtained in exchange for services rendered. You will recall from an earlier section that government transfer payments are made to welfare recipients, people receiving unemployment compensation or Social Security, and so forth. Also, there are business transfer payments—pensions and other payments made by firms that are not in exchange for current productive services.

[6] Two other small items must also be taken into account. As shown in Table 8.6, we must subtract *business transfer payments*—pensions and other payments made by firms that are transfer payments—and add *subsidies less surpluses of government enterprises,* which corrects for the fact that some government agencies pay out more to income recipients than they produce in value-added. In addition, of course, there is a statistical discrepancy that must be recognized. It is purely a statistical matter.

Table 8.6

Gross National Product, Net National Product, National Income, Personal Income, and Disposable Income, United States, 1972

Measure		Amount (billions of dollars)
Gross national product		1,155
Subtract:	Depreciation	102
Net national product		1,053
Subtract:	Indirect business taxes	109
	Business transfers	5
	Statistical discrepancy	−1
Add:	Subsidies less surpluses of government enterprises	2
National income		942
Subtract:	Corporate profits	91
	Contributions for social insurance	74
Add:	Government transfers to persons	98
	Dividends	26
	Interest paid by government	33
	Business transfers	5
Personal income		939
Subtract:	Personal taxes	142
Disposable personal income		797

Source: Survey of Current Business, July 1973.

If you know national income, it is easy to derive personal income. You begin by subtracting profits from national income and adding dividends to the result. This will correct for the fact that profits not distributed as dividends do not actually enter people's hands. Then you must deduct contributions for social insurance, and add government and business transfer payments. (Note that interest paid by governments on their debt is regarded as a transfer payment, on the grounds that it is not a payment for current goods and services.) These calculations are shown in detail in Table 8.6.

Finally, it is also useful for many purposes to know how much the people of a nation receive in income and get to keep after personal income taxes. This is ***disposable income.*** If you know what personal income is, you can easily obtain disposable income by deducting personal income taxes from personal income, as shown in Table 8.6. Disposable income plays a very important role in subsequent chapters because it has a major influence on how much consumers spend. According to Table 8.6, disposable income equaled about 69 percent of gross national product (gross national income) in 1972.

Consumption, Investment, and Government Expenditure

Up to this point, we have been concerned with national output and national income, Now we take up ***national expenditure.*** At the outset, note that, if we include business spending for increased inventories as a form of expenditure, *the total amount spent on final goods and services must equal the total value of final goods and services produced.* In other words, *gross national expenditure must equal gross national product,* because all goods produced must either be bought by someone or added to the producer's inventories. In either case, the value of the goods is included in gross national expenditure.

The total amount spent on final goods and services is generally broken down into four parts. First, there is ***consumption,*** the amount spent by households on durable goods, nondurable goods, and services. For example, consumption includes your expenditures on meals and clothing, and your parents' expenditures on the family car or on an electric washer and dryer. Table 8.7 shows that in 1972 consumption accounted for about 63 percent of the total amount spent on final goods and services in the United States. Expenditure on consumer durable goods is clearly much less than on consumer nondurable goods or services.

Second, there is ***investment,*** the amount spent by firms for new plant and equipment, new housing, and increases in inventories, as well as the

Table 8.7

Expenditure on Final Goods and Services, United States, 1972

Type of Expenditure		Amount (billions of dollars)
Personal consumption		727
Durable goods	118	
Nondurable goods	300	
Services	309	
Gross private domestic investment		178
Expenditures on plant and equipment	118	
Residential structures	54	
Increase in inventories	6	
Net exports		−5
Exports	73	
Imports	78	
Government expenditures		255
Federal	104	
State and local	151	
Gross national product		1,155

Source: Survey of Current Business, July 1973.

amount spent by households for new housing. (Owner-occupied houses are treated as investment goods because they can be rented out.) Table 8.7 shows that in 1972 investment accounted for about 15 percent of the total amount spent on final goods and services in the United States. This is ***gross investment,*** the gross amount of money spent on new plant, equipment, buildings, and extra inventory, not the net amount. Why? Because during the period in question, some plant, equipment, and so forth wore out: there was depreciation. Thus, to determine net investment we must deduct depreciation from gross investment. Net investment is a good measure of how fast the nation's capital goods are increasing. If net investment is positive, the nation's productive capacity, as gauged by its capital stock, is growing. If net investment is negative, the nation's productive capacity, as gauged by its capital stock, is declining.

Third, there are ***government purchases of goods and services.*** They include the expenditures of the federal, state, and local governments for the multitude of functions they perform: defense, education, police protection, and so forth. They do not include transfer payments, since they are not payments for current production. Table 8.7 shows that government spending in 1972 accounted for about 22 percent of the total amount spent on final goods and services in the United States. State and local expenditures are bigger than federal expenditures. As you recall from Chapter 5, much of the expenditures of the federal government are connected with national defense, while at the state and local levels the biggest expenditure is for education.

Finally, there are ***net exports of goods and services,*** which equal the amount spent by foreigners on our goods and services less the amount we spent on other nations' goods and services. Obviously, this factor must be included since some of our national output is destined for foreign markets, and since we import some of the goods and services we consume. There is no reason why this component of spending cannot be negative, since imports can exceed exports. The quantity of net exports tends to be quite small. Table 8.6 shows that net exports in 1972 were negative, and equal to about $\frac{4}{10}$ of 1 percent of the total amount spent on final goods and services in the United States. Because net exports are so small, we shall generally ignore them until Chapters 30 to 32, when we shall focus attention exclusively on international trade and finance.

Three Basic Facts

The measures of national output, national income, and national expenditure discussed above are some of the basic figures economists look at when trying to analyze the state of the economy. Using these measures, it is easy to demonstrate the following three facts, each of which will be needed in succeeding chapters. First, disposable income, although it goes up and down with gross national product, does not fluctuate as much as gross national product. This is shown in Figure 8.7. As we shall soon see, disposable income has a smoother path because our tax system and our social insurance programs, as well as other mechanisms, tend to dampen the effect of changes in gross national product on disposable income. When total output declines, the amount of aftertax income people receive does not go down so much; and when total output increases, the amount of aftertax income they receive does not go up so much. This, of course, cushions the effect of changes in gross national product.

Second, consumption expenditure seems to depend closely on—and vary directly with—disposable income. This observation, shown in Figure 8.8, is neither strange nor surprising. On the contrary, it would be odd if the amount households spend on goods and services were *not* closely related to their aftertax income, for consumers can do only two things with their aftertax income: spend it or save it.

Third, investment varies much more than the other components of total spending. Figure 8.9 shows that investment goes up and down, while

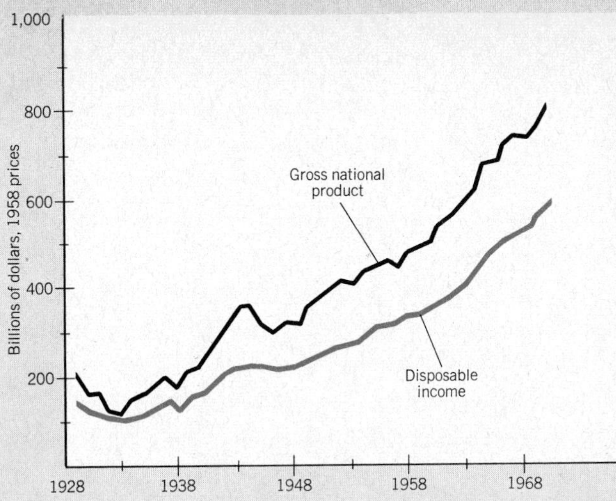

Figure 8.7
Relationship between Disposable Income and Gross National Product, United States, 1929–72

Disposable income, although it goes up and down with gross national product, does not fluctuate as much as GNP.

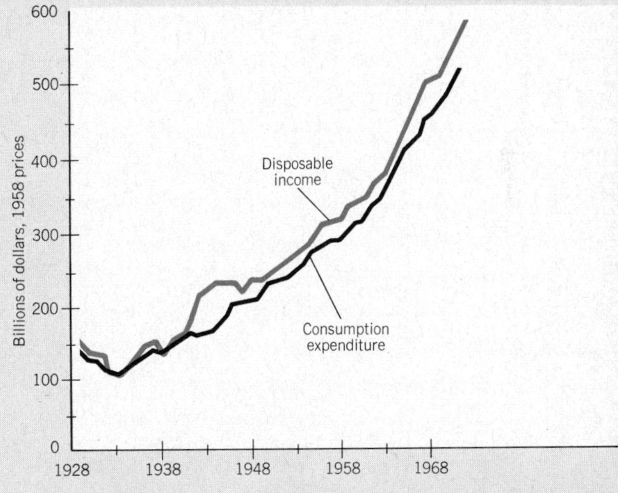

Figure 8.8
Relationship between Consumption and Disposable Income, United States, 1929–72

Consumption expenditure seems to depend closely on, and vary directly with, disposable income.

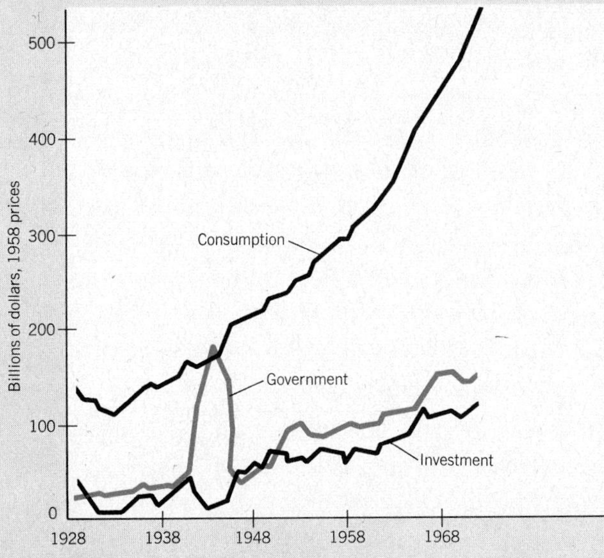

Figure 8.9
Consumption Expenditure, Gross Private Domestic Investment, and Government Expenditures, United States, 1929–72

Investment varies more than the other components of total spending. Also, because of wars, government spending moves up and down rather erratically.

consumption moves along with only slight bumps and dips, and government expenditures do not move up and down very much except when war breaks out.[7] (Note the bulges in government spending during World War II, the Korean war, and the Vietnamese war.) The volatility of investment is an important factor in explaining the changes in national output over time. Also, the wartime bulges in government spending have been major causes of changes in national output. We shall have considerably more to say on this score in the next few chapters.

The Gap between Actual and Potential Output

Gross national product is a measure of the value of final goods and services produced in a given period: in other words, GNP measures actual output. Besides being concerned about actual output, economists are also interested in potential output. Specifically, they are interested in estimating how high the gross national product could have been *if the unemployment rate had been quite low, say 4 percent* (which is a common definition of full employment)? An economy's potential output is determined by the size of its labor force, the average number of hours a worker is on the job per year, and the average amount of goods and services a worker can produce per hour. The average amount of goods and services a worker can produce per hour depends in turn on the extent and quality of the capital he has to work with, the level of technology, and his skill and schooling.

More specifically, the ***potential GNP*** is estimated by multiplying 96 percent of the labor force times the normal hours of work per year times the average output per manhour at the relevant time. In the past few years, there has been some criticism of this definition of potential GNP on the grounds that an unemployment rate of 4.5 or 5 percent is a more realistic measure of full employment than 4 percent because there now are more young people, women, and minority workers in the labor force. All of these groups find it relatively difficult to find jobs. Since this debate is unresolved, we shall stick with the conventional definition, but the apparent difficulties in this measure should be noted.

If potential GNP is defined in this way, the gap between actual and potential GNP depends on the difference between the actual unemployment rate and 4 percent. Specifically, the gap will grow larger and larger as the unemployment rate exceeds 4 percent by greater and greater amounts. According to Arthur Okun, who served as chairman of the Council of Economic Advisers under President Johnson, the relationship is as follows:

$$\text{potential GNP} - \text{actual GNP} = 3 \times (\text{unemployment rate} - .04) \times \text{actual GNP}.$$

In this equation, the number 3 in the formula is derived by fitting the equation to historical data.[8]

Needless to say, it is not easy to measure potential GNP. Consequently, as Okun is the first to emphasize, one should view this equation as only a rough predictor. But rough predictors are better than none, and this equation is a handy device to estimate the gap between actual and potential output at various levels of unemployment. For example, if the unemployment rate were 7 percent, the gap between actual and potential output would be 3 times .03 (the difference between .07 and .04) times the actual gross national product. In other words, the gap would equal 9 percent of actual gross national product. Figure 8.10 shows the estimated size of the gap between actual and potential GNP from 1955 to 1972. Note that both actual and potential GNP are expressed in 1958 prices.

The gap between actual and potential output is an extremely important measure of what it costs society to tolerate an unemployment rate above 4 percent. Besides the psychic costs of unemployment described in a previous section, society produces less than it could, so that human wants

[7] Net exports are excluded from Figure 8.9. They were almost always under $10 billion during this period.

[8] Arthur Okun, *The Political Economy of Prosperity*, New York: Norton, 1970.

Figure 8.10
Actual and Potential Output, United States, 1955–72

The gap measures what it costs society each year, in output forgone, to tolerate an unemployment rate above 4 percent.

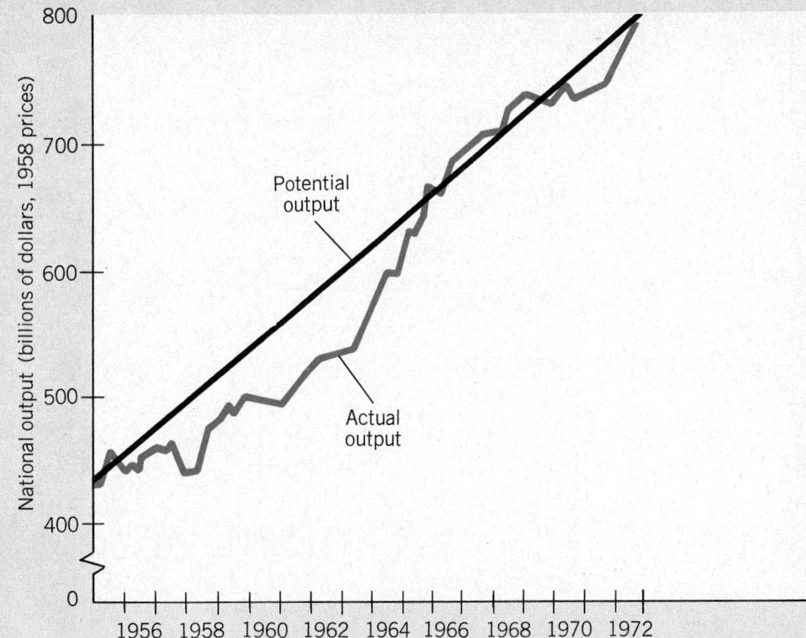

are less effectively fulfilled than they could be. For example, consider the period from 1958 to 1963. During this period, unemployment tended to be relatively high, and actual GNP was considerably less than potential GNP. Using Okun's equation, it is possible to estimate the gap between actual and potential GNP in each of these years. All one needs to do is insert the actual unemployment rates and actual figures for GNP in the equation. Based on such calculations, Okun has concluded that

> The United States could have produced a total of nearly $200 billion more output [if there had been a] 4% unemployment rate. This is two-thirds of the amount spent for national defense in the period and far more than the expenditure for public education. It is fair to conclude that tolerance of idle resources has been America's outstanding extravagance and waste [during this period.][9]

[9] Arthur Okun, *The Battle Against Unemployment,* New York: Norton, 1965, p. 22.

Clearly we must learn to curb the forces responsible for such waste. The following chapters will discuss some of the basic factors that cause excessive unemployment and excessive inflation, as well as various measures that can be taken to combat them.

Summary

Unemployment inflicts enormous social costs. Recognizing this fact, the Congress passed the Employment Act of 1946, which commits the federal government to combat excessive unemployment. Inflation is a general upward movement of prices. Since inflation results in an arbitrary and often inequitable redistribution of income, government policymakers attempt to curb inflation. Unfortunately, there appears to be an inverse relationship between the unemployment rate and the rate of inflation, because it is easier for unions and unorganized labor to increase wages and for firms to increase prices when there is little unemployment. Thus government policymakers, if they reduce unemployment, often create inflationary pressures, whereas if they attack inflation, they often increase unemployment. What you regard as the optimal combination of unemployment and inflation depends on your political preferences and values. The relationship between unemployment and inflation is by no means fixed, and one way out of this difficulty is for the government to try to shift this relationship downward and to the left.

Besides unemployment and inflation, another very important indicator of the health of any economy is its gross national product, which measures the total value of the final goods and services it produces in a particular period. Since gross national product is affected by the price level, it must be deflated by a price index to correct for price level changes. Gross national product is the sum of value-added by all industries. Net national product is gross national product minus depreciation. It indicates the value of net output when account is taken of capital used up.

Gross national product equals gross national income. Gross national income equals the sum of the total claims against output, including indirect business taxes and depreciation. National income is the total amount of income paid out (or owed) by employers; personal income is the total amount people actually receive in income; and disposable income is the total amount they get to keep after taxes.

Gross national product also equals gross national expenditure. Gross national expenditure equals the total amount spent on final goods and services, including business spending for increased inventories. The total amount spent on final goods and services is generally broken down into four parts: consumption, investment, government purchases, and net exports.

Based on the official data, investment appears to vary much more over time than other types of expenditure. As we shall see, this volatility is an important clue to the causes of change in national output. Also, there have been large variations in government expenditures associated with wars; these too have caused major changes in national output.

Estimates have been made of how the gap between actual and potential output is related to the unemployment rate. For example, if Okun's results are accepted, output could be expanded about 9 percent if the unemployment rate is reduced from 7 to 4 percent. Clearly, one of the major social costs of unemployment is the fact that less goods and services are produced than could be produced with full employment. According to Okun, this cost totaled nearly $200 billion over the 5-year period 1958–63 alone.

CONCEPTS FOR REVIEW

Frictional unemployment
Structural unemployment
Cyclical unemployment
Gross national product
Intermediate good
Current dollars
Constant dollars
Price index
Value added
Net national product
Gross national income
Personal income
Transfer payments
Disposable income
Inflation
National income
Consumption
Investment
Net exports

QUESTIONS FOR DISCUSSION AND REVIEW

1. According to the September 1932, issue of *Fortune* magazine, "About 1,000,000 out of [New York City's] 3,200,000 working population are unemployed." What effect did this have on the city's population? During the past 30 years, has this experience been repeated? About how many New Yorkers are presently unemployed?

2. Suppose that you were given the job of estimating the gross national product of Monaco. How would you proceed?

3. Inflation occurs whenever the price of an individual commodity moves up significantly. True or False?

4. The type of unemployment where jobs are available for qualified workers, but the unemployed do not have the necessary qualifications is called
   a. frictional. b. cyclical. c. structural.

CHAPTER 9

The Determination of National Output

In early 1973, the American economy was in the midst of a boom. Gross national product was moving ahead rapidly, the unemployment rate was receding, and inflationary pressures were evident practically everywhere. In 1970, on the other hand, GNP was declining, the unemployment rate was increasing, and there was less upward pressure on the price level. Why the pronounced difference between these two periods? To answer this question, as well as to understand the causes of severe unemployment and inflation, and what can be done to avoid these problems, we must understand how the level of a nation's output is determined.

In this chapter, we show how national output is determined in a purely market economy without government spending or taxation. The resulting model is interesting in its own right, as well as a useful step toward the more complete analysis provided in Chapter 10. In this chapter, national output is defined as net national product, since it is the best measure of how much the economy is producing when depreciation is taken into account. But since net national product and gross national product differ by relatively little, and since they move up and down together, this theory is also useful in explaining movements in gross national product. Indeed, as we shall see, it has been used to help forecast GNP.

The Classical View of Unemployment

Until the 1930s, most economists were convinced that the price system, left to its own devices, would hold unemployment to a reasonable minimum. Thus, most of the great names of economics in the nineteenth and early twentieth centuries—including John Stuart Mill, Alfred Marshall, and A. C. Pigou[1]—felt that there was no need for government intervention to promote a high level of employment. To be sure, they recognized that unemployment was sometimes large, but they regarded these lapses from high employment as temporary aberrations that the price system would cure automatically. Although economists today look at this matter differently, we must understand why the classical economists felt that this was the case.

Basically, their view was founded on the assertion that total spending was unlikely to be too small to purchase the high-employment level of output, because of the operation of a law propounded by the nineteenth-century French economist, J. B. Say. According to ***Say's Law,*** the production of a certain amount of goods and services results in the generation of an amount of income precisely sufficient to buy that output. In other words, supply creates its own demand, since the total amount paid out by the producers of the goods and services to resource owners must equal the value of the goods and services. (Recall the circular flow discussed in Chapter 4.) However, as the classical economists recognized, there could be a fly in the ointment. If some of the owners of resources did not spend their income, but saved some of it instead, how would the necessary spending arise to take all the output off the market?

The answer the classical economists offered is that each dollar saved will be invested. Therefore, investment (made largely by business firms) will restore to the spending stream what resource owners take out through the saving process. Recall that the economist's definition of investment is different from the one often used in common parlance. To the economist, investment means expenditure on plant, equipment, and other productive assets. The classical economists believed that the amount invested would automatically equal the amount saved because the interest rate—the price paid for the use of money—would fluctuate in such a way as to maintain equality between them. In other words, there is a market for loanable funds, and the interest rate will vary so that the quantity of funds supplied equals the quantity demanded. Thus, since funds are demanded to be used—that is, invested—the amount saved will be invested.

Further, the classical economists said that the amount of goods and services businessmen can sell depends upon the prices businessmen charge, as well as on total spending. For example, $1 million in spending will take 400 cars off the market if the price is $2,500 per car, and 500 cars off the market if the price is $2,000 per car. Recognizing this, the classical economists argued that firms would cut prices to sell their output. Competition among firms would prod them to reduce their prices in this way, with the result that the high-employment level of output would be taken off the market.

Looking at this process more closely, it is obvious that the prices of resources must also be reduced under such circumstances. Otherwise firms would

[1] The ideas of John Stuart Mill (1806–73) and his arguments in support of individual freedom are particularly famous. He was one of the great philosophers of the nineteenth century. He was also a great economist, his *Principles of Political Economy* (1848) being his best-known work. He advocated many social reforms, including shorter working hours and tax reform.

Alfred Marshall (1842–1924) played an important role in the construction of the theories of supply and demand, the use of partial equilibrium techniques, and other major developments in economics. His *Principles of Economics* (1890), which had eight editions, was a leading economics text for many years.

A. C. Pigou (1877–1959) a student of Marshall, was Professor of Economics at Cambridge University from 1908 to 1943. His *Economics of Welfare* (1932) was a pathbreaking work that dealt in an important way with various aspects of welfare economics.

incur losses because they would be getting less for their product, but paying no less for resources. The classical economists believed that it was realistic to expect the prices of resources to decline in such a situation. Indeed they were quite willing to assume that the wage rate—the price of labor—would be flexible in this way. They expected this flexibility because of competition among laborers. Through the processes of competition, they felt that wage rates would be bid down to the level where everyone who really wanted to work could get a job.

The Views of Karl Marx

Quite a different view of unemployment was held by Karl Marx (1818–83), the intellectual father of communism. A man of unquestioned genius, he became an object of quasi-religious devotion to a large part of the world and a hated (and sometimes feared) revolutionary figure to another large part of the world. Because Marx the revolutionary has had such an enormous effect on modern history, it is difficult to discuss Marx the economist. But he was a very profound and influential economist. A meticulous German scholar who spent much of his life in poverty-ridden circumstances in Britain, he wrote a huge, four-volume work on economics, *Das Kapital*.[2] Eighteen years in the making, it is one of the most influential books ever written.

To understand Marx, we need to know something about the times in which he lived. The period was characterized by revolutionary pressures against the ruling classes. In most of the countries of Europe, there was little democracy, as we know it. The masses participated little, if at all, in the world of political affairs, and very fully in the world of drudgery. For example, at one factory in Manchester, England, in 1862, people worked an average of about 80 hours per week. For these incredibly long hours of toil, the workers generally received small wages. They often could do little more than feed and clothe themselves. Given the circumstances of the times, it is little wonder that revolutionary pressures were manifest.

Marx, viewing the economic system of his day, believed that capitalism was doomed to collapse. He believed that the workers were exploited by the capitalists—the owners of factories, mines, and other types of capital. And he believed that the capitalists, by introducing new labor-saving technology, would throw more and more workers into unemployment. This army of unemployed workers, by competing for jobs, would keep wages at a subsistence level. As machinery was substituted for labor, Marx felt that profits would fall. Unemployment would become more severe. Big firms would absorb small ones. Eventually the capitalistic system was bound to collapse.

To get the flavor of his reasoning and emotions, consider the following passage from *Das Kapital*, a famous passage describing his vision of the death knell of the capitalist system:

> Along with the constantly diminishing number of the magnates of capital, who usurp and monopolize all advantages of this process of transformation, grows the mass of misery, oppression, slavery, degradation, exploitation; but with this too grows the revolt of the working-class, a class always increasing in numbers, and disciplined, united, organized by the very mechanism of the process of capitalist production itself . . . Centralization of the means of production and socialization of labor at last reach a point where they become incompatible with their capitalist integument. This integument bursts asunder. The knell of capitalist private property sounds. The expropriators are expropriated.[3]

According to Marx, the inevitable successor to capitalism would be socialism, an economic system with no private property. Instead, property would be owned by society as a whole. Socialism, constituting a "dictatorship of the proletariat," would be only a transitional step to the promised land of communism. Marx did not spell out the characteristics of communism in detail. He was sure that it

[2] Karl Marx, *Das Kapital*, New York: Modern Library, 1906.

[3] Karl Marx, *Das Kapital, op. cit.*, pp. 836–7, reprinted in E. Mansfield, *Economics: Readings, Issues, and Cases*, New York: Norton, 1974.

would be a classless society where everyone worked and no one owned capital, and he was sure that the state would "wither away," but he did not attempt to go much beyond this in his blueprint for communism. In Chapter 34, we shall discuss Marx's doctrines, and their limitations, in detail. The important point here is that, although the classical view was the dominant one, it did not go unchallenged, even in the nineteenth century.

John Maynard Keynes and the Great Depression

The man who was responsible for much of the modern theory of the determination of national product was John Maynard Keynes (1883–1946). Son of a British economist who was justly famous in his own right, Keynes was enormously successful in a variety of fields. He published a brilliant book on the theory of probability while still a relatively young man. Working for a half-hour in bed each morning, he made millions of dollars as a stock market speculator. He was a distinguished patron of the arts and a member of the Bloomsbury set, a group of London intellectuals who were the intellectual pace-setters for British society. He was a faculty member at Cambridge University, and a key figure at the British Treasury. In short, he was an extraordinarily gifted and accomplished man.

Keynes lived and worked almost a century after Marx. His world was quite different from Marx's world; and Keynes himself—polished, successful, a member of the elite—was quite different from the poverty-stricken, revolutionary Marx. But the two great economists were linked in at least one important respect: both were preoccupied with unemployment and the future of the capitalistic system. As we saw in the previous section, Marx predicted that unemployment would get worse and worse, until at last the capitalist system would collapse. In the 1930s, when Keynes was in his heyday, the Great Depression seemed to many people to be proving Marx right.

In 1936, while the world was still in the throes of this economic disaster, Keynes published his masterpiece, *The General Theory of Employment, Interest, and Money*.[4] His purpose in this book was to explain how the capitalist economic system could get stalled in the sort of depressed state of equilibrium that existed in the 1930s. He also tried to indicate how governments might help to solve the problem. Contrary to the classical economists, Keynes concluded that no automatic mechanism in a capitalistic society would generate a high level of employment—or, at least, would generate it quickly enough to be relied on in practice. Instead, the equilibrium level of national output might for a long time be below the level required to achieve high employment. His reasons for believing that this could be the case are discussed in detail in this and subsequent chapters.

To push the economy toward a higher level of employment, Keynes advocated the conscious, forceful use of the government's power to spend and tax. As we shall see in Chapter 10, many years passed before these powers became accepted tools of national economic policy, but it was Keynes who provided much of the intellectual stimulus. And in so doing, he helped falsify the predictions of Marx. Keynes and his many followers showed how severe unemployment could be tamed, and how a capitalistic economy could be managed to avoid the sorts of debacles Marx predicted. It is no exaggeration to say that Keynes made a major contribution to saving the capitalist system.

Flaws in the Classical View

There were at least two basic flaws in the classical model, as Keynes and his followers pointed out. First, *the people and firms who save are often not the same as the people and firms who invest, and they often have quite different motivations.* In particular, a considerable amount of saving is done by families who want to put something aside for a

[4] John Maynard Keynes, *The General Theory of Employment, Interest, and Money,* New York: Harcourt, Brace, 1936.

Figure 9.1
Relation between Family Expenditures on Consumption and Family Disposable Income, United States, 1960

Families with higher incomes spend more on consumption than families with lower incomes.

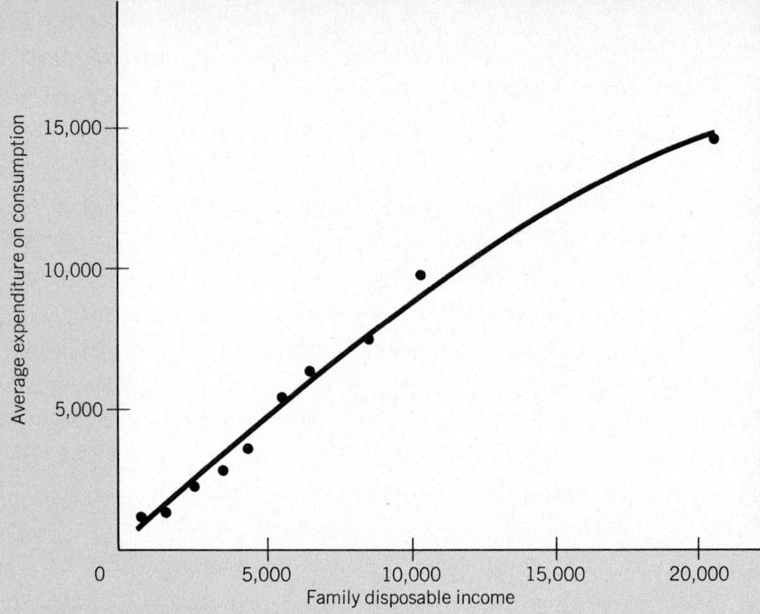

rainy day or for a car or appliance. On the other hand, a considerable amount of investment is done by firms that are interested in increasing their profits by expanding their plants or by installing new equipment. There is no assurance that desired saving will equal desired investment at a level insuring high employment. For one thing, saving may be used to increase money balances, not to support investment. Thus a purely capitalist economic system, in the absence of appropriate government policies, has no dependable rudder to keep it clear of the shoals of serious unemployment or of serious inflation.

Second, *Keynes and his followers pointed out the unreality of the classical economists' assumption that prices and wages are flexible.* Contrary to the classical economists' argument, the modern economy contains many departures from perfect competition that are barriers to downward flexibility of prices and wages. In particular, many important industries are dominated by a few producers who try hard to avoid cutting price. Even in the face of a considerable drop in demand, such industries have sometimes maintained extraordinarily stable prices. Moreover, the labor unions fight tooth and nail to avoid wage cuts. In view of these facts of life, the classical assumption of wage and price flexibility seems unrealistic indeed. And it seems unlikely that price and wage reductions can be depended on to maintain full employment.

The Great Depression of the 1930s struck a severe blow against the classical view. When it continued for years, and millions and millions of people continued to be unemployed, it became increasingly difficult to accept the idea that unemployment was only a temporary aberration that the market economy would cure automatically in a reasonable length of time. Nonetheless, the classical economists did not change their tune. They claimed that the economy would get back to high employment if the labor unions would allow more wage flexibility, if the big corporations would allow more price flexibility, and if President Franklin D. Roosevelt and his New Dealers would quit interfering with free markets.

Finally, when Keynes's *General Theory* appeared in 1936, it seemed to offer a more satisfactory model, even though, at first, only a minority of the econom-

Figure 9.2
Relationship between Consumption Expenditure and Disposable Income, United States, 1929–72

There is a very close relationship between consumption expenditure and disposable income in the United States.

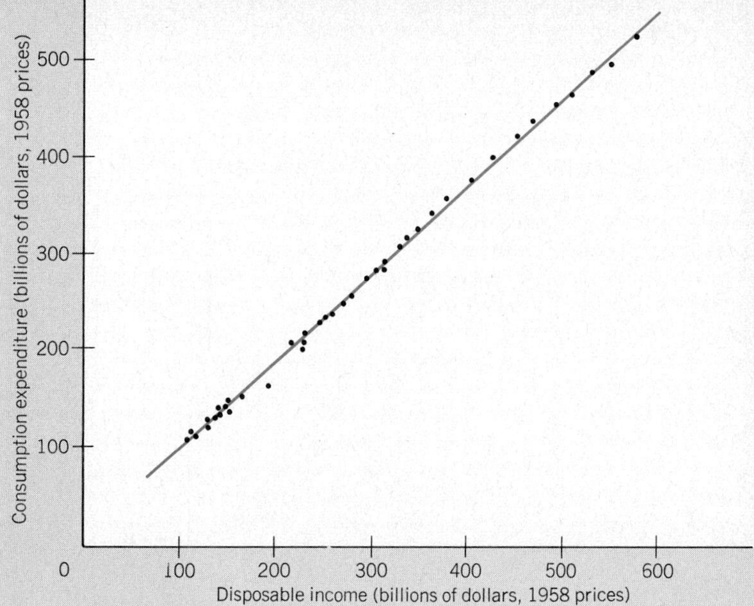

ics profession was converted to the Keynesian view. Within 10 or 15 years of its publication, most economists were convinced that Keynes's theory was essentially sound; and his ideas now are generally accepted, although they have been refined and extended by his followers. Whether Republican or Democrat, any modern economist relies heavily on Keynesian ideas and concepts. But, of course, not all economists share Keynes's views on proper public policy. Moreover, as we shall see in subsequent chapters, under certain circumstances, more complicated models are likely to outperform the simple Keynesian model presented in this and the following chapters.

The Modern Theory: The Consumption Function

Keynes's *General Theory of Employment, Interest, and Money* is impenetrable for the general reader. Even among professional economists, it is not noted for its lucidity or liveliness. But the basic ideas that Keynes presented—and that subsequent economists have refined, extended, and reworked—are really quite simple. In the remainder of this chapter, we shall describe and discuss the determinants of national output, according to the modern view. The first thing to note is that *consumption expenditures—whether those of a single household or the total consumption expenditures in the entire economy—are influenced heavily by income.* For individual households, Figure 9.1 shows that families with higher incomes spend more on consumption than families with lower incomes. Of course, individual families vary a good deal in their behavior; some spend more than others even if their incomes are the same. But, on the average, a family's consumption expenditure is tied very closely to its income.

What is true for individual families also holds for the entire economy: total consumption expenditures are closely related to disposable income. This fact, noted in the previous chapter, is shown in detail in Figure 9.2, a "scatter diagram" that plots total consumption expenditure in each year (from 1929 to 1972) against disposable income in the

Figure 9.3
Shift in the Consumption Function

The consumption function describes the total amount of consumption expenditure at each level of disposable income. The consumption function may shift upward (from *A* to *B*) if changes occur in the public's assets, its expectations, or in other variables.

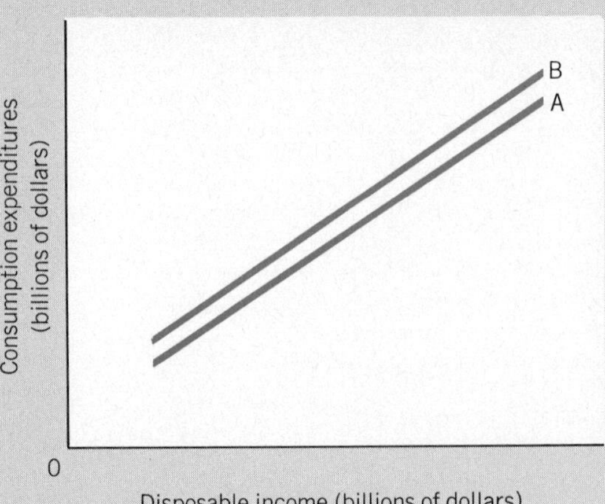

same year (from 1929 to 1972). The points fall very near the straight line drawn in Figure 9.2, but not right on it. For most practical purposes, however, we can regard the line drawn in Figure 9.2 as representing the relationship between total consumption expenditures and disposable income.

This relationship between consumption spending and disposable income is the ***consumption function.*** The consumption function, the importance of which was stressed by John Maynard Keynes, is at the heart of the modern theory of the determination of national output. It is a working tool that is used widely and often by economists to analyze and forecast the behavior of the economy. There have been many statistical studies of the consumption function. Some of these studies have been based on cross-section data—comparisons of the amount spent on consumption by families at various income levels. (Figure 9.1 is based on cross-section data.) Others have been based on time-series data—comparisons of the total amount spent on consumption in the economy with total income over various periods of time. (Figure 9.2 is based on time-series data.)

Like most things in the world, the consumption function does not remain fixed, but changes from time to time, because variables other than disposable income affect consumption expenditures. Some of the most important of these variables are changes in income distribution, changes in population, changes in the amount of assets in the hands of the public, changes in the ease and cheapness with which consumers can borrow money, and changes in their price expectations. For example, consumption expenditure is likely to be higher—holding disposable income constant—if income is more equally distributed, if the population is greater, if people are holding large amounts of government bonds and other liquid assets, or if consumers can borrow money easily and cheaply. Under any of these conditions, the consumption function is likely to shift upward, as indicated by the movement from position *A* to position *B* in Figure 9.3.

The Marginal Propensity to Consume

Suppose that we know what the consumption function for a given society looks like at a particular point in time. For example, suppose that it is given by the figures for disposable income and consumption expenditure in the first two columns of Table 9.1. Based on our knowledge of the consumption function, we can determine the *extra* amount families will spend on consumption if they receive an *extra* dollar of disposable income. *This amount—the fraction of an extra dollar of income that is spent on consumption—is called the* ***marginal propensity to consume.*** For reasons discussed in subsequent sections of this chapter, the marginal propensity to consume, shown in column 4 of Table 9.1, plays a major role in the modern theory of national output determination.

To make sure that you understand exactly what the marginal propensity to consume is, consult Table 9.1. What is the marginal propensity to consume when disposable income is between $1,000 billion and $1,050 billion? The second column shows that, when income rises from $1,000 billion to $1,050 billion, consumption rises from $950 billion to $980 billion. Consequently, the fraction of the extra income—$50 billion—that is consumed is $30 billion ÷ $50 billion, or 0.60. Thus, the marginal propensity to consume is 0.60.[5] Based on similar calculations, the marginal propensity to consume when disposable income is between $1,050 billion and $1,100 billion is 0.60; the marginal propensity to consume when disposable income is between $1,100 billion and $1,150 billion is 0.60; and so forth.

[5] Students with some knowledge of mathematics will recognize that this is an approximation since $50 billion is a substantial change in income, whereas the marginal propensity to consume pertains to a small change in income. But this is an innocuous simplification. Similar simplifications are made below.

Table 9.1

The Consumption Function

Disposable income (billions of dollars)	Consumption expenditure	Average propensity to consume	Marginal propensity to consume	Saving (billions of dollars)	Marginal propensity to save
1,000	950	.95		50	
			$\frac{30}{50} = .60$		$\frac{20}{50} = .40$
1,050	980	.93		70	
			$\frac{30}{50} = .60$		$\frac{20}{50} = .40$
1,100	1,010	.92		90	
			$\frac{30}{50} = .60$		$\frac{20}{50} = .40$
1,150	1,040	.90		110	
			$\frac{30}{50} = .60$		$\frac{20}{50} = .40$
1,200	1,070	.89		130	
			$\frac{30}{50} = .60$		$\frac{20}{50} = .40$
1,250	1,100	.88		150	
			$\frac{30}{50} = .60$		$\frac{20}{50} = .40$
1,300	1,130	.87		170	

There are several things to note about the marginal propensity to consume. First, it can differ, depending on the level of disposable income. Only if the consumption function is a straight line, as in Figure 9.2 and Table 9.1, will the marginal propensity to consume be the same at all levels of income. Second, the marginal propensity to consume will not in general equal the ***average propensity to consume***, which is the proportion of disposable income that is consumed. For example, in Table 9.1, the average propensity to consume when disposable income is $1,100 billion is 0.92; but the marginal propensity to consume when disposable income is between $1,050 billion and $1,100 billion is 0.60. The point is that the marginal propensity to consume is the proportion of *extra* income consumed, and this proportion generally is quite different from the proportion of *total* income consumed. Third, the marginal propensity to consume can be interpreted geometrically as the slope of the consumption function. The slope of any line is, of course, the ratio of the vertical change to the horizontal change when a small movement occurs along the line. Thus, the steeper the consumption function, the higher the marginal propensity to consume.

The Saving Function and the Marginal Propensity to Save

If people don't devote their disposable income to consumption expenditure, what else can they do with it? Of course, they can save it. When families refrain from spending their income on consumption goods and services—that is, when they forgo present consumption to provide for larger consumption in the future—they save. Thus we can derive from the consumption function the total amount people will save at each level of disposable income. All we have to do is subtract the total consumption expenditure at each level of disposable income from disposable income. This will give us the total amount of saving at each level of disposable income, as shown in Table 9.1. Then we can plot the total amount of saving against disposable income, as shown in Figure 9.4. The resulting relationship between total saving and disposable income is called the ***saving function.*** Like the consumption function, it plays a major role in the modern theory of national output determination.

If we know the saving function, we can calculate the marginal propensity to save at any level of disposable income. The ***marginal propensity to save*** *is the proportion of an extra dollar of disposable income that is saved.* To see how to calculate it, consult Table 9.1 again. The fifth column shows that, when income rises from $1,000 billion to $1,050 billion, saving rises from $50 billion to $70 billion. Consequently, the fraction of the extra income—$50 billion—that is saved is $20 billion ÷ $50 billion, or 0.40. Thus, the marginal propensity to save is 0.40. Similar calculations show that the marginal propensity to save when disposable income is between $1,050 billion and $1,100 billion is 0.40; the marginal propensity to save when disposable income is between $1,100 billion and $1,150 billion is 0.40; and so forth.

Note that, at any particular level of disposable income, the marginal propensity to save plus the marginal propensity to consume must equal one. By definition, the marginal propensity to save equals the proportion of an extra dollar of disposable income that is saved, and the marginal propensity to consume equals the proportion of an extra dollar of income that is consumed. The sum of these two proportions must equal one, for, as stated above, the only things that people can do with an extra dollar of disposable income are consume it or save it. Table 9.1 shows this fact quite clearly. At every level of disposable income, the marginal propensity to consume plus the marginal propensity to save equals one. Finally, it is worth noting that the marginal propensity to save equals the slope of the saving function—just as the marginal propensity to consume is the slope of the consumption function. As pointed out above, the slope of a line equals the vertical distance between

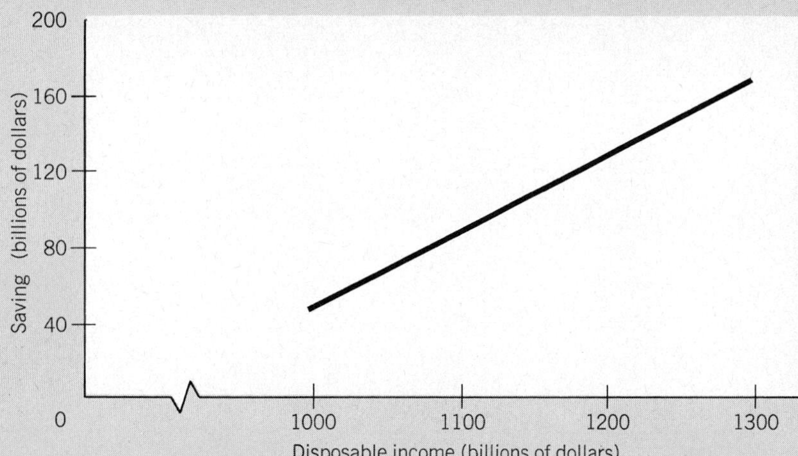

Figure 9.4
The Saving Function

The saving function describes the total amount of saving at each level of disposable income.

any two points on the line divided by the horizontal distance between them.

Determinants of Investment

Next, consider the factors determining the level of net investment. As you recall from the previous chapter, investment consists largely of the amount firms spend on new buildings and factories, new equipment, and increases in inventories. Net investment equals gross investment less depreciation. A host of factors influence the level of net investment. First, there is the ***rate of technological change.*** When new products are developed, firms often must invest in new plant and equipment in order to produce them. For example, Du Pont, after successfully developing nylon in 1938, had to invest millions of dollars in new plant and equipment to produce it. Moreover, the invention of new processes, as well as products, makes it profitable for firms to invest in new plant and equipment. For example, after the invention of the continuous wide strip mill by Armco in the 1920s, American steel producers invested huge sums in new rolling mills to replace the old hand mills.

Second, the level of investment is influenced by *the level of sales and the stock of capital goods needed to produce the output to be sold.* As a firm's sales go up, its need for plant, equipment, and inventories clearly goes up as well. Beyond some point, increases in sales result in pressure on the capacity of existing plant and equipment, so that the firm finds it profitable to invest in additional plant and equipment. Clearly, the crucial relationship is between a firm's sales and its stock of capital goods—that is, its stock of plant, equipment, and inventories. If its sales are well below the amount it can produce with its stock of capital goods, there is little pressure on the firm to invest in additional capital goods. But if its sales are at the upper limit of what can be produced with its capital goods, the firm is likely to view the purchase of additional capital goods as profitable.

Third, the level of investment is influenced heavily by the *expectations of businessmen.* If businessmen believe that their sales are about to drop, they will be unlikely to invest much in additional capital goods. On the other hand, if they believe that their sales are about to increase greatly, they may be led to invest heavily in capital goods. Firms must make investment decisions on the basis of forecasts. There is no way any firm can tell exactly what the future will bring, and the investment decisions it makes will be influenced by how optimistic or pessimistic its forecasts are. This in turn will depend on existing business conditions, as well as on many other factors. Sometimes government actions and political developments have an important impact on business expectations. Sometimes unexpected changes in the fortune of one industry have a major effect on expectations in other industries.

Fourth, the level of investment is affected by the ***rate of interest,*** the price an investor must pay for the use of money. Since the cost of an investment is bound to increase with increases in the rate of interest, a given investment will be less profitable when the interest rate is high than when it is low. For example, a firm may find it profitable to invest in a new machine if it can borrow the money needed to purchase the machine at 8 percent interest per year, but it may not find it profitable if the interest rate is 15 percent.

In most of the rest of this chapter, we shall assume that the total amount of desired investment is independent of the level of net national product. This, of course, is only a rough simplification, since, as we noted above, the amount firms invest will be affected by the level of output in the economy. But this simplification is very convenient and not too unrealistic. Moreover, as we shall show at the end of this chapter, it is relatively easy to extend the model to eliminate this assumption.

The Determination of the Equilibrium Level of National Output

We are now ready to show how net national product is determined. At the outset, however, we must make several assumptions. First, we assume that there are no government expenditures and that the economy is closed (no exports or imports). Thus *total spending on final output—that is, net national product—in this simple case equals consumption expenditure plus net investment.* Needless to say, in subsequent chapters we shall relax the assumptions that there are no government expenditures and that the economy is closed. Second, we assume that there are no taxes and no government transfer payments (and no undistributed corporate profits). Thus, *net national product equals disposable income in this simple case.* In subsequent chapters, we shall also relax this assumption.

Under these assumptions, suppose that firms decide that they want to invest $90 billion (net of depreciation) next year regardless of the level of net national product. Suppose too that the consumption function is as shown in Table 9.1. What will be the equilibrium level of net national product—the level of net national product that eventually will be attained, allowing some time for the basic forces to work themselves out? To answer this question, let's construct a table showing the amount consumers and firms desire to spend at various levels of NNP. Since NNP equals disposable income in this simple case, the consumption function in Table 9.1 shows the level of desired consumption expenditure at each level of NNP. These data are shown in columns 1 and 2 of Table 9.2. The level of desired saving at each level of NNP, which can be derived by subtracting desired consumption expenditures from NNP in this simple case, is shown in column 3. Desired investment expenditure is shown in column 4, while total desired spending, which equals desired consumption expenditure plus desired investment, is shown in column 5.

The equilibrium level of net national product will be at the point where desired spending on NNP equals NNP: no other level of NNP can be maintained for any considerable period of time. Let's see why this very important statement is true.

The easiest way to show this is to show that, if desired spending on NNP is *not* equal to NNP,

Table 9.2

Determination of Equilibrium Level of Net National Product

(1) Net national product (= disposable income)	(2) Desired consumption expenditure	(3) Desired saving	(4) Desired investment	(5) Total desired spending (2) + (4)	(6) Tendency of national output
1,000	950	50	90	1,040	Upward
1,050	980	70	90	1,070	Upward
1,100	1,010	90	90	1,100	No change
1,150	1,040	110	90	1,130	Downward
1,200	1,070	130	90	1,160	Downward
1,250	1,100	150	90	1,190	Downward

NNP is *not* at its equilibrium level. If desired spending on NNP is greater than NNP, what will happen? Since the total amount that will be spent on final goods and services exceeds the total amount of final goods and services produced (the latter being, by definition, NNP), firms' inventories will be reduced. Consequently, firms will increase their output rate to restore their inventories to their normal level and to bring their output into balance with the rate of aggregate demand. Since an increase in the output rate means an increase in NNP, it follows that NNP will tend to increase if desired spending on NNP is greater than NNP —reflecting the fact that NNP is not at its equilibrium level.

On the other hand, what will happen if desired spending on NNP is less than NNP? Since the total amount that will be spent on final goods and services falls short of the total amount of final goods and services produced (the latter being, by definition, NNP), firms' inventories will increase. As inventories pile up unexpectedly, firms will cut back their output to bring it into better balance with aggregate demand. Since a reduction in output means a reduction in NNP, it follows that NNP will tend to fall if desired spending on NNP is less than NNP—reflecting the fact that NNP is not at its equilibrium level.

Thus, if NNP tends to increase when desired spending on NNP is greater than NNP, and if NNP tends to decrease when desired spending on NNP is less than NNP, clearly NNP will be at its equilibrium level only if desired spending on NNP is equal to NNP.

The Process Leading Toward Equilibrium: A Tabular Analysis

In the previous section, we described the general nature of the process leading toward equilibrium. But this process is much clearer if we consider a specific numerical example, such as that contained in Table 9.2. To get a better idea of why NNP tends to the level where desired spending on NNP equals NNP, consider three possible values of NNP—$1,050 billion, $1,100 billion, and $1,150 billion—and see what would happen in our simple economy if these values of NNP prevailed. First, let's consider an NNP of $1,050 billion. What would happen if firms were to produce $1,050 billion of final goods and services? Given our assumptions, disposable income would also equal $1,050 billion (since disposable income equals NNP), so that consumers would spend $980 billion on consumption goods and services. (This follows from the nature of the consumption function: see column 2 of Table 9.2). Since firms want to invest $90 billion, total desired spending would be $1,070 billion ($980 billion + $90 billion, as shown in column 5). But the total amount spent on final goods and services under these circumstances would exceed the total value of final goods and services produced by $20 billion ($1,070 billion – $1,050 billion), so that firms' inventories would be drawn down by $20 billion. Clearly, this situation could not persist very long. As firms become aware that their inventories are becoming depleted, they would step up their production rates, so that the value of output of final goods and services—NNP—would increase.

Second, what would happen if $1,150 billion were the value of NNP—if firms were to produce $1,150 billion of final goods and services? Given our assumptions, disposable income would also equal $1,150 billion (since disposable income equals NNP), with the result that consumers would spend $1,040 billion on consumption goods and services. (This follows from the consumption function: see column 2 of Table 9.2.) Since firms want to invest $90 billion, total spending would be $1,130 billion ($1,040 billion + $90 billion, as shown in column 5). But the total amount spent on final goods and services under these circumstances would fall short of the total value of final goods and services produced by $20 billion ($1,150 billion – $1,130 billion), so that firms' inventories would increase by $20 billion. Clearly, this situation, like the previous one, could not continue very long. When firms see that their inventories are increasing, they reduce their production rates, causing the value of output of final goods and services—NNP—to decrease.

Finally, consider what would happen if NNP were $1,100 billion—if firms were to produce $1,100 billion of final goods and services? Disposable income would also equal $1,100 billion (since disposable income equals NNP), so that consumers would spend $1,010 billion on consumption goods and services. (This follows from the consumption function: see column 2 of Table 9.2.) Since firms want to invest $90 billion, total spending would be $1,100 billion ($1,010 billion + $90 billion, as shown in column 5). Thus, the total amount spent on final goods and services under these circumstances would exactly equal the total value of final goods and services produced. Consequently, there would be no reason for firms to alter their production rates. Thus, this would be an equilibrium situation—a set of circumstances where there is no tendency for NNP to change—and the equilibrium level of NNP in this situation would be $1,100 billion.

These three cases illustrate the process that pushes NNP toward its equilibrium value. So long as NNP is below its equilibrium value, the situation is like that described in our first case. So long as NNP is above its equilibrium value, the situation is like that described in our second case. Whether NNP is below or above its equilibrium value, there is a tendency for production rates to be altered so that NNP moves toward its equilibrium value. Eventually, NNP will reach its equilibrium value, and the situation will be like that described in our third case. The important aspect of the third case—the equilibrium situation—is that, for it to occur, desired spending on NNP must equal NNP. (Of course, the equilibrium value of NNP will change if the consumption function or the level of desired investment changes.)

A Graphical Analysis

Some people see things more clearly when they are presented in graphs rather than tables. Let's show again that the equilibrium level of NNP is at the point where desired spending on NNP equals NNP, but now using a graph. Since disposable income equals net national product in this simple case, we can plot consumption expenditure (on the vertical axis) versus net national product (on the horizontal axis), as shown in Figure 9.5. This is the consumption function. Also, we can plot the sum of consumption expenditures and investment expenditures against NNP, as shown in Figure

Figure 9.5
Determination of Equilibrium Value of Net National Product

The consumption function is C, and the sum of consumption and investment expenditure is $C + I$. The equilibrium value of NNP is at the point where the $C + I$ line intersects the 45-degree line, here \$1,100 billion. The $C + I$ line shows aggregate demand and the 45-degree line shows aggregate supply.

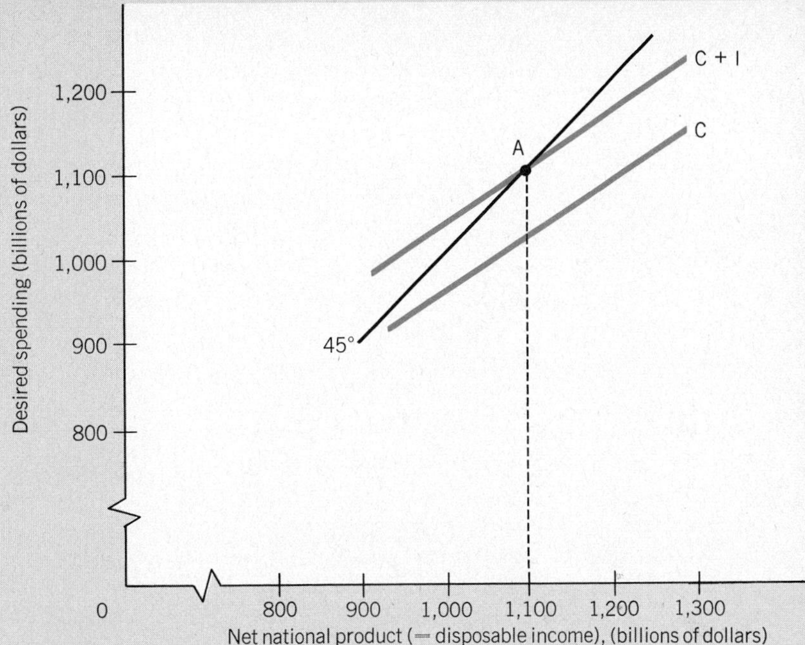

9.5. This relationship, shown by the $C + I$ line, indicates the level of total desired spending on net national product for various amounts of NNP. Finally, we can plot a 45-degree line, as shown in Figure 9.5. This line contains all points where total desired spending on net national product equals net national product.

The equilibrium level of net national product will be at the point where total desired spending on NNP equals NNP. Consequently, the *equilibrium level of NNP will be at the point on the horizontal axis where the $C + I$ line intersects the 45-degree line—\$1,100 billion in Figure 9.5.* Under the conditions assumed here, no other level of NNP can be maintained for any considerable period of time. Let's begin by proving that the point where the $C + I$ line intersects the 45-degree line is indeed the point where desired spending on NNP equals NNP. This is easy, since a 45-degree line is, by construction, a line that includes all points where the amount on the horizontal axis equals the amount on the vertical axis. In this case, desired spending on NNP is on the vertical axis and NNP is on the horizontal axis. Thus, at point A, the point where the $C + I$ line intersects the 45-degree line, desired spending on NNP must equal NNP, because such a point is on the 45-degree line.

Next, let's see why the equilibrium level of NNP must be at \$1,100 billion, the point on the horizontal axis where the $C + I$ line intersects the 45-degree line. If NNP exceeds \$1,100 billion, the $C + I$ line lies below the 45-degree line. Since the $C + I$ line shows how much people desire to spend with a particular level of disposable income, this shows that total desired spending on NNP is less than NNP. Consequently, some production will not be sold, inventories will build up, production will be cut back, and NNP will decrease. If NNP is less than \$1,100 billion, the $C + I$ line lies above the 45-degree line, which shows that total desired spending on NNP is greater than NNP. Consequently, inventories will decrease, production will be stepped up, and NNP will increase. Thus, since NNP tends to fall when it exceeds $1,100 billion, and to rise when it falls short of $1,100 billion, its equilibrium value must be $1,100 billion.

Saving and Investment: Desired and Actual

Another way to describe the conditions under which NNP is at its equilibrium level is to say that *desired saving must equal desired investment.* This is just another way to say that desired spending on NNP must equal NNP. To see this, note that desired spending on NNP equals desired consumption plus desired investment. This is obvious from Figure 9.5, since the desired spending line ($C + I$) equals the desired consumption line (C) + the desired investment line (I). Thus, if we subtract desired consumption from desired spending on NNP, we get desired investment. Next, note that NNP equals desired consumption plus desired saving. This is obvious from the fact, noted in a previous section, that people must save whatever amounts of their income they do not consume. Thus, if we subtract desired consumption from NNP, we get desired saving. Consequently, if desired spending on NNP equals NNP, it follows that desired spending on NNP minus desired consumption must equal NNP minus desired consumption—which means that desired investment must equal desired saving.

From this proposition, it follows that we can find the equilibrium value of NNP by plotting the saving function and finding the value of NNP where desired saving equals desired investment. For example, based on the situation described in Table 9.2, the savings function (SS') is as shown in Figure 9.6. The value of desired investment is $90 billion, which is represented by the horizontal line II'. Clearly, desired saving is equal to desired investment at point B, where NNP is equal to $1,100 billion. Of course, whether we use the sort of analysis shown in Figure 9.5 (based on the equilibrium condition that desired spending on NNP must equal NNP) or the sort shown in Figure 9.6 (based on the equilibrium condition that desired investment must equal desired saving), the answer —the equilibrium level of NNP—must be the

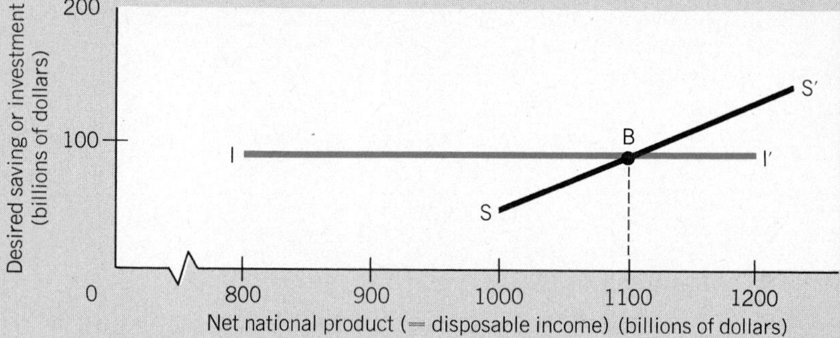

Figure 9.6
Determination of Equilibrium Value of Net National Product

The saving function is SS' and the investment function is II'. The equilibrium value of NNP is at the point where SS' interects II', which here is $1,100 billion.

same (in this case, $1,100 billion).[6]

Why bother to look at the determination of NNP in terms of desired saving and desired investment? After all, as we just stated, we can get the same answer by comparing desired spending on NNP with actual NNP. One important reason for looking at the determination of NNP in terms of desired saving and desired investment is that it helps to lay bare the reasons why equilibrium NNP may be different from the level of NNP that would result in reasonably full employment at reasonably stable prices. As we pointed out in our discussion of the flaws in the classical view of unemployment, these reasons revolve about the fact that desired saving and desired investment are carried out by different parts of society and for different reasons. Households do much of the saving. They abstain from consuming now in order to provide for retirement, college educations for their children, emergencies, and other ways of consuming later. Firms, on the other hand, do most of the investing. They build plants and equipment and expand their inventories in response to profit opportunities. Because of this cleavage between the savers and the investors, there is no assurance that desired saving will equal desired investment at a level of NNP that results in reasonably full employment at reasonably stable prices.

Finally, it must be recognized that, whether or not desired saving equals desired investment, *actual saving must always equal actual investment.* In other words, although the amount people *set out to save* during a particular year may not equal the amount firms *set out to invest,* the *actual amount saved* will always equal the *actual amount invested.* This must be true because, as pointed out in the previous chapter, NNP has to equal consumption plus net investment;[7] and it also has to equal consumption plus saving. Subtracting consumption from each of these expressions for NNP, saving must equal investment. To see why, consider the case where NNP is $1,050 billion. In this case, desired saving is $70 billion but desired investment is $90 billion. How does it turn out that actual saving equals actual investment? As pointed out in the previous section, there is an unintended ***disinvestment*** (i.e., negative investment) of − $20 billion in inventories if NNP is $1,050 billion. (Recall from Chapter 8 that a buildup of inventories is a form of investment, so a $1 billion increase in inventories equals $1 billion of investment.) Thus, the actual investment is $90 billion (in intended investment) minus $20 billion (in unintended disinvestment), or $70 billion. Actual saving equals desired saving, or $70 billion. Thus, actual saving equals actual investment.

To check your understanding, see if you can describe the process whereby actual investment is brought into equality with actual saving in the case where NNP is $1,150 billion. The answer is given below (footnote 8).[8] If you arrived at the right solution, you worked out for yourself one of the important conclusions of national income theory: actual saving must equal actual investment even though desired saving does not equal desired investment.

[6] To prove to yourself that this must be the case, note three things. (1) The saving function in Figure 9.6 plots the vertical distance between the 45-degree line and the consumption function in Figure 9.5, since saving here equals NNP less consumption. (2) The investment function in Figure 9.6 plots the vertical distance between the $C + I$ line and the consumption function in Figure 9.5, since $C + I$ less C obviously is I. (3) In Figure 9.5, the equilibrium value of NNP is at the point where these two vertical distances are equal, which means it must be at the point where the saving and investment functions intersect.

[7] Recall from Chapter 8 that net national product equals consumption plus government expenditures plus net exports plus net investment. Since government expenditures and net exports are assumed to be zero, it follows that net national product equals consumption plus net investment.

[8] In the case where NNP equals $1,150 billion, desired saving is $110 billion. This is shown in Table 9.2. Desired investment is $90 billion, but there is an unintended increase in inventories of $20 billion. Thus, actual investment turns out to equal $110 billion, which equals actual saving.

Note that we assume here that actual saving will equal desired saving and that unintended changes in inventories will make actual investment conform to actual and desired saving. There are other ways for adjustments to take place. The important thing is that, one way or another, actual saving will equal actual investment.

The Multiplier: A Geometric Formulation

In Chapter 8, we pointed out that investment is a particularly volatile form of expenditure. It is subject to large variations from year to year. For example, in 1955, net private investment was close to \$80 billion, and in 1958, it fell to about \$60 billion. Looking at the highly simplified model we have constructed, what is the effect of a change in the amount of desired investment? Specifically, if firms increase their desired investment by \$1 billion, what effect will this increase have on the equilibrium value of net national product?

Let's begin by noting once again that, if NNP is at its equilibrium level, desired saving must equal desired investment. Then let's apply the sort of graphical analysis that we used in the previous section to determine equilibrium NNP. If the saving function in our simplified economy is *SS′* in Figure 9.7 and desired investment is shown by the horizontal line *II′*, what will be the effect of a \$1 billion increase in desired investment on equilibrium NNP? Before the increase in desired investment, equilibrium NNP was equal to Y_O. The increase of \$1 billion in desired investment will shift the *II′* line up by \$1 billion, to the new position shown in Figure 9.7. This shift in the *II′* line will increase the equilibrium level of NNP, but by how much?

The resulting increase in equilibrium NNP, ΔY, can be derived by the following geometrical reasoning. First, the slope of *SS′* times the change in equilibrium NNP must equal the increase in desired investment, \$1 billion. This follows from the definition of the slope of a line: The slope of *SS′* equals the vertical distance between any two points on *SS′* divided by the horizontal difference between them. The vertical distance between points *A* and *B* in Figure 9.7 is the increase in desired investment (ΔI), and the horizontal distance between points *A* and *B* is the change in equilibrium NNP (ΔY). Consequently, the change in equilibrium NNP must equal the increase in desired investment divided by the slope of *SS′*. Since the slope of *SS′* is the marginal propensity to save—as pointed out in a previous section—it follows that *the change in equilibrium NNP equals the increase in desired investment divided by the marginal propensity to save. Thus, a \$1 billion increase in desired invest-*

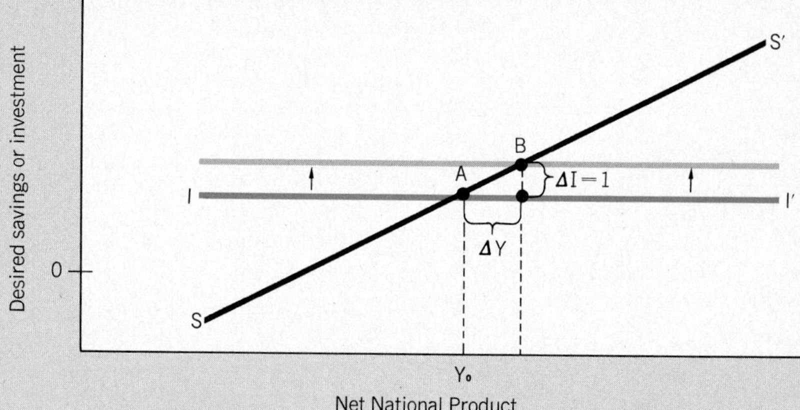

Figure 9.7
The Multiplier

If investment increases by ΔI, the equilibrium value of NNP increases by ΔY. Clearly $\frac{\Delta I}{\Delta Y}$ equals the slope of the saving function between *A* and *B*. Since this slope equals the marginal propensity to save (*MPS*), $\frac{\Delta I}{\Delta Y} = MPS$. Thus, $\Delta Y = \frac{\Delta I}{MPS}$ and if $\Delta I = 1$, $\Delta Y = \frac{1}{MPS}$.

ment will result in an increase in equilibrium NNP of $\left(\frac{1}{MPS}\right)$ *billions of dollars, where MPS is the marginal propensity to save.*

This is a very important conclusion. To understand more clearly what it means, let's consider a couple of numerical examples. For example, if the marginal propensity to save is ⅓, a $1 billion increase in desired investment will increase equilibrium NNP by 1 ÷ ⅓ billion dollars; that is, by $3 billion. Or take a somewhat more complicated case. If the consumption function is as shown in Table 9.1, what is the effect of an increase in desired investment from $90 billion to $91 billion? The first step in answering this question is to determine the marginal propensity to consume—which is 0.60 in Table 9.1. Then it is a simple matter to determine the marginal propensity to save—which must be 1 – 0.60 or 0.40. Finally, since the marginal propensity to save is 0.40, it follows from the previous paragraph that a $1 billion increase in desired investment must result in an increase in equilibrium NNP of $\frac{1}{0.40}$ billion dollars. That is, equilibrium NNP will increase by $2½ billion.

Since a dollar of extra desired investment results in $\left(\frac{1}{MPS}\right)$ dollars of extra NNP, $\left(\frac{1}{MPS}\right)$ is called the ***multiplier.*** If you want to estimate the effect of a given increase in desired investment on NNP, all you have to do is multiply the increase in desired investment by $\left(\frac{1}{MPS}\right)$: the result will be the resulting increase in NNP. Moreover, it is easy to show that the same multiplier holds for decreases in desired investment as well as for increases. That is, a dollar less of desired investment results in $\left(\frac{1}{MPS}\right)$ dollars less of NNP. Consequently, if you want to estimate the effect of a given change in desired investment (positive or negative) on NNP, all you have to do is multiply the change in desired investment by $\left(\frac{1}{MPS}\right)$.

It is important to note that, since *MPS* is less than one, the *multiplier must be greater than one.* In other words, an increase in desired investment of $1 will result in an increase in NNP of more than $1. This means, of course, that NNP is relatively sensitive to changes in desired investment. Moreover, since the multiplier is the reciprocal of the marginal propensity to save, the smaller the marginal propensity to save, the higher the multiplier—and the more sensitive is NNP to changes in desired investment. As we shall see, this result has important implications for public policy. For example, because our system of taxes and transfer payments tends to increase the marginal propensity to save out of NNP, the destabilizing effect of a sharp change in investment expenditures is reduced.

The Multiplier: An Algebraic Interpretation[9]

Equations speak more clearly to some than words, and so for those with a taste for (elementary) algebra, we will show how the results of the previous section can be derived algebraically. If you have trouble with equations, or if you feel that you already understand the material, go on to the next section. We begin by recalling that the equilibrium value of NNP is attained at the point where NNP equals desired spending on NNP. This condition can be expressed in the following equation:

$$NNP = C + I, \tag{9.1}$$

which says that NNP must equal desired expenditure on consumption goods (C) plus desired investment (I). Since desired consumption expenditures plus desired investment equals desired spending on NNP, it follows that this equation states that NNP must equal desired spending on NNP.

Next, let's introduce a friend from a few pages back, the consumption function. The consumption function in Table 9.1 can be represented by the

[9] This section is optional and can be omitted without loss of continuity.

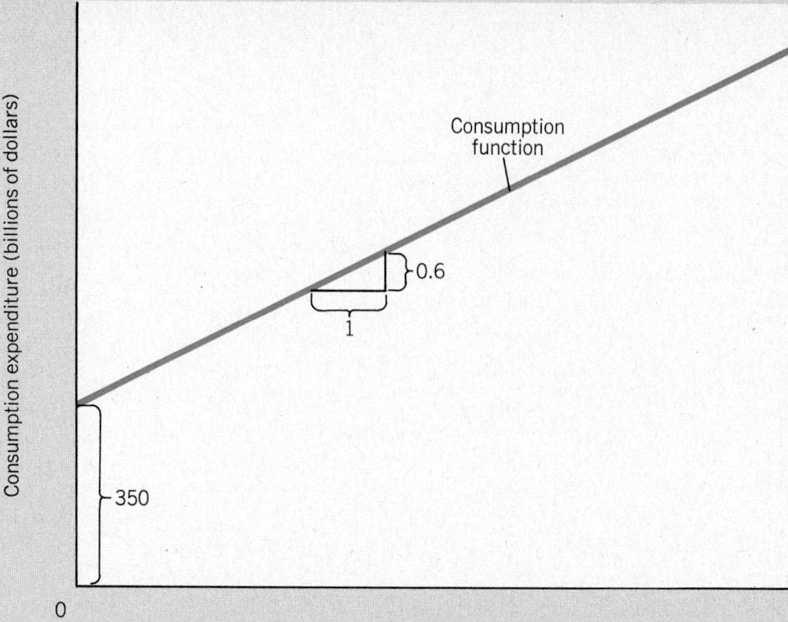

Figure 9.8
Consumption Function

The consumption function is derived from the data in Table 9.1. The marginal propensity to consume is 0.6, so the slope is 0.6.

following equation:

$$C = 350 + 0.6D \tag{9.2}$$

which says that desired consumption equals \$350 billion plus 0.6 times disposable income (D). Figure 9.8 shows the consumption function. As you can see, \$350 billion is the intercept on the vertical axis, while 0.6 is the slope of the consumption function. Since—as we noted in a previous section—the slope of the consumption function equals the marginal propensity to consume, 0.6 equals the marginal propensity to consume.

The next step is to substitute the right-hand side of equation (9.2)—$350 + .6D$—for C in Equation (9.1). The result is:

$$NNP = 350 + 0.6D + I. \tag{9.3}$$

But recall that disposable income is equal to NNP in our simplified economy. Consequently, we can substitute NNP for D in this equation, to get

$$NNP = 350 + 0.6NNP + I. \tag{9.4}$$

And going a step further, we can subtract 0.6 times NNP from both sides of Equation (9.4), which gives

$$NNP - 0.6NNP = 350 + I, \tag{9.5}$$

or, collecting terms,

$$0.4NNP = 350 + I. \tag{9.6}$$

Finally, dividing both sides by 0.4, we have

$$NNP = \frac{350}{0.4} + \frac{I}{0.4}. \tag{9.7}$$

Now we can see what happens to NNP if there is a \$1 billion increase in I. In other words, suppose that I is increased from some amount, \$$X$ billion, to $(X + 1) billion. How much will this increase NNP? From Equation (9.7), it is clear that NNP will equal

$$\frac{350}{0.4} + \frac{X}{0.4}$$

if desired investment equals $X billion. It is also clear from Equation (9.7) that NNP will equal

$$\frac{350}{0.4} + \frac{(X + 1)}{0.4}$$

if desired investment is equal to $(X + 1) billion. Consequently the increase in NNP due to the $1 billion increase in desired investment is equal to

$$\left[\frac{350}{0.4} + \frac{(X + 1)}{0.4}\right] - \left[\frac{350}{0.4} + \frac{X}{0.4}\right]$$
$$= \frac{X + 1}{0.4} - \frac{X}{0.4} = \frac{X}{0.4} + \frac{1}{0.4} - \frac{X}{0.4} = \frac{1}{0.4}$$

That is, a $1 billion increase in desired investment will result in an increase of $\frac{1}{0.4}$ billion dollars in NNP. Recalling that 0.6 is the marginal propensity to consume—and that the sum of the marginal propensity to consume and the marginal propensity to save equals one—it follows that *a $1 billion increase in desired investment will result in an increase of* $\left(\frac{1}{MPS}\right)$ *billions of dollars in NNP, where MPS is the marginal propensity to save—0.4 in this case.*

This is precisely the same conclusion we arrived at in the previous section. Thus, we have derived the value of the multiplier by an algebraic route rather than the geometric route used before.

The Multiplier and the Spending Process

Having shown in two ways that the multiplier equals $\frac{1}{MPS}$, we are in danger of beating a dead horse to death if we show it in still a third way. However, we don't yet have much feel for the process that results in the multiplier's being what it is. In other words, leaving the realm of graphs and equations, what process in the real world insures that a $1 billion change in desired investment results in a change of $\left(\frac{1}{MPS}\right)$ billions of dollars in equilibrium NNP? It is worthwhile spelling this out in some detail.

If there is a $1 billion increase in desired investment, the effects can be divided into a number of stages. In the first stage, firms spend an additional $1 billion on plant and equipment. This extra $1 billion is received by workers and suppliers as extra income, which results in a second stage of extra spending on final goods and services. How much of their extra $1 billion in income will the workers and suppliers spend? If the marginal propensity to consume is 0.6, they will spend 0.6 times $1 billion, or $.6 billion. This extra expenditure of $.6 billion is received by firms and disbursed to workers, suppliers, and owners as extra income, bringing about a third stage of extra spending on final goods and services. How much of this extra income of $.6 billion will be spent? Since the marginal propensity to consume is 0.6, they will spend 60 percent of this $.6 billion, or $.36 billion. This extra expenditure of $.36 billion is received by firms and disbursed to workers, suppliers, and owners as extra income, which results in a fourth stage of spending, then a fifth stage, a sixth stage, and so on.

Table 9.3 shows the total increase in expenditure on final goods and services arising from the original $1 billion increase in desired investment. The total increase in expenditures is the increase in the first stage, plus the increase in the second stage, plus the increase in the third stage, etc. Since there is an endless chain of stages, we cannot list all the increases. But because the successive increases in spending get smaller and smaller, we can determine their sum, which in this case is $2.5 billion. Thus, the $1 billion increase in desired investment results—after all stages of the spending

Table 9.3

The Multiplier Process

Stage	Amount of extra spending
1	\$1.00 billion
2	.60 billion
3	.36 billion
4	.22 billion
5	.13 billion
6	.08 billion
7	.05 billion
8	.03 billion
9 and beyond	.03 billion
Total	\$2.50 billion

and re-spending process have worked themselves out—in a \$2.5 billion increase in total expenditures on final goods and services. In other words, it results in a \$2.5 billion increase in NNP.

It is important to note that this spending and re-spending process results in the same multiplier as indicated in previous sections. This happens because, if 0.6 is the marginal propensity to consume, a \$1 billion increase in desired investment will result in increased total spending of $(1 + .6 + .6^2 + .6^3 + \ldots)$ billions of dollars. This is evident from Table 9.3, which shows that the increased spending in the first stage is \$1 billion, the increased spending in the second stage is \$.6 billion, the increased spending in the third stage is $\$.6^2$ billion, and so on. But it can be shown that $(1 + .6 + .6^2 + .6^3 + \ldots) = \frac{1}{1 - .6}$.[10] Consequently, since $(1 - .6)$ is equal to the marginal propensity to save, a \$1 billion increase in desired investment results in an increase of $\left(\frac{1}{MPS}\right)$ billions of dollars in NNP. Thus, however we look at it, the answer remains the same: the multiplier equals $\left(\frac{1}{MPS}\right)$.

Application of the Multiplier: A Case Study[11]

Having discussed the modern theory of the determination of NNP in the abstract, it is time to look at a specific application of this theory. Consider a famous incident that occurred at the end of World War II. Economists, using the best models then available, had been able to forecast the pace of the economy reasonably well during the war. When the war was coming to an end, they were charged with forecasting the level of national product in 1946, the year immediately after the war. This was an important task, since the government was worried that the economy might suffer severe postwar unemployment. The Great Depression of the 1930s was a recent—and still bitter—memory.

A group of economists in Washington was given the responsibility for this forecast. They made it in terms of gross national product, not net national product, but they used essentially the same theory as that discussed in previous sections. To forecast

[11] This account is based on Michael Sapir, "Review of Economic Forecasts for the Transition Period," *Conference on Research in Income and Wealth,* Volume XI, National Bureau of Economic Research, 1949; and Lawrence Klein, "A Post-Mortem on Transition Predictions of National Product," *Journal of Political Economy,* August 1946.

[10] To see this, let's divide 1 by $(1 - m)$, where m is less than 1. Using the time-honored rules of long division, we find that

$$
\begin{array}{r|l}
 & 1 + m + m^2 + m^3 + \cdots \\
1 - m & 1 \\
 & 1 - m \\
 & \quad m \\
 & \quad m - m^2 \\
 & \qquad m^2 \\
 & \qquad m^2 - m^3 \\
 & \qquad\quad m^3 \\
 & \qquad\quad m^3 - m^4 \\
 & \qquad\qquad m^4 \\
 & \qquad\qquad \vdots
\end{array}
$$

Thus, letting $m = 0.6$, it follows that 1 divided by $(1 - .6)$ equals $1 + .6 + .6^2 + .6^3 + \ldots$

gross national product in 1946, these Washington economists began by using prewar data to estimate the consumption function. Then they estimated the amount of investment that would take place in 1946. Finally, to forecast gross national product in 1946, they performed the sort of calculations shown in Equation (9.7). In other words, they computed the multiplier $\left(\frac{1}{MPS}\right)$ and multiplied it by their estimate of investment for 1946. Then they added an amount analogous to the first term on the right-hand side of Equation (9.7); and since their model—unlike ours—included government spending and taxes, other calculations, which will be discussed in Chapter 10, had to be made as well. The result was a forecast of a gross national product in 1946 of about $170 billion. This forecast received considerable attention and publicity inside and outside the government.

Before discussing the accuracy of this forecast, an important empirical question must be considered: in real-world studies like this, what is the estimated value of the multiplier? Judging from our findings in the previous sections, we would guess a figure of at least 2½, since the marginal propensity to consume should be at least 0.6. But these results are based on the assumption of no taxation. For reasons discussed in Chapter 10, the multiplier will be lower if there is taxation. Including the effects of taxation, most estimates of the multiplier seem to center around a value of 2. But these estimates can vary considerably, depending, of course, on the shape of the consumption function and other factors.

Multiplier Effects of Shifts in the Consumption Function

Before discussing the accuracy of this forecast, we must also look at the effects of shifts in the consumption function. So far, we have been concerned only with the effects of changes in desired investment on NNP. We have shown—repeatedly and in various ways—that changes in desired investment have an amplified effect on NNP, the extent of the amplification being measured by the multiplier. But it is important to note at this point that a shift in the consumption function will also have such an amplified effect on NNP. For example, in Figure 9.9, if the consumption function shifts from CC' to $\phi\phi'$, this means that, at each level of disposable income, consumers desire to spend $1 billion more on consumption goods and services than they did before. It is easy to show that *this $1 billion upward shift in the consumption function will have precisely the same effect on equilibrium NNP as a $1 billion increase in desired investment.*

For those of more mathematical bent, it may be worthwhile to prove that this is the case. Others can skip this paragraph without loss of continuity. Let's recall that in Equation (9.7), we showed that the equilibrium value of NNP equals

$$\frac{350}{0.4} + \frac{I}{0.4},$$

where 350 is the intercept on the vertical axis of the consumption function, 0.4 is the marginal propensity to save, and I is desired investment. A $1 billion shift upward in the consumption function causes the intercept to increase from its former amount, $350 billion, to $351 billion. What is the effect of this increase in the intercept on the equilibrium value of NNP? If the intercept is $350 billion, the equilibrium value of NNP will equal

$$\frac{350}{0.4} + \frac{I}{0.4}.$$

If the intercept is $351 billion, the equilibrium value of NNP will equal

$$\frac{351}{0.4} + \frac{I}{0.4}.$$

Consequently, the increase in NNP from the $1 billion upward shift in the consumption function is

Figure 9.9
Shift in the Consumption Function

If the consumption function shifts from CC' to $\phi\phi'$ this means that, at each level of disposable income, consumers desire to spend \$1 billion more on consumption goods and services. Such a *shift* is quite different from a *movement along* a given consumption function, such as from A to B.

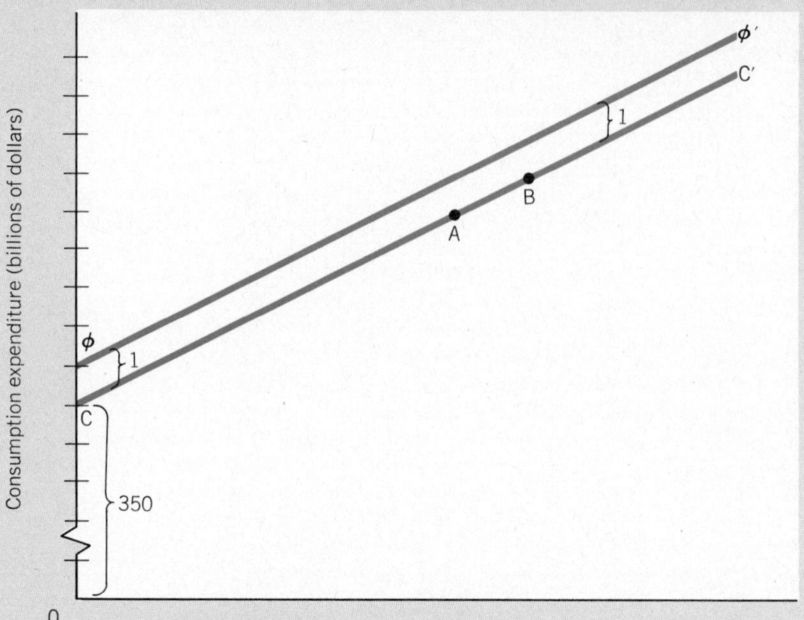

$$\left[\frac{351}{0.4} + \frac{I}{0.4}\right] - \left[\frac{350}{0.4} + \frac{I}{0.4}\right] = \frac{351}{0.4} - \frac{350}{0.4} = \frac{1}{0.4}.$$

That is, a \$1 billion upward shift in the consumption function results in an increase of $\frac{1}{0.4}$ billions of dollars in NNP. Recalling that 0.4 = MPS, it follows that *a \$1 billion upward shift in the consumption function will result in an increase of* $\left(\frac{1}{MPS}\right)$ *billions of dollars in NNP.*

Since a \$1 billion increase in desired investment also results in an increase of $\left(\frac{1}{MPS}\right)$ billions of dollars in NNP, the effect of a \$1 billion change in desired investment is the same as a \$1 billion shift in the consumption function. Both have the same multiplier effects. Thus, shifts in the consumption function—from changes in tastes, assets, prices, population, etc.—will have a magnified effect on NNP. In other words, NNP is sensitive to shifts in the consumption function in the same way that it is sensitive to changes in desired investment. This is an important point. Finally, to prevent misunderstanding, it must be clear that a *shift* in the consumption function is quite different from a *movement along* a given consumption function. (An example of the latter would be the movement from point A to point B in Figure 9.9.) We are concerned here with shifts in the consumption function, not movements along a given consumption function.

The Accuracy of the Postwar Forecasts

We can now pick up the account of the GNP forecasts in 1946 where we left off several paragraphs back. The government forecasters' estimate of a GNP of about \$170 billion caused a severe chill in many parts of the government, as well as among businessmen and consumers. A GNP of only about $170 billion would have meant a great deal of unemployment in 1946. Indeed, according to some predictions, about 8 million people would have been unemployed in the first quarter of 1946.

Unfortunately for the forecasters—but fortunately for the nation—the GNP in 1946 turned out to be not $170 billion, but about $190 billion. And unemployment was only about ⅓ of the forecasted amount. These are very large errors in practically anyone's book—so big that they continue to embarrass the economics profession 30 years later. Of course, our knowledge of the economy has expanded considerably over the past 30 years, and an error of this magnitude is much less likely now. Moreover, even at the end of World War II, some economists forecasted GNP in 1946 pretty well. Not everyone, by any means, agreed with the forecast of $170 billion. But it is worth bearing this notable mistake in mind when considering economic forecasts of this sort. Economics is not as exact a science as physics or chemistry—and mischief can result if one assumes otherwise.

What went wrong in the Washington economists' forecasts? To a considerable extent, the answer lies in the topic of the previous section: a shift in the consumption function. When World War II ended, households had a great deal of liquid assets on hand. They had saved money during the war. There had been rationing of many kinds of goods, and other goods—like automobiles or refrigerators—could not be obtained at all. When the war ended and these goods flowed back on the market, consumers spent more of their income on consumption goods than in the previous years. In other words, there was a pronounced upward shift of the consumption function.

To see why this shift in the consumption function caused the forecasters to underestimate GNP in 1946, recall from the previous section that an upward shift of $1 billion in the consumption function will result in an increase of $\left(\frac{1}{MPS}\right)$ billions of dollars in national product. Bearing this in mind, suppose the forecasters assumed that the consumption function remained fixed, when in fact there was a $8 billion shift upward. Then if the multiplier—$\frac{1}{MPS}$—were 2½, national product would turn out to be $20 billion higher than the forecasters would expect. (Since $\frac{1}{MPS}$ is assumed to be 2½, national product will increase $2.5 billion for every $1 billion shift in the consumption function, so an $8 billion shift in the consumption function will result in a $20 billion increase in national product.) Of course, these figures—a multiplier of 2½ and an $8 billion shift in the consumption function—are only illustrative, not precise estimates of the actual situation. For one thing, as noted above, the multiplier is wrong because it assumes no taxation. But they indicate the sort of thing that occurred, and they show dramatically the effects of a shift in the consumption function.

Induced Investment

Before concluding this chapter, one final point is worth noting. In previous sections, we have assumed that desired net investment is a certain amount, regardless of the level of NNP. This assumption has been reflected in the fact that the investment function—for example, in Figures 9.6 and 9.7—is horizontal. Although this assumption may be a useful first approximation, it neglects the fact that firms are much more likely to invest in plant and equipment when NNP is high than when it is low. After all, NNP measures output; and the greater the output of the economy, the greater the pressure on the capacity of existing plant and equipment—and the greater the pressure to expand this capacity by investing in additional plant and equipment.

It is relatively simple to extend the theory to take account of the fact that, to some extent, increases in NNP may increase desired investment. Rather than portraying the investment function

Figure 9.10
Determination of Equilibrium Value of Net National Product, with Induced Investment

If the level of investment depends on NNP, the investment function, *II′*, is positively sloped, and the equilibrium level of NNP is at the point where *II′* intersects *SS′*, the saving function.

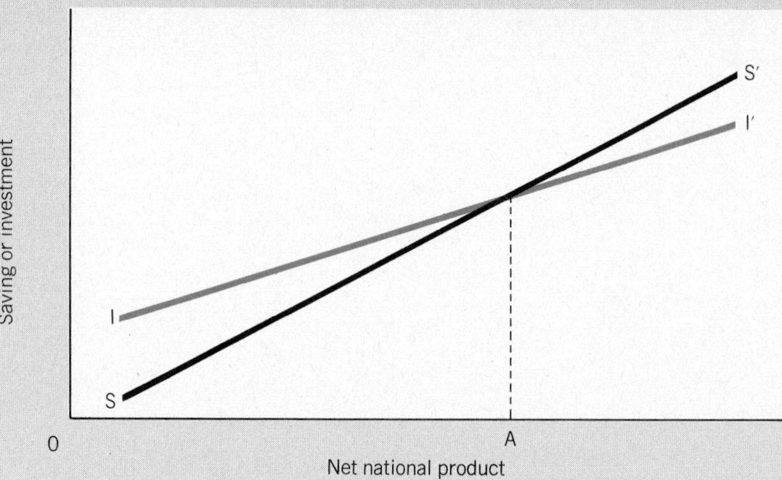

as a horizontal line, we need only assume that it is positively sloped, as in Figure 9.10. Then, as before, the equilibrium level of NNP is at the point where the saving function intersects the investment function—that is, at point A, the point where desired saving equals desired investment. Much more will be said about *induced investment* —investment stimulated by increases in NNP— in Chapter 11.

Summary

Until the 1930s, most economists were convinced that the price system, left to its own devices, would insure the maintenance of full employment. They thought it unlikely that total spending would be too small to purchase the full-employment level of output, and argued that prices would be cut if any problem of this sort developed. A notable exception was Karl Marx, who felt that the capitalistic system would suffer from worse and worse unemployment, leading to its eventual collapse. John Maynard Keynes, in the 1930s, developed a theory to explain how the capitalist economic system remained mired in the Great Depression, with its tragically high levels of unemployment. Contrary to the classical economists, Keynes concluded that there was no automatic mechanism in a capitalistic system to generate and maintain full employment— or, at least, to generate it quickly enough to be relied on in practice. Keynes's ideas form the core of the modern theory of output and employment.

The consumption function—the relation between consumption expenditures and disposable income— is at the heart of this theory. There have been many studies of the consumption function, some based on cross-section data, some based on time-series data. From the consumption function, one can determine the marginal propensity to consume, which is the proportion of an extra dollar of income that is spent on consumption, as well as the saving function (the relationship between total saving and disposable income) and the marginal propensity to save (the proportion of an extra dollar of income that is saved).

The equilibrium level of net national product will be at the point where desired spending on NNP equals NNP. If desired spending on NNP exceeds NNP, NNP will tend to increase. If desired spending on NNP falls short of NNP, NNP will tend to fall. Another way to describe this equilibrium condition is to say that NNP is at its equilibrium level if desired saving equals desired investment. Because of the cleavage between savers and investors, there is no assurance that desired saving will equal desired investment at a level of NNP that results in reasonably full employment at stable prices. But actual saving and actual investment always must turn out to be equal.

A \$1 billion change in desired investment will result in a change in equilibrium NNP of $\left(\frac{1}{MPS}\right)$ billions of dollars, where MPS is the marginal propensity to save. In other words, the multiplier is $\frac{1}{MPS}$. The multiplier can be interpreted in terms of—and derived from—the successive stages of the spending process. An example of the use of the multiplier was the formulation at the end of World War II of GNP forecasts for 1946. A shift in the consumption function will also have an amplified effect on NNP, a \$1 billion shift in the consumption function resulting in a change of $\left(\frac{1}{MPS}\right)$ billions of dollars in NNP. To a considerable extent, the large error in government forecasts of GNP in 1946 was due to an unanticipated shift in the consumption function. Responding to large accumulated wartime savings and pent-up wartime demands, consumers spent more of their income on consumption goods than in previous years.

CONCEPTS FOR REVIEW

Consumption function
Marginal propensity to consume
Average propensity to consume
Saving function
Marginal propensity to save
Multiplier
Induced investment
Shifts in the consumption function
Investment function
45-degree line

QUESTIONS FOR DISCUSSION AND REVIEW

1. Describe in detail the mechanisms that push NNP toward its equilibrium value. Must the equilibrium value be such that full employment results? Why or why not?

2. What assumptions are made in this chapter concerning the economy's position on the aggregate supply curve? Explain the significance of these assumptions.

3. Assume that the consumption function is as follows:

Disposable Income (billions of dollars)	Consumption Expenditure (billions of dollars)
900	750
1,000	800
1,100	850
1,200	900
1,300	950
1,400	1,000

a. How much will be saved if disposable income is $1,000 billion?
b. What is the average propensity to consume if disposable income is $1,000 billion?
c. What is the marginal propensity to consume if disposable income is between $1,000 billion and $1,100 billion?
d. What is the marginal propensity to save if disposable income is between $1,000 billion and $1,100 billion?

4. Including the effects of taxation, most estimates of the multiplier are around 5. True or False?

CHAPTER 10

Fiscal Policy and National Output

During the past 40 years, the idea that the government's power to spend and tax should be used to stabilize the economy—that is, to reduce unemployment and fight inflation—has gained acceptance throughout the world. In many countries, including the United States, this acceptance was delayed by a fear of government deficits and of increases in the public debt, but with the passage of time these fears have receded or been put in proper perspective. However, time has also revealed that fiscal policy is no panacea. Witness the severe inflationary pressures that have plagued the American economy in recent years. Both the power and the limitations of fiscal policy must be recognized.

This chapter presents a first look at fiscal policy, in the context of the simplest Keynesian model. In effect, we assume here that the money supply is fixed, and that the interest rate is not affected by changes in total desired spending (or that, if it is affected, it has little effect on total desired spending). In Chapter 15, a more sophisticated analysis of fiscal policy is presented, money and financial assets being included in the model.

Government Expenditures and Net National Product

In the previous chapter, we showed how the equilibrium level of net national product was determined in a simplified economy without government spending or taxation. We must now extend this theory to include government spending and taxation, an important extension in view of the large amounts of government spending and taxes in the modern economy. As we shall see, the results form the basis for much of our nation's past and present economic policy. In this section, we incorporate government spending into the theory of the determination of net national product. In so doing, we assume that government spending will not affect the consumption function or the level of desired investment. In other words, we assume that government spending does not reduce or increase private desires to spend out of each level of income. (Government includes here federal, state, and local.)

Suppose that the government purchases \$50 billion worth of goods and services and that it will purchase this amount whatever the level of NNP. (Note that only government purchases, not transfer payments, are included here.) Clearly, adding this public expenditure to the private expenditures on consumption and investment results in a higher total level of desired spending. In an economy with government spending (but no net exports), total desired spending on NNP equals desired consumption expenditure plus desired in-

Figure 10.1 Determination of Net National Product, Including Government Expenditure

The consumption function is C, the sum of consumption and investment expenditures is $C + I$, and the sum of consumption, investment, and government expenditures is $C + I + G$. The equilibrium value of NNP is at the point where the $C + I + G$ line intersects the 45-degree line, which here is \$1,225 billion. The $C + I + G$ line shows aggregate demand, and the 45-degree line shows aggregate supply.

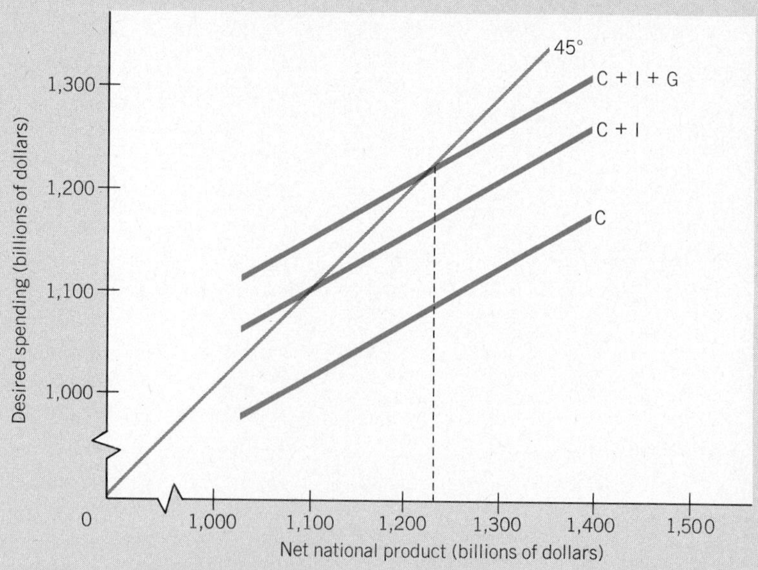

Figure 10.2
Effects on Equilibrium Net National Product of $5 Billion Increase and Decrease in Government Expenditure

A $5 billion increase raises the equilibrium value of NNP from $1,225 billion to $1,237.5 billion. A $5 billion decrease reduces the equilibrium value of NNP from $1,225 billion to $1,212.5 billion.

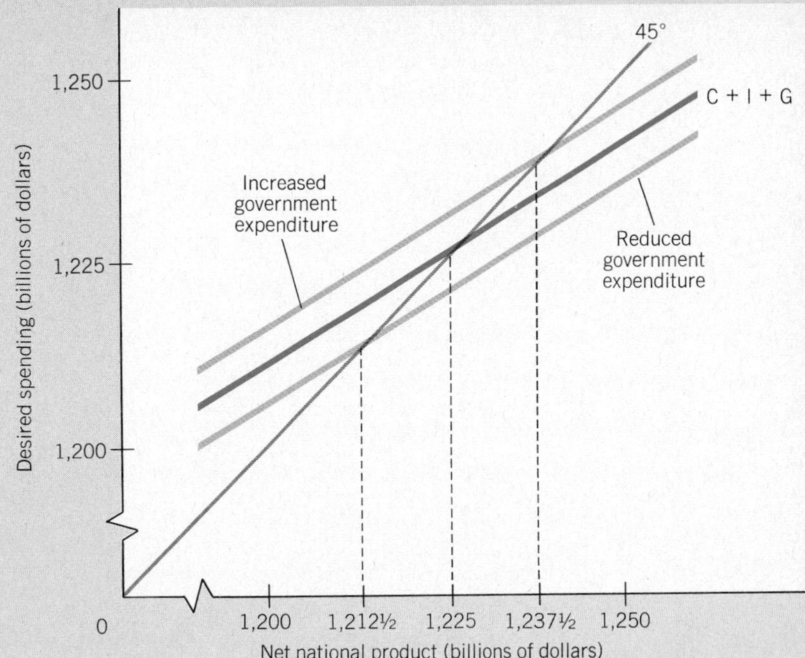

vestment expenditure plus desired government expenditure. Thus, since an increase in government expenditure (like increases in consumption or investment expenditure) results in an increase in desired spending on NNP, and since the equilibrium value of net national product is at the point where desired spending on NNP equals NNP, it follows that an increase in government expenditure, as well as the induced increase in private spending, brings about an increase in the equilibrium value of NNP.

To see the effects of government expenditure on the equilibrium value of NNP, we can use a simple graph similar to those introduced in the previous chapter. We begin by plotting the consumption function, which shows desired consumption expenditure at each level of NNP (since NNP equals disposable income under our assumptions): the result is line C in Figure 10.1. Then, as in Figure 9.5, we can plot the sum of desired consumption expenditure and investment expenditure at each level of NNP: the result is line $C + I$. Next, we plot the sum of desired consumption expenditure, investment expenditure, and government expenditure at each level of NNP, to get line $C + I + G$. Since the $C + I + G$ line shows total desired spending on NNP, and since, as we stressed in the previous chapter, the equilibrium value of NNP is at the point where desired spending on NNP equals NNP, it follows that the equilibrium value of NNP is $1,225 billion, since this is the point at which the $C + I + G$ line intersects the 45-degree line.

What happens to the equilibrium level of NNP if government expenditure increases? Figure 10.2 shows the results of a $5 billion increase in government spending. Obviously, the increased government expenditure will raise the $C + I + G$ line by $5 billion, as the figure shows. Since the $C + I + G$ line must intersect the 45-degree line at a higher level of NNP, increases in government expenditure result in increases in the equilibrium level of NNP. In Figure 10.2, the \$5 billion increase in government expenditure raises the equilibrium value of NNP from \$1,225 billion to \$1,237.5 billion. Figure 10.2 also shows what happens when government spending goes down by \$5 billion. Obviously, the $C + I + G$ line must be lowered by \$5 billion. Since the $C + I + G$ line must intersect the 45-degree line at a lower level of NNP, decreases in government expenditure result in decreases in the equilibrium level of NNP. In Figure 10.2, the \$5 billion decrease in government expenditure reduces the equilibrium value of NNP from \$1,225 billion to \$1,212.5 billion.

It is essential to learn how sensitive the equilibrium level of NNP is to changes in government spending. In the previous chapter, we found that a \$1 billion change in desired investment—or a \$1 billion shift in the consumption function—results in a change in equilibrium NNP of $\left(\frac{1}{MPS}\right)$ billions of dollars, where MPS is the marginal propensity to save. The effect of a \$1 billion change in government expenditure is exactly the same. In other words, *it will result in a change in equilibrium NNP of* $\left(\frac{1}{MPS}\right)$ *billion dollars.* Thus, *a change in government expenditure has the same multiplier effect on NNP as a change in investment or a shift in the consumption function.* For example, if the marginal propensity to consume is 0.6, an extra \$1 billion in government expenditure will increase equilibrium NNP by \$2.5 billion.

The mathematically inclined reader may be interested in proving that a \$1 billion change in government expenditure will result in a change in equilibrium NNP of $\left(\frac{1}{MPS}\right)$ billions of dollars: Others can skip to the next section without loss of continuity. To prove this proposition, recall that the equilibrium value of NNP is at the point where desired spending—$C + I + G$—equals NNP. Thus,

$$NNP = C + I + G. \tag{10.1}$$

Assuming that the consumption function is as given in Table 9.1, it follows that

$$C = 350 + 0.6\ NNP \tag{10.2}$$

where 0.6 is the marginal propensity to consume.[1] Substituting the right-hand side of Equation (10.2) for C in Equation (10.1), we have

$$NNP = 350 + 0.6\ NNP + I + G \tag{10.3}$$

Thus,

$$(1 - 0.6)\ NNP = 350 + I + G$$

$$NNP = \frac{350}{0.4} + \frac{I}{0.4} + \frac{G}{0.4}. \tag{10.4}$$

What happens to NNP when G increases from \$$X$ billion to \$$(X + 1)$ billion? How much will this increase the equilibrium value of NNP? From Equation (10.4), it is clear that equilibrium NNP will be

$$\frac{350}{0.4} + \frac{I}{0.4} + \frac{X}{0.4}$$

if government expenditure equals \$$X$ billion. And it is equally clear from Equation (10.4) that NNP will equal

$$\frac{350}{0.4} + \frac{I}{0.4} + \frac{(X + 1)}{0.4}$$

if government expenditure is \$$(X + 1)$ billion. Consequently the increase in NNP due to the \$1 billion increase in government spending is

$$\left[\frac{350}{0.4} + \frac{I}{0.4} + \frac{(X+1)}{0.4}\right] - \left[\frac{350}{0.4} + \frac{I}{0.4} + \frac{X}{0.4}\right],$$

which equals

$$\frac{X+1}{0.4} - \frac{X}{0.4} = \frac{1}{0.4}.$$

That is, a \$1 billion increase in government expenditure will result in an increase of $\frac{1}{0.4}$ billion dollars of NNP—which is equal to $\left(\frac{1}{MPS}\right)$ billions

[1] Note that NNP equals disposable income. This is because there are no taxes, no transfer payments, and no undistributed corporate profits. Taxes are brought into the picture in the next section.

Figure 10.3
Relationship between Consumption Expenditure and Net National Product, Given Three Tax Rates

If taxes are zero, C_0 is the relationship betwen consumption expenditure and NNP. If consumers pay 16⅔ percent of their income in taxes, C_1 is the relationship; and if consumers pay 33⅓ percent of their income in taxes, C_2 is the relationship. Clearly, the higher the tax rate, the less consumers spend on consumption from a given NNP.

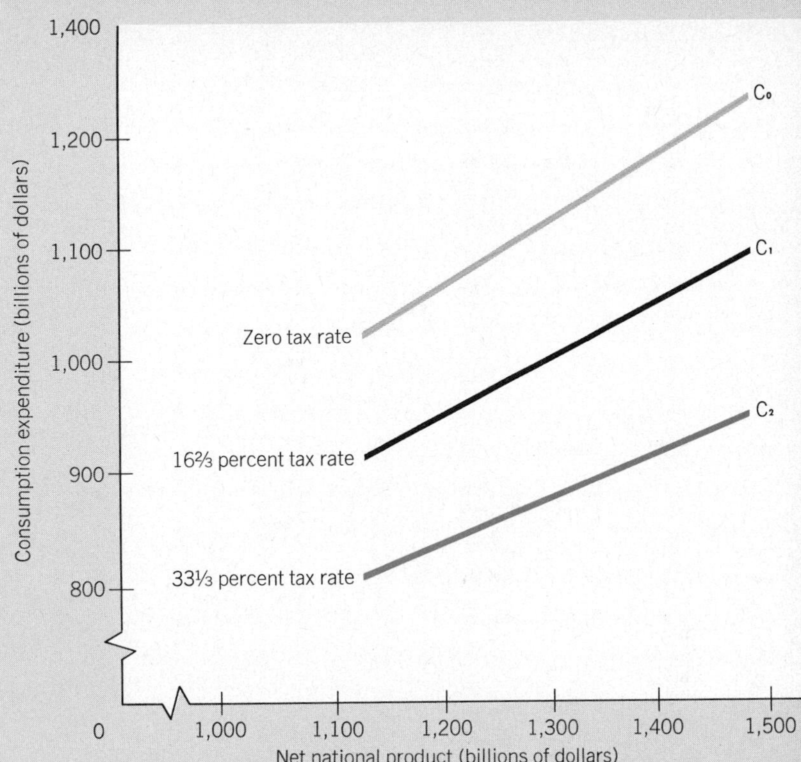

of dollars of NNP, since 0.4 = *MPS*. This is what we set out to prove.

Taxation and Net National Product

The previous section added government expenditures to our theory, but it did not include taxes. Here we assume taxes to be net of transfer payments. For simplicity, it is assumed that all tax revenues stem from personal taxes. How do tax collections influence the equilibrium value of net national product? For example, if consumers pay 16⅔ percent of their income to the government in taxes, what effect does this have on NNP? Clearly, the imposition of this tax means that, for each level of NNP, people have less disposable income than they would with no taxes. In particular, disposable income now equals 83⅓ percent of NNP, whereas without taxes it equaled NNP. Thus, the relationship between consumption expenditure and NNP is altered by the imposition of the tax. Before the tax was levied, the relationship was given by line C_0 in Figure 10.3; after the imposition of the tax, it is given by line C_1.

The relationship between consumption expenditure and NNP changes in this way because consumption expenditure is determined by the level of disposable income. For instance, in the case in Figure 10.3, consumption expenditure equals $350 billion plus 60 percent of disposable income. Thus, since the tax reduces the amount of disposable income at each level of NNP, it also reduces the amount of consumption expenditure at each level of NNP. In other words, since people have less aftertax income to spend at each level of NNP, they spend less on consumption goods and services at each level of NNP. This seems eminently reasonable. It is illustrated in Figure 10.3, where, at each level of NNP, consumption expenditure after the tax (given by line C_1) is less than before the tax (given by line C_0).

Because the imposition of the tax influences the relationship between consumption expenditure and NNP, it also influences the equilibrium value of NNP. As we have stressed repeatedly, the equilibrium value of NNP is at the point where desired spending on NNP equals NNP. Lines C_0 and C_1 in Figure 10.3 show desired consumption expenditure at each level of NNP, before and after the tax. Adding desired investment and government expenditure to each of these lines, we get the total desired spending on NNP before and after the tax. The results are shown in Figure 10.4, under the assumption that the sum of desired investment and government spending equals $140 billion. The $C_0 + I + G$ line shows desired spending on NNP before the tax, while the $C_1 + I + G$ line shows desired spending on NNP after the tax.

Note that the equilibrium level of NNP is lower after the imposition of the tax than before. Specifically, as shown in Figure 10.4, it is $980 billion after the imposition of the tax and $1,225 billion before. The tax reduced the equilibrium level of NNP because it lowered the $C + I + G$ line from $C_0 + I + G$ to $C_1 + I + G$. It did this because, as pointed out above, it reduced the amount people

Figure 10.4
Determination of Equilibrium Value of Net National Product, with Zero and 16⅔ Percent Tax Rates

The tax rate influences the relationship between consumption expenditure and NNP. (C_0 is this relationship with a zero tax rate, while C_1 is the relationship with a 16⅔ percent tax rate. See Figure 10.3.) The $C_0 + I + G$ line shows total desired spending at each level of NNP if the tax rate is zero, and the $C_1 + I + G$ line shows total desired spending at each level of NNP if the tax rate is 16⅔ percent. Consequently, the equilibrium value of NNP is $1,225 billion if the tax rate is zero, and $980 billion if it is 16⅔ percent.

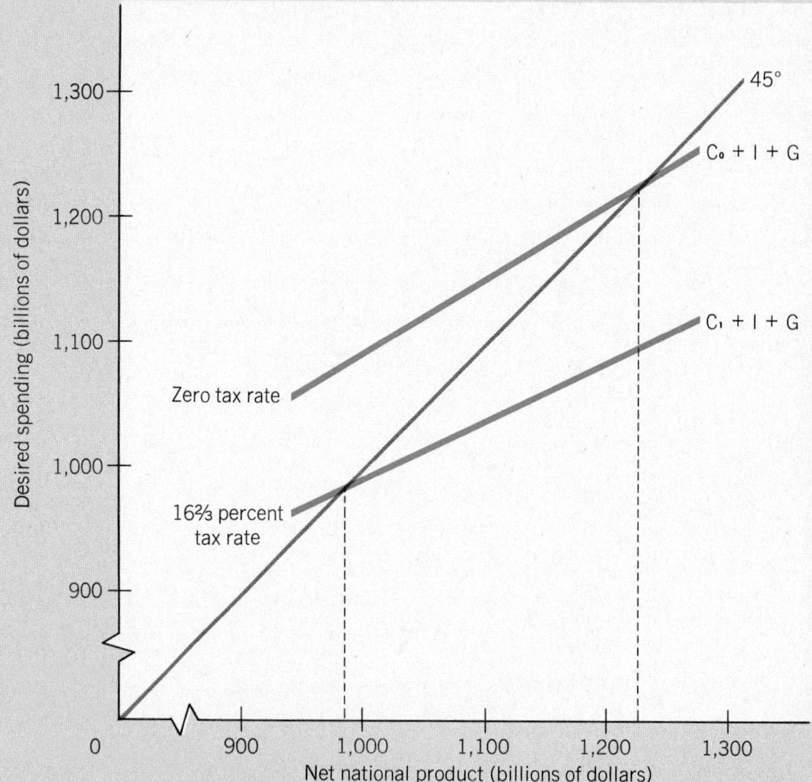

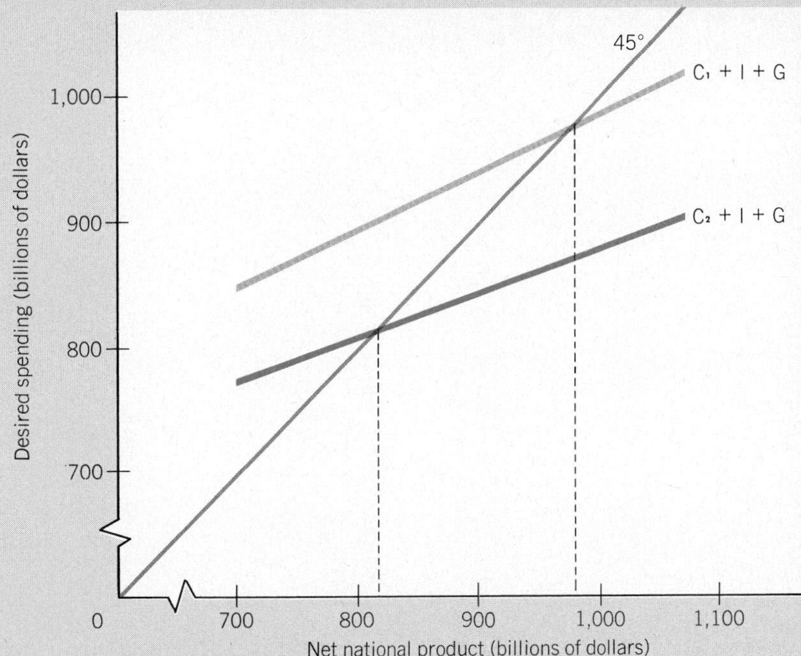

Figure 10.5
Determination of Equilibrium Value of Net National Product, with 16⅔ Percent and 33⅓ Percent Tax Rates

The $C_1 + I + G$ line shows total desired spending at each level of NNP if the tax rate is 16⅔ percent, and the $C_2 + I + G$ line shows total desired spending at each level of NNP if the tax rate is 33⅓ percent. Consequently, the equilibrium value of NNP is \$980 billion if the tax rate is 16⅔ percent and \$816⅔ billion if it is 33⅓ percent.

wanted to spend on consumption goods at each level of NNP. People still wanted to spend the same amount *from each (after-tax) income level,* but because of the tax their spending decisions had to be based on a *reduced (after-tax) income,* so that they spent less on consumption goods and services at each level of NNP.

Going a step further, *the higher the tax rate, the lower the equilibrium value of NNP; and the lower the tax rate, the higher the equilibrium value of NNP.* This is a very important proposition, as we shall see in subsequent sections. To demonstrate it, let's see what will happen to the equilibrium value of NNP when the tax rate is increased from 16⅔ percent of NNP to 33⅓ percent of NNP. If the tax rate is 33⅓ percent, the desired spending on NNP at each level of NNP will be given by line $C_2 + I + G$ in Figure 10.5. Since the equilibrium value of NNP will be at the point where the $C_2 + I + G$ line intersects the 45-degree line, the equilibrium value of NNP will be \$816⅔ billion, rather than \$980 billion (which was the equilibrium value when the tax rate was 16⅔ percent). Thus, the increase in the tax rate will reduce the equilibrium value of NNP. By reducing the amount people want to spend on consumption at each level of NNP, it will lower the $C + I + G$ line from $C_1 + I + G$ to $C_2 + I + G$.

On the other hand, suppose that the tax rate is lowered from 16⅔ percent of NNP to a lesser amount. What will happen to the equilibrium value of NNP? If the tax rate is less than 16⅔ percent, the desired spending on NNP at each level of NNP will be given by a $C + I + G$ line that lies between $C_0 + I + G$ and $C_1 + I + G$ in Figure 10.4. Since the equilibrium value of NNP will be at the point where this line intersects the 45-degree line, the equilibrium value of NNP will be greater than \$980 billion. Thus, the decrease in the tax rate will increase the equilibrium value of NNP. By increasing the amount people want to spend on consumption at each level of NNP, it will raise the $C + I + G$ line from $C_1 + I + G$ to a higher level.[2]

The Nature and Objectives of Fiscal Policy

Our discussions in previous sections make it easy to understand the basic ideas underlying modern fiscal policy. For example, suppose that the economy is suffering from an undesirably high unemployment rate. What should the government do? Since actual NNP is too low to result in full employment, the economy needs increased spending. In other words, as shown in Figure 10.6, the economy needs an upward shift of the $C + I + G$ line, which by increasing NNP will increase employment as well. There are three ways that the government can try to bring this about. First, it can reduce taxes, which, as shown in a previous section, will shift the relation between consumption expenditure and NNP—and consequently the $C + I + G$ line—upward. Second, it can increase government expenditures, which will also shift the $C + I + G$ line upward. Third, the government can encourage firms to invest more, perhaps by enacting tax credits to make investment more profitable for them; an increase in desired investment will shift the $C + I + G$ line upward too.

On the other hand, perhaps we are suffering from an undesirably high rate of inflation. What should the government do? Since total spending

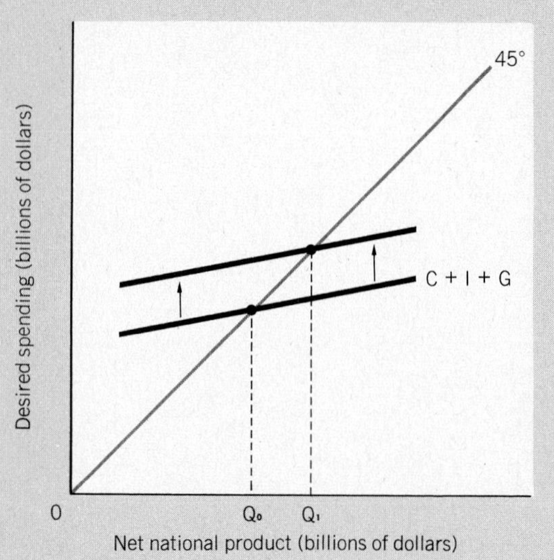

Figure 10.6
Expansionary Fiscal Policy

At Q_0, NNP is too low to result in high employment. By pushing the $C + I + G$ line upward, the government can increase NNP to Q_1, thus increasing real output and reducing unemployment.

[2] Note that the slope of the relationship between consumption and NNP increases as the tax rate decreases. This means that the "marginal propensity to consume out of NNP" increases as the tax rate decreases. Consequently, the multiplier—the amount by which NNP changes if desired investment changes (or the consumption function shifts, or government expenditures change)—increases as the tax rate goes down, and conversely decreases as the tax rate goes up. In other words, as the tax rate increases, NNP becomes less sensitive to changes in investment, government spending, and the consumption function.

To see this, the mathematically inclined reader is encouraged to work through the following proof. Suppose that the consumption function is a straight line:

$$C = \alpha + \beta(1 - T)Y,$$

were $Y =$ NNP and T equals the tax rate, i.e., the proportion of NNP consumers pay in taxes. Also, by definition,

$$Y = C + I + G.$$

Thus, substituting for C,

$$Y = \alpha + \beta(1 - T)Y + I + G,$$

which means that

$$[1 - \beta(1 - T)]Y = \alpha + I + G,$$

or

$$Y = \frac{\alpha}{1 - \beta(1 - T)} + \frac{I}{1 - \beta(1 - T)} + \frac{G}{1 - \beta(1 - T)}.$$

Thus, a \$1 billion increase in α, I, or G results in an increase of $\left[\frac{1}{1 - \beta(1 - T)}\right]$ billions of dollars in NNP. In other words, the multiplier is $\left[\frac{1}{1 - \beta(1 - T)}\right]$. But $\left[\frac{1}{1 - \beta(1 - T)}\right]$ gets bigger as T gets smaller; and conversely, $\left[\frac{1}{1 - \beta(1 - T)}\right]$ gets smaller as T gets bigger. This completes the proof.

exceeds the value at initial prices of maximum output, the economy needs reduced spending. In other words, what is required is a downward shift of the $C + I + G$ line, as shown in Figure 10.7. The government has three ways to try to bring this about. First, it can increase taxes; this, as shown in a previous section, will shift the relation between consumption expenditure and NNP—and consequently the $C + I + G$ line—downward. Second, it can cut government expenditures, which will also shift the $C + I + G$ curve downward. Third, it can change the tax laws and do other things to discourage firms from investing in plant and equipment or inventories; a decrease in desired investment will shift the $C + I + G$ line downward too.

Certainly, these ideas do not seem very hard to understand. Put bluntly, all we are saying is that, *if there is too much unemployment, the government should promote, directly or indirectly, additional public and/or private spending, which will result in additional output and jobs.* On the other hand, *if there is too much inflation, the government should reduce, directly or indirectly, spending (public and/or private); this will curb the inflationary pressure on prices.* Surely these propositions seem reasonable enough. And they are useful —although by themselves they cannot deal as effectively as one would like with times like the early 1970s, when excessive unemployment and inflation have occurred together. We shall discuss such situations in detail in Chapter 15.

Perhaps the most surprising thing about these ideas is that they have been understood and accepted only very recently. Until the appearance of John Maynard Keynes's work in the 1930s, the economics profession really did not understand the effects of fiscal policy at all well. And once Keynes showed his fellow economists the way, it took over 20 years to convince congressmen, presidents, and other officials that these ideas were valid. Moreover, the educational process is still going on. Per-

Figure 10.7
Contractionary Fiscal Policy

For simplicity, assume that Q_2 is the *maximum* value of *real* NNP (*in initial prices*) that can be achieved; thus, any increase of *money* NNP above Q_2 is due entirely to inflation. The existing $C + I + G$ line is too high, resulting in a money NNP of Q_3, which means considerable inflation. (A money NNP of Q_3 can be achieved only by an increase in prices since at initial prices Q_2 is the maximum value of money NNP.) By pushing the $C + I + G$ line downward, the government can ease the upward pressure on prices.

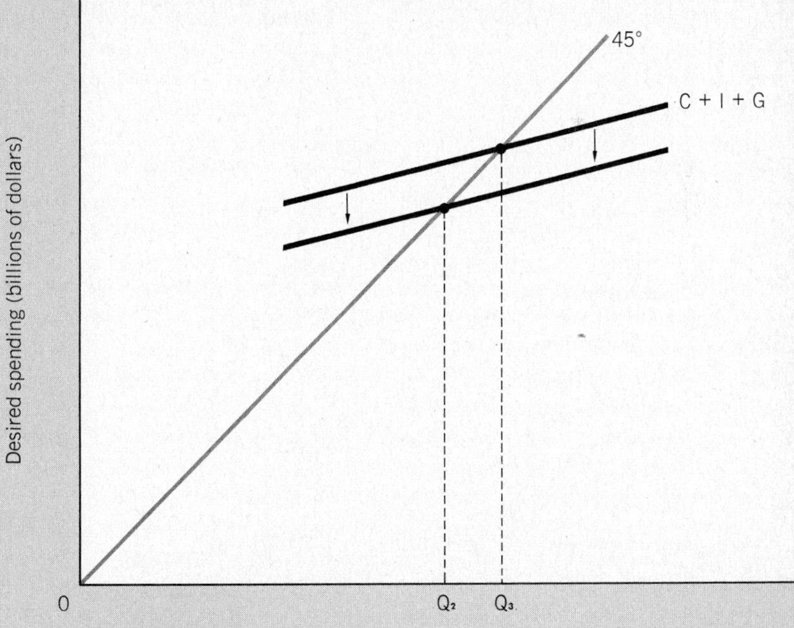

haps the most important reason why it has been so difficult to get across such simple ideas is that, until recently, the conventional wisdom passed down from father to son was that the government should balance its budget. In other words, it should spend no more than what it collects in taxes. This proposition is at odds with the ideas presented above. If those ideas are accepted, it may be necessary for the government to run a deficit or a surplus, depending on the economic situation. A ***deficit*** occurs when the government spends more than it collects in taxes; a ***surplus*** occurs when it spends less. It has taken a long time to convince people that full employment and stable prices—not a balanced budget—should be our goals. Some people still believe that the road to economic destruction is lined with unbalanced budgets.

Makers of Fiscal Policy

When you go to a ball game, you generally get a program telling you who on each team is playing each position. To understand the formulation and implementation of fiscal policy in the United States we need the same kind of information. Who are the people who establish our fiscal policy? Who decides that, in view of the current and prospective economic situation, tax rates or government expenditures should be changed? This is not a simple question because lots of individuals and groups play an important role. In the Congress, the House and Senate appropriations committees—as well as their numerous subcommittees—have enormous power over the size and direction of federal expenditure. The House Ways and Means Committee and the Senate Finance Committee have the same sort of power over federal tax matters. In addition, another congressional committee is of great importance—the Joint Economic Committee of Congress. Established by the Employment Act of 1946, this committee goes over the annual Economic Report of the President on the state of the economy, and, through its hearings, provides an important forum for review of economic issues.

In the executive branch of government, the most important person in the establishment of fiscal policy is, of course, the president. Although he must operate in the context of the tax and expenditure laws passed by Congress, he and his advisers are the country's principal analysts of the need for fiscal expansion or restraint and its leading spokesmen for legislative changes to meet these needs. Needless to say, he doesn't pore over the latest economic data and make the decisions all by himself. The Office of Management and Budget, which is part of the Executive Office of the President, is a very powerful adviser to the president on expenditure policy, as is the Treasury Department on tax policy. In addition, there is the ***Council of Economic Advisers,*** which is part of the Executive Office of the President. Established by the Employment Act of 1946, its job is to help the president carry out the objectives of that act.

During the past 20 years, the Council of Economic Advisers, headed by a series of very distinguished economists who left academic and other posts to contribute to public policy, has become a very important economic adviser to the president. Its position has been well described by Stanford's G. L. Bach:

> Fundamentally, it is responsible for overseeing the state of the economy, for continually checking on the appropriateness of government policies for stable economic growth, and for working intimately with the President and other parts of the executive branch in developing overall legislative policy in the economic field. Some Council chairmen have worked closely with Congressional committees; others have remained more in the background as Presidential advisers. But for macroeconomic policy, the Council is now perhaps the President's most important single advisory group. It is *his* council and more specifically *his* part of the government than are the regular executive branch departments.[3]

[3] G. L. Bach, *Making Monetary and Fiscal Policy,* Washington, D.C.: Brookings Institution, 1971, pp. 30–31. The Chairmen of the Council of Economic Advisers have been Herbert Stein, Paul McCracken, Arthur Okun, Gardner Ackley, Walter Heller, Raymond Saulnier, Arthur Burns, Leon Keyserling, and Edwin Nourse.

The Council of Economic Advisers

Before World War II, there was relatively little place in the government for economists. The Treasury had a small number, the antitrust division of the Justice Department a handful, but there was no place for economists who aspired to give advice on broad policy matters. The Employment Act of 1946 changed that situation by creating a council to "gather timely and authoritative information . . . to develop and recommend to the President national economic policies . . . and to make and furnish studies . . . as the President may request."

But, as demonstrated by the first chairman, Edwin Nourse, the Act was really a hunting license for a chairman to peddle his good counsel. Nourse, who believed that the Council's role was to "interpret literal facts . . . without becoming involved in any way in the advocacy of particular measures," found that such services were rarely required by the president. It is hard to find any trace of the Nourse era on the economic policies of the late forties.

THE FIRST COUNCIL OF ECONOMIC ADVISERS. EDWIN NOURSE, CHAIRMAN, AT LEFT.

Nourse's successor, Leon Keyserling, hunted so avidly that Congress almost suspended his license. Keyserling was temperamentally and politically inclined to activism. His advocacy of expansionist policies to a conservative Congress and a president concerned primarily with containing the Korean war inflation led to a bill reducing the CEA's budget by 25 percent. The Council was saved by the persuasiveness of a new chairman, Arthur F. Burns, and the support of a few senators. But the limits of independent advocacy had been established.

The Eisenhower years were quiet years for the Council. Even the election of John F. Kennedy, who was eager to increase the U.S. rate of economic growth, did not insure the Council's future. Kennedy, a C-student in economics at Harvard, was inclined to fiscal conservatism and less interested in domestic than in foreign affairs. It was Walter Heller, the new chairman under Kennedy, who made the CEA an integral part of the New Frontier. The tax cut of 1964, which Heller sold to a president committed to balanced budgets, is a tribute to his success in making a body without formal powers or legislative prerogatives an integral part of the policy-making process. The new-found status of the Council was acknowledged in Washington by the establishment of a Quadriad, made up of representatives of the Council, the Bureau of the Budget, the Treasury, and the Federal Reserve, which met periodically to discuss economic affairs.

The Council's influence has risen and ebbed in recent years with both the state of the economy and with other pressures on the president. In 1966, as Vietnam heated up, the Council urged a tax increase; Lyndon Johnson, more attuned to the political realities, did not take action on the proposal until 1967. The Council's position in the Nixon administration further exemplified this process. Led by Paul McCracken and Herbert Stein, the Council successfully championed restraint in fiscal and monetary policies early in Nixon's first term, and let the Kennedy-Johnson price-wage guideposts lapse. But faced with mounting inflationary pressures, the Council members reluctantly joined other administration economists in setting up wage and price controls. As one economic game plan after another was tried and modified, economists who had favored relaxing government reins on the economy found themselves tugging hard to keep inflation in check.

E.A.

Automatic Stabilizers

Now that we have met some of the major players, we must point out that they get help from some ***automatic stabilizers***—some structural features of our economy that tend to stabilize NNP. Although these automatic stabilizers cannot do all that is required to keep the economy on an even keel, they help a lot. As soon as the economy turns down and unemployment mounts, they give the economy a helpful shot in the arm. As soon as the economy gets overheated and inflation crops up, they tend to restrain it.

There are several automatic stabilizers. First, there are automatic changes in tax revenues. One of the major points emphasized in Chapter 5 was that our federal tax system relies heavily on the income tax. The amount of income tax collected by the federal government goes up with increases in NNP and goes down with decreases in NNP. Moreover, because the income tax is progressive, the average tax rate goes up with increases in NNP, and goes down with decreases in NNP. This, of course, is just what we want to occur! When NNP falls off and unemployment mounts, tax collections fall off too, so disposable income falls less than NNP. This means less of a fall in consumption, which tends to brake the fall in NNP. When NNP rises too fast and the economy begins to suffer from serious inflation, tax collections rise too—which tends to brake the increase in NNP. Of course, corporation income taxes, as well as personal income taxes, play a significant role here.

Second, there are unemployment compensation and welfare payments. Unemployment compensation is paid to workers who are laid off, according to a system that has evolved over the past 40 years. When an unemployed worker goes back to work, he stops receiving unemployment compensation. Thus, when NNP falls off and unemployment mounts, the tax collections to finance unemployment compensation go down (because of lower employment), while the amount paid out to unemployed workers goes up. On the other hand, when NNP rises too fast and the economy begins to suffer from serious inflation, the tax collections to finance unemployment compensation go up, while the amount paid out goes down because there is much less unemployment. Again, this is just what we want to see happen! Spending is bolstered when unemployment is high and curbed when there are serious inflationary pressures. Various welfare programs have the same kind of stabilizing effect on the economy.

Third, there are corporate dividends and family saving. Since corporations tend to maintain their dividends when their sales fall off, and moderate the increase in their dividends when their sales soar, their dividend policy tends to stabilize the economy. This is very important. Also, to the extent that consumers tend to be slow to raise or lower their spending in response to increases or decreases in their income, this too tends to stabilize the economy. Finally, there are the agricultural support programs, described in Chapter 5. The government has buttressed farm prices and incomes when business was bad and unemployment was high. When output was high and inflation occurred, the government distributed the commodities in its warehouses and received dollars. In both cases, these programs acted as stabilizers.

Having painted such a glowing picture of the economy's automatic stabilizers, we are in danger of suggesting that they can stabilize the economy all by themselves. It would be nice if this were true, but it isn't! All the automatic stabilizers do is *cut down* on variations in unemployment and inflation, not *eliminate* them. Discretionary programs are needed to supplement the effects of these automatic stabilizers. Some economists wish strongly that it were possible to set well-defined rules for government action, rather than leave things to the discretion of policy makers. Indeed, Milton Friedman, among others, forcefully argues for greater reliance on such rules, but most economists feel that it is impossible to formulate a set of rules flexible and comprehensive enough to let us do away with the discretionary powers of policy makers.

The Tools of Discretionary Fiscal Policy

Having discussed the automatic stabilizers, let's get back to the players—the people responsible for the formulation and implementation of discretionary fiscal policy—and the tools they have to work with. For example, suppose that the Council of Economic Advisers, on the basis of information concerning recent economic developments, believes that NNP may decline soon and that serious unemployment is likely to develop. Suppose that other agencies, like the Treasury and the Federal Reserve System (discussed in Chapter 14), agree. What specific measures can they recommend that the government take under such circumstances?

First, the government can vary its expenditure for public works and other programs. If increased unemployment seems to be in the wind, it can step up expenditures on roads, urban reconstruction, and other public programs. Of course, these programs must be well thought out and socially productive. There is no sense in pushing through wasteful and foolish public works programs merely to make jobs. Or if, as in 1969, the economy is plagued by inflation, it can (as President Nixon ordered) stop new federal construction programs temporarily.

Second, the government can vary welfare payments and other types of transfer payments. For example, a hike in Social Security benefits may provide a very healthy shot in the arm for an economy with too much unemployment. An increase in veterans' benefits or in aid to dependent children may do the same thing. The federal government has sometimes helped the states to extend the length of time that the unemployed can receive unemployment compensation; this too will have the desired effect. On the other hand, if there is full employment and inflation is a dangerous problem, it may be worthwhile to cut back on certain kinds of transfer payments. For example, if it is agreed that certain kinds of veterans' benefits should be reduced, this reduction might be timed to occur during a period when inflationary pressures are evident.

Third, the government can vary tax rates. For example, if there is considerable unemployment, the government may cut tax rates, as it did in 1964. Or if inflation is the problem, the government may increase taxes, as it did in 1968 when, after considerable political maneuvering and buck-passing, the Congress was finally persuaded to put through the 10 percent tax surcharge to try to moderate the inflation caused by the Vietnam war. We shall show in the next sections the processes leading up to the 1964 tax cut and the 1968 tax increase.

Of course there are advantages and disadvantages in each of these tools of fiscal policy. One of the big disadvantages of public works and similar spending programs is that they take so long to get started. Plans must be made, land must be acquired, and preliminary construction studies must be carried out. By the time the expenditures are finally made and have the desired effect, the dangers of excessive unemployment may have given way to dangers of inflation, so that the spending, coming too late, does more harm than good. To some extent, this problem may be ameliorated by having a backlog of productive projects ready to go at all times. In this way, at least a portion of the lag can be eliminated. But it is necessary to recognize that the supply of public services should be determined by public demand, and that considerations of stabilization policy are only one of many factors to be considered.

In recent years, there has been a widespread feeling that government expenditures should be set on the basis of their long-run desirability and productivity and not on the basis of short-term stabilization considerations. The optimal level of government expenditure is at the point where the value of the extra benefits to be derived from an extra dollar of government expenditure is at least equal to the dollar of cost. This optimal level is unlikely to change much in the short run, and it would be wasteful to spend more—or less—than this amount for stabilization purposes when tax changes could be used instead. Thus, many economists believe that tax cuts or tax increases should be the primary fiscal weapons to fight unemployment or inflation.

However, one of the big problems with tax changes is that it is difficult to get Congress to take speedy action. There is often considerable debate over a tax bill, and sometimes it becomes a political football. Another difficulty with tax changes is that it generally is much easier to reduce taxes than it is to get them back up again. To politicians, lower taxes are attractive because they are popular, and higher taxes are dangerous because they may hurt a politician's chances of reelection. In discussing fiscal policy (or most other aspects of government operations, for that matter), to ignore politics is to risk losing touch with reality.

The Tax Cut of 1964: An Application of Modern Economic Analysis

Knowing something about the players and the plays they can call, we can look now at two examples of fiscal policy in action. When the Kennedy administration took office in 1961, it was confronted with a relatively high unemployment rate—about 7 percent in mid-1961. By 1962, although unemployment was somewhat lower (about 6 percent), the president's advisers, led by Walter W. Heller, Chairman of the Council of Economic Advisers, pushed for a tax cut to reduce unemployment further. The president, after considerable discussion of the effects of such a tax cut, announced in June 1962 that he would propose such a measure to the Congress; and in January 1963, the bill was finally sent to Congress.

The proposed tax bill was a victory for modern ideas on fiscal policy. Even though it would mean a deliberately large deficit, the president had been convinced to cut taxes to push the economy closer to full employment. But the Congress was not so easily convinced. Many congressmen labeled the proposal irresponsible and reckless. Others wanted to couple tax reform with tax reduction. It was not until 1964, after President Kennedy's death, that the tax bill was enacted. It took a year from the time the bill was sent to Congress for it to be passed, and during this interval, there was a continuous debate in the executive branch and the Congress. The Secretary of the Treasury, Douglas Dillon, the Chairman of the Federal Reserve Board, William M. Martin, and numerous congressmen—all powerful and all initially cool to the proposal—were eventually won over. The result was a tax reduction of about $10 billion per year.

The effects of the tax cut are by no means easy to measure, but in line with the theory presented in earlier sections, consumption expenditure did increase sharply during 1964. Moreover, the additional consumption undoubtedly induced additional investment. According to estimates provided by Arthur Okun, Chairman of the Council of Economic Advisers under President Johnson, the tax cut resulted in an increase in GNP of about $24 billion in 1965 and more in subsequent years.[4] The unemployment rate, which had been about 5½ to 6 percent during 1962 and 1963, fell to 5 percent during 1964 and to 4.7 percent in the spring of 1965. It is fair to say that most economists were extremely pleased with themselves in 1965. Fiscal policy based on their theories seemed to work very well indeed! Unfortunately, however, this pleasure did not last very long, there being another, and sadder, tale to tell.

The Impact of Vietnam: Another Case Study

In late July 1965, President Johnson announced that the United States would send 50,000 more men to Vietnam. From fiscal 1965 to fiscal 1966, defense expenditures rose from $50 billion to $62

[4] Arthur Okun, "Measuring the Impact of the 1964 Tax Reduction," in Walter W. Heller, *Perspectives on Economic Growth,* New York: Random House, 1968, p. 33.

billion—a large increase in government expenditure, and one that took place at a time of relatively full employment. Clearly, on the basis of the theory presented earlier in this chapter, such an increase in government expenditure would be expected to cause inflationary pressures. Equally clearly, one way to eliminate undesirable pressures of this sort was to raise taxes (and, where possible, cut other kinds of government expenditure). The president was told by his economic advisers in late 1965 that an increase in income taxes was desirable to cut down on inflationary pressures, but he would not ask for such an increase at that time.

In fiscal 1967, the situation got no better. Because of the large military buildup in that year, military expenditure was $10 billion higher than estimated in the January 1966 budget. This was a large increase in government spending at a time when inflationary pressures were strong. The effects of these pressures were becoming clearer and clearer. During 1965, the general price level—as measured by the GNP deflator—had gone up by about 3 percent; during 1966, it had gone up by about 4 percent; and during 1967, it rose again by about 4 percent. The inflation was bubbling along merrily . . . and unfortunately, little was being done by fiscal policy makers to stop it.

Even in 1967, the Congress was unwilling to raise taxes. The case for fiscal restraint was, it felt, not clear enough. Moreover, the pressure from the general public was certainly not for an increase in the amount they would have to pay Uncle Sam. As for the president, he recognized that the Vietnam war was not popular. Consequently, as he himself put it, "It is not a popular thing for a President to do . . . to ask for a penny out of a dollar to pay for a war that is not popular either."[5] Finally, in mid-1968, when prices were rising by well over 4 percent per year, a 10 percent surcharge on income taxes, together with some restraint on government spending, was enacted. This was almost a year after the surtax had been requested.

[5] Arthur Okun, *The Political Economy of Prosperity,* New York: Norton, 1970, p. 88.

This increase in taxes was obviously the right medicine, but it was at least two years too late, and its effects were delayed. Certainly, the record of 1965–68 was disappointing. Government spending was highly destabilizing, and tax changes were painfully slow to come. One moral of this episode is that, although we know a great deal more than we used to about how fiscal policy should be used to avoid inflation or considerable unemployment, there is no guarantee that it will be used in this way. In the early 1960s, policy makers seemed to make the right choices; in the later 1960s, they did not.

Deficit and Surplus Financing

Now that you have studied the basic elements of fiscal policy, let's see how well you would fare with some of the problems that confront our nation's top policy makers. Suppose that, through some inexplicable malfunctioning of the democratic process, you are elected President of the United States. Your Council of Economic Advisers reports to you that, on the basis of various forecasts (based on models like those discussed in Chapter 11), NNP is likely to drop next year, and unemployment is likely to be much higher. Naturally, you are concerned; and having absorbed the ideas presented in this chapter, you ask your advisers—the Council of Economic Advisers, the Treasury, and the Office of Management and Budget—what sort of fiscal policy should be adopted to head off this undesirable turn of events. On the basis of their advice, you suggest to Congress that taxes should be cut and government expenditures should be increased.

When they receive your message, a number of key congressmen point out that if the government cuts taxes and raises expenditures it will operate in the red. In other words, government revenue will fall short of government spending—there will be a deficit. They warn that such fiscal behavior is irresponsible, since it violates the fundamental tenet of public finance that the budget should be balanced: income should cover outgo. For further clarification on this point, you call in your advisers, who deny that the budget should be balanced each year. They point out that if a deficit is run in a particular year, the government can borrow the difference; and they claim that the national debt is in no sense dangerously large in the United States at present. Whose advice would you follow—that of your economic advisers or that of the congressmen?

Or suppose your advisers tell you that inflation is a growing problem and that you should cut back government spending and raise taxes. Since this advice seems eminently sensible, based on the principles set forth in this chapter, you propose this course of action to Congress. Some prominent newspapers point out that by raising taxes and cutting expenditures, the government will take in more than it spends. In other words, there will be a surplus. They say that there is no reason for the government to take more money from the people than it needs to pay for the services it performs, and argue that taxes should not be increased because the government can cover its expenditures without such an increase. Whose advice would you follow—that of your economic advisers or that of the newspapers?

You would be wise to go along with your economic advisers in both cases. Why? Because there is nothing particularly desirable about a balanced budget. Although it may well be prudent for individuals and families not to spend more than they earn, this does not carry over to the federal government. When we need to stimulate the economy and raise NNP, it is perfectly legitimate and desirable for the federal government to run a deficit, provided it gets its full money's worth for what is spent. All that happens is that the government borrows the difference, and—as we pointed out in Chapter 6—there is no indication that the national debt is dangerously large. Thus, in the first case, you should not have been worried by the fact that a deficit would result. And in the second case, while it is true that the government could support its expenditures with lower taxes, this would defeat your purpose. What you want to do is to cut total spending, public and private, and raising taxes will cut private spending.

Deficit Spending in the 1930s: A Case Study

Some people—fewer than there used to be, but still some—are dead set against deficit spending by the government. Many, when pressed to explain their opposition, retort that it was tried by Franklin D. Roosevelt during the Great Depression of the 1930s and that it failed to eliminate the high levels of unemployment that prevailed then. This is both bad history and bad economics. The federal government did spend more than it took in during the Roosevelt administration, but the deficit was far too small to have much effect. GNP fell from about $100 billion in 1929 to less than $60 billion in 1933. Federal deficits in the 1930s were only a few billion dollars per year at most, and in many years these deficits were offset by surpluses run by the state and local governments. The situation somewhat resembled that described by the columnist Heywood Broun, when he wrote: "I have known people to stop and buy an apple on the corner and then walk away as if they had solved the whole unemployment problem."[6]

In a careful study of the effects of fiscal policy in the 1930s, Professor E. Cary Brown of M.I.T. concluded that fiscal policy "seems to have been an unsuccessful recovery device in the thirties—not because it did not work, but because it was not tried."[7] For those who know something of the political history of the period, this is not surprising.

[6] Heywood Broun, *It Seems to Me,* 1933. Of course, I am not implying that the Roosevelt administration did not attempt to reduce unemployment. What I am saying is that the history of the period is not a very good test of the effectiveness of deficit spending.

[7] E. Cary Brown, "Fiscal Policy in the Thirties: A Reappraisal," *American Economic Review,* December 1956, pp. 865–66.

Few government officials of that day understood the power and effects of fiscal policy. The federal government did run a deficit, but largely in spite of itself. In that era, the golden rule of fiscal responsibility was a balanced budget, and deficits were regarded as unfortunate aberrations. If you contrast this attitude with the attitude of the federal government toward the tax cut of 1964, you will see how far the nation has come in its understanding of fiscal policy.

Alternative Budget Policies

At least three policies concerning the government budget are worthy of detailed examination. The first policy says that the government's budget should be balanced each and every year. This is the philosophy that generally prevailed, here and abroad, until the advent of Keynesian economics in the 1930s. Superficially, it seems eminently reasonable. After all, won't a family or firm go bankrupt if it continues to spend more than it takes in? Why should the government be any different? However, the truth is that the government has economic capabilities, powers, and responsibilities that are entirely different from those of any family or firm, and it is misleading—sometimes even pernicious—to assume that what is sensible for a family or firm is also sensible for the government.

If this policy of balancing the budget is accepted, the government cannot use fiscal policy as a tool to stabilize the economy. Indeed, if the government attempts to balance its budget each year, it is likely to make unemployment or inflation worse rather than better. For example, suppose that severe unemployment occurs because of a drop in NNP. Since incomes drop, tax receipts drop as well. Thus if the government attempts to balance its budget, it must cut its spending and/or increase tax rates, both of which will tend to lower, not raise, NNP. On the other hand, suppose that inflation occurs because spending increases too rapidly. Since incomes increase, tax receipts increase too. Thus, for the government to balance its budget, it must increase its spending and/or decrease tax rates, both of which will tend to raise, not lower, spending.[8]

A second budgetary philosophy says that the government's budget should be balanced over the course of each "business cycle." As we shall see in Chapter 11, the rate of growth of NNP tends to behave cyclically. As shown in Figure 8.6, it tends to increase for a while, then drop, increase, then drop. Unemployment also tends to ebb and flow in a similar cyclical fashion. This is the so-called business cycle. According to this second budgetary policy, the government is not expected to balance its budget each year, but is expected to run a big enough surplus during periods of high employment to offset the deficit it runs during the ensuing period of excessive unemployment. This policy seems to give the government enough flexibility to run the deficits or surpluses needed to stabilize the economy, while at the same time allaying any public fear of a chronically unbalanced budget. It certainly seems to be a neat way to reconcile the government's use of fiscal policy to promote noninflationary full employment with the public's uneasiness over chronically unbalanced budgets.

Unfortunately, however, it does contain one fundamental flaw: there is no reason to believe that the size of the deficits required to eliminate excessive unemployment will equal the size of the surpluses required to moderate the subsequent inflation. For example, suppose that NNP falls

[8] In sophisticated circles, there is some support for this philosophy of a balanced budget, based on the idea that it makes it much easier for the Office of Management and Budget to keep expenditures within reasonable limits. Once this philosophy is abandoned completely, it is feared that the individual departments and agencies of the government can challenge OMB's estimate of how big a surplus or deficit is appropriate, and argue that more spending on their part would be a good thing. In other words, it makes it easier to control spending.

Another point that is frequently made is that the government, through inappropriate fiscal or monetary policies, is often responsible for problems of unemployment and inflation. To many economists, the practical problem seems to be how to prevent the government from creating disturbances, rather than how to use the government budget (and monetary policy) to offset disturbances arising from the private sector. Unfortunately, as we noted in connection with the inflation arising from the Vietnam war, there is sometimes a good deal of truth to this.

sharply, causing severe and prolonged unemployment; then regains its full-employment level only briefly; then falls again. In such a case, the deficits incurred to get the economy back to full employment are likely to exceed by far the surpluses run during the brief period of full employment. Thus there would be no way to stabilize the economy without running an unbalanced budget over the course of this business cycle. If this policy were adopted, and if the government attempted to balance the budget over the course of each business cycle, this would interfere with an effective fiscal policy designed to promote full employment with stable prices.

Finally, a third budgetary policy says that the government's budget should be set so as to promote whatever attainable combination of unemployment and inflation seems socially optimal, even if this means that the budget is unbalanced over considerable periods of time. This policy is sometimes called ***functional finance.***[9] Proponents of functional finance point out that, although this policy may mean a continual growth in the public debt, the problems caused by a moderate growth in the public debt are small when compared with the social costs of unemployment and inflation.

Certainly, the history of the past 40 years has been characterized by enormous changes in the nation's attitude toward the government budget. Forty years ago, the prevailing attitude was that the government's budget should be balanced. The emergence of the modern theory of the determination of national output and employment shook this attitude, at least to the point where it became respectable to advocate a balanced budget over the business cycle, rather than in each year. Then, as modern ideas regarding fiscal policy have become accepted by more and more people, the idea that the budget should be balanced over the business cycle has been largely abandoned, and the government budget is now viewed as a means to reduce undesirable unemployment and inflation.

[9] See Abba Lerner, *Economics of Control,* New York: Macmillan, 1944.

The Full-Employment Budget

Some of the misconceptions about budget deficits and surpluses can be avoided by the use of the ***full-employment budget,*** which shows the difference between tax revenues and government expenditures that would result if we had full employment, which is generally defined as 4 percent unemployed. For example, in 1958, the Eisenhower administration ran a deficit of over $10 billion—a reasonably large deficit by historical standards. Basically, the reason for this deficit was that, with the unemployment rate at about 7 percent, there was a substantial gap between actual and potential output. Net national product fell from 1957 to 1958, and, as a result, incomes and federal tax collections fell, and the government ran a deficit. But this $10 billion deficit was entirely due to the high level of unemployment the country was experiencing.

Had we been at full employment, there would have been a surplus of about $5 billion in 1958. NNP, incomes, and federal tax receipts would all have been higher. Government spending and the tax rates in 1958 were not such as to produce a deficit if full employment had been attained. On the contrary, the full-employment budget shows that, if full employment had prevailed, tax receipts would have increased so that federal revenues would have exceeded expenditure by about $5 billion. It is important to distinguish between the full-employment budget and the actual budget. When, as in 1958, the actual budget shows a deficit but the full-employment budget does not, most economists feel that fiscal policy is not too expansionary, since at full employment the federal government would be running a surplus.

Recognizing these considerations, President Nixon officially adopted the full-employment budget as his measure of the stabilization impact of the budget. As you can see in Figure 10.8, he ran a full-employment surplus during his first term in office to combat inflation. During the late 1950s and early 1960s there was also a substantial full-employment surplus because, with continued

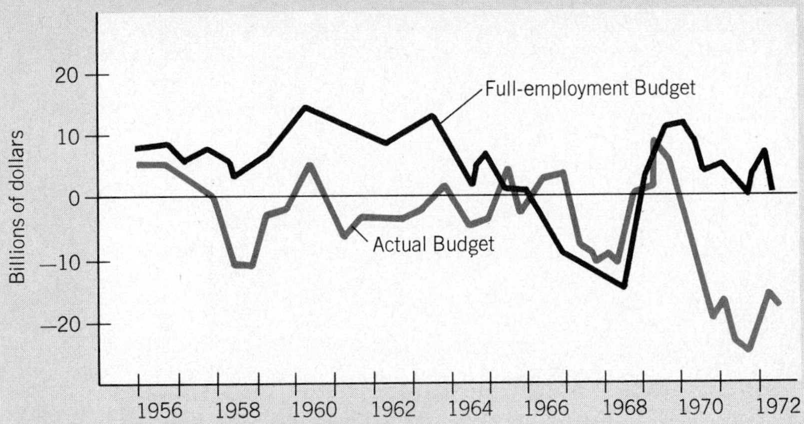

Figure 10.8
Full-Employment and Actual Budget Deficits and Surpluses, 1956–72

The full-employment budget shows the difference between tax revenues and government expenditures that would result if there was full employment, which is generally defined as 4 percent unemployed. The Nixon administration has officially adopted the full-employment budget as a measure of the stabilization impact of the budget.

growth in NNP, federal tax receipts grew each year—and this growth in tax receipts was considerable! Unless taxes are reduced or government expenditures increase, a full-employment surplus will develop and grow, with deflationary results. This automatic growth in tax receipts in a growing economy with progressive taxes is called ***fiscal drag.*** This drag is beneficial if there are inflationary pressures (as in the late 1960s and early 1970s), but under healthy full-employment conditions, it tends to push the economy toward less than full employment. One way to look at the 1964 tax cut is as a device to eliminate the effects of fiscal drag. (As you can see in Figure 10.8, the full-employment surplus was largely eliminated by the tax cut.) Unfortunately, the Vietnam war resulted in a large—and inflationary—full-employment deficit in 1966–68.

Recent American Experience with Fiscal Policy

It should be evident by now that much more is known today about the impact of fiscal policy than at the time when the economy was staggered by the Great Depression. During the 1930s, the ideas presented here were relatively new and by and large not accepted. In fact, the federal government did run a deficit, but—as we saw in a previous section—it was far too small to make a significant dent in the high unemployment levels of the Great Depression. During the 1940s, the ideas presented here began to gain wider acceptance. World War II showed beyond any reasonable doubt the power of government spending to increase output and generate full employment. Unfortunately, it also showed that an expansionary fiscal policy can produce inflation.

During the 1950s, modern ideas on fiscal policy had become strongly entrenched in the intellectual community, but were less accepted in the business community and some parts of the government. However, the makers of fiscal policy took these ideas into account in responding to the increases in unemployment during 1953–54 and 1957–58. During the 1960s, modern views on fiscal policy came to be widely accepted by practically all parts of the community. The tax cut of 1964 was a major victory for modern economics, but as we have observed, the later 1960s were marred by the destabilizing effects of greatly increased military spending on Vietnam, and the inflationary consequences remained with us afterward.

The hard choices faced by economists in the top councils of government can be demonstrated by a close inspection of the recent efforts to keep the economy on an even keel. When the Nixon administration took office, it inherited an economy suffering from considerable inflation, in part because of the fiscal policies pursued in the mid-1960s. In response to this inflation, the administration pursued a restrictive fiscal policy designed to keep a tight rein on spending. During 1969 and 1970, the administration restricted government expenditures and tried to run a surplus. For example, in his Economic Report in 1970, President Nixon said: "Our purpose has been to slow down the rapid expansion of demand firmly and persistently, but not to choke off demand so abruptly as to injure the economy. . . . The growth of total spending, public and private, which was the driving force of the inflation, slowed markedly, from 9.4 percent during 1968 to 6.8 percent during 1969."[10]

As the administration's restrictive fiscal policies took hold, the nation's level of real output began to rise more slowly; and in 1970, gross national product in constant dollars fell below its 1969 level. Unemployment, which had been only 3.5 percent of the civilian labor force in 1969, rose to 4.9 percent in 1970 and to 5.9 percent in 1971. During 1970 and 1971, many liberal economists criticized the administration's fiscal policies on the grounds that they were too restrictive. They accused the administration of being so absorbed with reducing inflation that it was creating serious unemployment. Yet despite the administration's efforts, the rate of inflation was not decreasing as fast as desired. Between 1969 and 1970, the index of consumer prices rose by about 6 percent. During the first half of 1971, it rose at an annual rate of about 4½ percent. Although there was improvement, the inflationary process was proving difficult to quell.

In August 1971, the Nixon administration, reversing its previous attitudes, established controls on prices, wages, and rents. At the same time, the administration switched to a more expansionary fiscal policy in order to reduce the relatively high level of unemployment. Specifically, the president called for a tax reduction of about $7 or $8 billion. Included in his tax package was an investment tax credit, which encouraged investment by business firms, as well as a reduction in personal income taxes. Commenting on his fiscal policy decisions, the president said in 1972:

> 6 percent unemployment is too much, and I am determined to reduce that number significantly in 1972. To that end I proposed the tax reduction package of 1971. Federal expenditures will rise by $25.2 billion between last fiscal year and fiscal 1972. Together these tax reductions and expenditure increases will leave a budget deficit of $38.8 billion this year. If we were at full employment in the present fiscal year, expenditures would exceed receipts by $8.1 billion. This is strong medicine, and I do not propose to continue its use, but we have taken it in order to give a powerful stimulus to employment.[11]

Of course, this New Economic Policy also was the subject of criticism, both from the left and the right. Some economists welcomed the shift to a more expansionary policy as long overdue; others viewed it as a mistake. Also, both the tax reduction and the controls were criticized on the grounds that they benefited business more than labor. Fortunately, both the rate of inflation and the unemployment rate fell during 1972. This was good news. But both remained undesirably high: the unemployment rate was about 5½ percent in late 1972 and the rate of inflation was about 3 percent during the year.

After his reelection in November 1972, President Nixon indicated that he wanted to keep a tight lid on government spending, both to reduce inflation and to trim some programs that he regarded as secondary or of dubious value. In particular, he stressed the desirability of a $250 billion ceiling on federal spending. Critics of the president's economic policies claimed that his emphasis on restricting public expenditures was a mistake. In

[10] *Economic Report of the President,* 1970, Washington, D.C.: Government Printing Office, p. 6.

[11] *Economic Report of the President,* 1972, *op cit.,* p. 5.

early 1973, the president phased out the wage and price controls he had imposed in 1971. Inflation, which never had been quelled, increased after the phaseout of the controls, and during early 1973 the economy was in the midst of a boom. In June 1973, the president imposed another price freeze, this time for 60 days. Then he instituted the so-called "Phase IV" program which attempted to limit price increases to an amount equal to cost increases.

Clearly, judging from our recent history, fiscal policy is no panacea. Policy makers are continually confronted with difficult choices, and the tools of fiscal policy, at least as they are currently understood and used, are not sufficient to solve or dispel many of the problems at hand. However, it is important to recognize that fiscal policy is not the only available means by which policy makers attempt to stabilize the economy. There is also monetary policy, which we shall discuss in detail in Chapter 14. Really, a sensible fiscal policy can be formulated only in conjunction with monetary policy, and although it is convenient to discuss them separately, in real life they must be coordinated. Also, lest you become overly pessimistic, you should note that, despite the problems that remain unsolved, our improved understanding of fiscal and monetary policy has enabled us to steer a better and more stable course than in the days before World War II. So far at least, we have managed to avoid either disastrous unemployment or disastrous inflation.

Improving the Workings of Fiscal Policy[12]

What measures might be adopted to improve the workings of fiscal policy? Several have been widely discussed. First, tax rates might vary automatically in response to changes in economic conditions. For example, tax rates might fall by a specified amount if unemployment exceeded a certain percentage of the labor force, or if industrial production fell from one quarter to the next. Similarly, tax rates might increase by a specified amount if the index of consumer prices rose by more than a certain amount during a year. The advantage of such an automatic change in tax rates would be in eliminating the long lag that often occurs while a change in fiscal policy is being pushed through.

Despite the apparent attractiveness of such an approach, critics have pointed out that it suffers from a number of problems. For one, it is difficult to develop rules that can be counted on to be sensible. For another, in some situations these rules could indicate contradictory signals. For example, if we applied such rules to the early 1970s, unemployment might be high enough to trigger a tax cut, while inflation might be high enough to trigger a simultaneous tax increase. For still another thing, there is no indication that Congress would be willing to give up some of its power over taxation. After all, such automatic changes in tax rates would have to be approved by Congress, which thereafter would have less discretionary power over taxes.

Second, Congress might give the president some discretionary power over taxes. For example, the president might be empowered to reduce or stop tax collections for a specified period of time, or to establish increases in tax rates of up to a certain percentage. This too might eliminate the long lag that often occurs while a change in fiscal policy is being pushed through. But it runs into the same difficulty as the previous suggestion: there is no indication that the Congress will give up any substantial portion of its power over the purse. On the contrary, the Congress seems very intent on keeping its existing power in this area.

Third, Congress might revise the way it makes fiscal decisions. Some people argue that the Congress should play a more active role in fiscal policy, rather than merely react to initiatives from the executive branch. Others point to the fragmented nature of the decision-making process in Congress. As we saw in a previous chapter, deci-

[12] Much of this section is based on Dernburg and McDougall, *op. cit.*, pp. 420–23.

sions on government expenditures are made by a number of separate appropriations subcommittees that set the level of spending for individual government agencies. The decisions made by these subcommittees are largely uncoordinated, and the total level of expenditure may not correspond with what is appropriate from the point of view of rational fiscal policy.

According to some conservative economists, this fragmentation of congressional decision making results in excessive government spending. For example, Herbert Stein, chairman of President Nixon's Council of Economic Advisers, believes that "our biggest difficulties in achieving a stabilizing budget policy lie in Congress. Every candid Congressman will agree with that. The whole Congressional procedure is so fragmented that Congress is permitted and encouraged to escape any discipline on total spending. . . . The great need is for improved procedure within the Congress that will force more disciplined action." Needless to say, liberal economists do not agree that there is any tendency toward excessive government spending: witness the views of John Kenneth Galbraith. But conservatives and liberals alike seem to see a need for congressional reform in this area.

Summary

The equilibrium level of net national product is the level where desired consumption plus desired investment plus desired government spending equals net national product. A $1 billion change in government expenditure will result in a change in equilibrium NNP of the same amount as a $1 billion change in desired investment or a $1 billion shift in the relation between consumption expenditures and NNP. In any of these cases, there is a multiplier effect. An increase in the tax rate shifts the relationship between consumption expenditure and NNP downward, thus reducing the equilibrium value of NNP. A decrease in the tax rate shifts the relationship upward, thus increasing the equilibrium value of NNP.

Policy makers receive a lot of help in stabilizing the economy from our automatic stabilizers—automatic changes in tax revenues, unemployment compensation and welfare payments, corporate dividends, family saving, and farm aid. However, the automatic stabilizers can only cut down on variations in unemployment and inflation, not eliminate them. Discretionary programs are needed to supplement the effects of these automatic stabilizers. Such discretionary actions include changing government expenditure on public works and other programs, changing welfare payments and other such transfers, and changing tax rates. An important problem with some of these tools of fiscal policy is the lag in time before they can be brought into play.

At least three policies concerning the government budget have received considerable attention. First, the budget can be balanced each and every year. Second, the budget can be balanced over the course of the business cycle. Third, the budget can be set in a way that will promote full employment with stable prices whether or not this means that the budget is unbalanced over considerable periods of time. The history of the past 40 years has seen enormous changes in the public's attitude toward the government budget. Forty years ago, the prevailing doctrine was that the budget should be balanced each year; now the attitude seems to be that the budget should be used as a tool to reduce unemployment and inflation. Some of the popular misconceptions concerning budget deficits and budget surpluses can be avoided by the use of the full-employment budget, which shows the difference between tax revenue and government expenditure that would result if we had full employment.

CONCEPTS FOR REVIEW

$C + I + G$ line
Deficit
Surplus
Automatic stabilizers
Full-employment budget
Fiscal drag
Functional finance
Discretionary fiscal policy
Balanced budget

QUESTIONS FOR DISCUSSION AND REVIEW

1. According to Joseph Pechman, "Among taxes, the federal individual income tax is the leading [automatic] stabilizer." Explain why, and discuss the significance of this fact. He also says that "on the expenditure side, the major built-in stabilizer is unemployment compensation." Again, explain why, and discuss the significance of this fact.

2. According to Maurice Stans, "The federal government should have a balanced budget; its expenditures, especially in times like these, should not exceed its income." Do you agree?

3. A $1 billion change in government expenditures will result in a change in equilibrium NNP of $\frac{1}{MPS}$ billions of dollars. True or False?

4. Most economists would feel that fiscal policy is not too expansionary when
a. the actual budget shows a deficit, but the full-employment budget shows no deficit.
b. both the actual and full-employment budgets show huge deficits.
c. the price level is increasing at 10 percent per year.
d. the actual and full-employment budgets both show deficits of $20 billion.

CHAPTER 11

Business Fluctuations and Economic Forecasting

The American economy has not grown at a constant rate: instead, output has grown rapidly in some periods, and little, if at all, in others. Our history indicates that national output, employment, and the price level tend to fluctuate. These fluctuations, often mild, sometimes violent, are frequently called business cycles. The average citizen, as well as the government official or the business executive, needs to know why these fluctuations occur and whether they can be avoided. This chapter summarizes some of the leading theories advanced to answer these questions.

We also take up a related question of great practical importance: can business fluctuations be forecasted? More and more, economic models are being used by government and industry to forecast changes in GNP and other economic variables. Economic forecasting has become a very important part of the economist's job. Although no reputable economist would claim that economic forecasting is very precise or reliable, some of the more sophisti-

Figure 11.1
Gross National Product (in 1958 Dollars), United States, 1918–72, Excluding World War II

Real GNP has not grown steadily. Instead, it has tended to approach its full-employment level, then to falter and fall below this level, then to rise once more, and so on. This movement of national output is sometimes called the business cycle.

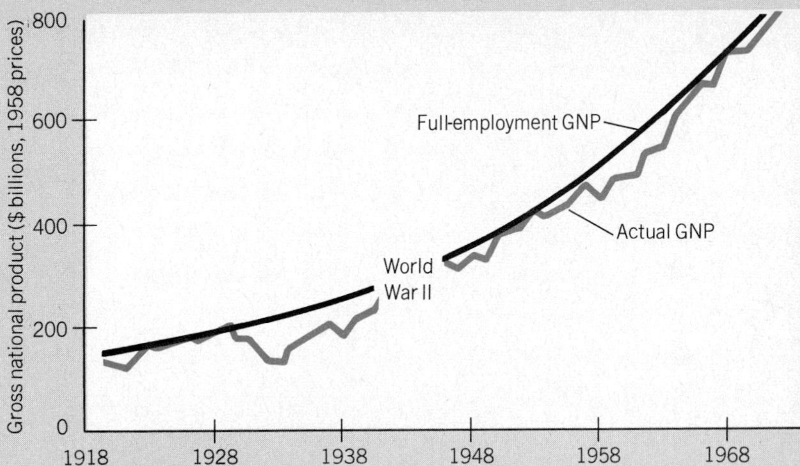

cated models have forecasted quite well in recent years. In the latter part of this chapter, we describe some of the more widely used forecasting techniques, and see how accurate they have proved in the past.

Business Fluctuations

To illustrate what we mean by "business fluctuations"—or the "business cycle"—let's look at how national output has grown in the United States since World War I. Figure 11.1 shows the behavior of real GNP (in constant dollars) in the United States since 1919. It is clear that output has grown considerably during this period; indeed, GNP is more than 5 times what it was 50 years ago. It is also clear that this growth has not been steady. On the contrary, although the long-term trend has been upward, there have been periods—like 1919–21, 1929–33, 1937–38, 1944–46, 1948–49, 1953–54, 1957–58, and 1969–70—when national output has declined.

Let's define the full employment-level of GNP as the total amount of goods and services that could have been produced if there had been full employment. Figure 11.1 shows that national output tends to rise and approach its full-employment level for a while, then falter and fall below this level, then rise to approach it once more, then fall below it again, and so on. For example, output remained close to the full-employment level in the prosperous mid-1920s, fell far below this level in the depressed 1930s, and rose again to this level once we entered World War II. This movement of national output is sometimes called the ***business cycle,*** but it must be recognized that these cycles are far from regular or consistent. On the contrary, they are very irregular.

Each cycle can be divided by definition into four phases, as shown in Figure 11.2. The ***trough*** is the point where national output is lowest relative to its full-employment level. ***Expansion*** is the subsequent phase during which national output rises. The ***peak*** occurs when national output is highest relative to its full-employment level. Finally, ***recession*** is the subsequent phase during which national output falls.[1] Besides these four phases, two other

[1] More precisely, the peak and trough are generally defined in terms of deviations from the long-term trend of NNP, rather than in terms of deviations from the full-employment level of NNP. But the latter definition tends to be easier for beginners to grasp.

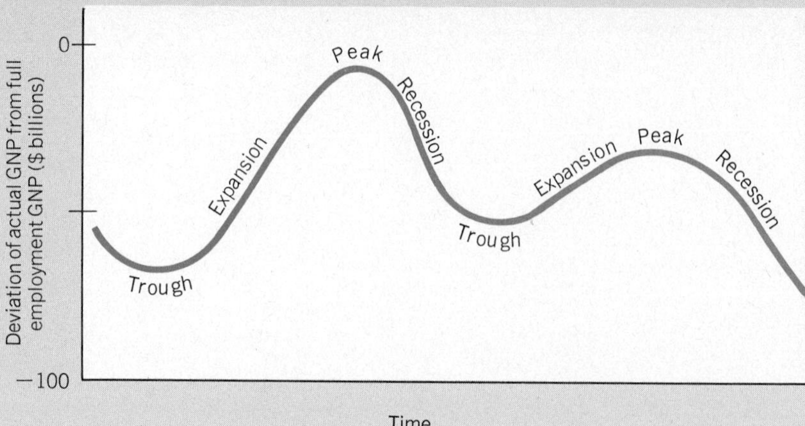

Figure 11.2
Four Phases of Business Fluctuation

Each cycle can be divided into four phases: trough, expansion, peak, and recession.

terms are frequently used to describe stages of the business cycle. A ***depression*** is a period when national output is well below its full-employment level; it is a severe recession. Depressions are, of course, periods of excessive unemployment. ***Prosperity*** is a period when national output is close to its full-employment level. Prosperity, if total spending is too high relative to potential output, can be a time of inflation. Of course, in some business cycles, the peak may not be a period of prosperity because output may be below its full-employment level, or the trough may not be a period of depression because output may not be far below its full-employment level.

Since World War II, peaks have occurred in 1948, 1953, 1957, 1960, and 1969, while troughs have occurred in 1949, 1954, 1958, 1961, and 1970. None of these recessions has been very long or very deep. We have done better since the war at avoiding and cushioning recessions, partly because of improvements in economic knowledge of the causes and cures of business cycles. Note that, although these cycles have certain things in common, they are highly individualistic. For certain classes of phenomena, it may be true that "if you've seen one, you've seen them all," but not for business cycles; they vary too much in length and nature. Moreover, the basic set of factors responsible for the recession and the expansion differs from cycle to cycle.[2] This means that any theory designed to explain them must be broad enough to accommodate their idiosyncracies.

It is also worth stressing that investment seems to be the component of total spending that varies most over the course of a business cycle. Investment goes down markedly during recessions and increases markedly during expansions; on the other hand, consumption generally moves along with only slight bumps and dips.[3] The volatility of investment, together with the reasons for this volatility, are important clues to the cause of many business cycles. We shall see that this variation in

[2] For example, there is some evidence that every so often, a business boom, or peak, takes place at about the same time as a boom in building construction; thus such a peak is buoyed further by this favorable conjuncture—and every so often, a trough is lowered by it. These long swings in building (and other phenomena), lasting 15 to 25 years, are called Kuznets cycles after Harvard's Nobel Laureate, Simon Kuznets, who has devoted considerable study to them. See Alvin Hansen, *Business Cycles and National Income,* New York: Norton, 1962.

[3] However, expenditure on consumer durables is more volatile than other consumption expenditure. Moreover, the consumption function can shift, as it did after World War II. (Recall the discussion of this shift in Chapter 9.)

investment plus our old friend (of Chapter 9), the multiplier, can produce the sorts of business fluctuations that have occurred in the United States.

Government Spending and Expectations

Government expenditures too can sometimes cause business fluctuations. When we discussed fiscal policy, we described how government spending might be used to stabilize the economy. The unfortunate fact is that in the past the government's spending—particularly during and after wars—has sometimes been a major destabilizing force, resulting in business fluctuations. Recall from Chapter 8 the great bulge in government spending during World War II and the lesser bulges during the Korean and Vietnamese wars. These increases in spending produced strong inflationary pressures. The price level rose over 50 percent during 1940–46 (World War II), and major inflationary spurts also occurred during the wars in Korea and Vietnam. In Chapter 10, we discussed in some detail the destabilizing effects of the Vietnamese military buildup.

Government spending has been a destabilizing force after, as well as during, wars. The recession in 1953–54 was caused primarily by the reduction in government expenditures when the Korean war came to a close. When hostilities terminated, government expenditures were reduced by more than $10 billion. Government spending sometimes has also had the same destabilizing effect in other than wartime or postwar situations. The recession in 1957–58 was aggravated by a drop in defense expenditures in late 1957. Faced with this drop, the defense contractors cut their inventories and expenditures for plant and equipment.

Another factor is the nature and behavior of expectations. For example, in the recession of 1957, businessmen's expectations became decidedly more pessimistic. Capital spending was cut by over $7 billion and inventory investment by over $8 billion. (Fortunately, the recession was short, and the economy began to move upward in late 1958.) Such expectations play a significant role in business fluctuations. Decisions made at any point in time depend on expectations concerning the future. For example, when a firm builds a new warehouse, it has certain expectations concerning the extent of its sales in the future, the price it will have to pay for labor and transportation, and so on. In forming their expectations, businessmen often tend to follow the leader. As more and more businessmen and analysts predict a rosy future, others tend to jump on the bandwagon. This means that, as the economy advances from a trough, optimistic expectations concerning sales and profits tend to spread, slowly at first, then more and more rapidly. These expectations generate investment, which in turn increases NNP. Thus, the rosy expectations are self-fulfilling, at least up to a point. (In this area, even if "wishing won't make it so," expecting may turn the trick!) The result is that the expansion is fueled by self-fulfilling and self-augmenting expectations.

Eventually, however, these expectations are not fulfilled, perhaps because full-employment ceilings cause NNP to grow at a slower rate, perhaps because the government cuts back its spending (as in 1953–54), perhaps for some other reason. Now the process goes into reverse. Pessimistic expectations appear; and as NNP begins to decline, these expectations spread more and more rapidly. These expectations also tend to be self-fulfilling. Businessmen, feeling that the outlook for sales and profits is unfavorable, cut back on their investing, which in turn reduces NNP. Thus, the recession is made more serious by the epidemic of gloom. In any theory of business fluctuations, it is necessary to recognize the importance of expectations.

The Acceleration Principle

Investment in plant and equipment, as we know, varies considerably over the course of the business cycle. One of the most important reasons for this variation is illustrated by the following example. Suppose that the Johnson Shoe Corporation, a maker of women's shoes, requires 1 machine to make 50 pairs of shoes per year. Since each machine (and related plant and facilities) costs $1,000 and each pair of shoes costs $10, it takes $2 worth of plant and equipment to produce $1 worth of output per year. In 1965, we suppose that the quantity of the firm's plant and equipment was exactly in balance with its output. In other words, the firm had no excess capacity; sales were $10,000 and the actual stock of capital was $20,000. The firm's sales in subsequent years are shown in Table 11.1. For example, in 1966 its sales increased to $12,000; in 1967 they increased to $14,000; and so forth.

Table 11.1 also shows the amount the firm will have to invest each year in order to produce the amount it sells. Let's begin with 1966. To produce $12,000 worth of product, the firm must have $24,000 worth of capital. This means that it must increase its stock of capital from $20,000—the amount it has in 1965—to $24,000.[4] In other words, it must increase its stock of capital by $4,000, which means that its net investment in plant and equipment must equal $4,000. But this is not the same as its gross investment—the amount of plant and equipment the firm must buy—because the firm must also replace some plant and equipment that wears out. Suppose that $1,000 of plant and equipment wear out each year: then gross investment in 1966 must equal net investment ($4,000) plus $1,000, or $5,000.

Next, let's look at 1967. The firm's sales in that year are $14,000. To produce this much output, the firm must have $28,000 of capital, which means that it must increase its stock of capital by $4,000—from $24,000 to $28,000. In addition, there is $1,000 of replacement investment to replace plant and equipment that wear out in 1967. In all, the firm's gross investment must be $5,000. In 1968, the firm's sales are $15,000. To produce this output,

[4] Note that the firm's stock of capital is an entirely different concept than its common stock or preferred stock. See Chapter 7.

Table 11.1

Relationship between Sales and Investment, Johnson Shoe Corporation

Year	Sales (thousands of dollars)	Needed stock of capital (thousands of dollars)	Actual stock of capital (thousands of dollars)	Replacement investment (thousands of dollars)	Net investment (thousands of dollars)	Gross investment (thousands of dollars)
1965	10	20	20	1	0	1
1966	12	24	24	1	4	5
1967	14	28	28	1	4	5
1968	15	30	30	1	2	3
1969	16	32	32	1	2	3
1970	16	32	32	1	0	1
1971	15	30	31	0	0	0
1972	15	30	30	0	0	0
1973	15	30	30	1	0	1
1974	17	34	34	1	4	5

the firm must have $30,000 of capital, which means that it must increase its stock of capital by $2,000—from $28,000 to $30,000. In addition, there is $1,000 of replacement investment. In all, the firm's gross investment must be $3,000. Table 11.1 shows the results for subsequent years.

What conclusions can be drawn from Table 11.1? First, *changes in sales can result in magnified percentage changes in investment.* For example, between 1965 and 1966 sales went up by 20 percent, whereas gross investment went up by 400 percent. Between 1973 and 1974, sales went up by about 13 percent, whereas gross investment went up by 400 percent. The effect of a decrease in sales is even more spectacular because it tends to drive net investment to zero. Indeed, even gross investment may be driven to zero, as in 1971, if the firm wants to reduce the value of its plant and equipment. To accomplish this, the firm simply does not replace the plant and equipment that wear out.

Second, *the amount of gross investment depends on the rate of increase of sales.* In particular, for gross investment to remain constant year after year, the rate of increase of sales must also remain constant. You can see this in 1966 and 1967. In each of these years, since sales increased from the previous year by the same amount ($2,000), gross investment remained constant at $5,000 per year. It is very important to note that *gross investment will fall when sales begin to increase at a decreasing rate.* The fact that sales are increasing does not insure that gross investment will increase; on the contrary, if sales are increasing at a decreasing rate, gross investment will fall. This is a very important point.

This effect of changes in sales on gross investment is often called the ***acceleration principle,*** since changes in sales result in accelerated, or magnified, changes in investment, and since an increase in investment results from an increase in the growth rate (an ***acceleration***) of sales. The acceleration principle applies to kinds of investment other than plant and equipment. For example, it is easy to show that it applies to inventories and housing as well. Thus, firms often try to maintain a certain amount of inventory for each dollar of sales—just as they often maintain a certain amount of plant and equipment for each dollar of sales.

The Interaction between the Acceleration Principle and the Multiplier

Economists—led by Nobel Laureates Paul Samuelson and Sir John Hicks[5]—have shown that the acceleration principle combined with the multiplier may produce business cycles like those experienced in the real world. The basic idea is easy. Suppose that the economy is moving up toward full employment, NNP is increasing, and sales are increasing at an increasing rate. Because of the acceleration principle, the increases in sales result in a high level of investment. And via the multiplier, the high level of investment promotes further increases in NNP. Thus, the accelerator and multiplier tend to reinforce one another, resulting in a strong upward movement of NNP. The economy is in an expansion. It is a good time to be president of the United States, president of a major corporation, or an average citizen.

Eventually, however, the economy nears full employment; and since we have only a certain amount of land, labor, and capital, it simply is impossible to increase NNP at the rate experienced during the recovery. Consequently, sales cannot increase forever at the same rate; instead, they begin to increase more slowly. But as we saw in the previous section, the reduction in the rate of increase of sales is the kiss of death for investment. Even though sales continue to increase, the drop in the rate of increase means decreasing investment. And this reduction in investment sounds the death

[5] Paul A. Samuelson, "The Interaction between the Multiplier Analysis and the Acceleration Principle," *Review of Economics and Statistics,* 1939; and John Hicks, *A Contribution to the Theory of the Trade Cycle,* Oxford, 1950. Also, see R. F. Harrod, *The Trade Cycle,* Oxford, 1936.

knell for the boom, since it reduces NNP directly and via the multiplier. The reduction in NNP means a reduction in sales, and the reduction in sales means a drastic reduction in investment, through the acceleration principle. The drastic reduction in investment means a further reduction in NNP. The economy is in a recession. Everything is moving downward, with the notable exception of unemployment. People are getting increasingly nervous—including the president of the United States, the presidents of major corporations, and many average citizens.

Eventually, however, firms reduce their stock of capital to the point where it is in balance with their reduced sales. In other words, they go through the sort of process shown in Table 11.1 during 1971–72, when the Johnson Shoe Corporation reduced its stock of capital by refusing to replace worn-out plant and equipment. At the end of this process, the stock of capital is in balance with sales. To keep this balance, firms must now replace worn-out equipment, which means an increase in gross investment. Via the multiplier, this increase in investment results in an increase in national product, which means an increase in sales. Via the acceleration principle, this increase in sales results in an increase in investment, which in turn increases national product. The economy is once again in the midst of a recovery. It is again a good time to be president of the United States, president of a major corporation, or an average citizen. As moviegoers put it, this is where we came in.

This theory, although highly simplified, provides a great many insights into the nature of business fluctuations. One aspect of the theory in particular should be noted: business cycles are self-starting and self-terminating. Recession, trough, recovery, peak—each phase of the business cycle leads into the next. This theory shows that one need not look outside the economic system for causes of the upper and lower turning points—that is, the points where the economy begins to turn down after a recovery or begins to turn up after a recession. These turning points can occur for the reasons we have just indicated.

Inventory Cycles

Inventories also play an important role in business fluctuations. Indeed, the "minor" or "short" business cycle, lasting about 2 to 4 years, is sometimes called an ***inventory cycle*** because it is often due largely to variations in inventories. This cycle proceeds as follows. Businessmen, having let their inventories decline during a business slowdown, find that they are short of inventories. They increase their inventories, which means that they produce more than they sell. This investment in inventories has a stimulating effect on NNP. So long as the rate of increase of their sales holds up, firms continue to increase their inventories at this rate.[6] Thus, inventory investment continues to stimulate the economy. But when their sales begin to increase more slowly, firms begin to cut back on their inventory investment. This reduction in inventory investment has a depressing effect on NNP. As their sales decrease, firms cut back further on their inventory investment, further damping NNP. Then when inventories are cut to the bone, the process starts all over again.

As an illustration, consider the recession of 1948–49, which was primarily the result of reduction of inventory investment. After World War II, there was a period of stockpiling. Inventories were built up very substantially during 1948: indeed, they increased by $5 billion during that year. In 1949, on the other hand, inventories were cut by about the same amount. Thus, there was a $10 billion decrease in inventory investment between 1947 and 1948. This meant a considerable cutback in production. Not only did firms stop producing more—$5 billion more—than they sold, they started producing less—$5 billion less—than they sold, and they cut wages and income. This was a major cause of the recession of 1948–49.

[6] As noted above, the acceleration effect discussed in previous sections applies to inventories as well as plant and equipment, since firms often try to maintain inventories equal to a certain percentage of sales. Thus, the *rate of increase* of sales will affect the rate of investment in inventories as well as plant and equipment.

Innovations and Random External Events

Let's turn now to a different sort of explanation of business fluctuations. Clearly, the acceleration principle is only one factor influencing gross investment. Since a firm will invest in any project where the returns exceed the costs involved, many investment projects are not triggered by changes in sales. For example, a new product may be invented, and large investments may be required to produce, distribute, and market it. Consider the automobile industry, currently one of America's largest industries. It took big investments by the pioneers in the auto business to get the automobile to the point where it was an important item in the average consumer's budget. Or consider nylon, which Du Pont spent several million dollars to develop. It took large investments before nylon was on its way.

Major innovations do not occur every day; neither do they occur at a constant rate. There are more in some years than in others, and sheer chance influences the number of innovations in a given year. Similarly, chance greatly influences the timing of many other types of events that bear on the level of output and investment. These include crop failures, hurricanes, and other such natural disasters, as well as man-made events, like strikes in major industries and financial panics, which also affect output and investment.

Let's suppose that these events—innovations and other occurrences that have a major effect on investment—occur more or less at random. Because so many factors influence the timing of each such event, we cannot predict how many will occur in a particular year. Instead, the number is subject to chance variation, like the number thrown in a dice game or the number of spades in a poker hand. In particular, suppose that the chance that one of these events occurs in one year is about the same as in another year.

If this is the case, economists—led by Norway's Nobel Laureate, Ragnar Frisch[7]—have shown that business cycles are likely to result. The basic idea is simple enough. The economy, because of its internal structure, is like a pendulum or rocking chair. If it is subjected to random shocks—like pushing a rocking chair every now and then—it will move up and down. These random shocks are the bursts of investment that arise as a consequence of a great new invention or of the development of a new territory, or for some other such reason. These bursts play the role of the forces hitting the pendulum or the rocking chair. To a considerable extent, they may be due to noneconomic events or forces, but whatever their cause, they bang into the economy and shove it in one direction or another.

Of course, the occurrence of these shocks is not the whole story. Business fluctuations in this model do not occur only because of the random events that affect investment. In addition, the economy must respond to—and amplify—the effects of these stimuli. The economy must be like a rocking chair, not a sofa. (If you whack a sofa every now and then, you are likely to hurt your hand, but not to move the sofa much.) Frisch showed that the economy is likely to respond to, and amplify, these shocks. This model explains the fact, stressed in a previous section, that although cycles bear some family resemblance, no two are really alike. Thus the model has the advantage of not explaining more than it should. It does not imply that business fluctuations are more uniform and predictable than they are.

This theory provides valuable insight into the nature of business fluctuations. Like the theory of the interaction of the acceleration principle and the multiplier, it contains important elements of truth, although it obviously is highly simplified. Each of these theories focuses on factors that may be partly responsible for business fluctuations. They complement one another, in the sense that both processes—the interaction of the multiplier and the acceleration principle, and the random external stimuli to investment—may be at work. There is

[7] Ragnar Frisch, "Propagation Problems and Impulse Problems in Dynamic Economics," *Economic Essays in Honor of Gustav Cassel,* London: George Allen and Unwin, 1933.

no need to choose between these theories: both help to explain business fluctuations, and both are far from the whole truth.

Monetary Factors

Finally, we must stress that *monetary factors are of great importance in causing business fluctuations.* For example, monetary factors were of the utmost importance in slowing down the boom of the late 1960s, as we shall see in Chapter 14. The fact that we have not yet taken up these factors is no indication that they are unimportant. On the contrary, they are so important that we shall devote the next several chapters entirely to them. For pedagogical reasons, it seems advisable to discuss them after the topics taken up in Chapters 9–11. You should constantly bear in mind that monetary policy can be of enormous importance in moderating business fluctuations and in promoting reasonably full employment with reasonably stable prices. In economics as in other aspects of life, money counts.

Can Business Fluctuations Be Avoided?

Having looked at some theories designed to explain business fluctuations, we are led to ask whether they (the fluctuations, not the theories) can be avoided in the future. To some extent, a discussion of this question is premature, since we have not yet taken up monetary policy. But there is no reason to postpone answering it in general terms, waiting for subsequent chapters to provide more detailed discussions of various aspects of the answer.

On the basis of our increased knowledge of the reasons for business fluctuations and the growing acceptance of modern monetary and fiscal policy, some people seem to think the business cycle has been licked. That is, they feel that we can now use monetary and fiscal policy to head off a recession or a boom, and in this way offset the processes and events that destabilize the economy. This is a rather optimistic view, although the evidence does indicate that we have been able to reduce the severity and frequency of major recessions in recent years. Our record in this regard has been distinctly better than in pre-World War II days.

In particular, the fact that we managed to maintain uninterrupted economic expansion for most of the 1960s was an unparalleled achievement—although, as pointed out in previous chapters, our record on inflation during the later 1960s was not so awe-inspiring. This improvement in performance must be attributed partly to better economic knowledge and partly to the fact that the nation, recognizing that depressions are not inevitable, expects the government to take the actions required to prevent them.

Unfortunately, this does not mean that a major depression—like that experienced in the 1930s—is impossible, although the chance of its occurrence must be regarded as very small. Even though we now know how to prevent a depression, one could still occur through stupidity or some weird sequence of events. But the probability of such a depression is very, very small, given our automatic stabilizers and the fact that policy makers—and the electorate—know now that fiscal policy (Chapter 10) and monetary policy (Chapter 14) can be used to push the economy toward full employment.

It seems unlikely, however, that the small recessions—the "dips" and "pauses"—are a thing of the past. There will be ups and downs in spending on plant and equipment, there will be fluctuations in inventories, there will be military buildups and cutbacks, and changes in government spending and in tax rates. All these things can be destabilizing, and existing economic knowledge is not sufficiently precise to allow policy makers to iron out the resulting small deviations of NNP from its long-term upward trend. Although there has been a certain amount of optimistic talk about "fine-tuning" of the economy, the truth is that we lack the knowledge or the means to do it.

Finally, the prospect for inflation is not so bright. The recent record of the United States has not been particularly encouraging. We have just about learned that a balanced budget is not the touchstone of fiscal policy, but we have not yet learned how to maintain reasonably full employment with reasonably stable prices. This is a very difficult problem, and an important one, which we shall discuss in much greater detail in Chapters 12, 14, and 15.

Can Business Fluctuations Be Forecasted?

Having studied important aspects of the modern theory of the determination of national product, as well as various reasons for business fluctuations, you may well ask how useful these theories are in forecasting NNP. This is a perfectly reasonable question. After all, when you study physics or chemistry, you want to come away with certain theories or principles that will enable you to predict physical or chemical phenomena. To the extent that economics is a science, you have a right to expect the same thing, since an acid test of any science is how well it predicts.

This question is also of great practical importance. Government officials are enormously interested in what NNP is likely to be in the next year or so, since they must try to anticipate whether excesive unemployment or serious inflationary pressures are developing. Business executives are equally interested, since their firms' sales, profits, and needs for equipment depend on NNP. For these reasons, forecasting is one of the principal jobs of economists in government and industry.

The first thing that must be said is that, in forecasting as in most other areas, economics is not an exact science. If an economist tells you he can predict exactly what NNP will be next year, you can be pretty sure that he is talking through his hat. Of course, by luck, he may be able to predict correctly, but lucky guesses do not a science make. However, although economic forecasting is not perfectly accurate, economic forecasts are still useful. Since governments, firms, and private individuals must continually make decisions that hinge on what they expect will happen, there is no way that they can avoid making forecasts, explicit or implicit. Really the only question is how best to make them.

There is considerable evidence that, even though forecasts based on economic models are sometimes not very good, they are better—on the average—than those made by noneconomists. There is no substitute for economic analysis in accurate forecasting over the long haul. Of course, this really isn't very surprising. It would be strange if economists, whose profession it is to study and predict economic phenomena, were to do worse than those without this training—even if the others are tycoons or politicians. Further, it would be strange if government and industry were to hire platoons of economists at fancy prices—which they do—if they couldn't predict any better than anyone else.

In the realm of economic forecasting, what is a good batting average? According to M.I.T.'s Paul Samuelson,

> In economic forecasting of the direction of change, we ought to be able to do at least .500 just by tossing a coin. And taking advantage of the undoubted upward trend in all modern economies, we can bat .750 or better just by parrot-like repeating, "Up, Up." The difference between the men and the boys, then, comes between an .850 performance and an .800 performance. Put in other terms, the good forecaster, who must in November make a point-estimate of GNP for the calendar year ahead, will over a decade, have an average error of perhaps one percent, being in a range of $12 billion with reality being $6 billion on either side of the estimate. And a rather poor forecaster may, over the same period, average an error of 1½ percent. When we average the yearly results for a decade, it may be found that in the worst year the error was over 2 percent, compensated by rather small errors in many of the years not expected to represent turning points.[8]

[8] Paul A. Samuelson, "Economic Forecasting and Science," in his *Readings in Economics*, New York: McGraw-Hill, 1970, pp. 112–113, and reprinted in E. Mansfield, *Economics: Readings, Issues, and Cases*, New York: Norton, 1974.

Economists have no single method for forecasting NNP or GNP. They vary in their approach just as physicians, for example, differ in theirs. But reputable economists tend to use one of a small number of forecasting techniques, each of which is described in a subsequent section. Of course, many economists do not restrict themselves to one technique, but rely on a combination of several, using one to check on another.

Leading Indicators

Perhaps the simplest way to forecast business fluctuations is to use ***leading indicators,*** which are certain economic series that typically go down or up before NNP does. The National Bureau of Economic Research, founded by Wesley C. Mitchell (1874–1948), has carried out detailed and painstaking research to examine the behavior of various economic variables over a long period of time, in some cases as long as 100 years. The Bureau has attempted to find out whether each variable goes down before, at, or after the peak of the business cycle, and whether it turns up before, at, or after the trough. Variables that go down before the peak and up before the trough are called ***leading series.*** Variables that go down at the peak and up at the trough are called ***coincident series.*** And those that go down after the peak and up after the trough are called ***lagging series.***

It is worthwhile examining the kinds of variables that fall into each of these three categories, since they give us important facts concerning the anatomy of the cycle. According to the Bureau, some important leading series are business failures, new orders for durable goods, average work week, building contracts, stock prices, certain wholesale prices, and new incorporations. These are the variables that tend to turn down before the peak and turn up before the trough.[9] Coincident series include employment, industrial production, corporate profits, and gross national product, among many others. Some typical lagging series are retail sales, manufacturers' inventories, and personal income.

Economists sometimes use leading series as forecasting devices. There are good economic reasons why these series turn down before a peak or up before a trough. In some cases, they indicate changes in spending in strategic areas of the economy, while in others they indicate changes in businessmen's and investors' expectations. Both to guide the government in determining its economic policies and to guide firms in their planning, it is important to try to spot turning points—peaks and troughs—in advance. This, of course, is the toughest part of economic forecasting. Economists sometimes use these leading indicators as evidence that a turning point is about to occur. If a large number of leading indicators turn down, this is viewed as a sign of a coming peak. If a large number turn up, this is thought to signal an impending trough.

Unfortunately, the leading indicators are not very reliable. It is true that the economy has never turned down in recent years without a warning from these indicators. This is fine. But unfortunately these indicators have turned down on several occasions—1952 and 1962, for example—when the economy did not turn down subsequently. Thus, they sometimes provide false signals. Also, in periods of expansion, they sometimes turn down too long before the real peak. And in periods of recession, they sometimes turn up only a very short while before the trough, so that we've turned the corner before anything can be done. Nonetheless, these indicators are not worthless. They are watched closely and used to supplement other, more sophisticated forecasting techniques.

Simple Keynesian Models

Leading indicators are used primarily to spot turning points—peaks and troughs. They are of little or no use in predicting GNP (or NNP). To forecast GNP, we need a more sophisticated approach,

[9] Of course, business failures turn *up* before the peak and *down* before the trough.

one more firmly rooted in economic theory. (Leading indicators are largely the product of strictly empirical analysis.) To forecast GNP, it is worthwhile bringing into play the theory we described in Chapters 9 and 10. After all, if the theory is any good, it should help us to forecast GNP. This theory can be used in a variety of ways to help prepare such forecasts, and a first course in economics can provide no more than the most basic introduction to these methods.

One simple way of trying to forecast GNP is to treat certain components of total spending as given and to use these components to forecast the total. This method is sometimes used by the Council of Economic Advisers, among others. For example, suppose that we decide to forecast private investment and government expenditures as a first step, after which we will use these forecasts to predict GNP.[10] Private investment is made up of three parts: expenditures on plant and equipment, residential construction, and changes in inventories. The most important of these parts is expenditure on plant and equipment. To forecast it, the results of surveys of firms' expenditure plans for the next year are helpful. The Department of Commerce and the Securities and Exchange Commission send out questionnaires at the beginning of each year to a large number of firms, asking them how much they plan to spend on plant and equipment during the year. The results, which appear in March in the *Survey of Current Business,* are pretty accurate. For example, the average error in 1951–63 was only about 3 percent.

This survey can help us forecast business expenditures on plant and equipment, but what about the other parts of private investment—residential construction and changes in inventories? Lots of techniques are used to forecast them. Some people use construction contracts and similar indicators as the basis for forecasts of residential construction. For inventory changes, some people watch the surveys carried out by *Fortune* magazine and the Commerce Department, which ask companies about their inventory plans.

Next, we need a forecast of government expenditures. At the federal level, it is possible to forecast government expenditures on the basis of the president's proposed budget or Congress's appropriations (although, as indicated by our discussion of the Vietnam buildup in Chapter 10, these forecasts can sometimes be quite wrong). At the state and local level, it is often possible to extrapolate spending levels reasonably well.

Suppose that, having studied as many relevant factors as we can, we finally conclude that in our best estimate private investment plus government expenditure will equal $400 billion next year. How do we go from this estimate to an estimate of GNP? Suppose that consumers in the past have devoted about 90 percent of their disposable income to consumption expenditure, and that disposable income has been about 70 percent of GNP. Assuming that this will also be true again next year, it follows that consumption expenditure will equal 63 percent (90 percent times 70 percent) of GNP. In other words,

$$C = .63Y, \tag{11.1}$$

where C is consumption expenditure and Y is GNP. Also, by definition,

$$Y = C + I + G,$$

where I is gross private investment and G is government expenditure. Since $I + G = 400$, it follows that

$$Y = C + 400. \tag{11.2}$$

Substituting the right-hand side of Equation (11.1) for C,

$$Y = .63Y + 400,$$

[10] We continue to ignore net exports in this part of the book because they are quite small. Chapters 30–32 will study them in some detail.

or

$$\begin{aligned} Y - .63Y &= 400 \\ .37Y &= 400 \\ Y &= \frac{400}{.37} \\ &= 1081. \end{aligned}$$

Thus, our forecast for GNP next year is $1,081 billion.

At this point, our job may seem to be over. But it really isn't; we must check this forecast in various ways. For example, it implies that consumption expenditures next year will be $681 billion. (Since $C = .63Y$, according to Equation (11.1), and Y equals 1081, C must equal 681.) Does this seem reasonable? For example, how does it compare with the latest results of the survey of consumer buying plans carried out at the Survey Research Center at the University of Michigan? Also, the forecasted level of GNP must be compared with the physical capacity of the economy. Do we have the physical capacity to produce this much at stable prices? To what extent will the general price level be pushed upward? Moreover, our assumptions concerning I and G must be reexamined in the light of our forecast of GNP. If GNP is $1,081 billion, is it reasonable to assume that I will be the amount we initially forecasted? Or do we want to revise our forecast of I? A great many steps must be carried out before we finally put forth a GNP forecast, if we are conscientious and professional in our approach. Moreover, even after the forecast is made, it is often updated as new information becomes available, so the process goes on more or less continuously.

Econometric Models

In recent years, more and more emphasis has been placed on econometric models. Twenty years ago, econometric models were in their infancy, but now the Council of Economic Advisers, the Treasury, the Federal Reserve Board, and other parts of the federal government pay attention to the forecasts made by econometric models—and sometimes construct their own econometric models. Business firms too hire economists to construct econometric models for them, to forecast both GNP and their own sales. ***Econometric models*** are systems of equations estimated from past data that are used to forecast economic variables. There are many kinds of econometric models. For example, some are designed to forecast wage rates; others are designed to forecast the sales of a new product; and still others are designed to forecast a particular company's share of the market. We are concerned here only with econometric models designed to forecast GNP.

The essence of any econometric model is that it blends theory and measurement. It is not merely a general, nonquantitative theory. Useful as such a theory may be, it does not in general permit quantitative or numerical forecasts. Nor is an econometric model a purely empirical result based on little or no theoretical underpinning. Useful as such results may be, they generally are untrustworthy once the basic structure of the economic situation changes. Most econometric models designed to forecast GNP are built, at least in part, on the theoretical foundations described in previous chapters. In other words, they contain a number of equations, one of which is designed to explain consumption expenditures, one to explain investment expenditures, and so forth.

To see what is involved in the construction of an econometric model, let's consider just one of the equations, the consumption equation. The first step in formulating this equation is to ask ourselves what variables influence consumption expenditure. We know from Chapter 9 that one important determinant of consumption expenditure is disposable income. Thus, if the ratio of disposable income to GNP remains constant, consumption expenditure should be closely related to GNP. To keep things simple, let's suppose that this is the only factor determining consumption expenditure. Needless to say, this is not the case, but it makes it easier to see what is involved in constructing an

Figure 11.3
Relationship between Consumption Expenditure and Gross National Product, 1950–70

The line $C = -15 + \frac{2}{3}Y$ fits the data (indicated by the dots) far better than the line $C = -800 + 2Y$. (C is consumption expenditure and Y is GNP.) No one needs a Ph.D. in mathematical statistics to see this.

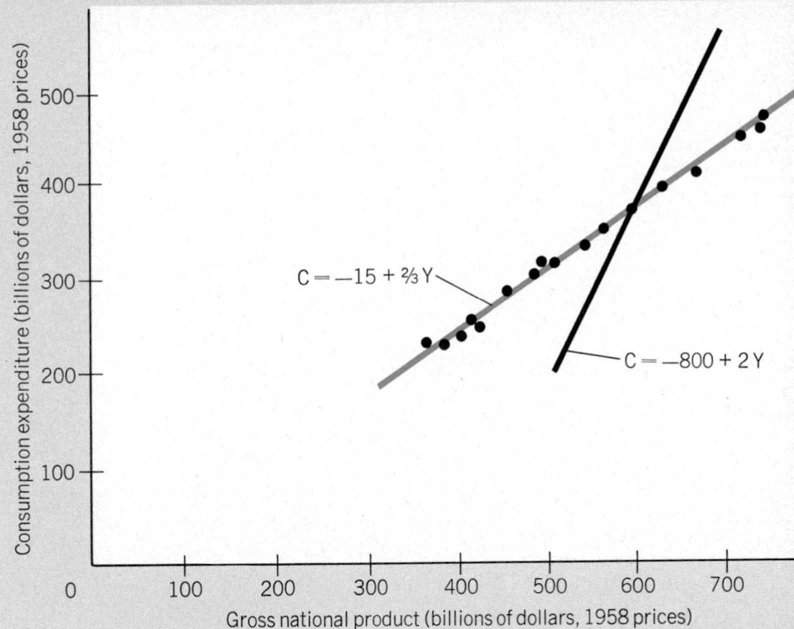

econometric model.

Economic theory—and hunch and intuition based on experience and insight—suggest the explanatory variables to be used in an equation, but they alone cannot supply the numbers to be used. For example, if the relationship between consumption expenditure and GNP is linear, it follows that

$$C = a + bY, \tag{11.3}$$

where C is consumption expenditure and Y is gross national product. But what are the numerical values of a and b? At this point, statistical techniques of various sorts come into play. In the simple case considered here, we can plot consumption expenditure (C) against gross national product (Y) in various years in the past, as shown in Figure 11.3. Then we can pick the values of a and b that fit the data best. For example, as shown in Figure 11.3, an equation based on $a = -800$ and $b = 2$ does not fit the data at all well, while an equation based on $a = -15$ and $b = \frac{2}{3}$ does much better. There are standard statistical methods, known as regression techniques, that can be used to determine which values of a and b fit the data best. These values, once determined, can be inserted into Equation (11.3).

A Small Econometric Model[11]

Econometric models, like many of the good things in life, come in various sizes. Some are composed of lots of equations; some contain only a few. Bigger models are not necessarily to be preferred to smaller ones, or vice versa. The sort of model that is best for a particular purpose depends on which one predicts best and how costly it is to operate. The best way to get a feel for the nature of an

[11] This section, and the following one, are optional and can be omitted without loss of continuity.

econometric model is to examine one. Let's take a look at a small one designed by Wharton's Irwin Friend and Paul Taubman.[12] Because it contains only 5 equations, it is an easy one for a student to begin on. More complicated models are discussed in the next section.

Although the discussion in this section and the next one is at an elementary level, the nature of the analysis requires familiarity with the idea of, and notation for, a set of equations. Readers who do not have this familiarity can skip these two sections without losing the thread of the argument.

One of the hardest things to keep track of in econometric models is what each symbol stands for. Let's begin by spelling this out for the Friend-Taubman model. There are 9 variables used in the model, and the symbol for each is as follows:

Y = gross national product
C = consumption expenditure
E = plant and equipment expenditures
E^e = expected plant and equipment expenditures, according to surveys
H = residential construction expenditure
L = housing starts (lagged a quarter)
I = inventory investment
S^e = expected business sales, according to surveys
G = government expenditure plus net exports.

Y, C, E, E^e, H, I, G, and S^e are measured in billions of 1954 dollars. L is measured in hundreds of thousands of units. Another symbol that must be explained is Δ, which means the change in a particular variable. For example, ΔY means "the change in Y," or since Y is GNP, it means "the change in GNP." Still another symbol is the subscript $_{-1}$. Any variable with a subscript $_{-1}$ means the value of the variable in the preceding period. Thus, a change with a subscript $_{-1}$ means a change occurring between the previous two periods. For example, ΔC_{-1} means the change in consumption expenditure between the last period and the period before. In this model, each period is 6 months.

Having disposed of the preliminaries, let's look at the model. The first equation explains ΔC, the change in consumption expenditure between this period and last period. According to this equation,

$$\Delta C = 2.18 + .37\Delta Y + .10\Delta C_{-1}. \qquad (11.4)$$

In other words, the change in consumption expenditures equals 2.18 billion (1954) dollars plus .37 times the change in GNP between this period and last period plus .10 times the change in consumption expenditures between last period and the period before. Certainly it is reasonable to expect that the change in consumption will be directly related to the change in GNP. This follows from our discussion of the consumption function in Chapter 9. It is also reasonable to expect that the change in consumption between this period and the last will depend on the change in consumption between the last period and the one before. Basically the reason for this is that there is likely to be a lag in adjustment. The numbers in Equation (11.4), like those in all the equations in the model, were estimated from past data.

The second equation explains ΔE, the change in expenditures on plant and equipment between this period and the last period. According to this equation,

$$\Delta E = -.82 + .63(E^e - E_{-1}) + .08(\Delta Y + \Delta Y_{-1}). \qquad (11.5)$$

In other words, the change in expenditure on plant and equipment equals −.82 billion (1954) dollars plus .63 times the difference between expected expenditure on plant and equipment (based on surveys) and actual expenditure on plant and equipment in the previous period, plus .08 times the sum of the change in GNP between this period and the last period and the change in GNP between the last period and the previous period. One would suppose, of course, that the change in actual expenditure on plant and equipment would

[12] Irwin Friend and Paul Taubman, "A Short-Term Forecasting Model," *Review of Economics and Statistics*, August 1964. This model has been revised since publication, and is presented for illustrative purposes only.

be directly related to the change indicated by businessmen's expectations concerning their expenditures on plant and equipment. Also, based on the acceleration principle, one would suppose that the amount spent on plant and equipment would be directly related to the rate of change of GNP. Both suppositions are included in Equation (11.5) because neither theory by itself does as well historically as a mixture of both.

The third equation explains ΔH, the change in residential construction between this period and last period. According to this equation,

$$\Delta H = .35 + .58\Delta L + .06(\Delta Y - \Delta Y_{-1}) - .16(E^e - E_{-1}). \quad (11.6)$$

In other words, the change in expenditure on residential construction equals .35 billion (1954) dollars plus .58 times the change in housing starts (lagged a quarter) plus .06 times the change in the rate of change of GNP minus .16 times the expected change in expenditure on plant and equipment (based on surveys). One would suppose, of course, that the change in expenditure on construction would be directly related to the change in housing starts (lagged a quarter). Also, from the acceleration principle, one would suppose that the amount spent on residential construction would be directly related to the rate of change of GNP. Thus, the change in the amount spent on residential construction would be assumed to vary directly with the change in the rate of change of GNP, which of course equals $\Delta Y - \Delta Y_{-1}$. Finally, the change in residential construction is likely to be inversely related to the change in expected expenditures on plant and equipment because if there is a great increase (decrease) in the latter, this will mean higher (lower) interest rates and greater (less) competition for resources which may discourage (encourage) residential construction.

The fourth equation explains ΔI, the change in inventory investment between this period and the last period. According to this equation,

$$\Delta I = 1.51 + .025\Delta S^e + 1.70(E^e - E_{-1}) - 1.15I_{-1}. \quad (11.7)$$

In other words, the change in inventory investment equals 1.51 billion (1954) dollars plus .25 times the change in total sales expected by businessmen (as given by surveys) plus 1.70 times the difference between expected expenditure on plant and equipment (as given by surveys) and actual expenditure on plant and equipment in the previous period minus 1.15 times the inventory investment in the previous period. The authors of the model argue that the change in inventory investment will be directly related to the change in expected sales, since firms generally want to keep their inventories more or less proportional to their sales. Also, they believe that the change in inventory investment will be directly related to the expected change in expenditure on plant and equipment, since the latter is a good indicator of the general economic outlook. In addition, they state that the change in inventory investment will be inversely related to the level of inventory investment in the previous period. According to their model, if inventory investment was high (low) in the previous period, there will be a smaller (bigger) change in inventory investment than if it was low (high) in the previous period.

Finally, the fifth equation merely states the obvious fact that the change in GNP must equal the change in consumption expenditures plus the change in each of the parts of gross private investment (expenditures on plant and equipment, residential construction, and inventories) plus the change in government expenditures (plus net exports). In other words,

$$\Delta Y = \Delta C + \Delta E + \Delta H + \Delta I + \Delta G. \quad (11.8)$$

This must be true because Y = consumption + gross private investment + government expenditures (plus net exports). Since gross private investment equals $E + H + I$, it follows that $Y = C + E + H + I + G$. Thus, the change in Y must equal the sum of the changes in C, E, H, I, and G.

Econometric models—even small ones like this—are fairly complicated. It is easy to get so engrossed in the details of each equation that we lose sight of the basic purpose of the model—to forecast GNP, in this case. How can we use this model to forecast GNP? As a first step, let's substitute the right-hand side of Equation (11.4) for ΔC in Equation (11.8). Also, let's substitute the right-hand side of Equation (11.5) for ΔE in Equation (11.8). Let's substitute the right-hand side of Equation (11.6) for ΔH in Equation (11.8), and the right-hand side of Equation (11.7) for ΔI in Equation (11.8). All of these substitutions give us an expression for ΔY. In particular,

$$\Delta Y = 3.22 + 2.00\Delta G + 4.34(E^e - E_{-1}) - 2.30I_{-1} + .05\Delta S^e + 1.15\Delta L + .037\,\Delta Y_{-1} + .19\Delta C_{-1}. \quad (11.9)$$

This equation can be used to forecast ΔY—the change in gross national product between the *next* period and the *present* period. To do so, one must insert the appropriate values of ΔC_{-1}, ΔY_{-1}, $(E^e - E_{-1})$, ΔL, ΔS^e, I_{-1}, and ΔG into Equation (11.9). For example, if the change in consumption between this period and the last period was $1 billion, we would substitute 1 for ΔC_{-1} in Equation (11.9). And if the change in gross national product between this period and the last period was $2 billion, we would substitute 2 for ΔY_{-1}, and so on for the other variables on the right-hand side of Equation (11.9). When the value of each of the variables has been inserted into Equation (11.9), we are the proud possessor of a forecast of ΔY—the change in gross national product between the next period and the present period.

Econometric Models, Big and Bigger

The econometric model just presented is a small one designed to forecast changes in GNP over the next 6 months. The economists who constructed it did not intend it to be used to estimate the effects of government policy—for example, changes in tax rates or government expenditures—or to forecast prices, income distribution, unemployment, capital utilization, and so forth. In recent years, there has been a remarkable amount of activity in the economics profession here and abroad, aimed at the construction of larger econometric models, which may be able to represent the behavior of the economy in richer and more complete detail. The leading figure in the development of such models has been Lawrence Klein of the University of Pennsylvania. Two of the models that he has constructed—or helped to construct—are known as the Wharton model and the Brookings model.

The Wharton model, published in 1967, contained about 50 equations: 3 equations that explain various components of consumer spending (consumer nondurable goods, automobiles, and other consumer durable goods), 6 equations to explain various components of private investment (expenditure on plant and equipment, residential housing, and inventory changes), 4 explaining depreciation, 4 explaining tax receipts and transfer payments, 5 explaining the level of output in various sectors of the economy, 7 explaining price level changes in various sectors of the economy, and other equations explaining hours worked, wage rates, unemployment, interest rates, profits, and other variables. This model was used to make quarterly forecasts of GNP, unemployment, changes in the price level, and other variables a year or more ahead. It was also used to forecast the effects on the economy of alternate government policies—for example, to estimate the effects of changes in tax rates on GNP and unemployment. Its forecasts were watched closely and publicized widely in the business community and in government.[13] In recent years, the Wharton model has been extended and refined in numerous ways.

The Brookings model—more formally, the Brookings Quarterly Econometric Model of the United States—was the "big daddy" of the econometric models. Composed of well over 200 equa-

[13] Michael Evans and Lawrence Klein, *The Wharton Econometric Forecasting Model,* Philadelphia: University of Pennsylvania, 1967.

Table 11.2

Predictive Record of Some Leading Economic Forecasting Techniques

		Error (in billions of dollars)				
Year	Actual GNP	Average general forecast (Federal Reserve Bank of Philadelphia)	Council of Economic Advisers	Michigan model	Friend-Taubman model	Wharton model
1959	484	−13	—	−19	—	
1960	504	4	—	−10	—	
1961	520	− 7	—	2	—	
1962	560	4	14	4	—	
1963	591	−11	− 6	− 6	4	1
1964	632	− 7	− 4	− 4	5	1
1965	685	−10	− 6	−14	−3	−4
1966	748	− 7	−10	− 7	—	−4
1967	790	4	6	13	—	3
Average error (1963–67)		7.8	6.4	8.8	4.0	2.8

Source: Michael Evans, *Macroeconomic Activity,* New York: Harper & Row, 1969, p. 516.

tions, it was the product of a team of over 20 well-known economists, headed by Klein and Harvard's James Duesenberry. Work on this model went on for over 10 years, and although it was designed largely for experimental purposes, it provided economists with many useful results.[14] Another very large model was the Federal Reserve Board–Massachusetts Institute of Technology–Pennsylvania model, which contained over 125 equations. It too was largely experimental in nature, although it has been used to generate some forecasts of the effects of alternate government policies.[15]

[14] J. Duesenberry, G. Fromm, L. Klein, and E. Kuh, *The Brookings Quarterly Econometric Model of the United States,* Chicago: Rand McNally, 1965.

[15] Some econometric models, such as those developed at the Federal Reserve Bank of St. Louis, have been built largely on monetary factors. In the following three chapters, we shall discuss the effects of monetary factors on national output, employment, and the price level.

Econometric Forecasts: The Track Record

How well can econometric models forecast? Table 11.2 compares the success of the Wharton model, the Friend-Taubman model, and a model constructed at the University of Michigan's Research Seminar in Quantitative Economics in predicting GNP during 1959–67 with the forecasts of the Council of Economic Advisers and a composite forecast of GNP from about 50 economists which is tabulated each year by the Federal Reserve Bank of Philadelphia. With the exception of the Friend-Taubman model, these forecasts were made at the end of the previous year. The Friend-Taubman forecasts were made in mid-March.

In this period, the econometric models seemed to do better than the average forecast of general economists. While the general economists were off, on the average, by about $8 billion during the period, the econometric models were off by an average of about $5 billion. The performance of the Wharton model in this period was particularly impressive. Its average error was only about $3 billion—or less than ½ of 1 percent. In this ball game, that is a very fancy batting average: recall Samuelson's remarks quoted earlier.

However, before you jump to the conclusion that the problem of economic forecasting is now solved, note several things. First, it is much easier to forecast GNP during a period of sustained prosperity like 1963–67—or a sustained downswing—than at a turning point of the business cycle. Unfortunately, the turning points are most significant to policy makers. Second, for some purposes, the components of GNP—like inventory changes or expenditures on consumer durables—are more important than GNP. Unfortunately, it is easier to forecast GNP than to forecast components of GNP. Third, the assumption underlying any econometric model is that the basic structure of the economy—the numbers in the equations of the model—will not change. If this assumption does not hold, the model is in trouble. After all, any econometric model is powered by past data, not magic.

The Economic Forecasts for 1972: A Case Study

To illustrate the nature, accuracy, and impact of economic forecasts, consider the situation at the end of 1971. The federal government was faced with both excessive unemployment and excessive inflation. With an election approaching in November 1972, the administration was clearly concerned about the economic picture in 1972. Would GNP grow rapidly enough to reduce the unemployment rate? Would it grow too rapidly, and provoke further inflationary pressures? The best answers available were the forecasts made by leading economists, inside and outside the government. As you can see in Table 11.3, these forecasts tended to agree with one another: the outlook was for a 1972 GNP in current dollars of about $1,150 billion, which would mean an unemployment rate of about 5½ percent.

Businessmen, as well as government officials, were vitally interested in what GNP would be. From past experience, firms have a pretty good idea of the relationship between GNP and their own sales and profits. Thus, if they know what GNP is likely to be, they can make better estimates of what their sales and profits will be. As an indication of the importance of such forecasts to business executives, leading business magazines and newspapers are continually keeping the business community informed of the latest forecasts. For example, *Business Week* published the forecasts in Table 11.3 in its December 25, 1971 issue, together with a long article on what they added up to.

As it turned out, GNP in 1972 was about $1,155 billion, unemployment was about 5.6 percent, and the price level increased by about 3.4 percent, which meant that these forecasts were darned good. Further, most private economists predicted GNP in the previous year, 1971, quite accurately, even though the official government forecast was far too optimistic. At the end of 1970, practically all economists, conservative or liberal, predicted that GNP in 1971 would be about $1,050 billion, although the administration insisted that it would be $1,065 billion. In part, the administration's forecast may have been wishful thinking because it wanted a more vigorous expansion to reduce unemployment. In any event, the economists' forecasts were very close to the mark. In contrast to the administration's expectations, GNP in 1971 was $1,047 billion.

Economic forecasts play an important role in the decision-making process, both in government and industry. For example, in the recession of 1953–54, President Eisenhower asked Arthur Burns, Chairman of the Council of Economic Advisers, to appear at every meeting of the Cabinet until further notice, and summarize developments and prospects. During the 1960s and 1970s, Presidents Kennedy, Johnson, and Nixon also paid close at-

Table 11.3

Forecasts of Gross National Product in 1972, as well as Price Increase and Unemployment

	1972 GNP (billions of current dollars)	1972 price increase	1972 average unemployment
Economists:			
Robert Johnson—Paine, Webber, Jackson & Curtis	$1,159	4.0%	5.4%
James O'Leary—U.S. Trust	1,157	4.0	5.3
A. Gary Shilling—Estabrook	1,156	2.7	5.0
Eleanor Daniel—Mutual of New York	1,154	3.8	5.4
Donald R. Conlan—Dean Witter	1,150	3.5	5.4
William Freund—New York Stock Exchange	1,150	3.5	5.5
Tilford C. Gaines—Manufacturers Hanover	1,150	3.2	5.6
Walter W. Heller—University of Minnesota	1,150	3.3	5.6
Raymond Jallow—United California Bank	1,150	2.9	5.4
Roy L. Reierson—Bankers Trust	1,150	4.0	5.6
Daniel Suits—University of California (Santa Cruz)	1,150	3.8	5.0
Robert Ortner—Bank of New York	1,149	3.5	5.6
Robert Parks—Eastman Dillon, Union Securities	1,148	3.0	5.5
Albert T. Sommers—The Conference Board	1,148	3.4	5.4
Guy E. Noyes—Morgan Guaranty	1,147	3.0	5.3
Bohdan Kekish—Moody's	1,146	3.2	5.5
Morris Cohen—Schroder, Naess & Thomas	1,145	3.0	5.5
Martin Gainsbrugh—The Conference Board	1,145	3.3	5.4
Saul Klaman—National Association of Mutual Savings Banks	1,145	3.5	5.1
Francis Schott—Equitable Life	1,145	3.5	5.4
Beryl Sprinkel—Harris Trust & Savings	1,145	3.1	5.4
Kenneth Wright—Life Insurance Association of America	1,145	3.2	5.6
Raymond J. Saulnier—Barnard College	1,140	3.0	5.5
George W. McKinney, Jr.—Irving Trust	1,139	3.9	5.4
Sally Ronk—Drexel Firestone	1,139	3.3	6.0
Leonard Santow—Aubrey G. Lanston	1,137	3.3	5.5
Econometric models:			
General Electric, MAPCAST	1,151	3.3	5.6
Wharton, EFA	1,150	3.6	5.4
University of California (Los Angeles)	1,148	3.7	5.5
Data Resources	1,147	3.2	5.7
Townsend-Greenspan	1,147	3.1	5.5
Chase Econometrics	1,152	3.1	5.4
University of Michigan, RSQE	1,144	2.9	5.3

Source: Business Week, December 25, 1971.

tention to economic forecasts. So do most corporation presidents. This isn't because these forecasts are always very good. It's because they are the best available. As Thomas Huxley put it, "If a little knowledge is dangerous, who is the man who has so much as to be out of danger?"

Summary

Changes in sales can result in magnified or accelerated changes in investment, the amount of gross investment depending on the rate of increase of sales. The fact that sales are increasing does not insure that gross investment will increase. On the contrary, if sales are increasing at a decreasing rate, gross investment is likely to fall. This effect of sales on investment is called the acceleration principle. The interaction of the acceleration principle with the multiplier can cause business cycles. Thus, turning points can be generated within the economic system. Investment is also determined by many events that occur more or less at random, like innovations, wars, and so on. The effects of these random shocks can also cause business fluctuations. The short cycles are generally inventory cycles. The acceleration principle also applies to inventories.

Although we are not in a position to erase the small dips and pauses in economic activity, it seems extremely unlikely that we will have another depression of the severity of the 1930s. The reason is that policy makers—and the electorate—know that monetary and fiscal policy can be used to push the economy back toward full employment. However, the prospect for price stability is not so bright. Although economics is by no means an exact science, economic forecasts are useful for many purposes. This does not mean that these forecasts are always very accurate. It means only that they are better than noneconomists' forecasts.

Economists have a number of techniques for forecasting. One makes use of leading indicators—variables that historically have turned up or down before GNP. Although of some use, these leading indicators are not very reliable. Another technique is based on the use of simple Keynesian models plus surveys and other data. For example, investment and government expenditures (and net exports) are sometimes estimated as a first step. Then, using the historical relationship between consumption and GNP, it is possible to forecast GNP. A third technique is based on econometric models, which are systems of equations estimated from past data. Econometric models blend theory and measurement.

Econometric models may be big or small. An example of a small model is the Friend-Taubman model; an example of a fairly large model is the Wharton model; and an example of a very large model is the Brookings model. During the period for which comparisons have been made, econometric models seemed to do somewhat better than the average forecasts of general economists. Some did very well indeed. However, it is important to recognize that econometric models—like any forecasting device in the social sciences—are quite fallible. We should also note that economic forecasts receive considerable attention from heads of state and heads of firms. This isn't because these forecasts are always very good: it's because they are the best available.

CONCEPTS FOR REVIEW

Business cycle
Trough
Expansion
Peak
Recession
Depression
Prosperity
Inventory cycle
Net investment
Gross investment
Acceleration principle
Leading indicators
Coincident series
Lagging series
Econometric models
Expectations

QUESTIONS FOR DISCUSSION AND REVIEW

1. Suppose that the president gave you the job of forecasting GNP for the next year. What techniques would you use? What range of probable error would you expect? Use these techniques as best you can to produce an actual numerical forecast.

2. According to Paul Samuelson, "A good scientist should be good at *some* kind of prediction. But it need not be flat prediction about future events." Do you agree? Why or why not?

3. It is much easier to forecast GNP during a turning point of the business cycle than during periods of sustained prosperity or sustained downswing. True or False?

4. Important factors in business fluctuations are:
a. inventories
b. expectations
c. innovations
d. changes in money supply and interest rates
e. all of the above

PART FOUR

Money, Banking, and Stabilization Policy

CHAPTER 12

The Role and Importance of Money

According to the maxim of an ancient Roman, "Money alone sets all the world in motion." Although a statement that leaves so little room for the laws of physics or astronomy may be a mite extravagant, no one would deny the importance of money in economic affairs. The quantity of money is a very significant factor in determining the health and prosperity of any economic system. Inadequate increases in the quantity of money may bring about excessive unemployment, while excessive increases in the quantity of money may result in serious inflation. To some economists, a discussion of business fluctuations and economic stabilization that ignores the money supply is like a performance of *Hamlet* that omits the prince. Most economists would not go quite that far, but almost all would agree that the money supply is very important.

In this chapter, we are concerned with the nature and value of money, as well as with the relationship between a nation's money supply and the extent of unemployment and inflation. In particular, we consider questions like: What is money? What determines its value? What factors influence the demand for money, and what factors influence its quantity? What is the relationship between the quantity of money and the price level? What is the relationship between the quantity of money and the level of net national product? To understand the workings of our economy and the nature of our government's economic policies, you must be able to answer these questions.

What Is Money?

We must begin by defining money. At first blush, it may seem natural to define it by its physical characteristics. You may be inclined to say that money consists of bills of a certain size and color with certain words and symbols printed on them, as well as coins of a certain type. But this definition would be too restrictive, since money in other societies has consisted of whale teeth, wampum, and a variety of other things. Thus it seems better to define money by its functions than by its physical characteristics. Like beauty, money is as money does.

Money's first function is to act as a *medium of exchange.* People exchange their goods and services for something called money, and then use this money to buy the goods and services they want. To see how important money is as a medium of exchange, let's suppose that it did not exist. To exchange the goods and services they produce for the goods and services they want to consume, people would resort to *barter,* or direct exchange. If you were a wheat farmer, you would have to go to the people who produce the meat, clothes, and other goods and services you want, and swap some of your wheat for each of these goods and services. Of course this would be a very cumbersome procedure, since it would take lots of time and effort to locate and make individual bargains with each of these people. To get some idea of the extent to which money greases the process of exchange in any highly developed economy, consider all the purchases your family made last year—cheese from Wisconsin and France, automobiles from Detroit, oil from Texas and the Middle East, books from New York, and thousands of other items from all over the world. Imagine how few of these exchanges would have been feasible without money.

Second, money acts as a *standard of value.* It is the unit in which the prices of goods and services are measured. How do we express the price of coffee or tea or shirts or suits? In dollars and cents, of course. Thus money prices tell us the rates at which goods and services can be exchanged. For example, if the money price of a shirt is $5 and the money price of a tie is $1, a shirt will exchange for 5 ties. Put differently, a shirt will be "worth" 5 times as much as a tie.

Money also acts as a *store of value.* A person can hold on to money and use it to buy things later. You often hear stories about people who hoard a lot of money under their mattresses or bury it in their back yards. These people have an overdeveloped appreciation of the role of money as a store of value. But even those of us who are less miserly often use this function of money by carrying some money with us, and keeping some in the bank to make future purchases.

Finally, it should be recognized that money is a social invention. It is easy to assume that money has always existed, but this is not the case. Someone had to get the idea, and people had to come to accept it. Nor has money always had the characteristics it has today. In ancient Greece and Rome, money consisted of gold and silver coins. By the end of the seventeenth century, paper money was established in England; but this paper currency, unlike today's currency, could be exchanged for gold. Only recently has the transition been made to money that is not convertible into gold or silver. But regardless of its form or characteristics, anything that is a medium of exchange, a standard of value, and a store of value is money.

Three Kinds of Money

Like Caesar's Gaul, all money in modern economies is divided into three parts—coins, currency, and demand deposits. ***Coins*** are not really a very large proportion of the total quantity of money in the United States. In all, they amount to only about $6 billion, or about 2 percent of the total money supply. This is mainly because coins come in such small denominations. It takes a small mountain of pennies, nickels, dimes, quarters, and half-dollars to make even a billion dollars. Of course, the metal in each of these coins is worth less than the face value of the coin; otherwise people would melt them down and make money by selling the metal. In the 1960s, when silver prices rose, the government stopped using silver in dimes and quarters to prevent coins from meeting this fate.

Currency—paper money like the $5 and $10 bills everyone likes to have on hand—constitutes a far larger share of the total money supply than coins. Together, currency and coins outstanding totaled about $50 billion in 1972, as shown in Table 12.1. The Federal Reserve System, described in a later section, issues practically all of our currency in the form of Federal Reserve Notes. Before 1933, it was possible to exchange currency for gold, but this is no longer the case. All American currency (and coin) is presently "fiat" money. It is money because the government says so and because the people accept it. There is no real metallic backing of the currency anymore. But this does not mean that we should be suspicious of the soundness of our currency, since gold backing is not what gives money its value. (In fact, to some extent, cause and effect work the other way: the use of gold to back currencies has in the past increased the value of gold.) Basically, the value of currency depends on its acceptability by people and on its scarcity.

Table 12.1

Money Supply, December 31, 1972, Seasonally Adjusted

	Amount (billions of dollars)
Demand deposits	$190.0
Currency and coins	56.9
Total	$246.9

Source: Economic Report of the President, 1973.

Third, bank deposits subject to payment on demand—so-called ***demand deposits***—are quantitatively by far the biggest part of our money supply, as shown in Table 12.1. At first you may question whether these demand deposits—or checking accounts, as you probably call them—are money at all. In everyday speech, they often are not considered money. But economists include demand deposits as part of the money supply, and for good reason. After all, you can pay for goods and services just as easily by check as with cash. Indeed, the public pays for more things by check than with cash. This means that checking accounts are just as much a medium of exchange—and just as much a standard of value and a store of value—as cash. Thus, since they perform all of the functions of money, they should be included as money.

Figure 12.1 shows how the money supply—the sum total of coins, paper currency, and demand deposits—has behaved since World War II. You can see that the quantity of money has generally increased from one year to the next, and that the increase has been at an average rate of about 3 percent per year. However, the rate of increase of the quantity of money has by no means been constant. In some years, like 1968, the quantity of money increased by about 8 percent; in others, like 1960, it decreased slightly. A great deal will be said later about the importance and determinants of changes in the quantity of money.

Figure 12.1
Behavior of Money Supply, United States, 1947–72

The money supply, about $250 billion in 1972, has generally increased from year to year, but the rate of increase has by no means been constant.

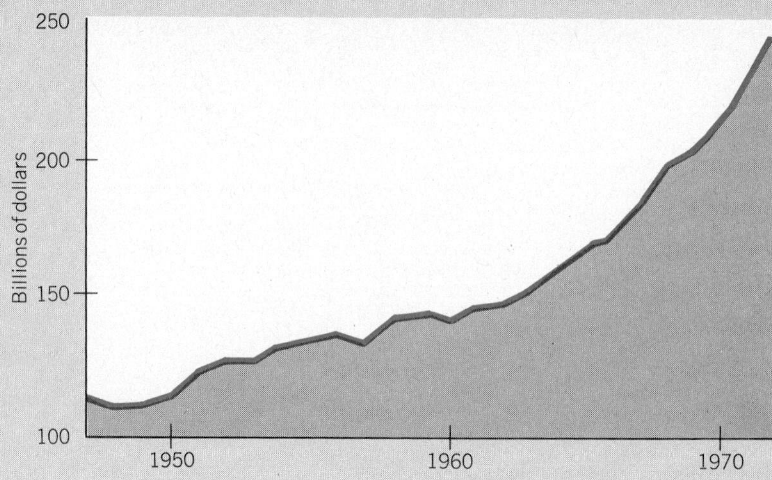

Near-Monies

We have just stated that all money is of three kinds—coins, currency, and demand deposits. This is the money supply, narrowly defined. It is not the only definition. There is also the money supply, broadly defined, which includes time or savings deposits as well as coins, currency, and demand deposits. The money supply, narrowly defined, is often called M_1, while the money supply, broadly defined, is often called M_2. Although economists usually use the narrow definition—and when we refer to the money supply in this book, we shall mean this definition—it is sometimes useful to work with the broad definition as well.

Time or savings deposits are excluded from the narrow definition of money because you cannot pay directly for anything with them. For example, suppose that you have a savings account at a commercial bank. You cannot draw a check against it, as you can with a demand deposit. To withdraw your money from the account, you may have to give the bank a certain amount of notice (although in practice this right may be waived and the bank will ordinarily let you withdraw your money when you want).

On the other hand, economists who use the broad definition feel that time or savings deposits should be included in the money supply because time or savings deposits can so readily be transformed into cash. You may intend to buy a house sometime in the next year and you may want to keep $5,000 on hand to use as a down payment. You could leave this $5,000 in your checking account, or you could put it in a savings account, where it would earn some interest. Because ordinarily you can withdraw the money from a savings account on short notice, you may decide on this alternative. Since this savings account can so readily be transformed into cash, it is almost like a checking account. Not quite, but almost. Although time deposits or savings deposits cannot be used as a medium of exchange, they can be transformed into cash quite readily.

Many other assets can also be transformed into cash without much difficulty—though not quite as easily as savings deposits. For example, it is not difficult to convert government bonds into cash. There is no simple way to draw a hard-and-fast dividing line between money and nonmoney, since many assets have some of the characteristics of money. Consequently, there are still other definitions of the money supply that are more inclusive than M_2. But most economists feel that, although assets like government bonds have some of the properties of money, it would be stretching things too far to include them in the money supply. (For one thing, their price varies as interest rates change.)

Economists call such assets ***near-money,*** and recognize that the amount of near-money in the economy has an important effect on spending habits. There is some disagreement among economists as to exactly what is and what isn't near-money, but this needn't concern us here. The major point we want to make is that any dividing line between money and nonmoney must be arbitrary.

The Value of Money

Let's go back to one very important point that was mentioned briefly in a previous section: there is no gold backing for our money. In other words, there is no way that you can exchange a $10 bill for $10 worth of gold. If you look at a $10 bill, you will see that it says that the United States will pay the bearer on demand ten dollars. But all this means is that the government will give you another $10 bill in exchange for this one. Currency and demand deposits are really just debts, or IOUs. Currency is the debt of the government, while demand deposits are the debts of the commercial banks. Intrinsically, neither currency nor demand deposits have any real value. A $10 bill is merely a small piece of paper, and a demand deposit is merely an entry in a bank's accounts. And, as we have seen, even coins are worth far less as metal than their monetary value.

All this may make you feel a bit uncomfortable. After all, if our coins, currency, and demand deposits have little or no intrinsic value, doesn't this mean that they can easily become worthless? To answer this question, we must realize that basically, *money has value because people will accept it in payment for goods and services.* If your university will accept your check in payment for your tuition, and your grocer will accept a $20 bill in payment for your groceries, your demand deposit and your currency have value. You can exchange them for goods and services you want. And your university or your grocer accepts this money only because they have confidence that they can spend it for goods and services they want.

Thus, money is valuable because it will buy things. But how valuable is it? For example, how valuable is $1? Clearly, *the value of a dollar is equivalent to what a dollar will buy. And what a dollar will buy depends on the price level.* If all prices doubled, the value of a dollar would be cut in half, because a dollar would be able to buy only half as many goods and services as it formerly could. On the other hand, if all prices were reduced by 50 percent, the value of a dollar would double, because a dollar would be able to buy twice as many goods and services as it formerly could. You often hear people say that today's dollar is worth only $.50. What they mean is that it will buy only half what a dollar could buy at some specified date in the past.

It is interesting and important to see how the value of the dollar, as measured by its purchasing power, has varied over time. Figure 12.2 shows how an index of the price level in the United States has changed since 1779. Over time, prices have fluctuated sharply, and the greatest fluctuations have resulted from wars. For example, the price level fell sharply after the Revolutionary War, and our next war—the War of 1812—sent prices skyrocketing, after which there was another postwar drop in prices. The period from about 1820 to about 1860 was marked by relative price stability, but the Civil War resulted in an upward burst followed by a postwar drop in prices. After a period of relative price stability from 1875 to 1915, there was a doubling of prices during World War I and the usual postwar drop. World War II also caused an approximate doubling, but there was no postwar drop in prices.

Clearly, the value of money is inversely related to the price level. The value of money decreases when the price level increases, and increases when the price level decreases. Thus, the wartime periods when the price level rose greatly were periods when the value of the dollar decreased greatly. The doubling of prices during World War II meant

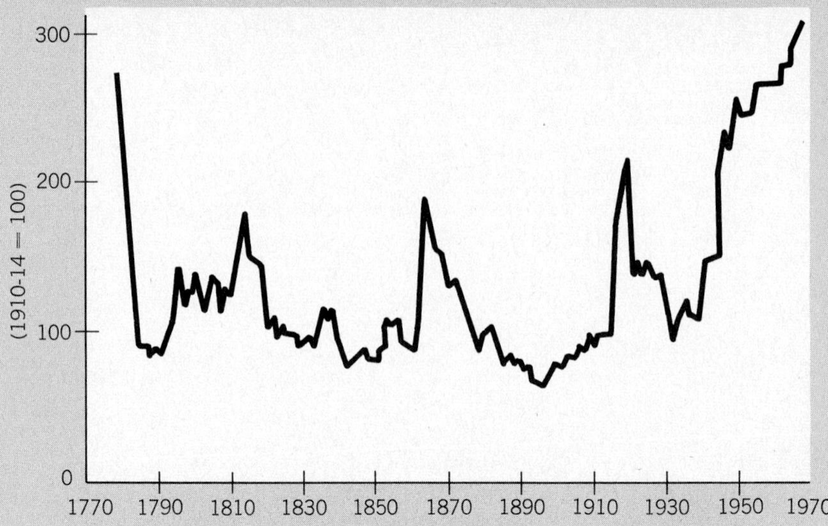

Figure 12.2
Index of Wholesale Prices, United States, 1779–1970 (1910–14 = 100)

The price level has fluctuated considerably, sharp increases generally occurring during wars. Since World War II, the price level has tended to go only one way—up.

that the value of the dollar was chopped in half. Similarly, the postwar periods when the price level fell greatly were periods when the value of the dollar increased. The 50 percent decline in prices after the Civil War meant a doubling in the value of the dollar. Given the extent of the variation of the price level shown in Figure 12.2, it is clear that the value of the dollar has varied enormously during our history.

Runaway Inflation and the Value of Money

In periods of inflation, the value of money is reduced. Since inflation means an increase in the price level, and since an increase in the price level means a reduction in the value of money, this proposition seems clear enough. But remember that inflations vary in severity: ***runaway inflations*** wipe out the value of money quickly and thoroughly, while ***creeping inflations*** erode its value gradually and slowly. There is a lot of difference between a runaway inflation and a creeping inflation.

The case of Germany after World War I is a good example of runaway inflation. Germany was required to pay large reparations to the victorious Allies after the war. Rather than attempting to tax its people to pay these amounts, the German government merely printed additional quantities of paper money. This new money increased total spending in Germany, and the increased spending resulted in higher prices because the war-devastated economy could not increase output substantially. As more and more money was printed, prices rose higher and higher, reaching utterly fantastic levels. By 1923, it took a *trillion* marks (the unit of German currency) to buy what one mark would buy before the war. The effect of this runaway inflation was to disrupt the economy. Prices had to be adjusted from day to day. People rushed to the stores to spend the money they received as soon as possible, since very soon it would buy much less. Speculation was rampant. This inflation was a terrible blow to Germany. The middle class was wiped out; its savings became completely worthless.

It is no wonder that Germany has in recent years been more sensitive than many other countries to the evils of inflation.

Needless to say, this is not the only case in history of runaway inflation. Our own country suffered from runaway inflations during the Revolutionary War and the Civil War. You may have heard the expression that something is "not worth a continental." It comes from the fact that the inflated dollars in use during the Revolutionary War were called "continentals." There have also been runaway inflations in China and Eastern Europe and other parts of the world. Generally, such inflations have occurred because the government increased the money supply at an enormously rapid rate. It is not hard to see why a tremendous increase in the quantity of money will result in a runaway inflation. Other things held constant, increases in the quantity of money will result in increases in total desired spending, and once full employment is achieved, such increases in desired spending will bring about more and more inflation. Eventually, when the inflation is severe enough, households and businesses may refuse to accept money for goods and services because they fear that it will depreciate significantly before they have a chance to spend it. Instead, they may insist on being paid in merchandise or services. Thus, the economy will turn to barter, with the accompanying inconveniences and inefficiency.

To prevent such an economic catastrophe, the government must manage the money supply responsibly. As we have stressed in previous sections, the value of money depends basically on the public's willingness to accept it, and the public's willingness to accept it depends on money's being reasonably stable in value. If the government increases the quantity of money at a rapid rate, thus causing a severe inflation and an accompanying precipitous fall in the value of money, public confidence in money will be shaken, and the value of money will be destroyed. The moral is clear: *The government must restrict the quantity of money, and conduct its economic policies so as to maintain a reasonably stable value of money.*

Creeping Inflation and the Value of Money

For the past 40 years, the price level in the United States has tended to go one way only—up. Year after year, prices have risen. Since 1950, there hasn't been a single year when the price level has fallen, and in the 1940s it fell only in 1949. Certainly, this has not been a runaway inflation, but it has resulted in a very substantial erosion in the value of the dollar. Like a beach slowly worn away by the ocean, the dollar has slowly lost a considerable portion of its value. Specifically, prices now tend to be over 3 times what they were about 40 years ago. Thus, the dollar now is worth less than ⅓ of what it was worth then. Although a creeping inflation of this sort is much less harmful than a runaway inflation, it has a number of unfortunate social consequences.

For one thing, people with fixed incomes are hit hard by inflation. Although a creeping inflation does not hurt them as much as a runaway inflation, its cumulative effect over a period of years can be substantial. Old people often suffer, since they tend to have fixed incomes derived from Social Security, private pensions, and interest on their savings. In addition, as we pointed out in Chapter 8, inflation hurts lenders and savers. The results can be both devastating and inequitable. The family that works hard and saves for retirement (and a rainy day) finds that its savings are worth far less, when it finally spends them, than the amount it saved. For example, consider the well-meaning souls who invested $1,000 of their savings in United States savings bonds in 1939. By 1949, these bonds were worth only about 800 1939 dollars, including the interest received in the 10-year period. Thus, these people had $200 taken away from them, in just as real a sense as if someone picked their pockets.

Although a mild upward creep of prices at the rate of 1 or 2 percent per year is not likely to result in very disastrous social consequences, any major inflation is a real social problem. In recent years, because it has proved difficult to bring inflation under control, some people have argued that inflation is not as bad as it looks. This, of course, seems quite sensible to those who have gained from inflation. But it does not do justice to the many people, including a disproportionate number of the elderly, who have been "suckered" by inflation. Why should these people have been subjected to such an arbitrary and inequitable tax on their savings and incomes? Moreover, this is not the only consideration. According to some respected economists, inflation tends to feed on itself. That is, a 2 percent rate of inflation tends to grow to a 3 percent rate of inflation, which tends to grow to a 4 percent rate of inflation, and so on. Although the available evidence is too weak to demonstrate this proposition, the possibility should nonetheless be borne in mind.

Inflation has a bad name, both among economists and with the general public. The novelist Ernest Hemingway, overstating his case more than a bit, wrote: "The first panacea for a mismanaged nation is inflation of currency: the second is war. . . . Both are the refuge of political and economic opportunists."[1] Yet we must recognize that, under some conditions, full employment can be achieved only if a moderate amount of inflation is tolerated. For example, as we shall see, this seems to have been the case in the early 1970s. Under such circumstances, the nation is faced with a painful decision: should it allow a moderate amount of inflation in order to promote full employment? The importance of maintaining full employment was described in detail in Chapter 8. The answer you give to this question will depend on your own ethical values and political preferences.

Unemployment and the Quantity of Money

In the last two sections, we have been concerned primarily with what happens when the quantity of money grows too rapidly. As we have seen, the result is inflation. But this is only part of the story. The quantity of money can grow too slowly as well as too rapidly; and when this happens the result is increased unemployment. If the money supply grows very slowly, or decreases, there will be a tendency for total desired spending to grow very slowly or decrease. This in turn will cause NNP to grow very slowly or decrease, thus causing unemployment to increase. The result will, of course, be the social waste and human misery associated with excessive unemployment.

Looking back over past business fluctuations, many economists believe that an inadequate rate of increase in the quantity of money was responsible, at least in part, for many recessions. For example, according to Harvard's James Duesenberry: "Every major depression has been accompanied by a substantial decline in the money supply, and often by a complete collapse of the banking system. Among the many causes responsible for our major depressions, money and banking difficulties have always been prominent."[2] Recall that in our discussion of business fluctuations in the previous chapter, we stressed the importance of monetary factors. In this chapter, as well as Chapters 13–15, we will study these factors in detail.

Determinants of the Quantity of Money

Judging from our discussion thus far, it is clear that to avoid excessive unemployment or excessive inflation, the quantity of money must not grow too slowly or too fast. But what determines the quantity of money? We have already seen that money is of three types: coins, paper currency, and demand deposits. Let's begin by considering the quantity of coins and paper currency in circulation. They make up about 1/5 of the total, a pro-

[1] Ernest Hemingway, "Notes on the Next War," *Esquire,* September 1935.

[2] J. S. Duesenberry, *Money and Credit: Impact and Control,* Englewood Cliffs, N.J.: Prentice-Hall, 1972, p. 3.

portion that has remained fairly stable over time. Practically all the currency is Federal Reserve Notes, issued by the Federal Reserve Banks. When the United States was on the gold standard, the amount of money in circulation was determined by the amount of monetary gold in the country. When gold flowed into the country, the money supply increased; when it flowed out, the money supply decreased. This is no longer the case, since we are no longer on the gold standard—and neither is any other major nation.

If gold doesn't determine the amount of coins and currency in circulation, what does? The answer is that this amount responds to the needs of firms and individuals for cash to use or hoard. When people want more coins and currency, they go to their banks and exchange their demand deposits for coins and currency: in other words, they convert part of their checking accounts into cash. When they want less coins and currency, they take their cash to the banks and exchange it for demand deposits, thus converting some of their cash into checking accounts. The government allows the share of money in coin and currency to be determined by the public's wishes.

Next, consider the quantity of demand deposits, which is of obvious importance, since the bulk of our money supply is composed of demand deposits, not coin and paper currency. Demand deposits are created by commercial banks.[3] The question of how much money banks can create is both fundamental and complicated, and most of the next chapter will be required to present an adequate answer. For the moment, it is sufficient to say that the Federal Reserve System and other government agencies limit the amount of demand deposits the banks can create.

[3] Of course, banks do not create money all by themselves. The public's preferences and actions, as well as bank behavior, influence the amount of demand deposits. Also, commercial banks may not be as unique in this respect as it appears at first sight. See James Tobin, "Commercial Banks as Creators of Money" in D. Carson (ed.), *Banking and Monetary Studies,* Homewood, Ill. Richard D. Irwin, 1963.

The Federal Reserve System

The Federal Reserve System—or "Fed," as it is called by the cognoscenti—plays a central role in the American banking system and in the economy as a whole. After a severe financial panic in 1907, when a great many banks failed, there was strong public pressure to do something to strengthen our banking system. At the same time, there was great fear of centralized domination of the nation's banks. The result—after 6 years of negotiation and discussion—was the establishment by Congress of the ***Federal Reserve System*** in 1913. As shown in Figure 12.3, the organization of this system can be viewed as a triangle. At the base are the commercial banks that belong to the system—the ***member banks.*** All ***national banks*** (so called because they receive their charter from the federal government) have to be members, and many of the larger ***state banks*** (chartered by the states) are members too. Member banks, which number about 6,000 out of the nation's 14,000 commercial banks, hold about 85 percent of the nation's demand deposits.

In the middle of the triangle in Figure 12.3 are the 12 Federal Reserve Banks, each located in a Federal Reserve district. The entire nation is divided into 12 Federal Reserve districts, with Federal Reserve Banks in New York, Chicago, Philadelphia, San Francisco, Boston, Cleveland, St. Louis, Kansas City, Atlanta, Richmond, Minneapolis, and Dallas. Each of these banks is a corporation owned by the member banks, but, despite this fact, the member banks do not in any sense act as "owners" of the Federal Reserve Bank in their district. Instead, each Federal Reserve Bank is a public agency. These Federal Reserve Banks act as "bankers' banks," performing much the same sorts of functions for commercial banks that commercial banks perform for the public. That is, they hold the deposits of member banks and make loans to them. In addition, as noted in previous sections, the Federal Reserve Banks perform a function no commercial bank can perform: they issue Federal

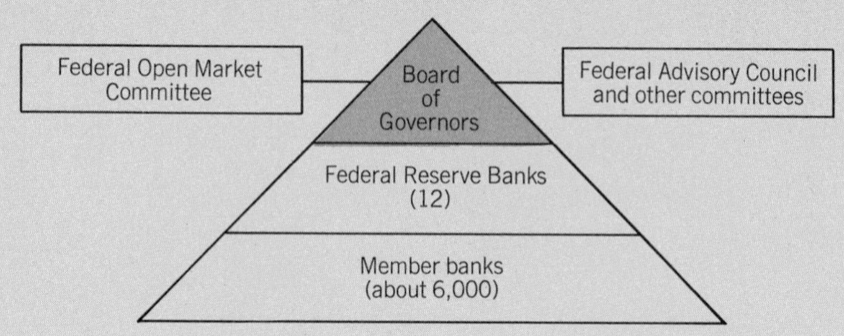

Figure 12.3
Organization of Federal Reserve System

The Federal Reserve System contains over 6,000 commercial banks, the 12 regional Federal Reserve Banks, and the Board of Governors, as well as the Federal Open Market Committee and various advisory councils and committees.

Reserve Notes, which are the nation's currency.

At the top of the triangle in Figure 12.3 is the Board of Governors of the Federal Reserve System. Located in Washington, this board—generally called the Federal Reserve Board—has 7 members appointed by the president for 14 year terms. The board, which coordinates the activities of the Federal Reserve System, is supposed to be independent of partisan politics and to act to promote the nation's general economic welfare. It is responsible for supervising the operation of the money and banking system of the United States. The board is assisted in important ways by the Federal Open Market Committee, which establishes policy concerning the purchase and sale of government securities. The Federal Open Market Committee is composed of the board plus 5 presidents of Federal Reserve Banks. The Board is also assisted by the Federal Advisory Council, a group of 12 commercial bankers that advises the board on banking policy.

The Federal Reserve Board, with the 12 Federal Reserve Banks, constitute the "central bank" of the United States. Every major country has a central bank: for example, England has the Bank of England, and France has the Bank of France. ***Central banks*** are very important organizations, whose most important function is to help control the quantity of money. One interesting feature of our central bank is that its principal allegiance is to Congress, not to the executive branch of the federal government. This came about because Congress wanted to protect the Fed from pressure by the president and the Treasury Department. Thus, the Fed was supposed to be independent of the executive branch. In fact, although the Fed has sometimes locked horns with the president, it has generally cooperated with him and his administration, as we shall see in Chapter 14.

To repeat, any central bank's most important function is to control the money supply. But this is not its only function: a central bank also handles the government's own financial transactions, and coordinates and controls the country's commercial banks. Specifically, the Federal Reserve System is charged with these responsibilities: First, the Federal Reserve Banks hold deposits, or reserves, of the member banks. As we shall see in the following chapters, these reserves play an important role in the process whereby the Fed controls the quantity of money. Second, the Federal Reserve System provides facilities for check collection. In other words, it enables a bank to collect funds for checks drawn on other banks. Third, the Federal Reserve Banks supply the public with currency. As we have already pointed out, they issue Federal Reserve Notes. Fourth, the Federal Reserve Banks act as fiscal agents for the federal government—

they hold some of the checking accounts of the U.S. Treasury, and aid in the purchase and sale of government securities. Finally, the Federal Reserve Banks supervise the operation of the member commercial banks. More will be said about the nature of bank supervision and regulation in the next chapter.

Commercial Banks in the United States

In 1970, there were over 13,000 commercial banks in the United States. This testifies to the fact that, in contrast to countries like England, where a few banks with many branches dominate the banking scene, the United States has promoted the growth of a great many local banks. In part, this has stemmed from a traditional suspicion in this country of "big bankers." ("Eastern bankers" are a particularly suspect breed in some parts of the country.) Most of our banks are state, not national, banks: there are about 9,000 state banks, but only about 4,600 national banks.

Commercial banks have two primary functions. First, *banks hold demand deposits and permit checks to be drawn on these deposits.* This function is familiar to practically everyone. Most people have a checking account in some commercial bank, and draw checks on this account. Second, *banks lend money to industrialists, merchants, homeowners, and other individuals and firms.* At one time or another, you will probably apply for a loan to finance some project for your business or home. Indeed, it is quite possible that some of the costs of your college education are being covered by a loan to you or your parents from a commercial bank.

In addition, commercial banks perform a number of other functions. Often they hold time or savings accounts. You will recall that these accounts bear interest and, although technically one must give a certain amount of notice before withdrawal, in practice they can usually be withdrawn whenever their owner likes. Commercial banks also sell money orders and traveler's checks, and handle estates and trusts. Because of their work with trusts, some banks—for example, the First Pennsylvania Bank and Trust Company, a large Philadelphia bank—include the word "trust" in their title. In addition, commercial banks rent safe-deposit boxes and provide a variety of services for customers.

Despite the number of these subsidiary activities, the principal functions of a commercial bank are to accept deposits and to make loans and investments. It is essential that these loans and investments be safe and reasonably easily turned into cash, because the bank must be able to meet its depositors' demands for cash. Otherwise it will be insolvent and fail. Until about 40 years ago, banks used to fail in large numbers during recessions, causing depositors to lose their money. Even during the prosperous 1920s, over 500 banks failed per year. It is no wonder that the public viewed the banks with less than complete confidence. Since the mid-1930s, bank failures have been rare, in part because of tighter standards of regulation by federal and state authorities. For example, bank examiners audit the books and practices of the banks. In addition, confidence in the banks was strengthened by the creation in 1934 of the Federal Deposit Insurance Corporation, which insures over 99 percent of all commercial bank deposits. At present, each deposit is insured up to $20,000.

Needless to say, commercial banks are not the only kind of financial institution. Mutual savings banks and savings and loan associations hold savings and time deposits; "consumer finance" companies lend money to individuals; insurance companies lend money to firms and governments; "factors" provide firms with working capital; and investment bankers help firms sell their securities to the public. All these types of financial institutions play an important role in the American economy. In general, they all act as intermediaries between savers and investors; that is, they all turn over to investors moneys that they received from savers. As we saw in Chapter 9, this process of converting savings into investment is very important in determining net national product.[4]

The Demand for Money

Turning now to the demand for money, let us recall money's various functions: it is a medium of exchange, a standard of value, and a store of value. Consider money from the point of view of the individual family or firm. Why does a family or firm want to hold money? Clearly, a family can be wealthy without holding much money. We all know stories about very rich men who have very little money, since virtually all of their wealth is tied up in factories, farms, and other nonmonetary assets. So why do people and firms want to hold money, rather than these other kinds of assets?

First, there is the ***transactions demand*** for money. People and firms like to keep some money on their person and in their checking accounts to buy things. (It is extremely inconvenient to want to buy something and not to have any money—even if you are rich.) Of course, the higher a person's annual income—in dollar, not real terms—the more money he will want to hold for transaction purposes. For example, in 1973, when a doctor makes about $50,000 a year, the average physician will want to keep more money on hand for transaction purposes than in the days—many, many years ago—when a doctor made perhaps $10,000 a year.

Second, there is a ***precautionary demand*** for money. Unpredictable events require money: for example, people get sick, and houses need repairs. To meet such contingencies, people and firms like to put a certain amount of their wealth into money and near-money. Also, there is a ***speculative demand*** for money. People and firms like to keep a certain amount of their wealth in a form in which they can be sure of its monetary value and can take advantage of future price reductions. The amount of money individuals or firms keep on hand for precautionary or speculative purposes will vary with the extent to which they feel that prices and interest rates will go up or down in the future, the degree to which they are uncertain about future income or expenses, and their aversion to or preference for risk.

Up to this point, we have discussed why individuals and firms want to hold money. But we must recognize that there are disadvantages, as well as advantages, in holding money. One is that the real value of money will fall if inflation occurs. Another is that an important cost of holding money is the interest or profit one loses, since instead of holding the money, one might have invested it in assets that would have yielded interest or profit. For example, the cost of holding $5,000 in money for one year, if one can obtain 6 percent on existing investments, is $300, the amount of interest or profit forgone.

Figure 12.4 shows the demand curve for money, with the interest rate as the "price" of holding money. Like other demand curves, this one slopes downward to the right, because the cost of holding money increases as the interest rate or yield on existing investments increases. For example, if the interest rate were 7 percent rather than 6 percent, the cost of holding $5,000 in money for one year would be $350 rather than $300. Thus, as the interest rate or profit rate increases, people try harder to minimize the amount of money they hold. So do firms: big corporations like General Motors or U. S. Steel are very conscious of the cost of holding cash balances. Consequently, with NNP constant, *the amount of money held by individuals and firms is inversely related to the interest rate: the higher the interest rate, the smaller the amount of money demanded.* The demand curve for money, shown in Figure 12.4, is often called the ***liquidity preference function.***

[4] If President Nixon's recommendations (of August 1973) are accepted, some of the differences between commercial banks and other financial institutions will narrow. According to his recommendations (based on the report of the so-called Hunt Commision), federally chartered thrift institutions could offer checking accounts. Also, the interest ceilings on time and savings deposits would be removed (over a 5½ year period).

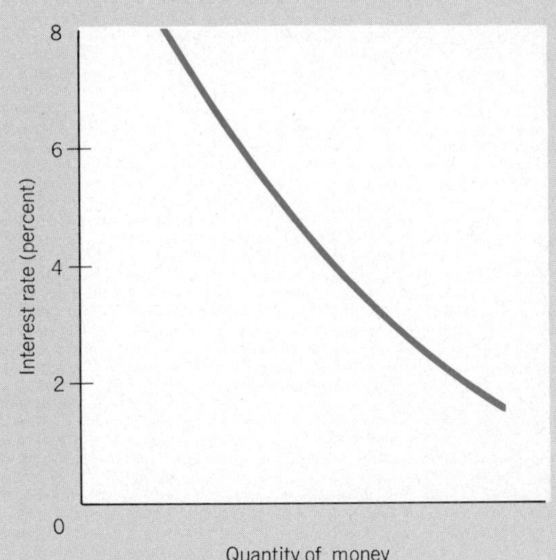

Figure 12.4 The Demand Curve for Money, or Liquidity Preference Function

Holding NNP constant, the amount of money demanded by individuals and firms is inversely related to the interest rate, since the cost of holding money is the interest or profit forgone.

The Role of Money in the Keynesian Model

We began this chapter by saying that the quantity of money has an important effect on the health and prosperity of the economy. Now we can show how changes in the quantity of money affect net national product. Recall our conclusion that the amount of money people want to hold is inversely related to the interest rate. Thus, if the money supply increases, the interest rate will tend to fall, in order to induce people to hold the extra money, since at the existing interest rate they would not have been willing to hold more money. (They would have spent it instead.) Similarly, if the money supply decreases, interest rates will tend to rise. The relationship between the interest rate and the quantity of money is shown in the liquidity preference function in Figure 12.4.[5]

Given the liquidity preference function, it is a simple matter to show how the money supply can be inserted into the Keynesian models in Chapters 9 and 10. For example, let's trace the effects of an increase in the money supply from $200 billion to $250 billion. The first effect is to decrease the interest rate from *d* percent to *c* percent, as shown by the liquidity preference function in panel A of Figure 12.5. This decrease in the interest rate in turn affects the investment function. Because it is less costly to invest—and because credit is more available[6]—the investment function will shift upward, as shown in panel B of Figure 12.5. This occurs because at each level of net national product, firms will want to invest more, since investment is more profitable (because of the cut in the interest rate) and funds are more readily available. This shift in the investment function then affects the equilibrium level of net national product. As shown in panel C of Figure 12.5, the equilibrium level of net national product will increase from D to E, in accord with the principles discussed in Chapter 9. (Recall that the equilibrium value of NNP is at the point where the $C + I + G$ line intersects the 45° line.) Thus, *the effect of the increase in the money supply is to increase net national product.*

Next, let's trace the effects of a decrease in

[5] However, this relationship between the quantity of money and the interest rate is only short-run. In the long run, increases in the money supply, if they result in increased inflation, may *raise* interest rates, because lenders will require a greater return to offset the greater rate of depreciation of the real value of the dollar. Still, however, the *real* rate of interest—the rate of interest adjusted for inflation—may decline.

[6] Note that it is not just a matter of interest rates: Availability of credit is also important. In times when money is tight, some potential borrowers may find that they cannot get a loan, regardless of what interest rate they are prepared to pay. In times when money is easy, people who otherwise might find it difficult to get a loan may be granted one by the banks. To repeat, both availability and interest rates are important.

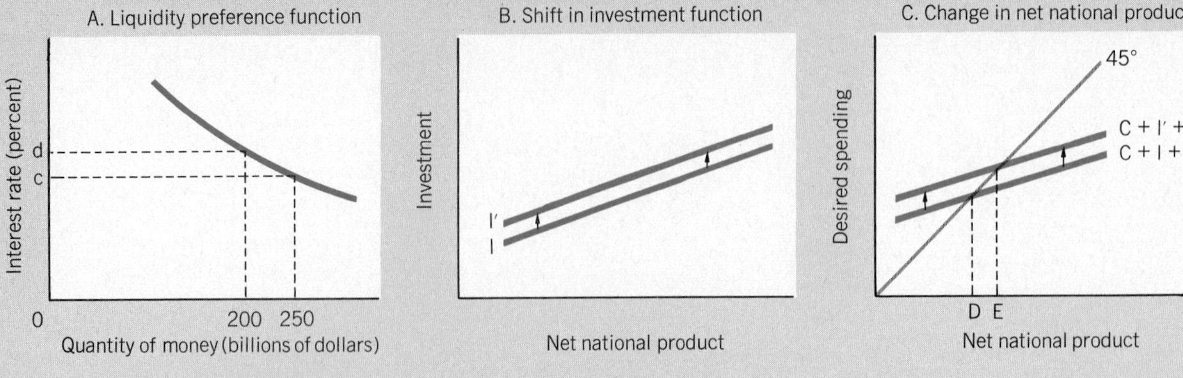

Figure 12.5 Effect of an Increase in the Money Supply.

If the money supply increases from $200 billion to $250 billion, the interest rate drops from *d* percent to *c* percent (panel A). Because of the decrease in the interest rate, the investment function shifts upward (panel B), and the equilibrium level of NNP increases from *D* to *E* (panel C).

the money supply from $200 billion to $160 billion. The first effect is to increase the interest rate from *d* percent to *e* percent, as shown by the liquidity preference function in panel A of Figure 12.6. This increase in the interest rate affects the investment function. Because it is more costly to invest—and more difficult to obtain credit—the investment function will shift downward, as shown in panel B of Figure 12.6. This shift occurs because, at every level of net national product, firms want to invest less. This shift in the investment function has an effect in turn on the equilibrium level of net national product. As shown in panel C of Figure 12.6, the equilibrium level of net national product will decrease from D to F. Thus, *the effect of the decrease in the money supply is to decrease net national product.*[7]

This, in simplified fashion, is how changes in the money supply affect NNP, according to the Keynesian model.[8] To summarize, increases in the money supply tend to increase NNP, and decreases in the money supply tend to reduce NNP. Obviously, these results are of great importance in understanding why our economy behaves the way it does. For example, we can now understand more completely why vast increases in the quantity of money will result in runaway inflation. Total spending will be pushed upward at a very rapid rate, driving the price level out of sight. Similarly, we can now see that an inadequate rate of growth of the money supply can lead to excessive unemployment, for an insufficient growth of the money supply prevents NNP from reaching its full employment level.

[7] Many firms depend to a considerable extent on retained earnings to finance their investment projects. Thus, since they do not borrow externally, the effect on their investment plans of changes in interest rates and credit availability is slight. This factor may reduce the effects of changes in the money supply.

[8] Changes in the money supply, interest rates, and credit availability affect the consumption function and government spending, as well as the investment function. For example, *increases (decreases) in interest rates shift the consumption function and the level of government spending downward (upward).* These factors augment the effect of monetary policy described in the text. We focus attention on the investment function in Figures 12.5 and 12.6 merely because this simplifies the exposition.

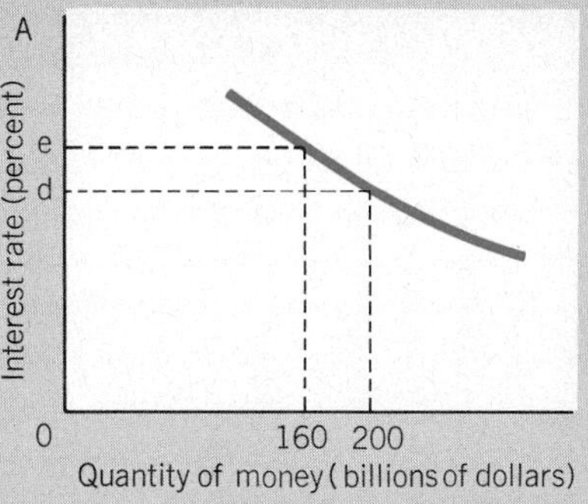

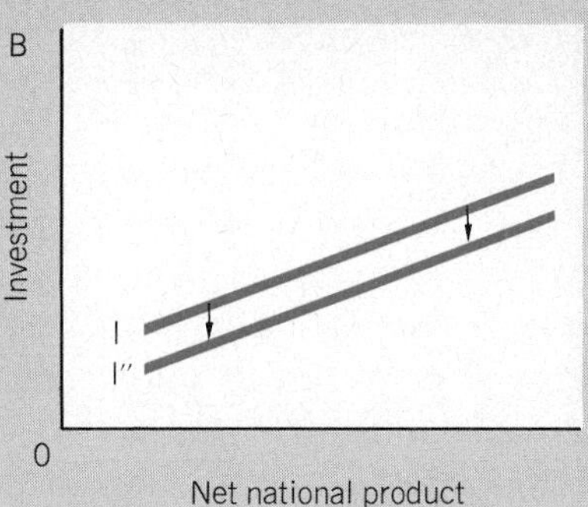

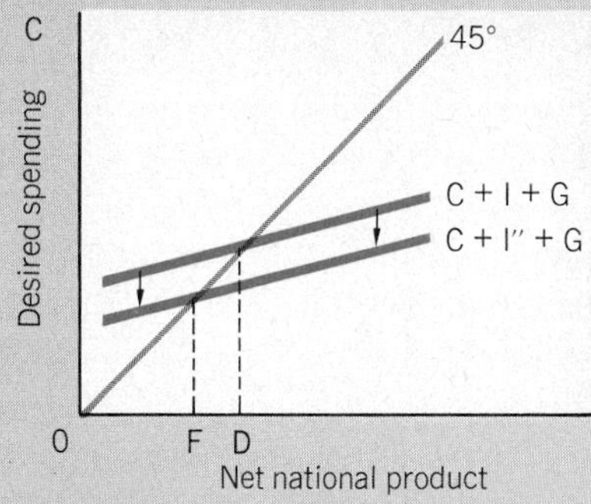

Figure 12.6 Effect of a Decrease in the Money Supply

If the money supply decreases from $200 billion to $160 billion, the interest rate increases from *d* percent to *e* percent (panel A). Because of the increase in the interest rate, the investment function shifts downward (panel B) and the equilibrium level of NNP decreases from *D* to *F* (panel C).

Money Makes a Comeback

Economists in the late 1930s, 1940s, and 1950s tended to play down the importance of the money supply as a determinant of net national product and to rely exclusively on the Keynesian model, in which the quantity of money plays a part, but the starring roles go to investment, government spending, and the multiplier. The quantity of money, which before the Keynesian revolution had occupied the center of the stage in economic models of this sort, was largely pushed to the wings. In recent years, however, there has been a great revival of interest in it. Some prominent economists, led by Milton Friedman of the University of Chicago, have emphasized the importance of the relationship between the quantity of money and nominal, or money, NNP. Undoubtedly this has been a healthy development; the significance of money was underestimated 20 or 30 years ago.

However, the monetarists—the name commonly given to Professor Friedman and his followers—go beyond saying that money matters. In their view, the quantity of money is a much more effective tool for forecasting or controlling nominal NNP than the Keynesian model described in Chapters 9 and 10. They view the rate of growth of the money supply as the principal determinant of nominal, or money, net national product. Indeed, they go so far as to say that fiscal policy, although it will alter the composition of net national product, will have no permanent effect on the size of nominal NNP unless it influences the money supply. This latter view, explained in more detail in Chapter 15, is not now accepted by most economists.

The monetarists have had a great impact on economic thought in the postwar period, even though theirs remains a minority view. Professor Friedman's most severe critics admit that his research in this area has been path-breaking and extremely important. According to his findings,

> the rate of change of the money supply shows well-marked cycles that match closely those in economic activity in general and precede the latter by a long interval. On the average, the rate of change of the money supply has reached its peak nearly 16 months before the peak in general business and

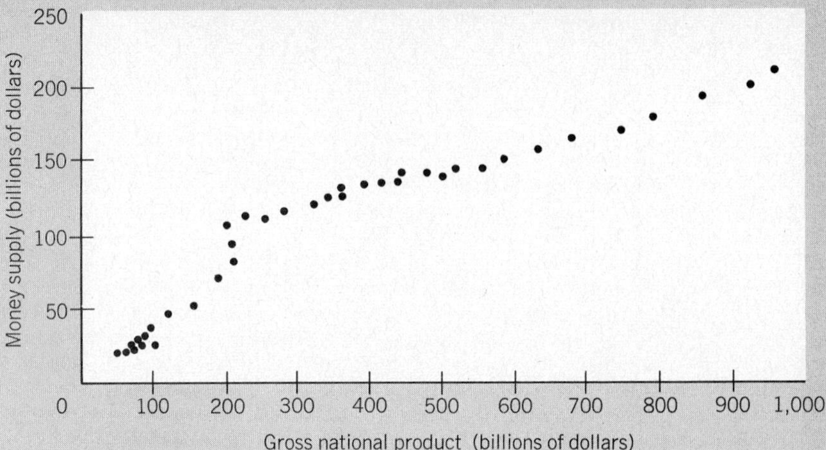

Figure 12.7
Relationship between Money Supply and National Product, United States, 1929–70

There is a reasonably close relationship between the money supply and the money value of national product. As one goes up, the other tends to go up too.

has reached its trough over 12 months before the trough in general business.[9]

Clearly, findings of this sort must be taken seriously. Moreover, research carried out at the Federal Reserve Bank of St. Louis has shown a close relationship between short-run changes in the quantity of money and short-run changes in NNP. Based on this relationship, the St. Louis Bank has constructed some simple econometric models that have had some success in forecasting NNP. These results have also strengthened the hand of the monetarists.

The Velocity of Money and the Equation of Exchange

The monetarists have revived interest in the so-called quantity theory of money. In previous sections, we defined the money supply; and in Figure 12.1, we saw how the money supply has varied over time. Now let's look at the money supply and nominal, or money, national product to determine what, if any, is the relationship between these two variables. Figure 12.7 shows that *there is a definite relationship between the money supply in the United States and our nominal national product.*[10] *In general, as the money supply has increased, national product has increased as well.* Indeed, the rate of increase of national product during 1929–70 was about the same as the rate of increase of the money supply: both increased by about 700 or 800 percent.

To see why this relationship exists, it is useful to begin by defining a new term: the velocity of circulation of money. The ***velocity of circulation of money*** is the rate at which the money supply is used to make transactions for final goods and services. That is, it equals the average number of times per year that a dollar was used to buy the final goods and services produced by the economy. In other words,

$$V = \frac{NNP}{M}, \tag{12.1}$$

where V is velocity, NNP is the nominal net national product, and M is the money supply. For example, if our nominal net national product is

[9] Milton Friedman, testimony before the Joint Economic Committee, The Relationship of Prices to Economic Stability and Growth, 85th Congress, 2nd Session, 1958.

[10] In Figure 12.7, the data refer to gross national product, not net national product. But, as noted in previous chapters, there is little difference between them and they are highly correlated.

$1 trillion and our money supply is $200 billion, the velocity of circulation of money is 5, which means that, on the average, each dollar of our money consummates $5 worth of purchases of net national product.[11]

Nominal net national product can be expressed as the product of real net national product and the price level: In other words,

$$NNP = P \times Q, \tag{12.2}$$

where P is the price level—the average price at which final goods and services are sold—and Q is net national product in real terms. Substituting this expression for NNP in Equation (12.1), we have

$$V = \frac{P \times Q}{M}. \tag{12.3}$$

That is, velocity equals the price level (P) times real NNP (Q) divided by the money supply (M). This is another way to define the velocity of circulation of money—a way that will prove very useful.

At the beginning of this section, we set out to explain why nominal national product is related to the money supply. Having defined the velocity of circulation of money, our next step is to present the so-called equation of exchange. The ***equation of exchange*** is really nothing more than a restatement, in somewhat different form, of our definition of the velocity of circulation of money. To obtain the equation of exchange, all we have to do is multiply both sides of Equation (12.3) by M. The result, of course, is

$$MV = PQ. \tag{12.4}$$

To understand exactly what this equation means, let's look more closely at each side. Clearly, the right-hand side equals the amount received for final goods and services during the period, because Q is the output of final goods and services during the period and P is their average price. Thus, the product of P and Q must equal the total amount received for final goods and services during the period—or nominal NNP.

Whereas the right-hand side of Equation (12.4) equals the *amount received for* final goods and services during the period, the left-hand side equals the *amount spent on* final goods and services during the period, since the left-hand side equals the money supply—M—times the average number of times during the period that a dollar was spent on final goods and services—V. Obviously, the result—$M \times V$—must equal the amount spent on final goods and services during the period. Thus, since the *amount received* for final goods and services during the period must equal *the amount spent* on final goods and services during the period, the left-hand side must equal the right-hand side.

The equation of exchange—Equation (12.4)—is what logicians call a tautology: it holds by definition. As pointed out above, it is nothing more than a restatement of the definition of the velocity of circulation of money. Yet it is not useless. On the contrary, economists regard the equation of exchange as very valuable, because it sets forth some of the fundamental factors that influence net national product and the price level.

The Crude Quantity Theory of Money and Prices

The classical economists discussed in Chapter 9 assumed that both V and Q were constant. They believed that V was constant because it was determined by the population's stable habits of holding money, and they believed that Q would remain constant at its full employment value. On the basis of these assumptions, they propounded

[11] This concept of velocity is often called the *income velocity of money*. Another velocity concept is the *transactions velocity of money,* defined as the ratio of the total volume of transactions per year to the quantity of money.

the ***crude quantity theory*** of money and prices, a theory that received a great deal of attention and exerted considerable influence in its day. If these assumptions hold, it follows from the equation of exchange—Equation (12.4)—that the price level (P) must be proportional to the money supply (M), because V and Q have been assumed to be constant. (In the short run, the full employment level of real net national product will not change much.) Thus, we can rewrite Equation (12.4) as

$$P = \left(\frac{V}{Q}\right) M, \tag{12.5}$$

where (V/Q) is a constant. So P must be proportional to M if these assumptions hold.

The crude quantity theory is true to its name: it is only a crude approximation to reality. One important weakness is its assumption that velocity is constant. Another is its assumption that the economy is always at full employment, which we know from previous chapters to be far from true. But despite its limitations, the crude quantity theory points to a very important truth: if the government finances its expenditures by a drastic increase in the money supply, the result will be drastic inflation. For example, if the money supply is increased tenfold, there will be a marked increase in the price level. If we take the crude quantity theory at face value, we would expect a tenfold increase in the price level; but that is a case of spurious accuracy. Perhaps the price level will go up only eightfold. Perhaps it will go up twelvefold. The important thing is that it will go up a lot!

There is a great deal of evidence to show that the crude quantity theory is a useful predictor during periods of runaway inflation, such as in Germany after World War I. The German inflation occurred because the German government printed and spent large bundles of additional money. You often hear people warn of the dangers in this country of the government's "resorting to the printing presses" and flooding the country with a vast increase in the money supply. It is a danger in any country. And one great value of the crude quantity theory is that it predicts correctly what will occur as a consequence: rapid inflation.

There is also considerable evidence that the crude quantity theory works reasonably well in predicting long-term trends in the price level. For example, during the sixteenth and seventeenth centuries, gold and silver were imported by the Spanish from the New World, resulting in a great increase in the money supply. The crude quantity theory would predict a great increase in the price level, and this is what occurred. Or consider the late nineteenth century, when the discovery of gold in the United States, South Africa, and Canada brought about a considerable increase in the money supply. As the crude quantity theory would lead us to expect, the price level rose considerably as a consequence.

A More Sophisticated Version of the Quantity Theory

The crude quantity theory was based on two simplifying assumptions, both of which are questionable. One assumption was that real net national product (Q) remains fixed at its full employment level; the other was that the velocity of circulation of money (V) remains constant. A more sophisticated version of the quantity theory can be derived by relaxing the first assumption. This version of the quantity theory recognizes that the economy is often at less than full employment and consequently that real net national product (Q) may vary a good deal for this reason.

So long as velocity remains constant, the equation of exchange—Equation (12.4)—can be used to determine the relationship between net national product in current dollars and M, even if Q is allowed to vary. On the basis of the equation of exchange, it is obvious that $P \times Q$ should be proportional to M, if the velocity of circulation of money (V) remains constant. Since $P \times Q$ is the net national product *in current dollars,* it follows that, if this assumption holds, *the nominal net national product should be proportional to the money supply*. In other words,

$$NNP = aM, \tag{12.6}$$

where NNP is the nominal net national product and V is assumed to equal a constant—a.

If velocity is constant, this version of the quantity theory should enable us to predict nominal net national product if we know the money supply. Also, if velocity is constant, this version of the quantity theory should enable us to control nominal net national product by controlling the money supply. Clearly, if velocity is constant, Equation (12.6) is an extremely important economic relationship—one that will go a long way toward accomplishing the goals of Chapters 9, 10, and 11, which were to show how net national product could be forecasted and controlled. But is velocity constant? Since Equation (12.6) is based on this assumption, we must find out.

Figure 12.8[12] shows how the velocity of circulation of money has behaved since 1920. Obviously velocity has not been constant. But on the other hand, it has not varied enormously. Excluding the war years, it has generally been between 2.5 and 4.5 in the United States. Over the long run, it has been reasonably stable, but it has varied a good deal over the business cycle. As shown in Figure 12.8, velocity tends to decrease during depressions and increase during booms. *All in all, one must certainly conclude that, although velocity is fairly stable over the long run, it is not so stable that Equation (12.6) alone can be used in any precise way to forecast or control net national product.*

However, this does not mean that Equation

[12] The velocity figures in Figure 12.8 are based on gross national product, not net national product. But for the reasons given in note 10, this makes little real difference.

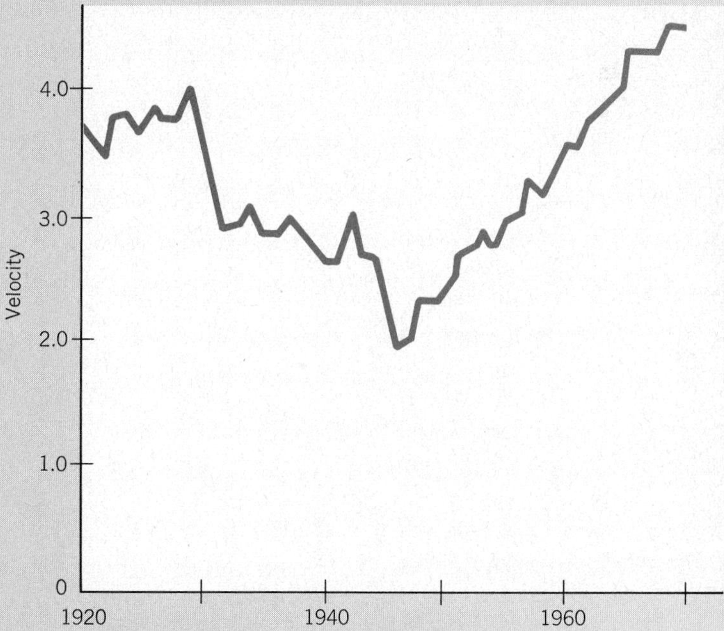

Figure 12.8
Velocity of Circulation of Money, United States, 1920–70

The velocity of circulation of money has generally been between 2.5 and 4.5, except during World War II.

(12.6) is useless, or that the more sophisticated quantity theory is without value. On the contrary, this version of the quantity theory points out a very important truth, which is that *the money supply has an important effect on net national product (in money terms): increases in the quantity of money are likely to increase net national product, while decreases in the quantity of money are likely to decrease net national product.* Because velocity is not constant, the relationship between the money supply and net national product is not as neat and simple as that predicted by Equation (12.6), but there is a relationship. And it may be possible to predict V as a function of other variables, like the frequency with which people are paid and the level of business confidence. Time will tell how far this tack may take us. (At present, most economists feel that changes in V reflect, rather than cause, changes in NNP.)

Now let's return to our original question: why is there a relationship (in Figure 12.7) between the money supply and national product (in money terms)? Given the discussion in the last few sections, the answer is obvious: the velocity of circulation of money has remained relatively stable over the long run—not so stable that the money supply and national product moved in locked steps, but stable enough so that there is a reasonably close relationship.

Two Alternative Models

At this point, you may have the uneasy feeling that two theories have been dished up to explain the same thing. If so, you are right. Earlier in this chapter when we discussed Figures 12.5 and 12.6, as well as in Chapters 9–11, we presented the Keynesian model, which uses changes in income and expenditure to explain changes in NNP. In the last few sections, we have presented the quantity theory, which uses changes in the money supply to explain changes in NNP. You have a perfect right to ask which model is better. At present, there is a controversy over this question. The monetarists believe that the latter theory is better, while the Keynesians argue for the former theory. This is one of the most important debates in economics at present.

While recognizing the existence and importance of this debate, we must underscore one major point on which these two alternative models agree: *the effect of the money supply on net national product is qualitatively the same in both the Keynesian and monetarist models.* More specifically, whatever theory you look at, you get the same result: increases in the money supply would be expected to increase nominal net national product, and decreases in the money supply would be expected to decrease nominal net national product. Thus, whether the Keynesian (majority) view of the world or the monetarist (minority) view of the world is correct, it is important that you understand the topics taken up in the next two chapters—the banking system, the factors determining the money supply, and the ways the government tries to alter the money supply in order to promote full employment with stable prices.

Also, no matter which view is accepted, if the economy is at considerably less than full employment, increases in the money supply would be expected to increase real national product, while decreases in the money supply would be expected to reduce real national product. However, once full employment is approached, increases in the money supply result more and more in increases in the price level, as distinct from increases in real output. These expectations are shared both by the monetarists and the Keynesians, which is fortunate since they underlie a great deal of monetary theory.

In Chapter 15 we shall discuss the theoretical and policy differences between the monetarists and the Keynesians in considerable detail. Before we do, we must describe how banks create money and how the Federal Reserve controls the money supply. These are the principal topics of the next two chapters.

Summary

Money performs several basic functions. It serves as a medium of exchange, a standard of value, and a store of value. There are three kinds of money —coins, currency, and demand deposits. Economists include demand deposits as part of the money supply because you can pay for goods and services about as easily by check as with cash. Besides this narrow definition of money, a broader definition includes saving and time deposits. Of course, there are lots of other assets—for example, government bonds—that can be transformed without much difficulty into cash. It is not easy to draw a line between money and nonmoney, since many assets have some of the characteristics of money.

America's history has seen many sharp fluctuations in the price level. Wars have generally been periods of substantial inflation, and prices have dropped in the postwar periods. Since World War II, prices have tended to go one way only—up. Although a mild upward creep of prices at the rate of 1 or 2 percent per year is not likely to result in very disastrous social consequences, runaway inflation is a real social evil that disrupts the economy very seriously. Generally, such inflations have occurred because the government expanded the money supply far too rapidly. However, too small a rate of growth of the money supply can also be a mistake, resulting in excessive unemployment.

The Federal Reserve System is responsible for regulating and controlling the money supply. Established in 1913, the Fed is composed of the member banks, twelve regional Federal Reserve Banks, and the Federal Reserve Board, which coordinates the activities of the system. The Federal Reserve System is the central bank of the United States. Commercial banks have two primary functions. First, they hold demand deposits and permit checks to be drawn on them. Second, they lend money to firms and individuals. In the course of carrying out these activities, banks create and destroy money.

Most economists believe that the lower the interest rate, the greater the amount of money demanded. Thus, increases in the quantity of money result in lower interest rates, which result in increased investment (and other types of spending), which results in a higher NNP. Conversely, decreases in the quantity of money result in higher interest rates, which result in decreased investment (and other types of spending), which results in a lower NNP. This is the Keynesian approach. Another, contrasting approach is based on the equation of exchange. The equation of exchange is $MV = PQ$, where M is the money supply, V is velocity, P is the price level, and Q is net national product in real terms. The velocity of circulation of money is the rate at which the money supply is used to make transactions for final goods and services. Specifically, it equals NNP in money terms divided by the money supply.

If the velocity of circulation of money remains constant and if real net national product is fixed at its full employment level, it follows from the equation of exchange that the price level will be proportional to the money supply. This is the crude quantity theory, which is a reasonably good approximation during periods of runaway inflation, and works reasonably well in predicting long-term trends in the price level. A more sophisticated version of the quantity theory recognizes that real net national product is often at less than full employment, with the result that Q is not fixed. Thus, if velocity remains constant, net national product in money terms should be proportional to the money supply. In fact, nominal net national product has been fairly closely related to the money supply. However, velocity has by no means remained stable over time. The monetarists, led by Milton Friedman, adopt the more sophisticated version of the quantity theory. There are many important disagreements between the monetarists and the Keynesians, but both approaches agree that increases in the money supply will increase NNP (in money terms) while decreases in the money supply will decrease NNP (in money terms).

CONCEPTS FOR REVIEW

Demand deposits
Currency
Time deposits
Near-money
Runaway inflation
Transactions demand
Precautionary demand
Speculative demand
Velocity of circulation
Equation of exchange
Crude quantity theory
Liquidity preference function
Federal Reserve Notes
Federal Reserve System
Federal Reserve Board
Federal Deposit Insurance Corporation

QUESTIONS FOR DISCUSSION AND REVIEW

1. According to Milton Friedman, the monetarists "have always stressed that money matters a great deal for the development of nominal [i.e., money] magnitudes, but not over the long run for real magnitudes." What does he mean? Do you agree or disagree?

2. Describe how the quantity of money influences nominal and real NNP according to (a) the Keynesion model, (b) the crude quantity theory, and (c) the more sophisticated quantity theory. What sorts of tests might be performed to determine which of these models works best?

3. Once full employment is reached, increases in the money supply result primarily in increases in the price level. True or False?

4. $MV = PQ$ is called
a. the equation of exchange.
b. a tautology.
c. a restatement of the velocity of circulation.
d. all of the above.
e. none of the above.

CHAPTER 13

The Banking System and the Quantity of Money

Banking is often viewed as a colorless, dull profession whose practitioners are knee-deep in deposit slips and canceled checks. Also, when the time comes to reject a loan application, the banker is often viewed as a heartless skinflint—even if he advertises that "you have a friend at Chase Manhattan." Yet despite these notions, most people recognize the importance of the banks in our economy, perhaps because the banks deal in such an important and fascinating commodity—money.

In this chapter, we look in detail at how commercial banks operate. We begin by discussing the nature of their loans and investments, as well as the important concept of reserves. Then, after looking into legal reserve requirements, we describe how commercial banks create money—a very important and commonly misunderstood process. Finally, we take up the effects of currency withdrawals and excess reserves on our results. The purpose of this chapter is to introduce you to the operations of the banking system, which is neither as colorless nor as mysterious as is sometimes assumed.

The Bank of America: A Case Study

We can learn something about banking in the United States from the history of a particular bank—the Bank of America, the nation's largest commercial bank. In 1904, Amadeo Peter Giannini, a 34-year-old son of an Italian immigrant, founded the Bank of Italy in the Italian district of San Francisco. Giannini was a man of enormous energy and drive. At the age of 12, he had gone to school by day, while working in his stepfather's produce firm for much of each night. At 19, he was a full-fledged member of the produce firm, and at 31 had become rich enough to retire from the produce business—and eventually to turn to banking.

Giannini showed the sort of entrepreneurial zeal in banking that would be expected from his previous track record. As an illustration, consider the following episode:

> In 1906, the city of San Francisco was rocked by earthquake and swept by fire. As the flames approached the little Bank of Italy, the young banker piled his cash and securities into a horse-drawn wagon and with a guard of two soldiers took them to his home at San Mateo, twenty miles from San Francisco, where he buried them in the garden; and then while the ruins of the city were still smoking he set up a desk in the open air down by the waterfront, put up a sign over the desk which read BANK OF ITALY, and began doing business again—the first San Francisco bank to resume.[1]

Clearly, Giannini was a banker who did not observe banker's hours.

Giannini's bank prospered and grew. By the time he was 50, it had over 25 branches. During the 1920s, he acquired more and more branches, until old-line California bankers began to realize that the Bank of Italy had become a factor to be reckoned with. They did their best to prevent its further expansion, but to no avail. A man who can turn an earthquake to his advantage is unlikely, after all, to submit to such pressures. Indeed, by 1929, Giannini had 453 banking offices in California alone, as well as a considerable number elsewhere. His was the fourth largest commercial bank in the country.

In 1930, Giannini's bank was renamed the Bank of America. The 1930s were not particularly kind to it, any more than they were to the rest of the economy. But in the past 35 years, the Bank of

Table 13.1

The Ten Largest Commercial Banks in the United States in Terms of Deposits, December 31, 1971

Bank and location	Deposits (billions of dollars)
Bank of America, San Francisco	29.0
First National City Bank, New York	24.4
Chase Manhattan Bank, New York	20.4
Manufacturers Hanover Trust Company, New York	12.2
Morgan Guaranty Trust Company, New York	10.7
Chemical Bank, New York	10.5
Bankers Trust Company, New York	8.9
Security Pacific National Bank, Los Angeles	8.5
Continental Illinois National Bank and Trust Company, Chicago	8.5
First National Bank, Chicago	7.2

Source: Moody's, 1972.

[1] Frederick Lewis Allen, *The Lords of Creation*, New York: Harper and Bros., 1935, p. 320. Much of this section is based on Allen's account.

America has grown and grown. In 1940, its loans (and discounts) totaled $778 million; in 1950, $3,257 million; in 1960, $6,699 million; and in 1970, $15,951 million. Clearly, the Bank of America was on the move. By the end of 1971, it had deposits of almost $30 billion, and was the largest commercial bank in the United States. (The 10 largest banks in the United States, in terms of deposits, are listed in Table 13.1.) Certainly it had come a long way since the days of the open-air desk on the waterfront.

How Banks Operate

The Bank of America, the biggest in the country, is hardly a typical commercial bank. It has had a remarkable history and a gifted founder. Many commercial banks are very small, as you would guess from the fact that there are over 13,000 of them in the United States. But regardless of their size, what do banks do? Their function and activities vary considerably. Some are principally for firms; they do little business with individuals. Others are heavily engaged in lending to consumers. Nonetheless, although it is difficult to generalize about the operations of commercial banks because they vary so much, certain principles and propositions generally hold.

First, *banks generally make loans to both firms and individuals, and invest in securities, particularly the bonds of state and local governments, as well as federal government bonds.* The relationship between a business firm and its bank is often a close and continuing one. The firm keeps a reasonably large deposit with the bank for long periods of time, while the bank provides the firm with needed and prudent loans. The relationship between an individual and his or her bank is much more casual, but banks like consumer loans because they tend to be relatively profitable. In addition, besides lending to firms and individuals, banks buy large quantities of government bonds. For example, in the early 1970s, commercial banks held about $60 billion of state and local government bonds.

Second, *banks, like other firms, are operated to make a profit.* They don't do it by producing and selling a good, like automobiles or steel. Instead, they perform various services, including lending money, making investments, clearing checks, keeping records, and so on. They manage to make a profit from these activities by lending money and making investments that yield a higher rate of interest than they must pay their depositors. For example, the Bank of America may be able to get 9 percent interest on the loans it makes, while it must pay only 5 percent interest to its depositors. (Commercial banks do not pay interest on demand deposits, but they do pay interest on time deposits. Also, they provide services at less than cost to holders of demand deposits.) If so, it receives the difference of 4 percent, which goes to meet its expenses—and to provide it with some profits.

Third, *banks must constantly balance their desire for high returns from their loans and investments against the requirement that these loans and investments be safe and easily turned into cash.* Since a bank's profits increase if it makes loans or investments that yield a high interest rate, it is clear why a bank favors high returns from its loans and investments. But those that yield a high interest rate often are relatively risky, which means that they may not be repaid in full. Because a bank lends out its depositors' money, it must be careful to limit the riskiness of the loans and investments it makes. Otherwise it may fail.

The Balance Sheet of an Individual Bank

A good way to understand how a bank operates is to look at its balance sheet. Figure 13.1 shows the Bank of America's balance sheet as of the beginning of 1970. The left-hand side shows that the total assets of the Bank of America were $25.6 billion, and that these assets were made up as fol-

Figure 13.1 Balance Sheet, Bank of America, January 1, 1970

Assets ($ billions)		Liabilities and net worth ($ billions)	
Cash	4.8	Demand deposits	9.1
Securities	4.2	Savings and time deposits	13.1
Loans	14.6	Other liabilities	2.0
Other assets	2.0	Net worth	1.4
Total	25.6	Total	25.6

Source: Bank of America.

lows: $4.8 billion in cash, $4.2 billion in bonds and other securities, $14.6 billion in loans, and $2.0 billion in other assets. In particular, note that the loans included among the assets of the Bank of America are the loans it made to firms and individuals. As we just said, lending money is one of the major functions of a commercial bank.

The right-hand side of the balance sheet says that the total liabilities—or debts—of the Bank of America were $24.2 billion, and that these liabilities were made up of $22.2 billion in deposits (both demand and time), and $2.0 billion in other liabilities. Note that the deposits at the Bank of America are included among its liabilities, since the Bank of America owes the depositors the amount of money in their deposits. It will be recalled from the previous chapter that maintaining these deposits is one of the major functions of a commercial bank. Returning to the balance sheet of the Bank of America, the difference between its total assets and its total liabilities—$1.4 billion—is, of course, its net worth.

One noteworthy characteristic of any bank's balance sheet is the fact that *a very large percentage of its liabilities must be paid on demand.* For example, if all the depositors of the Bank of America withdrew their demand deposits, over ⅓ of its liabilities would be due on demand. Of course, the chance of everyone wanting to draw out his or her money at once is infinitesimally small. Instead, on a given day some depositors withdraw some money, while others make deposits, and most neither withdraw nor deposit money. Consequently, any bank can get along with an amount of cash to cover withdrawals that is much smaller than the total amount of its demand deposits. For example, the Bank of America's cash equaled about ½ of its total demand deposits. Note that "cash" here includes the bank's deposit with the Federal Reserve System and its deposits with other banks, as well as cash in its vault.

The Bank of America's practice of holding an amount of cash—including its deposits with the Federal Reserve and with other banks—much less than the amount it owes its depositors may strike you as dangerous. Indeed, if you have a deposit at the Bank of America, you may be tempted to go over and withdraw the money in your account and deposit it in some bank that does have cash equal to the amount it owes its depositors. But you won't be able to do this because *all banks hold much less cash than the amount they owe their depositors.* Moreover, this is a perfectly sound banking practice, as we shall see.

Fractional-Reserve Banking

To understand the crucial significance of ***fractional-reserve banking,*** as this practice is called,

Figure 13.2 Bank Balance Sheet: Case where Reserves Equal Demand Deposits

Assets		Liabilities and net worth	
Reserves	$2,000,000	Demand deposits	$2,000,000
Loans and investments	500,000	Net worth	500,000
Total	$2,500,000	Total	$2,500,000

let's compare two situations—one where a bank must hold as reserves an amount equal to the amount it owes its depositors, another where its reserves do not have to match the amount it owes its depositors. In the first case, the bank's balance sheet might be as shown in Figure 13.2, if demand deposits equal $2 million. The bank's loans and investments in this case are made entirely with funds put up by the owners of the bank. To see this, note that loans and investments equal $500,000, and that the bank's net worth also equals $500,000. Thus, if some of these loans are not repaid or if some of these investments lose money, the losses are borne entirely by the bank's stockholders. The depositors are protected completely because every cent of their deposits is covered by the bank's reserves.

Now let's turn to the case of fractional-reserve banking. In this case, the bank's balance sheet might be as shown in Figure 13.3, if deposits equal $2 million. Some of the loans and investments made by the bank are not made with funds put up by the owners of the bank, but with funds deposited in the bank by depositors. Thus, though depositors deposited $2 million in the bank, the reserves are only $400,000. What happened to the remaining $1.6 million? Since the bank (in this simple case) only has two kinds of assets, loans (and investments) and reserves, the bank must have lent out (or invested) the remaining $1.6 million.

The early history of banking is the story of an evolution from the first to the second situation. The earliest banks held reserves equal to the amounts they owed depositors, and were simply places where people stored their gold. But as time went on, banks began to practice fractional-reserve banking. It is easy to see how this evolution could take place. Suppose that you owned a bank of the first type. You would almost certainly be struck by the fact that most of the gold entrusted to you was not demanded on any given day. Sooner or later, you might be tempted to lend out some of the gold and obtain some interest. Eventually, as

Figure 13.3 Bank Balance Sheet: Fractional Reserves

Assets		Liabilities and net worth	
Reserves	$400,000	Demand deposits	$2,000,000
Loans and investments	2,100,000	Net worth	500,000
Total	$2,500,000	Total	$2,500,000

experience indicated that this procedure did not inconvenience the depositors, you and other bankers might make this practice common knowledge.

You might use several arguments to defend this practice. First, you would probably point out that none of the depositors had lost any money. (To the depositors, this would be a rather important argument!) Second, you could show that the interest you earned on the loans made it possible for you to charge depositors less for storing their gold. Consequently, you would argue that it was to the depositors' advantage (because of the savings that accrued to them) for you to lend out some of the gold. Third, you would probably argue that putting the money to work benefited the community and the economy. After all, in many cases, firms can make highly productive investments only if they can borrow the money, and by lending out your depositors' gold, you would enable such investments to be made.

Legal Reserve Requirements

Arguments of this sort have led society to permit fractional-reserve banking. In other words, a bank is allowed to hold less in reserves than the amount it owes its depositors. But what determines the amount of reserves banks hold? For example, the Bank of America, according to Figure 13.1, held cash equal to about 20 percent of its total deposits. Probably it could get away with holding much less in reserves, so long as there is no panic among depositors and it makes sound loans and investments. One reason why the Bank of America held this much cash is very simple: *the Federal Reserve System requires every commercial bank that is a member of the system to hold a certain percentage of its deposits as reserves.* This percentage varies with the size of the bank. As of late 1973, each member bank had to hold as reserves 8 percent of its first $2 million of demand deposits, 10½ percent of its next $8 million, 12½ percent of its next $90 million, 13½ percent of its next $300 million, and 18 percent of its demand deposits in excess of $400 million. These are ***legal reserve requirements;*** they exist for time deposits too, but are lower than for demand deposits.

The Federal Reserve System in recent years has dictated that the average bank should hold about $1 dollar in reserves for every $6 of demand deposits. Most of these reserves are held in the form of deposits by banks at their regional Federal Reserve Bank. Thus, for example, a great deal of the Bank of America's reserves are held in its deposit with the Federal Reserve Bank of San Francisco. In addition, some of any bank's reserves are held in cash on the bank's premises. However, its legal reserves are less than the "cash" entry on its balance sheet since its deposits with other banks do not count as legal reserves. Of course, these legal reserve requirements are binding only on members of the Federal Reserve System, and, as we noted in the previous chapter, although all national banks are members, not all state banks are. But the banks outside the Federal Reserve System hold only a small percentage of the nation's deposits, and the Fed seems to believe that it includes a large enough proportion of the banks to accomplish its goals.

The most obvious reason why the Fed imposes these legal reserve requirements would seem to be to keep the banks safe, but in this case the obvious answer isn't the right one. Instead, *the most important reason for legal reserve requirements is to control the money supply.* It will take some more discussion before this becomes clear.

To close with a historical sidelight, until 1972 legal reserve requirements were higher for big-city banks than for small-town banks. Back when the Federal Reserve System was formed, big-city banks often held the reserves of the small-town banks, and thus it seemed reasonable to enforce higher reserve requirements for the big-city banks. But nowadays reserves of all member banks—in big cities or in small towns—are held by the Federal Reserve Banks. Consequently, this difference in legal reserve requirements was like the human appendix and wisdom teeth: a somewhat illogical and useless inheritance from the past. Finally, in 1972, it was jettisoned.

The Safety of the Banks

We have just argued that the reserve requirements imposed by the Federal Reserve System exceed what would be required under normal circumstances to insure the safety of the banks. To support our argument, we might cite some authorities who claim that a bank would be quite safe if it only had reserves equal to about 2 percent of its deposits. Under these circumstances it would be able to meet its depositors' everyday demands for cash. Obviously this level of reserves is much lower than the legally required level. We must, however, recognize that the safety of a bank depends on many factors besides the level of its reserves. In particular, a bank must make prudent investments.

For example, suppose that a bank lends money to every budding inventor with a scheme for producing perpetual-motion machines—and that it grants particularly large loans to those who propose to market these machines in the suburbs of Missoula, Montana. This bank is going to fail eventually, even if it holds reserves equal to 20 percent—or 50 percent for that matter—of its demand deposits. It will fail simply because the loans it makes will not be repaid, and eventually these losses will accumulate to more than the bank's net worth. In other words, if the bank is sufficiently inept in making loans and investments it will lose all the owners' money and some of the depositors' money besides.

In addition, even if the bank makes sensible loans and investments, it must protect itself against short-term withdrawals of large amounts of money. Although larger-than-usual withdrawals are not very likely to occur, the bank must be prepared to meet a temporary upswing in withdrawals. One way is to invest in securities that can readily be turned into cash. Such securities are near-money, in the jargon of the previous chapter. For example, the bank may invest in short-term government securities that can readily be sold at a price that varies only moderately from day to day.

There can be no doubt that banks are much safer today than they were 50 or 100 years ago. The reason is that the government has put its power squarely behind the banking system. It used to be that "runs" occurred on the banks. Every now and then, depositors, frightened that their banks would fail and that they would lose some of their money, would line up at the tellers' windows and withdraw as much money as they could. Faced with runs of this sort, banks were sometimes forced to close because they could not satisfy all demands for withdrawals. Needless to say, no fractional-reserve banking system can satisfy demands for total withdrawal of funds.

Runs on banks are a thing of the past, for several reasons. One is that the government—including the Federal Deposit Insurance Corporation (FDIC), the Fed, and other public agencies—has made it clear that it will not stand by and tolerate the sorts of panics that used to occur periodically in this country. The FDIC insures the accounts of depositors in practically all banks so that, even if a bank fails, the depositor will get his money back—up to $20,000. Another reason is that the banks themselves are better managed and regulated. For example, bank examiners are sent out to look over the bankers' shoulders and see whether they are solvent. It is a far cry from the situation sixty-odd years ago that led to the creation of the Federal Reserve System.

The Lending Decision: A Case Study

To get a better feel for the workings of a bank, let's look at an actual decision faced by Robert Swift, the assistant vice president of the Lone Star National Bank of Houston, Texas. Mr. Swift received a call from Ralph Desmond, president of the Desmond Engineering Corporation. Mr. Desmond wanted to change his bank; he was dissatisfied with the amount he could borrow from his present bank. He wanted to borrow $30,000 from the Lone Star to pay what he owed to his present bank, pay some bills coming up, and buy some material needed to fulfill a contract. Mr. Swift asked Mr. Desmond to come to his office with various financial statements regarding the Desmond Engineering Corporation and its prospects. These included recent profit and loss statements and balance sheets, as well as a variety of other data, including information indicating how rapidly the firm collected its bills and the quality of the debts owed the firm.

Mr. Swift forwarded Mr. Desmond's loan application to the credit department of the bank for further analyses. The credit department added comments on the Desmond Engineering Corporation's solvency and prospects. Besides being secured by a mortgage on some equipment owned by the Desmond Engineering Corporation, this loan was to be personally endorsed by Mr. Desmond and another principal stockholder in the firm. Consequently, Mr. Swift obtained information on the extent and nature of the personal assets of Mr. Desmond and the other stockholder. This information was used, together with all the other data on the firm, to determine whether the bank would make the loan. After a reasonable amount of time, Mr. Swift recommended the acceptance of Mr. Desmond's loan application. In his view, Mr. Desmond had a very good chance of repaying the loan.[2]

Note two things about this decision. First, if the bank grants Mr. Desmond the loan, it will create a demand deposit for him. In other words, it will create some money. Second, the bank can do this only if it has reserves exceeding the legal reserve requirements. Both of these points are important enough to dwell on for a while.

[2] This case comes from Leonard Marks and Alan Coleman, *Cases in Commercial Bank Management,* New York: McGraw-Hill, 1962, pp. 168–76. However, the outcome is purely conjectural.

Two Ways Banks Cannot Create Money

Genesis tells us that God created heaven and earth. Economists tell us that banks create money. To many people, the latter process is at least as mysterious as the former. Even bankers themselves have been known to fall into serious error by claiming that they do not create money. Yet the way banks create money is a relatively simple process, which the next few sections will describe in detail. Suppose that someone receives $10,000 in newly printed currency and deposits it in his local bank. Before we see how the bank can create more than $10,000 from this deposit, we will describe two ways in which banks *cannot* create new money. Since people often jump to the conclusion that one or the other of these two processes is the correct one, it is a good idea to kill off these heresies at the outset.

First, suppose that ours is not a fractional-reserve banking system. In other words, assume that every bank has to maintain reserves equal to its deposits. In this case, the bank receiving the $10,000 deposit cannot create any new money. You may be inclined to think that it can be done, but it can't. To see why not, consider the changes in the bank's balance sheet, shown in Figure 13.4. When the $10,000 is deposited in the bank, the bank's deposits go up by $10,000. Since the bank must hold $10,000 in reserves to back up the new 10,000 deposit, it must put the $10,000 it receives from the depositor into its reserves. Thus, the bank's demand deposits go up by $10,000, and its reserves go up by $10,000. Since demand deposits are on the right-hand side of the balance sheet and reserves are on the left-hand side, the balance sheet continues to balance. *No new money is created. All that happens is that the depositor gives up $10,000 in one form of money—currency—and receives $10,000 in another form of money—a demand deposit.*

Next, let's turn to a second way banks cannot create money. Suppose that we have a fractional-reserve banking system and that the legal reserve requirement is 16⅔ percent. In other words, the bank must hold $1 in reserves for every $6 of demand deposits. Suppose that the bank decides to take the crisp, new $10,000 in currency that is deposited and add it to its reserves, thus increasing its reserves by $10,000. Then suppose it reasons (incorrectly) that it can increase its deposits by $50,000, since it has $10,000 in additional reserves. Why $50,000? Because the $10,000 in additional reserves will support $60,000 in demand deposits; and since the person who deposited the $10,000 has a demand deposit of $10,000, this means that it can create additional demand deposits of $60,000 minus $10,000, or $50,000.

The bank will create these additional demand deposits simply by making loans or investments. Thus, when a person comes in to the bank for a loan, all the banker has to do is give him a demand deposit—a checking account—that didn't exist before. In other words, the banker can say to his staff: "Establish a checking account of $50,000 for Mr. Smith. We have just lent him this amount to buy a new piece of equipment to be used in his business." At first, this whole process looks a bit like black magic, perhaps even larceny. After all, how can checking accounts be established out of thin air? But they can, and are. In essence, this is how banks create money.

But we prefaced this example by saying that it contains an error: the error is the supposition that the bank can create an additional $50,000 of demand deposits on the basis of the $10,000 deposit. To see why this won't work, consider the changes in the bank's balance sheet, shown in Figure 13.5. After the bank received the $10,000 deposit, its demand deposits and its reserves both increased by $10,000, as shown in the first panel of Figure 13.5. Then, as we noted above, the bank made a $50,000 loan and (in the process of making the loan) created $50,000 in new deposits, as shown in the second panel. So far, so good. The bank's balance sheet continues to balance—in accord with common sense and accounting (in that order). The bank's reserves are ⅙ of its demand deposits; they satisfy the legal reserve requirements established by the Fed.

So what is the problem? None, unless the money lent by the bank is spent. If the man who received the loan—Mr. Smith—never used the money he borrowed, the bank could act this way and get away with it. But people who borrow money are in the habit of spending it; why pay interest on money one doesn't use? Even if Mr. Smith, the recipient of this loan, spent the money, the bank could act in accord with this example and get away with it if the people who received the money from Mr. Smith deposited it in this same bank. But the chances of this occurring are very small. The equipment Mr. Smith plans to buy is likely to be produced by a firm in some other city; and even if it is located in the same city, the firm may well have an account at another bank.

To see the problem that results when the loan

Figure 13.4 Changes in Bank Balance Sheet, where Reserves Equal Demand Deposits

Assets		Liabilities and net worth	
Reserves	+$10,000	Demand deposits	+$10,000
Loans and investments	No change	Net worth	No change
Total	+$10,000	Total	+$10,000

Figure 13.5 Changes in Bank Balance Sheet: Fractional Reserves

	Assets		Liabilities and Net Worth	
Bank receives deposit	Reserves	+$10,000	Demand deposits	+$10,000
	Loans and investments	No change	Net worth	No change
	Total	+$10,000	Total	+$10,000
Bank makes loan	Reserves	No change	Demand deposits	+$50,000
	Loans and investments	+$50,000	Net worth	No change
	Total	+$50,000	Total	+$50,000
Mr. Smith spends $50,000	Reserves	−$50,000	Demand deposits	−$50,000
	Loans and investments	No change	Net worth	No change
	Total	−$50,000	Total	−$50,000
Total effect	Reserves	−$40,000	Demand deposits	+$10,000
	Loans and investments	+ 50,000	Net worth	No change
	Total	+$10,000	Total	+$10,000

is spent in this way, suppose that Mr. Smith spends the $50,000 on a machine produced by the Acme Corporation, which has an account at the First National Bank of Boston. He sends the Acme Corporation a check for $50,000 drawn on our bank. When the Acme Corporation receives Mr. Smith's check, it deposits this check to its account at the First National Bank of Boston, which, using the facilities of the Federal Reserve System, presents the check to our bank for payment. Our bank must then fork over $50,000 of its cash—its reserves—to the First National Bank of Boston. Consequently, once the $50,000 check is paid, the effect on our bank's balance sheet is as shown in the third panel of Figure 13.5. Taken as a whole, the bank's demand deposits have increased by $10,000, and its reserves have decreased by $40,000, as shown in the bottom panel of Figure 13.5.

At this point, the error in this example is becoming clear. *If the bank was holding $1 in reserves for every $6 in demand deposits before the $10,000 deposit was made, these transactions must cause the bank to violate the legal reserve requirements.* This is simple to prove. Suppose that, before the $10,000 deposit, our bank had $X in demand deposits and $\$\frac{X}{6}$ in reserves. Then, after the transactions described above, it must have ($X + $10,000) in demand deposits and $\left(\$\frac{X}{6} - \$40{,}000\right)$ in reserves. Certainly, the reserves—$\$\frac{X}{6} - \$40{,}000$—are now less than 1/6 of the demand deposits—$X + $10,000. This must be true whatever value X has. (Try it and see.) Thus, no bank can create money in this way because, if it did, it would violate the legal reserve requirements after the newly created demand deposits were used. However, as we shall see later, a monopoly bank—that is, the only bank in the country—could create money like this. But monopoly banks do not exist in the United States.

How Banks Can Create Money

Now that you have learned two ways that banks *cannot* create money, let's describe how they *can* create money. Imagine the following scenario. First, suppose once again that someone deposits $10,000 of newly printed money in our bank, which we'll call Bank A. Second, suppose that Bank A lends Mr. Smith $8,333, and that Mr. Smith uses this money to purchase some equipment from Mr. Jones, who deposits Mr. Smith's check in his account at Bank B. Third, Bank B buys a bond for $6,941 from Mr. Stone, who deposits the check from Bank B to his account at Bank C. Fourth, Bank C lends $5,784 to Mr. White, who uses the money to buy a truck from the local General Motors dealer, Mr. Black, who deposits Mr. White's check for $5,784 to his account at Bank D. Fifth, Bank D lends Mr. Cohen $4,820 which Mr. Cohen uses to buy some lumber from Mr. Palucci, who deposits Mr. Cohen's check to his account at Bank E. Admittedly, this is a somewhat complicated plot with a substantial cast of characters, but life is like that.

The first step in our drama occurs when someone deposits $10,000 in newly printed money in Bank A. The effect of this deposit is shown in the first panel of Figure 13.6: Bank A's demand deposits

Figure 13.6 Changes in Bank A's Balance Sheet

	Assets		Liabilities and net worth	
Bank receives deposit	Reserves	+$10,000	Demand deposits	+$10,000
	Loans and investments	No change	Net worth	No change
	Total	+$10,000	Total	+$10,000
Bank makes loan	Reserves	No change	Demand deposits	+$ 8,333
	Loans and investments	+$ 8,333	Net worth	No change
	Total	+$ 8,333	Total	+$ 8,333
Mr Smith spends $8,333	Reserves	−$ 8,333	Demand deposits	−$ 8,333
	Loans and investments	No change	Net worth	No change
	Total	−$ 8,333	Total	−$ 8,333
Total effect	Reserves	+$ 1,667	Demand deposits	+$10,000
	Loans and investments	+$ 8,333	Net worth	No change
	Total	+$10,000	Total	+$10,000

and its reserves both go up by $10,000. Now Bank A is far too smart to pull the sort of trick described in the last section. It does not try to make a $50,000 loan, lest it wind up with less reserves than dictated by the legal reserve requirements. When Mr. Smith asks one of the loan officers of the bank for a loan to purchase equipment, the loan officer approves a loan of $8,333, not $50,000. Mr. Smith is given a checking account of $8,333 at Bank A.

How can Bank A get away with this loan of $8,333 without winding up with less than the legally required reserves? The answer to this question lies in the second panel of Figure 13.6, which shows what happens to Bank A's balance sheet when Bank A makes the $8,333 loan and creates a new demand deposit of $8,333. Obviously, both demand deposits and loans go up by $8,333. Next, look at the third panel of Figure 13.6, which shows what happens when Mr. Smith spends the $8,333 on equipment. As pointed out above, he purchases this equipment from Mr. Jones. Mr. Jones deposits Mr. Smith's check to his account in Bank B which presents the check to Bank A for payment. After Bank A pays Bank B (through the Federal Reserve System), the result—as shown in the third panel—is that Bank A's deposits go down by $8,333 since Mr. Smith no longer has the deposit. Bank A's reserves also go down by $8,333 since Bank A has to transfer these reserves to Bank B to pay the amount of the check.

As shown in the bottom panel of Figure 13.6, the total effect on Bank A is to increase its deposits by the $10,000 that was deposited originally and to increase its reserves by $10,000 minus $8,333, or $1,667. In other words, reserves have increased by ⅙ as much as demand deposits. This means that Bank A will meet its legal reserve requirements. To see this, suppose that before the deposit of $10,000, Bank A had demand deposits of $X and reserves of $\$\frac{X}{6}$. Then after the full effect of the transaction occurs on Bank A's balance sheet, Bank A's demand deposits will equal ($X + $10,000) and its reserves will equal $\left(\$\frac{X}{6} + \$\frac{10{,}000}{6}\right)$, since $\$1{,}667 = \frac{\$10{,}000}{6}$. Thus Bank A continues to hold $1 in reserves for every $6 in demand deposits, as required by the Fed.

Impact on Other Banks

It is important to recognize that *Bank A has now created* $8,333 *in new money*. To see this, note that Mr. Jones winds up with a demand deposit of this amount that he didn't have before; and this is a net addition to the money supply, since the person who originally deposited the $10,000 in currency still has his $10,000, although it is in the form of a demand deposit rather than currency. But this is not the end of the story. The effects of the $10,000 deposit at Bank A are not limited to Bank A. Instead, as we shall see, other banks can also create new money as a consequence of the original $10,000 deposit at Bank A.

Let's begin with Bank B. Recall from the previous section that the $8,333 check made out by Mr. Smith to Mr. Jones is deposited by the latter in his account at Bank B. This is a new deposit of funds at Bank B. As pointed out in the previous section, Bank B gets $8,333 in reserves from Bank A when Bank A pays Bank B to get back the check. Thus the effect on Bank B's balance sheet, as shown in the first panel of Figure 13.7, is to increase both demand deposits and reserves by $8,333. Bank B is in much the same position as was Bank A when the latter received the original deposit of $10,000. Bank B can make loans or investments of $6,941. (The way we derive $6,941 is explained in the next paragraph.) Specifically, it decides to buy a bond for $6,941 from Mr. Stone, who deposits the check from Bank B to his account in Bank C. Thus, as shown in the second panel of Figure 13.7, the effect of this transaction is to increase Bank B's investments by $6,941 and to increase its demand deposits by $6,941 when

Figure 13.7 Changes in Bank B's Balance Sheet

	Assets		Liabilities and net worth	
Bank receives deposit	Reserves	+$8,333	Demand deposits	+$8,333
	Loans and investments	No change	Net worth	No change
	Total	+$8,333	Total	+$8,333
Bank buys bond	Reserves	No change	Demand deposits	+$6,941
	Loans and investments	+$6,941	Net worth	No change
	Total	+$6,941	Total	+$6,941
Mr. Stone deposits money in Bank C	Reserves	−$6,941	Demand deposits	−$6,941
	Loans and investments	No change	Net worth	No change
	Total	−$6,941	Total	−$6,941
Total effect	Reserves	+$1,392	Demand deposits	+$8,333
	Loans and investments	+$6,941	Net worth	No change
	Total	+$8,333	Total	+$8,333

Bank B bought the bond. This transaction increases Bank B's demand deposits by $6,941 because the bank creates a demand deposit of $6,941 to pay for the bond. In other words, the bank in effect creates a deposit for itself and uses it to pay Mr. Stone for the bond. Then Bank B's demand deposits and its reserves are decreased by $6,941 when it transfers this amount of reserves to Bank C to pay for the check. When the total effects of the transaction are summed up, Bank B—like Bank A—continues to meet its legal reserve requirements, as shown in the bottom panel of Figure 13.7.

Bank B has also created some money—$6,941 to be exact. Mr. Stone has $6,941 in demand deposits that he didn't have before; and this is a net addition to the money supply since the person who originally deposited the currency in Bank A still has his $10,000, and Mr. Jones still has the $8,333 he deposited in Bank B. And this is still not the end of the story. Bank C has experienced an increase of $6,941 in its demand deposits and in its reserves. Thus it—like Banks A and B before it—can increase its loans and investments. By how much? At this point, the pattern is becoming clear: *it can lend the amount by which its reserves exceed the legally required reserves.* In other words, since Bank C must hold $\$\frac{6{,}941}{6}$, or $1,157, in legally required reserves against the new deposit of $6,941, it can lend $6,941 minus $1,157, or $5,784.

According to our plot, Bank C lends $5,784 to Mr. White, who buys a truck from the local General Motors dealer, Mr. Black. Mr. Black deposits Mr. White's check for $5,784 to his account at

Figure 13.8 Changes in Bank C's Balance Sheet

	Assets		Liabilities and net worth	
Bank receives deposit	Reserves	+$6,941	Demand deposits	+$6,941
	Loans and investments	No change	Net worth	No change
	Total	+$6,941	Total	+$6,941
Bank makes loan	Reserves	No change	Demand deposits	+$5,784
	Loans and investments	+$5,784	Net worth	No change
	Total	+$5,784	Total	+$5,784
Mr. White spends $5,784	Reserves	−$5,784	Demand deposits	−$5,784
	Loans and investments	No change	Net worth	No change
	Total	−$5,784	Total	−$5,784
Total effect	Reserves	+$1,157	Demand deposits	+$6,941
	Loans and investments	+ 5,784	Net worth	No change
	Total	+$6,941	Total	+$6,941

Bank D. Figure 13.8 traces out the effects on Bank C's balance sheet. The top panel shows the original increase in its demand deposits and in its reserves of $6,941. The second panel shows the increase of $5,784 in its loans stemming from its loan to Mr. White, as well as the accompanying increase in its demand deposits of $5,784 representing the demand deposit it gave to Mr. White. The third panel shows the $5,784 decrease in demand deposits when Mr. White checked out the whole of his account, and the $5,784 decrease in reserves when Bank C transferred this amount of reserves to Bank D to pay for the check. The bottom panel shows the total effect. As in the case of Banks A and B, Bank C continues to meet the legal reserve requirements when the full effects of the transaction have made themselves felt.

Bank C also has created some money—$5,784, to be exact. To see why, note that Mr. Black has $5,784 in demand deposits that he didn't have before; and this is a net addition to the money supply since the original depositor in Bank A still has his $10,000, Mr. Jones still has the $8,333 in Bank B, and Mr. Stone still has the $6,941 in Bank C. But this is still not the end of the story. Bank D has experienced an increase of $5,784 in its demand deposits and its reserves. Thus, it—like Banks A, B, and C before it—can increase its loans and investments by the amount of its ***excess reserves*** (those in excess of legal requirements). Since it must hold $\frac{\$5,784}{6} = \$964$ as legal reserves against its increase in deposits of $5,784, its excess reserves are $5,784 minus $964, or $4,820. Thus Bank D can increase its loans and investments by $4,820. As we saw at the beginning of this saga, it decides

Figure 13.9 Changes in Bank D's Balance Sheet

	Assets		Liabilities and net worth	
Bank receives deposit	Reserves		Demand deposits	
	Loans and investments		Net worth	
	Total		Total	
Bank makes loan	Reserves		Demand deposits	
	Loans and investments		Net worth	
	Total		Total	
Mr. Cohen spends $4,820	Reserves		Demand deposits	
	Loans and investments		Net worth	
	Total		Total	
Total effect	Reserves	+$ 964	Demand deposits	+$5784
	Loans and investments	+ 4820	Net worth	No change
	Total	+$5784	Total	+$5784

to lend Mr. Cohen $4,820 to buy some lumber from Mr. Palucci. Mr. Cohen pays Mr. Palucci with a check for $4,820 drawn on Bank D and Mr. Palucci deposits the check to his account at Bank E. As shown in Figure 13.9, Bank D winds up with no excess reserves after it transfers reserves to Bank E to pay for the check. (To check your grasp of the material in this section, see if you can fill in the numbers in the top three panels of Figure 13.9.)[3] But Mr. Palucci winds up with a demand deposit of $4,820 that he didn't have before. Thus *Bank D also creates some money—$4,820, to be exact.*

[3] The answer is:

	Assets		*Liabilities and net worth*	
Bank receives deposit	Reserves	+$5,784	Demand deposits	+$5,784
	Loans and investments	No change	Net worth	No change
	Total	+$5,784	Total	+$5,784
Bank makes loan	Reserves	No change	Demand deposits	+$4,820
	Loans and investments	+$4,820	Net worth	No change
	Total	+$4,820	Total	+$4,820
Mr. Cohen spends $4,820	Reserves	−$4,820	Demand deposits	−$4,820
	Loans and investments	No change	Net worth	No change
	Total	−$4,820	Total	−$4,820

The Total Effect of the Original $10,000 Deposit

How big an increase in the money supply can the entire banking system support as a consequence of the original $10,000 deposit in Bank A? Clearly, the effects of the original deposit spread from one bank to another, since each bank hands new reserves (and deposits) to another bank, which in turn hands them to another bank. For example, Bank E now has $4,820 more in deposits and reserves and so can create $4,017[4] in new money by making a loan or investment of this amount. This process goes on indefinitely, and it would be impossible to describe each of the multitude of steps involved. Fortunately, it isn't necessary to do so. We can figure out the total amount of new money the entire banking system can support as a consequence of the original $10,000 deposit in Bank A without going through all these steps.

We do this by computing how much new money each bank creates. Besides the original $10,000, Bank A creates $8,333—which is $5/6$ of $10,000. Then Bank B creates an additional $6,941—$(5/6)^2$ of $10,000. Then Bank C creates an additional $5,784—$(5/6)^3$ of $10,000. Then Bank D creates an additional $4,820—$(5/6)^4$ of $10,000. Then Bank E creates an additional $4,017—$(5/6)^5$ of $10,000. The amount of money created by each bank is less than that created by the previous bank, so that the total amount of new money created by the original $10,000 deposit—$10,000 + $8,333 + $6,941 + $5,784 + $4,820 + $4,017 + · · ·—tends to a finite limit as the process goes on and on. Elementary algebra tells us what this sum of terms will be. *When the process works itself out, the entire banking system can support $60,000 in money as a consequence of the original $10,000 deposit of new funds.*[5] For demonstrations of this fact, see Table 13.2 and Figure 13.10. Table 13.2 shows the amount of new demand deposits created at each stage of this process, while Figure 13.10 plots the cumulative expansion in demand deposits.

Table 13.2

Increase in Money Supply Resulting from $10,000 Increase in Reserves

Source	*Amount*
Original deposit	$10,000
Created by Bank A	8,333
Created by Bank B	6,941
Created by Bank C	5,784
Created by Bank D	4,820
Created by Bank E	4,017
Created by Bank F	3,347
Created by Bank G	2,789
Created by Bank H	2,324
Created by Bank I	1,937
Created by Bank J	1,614
Created by other banks	8,094
Total	60,000

We must note that the banking system as a whole has accomplished what we said in a previous section than an individual bank—Bank A—could not do. It has created an additional $50,000 of demand deposits on the basis of the original $10,000 deposit. In other words, given the additional $10,000 in reserves, the banking system can create $60,000 in money. Certainly this seems sensible, since each $1 of reserves can back up $6 in demand deposits. But for the reasons discussed in a previous section, an individual bank cannot do this, unless, of course, it is a monopoly bank. If it is, it need have no fear of losing reserves to other banks, because there are no other banks; so it can behave this way.

[4] Why $4,017? Because it must hold $\frac{\$4,820}{6} = \$803$ as reserves to support the new demand deposit of $4,820. Thus, it has excess reserves of $4,017, and it can create another new demand deposit of this amount.

[5] The proof of this is as follows: the total amount of money supported by the $10,000 in reserves is $10,000 + $8,333 + $6,941 + $5,784 + · · ·, which equals $10,000 + 5/6 × $10,000 + $(5/6)^2$ × $10,000 + $(5/6)^3$ × $10,000 + . . . , which equals $\$10,000 \times (1 + 5/6 + (5/6)^2 + (5/6)^3 + \ldots) = \$10,000 \times \frac{1}{1-(5/6)} = \$60,000$, since $1 + 5/6 + (5/6)^2 + (5/6)^3 + \ldots = \frac{1}{1-(5/6)}$.

However, banking in the United States is not monopolized.

In general, *if a certain amount of additional reserves is made available to the banking system, the banking system as a whole can increase the money supply by an amount equal to the amount of additional reserves multiplied by the reciprocal of the required ratio of reserves to deposits*. In other words, to obtain the total increase in the money supply that can be achieved from a certain amount of additional reserves, multiply the amount of additional reserves by the reciprocal of the required ratio of reserves to deposits—or, what amounts to the same thing, *divide the amount of additional reserves by the legally required ratio of reserves to deposits*. Putting it in still another way, the banking system as a whole can increase the money supply by $(1/r)$ dollars—where r is the required ratio of reserves to deposits—for every $1 increase in reserves.[6]

[6] The total amount of money supported by $1 of additional reserves is

$$1 + (1 - r) + (1 - r)^2 + (1 - r)^3 + \cdots = \frac{1}{1 - (1 - r)} = \frac{1}{r}$$

We reach this conclusion by the same method we used in note 5.

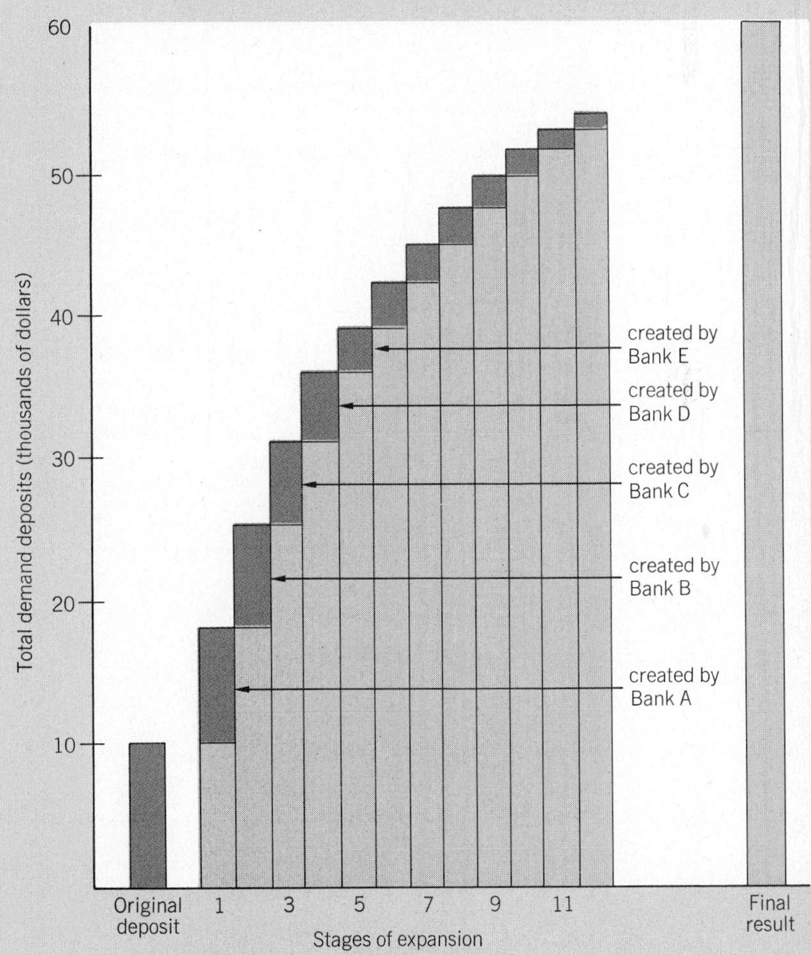

Figure 13.10
Cumulative Expansion in Demand Deposits on Basis of $10,000 of New Reserves and Legal Reserve Requirement of 16⅔ Percent

The original deposit was $10,000. In the first stage of the expansion process, Bank A created an additional $8,333. In the second stage, Bank B created an additional $6,941. In the third stage, Bank C created an additional $5,784. This process goes on until the final result is $60,000 of demand deposits.

Let's apply this proposition to a couple of specific cases. Suppose that the banking system's reserves increase by $10,000 and that the required ratio of reserves to deposits is 1/6. To determine how much the banking system can increase the money supply, we must divide the amount of the additional reserves—$10,000—by the required ratio of reserves to deposits—1/6—to get the answer, $60,000. Note, with proper satisfaction, that this answer checks with our earlier results. Now suppose that the required ratio of reserves to deposits is 1/5. By how much can the banking system increase the money supply? Dividing $10,000 by 1/5, we get the answer: $50,000. Note that the higher the required ratio of reserves to deposits, the smaller the amount by which the banking system can increase the money supply on the basis of a given increase in reserves. More will be said about this in the next chapter.

Finally, an increase in reserves generally affects a great many banks at about the same time. For expository purposes, it is useful to trace through the effect of an increase in the reserves of a single bank—Bank A in our case. But usually this is not what happens. Instead, lots of banks experience an increase in reserves at about the same time. Thus, they all have excess reserves at about the same time, and they all make loans or investments at about the same time. The result is that, when the people who borrow money spend it, each bank tends both to gain and lose reserves. Thus, on balance, each bank need not lose reserves. In real life the amount of bank money often expands simultaneously.

The Effect of a Decrease in Reserves

Up to this point, we have been talking only about the effect of an increase in reserves. What happens to the quantity of money if reserves decrease? For example, suppose that you draw $10,000 out of your bank and hold it in the form of currency, perhaps by sewing it in your mattress. You thus reduce the total reserves of the banking system by $10,000. Let us begin with the effect on your bank. Clearly, it will experience a $10,000 decrease in deposits (because of your withdrawal) and, at the same time, a $10,000 decrease in reserves. Thus, if it was holding $1 in reserves for every $6 in deposits before you withdrew the money, it now holds less than the legally required reserves. If its deposits go down by $10,000, its reserves must go down by $1,667, not $10,000, if the 6:1 ratio between deposits and reserves is to be maintained. To observe the legal reserve requirements, your bank must increase its reserves by $10,000 minus $1,667, or $8,333. It has several ways to get this money, one being to sell securities. It may sell a municipal bond to Mrs. Cherrytree for $8,333. To pay for the bond, she writes a check on her bank, Bank Q, for the $8,333. Thus, as shown in Figure 13.11, your bank's investments decrease by $8,333, and its reserves increase by $8,333 when Bank Q transfers this amount to your bank to pay for the check.

But this is not the end of the story. Because Bank Q has lost $8,333 in deposits and $8,333 in reserves, its reserves are now less than the legal minimum. Since its deposits have gone down $8,333, its reserves should have gone down $\frac{\$8,333}{6}$, or $1,392. Thus, Bank Q must increase its reserves by $8,333 minus $1,392, or $6,941. To do so, it might sell a bond it holds for $6,941. But when the person who buys the bond gives Bank Q his check for $6,941 drawn on Bank R, Bank R loses $6,941 in deposits and $6,941 in reserves. Thus, Bank R's reserves are now below the legal requirement. Since its deposits have gone down $6,941, its reserves should have gone down $\frac{\$6,941}{6}$, or $1,157. So Bank R must increase its reserves by $6,941 minus $1,157, or $5,784. And on and on the process goes.

Let us consider the overall effect on the money supply of the $10,000 decrease in reserves. Your bank's demand deposits decreased by $10,000, Bank Q's demand deposits decreased by $8,333 (5/6 of $10,000), Bank R's demand deposits decreased by $6,941 ($(5/6)^2$ of $10,000), and so on. The total de-

Figure 13.11 Change in Your Bank's Balance Sheet

	Assets		Liabilities and net worth	
You withdraw deposit	Reserves	−$10,000	Demand deposits	−$10,000
	Loans and investments	No change	Net worth	No change
	Total	−$10,000	Total	−$10,000
Bank sells bond and gets funds from Bank Q	Reserves	+$ 8,333	Demand deposits	No change
	Loans and investments	−$ 8,333	Net worth	No change
	Total	No change	Total	No change
Total effect	Reserves	−$ 1,667	Demand deposits	−$10,000
	Loans and investments	−$ 8,333	Net worth	No change
	Total	−$10,000	Total	−$10,000

crease in the money supply—$10,000 + $8,333 + $6,941 + · · · —tends to a finite limit as the process goes on and on. This limit is $60,000. Thus, *when the process works itself out, the entire banking system will reduce the money supply by $60,000 as a consequence of a $10,000 decrease in reserves.* More generally, *if the banking system's reserves decrease by a certain amount, the banking system as a whole will reduce demand deposits by an amount equal to the reduction in reserves multiplied by the reciprocal of the required ratio of reserves to deposits.*

In other words, to obtain the total decrease in demand deposits resulting from a reduction in reserves, *divide the reduction in reserves by the legally required ratio of reserves to deposits.* Putting it another way, the banking system as a whole will reduce demand deposits by $(1/r)$ dollars—where r is the required ratio of reserves to deposits—for every $1 decrease in reserves. Of course, there is often a simultaneous contraction of money on the part of many banks, just as there is often a simultaneous expansion. But this doesn't affect the result.

Let's apply this proposition to a particular case. Suppose that the banking system experiences a decrease in reserves of $10,000 and that the required ratio of reserves to deposits is ⅙. Applying this rule, we must divide the reduction in reserves—$10,000—by the required ratio of reserves to deposits—⅙—to get the answer, which is a $60,000 reduction in demand deposits. This answer checks with the result in the previous paragraph. The effect of a $1 decrease in reserves is equal in absolute terms to the effect of a $1 increase in reserves. Whether the change is an increase or a decrease, a $1 change in reserves leads to a $$(1/r)$ change in demand deposits. Or, more precisely, this is the case if certain assumptions, discussed in the next section, are true. To complete our discussion of how banks create money, we turn now to these assumptions.

Currency Withdrawals and Excess Reserves

In discussing the amount of additional demand deposits that can be created by the banking system as a result of injecting $10,000 of new reserves, we made the important assumption that everyone who received the new demand deposits—from Mr. Palucci back to the person who originally deposited his money in Bank A—wants to keep this money in the form of demand deposits rather than currency. However, this clearly may not be the case. Some people who receive new demand deposits may choose to withdraw some part of this money as currency. For example, Mr. Palucci may decide to withdraw $1,000 of his new demand deposit in cash.

It is fairly obvious what effect this withdrawal of currency will have on the amount of demand deposits the banking system can create. This withdrawal of currency from the entire banking system reduces the reserves of the banking system by $1,000. Applying the results of the previous section, this means that the banking system can create $6,000 less in demand deposits ($1,000 divided by ⅙) than it could if the currency had not been withdrawn. Consequently, the banking system can create $60,000 minus $6,000, or $54,000, from the combination of the original $10,000 injection of reserves and the $1,000 withdrawal of currency. In other words, the banking system can create an amount of demand deposits equal to the amount of additional reserves *left permanently with the banking system* ($10,000 minus $1,000, or $9,000 in this case) divided by the required ratio of reserves to demand deposits.

Similarly, in discussing how much demand deposits will be reduced as a consequence of a $10,000 reduction in reserves, we made the important assumption that everyone who buys a security from a bank pays the bank by check. But some people may pay partly or in full with currency, and this will affect how much the amount of demand deposits must be reduced by the banking system. If somebody pays $1,000 in currency to one of the banks, this restores $1,000 of the $10,000 in reserves that the banking system lost. Thus, the banking system really loses $9,000, not $10,000. Then, applying the rule set forth in the previous section, the banking system must reduce its demand deposits by $54,000 ($9,000 divided by ⅙), not $60,000 ($10,000 divided by ⅙). In general, whether the change in reserves is an increase or a decrease, the change in demand deposits equals the change in reserves *left permanently with the banking system* ($9,000 in these cases) divided by the required ration of reserves to demand deposits. Thus, *whether or not a change in reserves has the maximum effect on demand deposits depends on how much of these reserves the public leaves in the banking system.*[7]

Another important assumption lies behind our discussion of the effects of $10,000 of additional reserves—or a $10,000 reduction in reserves—on the amount of demand deposits: *we have assumed that no bank holds excess reserves.* In other words, we have assumed that, whenever a bank has enough reserves to make a loan or investment, it will do so. Recall Bank A, which received a new deposit of $10,000. The new deposit enabled Bank A to increase its loans and investments by $8,333 without winding up with less than the legally required reserves. Thus, we assumed that it would go ahead and make this much in additional loans and investments. In general, this seems to be a reasonable assumption, for the simple reason that loans and investments bring profits (in interest) into the bank while excess reserves bring none. But the matter is not as simple as all that. If a bank cannot find loans and investments it regards as attractive, it

[7] Note too that people can convert demand deposits into time deposits, and vice versa. There are legal reserve requirements against time deposits, but they are lower than those against demand deposits. The conversion of demand deposits into time deposits will influence how much money can be supported by a certain amount of reserves. Thus, the banking system can support an amount of demand deposits equal to the amount of additional reserves divided by the legally required ratio of reserves to demand deposits (no more, no less) only if there is no conversion of demand deposits into time deposits. In other words, we assume that all the demand deposits created by the banking system are converted into neither cash nor time deposits.

may decide to make no such loans. After all, there isn't much profit to be made on a loan that is not repaid. Also, if interest rates are very low, the bank may feel that it isn't losing much by not lending money. During the Great Depression of the 1930s, for example, banks held large excess reserves for this reason. In addition, banks can benefit by maintaining excess reserves, since they constitute insurance against deposit losses.

What difference does it make whether banks hold excess reserves? If, for example, Bank A decides to lend less than the full $8,333, this will mean that an increase in reserves will have a smaller effect on the amount of demand deposits than we indicated previously. Similarly, if banks hold excess reserves, a decrease in reserves is likely to have a smaller effect on the amount of demand deposits than we indicated above. Thus, *whether or not a change in reserves has the maximum effect on demand deposits depends on the lending policies of the bankers. If they do not lend out as much as they can, the effect on demand deposits will be diminished accordingly.*

Summary

Most of our money supply is not coin and paper currency, but bank money—demand deposits. This money is created by banks. Whereas the earliest banks held reserves equal to demand deposits, modern banks practice fractional-reserve banking: that is, their reserves equal only a fraction of their demand deposits. The Federal Reserve System requires every commercial bank that is a member of the system to hold a certain percentage of its demand deposits as reserves; the percentage varies with the size of the bank. Although they increase the safety of the banks, the major purpose of these legal reserve requirements is to control the money supply. Banks have become much safer in recent years, due in part to better management and regulation, as well as to the government's stated willingness to insure and stand behind their deposits.

A bank creates money by lending or investing its excess reserves. If banks had to keep reserves equal to their deposits, they could not create money. A bank cannot lend or invest more than its excess reserves, unless it is a monopoly bank, because it will wind up with less than the legally required reserves. However, the banking system as a whole can support demand deposits equal to its total reserves divided by the legally required ratio of reserves to deposits. Thus, if reserves somewhere in the banking system increase by a certain amount, the banking system as a whole can increase demand deposits by the amount of the increase in reserves divided by the legally required ratio of reserves to deposits.

Similarly, if there is a decrease in reserves somewhere in the banking system, the system as a whole must decrease demand deposits by the amount of the decrease in reserves divided by the legally required ratio of reserves to deposits. Demand deposits are decreased by banks' selling securities or refusing to renew loans, just as demand deposits are increased by banks' making loans and investments.

Our argument so far has assumed that when additional reserves were made available to the banking system, there was no withdrawal of part of them in the form of currency, and that when reserves are decreased, no currency is deposited in banks. If such changes in the amount of currency take place, the change in demand deposits will equal the change in reserves left permanently with the banking system divided by the legally required ratio of reserves to deposits. We have also assumed that the banks hold no excess reserves. Since banks make profits by lending money and making investments, this assumption is generally sensible. But when loans are risky and interest rates are low—for example, in the Great Depression of the 1930s—banks have been known to hold large excess reserves. Clearly, changes in reserves will not have their full, or maximum, effect on demand deposits if the banks do not lend and invest as much as possible.

CONCEPTS FOR REVIEW

Fractional-reserve banking
Legal reserve requirements
Excess reserves
Simultaneous expansion

QUESTIONS FOR DISCUSSION AND REVIEW

1. Describe the way in which the banking system can create money if there is a single monopoly bank in the nation.

2. Suppose that you were the president of the Bank of America. What rules would you ask your executives to follow in making loans? In other words, what information should they look at, and how should they use this information, to decide whether or not to grant a particular loan?

3. Demand deposits are increased by banks by their calling in loans and selling investments. True or False?

4. On the basis of additional reserves of $5,000, the banking system as a whole can support how much in demand deposits, if the legal reserve requirement is 20 percent of deposits?
a. $5,000 b. $10,000 c. $25,000 d. $50,000

CHAPTER 14

Monetary Policy

During the middle and late 1960s, strong inflationary pressures were generated by the increase in government expenditures associated with the Vietnam war and by the government's failure to increase taxes until 1968. Clearly, fiscal policy was a destabilizing rather than a stabilizing force in the economy. Under these circumstances, it was fortunate that government policy makers had other means to hold down the increasing price level and to stabilize the economy. As we shall see, monetary policy was ultimately called on to restrain an economy that seemed to be getting out of hand. Like fiscal policy, monetary policy is no panacea, but it is a very important tool for stabilization of the economy.

In this chapter, we are concerned with a variety of basic questions about monetary policy: Who makes monetary policy? What sorts of tools can be employed by monetary policy makers? How does monetary policy affect our national output and the price level? What are some of the problems involved in formulating effective monetary policy? What has been the nature of monetary policy in the United States in recent decades? These questions are very important, since the economic health of any nation depends on its monetary policies.

The Aims and Role of Monetary Policy

Monetary policy is concerned with the money supply and interest rates. We described in Chapter 12 how the money supply influences net national product and the price level. If the economy is at considerably less than full employment, increases in the money supply tend to increase real national product, and decreases in the money supply tend to decrease real national product, with little or no effect on the price level. As full employment is approached, increases in the money supply tend to affect the price level, as well as real output. Finally, once full employment is reached, increases in the money supply result primarily in increases in the price level, since real output cannot increase appreciably.

In formulating monetary policy, the government's objectives are to attain and maintain reasonably full employment without excessive inflation. In other words, when a recession seems imminent and business is soft, the monetary authorities are likely to increase the money supply and push down interest rates. That is, they will "ease credit" or "ease money," as the newspapers put it. This tends to increase net national product. On the other hand, when the economy is in danger of overheating and serious inflation threatens, the monetary authorities will probably rein in the money supply and push up interest rates—in newspaper terms, they will "tighten credit" or "tighten money." This tends to reduce spending, and thus curb the upward pressure on the price level.

At this point, you may be muttering to yourself: "But the aims of monetary policy are essentially the same as those of fiscal policy!" And, of course you are right. Monetary policy and fiscal policy are both aimed at promoting full employment without inflation. But they use different methods to attain this goal. Fiscal policy uses the spending and taxing powers of the government, whereas monetary policy uses the government's power over the money supply.

Before we go on, let us review the processes by which changes in the money supply affect national product and the price level. You will recall from Chapter 12 that there is a difference of view about these processes. On the one hand, monetarists use the quantity theory of money to link changes in the money supply directly with changes in nominal net national product. Although the velocity of circulation of money is by no means constant, nominal NNP does seem to have been fairly closely related to the money supply. Keynesians explain this relationship in different terms. They believe that an increase (decrease) in the money supply decreases (increases) the interest rate, which in turn shifts the investment function upward (downward). This shift in the investment function tends to increase (decrease) national product. They also recognize that spending by consumers and governments, as well as investment, is likely to be affected by changes in the quantity of money.

Let's be a little more specific about how the monetary authorities can promote their aims. In particular, how can they influence the money supply? The answer is: *by managing the reserves of the banking system*. For example, perhaps the monetary authorities think a recession is about to develop. To head it off, they want to increase the money supply more rapidly than they would otherwise. To realize this objective, they can increase the reserves of the banks. As we saw in the previous chapter, an increase in bank reserves enables the banks to increase the money supply. Indeed, we learned that if there were no excess reserves and no currency withdrawals, the banks could increase the money supply by $6 for every $1 of additional reserves.[1] The ways in which the monetary authori-

[1] Of course, this assumes that the legal reserve requirement is 16⅔ percent. If the legal reserve requirement were 20 percent, a $5 increase in the money supply could be supported by $1 of additional reserves. Also, this assumes that banks hold no excess reserves and that no currency is withdrawn. As pointed out in the previous chapter, a much smaller increase in the money supply may result from an extra dollar of reserves if banks hold excess reserves and if currency is withdrawn.

ties can increase the reserves of the banking system are discussed at length in subsequent sections.

On the other hand, suppose that the monetary authorities smell a strong whiff of unacceptable inflation in the economic wind, and so decide to cut back on the rate of increase of the money supply. To do so, they can slow down the rate of increase of bank reserves. As we saw in the previous chapter, this will force the banks to cut back on the rate of increase of the money supply. Indeed, if the monetary authorities go so far as to reduce the reserves of the banking system, this will tend to reduce the money supply. Under the assumptions made in the previous chapter, the banks must cut back the money supply by $6 for every $1 reduction in reserves.

Makers of Monetary Policy

Who establishes our monetary policy? Who decides that, in view of the current and prospective economic situation, the money supply should be increased (or decreased) at a certain rate? As in the case of fiscal policy, this is not a simple question to answer; many individuals and groups play an important role. Certainly, however, *the leading role is played by the Federal Reserve System—in particular, by the members of the Federal Reserve Board and the Federal Open Market Committee.* The Chairman of the Federal Reserve Board is often the chief spokesman for the Federal Reserve System. The recent chairmen—Arthur F. Burns and William McChesney Martin—undoubtedly have had considerable influence over monetary policy.

Although the Federal Reserve is responsible to Congress, Congress has established no clear guidelines for its behavior. Thus, the Federal Reserve has had wide discretionary powers over monetary policy. But the Federal Reserve System is a huge organization, and it is not easy to figure out exactly who influences whom and who decides what. Formal actions can be taken by a majority of the board and of the Federal Open Market Committee (which is composed of the 7 members of the board plus 5 of the presidents of the 12 regional banks). However, this obviously tells only part of the story.

To get a more complete picture, it is essential to recognize that many agencies and groups other than the Fed have an effect on monetary policy, although it is difficult to measure their respective influences. The Treasury frequently has an important voice in the formulation of monetary policy. Indeed, as we shall see, the Federal Reserve was largely subservient to the Treasury during the 1940s. Also, Congressional committees hold hearings and issue reports on monetary policy and the operations of the Federal Reserve. These hearings and reports cannot fail to have some effect on Fed policy. In addition, it is sometimes argued that the policies of the Fed are influenced by the commercial banks. In this connection, it is interesting to note that, of the 9 directors of each regional Bank, 3 may be bankers, 3 must represent industry and agriculture in the region, and 3 are appointed by the Federal Reserve Board to represent the general public. Finally, the President may attempt to influence the Federal Reserve Board. To keep the board as free as possible from political pressure, members are appointed for long terms—14 years—and a term expires every 2 years.

Tools of Monetary Policy: Open Market Operations

We know from a previous section that the Federal Reserve controls the money supply largely by controlling the quantity of member banks' reserves. The most important means the Federal Reserve has to exercise this control are ***open market operations,*** the purchase and sale by the Fed of U.S. government securities in the open market. As we saw in Chapter 6, the market for government securities is huge and well developed. The Federal Reserve is part of this market. Sometimes it buys government securities; sometimes it sells them. Whether it is buying or selling—and how much—can have a heavy impact on the quantity of bank reserves.

Figure 14.1 Effect of Fed's Purchasing $1 Million of Government Securities

A. Effect on Fed's balance sheet:

Assets		Liabilities and net worth	
Government securities	+$1 million	Member bank reserves	+$1 million

B. Effect on balance sheet of the Chase Manhattan Bank:

Assets		Liabilities and net worth	
Reserves	+$1 million	Demand deposits	+$1 million

Suppose that the Federal Reserve *buys* $1 million worth of government securities in the open market, and that the seller of these securities is General Motors.[2] To determine the effect of this transaction on the quantity of bank reserves, let's look at the effect on the balance sheet of the Fed and on the balance sheet of the Chase Manhattan Bank, General Motors' bank.[3] In this transaction, the Fed receives $1 million in government securities and gives General Motors a check for $1 million. When General Motors deposits this check to its account at the Chase Manhattan Bank, the bank's demand deposits and reserves increase by $1 million. Thus, as shown in Figure 14.1, the left-hand side of the Fed's balance sheet shows a $1 million increase in government securities, and the right-hand side shows a $1 million increase in bank reserves. The left-hand side of the Chase Manhattan Bank's balance sheet shows a $1 million increase in reserves, and the right-hand side shows a $1 million increase in demand deposits. Clearly, *the Fed has added $1 million to the banks' reserves.* The situation is entirely analogous to the $10,000 deposit at Bank *A* in the previous chapter.

Now consider the opposite situation, where the Federal Reserve *sells* $1 million worth of government securities in the open market. They are bought by Merrill Lynch, Pierce, Fenner, and Smith, a huge brokerage firm. What effect does this transaction have on the quantity of bank reserves? To find out, let's look at the balance sheet of the Fed and the balance sheet of Merrill Lynch's bank, which we again assume to be the Chase Manhattan. When Merrill Lynch buys the government securities from the Fed, the Fed gives Merrill Lynch the securities in exchange for Merrill Lynch's check for $1 million. When the Fed presents this check to the Chase Manhattan Bank for payment, Chase Manhattan's demand deposits and reserves decrease by $1 million. Thus, as shown in Figure 14.2, the left-hand side of the Fed's balance sheet shows a $1 million decrease in government securities, and the right-hand side shows a $1 million decrease in reserves. The left-hand side of the Chase Manhattan Bank's balance sheet shows a $1 million decrease in reserves, and the right-hand side shows a $1 million decrease in demand deposits. Clearly, *the Fed has reduced the reserves of*

[2] Large corporations often hold quantities of government securities.

[3] For simplicity, we assume that General Motors has only one bank, the Chase Manhattan Bank. Needless to say, this may not be the case, but it makes no difference to the point we are making here. We make a similar assumption regarding the investment firm of Merrill Lynch in the next paragraph.

Figure 14.2 Effect of Fed's Selling $1 Million of Government Securities

A. Effect on Fed's balance sheet:

Assets		Liabilities and net worth	
Government securities	−$1 million	Member bank reserves	−$1 million

B. Effect on balance sheet of the Chase Manhattan Bank:

Assets		Liabilities and net worth	
Reserves	−$1 million	Demand deposits	−$1 million

the banks by $1 million.

Thus, the Federal Reserve adds to bank reserves when it buys government securities and reduces bank reserves when it sells them. Obviously, the extent to which the Federal Reserve increases or reduces bank reserves depends on the amount of government securities purchased or sold. The greater the amount, the greater the increase or decrease in bank reserves. As noted above, open market operations are the Fed's most important technique for controlling the money supply. The power to decide on the amount of government securities the Fed should buy or sell at any given moment rests with the *Federal Open Market Committee.* This group wields an extremely powerful influence over bank reserves and the nation's money supply. Every few weeks, the Federal Open Market Committee meets to discuss the current situation and trends, and gives instructions to the Manager of the Open Market Account at the Federal Reserve Bank of New York, who actually buys and sells the government securities.

To get some insight into the nature of these discussions, consider the meeting of the Federal Open Market Committee (FOMC) that was held on May 26, 1970. According to Sherman Maisel, a former member of the Federal Reserve Board and one of the participants, much of the meeting was devoted to a discussion of whether the money supply was increasing too rapidly.

> The money supply and bank credit had grown far faster than appeared consistent with the 4 percent growth rate set as policy by prior votes [of the Committee]. The FOMC would now have to make a choice. . . . If the money supply were held to a 4 percent growth rate, interest rates would continue to rise and perhaps at an accelerating rate. . . . Was this what the Committee wanted, or would it prefer to allow reserves and money to grow more rapidly in order to avoid the unsettling effect of a still more rapid run-up in interest rates? . . . As in many similar situations, the Committee was sharply divided in its views. . . . The FOMC finally agreed that it would not change its basic policy stance. Monetary growth above 4 percent was not desirable.[4]

Although no single meeting can be regarded as typical, this brief description gives you some idea of the sort of discussion that takes place every few weeks in the meetings of the Federal Open Market Committee.

[4] Sherman Maisel, *Managing the Dollar,* New York: Norton, 1973. A section of this book dealing with Federal Reserve decision making is reprinted in E. Mansfield, *Economics: Readings, Issues, and Cases,* New York: Norton, 1974.

Changes in Legal Reserve Requirements

Open market operations are not the only means the Federal Reserve has to influence the money supply. Another way is *to change the legal reserve requirements.* In other words, *the Federal Reserve Board can change the amount of reserves banks must hold for every dollar of demand deposits.* In 1934, Congress gave the Federal Reserve Board the power to set—within certain broad limits—the legally required ratio of reserves to deposits for both demand and time deposits. From time to time, the Fed uses this power to change legal reserve requirements. For example, in 1960 it cut the legally required ratio of reserves to deposits in big-city banks from 17½ percent to 16½ percent, and the ratio remained there until 1968, when it was raised to 17 percent.

The obvious effect of an increase in the legally required ratio of reserves to deposits is that banks must hold larger reserves to support the existing amount of demand deposits. This in turn means that banks with little or no excess reserves will have to sell securities, refuse to renew loans, and reduce their demand deposits to meet the new reserve requirements. For example, suppose that a member bank has $1 million in reserves and $6 million in demand deposits. If the legal reserve requirement is 16 percent, it has excess reserves of $1 million minus $960,000 (.16 × $6 million), or $40,000. It is in good shape. If the legal reserve requirement is increased to 20 percent, this bank now needs $1,200,000 (.20 × $6 million) in reserves. Since it only has $1,000,000 in reserves, it must sell securities or refuse to renew loans.

Consider now what happens to the banking system as a whole. Clearly, an increase in the legally required ratio of reserves to deposits means that, with a given amount of reserves, the banking system can maintain less demand deposits than before. For example, if the banking system has $1 billion in total reserves, it can support $\frac{\$1 \text{ billion}}{.16}$, or $6.25 billion in demand deposits when the legal reserve requirement is 16 percent. But it can support only $\frac{\$1 \text{ billion}}{.20}$, or $5 billion in demand deposits when the legal reserve requirement is 20 percent. Thus, *increases in the legal reserve requirement tend to reduce the amount of demand deposits—bank money—the banking system can support.*

What is the effect of a decrease in the legally required ratio of reserves to deposits? Obviously, it means that banks must hold less reserves to support the existing amount of demand deposits, which in turn means that banks will suddenly find themselves with excess reserves. For example, if the banking system has $1 billion in reserves and $5 billion in demand deposits, there are no excess reserves when the legal reserve requirement is 20 percent. But suppose the Federal Reserve lowers the legal reserve requirement to 16 percent. Now the amount of legally required reserves is $800 million ($5 billion × .16), so that the banks have $200 million in excess reserves—which means that they can increase the amount of their demand deposits. Thus, *decreases in the legal reserve requirements tend to increase the amount of demand deposits—bank money—the banking system can support.*

Changes in legal reserve requirements are a rather drastic way to influence the money supply—they are to open market operations as a cleaver is to a scalpel, and so are made infrequently. For example, for over 7 years—from December 1960 to January 1968—no change at all was made in legal reserve requirements for demand deposits. Nonetheless, the Fed can change legal reserve requirements if it wants to. And there can be no doubt about the potential impact of such changes. Large changes in reserve requirements can rapidly alter bank reserves and the money supply.

Changes in the Discount Rate

Still another way that the Federal Reserve can influence the money supply is through changes in the discount rate. To understand this method, one needs to know that the commercial banks that are members of the Federal Reserve System can borrow from the Federal Reserve when their reserves are low (if the Fed is willing). This is one of the functions of the Federal Reserve. The interest rate the Fed charges the banks for loans is called the ***discount rate,*** and the Fed can increase or decrease the discount rate whenever it chooses. Increases in the discount rate discourage borrowing from the Fed, while decreases in the discount rate encourage it.

The discount rate can change substantially and fairly often. For example, take 1968: the discount rate was changed from 4½ to 5 percent in March, from 5 to 5½ percent in April, and from 5½ to 5¼ percent in August. When the Fed increases the discount rate, it obviously makes it more expensive for banks to augment their reserves in this way; hence it tightens up a bit on the money supply. On the other hand, when the Fed decreases the discount rate, it is cheaper for banks to augment their reserves in this way, and hence the money supply eases up a bit. However, note that the Fed is largely passive in these relations with the banks. It cannot make the banks borrow. It can only set the discount rate and see how many banks show up at the "discount window" to borrow. Also, it must be recognized that the Fed will not allow banks to borrow on a permanent or long-term basis. They are expected to use this privilege only to tide themselves over for short periods.

Most economists agree that changes in the discount rate have relatively little direct impact, and that the Fed's open market operations can and do offset easily the amount the banks borrow. Certainly changes in the discount rate cannot have anything like the direct effect on bank reserves of open market operations or changes in legal reserve requirements. *The principal importance of changes in the discount rate lies in their effects on people's expectations.* When the Fed increases the discount rate, this is generally interpreted as a sign that the Fed will tighten credit and the money supply. A cut in the discount rate is generally interpreted as a sign of easier money and lower interest rates. For example, when in 1969 the Federal Reserve announced an increase in the discount rate, the effect was a sharp drop in the prices of stocks and bonds. People interpreted this increase in the discount rate as a sure sign that the Fed was going to keep the money supply under tight reins to fight inflation.

Other Tools of Monetary Policy

In addition, the Federal Reserve has several other tools it can use. The first is ***moral suasion,*** a fancy term to describe various expressions of pleasure or displeasure by the Fed. In other words, the Fed tells the banks what it would like them to do or not do, and exhorts them to go along with its wishes. It may appeal to the patriotism of the bankers, or it may make some statements that could be regarded as threats. Of course, the Fed does not have the power to force banks to comply with its wishes, but the banks don't want to get into difficulties with the Fed. Consequently, moral suasion can have a definite impact, particularly for short periods. But banks are profit-oriented enterprises, and when the Fed's wishes conflict strongly with the profit motive, moral suasion may not work very well.

Second, the Fed can vary the maximum interest rates commercial banks can pay on time deposits. No commercial banks are permitted to pay interest on demand deposits, according to a law Congress passed during the depression of the 1930s.[5] For time or savings deposits, the Fed has the power, under ***Regulation Q,*** to establish a ceiling on the interest rates commercial banks can pay. And the level at which this ceiling is set can influence the flow of funds into time deposits, savings and loan associations, and other financial institutions. (For example, when savings and loan associations began

[5] Some people felt that many of the banks' problems in the 1920s and 1930s were due to too much competition: hence this law. It is easy to see why bankers felt that their earnings would be improved if none of them were allowed to compete for deposits by paying interest, but this is hardly consistent with a competitive philosophy.

to pay higher interest rates than commercial banks could pay on time deposits, people began to take their money out of time deposits and put it into savings and loan associations.) In recent years, the Fed, using Regulation Q, has increased the ceiling on interest rates on time deposits. In 1966 and 1970 this regulation had an important effect on interest rates and credit. Many economists would like to see such ceilings abolished because they interfere with the functioning of free markets for funds.

Another of the Fed's tools is to vary the margin requirements for the purchase of stocks. ***Margin requirements*** set the maximum percentage of the price of stocks that a person can borrow. For example, in the early 1960s, you could borrow 50 percent of the cost of such securities from your broker, but in late 1972, you could borrow only 35 percent from your broker. This is an example of a ***selective credit control***—a control aimed at the use of credit for specific purposes. It may seem odd that margin requirements for the purchase of stocks were singled out for special treatment, but the severity of the stock market crash in 1929 was attributed partly to the fact that people in those days could borrow a large percentage—sometimes even 90 percent—of the value of the stock they purchased. (When stock prices slid, their small equity vanished quickly, and they had to sell out.) Consequently, after the crash, margin requirements were imposed.

Finally, during and immediately after World War II, the Fed also had two other powers—regulation of mortgage terms and of installment contracts. Until 1953, the Fed could vary the size of down payments for houses and the number of years mortgages could run. This was an effective tool to influence the pace of residential construction. Increases in the size of down payments and decreases in the length of mortgages tended to discourage construction, while decreases in the size of down payments and increases in the length of mortgages tended to encourage construction. Until 1952, the Fed, under "Regulation W," could also establish minimum amounts a person had to put up when he bought appliances, automobiles, and other items; and it could impose other restrictions on installment buying. After the Korean war, these restrictions became unpopular, and this power of the Fed was not continued.

When Is Monetary Policy Tight or Easy?

Everyone daydreams about being powerful and important. It is a safe bet, however, that few people under the age of 21 daydream about being members of the Federal Reserve Board or the Federal Open Market Committee. Yet the truth is that the members of the board and the committee are among the most powerful people in the nation. Suppose you were appointed to the Federal Reserve Board. As a member, you would have to decide—month by month, year by year—exactly how much government securities the Fed should buy or sell, as well as whether and when changes should be made in the discount rate, legal reserve requirements, and the other instruments of Federal Reserve policy. How would you go about making your choices?

Obviously you would need lots of data. Fortunately, the Fed has a very large and able research staff to provide you with plenty of the latest information about what is going on in the economy. But what sorts of data should you look at? Clearly, one thing you would want is some information on the extent to which monetary policy is inflationary or deflationary—that is, the extent to which it is "tight" or "easy." This is not simple to measure, but there is general agreement that the members of the Federal Reserve Board—and other members of the financial and academic communities—have often used the following four variables as measures.

First, the Federal Reserve Board has looked at the level of short-term interest rates. High interest rates are interpreted as meaning that monetary policy is tight; low interest rates are usually thought to mean that monetary policy is easy. The Fed can influence the level of interest rates through its open market operations and other policies. The level of interest rates has been used by the Fed and by the financial and academic communities as a major indicator of the effect of monetary policy on the economy, and the Fed has set as a target increases, decreases, or stability in interest rates. However, to know what the proper interest rate is, you need a forecast of the strength or weakness of investment demand, and an estimate of the extent to which a high interest rate is required to offset inflation. Thus, the level of interest rates may be an ambiguous indicator.

Second, the Federal Reserve Board has looked at the rate of increase of the money supply. When the money supply is growing at a relatively slow rate (much less than 4 percent per year), this is often interpreted as meaning that monetary policy is tight. A relatively rapid rate of growth in the money supply (much more than 4 percent per year) is often taken to mean that monetary policy is easy. During the 1960s and 1970s, this has become an increasingly important indicator of the effects of monetary policy on the economy. Its popularity is due to the influence of the monetarists. This indicator has the disadvantage of being influenced by the decisions of the banks and the public about how they want to hold their assets.

Third, the Federal Reserve Board can also examine the rate of increase of the ***monetary base,*** which by definition equals bank reserves plus currency outstanding. The monetary base is important because the total money supply is dependent upon —and made from—it. Moreover, as an indicator of the effects of monetary policy, the monetary base has the advantage of being almost completely under the control of the Federal Reserve. A relatively slow growth rate in the monetary base (much less than 4 percent per year) is often interpreted as a sign of tight monetary policy. A relatively rapid rate of growth (much more than 4 percent per year) is often taken to mean that monetary policy is easy. This indicator is currently influential, particularly among the monetarists. Before 1960, it was seldom emphasized.

Fourth, the Federal Reserve Board has looked at ***free reserves,*** the excess reserves of the banks minus the amounts borrowed by the banks from the Federal Reserve.[6] When free reserves are negative, and the banks owe more to the Fed than they have in excess reserves, this has been used as an indicator that monetary policy is tight. Large and positive free reserves have been used as an indicator that monetary policy is easy. During the 1950s, the Fed used the amount of free reserves as its principal indicator of the effect of monetary policy on the economy, but this method is much less important today. Its shortcomings have been pointed out by many observers. In particular, the banks can influence the amount of free reserves by their lending and borrowing policies.

Decision Making at the Fed: A Case Study

Let's continue to assume that you have been appointed to the Federal Reserve Board, and that the economy suddenly is confronted with what seems to be a dangerously inflationary situation. What sort of action would you recommend? One appropriate action would be to sell a considerable amount of government securities, which would reduce bank reserves. You might also recommend an increase in the discount rate or even an increase in legal reserve requirements. To see how well you were doing, you would watch the variables discussed in the previous section. Specifically, you would look at the rate of increase of the money supply, as well as the rate of increase of the monetary base, and try to reduce both. At the same time you would try to increase interest rates.

Let's compare your recommendations with what the Fed really did in a similar situation. You will recall that the large military buildup associated

[6] Another measure of "money market conditions" is the interest rate on Federal funds, the interest rate banks receive when they make an overnight loan of reserves to another bank.

with the Vietnam war created strong inflationary pressures during the middle and late 1960s. Fiscal policy was not used to curb this inflation, since government spending was highly destabilizing and tax changes were painfully slow in coming. Consequently, much of the responsibility for fighting inflation fell to the Federal Reserve. What actions did it take?

In July 1965, when President Johnson announced that 50,000 more men would be sent to Vietnam, it was evident that inflationary pressures would mount unless appropriate fiscal or monetary policies were adopted. William M. Martin, chairman of the Federal Reserve Board, discussed these dangers with administration policy makers during the summer and fall of 1965, and argued publicly for a tax increase. But no such tax increase was in the cards. On December 4, 1965, the Fed decided to fire a highly visible volley against inflation. *The Federal Reserve Board voted to increase the discount rate from 4 to 4½ percent.* President Johnson and many Democrats in Congress were openly critical of this action, but many businessmen and economists agreed with the board's decision to act against inflation.

During 1965, the price level rose by 3 percent. During 1966, inflationary pressures continued unabated, and the government's large expenditures on Vietnam and domestic programs led to a huge budget deficit. As the hopes for a tax increase became dimmer, the Federal Reserve began to resort to sterner and more powerful measures to stem the inflationary tide. During early 1966, the Fed tried to tighten money, but there was a controversy within the Board over the proper indicator. Using interest rates as an indicator, money was tight; but the money supply seemed to indicate that money was easy.[7] By the summer of 1966, *the Fed allowed no increase in the monetary base, and the rate of increase in the money supply was cut to zero.* In other words, the Fed did not permit the money supply to increase at all. *Interest rates climbed to very high levels,* in part because of an increase in the demand for credit as people and firms began to fear that soon they would be unable to get credit. Money became extremely tight.

[7] For an interesting account of the controversy within the Fed by one of the members of the Federal Reserve Board at that time, see S. Maisel, *Managing the Dollar, op. cit.*

The effects on the financial and housing markets were devastating. Money for mortgages was extremely scarce, and for a time virtually no buyers could be found for municipal bonds. Knowledgeable people began to talk about an impending financial panic. By September 1966, when a crisis seemed imminent, the Fed assured all banks that it would lend them reserves so long as they made only legitimate and socially desirable loans. In addition, the Fed used its open market operations to increase bank reserves, and thus allow some increase in the money supply. By late September, the financial markets were operating reasonably well again.

Clearly, the Fed did pretty much what you would have recommended, and its policies had the intended effect. Indeed, this episode—the so-called "credit crunch of 1966"—indicates dramatically the potency of monetary policy. For that matter, according to some economists, the Fed may have gone too far. The job of the Fed is often described as "leaning against the wind," and in this case it leaned so heavily that it may almost have caused a panic. However, in its defense it must be pointed out that the Fed was faced with the problem of undoing the mischief caused by inadequate fiscal policies. It was dealt a very bad hand by the fiscal policy makers.

Monetary Policy in the 1950s and 1960s

For a more complete—and more balanced—picture of monetary policy in the United States, let's look briefly at the formulation of monetary policy in the past two decades. When the Eisenhower administration took office in 1952, the economy was prosperous, but the Korean war was ending and

William McChesney Martin and Arthur F. Burns

According to an old saying, "where you stand depends on where you sit." This is no less true at 20th and Constitution, the location of the Federal Reserve Board, than elsewhere in Washington. But while internal and external constraints determine the broad outlines of monetary policy, whatever baggage the chairman brings to the job weighs also in setting the Fed's stance vis-à-vis the rest of the government and its stand on specific issues. Consider, for example, former Chairman William McChesney Martin and present Chairman Arthur F. Burns.

Martin associated himself with the New York financial community. Indeed he had served as president of the New York Stock Exchange during the thirties. He believed that good monetary policy required a "feel" for credit markets, an instinct presumably inbred and possibly cultivated, but certainly not acquired by examining thousands of statistics on M_1 and M_2. More importantly, Martin held that the primary responsibility of the Fed was to preserve a sound currency: to stand firm while others were pandering to popular sentiment and calling for cheap money. While elected officials played to the crowd with promises of more employment, the Fed would fight the good fight—the fight against inflation. In order to assure the independence necessary to pursue such a course, Martin virtually removed the Fed from all but the most formal and infrequent contact with the Treasury, the CEA, and Budget Bureau during the Eisenhower administration.

WILLIAM MCCHESNEY MARTIN   ARTHUR F. BURNS

Burns brought a different set of baggage to his new job. Having spent much of his professional life as an economist at Columbia University and with the National Bureau of Economic Research, he was at home, not in a Wall Street club, but with a page of statistics. Thus, his chairmanship has meant much more systematic collection and analysis of data on money markets and interest rate movements. (One veteran banker commented, "They may not be making better policy now, but they can certainly tell you better why they're making it.") More significantly, under Burns the Fed became a more active member of the Quadriad and he himself has given informal economic counsel to President Nixon. In contrast to Martin, Burns has tried to maintain a more stable growth in money hoping that this would increase stability in GNP more than would large contracyclical swings in interest rates.

The Fed under Burns has taken the position that its proper role does not call for it to veto the official stance of the government. On several notable occasions, the Fed under Martin followed the opposite policy. For example, in June 1965 Martin spoke at Columbia University, drawing parallels between the 1965 economy and the pre-Depression economy, noting that "some experts seem resolved to ignore the lessons of the past!" (The Dow-Jones industrial stock average dropped 9 points after his speech.) In December, after his warnings had been ignored by the Johnson administration, the Federal Reserve took matters into its own hands, and against the wishes of the administration, raised the discount rate.

E.A.

the economy would soon have to adapt to peacetime conditions. At first, the Federal Reserve viewed inflation as the big danger, and in January 1953 it raised the discount rate and used open market operations to cut bank reserves. But by the middle of 1953, the Fed changed its course and increased bank reserves by its open market operations and by reducing the legal reserve requirements. This was fortunate because the reduction in government expenditures on the war helped to push the economy into a recession in mid-1953. During this recession, the Fed maintained a stimulative monetary policy.

The economy came out of the recession in 1954. By late 1954 and 1955, inflation began to reappear, and in late 1955 the Fed moved toward credit restraint. In the middle of 1957, the economy turned down again, partly because of a drop in investment and defense expenditures. Once this became evident, the Fed quickly eased credit. The money supply was permitted to increase more rapidly, and interest rates fell. The recession was short-lived, and by late 1958 the economy was rising once more. But almost as soon as the recovery was under way, both the monetary and fiscal authorities began to put on the brakes. Interest rates rose substantially during much of 1958 and all of 1959. As a consequence of these monetary (and fiscal) policies, the economy began to turn soft once more, and in 1960 another recession began. In early 1960, the Federal Reserve began to ease credit somewhat.

When the Kennedy administration took office in 1961, it inherited a soft economy. To stimulate it, the Federal Reserve added to bank reserves, thus permitting rapid growth in the money supply. However, monetary policy did not play a leading role in economic policy in the Kennedy years. Instead, as described in Chapter 10, the Kennedy administration pushed hard for the tax cut, which was the cornerstone of its economic policy. Monetary policy played a supporting role. Leading administration economists felt that the money supply should grow in such a way as to accommodate the desired growth in national product, but that the growth in national product was to be brought about largely by the tax cut.[8] In fact, the Federal Reserve expanded the money supply during the early 1960s at a substantially higher average annual rate than during the late 1950s. In later years, some monetarists—like Milton Friedman—were to argue that this increase in the money supply, and not the tax cut, was responsible for the growth of national product in the mid-1960s.

When government spending in Vietnam began to skyrocket in 1965, monetary policy began to push itself to the fore. As described in the previous section, the Federal Reserve Board, faced with strong inflationary pressures stemming from a highly destabilizing fiscal policy, committed itself to a strong deflationary stance. The result, as we have seen, was the "credit crunch of 1966," after which the Fed eased credit considerably. Indeed, in a rapid about-face, the Fed began to expand credit very rapidly in 1967 and 1968. In the latter part of 1967, the money supply was increasing at 10 percent per year. The tax surcharge was expected (incorrectly) to reduce spending so much that the Fed was encouraged to increase the money supply to offset it partially. Alarmed by this apparent shift to an inflationary posture, critics in Congress and elsewhere belabored the Fed for its "stop-go" policies.

Monetary Policy under the Nixon Administration

When the Nixon administration came into office in 1968, inflation was unquestionably the nation's principal economic problem. Moreover, it was generally agreed that the rapid increase in the

[8] During much of the 1960s, monetary policy was formulated with one eye on the balance of payments, discussed in Chapter 31. If the Fed had attempted to stimulate the economy, interest rates would have fallen, and capital would have gone abroad in response to higher yields there. The result would have been a worsening of our balance of payments problems. In Chapter 31, we discuss the effect of our balance of payments problems on our domestic economic policy.

money supply in 1968 had been a mistake. Thus, practically everyone, both Republicans and Democrats, agreed that monetary policy should be tight during 1969. In accord with this view, the Federal Reserve kept a close rein on the money supply during 1969. In the latter part of 1969, the quantity of money grew at an annual rate of only about 2 percent. Clearly, the nation's money managers were out to curb inflation. The result, however, was to slow the growth of national output and to increase unemployment (as would be expected from Figure 8.3).

Early in 1970, the Federal Reserve stated that it would adhere to a policy of maintaining steady growth in the money supply. Apparently the target was a 4 percent annual increase in the quantity of money. This decision was in part a reaction to the many criticisms of the Fed's previous "stop-go" policies. During most of 1970, the Fed succeeded in expanding the money supply at this relatively constant rate, but this meant that interest rates did not go down much. In the latter part of 1970, bank reserves increased considerably and interest rates fell sharply, but the money supply increased more slowly. Apparently, the Fed felt that money was sufficiently easy. During the first half of 1971, the money supply was allowed to expand rapidly: from January to June 1971, the quantity of money increased at a rate of 12 percent. But the second half of 1971 saw little growth in the money supply.

In August 1971, President Nixon announced his New Economic Policy, which, as you will recall from Chapter 10, entailed direct controls of prices, wages, and rents, as well as an expansionary fiscal policy. In line with the more expansionary tone of his economic policies, the president announced in early 1972, that "The Federal Reserve has taken steps to create the monetary conditions necessary for rapid economic expansion." Also, the Council of Economic Advisers stated in early 1972 that

> the steady, strong expansion we seek and expect will require support from monetary policy. An abundant supply of money and other liquid assets, and favorable conditions in money markets, should encourage an expansion of outlays by consumers, businesses, and State and local governments. This process would involve a more rapid rise of currency and demand deposits than occurred in the second half of 1971. Steps have been taken by the Federal Reserve System to start this acceleration.[9]

In fact, the money supply grew by about 8 percent in 1972.

After price and wage controls were largely removed in 1973, open inflation occurred with a vengeance. In the *single month* of June 1973, wholesale prices increased by 2.4 percent. President Nixon responded by slapping a 60-day freeze on most prices (but not wages) beginning in mid-June of 1973. And the Federal Reserve tightened money considerably. For example, on June 8, 1973, the Fed raised the discount rate to 6½ percent, its highest level since 1921. When it did this, the Fed announced that "the action was taken in recognition of increases that have already occurred in other short-term interest rates, the recent growth in money and bank credit, and the continuing rise in the general price level."

Problems in Formulating Monetary Policy

Before attempting to evaluate the Fed's record, we must recognize the three major problems it must confront. First, the Fed must continually try to figure out whether the economy is sliding into a recession, being propelled into an inflationary boom, or growing satisfactorily. As we saw in Chapter 11, there is no foolproof way to forecast the economy's short-term movements. Recognizing the fallibility of existing forecasting techniques all too well, the Fed must nonetheless use these techniques as best it can to guide its actions.

Second, having come to some tentative conclusion about the direction in which the economy is heading, the Fed must decide to what extent it

[9] *Economic Report of the President,* 1972, pp. 5 and 106.

should tighten or ease money. The answer depends on the Fed's estimates of when monetary changes will take effect and the magnitude of their impact, as well as on its forecasts of the economy's future direction. Also, the answer depends on the Fed's evaluation of the relative importance of full employment and price stability as national goals. If it regards full employment as much more important than price stability, it will probably want to err in the direction of easy money. On the other hand, if it thinks price stability is at least as important as full employment, it may want to err in the direction of tight money.

Finally, once the Fed has decided what it wants to do, it must figure out how to do it. Should open market operations do the whole job? If so, how big must be the purchase or sale of government securities? Should a change be made in the discount rate, or in legal reserve requirements? How big a change? Should moral suasion be resorted to? These are the operational questions the Fed continually must answer.

In answering these questions, the Fed must reckon with two very inconvenient facts, both of which make life difficult. First, *there is often a long lag between an action by the Fed and its effect on the economy.* Although the available evidence indicates that monetary policy affects some types of expenditures more rapidly than others, it is not uncommon for the bulk of the total effects to occur a year or more after the change in monetary policy.[10] Thus the Fed may act to head off an imminent recession, but find that some of the consequences of its action are not felt until later, when inflation—not recession—is the problem. Conversely, the Fed may act to curb an imminent inflation, but find that the consequences of its action are not felt until some time later, when recession, not inflation, has become the problem. In either case, the Fed can wind up doing more harm than good.

[10] For example, see Frank de Leeuw and Edward Gramlich, "The Channels of Monetary Policy: A Further Report on the Federal Reserve—MIT Econometric Model," *Federal Reserve Bulletin,* June 1969.

Second, *experts disagree about which of the available measures—such as interest rates, the rate of increase of the money supply, or the rate of increase of the monetary base—is the best measure of how tight or easy monetary policy is.* Fortunately, these measures often point in the same direction; but when they point in different directions, the Fed can be misled. For example, during 1967–68, the Fed wanted to tighten money somewhat. Using free reserves and interest rates as the primary measures of the tightness of monetary policy, it reduced free reserves and increased interest rates. However, at the same time, it permitted a substantial rate of increase in the money supply and the monetary base. By doing so, the Fed—in the eyes of many experts—really eased, not tightened, money.

The Fed's Relations with the Treasury

In making its decisions, the Federal Reserve must also take into account the problems of the Treasury, which is faced with the task of selling huge amounts of government securities each year. As you know from Chapter 6, the United States has a national debt of about $450 billion, and each year a part of this debt must be paid off. To pay off the bonds and notes that come due, as well as to borrow new amounts, the Treasury floats new securities on the market. Like any borrower, the Treasury has generally liked to reduce its interest costs; and in view of its responsibilities, it has had a major interest in finding a market for this vast amount of government securities. As a public body, the Federal Reserve System has worked closely with the Treasury, and the Treasury's interest in financing the public debt has sometimes had an important effect on Federal Reserve policy making.

During World War II, the government financed only about ⅓ of the cost of the war through taxes. The rest was financed by borrowing, much of it from the banks. The Federal Reserve used open market operations—that is, it bought government securities in the open market—to provide the banks with added reserves. Then the banks could increase their demand deposits by a multiple of the added reserves (such being the nature of a fractional-reserve banking system), and use the new demand deposits to pay for government securities. This, of course, was inflationary: the Fed was creating new money—new bank money—to be used by the Treasury. This creation of new money was just as real as if the Fed had printed up lots of new currency, but policy makers felt that wartime pressures justified this procedure.

After the war, the Fed was faced with an enormous headache. Inflationary forces were strong, and it would have liked to cut bank reserves and increase interest rates. But this would have caused the price of government securities to drop; and both the Treasury and President Truman, recalling that the drop in government bond prices after World War I had caused a considerable public outcry, were dead set against such a development. However, if the Fed maintained the price of government securities (by buying them whenever their price fell), banks could readily turn their vast holdings of government securities into reserves. Thus, so long as it maintained the price of government securities, the Fed really could not fight inflation.

Until 1951, the Fed supported the price of government securities, but by 1951 the Fed and the Treasury were in open conflict. On January 21, 1951, President Truman asked the Federal Open Market Committee to come to the White House to discuss the situation. This meeting created further conflict. On March 4, 1951, a so-called "accord" was worked out, stating that the Fed would no longer support the price of government securities. Thus the Fed was much freer to use monetary policy to tighten money and credit, and as we have seen in previous sections, it has used this power repeatedly in the 20 years since then. But this does not mean that the Fed turns its back on the Treasury's financing problems. On the contrary, in formulating monetary policy, the Fed must continually take account of the Treasury's problems. But the days are long gone when the Fed's policies are dictated by the Treasury's financing needs. Witness, for example, the "credit crunch of 1966!"

How Well Has the Fed Performed?

Given the difficult problems the Federal Reserve faces and the fact that its performance cannot be measured by any simple standard, it would be naive to expect that its achievement could be graded like an arithmetic quiz. Nonetheless, just as war is too important to be left to the generals, so monetary policy is too important to be left unscrutinized to the monetary authorities. According to recent studies of Federal Reserve policy making, what have been the strengths and weaknesses of the Fed's decisions?

First, if one takes into account the limitations in existing forecasting techniques, the Fed seems to have done a reasonably good job in recent years of recognizing changes in economic conditions. As noted in previous sections, it sometimes was a bit slow to see that the economy was sinking into a recession, or that inflationary pressures were dominant. But hindsight is always much clearer than foresight, which is why Monday morning quarterbacks make so few mistakes—and get paid so little. The lag between changes in economic conditions and changes in policy was consequently rather short, particularly when compared with the lag for fiscal policy.

Second, the Fed does not seem to have taken much account of the long—and seemingly quite variable—lags between changes in monetary policy and their effects on the economy. Instead, it simply reacted quickly to changes in business conditions. As pointed out in a previous section, such a policy can in reality be quite destabilizing. For example, the Fed may act to suppress inflationary pressures, but find that the consequences of its action are not felt until some time later when recession—not

Is There an Independent Federal Reserve? Should There Be?

A MEETING OF THE FEDERAL OPEN MARKET COMMITTEE.

Some say the Fed is responsible to Congress. Its enabling legislation was passed by Congress in 1913, and it could presumably be reorganized should it sufficiently rouse Congress's wrath. But Congress moves with nothing if not deliberate speed, and not since 1935 has it sought to influence the Federal Reserve through new legislation. The president fills vacancies on the Board of Governors, but since terms on the Board run for 14 years, presidents have had to wait until their second terms to appoint a majority of the Board.

In fact, as knowledgeable observers often agree, there are two groups that, without appearing prominently on the organization chart, exercise considerable influence over the policies of the Fed. One is the business community—a group with a definite interest in preserving the value of a dollar. The second is the Board's professional staff of senior economists. Administrations come and go, but the staff economist remains, and his uniquely detailed knowledge of the workings of the Fed assures him a hearing at 20th and Constitution.

Does it matter that the Fed is a focal point for the forces in the economy who fear inflation and are willing to accept somewhat higher unemployment in the hopes prices will not rise as rapidly? It may matter less than the formal structure suggests. Virtually since its inception, the Federal Reserve has had a crop of antagonistic observers in Congress. Former Secretary of the Treasury John Connally compared one of the Fed's perennial congressional foes to a cross-eyed discus thrower: "He'll never set any records for distance but he certainly keeps the crowd on its toes."

Both William McChesney Martin and the present chairman, Arthur Burns, have been sensitive to the ultimate vulnerability of the Fed's independence, and so have been reluctant to buck administration policy too dramatically. The slow increase in interest rates in the 1973 inflation was a compromise between the banker's feeling for sound money and a politician's unwillingness to be the "fall guy" in the fight against inflation. Whether the Federal Reserve's current procedures can survive the general call for more accountability is an open question. E.A.

inflation—is the problem. Unfortunately, the truth is that, despite advances in knowledge in the past decade, economists do not have a firm understanding of these lags. Thus, the Fed is only partly to blame.

Third, with a few notable exceptions, there generally seems to have been reasonably good coordination between the Federal Reserve and the executive branch (the Treasury and the Council of Economic Advisers, in particular). This is important because monetary policy and fiscal policy should work together, not march off in separate directions. Of course, the fact that the Fed and the executive branch have generally been aware of one another's views and probable actions does not mean that there has always been agreement between them. Nor does it mean that, even when they agreed, they could always point monetary and fiscal policy in the same direction. But at least the left hand had a pretty good idea of what the right hand was doing.

Fourth, the Fed has been criticized for paying too much attention during the 1950s to free reserves and interest rates as measures of the tightness or looseness of monetary policy, and giving too little attention to the rate of growth of the money supply and the monetary base. During the 1960s and 1970s, however, the Fed has paid much more attention to the rate of growth of the money supply and the monetary base. Again, the fault is only partly the Fed's, since the experts cannot agree on the relative importance that should be attached to each measure. But wherever the fault, if any, may lie, the Fed's performance is bound to suffer if it acts on the basis of unreliable measures.

Fifth, the Fed is often criticized for putting too much emphasis on preventing inflation and too little on preventing unemployment. According to various studies, it probably is true that the Fed has been more sensitive to the dangers of inflation than has the Congress or the administration. Liberals, emphasizing the great social costs of excessive unemployment, tend to denounce the Fed for such behavior. Without question, the costs of unemployment are high, as stressed in Chapter 8. Conservatives, on the other hand, often claim that governments are tempted to resort to inflation in order to produce short-term prosperity. In the short run (which is when the next election is decided), unemployment is much more likely than inflation to result in defeat at the polls. Whether you think that the Fed has put too much emphasis on restraining inflation will depend on the relative importance that you attach to reducing unemployment, on the one hand, and reducing inflation, on the other.[11]

Should the Fed Be Governed by a Rule?

As we have just seen, important criticisms can be made of Federal Reserve policy making. The monetarists, led by Milton Friedman, go so far as to say that the Fed's attempts to "lean against the wind"—by easing money when the economy begins to dip and tightening money when the economy begins to get overheated—really do more harm than good. In their view, the Fed actually intensifies business fluctuations by changing the rate of growth of the money supply. Why? Partly because the Fed sometimes pays too much attention to interest rates (and free reserves) rather than to the money supply or the monetary base. But more fundamentally, because the Fed tends to overract to ephemeral changes, and because the effects of changes in the money supply on the economy occur with a long and highly variable lag. In their view, this lag is so unpredictable that the Fed—no matter how laudatory its intent—tends to intensify business fluctuations.

Instead, Professor Friedman and his followers want the Fed to abandon its attempts to "lean

[11] For a good discussion of recent monetary and fiscal policy, see G. L. Bach, *Making Monetary and Fiscal Policy,* Washington: Brookings Institution, 1971. Also, see the papers by Milton Friedman and Walter W. Heller in E. Mansfield, *Economics: Readings, Issues and Cases,* New York: Norton, 1974.

against the wind." *They propose that the Fed conform to a rule that the money supply should increase at some fixed, agreed-upon rate, such as 4½ percent per year. The Fed's job would be simply to see that the money supply grows at approximately this rate.* The monetarists do not claim that a rule of this sort would prevent all business fluctuations, but they do claim that it would work better than the existing system. In particular, they feel that it would prevent the sorts of major depressions and inflations we have experienced in the past. Without major decreases in the money supply (such as occurred during the crash of 1929–33), major depressions could not occur. Without major increases in the money supply (such as occurred during World War II), major inflations could not occur. Of course, it would be nice if monetary policy could iron out minor business fluctuations as well, but in their view this simply cannot be done at present.

This proposal has received considerable attention from both economists and politicians. A number of studies have been carried out to try to estimate what would have happened if Friedman's rule had been used in the past. The results, although by no means free of criticism, seem to indicate that such a rule might have done better than discretionary action did in preventing the Great Depression of the 1930s and the inflation during World War II. But in the period since World War II, the evidence in favor of such a rule is less persuasive. Most economists seem to believe that it would be a mistake to handcuff the Fed to a simple rule of this sort. They think that a discretionary monetary policy can outperform Friedman's rule.

Nonetheless, the debate over rules versus discretionary action goes on, and the issues are still very much alive. Professor Friedman has been able to gain important converts, including the Federal Reserve Bank of St. Louis and members of the Joint Economic Committee of Congress. Indeed, after the Fed's "stop-go" policies of 1966–68 (when the Fed tightened money sharply in 1966 and loosened it rapidly in 1967–8), the Joint Economic Committee urged the Fed to adopt a rule of the sort advocated by Friedman. In 1968, the committee complained that its advice was not being followed, and special hearings were held. The Council of Economic Advisers and the Secretary of the Treasury sided with the Fed against adopting such a rule. Some academic economists favor such a rule, others oppose it, and considerable economic research is being carried out to try to clarify and resolve the questions involved.

Monetary Policy: Advantages and Disadvantages

Just as sensible wine drinkers value both Bordeaux and Burgundy (and both France and California), so most economists believe that both monetary and fiscal policy can and should play an important role in our nation's economic stabilization policies. However, this does not mean, of course, that monetary policy does not have certain advantages over fiscal policy, and vice versa. One disadvantage of monetary policy, according to many economists, is that it may be less dependable than fiscal policy when the government wants to stimulate the economy. All that monetary policy can do is to increase bank reserves. The monetary authorities cannot make the banks lend out the excess reserves—as illustrated by the situation during the 1930s when banks held huge excess reserves. And if the banks don't lend them out or invest them, there is little or no stimulation to the economy. Thus, monetary policy may be less effective as a stimulant than as a rein on the economy. However, under current circumstances (not the 1930s), this assymetry may be less pronounced than has sometimes been assumed.

On the other hand, one of the most important advantages of monetary policy is that the monetary authorities can react much more quickly to changed economic conditions than can the fiscal authorities. Changes in monetary policy can be put into effect relatively quickly if the Fed wants to do so, but no matter what the Treasury, the Council of Economic Advisers, and other administration officials want to do, changes in tax and expenditure policy must be approved by the Congress. Proposed fiscal policies can be delayed and even made into a political football, as happened to the tax surcharge of 1968, which had been kicked around for a couple of years before it finally was enacted.

According to some observers, another advantage of monetary policy is that it is nondiscriminatory. In other words, the Fed does not favor particular classes of borrowers or activities; it just tightens or eases money and credit, and lets the market determine which people and industries will be benefited or hurt. But other observers retort that monetary policy is highly discriminatory, since it can hit a particular group or industry or type of borrower harder than anyone would intend. For example, the home construction industry has sometimes been clobbered by tight monetary policy. Because of the importance of mortgage funds to the construction industry, tight money can really have a big impact on its output and profits.

Monetary Policy and Private Decision Making

Up to this point, we have discussed monetary policy strictly from the point of view of society as a whole. It is important to look at things from this vantage point, but it must also be recognized that an understanding of monetary policy is a great help, and sometimes absolutely essential, in making decisions about your personal finances and your firm's problems. For example, suppose that you have $10,000 in cash and are thinking about investing it in bonds, which currently yield a return of 7 percent per year. Should you invest it now, or wait? The answer depends on whether you think interest rates will rise. If so, you may be better off to hold the $10,000 in cash, and invest it in bonds later, when you can get a higher return.

But whether or not interest rates will rise depends upon the sort of monetary policy pursued by the Fed. Thus, to make an informed judgment about whether you should invest now or wait, you have to have some understanding of what the Fed is likely to do. Will it tighten money, and push interest rates up? Or will it ease money, and push interest rates down? Based on your appraisal of the current economic climate, as well as the published opinions of experts, you should be able to come to a reasoned conclusion on this score.

Or take another example. Suppose you own a small business, and will soon need to borrow some money to buy some new equipment. Is this a good time to apply for a bank loan? The answer depends in part on how tight money is now, and on how tight it is likely to be in the future. But to understand the current monetary situation, and the likely changes in the near future, you must understand what monetary policy is all about. You must be able to understand what the Federal Reserve has been doing in the recent past, and what it is likely to do in the future.

Or suppose that you are thinking of buying a house. The rate of interest you pay on the mortgage has a big effect on the total cost of the house. For example, the payments on a $40,000 mortgage are almost $4,000 higher over the 25-year life of the mortgage if the interest is 7½ percent than if it is 7 percent. Thus, since interest rates are influenced by monetary policy, an understanding of monetary policy is useful in figuring out whether and when it is a good time to buy.

Summary

Monetary policy is concerned with the money supply and interest rates. Its purpose is to attain and maintain full employment without inflation. When a recession seems imminent and business is soft, the monetary authorities are likely to increase the money supply and reduce interest rates. On the other hand, when the economy is in danger of "overheating" and inflation threatens, the monetary authorities are likely to rein in the money supply and push up interest rates. Monetary policy and fiscal policy are aimed at much the same goals, but they use different methods to promote them. One advantage of monetary policy is that the lag between decision and action is relatively short. In view of the time involved in getting tax (and spending) changes enacted, this is an important point.

Although monetary policy is influenced by Congress, the Treasury, and other parts of the government and the public at large, the chief responsibility for the formulation of monetary policy lies with the Federal Reserve Board and the Federal Open Market Committee. To a considerable extent, monetary policy operates by changing the quantity of bank reserves. The most important tool of monetary policy is open market operations, which involve the buying and selling of government securities in the open market by the Federal Reserve. When the Fed buys government securities, this increases bank reserves. When the Fed sells government securities, this reduces bank reserves. The Fed can also tighten or ease money by increasing or decreasing the discount rate or by increasing or decreasing legal reserve requirements. In addition, the Fed can use moral suasion, and it has power over maximum interest rates on time deposits and margin requirements for the purchase of stock.

As indicators of how tight or easy monetary policy is, the Fed has looked at the level of short-term interest rates, the quantity of free reserves, the rate of growth of the money supply, and the rate of growth of the monetary base. During the 1950s, the Fed paid most attention to the first two indicators; in the 1960s and 1970s, the Fed increased the amount of attention paid to the last two. To provide some idea of how monetary policy has been used, we presented a brief description of the nature and course of monetary policy during the past two decades. Also, to provide a richer picture of the use of monetary policy to stem inflation, we described in some detail the "credit crunch of 1966." This episode is a dramatic example of the potency of monetary policy.

The Federal Reserve is faced with many difficult problems in formulating and carrying out monetary policy. It must try to see where the economy is heading, and whether—and to what extent—it should tighten or ease money to stabilize the economy. This task is made very difficult by the fact that there is often a long—and highly variable—lag between an action by the Fed and its effect on the economy. There is also considerable disagreement over the best way to measure how tight or easy monetary policy is. In addition, the Fed's job is complicated by the fact that, although it is independent of the executive branch, it must take account of the Treasury's problems in financing the public debt. During the 1940s and early 1950s, the Fed's policies were dictated largely by such financing matters.

There has been criticism of various kinds regarding the performance of the Federal Reserve. Often, the Fed is criticized for paying too little attention to the long lags between its actions and their effects on the economy. Also, some critics claim that the Fed puts too much emphasis on fighting inflation and too little on preventing unemployment. Some monetarists, led by Milton Friedman, believe that monetary policy would be improved if discretionary policy were replaced by a rule that the Fed should increase the money supply at some fixed, agreed-on rate, such as 4½ percent per year. The Fed, the Council of Economic Advisers, the Treasury, and many academic economists have argued against the adoption of such a rule, but Friedman's proposal has won some support in the Joint Economic Committee and elsewhere. The debate over rules versus discretionary policy goes on, and is one of the liveliest in present-day economics.

CONCEPTS FOR REVIEW

Monetary policy
Federal Reserve Board
Federal Open Market Committee
Open market operations
Discount rate
Changes in legal reserve requirements
Easing money
Moral suasion
Selective credit control
Free reserves
Monetary base
Margin requirements
Credit crunch
Tightening money

QUESTIONS FOR DISCUSSION AND REVIEW

1. According to Henry Wallich, although "monetary policy has so often been wrong that it [may seem] preferable to deprive it of discretion and subject it to a fixed rule, . . . this reasoning is fallacious." Do you agree? Why or why not? How would you go about testing this proposition?

2. According to Sherman Maisel, William McChesney Martin, former Chairman of the Federal Reserve Board, felt "that the primary function of the Federal Reserve Board was to determine what was necessary to maintain a sound currency . . . [To Martin] it is as immoral for a country today to allow the value of its currency to fall as it was for kings of old to clip coinage." Do you agree with Martin's views? Why or why not?

3. The Fed's task is made more difficult by the fact that there is often a long lag between an action by the Fed and its effect on the economy. True or False?

4. In order to decide whether monetary policy is inflationary or deflationary and what should be done in this regard, the Federal Reserve Board would probably *not* consider

a. short-term interest rates.
b. the size of the national debt.
c. the rate of increase of the money supply.
d. the rate of increase of the monetary base.

CHAPTER 15

Problems of Economic Stabilization Policy

Despite the advances in economic knowledge during the past 40 years, we, like other countries, find it very difficult to achieve full employment with stable prices. Monetary policy is an important means toward that end. And in the eyes of most economists, so is fiscal policy. Yet, despite the power of monetary and fiscal policies, we are still a long way from the desired degree of economic stability. Judging from the experience of the past 40 years, we have learned how to avoid very serious depressions, but we have not yet learned how to attain full employment with stable prices. Excessive unemployment and excessive inflation persist.

Two important reasons why our performance has been less than satisfactory are evident. First, economists are still uncertain about many effects of monetary and fiscal policies. For one thing, as pointed out in previous chapters, the views of the monetarists differ from those of the Keynesians. Second, if some of the inflationary pressures in our society stem from an upward push of costs (or profits), some form of incomes policy may be needed to quell undesirable inflation. In this chapter, we discuss both of these problems at length.

The General Problem of Achieving Economic Stability

As a first step, let's review how fiscal and monetary policies can be used to promote full employment without inflation. We begin with fiscal policy. With a given level of potential output or capacity, actual net national product is determined by desired spending. Fiscal policy uses the government's expenditures and taxes to influence desired spending. Specifically, when NNP is at less than its full-employment level, increases in government expenditures or reductions in taxes can be used to push it up to this level, and thus reduce excessive unemployment. Or when there is excessive inflation, decreases in government expenditures or increases in taxes can reduce total spending, and thus curb inflation.

Monetary policy uses the government's power over the quantity of money to influence NNP. Increases in the money supply tend to increase the money value of NNP, whereas reductions in the money supply tend to reduce the money value of NNP. The route by which the quantity of money has this effect on NNP is a subject of controversy. The majority, or Keynesian, view is that increases in the money supply reduce interest rates, which stimulates investment, which increases NNP. Conversely, decreases in the money supply increase interest rates, which cuts investment, which reduces NNP. Many Keynesians, at least in more recent years, also recognize that changes in the money supply influence the net worth of consumers, and thus have an impact on consumption expenditures. Monetarists, relying heavily on the quantity theory of money, relate changes in the money supply more directly to changes in nominal, or money, NNP.

The controversy between the monetarists and the Keynesians has received so much attention in recent years that one might think that, if it were resolved, the problem of formulating monetary and fiscal policies to achieve full employment with stable prices would be licked. This is by no means true. However the controversy is resolved, no existing economic model can give policy makers reliable quantitative estimates of how much the money supply should be altered, or government expenditures should be changed, or tax rates should be modified, to achieve full employment with stable prices. To a considerable extent, the knowledge we have is qualitative, not quantitative. Until we can better estimate the quantitative effects of policy changes of various magnitudes, it will be unreasonable to expect that monetary and fiscal policies can be used with precision to achieve our national goals.

In addition, it must be emphasized that both the Keynesian and the monetarist models are just that—models. In other words, they are convenient and useful simplifications; and, as such, they abstract from many important aspects of reality. In particular, they take little or no notice of the possibility that inflation may arise because of an upward push of costs, and they tell us very little about what to do when there is both excessive unemployment and excessive inflation. Nor do they say much about the extent of the lags between the time when policy makers want to act and the time when such action is approved and taken, or the lags between the time when action is taken and the time when its economic effects are felt.

Further, it must be recognized that government decisions are not dictated by considerations of economic stabilization alone. Thus, even if economic models were completely accurate and the government knew how to achieve full employment at stable prices, it would not always choose to do so. For example, the political party in power may be committed to a particular policy designed to alleviate a certain social ill, like poverty or discrimination. To carry out this objective, it may increase government expenditures at a time when, from the point of view of economic stabilization, it would be better to reduce them. Or in wartime, modern military needs require enormous outlays, but the political party in power may not be willing to take the unpopular step of raising taxes, even though this would be desirable for economic stabilization. Or consider an upcoming presidential election. The incumbent president may initiate or expand programs to make people feel prosperous in the short run, even though this may be destabilizing in the longer run. After all, the important thing is to win the election and prevent that other fellow, whoever he may be, from ruining the country!

Monetarists versus Keynesians

The debate between the monetarists and the Keynesians has not been limited to the classroom and scholarly gatherings. It has spilled over onto the pages of the daily newspapers and aroused considerable interest in Congress and other parts of the government. At heart, the argument is over what determines the level of output, employment, and prices. The Keynesians put more emphasis on the federal budget than do the monetarists, who put more emphasis on the money supply than do the Keynesians. To understand this debate fully, we need to know something about the recent development of economic thought. Up until the Great Depression of the 1930s, the prevailing theory was that NNP, expressed in real terms, would tend automatically to its full-employment value. (Recall from Chapter 9 the classical economists' reasons for clinging to this belief.) Moreover, the prevailing theory was that the price level could be explained by the crude quantity theory of money. In other words, the price level, P, was assumed to be proportional to the quantity of money, M, because $MV = PQ$, and real NNP, Q, and the velocity of money, V, were thought to be essentially constant.

During the Great Depression of the 1930s, this body of theory was largely discredited and abandoned. Clearly, NNP was not tending automatically toward its full-employment level. And the crude quantity theory seemed to have little value. In contrast, Keynes's ideas, which stressed the importance of fiscal policy, seemed to offer the sort of theoretical guidance and policy prescriptions that were needed. Keynesians did not neglect the use of monetary policy entirely, but they felt that it played a subsidiary role. Particularly in depressions, monetary policy seemed to be of relatively little value, since "you can't push on a string." In other words, monetary policy can make money available, but it cannot insure that it will be spent.

During the 1940s, 1950s, and early 1960s, the Keynesian view was definitely predominant, here and abroad. But by the mid-1960s, it was being challenged seriously by the monetarists, led by Professor Milton Friedman and his supporters. The monetarist view harked back to the pre-Keynesian doctrine in many respects. In particular, it emphasized the importance of the equation of exchange as an analytical device and the importance of the quantity of money as a tool of economic policy. The monetarist view gained adherents in the late 1960s. Partly responsible was the long delay in passing the surtax of 1968, for the reluctance of the administration to propose and of Congress to enact the new levy vividly illustrated some of the difficulties in using fiscal policy for stabilization. In contrast, monetary policy seemed to assure only a short lag between policy decisions and their implementation. Another factor favoring the monetarists was that the economy was plagued by inflation, not unemployment. Monetary policy, by controlling the quantity of money, can quite effectively restrain inflation, even if, under certain circumstances, it may not be so effective in reducing unemployment. "You may be able to pull on a string," even if "you can't push on a string."

The Monetarist View of the Role of Money

Given its recent prominence, the monetarist view deserves a closer look. The monetarists believe that the velocity of money, V, is relatively stable or so predictable that changes in M will have a predictable effect on PQ. Suppose that people and firms want to hold a quantity of money equal to 20 percent of nominal, or money, NNP. Then if NNP is \$1,000 billion, they will want to hold \$200 billion of money; if NNP is \$1,200 billion, they will want to hold \$240 billion of money; and if NNP is \$1,400 billion, they will want to hold \$280 billion of money. According to the monetarists, there is a stable and predictable relationship of this sort between NNP and the quantity of money people and firms want to hold.

To the monetarists, this relationship determines the equilibrium level of NNP. Continuing our example (where firms and people want to hold 20 percent of NNP in the form of money), suppose that NNP is \$1,000 billion (which means that the public wants to hold \$200 billion in money), but that the Federal Reserve makes \$240 billion in money available. What will happen? Since the public has more money on hand than it wants, it will spend away its unwanted excess cash. Firms will invest in plant, equipment, inventories, or other items. Individuals too, having more cash on hand than they want, will step up their spending. The result, of course, will be an increase in NNP, since the increased spending will boost NNP.

By how much will NNP increase? So long as NNP is less than \$1,200 billion, the public will have more money than it wants to hold. Its \$240 billion of money is more than the 20 percent of NNP it wants to hold in money. Consequently, for the amount of money to be the amount people want to hold, NNP must be five times the quantity of money, or 5 × \$240 billion in this case. Thus, NNP must rise to \$1,200 billion. So long as NNP is less than \$1,200 billion, there is a disequilibrium, since people have more money than they want to hold. The result will be that they spend the excess cash and increase NNP. Only when NNP rises to \$1,200 billion will an equilibrium be achieved.

Similarly, suppose that NNP is \$1,000 billion, but that the Federal Reserve makes only \$160 billion of money available. Since NNP is \$1,000 billion, the public would like to hold \$200 billion (20 percent of NNP) in money. The public holds less money than it wants to; and in order to return to its desired relationship between NNP and the quantity of money furnished by the Fed, the public cuts down its spending. In other words, firms reduce their expenditures on plant, equipment, and other items in an attempt to build up their money balances. Similarly, individuals reduce their spending to try to build up their money balances. The result, of course, is a decline in NNP, since the reduced spending will reduce NNP.

By how much will NNP fall? For the amount of money to be the amount people want to hold, NNP must be five times the quantity of money, or 5 × \$160 billion in this case. Thus, NNP must fall to 800 billion. So long as NNP is above \$800 billion, there is a disequilibrium, since people have less money than they want to hold. Consequently, they will cut back on their spending in an effort to build up their money balances, and NNP is reduced. Only when NNP falls to \$800 billion will an equilibrium be achieved.

Following this line of reasoning, the monetarists conclude that increases in the quantity of money will increase NNP. If the economy is not at full employment, much of this increase in NNP will represent an increase in real output; but if full employment exists, it will represent an increase in the price level. Similarly, the monetarists conclude that decreases in the quantity of money will decrease NNP. Unless such a decrease in NNP offsets existing inflationary pressures, it will, of course, represent a decrease in real output. The monetarists provide considerable statistical evidence that, in their eyes at least, backs up these conclusions. For example, they point out that the money supply seemed to fall just before various depressions of the past. And they explain why the increase in taxes in 1968 had less than the expected contractionary effect on NNP by citing the fact that the money supply continued to increase at a relatively rapid rate.

The Debate over Stabilization Policy

From these theoretical and empirical foundations, the monetarists and the Keynesians reach quite different conclusions about how economic stabilization policies should be carried out. For one thing, the monetarists attack the Keynesian view that fiscal policy works in the way we described in Chapter 10. According to the monetarists, whether the government runs a surplus or a deficit has no permanent effect on NNP, except insofar as the government finances the surplus or deficit in a way that affects the stock of money.

For example, if the government runs a deficit and finances it by borrowing from the public, the money supply will be unchanged. Thus the monetarists would argue that such a deficit has no expansionary effect on NNP. On the other hand, if the government finances its deficit by increasing the money supply, the monetarists would expect NNP to increase, but as a result of the expansion of the money supply, not of the deficit. Thus, the monetarists claim that the expansion of NNP after the tax cut of 1964 was due to considerable increases in the money supply, not to the tax cut.

Another important difference between the monetarists and the Keynesians is that many, but not all, leading monetarists advocate the establishment of a rule to govern monetary policy. In the previous chapter, we discussed the arguments of Friedman and his supporters for such a rule. You will recall their charge that the Federal Reserve's monetary policies have often caused economic instability. Because of the difficulties in forecasting the future state of the economy and the fairly long and variable time lag in the effect of changes in the money supply, the Fed, in the eyes of many leading monetarists, has caused excessive inflation or unemployment by its discretionary policies. According to the monetarists, we would be better off with a rule stipulating that the money supply should grow steadily at a rate fixed somewhere between 4 and 5 percent per year.

Needless to say, the Keynesians—or the New Economists, as they have sometimes been called—have plenty of counterarguments against the monetarists. They believe that the monetarists take too simple and highly aggregated a view of the economy. The Keynesians point out that many factors impinge significantly on the economy and that, in their view, it is overly simplistic to concentrate so single-mindedly on one variable, the quantity of money. For example, desired spending may be influenced heavily by people's expectations, which may be unrelated to the quantity of money. The Keynesians also believe that the monetarists sometimes tend to mix up cause and effect. Changes in desired spending may bring about a greater demand for money, which in turn causes the money supply to increase. Under these circumstances, the line of causation may be the opposite of that posited by the monetarists.

In addition, the Keynesians tend to feel that the interest rate is far more important than the monetarists realize. According to the Keynesians, the money supply has an important influence on NNP, but its influence is felt largely through its impact on the interest rate, which in turn affects spending. Thus the Keynesians are more inclined than the monetarists to use the level of interest rates to measure whether money is tight or easy. To the monetarists, the change in the quantity of money, not the level of interest rates, is important. The Keynesians have presented evidence of various kinds to demonstrate, at least to their own satisfaction, that their view is the correct one.[1]

The Keynesians have also attacked the monetarists' contention that the velocity of money is relatively stable. Data we have seen (recall Figure 12.8) confirm that velocity is far from constant. For one thing, it varies with interest rates and with people's expectations. However, sophisticated monetarists would say that the velocity function—a functional relationship derived from the demand for money—is stable. This is different from saying that velocity as a calculated number is stable.

[1] For some of the arguments on both sides, see the papers by Walter W. Heller, Milton Friedman, and Arthur Okun in E. Mansfield, *Economics: Readings, Issues, and Cases*, New York: Norton, 1974.

Milton Friedman versus Walter W. Heller

Seldom do the *New York Times,* the *Wall Street Journal,* and *Vogue* cover a debate between two economists. That they covered the seventh annual Arthur K. Salomon Lecture at New York University in November 1968 is a tribute to the impact each of the protagonists—Milton Friedman and Walter W. Heller—has had on presidents, potential presidents, and public opinion in the monetary versus fiscal debate.

Friedman, a professor at the University of Chicago, has written on as wide a range of subjects as any living economist. A staunch conservative, he nevertheless originated such "liberal" proposals as the educational voucher (now being used experimentally in Vermont and North Dakota districts) and the negative income tax. In keeping with his conservative philosophy, he has attacked the evils of Social Security and the minimum wage, praised the virtues of abolishing licensing of professions, and argued the intimate connection between capitalism and freedom. Although never a full-time government employee since his World War II stint with the Treasury Department, he has served in his spare time as economics adviser to presidential candidate Barry Goldwater and to President Nixon (before Nixon left the faith and imposed price and wage controls).

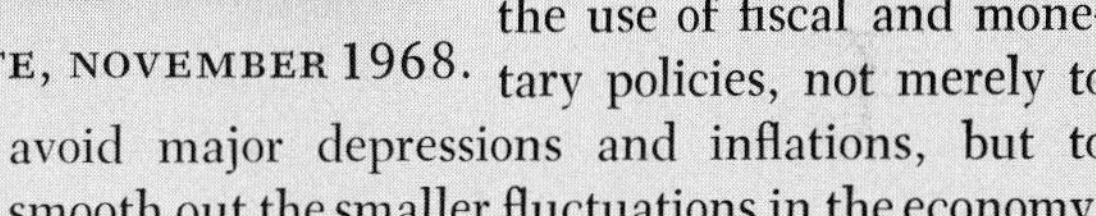

FRIEDMAN—HELLER DEBATE, NOVEMBER 1968.

But Friedman is most prominently identified, at least within the economics profession, as the defender (and in large part the creator) of monetarism. While Keynesianism triumphant swept the economics profession in the postwar years, Friedman and a few University of Chicago colleagues were investigating the historical connection between money and U.S. economic history, eventually persuading the Federal Reserve Bank of St. Louis to gather and publish statistics using their concepts and fortifying the monetarist arguments until the inflation of the late sixties made monetarism fashionable again.

By contrast, Walter W. Heller, a professor at the University of Minnesota, has been a liberal and a political activist (at least by economists' standards). As chairman of the Council of Economic Advisers under both Presidents Kennedy and Johnson, he was a principal architect of the 1962 investment tax credit and the 1964 tax cut. He enjoyed a close and sympathetic relationship with the New Frontiersmen, and as a consequence, the Council assumed a broader, more activist role than it has enjoyed before or since. He was a leading spokesman for the use of fiscal and monetary policies, not merely to avoid major depressions and inflations, but to smooth out the smaller fluctuations in the economy.

In their debate, Heller posed many basic questions concerning monetarism: "Which money-supply indicator do you believe? Can one read enough from money supply without weighing also shifts in demand and interest rates? Don't observed variations in monetary time lags and velocity cast serious doubt on any simple relation between money supply and GNP? Can a rigid monetary rule find happiness in a world beset with rigidities and rather limited adjustment capabilities? That is, is the rigid Friedman rule perhaps a formula made in heaven, that will work only in heaven?" These questions are of great importance, and they continue to be debated, here and abroad.

E.A.

As for the monetarists' contention that monetary policy should be governed by a rule, the Keynesians retort that such a rule would handcuff the monetary authorities and contribute to economic instability, since discretionary monetary policies are required to keep the economy on a reasonably even keel. The Keynesians grant that the Fed sometimes makes mistakes, but they assert that things would be worse if the Fed could not pursue the policies that a given set of circumstances seems to call for.

The debate between the monetarists and the Keynesians is important and illuminating. It has forced the entire economics profession to review its thinking about the effects of monetary and fiscal policies. This is the sort of ferment that keeps a discipline healthy and vital. Chances are that it will be many years before the issues are completely resolved, but in the past decade, considerable strides have been taken toward achieving a synthesis of these two views. Having focused attention on the differences between them, let's look now at this new synthesis.

Elements of a New Synthesis

The Keynesian theory says that the economy will be in equilibrium only when consumers are spending at the rate they desire, given their income, and when firms are investing at the rate they desire. The monetarist theory says that the economy will be in equilibrium only when consumers and firms are willing to hold the existing quantity of money, given their income and the quantity of other assets that they hold. In truth, of course, both these conditions for equilibrium must be fulfilled: neither alone is sufficient to guarantee equilibrium. This fact suggests that a more complete model than either the Keynesian or the monetarist model may be needed to analyze many problems effectively.

For example, what happens when the government increases the quantity of money by handing out some newly printed money to the public? Let's begin with the public's asset holdings. Since the public has more money than before, it will rearrange its portfolio of assets, assuming that it had the portfolio it desired prior to the increase in the money supply. Consumers and firms, finding themselves with more money than they want to hold, will exchange money for other types of assets. In other words, they will spend some of their money holdings—and will continue to spend money until, once again, their portfolio of assets is balanced so as to maximize their satisfaction.

Second, consider how the increase in the public's income due to the increase in the money supply will affect spending. The people who receive the newly printed money, finding that their disposable incomes have risen, want to spend more on consumption goods. Firms that receive the new money are also likely to want to increase their investment expenditures. Both consumers and firms will continue to spend more until, once again, their expenditures are in the desired relationship to their incomes. Note that this adjustment process, stressed by Keynesian theory, goes on simultaneously with the adjustment process described in the previous paragraph, which is related to the monetarist theory.

Once one recognizes that both processes go on simultaneously, it is easy to see that much of the debate between the Keynesians and monetarists is really over which of two simplifications is more fruitful—or does less violence to reality. According to the Keynesians, the multiplier is more stable than the velocity of money, so that changes in taxes or government spending have a more predictable effect on total spending than changes in the quantity of money. According to the monetarists, the velocity of money is more predictable than the multiplier, which means that the effects of changes in the quantity of money on total spending are more predictable than changes in taxes or government spending. Much econometric work is being done at present to try to resolve this issue. Although the evidence as yet is inconclusive, it is reasonable to expect that in the foreseeable future we will be much better able to answer this question.

Figure 15.1
The *IS* Curve

The *IS* curve shows, for each level of the interest rate, the level of NNP that will satisfy the equilibrium condition that desired saving must equal desired investment.

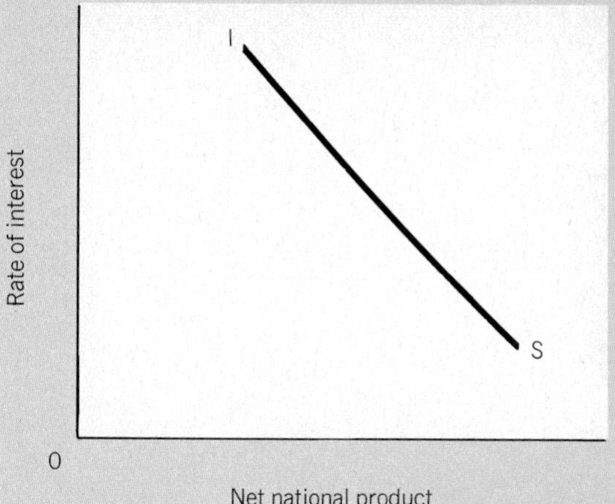

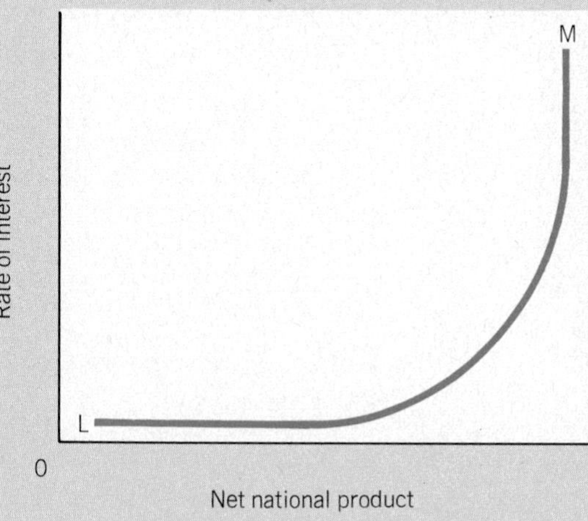

Figure 15.2
The *LM* Curve

The *LM* curve shows, for each level of the interest rate, the level of NNP that will satisfy the equilibrium condition that the public be satisfied to hold the existing quantity of money.

The IS and LM Curves[2]

Now that we recognize that equilibrium requires both that households and firms be spending the desired amount relative to their incomes and that they be satisfied to hold the existing quantity of money, it is worthwhile to show, in somewhat more detail, how net national product is determined. To do this, we draw two curves, *IS* and *LM*, both of which are constructed on the assumption that the money supply and the price level are fixed and that the public has a fixed demand curve for real money balances, a fixed consumption function, and a fixed investment function.

[2] This section, which is somewhat more advanced than the rest of this chapter, can be omitted without losing the thread of the argument.

The *IS* curve in Figure 15.1 shows, for each possible level of the interest rate, the level of NNP that will satisfy the equilibrium condition that desired saving equal desired investment (see Chapter 9). This equilibrium condition is equivalent to saying that the public must be spending the desired amount relative to its income. The *IS* curve slopes downward to the right because the higher the interest rate, the lower the amount of investment (as we know from Chapter 9); and the lower the amount of investment, the lower the equilibrium level of NNP (as we also know from Chapter 9). If the level of NNP is to satisfy the equilibrium condition that desired saving must equal desired investment, it must fall on the *IS* curve in Figure 15.1.

The *LM* curve, provided in Figure 15.2, shows,

for each possible level of the interest rate, the level of NNP that will satisfy the equilibrium condition that the public be satisfied to hold the existing quantity of money. The *LM* curve slopes upward to the right because the higher the interest rate, the less money the public will want to hold (as we know from Chapter 12). So the level of NNP will have to rise to offset this effect (since increases in NNP raise the amount of money the public wants to hold). If the level of NNP is to satisfy the equilibrium condition that the public be satisfied to hold the existing quantity of money, it must fall on the *LM* curve in Figure 15.2.

Since the equilibrium level of NNP must fall on both the *IS* and *LM* curves, *the equilibrium level of NNP must be at the intersection of the IS and LM curves,* as shown in Figure 15.3. That is, the equilibrium level of NNP must be *X,* and the equilibrium level of the interest rate must be *i.* This is the only combination of NNP and interest rate that will satisfy both equilibrium conditions, given that the money supply, the public's demand curve for money, its consumption function, and its investment function remain fixed.

Suppose, however, that all these conditions do not remain fixed. In particular, assume that fiscal policy is expansionary, thus stimulating spending by the public. This will shift the *IS* curve to the right, because spending at each level of the interest rate will be greater than before. As Figure 15.4 indicates, the result will be a higher equilibrium level of NNP and a higher rate of interest, so long as NNP is between X_0 and X_2. (Specifically, the equilibrium point shifts from *A* to *B*.) If NNP is at X_2, a shift of the *IS* curve to the right only increases the interest rate; it does not affect NNP. (The equilibrium point shifts from *C* to *D*.) This is the so-called ***classical range,*** where fiscal policy cannot increase NNP because the velocity of money is constant at its upward limit. Most economists do not consider such a situation very likely. If NNP is below X_0, a rightward shift of the *IS*

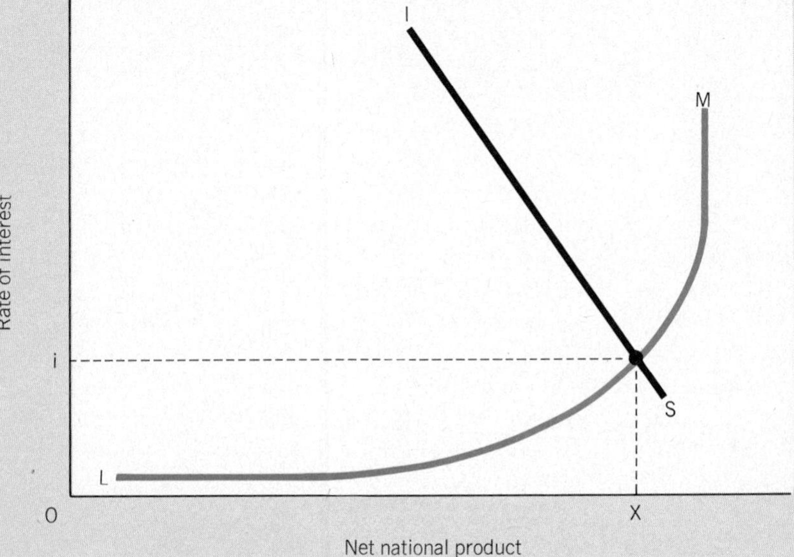

Figure 15.3
Determination of Equilibrium NNP and Interest Rate

The equilibrium level of NNP (and of the interest rate) must be at the intersection of the *IS* and *LM* curves. The equilibrium NNP equals *X*, and the equilibrium interest rate equals *i*.

Figure 15.4
Effects of an Expansionary Fiscal Policy

An expansionary fiscal policy shifts the *IS* curve to the right, resulting in a higher equilibrium level of NNP and of the interest rate, so long as NNP is between X_0 and X_2. For example, if I_1S_1 is the existing curve, which shifts to the right, the equilibrium shifts from *A* to *B*. On the other hand, if I_2S_2 is the existing curve, which shifts to the right, the equilibrium shifts from *C* to *D*. This is the *classical range*. Or if I_0S_0 is the existing curve, which shifts to the right, the equilibrium shifts from *E* to *F*. This is the *liquidity-trap range*.

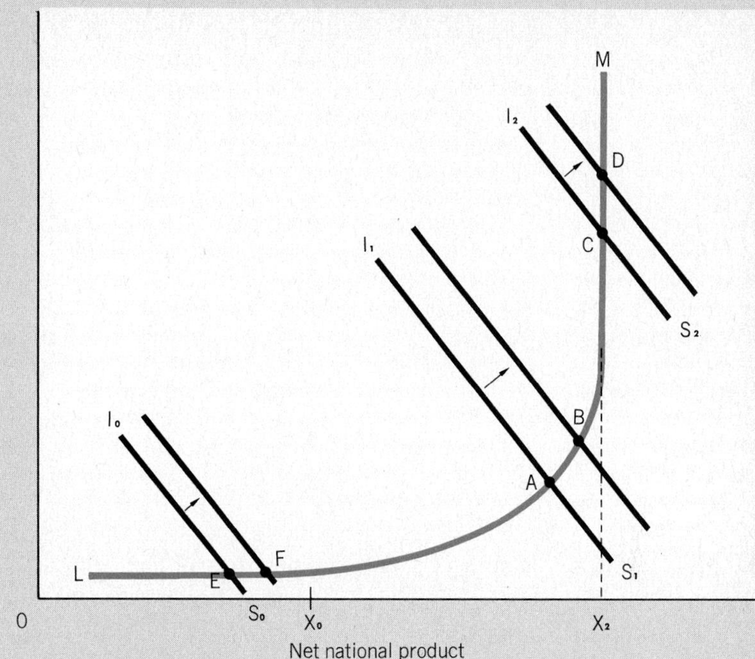

curve will not affect the interest rate, although it will increase NNP. (The equilibrium point shifts from *E* to *F*.) This is the so-called ***liquidity-trap range***, which is also unlikely to occur, except in severe depressions.

Assume next that the monetary authorities increase the money supply. Since the interest rate that equates the demand and supply of money (at any given level of NNP) must be lower if the quantity of money increases, this expansionary monetary policy results in a shift of the *LM* curve downward and to the right. As shown in Figure 15.5, the result will be a higher equilibrium level of NNP and a lower rate of interest, as long as the economy is not in the range of the liquidity trap. (Specifically, the equilibrium point shifts from *G* to *H*.) If we are in the liquidity trap, although the *LM* curve shifts, the portion of the curve below X_0 remains fixed, with the result that the equilibrium level of NNP and the interest rate are unchanged (at point *K*). A liquidity trap occurs when the interest rate is so low that people expect it to rise, and they are willing to hold more cash at existing interest rates. Such a situation is very unlikely to occur, except perhaps in very deep depressions. But if it does occur, monetary policy is unable to influence NNP.

Figures 15.4 and 15.5 show that the effects of monetary or fiscal policy on NNP depend on the shape of the *IS* and *LM* curves. For example, the closer the *LM* curve is to being vertical in the relevant range, the less impact fiscal policy will have, and the closer the economy is to the liquidity trap, the less effect monetary policy will have. These diagrams, originated by Oxford's Nobel Laureate, Sir John Hicks, are extremely useful in putting the debate between the monetarists and the Keynesians into proper perspective. To a considerable extent, this debate, when stripped of its semantic and rhetorical aspects, is over the shape of the *IS* and *LM* curves. This, of course, is an empirical question that requires careful statistical and

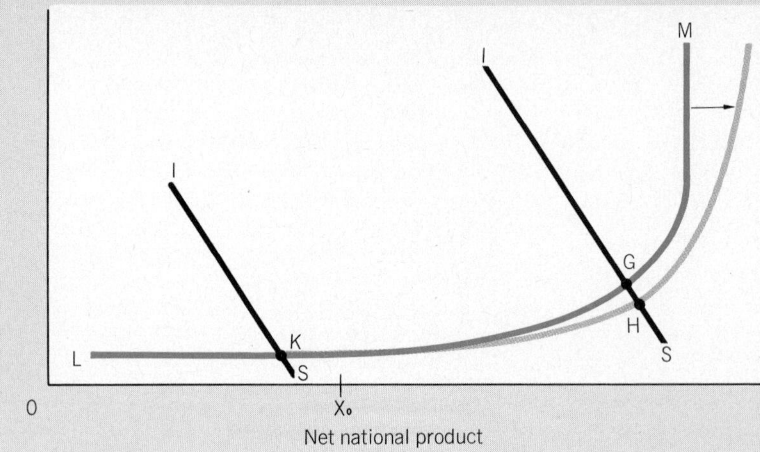

Figure 15.5
Effects of an Expansionary Monetary Policy

An expansionary monetary policy shifts the *LM* curve downward and to the right, the result being a higher equilibrium level of NNP and a lower rate of interest, so long as the economy is not in the liquidity trap. Specifically, the equilibrium shifts from *G* to *H*. If we are in the liquidity trap, the equilibrium remains at *K*.

econometric work to resolve. As we noted, considerable work of this sort is currently in progress. Regardless of how this work turns out, an understanding of the *IS* and *LM* curves provides us with much additional insight into the real differences and similarities between the monetarists and Keynesians.

Demand-Pull and Cost-Push Inflation

Whether they lean toward the monetarist or the Keynesian route to economic stability, policy makers have found inflation to be a stubborn foe. In previous chapters, we described ***demand-pull inflation,*** a situation in which there is too much aggregate spending. The $C + I + G$ line is too high, resulting in inflationary pressure. Or, put in terms of the equation of exchange, $M \times V$ is too high, so that P is pushed up: too much money is chasing too few goods. This kind of inflation stems from the demand or spending behavior of the nation's consumers, firms, and government. We have had many inflations of this kind. The major inflations during the Revolutionary and Civil wars were basically caused by demand-pull factors; and so, much more recently, was the inflation arising from the Vietnam war.

However, in the view of many economists, demand-pull inflation is not the only kind of inflation. There is also a different kind—***cost-push inflation.*** The process underlying cost-push inflation is not as well understood as it should be, but, according to many economists, it works something like this: costs are increased, perhaps because unions push up wages, and in an attempt to protect their profit margins, firms push up prices. These price increases affect the costs of other firms and the consumer's cost of living. As the cost of living goes up, labor feels entitled to, and obtains, higher wages to offset the higher living costs. Firms again pass on the cost increase to the consumer in the form of a price increase. This so-called ***wage-price spiral*** is at the heart of cost-push inflation.

Basically, in cost-push inflation, *the culprits are unions and firms with considerable market power.* In a world of perfect competition, both in product and input markets, cost-push inflation could not occur. In such a world, labor could not increase wages in the face of appreciable unemployment. If it tried, competition would bring wages back down. Nor could firms increase prices to protect their profits. Competition would put a tight ceiling on their pricing policy. Under perfect competition, inflation could occur (make no mistake about that), but it would have to be of the demand-pull type. Whether big labor or big business initiates the wage-price spiral is very difficult to determine in practice, and may well vary from case to case. But whoever makes the first move, the result is inflation.

Generally it is difficult, if not impossible, to sort out cost-push inflation from demand-pull inflation. However, one case of fairly pure cost-push inflation occurred in the late 1950s. This was a period of considerable slack in the economy. You will recall from Chapter 11 that a recession occurred in 1957–58. By 1958 6.8 percent of the labor force was unemployed. Nonetheless, wage increases took place during the late 1950s—and at a rate in excess of the rate of increase of labor productivity (output per manhour).[3] For example, average earnings (outside agriculture) went up by 4 percent between 1957 and 1961, while labor productivity went up by 2½ percent. Moreover, prices increased each year—by 3 percent from 1956 to 1957, and by 2 percent from 1957 to 1958.

Certainly this seemed to be a different phenomenon than the demand-pull inflation described in previous chapters. There was no evidence that too much money was chasing too few goods. Instead, this was apparently a case of cost-push inflation. Commenting on the situation in the middle and late 1950s, the Council of Economic Advisers concluded: "The movement of wages during this period reflected in part the power exercised in labor markets by strong unions and the power possessed by large companies to pass on higher wage costs in higher prices."[4]

The Phillips Curve

What determines the rate at which labor can push up wages? If you think about it for a while, you will probably agree that *labor's ability to increase wages depends on the level of unemployment. The more unemployment, the more difficult it is for labor to increase wages.* Although perfect competition by no means prevails in the labor market, there is enough competition so that the presence of a pool of unemployed workers puts some damper on wage increases. In nonunion industries and occupations, workers are much less inclined to push for wage increases—and employers are much less inclined to accept them—when lots of people are looking for work. In unionized industries and occupations, unions are less likely to put their members through the hardship of a strike—and firms have less to lose from a strike—when business is bad and unemployment is high.

Because wages tend to be increased at a greater rate when unemployment is low, one would expect the rate of increase of wages in any year to be inversely related to the level of unemployment. This expectation is borne out by the available evidence. Figure 15.6 shows how the rate of increase in wages in a particular period tends to be related to the level of unemployment. According to this figure, which is based on hypothetical, but reasonable, numbers, wages tend to rise by about 3 percent per year when 7 percent of the labor force is unemployed, by about 4½ percent per year when 5 percent of the labor force is unemployed, and by about 6 percent per year when 4 percent of the labor force is unemployed. *The relationship between the rate of increase of wages and the level of unemployment is the* ***Phillips curve.*** It was named after A. W. Phillips, the British economist who first called attention to it.

Given the Phillips curve in Figure 15.6 it is a simple matter to determine the relationship between the rate of inflation and the level of unemployment. It can easily be shown that the rate of increase of prices equals the rate of increase of total cost per manhour minus the rate of increase of labor productivity. If C is the total cost—wage and nonwage—per manhour, the total cost per unit of output equals $C \times M \div O$, where M is the total number of manhours worked and O is total output.

[3] In the next section, we shall discuss the importance of the rate of increase of output per manhour. For present purposes, it is sufficient to note that the greater the rate of increase of output per manhour, the larger the rate of increase of cost per manhour that can be absorbed without an increase in unit cost.

[4] 1962 *Annual Report of the Council of Economic Advisers,* Washington, D.C.: Government Printing Office, p. 175.

Figure 15.6
The Phillips Curve

The Phillips curve shows the relationship between the rate of increase of wages and the level of unemployment.

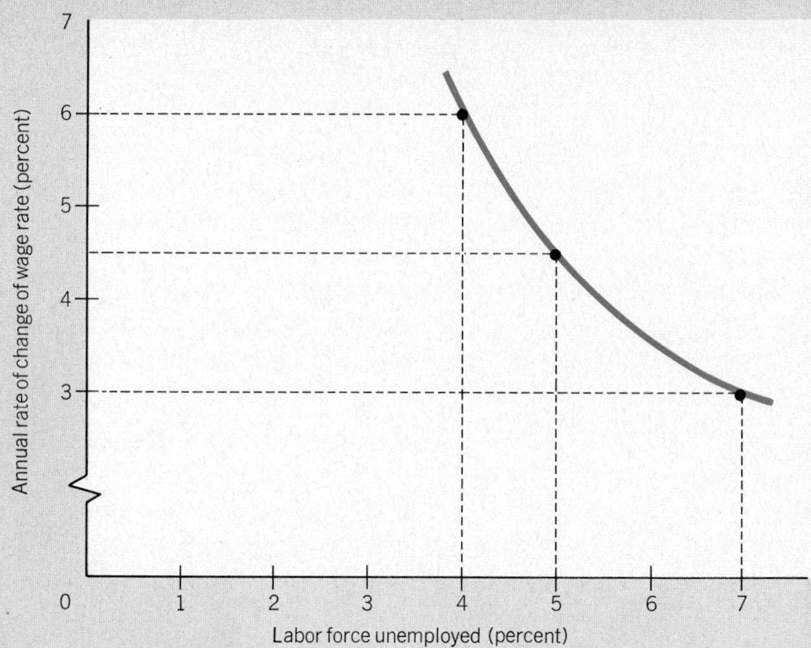

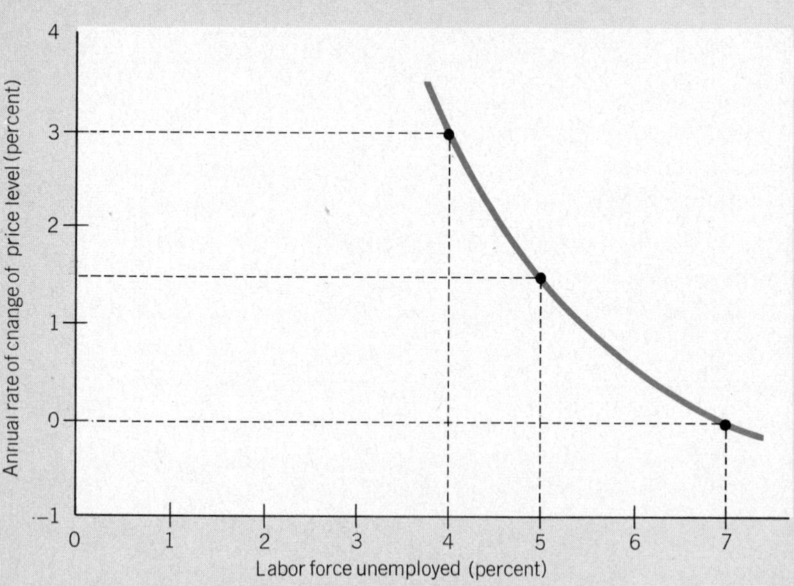

Figure 15.7
Relationship between Unemployment Rate and Rate of Inflation

This relationship can, under the conditions specified in the text, be deduced from the Phillips curve.

This says no more than that total cost per unit of output equals total cost per manhour times the number of manhours divided by the number of units of output. But $C \times M \div O$ equals $C \div (O/M)$. Thus, total cost per unit of output equals total cost per manhour divided by output per manhour.

Since the rate of increase of a ratio is the rate of increase of the numerator minus the rate of increase of the denominator, it follows that the rate of increase of total cost per unit of output equals the rate of increase of total cost per manhour minus the rate of increase of output per manhour. To see the implications of this result suppose that the rate of increase of total cost per manhour equals the rate of increase of wages, and that the rate of increase of labor productivity is 3 percent per year. Then the rate of increase of prices equals the rate of increase of wages minus 3 percent. Consequently, the relationship between the rate of increase in prices and the level of unemployment is as shown in Figure 15.7.

There is, of course, a simple relationship between the curve in Figure 15.6 and the curve in Figure 15.7. The curve in Figure 15.7 (which shows the relationship between *price* increases and unemployment) is always 3 percentage points below the curve in Figure 15.6 (which shows the relationship between *wage* increases and unemployment). Why? Because the rate of increase of prices—under the assumptions set forth above—always equals the rate of increase of wages minus 3 percent.

At this point it should be clear that the curve in Figure 15.7 is none other than the curve encountered before, in Figure 8.3. Our present discussion has added an account of how this relationship is related to, and based on, the Phillips curve.

Shifts in the Phillips Curve

Before we get too impressed by the apparent accuracy of the Phillips curve, we must remind ourselves that the world is more complicated than Figure 15.7 indicates. In fact, predictions based on this curve may be quite wrong. Why? Because the Phillips curve can shift over time. For example, it may shift from position 1 to position 2 in Figure 15.8, (on the next page) thus causing the relationship between the rate of price increase and unemployment to shift from position 1 to position 2 in Figure 15.9. If you make a prediction based on the curve's being in position 1 in Figure 15.9, when in fact it is in position 2, you can make a substantial mistake. For example, suppose that you want to predict the rate of price increase if unemployment is 5 percent. Assuming that the curve is in position 1, you will predict a 1 percent increase in prices, but in fact there will be a 3 percent increase. The moral is clear enough: we need to look at the factors that can cause the Phillips curve to move.

One of the most important factors that can shift the Phillips curve is education or training. As more and more of the labor force is trained and equipped with relevant and basic skills, there is less upward pressure on wages at any level of unemployment. An important reason why wages are pushed upward as unemployment falls is that the economy tends to run out of skilled workers, so that poorly educated and untrained workers constitute a large percentage of the unemployed. When aggregate demand gets strong enough to absorb these workers, other workers experience so strong a demand that their wages are pushed up. Thus it follows that programs to train the labor force, particularly the unemployed, will shift the Phillips curve downward. That is, the rate of increase of wages associated with a given level of unemployment will fall.

Increased mobility of workers will also shift the Phillips curve. As the labor force becomes able and willing to move from place to place, there is less pressure on wages at any level of unemployment. Thus it follows that measures designed to increase the mobility of workers—such as employment services and preferential tax treatment of moving expenses—tend to shift the Phillips curve downward. Still another factor that will shift the Phillips curve is reduced discrimination against blacks, women, and others who historically have fared poorly in the labor force. With intense discrimina-

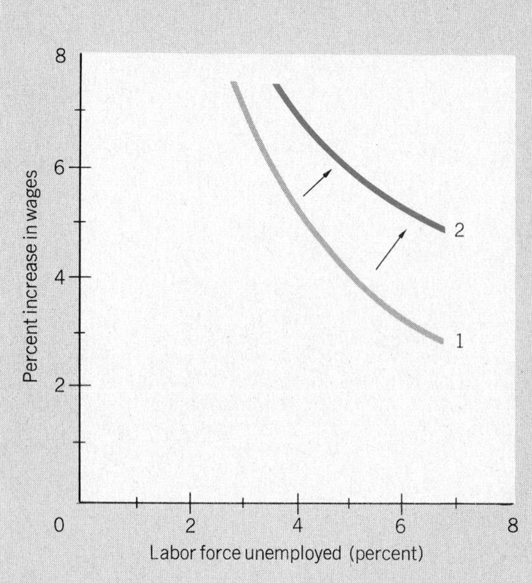

Figure 15.8
Shift in Phillips Curve

The Phillips curve can shift over time, as from position 1 to position 2.

tion, labor markets must be very tight (and wages must be under considerable upward pressure) to make employers willing to hire women, blacks, and other minorities. With less discrimination, there is less upward pressure on wages at any level of unemployment, because the minorities are now in a position to compete on a more equal basis with other workers. Thus, reductions in discrimination tend to shift the Phillips curve downward. The Phillips curve can also be shifted by changes over time in the demographic composition of the labor force (such as the proportion of women, teenagers, or blacks), as well as by changes in the bargaining power of unions.

Last but by no means least, another important factor in shifting the Phillips curve is the nature of people's expectations. If people expect a great deal of inflation, this will be reflected in the wage demands of labor (and the pricing policies of management). Thus, wages will rise more rapidly at a given unemployment level than if people expect less inflation. In other words, the more inflation people expect, the further upward and out from the origin the Phillips curve is likely to be. And the less inflation people expect, the further downward and close to the origin the Phillips curve will be. If we experience a great deal of inflation—as we did in the late 1960s—the Phillips curve is likely to be pushed upward because it is likely that people will come to expect inflation to continue. This phenomenon undoubtedly was important in explaining our experience with high unemployment and high rates of inflation in the early 1970s.

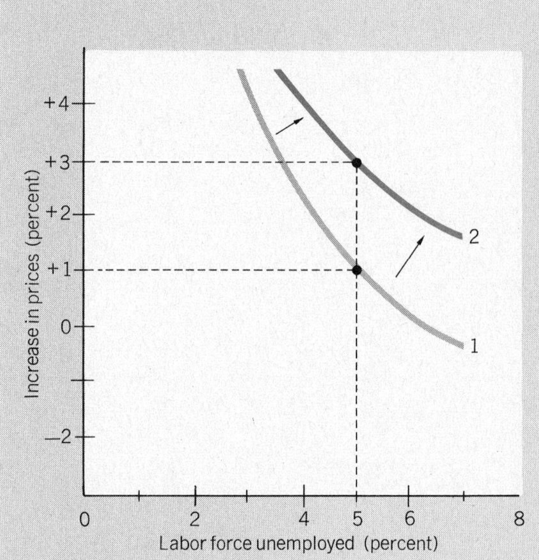

Figure 15.9
Shift in Relationship between Price Increase and Unemployment Rate.

If the Phillips curve shifts, as in Figure 15.8, the relationship between the unemployment rate and the rate of inflation will shift from position 1 to position 2.

Given these and other factors, the Phillips curve in one economy is likely to differ from that in another economy. It is interesting that, during the early 1960s, the annual rate of increase of prices was about 5 percent in Italy, about 3½ percent in Austria, and about 2 percent in Belgium. Yet all three countries had about 3 or 4 percent of the labor force unemployed. Apparently, the Phillips curve was higher in Italy than in Austria, and higher in Austria than in Belgium, in part because of the effects of the factors discussed in this section.

The Phillips Curve: Short versus Long Run

According to some economists, among them Milton Friedman of the University of Chicago and Edmund Phelps of Columbia, the Phillips curve in Figure 15.6 is only a short-run relationship. In the long run, the Phillips curve is vertical, as shown in panel A of Figure 15.10. Thus, expansionary monetary and fiscal policies that result in inflation will only reduce unemployment temporarily. The only permanent way to reduce it is through manpower and training policies that will make the unemployed better suited to the available jobs. This is because labor comes to recognize that its wage gains are being eroded by inflation, so that it builds its expectations of inflation into its wage demands, thus pushing the Phillips curve upward and outward from the origin. Eventually, labor bargains with reference to the real, not the money wage.

This challenge to the conventional Phillips curve has itself been challenged by many economists. (This entire area is one of continuing controversy.) As indicated by panel B of Figure 15.10, there may be a range of unemployment, perhaps above 5 percent, where an inverse relationship exists in the long run betweeen unemployment and inflation; but below this range, the Phillips curve may be essentially vertical. This view has been put forth by Yale's James Tobin and Northwestern University's Robert Gordon, among others. According to Gordon, "There is a danger zone, perhaps between 4 and 5 percent unemployed. In that zone, monetary and fiscal policies are no longer the right tools to reduce unemployment." Manpower and retraining programs should be used instead.

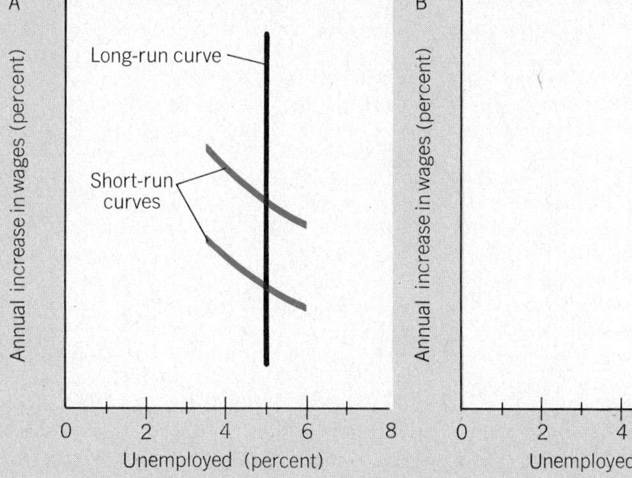

Figure 15.10
The Phillips Curve, Short and Long Run

Some economists argue that the long-run Phillips curve is vertical, as in panel A; others argue that it is shaped like that in panel B.

Price Controls and the Reduction of Market Power: Two Suggested Remedies

The government would, of course, like to shift the Phillips curve downward, for example from position *C* to position *D* in Figure 15.11. Programs to train manpower, increase labor mobility, reduce discrimination, and change expectations can have this effect. Unfortunately, however, programs of this sort take a considerable amount of time to make an impact, and the evidence of recent years seems to indicate that because young people and women make up a larger share of the labor force, the Phillips curve may have shifted upward, not downward. Consequently, the government has been forced to take more direct action in an attempt to shift the Phillips curve.

During World War II—and other wartime emergencies—the government has imposed controls on wages and prices. In other words, the government intervened directly in the market place to see that wages and prices did not increase by more than a certain amount. Some distinguished economists argue that price and wage controls should also be used to control cost-push inflation in peacetime. According to a former president of the American Economic Association:

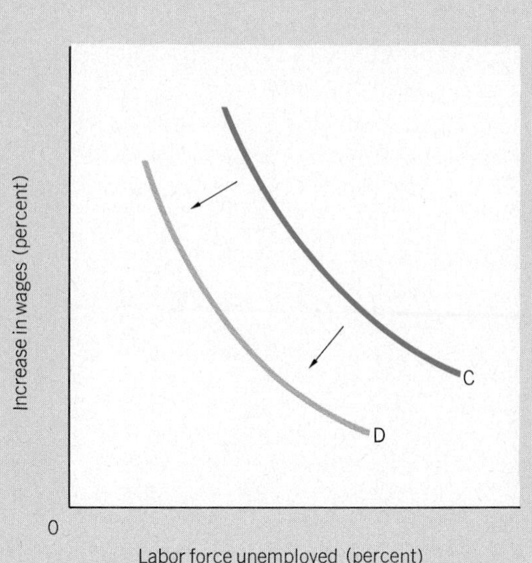

Figure 15.11
Shift in Phillips Curve

The government would like to shift the Phillips curve downward, as from position *C* to position *D*.

> A complete attack on inflation requires that both causes of inflation—both the excess of demand or spending, and the wage-price spiral—be brought under control. . . . The defense against the wage-price spiral (i.e., cost-push inflation) . . . is the direct control over prices and wages. These direct controls are not a substitute for a strong fiscal policy; they perform a different task. . . . To tie down the wage-price spiral, with reasonable justice and equity, we need to do three things. They are (1) Effectively stabilize basic living costs. This is necessary if wages are to be stabilized. (2) Maintain a general ceiling on wages and prices in that part of the economy where wages are determined by collective-bargaining contracts and where prices normally move in response to wage movements. I have reference here to what may properly be called the great industrial core of the American economy—the steel, automobile, electrical goods, construction, transport, and like industries. (3) As a contribution to over-all stability, place firm ceiling prices on basic raw materials.[5]

But most economists do not share this view. The economics profession has little enthusiasm for direct controls of wages and prices, for several reasons. First, such controls are likely to result in a distortion of the allocation of resources. Recall from Chapter 3 our discussion of the functions of the price system in allocating resources. Price and wage controls do not permit prices to perform these functions, and the result is inefficiency and waste.

[5] J. Kenneth Galbraith, Testimony before the Joint Committee on the Economic Report, 82nd Congress, 1st Session.

Second, such controls are likely to be expensive to administer. For example, during the Korean war, the Economic Stabilization Agency had 16,000 employees; and even so, it was difficult to prevent violation or evasion of the controls. Third, there is widespread opposition to detailed government regulation and control of this sort, on the grounds that it impairs our economic freedom. The Council of Economic Advisers undoubtedly spoke for most of the economics profession when it said in 1968:

> The most obvious—and least desirable—way of attempting to stabilize prices is to impose mandatory controls on prices and wages. While such controls may be necessary under conditions of an all-out war, it would be folly to consider them as a solution to the inflationary pressures that accompany high employment under any other circumstance. . . . Although such controls may be unfortunately popular when they are not in effect, the appeal quickly disappears once people live under them.[6]

Another approach to the problem of cost-push inflation is to reduce the market power of unions and firms. Since this market power is the basic cause of cost-push inflation, it would seem logical to attack cost-push inflation in this way. To some extent, the government is, of course, committed to a policy of this sort. Antitrust policy is a basic part of our nation's economic policy. But as we shall see in Chapter 25, antitrust policy is not designed to root out market power in all forms and degrees. This would be foolish in any case, because economies of scale and other considerations require that firms in many industries—to be efficient and innovative—must have a certain amount of market power. Moreover, even when the existing size of firms or concentration of industries cannot be defended on these grounds, the government is not seriously attempting to break up existing firms. Some economists would favor such a policy, both to quell cost-push inflation and to obtain the other advantages (discussed in Chapters 25 and 29) of a competitive economy. But it does not seem at all likely that such a radical—and politically difficult—policy will be adopted.

[6] 1968 *Annual Report* of the Council of Economic Advisers, Washington, D.C.: Government Printing Office, p. 119.

Peacetime Wage and Price Controls under the Nixon Administration

Despite the disadvantages of price controls, the United States was forced to adopt them in the summer of 1971 to stem an inflationary surge that threatened to get out of hand. Though the Nixon administration had been trying to use monetary and fiscal policies to halt inflation, wholesale prices were rising at about 5 percent per year. The wage-price spiral was very much in evidence. Collective bargaining agreements were reached calling for wage increases far in excess of productivity increases, and there was no question but that firms would boost prices in an attempt to cover the resulting increase in costs. Since it took office in 1969, the Nixon administration had been opposed to wage and price guidelines, or wage and price controls, although a number of congressmen and others had suggested the adoption of controls or some form of incomes policy.

However, in August 1971, President Nixon reversed his previous stand. He froze wages and prices for a 3-month period. Then he appointed a 15-member Pay Board and a 7-member Price Commission, both of which were supervised by the government's Cost of Living Council. The Pay Board was given the responsibility of administering wage controls, and the Price Commission was to administer price controls. In November 1971, these two bodies announced their initial policies. The Pay Board stated that pay increases had to be kept under 5.5 percent per year. A company could increase some employees' pay by more than this amount, but other employees would have to get less since total increases could not exceed this figure. The Price Commission ruled that price increases had to be kept under 2.5 percent. Both for prices and wages, exceptions could be made in some areas. Large firms were required to notify the Pay Board and Price Commission of intended wage or price increases. The government tried to avoid constructing a large bureaucracy to enforce the controls by giving the task of enforcing them to the Internal Revenue Service.

During the wage and price freeze in the latter part of 1971, both wages and prices continued to rise, but much more slowly than during early 1971. After the freeze ended, and the system of wage and price controls began to function, inflation seemed to go on at a lower rate than before the freeze. It was by no means stopped (the consumer price index rose by about 3 percent during 1972); but it was less severe than during 1970 or the early part of 1971.[7] In January 1973, the Pay Board and the Price Commission became part of the Cost of Living Council, headed by Harvard's labor economist, John Dunlop. And controls were eliminated or relaxed for most prices and wages, with the major exceptions of health, food, and construction industries. To a considerable extent, the Nixon administration phased out the first peacetime wage and price controls in our history.

Unfortunately, inflation occurred subsequently at a bewildering pace. During the first half of 1973, wholesale prices of farm products and processed foods and feeds rose at the unbelievable rate of 48 percent per year. At the same time, the prices of lumber, fuel, and other industrial goods rose at alarming rates. President Nixon responded by imposing a 60-day freeze on prices (but not wages), beginning in mid-June of 1973. This was only a breather, an interim measure designed to give the administration some time to deal with the serious inflationary pressures that were evident throughout the economy. In August 1973, the administration unveiled its so-called Phase IV program which said that price increases could not exceed cost increases. And in September 1973, steel and auto executives, among others, appeared before the Cost of Living Council to try to justify price increases. How much effect the Phase IV program will have on inflation is difficult at present to say.

[7] In particular, see B. Bosworth, "Phase II: The U.S. Experiment with an Incomes Policy" and R. Gordon, "Wage-Price Controls and the Shifting Phillips Curve" in *Brookings Papers on Economic Activity,* 1972, No. 2.

Incomes Policies

Most economists regard neither direct controls nor the reduction of market power as effective, practical devices to fight cost-push inflation. Faced with this fact, there has been considerable interest, both here and abroad, in using incomes policies to stem cost-push inflation. According to one common definition, an ***incomes policy*** contains three elements. *First, it has some targets for wages (and other forms of income) and prices for the economy as a whole.* For example, the target may be to stabilize the price level, or to permit the consumer price index to increase by less than 2 percent per year, or to allow wage increases not exceeding a certain percentage.

Second, an incomes policy gives particular firms and industries some more detailed guides for decision making on wages (and other forms of income) and prices. These guides are set in such a way that the overall targets for the entire economy will be fulfilled. For example, if the aim is price stability, these guides tell firms and unions what kinds of decisions are compatible with this target. To be useful, the guides must be specific and understandable enough to be applied in particular cases. There obviously is little point in telling firms and unions to avoid "inflationary" wage and price decisions if they don't know whether a particular decision is "inflationary" or not.

Third, an incomes policy contains some mechanisms to get firms and unions to follow the guides. An incomes policy differs from price and wage controls in that it seeks to induce firms and unions to follow these guides voluntarily. But if it is to have any effect, clearly the government must be prepared to use certain forms of "persuasion" beyond moral suasion. In fact, governments sometimes have publicly condemned decisions by firms and unions that were regarded as violating the guides. Government stockpiles of materials and government purchasing policies have also been used to penalize or reward particular firms and industries. Other pressures too have been brought to bear in an attempt to induce firms to follow the established guides.

An example of an incomes policy in the United States was the so-called Kennedy-Johnson guidelines. Although earlier administrations (for example, the Eisenhower and Truman administrations) had often appealed to business and labor to limit wage and price increases, the first systematic attempt at a fairly specific incomes policy in the United States occurred during the Kennedy administration. In 1961, President Kennedy's Council of Economic Advisers issued the following wage-price guidelines:

> The general guide for noninflationary wage behavior is that the rate of increase in wage rates (including fringe benefits) in each industry be equal to the trend rate of *over-all productivity advance.* General acceptance of this guide would maintain stability of labor cost per unit of output for the economy as a whole—though not of course for individual industries. The general guide for noninflationary price behavior calls for price reduction if the industry's rate of productivity increase exceeds the overall rate—for this would mean declining unit labor costs; it calls for an appropriate increase in price if the opposite relationship prevails; and it calls for stable prices if the two rates of productivity increase are equal.[8]

To see just what this meant, let's consider prices and wages in the auto industry. Suppose that labor productivity in the economy as a whole was increasing at 3.2 percent per year. Then according to the guidelines, *wages in the automobile industry should increase by 3.2 percent per year.* If labor productivity in the auto industry increased by 4.2 percent per year, then, applying the results of a previous section, the labor cost of producing a unit of output would decrease by 1 percent per year in the auto industry (since the 3.2 percent rate of increase of wages minus the 4.2 percent rate of increase of labor productivity equals −1 percent). Thus, the guidelines specified that *prices in the auto industry should decrease,* perhaps by about 1 percent per year.

The Council of Economic Advisers specified several situations where these general guidelines would have to be modified. In particular, if there was a shortage of labor in a particular industry or if an industry's wages were lower than those earned elsewhere by similar labor, higher wage increases (than specified in general) would be warranted. Or if an industry's profits were insufficient to attract needed infusions of capital, or if an industry's nonwage costs rose greatly, higher price increases than specified in general would be justified. However, the Council did not attempt to set forth detailed, quantitative provisions about the extent to which higher wages or prices would be warranted under these circumstances.

The Steel Price Increase of 1962: A Case Study

To conform to our definition of an incomes policy, the Kennedy-Johnson wage-price policy had to have an overall target, more detailed guides for wage and price decisions, and a mechanism to get firms and unions to observe these guides. The overall target was the stabilization of prices, and the more detailed guides for price and wage decisions were described in the previous section. But what about the mechanisms to induce acceptance of these guides? How did the government get industry and labor to go along?

The famous confrontation in 1962 between President Kennedy and the steel industry is an interesting case study of how pressure was brought to bear. Before the wage-price guidelines were issued, President Kennedy asked the major steel companies to avoid raising prices, and no price increases occurred. Then after the issuance of the

[8] 1962 *Annual Report of the Council of Economic Advisers,* Washington, D.C.: Government Printing Office, p. 189.

guidelines, he asked the steel union for restraint in the wage negotiations coming up in March 1962. Arthur Goldberg, Kennedy's Secretary of Labor, played an important role in persuading the union to accept a 2.5 percent increase in compensation, which was clearly noninflationary. At this point, government and the press felt quite optimistic about the apparent success of the President's program.

In the week following the wage agreement, however, the United States Steel Corporation increased all its prices by 3½ percent, and most of the major steel companies followed suit. The price increase was clearly a violation of the president's guidelines. It almost seemed as if the steel companies were trying to demonstrate once and for all that pricing was up to them, and them alone. Their action elicited a wrathful speech by the president publicly denouncing them. Roger M. Blough, chairman of the United States Steel Corporation, tried to rebut the president's arguments by claiming that U. S. Steel's profits were too low to attract new capital.

Three of the major steel producers—Armco, Inland, and Kaiser—did not follow U. S. Steel's lead in the day or so after its price increase. Government officials, noting this fact as well as prior public arguments against price increases by Inland officials, quickly began to apply pressure on these three producers to hold their prices constant. Government officials who knew executives of these firms called them and tried to persuade them to do so. The firms were also informed that government contracts would be directed to firms that held their prices constant. Apparently, the government's campaign succeeded. Inland and Kaiser made public statements that they would not raise prices. Faced with this fact, the other steel companies had no choice but to rescind the price increase.

This is an example of how presidential pressure can induce firms to go along with the guidelines. Often the Council of Economic Advisers tried to head off price increases before they were announced. In one way or another, sometimes from the companies themselves, the Council often learned of an impending price increase. The Council then asked the firms to meet to discuss the situation. In these meetings, the Council explained the importance of price stability and both parties discussed the proposed increase. It is difficult, of course, to measure the impact of such discussions, but, according to the Council, they sometimes resulted in the postponement or reduction of the planned price increases.

The Kennedy-Johnson Guidelines: Criticism and Experience

Soon after the announcement of the guidelines, critics began to point out problems in them. The criticism was of several types. First, some observers feared that the guidelines would result in inefficiency and waste. In a free-enterprise economy, we rely on price changes to direct resources into the most productive uses and to signal shortages or surpluses in various markets. If the guidelines were accepted by industry and labor, prices would not be free to perform this function. Of course, the guidelines specified that modifications of the general rules could be made in case of shortages, but critics of the guidelines felt that this escape hatch was too vague to be very useful.

Second, many observers were concerned about the reduction in economic freedom. Of course, the guidelines were presented in the hope that they would be observed voluntarily. But a time was sure to come when they would be in serious contradiction with the interests of firms and unions. In such a situation, what would happen if the firms or unions decided not to follow them? To the extent that the government applied pressure on the firms or unions, there would certainly be a reduction in economic freedom; and to some observers, it seemed likely that the next step might well be direct government controls. Moreover, the non-legislated character of the guidelines and the arbitrary choice of whom to pursue by the government raised important questions of a political nature.

Third, many people felt that the guidelines really

were not workable. In other words, even if the public would go along with them, in many cases they would be impossible to use, because accurate and relevant data on changes in labor productivity in particular industries were often unobtainable, and the situations where exceptions were allowed were so vaguely specified.

Fourth, some economists felt that reliance on the guidelines was dangerous because it focused attention on symptoms rather than causes, of inflation. In their view, inflation was largely the result of improper monetary and fiscal policies. In other words, the basic causes had to be laid at the government's own door. But by setting up guidelines, the government seemed to be saying that the fault lay with industry and labor. Thus, some critics felt that the guidelines tended to cloud the real issues and to let the government escape responsibility for its actions.

After the government's bout with the steel industry in 1962, there was no major public fight over wages and prices for a couple of years; and the government claimed that the guideposts were working well. To a considerable extent, this may have been because the economy still had considerable slack, as well as because of the noninflationary expectations of firms and individuals engendered by several years of relative price stability. By 1965, as labor markets tightened and prices rose in response to the Vietnam buildup (see Chapter 10), it became much more difficult to use the guidelines. Union leaders fought the guidelines tooth and nail, mainly because consumer prices were rising. In various important labor negotiations, unions demanded and got higher wage increases than the guidelines called for. For example, the airline machinists got a 4.9 percent increase in 1966. By 1968, the guidelines were dead: no one was paying any attention to them.

What effect did the guidelines have? Some people claim that they had no real effect at all, while others claim that they reduced cost-push inflation in the early 1960s by a considerable amount. Since it is difficult to separate the effects of the guidelines from the effects of other factors, there is considerable dispute over the question. Considering the level of unemployment in the early 1960s, wages increased less rapidly then than in earlier or later periods. Prices too increased less rapidly during that period—holding unemployment constant—than earlier or later. But whether these developments were due to the guidelines, or to noninflationary expectations or some other factor, is very hard to say.

Perhaps the most important reason why the guidelines broke down was that they could not deal with the strong demand-pull inflation of the late 1960s. Even the strongest defenders of the guidelines are quick to point out that they were no substitute for proper monetary and fiscal policy. *If fiscal or monetary policy is generating strong inflationary pressures, such as existed in the late 1960s, it is foolish to think that guidelines can save the situation.* Perhaps they can cut down on the rate of inflation for a while; but in the long run, the dike is sure to burst. If the guidelines are voluntary, as in this case, firms and unions will ignore them, and the government will find it difficult, if not impossible, to do anything about it. *Even price and wage controls are no adequate antidote to strong inflationary pressures generated by an overly expansive fiscal or monetary policy. Such controls may deal temporarily with the symptoms of inflation, but over the long haul these inflationary pressures will have an effect.*

Economic Stabilization: Where We Stand

Where do we stand in the struggle to achieve full employment without inflation? Clearly, we know much more than we did 40 years ago about how to use monetary and fiscal policies to attain this objective. Given the more advanced state of economics, it is very, very unlikely that a catastrophe like the Great Depression of the 1930s will occur again. But on the other hand, economists were overly optimistic in the mid-1960s when they talked about "fine-tuning" the economy. Our experience since then makes it clear that we have a long way to go before we understand the workings of the economy well enough to achieve continuous full employment without inflation. Equally important, we have seen that, even if the advice of its economists were always correct, the government might still pursue destabilizing policies, as it did in the late 1960s.

Pressed by events, government policy makers have turned to some form of incomes policy to supplement monetary and fiscal policy. Very little is known about the effects of various kinds of incomes policies, and what little we know is not very encouraging. As M.I.T.'s Robert Solow puts it, they "are not the sort of policy you would invent if you were inventing policies from scratch. They are the type of policy you back into as you search for ways to protect an imperfect economy from the worst consequences of its imperfect behavior."[9] Much more research is needed to illuminate the effects of various kinds of incomes policies, as well as the nature of cost-push inflation. In addition, we need more research to clarify the debate between the monetarists and the Keynesians on the effects of monetary and fiscal policy.

Finally, it must be reiterated that the game is well worth the candle. In recent years, it has become fashionable to say that our society's most pressing economic problems are not the attainment of full employment without inflation, but our urban problems, our pollution problems, our racial problems, and our poverty problems. Clearly, these are more visible, but it is hard to see how we can go about solving them with more than patchwork measures if we cannot achieve reasonably full employment with reasonably stable prices. In other words, economic stabilization, although it will not solve all our economic and social problems, is a necessary condition for solving many of them.

[9] R. Solow, "The Case Against the Case Against the Guideposts," reprinted in E. Mansfield, *Economics: Readings, Issues, and Cases,* New York: Norton, 1974. Also, see the papers by Friedman and Burns in the same volume.

Summary

There are many important differences between the policy recommendations of the monetarists and the Keynesians. The monetarists attack the Keynesian view that fiscal policy works as described in Chapter 10. According to the monetarists, whether the government runs a surplus or a deficit does not affect NNP, except insofar as the government finances the deficit or surplus in a way that alters the quantity of money. Also, many leading monetarists favor the establishment of a rule to govern monetary policy, an idea most Keynesians oppose. The Keynesians, on the other hand, attack the monetarist contention that the velocity of money is relatively stable, and argue that the interest rate is more important than the monetarists realize. In general, the Keynesians believe that the monetarists take too simple a view of the economy and that they tend to mix up cause and effect.

An important barrier to achieving economic stability through monetary and fiscal policy is cost-push inflation. The Phillips curve shows the relationship between the rate of increase of wages and the level of unemployment. As might be expected, the rate of increase of wages in any year seems to be inversely related to the level of unemployment. Given the Phillips curve, it is a simple matter to determine the relationship between the rate of inflation and the level of unemployment. If the Phillips curve remains fixed, it poses an awkward dilemma for policy makers. To the extent that they use fiscal and monetary policy to fight unemployment, they fuel the fires of inflation; to the extent that they use monetary and fiscal policy to fight inflation, they contribute to greater unemployment.

The only escape from this dilemma is, of course, to shift the Phillips curve, which is easier said than done. The Phillips curve shifts in response to increased education or training of the work force, increased mobility of workers, reduced discrimination, demographic changes, changes in union bargaining power, and changes in people's expectations. Also, it can shift, at least temporarily, in response to various government policies, such as wartime controls on wages and prices. Although a few economists favor such controls during peacetime, most do not agree. Such controls are likely to distort the allocation of resources, to be difficult and expensive to administer, and to run counter to our desire for economic freedom.

Another way to shift the Phillips curve is to attack market power, but although many economists favor some such action, it does not seem practically or politically feasible. In addition, many countries have experimented with various kinds of incomes policies. An incomes policy contains targets for wages and prices for the economy as a whole, more detailed guides for wage and price decisions in particular industries, and some mechanisms to get firms and unions to follow these guides. The Kennedy-Johnson guidelines were one form of incomes policy.

In the summer of 1971, President Nixon imposed a 3-month freeze on wages and prices. This was the first time the United States had resorted to direct wage and price controls in peacetime. After the freeze, he appointed a Pay Board to administer wage increases and a Price Commission to administer price increases. In the period after the freeze, inflation continued, but at a more modest rate than in previous years. This experiment with price and wage controls was an attempt to shift the Phillips curve. In January 1973, the Nixon administration dismantled most of this system of direct controls over prices and wages. But inflation accelerated at a rapid rate in the first half of 1973, causing the administration to impose another price freeze in June 1973. In August 1973, the administration began its so-called Phase IV program which said that price increases are not supposed to exceed cost increases.

CONCEPTS FOR REVIEW

Monetarists	Classical range	Wage-price spiral	Pay Board
Keynesians	Liquidity trap	Phillips curve	Cost of Living Council
IS curve	Demand-pull inflation	Incomes policy	Price freeze
LM curve	Cost-push inflation	Price Commission	

QUESTIONS FOR DISCUSSION AND REVIEW

1. According to Juanita Kreps, "It is the function of manpower programs to improve the terms of the tradeoff—that is, to shift the Phillips curve to the left." Suggest as many kinds of manpower programs as you can that might help in this regard. What sorts of manpower programs have been launched in this country?

2. According to Milton Friedman, "It is far better that inflation be open than that it be suppressed [by price guidelines]." Do you agree? Why or why not?

3. The Kennedy-Johnson guidelines for noninflationary price behavior called for price reduction if the industry's rate of productivity increase exceeded the overall rate. True or False?

4. The inflations arising from the Revolutionary, Civil, and Vietnam wars were largely a. cost-push. b. demand-pull. c. liquidity-trap.

5. According to *Business Week*, monetarists believe "that the economy itself is inherently stable, that as long as interest rates are kept relatively stable the demand for money will remain stable. . . ." Do you agree? Suggest ways to test this proposition.

PART FIVE

Economic Growth and the Environment

CHAPTER 16

Economic Growth

Until fairly recently in human history, poverty was the rule, not the exception. As Sir Kenneth Clark puts it in his famous lectures on *Civilization:*

> Poverty, hunger, plagues, disease: they were the background of history right up to the end of the nineteenth century, and most people regarded them as inevitable—like bad weather. Nobody thought they could be cured: St. Francis wanted to sanctify poverty, not abolish it. The old Poor Laws were not designed to abolish poverty but to prevent the poor from becoming a nuisance. All that was required was an occasional act of charity.[1]

Clearly, the human condition has changed considerably during the past century, at least in the industrialized nations of the world. Rising living standards have brought a decline in poverty, though by no means its disappearance. How has this increase in per capita output been achieved?

[1] K. Clark, *Civilization,* New York: Harper & Row, 1970.

This question has fascinated economists for a long time. Although we still are far from completely understanding the process of economic growth, our knowledge has increased considerably through the efforts of economic researchers, here and abroad. In this chapter, we discuss the process of economic growth in industrialized countries. A discussion of economic growth in less developed countries will be presented in Chapter 33.

What Is Economic Growth?

There are two common measures of the rate of economic growth. The first is the rate of growth of a nation's real gross national product (or net national product),[2] which tells us how rapidly the economy's total real output of goods and services is increasing. The second is the rate of growth of *per capita* real gross national product (or net national product), which is a better measure of the rate of increase of a nation's standard of living. We shall use the second measure unless we state otherwise.

Two aspects of the rate of growth of per capita real gross national product should be noted from the start. First, *this measure is only a very crude approximation to the rate of increase of economic welfare.* For one thing, gross national product does not include one good that people prize most highly—leisure. For another, gross national product does not value at all accurately new products and improvements in the quality of goods and services, and does not allow properly either for noneconomic changes in the quality of life, nor for the costs of environmental pollution. Nor does gross national product take account of how the available output is distributed. Clearly, it makes a difference whether the bulk of the population gets a reasonable share of the output, or whether it goes largely to a favored few.

Second, *small differences in the annual rate of economic growth can make very substantial differences in living standards a few decades hence.* For example, per capita GNP in the United States was about $4,800 in 1970. If it grows at 2 percent per year, it will be about $8,700 (1970 dollars) in the year 2000, whereas if it grows at 3 percent per year, it will be about $11,600 (1970 dollars) in the year 2000. Thus an increase of 1 percentage point in the growth rate means a $2,900—or 30 percent—increase in per capita GNP in the year 2000. Even an increase of ¼ of 1 percentage point can make a considerable difference. If the growth rate increases from 1¾ percent to 2 percent per year, per capita GNP in the year 2000 will increase from $8,100 to $8,700. Of course, this is no more than simple arithmetic, but that doesn't make it any less important.

Economic Growth as a Policy Objective

Following World War II, governments throughout the world became much more involved in trying to stimulate economic growth. In the United States, the government was not much inclined to influence the growth rate before the war. Of course, the government did many things that had some effect on the rate of economic growth, and in a general sort of way was interested in promoting economic growth. But it was normally taken for granted that, left to its own devices, our economy would manage to grow at more or less the proper rate. In the late 1950s and early 1960s, the climate of opinion began to change. To a considerable extent, this was because the U.S. rate of economic growth during the 1950s was rather low compared to that of other industrialized nations. From 1950 to 1959, per capita GNP grew by about 2 percent per year in the United States, whereas it grew by about 6 percent in Japan, 5 percent in Italy and Germany, 4 percent in France, and 3 percent in the

[2] Either net national product or gross national product will do. As pointed out in Chapter 8, NNP has certain conceptual advantages, but GNP is more frequently used. It makes little difference since they do not differ by much. We use gross national product in this chapter, because data on GNP are more easily available.

Netherlands, Norway, and Sweden. Moreover, our growth rate seemed to be less than that of the Soviet Union, the leading economic power in the Communist world.

During the late 1950s and early 1960s, many American economists and politicians drew attention to these facts, and called for an explicit public policy designed to increase our growth rate. In response, President Kennedy set as a target the attainment of a 4½ percent annual increase in total output during the 1960s. Three principal arguments were given at that time for government stimulation of the rate of economic growth. First, it was argued that we had to increase our rate of economic growth to stay ahead of the Communist countries, the Soviet Union in particular. Economic growth was regarded as important for national defense and national prestige. In 1958, a report by the Rockefeller Brothers Fund concluded that growth was the most feasible way to provide for the defense outlays it envisioned as necessary in the future.

Second, it was argued that we should increase our rate of economic growth in order to increase public expenditures for schools, urban renewal, transportation, hospitals, and other such services. As we saw in Chapter 6, some observers, led by John Kenneth Galbraith, believe that there is serious underinvestment in the public sector. Since it is very difficult politically to increase the percentage of GNP devoted to such services, it was felt that the only realistic way to remedy the situation was to increase the GNP. Then the absolute amount spent on the public sector could increase even if its percentage of GNP remained much the same.

Third, it was argued that we should increase our rate of economic growth in order to impress the neutral nations, many of which are relatively poor, with the benefits of our type of society. The emphasis here, as in the first argument, was on economic competition with the Communist world. According to many observers, the neutral countries were watching the growth rates of the Communist and capitalist countries, and the results would help decide which way these countries jumped. As the Council of Economic Advisers put it in 1962, "The less developed nations . . . need a further demonstration of the ability of a free economy to grow."[3]

Not all economists and policy makers agree that the government should alter the growth rate. Particularly in the past few years, there has been a growing feeling among economists (as well as the public at large) that economic growth should not be force-fed. Those who feel this way fall into two broad groups. One school of economists—including people like the University of Rochester's W. Allen Wallis, a prominent adviser to Presidents Nixon and Eisenhower—believes that the proper rate of economic growth is that which would emerge from private decisions. In their view, there is no reason to "force" growth on the economy, since there is no real possibility that the USSR will catch up with us soon, and the "unmet social needs" argument is little more than a slogan.

Another group of economists—led by E. J. Mishan of the London School of Economics—feels that economic growth, as usually measured, is a mirage. In their view, it has resulted in the degradation of the environment, the congestion and noise of our cities, the ugliness of some of the countryside, and the dullness of much of our work. They argue that the added production is not really of much value to society, and that people must be convinced by producers (through advertising and other sales techniques) that they want it. This viewpoint has appealed to many young people in recent years. However, it should be noted that if we are to reduce poverty, clean up the environment, and improve the quality of life, we shall need productive capacity, and economic growth is an important way to get it.

Whether or not the government should increase the rate of economic growth is, of course, a political decision; and your opinion of such a government policy will depend on many things, including

[3] 1962 *Annual Report of the Council of Economic Advisers,* Washington, D.C.: Government Printing Office, p. 110.

your attitude toward present sacrifice for future material gain. As we shall see in subsequent sections, *a more rapid rate of growth can often be achieved only if consumers are willing to give up some consumption now so that they and their children can have more goods and services in the future.* To the extent that you believe that private decisions place too little weight on the future and too much weight on the present, you may be inclined to support a government policy designed to increase the growth rate. Otherwise you may not favor such a policy. In the next chapter, we shall discuss the pros and cons of economic growth in much more detail. Here we are concerned with its determinants.

Economic Growth, the Product Transformation Curve, and the Aggregate Production Function

To represent the process of economic growth, it is convenient to use the product transformation curve which, as you will recall from Chapter 3, shows all efficient combinations of output an economy can produce. For example, suppose that a society produces only two goods, food and tractors. Then if this society has at its disposal a fixed amount of resources and if technology is fixed, the product transformation curve (like the one in Figure 16.1) shows the maximum quantity of food that can be

Figure 16.1
Product Transformation Curve

The product transformation curve shows all efficient combinations of output an economy can produce.

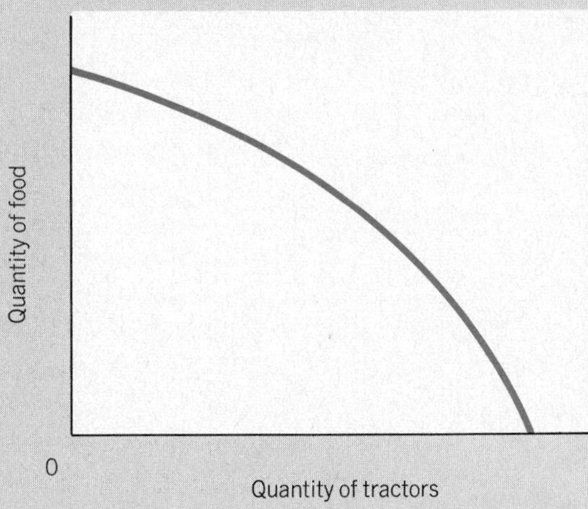

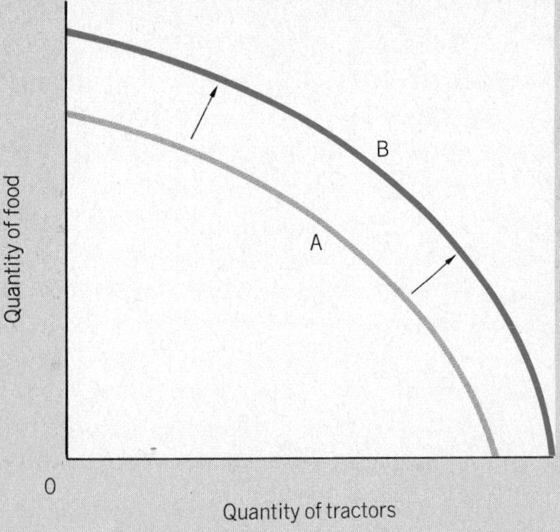

Figure 16.2 Outward Shift of Product Transformation Curve

A nation's potential output increases when its product transformation curve shifts outward, for example, from position *A* to position *B*.

produced, given each amount of tracters produced.

Clearly, *a nation's potential output increases when its product transformation curve shifts outward,* for example, from position A to position B in Figure 16.2. This happens because the society can produce (and consume) more of one good without having to produce (and consume) less of the other good. Thus, its productive capacity must be greater. If the product transformation curve shifts outward, if the economy is efficient, and if population remains constant, per capita GNP increases and economic growth occurs. Moreover, the faster the product transformation curve shifts outward, the greater the rate of economic growth.

In addition, economic growth can occur if unemployment or inefficiency is reduced. If a nation allows some of its resources to be unemployed or under-utilized because of an insufficiency of desired spending, this will cause the economy to operate at a point *inside* the product transformation curve rather than *on* the curve. The same thing will happen if a nation allocates its resources inefficiently. Clearly, a nation can achieve some economic growth by getting closer to the product transformation curve through a reduction in unemployment or inefficiency.

A nation's potential output is directly related to the amount of resources it possesses and the extent to which they are used. These resources, or inputs, are of various kinds, including labor, capital, and land. The relationship between the amount used of each of these inputs and the resulting amount of potential output is often called the ***aggregate production function.*** It is analogous to the production function discussed in Chapter 7, which is the relationship between a firm's inputs and its output. However, the aggregate production function pertains to the entire economy, not a single firm.

Given that a nation's potential output depends on the amount of labor, capital, and land it uses, then the rate of growth of a nation's potential output must depend, in part at least, on the changes that occur in the amount of each of these inputs that is used. For example, if a nation invests heavily in additional capital, we would expect this to result in a substantial increase in potential output. Thus, *a nation's rate of economic growth depends on the extent of the changes in the amounts of the various inputs used.* In addition, *a nation's rate of economic growth depends on the rate of technological change.* The aggregate production function is constructed on the assumption that technology is fixed. Changes in technology result in shifts in the production function, since more output is obtained from a given amount of resources.

The Law of Diminishing Marginal Returns

If a nation's land, labor, and capital increase, one would certainly expect its output to increase as well. But suppose the nation cannot increase the amount used of all of its resources at the same rate. Instead, suppose it can increase the quantity of one resource, say labor, while the amount of other resources, like land, is held constant. In this situation, what will be the effect on output of more and more increases in the amount of the resource that can be augmented? This is an important question, which occurs both in the present context and in the study of the production processes of the business firm.

To help answer it, economists have formulated the famous law of ***diminishing marginal returns,*** which states that, *if more and more of a resource is used, the quantities of other resources being held constant, the resulting increments of output will decrease after some point has been reached.* Note several important things about this law. First, at least one resource must be fixed in quantity. The law of diminishing marginal returns does not apply to cases where there is a proportional increase in all resources. Second, technology is assumed to be fixed. Third, the law of diminishing marginal returns is an empirical generalization that seems to hold in the real world, not a deduction from physical or biological laws.

Table 16.1

The Law of Diminishing Marginal Returns

(1) Manhours of labor (millions)	(2) Bushels of corn (millions)	(3) Marginal product of labor (bushels per manhour)	(4) Average product of labor (bushels per manhour)
1	1.5		1.50
		2.0	
2	3.5		1.75
		2.5	
3	6.0		2.00
		3.0	
4	9.0		2.25
		2.0	
5	11.0		2.20
		2.0	
6	13.0		2.17
		1.0	
7	14.0		2.00
		0.0	
8	14.0		1.75

To illustrate the workings of this law, consider Table 16.1, which shows the total output—or GNP—of a simple agricultural society under a set of alternative assumptions concerning the number of manhours of labor used. For simplicity, we assume that this society produces only one product, corn, so that total output can be measured in bushels of corn. Also, we assume that the amount of land and capital that can be used is fixed in quantity. Column 1 in the table shows various alternative numbers of manhours of labor that can be used with this fixed amount of land and capital. Column 2 shows the total output in each case.

Column 3 shows the additional output resulting from the addition of an extra manhour of labor; this is called the ***marginal product of labor.*** For example, if the quantity of labor is between 2 million manhours and 3 million manhours, the marginal product of labor is 2.5 bushels per manhour of labor, because each extra manhour of labor results in an extra 2.5 bushels of output.

In Table 16.1, the marginal product of labor increases as more and more labor is used, but only up to a point: beyond 4 million manhours of labor, the marginal product of labor goes down as more and more labor is used. Specifically, the marginal product of labor reaches a maximum of 3.0 bushels per manhour when between 3 and 4 million manhours of labor are used. Then it falls to 2.0 bushels per manhour when between 4 and 5 million manhours of labor are used, remains at 2.0 bushels per manhour when between 5 and 6 million manhours of labor are used, and falls once again to 1.0 bushel per manhour when between 6 and 7 million manhours of labor are used.

Thus, as predicted by the law of diminishing marginal returns, the marginal product of labor eventually declines. Moreover, as shown in Column 4 of Table 16.1, the ***average product*** of labor, which is defined as total output per manhour, also falls beyond some point as more and more labor is used with a fixed amount of other resources. This too stems from the law of diminishing marginal returns.

It is easy to see why the law of diminishing marginal returns must be true. For example, imagine what would happen in the simple economy of Table 16.1 if more and more labor were applied to a fixed amount of land. Beyond a point, as more and more labor is used, the extra labor has to be devoted to less and less important tasks, and it is increasingly difficult to prevent the workers from getting in one another's way. For such reasons, one certainly would expect that, beyond some point, extra amounts of labor would result in smaller and smaller increments of output. This is true as well as sensible: there is a lot of evidence for the validity of the law of diminishing marginal returns.

Thomas Malthus and Population Growth

A nation's rate of economic growth depends on, among other things, how much the quantities of inputs of various kinds increases. To illuminate the nature of the growth process, we discuss the effect on the rate of economic growth of increasing each kind of input, holding the others constant. We begin by looking at the effects of changes in the quantity of labor. Economists have devoted a great deal of attention to the effects of population growth on the rate of economic growth. The classic work was done by Thomas Malthus (1776–1834), a British parson who devoted his life to academic research. The first professional economist, he taught at a college established by the East India Company to train its administrators—and was called "Pop" by his students behind his back. Whether "Pop" stood for population or not, Malthus's fame is based on his theories of population growth.

Malthus believed that the population tends to grow at a geometric rate. In his *Essay on Population,* published in 1798, he pointed out the implications of such a constant rate of growth:

> If any person will take the trouble to make the calculation, he will see that if the necessities of life could be obtained without limit, and the number of people could be doubled every twenty-five years, the population which might have been produced from a single pair since the Christian era, would have been sufficient, not only to fill the earth quite full of people, so that four should stand in every square yard, but to fill all the planets of our solar system in the same way, and not only them but all the planets revolving around the stars which are visible to the naked eye, supposing each of them . . . to have as many planets belong to it as our sun has.[4]

In contrast to the human population, which tends to increase at a geometric rate,[5] the supply of land can increase slowly if at all. And land, particularly in Malthus's time, was the source of food. Consequently, it seemed to Malthus that the human population was in danger of outrunning its food supply: "Taking the whole earth," he wrote, ". . . and supposing the present population to be equal to a thousand millions, the human species would increase as the numbers 1, 2, 4, 8, 16, 32, 64, 128, 256, and subsistence as 1, 2, 3, 4, 5, 6, 7, 8, 9. In two centuries, the population would be to the means of subsistence as 256 to 9; in three centuries as 4096 to 13, and in two thousand years the difference would be incalculable."[6]

Certainly, Malthus's view of humanity's prospects was bleak, as he himself acknowledged (in a masterpiece of British understatement) when he wrote that "the view has a melancholy hue." Gone is the optimism of Adam Smith: according to Malthus, the prospects for economic progress are very limited. Given the inexorable increase in human numbers, the standard of living will be kept at the minimum level required to keep body and soul together. If it exceeds this level, the population will increase, driving the standard of living back down. On the other hand, if the standard of living is less than this level, the population

[4] T. Malthus, *Essay on Population,* as quoted by R. Heilbroner, *The Worldly Philosophers,* New York: Simon and Schuster, 1961, p. 71. For those who would like to read more concerning the history of economic thought, Heilbroner's book is highly recommended.

[5] Of course, it does not matter to Malthus's argument whether the population doubles every 25 years or every 40 years: the important thing is that it increases at a geometric rate.

[6] T. Malthus, "The Principle of Population Growth," as reprinted in E. Mansfield, *Economics: Readings, Issues, and Cases,* New York: Norton, 1974.

Thomas Malthus
on Population

Throughout the animal and vegetable kingdoms Nature has scattered the seeds of life abroad with the most profuse and liberal hand; but has been comparatively sparing in the room and the nourishment necessary to rear them.... Necessity, that imperious, all-pervading law of nature, restrains them within the prescribed bounds. The race of plants and the race of animals shrink under this great restrictive law; and man cannot by any efforts of reason escape from it.

In plants and irrational animals, the view of the subject is simple.... The effects of this check on man are more complicated.

It may safely be pronounced that population, when unchecked, goes on doubling itself every twenty-five years, or increases in a geometrical ratio. The rate according to which the productions of the earth may be supposed to increase, will not be so easy to determine. Of this, however, we may be perfectly certain, that the ratio of their increase in a limited territory must be of a totally different nature from the ratio of the increase of population. A thousand millions are just as easily doubled every twenty-five years by the power of population as a thousand. But the food to support the increase from the greater number will by no means be obtained with the same facility. Man is necessarily confined in room. When acre has been added to acre til all the fertile land is occupied, the yearly increase of food must depend upon the melioration of the land already in possession. This is a fund, which, from the nature of all soils, instead of increasing, must be gradually diminishing. But population, could it be supplied with food, would go on with unexhausted vigor; and the increase of one period would furnish the power of a greater increase the next, and this without any limit....

It may be fairly pronounced, therefore, that considering the present average state of the earth, the means of subsistence, under circumstances the most favorable to human industry, could not possibly be made to increase faster than in an arithmetical ratio.... The ultimate check to population appears then to be a want of food, arising necessarily from the different ratios according to which population and food increase.

Thomas Malthus, *An Essay on the Principle of Population*, London: Reeves and Turner, 1888, pp. 4–6. Originally published in 1798.

Figure 16.3
Diminishing Marginal Returns and the Effect of Population Growth

According to Malthus, the labor force will tend to *OP* because, if output per worker exceeds *OA*, population will increase, and if output per worker is less than *OA*, starvation will reduce the population.

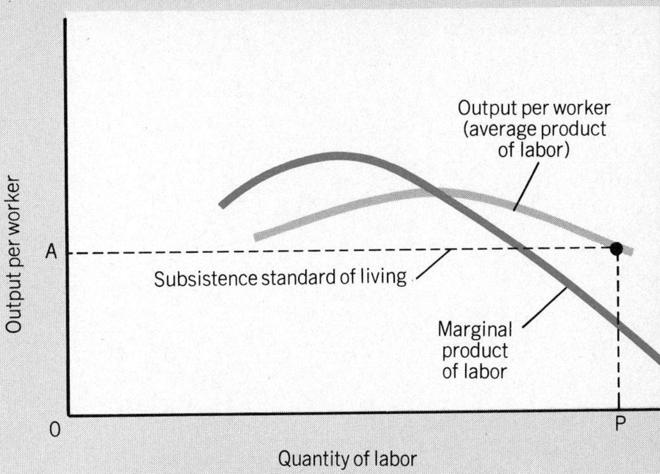

will decline because of starvation. Certainly, the long-term prospects were anything but bright. Thomas Carlyle, the famous historian and essayist, called economics "the dismal science." To a considerable extent, economics acquired this bad name through the efforts of Parson Malthus.

Malthus's theory can be interpreted in terms of the law of diminishing marginal returns. Living in what was still largely an agricultural society, he emphasized the role of land and labor as resources, and assumed a relatively fixed level of technology. Since land is fixed, increases in labor—due to population growth—will eventually cause the marginal product of labor to get smaller and smaller because of the law of diminishing marginal returns. In other words, because of this law, the marginal product of labor will behave as shown in Figure 16.3, with the result that continued growth of the labor force will ultimately bring economic decline —that is, a reduction in output per worker. This happens because as the marginal product of labor falls with increases in the labor force, the average product of labor will eventually fall as well—and the average product of labor is another name for output per worker.

Of course, Malthus recognized that various devices could keep the population down—war, famine, birth control measures, among others. In fact, he tried to describe and evaluate the importance of various checks on population growth. For example, suppose that population tends to grow to the point where output per worker is at a subsistence level—just sufficient to keep body and soul together. If this is the case, and if the subsistence level of output per worker is *OA*, then the labor force will tend to equal *OP* in Figure 16.3. Why? Because, as noted above, Malthus believed that if the standard of living rises appreciably above *OA*, population will increase, thus forcing it back toward *OA*. On the other hand, if the standard of living falls below *OA*, some of the population will starve, thus pushing it back toward *OA*.

Effects of Population Growth

Was Malthus right? Among the less developed nations of the world, his analysis seems very relevant today. During the past 30 years, the population of the less developed nations has grown very rapidly, in part because of the decrease in death rates attributable to the transfer of medical advances from the industrialized countries to the less developed coun-

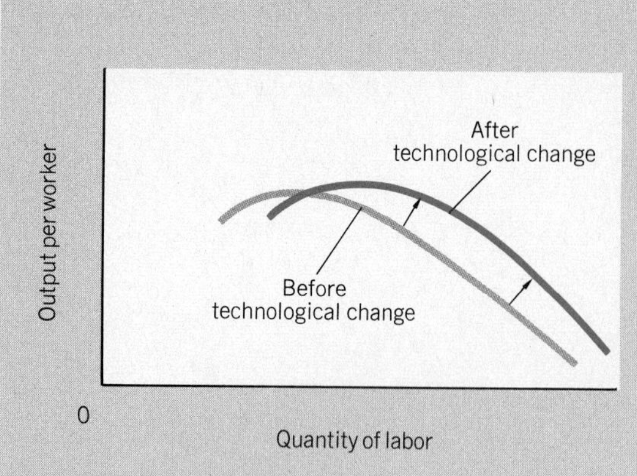

Figure 16.4
Shift over Time in the Marginal Product of Labor

Technological change has shifted the marginal-product-of-labor curve to the right.

tries. Between 1940 and 1970, the total population of Asia, Africa, and Oceania almost doubled. There has been a tendency for growing populations to push hard against food supplies in some of the countries of Africa, Latin America, and Asia; and the Malthusian model can explain important elements of the situation.

However Malthus's theory seems far less relevant or correct for the industrialized countries. In contrast to his model, population has not increased to the point where the standard of living has been pushed down to the subsistence level. On the contrary, the standard of living has increased dramatically in all of the industrialized nations. The most important mistake Malthus made was to underestimate the extent and importance of technological change. Instead of remaining fixed, the marginal-product-of-labor curve in Figure 16.3 moved gradually to the right, as new methods and new products increased the efficiency of agriculture. In other words, the situation was as shown in Figure 16.4. Thus, as population increased, the marginal product of labor did not go down. Instead, technological change prevented the productivity of extra agricultural workers from falling.

Among the industralized nations, have countries with relatively high rates of growth of population had relatively low—or relatively high—rates of economic growth? In general, there seems to be little or no relationship between a nation's rate of population increase and its rate of economic growth. For example, Figure 16.5 plots the rate of population increase against the rate of growth of output per manyear in 11 industrialized nations between 1913 and 1959. The results suggest that there is little or no relation between them; and the relationship that exists appears to be direct rather than inverse.

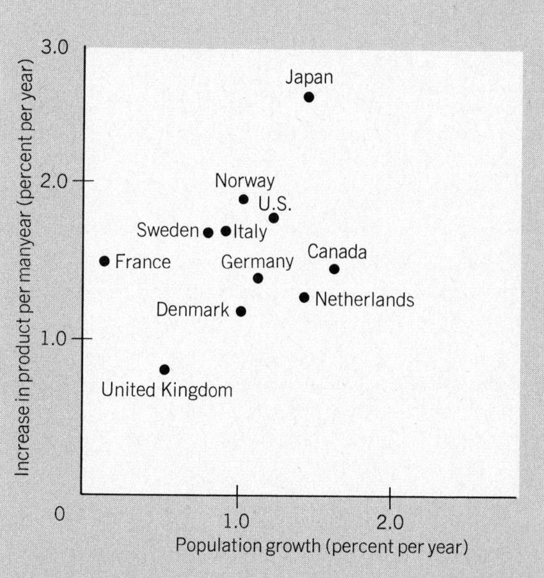

Figure 16.5
Relationship between Population Growth and Increases in National Product per Manyear, 11 Industrialized Nations, 1913–59

In industrialized nations, there is little or no relationship between a nation's rate of population growth and its rate of economic growth.

David Ricardo: Trade and Economic Growth

A contemporary and good friend of Malthus who also contributed to the theory of economic growth was David Ricardo (1772–1823). Of all the titans of economics, he is probably least known to the general public. Smith, Malthus, Marx, and Keynes are frequently encountered names. Ricardo is not, although he made many brilliant contributions to economic thought. An extremely successful stockbroker who retired at the age of 42 with a very large fortune, he devoted much of his time to highly theoretical analyses of the economic system and its workings. In contrast to Malthus, who was reviled for his pessimistic doctrines, Ricardo and his writings were widely admired in his own time. He was elected to the House of Commons and was highly respected there.

Ricardo was concerned in much of his work with the distribution of income. Unlike Adam Smith, who paid much less attention to the conflict among classes, Ricardo emphasized the struggle between the industrialists—a relatively new and rising class in his time—and the landowners—the old aristocracy that resisted the rise of the industrial class. This clash was reflected in the struggle in Britain around 1800 over the so-called Corn Laws ("corn" being a general term covering all types of grain). Because of the increase in population, the demand for grain increased in Britain, causing the price of grain to rise greatly. This meant higher profits for the landowners. But the industrialists complained bitterly about the increase in the price of food, because higher food prices meant that they had to pay higher wages. As the price of grain increased, merchants began to import cheap grain from abroad. But the landowners, who dominated Parliament, passed legislation—the Corn Laws—to keep cheap grain out of Britain. In effect, the Corn Laws imposed a high tariff or duty on grain.

According to Ricardo's analysis, the landlords were bound to capture most of the benefits of economic progress, unless their control of the price of grain could be weakened. As national output increased and population expanded, poorer and poorer land had to be brought under cultivation to produce the extra food. As the cost of producing grain increased, its price would increase too—and so would the rents of the landlords. The workers and the industrialists, on the other hand, would benefit little, if at all. As the price of grain increased, the workers would have to get higher wages—but only high enough to keep them at a subsistence level (since Ricardo agreed entirely with his friend Malthus on the population issue). Thus, the workers would be no better off; and neither would the industrialists, who would wind up with lower profits because of the increase in wage rates.

Ricardo felt that the Corn Laws should be repealed and that free trade in grain should be permitted. In a beautiful piece of theoretical analysis that is still reasonably fresh and convincing 150 years after its publication, he laid out the basic principles of international trade and pointed out the benefits to all countries that can be derived by specialization and free trade. For example, suppose that England is relatively more efficient at producing textiles, and France is relatively more efficient at producing wine. Then, on the basis of Ricardo's analysis, it can be shown that each country is likely to be better off by specializing in the product it is more efficient at producing—textiles in England, wine in France—and trading this product for the one the other country specializes in producing. In Chapter 30, we shall discuss this argument in considerable detail; it is a very important part of economics.

Ricardo's View of Capital Formation

Let's turn now to the effect on economic growth of increases in physical capital, holding other inputs and technology fixed. Ricardo constructed some interesting theories concerning the effects of capi-

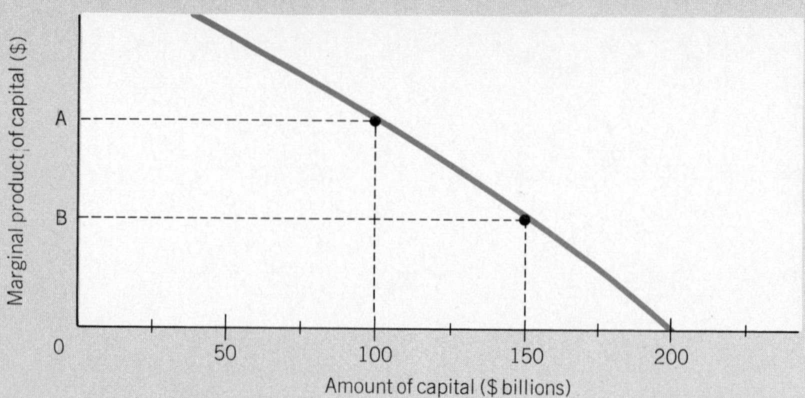

Figure 16.6
Marginal Product of Capital

This curve shows the marginal product of capital, under various assumptions concerning the total amount of capital. For example, if there is $100 billion of capital, the marginal product of capital is $*A*, whereas if there is $150 billion of capital, the marginal product of capital is $*B*.

tal formation—i.e., investment in plant and equipment—on economic growth. Other things held constant, a nation's output depends on the amount of plant and equipment that it has and operates. Moreover, one can draw a curve showing the marginal product of capital—the extra output that would result from an extra dollar's worth of capital—under various assumptions about the total amount of capital in existence. This curve will slope downward to the right, as shown in Figure 16.6, because of the law of diminishing marginal returns. As more and more capital is accumulated, its marginal product eventually must decrease. For example, if $100 billion is the total investment in plant and equipment (or total capital), the extra output to be derived from an extra dollar of investment is worth $*A*; whereas if the total investment is increased to $150 billion, the economy must resort to less productive investments, and the extra output to be derived from an extra dollar of investment is only worth $*B*.

The curve in Figure 16.6 leads to the conclusion that investment in plant and equipment, although it will increase the growth rate up to some point, will eventually be unable to increase it further. As more and more is invested in new plant and equipment, less and less productive projects must be undertaken. Moreover, when all the productive projects have been carried out, further investment in plant and equipment will be useless. At this point—$200 billion of total capital in Figure 16.6—further investment in plant and equipment will not increase output at all.

This kind of analysis led Ricardo to the pessimistic conclusion that the economy would experience decreases in the profitability of investment in plant and equipment, and eventual termination of economic growth. Also, he expected increases in the ratio of capital to output, because he expected increases in the total amount of capital to be accompanied by decreases in the marginal product of capital. To illustrate this, suppose that an economy's output equals $1 trillion and its total capital is $3 trillion. Suppose too that $100 billion of extra capital will result in $30 billion in extra output, another $100 billion of extra capital will result in $20 billion in extra output, and still another $100 billion in extra capital will result in $10 billion in extra output. Then the capital-output ratio will be (3,000 + 100)/(1,000 + 30) if $100 billion is invested, (3,000 + 200)/(1,000 + 50) if $200 billion is invested, and (3,000 + 300)/(1,000 + 60) if $300 billion is invested. Since the marginal product of capital is decreasing, the capital-output ratio is increasing—from 3 to 3.01 to 3.05 to 3.11.

Was Ricardo right? Have we experienced increases in the capital-output ratio, decreases in the profitability of investment in plant and equipment, and eventual termination of economic growth? Clearly, no. Ricardo, like Malthus, was led astray by underestimating the extent and impact of future changes in technology. Suppose that, because of the development of major new products and processes, lots of new opportunities for profitable investment arise. Obviously, the effect on the curve in Figure 16.6 is to shift it to the right, because there are more investment opportunities than before above a certain level of productivity. But if this curve shifts to the right, as shown in Figure 16.7, we may be able to avoid Ricardo's pessimistic conclusions.

To see how this can occur, note that, if *XX′* in Figure 16.7 is the relevant curve in a particular year and if $100 billion is the total amount of capital, an extra dollar of investment in plant and equipment would have a marginal product of $*C*. A decade later, if *YY′* is the relevant curve and if the total amount of capital has grown to $150 billion, the marginal product of an extra dollar of investment in plant and equipment is still $*C*. Thus, there is no reduction in the productivity of investment opportunities despite the 50 percent increase in the total amount of capital. Because of technological change and other factors, productive and profitable new investment opportunities are opened up as fast as old ones are invested in.

The history of the United States is quite consistent with this sort of shift in investment opportunities over time. Even though we have poured an enormous amount of money into new plant and equipment, we have not exhausted or reduced the productivity or profitability of investment opportunities. The rate of return on investment in new plant and equipment has not fallen. Instead, it has fluctuated around a fairly constant level during the past 70 years. Moreover, the capital-output ratio has remained surprisingly constant. It has not increased.

Effects of Capital Formation

To see more clearly the role of investment in the process of economic growth, let's extend the Keynesian model we discussed in Chapter 9. Suppose we ignore the government and consider only the private sector of the economy. Suppose that the full-employment, noninflationary NNP this year

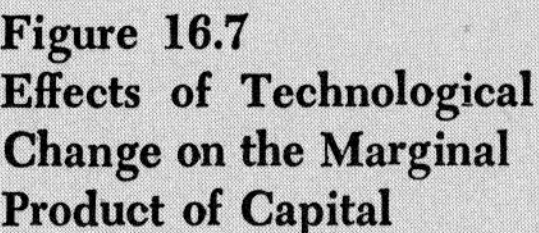

Figure 16.7
Effects of Technological Change on the Marginal Product of Capital

Technological change has shifted the marginal-product-of-capital curve to the right.

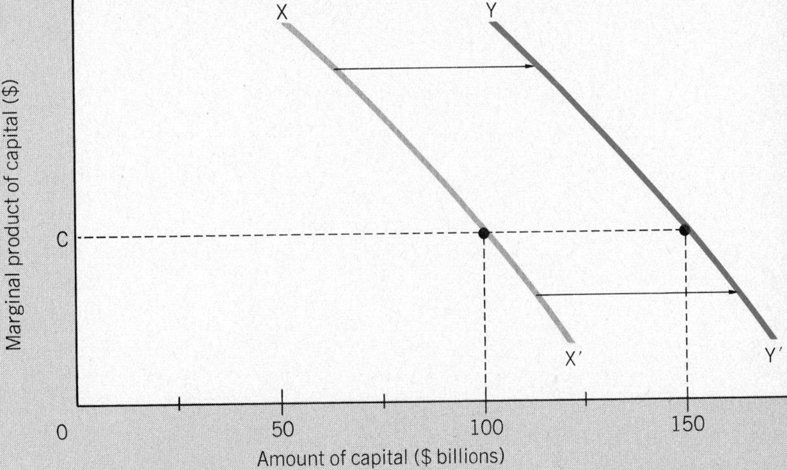

is $1,000 billion, and that the consumption function is such that consumption expenditure is $900 billion if NNP is $1,000 billion. If desired investment this year is $100 billion, with the result that NNP is in fact $1,000 billion, *next year's full-employment NNP will increase because this year's investment will increase the nation's productive capacity*. In other words, this year's investment increases next year's full-employment NNP. The amount of the increase in full-employment NNP depends on the ***capital-output ratio,*** which is the number of dollars of extra investment required to produce an extra dollar of output. For example, if the capital-output ratio is 2, $2 of investment is required to increase full-employment NNP by $1.

Let's look more closely at the effect of investment on full-employment NNP. If the capital-output ratio is 2, full-employment NNP will increase by $50 billion as a consequence of the $100 billion of investment: thus, full-employment NNP next year is $1,050 billion. On the other hand, suppose that this year's investment is $200 billion rather than $100 billion, and that the consumption function is such that consumption expenditure is $800 billion rather than $900 billion if NNP is $1,000 billion. What will full-employment NNP be next year? If the capital-output ratio is 2, it will be $1,100 billion. Thus, the full-employment NNP will be larger if investment is $200 billion than if it is $100 billion.

In general, the greater the percent of NNP that the society devotes to investment this year, the greater will be the increase in its full-employment NNP. Thus, *so long as the economy sustains noninflationary full employment and the capital-output ratio remains constant, the rate of growth of national output will be directly related to the percent of NNP devoted to investment.*[7]

[7] It can be shown that the rate of growth of NNP equals s/b, where s is the proportion of NNP that is saved (and invested), and b is the capital-output ratio, assuming that both s and b are constant and that full employment is maintained. For example, if b is 2 and $s = .10$, NNP will grow at 5 percent per year, since $.10/2 = .05$. This result is part of the so-called Harrod-Domar growth model developed by Sir Roy Harrod of Oxford and Evsey Domar of M.I.T. Although useful, this result must be used with caution since it is based on highly simplified assumptions.

Table 16.2

Rate of Growth of Output per Man and Percent of GNP Invested in Physical Capital, 1955–64

Nation	Rate of growth of output per man	Percent of GNP invested
	Annual Average	
France	4.7%	15.7%
Germany	4.4	20.1
Italy	5.7	16.9
Japan	8.8	30.2
United Kingdom	2.6	13.7
United States	1.9	13.9

Source: Angus Maddison, *Lloyds Bank Review,* January 1966 and E. Phelps, *The Goal of Economic Growth,* revised edition, Norton, 1969.

Certainly, this result seems sensible enough. If a country wants to increase its growth rate, it should produce more blast furnaces, machine tools, and plows, and less cosmetics, household furniture, and sports cars. But all this is theory. What do the facts suggest? Table 16.2 shows the rate of investment and the growth rate in the six major industrialized nations of the non-Communist world in 1955–64. The growth rate was highest in Japan, so was the investment rate. The growth rates were lowest in the United States and the United Kingdom, and so were the investment rates. Of course, this does not prove that there is any simple cause-and-effect relationship between the investment rate and the growth rate, but it certainly is compatible with the view that investment influences growth.

Turning to the historical record of the United States, between 1929 and 1947 the amount of U.S. plant and equipment increased at about the same rate as the labor force. On the other hand, between 1947 and 1965, the amount of U.S. plant and equipment increased much more rapidly than the labor force. These facts would lead one to expect that the rate of economic growth would be more rapid in the latter period; and, in keeping with the theory, this turns out to be true. Again, one must be cautious about interpreting such comparisons. Lots of other things besides the investment rate were different in 1947–65 than in 1929–47, and these other things, not the investment rate, may have been responsible for the difference in growth rates. However, it seems likely that the difference in investment rates was at least partially responsible.

The Role of Human Capital

A nation's rate of economic growth is influenced by the rate at which it invests in human capital as well as physical capital. It may seem odd to speak of *human* capital, but every society builds up a certain amount of human capital through investments in formal education, on-the-job training, and health programs. You often hear people talk about investing in their children's future by putting them through college. For the economy as a whole, the expenditure on education and public health can also be viewed—at least partly—as an investment, because consumption is sacrificed in the present in order to make possible a higher level of per capita output in the future.

The United States invests in human capital on a massive scale. For example, in 1960 expenditures for schools at all levels of education were about $25 billion, or about 5 percent of our gross national product. Moreover, our total investment in the education of the population—the "stock" of educational capital—has grown much more rapidly than has the stock of plant and equipment. For example, whereas the stock of physical capital was about 4 times as big in 1956 as in 1900, the stock of educational capital was about 8 times as big. These enormous and rapidly growing investments in human capital have unquestionably increased the productivity, versatility, and adaptability of our labor force. They have certainly made a major contribution to economic growth.

Income tends to rise with a person's education. Using this relationship to measure the influence of education on a person's productivity, some economists, notably the University of Chicago's Theodore Schultz and Gary Becker, have tried to estimate the profitability, both to society and to the person, of an investment in various levels of education. For example, Becker has tried to estimate the rate of return from a person's investment in a college education. According to his estimates, the typical urban white male in 1950 received about a 10 percent return (after taxes) on his investment in tuition, room, books, and other college expenses (including the earnings he gave up by being in college rather than at work). This was a relatively high return—much higher, for example, than if the student (or his family) simply put the equivalent amount of money in a savings bank or in government bonds.

The Role of Technological Change

A nation's rate of economic growth depends on the rate of technological change, as well as on the extent to which quantities of inputs of various kinds increase. Indeed, the rate of technological change is perhaps the most important single determinant of a nation's rate of economic growth. Recall from Chapter 3 that technology is knowledge concerning the industrial and agricultural arts. Thus, technological change often takes the form of new methods of producing existing products, new designs that make it possible to produce goods with important new characteristics, and new techniques of organization, marketing, and management. Two examples of technological change are new ways of producing power (for example, atomic energy) and new fibers (for example, nylon or dacron).

We have already seen that technological change can shift the curves in both Figure 16.4 and 16.7, thus warding off the law of diminishing marginal returns. But note that new knowledge by itself has little impact. *Unless knowledge is applied, it has little effect on the rate of economic growth.* A change in technology, when applied for the first time, is called an ***innovation,*** and the firm that first applies it is called an ***innovator.*** Innovation is a key stage in the process leading to the full evaluation and utilization of a new process or product. The innovator must be willing to take the risks involved in introducing a new and untried process, good, or service; and in many cases, these risks are high. Once a change in technology has been applied for the first time, the ***diffusion process***—the process by which the use of the innovation spreads from firm to firm and from use to use—begins. How rapidly an innovation spreads depends heavily on its economic advantages over older methods or products. The more profitable the use of the innovation is, the more rapidly it will spread.

Joseph Schumpeter, Harvard's distinguished economist and social theorist, stressed the important role played by the innovator in the process of economic growth. In Schumpeter's view, the innovator is the mainspring of economic progress, the man with the foresight to see how new things can be brought into being and the courage and resourcefulness to surmount the obstacles to change. For his trouble, the innovator receives profit; but this profit eventually is whittled down by competitors who imitate the innovator. The innovator pushes the curves in Figure 16.4 and 16.7 to the right, and once his innovation is assimilated by the economy, another innovator may shove these curves somewhat further to the right. For example, one innovator introduces vacuum tubes, a later innovator introduces semiconductors, one innovator introduces the steam locomotive, a later innovator introduces the diesel locomotive. This process goes on and on —and is a main source of economic growth.

The Electronic Computer: A Case Study[8]

To get a better feel for the nature of technological change and the process of innovation, let's consider one of the most important technological advances of the twentieth century—the electronic computer. Many of the basic ideas underlying the computer go back to Charles Babbage, a brilliant nineteenth-century British inventor; but not until 1946 was the first electronic computer, the ENIAC, designed and constructed. John Mauchly and J. Presper Eckert, both professors at the Moore School of Electrical Engineering at the University of Pennsylvania, were responsible for the ENIAC's design and construction. The work was supported by the U.S. Army. John von Neumann, a famous mathematician at the Institute for Advanced Study at Princeton, added the important concepts of stored programming and conditional transfer.

After the war, Mauchly and Eckert established a small firm to produce electronic computers. Their firm was acquired by Remington Rand, which in 1951 marketed the Univac I, a machine used by the Census Bureau. The International Business Machines Corporation (IBM), the leading company in office machinery and data processing, which before this had been cautious about the potential market for computers, was spurred into action by Remington Rand's success. Once it entered the field, IBM's financial resources, strong marketing organization, and engineering strength enabled it to capture a very large share of the computer market, here and abroad. In the United States, IBM's share of the market grew to about 90 percent during the 1960s.

The electronic computer has been an extremely important stimulus to economic growth. By 1966, the total number of computers installed in the Western world exceeded 50,000 at a total value of about $20 billion. These computers have had important effects on production techniques in many industries. For example, in the chemical, petroleum, and steel industries, digital computers are the latest step in the evolution of control techniques. Com-

[8] This and the following section are based to a considerable extent on E. Mansfield, *The Economics of Technological Change,* New York: Norton, 1968; and my paper in the International Economic Association's *Science and Technology in Economic Growth,* London: Macmillan, 1973.

puters help to determine and enforce the best conditions for process operation, as well as act as data loggers. They can also be programmed to help carry out the complex sequence of operations required to start up or shut down a plant. They have increased production, decreased waste, improved quality control, and reduced the chance of damage to equipment. In another quite different industry, banking, computers have had an important effect too. They have made it possible to eliminate conventional machines and processes for sorting checks, balancing accounts, and computing service charges. With high-speed sorters, it is possible now to process more than 1,500 checks per minute.

Obviously, the electronic computer has enabled us to produce more output from a given amount of resources. In other words, it has enabled us to push the product transformation curve outward, thus increasing our rate of economic growth. But it must be recognized that the process by which the computer has had this effect has by no means been simple or straightforward. Many people in many countries were involved in the development of the basic ideas. Many organizations, public and private, funded the experimental work. Firms of various types were the innovators with respect to particular aspects of the modern computer. And countless individuals and organizations had to be willing to accept, work with, and invest in computers.

Technological Change: Determinants and Measurement

What determines the rate of technological change and the rate at which changes in technology are applied and spread? Clearly, the nature and extent of a nation's scientific capability, and the size and quality of its educational system are of fundamental importance. The first thing that must be said about the influence of a nation's scientific capability on its rate of technological change is that science and technology are two quite different things that have drawn together only recently. Until the twentieth century, it simply was not true that technology was built on science. Even today, many technological advances rely on little in the way of science. However, in more and more areas of the economy (such as aircraft, electronics, and chemicals), the rapid application of new technology has come to depend on a strong scientific base. Merely to imitate or adapt what others have developed, a firm in these areas needs access to high-caliber scientists.

A nation's educational system also has a fundamental influence on the rate of technological change. First, and perhaps most obviously, it determines how many scientists and engineers are graduated, and how competent they are. Clearly, the rate of technological change depends on the quantity and quality of scientific and engineering talent available in the society. Second, the educational system influences the inventiveness and adaptability of the nation's work force. The effective use of modern technology depends on the skills and educational level of the work force; so does the extent to which inventions and improvements are forthcoming from the labor force. The closer links between technology and science should not lead one to believe that workers and independent inventors are no longer important sources of invention. On the contrary, they remain very important in many areas. The educational system also influences the rate of technological change and innovation via the training of managers.

Industrial managers are a key agent in the innovative process. We must emphasize that the proper management of innovation is much more than establishing and maintaining a research and development laboratory that produces a great deal of good technical output. In many industries, most important innovations are not based in any significant degree on the firms' research and development. And even when the basic idea does come from a firm's own R and D, the coupling of R and D with marketing and production is crucial. Many good ideas are not applied properly because the potential users do not really understand them, and many R and D projects are technically successful but commercially irrelevant because they were not designed with sufficient comprehension of market realities. Typically, successful technological innovations seem to be stimulated by perceived production and marketing needs, not by technological opportunities. In other words, most of the time it takes a market-related impetus to prompt work on a successful innovation.

In addition, the rate of technological change depends on the organization of industry and the nature of markets. Although a certain amount of industrial concentration may promote more rapid technological change, increases in concentration beyond a moderate level probably reduce rather than increase the rate of technological change. The rate of technological change also depends on the scale and sophistication of available markets. The scale of the market influences the extent to which a firm can spread the fixed costs of developing and introducing an innovation. This factor has often been cited as a reason for America's technological lead over many other countries. Finally, it is extremely important to note that a country that is not a technological leader can still achieve considerable technological change by borrowing and transferring technology from the leaders.

It is difficult to measure the rate of technological change. Perhaps the most frequently used measure is the rate of growth of labor productivity—that is, the rate of growth of output per manhour. Unfortunately, this measure is influenced by lots of other factors besides the rate of technological change. Nonetheless, despite its inadequacies, it is worthwhile to look briefly at how rapidly productivity has increased in the United States over the long run. Since about 1890, the nation's real output per manhour increased by about 2 percent per year—and these productivity gains were widely diffused, real hourly earnings growing about as rapidly, on the average, as output per manhour.

In part because of differing rates of technological change, there have been considerable differences among industries in the rate of growth of output per manhour. As shown in Table 16.3, labor productivity increased in some industries—like rubber—by more than 4 percent per year, and in other industries—like lumber products—by only about 1 percent per year. To some extent, these differences can be explained by interindustry differences in the amount spent on *research and development*. In addition, a number of other factors—like the amount spent by *other industries* to improve the capital goods and other inputs the industry uses, the extent of *competition* in the industry, the attitudes of *unions* toward change, and the quality of *management*—undoubtedly played an important role too in explaining these interindustry differences in productivity increase.

Table 16.3

Average Annual Rates of Increase of Labor Productivity, Manufacturing Industries, 1899–1953

Industry	Productivity increase (percent per year)
Foods	1.8
Beverages	1.6
Tobacco	5.1
Textiles	2.5
Apparel	1.9
Lumber	1.2
Furniture	1.3
Paper	2.6
Printing	2.7
Chemicals	3.5
Petroleum	3.8
Rubber	4.3
Leather	1.3
Glass	2.7
Primary metals	2.3
Fabricated metals	2.7
Machinery, nonelectric	1.8
Machinery, electric	2.4
Transportation equipment	3.7

Source: John Kendrick, *Productivity Trends in the United States,* Princeton University Press, 1961.

Entrepreneurship and the Social Environment

Still another set of basic factors influencing a nation's level of potential output and its rate of economic growth is the economic, social, political, and religious climate of the nation. It is difficult, if not impossible, to measure the effect of these factors, but there can be no doubt of their importance. Some societies despise material welfare and emphasize the glories of the next world. Some societies are subject to such violent political upheavals that it is risky, if not foolish, to invest in the future. Some societies are governed so corruptly that economic growth is frustrated. And some societies look down on people engaged in industry, trade, or commerce. Obviously, such societies are less likely to experience rapid economic growth than others with a more favorable climate and conditions.

The relatively rapid economic growth of the United States was undoubtedly stimulated in part by the attitude of its people toward material gain. It is commonplace to note that the United States is a materialistic society, a society that esteems business success, that bestows prestige on the rich, that accepts the Protestant ethic (which, crudely stated, is that work is good), and that encourages individual initiative. The United States has been criticized over and over again for some of these traits—often by nations frantically trying to imitate its economic success. Somewhat less obvious is the fact that, because the United States is a young country whose people came from a variety of origins, it did not inherit many feudal components in the structure of society. This too was important.

The United States has also been characterized by great economic and political freedom, by institutions that have been flexible enough to adjust to change, and by a government that has encouraged competition in the marketplace. This has meant fewer barriers to new ideas. Also, the United States has for a long time enjoyed internal peace, order, and general respect for property rights. There have been no violent revolutions since the Civil War, and for many years we were protected from strife in other lands by two oceans—which then seemed much broader than they do now. All these factors undoubtedly contributed to rapid economic growth.

The American economy also seems to have been able to nurture a great many entrepreneurs and a vast horde of competent businessmen. During the nineteenth century, American entrepreneurs were responsible for such basic innovations as the system of interchangeable parts, pioneered by Eli Whitney and others. In many areas, the United States gained a technological lead over other nations, and the available evidence seems to indicate that, to a significant extent, this lead has been maintained. It must be recognized that much of this lead has come from superior management as well as superior technological resources. For example, the Organization for Economic Cooperation and Development recently concluded: "In the techniques of *management,* including the management of research, and of combined technological and market forecasting, the United States appears to have a significant lead."[9]

The Gap between Actual and Potential Output

Up to this point, our discussion of economic growth has centered on the factors that determine how rapidly a nation's potential output grows—factors like technological change, increased education, investment in plant and equipment, and increases in the labor force. Now we must examine the factors that determine how close a nation's actual output comes to its potential output. As we already know, a nation's potential output is its output under full employment. Thus, as we also know, whether or not the economy operates close to full employment is determined by the level of $C + I + G$. If the $C + I + G$ line is too low, the economy will operate with considerable unemploy-

[9] Organization for Economic Cooperation and Development, *Technology Gap: General Report,* Paris, 1968, p. 25.

ment, and actual output will be substantially below potential output. Or, in terms of the equation of exchange, if $M \times V$ is too small, the economy will operate with considerable unemployment, and actual output will be substantially below potential output.

From previous chapters, we also know how the government can use fiscal and monetary policies to push actual output close to potential output. Cuts in tax rates, increases in government spending, incentives for private investment in plant and equipment, increases in the money supply, reductions in interest rates; all these devices can be used to push actual output closer to potential output. Such devices promote economic growth, in the sense that actual per capita output is increased. However, only so much growth can be achieved by squeezing the slack out of the economy. For example, if there is a 7 percent unemployment rate, output per capita can be increased by perhaps 9 percent simply by reducing the unemployment rate to 4 percent, as we saw in Chapter 8. *But this is a one-shot improvement.* To get any further growth, the nation must increase its potential output.

Of course this doesn't mean that it isn't important to maintain the economy at close to full employment. On the contrary, as we stressed in Chapter 8, one of the major objectives of public policy must be full employment, and a reduction of unemployment will have a significant effect on the rate of economic growth in the short run. (Much of the economic growth in the United States in the early 1960s was caused by the transition to full employment.) But the point we are making is that, once the economy gets to full employment, no further growth can occur by this route. If a nation wants further growth, it must influence the factors responsible for the rate of growth of potential output.

Japan: A Case Study of Rapid Economic Growth

Japan has experienced a very high rate of economic growth for a long time. Especially after World War II, the Japanese economy increased per capita GNP very rapidly. For example, between 1955 and 1964 gross national product per man increased at an average rate of 8.8 percent per year. Some of the most important reasons for this rapid growth are as follows:[10]

First, after World War II, the rate of investment in plant and equipment was extremely high. For example, in 1954 the Japanese devoted over 20 percent of their GNP to the formation of physical capital; and in 1961 and 1964, they devoted 35 and 33 percent, respectively. While this high rate of capital formation was due, particularly in the early postwar years, to the dislocations caused by the war, this was not the only reason. To a considerable extent, the rate was high because Japan was catching up with technological developments elsewhere in the world. Japan invested heavily in newer industries based on innovations in other countries—television, electronic devices, synthetics, and others—as well as in older industries like steel, machinery, and chemicals.

A second very important contributor to Japan's economic growth was the borrowing and application of technology developed in other countries. The Japanese were skilled borrowers of Western technology. Their success illustrates a very important point often overlooked by nations interested in increasing their growth rates. To benefit from technology, a nation does not have to develop or invent it. Conversely, because a country develops or invents a new product or process, it does not follow that the product or process will do much for its rate of economic growth. If another country is quicker to apply and exploit the innovation, it may get more of the economic benefits. The Japanese concentrated their energies and resources on transferring Western technology rather than developing or inventing their own. This strategy paid off well.

Japan has also had an abundant supply of edu-

[10] For further discussion, see K. Ohkawa and H. Rosovsky, "Recent Japanese Growth in Historical Perspective," *American Economic Review*, May 1963, pp. 578–88.

cated labor, which has made it much easier to assimilate new technology. The importance of such an investment in human capital has been emphasized in previous sections. And Japan undoubtedly benefited from the fact that its burden of national defense was largely assumed by the United States, so that Japanese resources could be devoted to economic development rather than to defense. Last, Japan's level of per capita GNP was lower than that of most of the nations with which it is generally compared. It is often argued that countries at a relatively low level of economic development find it easier to achieve a high growth rate than do more affluent societies. In other words, a high rate of growth may be easier to achieve from a low economic base.

Summary

Economic growth is measured by the increase of per capita real gross national product, an index that does not measure accurately the growth of economic welfare, but is often used as a first approximation. In recent years, many economists and politicians have called for an explicit public policy designed to increase our growth rate. A nation's rate of economic growth depends on the increase in the quantity and quality of its resources (including physical and human capital) and the rate of technological change. In addition, the rate of economic growth depends on the extent to which a society maintains full employment and on the efficiency with which its resources are allocated and managed.

One factor that may influence a nation's rate of economic growth is the rate at which its population grows. In Malthus's view, population growth, unless checked in some way, ultimately meant economic decline, since output could not grow in proportion to the growth in population. The law of diminishing marginal returns insured that beyond some point, increases in labor, holding the quantity of land constant, would result in smaller and smaller increments of output. However, Malthus underestimated the extent and importance of technological change, which offset the law of diminishing marginal returns.

Another factor that determines whether per capita output grows rapidly or slowly is the rate of expenditure on new plant and equipment. Without technological change, more and more of this sort of investment would result in increases in the capital-output ratio and decreases in the profitability of investment in plant and equipment, as Ricardo pointed out. But because of technological change, none of these things has occurred. According to the available evidence, a nation's rate of economic growth seems directly related to its rate of investment in plant and equipment.

To a considerable extent, economic growth here and abroad has resulted from technological change. A change in technology, when applied for the first time, is called an innovation, and the firm that first applies it is called an innovator. Innovation is a key stage in the process leading to the full evaluation and utilization of a new process or product. Unless knowledge is used, it has little effect on the rate of economic growth. The rate of technological change and the rate at which new technology is applied depend on a number of factors, including the nature and extent of a nation's scientific capability, the size and quality of its educational system, the quality of its managers, the attitude and structure of its firms, the organization of its industries, and the nature of its markets.

Another factor with an important effect on a nation's rate of economic growth is the rate at which it invests in human capital. The United States invests in human capital on a massive scale, and these enormous and rapidly growing investments have unquestionably increased the productivity, versatility, and adaptability of our labor force. Still another set of basic factors influencing the rate of economic growth is the economic, social, and political climate of the nation. Some societies despise material welfare, are subject to violent political upheavals, and are governed by corrupt groups. Such societies are unlikely to have a high rate of economic growth. Finally, the rate of economic growth is also affected by the extent and behavior of the gap between actual and potential GNP. However, once a nation gets to full employment, it cannot grow further by reducing this gap.

CONCEPTS FOR REVIEW

Economic growth	Average product of labor	Innovation
Capital formation	Law of diminishing marginal returns	Innovator
Population increase	Technological change	Diffusion process
Marginal product of labor		Aggregate production function

QUESTIONS FOR DISCUSSION AND REVIEW

1. In 1971, Herbert Stein wrote, "During the past 4 years the rates of growth in productivity . . . slowed down." What are some possible reasons why this occurred? What is the significance of this slowdown?

2. Describe in as much detail as you can the ways in which capital formation, population growth, technological change, and education are interrelated. Show how these interrelationships make it difficult to sort out the effect of each of these factors on the rate of economic growth.

3. Malthus thought that output would increase only in proportion to the growth in population. True or False?

4. In the United States during the twentieth century the capital-output ratio has a. increased steadily. b. remained fairly constant. c. decreased steadily. d. fluctuated markedly up and down.

CHAPTER 17

American Economic Growth: History, Policies, Problems, and Prospects

About a century ago, Benjamin Disraeli, the famous British prime minister, said that "increased means and increased leisure are the two civilizers of man." Although one might add to Disraeli's list of "civilizers," there can be little doubt that economic growth has helped to improve man's lot. Since World War II, the rate of economic growth has become a major index, both here and abroad, of how well an economy is performing; and many governments have tried to increase their rate of economic growth. In 1960 John F. Kennedy ran for president on a platform emphasizing the need for faster economic growth in the United States; and in subsequent elections—here and abroad—economic growth frequently has been a campaign issue.

However, bigger may not always be better. More and more often, observers in recent years have stressed that economic growth may not be an unalloyed blessing. It too has its costs. Indeed, the pros and cons of more rapid economic growth have been the subject of much debate. In this chapter, we are concerned with four basic questions about economic growth in the United States. What has been our rate of economic growth in the past? What are the advantages and disadvantages of a faster rate of economic growth? If faster growth is desired, what measures can the government take to promote it? And, assuming that present trends continue, what rate of economic growth can we expect in the future?

Economic Growth in the United States

Let's begin by looking at the salient facts about the rate at which the American economy has grown in the past. Soon after its emergence as an independent nation, the United States reached a relatively high level of economic development. By 1840, it ranked fourth in per capita income, behind England, France, and Germany. During the next 30 years, the United States experienced relatively rapid economic growth. By 1870, it ranked second only to England in per capita income. In the next 40 years, the American economy continued to grow rapidly. National product per person employed grew by about 2.2 percent per year between 1871 and 1913. This growth rate was higher than for practically any other major industrialized nation; and well before the turn of the century, income per capita was greater in the United States than in any other nation in the world.

Between 1913 and 1959, the American growth rate was somewhat lower than in previous years. National product per person employed grew by about 1.8 percent per year. Nonetheless, although we grew less rapidly than in earlier years, we pulled further ahead of most other industrialized countries, because we continued to grow faster than they did. Of course, our rate of economic growth varied from decade to decade: economic growth does not proceed at a steady rate. In some decades (like the 1920s), our economy grew rapidly, while in others (like the 1930s), it grew little, if at all. During periods of recovery and prosperity, the growth rate was high; during depressions, it was low. In the 1950s, the growth rate in the United States was lower than in many other countries. As pointed out in the previous chapter, this caused considerable controversy and some alarm.

During the 1960s, our growth rate increased perceptibly. But our present growth rate is by no

Table 17.1

Average Annual Growth Rates of Per Capita Real GNP, Selected Industrialized Countries

Country	1870–1964	1929–1964	1950–1964
United States	1.9%	1.7%	1.8%
Canada	1.7	1.8	1.8
France	1.5	1.4	3.8
Germany	1.7	2.8	5.9
Italy	1.4	2.2	5.2
Japan	—	—	8.7
United Kingdom	1.3	1.7	2.4

Source: U.S. Department of Commerce, *Long-Term Economic Growth,* 1966.

means the highest among the major industrialized nations. That honor belongs to Japan, which, as we saw in the previous chapter, has long experienced rapid economic growth. Table 17.1 shows the annual rates of growth of per capita real GNP in the United States and other major industrialized countries during various periods in the last century. You can see that, for the period as a whole, per capita real GNP in the United States grew at an average rate of about 2 percent per year. Compared with Germany, France, Italy, Canada, and the United Kingdom, our growth rate was quite impressive. In recent years, however, many industrialized countries have shown growth rates larger than or equal to ours.

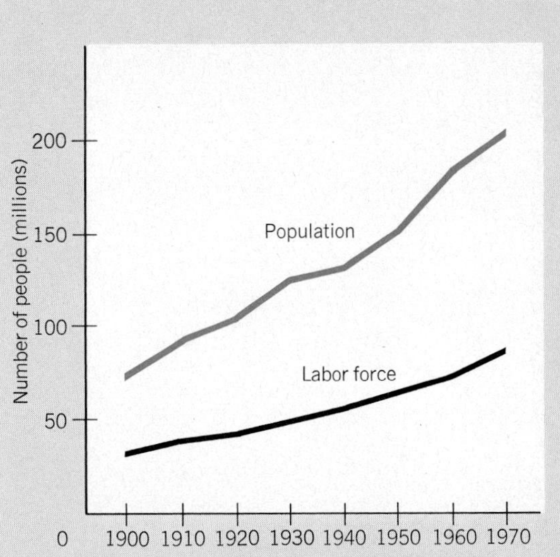

Figure 17.1
Population and Labor Force, United States, 1900–70.

The American population in 1970 was about double what it was in 1920, and almost triple what it was in 1900.

Population and Human Resources

As we have seen, a nation's rate of economic growth is influenced, among other things, by its rate of population growth and the extent of its investment in human capital. As shown in Figure 17.1, the population of the United States has grown substantially during our history, because of a fairly high birth rate as well as considerable immigration from other parts of the world.[1] Indeed, our population in 1970 was about double what it was in 1920, and almost triple what it was in 1900.

In the past 15 or 20 years, the birth rate has fallen considerably, due partly to changes in attitudes toward women's role in society. However, according to official forecasts, the American population will continue to grow for at least the next 10 or 20 years, and perhaps for much longer. Of course, increases in population do not necessarily bring about economic growth. As we saw in the previous chapter, population increases, carried beyond a certain point, can lower per capita GNP, unless they are offset by other factors, such as advances in technology.

Equally important, it is not sheer numbers alone that count. The quality as well as the quantity of the population determines how much is produced. Measured by its education and skill, the quality of the American population is among the highest in the world. Moreover, as indicated by Table 17.2, the educational level of the population has increased dramatically during the past 70 years. To a considerable extent, our economic growth seems to have been due to this large investment in human capital.

Is it possible to make any quantitative estimate of the contribution of increased education to eco-

[1] As shown in Figure 17.1, the percent of the population in the labor force does not remain constant over time, and changes in this percentage can, of course, influence a country's rate of economic growth. Increases in the number of years of schooling and more liberal attitudes toward working wives, as well as changes in the age distribution of the population and in income levels, will influence this percentage.

Table 17.2

Percent of 17-Year-Olds that Graduated from High School, United States, 1900–1980

Year	Percent graduated from high school
1900	6.4
1920	16.8
1940	50.8
1950	59.0
1960	65.1
1970	78.0
1980 (projected)	82.5

Source: Statistical Abstract of the United States, 1972.

Table 17.3

Estimated Sources of Growth in Real National Income in the United States, 1909–57

Source	Period 1909–29	1929–57
	[Percent of total growth]	
Increase in quantity of labor	39	27
Increase in quantity of capital	26	15
Improved education and training	13	27
Technological change	12	20
Other factors	10	11
Total	100	100

Source: E. Denison, *The Sources of Economic Growth in the United States,* Committee for Economic Development, 1962.

nomic growth in the United States? Because the effects of education, technological change, and investment in plant and equipment intertwine in various ways, it is very difficult to sort out any one of them. Yet it is worthwhile to give the best estimates currently available. According to Edward Denison of the Brookings Institution, increased education seemed to account for about ⅛ of the growth in real output in the United States during 1909–29, and for about ¼ of this growth during 1929–57. Thus, if these estimates, shown in Table 17.3, can be trusted, increased education has been a major contributor to economic growth in the United States.

Technological Change

America's economic growth has also been due in very considerable part to technological change. For example, as shown in Table 17.3, Denison concludes that the "advance of knowledge" contributed about ⅛ of the growth in real output during 1909–29, and about ⅕ of this growth during 1929–57. Such estimates are rough, but useful. It is very difficult to separate the effects on economic growth of technological change from those of investment in physical capital, since to a considerable extent new technology must be embodied in physical capital—new machines and equipment—to be used. For example, a nuclear power plant must obviously be built to take advantage of nuclear power plant technology. Nor can the effects of technological change easily be separated from those of education. After all, the returns from increased education are enhanced by technological change, and, as we saw in the previous chapter, the rate of technological change is influenced by the extent and nature of a society's investment in education.

In interpreting America's economic growth, we must recognize that the United States has long been a technological leader. Even before 1850, scattered evidence gives the impression that the United States was ahead of other countries in many technological areas. And after 1850, the available evidence indicates that productivity was higher in the United States than in Europe, that the United States had a strong export position in technically progressive industries, and that Europeans tended to imitate American techniques. Needless to say, the United States did not lead in all fields, but it appears to have held a technological lead in many important aspects of manufacturing. This was in contrast to pure science where, until World War II, the United States was not a leader.

Toward the end of the nineteenth century, as the connection between science and technology gradually became closer, commercial research laboratories began to appear. The first organized research laboratory in the United States was established by Thomas Edison in 1876. Eastman Kodak (1893), B. F. Goodrich (1895), General Electric (1900), DuPont (1902), and the Bell Telephone System (1907) were some of the earliest firms to establish laboratories. The industrial R and D laboratory constituted a significant departure from the past, when invention was mainly the work of independent inventors like Eli Whitney (interchangeable parts and cotton gin), Robert Fulton (steamboat), Samuel Morse (telegraph), Charles Goodyear (vulcanization of rubber), and Cyrus McCormick (reaper). These men were responsible for a very rich crop of inventions, some of which established whole new industries. Since the advent of the industrial laboratory, the relative importance of independent inventors seems to have declined, but they continue to produce a significant share of the important inventions in many areas. For example, xerography was invented by an independent inventor, Chester Carlson.

Recent decades have witnessed a tremendous growth in the amount spent on research and development. Table 17.4 shows that R and D expenditures in the United States in 1972 were about 19 times what they were in 1945. Although the bulk of these expenditures go for rather minor improvements rather than major advances, this vast increase in research and development has generated much economic growth. But, as the table shows, the federal government is the source of most R and D funds, which are heavily concentrated on defense and space technology. In the eyes of many economists, this vast investment in R and D would

Table 17.4

Expenditures on Research and Development, United States, 1945–70

		Sources of funds		
Year	Total R and D expenditure	Government	Industry	Universities and nonprofit institutions
		(millions)		
1945	$ 1,520	$ 1,070	$ 430	$ 20
1950	2,870	1,610	1,180	80
1955	6,270	3,490	2,510	270
1960	13,710	8,720	4,510	480
1965	20,439	13,033	6,539	867
1972*	28,000	15,210	11,320	1,470

Source: Statistical Abstract of the United States, 1970, and National Science Foundation, *National Patterns of R and D Resources,* 1972.
* Estimated by National Science Foundation.

probably have had a bigger impact on the rate of economic growth if more of it had been directed at civilian rather than military and political objectives.

Capital Formation and Natural Resources

As pointed out in the previous chapter, a nation's rate of economic growth depends partially on how much of its GNP is invested in new plant and equipment. In recent years, we have devoted over 10 percent of our GNP to this purpose. In the United States, the average worker has more equipment to work with than his counterpart in any other country of the world. In manufacturing, for example, the average American worker has at his disposal about $30,000 worth of plant and equipment. Moreover, the government has invested huge amounts in highways, harbors, dams, and other forms of social capital; and the public has invested heavily in residential construction.

America's great natural resources have also been an important factor underlying our economic growth. We have an abundance of fertile soil and of various kinds of ores and minerals, a reasonably good climate, and coal, oil, and other sources of power. Few nations have as plentiful a supply of natural resources, and obviously they have been a great boon to our economic development. Although countries with limited natural resources can offset this limitation by importing raw materials, by irrigation and drainage projects, and by the use of modern technology, a good supply of natural resources is a valuable asset in achieving rapid economic growth.

In recent years, some fear has been expressed that, if the world economy continues to grow at current rates, we shall begin to run out of basic raw materials. For example, in 1972 Jay Forrester and his colleagues at M.I.T. conducted a study sponsored by the Club of Rome on *The Limits of Growth,*[2] in which they concluded that unless we curb our growth rate the world will run out of raw materials in the foreseeable future. However, this ignores the fact that the price system encourages producers to conserve raw materials as they become increasingly scarce, and that it provides a strong incentive for producers to invent and adopt new techniques that use less of these resources. The price system accomplishes these things simply by seeing to it that the price of a raw material increases as it becomes scarcer.

The history of technology seems to indicate that Forrester's view is oversimplified and overly pessimistic. As Peter Passell and Leonard Ross of Columbia University point out

> Before we run out of Arabian oil, we will begin extracting petroleum from the vast reserves of oil-shale rocks and tar sands. And long before we run out of those reserves, cars will be powered with other sources of energy. Appeals to faith in technical change are more than a cheap debating trick to counter the Forrester school. The technology of substituting plentiful materials for scarce ones grows every day. Silicates made from sand replace copper and silver radio circuitry; European cattle feeds are enriched with nutrients made of natural gas converted by bacteria; mattresses are filled with polyurethane which never was closer to a Liberian rubber tree than Bayonne, N.J.[3]

The Social and Entrepreneurial Environment, the GNP Gap, and Allocative Efficiency

As we stressed in the previous chapter, America's relatively rapid long-term economic growth has also been a result of its social and entrepreneurial environment. In general, American society places con-

[2] For example, see Donella Meadows, Dennis Meadows, J. Randers, and William Behrens, "The Limits to Growth," reprinted in E. Mansfield, *Economics: Readings, Issues, and Cases,* New York: Norton, 1974.

[3] P. Passell and L. Ross, "Don't Knock the $2-Trillion Economy," *New York Times,* March 5, 1972.

siderable emphasis on materialistic considerations, values hard work, allows a great deal of economic and political freedom, and is flexible enough to adjust to change. Also, the United States has not been wracked (in the past century) by internal armed conflict or widespread confiscation of private property. These factors have been important in promoting economic growth. In addition, the price system, which has been relied on to channel resources into the proper uses, seems to have worked quite well. It has provided the incentives required to get labor, land, and capital to move from less productive to more productive uses.

However, not all aspects of the American economy have been conducive to rapid economic growth. For one thing, as we saw in Chapter 8, in many periods actual GNP fell short of potential GNP because desired spending was too low. For example, in the Great Depression of the 1930s, actual GNP was far below our potential GNP. When a large gap develops between actual and potential GNP, this reduces the growth rate, as we saw in the previous chapter. Moreover, it has indirect as well as direct effects. As this gap grows, and there is substantial unemployment, firms are discouraged from investing in new technology or capital formation, and unions are more inclined to resist adopting new techniques that might replace men with machines, so that the growth rate in subsequent years may be reduced as well.

Another factor that can reduce our economic growth rate is the growth of monopolistic elements that prevent resources from being allocated efficiently. For example, some labor unions resist the adoption of new techniques that would increase productivity and growth. Thus, the compositors' union has restricted the use of the teletypesetter by requiring that the machine be operated by a journeyman printer or apprentice. Also, groups that are adversely affected by changes that would promote economic growth often try to convince the government to stop or offset them. For example, the farm programs discussed in Chapter 5 impeded past economic growth by making it more difficult to transfer resources out of agriculture and into more productive uses. Also, many industries that cannot compete with foreign producers lobby for and obtain tariffs, with the result that resources are misallocated.

Finally, if resources tend to be more immobile, this too will hamper economic growth. As tastes, technology, and population change, resources often should move from one use or location to another, if society's output is to be maximized. But there are many barriers to the mobility of resources. In the case of labor, people often are reluctant to pick up stakes, sever their ties to friends, family, and neighbors, and move to another location. Similarly, they often are unwilling or unable to learn a new occupation or trade, even though it might increase their income. The immobility of capital is even more obvious. A particular piece of capital is built for specific purposes—for example, to cut metal or to refine oil—and cannot be used for other purposes. However, when this piece of capital wears out, it can be replaced with capital of another type.

Past and Present Views of Economic Growth

Despite an imperfect record, the American economy has strongly adhered to a pattern of growth. Should we try to increase our rate of economic growth? Some economists answer yes, some answer no. Before presenting the issues, several points should be noted about the attitudes of economists, past and present, toward economic growth. First, the great economists of the past were deeply concerned with the poverty and economic misery of their times; and they tried in various ways to help set humanity on a course whereby output per capita might rise. Smith, Malthus, and Ricardo all wanted to ameliorate the meager lot of the average Englishman of their day; Marx was distressed and angered by the misery of the working classes; and Keynes spent much of his time and energy trying to find a way out of the poverty and misery arising from the Great Depression.

Second, except for Smith and Keynes, these great economists of the past were not very optimistic about how much output per capita could be increased. Malthus and Ricardo were about as pessimistic as one reasonably could get. In their view, population would expand whenever the standard of living poked its head above the subsistence level, with the result that more and more people would be working a relatively fixed amount of land. Given the law of diminishing marginal returns, it appeared certain to them that output per capita would eventually fall. As for Marx, we have seen that he believed the capitalistic system was headed for collapse, and that the bulk of the population was doomed to increased misery so long as capitalism survived.

With all the advantages of hindsight, it is relatively easy to see where the pessimists went wrong, at least for the industrialized nations. As pointed out in the previous chapter, Malthus and Ricardo vastly underestimated the power of technological change. They could not visualize the sorts of innovations that were to occur. New techniques and new products were destined to offset the dreaded law of diminishing marginal returns and to allow food supplies to more than keep pace with increases in population. Moreover, because of innovations in birth control and changes in attitudes, population has not grown as rapidly as many people forecasted. Marx could not visualize the sorts of changes that were to occur in capitalism. Nor could he avoid the consequences of the basic flaws in his economic theories, which are discussed further in Chapter 34.

It is important to recognize that, for a variety of reasons, the attitude of most economists today is quite different from the attitudes of their great predecessors. Of course, the difference does not lie in a lack of concern for the underprivileged. Most economists today are just as interested in eradicating poverty as were Smith or Marx. *The big difference is that today's economists are reasonably confident that we can increase output per capita. Indeed, they expect, almost as a matter of course, that output per capita will increase in the industrialized nations of the world.* Of course, some wish that it could be made to increase a little faster (and some would like to slow it down) but, in general, the present view is decidedly optimistic.

The Case for Economic Growth

Having reached a level of affluence that would have astonished Smith, Ricardo, Malthus, or Marx (but not Keynes), the industrialized nations are now at a point where some observers question the wisdom of further economic growth. For example, in the United States, the attitude toward economic growth has changed perceptibly in the decade or so since President Kennedy made it a target of public policy. More emphasis is placed today on the "costs" of economic growth. There are more statements to the effect that we really are rich enough, and more questions about the desirability of technological change, which is one of the principal mainsprings of economic growth.

In making the case for rapid economic growth, three basic arguments are employed. First, it is argued that economic growth means a higher standard of living, which is important in and of itself. But before accepting this uncritically, one should stress the limitations of the customary growth measures. A decade or so ago, people tended uncritically to accept increases in per capita GNP as a measure of increases in economic welfare, despite the many warnings of economists. People now are more conscious of the frailties of the GNP—the fact that it does not count as "product" many benefits that are provided as part of the productive process (such as increased leisure) and that it does not count as "costs" many problems (such as the human and environmental costs) that arise as a consequence of the productive process. Some economists are currently trying to improve the statistics to take better account of some of these factors, such as environmental pollution (see Chapter 8). But since it is unlikely that we will ever have very precise measures of economic welfare, the available figures need to be treated with caution.

Second, it is argued that economic growth provides the means to reduce poverty and attain other national objectives. In the words of Peter Passell and Leonard Ross, "Growth is the only way that America will ever reduce poverty. . . . While the relative share of income that poor people get seems to be frozen, their incomes do keep pace with the economy. . . . Even allowing for inflation, the average income of the bottom 10th of the population has increased about 55 percent since 1950. Twenty more years of growth could do for the poor what the Congress won't do."[4] Also, it is argued that economic growth makes it easier to achieve other national goals, because they can be achieved without reducing the production and consumption of other goods and services.

Third, many maintain that economic growth contributes to national prestige and national defense. As pointed out in the previous chapter, this was one of the most important reasons for the emphasis on economic growth in the early 1960s. People were worried that we were losing the "growth race" to the Soviet Union, and that Premier Khrushchev's claim that the Russians would "bury" us economically might be more than an idle boast. In recent years, as our relations with the Communist countries have improved, these reasons for economic growth have been given less importance, but they still are cited by some proponents of economic growth.

The Case against Economic Growth

Basically, there are four arguments made by those who question the wisdom of further economic growth in our society. First, it is argued that increases in per capita GNP really will not make us any happier: on the contrary, they will only be achieved by reducing the quality of our lives. For example, according to E. J. Mishan of the London School of Economics, economic growth results in "the appalling traffic congestion in our towns, cities, and suburbs, . . . the erosion of the countryside, the 'uglification' of coastal towns, . . . and a wide heritage of natural beauty being wantonly destroyed."[5] In his view, to strain for further economic growth is simply to put ourselves on a meaningless treadmill, since it prevents us from enjoying what we have. Relatively few economists share this rather extreme view.

[4] Passell and Ross, *op. cit.*

Second, it is argued that economic growth is likely to result in additional environmental pollution. Of course, increases in per capita GNP do not necessarily have to entail increases in pollution. On the contrary, as we shall see in the next chapter, it is possible to increase output without increasing pollution. Nonetheless, the fact seems to be that economic growth in the past has been associated with increases in pollution, and some observers feel that this association is likely to persist in the future. Thus they regard increases in environmental pollution as a likely "cost" of economic growth. Among those who argue against further economic growth on environmental grounds is biologist Barry Commoner of Washington University, who concludes that:

> In most of the technological displacements which have accompanied the growth of the economy since 1946, the new technology has an appreciably greater environmental impact than the technology which it has displaced, and the postwar technological transformation of productive activities is the chief reason for the present environmental crisis. . . . If we are to survive economically as well as biologically, much of the technological transformation of the United States economy since 1946 will need to be, so to speak, redone in order to bring the nation's productive technology much more closely into harmony with the inescapable demands of the ecosystem.[6]

[5] E. Mishan, *Technology and Growth,* New York: Praeger, 1969.

[6] B. Commoner, "The Environmental Costs of Economic Growth," in R. and N. Dorfman, *Economics of the Environment,* New York: Norton, 1972.

Third, it is argued that economic growth is not the solver of social problems that its proponents claim. For example, critics point out that we are rich enough now to solve the problem of poverty in the United States. In their view, what we need is the will and courage to eliminate poverty, not extra output. In reply to the argument that economic growth is needed for reasons of national prestige and defense, the critics retort that it is not the size of a country's GNP, but its composition, that counts in determining military strength. For example, the Soviet Union's military strength is roughly equal to ours, although its GNP is about 50 percent smaller. Moreover, the critics question whether the less developed countries are much impressed by a simple comparison of our growth rate with that of the Soviet Union.

Fourth, it is pointed out that, to increase our growth rate, it may be necessary for us to make sacrifices now. For example, we may have to sacrifice leisure or postpone the consumption of goods and services in order to invest in capital goods. Many economists have stressed that one cannot make the naive assumption that more growth is costless, or that it will always be worth the sacrifices involved. According to some economists, there is no reason to "force" growth on the economy. To them, the proper rate of economic growth is that which would emerge from private decisions. Whether the increase in the growth rate is worth the sacrifices depends upon the tastes and preferences of the people: it is a political issue.

Public Policies to Stimulate Economic Growth

Although the critics of growth have made some headway, there has been no renunciation of economic growth as a goal of public policy. On the contrary, most government officials, in the United States and elsewhere, continue to press for further economic growth. All nations have important social objectives that seem more likely to be attained if they can increase per capita output. Thus, most would like to effect such an increase, notwithstanding Mishan's views concerning the hollowness of it all. But the more sophisticated question of how far the government should go in promoting or forcing growth is not easy to answer. And as you would expect, there are very substantial differences of opinion on this score among politicians in this country (and other countries as well).

Whether or not we should stimulate growth is essentially a political question, and your own view will depend on your political preference. As Robert Solow puts it, "The pro-growth-man is someone who is prepared to sacrifice something useful and desirable right now so that people should be better off in the future; the anti-growth-man is someone who thinks that is unnecessary or undesirable."

But whether you are for or against the stimulation of growth, you should know how the government's policies can influence the growth rate. Suppose that the American people, registering their opinions through the proper democratic process, indicate that they want to increase the nation's rate of economic growth. Suppose that you are a United States Senator and that you feel that, regardless of your own preferences, you should advocate programs to further the people's objectives—in this case, to increase the nation's rate of economic growth. What sorts of programs would you support?

First, you would probably want to *increase expenditures on research and development* (R and D), since increases in such expenditures are likely to increase the rate of technological change, which in turn will increase the growth rate.[7] The government can either increase R and D expenditures by directly financing more R and D, or it can provide tax credits or other inducements to get private firms to increase their R and D expenditures. It is important to recognize, however, that the added R and D must be carried out in areas

[7] It is interesting to contrast this attitude toward R and D with the view of the French revolutionaries, who said, as they led the famous scientist, Lavoisier, to the guillotine: "The Republic has no need of scientists." Clearly, scientists are viewed differently—and treated more gently—today.

where the social payoffs are high: otherwise there will be little impact on the growth rate. Moreover, we must also note that the government can stimulate the growth rate by encouraging the application and diffusion of existing technology, as well as by encouraging the development of new technology.

Second, you would probably want to *increase investment in education and training.* We saw in the previous chapter that, according to various experts, there may be a high rate of return from such an investment. Increased education and training may increase the nation's potential output considerably. To foster such increases, the federal government could spend larger amounts on scholarships and provide loans for potential students. Many people argue that loans should be made available to students who plan to enter highly paid occupations, since the student could pay back the loan from his extra earnings. Also, the government could provide more financial support to the nation's colleges and universities.

Third, you would probably want to *increase aggregate investment in plant and equipment.* Increases in such investment will increase the growth rate, assuming, of course, that the extra investment is in areas of high productivity. Again, we must recognize that this policy, like the others described above, imposes costs. Increases in investment can occur—under full employment—only at the expense of current consumption. Assuming that the people understand these costs and are willing to pay them, the government can increase investment in plant and equipment by keeping interest rates low (to encourage investment) and personal tax rates high (to choke off consumption). Also, the government can give tax credits for investment in plant and equipment and allow firms to depreciate their plant and equipment more rapidly.[8]

[8] A tax credit is a device whereby a firm's income tax liability is smaller if it invests a great deal in plant and equipment than if it invests little. Obviously, such a tax credit increases the profitability of investing in plant and equipment. More rapid depreciation of plant and equipment also encourages investment because, if a firm can write off a new piece of equipment more rapidly for tax purposes, the new piece of equipment is more profitable to the firm than it otherwise would be.

Fourth, if the economy is operating at considerably less than full employment, you would probably want *to narrow the gap between actual and potential output.* As we saw in the previous chapter, this can be a very effective way to grow, at least in the short run. To do it, the government must use its fiscal and monetary policies to reduce unemployment. The goal of full employment is widely accepted—more widely, for that matter, than the goal of increasing the rate of economic growth. Unfortunately, however, when the economy approaches full employment, there is a tendency for the goal of full employment to conflict with the goal of price stability, as we saw in Chapter 8. Thus, an attempt to close completely the gap between actual and potential output may lead to undesirable inflationary pressures.

Policies for Economic Growth in the Early 1960s: A Case Study

As we have noted, in the early 1960s, the Kennedy administration set out to spur the rate of economic growth in the United States. We now can take a closer look at the set of economic policies designed to accomplish this goal. These policies were formulated by members of the Council of Economic Advisers, and others, inside and outside the government. To be put into effect, some of these policies and programs had to be approved by the Congress.

For research and development, the Kennedy administration proposed a Civilian Industrial Technology program to encourage and support additional R and D in industries that it regarded as lagging technologically. It also proposed an industrial extension service—analogous to the agricultural extension service that distributes technological information and advice—to increase the rate of diffusion of innovations. Congress eventually approved the industrial extension service,[9] but not the Civilian

[9] The industrial extension service, embodied in the State Technical Services Act, was passed in 1965, but was later killed.

Industrial Technology program. An important reason for its defeat was that some industrial groups feared that government sponsorship of industrial R and D could upset existing competitive relationships.

In the field of education too, the administration proposed new measures. For example, in his 1962 Economic Report, President Kennedy stated:

> Public education has been the great bulwark of equality of opportunity in our democracy for more than a century. . . . There can be no better investment in equity and democracy—and no better instrument for economic growth. For this reason, I urge action by the Congress to provide Federal aid for more adequate public school facilities, higher teachers' salaries, and better quality in education. I urge early completion of congressional action on the bill to authorize loans for construction of college academic facilities and to provide scholarships for able students who need help. The talent of our youth is a resource which must not be wasted.[10]

To encourage investment in plant and equipment, the administration pushed through an "investment tax credit" that permitted firms to deduct from their income tax statements 7 percent of the amount they invested in new plant and equipment. Obviously, this made such investment more profitable. Also, the administration revised the depreciation schedules so that firms could write off such investments more quickly for tax purposes, thus increasing their profitability still more. But it did not lower interest rates or increase taxes to choke off consumption. In its 1962 Annual Report, the Council of Economic Advisers recognized that such actions might promote growth, but felt that other considerations, such as our balance of payments (discussed in Chapter 31), ruled them out.

Finally, turning to the reduction of the gap between actual and potential output, the administration used fiscal and monetary policies to push the economy toward full employment. An important part of this policy in the eyes of most economists was the tax cut of 1964, described in Chapter 10. Between 1962 and 1966, the United States achieved a high rate of growth, in considerable part because of the reduction of the gap between actual and potential output.

Thus, taken as a whole, the Kennedy administration's policies to stimulate economic growth conformed to the elementary principles discussed in this and the previous chapter. In the area of growth policy—just as in fiscal, monetary, and incomes policy—the basic principles of economics take you a long way toward understanding the policies of government, whether Democratic or Republican.

Technological Unemployment

Up to now, we have stressed that rapid technological change is an important stimulus to economic growth. But this stimulus to growth can be offset, at least partially, if rapid technological change results in technological unemployment. Economists have long recognized that new technology can throw people out of work. Karl Marx, in particular, gave technological change—and technological unemployment—a significant role in his theoretical system. (As we saw in Chapter 9, he believed that capitalists would adopt new technologies that would result in more and more technological unemployment.) Workers too have long recognized and feared technological unemployment. As long ago as the mid-1700s, a mob of worried English spinners entered James Hargreaves's mill and smashed the first workable multispindle frames.

Although the dread of technology-induced mass unemployment is not new, it was revived with great effect in the late 1950s and early 1960s. The new scare word was "automation." For example, Professor Crossman of Oxford University, addressing an international conference in 1964, said that "unemployment due to automation will grow steadily over the next four decades, perhaps centuries, and in the end it is likely to reach a very high figure, say 90 percent of the labor force, unless radical changes are made in the present

[10] *Economic Report of the President,* 1962, Washington, D.C.: Government Printing Office, p. 10.

pattern of working."[11] Although ***automation*** means different things to different people, it generally refers to processes designed to mechanize the human cognitive, conceptual, and informational processes.

Do increases in the rate of technological change necessarily result in increases in aggregate unemployment? To make a long story short, the answer is *no.* Rapid technological change need not have this effect if the government increases total spending at the proper rate. When total spending rises too slowly, increased aggregate unemployment takes place. If it rises too rapidly and resources are already fully employed, inflation will result. As we know, the job of choosing and carrying out appropriate fiscal and monetary policies is not easy; but used with reasonable finesse, such policies should prevent any large increase in aggregate unemployment from technological change.

To see how large-scale technological unemployment can occur—and how it can be avoided—consider Figure 17.2, which shows the $C + I + G$ line at a particular point in time. (If you are a bit hazy about the meaning and significance of this line, review Chapter 10.) Since this line intersects the 45-degree line at point *A,* the equilibrium level of net national product is $400 billion. If the high-employment level of net national product is also $400 billion, the economy enjoys a high level of employment. Now suppose that there is a significant amount of technological change. What will be the result? To begin with, the advance in technology will almost certainly result in an increase in productivity. In other words, it will enable the labor force to produce more than it formerly could. Thus, the high-employment level of net national product will increase—say to $450 billion. Given this increase, it is obvious that there will be substantial unemployment if the $C + I + G$ line stays put. This is obvious enough. After all, if output remains the same and output per manhour increases, fewer workers will be needed and there

[11] Organization for Economic Cooperation and Development, *The Requirements of Automated Jobs,* Paris, 1965, p. 21.

Figure 17.2

Possible Effects of Technological Change on Equilibrium Level of Net National Product.

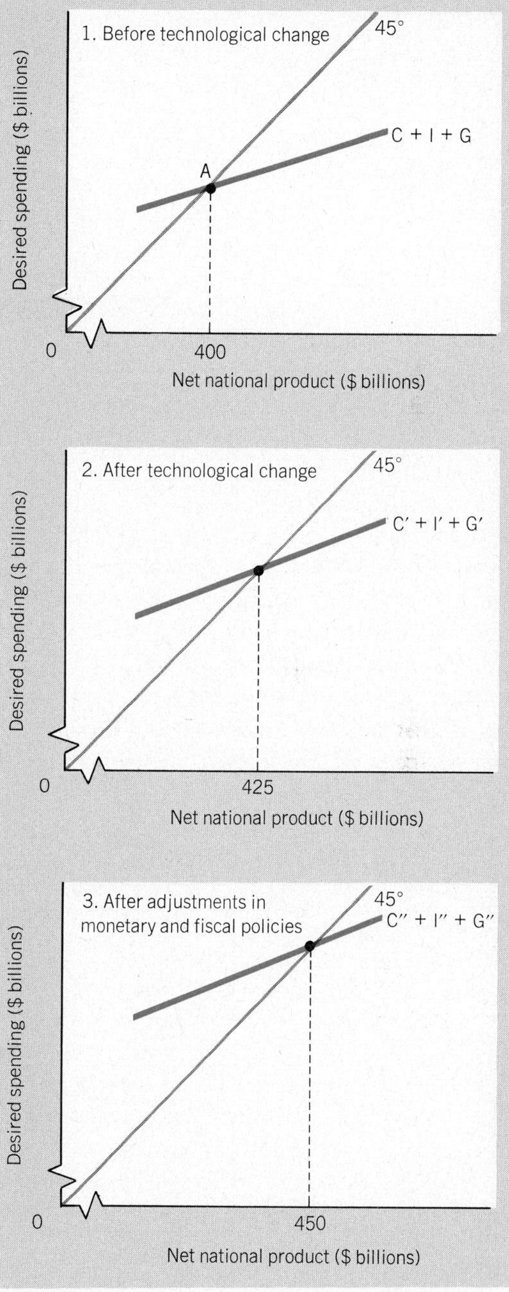

will be unemployment.

But there is no reason why the $C + I + G$ *line should remain constant.* The advance in technology itself may increase the profitability of investment, thus raising I. Moreover, the advance in technology may result in new consumer products, which prompt consumers to spend more of a given level of income, thus raising C. Suppose that, by virtue of these changes in C and I, the $C + I + G$ line shifts to $C' + I' + G'$ (shown in panel 2 of Figure 17.2). The new equilibrium level of net national product is \$425 billion, as shown in panel 2. Unfortunately, in this particular case (but not necessarily in other cases), the new equilibrium level of NNP is less than the new high-employment level of NNP. Thus, without some change in public policy, there would be some technological unemployment. But as we know, the Federal Reserve can increase I by increasing the money supply and reducing interest rates, and the government can push C upward by reducing tax rates and increase G by increasing its own expenditures. Thus, there is no reason why the government cannot raise the $C + I + G$ line to the point where it intersects the 45-degree line at \$450 billion. For example, the government might nudge the $C + I + G$ line up to $C'' + I'' + G''$ in panel 3 of Figure 17.2. And if it does this, the equilibrium level of net national product equals the high-employment level of net national product. Thus it should be possible to avoid large amounts of technological unemployment, although transitional problems, discussed in a subsequent section, will remain.

Structural Unemployment

The considerable concern during the 1950s and early 1960s that technological change would result in massive technological unemployment was heightened by fears that workers and jobs were becoming more and more mismatched. According to one group of economists, technological change and other factors were increasing the skill and educational requirements of available jobs, and making it more likely that shortages of highly educated workers would coexist with unemployed pools of unskilled workers. Unemployment of this sort—unemployment that occurs because the workers available for employment do not possess the qualities that employers require—is called ***structural unemployment.*** The economists who asserted that structural unemployment was growing in the late 1950s and early 1960s were often called the structuralists.

In opposition to the structuralists, another large group of economists denied that structural unemployment was increasing. An important and lively debate took place, both inside and outside the government, over the important question of how unemployment would respond to an increase in total spending. If an increase in total spending would reduce unemployment, then evidently at least that much unemployment was not structural. If it would fail to reduce unemployment, then the unemployment that remained could be called structural. To put the issue to a test, attempts were made to compare various periods when the general pressure of total spending was about the same, to see whether the level of unemployment was higher or more strongly concentrated in certain skill categories, industries, or regions in more recent periods than in the past.

Although neither side had a monopoly on the truth, the results of these tests, as well as the course of events since the 1964 tax cut, provided little support for the structuralist view. There was no evidence that unemployment was becoming more concentrated in particular geographic regions. Moreover, after adjusting for the effect of the overall unemployment rate on the unemployment rate in particular occupations and industries, very few occupations or industries showed an unambiguous tendency for unemployment to increase with time. Also, after adjusting for the effects of the overall unemployment rate, there was no significant tendency for unemployment rates among blacks to rise during the late 1950s and early 1960s. Thus, although a substantial portion of all unemployment may have been structural, there was no evidence that unemployment of this type increased greatly during that period.

Labor Displacement

Economic growth often occurs as a consequence of innovation and the redeployment of resources, which in turn means that *people*—workers, managers, owners of capital—*must adapt to these innovations and redeployments of resources.* Some people lose their jobs, some must move to other places, and some must enter new occupations. For example, consider the movement of people from agricultural to urban areas in the United States—a movement that has been part of the process of economic growth. During the postwar period, the number of farm owners and farm workers declined by over 40 percent. Innovations in agriculture—ranging from chemical fertilizers and insecticides to the mechanical cotton picker and huge harvesting combines—have contributed to this exodus, although they are by no means the only reason. Of those who left agriculture, many wound up in urban ghettos, many lacked the skills and education needed to fill urban jobs, and many who adapted to their new surroundings did so at considerable cost in psychological and emotional terms. Such human costs do not show up in the gross national product. Yet they are important costs, or disadvantages, of economic growth.

Although an adequate level of total spending can go a long way toward assuring that aggregate unemployment will not exceed a socially acceptable minimum, it cannot prevent labor from being displaced from particular occupations, industries, and regions, and being drawn to others. Nor would we want to eliminate all such movements of labor, without which it would be impossible to adjust to changes in technology, population, and consumer tastes. However, regardless of the long-run benefits of this adjustment process, important problems may arise in the short run, and great distress may be imposed on the workers who are displaced. These movements of labor must be carried out as efficiently and painlessly as possible.

The most serious adjustment problems have occurred when massive displacement has occurred in isolated areas among workers with specialized skills and without alternative sources of employment. Coal miners are a good example. About ⅔ of the nation's bituminous coal miners in 1960 were located in West Virginia, Pennsylvania, and Kentucky, and most of the coal mining was concentrated in isolated towns. Employment in bituminous coal started to decline after World War II, partly because of shifting demand and the adoption of new techniques. Between 1947 and 1959, total employment in the industry declined by more than 60 percent, leading to an unemployment rate of roughly 10 percent of the labor force in 5 major bituminous coal areas during most of the 1950s. In 25 smaller areas where there were few job opportunities outside coal mining, the unemployment rate was even higher.

Displaced older workers have encountered particularly serious problems. Seniority rights have helped hold down the displacement of older workers; but once unemployed, they are less likely than younger workers to be reemployed. For example, one year after the shutdown of the Packard automobile plant in Detroit, 77 percent of the workers under 45 were working at another job, whereas the percentages were 67 for the 45-to-54 age group and 62 for the 55-to-64 age group. Even if skill is held constant, the older workers had more serious unemployment problems than the younger workers, at least as measured by length of unemployment. Another study obtained similar results for a period when the general level of employment was higher than in the Packard case. It is easy to understand why older workers have more trouble finding another job. Many of their skills are specific to a particular job, and much of their income and status may be due to seniority, so that they cannot command as high a wage on the open market as they previously earned. Moreover, employers naturally are reluctant to invest in hiring and training a worker who will only be available for a relatively few years and who often has relatively limited education. Finally, because of their roots in the community, older workers are less likely to move to other areas where jobs are more plentiful.

Displaced black workers seem to find it even more difficult than older workers to obtain suitable reemployment at their previous status and earnings. For example, among workers who had been earning the same wage at Packard, blacks experienced a higher average length of unemployment than whites. Moreover, the prestige and economic level of the new job were more likely to be lower for blacks than whites. Needless to say, prejudice often plays an important role in preventing displaced blacks from obtaining new jobs.

Manpower and Training Policies

Beyond insuring an adequate level of total spending, perhaps the most important way that the government can facilitate adjustment to the adoption of new techniques is by promoting the necessary adaptability of the labor force through education and training. Education can increase the versatility and flexibility of the work force and increase its ability to adjust to change. It can open up greater opportunities and improve the productivity of workers at any level of skill or ability. The available evidence indicates the importance of a broad-based secondary education rather than a narrow vocational education. The training for many—perhaps most—specific jobs can and should be done on the job.

Turning from the education of tomorrow's work force to the retraining of today's, it is generally agreed that the government should help workers who are casualties of technological (and other) change to obtain the skills required to return to productive employment. A coordinated, integrated system of adult retraining, which takes proper account of nationwide needs and supplies and reaches the underprivileged and hard-core unemployed, is useful and important. However, it should be recognized that industry quite properly plays the predominant role in the vocational training and retraining of the work force, and that the government plays only a residual role. The difficulties faced by government-sponsored training programs are considerable, given the limitations of capacity of the vocational education system and the lack of basic education among the trainees.

The government can also promote greater efficiency of labor markets and better adjustment to change by providing better labor market information and by experimenting, in its role as employer, with new adjustment techniques. Job seekers typically have relatively little information about alternative job openings. The federal government should do what it can to expand the amount and quality of available information—keeping in mind that the costs incurred must bear a reasonable relationship to the benefits attained. As well as exploring new ways of disseminating information to those who need and want work, the government might also investigate new education technologies to recognize individual potential and to promote faster and better learning.

Visions of the Economic Future

Finally, let's turn to the rate of economic growth in the future. What sort of economic growth rate is the United States likely to experience between now and the year 2000? Long-range economic forecasting is a hazardous business—unless, of course, the forecaster is so old and the forecast so far in the future that he can be sure of being dead before anyone can tell whether the forecast was right or wrong. As we saw in Chapter 11, it is difficult enough to forecast what will happen next year, let alone 25 years from now. Nonetheless, for some purposes, long-range economic forecasts are useful and need to be made. What do they indicate about the future rate of economic growth in the United States?

In 1967, Herman Kahn, the well-known physicist and strategic theorist, collaborated with sociolo-

John Maynard Keynes

on "Economic Possibilities for Our Grandchildren"

Let us, for the sake of argument, suppose that a hundred years hence we are all of us, on the average, eight times better off in the economic sense than we are today. Assuredly there need be nothing here to surprise us.

Now it is true that the needs of human beings may seem to be insatiable. But they fall into two classes—those needs which are absolute in the sense that we feel them whatever the situation of our fellow human beings may be, and those which are relative in the sense that we feel them only if their satisfaction lifts us above, makes us feel superior to, our fellows. Needs of the second class, those which satisfy the desire for superiority, may indeed be insatiable; for the higher the general level, the higher still are they. But this is not so true of the absolute needs—a point may soon be reached, much sooner perhaps than we are all of us aware of, when these needs are satisfied in the sense that we prefer to devote our further energies to non-economic purposes.

Now, for my conclusion, which you will find, I think, to become more and more startling to the imagination the longer you think about it.

I draw the conclusion that, assuming no important wars and no important increase in population, the *economic problem* may be solved, or be at least within sight of solution, within a hundred years. This means that the economic problem is not—if we look into the future—*the permanent problem of the human race.*

Why, you may ask, is this so startling? It is startling because—if, instead of looking into the future we look into the past—we find that the economic problem, the struggle for subsistence, always has been hitherto the primary, most pressing problem of the human race—not only of the human race, but of the whole of the biological kingdom from the beginnings of life in its most primitive forms.

Thus we have been expressly evolved by nature —with all our impulses and deepest instincts— for the purpose of solving the economic problem. If the economic problem is solved, mankind will be deprived of its traditional purpose.

Will this be a benefit? If one believes at all in the real values of life, the prospect at least opens up the possibility of benefit. Yet I think with dread of the readjustment of the habits and instincts of the ordinary man, bred into him for countless generations, which he may be asked to discard within a few decades.

John Maynard Keynes, *Essays in Persuasion*, London: Macmillan, 1933. Originally published in 1930.

gist Anthony Wiener to produce some forecasts of what the world will be like by the year 2000. In their view, economic growth will probably have resulted in a per capita gross national product of at least $10,000 (in terms of 1965 prices) in the United States. This is a very, very high standard of living. For comparison, recall that per capita GNP in 1970 was about $4,800. Thus, Kahn and Weiner believe that per capita GNP will be more than twice as high in 2000 as in 1970. In their view the United States will have become a "post-industrial society". There will be a reduction in society's emphasis on efficiency and production, less attention paid to traditional work-oriented values, much more leisure, and a much looser relationship between work and income.[12]

Certainly, if these are truly the characteristics of the future, it is not at all what was anticipated by many of the great economists of the past. Malthus and Ricardo never dreamed of such affluence, and Marx never dreamed it could happen under capitalism. Only Keynes, who lived much later than the others, could see the handwriting on the wall. In a famous article written in 1930, he concluded that, "assuming no important wars and no important increase in population, the *economic problem* may be solved, or be at least within sight of solution, within a hundred years."[13] Specifically, he hazarded the guess that we might then be 8 times better off economically than at the time he was writing.

At first glance, it may seem that if Keynes and Kahn and Wiener are right, we are on the threshold of solving practically all our problems. But upon closer examination, one cannot escape the feeling that there are likely to be important problems in adjusting to such a level of affluence. As Keynes put it so well:

> I think with dread of the readjustment of the habits and instincts of the ordinary man, bred into him for countless generations, which he may be asked to discard within a few decades. . . . (For) the first time since his creation man will be faced with his real, his permanent problem—how to use his freedom from pressing economic cares, how to occupy his leisure, which science and compound interest will have won for him, to live wisely and agreeably and well.

Nonetheless, one must be very pessimistic about the intelligence and imagination of our people if he regards such problems as outweighing the benefits of this economic freedom. Admittedly, the rich have their problems, but there are few poor people who wouldn't trade places with them. In time, is it too much to expect that we will learn how to use these riches to build a better life than we, or others, have known before? I think not. In time, is it too much to expect that we will become more willing and able to share these riches with the poorer nations of the world? I hope not. On this latter point, it is important to understand that the forecasts of milk and honey by the year 2000 are for the industrialized countries, not the less developed countries. The prospects for the latter are less cheerful, as we shall see in Chapter 33.

Summary

Compared with that of other major industrial countries, America's rate of economic growth has been quite impressive over the past century, although in recent years many industrialized countries have experienced higher growth rates than we have. Our relatively rapid economic growth has been due to a variety of important factors, such as rapid technological change, increases in education and training, investment in plant and equipment, plentiful natural resources, and our social and entrepreneurial climate. However, not all aspects of the American economy have been conducive to rapid economic growth. Actual GNP has fallen short of potential GNP, and monopolies and immobilities have prevented efficient resource allocation.

Having reached a level of affluence that would have astonished Smith, Ricardo, Malthus, or Marx (but not Keynes), the industrialized nations are

[12] Herman Kahn and Anthony J. Weiner, *The Year 2000*, New York: Macmillan, 1967.
[13] John Maynard Keynes, "Economic Possibilities for our Grandchildren," reprinted in *Essays in Persuasion*, London: Macmillan, 1933.

now at a point where some observers question the wisdom of further economic growth. The critics of growth assert that more output does not bring more happiness, that economic growth is likely to result in additional environmental pollution, that we are rich enough now to solve our major social problems, and that extra growth is not worth the sacrifices it requires. On the other hand, the proponents of growth argue that it will bring higher living standards, that it will enable us to solve such national problems as poverty, and that it is important for reasons of national defense and national prestige. Although the critics of growth have made some headway, there has been no renunciation of economic growth as a goal of public policy. To stimulate the rate of economic growth, governments can encourage investment in technology, education, and plant and equipment, as well as reduce the gap between actual and potential GNP.

Although rapid technological change is an important stimulus to economic growth, it can also result in technological unemployment. If the government increases total spending at the proper rate, there is no reason why technological unemployment should be large. But an adequate level of total spending cannot prevent labor from being displaced from particular occupations, industries, and regions, and being drawn to others. This adjustment process, which results in long-run benefits, may impose great distress on the workers who are involved. It is important than these movements of labor be carried out as efficiently and painlessly as possible. Through its manpower and training policies, the government can help to distribute the "costs of change" more equitably. According to various long-term forecasts, per capita real GNP in the United States is likely to be more than twice as high in 2000 as in 1970. If this turns out to be true, many economic problems will be solved, but many will still remain.

CONCEPTS FOR REVIEW

Benefits from economic growth
Costs of economic growth
Limits to economic growth
Automation
Structural unemployment
Technological unemployment
Investment tax credit

QUESTIONS FOR DISCUSSION AND REVIEW

1. According to E. J. Mishan, "If the moving spirit behind economic growth were to speak, its motto would be 'Enough does not suffice.'" Do you agree?

2. According to Robert Solow, "The Doomsday Models [by Forrester et al., say that continued economic growth is, possible . . . because (a) the earth's natural resources will soon be used up; (b) increased industrial production will soon strangle us in pollution; and (c) increased population will eventually outrun the world's capacity to grow food." Do you agree with these models?

3. Increases in the rate of technological change necessarily result in increases in aggregate unemployment. True or False?

4. In order to stimulate economic growth the government probably would *not*
a. increase expenditures on research and development.
b. increase investment in education and training.
c. decrease aggregate investment in plant and equipment.
d. decrease the gap between actual and potential output.

CHAPTER 18

Environmental Pollution

According to many scientists and social observers, one of the costs of economic growth is environmental pollution. For many years, people in the United States paid relatively little attention to the environment and what they were doing to it, but this attitude has changed markedly in the last decade. Now the public seems genuinely concerned about environmental pollution. Even television stars ask that we be kind to the environment. However, in the effort to clean up the environment, choices are not always clear, nor solutions easy. For example, the "energy crisis" that surfaced in the fall of 1973 has brought home the fact that a cleaner environment is not costless. There are major tasks here for the economist, since most environmental issues ultimately come down to questions of economics.

In this chapter, we discuss the nature and causes of environmental pollution, as well as its relationship to the rate of economic growth. After describing the extent of the various kinds of pollution today, we show that excessive pollution results from certain defects in the economic system. Basically, as we shall see, it occurs because of external diseconomies in waste disposal. We also discuss various ways in which public policy might help to solve the problem, with particular attention to direct regulation, effluent fees, and tax credits. Finally, we describe the nature and extent of existing pollution control programs in the United States.

The Nature and Extent of Environmental Pollution

To see what we mean by environmental pollution, let's begin with one of the most important parts of man's environment, our water supplies. As a result of human activities, large amounts of pollutants are discharged into streams, lakes, and the sea. Chemical wastes are released by industrial plants and mines, as well as by farms and homes when fertilizers, pesticides, and detergents run off into waterways. Oil is discharged into the waters by tankers, sewage systems, oil wells, and other sources. (A spectacular example occurred in California in 1969, when an offshore oil well blew out in the Santa Barbara channel, fouling beaches and killing fish and birds for miles around.) Organic compounds enter waterways from industrial plants and farms, as well as from municipal sewage plants; and animal wastes, as well as human wastes, contribute substantially to pollution.

To reduce the ill effects of water pollution, waste water is sometimes subjected to a treatment process, in which the water is separated from the solid waste, and both are treated so as to protect public health and in-stream life. Generally, the treatment occurs in one or two phases. Primary treatment takes large particles out of the water and lets some of the smaller particles settle out as sludge before releasing the water to a nearby stream or river. Secondary treatment employs a controlled sequence of aeration and settling processes. According to a 1962 survey, 20 percent of the waste water in communities with sewage systems was untreated, and 28 percent received only primary treatment.

Obviously, we cannot continue to increase the rate at which we dump wastes into our streams, rivers, and oceans. A river, like everything else, can bear only so much. The people of Cleveland know this well: in 1969, the Cuyahoga River, which flows through Cleveland, literally caught fire, so great was its concentration of industrial and other wastes. Of course, the Cuyahoga is an extreme case, but many of our rivers, including the Hudson and the Ohio, are badly polluted, as Table 18.1 shows. Water pollution is a nuisance and perhaps a threat: for example, according to the Public Health Service, we may be approaching a crisis with respect to drinking water.[1]

If clean water is vital to man's survival, so too is clean air. Yet the battle being waged against air pollution in most of our major cities has not been won. Particles of various kinds are spewed into the air by factories that utilize combustion processes, grind materials, or produce dust. Motor vehicles release lead compounds from gasoline and rubber particles worn from tires, helping to create that unheavenly condition known as smog. Citizens of Los Angeles are particularly familiar with smog, but few major cities have escaped at least periodic air pollution. No precise measures have been developed to gauge the effects of air pollution on public health and enjoyment, but some rough estimates suggest that perhaps 25 percent of all deaths from respiratory disease could be avoided by a 50 percent reduction in air pollution.

One of the most important contributors to air pollution is the combustion of fossil fuels, particularly coal and oil products: by-products of combustion comprise about 85 percent of the total amount of air pollutants in the United States. Most of these pollutants result from impure fuels or inefficient burning. Among the more serious pollutants are sulfur dioxide, carbon monoxide, and various

[1] See *Fortune,* February 1970, and D. Rohrer, D. Montgomery, M. Montgomery, D. Eaton, and M. Arnold, *The Environment Crisis,* Skokie, Ill.: National Textbook Company, 1970.

Table 18.1

Water Pollution for Major Drainage Areas, United States, 1970 and 1971

Major watershed	Stream miles	Polluted miles 1970	Polluted miles 1971	Polluted miles Change
Ohio	28,992	9,869	24,031	+14,162
Southeast	11,726	3,109	4,490	+ 1,381
Great Lakes	21,374	6,580	8,771	+ 2,191
Northeast	32,431	11,895	5,823	− 6,072
Middle Atlantic	31,914	4,620	5,627	+ 1,007
California	28,277	5,359	8,429	+ 3,070
Gulf	64,719	16,605	11,604	− 5,001
Missouri	10,448	4,259	1,839	− 2,420
Columbia	30,443	7,443	5,685	− 1,758
United States	260,324	69,739	76,299	+ 6,560

Source: Council on Environmental Quality, *Third Annual Report,* August 1972.

oxides of nitrogen. Table 18.2 shows the total amount of major air pollutants emitted by various sources, and Figure 18.1 shows the upward trend in the amount of these emissions. According to some observers, the worst air pollution threat for the future lies in the tremendous growth of the electric power industry. Some technologists hope that nuclear energy, which does not pollute the air, will provide the power the American economy needs. However, it will be a long time before nuclear energy is likely to supply most of the nation's energy, and even then, the environment may be subjected to hazards. Nuclear reactors can cause thermal pollution of rivers and streams, and radiation may be a threat despite various preventive measures.

At present, the automobile is the principal source of air pollution in the United States. According to some estimates, human activities pump into the air over 200 million tons of waste each year, and automobiles can be credited with the dubious honor of contributing about 40 percent of this figure. Spurred on by the public interest in pollution control, some technologists have been hard at work on substitutes for the internal combustion engine. Attempts have been—and are being—made to devise economical and convenient electric and steam-driven automobiles. To date, however, these efforts have not succeeded. Thus it seems likely that, in the near future at least, we shall have to rely heavily on modifications of the internal combustion engine and its fuel to reduce air pollution.[2] (More use of nonpolluting transport like bicycles and feet would help too.)

Unfortunately, the air and water are not the only parts of man's environment that are being polluted. Each year, we produce an enormous amount of solid waste. Junk heaps testify to the quantity of superannuated cars left, like mechanical corpses, to mar the scenery. Each year industry produces literally mountains of waste and refuse. And picnic lovers and beer drinkers the world over are engaged in what sometimes seems a conspiracy to distribute cans, bottles, and other trash in every conceivable quarter. (Indeed, they sometimes even deposit some in a trash basket!) And it must be noted that the problem is not merely an aesthetic one. Our nation's cities are buckling under the

[2] Ibid. Also, see L. Lave and E. Seskin, "Air Pollution and Human Health," *Science,* August 21, 1970.

Table 18.2

Estimated Emissions of Air Pollutants by Weight, Nationwide, 1970

Source	Carbon monoxide	Particulates	Sulfur oxides	Hydrocarbons	Nitrogen oxides
	(millions of tons per year)				
Transportation	110.0	0.7	1.0	19.5	11.7
Fuel combustion in stationary sources	0.8	6.8	26.5	0.6	10.0
Industrial processes	11.4	13.1	6.0	5.5	0.2
Solid waste disposal	7.2	1.4	0.1	2.0	0.4
Miscellaneous	16.8	3.4	0.3	7.1	0.4
Total	147.2	25.4	33.9	34.7	22.7

Source: Council on Environmental Quality, *Third Annual Report,* August 1972.

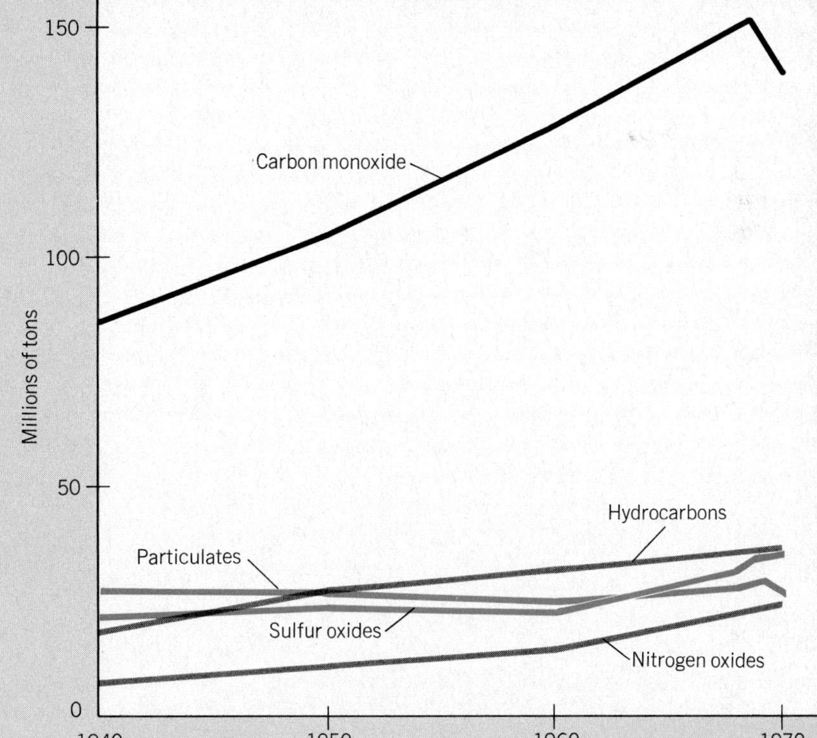

Figure 18.1
Weight of Emission of Air Pollutants, United States, 1940–70

Among the most serious air pollutants are carbon monoxide, sulfur oxides, nitrogen oxides, particulates, and hydrocarbons. In the past 30 years, the amount of these pollutants emitted in the United States has increased.

strain of disposing of all the solid waste generated by the affluent society.

There are other problems too. In many of our cities, the noise level is annoying and perhaps dangerous. Then there is thermal pollution. Water is used to cool machinery, particularly in electric power plants; in the process, the water is heated and when discharged, raises the water temperature in the stream or lake into which it flows. Thus, the solubility of certain substances may rise, the water may become more toxic and unable to hold as much oxygen, and the behavior patterns and reproductive capacities of fish may be altered. As for fish, so perhaps for man. There are questions about the extent to which man's production and disposal of wastes may render the earth uninhabitable for various kinds of life. To be sure, many of the most pessimistic and shocking predictions are probably little more than science fiction, but the questions are too important to be dismissed without careful consideration.

The Important Role of External Diseconomies

The reason why our economic system has tolerated pollution of the environment lies largely in the concept of external diseconomies, which we mentioned in Chapter 5. An ***external diseconomy*** occurs when one person's (or firm's) use of a resource damages other people who cannot obtain proper compensation. When this occurs, a market economy is unlikely to function properly. The price system is based on the supposition that the full cost of using each resource is borne by the person or firm that uses it. If this is not the case and if the user bears only part of the full costs, then the resource is not likely to be directed by the price system into the socially optimal use.

To understand why, we might begin by reviewing briefly how resources are allocated in a market economy. As we saw in Chapter 4, resources are used in their socially most valuable way because they are allocated to the people and firms who find it worthwhile to bid most for them, assuming that prices reflect true social costs. For example, under these circumstances, a paper mill that maximizes its profits will produce the socially desirable output of paper and use the socially desirable amounts of timber, labor, capital, and other resources.

Suppose, however, that because of the presence of external diseconomies people and firms do not pay the true social costs for resources. For example, suppose that some firms or people can use water and air for nothing, but that other firms or people incur costs as a consequence of this prior use. In this case, the ***private costs*** of using air and water differ from the ***social costs:*** *the price paid by the user of water and air is less than the true cost to society.* In a case like this, users of water and air are guided in their decisions by the private cost of water and air—by the prices they pay. Since they pay less than the true social costs, water and air are artificially cheap to them, so that they will use too much of these resources, from society's point of view.

Note that the divergence between private and social cost occurs if and only if the use of water or air by one firm or person imposes costs on other firms or persons. Thus, if a paper mill uses water and then treats it to restore its quality, there is no divergence between private and social cost. But when the same mill dumps wastes into streams and rivers (the cheap way to get rid of its by-products), the towns downstream that use the water must incur costs to restore its quality. The same is true of air pollution. An electric power plant uses the atmosphere as a cheap and convenient place to dispose of wastes, but people living and working nearby may incur costs as a result, since the incidence of respiratory and other diseases may increase.

We said above that pollution-causing activities that result in external diseconomies represent a malfunctioning of the market system. Let's examine this statement at greater length. *Firms and people dump too much waste material into the water and the atmosphere. The price system does not provide the proper signals because the polluters are induced to use our streams and atmosphere in this socially undesirable way by the artificially low price of disposing of wastes in this manner. Moreover, because the polluters do not pay the true cost of waste disposal, their products are artificially cheap, so that too much is produced of them.*

Consider two examples. Electric power companies do not pay the full cost of disposing of wastes in the atmosphere. They charge an artificially low price, and the public is induced to use more electric power than is socially desirable. Similarly, since the owners of automobiles do not pay the full cost of disposing of exhaust and other wastes in the atmosphere, they pay an artificially low price for operating an automobile, and the public is induced to own and use more automobiles than is socially desirable.[3]

The Polluted Hudson and the Tin Can: Two Case Studies[4]

Richmond is a village of about 2,000 people about 10 miles south of Albany. It is situated at a very badly polluted place on the Hudson River. The water is brown with the human and industrial wastes of Albany, Troy, and other cities upstream, as well as with the wastes dumped into the river locally. In the area immediately around Richmond, two of the principal polluters are the village of Richmond itself and the Smith Paper Company. The village's sewer mains dump their contents into the river, and the Smith Paper Company discharges its untreated wastes into a creek that flows into the river.

[3] L. Ruff, "The Economic Common Sense of Pollution," *The Public Interest,* Spring 1970; R. Solow, "The Economist's Approach to Pollution and Its Control," *Science,* August 6, 1971; and M. Goldman, *Controlling Pollution,* Englewood Cliffs, N.J.: Prentice-Hall, 1967.

[4] The names Richmond and Smith are fictitious, but otherwise the case study given in the first part of this section, taken from an article in the *New York Times,* May 4, 1970, is factual.

The people of Richmond have dragged their heels about building a sewage treatment system because they have felt that unless towns upstream took action, their own efforts would be fruitless. After some prodding by New York State, a referendum was held in 1968 to vote on a sewer district, but it was turned down by the voters. Needless to say, part of the reason was that the people of the village would have to pay about $85 per family per year for the water treatment system. Despite the state's nudging, the officials of Richmond admit that it will be a long time before the problem is taken care of.

The Smith Paper Company has also been slow to do anything about water pollution. State health officials ordered it to clean up its effluent by July 1970, but the Company did not formulate a preliminary plan for a treatment system until April 1970. According to many reports, the Company was not in healthy financial condition, and Smith's treatment costs, according to some of its engineers, could run as high as $300,000—or about 10 percent of the value of its plant. Obviously, one reason why this plant remains in business is that it does not pay the full social costs of waste disposal. Obviously, too, the price of its paper is artificially low for this reason. This is no criticism of the Company. In a free enterprise economy, firms are expected to be motivated by profit. The problem is that, because of external diseconomies, the market system does not insure that the private costs of waste disposal equal the social costs. The result is a polluted river.

Richmond is an example of one type of pollution. To understand how external diseconomies can result in another type of pollution, consider the cans and bottles that are so conspicuous a part of our nation's litter problem. Years ago, beer, soft drinks, and other such liquids came in relatively expensive bottles on which there was a deposit. Typically, when you purchased a bottle of beverage, you had to deposit $.05 for the bottle. If you didn't bring back the bottle, you didn't get the $.05 back. If someone else found—or stole—your bottle, he could take it back and get the

Figure 18.2
Beer Containers by Type, United States, 1957–76

In recent years, metal cans and nonreturnable bottles have captured a much larger share of the market, while returnable bottles, which result in less trash and litter, have become far scarcer.

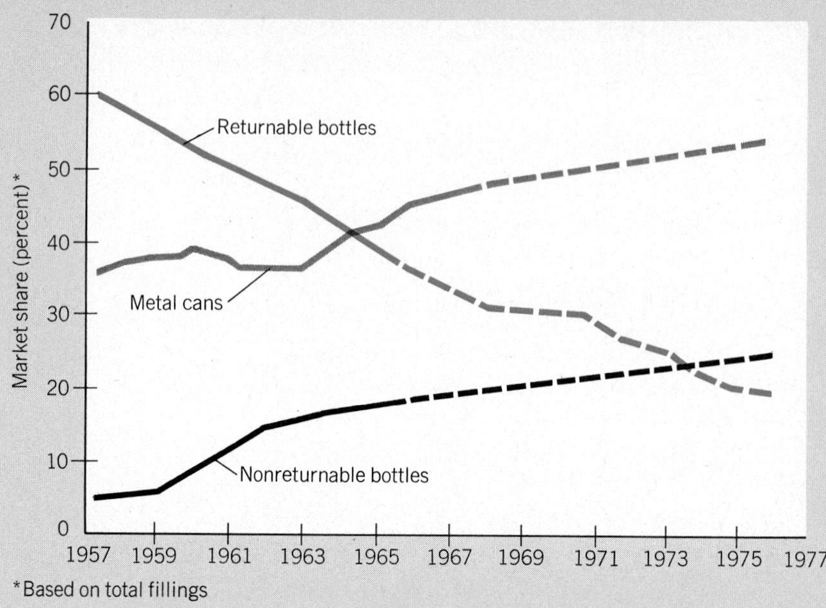

money. Since $.05 was a significant amount in those days, there were few bottles lying around as unsightly litter. Kids—and more than a few adults—were only too glad to pick them up and take them back to the store to get the deposit. Thus, in those days, the system worked in such a way that the purchaser of the beverage paid for the cost of bringing the bottle back to the store. Either he took it back himself (and got his deposit back), or in effect he paid someone else $.05 to do it for him.

But this situation changed abruptly about 40 years ago, when producers of beer and soft drinks introduced a packaging innovation: the can. Unlike the old-fashioned bottle, there was no deposit on the can. Indeed, one of the advantages to consumers was that they didn't have to bother to take the cans back; they could simply throw them away. Consumers preferred the can for its convenience, and bottle manufacturers were forced to develop a cheaper no-deposit bottle to compete with cans. (Figure 18.2 shows the increase in recent years in the percentage of beer containers that are metal cans or nonreturnable bottles.) The result has been trash and litter, because there is no longer the same incentive to pick up cans and bottles or to return them to stores or manufacturers. Moreover, since bottles are no longer used over and over, there are more bottles and cans to dispose of.

It is important to note that, once the cans and no-deposit bottles were introduced, the consumer of beverages no longer had to pay for the cost of disposing of the cans or bottles. Basically, this was the reason for the litter problem. In other words, there was now an external diseconomy, since purchasers and consumers of beverages imposed costs on other people, who had to bear the expense of disposing of the litter. Of course, this was not always the case, since many people were public-spirited enough to dispose of their own cans and bottles, even without financial incentive. But our highways and parks testify to the fact that many people are not so public-spirited; as a result, certain states and localities have recently passed laws requiring the sale of deposit bottles.

Economic Growth and Environmental Pollution

According to many authorities, economic growth—defined as increases in total economic output per capita—has been associated with increases in the level of environmental pollution. This is not very surprising, since practically all the things that are produced must eventually be thrown away in one form or another. Thus, as output per capita goes up, the level of pollution is likely to go up as well. For example, as we grow more affluent and increase the number of automobiles per capita, we also increase the amount of such air pollutants as nitrogen oxide and tetraethyl lead, both of which are emitted by automobiles. We also increase the number of automobiles that eventually must be scrapped.

But it is important to recognize that pollution is not tied inextricably to national output. Although increases in national output in the past have been associated with increases in pollution, there is no reason why this correlation must continue unchanged in the future. Clearly, we can produce things that are heavy polluters of the environment—like electric power and automobiles—or we can produce things that do not pollute the environment nearly so much—like pianos and bicycles.

In recent years, some people have suggested that we curtail our economic growth in order to reduce pollution: ***Zero Economic Growth*** is their goal. Very few economists seem to favor such a policy. Opponents of Zero Economic Growth point out that more productive capacity would help produce the equipment required to reduce pollution. As we shall see, this equipment will not be cheap. Moreover, with proper public policies, we should be able to increase output without increasing pollution, if this is what our people want. In addition, as pointed out by Walter Heller of the University of Minnesota:

> Short of a believable threat of extinction, it is hard to believe that the public would accept the tight controls, lowered material living standards, and large income transfers required to create and manage a [no-growth] state. Whether the necessary shifts could be accomplished without vast unemployment and economic dislocation is another question. It may be that the shift to a no-growth state would throw the fragile ecology of our economic system so out of kilter as to threaten its breakdown. Like it or not, economic growth seems destined to continue.[5]

Some people have also argued that technological change is the real villain responsible for pollution, and that the rate of technological change should be slowed. Certainly, technological change has made people more interdependent, and brought about more and stronger external diseconomies. Technological change also results in ecological changes, some of which are harmful. For example, detergents contain phosphate, which induces water pollution by causing heavy overgrowths of algae.

But technological change is also a potential hero in the fight against pollution, because the creation of new technology is an important way to reduce the harmful side effects of existing techniques—assuming, of course, that we decide to use our scientists and engineers to this end. Contrary to some people's views, pollution is not the product of some mindless march of technology, but of human action and inaction. There is no sense in blaming technology, when pollution is due basically to economic, social, and political choices and institutions.

Finally, it is frequently suggested that, as our population increases, we must expect more pollution. Many who advocate a policy of ***Zero Population Growth*** advance the argument that it would help reduce the level of pollution. The available evidence indicates some relationship between a nation's population and its pollution levels. But there are important differences in the amount of pollution generated by people in various countries. The average American is responsible for much more pollution than the average citizen of most other countries, because the average American is a much bigger user of electric power, detergents, pesticides,

[5] W. Heller, "Economic Growth and Ecology—An Economist's View," *Monthly Labor Review,* November 1971.

and other such products. It has been estimated that the United States, with less than 1/10 of the world's population, produces about 1/3 of the wastes discharged into the air and water. Clearly, much more than economics is involved in the discussion of the optimal level of population. Although it is only one of a number of important factors, a nation's population does affect the level of pollution; but as we shall see in subsequent sections, pollution can be reduced considerably even if our population continues to grow.[6]

Public Policy toward Pollution

Pollution is caused by defects in our institutions, not by malicious intent, greed, or corruption. In cases where waste disposal causes significant external diseconomies, economists generally agree that government intervention may be justifiable. But how can the government intervene? Perhaps the simplest way is to issue certain regulations for waste disposal. For example, the government can prohibit the burning of trash in furnaces or incinerators, or the dumping of certain materials in the ocean; and make any person or firm that violates these restrictions subject to a fine, or perhaps even imprisonment. Also, the government can ban the use of chemicals like DDT, or require that all automobiles meet certain regulations for the emission of air pollutants. Further, the government can establish quality standards for air and water.

The government can also intervene by establishing effluent fees. An ***effluent fee*** is a fee a polluter must pay to the government for discharging waste. In other words, a price is imposed on the disposal of wastes into the environment; and the more a firm or individual pollutes, the more he must pay. The idea behind the imposition of effluent fees is that they can bring the private cost of waste disposal closer to the true social costs. Faced with a closer approximation to the true social costs of his activities, the polluter will reduce the extent to which he pollutes the environment. Needless to say, many practical difficulties are involved in carrying out this seemingly simple scheme, but many economists believe that this is the best way to deal with the pollution problem.[7]

Still another way for the government to intervene is to establish tax credits for firms that introduce pollution-control equipment. There are, of course, many types of equipment that a plant can introduce to cut down on pollution—for example, "scrubbers" for catching poisonous gases, and electrostatic precipitators for decreasing dust and smoke. But such pollution-control equipment costs money, and firms are naturally reluctant to spend money on purposes where the private rate of return is so low. To reduce the burden, the government can allow firms to reduce their tax bill by a certain percentage of the amount they spend on pollution-control equipment. Tax incentives of this sort have been discussed widely in recent years, and some have been adopted.

Direct Regulation

Let's look more closely at the advantages and disadvantages of each of these major means by which the government can intervene to remedy the nation's pollution problems. At present we rely mostly on direct regulation of waste disposal (and the quality of the environment); and despite the many problems involved, it has undoubtedly done much good. As Allen Kneese, one of the country's top experts in this area, says about water pollution,

[6] It must also be noted that pollution is not confined to capitalist countries; the Soviet Union and other Communist countries are afflicted by serious pollution problems. Nor is pollution anything new: for example, the ancient Romans complained of water pollution.

[7] Another possibility is for the government to issue a certificate or license to pollute. The government might issue a limited number of certificates, to be auctioned off to the highest bidders. Although it has theoretical possibilities, this technique is not being used to any appreciable extent at present.

"The control of water discharges through administrative orders regulating individual waste disposers has been a useful device and cannot be abandoned until we have a better substitute."[8]

However, economists agree that direct regulation suffers from some serious disadvantages. First, such regulations have generally taken the form of general, across-the-board rules. For example, if two factories located on the same river dump the same amount of waste material into the river, such regulations would probably call for each factory to reduce its waste disposal by the same amount. Unfortunately, although this may appear quite sensible, it may in fact be very inefficient. Suppose, for example, that it is much less costly for one factory to reduce its waste disposal than for the other. Clearly, in such a case, it would be more efficient to ask the factory that could reduce its wastes more cheaply to cut down more on its waste disposal than the other factory. For reasons of this sort, reductions in pollution are likely to be accomplished at more than minimum cost, if they are accomplished by direct regulation.

Second, to formulate such regulations in a reasonably sensible way, the responsible government agencies must have access to much more information than they are likely to obtain or assimilate. Unless the government agencies have a detailed and up-to-date familiarity with the technology of hundreds of industries, they are unlikely to make sound rules. Moreover, unless the regulatory agencies have a very wide jurisdiction, their regulations will be evaded by the movement of plants and individuals from localities where regulations are stiff to localities where they are loose. In addition, the regulatory agencies must view the pollution problem as a whole, since piecemeal regulation may simply lead polluters to substitute one form of pollution for another. For example, New York and Philadelphia have attempted to reduce water pollution by more intensive sewage treatment. However, one result has been the production of a lot of biologically active sludge that is being dumped into the ocean—and perhaps causing problems there.[9]

[8] A. Kneese, "Public Policy Toward Water Pollution," in E. Mansfield, *Microeconomics: Selected Readings,* New York: Norton, 1971, p. 467.

Effluent Fees

The use of effluent fees is the approach most economists seem to prefer, for the following reasons. First, it obviously is socially desirable to use the cheapest way to achieve any given reduction in pollution. A system of effluent fees is more likely to accomplish this objective than direct regulation, because the regulatory agency cannot have all the relevant information (as we noted above), whereas polluters, reacting in their own interest to effluent fees, will tend to use the cheapest means to achieve a given reduction in pollution.

To see why this is the case, consider a particular polluter. Faced with an effluent fee—that is, a price it must pay for each unit of waste it discharges—the polluter will find it profitable to reduce its discharge of waste to the point where the cost of reducing waste discharges by one unit equals the effluent fee. Why? Because, if the cost of reducing its waste disposal (i.e., its pollution) by an additional unit is less than the effluent fee, the firm can increase its profits by discharging less waste. On the other hand, if the cost of reducing its waste disposal (i.e., its pollution) by an additional unit is greater than the effluent fee, the firm can increase its profits by discharging more waste. Thus, if the firm is maximizing profit, the cost of reducing its waste disposal by an additional unit must equal the effluent fee.

It follows that, since the effluent fee is the same for all polluters, the cost of reducing waste discharges by one extra unit must be the same for all polluters. But if this is so, the total cost of achieving the resulting decrease in pollution must be a minimum. Why? Because the total cost of achieving a certain decrease in pollution is a mini-

[9] Solow, *op. cit.*

mum if the decrease is carried out so that the cost of reducing waste discharges by one extra unit is the same for all polluters. To see this, suppose that the cost of reducing waste discharges by an additional unit is *not* the same for all polluters. Then there is a cheaper way to reduce pollution to its existing level—by getting polluters whose cost of reducing waste discharges by an additional unit is low to reduce their waste disposal by an additional unit, and by allowing polluters whose cost of reducing waste discharges by an additional unit is high to increase their pollution commensurately.

Economists also favor effluent fees because this approach requires far less information in the hands of the relevant government agencies than does direct regulation. After all, when effluent fees are used, all the government has to do is meter the amount of pollution a firm or household produces (which admittedly is sometimes not easy) and charge accordingly. It is left to the firms and households to figure out the most ingenious and effective ways to cut down on their pollution and save on effluent fees. This is also a spur to inventive activities aimed at developing more effective ways to reduce pollution. Also, economists favor the use of effluent fees because financial incentives are likely to be easier to administer than direct regulation. Witness the case of Richmond, which illustrates the gap between regulation and enforceable performance.

To illustrate how effluent fees can produce more efficient ways to reduce pollution, consider a recent proposal by the state of Washington for reducing emission of sulfur oxides. The proposed regulation would oblige copper smelters to control 90 percent of the sulfur content of ore entering smelters. There is considerable disagreement over the cost of the regulation. The state says it would cost the smelters about $.02 per pound of copper to comply, whereas the smelters say it is technologically impossible to comply. Some people have suggested that one way to resolve this controversy might be to impose a fee equivalent to $.03 per pound of copper if the emission of sulfur oxide were not controlled. Then if the smelters could achieve 90 percent control for $.02 per pound, they would have every incentive to do so, thus increasing their profits. If they could not reach the goal, they would have an incentive to adopt other control measures or to develop new and less costly control devices.

While economists tend to favor the use of effluent fees, they are not always against direct regulation. Some ways of disposing of certain types of waste are so dangerous that the only sensible thing to do is to ban them. For example, a ban on the disposal of mercury or arsenic in places where human beings are likely to consume them—and die—seems reasonable enough. In effect, the social cost of such pollution is so high that a very high penalty—imprisonment—is put on it. In addition, of course, economists favor direct regulation when it simply is not feasible to impose effluent fees—for example, in cases where it would be prohibitively expensive to meter the amount of pollutants emitted by various firms or households.

The Ruhr: A Case Study[10]

Let's consider a well-known case of effluent fees in use—the Ruhr valley in West Germany. The Ruhr is one of the world's most industrialized areas. It includes about ⅓ of West Germany's industrialized capacity, and about 70 to 90 percent of West Germany's coal, coke, and iron and steel outputs. It contains about 10 million people and about 4,300 square miles. Water supplies in the Ruhr are quite limited: five small rivers supply the area. The amazing amount of waste materials these rivers carry is indicated by the fact that the average annual natural low flow is less than the volume of effluent discharged into the rivers. Yet the local water authorities have succeeded in making this small amount of water serve the needs of the firms and households of this tremendous industrial area, and at the same time the streams

[10] This section is based on A. Kneese and B. Bower, *Managing Water Quality: Economics, Technology, Institutions* (Resources for the Future, 1968), Chapter 12.

have been used for recreation. Moreover, all this has been achieved at a remarkably low cost. The success of water management in the Ruhr seems to be due in considerable part to institutional arrangements that allowed the German water managers to plan and operate a relatively efficient regional system. Collective water quality improvement measures are used. Water quality is controlled by waste treatment in over 100 plants, regulation of river flow by reservoir, and a number of oxidation lakes in the Ruhr itself.

Effluent fees are an integral part of the institutional arrangements governing water quality. The amount a firm has to pay depends upon how much waste—and what kind—it pumps into the rivers. A formula has been devised to indicate how much a polluter must pay to dispose of a particular type of waste. In simple terms, the formula bases the charge on the amount of clean water needed to dilute the effluent in order to avoid harm to fish. Using this formula, the local authorities can determine, after testing the effluent of any firm, the amount the firm should pay. Specifically, the amount depends on the amount of suspended materials that will settle out of the effluent, the amount of oxygen consumed by bacteria in a sample of effluent, the results of a potassium permanganate test, and the results of a fish toxicity test. You need not understand the nature or specific purposes of these measurements and tests. The important thing is that you understand their general aim—which is to measure roughly the amount of pollution caused by various kinds of wastes. Having made these measurements and tests, the local authorities use their formula to determine how much a firm must pay in effluent fees.

Tax Credits for Pollution-Control Equipment

Many tax inducements to encourage firms and individuals to install pollution-control equipment have been proposed. A typical suggestion is that the government offer a tax credit equal to 20 percent of the cost of pollution-control equipment, and allow a firm to depreciate such equipment in only 1 to 5 years. In this way, the government would help defray some of the costs of the pollution-control equipment by allowing a firm that installed such equipment to pay less taxes than if no such tax inducements existed.

However, such schemes have a number of disadvantages. For one, subsidies to promote the purchase of particular types of pollution-control equipment may result in relatively inefficient and costly reductions in pollution. After all, other methods that don't involve special pollution-control equipment—such as substituting one type of fuel for another—may sometimes be a more efficient way to reduce pollution. Also, subsidies of this sort may not be very effective. Even if the subsidy reduces the cost to the firm of reducing pollution, it may still be cheaper for the firm to continue to pollute. In other words, subsidies of this sort make it a little less painful for polluters to reduce pollution; but unlike effluent fees, they offer no positive incentive.

Furthermore, it seems preferable on grounds of equity for the firms and individuals that do the polluting—or their customers—to pay to clean up the mess that results. Effluent fees work this way, but with tax credits for pollution-control equipment, the government picks up part of the tab by allowing the polluter to pay lower taxes. In other words, the general public, which is asked to shoulder the additional tax burden to make up for the polluters' lower taxes, pays part of the cost. But is this a fair allocation of the costs? Why should the general public be saddled with much of the bill?

Pollution-Control Programs in the United States

In recent years, there has been considerable growth in government programs designed to control pollution. To take but one example, federal expenditures to reduce water pollution increased in the period from the mid-1950s to 1970 from about $1 million to $300 million annually. In water pollution, the federal government has for many years operated a system of grants-in-aid to state, municipal, or regional agencies to help construct treatment plants; and grants are made for research on new treatment methods. In addition, the 1970 Water Quality Improvement Act authorizes grants to demonstrate new methods and techniques and to establish programs to train people in water control management. (The federal government has also regulated the production and use of pesticides.) The states, as well as the federal government, have played an important role in water pollution control. They have been primarily responsible for setting standards for allowable pollution levels, and many state governments have provided matching grants to help municipalities construct treatment plants.

For air pollution, the federal government has disbursed funds to promote research and development to prevent and control the pollution of the atmosphere. Federal agencies offer extensive technical advice about air pollution and air quality standards. The states, as well as the federal government, have played an important role in setting air quality standards. Most states have also established planning commissions and pollution control boards, and have provided tax incentives to industry for abatement. Further, in the area of solid wastes, the government has made grants for research, training, and surveys of disposal techniques.

In 1969, the Congress established a new agency—the Council on Environmental Quality—to oversee and plan the nation's pollution control programs. Modeled to some extent on the Council of Economic Advisers, the Council on Environmental Quality, which has three members, is supposed to gather information on considerations and trends in the quality of the environment, review and evaluate the federal government's programs in this area, develop appropriate national policies, and conduct needed surveys and research on environmental quality. The tasks assigned to the council are obviously important ones. The extent to which this relatively new agency can carry out these tasks is difficult to say. It will be some time before the council's effectiveness can be appraised.

In 1970, the federal government established another new agency, the Environmental Protection Agency. Working with state and local officials, this agency establishes standards for desirable air and water quality, and devises rules for attaining these goals. For example, the government has required various sources of pollution to reduce their emission of pollutants so that these goals can be reached. According to the amendments to the Clean Air Act of 1967, automobiles in 1975 were supposed to cut emissions of carbon monoxide and hydrocarbons by 90 percent from 1970 levels, but this requirement has been softened. Because direct regulation of this sort suffers from the disadvantages cited in a previous section, there also has been some study of the use of effluent fees. For example, the government has considered imposing a fee on the emission of sulfur oxide into the air.

Many people feel that public policy is not moving as rapidly as it should in this area. Certainly, however, it is not easy to determine how fast or how far we should go in attempting to reduce pollution. Those who will bear the costs of pollution control projects—towns like Richmond, firms like the Smith Paper Company—have an understandable tendency to emphasize (and perhaps inflate) the costs and discount the benefits of such projects. Those who are particularly interested in enjoying nature and outdoor recreation—like the Sierra Club—are understandably inclined to emphasize (and perhaps inflate) the benefits and discount the costs of such projects. Politics inevitably plays a major role in the outcome of such cases. The citizens of the United States must indicate, through the ballot box as well as the marketplace, how much they are willing to pay to reduce pollution. We must also decide at what level of government the relevant rules are to be made. Since many pollution problems are local, it often seems sensible to determine the appropriate level of environmental quality locally. (However, there are obvious dangers in piecemeal regulation, as pointed out above.)

Cost of Cleaning Up the Environment

One of the most fundamental questions about pollution control is: how clean do we want the air, water, and other parts of our environment to be? At first glance, it may seem that we should restore and maintain a pristine pure environment, but this is not a very sensible goal, since the costs of achieving it would be enormous. The Environmental Protection Agency has estimated that it would cost about $60 billion to remove 85 to 90 percent of water pollutants from industrial and municipal sources by 1982. This is hardly a trivial amount, but it is far less than the cost of achieving zero discharge of pollutants, which would be about $320 billion—a truly staggering sum.

Fortunately, however, there is no reason to aim at so stringent a goal. It seems obvious that, as pollution increases, various costs to society increase as well. Some of these costs were described at the beginning of this chapter. For example, we pointed out that increases in air pollution result in increased deaths, and that increases in water pollution reduce the recreational value of rivers and streams. Suppose that we could get accurate data on the cost to society of various levels of pollution. Of course, it is extremely difficult to get such data, but if we could, we could determine the relationship between the amount of these costs and the level of pollution. Clearly, it would look like the hypothetical curve in Figure 18.3: the greater the level of pollution, the higher these costs will be.

But these costs are not the only ones that must be considered. We must also take into account the costs of controlling pollution. In other words, we must look at the costs to society of maintaining a certain level of environmental quality. These costs are not trivial, as we saw at the beginning of this section. To maintain a very low level of pollution, it is necessary to invest heavily in pollution-control equipment and to make other economic sacrifices. If we could get accurate data on the cost to society of controlling pollution, we could find the relationship between the amount of these costs and the level of pollution. Clearly, it would look like the hypothetical curve in Figure 18.4; the lower the level of pollution, the higher these costs will be.

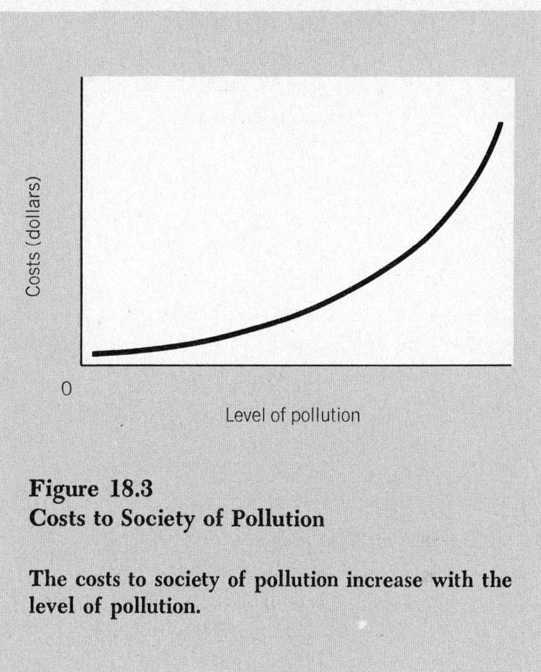

Figure 18.3
Costs to Society of Pollution

The costs to society of pollution increase with the level of pollution.

At this point, it should be obvious why we should not try to achieve a zero level of pollution. *The sensible goal for our society is to minimize the sum of the costs of pollution and the costs of controlling pollution.* In other words, we should construct a graph, as shown in Figure 18.5, to indicate the relationship between the sum of these two types of costs and the level of pollution. Then we should choose the level of pollution at which the sum of these two types of costs is a minimum. Thus, in Figure 18.5, we should aim for a pollution level of *A*. There is no point in trying for a lower level; such a reduction would cost more than it would be worth. For example, the cost of achieving a zero pollution level would be much more than it would be worth. Only when the pollution level exceeds *A* is the extra cost to society of the additional pollution greater than the cost of preventing it. For example, the cost of allowing pollution to increase from *A* to *B* is much greater than the cost of prevention.

It is easy to draw hypothetical curves, but not so easy actually to measure these curves. Unfortunately, no one has a very clear idea of what the curves in Figure 18.5 really look like—although we can be sure that their general shapes are like those shown there. Thus, no one really knows just how clean we should try to make the environment. Under these circumstances, expert opinion differs on the nature and extent of the programs that should be carried out, and the costs involved. Moreover, as pointed out in the previous section, political considerations and pressures enter in. Thus, while it is difficult to estimate how much the United States is likely to spend in the future

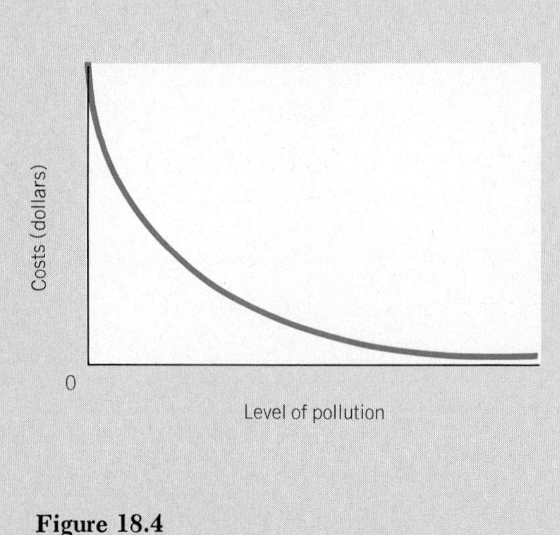

Figure 18.4
Costs to Society of Pollution Control

The more pollution is reduced, the higher are the costs to society of pollution control.

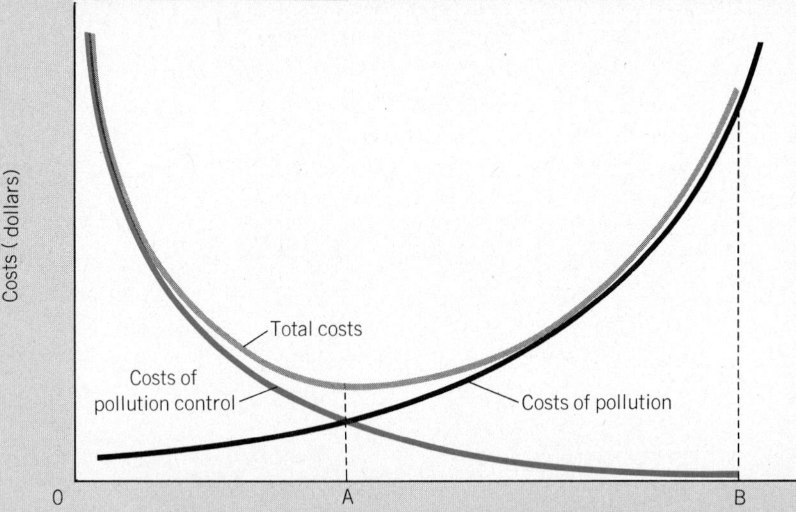

Figure 18.5
Determining Optimal Level of Pollution

The optimal level of pollution is at point *A*, since this is where the total costs are a minimum. Below point *A*, the cost to society of more pollution is less than the cost of preventing it. Above point *A*, the cost to society of more pollution is greater than the cost of preventing it.

Table 18.3

Costs to Industry of Pollution Control

Industry	Expenditures Actual 1971	Planned 1972	Planned 1975	Total investment required to meet 1972 standards
	(Millions of dollars)			
Electric utilities	565	1,027	1,188	6,190
Petroleum	527	542	462	2,690
Paper	257	494	224	1,980
Iron and steel	217	206	870	1,780
Nonferrous metals	111	269	149	1,670
Chemicals	282	445	419	1,250
Commercial	234	224	315	1,200
Stone, clay, and glass	112	173	195	780
Machinery	95	381	239	560
Food and beverages	101	158	208	550
Mining	61	192	157	470
Rubber	45	53	100	410
Fabricated metals	89	119	74	400
Instruments	60	74	119	260
Electrical machinery	70	70	91	240
Gas utilities	49	79	82	220
Total	3,245	4,906	5,378	22,760

Source: Business Week, May 13, 1972.

on pollution control, we can be sure that we will continue to live with considerable pollution—and that, for the reasons just given, this will be the rational thing to do.

According to a 1972 McGraw-Hill survey, American industry alone spent about $3.2 billion in 1971 and planned to spend about $4.9 billion in 1972 to control air and water pollution. To meet pollution control standards in effect as of January 1, 1972, industry would have to spend about $22.8 billion. (See Table 18.3.) It is important to recognize that the costs of pollution control extend far beyond the construction of more and better water treatment plants, or the more extensive control of gas emission, or other such steps. A serious pollution control program can put firms out of business, put people out of work, and bring economic trouble to communities that rely heavily on industries and farms that must pollute to compete. This is not to argue that polluters should be allowed to pay less than the true social cost of disposing of their wastes; but any pollution control program must allow firms and workers time to make the necessary adjustments.

We must also recognize that a pollution control system can result in a redistribution of income. For example, automobiles, electric power, and other goods and services involving considerable pollution are likely to increase in price relative to other goods and services involving little pollution. To the extent that polluting goods and services play a bigger role in the budgets of the poor than of the rich, pollution control hurt the poor and help the rich. This effect can be offset by using the tax system and the expenditures of the government, but, as we have seen, this is easier said than done.

How Should We Dispose of Materials?

In conclusion, it must be stressed that the entire pollution problem is basically concerned with how to dispose of materials in our society. Economists and others customarily speak of people "consuming" goods. The word "consume" suggests that nothing is left of the goods after "consumption," but in truth they are still very much with us. Sometimes they are transformed into waste materials; sometimes they are banged up and useless; sometimes they are changed from a solid state to a gaseous state. But they are still around, and they have to be disposed of somehow. Moreover, some ways of disposing of them are better from society's point of view than others. For example, it may be better to bury certain types of wastes in the ground than to pollute the air.

An interesting scheme to help solve this problem has been proposed by Princeton's Edwin Mills.[11] It is not yet at the stage of serious consideration for practical application, but it is nonetheless an interesting stimulus to further thought in this area. Mills proposes that the government collect from the original producer or importer of certain raw materials a fee equal to the cost to society if each material were disposed of in the most harmful way. Then the fee would be returned, in part or in full, when the material was returned to the environment—that is, disposed of. If it was disposed of in a socially innocuous way, the full fee would be returned, but the more harmful the method of disposal, the less the refund.

[11] E. Mills, *User Fees and the Quality of the Environment,* in preparation.

An advantage of this scheme is that prices of materials would tend to reflect their true social costs—including the costs of disposal. There are also lots of practical difficulties: for one, owners of some materials would be hit with a large financial loss. Whether or not Mills' scheme is practical, it has the considerable virtue of looking at the pollution problem in the right light—as how we are to dispose of materials. If you are concerned about the environmental issue, you would be well advised to study further the economic (and technological) aspects of this problem. The environment you save is bound to be your own.

Summary

One of the major social issues of the 1970s is environmental pollution. As a result of human activities, great quantities of chemicals, industrial wastes, pesticides, fertilizers, animal wastes, and human wastes are being dumped into the rivers, lakes, and oceans. Particles of various kinds are being spewed into the air by factories that utilize combustion processes, or that grind materials, or that produce dust. Lead compounds from gasoline and rubber particles worn from tires are being released into the atmosphere by motor vehicles. Each year we produce an enormous amount of solid waste—junked cars, garbage, cans, bottles, and other trash. In addition, noise pollution assaults our ears, and thermal pollution degrades our lakes and rivers. Many observers regard these various forms of pollution as a problem that must be dealt with much more effectively in the future than it has been in the past.

To a considerable extent, environmental pollution is an economic problem. Waste disposal and other pollution-causing activities result in external diseconomies. Specifically, the firms and individuals that pollute the water and air (and other facets of the environment) pay less than the true social costs of disposing of their wastes in this way. Part of the true social cost is borne by other firms and individuals who must pay to clean up the water or air, or who must live with the consequences. Because of the divergence of private from social costs, the market system does not result in an optimal allocation of resources. Firms and individuals create too much waste and dispose of it in excessively harmful ways. Because the polluters do not pay the full cost of waste disposal, their products are artificially cheap, with the result that too much is produced of them.

The government can intervene in several ways to help remedy the breakdown of the market system in this area. One way is to issue regulations for waste disposal and other activities influencing the environment. Another is to establish effluent fees, charges a polluter must pay to the government for discharging wastes. Two important advantages of effluent fees are that they are more likely to result in the use of the minimum-cost way to achieve a given reduction in pollution and that they require far less information in the hands of the relevant government agencies than direct regulation. Still another way for the government to intervene is to grant tax credits to firms that introduce pollution-control equipment. But this method is questionable on grounds of efficiency, effectiveness, and equity. Also, the federal government can, and does, help local governments meet the costs of waste treatment.

In recent years, there has been considerable growth in government programs designed to control pollution. In 1969, the Council on Environmental Quality was formed; and in 1970, the Environmental Protection Agency was added. It is extremely difficult to determine how clean the environment should be. Of course, the sensible goal for society is to permit the level of pollution that minimizes the sum of the costs of pollution and the costs of controlling pollution; but no one has a very clear idea of what these costs are, and to a large extent the choices must be made through the political process. Basically, the entire pollution problem is concerned with how materials are to be disposed of in our society, and economists and policy makers are beginning to view the problem in this light.

CONCEPTS FOR REVIEW

External diseconomies
Private costs
Social costs
Water pollution
Primary treatment
Secondary treatment
Air pollution
Thermal pollution
Noise pollution
Effluent fees
Council on Environmental Quality
Environmental Protection Agency

QUESTIONS FOR DISCUSSION AND REVIEW

1. The 1971 annual report of the Council of Economic Advisers states that: "New rules for use of the environment are bound to affect competitive relationships within and among industries, localities, and nations." Give examples of these effects, and ways that society can make the transition easier.

2. Smoke is a classic case of an external diseconomy. (It was cited by Alfred Marshall and others.) Describe what actions can and should be taken to eliminate socially undesirable effects of smoke.

3. It is generally agreed that in the long run we should try to reach a zero level of pollution. True or False?

4. Which of the following forms of government intervention in the pollution problem is most often favored by economists?
a. Direct regulations b. Effluent fees c. Tax credits d. Population control

PART SIX

Consumer Behavior and Business Decision Making

CHAPTER 19

Consumer Behavior and Rational Choice

To a considerable extent, consumers, voting with their pocketbooks, are the masters of our economic system. No wonder, then, that economists spend much of their time describing and analyzing how consumers act. In addition, economists are interested in determining how consumers, as well as other decision-making units, should go about making rational choices. In this chapter, we present the basic model economists use to analyze consumer behavior.

After describing this model, we shall show how it can be used to promote better decision making, both by consumers and by government agencies and other organizations. After all, as we stressed in Chapter 1, one of the reasons why anyone should take the trouble to study economics is that it helps him or her to make better decisions. These applications should make the basic economic theory more interesting and understandable, as well as provide concepts and data we will need in subsequent chapters.

Consumer Expenditures: The Walters of San Diego

Since we are concerned here with consumer behavior, perhaps the best way to begin is to look at the behavior of a particular consumer. It is hard to find any consumer who is "typical." There are hundreds of millions of consumers in the United States, and as we saw in Chapter 4, they vary enormously. (Recall the princely Onassises and the poverty-stricken Ríoses.) Nonetheless, it is instructive to look at how a particular American family—the Edward Walters of San Diego[1]—spends its money. The Walters are in their mid-thirties, have two children (ages 8 and 6), and have Mrs. Walter's younger brother living with them. They own their own home, and both work. Mr. Walter manages a small clothing firm in San Diego, and Mrs. Walter is a designer at the same firm. Together, the Walters make about $25,000 a year.

How do the Walters spend their money? For most consumers, we cannot answer this question with any accuracy, because the people in question simply do not tell anyone what they do with their money. But because the Walters and their buying habits were scrutinized in a series of articles in a national magazine, it is possible to describe quite accurately where their money goes. As shown in Table 19.1, the Walters, who own their own home, spend about $735 a month—about 35 percent of their income—on housing. In addition, they spend about $300 a month—about 14 percent of their income—on food and drink. Also, they spend about $150 a month—about 7 percent of their income—on domestic help, which is needed since both parents work.

In addition, as shown in Table 19.1, the Walters spend about $150 a month—about 7 percent of their income—on private school and other lessons for their children. Another $150 a month goes for entertainment and clothing. Because of the mild weather in San Diego (and perhaps because they can get clothing at a discount since they are in the clothing business), their expenditures on clothing are not very large. Medical, dental, and insurance expenses consume about $145 a month—again, about 7 percent of income—and $50 a month—or about 3 percent of their income—is spent on transportation. Finally, the Walters allocate about $420 a month—about 20 percent of their income—for taxes and savings.

This, in a nutshell, is how the Walters spend their money. The Walters exchange their resources—mostly labor—in the resource markets for $25,000 a year. They take this money into the product markets and spend about ⅘ of it for the goods and services described above. The remaining ⅕ of their income goes for taxes and saving. The

[1] For obvious reasons, we have changed the name and residence of the family in question. Otherwise, however, the facts given in the following paragraphs are as they were stated in a national magazine.

Table 19.1

Monthly Spending Pattern of Mr. and Mrs. Walter of San Diego, California, 1970

Item	Amount	Percent of income
Housing	$ 735	35
Food and drink	300	14
Domestic help	150	7
Private school and education	150	7
Entertainment and clothing	150	7
Medical, dental, and insurance expenses	145	7
Transportation	50	3
Taxes and savings[a]	420	20
Monthly income	$2,100	100

[a] Estimated by deducting other items from monthly income.

Walters, like practically every family, keep a watchful eye on where their money goes and what they are getting in exchange for their labor and other resources. So do we all: as stressed in Chapter 3, the basic purpose of our economic system is to satisfy the wants of consumers.

Table 19.2

Allocation of Income by U.S. Households, 1970

	Amount (billions of dollars)	Percent of total
Personal taxes	$116	15
Personal saving	50	6
Consumption expenditures		
Autos and parts	37	5
Furniture and household equipment	38	5
Other durable goods	14	2
Food and drink	132	17
Clothing and shoes	52	6
Gasoline and oil	23	3
Other nondurable goods	58	7
Housing	92	12
Household operations	36	5
Transportation	18	2
Other services	116	15
Total income[a]	783	100

[a] Personal income net of interest payments. See Chapter 8.

Source: Survey of Current Business, April 1970.

Consumer Expenditures: Aggregate Data for the United States

How does the way that the Walters spend their money compare with consumer behavior in general? In Table 19.2, we provide data on how all consumers allocated their aggregate income in 1970. These data tell us much more about the typical behavior of American consumers than our case study of the Walters. Note first of all that American households paid about 15 percent of their income in taxes. This, of course, is the price of the government services we described in Chapter 5. In addition, American households saved about 6 percent of their income. In other words, they refrained from spending 6 percent of their income on goods and services; instead, they put this amount into stocks, bonds, bank accounts, or other such channels for saving.

American consumers spent the remaining 79 percent of their income on goods and services. Table 19.2 makes it clear that they allocated much of their expenditures to housing, food and drink, and transportation. Spending on housing, household operations, and furniture and other durable household equipment accounted for about 10 percent of American consumers' total income. Spending on food and alcoholic beverages accounted for about 17 percent of total income. Spending on automobiles and parts, gasoline and oil, and other transportation accounted for about 10 percent of total income. Thus, taxes, savings, housing, food and drink, and transportation accounted for almost 60 percent of the total income of all households in the United States.

The data in Table 19.2 make it obvious that the Walter family is not very typical of American consumers. For example, it spends a much larger percentage of its income on housing, domestic help, and education than do consumers as a whole. To some degree, this is because the Walters are far more affluent than most American families, but this is only part of the reason. To a large extent, it simply reflects the fact that people want different things. Looking around you, you see considerable diversity in the way consumers spend their money. Take your own family as an example. It is a good bet that your family spends its money quite differently than the nation as a whole. If your parents like to live in a big house, your family may spend much more than the average on housing. Or if they like to go to sports events, their expenditures on such entertainment may be much higher than average.

A Model of Consumer Behavior

Why do consumers spend their money the way they do? The economist answers this question with the aid of a ***model of consumer behavior,*** which is useful both for analysis and for decision making, and which is not difficult to understand, despite some unfamiliar and strange-sounding terminology. We shall soon see how it can be used to help solve real problems in both the private and public sectors of the economy.

To construct this model, the economist obviously must consider the tastes of the consumer. As Henry Adams put it: "Everyone carries his own inch-rule of taste, and amuses himself by applying it, triumphantly, wherever he travels." Certainly, it takes no genius to figure out that the amount a consumer purchases of a particular commodity is influenced by his tastes. Some people like beef, others like pork. Some people like the opera, others would trade a ticket to hear Joan Sutherland for a ticket to the Dallas Cowboys game any day of the week. Three assumptions, which seem reasonable for most purposes, underlie the economist's model of consumer preferences.

First, it is assumed that the consumer, when confronted with two alternative market baskets, can decide whether he prefers the first to the second, the second to the first, or whether he is indifferent between them. For example, suppose Mrs. Walter, the San Diego designer, is confronted with a choice between a market basket containing 3 chocolate bars and a ticket to the movies and another market basket containing 2 chocolate bars and a record of the Tabernacle Choir singing Chopin's Minute Waltz. Despite the rather bizarre composition of these two market baskets, we assume that she can somehow decide whether she prefers the first market basket to the second, the second market basket to the first, or whether she is indifferent between them.

Second, it is assumed that the consumer's preferences are transitive. The meaning of transitive in this context is simple enough. Suppose that Mrs. Walter prefers an ounce of Chanel No. 5 perfume to an ounce of Blue Grass perfume, and that she prefers an ounce of Blue Grass perfume to an ounce of Sortilège perfume. Then, if her preferences are transitive, she must prefer an ounce of Chanel No. 5 perfume to an ounce of Sortilège perfume. The reason for this assumption is clear. If the consumer's preferences were not transitive, the consumer would have inconsistent or contradictory preferences. Although some people may have preferences that are not transitive, this assumption seems to be a reasonable first approximation—for the noninstitutionalized part of the population at least.

Third, it is assumed that the consumer always prefers more of a commodity to less. For example, if one market basket contains 3 bars of soap and 2 monkey wrenches and a second contains 3 bars of soap and 3 monkey wrenches, it is assumed that the second market basket is preferred to the first. To a large extent, this assumption is justified by the definition of a commodity as something the consumer desires. Of course, this does not mean that certain things are not a nuisance. For example, if one market basket contains 3 bars of soap and 2 rattlesnakes, we would not be at all surprised if the consumer did *not* prefer this market basket to one containing 3 bars of soap and no rattlesnakes. But to such a consumer, a rattlesnake would not be desired—and thus would not be a commodity. Instead, the absence of a rattlesnake would be desired—and would be a commodity.

Indifference Curves and Utility

In Chapter 2, we pointed out that a model, to be useful, must omit many unimportant factors, concentrate on the basic factors at work, and simplify in order to illuminate. So that we focus on the important factors at work here, let's assume that there are only two goods, food and clothing. This is an innocuous assumption, since the results we shall obtain can be generalized to include cases where any number of goods exists; but it allows us to use simple two-dimensional diagrams to illustrate the model. Since there are only two commodities, we can represent every possible combination of goods purchased by a consumer by a point in Figure 19.1, which measures the amount of food purchased along the vertical axis and the amount of clothing purchased along the horizontal axis. For simplicity, food is measured in pounds, and clothing is measured in number of pieces of clothing.

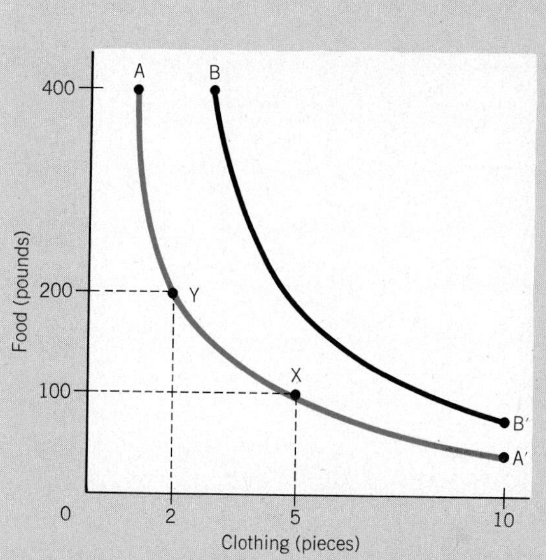

Figure 19.1
Two of Mrs. Walter's Indifference Curves

***AA′* and *BB′* are two of Mrs. Walter's indifference curves. Each shows market baskets that are equally desirable to Mrs. Walter. For example, she is indifferent between 200 pounds of food and 2 pieces of clothing (point *Y*) and 100 pounds of food and 5 pieces of clothing (point *X*).**

Consider Mrs. Walter, making choices for her family. If the three assumptions in the previous section hold, certain market baskets—that is, certain combinations of food and clothing (the only commodities)—will be equally desirable to her. For example, she may be indifferent between a market basket containing 100 pounds of food and 5 pieces of clothing and a market basket containing 200 pounds of food and 2 pieces of clothing. These two market baskets can be represented by two points, *X* and *Y*, in Figure 19.1. In addition, other market baskets—each of which can be represented by a point in Figure 19.1—are just as desirable to Mrs. Walter as those represented by points *X* and *Y*. If we connect all of these points, we get a curve that represents market baskets that are equally desirable to the consumer. In our case, Mrs. Walter is indifferent among all of the market baskets represented by points on *AA′* in Figure 19.1. *AA′* is therefore called an ***indifference curve.***

There are three important things to note about any consumer's indifference curve. First, any consumer has lots of indifference curves, not just one. If Mrs. Walter is indifferent among all the market baskets represented by points on *BB′* in Figure 19.1, *BB′* is another of her indifference curves. Moreover, one thing is certain: she prefers any market basket on *BB′* to any market basket on *AA′*, since *BB′* includes market baskets with as much clothing and more food (or as much food and more clothing) than the market baskets on *AA′*. (Remember that commodities are defined so that more of them are preferred to less.) Consequently, it must always be true that market baskets on higher indifference curves like *BB′* must be preferred to market baskets on lower indifference curves like *AA′*.

Second, every indifference curve must slope downward and to the right, to reflect the fact that

Figure 19.2
Intersecting Indifference Curves: A Contradiction

Indifference curves cannot intersect. If they did, the consumer would be indifferent between *D* and *E*, since both are on indifference curve *AA′*; and between *F* and *E*, since both are on indifference curve *BB′*. But this implies that he must be indifferent between *D* and *F*, which is impossible since *F* contains the same amount of food and 6 more pieces of clothing than *D*.

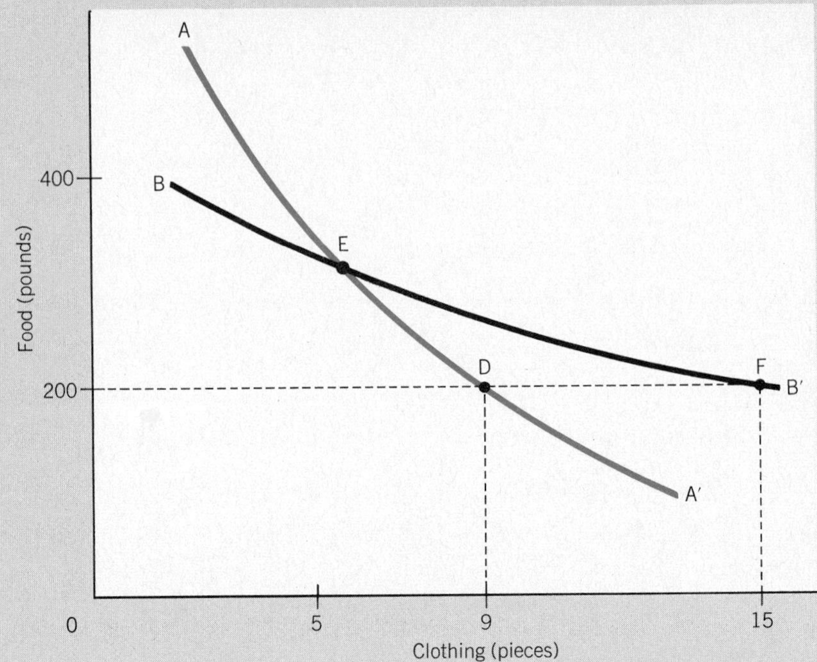

commodities are defined so that more of them are preferred to less. If one market basket has more of one commodity than a second market basket, it must have less of the other commodity than the second market basket—assuming that the two market baskets are to yield equal satisfaction to the consumer. You can prove this to yourself. Suppose that you have a choice between two snacks and that you are indifferent between them. One snack consists of 1 piece of apple pie and 2 glasses of milk. The other consists of 2 pieces of apple pie and a certain number of glasses of milk. If you prefer more apple pie to less, and if you prefer more milk to less, can the number of glasses of milk in the latter snack be as large as 2? Clearly, the answer must be no.

Third, indifference curves cannot intersect. If they did, this would contradict the assumption that more of a commodity is preferred to less. For example, suppose that *AA′* and *BB′* in Figure 19.2 are two indifference curves and that they intersect. If this is the case, the market basket represented by point *D* is equivalent in the eyes of the consumer to the one represented by point *E*, since both are on indifference curve *AA′*. Moreover, the market basket represented by point *F* is equivalent in the eyes of the consumer to the one represented by point *E*, since both are on indifference curve *BB′*. And this means that the market basket represented by point *F* must be equivalent in the eyes of the consumer to the one represented by point *D*. (Remember that consumer preferences are assumed to be transitive!) But this is impossible because market basket *F* contains the same amount of food and 6 more pieces of clothing than does market basket *D*. Since more of a commodity is preferred to less, market basket *F* must be preferred to market basket *D*.

To continue building our model of consumer behavior, we need now to bring in the concept of utility. *A **utility** is a number that represents the level of satisfaction the consumer derives from a* *particular market basket.* Since all market baskets on a particular indifference curve yield the same satisfaction to the consumer, they all must have the same utility. For example, all market baskets on indifference curve *AA′* in Figure 19.1 must have the same utility. Moreover, market baskets on higher indifference curves must have higher utilities than market baskets on lower indifference curves. For example, all market baskets on indifference curve *BB′* in Figure 19.1 must have higher utilities than market baskets on indifference curve *AA′*. We attach utilities to market baskets so that we can tell at a glance which market baskets the consumer will pick over other market baskets. Since market baskets on higher indifference curves are given higher utilities, and since market baskets on higher indifference curves are always preferred to market baskets on lower indifference curves, the consumer will always choose a market basket with a higher utility over a market basket with a lower utility.

Modern economists believe that no particular significance attaches to the scale used to measure utilities or to the differences between the utilities attached to a pair of market baskets. The only important thing is that market baskets with higher utilities are preferred over market baskets with lower utilities and that market baskets with equal utilities are equivalent in the eyes of the consumer. In other words, to modern economists, utility is measurable only in an *ordinal* sense. This is in contrast with earlier versions of utility theory, which viewed utility as measurable in the same sense as a man's height or weight. According to economists in the nineteenth and early twentieth centuries, a utility was measurable in a *cardinal* sense. It was felt that a curve could be drawn to represent the actual relationship between the amount of the commodity consumed and the consumer's total utility (Figure 19.3). For at least the past 40 years, economists have avoided relying on the assumption that utility is cardinally measurable, although this assumption is still used occasionally (particularly, as in some sections below, for expository purposes).

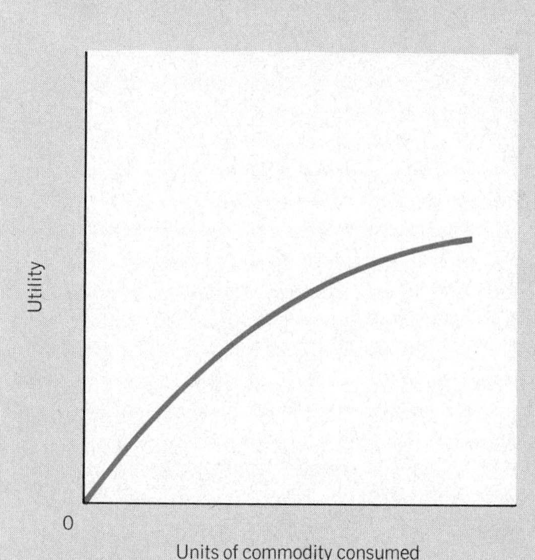

Figure 19.3
Total Utility Curve

In the nineteenth and early twentieth centuries, economists believed that utility was cardinally measurable, in the same sense as a person's height or weight, and that the relationship between the amount of a commodity consumed and the consumer's total utility was like that shown here.

The Consumer as a Rational Decision Maker

Preferences alone do not determine the consumer's actions. Besides knowing the consumer's preferences, we must also know his income and the prices of commodities to predict which market basket he will buy. The consumer's money income is the amount of money he can spend per unit of time. Clearly, his choice of a market basket is constrained by the size of his money income. For example, although Mr. Walter may regard a Jaguar as his favorite car, he may not buy it because he may have insufficient funds (as the bankers delicately put it). Also, the market basket the consumer chooses is influenced by the prices of commodities. For example, if a Jaguar were miraculously to become available at $500, rather than $5,000, Mr. Walter might purchase it after all.

Given the consumer's tastes, as reflected in his indifference curves, economists assume that he attempts to maximize utility. Put differently, it is assumed that he attempts to get on his highest possible indifference curve. In other words, the consumer is assumed to be rational in the sense that he chooses the market basket—or more generally, the course of action—that is most to his liking. Of course, as previously noted, the consumer is generally unable to reach the most preferred position—the market basket he would choose if his money income were unlimited and if prices did not matter. Instead, *he must maximize his utility subject to the constraints imposed by the size of his money income and the nature of commodity prices.*

Exactly what constraints are imposed on the consumer by the size of his money income and the nature of commodity prices? To make things concrete, let's return to Mrs. Walter. Suppose that her total income is $400 per month, and that she can spend this amount only on two commodities, food and clothing. Needless to say, it is unrealistic to assume that there are only two commodities in existence, but this, as we have seen, makes it easier to present the model, and the results can easily be generalized to cases where more than two commodities exist. Given these conditions, the answer to how much of each commodity Mrs. Walter can buy depends on the price of a pound of food and the price of a piece of clothing. Suppose the price of a pound of food is $1 and the price of a piece of clothing is $40. Then if she spent all of her income on food, she could buy 400 pounds of food per month. On the other hand, if she spent all of her income on clothing, she could buy 10 pieces of clothing per month. Or she could, if she wished, buy some food and some clothing. There are a large number of combinations of amounts of food and clothing that she could buy, and each such combination can be represented by a point on the line CC' in Figure 19.4. This line is called her ***budget line.***

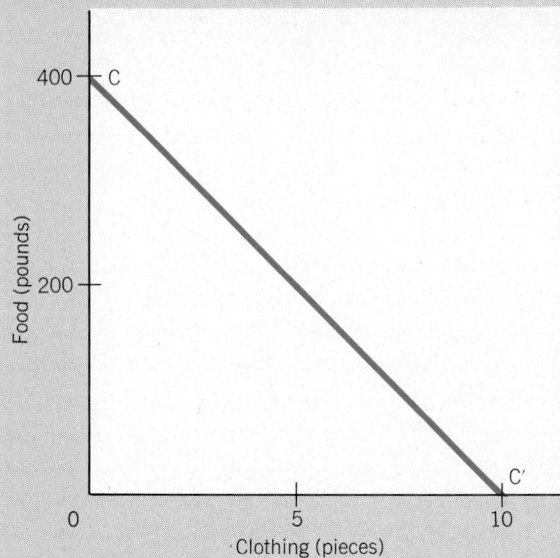

Figure 19.4
Mrs. Walter's Budget Line

The consumer's budget line shows the market baskets that can be purchased, given the consumer's income and prevailing commodity prices. This budget line assumes that Mrs. Walter's income is $400 per month, that the price of a pound of food is $1, and that the price of a piece of clothing is $40.

Of course, the consumer's budget line depends on the consumer's money income and on commodity prices. In particular, an increase in money income means that the budget line rises, and a decrease in money income means that the budget line falls. This is illustrated in Figure 19.5, which shows Mrs. Walter's budget line at money incomes of $200, $400, and $600 per month. As you can see, her budget line moves upward as her income rises.

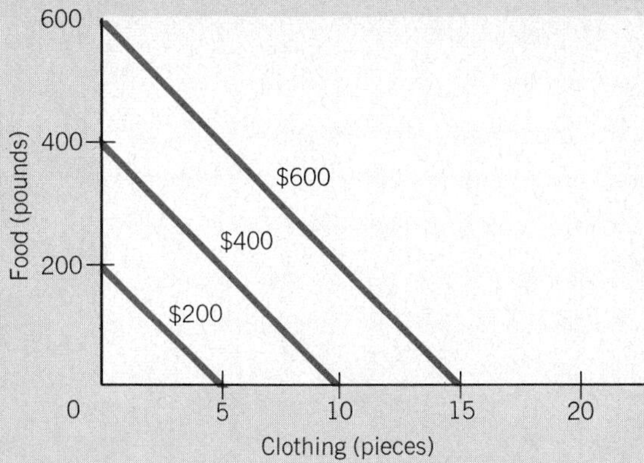

Figure 19.5
Mrs. Walter's Budget Line at Money Incomes of $200, $400, and $600 per Month

The higher the consumer's money income, the higher the budget line. Holding commodity prices constant, the budget line's slope remains constant.

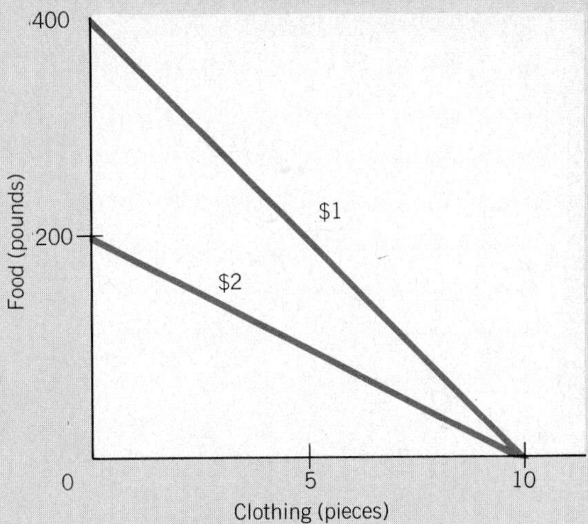

Figure 19.6
Mrs. Walter's Budget Line at Food Prices of $1 and $2 per Pound

Holding constant Mrs. Walter's money income at $400 per month and the price of a piece of clothing at $40, the budget line cuts the vertical axis farther from the origin when the price of food is $1 than when it is $2.

Commodity prices too affect the budget line: a decrease in a commodity's price causes the budget line to cut this commodity's axis at a point farther from the origin. Figure 19.6 shows Mrs. Walter's budget line when the price of a pound of food is $1 and when it is $2. You can see that the budget line cuts the vertical, or food, axis farther from the origin when the price of food is $1 per pound.

With information on the consumer's indifference curves and his budget line, we are in a position to determine the consumer's ***equilibrium market basket***—the market basket that, among all those his income and prices permit him to purchase, yields the maximum utility. The first step is to combine the indifference curves with the budget line on the same graph. For example, Figure 19.7 brings together Mrs. Walter's indifference curves (from Figure 19.1) and her budget line (from Figure 19.4). Given the information assembled in Figure 19.7, it is a simple matter to determine her equilibrium market basket. *Her indifference curves show what she wants:* specifically, she wants to attain the highest possible indifference curve. Thus, she would rather be on indifference curve *BB′* than on indifference curve *AA′*, and on indifference curve *DD′* than on indifference curve *BB′*. But, as we have pointed out repeatedly, she cannot choose any market basket she likes. *The budget*

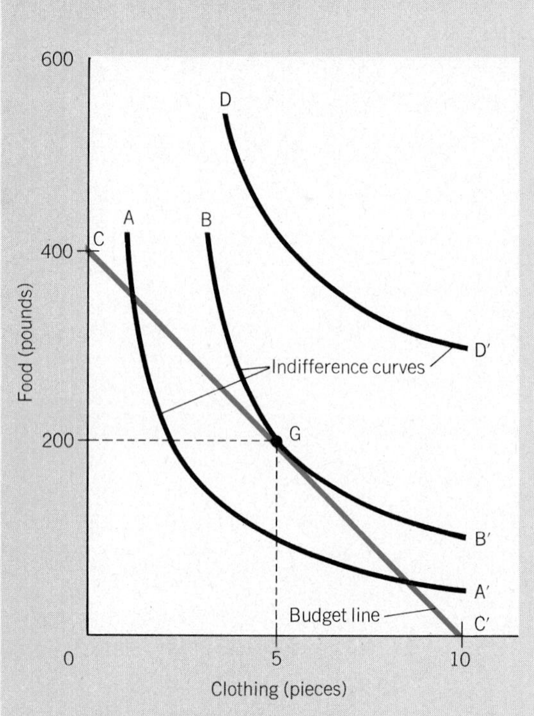

Figure 19.7
Mrs. Walter's Equilibrium Market Basket

Mrs. Walter's equilibrium market basket is at point *G*, containing 200 pounds of food and 5 pieces of clothing. This is the point on her budget line, *CC′*, that is on the highest indifference curve, *BB′*, she can attain.

line shows which market baskets her income and commodity prices permit her to buy. Thus, she must choose some market basket on her budget line, CC'.

Consequently, *the consumer's choice boils down to choosing that market basket on the budget line that is on the highest indifference curve. This is the equilibrium market basket.* For example, Mrs. Walter's equilibrium market basket is clearly at point G in Figure 19.7; it consists of 200 pounds of food and 5 pieces of clothing per month. This is her equilibrium market basket because any other market basket on the budget line CC' is on a lower indifference curve than point G is. But will the consumer choose this market basket? Admittedly, it may take some time and fumbling for the consumer to find out that this is the best market basket for him under the circumstances. Consumers, after all, do make mistakes. But they also learn, and eventually one would expect a consumer to come very close to acting in the predicted way.

An Overview of the Model and Its Uses

Sometimes, when a model of this sort is first described, you can spend so much time figuring out the details that you tend to lose sight of its overall structure and workings. So let's review the broad features and objectives of the model of consumer behavior. What is this model intended to do? Basically, its purpose is to predict the quantity of various commodities that a particular consumer will purchase during a particular time interval. Of course, our discussion assumed that there were only two commodities, food and clothing, but essentially the same model can be used for any number of commodities. Also, we spent a lot of time talking about Mrs. Walter, the designer and housewife from San Diego; but the same sort of model will work for any consumer. What sort of information and variables does the model use to carry out its purpose? First, it assumes that we know the tastes of the consumer and that these tastes can be represented by a series of indifference curves. Second, it assumes that we know the consumer's money income and the price of each commodity.

It is essential that you understand exactly what any model assumes that people are trying to do. In the case at hand, the model of consumer behavior assumes that consumers are trying to reach as high a level of satisfaction as possible. In other words, it assumes that the level of satisfaction the consumer attaches to a particular market basket can be gauged by the market basket's utility—or, in other words, by how high the indifference curve is that includes this market basket—and that the consumer, forced to choose a market basket on his budget line, will choose the one with the highest utility.

Of what practical use is this model, other than to help you pass courses in economics? In Chapter 20, we shall describe how this model of consumer behavior helps us interpret and analyze market demand curves, but for now we want to emphasize that, apart from its usefulness as a theoretical tool, this model of consumer behavior can be applied to practical decision making. Many problems people and organizations face are of the following type: *the person or organization has a certain amount of money to spend, and must decide how much to allocate to a number of different uses.* For example, a person may have a certain money income, and the problem is how much to spend on various goods and services. Or a philanthropic foundation like the Ford Foundation must determine how much of its money to allocate each year to various kinds of research and educational purposes. Or a government agency like the Department of Health, Education, and Welfare must allocate its funds to medical research, medical education, and so on.

Faced with a problem of this sort, the economist's model of consumer behavior is of enormous help. All these problems are basically the same as that facing the consumer, and the economist's model of consumer behavior shows the rational approach to their solution. Thus, this model does not apply only to consumers. It can be useful in any situation where a person or organization must allocate a fixed amount of money among alternative uses. *This model is much more than a theory of consumer behavior: it is a theory of rational choice.*

A model like this is useful because it shows what factors are important to the decision maker, and how these factors should be combined to come to a decision. At first glance, this statement may not mean much, but put yourself in the position of the person making the decision. There are lots of factors that he might weigh and try to measure in coming to a decision. There is a good chance that he will look at the wrong factors, or give some factors improper weight. The economist's model of consumer behavior can be very useful in indicating which factors are relevant and how they should be combined.

Purchasing a Sprinkler System: A Case Study

Consider a very simple decision, the sort that must be made frequently by practically everyone. Mr. Walter, whom we met earlier, must buy a sprinkler system for his lawn. He finds that there are two possibilities: either he can purchase a sprinkler system that will cost $500 and that will spray 500 gallons of water per hour on his lawn, or he can purchase a sprinkler system that will cost $300 and that will spray 200 gallons of water per hour on his lawn. The owner of the firm that sells sprinkler systems advises Mr. Walter to buy the more expensive system because the cost per gallon of water sprayed on his lawn per hour will be less than with the less expensive system. For this reason, the owner of the firm regards the more expensive system as the better buy.

You may find it difficult to see how the model of consumer behavior can help Mr. Walter come to a decision. But think for a moment about the choice he faces. If he buys the less expensive sprinkler system, he will save $200, but he will be able to put 300 fewer gallons of water on his lawn per hour. The more expensive sprinkler system will cost $200 more, but he will be able to put 300 more gallons of water on his lawn per hour. Clearly, according to the model, Mr. Walter should maximize his utility, not minimize the cost per gallon of water put on his lawn per hour. Thus, his decision should depend on whether the extra utility from the $200 is greater or less than the extra utility to be gained from being able to put 300 extra gallons of water on his lawn per hour. If he has a big lawn or if he wants to be able to water it quickly, the extra capability may be worth at least $200 to him. In this case, he should buy the more expensive system, since this will put him on a higher indifference curve. On the other hand, if he has a small lawn or if he doesn't care how long it takes to water it, the extra capability may not be worth $200 to him. In this case, he should buy the less expensive system, which will put him on a higher indifference curve.

In conclusion, then, Mr. Walter should not necessarily take the advice of the owner of the firm that sells sprinkler systems. The owner is using the wrong model. He is assuming that Mr. Walter wants to minimize the average cost of a gallon of water put on his lawn per hour, whereas Mr. Walter really wants to maximize utility. In a problem of this sort, the model of consumer behavior can provide the decision maker with the criteria or principles to guide his decision. Here it tells him his decision should depend on whether the capability of putting 300 extra gallons of water on the lawn per hour is worth the extra $200, not on whether one system has a lower cost per gallon per hour than the other system. In general, this is the sort of role this model can be expected to play—and it is an important role. Many important decisions (by consumers and others) are made improperly, often with wasteful and sometimes disastrous consequences, because people base their decisions on the wrong criteria.

The Optimal Budget Allocation

In contrast to the previous example, which involved a decision of no momentous importance by one consumer, this model is also applicable to the allocation of government expenditures, where decisions involve billions of dollars. Before discussing how this model can be useful in this area, we first must describe an important characteristic of the market basket that maximizes consumer satisfaction. To describe this characteristic, it is convenient (though by no means necessary) to assume that the consumer's utility—or satisfaction—is cardinally measurable. For example, suppose that the total utility the Walter family derives from the consumption of various amounts of food (per day) is given in Table 19.3. To measure the additional satisfaction derived from an additional unit of a commodity, economists use the concept of marginal utility. In this case, the ***marginal utility*** derived from a certain amount of food is the extra utility derived from this amount of food over and above the utility derived from one less pound of food. For example, as shown in Table 19.3, the marginal utility derived from 3 pounds of food is 2 utils, and the marginal utility derived from 2 pounds of food is 3 utils. (A util is the unit in which we shall assume that utility can be measured.)

It is generally assumed that, as a person consumes more and more of a particular commodity, there is, beyond some point, a decline in the commodity's marginal utility—that is, a decline in the extra satisfaction derived from the last unit of the commodity consumed. For example, if the Walters consume 1 pound of food in a particular period of time, it may be just what the doctor ordered. If they consume 2 pounds of food in the same period of time, the second pound of food is likely to yield

Table 19.3

Marginal Utility Derived by the Walters from Consuming Various Amounts of Food per Day

Pounds of food	Total utility	Marginal utility *
0	0	—
1	4	4 (= 4 − 0)
2	7	3 (= 7 − 4)
3	9	2 (= 9 − 7)
4	10	1 (= 10 − 9)

* These figures pertain to the interval between the indicated number of pounds of food and one pound less than the indicated number.

less satisfaction than the first. If they consume 3 pounds of food in the same period of time, the third pound of food is likely to yield less satisfaction than the second. And so on. This assumption —the so-called ***law of diminishing marginal utility***—is reflected in the figures in Table 19.3.

The market basket that maximizes the consumer's satisfaction has this important characteristic: *the consumer's income is allocated among commodities so that, for every commodity purchased, the marginal utility of the commodity is proportional to its price. In other words, the marginal utility per dollar spent is made equal for all commodities purchased.* Take a numerical example. Table 19.4 shows the marginal utility the Walters derive from various amounts of food and clothing. (Rather than measuring food and clothing in physical units, we measure them in terms of the amount of money spent on them.) Given the information in Table 19.4, how much of each commodity should Mrs. Walter buy if her money income is only $4 (a ridiculous assumption but one that will help make our point)? Clearly, the first dollar she spends should be on food since it will yield her a marginal utility of 20. The second dollar she spends should also be on food since a second dollar's worth of food has a marginal utility of 16. The marginal utility of the third dollar is 12 if it is spent on more food—and 12 too if it is spent for clothing. Suppose that she chooses more food. What about the final dollar? Its marginal utility is 10 if it is spent on more food and 12 if it is spent on clothing; thus she will spend it on clothing.

Clearly, Mrs. Walter, if she is rational, will allocate $3 of her income to food and $1 to clothing. This is the equilibrium market basket, the market basket that maximizes consumer satisfaction. The important thing to note is that this market basket demonstrates the principle set forth in the previous paragraph. As shown in Table 19.4, the marginal utility derived from the last dollar spent on food is equal to the marginal utility derived from the last dollar spent on clothing. (Both are 12.) Thus, this market basket has the characteristic described above: the marginal utility per dollar spent is made equal for all commodities purchased. It can be shown that this will always be the case for market baskets that maximize the consumer's utility. If it were not true, the consumer could obtain a higher level of utility by changing the composition of his market basket. This finding will prove useful in the next section, where we discuss the allocation of government expenditures.

Table 19.4

Marginal Utility Derived by the Walters from Various Quantities of Food and Clothing

	Dollars worth				
Commodity	1	2	3	4	5
	Marginal utility (utils)				
Food	20	16	12	10	7
Clothing	12	10	7	5	3

Allocating Government Expenditures: Another Case Study

Let's show how the model of consumer behavior and rational choice can be used by government decision makers to help allocate their budget. For example, decision makers in the Department of Health, Education, and Welfare must decide how much of the department's expenditures are to go for medical research, medical education, the promotion of good medical practices, and a host of other purposes. Billions of dollars are involved in these decisions. To what extent can our model be used by these decision makers?

Let's begin by examining how such decisions have often been made in the past. Many parts of the government have tended in the past to adopt a ***priorities approach*** to the allocation of a specified budget. That is, various items have been ranked according to the "urgency" with which they were needed. For example, the Department of Defense might have put a new supersonic bomber first on the list, indicating that it was to receive top priority.. A main battle tank might be second, indicating next highest priority, and so on. In recent years, the military services have sometimes formulated lists of this kind that included several hundred weapons and items. Since such decisions involve huge sums, it is fair to ask whether this is a sensible approach to the problem of allocating funds. Based on the model of consumer behavior and rational choice, the answer is no. As Charles Hitch and Roland McKean put it, in their well-known book on defense economics, "The 'priorities approach' does not solve the allocation problem and can even trap us into adopting foolish policies."[2]

What is wrong with the priorities approach? In the first place, it is not clear exactly what a priority ranking means. Does it mean that money should be spent on the highest priority item until no more is needed, then on the second highest priority item until no more is needed, and so on? Certainly not; one probably could continue spending on the highest priority item almost without limit and not reach the point where the usefulness of further units of the item was zero.

Nor does a list of priorities provide the information required to make a rational allocation of the budget. The information needed is precisely the sort required by the model of consumer behavior and rational choice—the "utility" to be derived from various amounts spent on particular items. Given this information, the principle that should be used to allocate the budget is precisely the one we discussed in the previous section: the amount spent on each item should be set in such a way that the marginal utility of the last dollar spent on each item is the same.

A government decision maker's problem in allocating an agency's budget is quite similar to that of our consumer, Mrs. Walter. The government decision maker is given a certain budget, which is analogous to the consumer's money income. He, like the consumer, is faced with prices attached to each of the items he is interested in buying. Like the consumer, he has indifference curves showing various combinations of items that have equal utility, in the sense that they make an equal contribution to the agency's goals. For example, if HEW's budget must be allocated between medical education and medical research, the indifference curves might be as shown in Figure 19.8, which also shows the budget line—determined by the prices of medical education and medical research, as well as the total amount the agency can spend. Thus, using the same reasoning as in the model of consumer behavior and rational choice, the government decision maker should support the education of *OB* physicians and the funding of *OM* medical research projects. Of course, it is not easy to measure the indifference curves in Figure 19.8; we do not pretend it is. But the approach is right.

During the 1960s, the federal government turned increasingly from priority lists and other such crude devices to more sophisticated economic analysis in the allocation of funds. According to many observers, this considerably improved decision making. Although much of this analysis is far too complicated to be presented here, the basic principles involved in the newer analysis were essentially those of the model of consumer behavior and rational choice. This model is a guide to rational allocation of funds, whether the funds are being spent by consumers or governments. As we have seen, the fundamental rule is: given a fixed budget to be spent, the amount spent on each item in the budget should be set so that the marginal utility of the last dollar spent on each item is the same.

This is a very useful and powerful rule. As Edmund Burke said two centuries ago, "Economy is a distributive virtue, and consists not in saving but in selection." In other words, the basic problem for decision makers in both the private and public sectors of the economy is how to select those things on which they should spend money, and to decide

[2] C. Hitch and R. McKean, *The Economics of Defense in the Nuclear Age,* Cambridge: Harvard University Press, p. 123.

Figure 19.8
Budget Allocation of Department of Health, Education, and Welfare

The optimal allocation of the budget between medical research and medical education is to support the education of *OB* physicians and the funding of *OM* medical research projects.

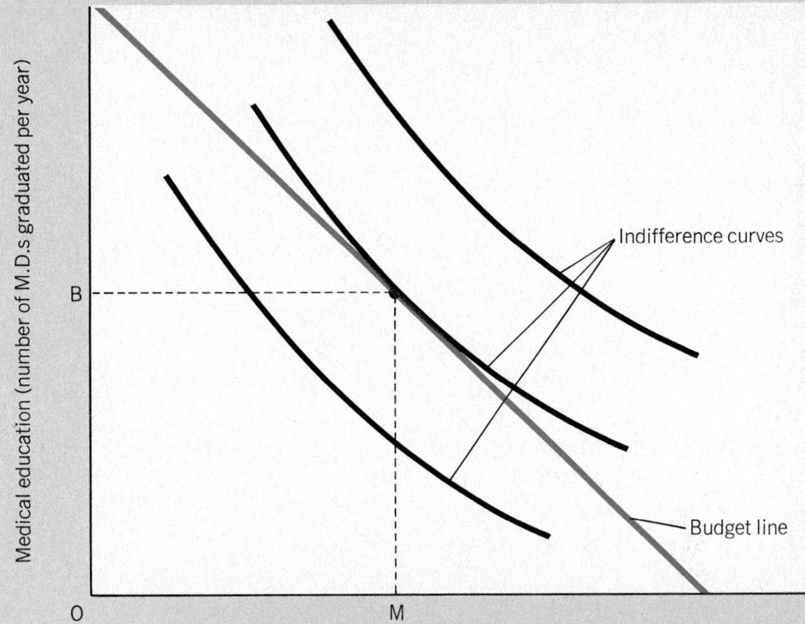

how much to spend on each. The model of consumer behavior and rational choice provides the fundamental principles on which such decisions should be based.

Protecting the Consumer

Finally, we must note a major assumption underlying the economist's model of consumer behavior and rational choice. It is that people know what they like and what they want. In general, this assumption is sensible, but sometimes the consumer is led to believe—by false advertising, improper grading of materials, and other such deceptive practices—that he is buying something he is not buying at all. The Federal Trade Commission has encountered practices of this sort in the lumber industry:

> The masquerading of low-grade lumber for high-grade lumber has bilked consumers of millions of dollars, has lowered the margin of structural safety in innumerable dwellings and, in the affected market areas, has impaired competitive mores among surviving wholesalers, retailers, and contractors.[3]

Similar improper practices have been discovered in other industries. For example, Ralph Nader testified before a Senate subcommittee concerning the packaging of sausage:

> What is on the labels is not all that is in the meat product. Last year, *Consumer Reports* tested fresh pork sausage—including leading brands—and found some distressing things. One-eighth of the federally inspected sausage and more than one-fifth of the

[3] R. Nader, Testimony before the Senate Subcommittee on Executive Reorganization of the Committee on Government Operations, 91st Congress, 1st Session, 1969, reprinted in E. Mansfield, *Economics: Readings, Issues, and Cases,* New York: Norton, 1974.

> nonfederally inspected sausage contained "insect fragments, insect larvae, rodent hairs, and other kinds of filth." In typical samples, *Consumer Reports* found that 30 percent of the federally inspected sausage and 40 percent of the sausage subject only to infrequent Illinois inspection failed the tests for absence of filth or acceptable low bacteria counts. *Consumer Reports* stated that such findings suggest "unclean packinghouses, unsanitary ingredients, and inadequate inspection."[4]

Of course, such practices are the exception, not the rule, but there are enough problems of this sort to warrant a government program of consumer protection. For example, as we saw in Chapter 5, the federal government has long been charged by the Pure Food and Drug Act with the responsibility of seeing that adulterated and misbranded drugs and foods are not put on the market. In addition, the Federal Trade Commission is supposed to act against misleading advertising, and the 1969 Truth in Lending Act requires lenders to state more clearly the exact costs of borrowing, thus protecting the consumer when he borrows money. Unless consumers know what they are buying, they cannot make the proper choices. In other words, they cannot maximize their satisfaction if they are lied to or misled about the nature of the goods and services for sale. For the price system to work well, the consumer must be protected against such deception and fraud.

Summary

In our economic system, consumer wants and desires are a basic determinant of the nature and quantity of the goods and services produced. As a first step toward understanding consumer behavior, it is useful to look at how consumers spend their income. Recent government figures show that consumers spend about 79 percent of their income on goods and services; the rest goes for taxes and saving. Much of their expenditures for goods and services go for housing, food and drink, and transportation. To explain how a particular consumer allocates his or her income among various commodities, economists have formulated a model of consumer behavior and rational choice. This model is very important both for theoretical purposes and as a guide to practical decision making.

The amount of a particular commodity a consumer purchases is clearly influenced by his preferences. The model of consumer behavior assumes that the consumer's preferences are transitive and that commodities are defined so that more of them are preferred to less. Given these assumptions, the consumer's preferences can be represented by a set of indifference curves. Every indifference curve must slope downward and to the right; indifference curves cannot intersect; and higher are preferred to lower indifference curves. Utility is a number that indexes the level of satisfaction derived by the consumer from a particular market basket. Market baskets with higher utilities are preferred over market baskets with lower utilities, and market baskets with equal utilities are on the same indifference curve.

The model of consumer behavior and rational choice recognizes that preferences alone do not determine the consumer's actions. Given the consumer's preferences, as reflected in his indifference curves, the choices open to him are dictated by the size of his money income and the nature of commodity prices. His income and the prices he pays determine his budget line, which includes all the market baskets he can afford to purchase. Whereas the consumer's indifference curves show what he wants, his budget line shows which market baskets his income and commodity prices permit him to buy. The consumer is assumed to choose the market basket on the relevant budget line that is on the highest indifference curve. This is the equilibrium market basket.

If the consumer maximizes his utility, his income is allocated among commodities so that, for every commodity he buys, the marginal utility of the commodity is proportional to its price. In other words, the marginal utility of the last dollar

[4] Ibid.

spent on each commodity is made equal for all commodities. This principle is a useful guide for practical decision making. For example, in the allocation of government expenditures, there has often been a tendency in the past to adopt a priorities approach. As has been recognized more and more in recent years, such an approach is likely to be less effective than an application of the simple principles underlying the model of consumer behavior and rational choice. Finally, we must remember that this model assumes that consumers know what they like and what they want. Sometimes consumers are misled by false advertising and other deceptive practices. For the price system to work well, the consumer must be protected against such deception and fraud.

CONCEPTS FOR REVIEW

Ordinal utility
Cardinal utility
Utility
Indifference curve
Transitive
Commodity
Budget line
Equilibrium market basket
Marginal utility
Law of diminishing marginal utility
Priorities approach
Consumer protection

QUESTIONS FOR DISCUSSION AND REVIEW

1. Faced with a number of alternative choices, people sometimes base their choice on the wrong criteria. According to Roland McKean, "One error, the use of the ratio of benefits to costs, is . . . a perennial favorite." What is wrong with using this ratio as a criterion?

2. According to Ralph Nader, "A negligently maintained, leaky pipeline blew up . . . , taking 41 lives and seriously burning over 100 other persons. . . . No law and no order was applied to the gas company and its induced violence." If consumers were misled concerning the safety of the pipeline, were their choices optimal? If not, in what way were they distorted?

3. If the marginal utility of one good is 3 and its price is $1, while the marginal utility of another good is 6 and its price is $3, is the consumer maximizing his or her satisfaction, given that he or she is consuming both goods? Why or why not?

4. Market baskets with equal utilities are on the same indifference curve. True or False?

CHAPTER 20

Market Demand

What do Corfam (Du Pont's synthetic leather) and the Edsel (the new make of automobile Ford introduced in the 1950s) have in common? Both were new products that were unsuccessful because the market demand for them was too small. In a capitalist economy, market demand is a fundamental determinant of what is produced and how. The market demand curve for a commodity plays an important role in the decision-making process within each firm producing the commodity, as well as in the economy as a whole. It is no exaggeration to say that firms spend enormous time and effort trying to cater to, estimate, and influence market demand.

In this chapter, we discuss the factors influencing the market demand curve for a commodity, as well as the measurement of market demand curves and their role in decision making by private business firms and government agencies. We consider questions like: How can we measure market demand curves? What is the price elasticity of demand? What role does the price elasticity of demand play in various practical problems facing the private and public sectors of the economy? What factors underlie the market demand curve for a commodity? How can we derive the market demand curve from the model of consumer behavior discussed in Chapter 19? These are important questions, from both a theoretical and a practical point of view.

Market Demand Curves: Role and Importance

Let's review what a market demand curve is. You will recall from Chapter 4 that a commodity's market demand curve shows how much of the commodity will be purchased during a particular period of time at various prices. Figure 20.1 ought to be familiar; it is the market demand curve for wheat in the early 1960s, which figured prominently in our discussion of the price system in Chapter 4. Among other things, it shows that during the early 1960s about 1,500 million bushels of American wheat would have been purchased per year if the price was $1.00 per bushel, that about 1,100 million bushels would have been purchased per year if the price was $1.40 per bushel, and that about 800 million bushels would have been purchased if the price was $1.80 per bushel.

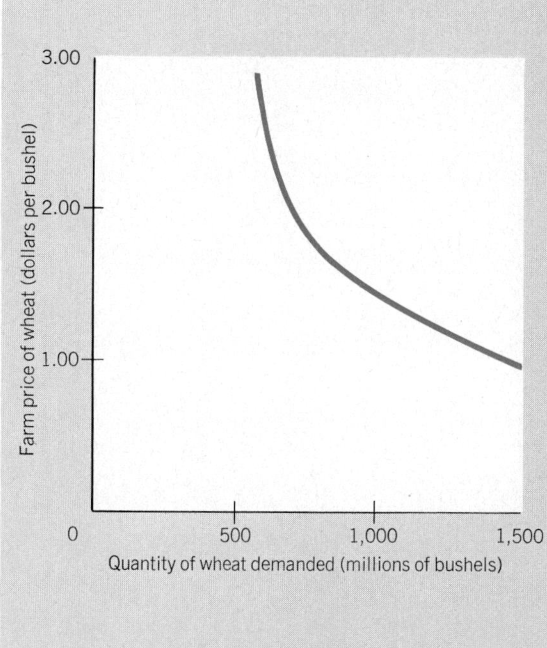

Figure 20.1
Market Demand Curve for Wheat, Early 1960s

This curve shows how much wheat would be purchased at various prices.

Since the market demand curve reflects what consumers want and are willing to pay for, when the market demand curve for wheat shifts upward to the right this indicates that consumers want more wheat at the existing price. On the other hand, when the curve shifts downward to the left, this indicates that consumers want less wheat at the existing price. Such shifts in the market demand curve for a commodity trigger changes in the behavior of the commodity's producers. When the market demand curve shifts upward to the right, the price of wheat will tend to rise. Thus, farmers will be induced to produce more wheat, because they will find that, given the price increase, their profits will increase if they raise their output levels. The same process occurs in other parts of the economy: shifts in the demand curve reflecting the fact that consumers want more (less) of a commodity set in motion a sequence of events leading to more (less) production of the commodity.

Beyond playing a central role in the functioning of the price system, market demand curves are of enormous importance to firms and industries. In some industries, like wheat, there are lots of producers, no one of whom has any real influence over the price. In such industries, firms must base many important decisions on the price they expect to receive in the future. To forecast this price, they have to estimate the market demand curve, explicitly or implicitly. In other industries, like steel or petroleum, there are few producers, and these firms have considerable influence over the price they charge. In such industries, firms cannot make rational pricing decisions unless they take proper account of the market demand curve for their product. In Chapters 23 and 24, we shall describe the specific way in which such decisions should be made if firms want to maximize their profits.

Market demand curves are also very important to government agencies. The Department of Agriculture is continually engaged in intensive and sophisticated studies to estimate the market demand curves for various farm products. This information is essential to the department's work. In the case of wheat, for example, to estimate how changes in price will affect the amount of wheat that is purchased by buyers (other than the government), the department must have estimates of the market demand curve for wheat. Many other government agencies are vitally interested in other market demand curves. For example, the Federal Power Commission is concerned with the market demand curves for natural gas, oil, and other fuels. And the Federal Communications Commission is concerned with the market demand curve for telephone service, among other products. Without some knowledge of these demand curves, they are in no position to regulate these industries.

Measuring Market Demand Curves

To be of practical use, market demand curves must be based on careful measurements. Let's look briefly at some of the techniques used to estimate the market demand curve for particular commodities. At first glance, a quick and easy way to estimate the demand curve might seem to be interviewing consumers about their buying habits and intentions. However, although more subtle variants of this approach sometimes may pay off, simply asking people how much they would buy of a certain commodity at particular prices does not usually seem very useful, since off-the-cuff answers to such questions are rarely very accurate. Thus, marketing researchers and econometricians interested in measuring market demand curves have been forced to use more complex procedures.

Another more useful technique is the ***direct market experiment.*** Although the designs of such experiments vary greatly and are often quite complicated, the basic idea is simple: to see the effects on the quantity demanded of actual variations in the price of the product. (Of course, researchers attempt to hold other market factors constant or to take into account whatever changes may occur.) For example, the Parker Pen Company conducted an experiment a number of years ago to estimate the demand curve for their ink, Quink. They increased the price from $.15 to $.25 in four cities, and found that the quantity demanded was quite insensitive to the price. Experiments like this are frequently made to try to estimate a product's market demand curve.

Still another technique is to use statistical methods to estimate demand curves from historical data on price and quantity purchased of the commodity. For example, one might plot the price of slingshots in various periods in the past against the quantity sold, as shown in Figure 20.2. Judging from the results, *DD′* seems a reasonable approximation to the demand curve. Although this simple analysis provides some insight into how statistical methods are used to estimate demand curves from historical data, it is a vast oversimplification. For one thing, the market demand curve may have shifted over time, so that *DD′* is not a proper estimate. Fortunately, modern statistical techniques recognize this possibility and allow us to estimate this curve at various times in spite of it.

Hundreds, perhaps thousands, of studies have been made to estimate the demand curves for particular commodities. In view of the importance of the results for decision making, this is not surprising. Businessmen need to be able to predict the effect of a change in price on the quantity demanded of their products. Clearly this will in-

Figure 20.2
Estimated Demand Curve for Slingshots

One very crude way to estimate the market demand curve is to plot the amount sold of a commodity in each year against its price in that year, and draw a curve, like *DD′*, that seems to fit the points reasonably well. However, this technique is generally too crude to be reliable.

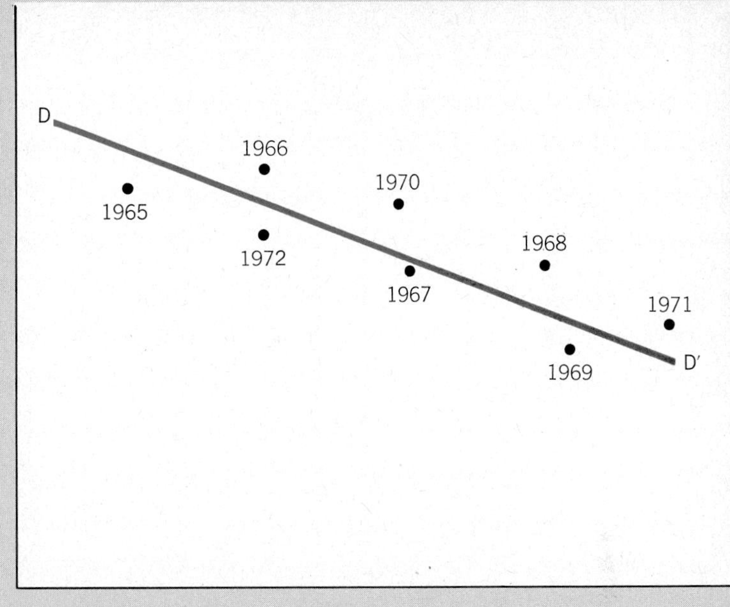

fluence their pricing and other policies. Also, government agencies often need to estimate the effects of price changes on the quantity demanded.

Railroad Transportation in Metropolitan Boston: A Case Study

As you will recall from Chapter 2, in the early 1960s the Boston and Maine Railroad wanted to discontinue passenger commuter service into Boston because it felt such service was unprofitable. In 1963, the Mass Transportation Commission of Massachusetts contracted with the Boston and Maine to establish a demonstration project to establish the effect of a lowering of fares on the quantity of commuter tickets sold. The Boston and Maine was requested not to file a petition for the discontinuance of commuter service into Boston until after the experiment. During the experiment, which lasted about a year, fares were reduced about 28 percent on the average. The result was, of course, an increase in the number of tickets sold. However, the more important thing to the railroad and the commission was the *extent* to which the fare cut would increase the number of tickets sold. *How great* would be the resulting increase in the number of tickets sold? This was the important question because to increase the railroad's profits, a fare cut had to increase the railroad's revenues more than it increased its costs. And unless the price cut increased the number of tickets sold by a greater percentage than the reduction in price, it would not increase the railroad's revenues at all.

A comparison of the Boston and Maine's commuter revenues in 1963 with those in 1962 showed that this large fare reduction resulted in only a 0.6 percent increase in the railroad's revenues. Thus, the price reduction increased the railroad's revenues by little or nothing. Since the reduction in fares increased the railroad's costs—because it was more costly to handle the larger volume of traffic—and increased its revenues scarcely at all, it did not increase the railroad's profits. Thus after the experiment the Boston and Maine decided to continue with its petition to terminate commuter service.[1] (Eventually, however, public subsidies were instituted to keep the service going.)

This is a fairly typical example of a direct market experiment designed to obtain information on relevant aspects of a market demand curve. Note the problems experiments of this sort must face. First, the experiment can be very costly if it alienates customers or reduces the firm's profits. Second, it is difficult to hold other relevant variables constant. For example, the effect of price changes was mixed up, to some extent, with the effect of increased service in the Boston and Maine case. Third, it is hard to conduct an experiment of this sort over a long enough period to estimate long-run effects. Thus, in the Boston and Maine case, the effect of the fare reduction on the number of tickets sold might have been much greater if the experiment had lasted longer. Nonetheless, despite these problems, experiments of this sort can produce useful evidence on the location and shape of a product's market demand curve. They are an important supplement to statistical analysis of historical data to estimate market demand curves.

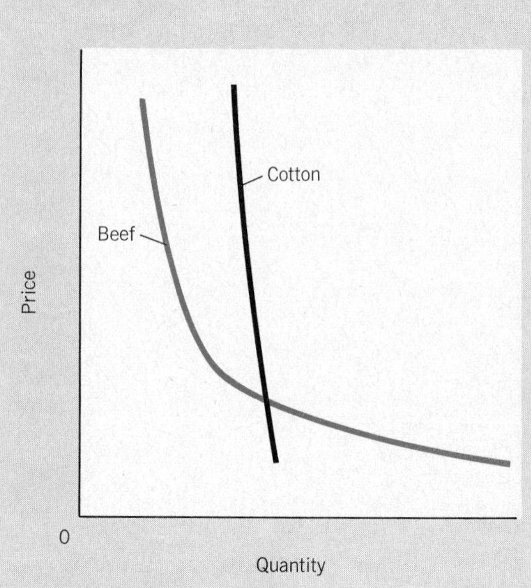

Figure 20.3
Market Demand Curves, Beef and Cotton

The quantity demanded of beef is much more sensitive to price than is the quantity demanded of cotton.

The Price Elasticity of Demand

Market demand curves, like people, do not all look alike. Clearly, the shape of a commodity's market demand curve will vary from commodity to commodity. For example, the quantity demanded of some commodities, like beef in Figure 20.3, is fairly sensitive to changes in the commodity's price. That is, changes in price result in significant changes in quantity demanded. On the other hand, the quantity demanded of other commodities, like cotton in Figure 20.3, is not at all sensitive to changes in the price. Large changes in price result in small changes in the quantity demanded. Economists, government officials, businessmen, and labor leaders are all interested in the sensitivity of the quantity demanded of a particular good to changes in its price. Indeed, even the Congress, in its hearings, has shown considerable interest in this subject. There have, for example, been Congressional investigations of the sensitivity of the quantity demanded of autos and steel to changes in their prices.

To promote unambiguous discussion of this subject, we must have some measure of the sensitivity of quantity demanded to changes in price. The measure customarily used for this purpose is

[1] See *Mass Transportation in Massachusetts,* Boston: Mass Transportation Commission, 1964.

the ***price elasticity of demand,*** defined as the percentage change in quantity demanded resulting from a 1 percent change in price. For example, suppose that a 1 percent reduction in the price of slingshots results in a 2 percent increase in the quantity demanded. Then, using this definition, the price elasticity of demand for slingshots is 2. (Convention dictates that we give the elasticity a positive sign even though the change in price is negative and the change in quantity demanded is positive.) Clearly, the price elasticity of demand is likely to vary from one point to another on the market demand curve. For example, the price elasticity of demand for slingshots may be higher when a slingshot costs a dollar than when it costs a quarter.

Note that the price elasticity of demand is expressed in terms of *relative*—i.e., proportional or percentage—changes in price and quantity demanded, not *absolute* changes in price and quantity demanded. Thus, in studying the slingshot market, we looked at the *percentage* change in quantity demanded resulting from a 1 *percent* change in price. This is because absolute changes are difficult to interpret. For example, suppose that a price goes up by a nickel. This is a lot for a newspaper but little for a car, a lot for a gallon of gasoline but little for 1,000 gallons.

Table 20.1

Market Demand for Wheat, Early 1960s

Farm price of wheat (dollars per bushel)	Quantity of wheat demanded (millions of bushels)
$1.00	1,500
1.20	1,300
1.40	1,100
1.60	900
1.80	800
2.00	700
2.20	675

Source: See Figure 4.1.

Calculating the Price Elasticity of Demand

The price elasticity of demand is a very important concept and one that economists use often, so it is worthwhile to spend some time explaining exactly how it is computed. Suppose that you have a table showing various points on a market demand curve. For example, Table 20.1 shows the quantity of wheat demanded at various prices, as estimated by Professor Karl Fox of Iowa State University during the early 1960s. Given these data, how do you go about computing the price elasticity of demand for wheat? Clearly, the price elasticity of demand for any product generally varies from point to point on its market demand curve; so you must first determine at what point on the demand curve you want to measure the price elasticity of demand.

Let us assume that you want to estimate the price elasticity of demand for wheat when the price of wheat is between \$2.00 and \$2.20 per bushel. One way is to use the following formula:

$$\text{price elasticity} = -\left(\frac{Q_2 - Q_1}{Q_1}\right) \div \left(\frac{P_2 - P_1}{P_1}\right), \quad (20.1)$$

where Q_2 is the quantity demanded when the price is P_2, and Q_1 is the quantity demanded when the price is P_1. If $P_2 = \$2.20$, it follows from Table 20.1 that $Q_2 = 675$, and if $P_1 = \$2.00$, it follows from Table 20.1 that $Q_1 = 700$. Thus, substituting these values into Equation (20.1), we have

$$\begin{aligned}\text{price elasticity} &= -\left(\frac{675 - 700}{700}\right) \div \left(\frac{2.20 - 2.00}{2.00}\right)\\ &= .36\,.\end{aligned}$$

Thus, the price elasticity of demand is estimated to be .36.

But we could just as well have estimated the price elasticity of demand in this range in a somewhat different way:

$$\text{price elasticity} = -\left(\frac{Q_1 - Q_2}{Q_2}\right) \div \left(\frac{P_1 - P_2}{P_2}\right), \quad (20.2)$$

where P_1, P_2, Q_2, and Q_1 are as defined above. The answer would be

$$\text{price elasticity} = -\left(\frac{700 - 675}{675}\right) \div \left(\frac{2.00 - 2.20}{2.20}\right)$$
$$= .41\,,$$

which is somewhat different from the answer we got in the previous paragraph.

To get around this difficulty, the generally accepted procedure is to use the average values of P and Q in place of Q_1 and P_1 in the denominators in Equation (20.1), and in place of P_2 and Q_2 in the denominators in Equation (20.2). In other words, we use as an estimate of the price elasticity of demand:

$$\text{price elasticity} = -\frac{(Q_2 - Q_1)}{\left(\frac{Q_1 + Q_2}{2}\right)} \div \frac{(P_2 - P_1)}{\left(\frac{P_1 + P_2}{2}\right)} \quad (20.3)$$

This is the so-called ***arc elasticity of demand.*** In the specific case we are considering, the arc elasticity is

$$\text{price elasticity} = -\frac{(675 - 700)}{\left(\frac{675 + 700}{2}\right)} \div \frac{(2.20 - 2.00)}{\left(\frac{2.20 + 2.00}{2}\right)}$$
$$= .38\,.$$

This is the answer to our problem.

Determinants of the Price Elasticity of Demand

Many studies have been made of the price elasticity of demand for particular commodities. Table 20.2 reproduces the results of some of them. Note the substantial differences among products. For example, the estimated price elasticity of demand for millinery (women's hats) is about 3.00, while for cotton it is only about 0.12. Think for a few minutes about these results, and try to figure out why these differences exist. If you rack your brains for a while, chances are that you will agree that the following factors are important determinants of whether the price elasticity of demand is high or low.

First, and most important, the price elasticity of demand for a commodity depends on the number and closeness of available substitutes. If a commodity has many close substitutes, its demand is likely to be highly elastic, i.e., the price elasticity

Table 20.2

Estimated Price Elasticities of Demand for Selected Commodities, United States

Commodity	Price elasticity
Beef	0.92
Millinery	3.00
Gasoline	0.52
Sugar	0.31
Corn	0.49
Cotton	0.12
Hay	0.43
Potatoes	0.31
Oats	0.56
Barley	0.39
Buckwheat	0.99

Source: H. Schultz, *Theory and Measurement of Demand,* Chicago: University of Chicago Press, 1938; and M. Spencer and L. Siegelman, *Managerial Economics,* Homewood, Ill.: Richard D. Irwin, 1959.

is likely to be high. If the price of the product increases, a large proportion of its buyers will turn to the close substitutes that are available. If its price decreases, a great many buyers of substitutes will switch to this product. Naturally, the closeness of the substitutes depends on how narrowly the commodity is defined. In general, one would expect that as the definition of the product becomes narrower and more specific, the product has more close substitutes and its price elasticity of demand is higher. Thus, the demand for a particular brand of oil is more price elastic than the overall demand for oil, and the demand for oil is more price elastic than the demand for fuel as a whole. If a commodity is defined so that it has perfect substitutes, its price elasticity of demand is infinite. Thus, if one farmer's wheat is exactly like that produced by other farmers and if he increases his price slightly (to a point above the market level), his sales will be reduced to nothing.

Second, it is often asserted that the price elasticity of demand for a commodity is likely to depend on the importance of the commodity in consumers' budgets. For example, the demand for commodities like pepper and salt may be quite inelastic. The typical consumer spends only a very small percentage of his income on pepper and salt, and the quantity he demands may not be influenced much by changes in price within a reasonable range.

Third, the price elasticity of demand for a commodity is likely to depend on the length of the period to which the demand curve pertains. (Every market demand curve pertains, you will recall, to a certain time interval.) In general, demand is likely to be more sensitive to price over a long period than over a short one. The longer the period, the easier it is for consumers and business firms to substitute one good for another. If, for example, the price of oil should decline relative to other fuels, oil consumption in the month after the price decline would probably increase very little. But over a period of several years, people would have an opportunity to take account of the price decline in choosing the type of fuel to be used in new and renovated houses and businesses. In the longer period of several years, the price decline would have a greater effect on the consumption of oil than in the shorter period of one month.

Price Elasticity and Total Money Expenditure

Many important decisions hinge on the price elasticity of demand for a commodity. Frequently, firms and government agencies must estimate, as best they can, the sensitivity of quantity demanded to changes in price. They need to know whether a price change will increase the amount of money spent on a commodity. This, for instance, was of basic importance in the case of the Boston and Maine Railroad.

It is customary to say that *the demand for a commodity is price elastic if the price elasticity of demand is greater than 1.* Suppose that the demand for a particular good is price elastic. Then, if the price of the commodity is reduced, the percentage increase in quantity demanded must be more than the percentage decrease in price. (After all, this follows directly from the supposition that the price elasticity of demand exceeds 1.) Since the total amount consumers spend on the commodity equals the quantity demanded times the commodity's price, it follows that under these circumstances a price decrease must lead to an increase in the total amount spent on the commodity. Similarly, if the demand for the commodity is price elastic, an increase in its price will lead to a decrease in the total amount spent by consumers on the commodity.

It is also customary to say that *the demand for a commodity is price inelastic if the price elasticity of demand is less than 1.* Suppose that the demand for a particular good is price inelastic. Under these circumstances, if the price is reduced, the percentage increase in quantity demanded must be less than the percentage decrease in price. Since the total amount spent on the commodity is the quantity demanded times its price, a price

Henry Ford and the Price Elasticity of Demand for Autos

HENRY FORD IN HIS FIRST AUTOMOBILE, 1903.

In 1905 the average automobile produced in the U.S. cost more than the average 1972 Datsun. Many of the firms in the auto industry were warmed-over buggy makers who handcrafted rich men's toys. But change was in the air. *Motor Age,* the industry's first trade magazine, prophesied that "the simple car is the car of the future—. A golden opportunity awaits some bold manufacturer of a simple car."

It remained for Henry Ford, the son of a Wisconsin farmer, to translate these words into a car—the Model T. Ford, commenting on his rural youth, declared, "It was life on the farm that drove me into devising ways and means to better transportation." Turning from the kid glove and checkbook set, he saw the potential market—at the right price—for car sales in the agricultural community.

The Model T was introduced in 1909. A few numbers indicate its phenomenal progress.

YEAR	PRICE	CARS SOLD
1909	$900	58,022
1914	$440	472,350
1916	$360	730,041

However, all good things come to an end. By the twenties, Ford's unwillingness to alter the Model T in any fashion (cosmetic or mechanical), as well as increased competition from other manufacturers, and the development of trade-in and installment buying (which reduced the price elasticity of demand for automobiles) brought the Model T to an end. But the record profits of the Ford Motor Company between 1910 and 1920 vindicated Henry Ford in his belief that: "it is better to sell a large number of cars at a reasonably small margin than to sell fewer cars at a larger margin of profit. Bear in mind that when you reduce the price of the car without reducing the quality you increase the possible number of purchases. There are many men who will pay $360 for a car who would not pay $440. I figure that on the $360 basis we can increase the sales to 800,000 cars for the year—less profit on each car, but more cars, more employment of labor and in the end, we get all the profit we ought to make."* E.A.

**Henry Ford*, edited by John B. Rae, Englewood Cliffs, N.J.: Prentice-Hall, 1969, p. 112.

decrease must lead to a decrease in the amount spent on the commodity. Similarly, a price increase will lead to an increase in the amount spent on the commodity if the demand for the product is price inelastic.

Finally, *if the price elasticity of demand for a commodity is equal to 1, its demand is said to be of unitary elasticity*. Clearly, under these circumstances a price increase or decrease results in no difference in the total amount spent on the commodity. Why? Because a price decrease (increase) of a certain percentage always results in a quantity increase (decrease) of the same percentage, so that the product of the price and quantity is unaffected.

The Farm Problem and the Price Elasticity of Demand

To illustrate the importance of the price elasticity of demand, let's return to the nation's farm problems. One of the most difficult problems for farmers is that, under a free market, farm incomes vary enormously between good times and bad, the variation being much greater than for nonfarm incomes. This is so because farm prices vary a great deal between good times and bad, whereas farm output is much more stable than industrial output. Why is agriculture like this?

The answer lies in considerable part with the price elasticity of demand for farm products. As we emphasized in Chapter 5, food is a necessity with few good substitutes. Thus, we would expect the demand for farm products to be price inelastic. And as Table 20.2 suggests, this expectation is borne out by the facts. Given that the demand curve for farm products is price inelastic —and that the quantity supplied of farm products is also relatively insensitive to price—it follows that relatively small shifts in either the supply curve or the demand curve result in big changes in price. This is why farm prices are so unstable. For example, Panel A of Figure 20.4 shows a market where the demand curve is much more inelastic than in Panel B. As you can see, a small shift in the demand curve from D_1D_1' to DD' results in a much bigger drop in price in Panel A than in Panel B.

This is not the only role the price elasticity of

Figure 20.4
Instability of Farm Prices and Incomes

Because the demand curve in panel A is much less elastic than that in panel B, a small shift in the demand curve has a much bigger impact on price in panel A than in panel B.

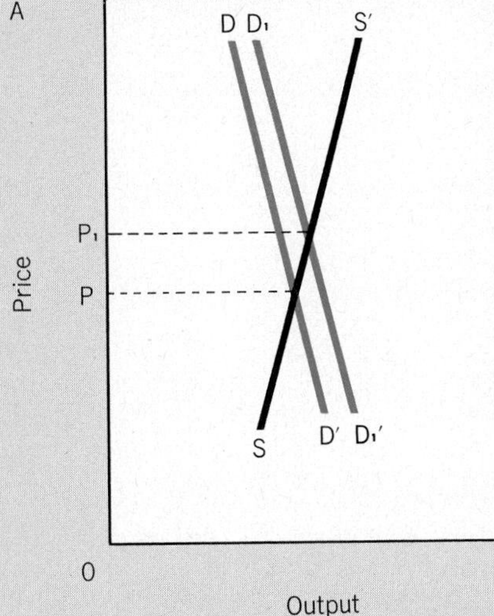

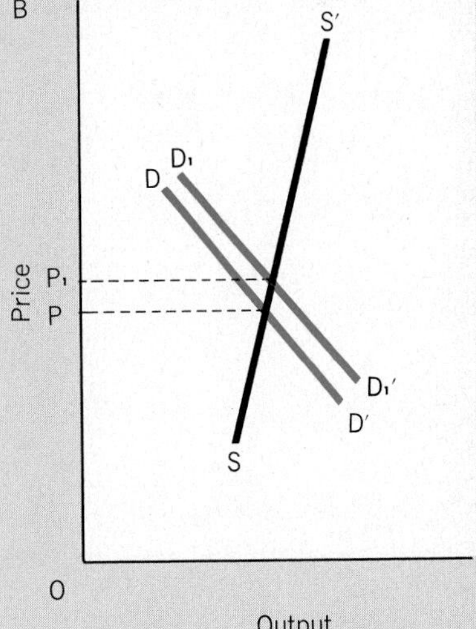

demand plays in our farm problems. Many other questions involve it. For example, consider the plan proposed after World War II by Charles Brannan who served as President Truman's Secretary of Agriculture. The plan was later supported in somewhat modified form by Ezra Taft Benson, Secretary of Agriculture in the Eisenhower administration. But it drew fire from many farmers, and not until 1973, after nearly three decades of controversy, was the plan approved by Congress.

According to the Brannan plan, a floor is established under the price received by farmers. Suppose that the market price is below this "target" level. If the target level is OP' in Figure 20.5, and if the output quota is OQ_3, this plan lets the competitive market alone, so that the output of OQ_3 is sold at a price of OP_2. Then according to this plan, the government issues subsidy checks to farmers to cover the difference between the market price and the target price, OP'.

Clearly, the cost to the government under the Brannan plan would be $(OP' - OP_2) \times OQ_3$. An important question is: will the cost to the U.S. Treasury under this plan be greater than under a system whereby the price is supported at OP', and the government buys the amount—$(OQ_3 - OQ_2)$—that private buyers do not purchase at that price? The answer can be shown to depend on our friend, the price elasticity of demand. The cost to the Treasury under the latter system is $OP'(OQ_3 - OQ_2)$. Thus, the cost under the Brannan plan would be greater than under the latter system if $(OP_2 \times OQ_3) < (OP' \times OQ_2)$. But since $OP_2 \times OQ_3$ is the total money expenditure at price OP_2 and $OP' \times OQ_2$ is the total money expenditure at price OP', it follows from the previous section that $OP_2 \times OQ_3$ will be less than $OP' \times OQ_2$ if the price elasticity of demand is less than 1. Thus, since the elasticity of demand for farm products is in fact less than 1, the cost to the Treasury will be greater under the Brannan plan than under a system whereby the price is supported at OP', with the government clearing the market of the farm products not purchased by the private sector at that price.

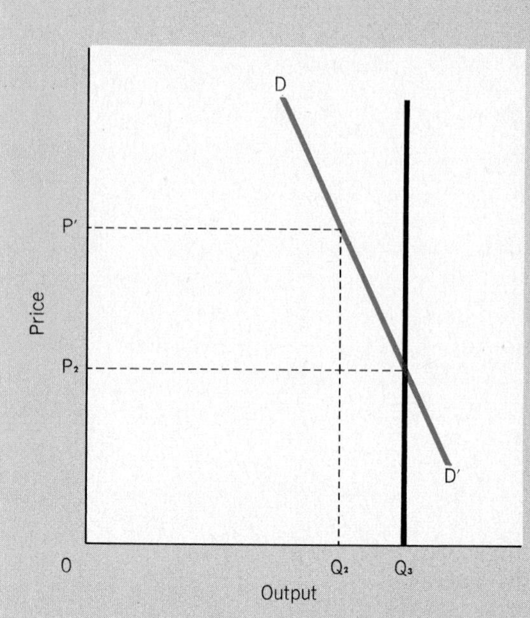

Figure 20.5
Effect of the Brannan Plan

Under the Brannan plan, the competitive market would be let alone, so that, if output were OQ_3, the price would be OP_2. Then the government would pay farmers the difference between this price and the target price, OP'.

Of course this is not necessarily an overwhelming argument against the Brannan plan. Clearly, the total cost to consumers and taxpayers is the same, whether the Brannan plan or the latter system is adopted. What is different is the burden on different segments of the population. The significant fact for present purposes is not whether the Brannan plan is good or bad, but the importance of the price elasticity of demand in discussing this plan, just as in discussing the instability of farm income and prices. Moreover, the price elasticity of demand is equally as important in problems concerning the industrial and service sectors of the economy as in problems concerning agriculture.

Derivation of the Consumer's Demand Curve

Up to this point, we have simply taken the market demand curve for a commodity as given. Let's look now at the factors underlying the market demand curve. We begin with the behavior of a particular consumer, Mrs. Walter, the San Diego designer we introduced in Chapter 19. Let's examine the relationship between the price of food and the amount of food she will buy per month. Applying the theory of consumer behavior presented in Chapter 19 makes it easy to derive this relationship, which economists call the consumer's ***individual demand curve.*** In this section, we show how we derive Mrs. Walter's individual demand curve for food.

Assuming that food and clothing are the only goods, that Mrs. Walter's monthly income is $400, and that the price of clothing is $40 per piece of clothing, Mrs. Walter's budget line is Budget Line 1 in Figure 20.6, when the price of food is $1 per pound. Thus, as we saw in the previous chapter, Mrs. Walter will buy 200 pounds of food per month under these conditions. If, however, the price of food increases to $2 per pound, her income and the price of clothing remaining constant, her budget line will be Budget Line 2 in Figure 20.6, and she will attain her highest indifference curve, *AA′*, by choosing the market basket corresponding to point *I*, a market basket containing 100 pounds of food per month. Thus, if the price of food is $2 per pound, she will buy 100 pounds of food per month.

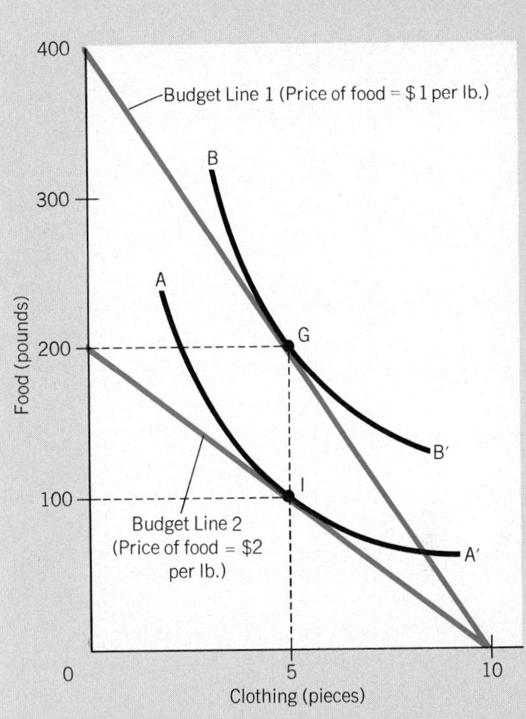

Figure 20.6
Effect of Change in Price of Food on Mrs. Walter's Equilibrium Market Basket

If the price of a pound of food is $1, Mrs. Walter's budget line is such that her equilibrium market basket is at point G, where she buys 200 pounds of food per month. If the price of a pound of food is $2, Mrs. Walter's budget line is such that her equilibrium market basket is at point I, where she buys 100 pounds of food per month.

We have derived two points on Mrs. Walter's individual demand curve for food—those corresponding to prices of $1 and $2 per pound. Figure 20.7 shows these two points, *X* and *Y*. It is no trick to obtain more points on her individual demand curve for food. All we have to do is assume a particular price for food, construct the budget line corresponding to this price (holding her income and the price of clothing constant), and find the market basket on this budget line that is on her highest indifference curve. Plotting the amount of food in this market basket against the assumed price of food, we obtain a new point on her individual demand curve for food. Connecting up all these points, we get her complete individual demand curve for food, shown in Figure 20.7.

Clearly, *the location and shape of an individual demand curve depend on the tastes of the consumer.* In other words, the shape of the consumer's indifference curves influences the location and shape of an individual demand curve. For example, if Mrs. Walter values food so much that she is determined to maintain her family's consumption of this commodity regardless of its price, her individual demand curve for food will look like GG' in Figure 20.8. But if she is less determined to maintain her family's food consumption, it may look like HH' in Figure 20.8.

Besides the consumer's tastes, other factors determining the location and shape of the consumer's individual demand curve are the income of the consumer and the prices of other goods. For example, Mrs. Walter's individual demand curve for food in Figure 20.7 is based on the assumption that her income is $400 per month and that the price of a piece of clothing is $40. If her income or the price of clothing changes, her individual demand curve for food will change as well. Thus, her individual demand curve for food may be D_0D_0' in Figure 20.9 if her income is $300 per month and the price of a piece of clothing is $40, D_1D_1' if her income is $500 per month and the price of a piece of clothing is $40, and D_2D_2' if her income is $500 per month and the price of a piece of clothing is $50.

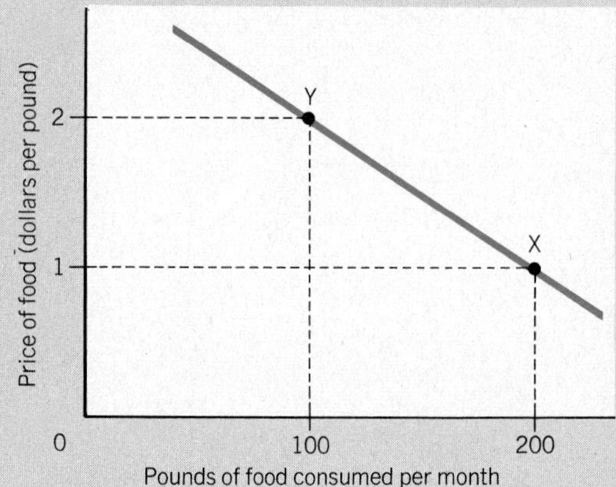

Figure 20.7
Mrs. Walter's Individual Demand Curve for Food

The consumer's individual demand curve for a commodity shows the amount of the commodity the consumer will buy at various prices. Points *X* and *Y* on Mrs. Walter's individual demand curve for food were derived in Figure 20.6.

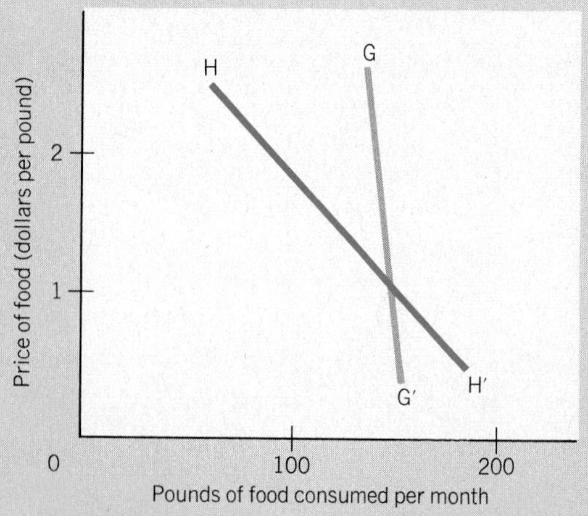

Figure 20.8
Hypothetical Individual Demand Curves

If Mrs. Walter values food so much that she is determined to buy much the same amount regardless of its price, her individual demand curve for food may look like GG'; but if she is less determined to maintain her family's food consumption, her individual demand curve for food may look like HH'.

Figure 20.9
Effect of Changes in Income and in Price of Clothing on Mrs. Walter's Individual Demand Curve for Food

The consumer's individual demand curve for a commodity depends on his money income and the price of other commodities. Mrs. Walter's individual demand curve for food may be D_0D_0' if her income is $300 per month and the price of a piece of clothing is $40, D_1D_1' if her income is $500 per month and the price of a piece of clothing is $40, and D_2D_2' if her income is $500 per month and the price of a piece of clothing is $50.

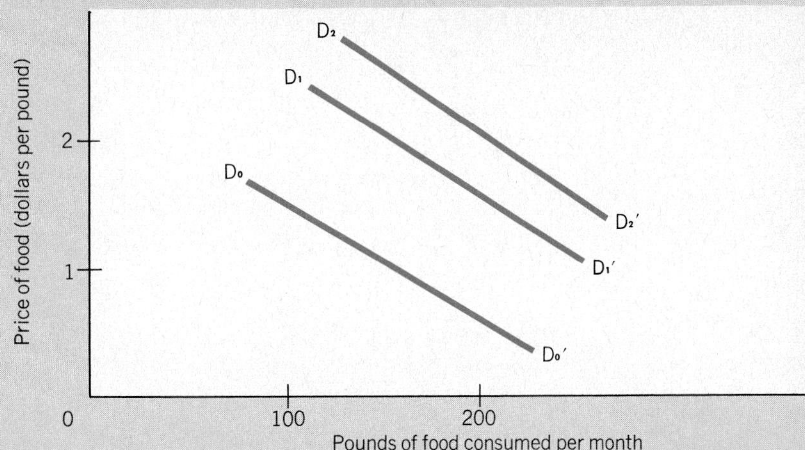

Transition to the Market Demand Curve

In Chapter 4, we discussed what we meant by a market. As a working definition, we decided that a market could be regarded as a group of firms and individuals that are in touch with each other in order to buy or sell some commodity. *The market demand curve for a commodity bears a very simple relationship to the individual demand curves of all the consumers in the market: it is the horizontal sum of all the individual demand curves.* In other words, to find the total quantity demanded in the market at a certain price, we add up the quantities demanded by the individual consumers at that price.

For example, Table 20.3 shows the individual demand curves for food of four families: the Walters, Joneses, Smiths, and Kleins. For simplicity, suppose that these four families constitute the entire market for food. (This assumption can easily be relaxed; it just makes things simple.) Then the market demand curve for food is shown in the last column of Table 20.3. Figure 20.10 shows the families' individual demand curves for food, as well as the resulting market demand curve.

Individual demand curves almost always slope downward to the right: that is, the consumer almost always responds to an increase in a commodity's price by reducing the amount of it he consumes. Or, put the other way around, a commodity's price almost always must be reduced to persuade the consumer to buy more of it. One way

Table 20.3

Individual Demand Curves and Market Demand Curve for Food

Price of food (per pound)	Individual demand				Market demand
	Jones	Klein	Smith	Walter	
	(hundreds of pounds per month)				
$1.00	50.0	45.0	5.0	2.0	102
1.20	43.0	44.0	4.2	1.8	93
1.40	36.0	43.0	3.4	1.6	84
1.60	30.0	42.0	2.6	1.4	76
1.80	25.0	41.4	2.4	1.2	70
2.00	20.0	41.0	2.0	1.0	64

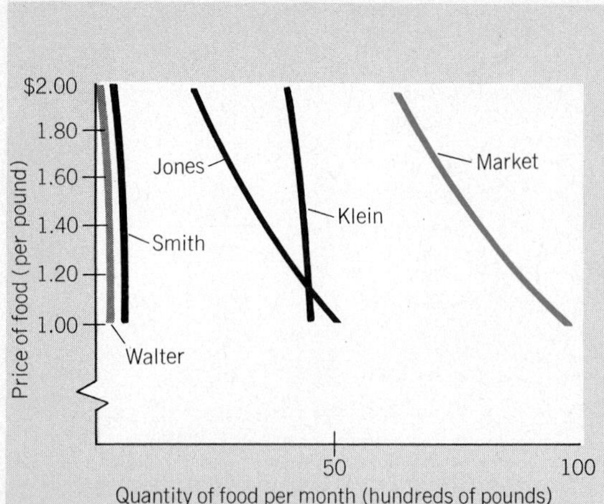

Figure 20.10
Individual Demand Curves and Market Demand Curves for Food

The market demand curve is the horizontal sum of all the individual demand curves.

to explain this fact is by an appeal to the law of diminishing marginal utility, which (you will recall from Chapter 19) states that, as a person consumes more and more of a particular commodity, the commodity's marginal utility declines. Since the marginal utility—the extra utility derived from an extra unit of the commodity—declines, the price the consumer is willing to pay for an extra unit of the commodity must decline too.

This explanation relies on the assumption that utility is cardinally measurable. Another way to explain the same thing makes no such assumption. According to this explanation, an increase in a commodity's price has two kinds of effects on the consumer—a substitution effect and an income effect. The ***substitution effect*** is what happens to the consumer's behavior if the commodity becomes dearer relative to other commodities: clearly, the consumer tends to buy less of the good. But this is not the only effect of the price increase. At the same time, there is also an ***income effect,*** the effect on the consumer's behavior of the fact that his real income is lower now that the price of the commodity has become higher. The income effect may prompt the consumer to buy more or less of the commodity. However, unless the income effect is very strange indeed—small increases in real income resulting in very large decreases in the consumption of the good—the total effect of a price increase (i.e., the substitution effect plus the income effect) will be a reduction of the quantity demanded of the commodity.

Since individual demand curves for a commodity almost always slope downward to the right, it follows that market demand curves too almost always slope downward to the right. However, as emphasized repeatedly here and in Chapter 4, the shape and location of the market demand curve vary greatly from commodity to commodity and from market to market. For example, the quantity demanded of some commodities is quite sensitive to changes in their price; for other commodities, the quantity demanded varies only slightly with price changes.

The reasons for this variation should be clearer now that we have shown how market demand curves depend on the indifference curves of consumers, the number of consumers in the market, the income of consumers, and the prices of other commodities. Having seen how market demand curves can be derived from the model of consumer behavior presented in Chapter 19, you should be more aware now of the factors underlying the market demand curve for a commodity. In addition, you should recognize that, as we pointed out in Chapter 19, the model of consumer behavior is a useful foundation for the interpretation and analysis of market demand curves.

The Demand Curve for Automobiles: A Case Study

Some congressional committees have asserted that important industries in the American economy have tended to underestimate the price elasticity of demand, so that they have not been sufficiently prone to reduce prices. According to the critics, the industries in question should, in their own interest as well as the public's, reduce their prices. Among those charged with such an underestimation is the automobile industry, unquestionably one of the biggest industries in the entire American economy.

How great is the price elasticity of demand for automobiles? This is a very important question both to the automobile industry and to those, like the congressional committees, who have some responsibility for evaluating our economy's overall performance. Perhaps the first major study of this question was carried out in 1939 by C. F. Roos and V. von Szeliski for the General Motors Corporation. On the basis of data for 1919–37, their statistical analysis indicated that the price elasticity of demand for new automobiles was about 1.5. In other words, a 1 percent reduction in price would result in about a 1.5 percent increase in the quantity demanded of new automobiles.

Several more recent studies of the price elasticity of demand for automobiles have been carried out by academic economists. Although there has been some controversy over particular aspects of these investigations, they seem to indicate that the price elasticity of demand for automobiles is at least 1.2. In other words, a 1 percent reduction in price brings about at least a 1.2 percent increase in the quantity demanded. Thus, these studies, carried out by L. J. Atkinson, Gregory Chow, and D. B. Suits, seem generally to agree rather well with the earlier study by Roos and von Szeliski.

Two aspects of these studies should be noted. First, in contrast to the case of the Boston and Maine Railroad, the estimates obtained by these researchers were based on detailed statistical analysis of past data on price, quantity demanded, income, and a variety of other variables, not on the sort of direct market experiment the Boston and Maine carried out. Second, because automobiles are durable goods, these investigators had to recognize that the basic demand is for automobile ownership, not new cars. As Princeton's Gregory Chow put it, "People buy automobiles because they want to use automobiles, and their wants are satisfied not only by the new cars that they have just bought but by the total number of cars in existence. So the demand for automobile services actually is a demand for automobile ownership rather than the demand for purchase. The demand for purchase is derived from the demand for automobile ownership."[2]

On the basis of the available evidence, it is difficult to tell conclusively whether the automobile manufacturers have tended to underestimate the price elasticity of demand for their product. But suppose for the sake of argument that they have. Why should anyone care? The answer is that both the automobile manufacturers and the general public should care, because, by underestimating the price elasticity of demand, the companies are underestimating the gain in sales from a price reduction. Thus, they are inclined to maintain the price at too high a level, to the detriment of their own profits as well as the consumer's pocketbook.

Industry and Firm Demand Curves

Up to this point, we have been dealing with the market demand curve for a commodity. *The market demand curve for a commodity is not the same as the market demand curve for the output of a single firm that produces the commodity, unless, of course, the industry is composed of only a single firm.* If the industry is composed of more than one firm, as is usually the case, the demand curve for the output of each firm producing the commodity will usually be quite different from the demand curve for the commodity. For example, the demand curve for the output of Farmer Brown's wheat is quite different from the market demand curve for wheat. *In particular, the demand curve for the output of a particular firm is generally more price elastic than the market demand curve for the commodity,* because the products of other firms in the industry are close substitutes for the product of

[2] Senate Subcommittee on Antitrust and Monopoly, "The Price Elasticity of Demand for Automobiles," reprinted in E. Mansfield, *Microeconomics: Selected Readings,* New York: Norton, 1971.

this firm. As we pointed out earlier, products with lots of close substitutes have relatively high price elasticities of demand.

If there are many, many firms selling a homogeneous product, the individual firm's demand curve becomes ***infinitely elastic.*** That is, the price elasticity of demand becomes infinite. To see this, suppose that 100,000 firms sell a particular commodity and that each of these firms is of equal size. If any one of these firms were to triple its output and sales, the total industry output would change by only .002 percent—too small a change to have any perceptible effect on the price of the commodity. Consequently, each firm can act as if variations in its output—within the range of its capabilities—will have no real impact on market price. In other words, the demand curve facing the individual firm is horizontal, as in Figure 20.11. And if the demand curve is horizontal, the price elasticity of demand must be infinite, because it is the percentage change in quantity demanded resulting from a 1 percent change in price. If the percentage change in quantity demanded resulting from a 1 percent change in price is infinite—as is indicated by a horizontal demand curve—the price elasticity of demand must be infinite too.

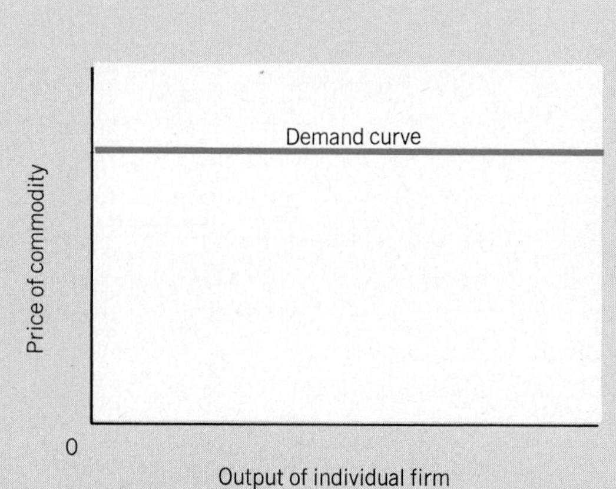

Figure 20.11
Demand Curve for Output of an Individual Firm: The Case of a Great Many Sellers of a Homogeneous Commodity

If there are many, many firms selling a homogeneous product, the demand curve facing an individual firm is horizontal.

Income Elasticity of Demand

So far this chapter has dealt almost exclusively with the effect of a commodity's price on the quantity demanded of it in the market. But price is not, of course, the only factor that influences the quantity demanded of the commodity. Another important factor is the level of money income among the consumers in the market. The sensitivity of the quantity demanded to the total money income of all of the consumers in the market is measured by the ***income elasticity of demand,*** which is defined as the percentage change in the quantity demanded resulting from a 1 percent increase in total money income (all prices being held constant).

A commodity's income elasticity of demand may be positive or negative. For many commodities, increases in income result in increases in the amount demanded: such commodities, like steak or caviar, have positive income elasticities of demand. For other commodities, increases in income result in decreases in the amount demanded: these commodities, like margarine and poor grades of vegetables, have negative income elasticities of demand. However, be careful to note that the income elasticity of demand of a commodity is likely to vary with the level of income under consideration. For example, if only families at the lowest income levels are considered, the income elasticity of demand for margarine may be positive.

Luxury items tend to have higher income elasticities of demand than necessities. Indeed, one way to define luxuries and necessities is to say that luxuries are commodities with high income elasticities of demand, and necessities are commodities with low income elasticities of demand.

Many studies have been made to estimate the

income elasticity of demand for particular commodities, since like the price elasticity of demand, it is of great importance to decision makers. In making long-term forecasts of industry sales, for example, firms must take the income elasticity of demand into account. Thus, if the income elasticity of demand for a product is high, and if incomes increase considerably during the next 20 years, the product's sales will tend to increase greatly during that period. On the other hand, if the income elasticity of demand for a product is close to zero, one would expect the product's sales not to increase very much on account of such increases in income.

To illustrate the findings of empirical studies in this area, consider the following results obtained by Herman Wold, a distinguished Swedish economist. According to his estimates, the income elasticity of demand is 0.37 for eggs, 0.34 for cheese, 0.42 for butter, 1.00 for liquor, −0.20 for margarine, 0.07 for milk and cream, and 1.48 for restaurant consumption of food. Certainly, these estimates seem reasonable. One would expect the income elasticity of demand to be negative for margarine, because consumers tend to view margarine as an inferior good, and as their incomes rise, they tend to switch from margarine to butter. Also, it is not surprising that the income elasticity of demand for milk and cream is close to zero, since people tend to view milk and cream as necessities, particularly for children. In addition, it is quite reasonable that the income elasticity of demand for liquor and restaurant consumption of food is higher than for the other commodities. Liquor and restaurant meals tend to be luxury items for most people.

Finally, let's look once again at the market demand for automobiles, considering the income elasticity of demand this time. To develop and exercise your economic intuition, think about the demand for automobiles, and try to guess what the income elasticity of demand for automobiles is likely to be. Is it likely to be positive or negative? If positive, is it likely to be above or below 1? This sort of exercise is extremely useful. Just as it is important that you be able to come up with a reasonable guess concerning the answer to an arithmetic problem, so you should be able to make a reasonable guess at a product's income elasticity of demand—or its price elasticity of demand, for that matter.

What are the facts? According to the early study by Roos and von Szeliski, the income elasticity of demand for automobiles is about 2.5: in other words, a 1 percent increase in income will result in about a 2.5 percent increase in the quantity demanded of automobiles. According to the later studies by Atkinson, Chow, and Suits, it is about 3.0: in other words, a 1 percent increase in income will result in about a 3.0 percent increase in the quantity demanded of automobiles. Needless to say, despite the advances that have been made in statistical and econometric methods, it is hard to estimate income elasticities or price elasticities with pinpoint accuracy. Fortunately, however, pinpoint accuracy seldom is necessary. In this case, the knowledge that the answer probably lies between 2.5 and 3.0 is of great value for many practical purposes.

Cross Elasticity of Demand

Besides the price of the commodity and the level of total money income—the factors discussed primarily in previous sections of this chapter—the quantity demanded of a commodity also depends on the prices of other commodities. For example, if the price of butter is held constant, the amount of butter demanded will be influenced by the price of margarine. The ***cross elasticity of demand,*** defined as the percentage change in the quantity demanded of one commodity resulting from a 1 percent change in the price of another commodity, is used to measure the sensitivity of the former commodity's quantity demanded to changes in the latter commodity's price.

Pairs of commodities are classified as ***substitutes*** or ***complements,*** depending on the sign of the cross elasticity of demand. If the cross elasticity of demand is positive, two commodities are substitutes. For example, butter and margarine are substitutes because a decrease in the price of butter will result in a decrease in the quantity demanded of margarine—many margarine eaters really prefer the "higher-priced spread." On the other hand, if the cross elasticity of demand is negative, two commodities are complements. For example, gin and tonic may be complements since a decrease in the price of gin may increase the quantity demanded of tonic. The reduction in the price of gin will increase the quantity demanded of gin, thus increasing the quantity demanded of tonic since gin and tonic tend to be used together.

Many studies have also been made of the cross elasticity of demand for various pairs of commodities. After all, it frequently is most important to know how a change in the price of one commodity will affect the sales of another commodity. For example, what would be the effect of a 1 percent increase in the price of pork on the quantity demanded of beef? According to Herman Wold's estimates, the effect would be a .28 percent increase in the quantity demanded of beef—since he estimates that the cross elasticity of demand for these two commodities is 0.28. What effect would a 1 percent increase in the price of butter have on the quantity demanded of margarine? According to Wold, the effect would be a .81 percent increase in the quantity demanded of margarine—since he estimates that the cross elasticity of demand for these two commodities is 0.81.

Criticisms and Extensions of the Model

The theory of consumer behavior and market demand has not been without its critics. Among the most articulate (and severe) is Harvard's John Kenneth Galbraith, who argues that it is naïve and misleading to assume that consumer tastes arise from within the consumer, and that producers dance to the tune of consumer preferences. Instead, in Galbraith's view, producers, through their advertising and other selling activities, play an important role in molding consumer tastes and in getting consumers to want more and more of whatever they are producing. The following quotation indicates the spirit (and wit) of Galbraith's attack:

> Were it so that a man on arising each morning was assailed by demons which instilled in him a passion sometimes for silk shirts, sometimes for kitchenware, sometimes for chamber pots, and sometimes for orange squash, there would be every reason to applaud the effort to find the goods, however odd, that quenched this flame. But should it be that . . . production creates the wants it seeks to satisfy, or if the wants emerge *pari passu* with the production, then the urgency of the wants can no longer be used to defend the urgency of the production. Production only fills a void that it has itself created.[3]

Of course, Galbraith is certainly correct in pointing out that consumer tastes are affected by advertising and other types of promotional efforts by producers. However most economists seem to feel that he goes too far in portraying the consumer as a docile animal producers lead around by the nose, and they are skeptical of his argument that acquired desires or tastes must be less important than those that are innate. For example, Friedrich von Hayek has stated:

> Professor Galbraith's argument could be easily employed, without any change of the essential terms, to demonstrate the worthlessness of literature or any form of art. Surely an individual's want for literature is not original with himself in the sense that he would experience it if literature were not produced. Does this then mean that the production of literature cannot be defended as satisfying a want because it is only the production which provokes the demand?[4]

Even such Marxist economists as Paul Baran feel that Galbraith goes too far. Baran writes that "to be sure, it does not follow, as some business economists like to assert, that the barrage of advertising and salesmanship to which the consumer is continually exposed has *no* influence on the formation of his wants. But neither is it true that these business practices constitute *the* decisive factor in

[3] J. K. Galbraith, *The Affluent Society*, Boston: Houghton Mifflin, 1958, reprinted in E. Mansfield, *Economics: Readings, Issues, and Cases*, New York: Norton, 1974.

making the consumer want what he wants."[5] To Baran, the crucial issue is over the kinds of values and preferences that are instilled into people by these processes, and whether they are good or bad, not whether such processes go on. Much more will be said on this score in Chapter 34.

Another criticism of the theory of consumer behavior and market demand is that it pays too little attention to the fact that what one consumer wants depends on what other consumers buy. In other words, the location and shape of one consumer's indifference curves depend on the purchases of other consumers. For example, if the Walters associate with people who have big houses and beach cottages, they may come to want them too. However, it is possible to extend the model of consumer behavior and market demand to include such interdependencies, or "demonstration effects," as they are called by economists. Moreover, it is possible to extend the model to include the fact that some people may prefer expensive goods to cheaper ones, either because they like to show off their wealth or because they judge quality by price. Also, it is possible to include the effects of advertising in such a model. Interested students are referred to more advanced textbooks, where these extensions properly belong.

Summary

The market demand curve, which is the relationship between the price of a commodity and the amount of the commodity demanded in the market, is one of the most important and frequently used concepts in economics. The market demand curve is the horizontal sum of the individual demand curves of all of the consumers in the market. Individual demand curves almost always slope downward to the right because of the so-called law of decreasing marginal utility. Or, to avoid the use of cardinal utility measures, one can explain this same thing in terms of the substitution and income effects of a price change. Since the individual demand curves almost always slope downward to the right, market demand curves will do so too.

The price elasticity of demand measures the sensitivity of the amount demanded to changes in price. Whether a price increase results in an increase or decrease in the total amount spent on a commodity depends on the price elasticity of demand. The income elasticity of demand measures the sensitivity of the amount demanded to changes in total income. A commodity's income elasticity of demand may be positive or negative. Luxury items are generally assumed to have higher income elasticities of demand than necessities. The cross elasticity of demand measures the sensitivity of the amount demanded to changes in the price of another commodity. If the cross elasticity of demand is positive, two commodities are substitutes; if it is negative, they are complements.

The market demand curve for a commodity is not the same as the demand curve for the output of a single firm that produces the commodity, unless the industry is composed of only one firm. In general, the demand curve for the output of a single firm will be more elastic than the market demand curve for the commodity. Indeed, if there are many, many firms selling a homogeneous commodity, the individual firm's demand curve becomes infinitely elastic. There are many techniques for measuring demand curves, such as interview studies, direct experiments, and the statistical analysis of historical data. An example of a direct experiment was the demonstration project carried out in 1963 by the Boston and Maine Railroad.

A consumer's individual demand curve for a commodity can be derived from the model of consumer behavior presented in Chapter 19. To obtain the point on this demand curve corresponding to a particular price, all we have to do is construct the budget line corresponding to this price (holding the consumer's income and all other prices constant), find the market basket on this budget line that is on the highest indifference curve, and plot

[4] F. A. Hayek, "The Non Sequitur of the Dependence Effect," *Southern Economic Journal,* April 1961, reprinted in E. Mansfield, *Economics: Readings, Issues, and Cases, op. cit.*

[5] Paul Baran, *The Political Economy of Growth,* New York: Monthly Review Press, 1957.

the amount of this commodity in that market basket against this price. Clearly the location and shape of the consumer's individual demand curve depends on his tastes, his income, and the prices of other commodities. And since the market demand curve is the horizontal sum of individual demand curves, it too depends on these factors, as well as on the number of consumers in the market.

CONCEPTS FOR REVIEW

Market demand curve	Individual demand curve
Arc elasticity of demand	Complement
Price elasticity of demand	Substitute
Income elasticity of demand	Infinitely elastic
Cross elasticity of demand	Brannon plan
Unitary elasticity	Substitution effect
Price elastic	Income effect
Price inelastic	

QUESTIONS FOR DISCUSSION AND REVIEW

1. On page 412, we saw that the quantity of Model T's sold increased from about 472,000 to about 730,000 when its price was reduced from $440 in 1914 to $360 in 1916. How can this fact be reconciled with recent studies which indicate that the price elasticity of demand for automobiles is about 1.2 to 1.5?

2. According to S. M. Sackrin's study for the Department of Agriculture of the demand for cigarettes, the price elasticity of demand is between 0.3 and 0.4, and the income elasticity of demand is about 0.5. If you were an economist at one of the major tobacco companies, how might you use these data?

3. Suppose that the relationship between the price of aluminum and the quantity of aluminum demanded is as follows:

Price ($)	*Quantity*
1	8
2	7
3	6
4	5
5	4

What is the arc elasticity of demand when price is between $1 and $2? Between $4 and $5?

4. According to the Department of Agriculture, the income elasticity of demand for coffee is about 0.23. If incomes rose by 1 percent, what effect would this have on the quantity demanded of coffee?

CHAPTER 21

Optimal Input Decisions and Cost Analysis

In economies based largely on free enterprise, like our own, the managers of business firms are given considerable responsibility for deciding where, when, and how various resources are used. Thus, the manager's job is a central one, from both a social and private point of view. Fortunately, the United States has been able to develop large cadres of effective managerial talent, in large part because management and business have been highly esteemed professions in the United States. As Calvin Coolidge put it, with characteristic brevity and uncharacteristic overstatement, "The business of America is business." This is quite a different sentiment from that expressed by the ancient Roman historian, Tacitus, who said that Sabinus "had talents equal to business, and aspired no higher."

In this chapter, we shall take a closer look at the decision-making process within the firm. Having discussed the organization, motivation, and technology of the firm in Chapter 7, we now discuss some of the central questions involved in its management and operation. In particular, if a firm attempts to maximize profits, what production technique—i.e., what combination of inputs—should it choose to produce a particular quantity of output? What are its costs? How do various types of costs vary with the firm's output rate? These questions are of the utmost importance, both for the managers of a firm and for society as a whole.

Average and Marginal Products

If the United States Steel Corporation decides to produce a certain quantity of steel, it can do so in many ways. It can use open hearth furnaces, or basic oxygen furnaces, or electric furnaces; it can use various types of iron ore; and it can use various types of coke. Which of these many ways will maximize U. S. Steel's profits? The management of U. S. Steel—and every business firm—devotes considerable time and energy to answering this kind of question. Let's restate it in the economist's terms: given that a firm is going to produce a certain quantity of output, what production technique—i.e., what combination of inputs—should it choose to maximize its profits?

As a first step toward answering this question, recall the characteristics of a firm's production function; namely, that it shows the most output that existing technology permits the firm to extract from each quantity of inputs. For example, the production function for an oil pipeline, described in Chapter 7, shows the maximum amount of oil a pipeline can carry, given that it has a certain diameter and that a certain number of horsepower are applied. From the production function, we can compute an input's average product and its marginal product. The ***average product of an input*** is the firm's total output divided by the amount of the input used to produce this amount of output. For example, consider the simple case of a wheat farm with 1 acre of land (a fixed input). The relationship between the amount of labor used per year by this farm (a variable input) and

Table 21.1

Relationship between Labor Input and Output of One-Acre Wheat Farm

Number of manyears of labor	Bushels of wheat produced per year
0	0
1	30
2	70
3	100
4	125
5	145

the farm's output are shown in Table 21.1. This is the farm's production function. And the average product of labor is 30 bushels per manyear of labor when 1 manyear of labor is used, 35 bushels per manyear of labor when 2 manyears are used, 33⅓ bushels per manyear of labor when 3 manyears are used, and so forth.

As the amount of labor used on the farm increases, so does the farm's output, but the amount of extra output from the addition of an extra manyear of labor varies depending on how much labor is already being used. The extra output from the addition of the first manyear of labor is 30 − 0 = 30 bushels per manyear of labor. The extra output due to the addition of the second manyear of labor is 70 − 30 = 40 bushels per manyear of labor. And the extra output from the addition of the fifth manyear of labor is 145 − 125 = 20 bushels per manyear of labor. The ***marginal product of an input*** is the addition to total output due to the addition of the last unit of input, the quantity of other inputs used being held constant. Thus, the marginal product of labor is 30 bushels when between 0 and 1 manyears of labor are used, 40 bushels when between 1 and 2 manyears of labor are used, and so on.

Table 21.2 shows the average and marginal products of labor at various levels of utilization of

Table 21.2

Average and Marginal Products of Labor, One-Acre Wheat Farm

Number of manyears of labor	Average product (bushels per manyear)	Marginal product* (bushels per manyear)
1	30	30
2	35	40
3	33⅓	30
4	31¼	25
5	29	20

* These figures pertain to the interval between the indicated number of manyears of labor and one manyear less than the indicated number.

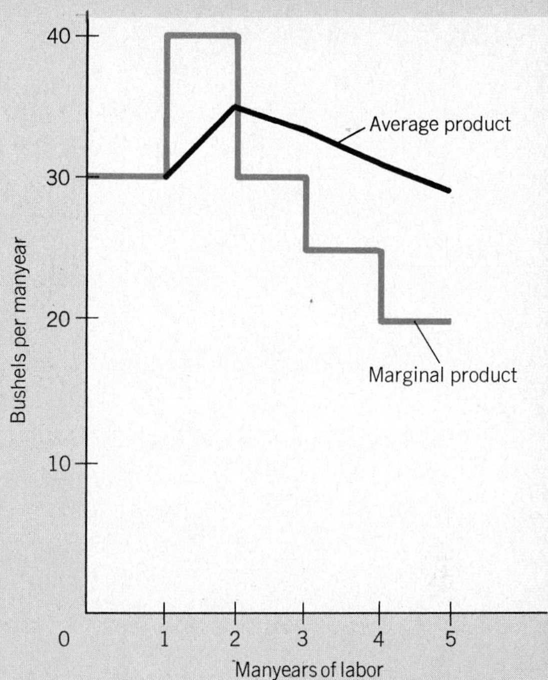

Figure 21.1
Average and Marginal Products of Labor, 1-Acre Wheat Farm

Both the average product and the marginal product of labor rise, reach a maximum, and fall. The marginal product curve intersects the average product curve when the latter is a maximum.

labor; Figure 21.1 shows the same thing graphically. As is generally the case for production processes, the average product of the variable input—labor in this case—rises, reaches a maximum, and then falls. The marginal product of labor also rises, reaches a maximum, and falls; this too is typical of many production processes. Also, it is noteworthy that the marginal product curve intersects the average product curve when the latter is a maximum. This will always be the case.[1]

[1] Marginal product must exceed average product when the latter is increasing, equal average product when the latter reaches a maximum, and be less than average product when the latter is decreasing. This is simply a matter of arithmetic: if the addition to a total is greater (less) than the average, the average is bound to increase (decrease).

The Law of Diminishing Marginal Returns

Perhaps the best-known—and certainly one of the least understood—laws of economics is the so-called ***law of diminishing marginal returns.*** Put in a single sentence, this law states that *if equal increments of an input are added, the quantities of other inputs held constant, the resulting increments of product will decrease beyond some point;* that is, the marginal product of the input will diminish. This law is illustrated by Table 21.2; beyond 2 manyears of labor, the marginal product of labor falls. Certainly, it seems entirely reasonable that, as more and more of a variable input (in this case, labor) is combined with a fixed amount of another input (in this case, land), the additional output to be derived from an additional unit of the variable input will eventually decrease. For example, in the case of Table 21.2, one would expect that, as more and more labor is added, the extra workers' functions eventually would become less and less important and productive.

This law plays a part in determining the firm's optimal input combination and the shape of the firm's cost functions, as we shall see below. To prevent misunderstanding and confusion, several points about this law should be stressed. First, it is assumed that technology remains fixed. If technology changes, the law of diminishing marginal returns cannot predict the effect of an additional unit of input. Second, at least one input must be fixed in quantity, since the law of diminishing marginal returns is not applicable to cases where there is a proportional increase in all inputs. Third, it must be possible, of course, to vary the proportions in which the various inputs are utilized. This is generally possible in industry and agriculture.

To illustrate how the law of diminishing marginal returns operates in real-life situations, let's return to the case of a 1,000-mile-long crude oil pipeline. Recall from Chapter 7 that the output of such a pipeline is the amount of oil carried per day, and that the two principal inputs are the diameter of the pipeline and the horsepower applied to the oil it carries. It makes sense, of course, that the pipeline's output will depend heavily on its diameter and the horsepower applied to the oil. The exact relationship between the quantities of these inputs and the quantity of output was given in the production function shown in Table 7.3. For convenience, this production function is reproduced in Table 21.3. Using the production func-

Table 21.3

Production Function, Crude Oil Pipeline

Line Diameter (inches)	Horsepower (thousands) 20	30	40	50	60
	Output rate (thousands of barrels per day)				
14	70	90	95	100	104
18	115	140	155	165	170
22	160	190	215	235	250
26	220	260	300	320	340

Source: See Table 7.3.

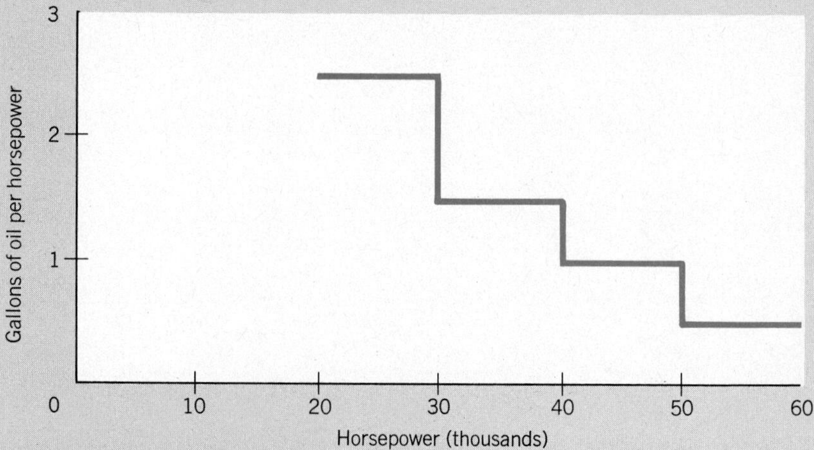

Figure 21.2
Marginal Product of Horsepower, Crude Oil Pipeline, 18-Inch Diameter

The graph shows the marginal product curve in an actual case. Note that the results agree with the law of diminishing returns.

Figure 21.3
Marginal Product of Line Diameter, Crude Oil Pipeline, 50,000 Horsepower

In this range, the marginal product of pipeline diameter does not decrease as the diameter increases, but this does not contradict the law of diminishing returns since the law states that the marginal product will decrease eventually, not in any particular range.

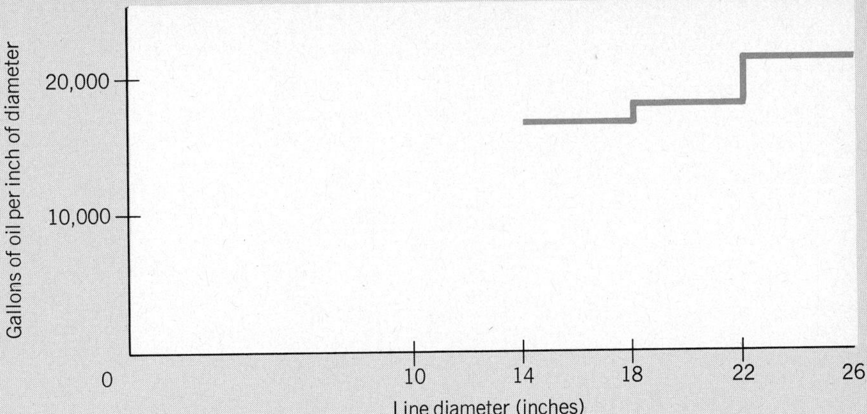

tion, we can estimate the marginal product of each input.

Figure 21.2 shows the marginal product of horsepower if the diameter of the pipeline is 18 inches. For example, when horsepower is between 20,000 and 30,000, the marginal product is (140,000 − 115,000) ÷ (30,000 − 20,000)—or 2.5 gallons of oil (per day) per horsepower. Why? Because in this range, an extra horsepower results in 2.5 extra gallons of oil carried per day. Similarly, the marginal product is 1.5 gallons when horsepower is between 30,000 and 40,000, 1.0 gallons when horsepower is between 40,000 and 50,000, and 0.5 gallons when horsepower is between 50,000 and 60,000. Thus, in accord with the law of diminishing marginal returns, the marginal product of horsepower decreases as more and more horsepower is used. Moreover, this is true for every pipe diameter, not just 18 inches.

Figure 21.3 shows the marginal product of pipeline diameter, given that the horsepower is 50,000. For example, when the diameter is between 14 and 18 inches, the marginal product is (165,000 − 100,000) ÷ (18 − 14)—or 16,250 gallons of oil (per day) per inch of pipeline diameter. This is so because in this range, an extra inch of diameter results in 16,250 extra gallons of oil carried per day. Similarly, the marginal product is 17,500 gallons when the diameter is between 18 and 22 inches, and 21,250 gallons when the diameter is between 22 and 26 inches. Thus, the marginal product of pipeline diameter does not decrease as the diameter increases. However, this does not contradict the law of diminishing marginal returns because the law states only that the marginal product will decrease *eventually,* not that it will decrease in any particular range. In other words, the law says that, if diameter in increased more and more (and if horsepower is held constant at 50,000), *eventually* the marginal product of pipeline diameter will decrease.[2]

Isoquants

In the case of a crude oil pipeline, a given amount of oil can be carried per day either by using a large diameter of pipe and relatively small horsepower or by using a smaller diameter of pipe and greater horsepower. Similar opportunities to vary inputs to achieve a given output rate exist in practically all industries. To describe these oppor-

[2] Also, the inputs associated with line diameter may be gauged more appropriately by measures other than diameter. This too may influence the results.

tunities, economists use the concept of an isoquant. An ***isoquant*** is a curve showing all possible efficient combinations of inputs capable of producing a certain quantity of output. An *inefficient* combination of inputs is one that includes more of at least one input, and as much of other inputs, as some other combination of inputs that can produce the same quantity of output. Inefficient combinations clearly cannot minimize costs or maximize profits. For example, it may be possible to produce 1 unit of output with 2 units of land and 3 units of labor. It may also be possible to produce 1 unit of output with 3 units of land and 3 units of labor. The second input combination—which is inefficient—cannot be the least-cost input combination, so long as land has a *positive* price. Only *efficient* input combinations are worth bothering with in the present circumstances, and they alone are included in an isoquant.

There is an isoquant pertaining to each level of production. Figure 21.4 shows some isoquants for the wheat farm cited above (assuming it can now vary its quantity of land). These isoquants show the various combinations of inputs that can produce 100, 200, and 300 bushels of wheat per period of time. For instance, consider the isoquant for 100 bushels of wheat per period of time. According to this isoquant, the farm can attain this output rate if OL_1 units of labor and OD_1 units of land are used per period of time. Alternatively, this output rate can be attained with OL_2 units of labor and OD_2 units of land—or OL_3 units of labor and OD_3 units of land—per period of time.

The shape and position of a firm's isoquants are derived from the firm's production function. Indeed, one way to represent the firm's production function is by showing its isoquants. Thus, the firm's isoquants, like its production function, show the firm's technological possibilities—the various efficient input-output combinations that can be achieved with existing technology. The shape of an isoquant is typically like that shown in Figure 21.4; that is, it slopes downward to the right, but *its slope becomes less and less steep.* This fact stems from the operation of the law of diminishing returns.

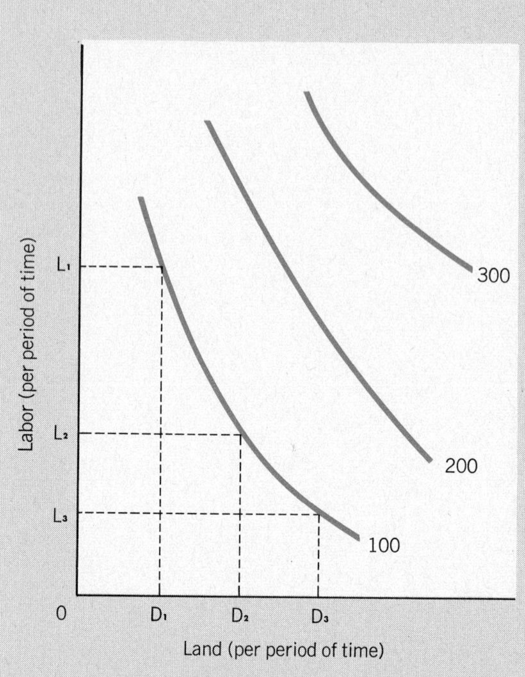

Figure 21.4
Isoquants, Wheat Farm

An isoquant shows all possible efficient combinations of inputs capable of producing a certain quantity of output. These isoquants show the various combinations of inputs that can produce 100, 200, and 300 bushels of wheat per period of time. For example, 100 bushels of wheat can be produced with OL_1 units of labor and OD_1 units of land, with OL_2 units of labor and OD_2 units of land, or with OL_3 units of labor and OD_3 units of land.

To illustrate what isoquants in an actual firm look like, consider once again our crude oil pipeline. Figure 21.5 shows the isoquants corresponding to 100,000, 200,000, and 300,000 barrels of crude oil carried per day. For example, the isoquant corresponding to 100,000 barrels per day shows all

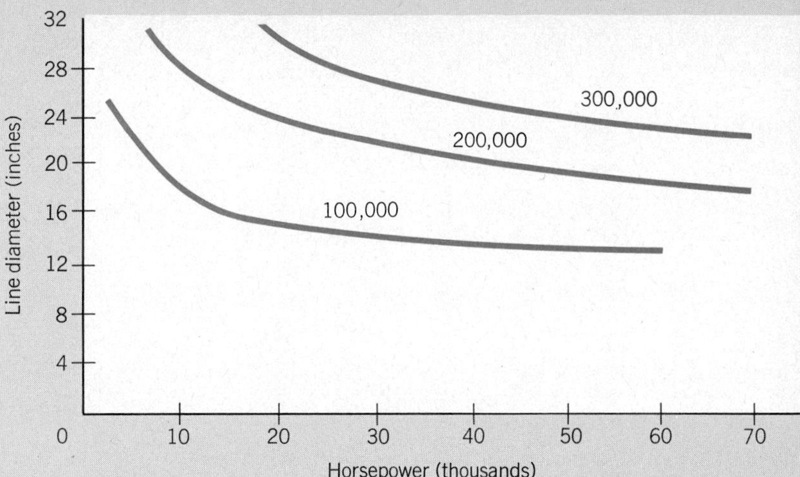

Figure 21.5
Isoquants for 100,000, 200,000, and 300,000 Barrels of Crude Oil Carried per Day, Crude Oil Pipeline

This graph shows the isoquants in an actual case. Note that they are shaped as economic theory would predict.

the combinations of line diameter and horsepower that permit a pipeline to carry 100,000 barrels per day (for 1,000 miles). Note that each of these isoquants slopes downward to the right. Moreover, comparing these isoquants with Table 21.3, you can readily see that, if Table 21.3 contained more detailed data on the production function, it would be simple to derive the isoquants from the data regarding the production function in Table 21.3. How? By determining from this more detailed version of Table 21.3 the various input combinations that can produce each output rate.

The Optimal Input Decision

Now we are in a position to answer the question posed at the beginning of this chapter: given that a firm is going to produce a particular quantity of output, what production technique—i.e., what combination of inputs—should it choose to maximize profits? Note first that, if the firm maximizes its profits, it must minimize the cost of producing this quantity of output. This seems obvious enough. But what combination of inputs (that will produce the required quantity of output) will minimize the firm's costs? The answer can be stated like this: *the firm will minimize cost by combining inputs in such a way that the marginal product of a dollar's worth of any one input equals the marginal product of a dollar's worth of any other input used.*

Another way to say the same thing is: *the firm will minimize cost by combining inputs in such a way that, for every input used, the marginal product of the input is proportional to its price.* To see what this means, let's take a numerical example from our wheat farm. Suppose that the farm can vary the amount of labor and land it uses. Table 21.4 shows the marginal product of each input when various combinations of inputs (all combinations being able to produce the specified quantity of output) are used. Suppose that the price of labor is $4,000 per manyear and that the annual price of using land is $1,000 per acre. (We assume that the firm takes the prices of inputs as given and that it can buy all it wants of the inputs at these prices.) Since the annual price of an acre of land is ¼ the price of a manyear of labor, our rule implies that the marginal product of land must be ¼ the marginal product of labor if costs are to be minimized. Thus, the optimal combination of inputs must be 4 acres of land and 1 manyear of labor, since this is

Table 21.4

Marginal Products of Labor and Land

Amount of input used		Marginal product		Total cost
Labor (Manyears)	Land (Acres)	Labor	Land	(dollars)
0.5	7	50	5	9,000
1.0	4	40	10	8,000
1.5	3	30	30	9,000
2.5	2	20	50	12,000

the only combination capable of producing the required output where this is the case. (See Table 21.4.)

Is this rule correct? Does it really result in a least-cost combination of inputs? Let's look at the cost of the other input combinations in Table 21.4. The first combination (0.5 manyears of labor and 7 acres of land) costs $9,000; the second combination (1.0 manyears of labor and 4 acres of land) costs $8,000; and so on. An examination of the total cost of each input combination shows that the input combination chosen by our rule—1.0 manyears of labor and 4 acres of land—is indeed the least-cost input combination, the one for the profit-maximizing firm to use.

Isocost Curves and Isoquants

Of course, one example really does not prove that the rule results in minimum costs; it only demonstrates that it does so in this particular case. Another way to determine the combination of inputs that will minimize the firm's costs is to use the isoquant concept. All input combinations that can efficiently produce the specified level of output can be represented by the isoquant corresponding to this level of output. For example, the isoquant in Figure 21.6 shows all the input combinations the wheat farm can use to produce the required amount of wheat. The optimal input combination must lie on this isoquant, but where? A simple way to determine the optimal input combination is to draw a number of ***isocost curves,*** as shown in Figure 21.6. Each isocost curve shows the input combinations the firm can obtain for a given expenditure. For example, the isocost curves corresponding to expenditures of $6,000, $8,000, and

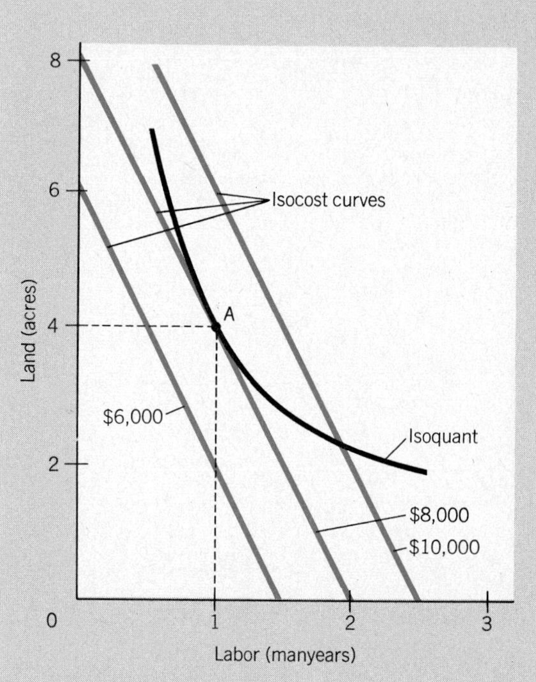

Figure 21.6
Least-Cost Input Combination

The least-cost input combination is at point *A*, where 4 acres of land and 1 manyear of labor are used. The isoquant shows all input combinations that can be used to produce the required amount of wheat, and the isocost curves show the input combinations costing $6,000, $8,000, and $10,000, respectively.

$10,000 are shown in Figure 21.6.

Given the price of each input, it is, of course, a simple matter to draw each of these curves. For example, take the case of the isocost curve corresponding to annual expenditures of $6,000. If this expenditure were devoted entirely to labor, 1½ manyears could be hired (since the price of labor is $4,000 per manyear). Thus, this isocost curve must cut the horizontal axis in Figure 21.6 at 1½ manyears of labor. Similarly, if this expenditure were devoted entirely to land, 6 acres of land could be hired (since the annual price of using land is $1,000). Thus, this isocost curve must cut the vertical axis at 6 acres of land. Finally, if we connect the point where the isocost curve cuts the vertical axis to the point where it cuts the horizontal axis, we obtain the entire isocost curve.

Given both the isoquant and the isocost curves, one can readily determine the input combination that will minimize the firm's costs. This input combination corresponds to *that point on the isoquant that lies on the lowest isocost curve*—in other words, point *A* in Figure 21.6. Input combinations on lower isocost curves (like that corresponding to $6,000) that lie below *A* are cheaper than *A*, but cannot produce the desired output. Input combinations on isocost curves (like that corresponding to $10,000) that lie above *A* will produce the desired output but at a higher cost than *A*.

Finally, what is the relationship between the input combination determined in this way and the input combination determined by means of the rule described in the previous section? Reassuringly enough, these input combinations are the same—1 manyear of labor and 4 acres of land. Moreover, we can be sure that the rule described in the previous section will always give the same answer as this geometric technique. In general, if you find the combination of inputs where the marginal product of a dollar's worth of any one input equals the marginal product of a dollar's worth of any other input used, this will give you the same answer as if you find the point on the isoquant that lies on the lowest isocost curve.

To prove that this is the case, suppose that this rule is violated, and the firm combines inputs so that the marginal product of a dollar's worth of one input does *not* equal the marginal product of some other input used. Specifically, suppose that the wheat farm combines labor and land in such a way that the marginal product of a dollar's worth of labor is *greater* than the marginal product of a dollar's worth of land. It is then easy to see that the wheat farm is not minimizing its costs. Since the marginal product of a dollar's worth of labor is greater than the marginal product of a dollar's worth of land, it must follow that the wheat farm could increase its output, *without increasing its costs,* if it substituted one dollar's worth of labor for one dollar's worth of land. A substitution of this sort would lead to increased output with no increase in cost.

Let's now introduce isoquants and isocost curves. If the marginal product of a dollar's worth of labor is greater than that of a dollar's worth of land, the firm can attain a higher isoquant, while staying on the same isocost curve. Thus, the firm is clearly not at the point on the relevant isoquant that lies on the lowest isocost curve. Similarly, if the marginal product of a dollar's worth of labor is less than that of a dollar's worth of land, the firm can attain a higher isoquant, while staying on the same isocost curve. (It can do this by substituting a dollar's worth of land for a dollar's worth of labor.) Thus, under these circumstances too, the firm is clearly not at the point on the relevant isoquant that lies on the lowest isocost curve.

Since the firm is not at the point on the relevant isoquant that lies on the lowest isocost curve when the marginal product of a dollar's worth of labor is greater than, or less than, that of a dollar's worth of land, it must be true that the firm is at this point only when the marginal product of a dollar's worth of labor equals that of a dollar's worth of land. This, of course, is what we set out to prove.

Our rule for the determination of the least-cost input combination follows directly from the rule of rational choice presented in Chapter 19. Recall that a rational allocation of expenditures is one where the marginal utility from a dollar spent for one commodity equals the marginal utility from a dollar spent for another commodity. If the firm maximizes profit, and if its total costs are held constant, its "utility" increases with its output level, because the firm prefers more output to less, so long as the extra output does not increase its costs and does increase its revenues. Thus, one can use its output level (under these special circumstances) as its "utility" function, with the result that the marginal product from a dollar's worth of an input is the same as the marginal "utility" from a dollar's worth of an input. Consequently, the rule presented in previous sections—allocate expenditures so that the marginal product of a dollar's worth of an input is the same for all inputs used—is essentially the same under these circumstances as the rule presented in Chapter 19—allocate expenditures so that the marginal utility of a dollar's worth of a commodity bought is the same for all commodities purchased. This, of course, is not surprising. Whether we are talking about consumers, firms, or other organizations, the same rules should apply to get the most out of a given amount of resources.

Determining the Optimal Input Combination: A Case Study

If by now you wonder about the practical payoff from this sort of analysis, consider how a distinguished agricultural economist, Earl Heady of Iowa State University has used these methods to help farmers make better production decisions. Figure 21.7 illustrates the sort of work Heady and his co-workers have done. The two inputs in this case are land and fertilizer, and the isoquant shows the various amounts of land and fertilizer that will produce 82.6 bushels of corn on Kansas Verdigras soil. According to the isoquant, this amount of corn can be produced if 1.19 acres of land and no fertilizer are used, or if 1.11 acres of land and 20 pounds of fertilizer are used, or if .99 acres of land

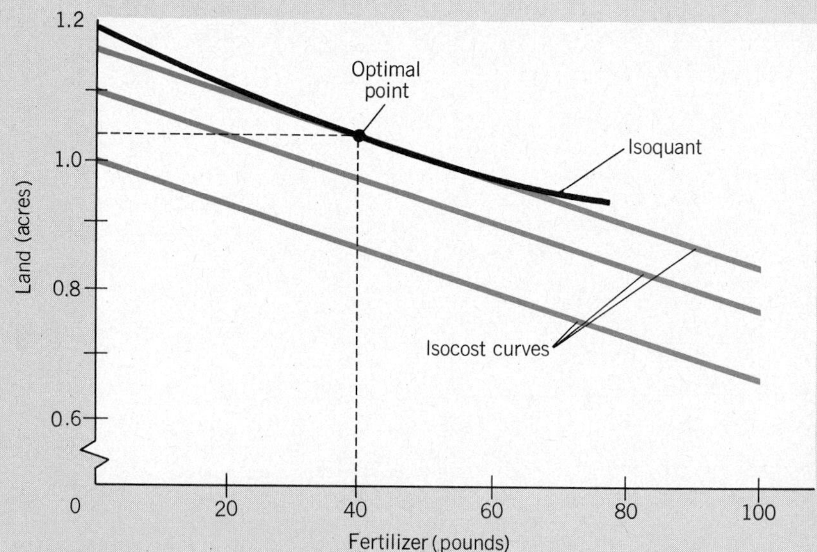

Figure 21.7
Isoquant for the Production of 82.6 Bushels of Corn in Kansas

This graph shows how economic analysis has been used to help farmers make better production decisions. Given the assumed conditions, the optimal input combination would be 40 pounds of fertilizer and 1.04 acres of land.

and 60 pounds of fertilizer are used, and so forth.[3]

After estimating isoquants of this sort, Heady and his coworkers derived the optimal input combinations farmers should use to minimize their costs. Suppose that a pound of fertilizer costs .003 times as much as an acre of land: then the isocost curves would be as shown in Figure 21.7. Clearly, under these circumstances, the minimum-cost input combination would be 40 pounds of fertilizer and 1.04 acres of land. No matter what the ratio of the price of fertilizer to the price of land may be, the least-cost input combination can be derived this way.

Clearly, such results are of considerable practical value to farmers. Moreover, this same kind of analysis can be used by organizations in other sectors of the economy, not just agriculture. Studies of how the Defense Department could reduce its costs utilize isoquants that show the various combinations of aircraft and missiles (or similar weapons systems) that provide the same defense capability. In a more peaceful vein, this same kind of analysis has been used in various kinds of manufacturing firms. For example, steel firms have made many such studies to determine least-cost ways to produce steel.

Note once again the strong similarity between the present model and the model of rational choice in Chapter 19. In the model of rational choice, indifference curves showed what the consumer wants; in the present analysis, the isoquants are analogous to the consumer's indifference curves. In both the model of rational choice and the present model, a budget line or isocost curve shows what can be purchased for a given outlay. The main difference is that in the model of rational choice the consumer is pictured as wanting to reach the highest indifference curve compatible with a given budget line, whereas in the present model the firm wants to reach the lowest isocost curve compatible with a given isoquant. But the basic structures of the two models are essentially the same.

[3] E. Heady and L. Tweeten, *Resource Demand and Structure of the Agricultural Industry,* Ames: Iowa State, 1963. It is assumed that a certain amount of labor is also used, this amount being proportional to the number of acres of land.

What Are Costs?

Previous sections have discussed how we can determine the input combination that minimizes costs. But what do we mean by costs? Although this question may seem foolishly simple, it is in fact tricky. *Fundamentally, the **cost** of a certain course of action is the value of the best alternative course of action that could have been adopted instead.* For example, the cost of producing automobiles is the value of the goods and services that could be obtained elsewhere from the manpower, equipment, and materials used currently in automobile production. The costs of inputs to a firm are their values in their most valuable alternative uses. This is the so-called ***alternative cost,*** or ***opportunity cost*** doctrine.

Suppose that a firm's owner devotes 50 hours a week to the firm's business, and that, because he is the owner, he pays himself no salary. According to the usual rules of accounting, as we saw in Chapter 7, the costs of his labor are not included in the profit and loss statement. But according to the economist's alternative cost doctrine, the cost of his labor is by no means zero! Instead, this cost equals whatever amount he could obtain if he worked 50 hours a week for someone else. Both economists and sophisticated accountants agree that alternative costs are the relevant costs for many types of problems, and that failure to use the proper concept of cost can result in serious mistakes.

Costs for the individual firm are the necessary payments to the owners of resources to get them to provide these resources to the firm. To obtain these resources as inputs, the firm must bid them away from alternative uses. The payments made to the owners of these resources may be either explicit or implicit costs. If a payment is made to a supplier, laborer, or some other resource owner besides the firm's owner, this is an explicit cost, which is paid for in an explicit way. But if a resource is owned by the firm's owner, there may be no explicit payment for it, as in the case of the labor of the owner who paid himself no salary. The costs of such owner-supplied resources are called ***implicit costs.*** As we stressed above, such implicit costs equal what these resources could bring if they were used in their most valuable alternative employments. And the firm's profits (or losses), as defined by the economist, are the difference between the firm's revenues and its total costs, both explicit and implicit.

It should also be noted that the ***social costs*** of producing a given commodity do not always equal the ***private costs.*** That is, *the costs to society do not always equal the costs to the individual producer.* When a chemical plant discharges waste products into a nearby river the cost to the plant of disposing of the wastes is simply the amount paid to pump them to the river. However, if the river becomes polluted and its recreational uses are destroyed and the water becomes unfit for drinking, additional costs are incurred by other people. Differences of this sort between social and private costs may call for remedial government action.

Table 21.5

Fixed, Variable, and Total Costs, Bugsbane Music Box Company

Number of music boxes produced per day	Total fixed cost	Total variable cost	Total cost
0	$1,000	$ 0	$1,000
1	1,000	40	1,040
2	1,000	70	1,070
3	1,000	105	1,105
4	1,000	145	1,145
5	1,000	190	1,190
6	1,000	240	1,240
7	1,000	300	1,300
8	1,000	400	1,400
9	1,000	720	1,720

Total Costs in the Short Run

In previous sections, we showed how to determine the least-cost combination of inputs to produce any quantity of output. With this information at our disposal, it is easy to determine the minimum cost of producing each quantity of output. Knowing the (minimum) cost of producing each quantity of output, we can define and measure the firm's ***cost functions,*** which show how various types of costs are related to the firm's output. A firm's cost functions will vary, depending on whether they are based on the short or long run. In the short run, the firm cannot vary the quantities of plant and equipment it uses. These are the firm's fixed inputs, and they determine the scale of its operations.

Three kinds of costs are important in the short run: total fixed cost, total variable cost, and total cost. ***Total fixed cost*** is the total expenditure per period of time by the firm for fixed inputs. Since the quantity of the fixed inputs is unvarying (by definition), the total fixed cost will be the same whatever the firm's level of output. Among the firm's fixed costs in the short run are property taxes and interest on bonds issued in the past. To inject a whimsical note into a subject not otherwise noted for its amusement value, consider a hypothetical firm: the Bugsbane Music Box Company. This firm produces a high-priced line of music boxes that, when opened, play your favorite aria, show tune, or hymn, and emit a deadly gas that kills all insects, rodents, or pests—and alas, occasionally a frail Chihuahua—within a 50-foot radius. Table 21.5 shows that Bugsbane's fixed costs are $1,000 per day; the firm's total fixed cost function is shown in Figure 21.8.

Total variable cost is the firm's total expenditure on variable inputs per period of time. Since higher output rates require greater utilization of

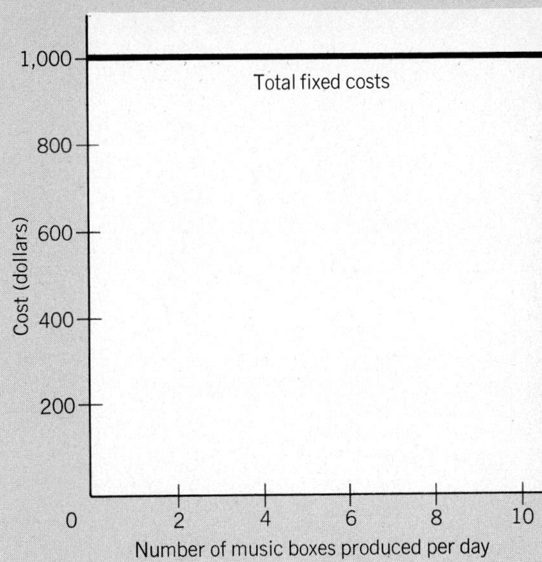

Figure 21.8
Total Fixed Costs, Bugsbane Music Box Company

The total fixed cost function is always a horizontal line, since fixed costs do not vary with output.

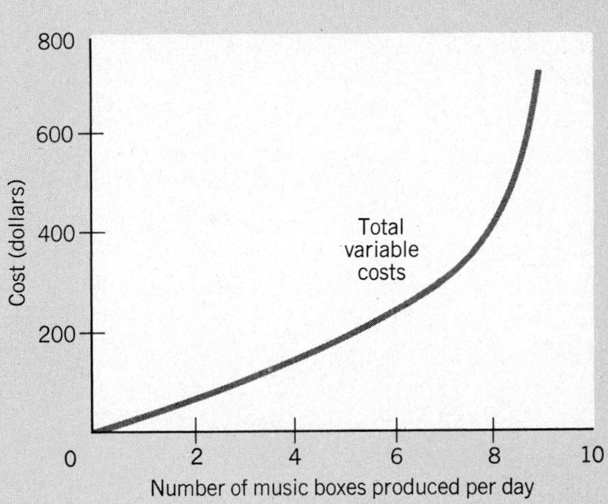

Figure 21.9
Total Variable Costs, Bugsbane Music Box Company

Total variable cost is the total expenditure per period of time on variable inputs. Due to the law of diminishing marginal returns, total variable cost increases first at a decreasing rate, then at an increasing rate.

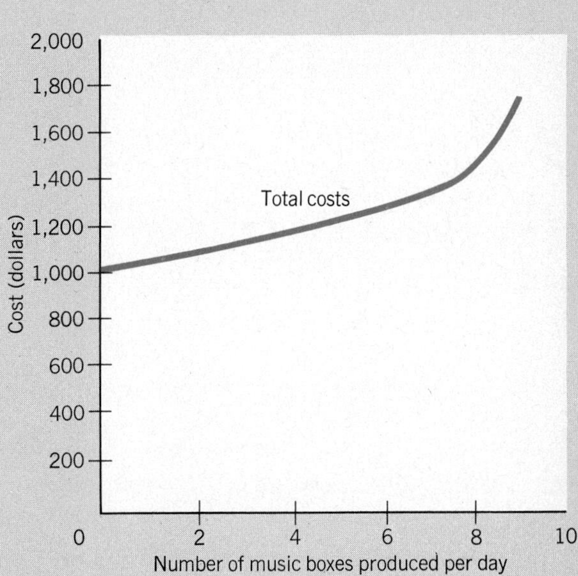

Figure 21.10
Total Costs, Bugsbane Music Box Company

Total cost is the sum of total fixed cost and total variable cost. It has the same shape as the total variable cost curve, since they differ by only a constant amount (equal to total fixed cost).

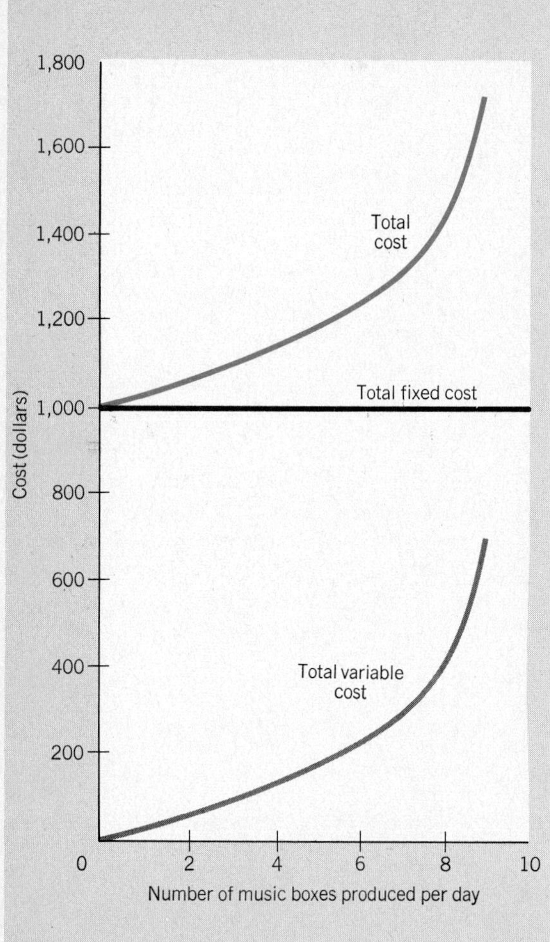

Figure 21.11
Fixed, Variable, and Total Costs, Bugsbane Music Box Company

All three total cost functions, presented in Figures 21.8–21.10, are brought back for a curtain call.

variable inputs, they mean a higher total variable cost. Thus, if Bugsbane increases its daily production of music boxes, it must increase the amount it spends per day on metal (for the components), wood (for the outside of the boxes), labor (for the assembly of the boxes), and other variable inputs. Table 21.5 shows Bugsbane's total variable costs at various output rates; Figure 21.9 shows the firm's total variable cost function.

Up to the output rate of 2 music boxes per day, total variable cost increases at a decreasing rate; beyond that output rate, total variable cost increases at an increasing rate. It is important to understand that this characteristic of the total variable cost function results from the operation of the law of diminishing marginal returns. At small output rates, increases in the utilization of variable inputs may bring about increases in their productivity, causing total variable cost to increase with output, but at a decreasing rate. Beyond a point, however, there are diminishing marginal returns from the variable input, with the result that total variable costs increase at an increasing rate.

Total cost is the sum of total fixed cost and total variable cost. Thus, to obtain the Bugsbane Company's total cost at a given output, we need only add its total fixed cost and its total variable cost at that output. The result is shown in Table 21.5, and the corresponding total cost function is shown in Figure 21.10. Since the total cost function and the total variable cost function differ by only a constant amount (equal to total fixed cost), they have the same shape, as shown in Figure 21.11, which brings together all three of the total cost functions (or curves as they are often called).

Average Costs in the Short Run

The president of Bugsbane unquestionably cares about the average cost of a music box as well as the total cost incurred; so do economists. Average cost tells you how much a product costs per unit of output. There are three average cost functions, one corresponding to each of the three total cost functions. Let's begin with ***average fixed cost,*** which is simply the total fixed cost divided by the

Table 21.6

Average Fixed Cost, Average Variable Cost, and Average Total Cost, Bugsbane Music Box Company

Number of music boxes produced per day	Average fixed cost	Average variable cost	Average total cost
1	$1,000 (= 1000 ÷ 1)	$40 (= 40 ÷ 1)	1,040 (= 1040 ÷ 1)
2	500 (= 1000 ÷ 2)	35 (= 70 ÷ 2)	535 (= 1070 ÷ 2)
3	333 (= 1000 ÷ 3)	35 (= 105 ÷ 3)	368 (= 1105 ÷ 3)
4	250 (= 1000 ÷ 4)	36 (= 145 ÷ 4)	286 (= 1145 ÷ 4)
5	200 (= 1000 ÷ 5)	38 (= 190 ÷ 5)	238 (= 1190 ÷ 5)
6	167 (= 1000 ÷ 6)	40 (= 240 ÷ 6)	207 (= 1240 ÷ 6)
7	143 (= 1000 ÷ 7)	43 (= 300 ÷ 7)	186 (= 1300 ÷ 7)
8	125 (= 1000 ÷ 8)	50 (= 400 ÷ 8)	175 (= 1400 ÷ 8)
9	111 (= 1000 ÷ 9)	80 (= 720 ÷ 9)	191 (= 1720 ÷ 9)

firm's output. Table 21.6 and Figure 21.12 show the average fixed cost function for the Bugsbane Music Box Company. Clearly, average fixed cost must decline with increases in output, since it equals a constant—total fixed cost—divided by the output rate.

The next type of average cost is ***average variable cost,*** which is total variable cost divided by output. For Bugsbane, the average variable cost function is shown in Table 21.6 and Figure 21.13. At first, increases in the output rate result in decreases in average variable cost, but beyond a point they result in higher average variable cost. This is because the law of diminishing marginal returns is in operation. As more and more of the variable inputs are utilized, the extra output they produce declines beyond some point, so that the amount spent on variable input per unit of output tends to increase.

The third type of average cost is ***average total cost,*** which is total cost divided by output. For Bugsbane, the average total cost function is shown in Table 21.6 and Figure 21.14. At any level of output, average total cost equals average fixed cost plus average variable cost. This is easy to prove:

$$\text{average total cost} = \frac{\text{total cost}}{\text{output}} = \frac{\text{total fixed cost} + \text{total variable cost}}{\text{output}},$$

since total cost = total fixed cost + total variable cost. Moreover,

$$\frac{\text{total fixed cost} + \text{total variable cost}}{\text{output}} = \frac{\text{total fixed cost}}{\text{output}} + \frac{\text{total variable cost}}{\text{output}}$$

and the right-hand side of this equation equals average fixed cost plus average variable cost. Thus, we have proved what we set out to prove.

The fact that average total cost is the sum of average fixed cost and average variable cost helps explain the shape of the average cost function. At those levels of output where both average fixed cost and average variable cost decrease, average total cost must decrease too. But eventually average total cost must increase because increases in

Figure 21.12
Average Fixed Costs, Bugsbane Music Box Company

Average fixed cost is total fixed cost divided by the firm's output. Since it equals a constant (total fixed cost) divided by the output rate, it must decline with increases in output.

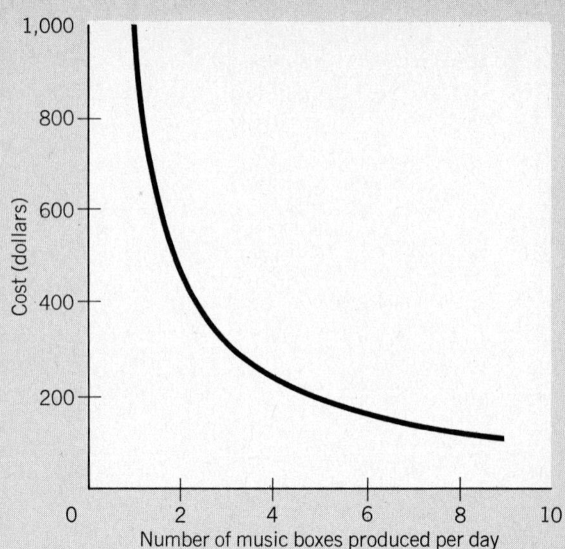

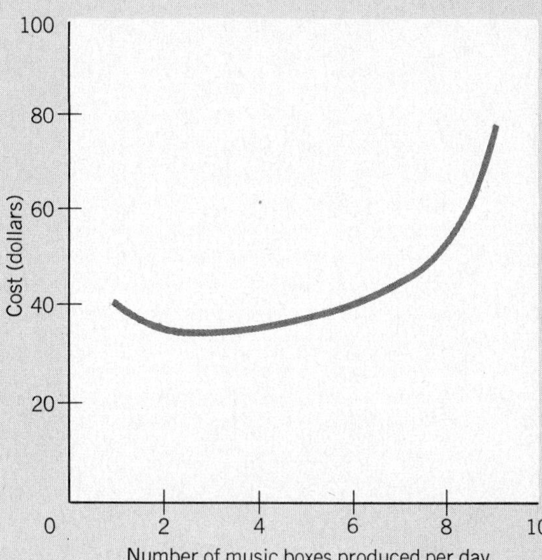

Figure 21.13
Average Variable Costs, Bugsbane Music Box Company

Average variable cost is total variable cost divided by the firm's output. Beyond a point, it increases as output increases because of the law of diminishing marginal returns.

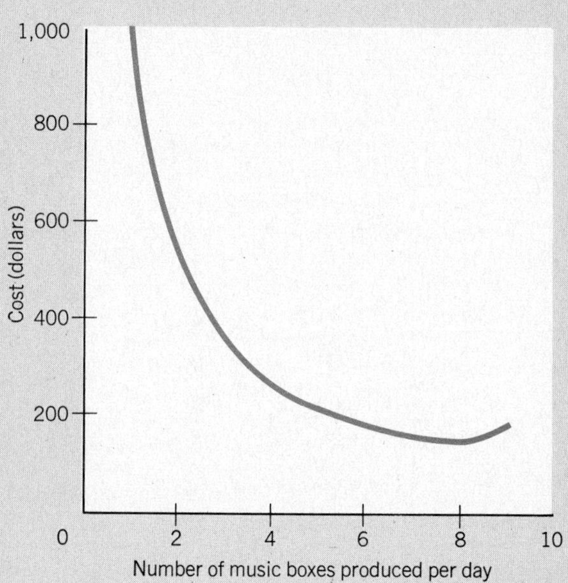

Figure 21.14
Average Total Costs, Bugsbane Music Box Company

Average total cost is total cost divided by output. It equals average fixed cost plus average variable cost; and beyond a point, it increases as output increases because of the law of diminishing marginal returns.

average variable cost eventually more than offset decreases in average fixed cost. Average total cost achieves its minimum after average variable cost, because the increases in average variable cost are for a time more than offset by decreases in average fixed cost. All the average cost functions are shown below in Figure 21.16 on page 442.

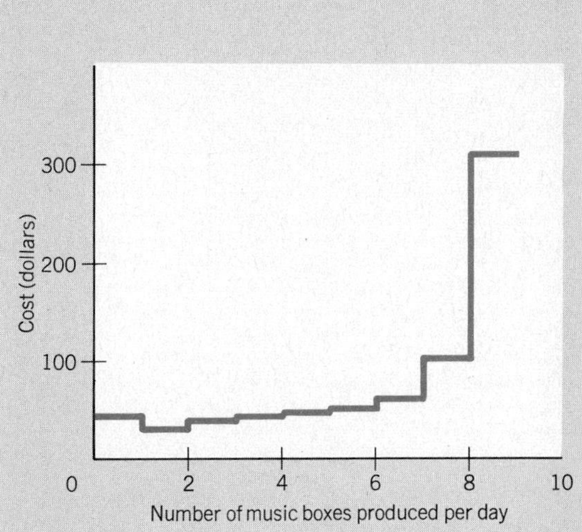

Figure 21.15
Marginal Costs, Bugsbane Music Box Company

Marginal cost is the addition to total cost resulting from the addition of the last unit of output. Beyond a point, it increases as output increases because of the law of diminishing marginal returns.

Marginal Cost in the Short Run

No one can really be said to understand the operations of a business firm without understanding the concept of ***marginal cost,*** the addition to total cost resulting from the addition of the last unit of output. To see how marginal cost is calculated, look at Table 21.7, which shows the total cost function of the Bugsbane Music Box Company. When output is between zero and one music box per day, the firm's marginal cost is $40, since this is the *extra cost* of producing the first music box per day. In other words, $40 equals marginal cost in this situation because it is the difference between the total cost of producing one music box per day ($1,040) and the total cost of producing zero music boxes per day ($1,000).

Table 21.7

Calculation of Marginal Cost, Bugsbane Music Box Company

Number of music boxes produced per day	Total cost	Marginal cost*
1	1,040	$ 40 (= 1040 – 1000)
2	1,070	30 (= 1070 – 1040)
3	1,105	35 (= 1105 – 1070)
4	1,145	40 (= 1145 – 1105)
5	1,190	45 (= 1190 – 1145)
6	1,240	50 (= 1240 – 1190)
7	1,300	60 (= 1300 – 1240)
8	1,400	100 (= 1400 – 1300)
9	1,720	320 (= 1720 – 1400)

* These figures pertain to the interval between the indicated output rate and one unit less than the indicated output rate.

In general, marginal cost will vary depending on the firm's output level. Thus, Table 21.7 shows that at Bugsbane marginal cost is $30 when the firm produces between 1 and 2 music boxes per day, $50 when the firm produces between 5 and 6 music boxes per day, and $320 when the firm produces between 8 and 9 music boxes per day. Table 21.7—and Figure 21.15, which shows the marginal cost function graphically—indicate that marginal cost, after decreasing with increases in output at low output levels, increases with further increases in output. In other words, beyond some point it becomes more and more costly for the firm to produce yet another unit of output.

The reason why marginal cost increases beyond some output level is to be found in the law of diminishing marginal returns. Clearly, if (beyond some point) increases in variable inputs result in less and less extra output, it follows that a larger and larger quantity of variable inputs must be added to produce an extra unit of output. For example, return for a moment to the wheat farm in Table 21.1. If it is producing 70 bushels of wheat, it requires an extra $\frac{1}{30}$ manyear of labor to produce an extra bushel of wheat—since Table 21.1 shows that the marginal product of a manyear of labor is 30 bushels of wheat if the farm's output is 70 bushels of wheat. But if it is producing 100 bushels of wheat, an extra $\frac{1}{25}$ manyear of labor is needed to produce an extra bushel of wheat, since Table 21.1 shows that the marginal product of a manyear of labor is 25 bushels of wheat if the farm's output is 100 bushels of wheat. Since more and more of the variable input is required to produce an extra unit of output, the cost of producing an extra unit of output increases as output rises.

In addition, the relationship between the marginal cost function and the average cost functions must be noted. Figure 21.16 shows the marginal cost curve together with the three average cost curves. *The marginal cost curve intersects both the average variable cost curve and the average total cost curve at their minimum points.* The reason for this is simple. If the extra cost of a unit of output is greater (less) than the average cost of the units of output already produced, the addition of the extra unit of output clearly must raise (lower) the average cost of production. Thus, if marginal cost is greater (less) than average cost, average cost must be rising (falling). And if this is so, average cost can be a minimum only when it equals marginal cost. (The same reasoning holds for both average total cost and average variable cost, and for the short and long runs.)

Finally, note the analogy between marginal cost and marginal utility, which we discussed in Chapter 19. Recall that marginal utility is the extra

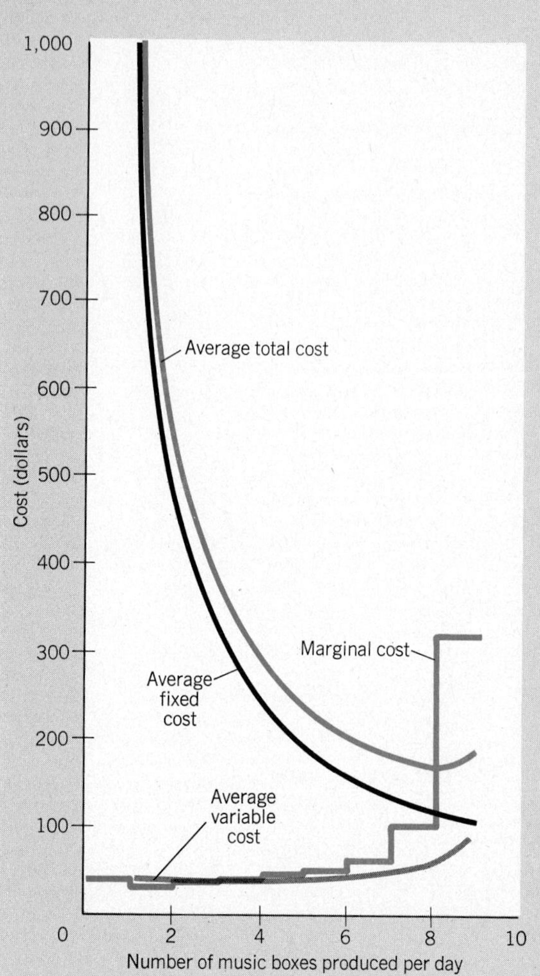

Figure 21.16
Average Fixed Costs, Average Variable Costs, Average Total Costs, and Marginal Costs, Bugsbane Music Box Company

All the curves presented in Figures 21.12–21.15 are brought together for review. Note that the marginal cost curve intersects both the average variable cost curve and the average total cost curve at their minimum points.

utility resulting from the consumption of an additional unit of a commodity. Substitute "cost" for "utility" and "production" for "consumption" in the previous sentence, and you get a perfectly valid definition of marginal cost. Economics is chock-full of marginal "thises" and marginal "thats", and you should be aware of their general family traits by now.

The Short-Run Cost Functions of a Crude Oil Pipeline: A Case Study

Cost functions are not academic toys, but eminently practical analytical devices that play a major role in decision making by business executives and government agencies. To illustrate the nature and use of short-run cost functions, we will take up the real-world case of crude oil pipelines where we left off (earlier in this chapter). In the short run, it is reasonable to assume that the diameter of a pipeline is fixed. Given the production function in Table 21.3, it is easy to figure out the total cost of carrying various amounts of oil per day, with a pipeline of given diameter. In other words, we assume that the company that owns the pipeline can vary the horsepower by varying the number and type of pumping stations, but that the diameter of the pipeline is fixed.[4] Under these circumstances, if the diameter of the pipeline is 18 inches, what will the pipeline's cost functions look like?

Figures 21.17 and 21.18 answer this question. Figure 21.17 shows the ***total cost function*** for an

[4] Because the number and type of pumping stations must be altered, Cookenboo refers to this as the "intermediate run." See Cookenboo, *op. cit.*

Figure 21.17
Total Cost Function, Crude Oil Pipeline, 18-Inch Diameter

This graph shows the total cost function in an actual case. Note that it is shaped as economic theory would predict.

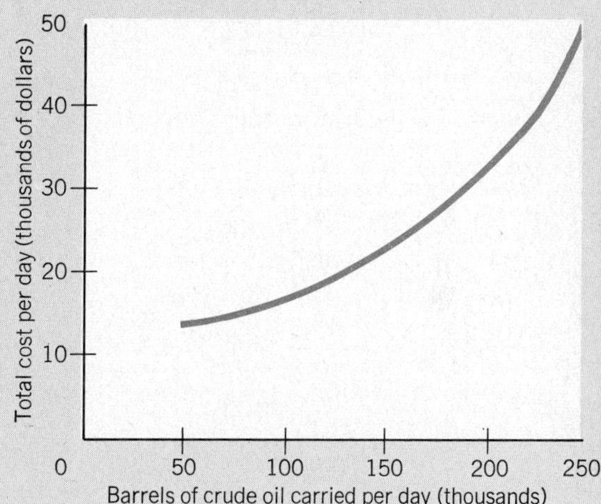

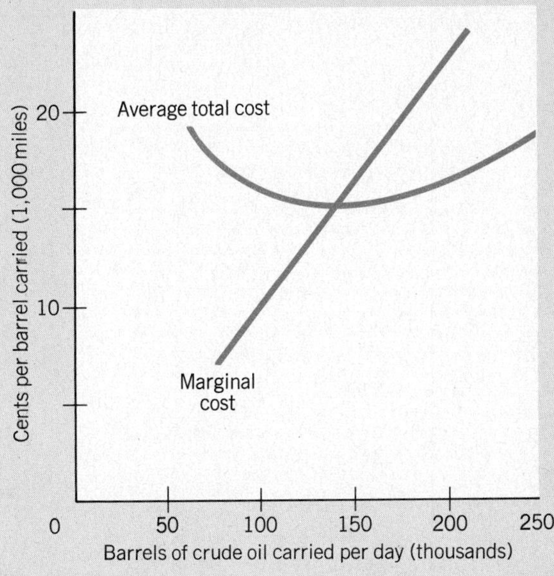

Figure 21.18
Average Total Cost Function and Marginal Cost Function, Crude Oil Pipeline, 18-Inch Diameter

This graph shows the average cost and marginal cost functions in an actual case. Note that their shape follows economic theory.

18-inch pipeline: the total daily cost of operating it, given that it carries various amounts of crude oil per day. If the pipeline carries 200,000 barrels of oil per day, the total daily cost is $33,000; if the amount of oil is increased to 250,000 barrels per day, the total daily cost rises to $48,000.

Figure 21.18 shows the ***average total cost function*** for an 18-inch pipeline: the total daily cost per barrel for the pipeline, given that it carries various amounts of crude oil per day. For example, according to Figure 21.18, the total daily cost per barrel for this pipeline to carry 200,000 barrels per day is $.16½, and the total daily cost per barrel for it to carry 250,000 barrels per day is $.19⅕. Figure 21.18 also shows the ***marginal cost function*** for such a pipeline: the additional daily cost of carrying an extra barrel of crude oil per day. For example, when this pipeline is carrying 200,000 barrels per day, the marginal cost runs to about $.23.

To the operators of the pipeline, a knowledge of these cost functions can mean the difference between profit and loss. For example, suppose that the operators of a particular 18-inch pipeline are thinking about increasing the amount of oil the pipeline will carry per day. Specifically, suppose that the pipeline can now carry 200,000 barrels per day and that the operators are thinking about adding enough horsepower so that it can carry 250,000 barrels per day. Suppose that according to the best estimates available, the pipeline can get $5 million in additional revenue each year if it carries the additional 50,000 barrels per day. Should the operators increase in this way the amount of oil the pipeline can carry?

If they want to increase profits, they should decide against this increase in the amount of horsepower. According to the total cost function in Figure 21.17, the pipeline's daily costs would increase by $15,000 per day if horsepower were increased so that 250,000, rather than 200,000, barrels of oil could be carried per day, while the extra oil carried would increase daily revenues by $5 million ÷ 365, or about $14,000 per day. Thus, the extra costs would exceed the extra revenue, which means that the pipeline's profit would be reduced by increasing the amount of horsepower. Clearly, in making decisions of this sort (and they must make them repeatedly!), managers must rely heavily on information about the relevant cost functions.

The Long-Run Average Cost Function

We have held to last one additional kind of cost function that plays a very important role in economic analysis. This is the firm's ***long-run average cost function,*** which shows the minimum average cost of producing each output level *when any desired type or scale of plant can be built.* Unlike the cost functions discussed in the previous three sections, this cost function pertains to the long run—to a period long enough that all inputs are variable and none is fixed. A useful way to look at the long run is to consider it a *planning horizon:* the firm must continually be planning ahead and trying to decide its strategy in the long run.

For example, a firm may be able to build plants of three sizes: small, medium, and large. The short-run average total cost functions corresponding to these plants are *AA′*, *BB′*, and *DD′* in Figure 21.19. If the firm is still in the planning stage of plant construction it can choose whichever plant has the lowest costs. Consequently, the firm will choose the small plant if it believes its output rate will be smaller than OQ_1, the medium plant if it believes its output rate will be above OQ_1 but below OQ_2, and the large plant if it believes that its output rate will be above OQ_2. Thus, the long-run average cost curve is *AUVD′*. And if, as is generally the case, there are many possible types of plants, the long-run average cost curve looks like *LL′* in Figure 21.20. (Only a few of the short-run average cost curves are shown in Figure 21.20.)

The usefulness of the long-run average cost function can be illustrated by the familiar case of crude oil pipelines. Figure 21.21 shows the long-run

Figure 21.19
Short-Run Average Cost Curves and Long-Run Average Cost Curve

The short-run average total cost functions for three plants—small, medium, and large—are *AA′*, *BB′*, and *DD′*. The long-run average cost function is *AUVD′*, if these are the only three types of plant that can be built.

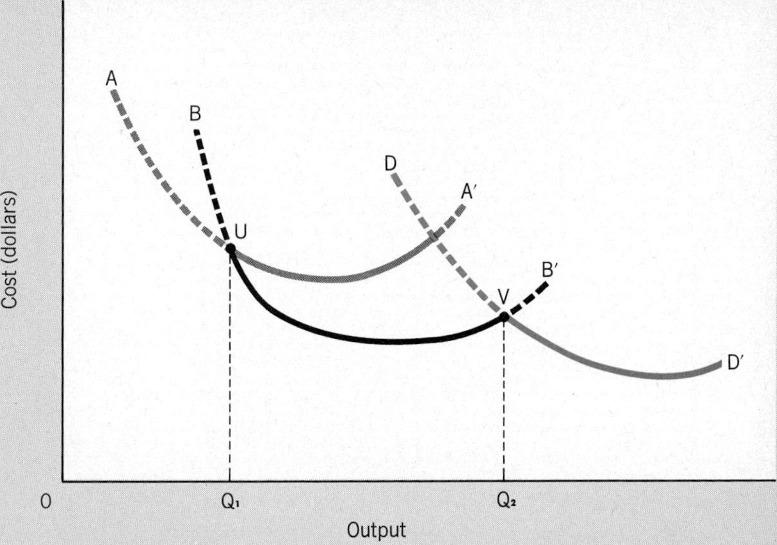

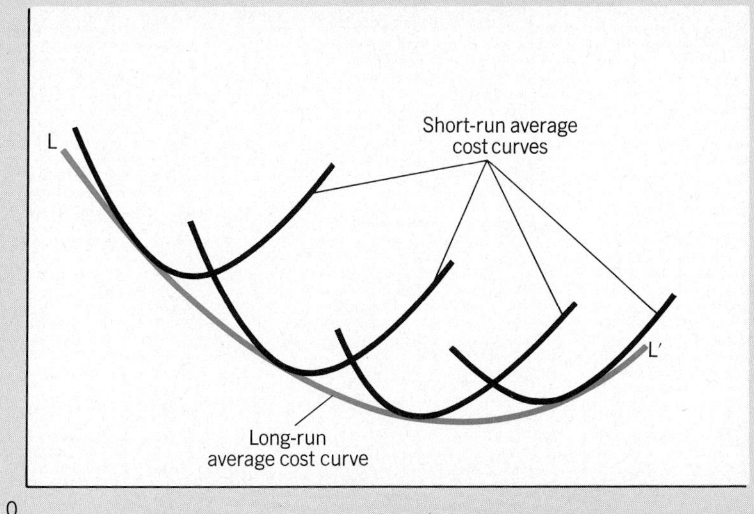

Figure 21.20
Long-Run Average Cost Curve

If many possible types of plants can be built, the long-run average cost function is *LL′*.

Figure 21.21
Costs per Barrel of Operating Crude Oil Trunk Pipelines

This graph shows the long-run average cost curve (and the revelant short-run average cost curves) in an actual case. Note that, in this range at least, long-run average cost decreases as output increases.

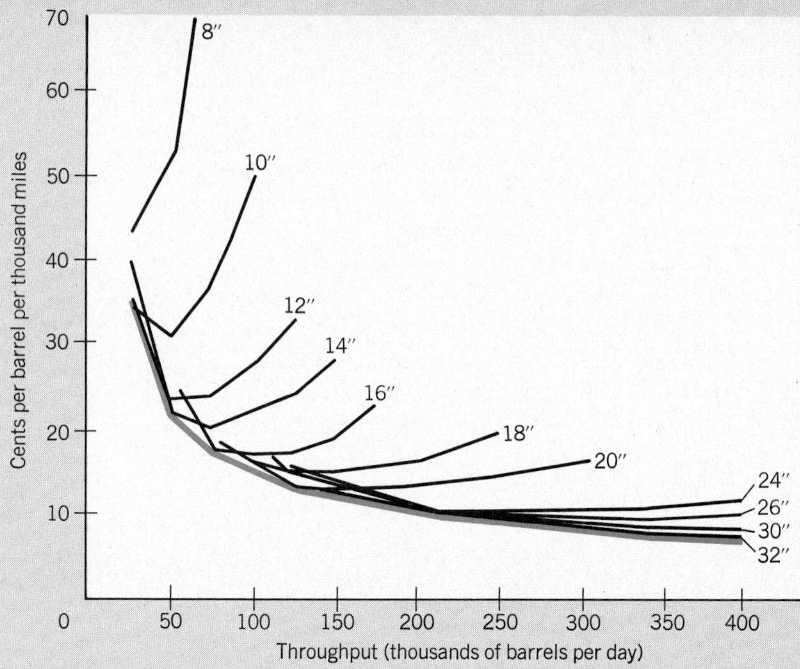

average cost function for these pipelines, as well as selected short-run average cost functions (corresponding to diameters of 8, 10, 12, 14, 16, 18, 20, 24, 26, 30, and 32 inches). Note that long-run average cost—that is, cost per barrel—decreases as more and more oil is carried per day, at least up to 400,000 barrels per day. Thus, it appears that costs are reduced when the greatest possible quantities of oil are transported in large-diameter pipelines. This fact is important in evaluating the effects of various kinds of market structure in the pipeline industry. If long-run average costs decrease with increases in output up to an output representing all, or nearly all, of the market, it is wasteful to force competition in such an industry, since costs would be greater if the industry output were divided among a number of firms than if it were produced by only one or two firms. More will be said on this score in Chapter 23.

Returns to Scale

What determines the shape of the long-run average cost function in a particular industry? Obviously, its shape must depend upon the characteristics of the production function—specifically, upon whether there are increasing, decreasing, or constant returns to scale. To understand what these terms mean, consider a long-run situation and suppose that the firm increases the amount of all inputs by the same proportion. What will happen to output? If output increases by a larger proportion than each of the inputs, this is a case of ***increasing returns to scale.*** If output increases by a smaller proportion than each of the inputs, this is a case of ***decreasing returns to scale.*** If output increases by the same proportion as each of the inputs, this is a case of ***constant returns to scale.***

There are many reasons why increasing returns

to scale may exist in a particular industry. For example, one large plant may be more efficient than two smaller plants of the same total capacity because it is big enough to use certain techniques that the smaller plants cannot use. Moreover, increasing returns can result from certain geometric relations. For example, since friction is related to the surface area of a pipeline, whereas the amount a pipeline can carry is related to its volume, there are increasing returns to scale in pipelines. Also, greater specialization can result in increasing returns to scale. For example, as more machines and men are used to perform a certain activity, it is possible to subdivide tasks and allow various inputs to specialize.

On the other hand, there also are reasons why decreasing returns to scale may occur. As a firm gets bigger and bigger, one would expect that the problems of coordinating activities and conveying information promptly and accurately would multiply, and that decreasing returns to scale would eventually set in. There is also the possibility of constant returns to scale, although it may not occur as frequently as many economic theorists would like. In constructing economic models, theorists often find it convenient to assume constant returns to scale, but it is by no means clear that this assumption is justifiable in many situations where it is made.

Whether there are increasing, decreasing, or constant returns to scale in a particular situation must be settled case by case. Moreover, the answer is likely to depend on the particular range of output considered. For example, there frequently are increasing returns to scale up to some level of output, then perhaps constant returns to scale up to a higher level of output, beyond which there may be decreasing returns to scale. This pattern is responsible for the U-shaped long-run average cost function in Figure 21.20. However, in many industries, there is little or no evidence that long-run average cost increases as output rises—at least within the range covered by the available data. Eventually, however, one would expect long-run average cost to rise because of problems of coordination, increased red tape, and reduced flexibility. Firms as large as General Motors or U. S. Steel are continually bedeviled by the very real difficulties of enormous size.

Measurement of Cost Functions and Break-Even Charts

Countless studies have been made to estimate cost functions in particular firms and industries. Many of these have been based on the relationship over time between cost and output. For example, Figure 21.22 shows the total costs of a hypothetical

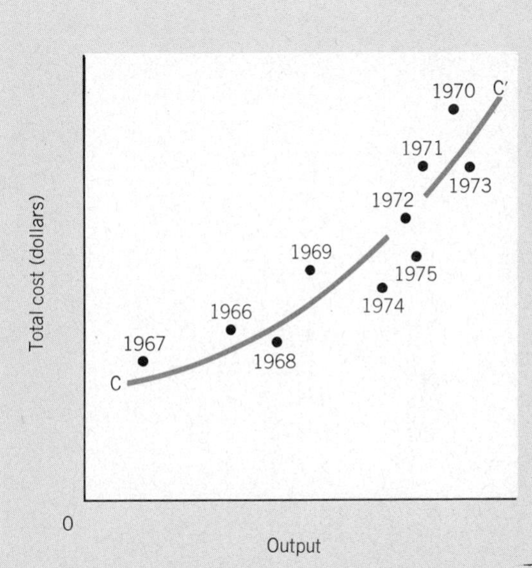

Figure 21.22
Relationship between Total Cost and Output: Time Series for a Particular Firm

One very crude way to estimate the total cost curve is to plot total cost in each year against total output in that year, and draw a curve, like *CC′*, that fits the points reasonably well. However, this technique is generally too crude to be reliable.

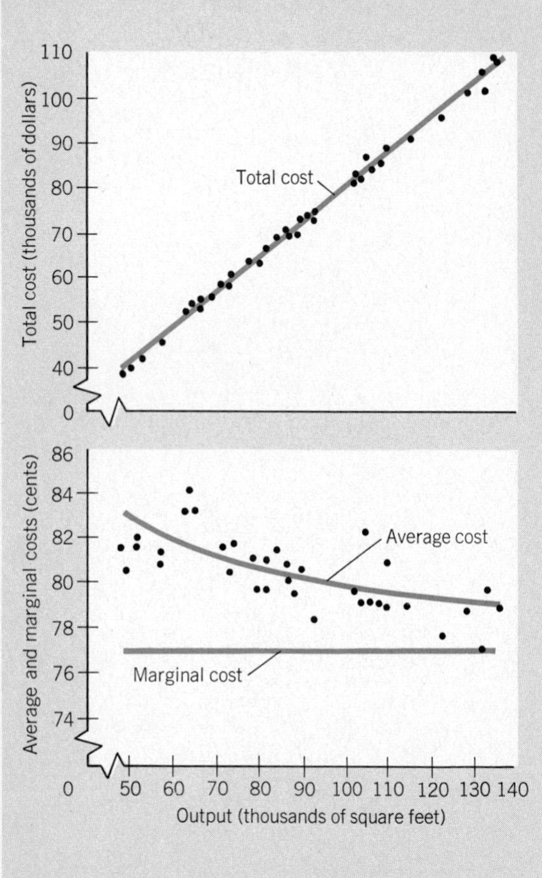

Figure 21.23
Total, Average, and Marginal Cost Functions of a Leather Belt Shop

This graph shows the short-run total, average, and marginal cost curves in an actual case. Note that marginal cost is constant in this case.

firm in various years plotted against the firm's output in these years. Based on these data, a reasonable approximation to the firm's total cost function might be *CC′*. However, there are a number of difficulties in this simple procedure. For one thing, the firm's cost function may not have remained fixed throughout this period. For another, accounting data on costs may not be as accurate as one would like.[5] For these and other reasons, economists and statisticians have devised more sophisticated techniques to estimate cost functions.

To illustrate the sorts of results that have been obtained, Figure 21.23 shows the total cost function, average total cost function, and marginal cost function for a leather belt shop. Note that the total cost function appears linear, that is, a straight line, in the relevant range. These results were obtained over 30 years ago by one of the pioneers in this field, Joel Dean of Columbia University.[6] Since

[5] Some of the difficulties are that the depreciation of an asset is often determined by the tax laws rather than economic criteria, many inputs are valued at historical, rather than alternative, cost, and accountants sometimes use arbitrary allocations of overhead and joint costs.
[6] Joel Dean, *The Relation of Cost to Output for a Leather Belt Shop*, New York: National Bureau of Economic Research, 1941.

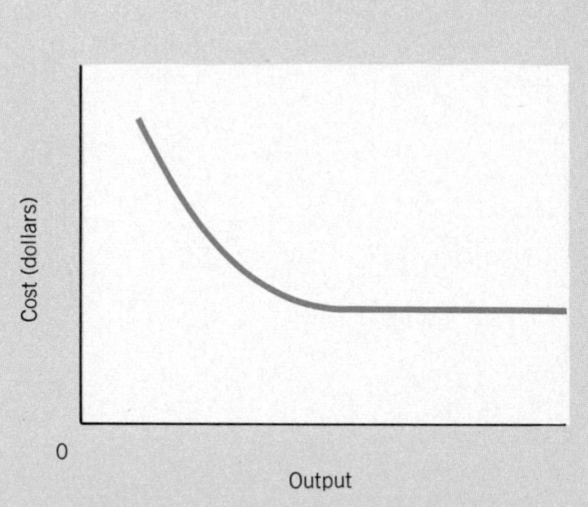

Figure 21.24
Apparent Shape of Many Long-Run Average Cost Curves

Within the range of observed data, there is no evidence in many industries that the long-run average cost curve turns upward, rather than remains horizontal, at high output levels.

that time, a great deal of evidence has been amassed on the shape of the cost functions of individual firms and industries. Two findings are particularly worth noting. First, within the range of observed data, the long-run average cost curve in many industries seems to be L-shaped (as in Figure 21.24), not U-shaped (as in Figure 21.20). That is, there is no evidence that it turns upward, rather than remains horizontal, at high output levels. Second, many empirical studies indicate that marginal cost in the short run tends to be constant in the relevant output range. However, this really does not contradict our assertions in previous sections, because the data used in these studies often do not cover periods when the firm was operating at peak capacity.

Estimated cost functions are used in a variety of ways by firms and government agencies. One important practical application of cost functions is to so-called ***break-even charts.*** To construct a break-even chart, the firm's total revenue must be plotted on the same chart with its total cost function. It is generally assumed that the price the firm receives for its product will not be influenced by the amount it sells, so that total revenue is proportional to output. Thus, the total revenue curve is a straight line through the origin. Also, it is generally assumed that the firm's average variable cost—and marginal cost—are constant *in the relevant output range,* meaning that the firm's total cost function is also assumed to be a straight line.

Panel A of Figure 21.25 shows the break-even chart for an actual cable manufacturing firm.[7] The sales price of each unit of its output was $200. The firm's fixed costs were $50,000 per month and its average variable cost per unit of output was $20. The break-even chart shows the monthly profit or loss that will result from each sales level. For example, Panel A (Figure 21.25) shows that

[7] See Charles Stokes, *Managerial Economics: A Case Book,* New York: Random House, 1969. However, I have changed the numbers to make them easy to work with.

Figure 21.25
Break-Even Chart, Cable Manufacturing Firm

In panels A and B, the sales price of each unit of output is $200. In panel A, the firm's fixed costs are $50,000 per month, and its average variable cost per unit of output is $20. In panel B, the firm's fixed costs are $60,000 per month, and its average variable cost per unit of output is $10. In panel A, the firm's break-even point is 278 units of output per month, whereas in panel B it is 316 units of output per month.

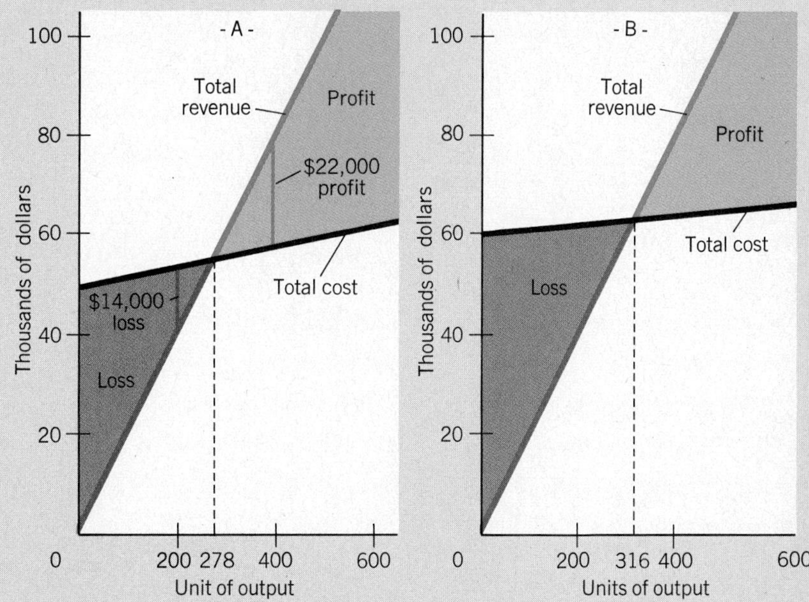

the firm would have lost $14,000 per month if it had sold 200 units per month. On the other hand, it would have made a profit of $22,000 per month if it had sold 400 units per month. The chart also shows the ***break-even point,*** the output level that must be reached if the firm is to avoid losses. In Panel A, the break-even point is 278 units of output per month.

Break-even charts are used very extensively by firms and other groups to estimate the effect of the sales rate on costs, receipts, and profits. A firm may use a break-even chart to determine the effect on profits of a projected increase in sales, or how many units of a particular product it must sell in order to break even. For instance, the cable manufacturing firm wanted to find out, among other things, how its break-even point would be affected if it installed new equipment that would increase its fixed costs to $60,000 per month and reduce its average variable cost to $10. Panel B of Figure 21.25 shows that under these circumstances the firm's break-even point would be 316, rather than 278, units of output per month. This information is, of course, of considerable value to the firm. It means that, if the firm installs the new equipment, it must sell at least 316 units of output per month to stay in the black.

Summary

If a firm is going to produce a certain output, what combination of inputs should it choose to maximize its profits? As a first step toward answering this question, we describe the law of diminishing marginal returns, which states that, if equal increments of an input are added, the quantities of other inputs held constant, the resulting increments of product will decrease beyond some point; that is, the marginal product of the input will diminish. The marginal product of an input is the addition to total output due to the addition of the last unit of the input, the amount of other inputs used being held constant. Also, it is useful to define an input's average product, which is the firm's total output divided by the amount of the input used to produce this amount of output. An isoquant is a curve showing all efficient combinations of inputs capable of producing a certain amount of output.

To minimize its costs (and maximize its profits) a firm must choose its input combination so that the marginal product of a dollar's worth of any one input equals the marginal product of a dollar's worth of any other input used. Put differently, the firm should combine inputs so that, for every input used, the marginal product of the input is proportional to its price. Put in still another way, the firm should pick the input combination corresponding to the point on the relevant isoquant that lies on the lowest isocost curve. As an illustration, we showed how this sort of model can be used to determine the optimal combination of fertilizer and land in the production of Kansas corn.

The cost of a certain course of action is the value of the best alternative course of action that could have been pursued instead. This is the doctrine of alternative, or opportunity, cost. Three kinds of total cost functions are important in the short run—total fixed cost, total variable cost, and total cost. In addition, there are three kinds of average cost functions (corresponding to each of the total cost functions)—average fixed cost, average variable cost, and average total cost. Also, marginal cost—the addition to total cost due to the addition of the last unit of output—is of enormous significance. Because of the law of diminishing marginal returns, marginal cost tends to increase beyond some output level. The firm's long-run average cost curve shows the minimum average cost of producing each output level when any desired type or scale of plant can be built. The shape of the long-run average cost curve is determined by whether there are increasing, decreasing, or constant returns to scale.

Cost functions play a very important practical role in economics and management. There have been countless studies to estimate cost functions in particular firms and industries. We have illustrated the sorts of results that have been obtained: for example, we have presented actual cost functions for a crude oil pipeline, as well as relevant aspects of the pipeline's production function. Also, we have indicated how the resulting cost functions can be used to help solve important sorts of managerial problems, as well as problems of public policy. In addition, we have shown how estimates of cost functions have been used to construct break-even charts, a commonly used practical application of cost functions. An actual case study of a cable manufacturing firm was employed to illustrate the use of these charts.

CONCEPTS FOR REVIEW

Marginal product	Opportunity cost	Average total cost
Average product	Fixed cost	Marginal cost
Law of diminishing marginal returns	Variable cost	Planning horizon
Isoquant	Average fixed cost	Break-even chart
	Average variable cost	

QUESTIONS FOR DISCUSSION AND REVIEW

1. Suppose that you were the president of a firm that operates a crude oil pipeline. Describe in detail the various ways in which the production and cost functions given in this chapter might be useful to you.

2. Suppose that you were given the job of estimating the cost functions for your college or university. How would you go about estimating the relationships between costs and number of students? Is there a difference between the long run and the short run? In this context, what is meant by variable and fixed costs? How might your results be used?

3. Suppose that a firm's short-run total cost function is as follows:

Output (number of units per year)	*Total cost per year*
0	$20,000
1	20,100
2	20,200
3	20,300
4	20,500
5	20,800

What are the firm's total fixed costs? What are its total variable costs when it produces 4 units per year?

4. In question 3, what is the firm's marginal cost when between 4 and 5 units are produced per year? Does marginal cost increase beyond some output level?

Optimal Output Decisions and Linear Programming

In the previous chapter, we showed how the profit-maximizing firm determines the input combination it uses to produce any specified quantity of output. We now ask the second question that must be answered if a firm desires to maximize profits: how should the firm decide the quantity to produce? We devote the first half of this chapter to the way the profit-maximizing firm answers this question and to the derivation of the firm's and the industry's supply curves. Following this discussion, we show how the firm's production decisions can be viewed from a somewhat different standpoint: that of linear programming, a relatively new economic technique. We describe the nature and objectives of linear programming, and illustrate the sorts of problems it can handle. Linear programming and other modern techniques help economists solve many important problems of industry and government that were beyond their reach only a few decades ago.

The Output of the Firm

What determines the output rate of a profit-maximizing firm? For simplicity, we will assume that the firm cannot affect the price of its product and that it can sell any amount it wants at this price. In other words, this is a ***perfectly competitive firm.*** Also, we will consider a short-run situation in which the firm can expand or contract its output rate by increasing or decreasing its utilization of variable inputs. The situation in the long run will be reserved for Chapter 23.

To illustrate the nature of the problem, suppose that your rich uncle dies and leaves you his business, the Allegro Piano Company. Once you take over the business, your first problem is to decide how many pianos the firm should produce per week. Having a good deal of economic intuition, you instruct your accountant to estimate the company's total revenue and total costs (as well as fixed and variable costs) at various output levels. The figures are given in Table 22.1, with the market price of one of the firm's pianos set at $1,000. The firm's total revenue at various output rates and its total cost function (as well as its total fixed cost function and total variable cost function) are as shown in Table 22.1. Subtracting the total cost at a given output rate from the total revenue at this output rate, you obtain the total profit at each output rate, which is shown in the last column of Table 22.1. Since the maximum profit is obtained at an output level of either 4 or 5 pianos per week, this is the output level you choose.

Figure 22.1 gives a somewhat more vivid picture of the firm's situation by plotting the relationship between total revenue and total cost on the one hand, and output on the other. The vertical distance between the total revenue curve and the total cost curve is, of course, the profit at a corresponding output rate. Below an output rate of 2 pianos per week and above a rate of 7 pianos per week, the total revenue curve lies *below* the total cost curve, indicating that profits are negative—that is, there are losses. Both Table 22.1 and Figure 22.1 show that the output rate that will maximize the firm's profits is either 4 or 5 pianos per week. At either of these rates, the firm will make a profit of $2,000 per week, which is more than it can make at any other output rate.

There is an alternative way to analyze the firm's

Table 22.1

Costs and Revenues, Allegro Piano Company

Output per week (pianos)	Price	Total revenue	Total fixed cost	Total variable cost	Total cost	Total profit
0	$1,000	$ 0	$1,000	$ 0	$1,000	−$1,000
1	1,000	1,000	1,000	200	1,200	− 200
2	1,000	2,000	1,000	300	1,300	700
3	1,000	3,000	1,000	500	1,500	1,500
4	1,000	4,000	1,000	1,000	2,000	2,000
5	1,000	5,000	1,000	2,000	3,000	2,000
6	1,000	6,000	1,000	3,200	4,200	1,800
7	1,000	7,000	1,000	4,500	5,500	1,500
8	1,000	8,000	1,000	7,200	8,200	− 200

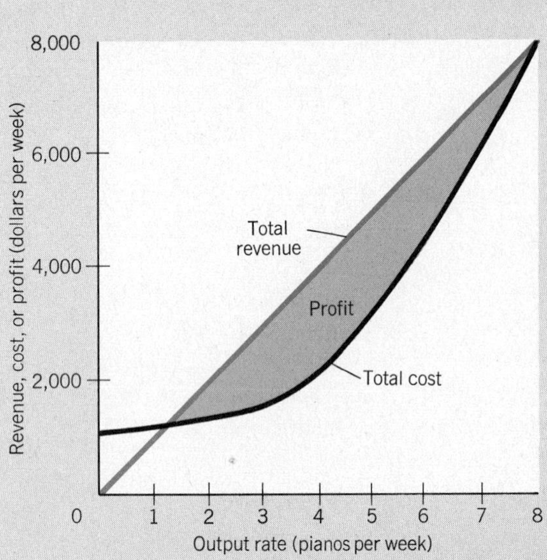

Figure 22.1
Costs, Revenue, and Profits, Allegro Piano Company

The output rate that will maximize the firm's profits is either 4 or 5 pianos per week.

Table 22.2

Marginal Cost and Price, Allegro Piano Company

Output per week (pianos)	Marginal cost*	Price
1	$ 200	$1,000
2	100	1,000
3	200	1,000
4	500	1,000
5	1,000	1,000
6	1,200	1,000
7	1,300	1,000
8	2,700	1,000

* This is the marginal cost between the indicated output level and 1 unit less than the indicated output level.

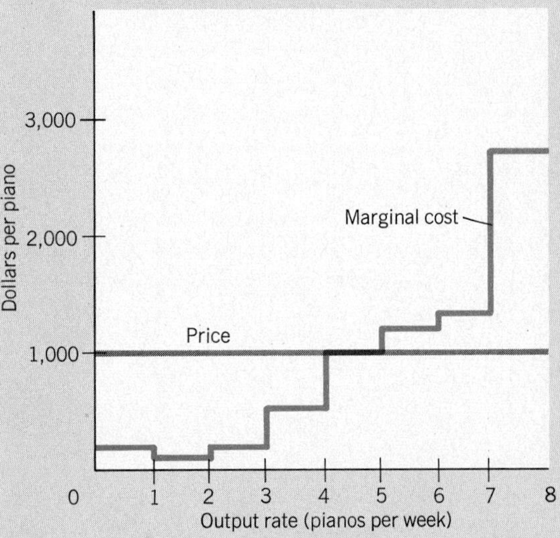

Figure 22.2
Marginal Cost and Price, Allegro Piano Company

At the profit-maximizing output rate of 4 or 5 pianos per week, marginal cost equals price.

situation. Rather than looking at total revenue and total cost, let's look at price and marginal cost. Table 22.2 and Figure 22.2 show the product price and marginal cost at each output rate. It turns out that the maximum profit is achieved at the output rate where price equals marginal cost. In other words, both Table 22.2 and Figure 22.2 indicate that price equals marginal cost at the profit-maximizing output rates of 4 or 5 pianos per week. This raises a question: will price usually equal marginal cost at the profit-maximizing output rate, or is this merely a coincidence?

The Golden Rule of Output Determination

Readers familiar with television scripts and detective stories will have recognized that the question just posed can only be answered in one way without ruining the plot. The equality of marginal cost and price at the profit-maximizing output rate is no mere coincidence. It will usually be true if the firm takes the price of its product as given. Indeed, the Golden Rule of Output Determination for a perfectly competitive firm is: choose the output rate at which marginal cost is equal to price.

To prove that this rule maximizes profits, consider Figure 22.3, which shows a typical short-run marginal cost function, MM'. Suppose that the price is OP_1. At any output rate less than OQ_1, price is greater than marginal cost.[1] This means that increases in output will increase the firm's profits since they will add more to total revenues than to total costs. Why? Because an extra unit of output adds an amount equal to price to total revenue and an amount equal to marginal cost to total cost. Thus, since price exceeds marginal cost, an extra unit of output adds more to total revenue than to total cost. For example, this is the case for the Allegro Piano Company when it is producing 3 pianos per week. As shown in Table 22.2, the extra cost of producing a fourth piano is $500, while the revenue brought in by producing and selling it is $1,000. Consequently, it pays the Allegro Piano Company to produce more than 3 pianos per week.

At any output rate above OQ_1, price is less than

[1] Except perhaps for an irrelevant range where marginal cost decreases with increases in output.

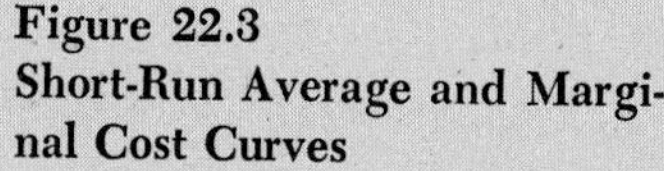
Figure 22.3
Short-Run Average and Marginal Cost Curves

If price is OP_1, the profit-maximizing output rate is OQ_1. If price is OP_2, the profit-maximizing output rate is OQ_2, even though the firm will incur a loss. If the price is below OP_3, the firm will discontinue production.

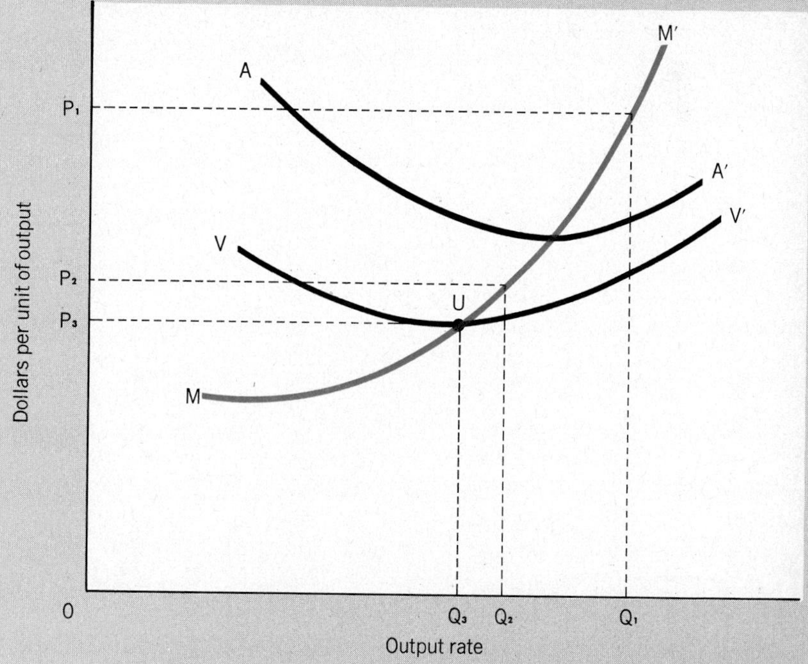

marginal cost. This means that decreases in output will increase the firm's profits since they will subtract more from total costs than from revenue. This happens because one less unit of output subtracts an amount equal to price from total revenue and an amount equal to marginal cost from total cost. Thus, since price is less than marginal cost, one less unit of output subtracts more from total cost than from total revenue. Such a case occurs, for instance, when the Allegro Piano Company is producing 7 pianos per week. As shown in Table 22.2, the extra cost of producing the seventh piano is $1,300, while the extra revenue it brings in is $1,000. So it pays the Allegro Piano Company to produce less than 7 pianos per week.

Since increases in output will increase profits if output is less than OQ_1, and decreases in output will increase profits if output is greater than OQ_1, it follows that profits must be maximized at OQ_1, the output rate at which price equals marginal cost. After all, if increases in output up to this output rate (OQ_1) result in increases in profit and further increases in output result in decreases in profit, OQ_1 must be the profit-maximizing output rate. For the Allegro Piano Company, this output rate is 4 or 5 pianos per week, as we just saw.

Does It Pay to Be a Dropout?

All rules—even the Golden Rule we just mentioned—have exceptions. Under some circumstances, the perfectly competitive firm will not maximize its profits if it sets marginal cost equal to price. Instead, it will maximize profits only if it becomes an economic dropout by discontinuing production. Let's demonstrate that this is indeed a fact. The first important point is that even if the firm is doing the best it can, it may not be able to earn a profit. For example, if the price is OP_2 in Figure 22.3, short-run average cost, AA', exceeds the price, OP_2, at all possible output rates. Thus the firm cannot earn a profit whatever output it produces. Since the short run is too short for the firm to alter the scale of its plant, it cannot liquidate its plant in the short run. Its only choice is to produce at a loss or discontinue production.

Under what conditions will the firm produce at a loss, and under what conditions will it discontinue production? *If there is an output rate where price exceeds average variable cost, it will pay the firm to produce, even though price does not cover average total cost. If there is no such output rate, the firm is better off to produce nothing at all.* This is true because even if the firm produces nothing, it must pay its fixed cost. Thus, if the loss resulting from production is less than the firm's fixed cost, the firm is better off producing than not producing. On the other hand, if the loss resulting from production is greater than the firm's fixed cost, the firm is better off not to produce.

In other words, the firm will find it advantageous to produce if

$$\text{total losses} < \text{total fixed cost, or if}$$
$$\text{total cost} - \text{total revenue} < \text{total fixed cost.}$$

Dividing each side of this inequality by output, the firm is better off to produce if

$$\frac{\text{total cost}}{\text{output}} - \frac{\text{total revenue}}{\text{output}} < \frac{\text{total fixed cost}}{\text{output}}$$

Since total revenue = price × output, this means that the firm is better off to produce if

$$\text{average total cost} - \text{price} < \text{average fixed cost,}$$

or (adding price to both sides)

$$\text{average total cost} < \text{average fixed cost} + \text{price,}$$

or (subtracting average fixed cost from both sides)

$$\text{average variable cost} < \text{price.}$$

Once again, we have proved what we set out to prove: that the firm will maximize profits by producing *nothing* if there is no output rate at which price exceeds average variable cost. Of course, if such an output rate does exist, the Golden Rule applies: the firm will set its output rate at the point where marginal cost equals price.

To illustrate the conditions under which it pays

Table 22.3

Costs and Revenues, Allegro Piano Company

Output per week (pianos)	Price	Total revenue	Total fixed cost	Total variable cost	Average variable cost	Total cost	Total profit
0	$1,000	$ 0	$1,000	$ 0	$ 0	$ 1,000	−$1,000
1	1,000	1,000	1,000	1,200	1,200	2,200	− 1,200
2	1,000	2,000	1,000	2,600	1,300	3,600	− 1,600
3	1,000	3,000	1,000	4,200	1,400	5,200	− 2,200
4	1,000	4,000	1,000	6,000	1,500	7,000	− 3,000
5	1,000	5,000	1,000	8,000	1,600	9,000	− 4,000
6	1,000	6,000	1,000	10,200	1,700	11,200	− 5,200
7	1,000	7,000	1,000	12,600	1,800	13,600	− 6,600
8	1,000	8,000	1,000	15,200	1,900	16,200	− 8,200

a firm to drop out, suppose that the cost functions of the Allegro Piano Company are as shown in Table 22.3. Clearly, in this case, there exists no output rate such that average variable cost is less than price—which, you will recall, is $1,000 per piano. Thus, according to the results of the last paragraphs, the Allegro Piano Company should discontinue production under these conditions. The wisdom of this course of action is shown by the last column of Table 22.3, which demonstrates that the profit-maximizing—or, what amounts to the same thing, the loss-minimizing—output rate is zero.

Sometimes, as in the present case, the best thing to do is nothing. The situation is analogous to the common experience of leaving a movie after the first ten minutes indicate that it is not going to be a good one, even though the admission price is not refundable. One ignores the fixed costs (the admission price), and finding that the variable cost (the pleasure gained from activities that would be forgone by seeing the rest of the show) is going to exceed the benefits of staying, one leaves.

In 1973, many meat-processing plants discontinued production for essentially this reason. The federal government, in an attempt to control inflation, froze the price of their product, but allowed the prices of the inputs they used to go up, with the result that their average variable costs exceeded price at all possible output levels. The consequence, as our theory would predict, was that many plants closed down. For example, in Chicago, the American Meat Institute announced that 16 plants closed down in the second quarter of 1973. As the president of Detroit's Crown Packing Company put it, "Frankly, we closed down so that we would lose less money."

Decision Making at Continental Air Lines: A Case Study

In showing how the profit-maximizing firm should determine its output rate, we have repeatedly used this simple principle: *undertake a particular activity if, and only if, the additional revenues stemming from the activity exceed the additional costs.* Clearly, this principle underlies our Golden Rule of Output Determination. Recall that the Golden Rule dictates that an extra unit of output be produced so long as its price exceeds its marginal cost. Since its price equals the additional revenue stemming from the production of the additional unit and since its marginal cost equals the additional cost stemming from the production of the additional unit, the Golden Rule can be derived from this principle. This principle also underlies our discussion of the conditions under which it pays a firm to discontinue production.

It is remarkable how often this simple principle can be helpful in real-life problems—and even more remarkable how often managers fail to apply it, with the result that their firms make less money than they could. This doesn't mean, of course, that business executives are stupid or incompetent. It does mean that they often receive information in a form that makes it difficult to apply this rule. Also, they sometimes have the habit of applying rules of thumb which, if carefully examined, violate this principle.

To illustrate the sorts of cases that arise, consider Continental Air Lines, the nation's tenth largest airline. Continental, like other airlines, must continually decide whether or not to run an extra flight from one city to another. For example, Continental may be contemplating an extra daily flight from Houston to Los Angeles. To reach its decision, Continental must compare the costs of the extra flight with the revenues it is likely to bring in. Suppose that the extra revenues are estimated to be $3,100, that the extra out-of-pocket costs are $2,000, and that the fully allocated costs of the flight are $4,500. If you were the president of Continental, would you decide to run the extra flight?

Obviously, the first thing you need is a clear definition of "out-of-pocket cost" and "fully allocated cost." Suppose your accountants tell you that the ***out-of-pocket costs*** of the extra flight are the actual dollars Continental has to pay out to run the flight: the costs of the extra crew, the extra fuel, and the other extra inputs. On the other hand, the ***fully allocated costs*** are the out-of-pocket costs plus a specified share of Continental's overhead, depreciation, insurance, and other fixed costs. Given these definitions, if you were a clear-headed profit maximizer, you would run the flight. The extra costs incurred by the flight are the out-of-pocket costs, not the fully allocated costs, and the out-of-pocket costs are less than the extra revenue the new flight will produce. Thus, the flight will increase the firm's profit—by $3,100 less $2,000, or $1,100 per day.

Why is the out-of-pocket cost, rather than fully allocated cost, the relevant measure of the flight's cost? Because the extra cost incurred by the flight is the out-of-pocket cost—and only that The firm's fixed costs (including overhead, depreciation, insurance, and so forth) will be the same whether the extra flight is run or not. (Remember that fixed costs are fixed *in the short run!*) Consequently, it is incorrect to use the fully allocated cost, which includes a share of the firm's fixed costs, to measure the extra costs of the flight.

The case described here was an actual one. And in accord with the principles described above, Continental made the proper decision: it ran the extra flight. Unfortunately, however, not all firms are as sophisticated in this regard, with the result that profitable opportunities are sometimes missed. Any aspiring executive would do well to bear in mind the simple principle that additional revenues should be compared with additional costs (and that out-of-pocket and fully allocated costs can be quite different). According to *Business Week,* a leading magazine for business executives, "Getting management to accept and apply . . . [this principle] is the chief contribution any economist can make to his company."[2] Perhaps this is an overstatement, but unquestionably it has a core of truth.

The Firm's Supply Curve and the Market Supply Curve

In Chapter 4, we described some of the factors underlying a commodity's market supply curve, but we could not go into much detail. Now we can, because our Golden Rule of Output Deter-

[2] *Business Week,* "An Airline Takes the Marginal Route," April 20, 1963.

mination underlies the market supply curve. As a first step, let's derive the firm's ***supply curve,*** which shows how much the firm will want to produce at each price. Assuming that the firm takes the price of its product as given (and can sell all it wants at that price), we know from the previous sections that the firm will choose the output level at which price equals marginal cost. Or if the price is below the firm's average variable cost curve at every output level, the firm will produce nothing. These results are all we need to determine the firm's supply curve.

For example, suppose that the firm's short-run cost curves are as shown in Figure 22.3. The marginal cost curve, MM', must, of course, intersect the average variable cost curve, VV', at the latter's minimum point, U. If the price of the product is less than OP_3, the firm will produce nothing, because there is no output level where price exceeds average variable cost. If the price of the product exceeds OP_3, the firm will set its output rate at the point where price equals marginal cost. Thus, if the price is OP_1, the firm will produce OQ_1; if the price is OP_2, the firm will produce OQ_2; and so forth. Consequently, it is obvious that *the firm's supply curve is exactly the same as the firm's marginal cost curve for prices above the minimum value of average variable cost* (OP_3). For prices at or below the minimum value of average variable cost, the firm's supply curve corresponds to the price axis, the desire to supply at these prices being uniformly zero. Thus, *the firm's supply curve is* OP_3UM'.

Our next step is to derive the market supply curve from the supply curves of the individual firms. If one assumption holds, *the market supply curve can be regarded as the horizontal summation of the supply curves of all the firms producing the product.* For example, if there were 3 firms in the industry and their supply curves were $OSBB'$, $OSDD'$, and $OSFF'$ in Figure 22.4, the market supply curve would be $OSGG'$, since $OSGG'$ shows the *total* amount of the product that all of the firms together would supply at various prices. Of course, if there were only 3 firms, the market would not be perfectly competitive, but we can

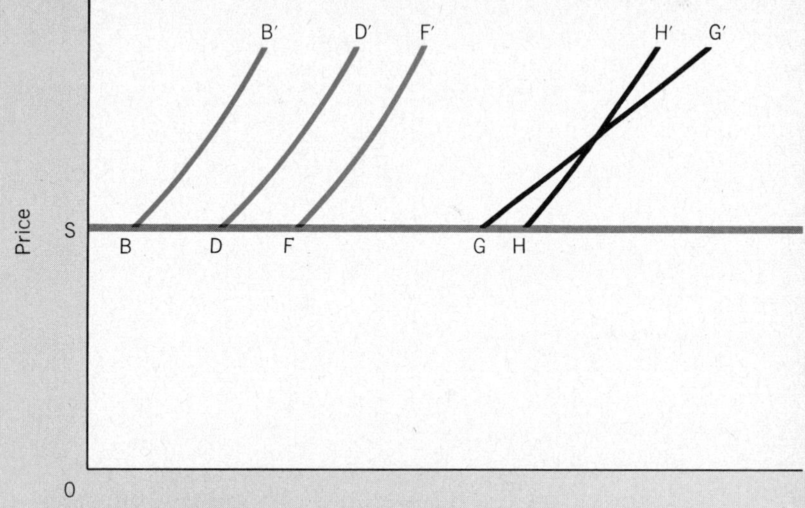

Figure 22.4
Horizontal Summation of Short-Run Supply Curves of Firms

The market supply curve is *OSGG′*, if the firm supply curves are *OSBB′*, *OSDD′*, and *OSFF′*. However, if input prices are influenced by the output of the industry, the market supply curve may be *OSHH′* rather than *OSGG′*.

ignore this inconsistency. Figure 22.4 is designed to illustrate the fact that the market supply curve is the horizontal summation of the firm supply curves, at least under one important assumption.

The assumption underlying this construction of the short-run market supply curve is that *increases or decreases in output by all firms simultaneously do not affect input prices*. This is a strong assumption. Although changes in the output of one firm alone often cannot affect input prices, the simultaneous expansion or contraction of output by all firms may well alter input prices, so that the individual firm's cost curves—and supply curve—will shift. For instance, an expansion of the whole industry may bid up the price of certain inputs, with the result that the cost curves of the individual firms will be pushed upward. In the aerospace industry, for example, a sudden expansion of the industry might well increase the price of certain inputs like the services of aerospace scientists and engineers.

If, contrary to the assumption underlying Figure 22.4, input prices *are* increased by the expansion of the industry, what will happen to the short-run market supply curve? The effect will be to make the amount supplied less sensitive to price changes than is indicated by *OSGG′*. In the relevant price range, the curve might be more like *HH′* than *GG′*. To see why, note that expansion of the industry causes the short-run average cost curve and the short-run marginal cost curve of each firm to move upward, because of the resulting increase in input prices. But if the marginal cost curve moves upward, price will equal marginal cost at a lower output than it would have if the marginal cost curve had not moved.

Returning now to the question posed at the beginning of this section, what factors determine the market supply curve? First, since the market supply curve is derived from the marginal cost curves of the firms in the industry, the shape of the short-run supply curve is determined by the size of the firm's plants, the level of input prices, the nature of technology, and the other factors determining the shape of the marginal cost curve for each firm. In particular, the short-run market supply curve generally slopes upward to the right because marginal cost curves (in the relevant range) generally slope upward to the right. Second, as we have seen in previous paragraphs, the shape of the supply curve is influenced by the effect of changes in industry output on input prices. Third, the shape of the short-run supply curve is determined by the number of firms in the industry. The supply curve in Figure 22.4 would be located farther to the right if there were more firms in the industry.

Measurement of Market Supply Curves and the Price Elasticity of Supply

In many situations, major decisions must be based on predictions of the effect of a commodity's price on the amount of the commodity that will be supplied. For example, recall the agricultural programs described in Chapter 5. Clearly, decision makers in the U.S. Department of Agriculture must be concerned with the market supply curve for many basic agricultural commodities. Nor is the importance of market supply curves confined to agriculture. In other parts of the economy, people must be vitally concerned with the location and shape of the market supply curve for various commodities.

Attempts to measure market supply curves have been aided greatly by modern advances in statistical and econometric techniques. Basically, these techniques rely on analyzing historical data on price and output to estimate the relationship between price and the quantity supplied. There are still many difficulties and hazards in estimating market supply curves, just as with market demand curves. It is not a business for the neophyte. But based on careful professional analysis, useful measurements can be made of market supply (and demand) curves.

Figure 22.5
Market Supply Curves for Watermelons, Periods of Varying Length

Panel A shows the market supply curve in a period of a few hours or a day. Panel B refers to a year or so. Panel C refers to 10 to 20 years.

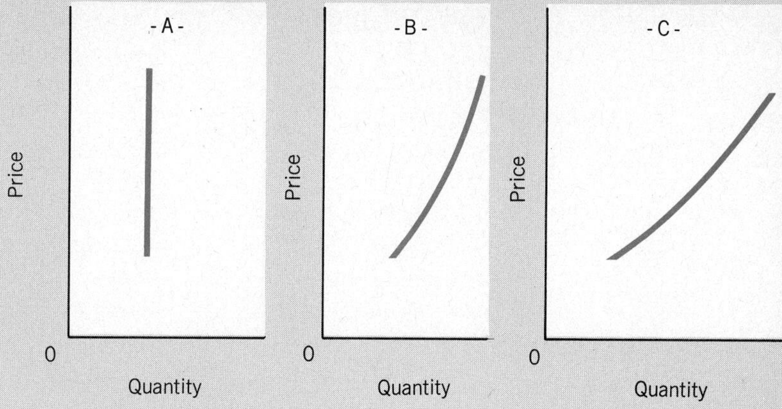

Market supply curves vary, of course, in their shape. For some commodities, the quantity supplied is very sensitive to changes in the commodity's price. For others, the quantity supplied is not at all sensitive to changes in price. To measure the sensitivity of quantity supplied to changes in price, economists use the ***price elasticity of supply,*** which is defined as the percentage change in quantity supplied resulting from a 1 percent change in price. For example, suppose that a 1 percent reduction in the price of slingshots results in a 1.5 percent reduction in the quantity supplied. Then the price elasticity of supply for slingshots (in the neighborhood of the existing price) is 1.5. Clearly, the price elasticity of supply is likely to vary from one point to another on the market supply curve. For example, the price elasticity of supply for slingshots may be higher when the price of a slingshot is $2 than when it is $1.

The same factors that influence the location and shape of the market supply curve also determine the price elasticity of supply. But to these factors previously mentioned—the number of plants, input prices, and the nature of technology, among others—another important factor should be added: the length of the time period to which the supply curve pertains. *Market supply curves, like market demand curves, tend to be more price elastic if the time period is long rather than short.* For example, consider the market for watermelons. If we are dealing with a very short period—a few hours or a day—the supply of watermelons may be fixed, as in panel A of Figure 22.5. That is, the market supply curve may be perfectly inelastic, the price elasticity of supply being zero, because the period is too short to grow any more watermelons or transport any more watermelons into the market.

Suppose now that we lengthen the period of time to a year or so. In this period, farmers can alter the size of their watermelon crop in response to variations in price. Thus, the price elasticity of supply will be higher than in the very short period of a few hours or a day. In this longer period, the price elasticity of supply has been estimated to be about .30; and the supply curve may be as shown in panel B of Figure 22.5.[3]

Finally, suppose that we lengthen the period further—to 10 or even 20 years. In this period, farmers can take land out of watermelon production or put land into watermelon production. Indeed, they can make all reasonable adjustments to changes in price. So the price elasticity of supply will be higher than in a period of a year or so—and much higher than in a period of a few hours

[3] D. Suits, "An Econometric Model of the Watermelon Market," *Journal of Farm Economics,* May 1955; and W. L'Esperance, "A Case Study in Prediction," *Econometrica,* 1964.

or a day. The supply curve may be as shown in panel c of Figure 22.5.

For various leading commodities, what are the best available estimates of the price elasticity of supply? Marc Nerlove of Northwestern University has done some important studies of the price elasticity of supply of agricultural commodities, in both the short and long runs. He concludes that, although the short-run price elasticity of supply for commodities like cotton and corn may be quite low, their price elasticity of supply in the long run is substantially higher. Specifically, estimates of the short-run price elasticities of supply are about 0.2 for cotton and about 0.1 for corn; but in the long run, Nerlove estimates the price elasticity of supply to be about 0.7 for cotton and about 0.2 for corn.[4]

Linear Programming[5]

Previous sections of this chapter have shown how the profit-maximizing firm chooses its output level in the short run, when it takes the price of each of its inputs and outputs as given. When the economist pairs his understanding of how much the firm will produce with his conclusions about the combination of inputs the firm will use to produce this quantity of output, he has a reasonably complete model of the behavior of a perfectly competitive firm in the short run.

At this point, it is useful to look at the theory of the firm from a somewhat different angle—that of ***linear programming.*** Linear programming is the most famous of the mathematical programming methods that have come into existence since World War II. It is a technique that permits decision makers to solve maximization and minimization problems where there are certain constraints on what can be done. First used shortly after World War II to help schedule the procurement activities of the United States Air Force, linear programming has become an extremely important part of economic theory and a very powerful tool for solving managerial problems. Its remarkable growth has been helped along by the development of computers, which can handle the many computations required to solve large linear programming problems.

There are at least two reasons why it is important to reexamine the theory of the firm in terms of linear programming. First, the programming analysis is more fundamental in one respect than the conventional analysis presented up to this point. The conventional theory is based on the production function, which assumes that the efficient production processes have been determined and given to the economist before he attacks the problem. But in the real world, the economist is usually confronted with a number of *feasible* production processes, and it is very difficult to tell which ones—or which combinations—are *efficient.* The choice of the optimal combination of production processes is an extremely important decision, and it can be analyzed more fully by linear programming.

Second, the programming analysis seems to conform more closely to the way businessmen view production. The language and concepts of linear programming, though abstract and by no means the same as those of management, seem to be closer to those of managers and engineers than the ones used by conventional theory. This means that often it is easier to apply linear programming to many types of production problems in industry and government.

The Linear-Programming View of the Firm

To the economist who uses linear programming, the technology available to a firm consists of a

[4] M. Nerlove, "Estimates of the Elasticities of Supply of Selected Agricultural Commodities," *Journal of Farm Economics,* May 1956.

[5] The rest of this chapter may be omitted without loss of continuity. An understanding of subsequent chapters does not depend on a reading of this material on linear programming.

finite number of ***processes,*** each of which uses inputs and produces one or more outputs. General Motors can choose among a number of different processes to manufacture an automobile, and U. S. Steel can use a number of processes to manufacture steel. Typically, a firm can use various alternative processes to do a particular job. An important assumption in linear programming is that each process uses inputs in fixed proportions. Consider the case of an automobile manufacturer that, among other things, assembles truck engines. Suppose that one process it can employ is Process X, which uses 10 hours of labor and 1 hour of machine time to assemble 1 truck engine. If this process uses inputs in fixed proportions—as assumed in linear programming—this 10:1 ratio of labor time to machine time must be maintained. It cannot be altered.

Any process can be operated at various activity levels; the ***activity level*** of a process is the number of units of output produced with the process. For example, if Process X is used to assemble 3 truck engines, its activity level is 3; if it is used to assemble 100 truck engines, its activity level is 100. If the output of any process is varied, it is assumed that the inputs used by the process vary proportionately with the output of the process. Consequently, the amount of any input used by a process equals the activity level of the process—i.e., the number of units of output produced with the process—times the number of units of input the process requires to produce a unit of output. In our example, the amount of labor used by Process X to assemble 5 truck engines is 50 manhours, since the process is operated at an activity level of 5, and Process X requires 10 manhours of labor to assemble each truck engine.[6]

Linear programming views the firm's production problem as follows: *The firm has certain fixed amounts of a number of inputs at its disposal. A manufacturing firm, for example, has available a limited amount of land, managerial labor, raw materials, and equipment of various kinds. (These limitations on the amounts of various inputs that the firm can use are called* **constraints.**) *Each unit of output resulting from a particular process yields the firm a certain amount of profit. This amount of profit varies in general from process to process. Knowing the profit to be made from a unit of output from each process and bearing in mind the limited amounts of inputs at its disposal, the firm must determine the activity level at which each process should be operated to maximize profit.* This is the firm's problem in a nutshell—a linear-programming nutshell, that is.

[6] It is also assumed that, when two or more processes are used simultaneously, they do not interfere with one another or make each other more productive.

Removing Defects from Sheet Metal: A Case Study

No general description of linear programming can give more than a very incomplete idea of the nature of linear programming and its power to solve real-life problems. We can get a somewhat better idea from a simple case study which concerns a metalworking firm that removes defects from sheet metal. Suppose that there are three processes the firm can use: Processes A, B, and C. Process A requires 2 manhours of labor and 1 hour of machine time to remove the defects from 1 square foot of sheet metal, Process B does the same job with 1.5 manhours of labor and 1.5 hours of machine time, and Process C requires 1.1 manhours of labor and 2.2 hours of machine time. The same kind of machine is used for each process.

Assume that the firm has contracted to remove the defects from 100 square feet of sheet metal per week, and that it will receive a price of $10 a square foot for this service. Also assume that the firm must pay $3 per manhour for labor and that the cost of an hour of machine time is $2. Given these circumstances, the firm must decide which process or processes it should use to satisfy this contract. Should it use any single process to remove the defects from all 100 square feet of sheet metal per week? If so, which process should it use? Should it use some combination of processes, such as Process A for 50 square feet and Process B for the rest? Which of the myriad of possibilities will maximize the firm's profits?

Given that the firm will receive $1,000 a week for the work (100 square feet × $10 per square foot) whatever processes it uses, the firm will clearly maximize its profit by minimizing its costs. Thus, in this simple case,[7] the problem boils down to determining which process or processes can do the job at least cost. We begin by assuming that the firm can hire all the labor that it wants and that it has plenty of the necessary machines. (This assumption is contrary to our earlier statement that linear programming views the firm as having limited amounts of certain inputs, but we relax this assumption in a later section.) Letting Q_1 be the number of square feet of sheet metal subjected to Process A, Q_2 be the number of square feet subjected to Process B, and Q_3 be the number of square feet subjected to Process C, the firm's problem can be regarded as the following simple linear programming problem: Choose the lowest possible value for

$$\text{total cost} = 8.0\ Q_1 + 7.5\ Q_2 + 7.7\ Q_3 \qquad (22.1)$$

subject to the constraints.

$$Q_1 + Q_2 + Q_3 = 100 \qquad (22.2)$$
$$Q_1 \geq 0;\ Q_2 \geq 0;\ Q_3 \geq 0. \qquad (22.3)$$

Why should the firm seek the lowest possible value for the expression in Equation 22.1? Because this expression equals the firm's total weekly costs of doing the job. The cost of each square foot of sheet metal subjected to Process A is $8.00, since Process A requires 2 manhours of labor (at $3 per manhour) and 1 hour of machine time (at $2 per hour). Thus the total cost of the sheet metal subjected to Process A is 8.0 Q_1. Similarly, the total cost of sheet metal subjected to Process B is 7.5 Q_2, since the cost of each square foot of sheet metal subjected to Process B is $7.50. And the total cost of the sheet metal subjected to Process C is 7.7 Q_3, since the cost of each square foot subjected to Process C is $7.70. Clearly, the total cost of the job is the sum of whatever costs are incurred using each of the processes, which is the expression in Equation 22.1.

Why must the firm conform to the constraints in Equation 22.2 and Inequality 22.3? Obviously, Equation 22.2 must hold if the firm is to meet its contract, since it states that the sum of the amounts of sheet metal subjected to each process must

[7] Of course, in general the problem of maximizing profit does not boil down to the minimization of cost because the firm's total revenue is not fixed as it is in this simple case.

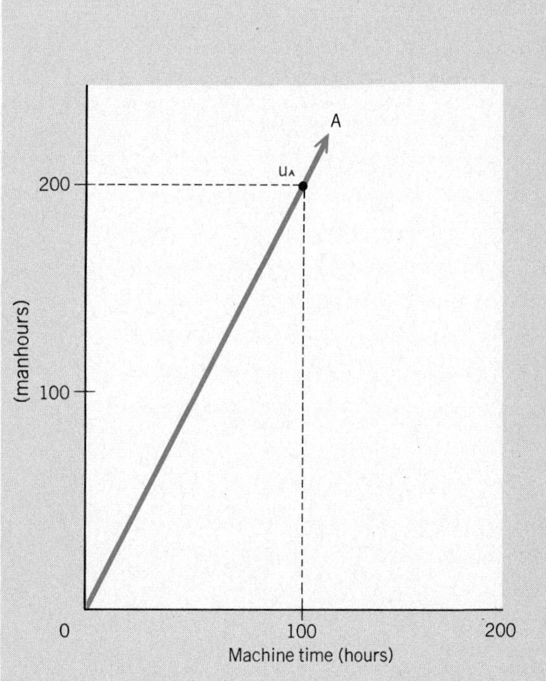

Figure 22.6
Graphical Representation of Process A

The ray *OA* includes all points where labor time is combined with machine time in the ratio of 2:1, since this is the ratio used by Process A. The point U_A corresponds to an output of 100 square feet of sheet metal per week.

equal 100 square feet. That is, $Q_1 + Q_2 + Q_3$ must equal 100. Also, the inequalities in (22.3) must hold: all they say is that the number of square feet of sheet metal subjected to each process must be either zero or more than zero, which certainly must be true. (If you wonder why such an obvious constraint must be specified, remember that electronic computers won't recognize it as being true unless they are told.)

Solving the Problem: No Constraints on Inputs

It is convenient to begin solving the problem by providing a graphic representation of each of the three processes. Since a process is defined to have fixed input proportions and since all points where input proportions are unchanged lie along a straight line through the origin, we can represent each process by such a line, or ***ray.*** In Figure 22.6, the ray OA represents process A. Process A uses 2 manhours of labor and 1 hour of machine time per square foot of sheet metal—in other words, 2 manhours of labor for every hour of machine time. Consequently, the ray OA includes all points where labor time is combined with machine time in the ratio of 2:1.

Two things should be noted about ray OA. First, each point on this ray implies a certain output level. For example, point U_A, where 200 manhours of labor and 100 hours of machine time are used, implies an output of 100 square feet of sheet metal per week. Second, every possible output rate corresponds to some point on this ray. This is true because all possible points at which labor time is combined with machine time in the ratio of 2:1 are included in the ray OA.

In Figure 22.7, we show the rays corresponding to all three processes: OA corresponds to Process A, OB to Process B, and OC to Process C. Each

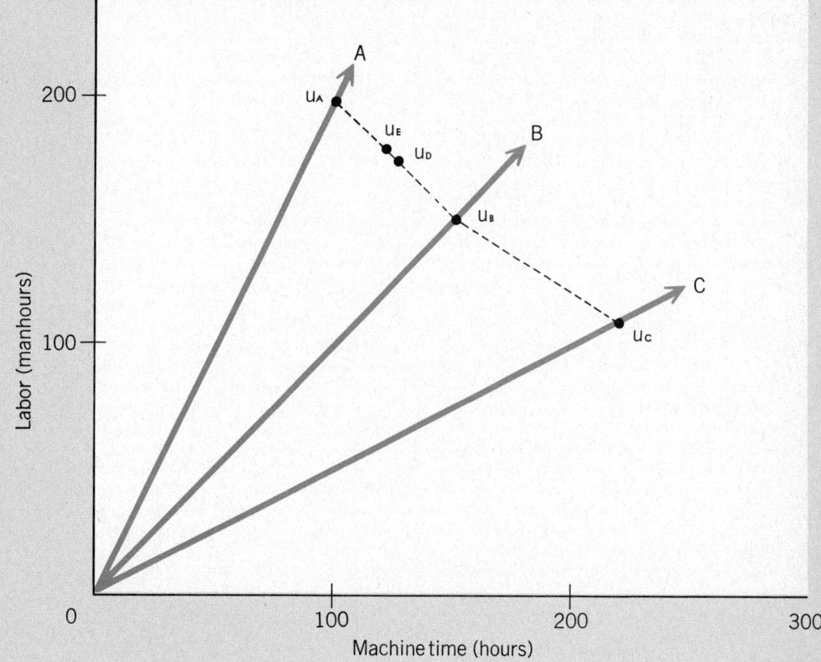

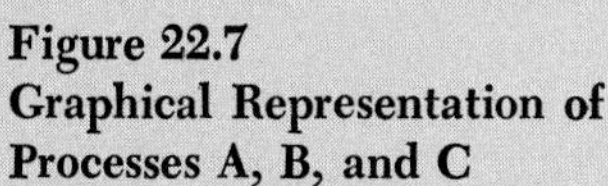

Figure 22.7
Graphical Representation of Processes A, B, and C

Ray *OA* pertains to Process A, ray *OB* to Process B, and ray *OC* to Process C. Based on these rays, we derive the isoquant corresponding to an output of 100 square feet per week, $U_AU_BU_C$.

ray is constructed in the same way. Using these rays, we can draw the isoquant corresponding to the output of 100 square feet of sheet metal processed—the curve that includes all input combinations that can produce this amount of output. Focusing first on Processes A and B, point U_A is the point corresponding to an output of 100 square feet of sheet metal with Process A, and point U_B corresponds to an output of 100 square feet with Process B. Thus U_A and U_B are points on the isoquant corresponding to an output of 100 square feet of sheet metal.

Moreover, any point on the line segment joining U_A and U_B is also on this isoquant, because the firm can simultaneously use both Process A and Process B to remove defects from a total of 100 square feet of sheet metal. For example, point U_D corresponds to the case in which Processes A and B are each used to remove defects from 50 square feet of the metal; and point U_E corresponds to the case in which Process A is used for 60 square feet and Process B for 40 square feet. By varying the proportion of the total output subjected to each of these two processes, one can obtain all points on the line segment that joins U_A to U_B.

To complete the isoquant, we must recognize the existence of Process C, too. In Figure 22.7, U_C is the point corresponding to the use of Process C to remove defects from 100 square feet of sheet metal. Thus, U_C is also a point on this isoquant. Moreover, any point on the line segment joining U_B and U_C is also on this isoquant, because the firm can simultaneously use both Process B and Process C to remove defects from a total of 100 square feet of sheet metal.[8] Consequently, the entire

[8] At first glance, one might wonder why the line segment joining U_A to U_C is not part of the isoquant. After all, it too represents various combinations of labor time and machine time that can remove the defects from 100 square feet of sheet metal. This line segment is excluded because the points on it are inefficient: they use as much of one input and more of the other input than some point on $U_AU_BU_C$. Recall from Chapter 21 that an isoquant contains only efficient combinations of inputs.

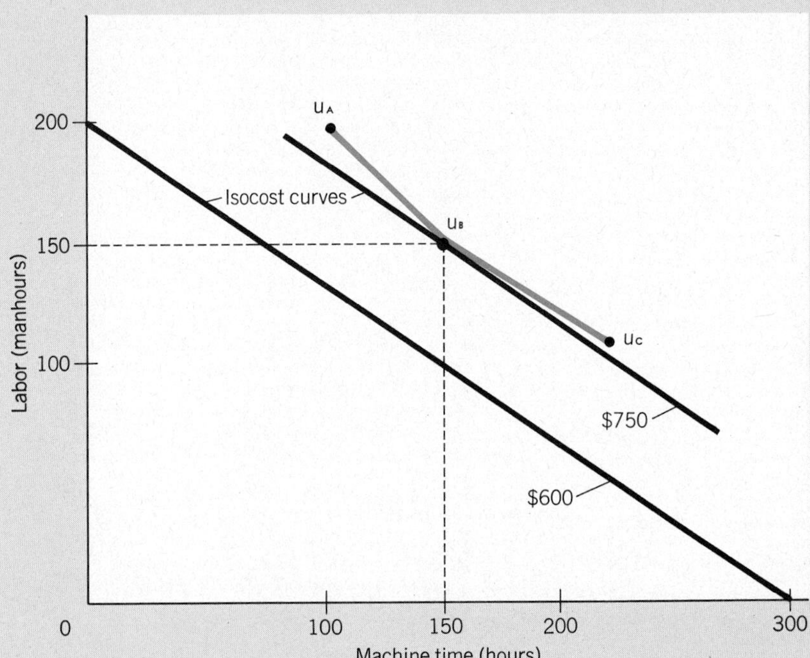

Figure 22.8
Isoquant and Isocost Curves

The point on the isoquant $U_AU_BU_C$ that is on the lowest isocost curve is point U_B.

isoquant is $U_A U_B U_C$. Note that this isoquant, like all in linear programming, consists of connected line segments, and, while not smooth, has the same basic shape as the isoquants of conventional theory.

Given the isoquant $U_A U_B U_C$, it is simple to solve the firm's problem. All we have to do is construct Figure 22.8, which contains this isoquant as well as some isocost curves, each of which shows all input combinations that cost the firm the same amount. The isocost curves corresponding to \$600 and \$750 are shown in Figure 22.8. To find the input combination that minimizes the cost of removing defects from 100 square feet of sheet metal, we need only follow a familiar procedure: finding the point on the isoquant that is on the lowest isocost curve. Clearly, this is U_B—the point corresponding to the use of Process B alone. Thus, the firm should use only Process B, its total costs will be \$750, and it will make a profit of \$250 per week on the contract—which is the best it can do.

Solving the Problem: Constraint on Machine Time

The foregoing problem is extremely simple—so simple that it can easily be solved outside the framework of linear programming.[9] Let's complicate the problem a bit and make it somewhat more realistic. In the previous section, we assumed that the firm could use all the machine time it wanted —at \$2 per hour. But in the short run, the firm is likely to have only a certain number of machines available. It therefore is constrained to use no more than a certain number of machine hours per week. Specifically, suppose that the firm can use no more than 120 hours of machine time per week; this is the maximum capacity of the machines it owns or to which it has access. Now which process or processes should be used to satisfy the contract?

This problem recognizes that the firm has limited amounts of certain inputs in the short run; thus, it contains constraints of the sort visualized in the linear-programming view of the firm. The objective is still to minimize the expression in Equation 22.1, and the constraints in Equation 22.2 and Inequality 22.3 must still be met, but there is now a new constraint:

$$Q_1 + 1.5\,Q_2 + 2.2\,Q_3 \leq 120 \qquad (22.4)$$

Why? Because the number of hours of machine time per week must be less than (or equal to) 120, and the total number of hours of machine time used per week equals $Q_1 + 1.5\,Q_2 + 2.2\,Q_3$.

To see that this is so, recall that the removal of defects from each square foot of sheet metal by Process A requires 1 hour of machine time; thus, since Q_1 is the number of square feet of sheet metal treated per week by Process A, the number of hours of machine time per week used on Process A must also equal Q_1. Similarly, the number of hours of machine time per week used on Process B must equal $1.5\,Q_2$ since the removal of defects from each square foot of sheet metal by Process B requires 1.5 hours of machine time. Moreover, the number of hours of machine time per week used on Process C must equal $2.2\,Q_3$ since Process C requires 2.2 hours of machine time per square foot of metal. Thus, the *total* amount of machine time used per week on *all* processes must be $Q_1 + 1.5\,Q_2 + 2.2\,Q_3$.

How can this problem be solved? The constraint in Inequality 22.4 means that many of the points in Figure 22.8 are no longer feasible, because they require more than 120 hours per week of machine time. These nonfeasible points are shown in the shaded area of Figure 22.9. To solve the problem, we must find that *feasible* point on the isoquant $U_A U_B U_C$ that is on the lowest isocost curve. The

[9] All this problem really entails is a choice among three methods of production, the average costs of production being constant for each process and no constraint being placed on the amount that can be produced with a certain process. In such a case, the answer is obvious: produce the required volume of output with the process with the lowest average cost. Of course, the simplicity of this case does not detract from its usefulness as a first step in the discussion of the nature of linear programming.

Figure 22.9
Isoquant (with Constraint on Machine Time) and Isocost Curves

If the firm cannot use more than 120 hours of machine time per week, the shaded area is no longer feasible, so the feasible point on the isoquant that is on the lowest isocost curve is U_E.

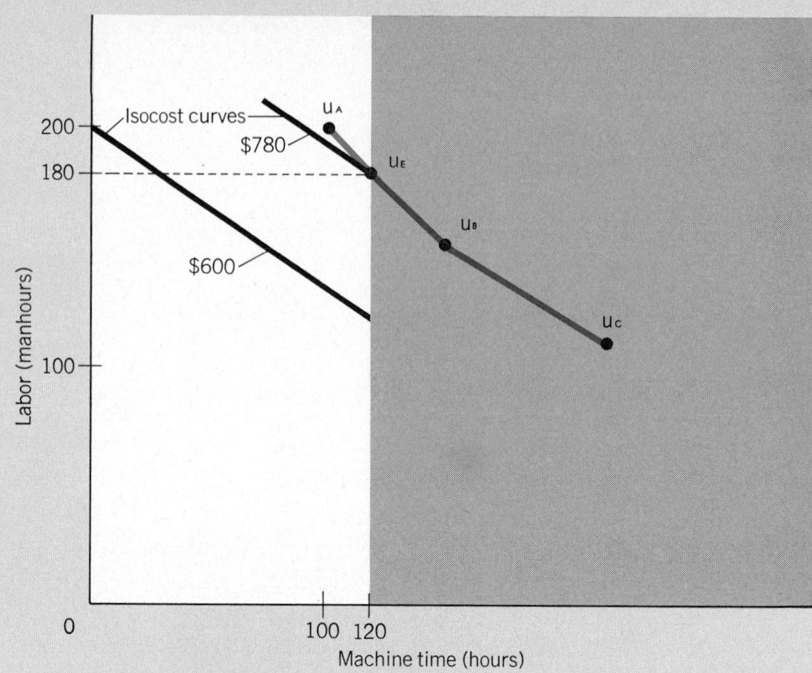

feasible points on this isoquant are all on line U_AU_E in Figure 22.9. Isocost curves representing costs of \$600 and \$780 are also shown in Figure 22.9. It is evident that the point on U_AU_E that is on the lowest isocost curve is U_E. Thus the firm should use 180 manhours of labor and 120 machine hours per week—which means that Process A should be used on 60 square feet of sheet metal per week and Process B on 40 square feet.[10] The firm's total cost is \$780, and it makes \$220 per week—which is the best it can do under these circumstances.

Applications of Linear Programming and Management Science

Since it is impossible to review all the many situations where linear programming has been applied, we restrict our attention here to two reasonably representative cases, as described by Robert Dorfman of Harvard. The first pertains to the petroleum refining industry; the second to the newsprint industry. Both are practical examples of how linear programming is actually used. Here are Dorfman's descriptions of these two cases:

> [In oil refining, one] application was to a moderate-sized refinery which produces premium and regular grades of automotive gasoline. The essential operation studied was blending. In blending, ten chemically distinct kinds of semirefined oil, called blending stocks, are mixed together. The result is a salable gasoline whose characteristics are approximately the weighted average of the characteristics of the blending stocks. For example, if 500 gallons

[10] Since the total amount of manhours used equals 180 hours, $2Q_1 + 1.5Q_2 = 180$. And since the total amount of machine time used equals 120 hours, $Q_1 + 1.5Q_2 = 120$. Solving these two equations simultaneously, $Q_1 = 60$ and $Q_2 = 40$. Thus Process A should be used on 60 square feet and Process B on 40 square feet.

of a stock with octane rating of 80 are blended with 1,000 gallons of a stock with octane rating of 86, the result will be 500 + 1,000 = 1,500 gallons of product with octane rating of $(\frac{1}{3} \times 80) + (\frac{2}{3} \times 86) = 84$.

The significant aspect of gasoline blending for our present purposes is that the major characteristics of the blend—its knock rating, its vapor pressure, its sulphur content, etc.—can be expressed as linear functions of the quantities of the various blending stocks used. So also can the cost of the blend if each of the blending stocks has a definite price per gallon. Thus the problem of finding the minimum cost blend which will meet given quality specifications is a problem in mathematical programming.

An entirely different kind of problem, also amenable to mathematical programming, arises in newsprint production. Freight is a major element in the cost of newsprint. One large newsprint company has six mills, widely scattered in Canada, and some two hundred customers, widely scattered in the United States. Its problem is to decide how much newsprint to ship from each mill to each customer so as, first, to meet the contract requirements of each customer, secondly, to stay within the capacity limits of each mill, and third, to keep the aggregate freight bill as small as possible. This problem involves 1,200 variables (6 mills × 200 customers), in contrast to the two- or four-variable problems we have been discussing. In the final solution most of these variables will turn out to be zero—the question is which ones. This problem is solved by mathematical programming and, though formidable, is not really as formidable as the count of variables might indicate.[11]

Of course, there is a great deal more to learn about linear programming than we can—or should—provide here. To understand the details, you must know some mathematics. Consequently, the detailed construction and solution of linear programming models are generally a matter for the expert, not the neophyte. But just as war is too important to be left to the generals, so linear programming is too useful to be left to the experts. In facing many problems, it is helpful to be familiar with the existence of linear programming and what it can reasonably be expected to do. Indeed, in many situations, this really is enough, since the rest can be delegated to others.

Linear programming is only one of a number of analytical tools that have been developed in the past 30 years to aid decision making in the private and public sectors of the economy. These techniques form the core of ***management science*** or ***operations research,*** a very rapidly growing and exciting field that draws on economics and other disciplines. Although management is still very much an art, the development and application of techniques like linear programming are making it more and more a science. Many problems that were "solved" only 10 or 20 years ago by guesswork and seat-of-the-pants judgment are now being handled by linear programming and other such techniques, with the result that decisions are better, firms are more efficient, and society gets more out of its available resources.

[11] R. Dorfman, "Mathematical, or 'Linear,' Programming," *American Economic Review,* December 1953, reprinted in Edwin Mansfield. *Microeconomics: Readings, Issues, and Cases,* New York: Norton, 1974.

Summary

Suppose that a firm takes as given the price of its product and that it can sell all it wants at this price. Then, if it maximizes profit, it should set its output rate in the short run at the level where marginal cost equals price, so long as price exceeds average variable cost. If there is no output rate at which price exceeds average variable cost, the firm should discontinue production. These are the basic rules the firm must follow to maximize profits. From these rules it follows that the firm's supply curve coincides with its marginal cost curve for prices exceeding the minimum value of average variable cost. For prices that are less than or equal to the minimum value of average variable cost, the firm's supply curve coincides with the price axis.

As a first approximation, the market supply curve

can be viewed as the horizontal summation of the supply curves of all of the firms producing the product. This assumes that increases or decreases in output by all firms simultaneously do not affect input prices—a strong assumption. In general, the market supply curve of a product is determined by the size of the firms' plants, the level of input prices, the nature of technology, and the other factors determining the shape of the firms' marginal cost curves, as well as by the effect of changes in the industry output on input prices and by the number of firms producing the product. The sensitivity of the quantity supplied to changes in price is measured by the price elasticity of supply, defined as the percentage change in quantity supplied resulting from a 1 percent change in price. In general, the price elasticity of supply is greater if the time interval is long rather than short.

Linear programming, the most famous of the mathematical programming methods that have come into existence since World War II, is a technique that permits decision makers to solve maximization and minimization problems where certain constraints limit what can be done. It is worthwhile reexamining the theory of the firm from the point of view of linear programming because linear programming is more fundamental in at least one respect than the conventional analysis and seems to conform more closely to the way businessmen tend to view production. Also, powerful computational techniques have been developed to find numerical solutions to linear programming problems.

Linear programming views the firm's production problem as follows. The firm has at its disposal certain fixed amounts of a number of inputs. Each unit of output resulting from a particular process yields a certain amount of profit. Knowing the amount to be made from a unit of output from each process and bearing in mind the limited amounts of inputs at its disposal, the firm must determine the activity level at which each process should be operated to maximize profit. To illustrate this approach to the theory of the firm, we discussed in some detail the way in which a metal-working firm should make a choice among alternative production techniques. Linear programming is one of a number of analytical techniques developed in the recent past to aid decision making in the private and public sectors of the economy. Unquestionably, these techniques have resulted in better decisions and more efficient and economical use of society's resources.

CONCEPTS FOR REVIEW

Supply curve of a firm
Market supply curve
Perfectly competitive firm
Linear programming
Activity level
Constraints
Ray
Management science
Operations research
Fully allocated cost
Out-of-pocket cost
Price elasticity of supply

QUESTIONS FOR DISCUSSION AND REVIEW

1. A merchant named Lapidus said that he lost money on every item that he sold, but that he made it up on volume. Does this seem reasonable? Why or why not?

2. Describe various ways that estimates might be made of the price elasticity of supply of wheat, and indicate how these estimates might be of practical use to the Department of Agriculture.

3. Suppose that the total costs of a perfectly competitive firm are as follows:

Output rate	*Total cost*
0	$ 40
1	60
2	90
3	130
4	180
5	240

If the price of the product is $50, what output rate should the firm choose?

4. If the price elasticity of supply for corn is about 0.1 in the short run, as estimated by Marc Nerlove of Northwestern University, a 1 percent increase in the price of corn would have approximately what impact on the quantity supplied?

PART SEVEN

Market Structure and Antitrust Policy

CHAPTER 23

Perfect Competition and Monopoly

Even a country as rich as the United States cannot afford to waste resources, particularly when many of its citizens are poor and much of the world is hungry. One of the important determinants of how a society's resources are used is how its markets are organized. Thus, if the market for wheat contained few sellers rather than many, it would certainly use resources quite differently. Or if 20 firms, rather than one, provided telephone service in New York City, resources would be used differently. Some forms of market organization tend to minimize social waste, whereas other forms promote it.

In this chapter, we examine the way resources are allocated and prices are set under perfect competition and monopoly. These two types of market organization—or market structures, as they are often called—are polar cases which seldom, if ever, occur in a pure form in the real world. But they are extremely useful models that shed much light on market structure's effects on resource allocation. Moreover, these models lie at the heart of many of our nation's policies toward business, including such important areas as our antitrust laws and the regulation of public utilities. Anyone who wants to understand how markets work in a capitalistic economy—or why our public policies toward business are what they are—must understand perfect competition and monopoly.

Market Structure and Economic Performance

It stands to reason that the way a market operates will be affected by the way it is organized. For example, suppose that the market for wheat were composed—as it is, for that matter—of a relatively large number of buyers and sellers. You would expect this market to operate differently than if there were only a single seller or buyer of wheat. In wheat, as in any other market, if there were only a single seller, he would have more power over the amount he sold than a lot of small sellers would. This certainly stands to reason—and the experience of generations of economists and businessmen bears it out.

Moreover, economists and other social observers generally have come to the conclusion, based on their studies of the workings of markets, that certain kinds of market organization are better, from society's point of view, than others. This is a much stronger statement than merely saying, as we did in the previous paragraph, that market structure influences market behavior. This statement is based on some set of values and preferences, explicit or implicit, and on certain economic models that predict that "better" behavior is more likely if markets are organized in certain ways than in other ways. In general, most economists believe that, from society's point of view, market structures should be as close as possible to perfect competition, for reasons given below.

Economists have generally found it useful to classify markets into four broad types: perfect competition, monopoly, monopolistic competition, and oligopoly. Each of these terms describes a particular type of market structure or organization, a classification based largely, but not completely, on the number of firms in the industry that supplies the product. In perfect competition and monopolistic competition, there are *many* sellers, each of which produces only a small part of the industry's output. In monopoly, on the other hand, the industry consists of only a *single* seller. Oligopoly is an intermediate case where there are a *few* sellers. Each of these terms will be defined in detail in subsequent sections of this and the following chapter.

Perfect Competition

When a businessman speaks of a highly competitive market, he often means one in which each firm is keenly aware of its rivalry with a few others and in which advertising, styling, packaging, and other such commercial weapons are used to attract business away from them. In contrast, the basic feature of the economist's definition of ***perfect competition*** is its *impersonality*. Because there are so many firms in the industry, no firm views another as a competitor, any more than one small tobacco farmer views another small tobacco farmer as a competitor.

More specifically, a market must satisfy the following three conditions to be perfectly competitive. First, *the product of any one seller must be the same as the product of any other seller*. This condition insures that buyers do not care from which seller they purchase the goods, so long as the price is the same. Second, *each participant in the market, whether buyer or seller, must be so small in relation to the entire market that he cannot affect the product's price*. That is, all buyers and sellers must be "price takers," not "price makers." Third, *all resources must be able to switch readily from one use to another, and consumers, firms, and resource owners must have complete knowledge of all relevant economic and technological data.*

Clearly, no industry in the real world, now or in the past, satisfies all these conditions completely; thus no industry is perfectly competitive. Some agricultural markets may be reasonably close, but even they do not meet all the requirements. But this does not mean that it is useless to study the behavior of a perfectly competitive market. The conclusions derived from the model of perfect competition have proved very helpful in explaining and predicting behavior in the real world. Indeed, as we shall see, they have permitted a reasonably accurate view of resource allocation in many important segments of our economy.

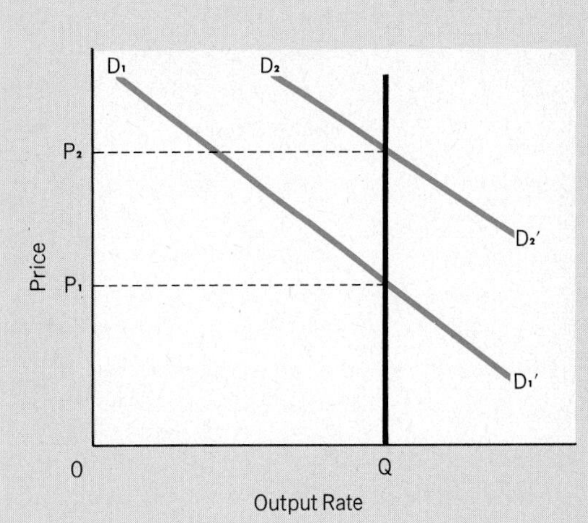

Figure 23.1
Price Determination in the Market Period

In the market period, supply is fixed at *OQ*. Equilibrium price is OP_1 if the demand curve is D_1D_1' and OP_2 if the demand curve is D_2D_2'.

Price and Output under Perfect Competition: The Market Period and the Short Run

How much of a particular product will be produced if the market is perfectly competitive, and what will the price be? The answers depend on the length of the time period. Besides the short run and the long run, there is also the ***market period,*** a length of time during which the supply of a good is fixed. The market period is generally quite short. As we saw in Chapter 22, the price elasticity of supply increases with the length of the time period. In the market period, the price of a good in a perfectly competitive market is determined by the market demand and market supply curves. However, the market supply curve is a vertical line, as shown in Figure 23.1.

In the market period, output is set by supply alone. In Figure 23.1, output is *OQ*—and regardless of price, it cannot be changed. *Given the supply, price is set by demand alone.* For example, price is OP_1 if the demand curve is D_1D_1', and OP_2 if the demand curve is D_2D_2'. The role of the price as a rationing device is particularly obvious in the market period, where this is the major function of price. The allocation of jam in the prisoner-of-war camp and the allocation of tickets to *My Fair Lady,* both taken up in Chapter 4, are among the examples you have encountered earlier of how price rations output in the market period. These cases can be regarded as taking place in the market period because the supply is fixed in each case.

Let's turn now to the short run, the period during which each firm's plant and equipment are fixed. What determines the price and output of a good in a perfectly competitive market in the short run? The answer once again is the market demand and market supply curves. However, the position and shape of these curves will generally be different in the short run than in the market period. In particular, the market supply curve in the short run will not be a vertical line; it will generally slope upward to the right, as in Figure 23.2. Thus, *in*

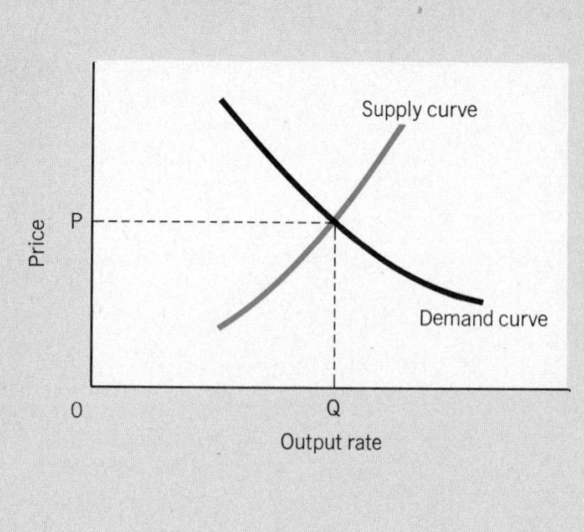

Figure 23.2
Price Determination in the Short Run

Equilibrium price is *OP*, and equilibrium output is *OQ*.

the short run, price influences, as well as rations, the amount supplied. In Figure 23.2, the equilibrium price and output in the short run are *OP* and *OQ*.

To illustrate the nature of the short-run supply curve, consider the bituminous coal industry, which in many respects comes reasonably close to perfect competition. According to Hubert Risser of the University of Kansas, the short-run supply curve for bituminous coal is very price elastic, so long as output stays within the range of existing capacity.[1] In other words, if output is less than existing capacity, small variations in price will result in large variations in output. Thus, the situation in the short run is quite different from that in the market period, where output is fixed and unaffected by price. But of course the basic fact remains that equilibrium price and equilibrium output are determined by the intersection of the relevant demand and supply curves, in both the market period and the short run.

[1] H. Risser, *The Economics of the Coal Industry,* Lawrence: University Press of Kansas, 1958, p. 155.

Price and Output under Perfect Competition: The Long Run

In the long run, what determines the output and price of a good in a perfectly competitive market? In the long run, a firm can change its plant size, which means that established firms may leave an industry if it has below-average profits, or that new firms may enter an industry with above-average profits. Equilibrium is achieved in the long run when enough firms—no more, no less—are in the industry so that "economic profits"—the excess of a firm's profits over what it could make with its resources in other industries—are zero. This condition is necessary for long-run equilibrium because new firms will enter the industry if there are economic profits, and existing firms will leave if there are economic losses.

Note that the existence of economic profits or losses in an industry brings about a shift in the industry's short-run supply curve. If there are economic profits, new firms will enter the industry, and so shift the short-run supply curve to the right. On the other hand, if there are economic losses in the industry (i.e., if the industry's profits are less than could be obtained elsewhere), existing firms will leave the industry, causing the short-run supply curve to shift to the left. Only if economic profits are zero will the number of firms in the industry—and the industry's short-run supply curve—be stable. Putting this equilibrium condition another way, the long-run equilibrium position of the firm is at the point at which its long-run average costs equal price. If price exceeds average total costs, economic profits are being earned; and if price is less than average total costs, economic losses are being incurred.

Going a step further, *long-run equilibrium requires that price equal the lowest value of long-run average total costs.* In other words, firms must

Figure 23.3
Long-Run Equilibrium of a Perfectly Competitive Firm

In long-run equilibrium, output is *OQ* and the firm's plant corresponds to short-run average and marginal cost curves, *AA′* and *MM′*. At *OQ*, long-run marginal cost equals short-run marginal cost equals price; also, long-run average cost equals short-run average cost equals price. These conditions assure that the firm is maximizing profits and that economic profits are zero.

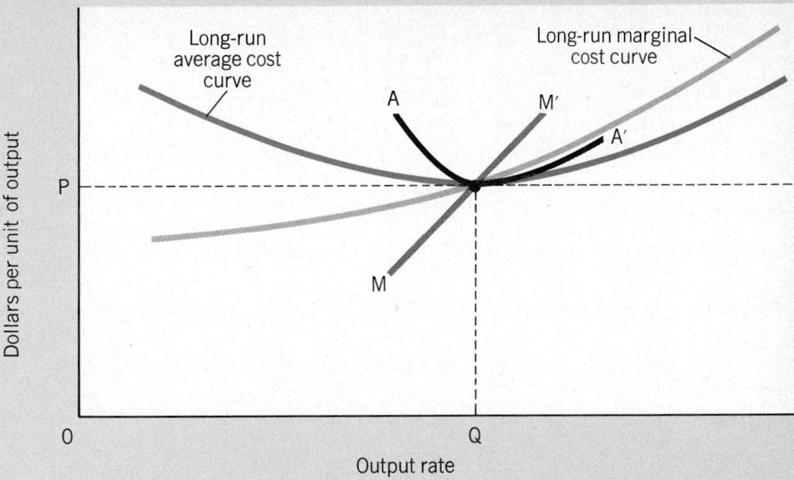

be producing at the *minimum point* on their long-run average cost curves, because to maximize their profits they must operate where price equals long-run marginal cost.[2] Also, we have just seen that they must operate where price equals long-run average cost. But if both these conditions are satisfied, long-run marginal cost must equal long-run average cost—since both equal price. And we know that long-run marginal cost equals long-run average cost only at the point at which long-run average cost is a minimum.[3] Consequently, if long-run marginal cost equals long-run average cost, the firm must be producing at the minimum point on the long-run average cost curve.

This equilibrium position is illustrated in Figure 23.3. When all adjustments are made, price equals *OP*. The equilibrium output of the firm is *OQ*, and its plant corresponds to short-run average and marginal cost curves *AA′* and *MM′*. At this output and with this plant, long-run marginal cost equals short-run marginal cost equals price: this insures that the firm is maximizing profit. Also, long-run average cost equals short-run average cost equals price: this insures that economic profits are zero. Since the long-run marginal cost and long-run average cost must be equal, the firm is producing at the minimum point on its long-run average cost curve.

To illustrate the process of entry and exit in an industry that approximates perfect competition, let's return to the bituminous coal industry. Entry into this industry is relatively easy, but exit is relatively difficult, for at least two reasons. First, it is costly to shut down a mine and reopen it later. Second, because of corrosion and water damage, it is hard to shut down a mine for longer than 2 years unless it is to be abandoned entirely. For these reasons, mines tend to stay open and produce even though short-term losses are incurred. For example, in the period before World War II, the demand for coal fell substantially, but although the industry suffered substantial losses, mines were slow to close down. Nonetheless, the competitive process had its way. Slowly, but surely,

[2] The reasons why marginal cost must be set equal to price, if profits are to be maximized, are given in Chapter 22.

[3] The previous discussion of this point on p. 442 concerned short-run cost functions, but the argument applies just as well to long-run cost functions.

the number of mines fell markedly in response to these losses.[4] Thus, despite the barriers to rapid exit, firms eventually left the industry, just as the model would predict.

Constant, Increasing, and Decreasing Cost Industries

Perfectly competitive industries can be categorized into three types: constant cost industries, increasing cost industries, and decreasing cost industries. In a ***constant cost industry*** an expansion of output does not result in a change in input prices. Figure 23.4 shows the long-run equilibrium in a constant cost industry. The left-hand panel shows the short- and long-run cost curves of a typical firm in the industry. The right-hand panel shows the demand and supply curves in the market as a whole, DD' being the original demand curve and SS' being the original short-run supply curve.

[4] J. B. Hendry, "The Bituminous Coal Industry" in W. Adams, *The Structure of American Industry,* New York: Macmillan, 1961.

It is assumed that the industry is in long-run equilibrium, with the result that the price line is tangent to the long-run (and short-run) average cost curve at its minimum point. The price is OP.

Let's assume that the demand curve shifts from DD' to D_1D_1'. In the short run, with the number of firms fixed, the price of the product will rise from OP to OP_1; each firm will expand output from OQ to OQ_1; and each firm will be making economic profits since OP_1 exceeds the short-run average costs of the firm at OQ_1. The consequence is that firms will enter the industry and shift the short-run supply curve to the right. In a constant cost industry, the entrance of the new firms does not affect the costs of the existing firms. The inputs used by this industry are used by many other industries as well, and the appearance of the new firms in this industry does not bid up the price of inputs (and consequently raise the costs of existing firms). Thus, *a constant cost industry has a horizontal long-run supply curve.* Since output can be varied by varying the number of firms producing OQ units at an average cost of OP, the long-run supply curve is horizontal at OP.

Most economists seem to regard increasing, not

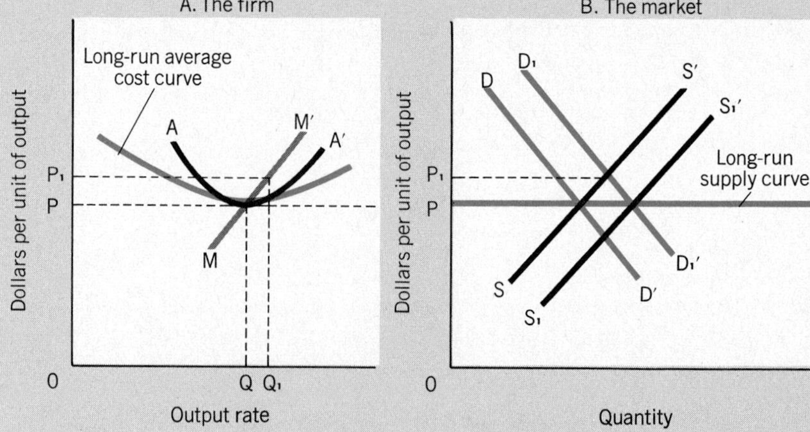

Figure 23.4
Long-Run Equilibrium: Constant Cost Industry

If the demand curve shifts from DD' to D_1D_1', the price will increase in the short run from OP to OP_1. Each firm will expand output from OQ to OQ_1, and entry will occur, thus shifting the supply curve from SS' to S_1S_1'. The long-run supply curve in a constant cost industry is horizontal.

Figure 23.5
Long-Run Equilibrium: Increasing Cost Industry

If the demand curve shifts from DD' to D_1D_1', the price will increase in the short run. Entry will occur, and the price of inputs will increase, thus pushing the long-run average cost curve upward (from LL' to L_1L_1'). The new short-run supply curve will be S_2S_2'. The long-run supply curve in an increasing cost industry slopes upward to the right.

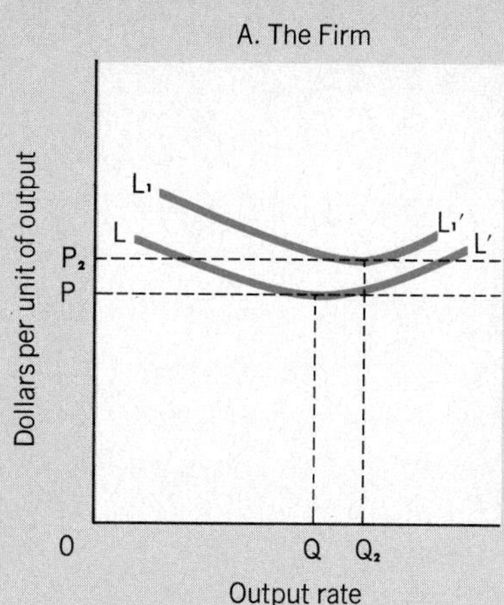

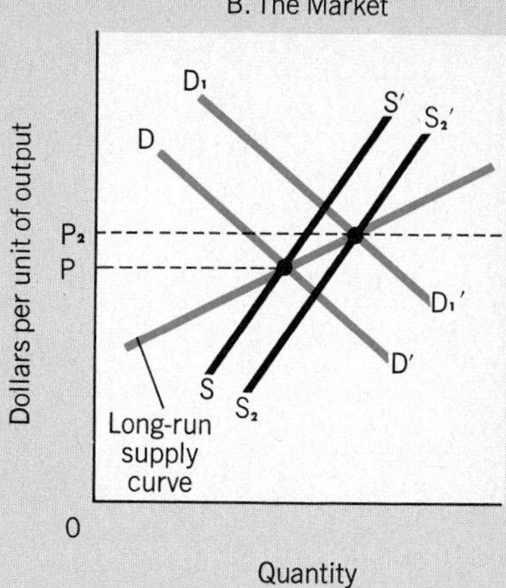

constant, cost industries as the most prevalent of the three types. An ***increasing cost industry*** is one where the price of inputs increases with the amount the industry uses. The situation in such an industry is shown in Figure 23.5. The original conditions are the same as those in Figure 23.4, and we suppose again that the demand curve shifts from DD' to D_1D_1', with the result that the price of the product increases and firms earn economic profits, thus attracting new entrants. More and more inputs are required by the industry, and in an increasing cost industry the price of inputs increases with the amount the industry uses. Consequently, the cost of inputs increases for the established firms as well as the new entrants. The long-run average cost curves are pushed up from LL' to L_1L_1'. Thus the new equilibrium price is OP_2 and each firm produces OQ_2 units, the new short-run supply curve being S_2S_2'. *An increasing cost industry has a positively sloped long-run supply curve,* as shown in Figure 23.5. That is, after long-run equilibrium is achieved, increases in output require increases in the price of the product.

Decreasing cost industries are the most unusual situation, although quite young industries may sometimes fall into this category. In a ***decreasing cost industry,*** the expansion of the industry results in a decrease in the costs of the established firms.[5] Thus, *a decreasing cost industry has a negatively sloped long-run supply curve.* That is, after long-run equilibrium is reached, increases in output are accompanied by decreases in price.

Whether an industry is a constant cost industry, an increasing cost industry, or a decreasing cost industry is an empirical question that must be settled case by case. In trying to determine whether a particular industry is an increasing or constant cost industry, one important consideration is whether it is a relatively large user of certain inputs. For example, because the automobile industry uses a great deal of the nation's steel, an expansion of the automobile industry might well cause an increase in the price of steel; but an expansion of the paper-clip industry, which uses very little of the nation's steel, would be unlikely to raise the price of steel.

[5] Certain *external economies,* which are cost reductions that occur when an industry expands, may be responsible for the existence of decreasing cost industries. An example of such an external economy is an improvement in transportation that is due to the expansion of an industry and that reduces the costs of each firm in the industry (see Chapter 5).

The Allocation of Resources under Perfect Competition: A More Detailed View

At this point, it is instructive to describe the process by which a perfectly competitive economy—one composed of perfectly competitive industries—would allocate resources. In Chapters 3 and 4, we stressed that the allocation of resources among alternative uses is one of the major functions of an economic system. Equipped with the concepts of this and previous chapters, we can now go much farther in describing how a perfectly competitive economy shifts resources in accord with changes in tastes, technology, and other factors.

To be specific, suppose that a change occurs in tastes. Consumers become more favorably disposed toward wheat and less favorably disposed toward corn than in the past.[6] In the short run, the increase in the demand for wheat increases the price of wheat, and results in some increase in the output of wheat. However, the output cannot be increased very substantially because the industry's capacity cannot be expanded in the short run. Similarly, the fall in the demand for corn reduces the price of corn, and results in some reduction in output. But the output will not be curtailed greatly because firms will continue to produce as long as they can cover variable costs.

The change in the relative prices of wheat and corn tells producers that a reallocation of resources is called for. Because of the increase in the price of wheat and the decrease in the price of corn, wheat producers are earning economic profits and corn producers are showing economic losses. This will trigger a new deployment of resources. If some variable inputs in corn production can be used as effectively in the production of wheat, they may be switched from corn production to wheat production. Even if no variable inputs are used in both wheat and corn production, adjustment can be made in various interrelated markets, with the result that wheat production gains resources and corn production loses resources. When short-run equilibrium is attained in both the wheat and corn industries, the reallocation of resources is not yet complete since there has not been enough time for producers to build new capacity or liquidate old capacity. In particular, neither industry is operating at minimum average cost. The wheat producers are operating at greater than the output level where average cost is a minimum; and the corn producers are operating at less than this level.

What will happen in the long run? The shift in consumer demand from corn to wheat will result in greater adjustments in production and smaller adjustments in price than in the short run. In the long run, existing firms can leave corn production and new firms can enter wheat production. Because of short-run economic losses in corn production, some corn land and related equipment will be allowed to run down, and some firms engaged in corn production will be liquidated. As firms leave corn production, the supply curve shifts to the left, causing the price to rise above its short-run level. The transfer of resources out of corn production will stop when the price has increased, and costs have decreased, to the point where losses are avoided.

While corn production is losing resources, wheat production is gaining them. The prospect of positive economic profits in wheat production will cause new firms to enter the industry. The increased demand for inputs will raise input prices and cost curves in wheat production, and the price of wheat will be depressed by the movement to the right of the supply curve because of the entry of new firms. Entry ceases when economic profits are no longer being earned. At that point, when long-run equilibrium is achieved, more resources will be used in the industry than in the short run.

Finally, long-run equilibrium is established in both industries, and the reallocation of resources is complete. It is important to note that this reallocation can affect industries other than wheat and corn. If corn land and equipment can be easily

[6] Since we assume here that the markets for wheat and corn are perfectly competitive, it is also assumed that there is no government intervention in these markets.

adapted to the production of wheat, corn producers can simply change to wheat production. If not, the resources used in corn production are converted to some use other than wheat, and the resources that enter wheat production come from some use other than corn production.

Bituminous Coal: A Case Study

To illustrate how resources are allocated in the long run, we will look in more detail at the bituminous coal industry. Although it does not have all the characteristics of a perfectly competitive industry, it has enough of them so that the perfectly competitive model predicts many aspects of its behavior reasonably well. From the turn of the century until about 1923, the bituminous coal industry expanded rapidly. Between 1903 and 1923, the price of coal increased from $1.24 to $2.68 per ton, in considerable part because of the marked upward shift to the right of the demand curve for coal, an important fuel in this period of general industrial growth. In addition, the high prices of the period were sometimes the result of temporary shortages caused by strikes and insufficient railroad transportation. Thus, temporary upward shifts to the left of the supply curve for coal, as well as shifts of the demand curve, were responsible for the increases in price.

Given the very high coal prices of 1917–23, coal mining was very profitable. Indeed, aftertax income in 1920 was about 20 percent of invested capital for all bituminous coal companies—and much higher for particular companies. These high profits signaled that more resources should be invested in the industry. And just as the perfectly competitive model would predict, more resources were invested; the number of bituminous coal firms increased by over 130 percent in 9 key states between 1903 and 1923, and the industry's capacity grew by over 50 percent between 1913 and 1923.

Unfortunately, the demand for coal dropped considerably from 1923 to 1933, plunging the industry into a severe economic crisis. The downward shift to the left of the demand curve for coal during the early 1930s was due in considerable part to the fall in national output during the Great Depression. It was accompanied by a marked decrease in the price of coal: from $2.68 in 1923, the price per ton fell to $1.34 in 1933. Needless to say, this tremendous drop meant losses for bituminous coal producers. Indeed, in every year between 1925 and 1940, the bituminous coal industry as a whole showed losses.

These economic losses signaled that resources should be withdrawn from the bituminous coal industry and used elsewhere in the economy where they could be more valuably employed. And as the perfectly competitive model would predict, resources were in fact taken out of bituminous coal. Between 1923 and 1933, there was a reduction of over 40 percent in the number of coal companies operating in 9 key states. And the industry's capacity fell by almost 40 percent between 1923 and 1933. Despite the difficulties in exit that we described in a previous section, the competitive process had its way. Its signals were heeded. Consequently, the industry began to move closer and closer to a position of long-run equilibrium, and although the industry remained on the nation's sick list, it began to show much smaller losses. By the onset of World War II, many of the basic adjustments had taken place.

Monopoly

At the opposite extreme from perfect competition is monopoly. Under a monopolistic market structure, what sort of behavior can we expect? How much of the product will be produced, and at what level will its price be set? To begin with, recall what is meant by ***monopoly:*** *a market where there exists one, and only one, seller*. Monopoly, like perfect competition, seldom corresponds more than approximately to conditions in real industries, but it is a very useful model.

In several respects, monopoly and perfect competition stand as polar opposites. The firm in a perfectly competitive market has so many rivals that competition becomes entirely impersonal. The firm is a price taker, an inconspicuous seller in a sea of inconspicuous sellers. The firm under monopoly has no direct competitors at all; it is the sole supplier. However, the monopolist is not entirely free of rivals. Even he is affected by certain indirect and potential forms of competition. For example, even if a firm managed to obtain a monopoly on wheat production, it would have to worry about competition from corn and other agricultural commodities that could be substituted for wheat. Moreover, the wheat monopolist would also have to take into account the possibility that new firms might arise to challenge its monopoly if it attempted to extract conspicuously high profits. Thus, even the monopolist is subject to some restraint imposed by competitive forces.

Causes of Monopoly

There are many reasons why monopolies, or market structures that closely approximate monopoly, may arise. First, a firm may acquire a monopoly over the production of a good by having patents on the product or on certain basic processes used in its production. The patent laws of the United States give an inventor the exclusive right to make a certain product or to use a certain process for 17 years. The purpose of the patent system is, of course, to encourage invention and innovation and to discourage industrial secrecy. Many firms with monopoly power achieved it in considerable part through patents. For example, the United Shoe Machinery Company became the sole supplier of certain important kinds of shoemaking equipment through control of basic patents. United Shoe was free to dominate the market until 1954, when, after prosecution under the antitrust laws, the firm was ordered to license its patents. And in 1968, when this remedy seemed insufficient, a divestiture program was agreed upon.

Second, a firm may become a monopolist by obtaining control over the entire supply of a basic input required to manufacture a product. For example, the International Nickel Company of Canada controls about $\frac{9}{10}$ of the proven nickel reserves in the world. Since it is hard to produce nickel without nickel, the International Nickel Company obviously has a strong monopoly position. Similarly, the Aluminum Company of America (Alcoa) kept its dominant position for a long time by controlling practically all the sources of bauxite, the ore used to make aluminum. However, as we shall see in Chapter 25, Alcoa's monopoly was broken in 1945 when the Supreme Court decided that Alcoa's control of practically all the industry's output violated the antitrust laws.

Third, a firm may become a monopolist because it is awarded a market franchise by a government agency. For example, the government may give a particular firm the franchise to sell a particular product in a public facility. Or it may give a particular company the right to provide a service, such as telephone service, to people in a particular area. In exchange for this right, the firm agrees to allow the government to regulate certain aspects of its operations. The form of regulation does not matter here; the important point for now is that the monopoly is created by the government.

Fourth, a firm may become a monopolist because the average costs of producing the product reach a minimum at an output rate that is large enough to satisfy the entire market (at a price that is profitable). In a case like this, a firm obviously has an incentive to expand until it produces all the market wants of the good. (Its costs fall as it continues to expand). Thus, competition cannot be maintained in this case. If there are a number of firms in the industry, the result is likely to be economic warfare—and the survival of a single victor, the monopolist.[7]

Cases where costs behave like this are called ***natural monopolies.*** When an industry is a natu-

[7] Note that economies of scale are different from the external economies discussed in note 5: The individual firm has no control over external economies.

Figure 23.6
Natural Monopoly

The industry is a natural monopoly if the demand curve is *DD′*, but not if it is *D₁D₁′*.

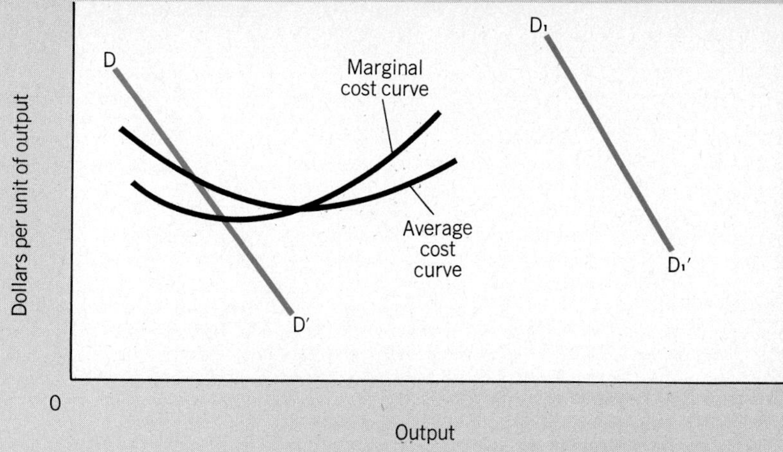

ral monopoly, the public often insists that its behavior be regulated by the government. For example, electric power is an industry where there seem to be great economies of scale—and thus decreasing average costs. Fuel consumed per kilowatt hour is lower in larger power generating units, and there are economies in combining generating units at a single site.[8] Because of these factors, it would be foolish to force competition in the industry, since it would be grossly wasteful. Instead, as we describe later, the market for electric power in a particular area is a regulated monopoly.

Naturally, the likelihood that the long-run average cost curve will decrease up to a point that satisfies the entire market depends on the size of the market. The smaller the market, the more likely it is. For example, in Figure 23.6, the industry is a natural monopoly if the demand curve is DD', but not if it is D_1D_1'. This is an important point. One of the disadvantages of tariffs is that they create separate little markets that can more easily be monopolized. Conversely, one of the advantages claimed for the Common Market in Europe was that it would create a larger market that could support more efficient production and more competitive industries. More will be said on this score in Chapter 30. For now, the important point to recognize is that, just as stagnant marshes breed mosquitos, so small, insulated markets breed monopoly.

[8] Leonard W. Weiss, *Case Studies in American Industry*, New York: Wiley, 1967, pp. 90–91.

Demand Curve and Marginal Revenue under Monopoly

Before we can make any statements about the behavior of a monopolistic market, we must point out certain important characteristics of the demand curve facing the monopolist. Since the monopolist is the only seller of the commodity, the demand curve facing him is, of course, the market demand curve for the product. Since the market demand curve is almost always downward-sloping to the right, the monopolist's demand curve must also be downward-sloping to the right. This is quite different from perfect competition, where the firm's demand curve is horizontal. To illustrate the situation faced by a monopolist, consider the hypothetical case in Table 23.1. The price at which each quantity (shown in column 1) can be sold by the monopolist is shown in column 2. The firm's ***total revenue***—its total dollar sales volume—is

Table 23.1

Demand and Revenue of a Monopolist

Quantity	Price	Total revenue	Marginal revenue*
1	$100	$100	—
2	90	180	$80
3	80	240	60
4	70	280	40
5	60	300	20
6	50	300	0
7	40	280	−20
8	30	240	−40

* These figures pertain to the interval between the indicated quantity of output and 1 unit less than the indicated quantity of output.

shown in column 3. Obviously, column 3 is the product of the first two columns. Column 4 contains the firm's ***marginal revenue***, defined as the addition to total revenue attributable to the addition of one unit to sales. (Thus if $R(q)$ is total revenue when q units are sold and $R(q-1)$ is total revenue when $(q-1)$ units are sold, the marginal revenue between q units and $(q-1)$ units is $R(q) - R(q-1)$.)

Marginal revenue is very important to the monopolist. We can estimate it from the figures in the first three columns of Table 23.1. Clearly, the marginal revenue between 1 and 2 units of output per month is $180 – $100, or $80; the marginal revenue between 2 and 3 units of output per month is $240 – $180; or $60; the marginal revenue between 3 and 4 units of output per month is $280 – $240, or $40; and so on. The results are shown in column 4 of the table. Note that marginal revenue is analogous to marginal cost (and marginal utility, for that matter). Recall that marginal cost is the extra cost resulting from an extra unit of production. Substitute "revenue" for "cost" and "sales" for "production" in the previous sentence, and what do you get? A perfectly acceptable definition of marginal revenue.

Two things should be noted about marginal revenue. First, it will always be less than price if the firm's demand curve is downward sloping (as it is under monopoly and other market structures that are not perfectly competitive). For example, in Table 23.1, the extra revenue from the second unit of output is $80 whereas the price of this unit is $90. The basic reason is that the firm must reduce the price of *all* units of output, not just the extra unit, in order to sell the extra unit. Thus, in Table 23.1, the extra revenue from the second unit of output is $80 because, while the price of the second unit is $90, the price of the first unit must be reduced by $10 in order to sell the second unit.

Second, marginal revenue will be positive at a point on the monopolist's demand curve where demand is price elastic and negative at a point on the monopolist's demand curve where demand is price inelastic. As we know, if demand is price elastic, a decrease in price will lead to an increase in the total amount spent on a commodity, which is equal to the monopolist's total revenue. Thus, since decreases in price are associated with increases in quantity sold, it follows that if demand is price elastic, an increase in the quantity sold by the monopolist will result in an increase in the monopolist's total revenue—which means that, if demand is price elastic, marginal revenue is positive. The same kind of reasoning can be used to show that, if demand is price inelastic, marginal revenue is negative.

Price and Output under Monopoly: The Short Run

We are now in a position to determine how output and price behave under monopoly. If the monopolist is free to maximize his profits, he will, of course, choose the price and output at which the difference between total revenue and total cost is

Table 23.2

Costs of a Monopolist

Quantity	Total variable cost	Fixed cost	Total cost	Marginal cost*
1	$ 40	$100	$140	$ 40
2	70	100	170	30
3	110	100	210	40
4	150	100	250	40
5	200	100	300	50
6	260	100	360	60
7	350	100	450	90
8	450	100	550	109

* These figures pertain to the interval between the indicated quantity of output and 1 unit less than the indicated quantity of output.

Table 23.3

Profits of a Monopolist

Quantity	Total revenue	Total cost	Total profit
1	$100	$140	−$40
2	180	170	10
3	240	210	30
4	280	250	30
5	300	300	0
6	300	360	−60
7	280	450	−170
8	240	550	−310

Table 23.4

Marginal Cost and Marginal Revenue of a Monopolist

Quantity	Marginal cost*	Marginal revenue*	Total profit
1	$ 40	—	−$40
2	30	$80	10
3	40	60	30
4	40	40	30
5	50	20	0
6	60	0	−60
7	90	−20	−170
8	100	−40	−310

* These figures pertain to the interval between the indicated quantity of output and one unit less than the indicated quantity of output.

greatest. For example, if the firm's costs are as shown in Table 23.2 and if the demand curve it faces is as shown in Table 23.1, the firm will choose an output of either 3 or 4 units per period of time and a price of $80 or $70. This is evident from Table 23.3, which shows the firm's total profit at each output rate. Figure 23.7 on the next page shows the same thing graphically.

In Chapter 22, we set forth the Golden Rule of Output Determination for a perfectly competitive firm. We can now formulate a Golden Rule of Output Determination for a monopolist: *set the output rate at the point where marginal revenue equals marginal cost.* Table 23.4 and Figure 23.8 show that this rule results in a maximum profit in this example. It is easy to prove that this is generally a necessary condition for profit maximization. At any output rate at which marginal revenue exceeds marginal cost, profit can be increased by increasing output, since the extra revenue will exceed the extra cost. At any output rate at which marginal revenue is less than marginal cost, profit can be increased by reducing output, since the decrease in cost will exceed the decrease in revenue. Thus, since profit will not be a maximum when marginal revenue exceeds marginal cost or falls short of marginal cost, it must be a maximum only when marginal revenue equals marginal cost.

Figure 23.7
Total Revenue, Cost, and Profit of Monopolist

The output rate that will maximize the firm's profits is either 3 or 4 units per period of time.

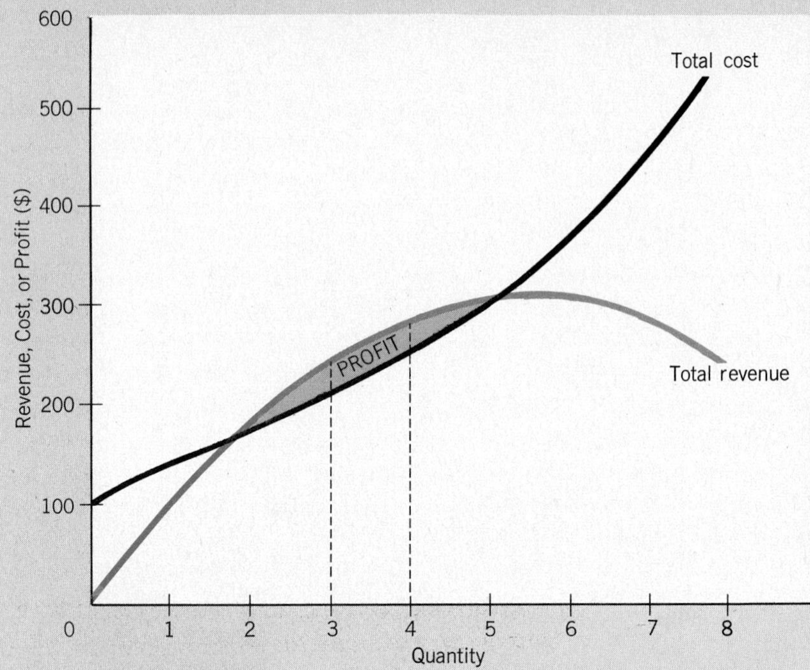

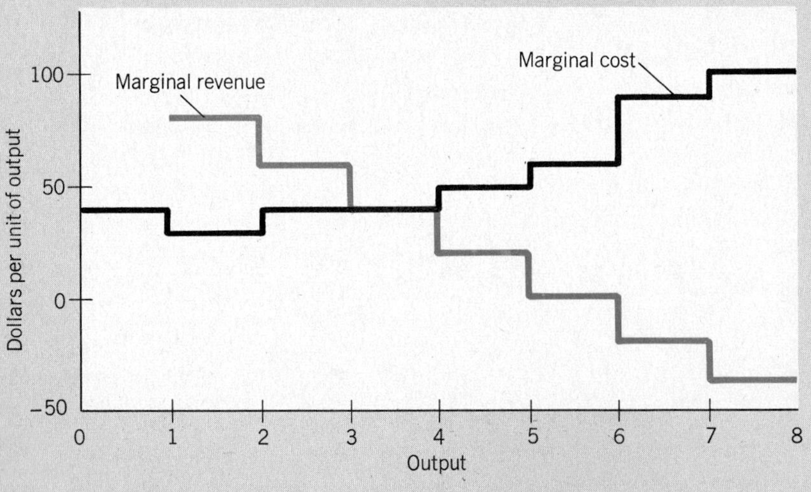

Figure 23.8
Marginal Cost and Marginal Revenue of Monopolist

At the profit-maximizing output rate of 3 or 4 units per period of time, marginal cost equals marginal revenue.

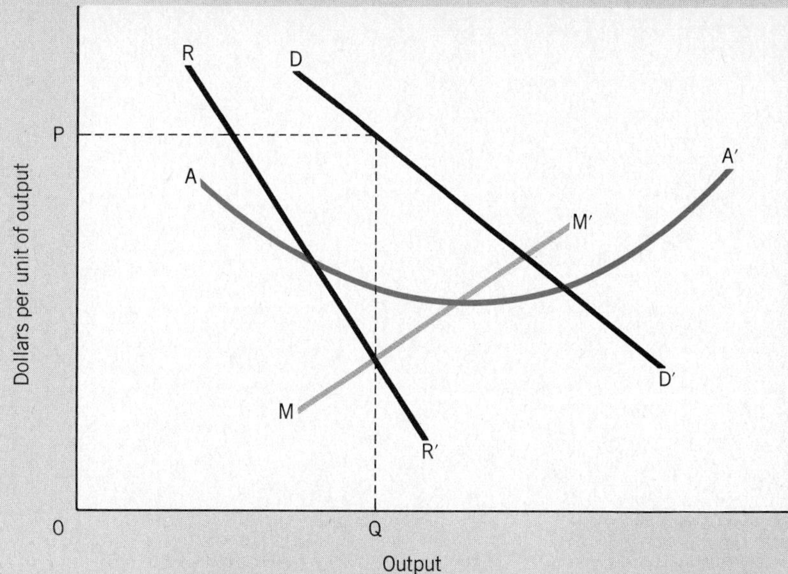

Figure 23.9
Equilibrium Position of Monopolist

The monopolist sets its output rate at *OQ*, where the marginal revenue curve *RR′* intersects the marginal cost curve *MM′*. At this output, price must be *OP*.

Figure 23.9 shows the equilibrium position of a monopolist in the short run, *DD′* being the demand curve for its product, *AA′* the firm's short-run average cost curve, and *MM′* the firm's short-run marginal cost curve. *RR′* is the marginal revenue curve—the curve that shows the firm's marginal revenue at each output level. Short-run equilibrium will occur at the output, *OQ*, where the *MM′* curve intersects the *RR′* curve. And if the monopolist is to sell *OQ* units per period of time, the demand curve shows that it must set a price of *OP*. Thus the equilibrium output and price are *OQ* and *OP*, respectively. It is interesting to compare the Golden Rule of Output Determination for a monopolist (Set the output rate at the point where marginal revenue equals marginal cost) with that for a perfectly competitive firm (Set the output rate at the point where price equals marginal cost). The latter is really the same as the former because, for a perfectly competitive firm, price equals marginal revenue. Since the perfectly competitive firm can sell all it wants at the market price, each additional unit sold increases the firm's total revenue by the amount of the price.

Thus, *for both the monopolist and the perfectly competitive firm, profits are maximized by setting the output rate at the point where marginal revenue equals marginal cost.* Also, harking back to the previous chapter, we know that perfectly competitive firms sometimes find it preferable to shut down rather than follow this rule; is this true for a monopolist as well? The answer is yes. *Just as a perfectly competitive firm will discontinue production if it will lose more money by producing than by shutting down, so a monopolist will do the same thing, and for the same reasons.* In other words, if there is no output such that price exceeds average variable costs, the monopolist, like a perfect competitor, will discontinue production. Certainly this makes sense. If by producing, the monopolist incurs greater losses than his fixed costs, he will "drop out," i.e., produce nothing.

Finally, note two misconceptions concerning monopoly behavior. First, it is sometimes said that a monopolist will charge "as high a price as he can get." Clearly, this is nonsense. For example, the monopolist in Table 23.1 could charge a higher price than $70 or $80, but to do so would be foolish since it would result in lower profits. Second, it is sometimes said that a monopolist will seek to maximize his profit per unit of output. This too is nonsense, since the monopolist is interested in his total profits and his return on capital, not on the profit per unit of output. A rational monopolist will not sacrifice his total profits to increase his profit per unit of output.

Price and Output under Monopoly: The Long Run

In contrast to the situation of perfect competition, the long-run equilibrium of a monopolistic industry may not be marked by the absence of economic profits. If a monopolist earns a short-run economic profit, he will not be confronted in the long run with competitors, unless the industry ceases to be a monopoly. The entrance of additional firms into the industry is, of course, incompatible with the existence of monopoly. Thus the long-run equilibrium of an industry under monopoly may be characterized by economic profits.

On the other hand, if the monopolist incurs a short-run economic loss, he will be forced to look for other, more profitable uses for his resources. One possibility is that his existing plant is not optimal and that he can earn economic profits by appropriate alterations to its scale and characteristics. If so, he will make these alterations in the long run and remain in the industry. However, if there is no scale of plant that will enable him to avoid economic losses, he will leave the industry in the long run. It should be obvious that the mere fact of having a monopoly over the production of a certain commodity does not mean that the firm must be profitable. For example, a monopoly over the production of cut-glass spittoons would be unlikely to catapult a firm into financial glory—or even allow it to avoid losses.

To illustrate the long-run behavior of a monopolist, consider the prewar policy of the Aluminum Company of America (Alcoa). Until after World War II, Alcoa was virtually the sole producer of aluminum in the United States. According to various observers, Alcoa recognized the dangers involved in potential competition, and adopted a policy of keeping its price low enough to ward off potential entrants. Naturally, it wanted to make money—and it did. But it was smart enough to see that, if it charged very high prices, it might encourage other firms to enter the aluminum industry. So it set a price high enough to permit it to make plenty of economic profits, but not so high that it would have to wrestle with competitors. Some other firms with monopoly power think the same way and act accordingly, but by no means all are so clever. On the contrary, some monopolists, like some newlyweds, think the status quo will last forever. And just as for newlyweds, sometimes it does, but sometimes it doesn't.

Perfect Competition and Monopoly: A Comparison

At the beginning of this chapter, we said that a market's structure would be likely to affect the behavior of the market; in other words, that a market's structure would influence how much was produced and the price that would be set. If we could perform an experiment in which an industry was first operated under conditions of perfect competition and then under conditions of monopoly (assuming that the demand for the industry's product and the industry's cost functions would be the same in either case[9]), we would find that the equilibrium price and output would differ under the two sets of conditions.

Specifically, if the product demand curve and the industry's cost functions are the same, *the output of a perfectly competitive industry tends to*

[9] However, the cost and demand curves need not be the same. For example, the monopolist may spend money on advertising, thus shifting the demand curve. It should be recognized that the assumption that they are the same is stronger than it appears at first glance.

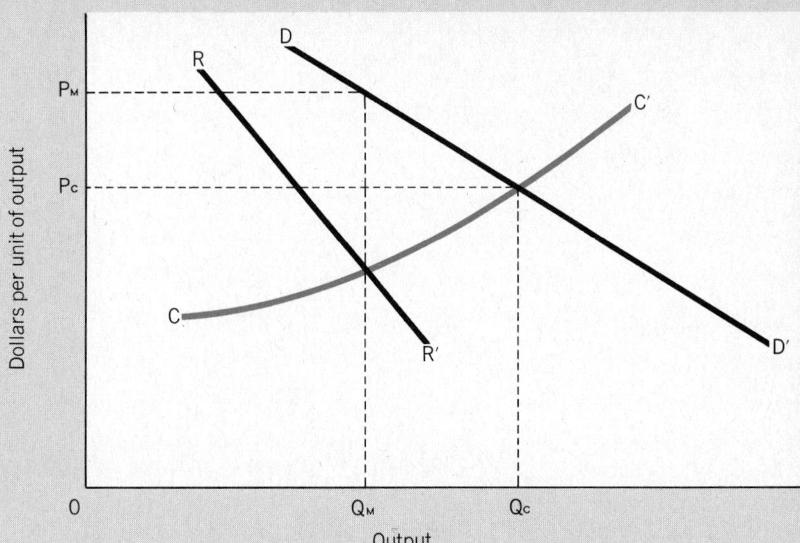

Figure 23.10
Comparison of Long-Run Equilibria: Perfect Competition and Monopoly

Under perfect competition, OQ_C is the industry output and OP_C is the price. Under monopoly, OQ_M is the industry output and OP_M is the price. Clearly, output is higher and price is lower under perfect competition than under monopoly.

be greater and the price tends to be lower than under monopoly. We see this in Figure 23.10, which shows DD', the industry's demand curve, and CC', the horizontal sum of the marginal cost curves of the perfectly competitive firms. If the industry is perfectly competitive, CC' is the industry supply curve. Since price and output under perfect competition are given by the intersection of the demand and supply curves, OQ_C is the industry output and OP_C is the price. But what if all of the competitive firms are bought up by a single firm, which operates as a pure monopolist? Under these conditions, CC' is the monopolist's marginal cost curve,[10] and DD' is the demand curve he faces. Moreover, RR' is his marginal revenue curve. Since the monopolist chooses the output where marginal cost equals marginal revenue, the industry output will be OQ_M and the price will be OP_M. Clearly, OQ_M is less than OQ_C, and OP_M is greater than OP_C—which is what we set out to prove.

[10] The monopolist will operate the various plants that would be independent under perfect competition as branches of a single firm. It can be shown that the marginal cost curve of a multiplant monopoly is the horizontal sum of the marginal cost curves of the individual plants.

Of course, all this is theory. But there is plenty of evidence that monopolists restrict output and charge higher prices than under competition. For example, take the case of tungsten carbide, which sold for $50 per pound until a monopoly was established in 1927 by General Electric. Then the price went to between $225 and $453 per pound, until the monopoly was broken by the antitrust laws in 1945. The price then dropped back to between $27 and $45 per pound.[11] This case was extreme, but by no means unique. Indeed, for centuries people have observed that when monopolies are formed, output tends to be restricted, and price tends to be driven up.

Moreover, it has long been felt that the allocation of resources under perfect competition is socially more desirable than under monopoly. In other words, society would be better off if more resources were devoted to producing the good in Figure 23.10, and if the competitive, not the monopolistic, output were produced. For example, in the *Wealth of Nations*, published about 200 years ago, Adam Smith stressed that when com-

[11] W. Adams, *op. cit.*, p. 537.

petitive forces are thwarted by "the great engine . . . of monopoly," the tendency for resources to be used "as nearly as possible in the proportion which is most agreeable to the interest of the whole society" is thwarted as well.

Why is the allocation of resources under perfect competition more socially desirable than that under monopoly? This is not a simple question, and like most such questions can be answered at various levels of sophistication. At the most basic level, most economists believe that resource allocation under perfect competition is preferable to that under monopoly because under perfect competition, consumers as a whole can attain a higher level of satisfaction than under monopoly. Why? Because firms under perfect competition are induced to produce quantities of goods that are more in line with consumer desires, and because firms under perfect competition are induced to use the least costly methods of production. In Chapter 25, we shall demonstrate that these things are true—and provide a much more complete discussion of the pros and cons of monopoly and competition.

Public Regulation of Monopoly

One way that society has attempted to reduce the harmful effects of monopoly is through ***public regulation.*** For example, suppose that the long-run cost curve in a particular industry is such that competition is not feasible. In such a case, society may permit a monopoly to be established, but a commission or some other public body is also established to regulate the monopoly's behavior. Among the many such regulatory commissions in the United States are the Federal Power Commission, the Federal Communications Commission, and the Interstate Commerce Commission. They regulate the behavior of firms with monopoly power in the electric power, telephone, transportation, and other industries. These industries are big as well as important, taking in about 8 percent of the national income. Thus, we need to know how these commissions operate and make decisions on prices and other matters.

Regulatory commissions often set the price—or the maximum price—at the level at which it equals average total cost, including a "fair" rate of return on the firm's investment. For example, in Figure 23.11, the price would be established by the commission at *OP*, where the demand curve, *DD′*, intersects the average total cost curve, *AA′*, the latter including what the commission regards as a fair profit per unit of output. Needless to say, there has been considerable controversy over what constitutes a fair rate of return. Generally, commissions have settled on 6 to 8 percent. In addition, there has been a good deal of controversy over what should be included in the company's "investment" on which the fair rate of return is to be earned. A company's assets can be valued at ***historical cost*** or at ***reproduction cost***—at what the company paid for them or at what it would cost to replace them. If the price level does not change much, these two approaches yield much the same answer. But if prices are rising—as they have been during most of the past 40 years—replacement cost will be greater than historical cost, with the result that the company will be allowed higher profits and rates if replacement cost is used. Most commissions now use historical cost.

To illustrate the public regulation of monopoly, consider the electric power industry in the United States. From its inception, the industry has been regulated, but this regulation has taken various forms. In the latter part of the nineteenth century, local governments issued franchises to attract power companies to their areas. As time went on, these franchises attempted to introduce more control over the companies, but city officials were often inexpert and corruption was frequent. At the turn of the century, there was a widespread cry for reform. Shortly before World War I, most of the states set up public utility commissions with the power to set rates and regulate service, the idea being to transfer control from the local governments to expert commissions. Most public utility regulation is in the hands of state commissions today.

Figure 23.11
Regulation of Monopoly

The price established by a commission might be *OP*, where the demand curve *DD′* intersects the average total cost curve *AA′*. Costs here include what the commission regards as a "fair" profit per unit of output.

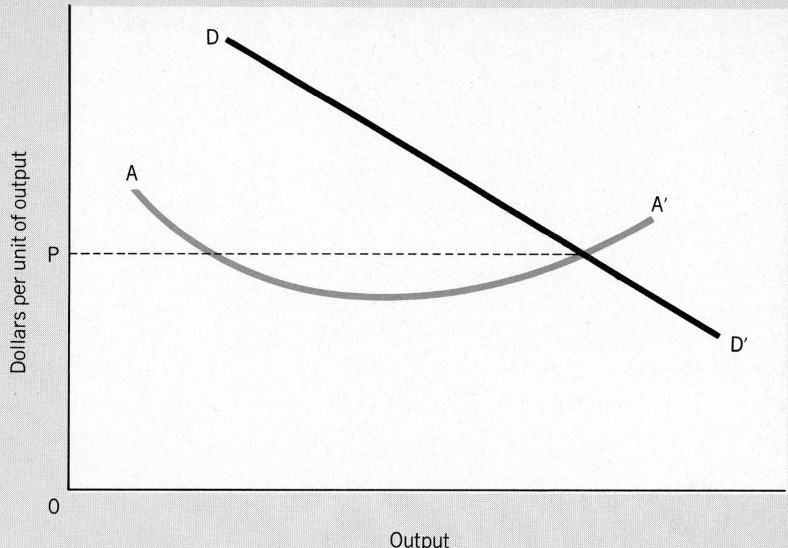

The federal government also has played an important role in regulating the electric power industry since 1935, when the Federal Power Commission (established in 1920) was given power over rates and service in interstate commerce. Also, the FPC was given considerable power over accounting and security issues in the wake of the financial problems of the 1920s and the relative impotence of the state commissions in handling them. Although state commissions still have the principal responsibility for regulating electric power companies, the FPC has introduced many important new policies and methods. For example, it has been stricter in various areas of accounting. Indeed, some firms have tried to get out from under federal regulations by getting rid of their interstate connections. Although conflicts have arisen between the FPC and the state commissions, the FPC's orders generally supplement, rather than override, those of the state commissions.[12]

The regulatory commissions and the principles they use have become extremely controversial. Many observers feel that the commissions are lax, and that they tend to be captured by the industries they are supposed to regulate. For these and other reasons, some economists believe that regulation has little effect on prices. For example, George Stigler and Claire Friedland of the University of Chicago found that the level of electricity prices in a state does not seem to be affected by whether or not the state has a regulatory commission.[13] Moreover, it is frequently charged that the regulated industries have too little incentive to cut costs and to develop and accept innovations, and that they tend to favor uneconomical techniques because of the way prices are regulated. It is extremely difficult to measure the effects of regulation, and equally difficult to specify reasonable alternatives to existing practices that are both politically feasible and likely to be a substantial improvement. The odds are that this problem will remain with us for many years to come.

[12] Weiss, *op. cit.,* pp. 96–98.

[13] G. Stigler and C. Friedland, "What Can Regulators Regulate? The Case of Electricity," *The Journal of Law and Economics,* 1962.

Natural Gas: A Case Study

One of the most interesting and important illustrations of the controversies swirling around the regulatory process is the case of natural gas. The regulation of natural gas prices has been quite unlike regulation in other areas. Only recently has the Federal Power Commission been required to set prices of gas producers in sales to pipelines. Before 1954, there was no such regulation. But in that year, the Supreme Court found that the Federal Power Commission should determine whether prices of gas sold in interstate commerce were "reasonable." Since then, there has been continual controversy over whether such regulation is really necessary or desirable, and if so, over what form it should take.

The Supreme Court ruled that the price of natural gas should be regulated because it felt that the price was not determined under competitive conditions. It believed that the producers of natural gas had appreciable monopoly power. However, this belief was not shared by many observers, including a number of distinguished academic economists. For example, Morris Adelman of Massachusetts Institute of Technology testified that "it is my conclusion that the production of natural gas is a competitive industry." In support of this conclusion, one can point to the fact that the industry contains thousands of producers and that there is relatively little concentration of employment or sales. Nonetheless, other eminent economists argued that the industry did contain serious monopolistic elements, and the court seemed to agree.

In response to its new responsibility, the Federal Power Commission established "area prices" for each of 23 natural gas producing regions of the United States. Any producer of gas was allowed to agree to a contract for a price less than or equal to the "area price" for his region. If he wanted a higher price, he had to prove its "necessity and convenience" to the commission. According to many observers, the commission set these "area prices" in such a way as to keep the price of natural gas artificially low. In other words, the commission has been accused of "freezing" the price at less than its equilibrium level. At first glance, this may seem to be a boon to the nation and the consumer. After all, who can be against low prices? But the truth is that a price that is too low can be just as bad for society as one that is too high.

To see what is wrong with a price that is too low, we must hark back to our discussion of how the price system works. Recall that a product's price influences how much of it firms will supply. Clearly, if the price set by the commission is lower than would be the case in a competitive market, firms will supply less natural gas in the long run than they would under competition. That is, they will invest fewer resources in exploring for natural gas, with the result that there may be a "shortage" of natural gas, in the sense that the quantity supplied may be less than the quantity demanded. According to some observers, such a shortage is one reason for the so-called energy crisis in this country in recent years. In 1973, the Commission approved much higher prices for natural gas. Nonetheless, the controversy continues over the adequacy of the prices set by the commission and the need for regulation in this industry. Only time will tell whether the natural gas industry will continue to be regulated in this way.[14]

Summary

Economists generally classify markets into four types: perfect competition, monopoly, monopolistic competition, and oligopoly. Perfect competition requires that the product of any seller be the same as the product of any other seller, that no buyer or seller be able to influence the price of the product, and that resources be able to switch readily from one use to another. Price and output under perfect competition are determined by the intersection of

[14] For a more complete discussion, see P. MacAvoy, *The Crisis of the Regulatory Commissions,* New York: Norton, 1970. In Chapter 29, we discuss the use of marginal-cost pricing by regulated industries.

the market supply and demand curves. In the market period, supply is fixed; thus price, which is determined by demand alone, plays the role of the allocating device. In the short run, price influences as well as rations the amount supplied.

In the long run, equilibrium is achieved under perfect competition when enough firms—no more, no less—are in the industry so that economic profits are eliminated. In other words, the long-run equilibrium position of the firm is at the point where its long-run average cost equals price. But since price must also equal marginal cost (to maximize profit), it follows that the firm must be operating at the minimum point on the long-run average cost curve. Perfectly competitive industries can be categorized into three types: constant cost industries (horizontal long-run supply curves), increasing cost industries (upward-sloping long-run supply curves), and decreasing cost industries (downward-sloping long-run supply curves). Finally, we described in some detail how perfectly competitive industries go about shifting resources in accord with changes in consumer demand.

A pure monopoly is a market with one, and only one, seller. Monopolies may occur because of patents, control over basic inputs, and government action, as well as because of decreasing average costs up to the point where the market is satisfied. If average costs reach their minimum at an output rate large enough to satisfy the entire market, perfect competition cannot be maintained; and the public often insists that the industry (a natural monopoly) be regulated by the government. Since the monopolist is the only seller of the product, the demand curve facing the monopolist is the market demand curve, which slopes downward (rather than being horizontal as in perfect competition). The unregulated monopolist will maximize profit by choosing the output where marginal cost equals marginal revenue, marginal revenue being defined as the addition to total revenue attributable to the addition of one unit to sales. This rule for output determination also holds under perfect competition, since price equals marginal revenue under perfect competition. However, if the monopolist cannot prevent losses from exceeding fixed costs, he, like a perfect competitor, will discontinue production. In contrast to the case in perfect competition, the long-run equilibrium of a monopolistic industry may not be marked by the absence of economic profits.

The output of a perfectly competitive industry tends to be greater and the price tends to be lower than under monopoly. Under various circumstances, it can be shown that society would be better off if more resources were devoted to the production of the good than under monopoly, the competitive output being best. One way that society has attempted to reduce the harmful effects of monopoly is through public regulation. Commissions often set price at the level at which it equals average total cost, including a "fair" rate of return on the firm's investment. To illustrate the public regulation of monopoly, we described briefly the history of electric power regulation in the United States, and discussed some of the issues regarding the regulation of the natural gas industry. There is a great deal of controversy over current practices of the regulatory commissions; many economists view them as lax and ineffectual.

CONCEPTS FOR REVIEW

Monopoly	**Market period**	**Patents**
Perfect competition	**Constant cost industry**	**Historical cost**
Monopolistic competition	**Increasing cost industry**	**Reproduction cost**
Oligopoly	**Natural monopoly**	**Economic profit**
		Marginal revenue

QUESTIONS FOR DISCUSSION AND REVIEW

1. Compare the long-run equilibrium of a perfectly competitive industry with that which would occur if all the firms were to be merged into a single monopolistic firm. Is there any reason for society to prefer one equilibrium over the other?

2. According to the 1970 annual report of the Council of Economic Advisers, "The American experience with regulation, despite notable achievements, has had its disappointing aspects." What are some of these disappointing aspects? How might they be improved?

3. If you were the president of a firm that had a monopoly on a certain product, would you choose an output level where demand for the product was price inelastic? Why or why not?

4. Perfect competition requires that each participant in the market be able to affect the product's price. True or False?

5. Under perfect competition equilibrium is achieved in the long run when there are enough firms so that "economic profits" are
a. negative. b. zero. c. positive but small. d. positive and sizable.

CHAPTER 24

Monopolistic Competition and Oligopoly

The industries encountered in the real world are seldom perfectly competitive or monopolistic. Although perfect competition and monopoly are very useful models that shed much valuable light on the behavior of markets, they are polar cases. Economists have developed other models that portray more realistically the behavior of many modern industries. The model of monopolistic competition, for example, helps to explain market behavior in such retail trades as gasoline stations and barber shops, while the model of oligopoly pertains to industries like steel, oil, and automobiles.

In this chapter, we examine how resources are allocated and prices are set under monopolistic competition and oligopoly. We also compare the behavior of monopolistically competitive and oligopolistic markets with the behavior of perfectly competitive and monopolistic markets. The results are of considerable significance, both because they give us a better understanding of how many markets work, and because they provide valuable information on the social desirability of monopolistic competition and oligopoly.

Monopolistic Competition and Oligopoly: Their Major Characteristics

A good way to begin studying monopolistic competition and oligopoly is to compare them with the market structures we have already encountered, perfect competition and monopoly. This we do in Table 24.1. According to this table, ***monopolistic competition*** *occurs where there are many sellers (as in perfect competition) but where there is product differentiation. In other words, the firms' products are not the same.* It does not matter whether the differences among products are real or imagined; what is important is that the consumer regards the products as different.

According to Table 24.1, ***oligopoly*** *occurs in markets where there are few sellers.* There are two types of oligopolies, one where all sellers produce an identical product, and one where the sellers produce somewhat different products. Examples of the first type—***pure oligopoly***—are the markets for steel, cement, tin cans, and petroleum. Examples of the second type—***differentiated oligopoly***—are the markets for automobiles and machinery. In contrast to the extremes of perfect competition and monopoly, monopolistic competition and oligopoly are intermediate cases that include an element of competition and an element of monopoly—an advantage from the point of view of realism.

Table 24.1

Types of Market Structure

Market structure	Number of producers	Product differentiation	Power over price	Marketing methods	Examples
1. Perfect competition	Many	None	None	Exchange or auction	Parts of agriculture are reasonably close
2. Monopolistic competition	Many	Considerable	Some	Advertising and product variation	Retail trade
3. Oligopoly	Few	Sometimes	Some	Advertising and product variation	Autos, steel, machinery
4. Monopoly	One	Unique product	Considerable	Institutional advertising	Public utilities

Monopolistic Competition

The key feature of monopolistic competition is ***product differentiation.*** In contrast to perfect competition, where all firms sell an identical product, firms under monopolistic competition sell somewhat different products. Each producer differentiates his product from that of the next producer. This, of course, is the case in many American markets. For example, in many parts of retail trade, each producer tries to make his product a little different, by altering the product's physical makeup, the services he offers, and other such variables. Other differences—which may be spurious—are based on brand name, "image" making, advertising claims, and so forth. In this way, each producer has some monopoly power, but it usually is small, because the products of other firms are very similar.

In perfect competition, the firms included in an industry are easy to determine because they all produce the same product. But if product differentiation exists, it is no longer easy to define an industry, since each firm produces a somewhat different product. Nevertheless, it may be useful to group together firms that produce similar products and call them a ***product group.*** For example, we can formulate a product group called "toothpaste" or "toilet soap" or "chocolate bars." Of course, the process by which we combine firms into product groups is bound to be somewhat arbitrary, since there is no way to decide how close a pair of substitutes must be to belong to the same product group. However, it is assumed that meaningful product groups can be established.

Besides product differentiation, other conditions must be met for an industry to qualify as a case of monopolistic competition. First, *there must be a large number of firms in the product group.* In other words, the product must be produced by perhaps 50 to 100 or more firms, with each firm's product a fairly close substitute for the products of the other firms in the product group. Second, *the number of firms in the product group must be large enough so that each firm expects its actions to go unheeded by its rivals and is unimpeded by possible retaliatory moves on their part.* If there is a large number of firms, this condition will normally be met. Third, *entry into the product group must be relatively easy, and there must be no collusion, such as price fixing or market sharing, among firms in the product group.* Of course, if there are a large number of firms, collusion generally is difficult, if not impossible.

Price and Output under Monopolistic Competition

Under monopolistic competition, what determines how much output a firm will produce, and what price it will charge? If each firm produces a somewhat different product, it follows that the demand curve facing each firm slopes downward to the right. That is, if the firm raises its price slightly it will lose some, but by no means all, of its customers to other firms. And if it lowers its price slightly, it will gain some, but by no means all, of its competitors' customers. This, of course, is in contrast to perfect competition, where the demand curve facing each firm is horizontal.

Figure 24.1 shows the short-run equilibrium of a monopolistically competitive firm. Its demand curve is DD', its marginal revenue curve is RR', its short-run marginal cost curve is MM', and its short-run average total cost curve is AA'. Given this demand curve and these cost curves, the firm in the short run will set its price at OP_0 and its output rate at OQ_0, since this combination of price and output will maximize its profits. We can be sure that this combination of price and output maximizes profit because marginal cost equals marginal revenue at this output rate. Economic profits will be earned because price, OP_0, exceeds average total costs, OC_0, at this output rate.

What will the equilibrium price and output be in the long run? Clearly, one condition for long-

Figure 24.1
Short-Run Equilibrium: Monopolistic Competition

The firm will set price at OP_o and its output rate at OQ_o since marginal cost, MM', equals marginal revenue, RR', at this output. It will earn a profit of C_oP_o per unit of output.

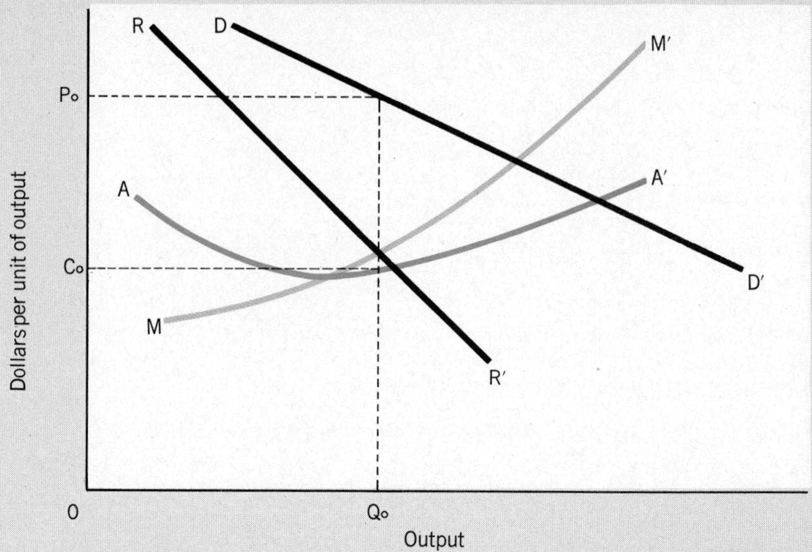

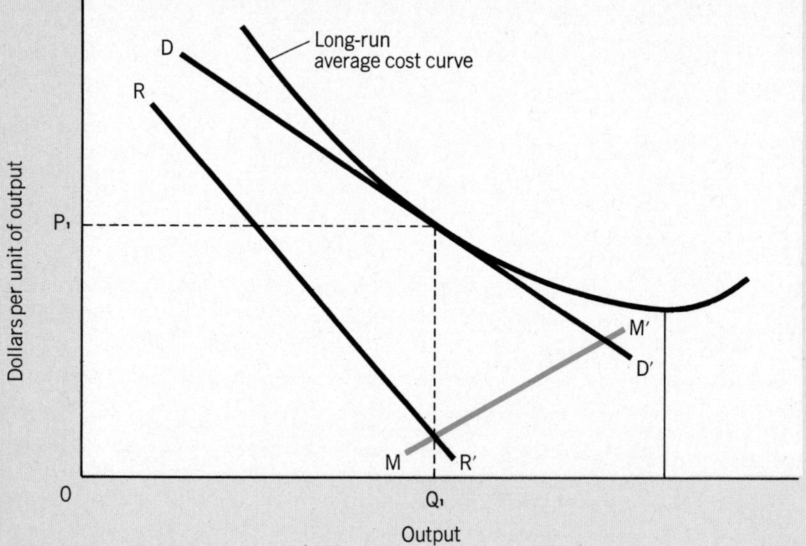

Figure 24.2
Long-Run Equilibrium: Monopolistic Competition

The long-run equilibrium is at a price of OP_1 and an output of OQ_1. There are zero profits since long-run average cost equals price. Profits are being maximized since marginal cost (MM') equals marginal revenue (RR') at this output.

run equilibrium is that each firm be making no economic profits or losses, since entry or exit of firms will occur otherwise—and entry and exit are incompatible with long-run equilibrium. Another condition for long-run equilibrium is, of course, that each firm be maximizing its profits. At what price and output will both these conditions be fulfilled? Figure 24.2 shows that the long-run equilibrium is at a price of OP_1 and an output of OQ_1. The zero-economic-profit condition is met at this combination of price and output since the firm's average cost at this output equals the price, OP_1. And the profit-maximization condition is met since the marginal revenue curve, RR', intersects the marginal cost curve, MM', at this output rate.

A famous conclusion of the theory of monopolistic competition is that a firm under this form of market organization will tend to operate with excess capacity. In other words, the firm will construct a plant smaller than the minimum-cost size of plant and operate it at less than the minimum-cost rate of output. Why? Because, as shown in Figure 24.2, the long-run average cost curve must be tangent in long-run equilibrium to the demand curve. Thus, since the demand curve is downward-sloping, the long-run average cost curve must also be downward-sloping at the long-run equilibrium output rate. Consequently, the firm's output must be less than OQ_2, the output rate at which long-run average costs are minimized, since the long-run average cost curve slopes downward only at output rates less than OQ_2.

This is a very important conclusion, since it suggests that monopolistically competitive industries will be over-crowded with firms. There will be too many firms (from society's point of view), each of which is smaller than required to minimize its unit costs. For this conclusion, as well as much of the entire theory of monopolistic competition, we are indebted to Edward Chamberlin of Harvard University, whose path-breaking book on the subject first appeared in 1933.[1]

[1] E. Chamberlin, *The Theory of Monopolistic Competition,* Cambridge: Harvard University Press, 1933.

Comparisons with Perfect Competition and Monopoly

Market structure is important because it influences market behavior. We need to know how the behavior of a monopolistically competitive industry differs from that of a perfectly competitive industry or a monopoly. For example, suppose that there exists a magician who can transform an industry's structure by a wave of his wand. (John D. Rockefeller was a real-life magician who transformed the structure of the oil industry in the late 1800s—but he seemed to favor mergers, mixed with some ungentlemanly tactics, over wands.) Suppose that the magician makes an industry monopolistically competitive, rather than perfectly competitive or monopolistic. What difference would it make in the behavior of the industry? Or, to take a less fanciful case, what difference would it make if government action or technological change resulted in such a change in an industry's market structure? Of course, it is difficult to say how the industry's behavior would be affected, because output would be heterogeneous in one case and homogeneous in the other, and its cost curves would probably vary with its organization. But many economists seem to believe that differences of the following kind can be expected.

First, *the firm under monopolistic competition is likely to produce less, and charge a higher price, than under perfect competition.* The demand curve confronting the monopolistic competitor slopes downward to the right. Consequently, as we saw in the previous chapter, marginal revenue must be less than price. Thus, under monopolistic competition, marginal cost must also be less than price, since marginal revenue must equal marginal cost at the firms' profit-maximizing output rate. But if marginal cost is less than price, the firm's output rate must be smaller—and the price higher—than if marginal cost equals price, which is the case under perfect competition. On the other hand, *relative to monopoly, monopolistically competitive firms are likely to have lower profits, greater output, and lower prices.* For example, the firms in a product group might obtain positive economic profits if they were to collude and behave as a monopolist. Of course, the increase in profits resulting from the monopoly would benefit the producers, but consumers would be worse off because of the higher prices and smaller output of goods.

Also, as noted in the previous section, *a firm under monopolistic competition may be somewhat inefficient because it tends to operate with excess capacity.* Each firm builds a smaller than minimum-cost plant and produces a smaller than minimum-cost output. More firms exist than if there were no excess capacity, resulting in some overcrowding of the industry. Of course, inefficiencies of this sort would not be expected under perfect competition. These inefficiencies may not be very great, since the demand curve confronting the monopolistically competitive firm is likely to be highly elastic; and the more elastic it is, the less excess capacity the firm will have. But many observers seem to believe that excess capacity of this sort is a serious problem in many important industries, including textiles.

Finally, *firms under monopolistic competition will, of course, offer a wider variety of styles, brands, and qualities than firms under perfect competition. Moreover, they will spend much more on advertising and other selling expenses than a perfectly competitive firm would.* Whether this diversity is worth its cost is hard to say. Some economists are impressed by the apparent waste in monopolistic competition. They think it results in too many firms, too many brands, too much selling effort, and too much spurious product differentiation. But if the differences among products are real and are understood by consumers, the greater variety of alternatives available under monopolistic competition may be very valuable to consumers. The proper evaluation of the social advantages and disadvantages of product differentiation is a problem economists have not solved.

Retailing: A Case Study[2]

To illustrate the case of monopolistic competition, consider retailing in the United States. An example of a retailer is, of course, Peter Amacher's drugstore, described in Chapter 4. Each retailer has a certain amount of monopoly power because his location, his product lines, his personality, and his salespeople are somewhat different from those of his competitors. In other words, his product is differentiated. But the extent and strength of his monopoly power is generally quite limited because he faces many competitors reasonably similar to himself in these respects. That is, lots of other firms sell products that are close substitutes for his own product. The goods carried by one drugstore, grocery store, or clothing shop are close substitutes for those carried by another drugstore, grocery store, or clothing shop. Moreover, entry into retail trade tends to be quite easy, as indicated by the fact that firms are continually entering various lines of retailing, and that the capital and skill required for entry are generally rather modest.

All in all, retailing seems to have many of the most important characteristics of monopolistic competition. Assuming that the retail industry can be approximated reasonably well by our model of monopolistic competition, we would expect that there would be some overcrowding of firms, that firms would try hard to differentiate their product through advertising and other selling expenses, and that long-run profits in the industry would tend to be low. Let us see to what extent these conditions do prevail.

There seems to be considerable evidence of overcrowding. More firms exist in retail trade than would be the case if each were operating at a point where unit costs were a minimum. But the extent of this excess capacity may not be very great, since the price elasticity of demand in retailing is normally very high—typically about 5.0, according to Leonard Weiss of the University of Wisconsin. Also, in accord with the model, firms in retail trade spend a great deal on various selling expenses, notably advertising. About ¼ of the total expendi-

[2] For a much more extensive discussion of retailing, see Leonard Weiss, *Case Studies in American Industry*, New York: Wiley, 1967.

ture on advertising in the United States is spent by retailers. Usually these ads are local and provide a valuable source of information on sales and specials in a particular neighborhood. (It is the exceptional person who does not spend some part of each week scanning the retail ads in a local newspaper.) Retail stores spend a lot on other selling expenses too—attractive decor, free parking, trading stamps, clerks to hover over the customer, and so forth. These expenses add to the prices they charge for the products they carry.

The level of profits in retail trade also accords with what theory would lead us to expect: it is low. Except for a few years right after World War II (when there was a relative scarcity of retail outlets), profits seem to have been consistently lower in retailing than in manufacturing. Moreover, this can hardly be attributed to less risk in retailing than in manufacturing, since retailing's bankruptcy rate has been exceptionally high—much higher than in other parts of the nonfarm economy. The facts seem to correspond quite well with the theory's prediction of no economic profits in the industry.[3]

Oligopoly

Oligopoly (domination by a few firms) is a common and important market structure in the United States; many industries, like steel, automobiles, oil, and electrical equipment, are oligopolistic. An example of an oligopolist is General Motors, described in Chapter 7. The key characteristic of oligopoly is interdependence, actual and perceived, among firms. Each oligopolist formulates his policies with an eye to their effect on his rivals. Since an oligopoly contains a small number of firms, any change in one firm's price or output influences the sales and profits of its competitors. Moreover, since there are only a few firms, each must recognize that changes in its own policies are likely to result in changes in the policies of its rivals as well.

What factors are responsible for oligopoly? First, in some industries, low production costs cannot be achieved unless a firm is producing an output equal to a substantial proportion of the total available market, with the consequence that the number of firms will tend to be rather small. Second, there may be economies of scale in sales promotion in certain industries, and this too may promote oligopoly. Third, entry into some industries may be blocked by the requirement that a firm build and maintain a large, complicated, and expensive plant, or have access to patents or scarce raw materials. Only a few firms may be in a position to obtain all these necessary prerequisites for membership in the club.

The automobile industry is a good example of the impact of economies of scale in production. According to studies made by Joe Bain of the University of California, an automobile plant of minimum efficient size can provide almost 10 percent of the total national market.[4] Thus, it simply is not economical to have a great many automobile firms. It might be possible to have a dozen automobile firms rather than the four we currently have without sacrificing productive efficiency, but because of economies of scale, it would not be feasible to have 50 or 100.

The automobile industry is also a good example of economies of scale in sales promotion. To be effective, advertising must often be carried out on a large scale, the result being that the advertising cost per unit of output decreases with increases in output, at least up to some point. For example, according to Leonard Weiss of the University of Wisconsin, General Motors and Ford each spent about $27 on advertising per car sold during 1954–57, whereas the smaller companies—Chrysler, Studebaker-Packard, and American Motors—spent about $50 or more per car sold. Also, car buyers

[3] Before leaving the subject of monopolistic competition, it should be recognized that Professor Chamberlin's theory has been subjected to considerable criticism. For example, the definition of the product group is ambiguous. See G. Stigler, *Five Lectures on Economic Problems,* London: Longmans Green, 1949.

[4] J. Bain, *Barriers to New Competition,* Cambridge: Harvard University Press, 1956.

like to deal with firms with a large, dependable dealer network. Since it takes a lot of money to establish such a network, and since the better dealers are attracted by the more popular brands, the smaller automobile manufacturers are at a substantial disadvantage.

In addition, the automobile industry offers a good example of barriers to entry due to large financial requirements. An automobile plant of minimum efficient size costs about $500 million to build and put into operation. This is an enormous amount of money, beyond the reach of practically all individuals. It takes the help of major financial interests and financial institutions to break into the automobile business. Since World War II, no new firms have obtained a foothold in the American automobile industry.

The availability of raw materials can also be a barrier to entry. Such is the case in the steel industry, where a few big firms have most of the available iron ore, partly through foresight and partly because they were the only organizations that could afford to spend the vast sums required to obtain the ore. Also, patents can be a very big barrier to entry. The electric light industry is a famous example: General Electric was able to dominate the industry from 1892 to 1930 through the acquisition of the basic Edison patents and then the acquisition of patents on the various improvements.[5]

Mergers and Oligopoly

Mergers between firms often contribute to the movement toward oligopoly in particular industries. There have been three major waves of mergers in the American economy. The first occurred between 1887 and 1904, the second between 1916 and 1929, and the third after World War II. The first wave in 1887–1904 saw the formation of such giants as United States Steel and John D. Rockefeller's Standard Oil. The mergers in this period tended to be ***horizontal;*** that is, among firms producing essentially the same product. Such was the case with U. S. Steel, formed in 1901 from a combination of about 785 plants. During the second wave of mergers in 1916–29, the emphasis was more on ***vertical mergers*** (mergers among firms at various stages in the production process) and ***conglomerate mergers*** (mergers among firms producing entirely different products). During the third wave of mergers in the 25 years following World War II, a very large number of firms were absorbed and assimilated by others. Of the 1,000 largest manufacturing firms in existence at the end of 1950, 216 had disappeared by merger by 1963.

There are a host of reasons why firms merge. Sometimes they do it to reduce competition. For example, Thomas Edison was forthright when he said in 1892 about the formation of General Electric: "The consolidation of the companies . . . will do away with a competition which has become so sharp that the product of the factories has been worth little more than ordinary hardware."[6] Other mergers are made so that promoters can earn profits from corporate marriages. In still other cases, mergers occur because firms need the people or ideas other firms have, or because the owners want to sell out, or because there appear to be beneficial synergetic effects arising from complementary resources owned by the merging firms.

Whatever the reasons, many oligopolies have been created by a series of mergers. For example, consider U. S. Steel, which, as we have seen, was formed by combining about 785 plants. Just before the turn of the century, a large number of mergers resulted in the consolidation of more than 200 iron and steel firms into 20 much bigger firms. Then J. P. Morgan, the famous financier, organized the merger of 12 of these bigger firms into U. S. Steel —and received about $62 million in promotional profits for his labor. Or consider the electrical equipment industry. In 1892, General Electric

[5] F. M. Scherer, *Industrial Market Structure and Economic Performance,* Skokie, Ill.: Rand McNally, 1970, pp. 391–2.

[6] Ibid., p. 113.

was formed through the merger of Edison General Electric (itself a product of a number of mergers) and Thomson-Houston (it too the product of numerous mergers).

Oligopoly Behavior and the Stability of Prices

Unlike perfect competition, monopoly, and monopolistic competition, there is no single unified model of oligopoly behavior. Instead, there are a number of models, each based on a somewhat different set of assumptions concerning the relationships among the firms that make up the oligopoly. Basically, no single model exists because economists have not yet been able to devise one that would cover all the relevant cases adequately. Economics, like all sciences, continues to grow; perhaps someone—indeed, perhaps someone reading this book—may be able to develop such a model before too long. However, it doesn't exist now.

Let's start with a model that sheds light on the stability of oligopolistic prices. Empirical studies of pricing in oligopolistic markets have often concluded that prices in such markets tend to be rigid. A classic example occurred in the sulfur industry. From 1926 to 1938, the price of sulfur remained at $18 a ton, despite great shifts in demand and production costs.[7] This example is somewhat extreme, but it illustrates the basic point: prices in oligopolistic industries commonly remain unchanged for fairly long periods. A well-known model designed to explain this price rigidity was advanced by Paul Sweezy, who asserted that, if an oligopolist cuts his price, he can be pretty sure that his rivals will meet the reduction. On the other hand, if he increases his price, his rivals may not change theirs.

Figure 24.3 shows the situation. The oligopolist's demand curve is represented by *DAD′* and the current price is *OP*. There is a "kink" in the demand curve because under the postulated circumstances the demand curve for the oligopolist's product is much less elastic for price decreases than for price increases. Because of the kink the marginal revenue curve is not continuous: it consists of two segments, *RX* and *YR′*. Given that the firm's marginal cost curve is *MM′*, the most profitable output is *OQ*, where the marginal cost curve intersects the vertical line, *XY*. Moreover, *OQ remains the most profitable output—and OP the most profitable price—even if the marginal cost curve shifts considerably (even to NN′ or GG′) or if the demand curve shifts (within limits).* One

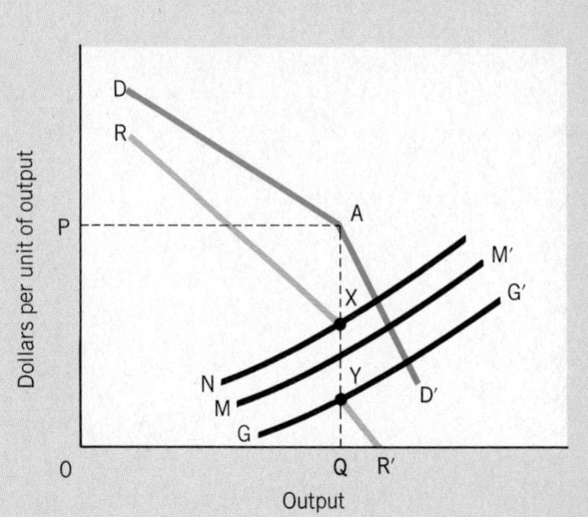

Figure 24.3
The Kinked Oligopoly Demand Curve

The oligopolist's demand curve is *DAD′*, the current price being *OP*. Because of the kink in the demand curve, the marginal revenue curve consists of two segments *RX* and *YR′*. Since the marginal cost curve is *MM′*, the most profitable output is *OQ*. Moreover, it remains the most profitable output—and *OP* the most profitable price—even if the marginal cost curve shifts to *NN′* or *GG′* or if the demand curve shifts considerably.

[7] Marshall Colberg, William Bradford, and Richard Alt, *Business Economics: Principles and Cases*, Homewood, Illinois: Richard D. Irwin, 1957, p. 276.

would expect price to be quite rigid under these circumstances, since many types of changes in cost and demand will not alter the price that maximizes profits.

This theory, although useful in explaining why price tends to remain at a certain level (*OP* in Figure 24.3), is of no use at all in explaining why this level, rather than another, currently prevails. It simply takes the current price as given; it does not explain why it is *OP* in Figure 24.3, for example. Thus, this theory is an incomplete model of oligopoly pricing. Nonetheless, it seems to square with many of the relevant facts. For this and other reasons, Sweezy's model certainly has a place in the theory of oligopoly.

The Theory of Games

Another useful model is one that stresses the gamelike characteristics of oligopoly. As in a game, in oligopoly each firm must take account of its rivals' reactions to its own actions. For this reason, an oligopolistic firm cannot tell what effect a change in its output will have on the price of its product and on its profits unless it can guess how its rivals will respond to the change. To understand game theory,[8] you have to know what a ***game*** is: a competitive situation where two or more persons pursue their own interests and no person can dictate the outcome. Poker is a game, and so is a situation in which two firms are engaged in competitive advertising campaigns. A game is described in terms of its players, rules, payoffs, and information conditions. These elements are common to all conflict situations.

More specifically, a ***player***, whether a single person or an organization, is a decision-making unit. Each player has a certain amount of resources, and the ***rules of the game*** describe how these resources can be used. For example, the rules of poker indicate how bets can be made and which hands are better than others. A ***strategy*** is a complete specification of what a player will do under each contingency in the playing of the game. For example, a corporation president might tell his subordinates how he wants an advertising campaign to start, and what should be done at subsequent times in response to various actions of competing firms. The game's outcome clearly depends on each player's strategies. A player's ***payoff*** varies from game to game: it is win, lose, or draw in checkers, and various sums of money in poker.

For simplicity we will restrict our attention to ***two-person games,*** i.e., those with only two players, and to ***zero-sum games,*** in which the amount one player wins exactly equals the amount the other player loses. The relevant features of a two-person, zero-sum game can be shown by constructing a ***payoff matrix.*** To illustrate, consider the case of two big soap producers, Procter and Gamble and Lever Brothers. Suppose that these two firms are about to stage rival advertising campaigns and that each firm has a choice of strategies. Procter and Gamble can choose to concentrate on either television ads or magazine ads; Lever Brothers has the same choice. Table 24.2 shows what will happen to the profits of each firm when each combination of strategies is chosen. For example, if both firms concentrate on TV ads, Procter and Gamble gains $3 million and Lever Brothers loses $3 million. If Procter and Gamble concentrates on TV ads and Lever Brothers concentrates on magazine ads, Procter and Gamble gains $2 million and Lever Brothers loses $2 million. And so on.

Given the payoff matrix in Table 24.2, there is a definite optimal choice for each firm. To see that this is the case, suppose that Procter and Gamble is allowed to select its strategy first and chooses to concentrate on magazine ads. Lever Brothers would respond by choosing to concentrate on TV ads to minimize its losses. Assuming that each firm knows the payoff matrix, this would therefore be a foolish move on Procter and Gamble's part. It

[8] One of the most interesting developments in the theory of oligopoly in the postwar period was the appearance of the classic volume, J. von Neumann and O. Morgenstern, *Theory of Games and Economic Behavior,* Princeton: Princeton University Press, 1944.

Table 24.2

Payoff Matrix

Possible strategies for Procter and Gamble	Possible strategies for Lever Brothers: Concentrate on TV	Concentrate on magazines	Row Minimum
	Gains for Procter and Gamble (= Losses for Lever Brothers)		
Concentrate on TV	$3 million	$2 million	$2 million
Concentrate on magazines	$1 million	$1.5 million	$1 million
Column maximum	$3 million	$2 million	

knows that, whatever strategy it chooses, Lever Brothers will choose its strategy so as to minimize its losses—and minimize Procter and Gamble's gains. Consequently, Procter and Gamble should focus its attention on the row minima (the lowest number in each row), and pick the strategy where the row minimum (shown in the last column in Table 24.2) is highest. Thus *Procter and Gamble, if it reasons this way, will choose the strategy of concentrating on TV ads,* since it provides Procter and Gamble with a greater gain than if it concentrates on magazine ads.

What strategy will Lever Brothers choose? Naturally, Lever Brothers will assume that, whatever strategy it picks, Procter and Gamble will respond by choosing the strategy that maximizes Procter and Gamble's profits. Thus, Lever Brothers, if it chooses a certain strategy, must bargain on incurring a loss equal to the greater of the two numbers in the column corresponding to this strategy. Consequently, Lever Brothers will choose the strategy where this loss (equal to the column maxima shown in Table 24.2) is as small as possible. Specifically, *Lever Brothers will choose the strategy of concentrating on magazine ads,* since it provides Lever Brothers with a smaller loss than if it concentrates on TV ads.

The solution of this game is quite simple. Procter and Gamble maximizes the row minima, Lever Brothers minimizes the column maxima. Procter and Gamble gains $2 million, Lever Brothers loses $2 million. By adopting these strategies, Procter and Gamble can guarantee itself a gain of this amount, and Lever Brothers can guarantee that its loss will not exceed this amount. Note that each firm is assumed to maximize its payoff under the assumption that its opponent will adopt the strategy most damaging to itself. Many economists feel that this is an unnecessarily pessimistic outlook for the firm, and wonder whether such an attitude is a realistic representation of how firms actually view competitive situations. The firm that adopts this viewpoint, while his competitor does not, is likely to forgo considerable profit. Despite this and other limitations, the theory of games is a useful addition to economic theory because it provides a suggestive framework for analysis. One can structure formerly intractable problems and think about them in terms of this theory. However, in its present state, game theory cannot be used to derive specific predictions of the behavior of oligopolists; the world is much more complicated than simple examples like this one.

Collusion and Cartels

Up to this point, we have assumed that oligopolists do not collude, but conditions in oligopolistic industries tend to promote collusion, since the number of firms is small and the firms recognize their interdependence. The advantages of collusion to the firms seem obvious: increased profits, decreased uncertainty, and a better opportunity to prevent entry. Not all collusion is disguised from the public or secret. In contrast to illicit collusion, a ***cartel*** is an open, formal collusive arrangement among firms. In many countries in Europe, cartels are common and legally acceptable. In the United States, most collusive arrangements, whether secret or open cartels, were declared illegal by the Sherman Antitrust Act, which was passed in 1890. However, this does not mean that such arrangements do not exist. For example, widespread collusion to fix prices occurred among American electrical equipment manufacturers during the 1950s, and when the collusion was uncovered a number of high executives were tried, convicted, and sent to jail. Moreover, collusion of this sort is not limited to a single country: some cartels, like that in quinine in the early 1960s, are international in scope.[9]

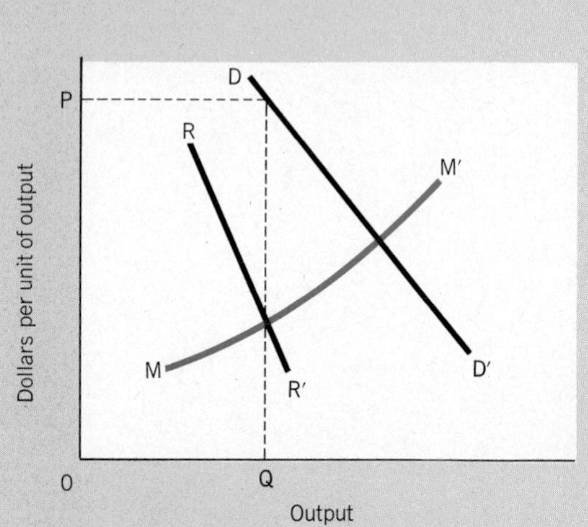

Figure 24.4
Price and Output of a Cartel

MM′ **is the horizontal sum of the marginal cost curves of the firms in the cartel. If** ***DD′*** **is the demand curve, and** ***RR′*** **is the marginal revenue curve, the output that maximizes the total profit of the cartel members is** ***OQ*****. The corresponding price is** ***OP*****.**

If a cartel is established to set a uniform price for a particular product, what price will it charge? As a first step, the cartel must estimate the marginal cost curve for the cartel as a whole. If input prices do not increase as the cartel expands its output, this marginal cost curve is the horizontal sum of the marginal cost curves of the individual firms. Suppose that the resulting marginal cost curve for the cartel is *MM′* in Figure 24.4. If the demand curve for the industry's product is *DD′*, the relevant marginal revenue curve is *RR′*, and the output that maximizes the total profit of the cartel members is *OQ*. Thus, if it maximizes cartel profits, the cartel will choose a price of *OP*, which, of course, is the monopoly price. In short, *the cartel acts like a monopolist with a number of plants or divisions, each of which is a member firm.*

How will the cartel allocate sales among the member firms? If its aim is to maximize cartel profits, it will allocate sales to firms in such a way that the marginal costs of all firms are equal. But this allocation is unlikely to occur in reality. The allocation process is a bargaining process, and firms with the most influence and the shrewdest negotiators are likely to receive the largest sales quotas, even though this decreases the total profits of the cartel. Moreover, high-cost firms are likely to receive larger sales quotas than would be the case if total cartel profits were maximized, since they would be unwilling otherwise to stay in the cartel. In practice, it appears that cartels often divide markets geographically or in accord with a firm's level of sales in the past.

To illustrate how firms collude, consider the electrical equipment manufacturers we mentioned

[9] See "Collusion among Electrical Equipment Manufacturers" and "Quinine: An International Cartel" in Edwin Mansfield, *Microeconomics: Selected Readings,* New York: Norton, 1971.

above. During the 1950s, there was widespread collusion among about 30 firms selling turbine generators, switchgear, transformers, and other products with total sales of about $1.5 billion per year. Representatives of these firms got together and agreed upon prices for many products. The available evidence indicates that both prices and profits tended to be increased by the collusive agreements—or at least until the firms were prosecuted under the antitrust laws by the Department of Justice. The following statement by F. M. Scherer of the International Institute of Management is a good description of some of the procedures used by these firms:

> Some of the most elaborate procedures were devised to handle switchgear pricing. As in the case of generators, book prices served as the initial departure point. Each seller agreed to quote book prices in sales to private buyers, and meetings were held regularly to compare calculations for forthcoming job quotations. Sealed-bid competitions sponsored by government agencies posed a different set of problems, and new methods were worked out to handle them. Through protracted negotiation, each seller was assigned a specified share of all sealed-bid business, e.g., General Electric's share of the high voltage switchgear field was set at 40.3 per cent in late 1958, and Allis-Chalmers' at 8.8 per cent. Participants then coordinated their bidding so that each firm was low bidder in just enough transactions to gain its predetermined share of the market. In the power switching equipment line, this was achieved for a while by dividing the United States into four quadrants, assigning four sellers to each quadrant, and letting the sellers in a quadrant rotate their bids. A "phases of the moon" system was used to allocate low-bidding privileges in the high voltage switchgear field, with a new seller assuming low-bidding priority every two weeks. The designated bidder subtracted a specified percentage margin from the book price to capture orders during its phase, while others added various margins to the book price. The result was an ostensibly random pattern of quotations, conveying the impression of independent pricing behavior.[10]

[10] F. M. Scherer, *op. cit.*, p. 160.

Barriers to Collusion

The fact that oligopoly often can lead to collusion is not new. Nor is it newly understood. Back in 1776, Adam Smith warned that "people of the same trade seldom meet together even for merriment and diversion, but the conversation ends in a conspiracy against the public, or in some contrivance to raise prices." However, it must be borne in mind that collusive arrangements are often difficult to accomplish and maintain for long. In particular, there are several important barriers to collusion. First, the antitrust laws forbid outright collusion and price fixing. Of course, this does not mean that firms do not break those laws; witness the electrical equipment manufacturers just described. But the antitrust laws are an important obstacle to collusion.

Second, collusion is often difficult to achieve and maintain because an oligopoly contains an unwieldy number of firms, or the product is quite heterogeneous, or the cost structures of the firms differ considerably. It is clear that a collusive agreement will be more difficult to achieve and maintain if there are a dozen oligopolists than if there are three or four. Moreover, if the products sold by the oligopolists differ substantially, it will probably be more difficult for them to find a common price strategy that will be acceptable to all. Similarly, if the firms' cost structures differ, it will be more difficult to get agreement, since the low-cost firms will be more inclined to cut price. For example, National Steel, after introducing low-cost continuous strip mills in the 1930s, became a price cutter in the steel industry.

Third, there is a constant temptation for oligopolists to cheat on any collusive agreement. If other firms stick to the agreement, any firm that cheats—by cutting its price below that agreed to under the collusive arrangement—can take a lot of business away from the other firms and increase its profits substantially, at least in the short run. This temptation is particularly great when an industry's sales are depressed and its profits are low. Every firm is hungry for business, and it is difficult to resist. Moreover, one firm may be driven to cheating because it hears that another firm is doing so, with the eventual result that the collusive agreement is torn apart.

To illustrate the problems of maintaining a collusive agreement, let's return to the electrical equipment manufacturers. As the *Wall Street Journal* summed it up, "One of the great ironies of the conspiracies was that no matter how hard the participants schemed, no matter how friendly their meetings and communications might be, there was an innate tendency to compete. Someone was always violating the agreements to get more business and this continually called for new illegal plans. For example, price-cutting in sales of power switching equipment to government agencies was getting out of hand in late 1958. This led to the 'quadrant' system of dividing markets [described in the previous section]." As one executive of General Electric complained, "No one was living up to the agreements and we . . . were being made suckers. On every job some one would cut our throat; we lost confidence in the group." Given that these agreements were illegal, it is remarkable that such a complaint was uttered with a straight face.

Price Leadership

In order to coordinate their behavior without outright collusion, some industries contain a ***price leader.*** It is quite common in oligopolistic industries for one or a few firms to set the price and for the rest to follow their lead. Two types of price leadership are the dominant-firm model and the barometric-firm model. The ***dominant-firm*** model applies to cases where the industry has a single large dominant firm and a number of small firms. The dominant firm sets the price for the industry, but it lets the small firms sell all they want at that price. The ***barometric-firm*** model applies to cases where one firm usually is the first to make changes in price that are generally accepted by other firms in the industry. The barometric firm may not be the largest, or most powerful, firm. Instead, it is a reasonably accurate interpreter of changes in basic cost and demand conditions in the industry as a whole.

In the past, the steel industry has been a good example of price leadership of the dominant-firm variety. The largest firm in the industry is U. S. Steel, which, as we know, was formed in 1901 by the merger of a number of companies. Judge Elbert Gary, the first chairman of the board of U. S. Steel, sought the cooperation of the smaller firms in the industry. He inaugurated a series of so-called "Gary dinners," attended by all the major steel producers, which made declarations of industry policy on pricing and other matters. Since any formal pricing agreements would have been illegal, they made no such agreements. But, generally speaking, U. S. Steel set the pricing pattern and other firms followed. Moreover, this relationship continued long after Judge Gary had gone to his reward. According to Walter Adams of Michigan State University, U. S. Steel typically set the pace, "and the other companies follow in lockstep—both in their sales to private customers and in their secret bids on government contracts."[11]

Illustrating the attitude of the other firms was the statement by the president of Bethlehem Steel to a congressional committee in 1939 that "in the main we . . . await the [price] schedules of the [U. S.] Steel Corporation." However, there was some secret price-cutting, particularly during depressions. On at least one occasion, U. S. Steel responded to such price-cutting by announcing publicly that it would meet any price reduction it heard of. In this way, it attempted to discourage under-the-counter price cutting. In more recent times, U. S. Steel no longer seems to be the price leader it once was. In 1962, it drew a great deal of criticism from President Kennedy for being the first steel firm to raise prices. Subsequently, smaller steel firms have often been the first. Indeed, in 1968 the world was treated to the amusing spectacle of Bethlehem announcing a price cut in order

[11] W. Adams, *The Structure of American Industry*, New York: Macmillan, 1961, p. 168.

to counter some secret price-cutting by the former price leader, U. S. Steel.[12]

Cost-Plus Pricing

There is one further model of oligopoly behavior to consider. According to studies of business behavior, ***cost-plus*** pricing is used by many oligopolists. It occurs in two steps. First, the firm estimates the cost per unit of output of the product. Since this cost will generally vary with the output rate, the firm must base this computation on some assumed output rate—often ⅔ or ¾ of the firm's capacity. Second, the firm adds a markup to the estimated average cost. This markup is meant to include certain costs that cannot be allocated to any specific product and to provide a return on the firm's investment. The size of the markup depends, of course, on the rate of profit the firm believes it can earn. Some firms, like General Electric and General Motors, have set a ***target rate-of-return*** figure they hope to earn, which determines the markup.

Unquestionably, many firms do compute prices on the basis of this sort of procedure. However, the cost-plus pricing model is incomplete unless it specifies more precisely what determines the size of the markup. Although firms may construct these markups to yield a certain target rate of return, the firms' profit-and-loss statements show that these markups do not prevail, since the firms' actual rates of return frequently vary considerably from the target rate of return. Moreover, to many economists this form of pricing seems naive, since it takes no account, explicitly at least, of the extent or elasticity of demand or of the size of marginal, rather than average, costs.

Consider General Motors, which has been using cost-plus pricing for over 40 years. General Motors starts by stating an objective of earning a profit of about 15 percent (after taxes) on total invested capital. Then it assumes that it will sell enough cars in the next year to operate at about 80 percent of its capacity; and on the basis of this assumption, it figures what its cost per car will be. Then it adds to this cost a markup big enough to produce the desired return on investment. The result is the so-called standard price. General Motors' high-echelon price policy committee takes this standard price as a first approximation, and makes small adjustments to reflect competitive conditions, long-run goals of the firm, and other things. Typically, these adjustments are quite small, and the actual price winds up close to the standard price.

Needless to say, there is no assurance that General Motors will earn the desired 15 percent of total invested capital. If it sells fewer cars than it needs to sell in order to operate at 80 percent of capacity, its unit costs will be higher than expected, and its profits—both total and per unit of output—will be less than expected. On the other hand, if it sells more cars than it needs to sell in order to operate at 80 percent of capacity, its profits will be higher than expected. In general, since World War II, General Motors has achieved sales levels that permitted it to operate at more than 80 percent of capacity, with the result that it has earned substantially more, on the average, than the target rate of 15 percent of invested capital.

Nonprice Competition

Oligopolists tend to compete more aggressively through advertising and product differentiation than through direct price reductions. In other words, when we observe the behavior of major oligopolies, we find that firms try hard to get business away from their rivals by outdoing them with better advertising campaigns and with improvements in the product; but it is less common for oligopolists to slug it out, toe to toe, with price reductions. This is an important characteristic of oligopoly. In contrast to the case of perfect competi-

[12] For a much more extensive discussion of the steel industry, see Weiss, *op. cit.*, Adams, *op. cit.*, and Scherer, *op. cit.*

tion, nonprice competition plays a central role in oligopoly. It is worthwhile, therefore, to note a few salient points about the advertising and product development strategies of oligopolists.

Advertising is a very big business: currently about $20 billion per year is spent on it in the United States. One important purpose of advertising is, of course, to convince the consumer that one firm's product is better than another's. In industries where there is less physical differentiation of the product, advertising expenditures often are larger than in industries where the product varies more. Thus, the cigarette, liquor, and soap industries spend over 10 percent of their gross revenues (excluding excise taxes) on advertising, whereas the automobile industry spends less than 1 percent of its gross revenues on advertising. The social desirability of much of this advertising is debatable, and much debated. While advertising can serve an important purpose by keeping the consumer better informed, some advertising is more misleading than informative. Unfortunately, it is difficult to make reliable estimates of the extent to which oligopolists may be overinvesting, from society's point of view, in advertising.

The development of new and improved products is also a very big business in the United States. Currently firms spend over $10 billion per year on research and development. In many industries, R and D is a central part of oligopolistic competition. For example, a spectacular case in the drug industry was the effect of American Cyanamid's Achromycin tetracycline, introduced in 1953, on sales of Aureomycin chlortetracycline, which had been marketed since late 1948. After an almost continuous upward trend in 1950–53, Aureomycin sales dropped by nearly 40 percent during the first full year of the sale of Achromycin. Hardly a typical case, this nonetheless illustrates how one firm can take sales away from its rivals through new product development.

It is important to add, however, that much of industry's R and D is aimed at fairly minor improvements in products and processes. Moreover, a good deal of the engineering efforts of many important industries is aimed largely at style changes, not basic improvements in the product. For example, the automobile industry spends an enormous amount to produce the model changes that are familiar to car buyers throughout the land. Specifically, according to three economists—Frank Fisher, Zvi Griliches, and Carl Kaysen—such model changes in the automobile industry cost about $5 billion per year during the late 1950s.[13] From society's point of view, it is not at all clear that such huge expenditures are justifiable.

Perhaps the main reason why oligopolists would rather compete through advertising and product differentiation than through price is that a firm's rivals can easily and quickly match a price reduction, whereas they may be unable to match a clever advertising campaign or an attractive product improvement. Thus, oligopolists tend to feel that they have a better chance of improving their long-run profits at the expense of their rivals in the arena of nonprice competition than in the arena of direct price competition.

The Automobile Industry: A Case Study

To see in more detail how oligopoly works, let's examine the automobile industry. Its history can be divided into three stages. First, there was the period of growth and experimentation, which lasted until about 1910. During this period, dozens of firms entered the automobile industry, and there was widespread experimentation with various kinds of car designs. No single firm dominated the market, which was growing by leaps and bounds. Second, there was the period from about 1911 to about 1918, during which a mass market for automobiles was developed, through the genius of Henry Ford, who developed the assembly-line technique of production that is commonplace today.

[13] F. Fisher, Z. Griliches, and C. Kaysen, "The Costs of Automobile Model Changes Since 1949," *Journal of Political Economy,* 1962.

Exploiting the great economies of scale associated with this production technique, Ford reduced costs substantially, and adopted a strategy of reducing the price to broaden the market, cutting the price of the Model T from $900 in 1909 to $290 in 1925. (Recall our discussion in Chapter 20.)

Following World War I, there began the third stage in the industry's history, during which the number of automobile firms declined and the industry became concentrated in the hands of a few firms. Firms other than the Big Three—General Motors, Ford, and Chrysler—found it difficult to stay alive, largely for lack of capital. Moreover, new firms were effectively barred from entering the industry by the substantial economies of scale (both for production and sales promotion) and large capital requirements described earlier. The result was a drastic decline in the number of firms, eventually producing the present industry structure. Today there are only four automobile firms, and the Big Three have over 90 percent of the market for domestic automobiles. General Motors, which took the lead away from Ford after World War I, leads the industry in sales.

How are prices determined in the automobile industry? According to Richard Caves of Harvard University, the answer is as follows:

> The automobile industry fits [the] pattern of "tacit collusion" exceptionally well. Its product differentiation is there for all to see. The 3 leading producers accounted for almost 90 per cent of domestic output of cars in the 1930's and for more than 90 per cent in the post-war period. Each firm seems to use the same basic type of formula in setting prices annually for its various models. [General Motors' formula is discussed in a previous section.] These prices, once announced, normally stay unchanged through a whole model year (except for standard discounts to dealers to "clean up" what remains at the end of the year).
>
> Each firm, figuring the prices to announce for forthcoming models, naturally looks at trends in its own production and model-change costs and at general developments in the economy. It also pays close attention to its rivals' costs and what they may be expected to charge. In this game the firm likely to prefer the lowest price has a good deal of leverage to determine the general range of prices announced for any given type of car. The firms in this industry, as in others, dislike getting caught with an overpriced model more than they fear being slightly under the market. In the 1930's Ford tended to prefer the lowest prices and hence drew close attention from its rivals. In more recent years General Motors has been closely watched.
>
> The prices announced for a given class of vehicle (e.g., full-size four-door sedans with the least luxurious trim) do not come out identical, nor is one firm among the Big Three (Ford, General Motors, Chrysler) typically either high or low. But the announced prices are close enough so that seldom does any adjustment occur after the first announcement. In both 1955 and 1956 (the 1956 and 1957 model years), however, Ford's prices missed those announced later by General Motors by a wide enough margin to lead Ford to make a change, down in 1955 and up in 1956. In each case it ended up within a few dollars of GM's announced price.[14]

Comparison of Oligopoly with Perfect Competition

We have seen that economists have constructed a number of types of models of oligopoly behavior—the Sweezy model, the game-theoretic models, cartel models, price leadership models, cost-plus pricing models, and others—but there is no agreement that any of these models is an adequate general representation of oligopoly behavior. For this reason, it is difficult to estimate the effects of an oligopolistic market structure on price, output, and profits. Nonetheless, if a perfectly competitive industry were turned overnight into an oligopoly, it seems likely that certain changes would occur.

First, *price would probably be higher than under perfect competition*. The difference between the oligopoly price and the perfectly competitive price will depend, of course, on the number of firms in

[14] R. Caves, *American Industry: Structure, Conduct, Performance*, Englewood Cliffs, N.J.: Prentice-Hall, 1967, p. 45.

the industry and the ease of entry: the larger the number of firms and the easier it is to enter the industry, the closer the oligopoly price will be to the perfectly competitive level. Also, prices will tend to be more inflexible under oligopolistic conditions than under perfect competition.

Second, if the demand curve is the same under oligopoly as under perfect competition, it also follows that *output will be less under oligopoly than under perfect competition*. However, it is not always reasonable to assume that the demand curve is the same in both cases, since the large expenditures for advertising and product variation incurred by some oligopolies may tend to shift the demand curve to the right. Consequently in some cases both price and output may tend to be higher under oligopoly than under perfect competition.

Third, *oligopolistic industries tend to spend more on advertising, product differentiation, and style changes than perfectly competitive industries*. The use of some resources for these purposes is certainly worthwhile, since advertising provides buyers with information, and product variation allows greater freedom of choice. Whether oligopolies spend too much for these purposes is by no means obvious. However, there is a widespread feeling among economists, based largely on empirical studies (and hunch), that in some oligopolistic industries such expenditures have been expanded beyond socially optimal levels.

Fourth, one would expect on the basis of the models presented in this chapter that the *profits earned by oligopolists would be higher, on the average, than the profits earned by perfectly competitive firms*. This conclusion is supported by substantial statistical evidence. For example, Joe Bain of the University of California has found that firms in industries in which the largest few firms had a high proportion of total sales tended to have higher rates of return than firms in industries in which the largest few firms had a small proportion of total sales.[15]

These conclusions would be accepted by most economists, though certainly not by all. For example, some distinguished economists are impressed by the fact that big oligopolists must constantly confront big labor and big government.[16] They emphasize the importance of ***countervailing power,*** the check on a big firm that arises from the fact that it deals with other big organizations. Put crudely, the idea is that big firms must sit across the negotiating table from other big firms, as well as big unions and big government. Confronted with these big customers and suppliers, the large oligopolistic firm is, according to this view, unable to capitalize on its market power, since it encounters countervailing power from its customers and suppliers. The result is that the behavior of the big oligopolist is closer to the behavior of a perfectly competitive firm than would otherwise be the case. Within the economics profession, this idea has been received skeptically, although it has had an undeniable impact. Critics have pointed out that it is not clear that entrenched power breeds countervailing power. Nor is it clear that two oligopolists confronting one another will act to eliminate, rather than redistribute, their oligopolistic gains.

Summary

Monopolistic competition occurs where there are many sellers whose products are not the same. Thus, the demand curve facing each firm slopes downward to the right. The conditions for long-run equilibrium are that each firm is maximizing profits and that economic profits are zero. A famous conclusion of the theory of monopolistic competition is that firms under this form of market organization will tend to operate with excess capacity. The firm under monopolistic competition is likely

[15] J. Bain, "Relation to Profit Rate to Industry Concentration: American Manufacturing, 1936–1940," *Quarterly Journal of Economics,* August 1951.

[16] John Kenneth Galbraith, *American Capitalism,* Boston: Houghton Mifflin, 1952.

to produce less, and charge a higher price, than under perfect competition. Relative to pure monopoly, monopolistically competitive firms are likely to have lower profits, greater output, and lower prices. Firms under monopolistic competition will, of course, offer a wider variety of styles, brands, and qualities than will firms under perfect competition. Retailing provides an interesting illustration of monopolistic competition.

Oligopoly is characterized by a small number of firms and a great deal of interdependence, actual and perceived, among them. Oligopoly is a common market structure in the United States. According to empirical studies, prices tend to be rigid in oligopolistic industries. A well-known theory designed to explain this phenomenon is Sweezy's model, based on the "kinked" demand curve. This theory is an incomplete model of oligopoly pricing even though it may be of use in explaining the rigidity of prices. One of the most interesting postwar developments in oligopoly theory is the theory of games, a suggestive framework for analysis in which one can structure formerly intractable problems. However, in its present state, game theory cannot be used to derive specific predictions concerning the behavior of oligopolists.

Conditions in oligopolistic industries tend to promote collusion. A cartel is an open, formal, collusive arrangement. A profit-maximizing cartel will act like a monopolist with a number of plants or divisions, each of which is a member firm. However, in practice, output is unlikely to be allocated among the member firms to minimize total costs, since the allocation process is basically a matter of bargaining. Collusive arrangements often occur, although there are important barriers to effective collusion. Price leadership is quite common in oligopolistic industries, one or a few firms apparently setting the price and the rest following their lead. Two types of price leadership are the dominant-firm model and the barometric-firm model. An example of the former kind of price leadership was the steel industry until a decade or so ago.

According to numerous studies of business behavior, cost-plus pricing is used by many oligopolists. However, a cost-plus model of pricing is incomplete unless it specifies more precisely the determinants of the size of the markup. Relative to perfect competition, it seems likely that price will be higher under oligopoly and that profits will be higher under oligopoly. Moreover, oligopolistic industries will tend to spend more on advertising, product differentiation, and style changes than perfectly competitive industries. Galbraith has emphasized the importance of countervailing power as a check on the power of the large oligopolistic firm.

CONCEPTS FOR REVIEW

Monopolistic competition
Oligopoly
Pure oligopoly
Differentiated oligopoly
Product differentiation
Product group
Game theory
Player
Strategy
Countervailing power
Payoff
Zero-sum game
Payoff matrix
Cartel
Collusion
Dominant firm
Barometric firm
Cost-plus pricing
Markup
Target rate of return

QUESTIONS FOR DISCUSSION AND REVIEW

1. Make a detailed comparison of the long-run equilbrium in (a) a perfectly competitive industry, (b) a monopolistic industry, (c) a monopolistically competitive industry, and (d) an oligopolistic industry. Are there any reasons for believing that society should prefer one of these equilibria over the others?

2. In 1973, the Federal Trade Commission accused the nation's eight largest oil firms of pursuing "a common course of action" that kept the profits from the sale of crude petroleum artificially high. Would such behavior be in accord with oligopolistic theories? How would you go about proving or disproving the FTC's accusation?

3. Monopolistic competiton occurs in markets where there are few sellers and oligopoly where there are many sellers. True or False?

4. There is general agreement that which of the following models is an adequate general representation of oligopoly behavior?
a. Sweezy model b. Game theory c. Cartel model d. Cost-plus pricing e. None of the above

CHAPTER 25

Industrial Organization and Antitrust Policy

"Monopoly" and "monopolist" have long been dirty words—or at least slightly derogatory ones. Economists have viewed monopolists with disapproval at least since Adam Smith's famous attack on monopolies in the eighteenth century. Smith preached and generations of economists since have taught that a monopolist charges a price in excess of the price that would prevail under perfect competition. But why is it so bad that price is higher, and output lower, than under perfect competition?

In this chapter we deal with this and other issues of public policy toward market structure and industrial organization. The opening sections present the case against monopoly power, as well as the defense made by some economists. Then, after describing the extent of industrial concentration in the United States, we discuss the nature, history, and effectiveness of antitrust policy in the United States, together with the problems in constructing standards for antitrust policy. Finally, we describe some laws in this country that restrict, rather than promote, competition.

Monopoly and the Misallocation of Resources

Many people oppose monopolies on the grounds that they "gouge" the consumers by charging a higher price than would otherwise exist—a price that can be sustained only because monopolists artificially limit the supply. In other words, these people claim that monopolists reap higher profits than would be possible under perfect competition and that these profits are at the expense of consumers, who pay higher prices than under perfect competition. Is their claim accurate? Certainly, as we saw in Chapter 23, a monopolist will reap higher profits than under perfect competition and consumers will pay higher prices under monopoly than under perfect competition. But is this bad?

To the extent that the monopolist is rich and the consumers are poor, we are likely to answer yes. Also, to the extent that the monopolist is less deserving than the consumers, we are likely to answer the same thing. But suppose the monopolist is a selfless philanthropist who gives to the poor: is monopoly still socially undesirable? The answer remains yes, because *monopoly imposes a burden on society by misallocating resources. In the presence of monopoly, the price system cannot be relied on to decide what is to be produced, how the output is to be produced, and to whom it should be distributed.*

To see more precisely how monopoly interferes with the proper functioning of the price system, suppose that all industries other than the shoe industry are perfectly competitive. The shoe industry, however, has been monopolized. How does this cause a misallocation of resources? Under fairly general circumstances, a good's price can be taken as a measure of the social value of an extra unit of the good. For example, if the price of a pair of socks is $1, the value to the consumer of an extra pair of socks can be taken to be $1. Moreover, under fairly general circumstances, a good's marginal cost can be taken as a measure of the cost to society of an extra unit of the good. For example, if the marginal cost of a pair of shoes is $30, the cost to society of producing an extra pair of shoes can be taken to be $30.

In perfectly competitive industries, price is set equal to marginal cost, as we saw in Chapter 23. Thus, each of the competitive industries produces up to the point where the social value of an extra unit of the good (which equals price) is set equal to the cost to society of producing an extra unit of the good (which equals marginal cost). This is the amount each of these industries should produce: the output rate that will result in an optimal allocation of resources.

To see that this is the optimal output rate, consider what happens when an industry produces up to the point where the social value of an extra unit of the good is *more* than the cost to society of producing an extra unit. This isn't the socially optimal output rate because a 1-unit increase in the output rate will increase the social value of output by more than the social cost of production. On the other hand, if an industry produces up to the point where the social value of an extra unit of the good is *less* than the cost to society of producing the extra unit, a decrease in the output rate will decrease the social value of output by less than the social cost of production. Consequently, this isn't the socially optimal output rate either. Thus it follows that the socially optimal output rate must be at the point where the social value of an extra unit of the good *equals* the social cost of producing an extra unit of the good.

But let's return to the shoe industry—the sole monopolist.[1] Is the shoe industry producing the optimal amount of shoes? The answer is no. Like any monopolist, it produces at the point where marginal revenue equals marginal cost, as we saw in Chapter 23. Thus, since marginal revenue is less than price (as was proved there), the monopo-

[1] Are puns really the lowest form of humor?

list produces at a point where price is greater than marginal cost. Consequently, *the monopolistic industry produces at a point where the social value of an extra unit of the good (which equals price) is greater than the cost to society of producing the extra unit (which equals marginal cost).* As we saw in the previous paragraph, this means that the monopolist's output rate is too small. A 1-unit increase in the output of shoes will increase the social value of output by more than the social cost of production.

Here lies the economist's principal complaint against monopoly: it results in a misallocation of resources. Too little is produced of the monopolized good. Society is less well off—in terms of its own tastes and potentialities—than it could be. The price system, which would not lead to, or tolerate, such waste if all industries were perfectly competitive, is not allowed to perform as it should. These inefficiencies caused by monopoly are described further and in more detail in Chapter 29.

Income Distribution and Efficiency

Misallocation of resources is only part of the economist's brief against monopoly. As we have already pointed out, *monopoly redistributes income in favor of the monopolists.* In other words, the monopolist can fatten his own purse by restricting his output and raising his price. Admittedly, there is no scientific way to prove that monopolists are less deserving than the rest of the population, but it is also pretty difficult to see why they are more deserving.

In addition, *since monopolists do not have to face direct competition, they are likely to be less diligent in controlling costs and in using resources efficiently.* As Sir John Hicks put it, "The best of all monopoly profits is a quiet life."[2] Certainly we all dream at times of being able to take life easy. It would be strange if the monopolist, having succeeded in insulating himself from direct competition, did not take advantage of the opportunity—not open to firms in perfectly competitive markets—to relax a bit and worry less about pinching pennies. For this reason, economists fear that, to use Adam Smith's pungent phrase, "Monopoly . . . is a great enemy to good management."

Further, *it is often claimed that monopolists are slow to innovate and adopt new techniques and products.* This lethargy stems from the monopolist's freedom from direct competition. Innovation tends to be disruptive, while old ways, like old shoes, tend to be comfortable. The monopolist may be inclined, therefore, to stick with "time-honored" practices. Without question, competition is an important spur to innovation and to the rapid diffusion of innovations. But there are well-known arguments on the other side as well: some economists argue that substantial monopoly power promotes innovation and technological change. Much more will be said below on this score.

[2] J. R. Hicks, "Annual Survey of Economic Theory: The Theory of Monopoly," *Econometrica,* 1935.

The Case against Oligopoly and Monopolistic Competition

Thus far, we have discussed the case against monopoly. Although economists are more concerned about monopoly than about oligopoly or monopolistic competition, this does not mean that they give either oligopoly or monopolistic competition a clean bill of health. Even though oligopoly has aroused less public indignation and opposition than out-and-out monopoly, an oligopoly can obviously be just as deleterious to social welfare. After all, if oligopolists engage in collusion, open or tacit, their behavior with regard to price and output may resemble a monopolist's. Only if there is real competition among the oligopolists can we expect price to be pushed closer to marginal cost under oligopoly than under monopoly. If oligopolists "cooperate" and "maintain orderly markets," the amount of social waste may be no less than under monopoly.

Also, the inflexibility of prices under oligopoly

tends to interfere with the effective functioning of the price system. In a perfectly competitive industry, price will decline when the demand curve shifts to the left, thus prompting resources to move out of the industry. (We examined this process in Chapter 23, using coal and corn as examples.) But in an oligopolistic industry, price tends to remain constant when demand shifts to the left, with the result that output falls and much of the industry's plant is left idle. Although resources leave the oligopolistic industry, as they should, the resources that are stuck in the industry in the short run are not utilized adequately. Moreover, the fact that prices are not allowed to decline contributes to cost-push inflation.

Monopolistic competition can also be a socially wasteful form of market organization. As we saw in Chapter 24, monopolistically competitive markets are characterized by overcrowding and excess capacity. There are more firms than would exist under perfect competition, and each firm produces less than the minimum-cost output rate. Thus, the industry's output is produced inefficiently. More resources are used than are really necessary. Of course, the extent of this waste may not be very great if the demand curve facing each firm is very elastic, but there is no reason to believe that the demand curve will always be so elastic as to insure that the waste is small.

In addition, price under monopolistic competition—as well as under monopoly and oligopoly—will exceed marginal cost, although the difference between price and marginal cost may be smaller than under monopoly or oligopoly. Thus, monopolistic competition, like monopoly and oligopoly, results in a misallocation of resources. The argument leading to this conclusion is exactly like that given earlier for monopoly. Also, monopolistic competition, as well as oligopoly, may allow waste arising from too much being spent (from society's point of view) on product differentiation, advertising, and other selling expenses. This is very difficult to prove, although many economists suspect it is so.

The moral is that economists look with disfavor on serious departures from perfect competition, whether these departures are in the direction of monopoly, oligopoly, or monopolistic competition. Judged against the perfectly competitive model, all are likely to lead to social waste and inefficiency. However, monopoly is generally presumed to be the greatest evil, with the result that economists usually look with most disfavor on markets dominated by one, or a very few, sellers—or buyers.[3]

The Defense of Monopoly Power

Not all economists agree that monopoly power is a bad thing. On the contrary, some respected voices in the economics profession have been raised to praise monopoly, not bury it. In the previous sections, we have assumed that technology is fixed and independent of an industry's market structure. Some economists like Joseph Schumpeter and John Kenneth Galbraith of Harvard University have asserted that the rate of technological change is likely to be higher in an imperfectly competitive industry (i.e., monopoly, oligopoly, etc.) than in a perfectly competitive industry. Since the rate of technological change affects productivity and living standards, in their view a perfectly competitive economy is likely to be inferior in a dynamic sense to an economy containing many imperfectly competitive industries.

But is their assertion true? This question has been debated at great length. On the one hand, Schumpeter and Galbraith argue that firms under perfect competition have fewer resources to devote to research and experimentation than do firms under imperfect competition. Because profits are at a relatively low level, it is difficult for firms under perfect competition to support large expenditures on research and development. Moreover, they argue that unless a firm has sufficient control over the market to reap the rewards from an innovation,

[3] Monopsony, where a single buyer exists, is taken up in Chapter 26.

the introduction of the innovation may not be worthwhile. If competitors can imitate the innovation very quickly, the innovator may be unable to make any money from it.

Defenders of perfect competition retort that there is likely to be less pressure for firms in imperfect markets to introduce new techniques and products, since such firms have fewer competitors. Moreover, firms in imperfect markets are better able to drive out entrants who, uncommitted to present techniques, are likely to be relatively quick to adopt new ones. Entrants, unlike established producers, have no vested interest in maintaining the demand for existing products and the profitability of existing equipment. Also, there are advantages in having a large number of independent decision-making units. There is less chance that an important technological advance will be blocked by the faulty judgment of a few men.

It is very difficult to obtain evidence to help settle the question, if it is posed in this way, since perfect competition is, of course, a hypothetical construct that does not exist in the real world. However, it does seem unlikely that a perfectly competitive industry (if such an industry could be constructed) would be able in many areas of the economy to carry out the research and development required to promote a high rate of technological change. Moreover, if entry is free and rapid, firms in a perfectly competitive industry will have little motivation to innovate. Although the evidence is not at all clear-cut, this much can probably be granted the critics of perfect competition.

Monopoly Power, Big Business, and Technological Change

But some economists go much further than the assertion that a certain amount of market imperfection will promote a more rapid rate of technological change. They say that an industry composed of or dominated by a few large companies is the best market structure for promoting rapid technological change. For example, Galbraith has said that the "modern industry of a few large firms [is] an almost perfect instrument for inducing technical change."[4] And in some circles, it is accepted as an obvious fact that giant firms with their financial strength and well-equipped laboratories are absolutely necessary to maintain a rapid rate of technological change.

Suppose that, for a market of given size, we could replace the largest firms by a larger number of somewhat smaller firms—and thus reduce the extent to which the industry is dominated by the largest firms. Is there any evidence that this would decrease the rate of technological change, as is sometimes asserted? The evidence currently available is much more limited than one would like, but the available studies—based on detailed data concerning research expenditures, patents, important inventions and innovations, and the diffusion of innovations—do not indicate that such a decrease in industrial concentration would reduce the rate of technological change in most industries.

Specifically, the available studies do not show that total research and development expenditures in most industries would decrease if the largest firms were replaced by somewhat smaller ones. Nor do they indicate that the research and development expenditures carried out by the largest firms are generally more productive (or more fundamental or more risky) than those carried out by somewhat smaller firms. Moreover, they do not suggest that greater concentration of an industry results in a faster diffusion of innovations. However, if innovations require a large amount of capital, they do suggest that the substitution of a larger number of smaller firms for a few large ones may lead to slower commercial introduction of the innovations.[5]

Thus, *contrary to the allegations of Galbraith and others, there is little evidence that industrial giants are needed in most industries to insure*

[4] John Kenneth Galbraith, *American Capitalism*, Boston: Houghton Mifflin, 1952, p. 91.

[5] Edwin Mansfield, *Technological Change*, New York: Norton, 1971, and the literature cited there.

rapid technological change and rapid utilization of new techniques. Of course this does not mean that industries composed only of small firms would necessarily be optimal for the promotion and diffusion of new techniques. On the contrary, there seem to be considerable advantages in a diversity of firm sizes. Complementarities and interdependencies exist among large and small firms. There is often a division of labor. Smaller firms may focus on areas requiring sophistication and flexibility and cater to specialized needs, while bigger firms concentrate on areas requiring large production, marketing, or technological resources. However, there is little evidence in most industries that firms considerably smaller than the biggest firms are not big enough for these purposes.

Monopoly, Big Business, and Economic Power

The discussion in previous sections makes it clear that the case against monopoly power is not open-and-shut. On the contrary, a certain amount of monopoly power is inevitable in practically all real-life situations, since perfect competition is a model that can only be approximated in real life. Moreover, a certain amount of monopoly power may be needed to promote desirable technological change. But it is one thing to say that a certain amount of monopoly power may be a good thing, and another thing to say that a lot of it is socially desirable. Few economists would lose sleep over the fact that an industry showed reasonably small departures from perfect competition, but most would be concerned if it were dominated by one firm, or even a small number of firms.

There also are important noneconomic arguments against monopoly power and big business. The public and its representatives have been concerned about the centralization of power in the hands of a relatively few firms. Economic power in the United States is distributed very unevenly; a few hundred corporations control a very large share of the total assets of the nonfarm economy. Moreover, within particular industries, there is considerable concentration of ownership and production, as we shall see in the next section. This concentration of power has been viewed with concern by observers like A. A. Berle, who asserted that the largest several hundred firms "each with its own dominating pyramid within it—represent a concentration of power over economies which makes the medieval feudal system look like a Sunday School party. In sheer economic power this has gone far beyond anything we have yet seen."[6]

It is important to note that this distrust of power leads to a distrust of giant firms, whether or not they have substantial monopoly power. Even if General Motors had little power over prices, it would still have considerable economic—and political—power because of its sheer size. Note too that a firm's size is not necessarily a good indicator of the extent of its monopoly power. A small grocery store in a remote community may be a monopolist, but a large merchandising firm with many rivals may have little monopoly power.

Let's look at the biggest 100 manufacturing firms in the United States. Recognizing that bigness is not the same as monopoly power, what percentage of the nation's assets do these firms control, and is this percentage increasing or decreasing over time? According to the latest available figures, the 100 largest manufacturing firms control about ½ of all manufacturing assets in the United States, and this percentage seems to have increased considerably since the end of World War II. For example, Willard Mueller of the University of Wisconsin points out that, of the total assets of manufacturing firms, "the share held by the top one hundred companies rose from 39.3 percent to 49.3 percent [between 1947 and 1968], and the share of the top 200 rose from 47.2 percent to 60.9 percent. In other words, by 1968 the top one hundred companies held a greater share than that held by

[6] A. A. Berle, *Economic Power and the Free Society,* New York: Fund for the Republic, p. 14.

the top 200 in 1947."[7] Thus, there can be no doubt about the vast economic power of the 100 largest firms—and no doubt that, since World War II, they have increased their share of the nation's manufacturing assets.

Industrial Concentration in the United States

Market structure influences market performance. Consequently, economists and policy makers are interested in market structure. But how can one measure an industry's market structure? How can one tell how close an industry is to being a monopoly or a perfectly competitive industry? An important measure economists have devised is the ***market concentration ratio,*** which shows the percentage of total sales or production accounted for by the biggest 4 firms. Clearly, the higher the market concentration ratio, the more concentrated the industry is in a very few hands. Of course, basing this measure on 4 firms is arbitrary. You can use 5, 6, 7, or any number of firms you like. But the figures issued by the government are generally based on 4 firms.

Table 25.1 shows the market concentration ratios for selected industries. Clearly, these ratios vary widely from industry to industry. For example, the automobile industry is clearly a tight oligopoly, with the concentration ratio about as high as it can get—99 percent. On the other hand, there is very little industrial concentration in the unupholstered wood furniture industry: its concentration ratio is only 11 percent. Table 25.2 shows the number and size of industries that have concentration ratios of various magnitudes. The bulk of the manufacturing industries in the United States seems to have concentration ratios of less than 40 percent, but a substantial number (which account for 12 percent of the total shipments) have concentration ratios of 80 percent or more.

Table 25.1

Concentration Ratios in Selected Manufacturing Product Markets

Industry	Market share of four largest firms (percent)
Automobiles	99
Aluminum	96
Cigarettes	80
Soap	72
Tires	70
Aircraft	59
Blast furnaces and steel plants	50
Watches and clocks	46
Petroleum refining	34
Cement	29
Shoes	25
Milk	23
Newspapers	15
Soft drinks	12
Wood furniture, unupholstered	11

Source: Concentration Ratios in Manufacturing Industry, Senate Judiciary Committee, 1967, as quoted in F. M. Scherer, *op. cit.*

Most economists who have studied trends in industrial concentration seem to agree that remarkably little change has occurred in the past 70 years in the average level of concentration in the United States. As Morris Adelman of M.I.T. puts it, "Any tendency either way, if it exists, must be at the pace of a glacial drift."[8] Also, the available evidence seems to indicate that the levels of market concentration are lower in the United States than in

[7] W. Mueller, *A Primer on Monopoly and Competition,* New York: Random House, 1970, p. 26.

[8] M. Adelman, "The Measurement of Industrial Concentration," *Review of Economics and Statistics,* 1951.

Table 25.2

Number and Relative Value of Shipments of Industries with Various Levels of Concentration

Concentration ratio (percent)	Number of industries	Percent of total shipments
80–100	27	11
60–79	47	10
40–59	92	20
20–39	161	38
Less than 20	89	21
Total	417	100

Source: *Concentration Ratios in Manufacturing Industry,* Senate Judiciary Committee, 1963, as quoted in F. M. Scherer, *op. cit.*

other major industrialized countries, with the possible exception of Great Britain and Japan.

Interestingly, there is a tendency for industries that have high (or low) levels of concentration in one country also to have high (or low) levels of concentration in another country. This suggests that certain basic factors, such as barriers to entry, play an important role in determining an industry's level of concentration in all countries. Very substantial barriers to entry, such as economies of scale and large capital requirements, tend to promote high levels of concentration. (Industries with low levels of concentration seldom have such substantial barriers to entry.) Just as barriers to entry promote oligopoly, so they promote high levels of concentration.

Finally, it is important to recognize that the concentration ratio is only a rough measure of an industry's market structure. Certainly, to provide a reasonably adequate description, it must be supplemented with data on the extent and type of product differentiation in the industry, as well as on barriers to entry. Moreover, even with these supplements, it is still a crude measure. (Among other things, it takes no account of competition from foreign suppliers.) Nonetheless, the concentration ratio has proved to be a valuable tool to economists, and it has turned out to have some predictive value. For example, in accord with the models described in Chapters 23 and 24, there is a definite relationship between the level of concentration in an industry and the industry's profit rate. As these models would predict, the profit rate tends to be higher in industries where the concentration ratio is higher.

The Antitrust Laws

National policies are too ambiguous and rich in contradictions to be summarized neatly and concisely. Consequently, it would be misleading to say that the United States has adopted a policy of promoting competition and controlling monopoly. To a large extent, it certainly is true that "competition is our fundamental national policy," as the Supreme Court said in 1963. But it is also true that we have adopted many measures to promote monopoly and to limit competition, as we shall see in subsequent sections. On balance, however, we probably have gone further in promoting competition than other major industrialized countries, and the principal pieces of legislation designed to further this objective are the ***antitrust laws.***

In 1890, the first antitrust law, the Sherman Act, was passed by Congress. Although the common law had long outlawed monopolistic practices, it appeared to many Americans in the closing years of the nineteenth century that legislation was required to discourage monopoly and to preserve and encourage competition. The formation of "trusts"—monopolistic combines that colluded to raise prices and restrict output—brought the matter to a head. The heart of the Sherman Act lies in the following two sections:

Sec. 1. Every contract, combination in the form

of trust or otherwise, or conspiracy, in restraint of trade or commerce among the several states or with foreign nations, is hereby declared to be illegal. Every person who shall make any such contract or engage in any such combination or conspiracy, shall be deemed guilty of a misdemeanor . . .

Sec. 2. Every person who shall monopolize, or attempt to monopolize or combine or conspire with any other person or persons, to monopolize any part of the trade or commerce among the several States, or with foreign nations shall be deemed guilty of a misdemeanor . . .

The first 20 years of experience with the Sherman Act were not very satisfying to its supporters. The ineffectiveness of the Sherman Act led in 1914 to passage by Congress of two additional laws: the Clayton Act and the Federal Trade Commission Act. The Clayton Act tried to be more specific than the Sherman Act in identifying certain practices that were illegal because they would "substantially lessen competition or tend to create a monopoly." In particular, the Clayton Act outlawed unjustified ***price discrimination,*** a practice whereby one buyer is charged more than another buyer for the same product. It also outlawed the use of a ***tying contract,*** which makes the buyer purchase other items to get the product he wants. Further, it outlawed mergers that substantially lessen competition; but since it did not prohibit one firm's purchase of a competitor's plant and equipment, it really could not stop mergers. In 1950, this loophole was closed by the Celler-Kefauver Anti-Merger Act.

The Federal Trade Commission Act created the Federal Trade Commission to investigate unfair and predatory practices and to issue cease-and-desist orders. The act stated that "unfair methods of competition in commerce are hereby declared unlawful." However, the commission—composed of 5 commissioners, each appointed by the president for a term of 7 years—was given the unenviable task of defining exactly what was "unfair." The courts took away much of the commission's power; but in 1938, the commission acquired the function of outlawing untrue and deceptive advertising. Also, the commission has authority to carry out economic investigations of the structure and conduct of American business.

The language of the antitrust laws does not tell you a great deal about their meaning or effect; the words are vague and slippery. What these laws mean must be determined by the courts, which obviously have considerable freedom in interpreting them. Nor do these laws enforce themselves. Thus, their effect is determined by the action or inaction of the Department of Justice, which is responsible for enforcing them.

The Courts and the Justice Department

The antitrust laws, like any laws, are enforced in the courts. Typically, charges are brought against a firm or group of firms by the Antitrust Division of the Department of Justice, a trial is held, and a decision is reached by the judge. In key cases, appeals are made that eventually reach the Supreme Court. Clearly, the real impact of the antitrust laws depends on how the courts interpret them. And the judicial interpretation of these laws has changed considerably over time. The first major set of antitrust cases took place in 1911 when the Standard Oil Company and the American Tobacco Company were forced to give up a large share of their holdings of other companies. In these cases, the Supreme Court put forth and used the famous ***rule of reason***—that only unreasonable combinations in restraint of trade, not all trusts, required conviction under the Sherman Act. In 1920, the rule of reason was used by the Supreme Court in its finding that U. S. Steel had not violated the antitrust laws even though it had tried to monopolize the industry—since the court said it had not succeeded. Moreover, U. S. Steel's large size and its potential monopoly power were ruled beside the point since "the law does not make mere size an offense. It . . . requires overt acts."

During the 1920s and early 1930s the courts, including a conservative Supreme Court, interpreted the antitrust laws in such a way that they were as toothless as a new-born babe. Although Eastman Kodak and International Harvester controlled very substantial shares of their markets, the court, using the rule of reason, found them innocent on the grounds that they had not built up their near-monopoly position through overt coercion or predatory practices. Moreover, the court reiterated that mere size was not an offense, no matter how great the unexerted monopoly power might be. However, this situation was not to last. Indeed, it changed greatly in the late 1930s, with the prosecution of the Aluminum Corporation of America (Alcoa). This case, decided in 1945 (but begun in 1937), reversed the decisions in the U. S. Steel and International Harvester cases. Alcoa had achieved its 90 percent of the market by means that would have been considered "reasonable" in the earlier cases—keeping its price low enough to discourage entry, building capacity to take care of increases in the market, etc. Nonetheless, the court decided that Alcoa, because it controlled practically all the industry's output, violated the antitrust laws. Thus, *the court used market structure rather than market conduct as a test of legality: monopoly, not just monopolizing, was declared illegal.*

The impact of the antitrust laws is determined by the vigor with which the Antitrust Division of the Justice Department prosecutes cases. If the Antitrust Division does not prosecute, the laws can have little effect. Like the judicial interpretation of the laws, the extent to which the Justice Department has prosecuted cases has varied from one period to another. Needless to say, the attitude of the political party in power has been an important determinant of how vigorously antitrust cases have been prosecuted. When the Sherman Act was first passed, it was of singularly little value. For example, President Cleveland's Attorney General did not agree with the law and would not prosecute under it. "Trust-busting" was truly a neglected art until President Theodore Roosevelt devoted his formidable energies to it. In 1903, he established the Antitrust Division of the Justice Department. Moreover, his administration started the major cases that led to the Standard Oil, American Tobacco, and U. S. Steel decisions.

Subsequently, there was a long lull in the prosecution of antitrust cases, reflecting the Supreme Court's rule of reason doctrine and a strong conservative tide in the nation. The lull continued for about 25 years, until 1937, when there was a significant upsurge in activity on the antitrust front. Led by Thurman Arnold, the Antitrust Division entered one of the most vigorous periods of antitrust enforcement to date. Arnold went after the glass, cigarette, cement, and other industries, the most important case being that against Alcoa. The Antitrust Division attempted in this period to reopen cases that were hopeless under the rule of reason doctrine. With the change in the composition of the Supreme Court and the less business-oriented administration, Arnold's activism turned out to be effective.

Post-World War II Developments

The period since World War II has been a vigorous one from the viewpoint of antitrust, with at least three notable developments. First, one of the biggest cases in the history of antitrust occurred in 1961 when, as you will recall from the previous chapter, the major electrical equipment manufacturers were convicted of collusive price agreements. Executives of General Electric, Westinghouse, and other firms in the industry admitted that they met secretly in hotels and communicated by mail in order to maintain prices, share the market, and eliminate competition. Some of the executives were sentenced to jail on criminal charges, and the firms had to pay large amounts to customers to make up for the overcharges. In particular, 1,800 triple damage suits against the firms resulted in payments estimated at between $400 and $600 million. Even the most zealous antitrusters will admit that this was no slap on the wrist!

Second, following the enactment of the Celler-Kefauver Anti-Merger Act, horizontal mergers—mergers of firms making essentially the same good—have become increasingly likely to run afoul of the antitrust laws. In 1962, Chief Justice Warren went so far as to say that a merger that resulted in a firm having 5 percent of the market might be undesirable. In the Von's Grocery case in 1965, the court disallowed a merger between two supermarkets that together had less than 8 percent of the Los Angeles market. In this case, the court emphasized the trend toward increasing concentration in grocery retailing in Los Angeles. Also, vertical mergers—mergers of firms that supply or sell to one another—have been viewed with a jaundiced eye by the courts. For example, in the Brown Shoe case, the Supreme Court said that the merger of Brown with R. G. Kinney would mean that other shoe manufacturers would be frozen out of a substantial part of the retail shoe market.

Third, one of the leading problems confronting the Justice Department in recent years has been conglomerate mergers—mergers of firms in unrelated industries. Conglomerate firms like Litton Industries, International Telephone, and Ling-Temco-Vought were regarded very highly by investors during the 1960s. Inspired by their apparent success, other firms began to merge with firms in other industries in order to become conglomerates themselves. Supporters of these mergers claimed that they enabled weak companies to be revitalized by superior management, bigger research facilities, and so on. However, this merger movement was opposed by many other observers on the grounds that conglomerates were obtaining too much power in the economy. To some extent, this problem has diminished in importance since the conglomerates began to show relatively disappointing earnings in the late 1960s. But the Justice Department continues to keep a watchful eye on conglomerate mergers. For example, in 1967 it succeeded in preventing a conglomerate merger between Procter and Gamble, the big soap manufacturer, and Clorox, a maker of liquid bleach.

Standards for Antitrust Policy

There are at least two fairly distinct approaches to antitrust policy. *The first looks primarily and directly at market performance—the industry's rate of technological change, efficiency, and profits, the conduct of individual firms, and so on.* Advocates of this approach argue that, in deciding antitrust cases, one should review in detail the performance of the firms in question to see how well they have served the economy. If they have served well, they should not be held in violation of the antitrust laws simply because they have a large share of the market. This test, as it is usually advocated, relies heavily on an evaluation of the technological "progressiveness" and "dynamism" of the firms in question. Although this approach seems quite sensible, it has a number of disadvantages. In particular, it is very difficult to tell at present whether a particular industry's performance is "good" or "bad." Economists simply do not have the sorts of measuring rods that would be required to obtain reasonably accurate and well-accepted readings on an industry's performance. In view of the vagueness of the criteria and the practical realities of the antitrust environment, adopting this approach would probably invite nonenforcement of the laws.

The second approach emphasizes the importance of an industry's market structure—the number and size distribution of buyers and sellers in the market, the ease with which new firms can enter, and the extent of product differentiation. According to this approach, one should look to market structure for evidence of undesirable monopolistic characteristics. The basic idea behind this approach, as George Stigler puts it, is that "an industry which does not have a competitive structure will not have competitive behavior." Two leading authorities on antitrust law, Carl Kaysen of the Institute for Advanced Study and Donald Turner of Harvard (and formerly head of the Antitrust Division under President Johnson), are strong advocates of this approach. They believe that, if for 5 years or more, one firm has accounted for 50 percent or more of annual sales in a market, or if 4 or fewer firms have accounted for 80 percent of such sales, it should be presumed that "market power" exists. And they propose that such "market power" be declared illegal, unless such concentration can be defended by economies of scale or some other such justification. If it cannot be defended, divestiture and dissolution would constitute possible remedies.[9]

Although respected economists favor each of these approaches, the second is probably preferred by most experts in this field. Moreover, the Justice Department adopted this approach in its 1968 merger guidelines, which stated that mergers would ordinarily be challenged when the firms involved had more than specified shares of the market.[10] However, this does not mean that the market structure approach does not have lots of critics. On the contrary, many economists and lawyers feel that the relationship between market structure and market performance is so weak that it is a mistake to choose, more or less arbitrarily, some level of concentration and to say that, if concentration exceeds this level, market performance is likely to be undesirable. For example, the editors of *Fortune Magazine* went so far in 1966 as to propose that Congress should amend the antitrust laws to make it clear that "it is not national policy to prefer any particular size, shape, or number of firms to any other size, shape, or number; and that mergers—horizontal, vertical, or conglomerate—are entirely legal unless they spring from a manifest attempt to restrain trade.[11]

[9] C. Kaysen and D. Turner, *Antitrust Policy,* Cambridge: Harvard University Press, 1959.

[10] For example, in the case of horizontal mergers, the guidelines stated that a horizontal merger would ordinarily be challenged when:

1. The 4-firm concentration ratio in the appropriate market is approximately 75 percent or more, and the firms involved in the merger account for the following percentages of the market:

Larger or acquiring firm	Smaller or acquired firm
4 percent	4 percent or more
10 percent	2 percent or more
15 percent	1 percent or more

2. The 4-firm concentration ratio is less than approximately 75 percent, and the firms involved in the merger account for the following percentages of the market:

Larger or acquiring firm	Smaller or acquired firm
5 percent	5 percent or more
10 percent	4 percent or more
15 percent	3 percent or more
20 percent	2 percent or more
25 percent	1 percent or more

(Under both 1 and 2, percentages not shown in the table should be interpolated between those given.)

3. In industries in which the concentration ratio for any group of firms from the 2 largest to the 8 largest has increased 7 percent or more in the last 5 to 10 years, the department will challenge any merger involving a firm whose market share is roughly 2 percent or more.

Source: U.S. Department of Justice, *Merger Guidelines* (mimeo) isued May 30, 1968.

[11] See "A New 'Worst' in Antitrust" and "The Antitrust Chief Replies", reprinted in E. Mansfield, *Economics: Readings, Issues, and Cases,* New York: Norton, 1974.

The Effectiveness of Antitrust Policy

How effective have the antitrust laws been? Obviously it is difficult to tell with any accuracy, since there is no way to carry out an experiment in which American history is rewritten to show what would have happened if the antitrust laws had not been on the books. Many experts seem to feel that the antitrust laws have not been as effective as they might—and should—have been, largely because they do not have sufficient public support and there is no politically powerful pressure group pushing for their enforcement. But this does not mean that they have not had an important effect. On the contrary, *the evidence, although incomplete and unclear, suggests that they have had a significant effect on business behavior and markets.* Their effectiveness has been described well by Edward Mason of Harvard University, who has said that it is due "not so much to the contribution that particular judgments have made to the restoring of competition as it is to the fact that the consideration of whether or not a particular course of action may or may not be in violation of the antitrust acts is a persistent factor affecting business judgment, at least in large firms."[12] This same idea is summed up in the old saying that the ghost of Senator Sherman sits as an *ex officio* member of every firm's board of directors.

Some indication of the effects of our antitrust laws can perhaps be obtained by looking at experience in other countries, since Britain, Germany, and many other European countries (as well as Japan) took a very tolerant view of monopoly power for a long time. After World War II, there was pressure to break up some of the powerful combines in Germany and Japan, but this pressure has been somewhat relaxed more recently—although antitrust practices seem to be gaining ground in the European Common Market. Foreign experience seems to indicate that the antitrust laws have helped prevent American firms from adopting many restrictive and predatory practices common elsewhere. However, this does not mean that antitrust legislation and enforcement have managed to break up many of our giant corporations. One of the most important problems is that it is more difficult to attack existing concentration in an industry than to stop further concentration firms attempt to bring about through merger. As John Kenneth Galbraith puts it, "If a firm is already large, it is substantially immune under the antitrust laws."[13]

Certainly, there is little prospect that our giant corporations will soon be broken up. In part, this reflects the fact that much of the public is not really sold on the idea of breaking up big oligopolists, even though it may not be quite comfortable with them. Also, the effectiveness of the antitrust laws is limited by the amount of resources the Antitrust Division is given to carry out its job. Until the 1930s, the Antitrust Division received an annual appropriation of less than $300,000, which permitted it to bring only a few cases to court a year. More recently, the division's budget has increased considerably—it was about $6 million in 1963—but it is still unable to bring more than about 50 cases annually, a small number by practically any standard. Moreover, most of these tend to be "open and shut" cases of price-fixing conspiracies, frequently in food processing and distribution, building materials, and the service trades.

[12] Edward Mason, preface to Carl Kaysen and Donald Turner, *Antitrust Policy*, (and reprinted in E. Mansfield, *Monopoly Power and Economic Performance*, New York: Norton, 1974).

[13] J. K. Galbraith, "The New Industrial State," in E. Mansfield, *Economics: Readings, Issues, and Cases, op. cit.*

The Pabst Case: Antitrust in Action

Perhaps the most effective way to learn certain things about the antitrust field is to try to decide an actual antitrust case. Suppose that, over the protests of the American Bar Association, you are appointed a District Court Judge and that your first job is to hear a case (actually brought by the government in 1958) to prevent Pabst Brewing Company from acquiring the Blatz Brewing Company. According to the government, the effect of this merger "may be substantially to lessen competition, or to tend to create a monopoly" in the production and sale of beer in the state of Wisconsin, the three-state area of Wisconsin, Illinois, and Michigan, and the United States. A fundamental issue in any case of this sort is the definition of market and industry boundaries. Market boundaries must be broad enough to include all relevant competitors but not so broad as to include products that are not reasonable substitutes. The delineation of market and industry boundaries—in terms of "line of commerce" and "section of the country"—is bound to involve judgment, there being no simple, mechanical rule to settle it.

In the Pabst case, both the government and Pabst agreed "that the line of commerce involved the production, sale, and distribution of beer and that the continental United States is a relevant geographic market." However, there was disagreement over the government's use of Wisconsin and the three-state area of Wisconsin, Illinois, and Michigan as separate geographical markets. Pabst and Blatz claimed that there was no good reason to single out these particular areas as distinct markets. The government, on the other hand, claimed that they were distinct markets because the two firms competed most intensively in these areas. Pabst was the nation's eleventh largest seller of beer; its sales were 2.67 percent of the national market and about 11 percent of the sales in Wisconsin. Blatz was the nation's thirteenth largest seller of beer, its sales being 2.04 percent of the national market and about 13 percent of the sales in Wisconsin. Thus, if you look at the smaller geographical area (Wisconsin and the three-state area), the two firms account for a substantial proportion of the market—about 24 percent in Wisconsin. But if you look at the national market as a whole, they account for a small proportion—less than 5 percent.

As the District Judge, how should you decide the case? Should you agree with the government that Wisconsin and the three-state area are relevant markets? Or should you agree with Pabst and Blatz that they are not relevant markets in themselves, but just parts of a market? Moreover, if you agree with the government concerning the market definition, should you also agree that two firms with a total of 24 percent of Wisconsin sales should not be allowed to merge? Or if you agree with Pabst and Blatz concerning the market definition, should you allow a merger between two firms that together account for about 5 percent of the national market? It is a tough problem, isn't it? To demonstrate just how tough it is, the District Judge decided one way, while the Supreme Court decided the other way. The District Court, agreeing with Pabst and Blatz that Wisconsin and the three-state area should not be treated as distinct relevant areas, dismissed the government's complaint. But the District Court's decision was reversed by the Supreme Court, which agreed with the government's position that the smaller areas should be treated as relevant, distinct markets.

The antitrust field is characterized by many complexities and uncertainties, as well as by legal and economic vagueness and ambiguity. This case illustrates how difficult it is even to decide what the relevant market is![14]

The Patent System

In a previous section, we pointed out that our national economic policies are by no means free of contradiction. In particular, although many of our policies are designed to promote competition and limit monopoly, one should not assume that all of them are meant to promote these objectives. On the contrary, quixotic as it may seem, some are designed to do just the opposite: to restrict competition. Among the most important of these policies are our laws concerning patents, which grant the inventor exclusive control over the use of his invention for 17 years. That is, the inventor is given a temporary monopoly over the use of his invention.

Since Congress passed the original patent act in 1790, the arguments used to justify the existence of the patent laws have not changed very much. First, these laws are regarded as an important incentive to induce the inventor to put in the work required to produce an invention. Particularly in the case of the individual inventor, it is claimed that patent protection is a strong incentive. Second, patents are regarded as a necessary incentive to induce firms to carry out the further work and make the necessary investment in pilot plants and other items that are required to bring the invention to commercial use. If an invention became public property when made, why should a firm incur the costs and risks involved in attempting to develop, debug, and perfect it? Another firm could watch, take no risks, and duplicate the process or product if it were successful. Third, it is argued that, because of the patent laws, inventions are disclosed earlier than otherwise, the consequence being that other inventions are facilitated

[14] For further discussion of the Pabst case, see Henry Einhorn and William Smith, *Economic Aspects of Antitrust: Readings and Cases,* New York: Random House, 1968.

by the earlier dissemination of the information. The resulting situation is often contrasted with the intense secrecy about processes that characterized the medieval guilds and which undoubtedly retarded technological progress and economic growth.

Not all economists agree that the patent system is beneficial. A patent represents a monopoly right, although as many inventors can testify, it may be a very weak one. Critics of the patent system stress the social costs arising from the monopoly. After a new process or product has been discovered, it costs little or nothing for other persons who could make use of this knowledge to acquire it. The patent gives the inventor the right to charge a price for the use of the information, with the result that the knowledge is used less widely than is socially optimal. Critics also point out that patents have been used to create monopoly positions, which were sustained by other means after the original patents had expired. They cite as examples the aluminum, shoe machinery, and plate glass industries. In addition, the cross-licensing of patents often has been used by firms as a vehicle for joint monopolistic exploitation of their market.

Critics also question the extent of the social gains arising from the system. They point out that the patent system was designed for the individual inventor, but that over the years most research and development has been institutionalized. They assert that patents are not really important as incentives to the large corporation, since it cannot afford to fall behind in the technological race, whether or not it receives a patent. They point out that, because of long lead times, most of the innovative profits from some types of innovations can be captured before imitators have a chance to enter the market. Moreover, they claim that firms keep secret what inventions they can, and patent those they cannot.

These questions concerning the effects and desirability of the patent system have proven extremely difficult to settle. But most observers seem to agree that, despite its faults, it is difficult to find a realistic substitute for the patent system. However, over the past 30 years, there has been a discernible trend for the courts and Congress to resolve conflicts between the patent system and antitrust policy more and more in favor of the latter. The courts have found more and more patents invalid. Congress has set higher standards of patentability, and the courts have curtailed the extension of the effects of the patent beyond the invention described in the patent claim.

Other Policies Designed to Restrict Competition

The reasons why laws are enacted to restrict, rather than promote, competition are not difficult to understand. Everyone wants competition for the other guy, but not for himself. Moreover, certain sectors of the economy seem to need help, and have the political muscle to get it—partly in the form of laws designed to take some of the competitive heat off them. A case of this sort is retail trade, where the small independent retailers felt threatened by the advent of the chain store. The chain stores were able to reduce the costs of distribution below those of the smaller retailers, with the result that the total number of grocery stores and drug stores fell considerably in the 1920s and 1930s. The small retailers charged that their smaller numbers were due to the predatory tactics by the chain stores. They took their charges to Congress and succeeded in getting the Robinson-Patman Act enacted in 1936.

The Robinson-Patman Act says that sellers must not discriminate in price among purchasers of similar grade and quality where the effect might be to drive competitors out of business. The act was aimed at preventing price discrimination in favor of chain stores that buy goods in large quantities. Most economists do not regard the Robinson-Patman Act with enthusiasm because it attempts to keep competitors in existence even if they are inefficient. Needless to say, the social virtues of the competitive system do not lie in maintaining a lot of inefficient small businessmen in operation. Moreover, most observers seem to believe that the act has had the effect of reducing the vigor of price competition in retail trade.

Another law designed to limit competition in retail trade was the Miller-Tydings Act of 1937, which exempted from the antitrust laws the use of resale price maintenance agreements in states permitting such agreements. ***Resale price maintenance agreements*** permit manufacturers of a trademarked or branded item to establish the retail price of the item by contracts with retailers. Moreover, the Miller-Tydings Act permitted the manufacturer to bind *all* retailers in a state to a contract simply by signing such a contract with *any one* of the retailers in the state. Of course, the result has been to reduce the amount of price competition in retail trade.

Finally, you should recognize that policies designed to limit competition are found in many other areas besides retail trade. In Chapter 5, we saw that our national farm policies have been aimed at keeping the prices of agricultural products at a level exceeding what they would be under competition. In Chapter 26, we shall see that the government has promoted the growth of strong labor unions, which try to raise wages above competitive levels. In the field of international trade, the Webb-Pomerene Act of 1918 allowed American exporters to get together to form export trade associations, which, according to some observers, may have tended to reduce competition. Even in the bituminous coal industry, which we looked at in some detail in Chapter 23, Congress passed the Bituminous Coal Act of 1937 to establish minimum prices and reduce "cutthroat" competition, though in 1943 the act was not renewed.

Thus, it simply is erroneous to think that the United States has opted decisively for competition. On the contrary, although the antitrust laws are clearly designed to promote competition and limit monopoly, a number of other laws are designed to do just the opposite. In many of the industries where laws designed to restrict competition have been enacted—for example, agriculture, retail trade, and bituminous coal—the basic problem has been that too many people and too much capital were tied up in the industry. Economists generally believe that it would be wiser to encourage people and capital to leave these industries than to attempt to limit competition. Recall, for example, our discussion in Chapter 5 of American farm policies.

Summary

The most important reason why economists oppose monopoly is that it imposes a burden on society by misallocating resources. A monopolistic industry produces up to the point where the social value of an extra unit of the good is greater than the cost to society of producing an extra unit of the good —which means that too little is produced of the monopolized good. Society is less well off than it could be. Oligopoly can be as bad as monopoly if oligopolists engage in collusion; and even if they don't collude, inefficiencies are likely to result. Monopolistic competition can also be a socially wasteful form of market organization. In defense of monopoly power, some economists have asserted that the rate of technological change is likely to be greater in an imperfectly competitive industry than under perfect competition. It does seem unlikely that a perfectly competitive industry would be able—and have the incentive—to carry out the research and development required to promote a rapid rate of technological change in many sectors of the economy. But contrary to the allegations of Galbraith and others, there is little evidence that giant firms are needed to insure rapid technological change and rapid utilization of new techniques. The situation is much more complex than such statements indicate, and the contributions of smaller firms are much greater than is commonly recognized.

Economic power in the United States is distributed very unevenly; 100 corporations control about ½ the total manufacturing assets of the economy. Moreover, many individual industries are dominated by a few firms. This concentration of power is viewed with concern by many economists and lawyers. In 1890, the Sherman Act was passed; it outlawed any contract, combination, or conspiracy in restraint of trade and made it illegal to monopolize or attempt to monopolize. In 1914, Congress passed the Clayton Act, and the Federal Trade Commission was created. A more recent antitrust development was the Celler-Kefauver Anti-Merger Act of 1950. The real impact of the antitrust laws depends on the interpretation placed on these laws by the courts. In its early cases, the Supreme Court put forth and used the famous rule of reason—that only unreasonable combinations in restraint of trade, not all trusts, required conviction under the Sherman Act. The situation changed greatly in the 1940s when the Court decided that Alcoa, because it controlled practically all of the nation's aluminum output, was in violation of the antitrust laws. The impact of the antitrust laws is also determined by the vigor with which the Antitrust Division of the Justice Department prosecutes cases. This too has varied from period to period.

There are at least two fairly distinct approaches to antitrust policy. One looks primarily and directly at market performance; the other emphasizes market structure. Although there are respected economists in favor of each of these approaches, the second is probably preferred by most experts in this field. Many observers seem to feel that the antitrust laws have not been as effective as they might—and should—have been, largely because they do not have sufficient public support. But this does not mean that they have not had an important effect. On the contrary, the evidence, although incomplete and unclear, suggests that they have had a significant effect on business behavior and markets. Finally, it is important to note that not all our laws are designed to promote competition and restrict monopoly. On the contrary, some laws are designed to do just the opposite. For example, the patent system confers a temporary monopoly on inventors. And the Robinson-Patman Act, the Miller-Tydings Act, and many other laws are designed to restrict competition. The truth is that, despite some protests to the contrary, our nation is by no means fully committed to promoting competition and preventing monopoly.

CONCEPTS FOR REVIEW

Concentration ratio
Rule of reason
Horizontal merger
Vertical merger
Conglomerate merger
Resale price maintenance
Market performance
Market structure
Line of commerce
Section of the country
Patent system
Robinson-Patman Act

QUESTIONS FOR DISCUSSION AND REVIEW

1. According to John Kenneth Galbraith, "The antitrust laws effectively protect the large business from social pressure or regulation by maintaining the myth that the market does the regulating instead." Do you agree? Why or why not?

2. According to *Fortune* magazine, "Congress should amend the antitrust statutes to make it clear . . . that it is not national policy to prefer any particular size, shape, or number of firms to any other size, shape, or number. . . ." Do you agree? Why or why not?

3. The real impact of the antitrust laws depends on judicial interpretation. True or False?

4. Mergers of firms in unrelated industries are called
a. horizontal. b. vertical. c. conglomerate. d. restraining.

PART EIGHT

Distribution of Income and General Equilibrium

CHAPTER 26

Determinants of Wages

Everyone has a healthy—indeed, sometimes an unhealthy—interest in income: organizations as holy as the church and as unholy as the Mob exhibit an interest in this subject. Surely we all need to look carefully at the social mechanisms underlying the distribution of income in our society. Most income is in the form of wages and salaries: that is, it is labor income. What determines the price paid for a particular kind of labor? For example, why is the wage rate for surgeons frequently in the neighborhood of $50 an hour, while the wage rate for relatively unskilled labor is frequently in the neighborhood of $2 or $3 an hour? Or why is the wage rate for a secretary higher in 1975 than in 1960?

Economists frequently classify inputs into three categories: labor, capital, and land. The disadvantage of this simple classification is that each category contains an enormous variety of inputs. For example, the services of labor include the work of a football star like Joe Namath, a salesman like

Willy Loman, and a knight like Don Quixote. But it does have the important advantage of distinguishing between quite different classes of inputs. In this chapter, we are concerned with the determinants of the price of labor. The next chapter will deal with the determinants of the prices of capital and land, as well as profits.

The Labor Force

At the outset it is important to note that, to the economist, labor includes a great deal more than the "organized labor" that belongs to trade unions. The secretary who works at General Motors, the young account executive at Merrill Lynch, the auto mechanic at your local garage, the professor who teaches molecular biology, all put forth labor. Table 26.1 shows the occupational distribution of the labor force in the United States. You can see that almost ⅔ of the people employed are white-collar workers (such as salesmen, doctors, secretaries, or managers) and service workers (such as waiters, bartenders, or cooks), while only about ⅓ are blue-collar workers (such as carpenters, mine workers, or foremen) and farm workers.

Labor Utilization by the Perfectly Competitive Firm

Let's begin by discussing the determinants of the price of labor under perfect competition. That is, we assume that firms take the prices of their products, as well as the prices of all inputs, as given; and we assume that owners of inputs take input prices as given. We first review some relevant material concerning the conditions for profit maximization under perfect competition; this material will be useful in deriving the firm's demand curve

Table 26.1

Occupational Composition of the Employed Labor Force, United States, 1971

	Percent of employed labor force	
White-collar workers		50.6
Professional and technical	14.6	
Managers and administrators	11.8	
Salesworkers	6.9	
Clerical workers	17.4	
Blue-collar workers		33.7
Craftsmen and foremen	13.5	
Operatives	15.8	
Nonfarm laborers	4.5	
Service workers		11.8
Farm workers		3.9
Total		100.0

Source: Statistical Abstract of the United States, 1972.

for labor. In particular, recall from Chapter 21 that the firm, if it minimizes costs, will pick a combination of inputs in which the ratio of each input's marginal product to its price is equal. That is, it will set

$$\frac{MP_A}{P_A} = \frac{MP_B}{P_B} = \cdots = \frac{MP_C}{P_C}, \qquad (26.1)$$

where MP_A is the marginal product of input A, P_A is the price of input A, MP_B is the marginal product of input B, P_B is the price of input B, and so on. If Equation (26.1) does not hold, the firm can always reduce costs by altering the utilization of certain inputs. For example, if the marginal product of a unit of input A is 2 units of output, the price of a unit of input A is \$1, the marginal product of a unit of input B is 6 units of output, and the price of a unit of input B is \$2, the firm can reduce its costs by using 1 unit less of input A—which reduces output by 2 units and cost by \$1—and by using ⅓ unit more of input B—which increases output by 2 units and cost by \$.67. This substitution of input B for input A has no effect on output but reduces the total cost of production by \$.33.

Going a step further, it can be shown that, if a firm minimizes cost, each of the ratios in Equation (26.1) equals the reciprocal of the firm's marginal cost. In other words,

$$\frac{P_A}{MP_A} = \frac{P_B}{MP_B} = \cdots = MC, \qquad (26.2)$$

where MC is its marginal cost.[1] At this point, it is important to recall from Chapter 22 that the perfectly competitive firm, if it maximizes profit, must be operating at a point at which marginal cost equals price. Thus it follows that

$$\frac{P_A}{MP_A} = \frac{P_B}{MP_B} = \cdots = P, \qquad (26.3)$$

where P is the product's price. Rearranging terms,

$$MP_A \cdot P = P_A \qquad (26.4a)$$
$$MP_B \cdot P = P_B \qquad (26.4b)$$
$$MP_C \cdot P = P_C \qquad (26.4c)$$

Thus we conclude that the profit-maximizing, perfectly competitive firm employs each input in an amount such that the input's marginal product multiplied by the product's price equals the input's price. This is a fundamental result, the basis of the firm's demand curve for an input. A further explanation of why this result must hold—and what it means—is given in the next section.

The Firm's Demand Curve for Labor

To show more clearly why the result in Equation (26.4) must hold and how it enables us to derive the firm's demand curve for labor, let us assume that we know the firm's production function, and that labor is the only variable input. Given the production function, we can determine the marginal product of labor when various quantities are used. The results of such a calculation are as shown in Table 26.2. If the price of the firm's product is \$10, let's determine the value to the firm of each additional worker it hires per day. According to Table 26.2, the firm increases its daily output by 7 units when it hires the first worker; and since each unit is worth \$10, this increases the firm's daily revenues by \$70. By hiring the second worker, the firm increases its daily output by 6 units; and since each unit is worth \$10, the resulting increase in the firm's daily revenues is \$60. Similarly, the increase in the firm's daily revenues from hiring the third worker is \$50, the increase

[1] To see this, consider any input, say input A. What is the cost of producing an extra unit of output if this extra unit of output is achieved by increasing the utilization of input A, while holding constant the utilization of other inputs? Since an extra unit of input A results in MP_A extra units of output, $(1/MP_A)$ units of input A will result in one unit of extra output. Since $(1/MP_A)$ units of input A will cost $(1/MP_A)P_A$, it follows that $P_A \div MP_A$ equals marginal cost. The same type of reasoning can be used for any input, not just input A.

Table 26.2

The Firm's Demand for Labor under Perfect Competition

Number of workers per day	Total output per day	Marginal product of labor	Value of marginal product
0	0		
		7	$70
1	7		
		6	60
2	13		
		5	50
3	18		
		4	40
4	22		
		3	30
5	25		

from hiring the fourth worker is $40, and so on.

How many workers should the firm hire per day if it wants to maximize profit? Clearly, it should hire more workers as long as each extra worker results in at least as great an addition to revenues as he does to costs. For example, if the price of a worker is $50 per day, it is profitable for the firm to hire the first worker since this adds $70 to the firm's daily revenues but only $50 to its daily costs. Also, it is profitable to hire the second worker, since this adds $60 to the firm's daily revenues but only $50 to its daily costs. The addition of the third worker does not reduce the firm's profits. But beyond 3 workers per day, it does not pay the firm to hire more labor. (The addition of a fourth worker adds $50 to the firm's daily costs but only $40 to its daily revenues.)

Thus the optimal number of workers per day for this firm is 3. Table 26.2 shows that this is the number of workers at which the value of the marginal product of labor is equal to the price of labor. This, of course, is exactly what we stated in Equation (26.4). This condition—that the value of the marginal product of an input be equal to the price of the input—must hold because if the value of the marginal product is *greater* than the input's price, the firm can increase its profit by increasing the quantity used of the input; while if the value of the marginal product is *less* than the input's price, the firm can increase its profit by reducing the quantity used of the input. Thus, profits must be at a maximum when the value of the marginal product is *equal* to the price of the input.

A firm's demand curve for an input is the relationship between the input's price and the amount of the input utilized by the firm. That is, it shows, for each price, the amount of the input that the firm will use. Given the results in this and the previous section, it is a simple matter to derive the firm's demand curve for labor. Specifically, its demand curve must be the value-of-marginal-product schedule in the last column of Table 26.2. For example, if the daily wage of a worker is between $51 and $60, the firm will demand 2 workers per day; if the daily wage of a worker is between $41 and $50, the firm will demand 3 workers per day; and so forth. Thus, *the firm's demand curve for labor is its value-of-marginal-product curve, which shows the value of labor's marginal product at each quantity of labor used.* This curve is shown in Figure 26.1.[2]

The Market Demand and Supply Curves for Labor

In the previous section, we were concerned with the demand curve of a single firm for labor. But many firms, not just one, are part of the labor market, and the price of labor depends on the demands of all of these firms. The situation is analogous to the price of a product, which depends on the demands of all consumers. *The market demand curve for labor shows the relationship between the price of labor and the total amount of*

[2] Strictly speaking, the firm's demand curve is the same as the curve showing the value of the input's marginal product only if this input is the only variable input. For a discussion of the more general case, see my *Microeconomics: Theory and Applications,* New York: Norton, 1970, Chapter 12.

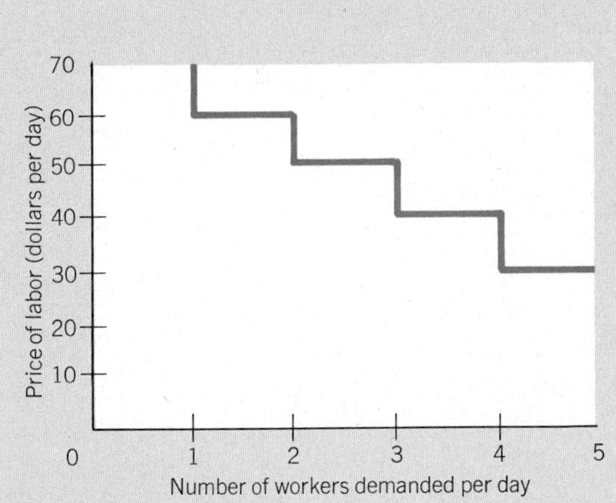

Figure 26.1
The Firm's Demand Curve for Labor under Perfect Competition

The firm's demand curve for labor is the firm's value-of-marginal-product curve, which shows the value of labor's marginal product at each quantity of labor used. The data for this figure come from Table 26.2.

labor demanded in the market: that is, it shows, for each price, the amount of labor that will be demanded in the entire market. The market demand curve for labor, like any other input, is quite analogous to the market demand curve for a consumer good, but there is at least one important difference. The demand for labor and other inputs is a *derived demand,* since inputs are demanded to produce other things, not as an end in themselves.

In Chapter 20 we pointed out that in the case of products the price elasticity of market demand varies enormously, since for some commodities the quantity demanded is very sensitive to price changes, while the quantity demanded of other products is quite insensitive to them. This is true of labor and other inputs as well. The quantity demanded of some inputs is very sensitive to price changes, whereas the quantity demanded of other inputs is not at all sensitive to them. Why is this, and what determines whether the price elasticity of demand for a particular input will be high or low? Several factors seem important. For one thing, the more easily other inputs can be substituted for a certain input, the more price-elastic will be the demand for the input. Also, the larger the price elasticity of demand for the product the input helps produce, the larger the price elasticity of demand for the input. In addition, the price elasticity of demand for an input is likely to be greater in the long run than in the short run.

We have already seen that a product's price depends on its market supply curve as well as its market demand curve. This is equally true for labor. Its *market supply curve* is *the relationship between the price of labor and the total amount of labor supplied in the market.* Many inputs are intermediate goods—goods that are bought from other business firms. For example, an important input in the aluminum industry is electric power, which is bought from the electric power industry. The supply curve for inputs of this kind is already familiar. However, labor is supplied by individuals, not firms. When an individual supplies labor, he is supplying something he himself can use, since the time that he does not work can be used for leisure activities. As Charles Lamb, the famous English essayist, put it, "Who first invented work, and bound the free and holiday-rejoicing spirit down . . . to that dry drudgery at the desk's dead wood?"[3]

An interesting feature of the market supply curve for labor is that, unlike the supply curve for inputs supplied by business firms, it may be ***backward bending,*** particularly for the economy as a whole. That is, *beyond some point, increases in price may result in smaller amounts of labor being supplied.* An example of a backward-bending supply curve is provided in Figure 26.2. What factors account for a curve like this? Basically, the reason is that as the price of labor is increased the

[3] The answer to Lamb's question is perhaps to be found in Genesis III, 19.

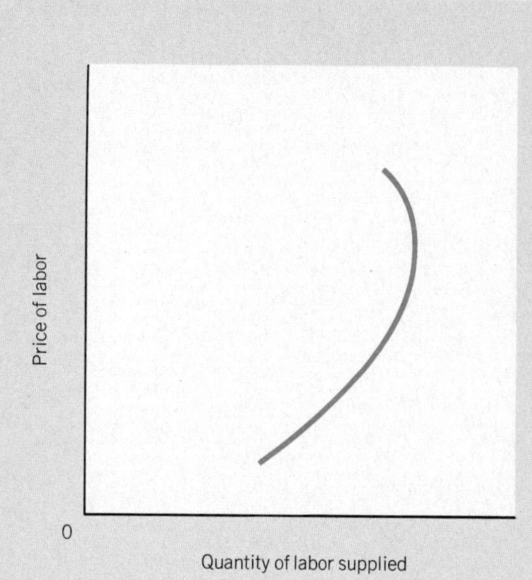

Figure 26.2
Backward-Bending Supply Curve for Labor

Beyond some point, increases in the price of labor may result in smaller amounts of labor being supplied. The reason for a supply curve of this sort is that, as the price of labor increases, the individual supplying the labor becomes richer and wants to increase his amount of leisure time.

individual supplying the labor becomes richer. And when he becomes richer, he wants to increase his amount of leisure time, which means that he wants to work less. Even though the amount of money per hour he gives up by not working is greater than when the price of labor was lower, he nonetheless chooses to increase his leisure time. This sort of tendency has shown up quite clearly in the last century. As wage rates have increased and living standards have risen, the average work week has tended to decline.

Note that there is no contradiction between the assumption that the supply of labor or other inputs to an individual firm is perfectly elastic under perfect competition and the fact that the market supply curve for the input may not be perfectly elastic. For example, unskilled labor may be available to any firm in a particular area at a given wage rate in as great an amount as it could possibly use. But the total amount of unskilled labor supplied in this area may increase relatively little with increases in the wage rate. The situation is similar to the sale of products. As we saw in Chapter 20, any firm under perfect competition believes that it can sell all it wants at the existing price. Yet the total amount of the product sold in the entire market can ordinarily be increased only by lowering the price.

Equilibrium Price and Quantity of Labor

Labor's price is determined under perfect competition in essentially the same way that a product's price is determined: by supply and demand. *The price of labor will tend toward equilibrium at the level where the quantity of labor demanded equals the quantity of labor supplied.* Thus, in Figure 26.3, the equilibrium price of labor is *OP*. If the price were higher than *OP*, the quantity supplied would exceed the quantity demanded and there would be downward pressure on the price. If the price were lower than *OP*, the quantity supplied would fall short of the quantity demanded and there would be upward pressure on the price. By the same token, *the equilibrium amount of labor utilized is also given by the intersection of the market supply and demand curves.* For example, in Figure 26.3, *OQ* units of labor will be utilized in equilibrium in the entire market.

Graphs such as Figure 26.3 are useful, but it is important to look behind the geometry. First, we must recognize that the price of labor includes a great many forms of remuneration other than what are commonly regarded as wages. Economists include as labor the services performed by professional people (such as lawyers, doctors, and professors) and self-employed businessmen (such as

Figure 26.3
Equilibrium Price and Quantity of Labor

The equilibrium price of labor is *OP*, and the equilibrium quantity of labor used is *OQ*.

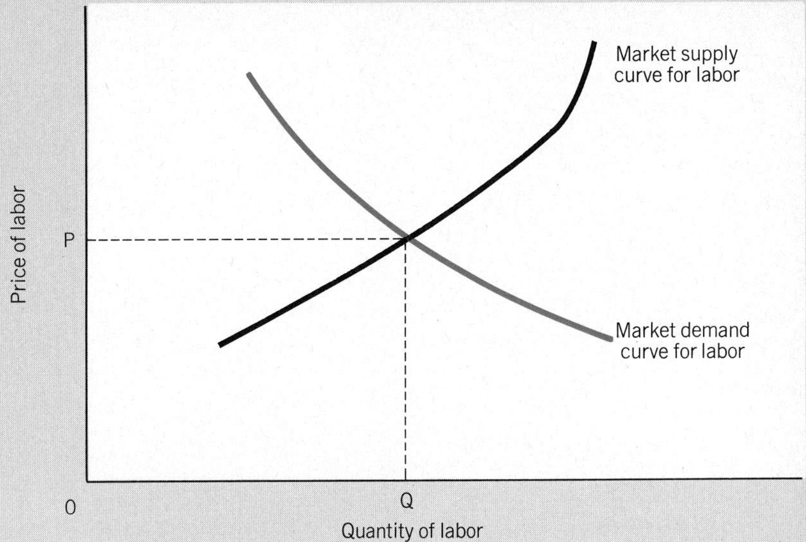

electricians, mechanics, and barbers). Thus, the amount such people receive per unit of time is included as a particular sort of price of labor. Also, it is important to distinguish between money wages and real wages. Whereas the money wage is the amount of money received per unit of time, the real wage is the amount of real goods and services that can be bought with the money wage. Obviously, the real wage depends on the price level for goods and services as well as on the level of the money wage. Since we assume that product prices are held constant, our discussion is in terms of real wages.

We must also recognize that labor productivity lies behind the demand curve and labor scarcity lies behind the supply curve. To illustrate this, consider the labor market for surgeons and that for unskilled labor. As shown in Figure 26.4, the demand curve for the services of surgeons is to the right of the demand curve for unskilled labor

Figure 26.4
The Labor Market for Surgeons and Unskilled Labor

The wage for surgeons is higher than for unskilled labor because the demand curve for surgeons is farther to the right and the supply curve for surgeons is farther to the left than the corre sponding curves for unskilled labor.

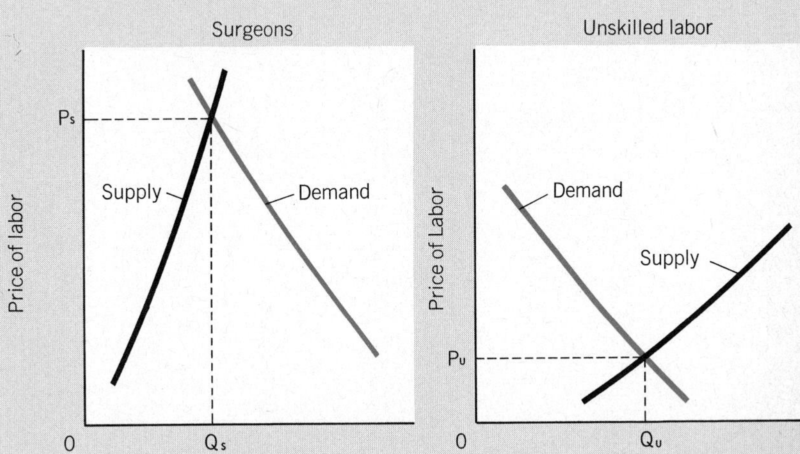

(particularly at high wage rates), because an hour of a surgeon's services is worth more to people than an hour of an unskilled laborer's services. In this sense, surgeons are more productive than unskilled laborers. Also, as shown in Figure 26.4, the supply curve for the services of surgeons is far to the left of the supply curve for unskilled labor. Very few people, after all, are licensed surgeons, whereas practically everyone can do unskilled labor. In other words, surgeons are much more scarce than unskilled laborers.

For these reasons, surgeons receive a much higher wage rate than do unskilled laborers. As shown in Figure 26.4, the equilibrium price of labor for surgeons is much higher than for unskilled labor. Of course, if unskilled laborers could quickly and easily turn themselves into competent surgeons, this difference in wage rate would be eliminated by competition, since unskilled workers would find it profitable to become surgeons. But unskilled workers lack the training and often the ability to become surgeons. Thus, surgeons and unskilled labor are examples of ***noncompeting groups.*** Wage differentials can be expected to persist among noncompeting groups because people cannot move from the low-paid to the high-paid jobs.

Wage Differentials

Everyone realizes that, even in the same occupation, some people get paid more than others. One reason for such wage differentials is that people differ in productive capacity. For example, some machinists are more skillful than others. Suppose that there are two types of machinists: class A and class B. Then, to maximize profit, a firm should hire each type of machinist up to the point at which

$$MP_A \cdot P = P_A \tag{26.5a}$$

$$MP_B \cdot P = P_B \tag{26.5b}$$

where MP_A is the marginal product of class A machinists, MP_B is the marginal product of class B machinists, P_A is the wage rate for class A machinists, P_B is the wage rate for class B machinists, and P is the price of the firm's product. This follows directly from Equation (26.4). Thus, the differential in wages between more skilled and less skilled machinists will equal the differential in their marginal products, since $P_A \div P_B = MP_A \div MP_B$.

In general, however, one cannot divide workers into two homogeneous groups, because each worker differs from the next in the value of his output. Under these circumstances, the difference in wages paid to workers will equal the difference in the total value of their output. For example, Arnold (together with the appropriate tools and materials) may produce output worth $1,000 per month and Leo (with the same tools and materials) may produce output worth $900 per month. In equilibrium, Arnold will earn $100 more per month than Leo. If the difference in wages were less than $100, Leo's employer would find it profitable to replace Leo with Arnold, since this would increase the value of output by $100 and cost less than $100. If the difference were more than $100, Arnold's employer would find it profitable to replace Arnold with Leo; although this would reduce the value of output by $100, it would reduce costs by more than $100.

This sort of analysis has been applied repeatedly to explain differences in land rents. According to the classical discussions of this subject, only the better tracts of land will be used at a given point in time. (The land not productive enough to earn a profit will not be in use.) The least productive lands in use earn neither a profit nor a loss. Consequently their price is zero, since no one would be willing to pay more for them. The rent of any other tract of land in use will equal the difference between its value yield and the value yield of this zero-priced marginal land (as long as the area of the plot remains constant). Consequently the tracts of land that are worked will rent at a variety of levels, but after subtracting rental costs they will earn an equal net profit for those who work them.

Besides differences in productive capacity and ability, there are many other reasons for wage differentials. Even if all workers were of equal ability, these differentials would still exist to offset differences in the characteristics of various occupations and areas. For example, some occupations require large investments in training, while other occupations require a much smaller investment in training. A chemist must spend about 8 years in undergraduate and graduate training. During each year of training, he incurs direct expenses for books, tuition, etc., and he loses the income he could make if he were to work rather than go to school. Clearly, if his net remuneration is to be as high in chemistry as in other jobs he might take, he must make a greater wage when he gets through than a person of comparable age, intelligence, and motivation whose job requires no training beyond high school. The difference in wages must be at least sufficient to compensate for his investment in extra training.

Similarly, members of some occupations must bear larger occupational expenses than others. For example, a psychologist may have to buy testing materials and subscribe to expensive journals. For net compensation to be equalized, such workers must be paid more than others. Also, some jobs are more unstable than others. For example, some types of construction workers are subject to frequent layoffs and have little job security, whereas many government employees (but not the top ones) are assured stable and secure employment. If the former jobs are to be as attractive as the latter, they must pay more. In addition, other differences among jobs must be offset by wage differentials if the net remuneration is to be equalized. For instance, there are differences among regions and communities in the cost of living. Living costs are generally lower in small towns than in big cities.

The All-Volunteer Army: A Case Study

In recent years, there has been considerable interest and controversy concerning the advantages and disadvantages of an all-volunteer army. Many economists have argued that it is more efficient and equitable to recruit an all-volunteer army than to rely on the draft, which through a complicated system of deferments and exemptions, as well as a lottery system, chooses a certain number of young men for military service. Proponents of an all-volunteer army point out that it is more compatible with freedom of choice than the draft. In addition, they say that military personnel can be used more effectively because the price of such personnel will be a more realistic indicator of its value in alternative uses. Further, they point out that the cost of military manpower will be distributed more equitably among the members of society. Under the draft a small group of draftees bears a large share of the cost, because they receive less in wages than would be required to induce them to volunteer.

Other economists and social observers oppose an all-volunteer army. They point out that it could hardly be expected to produce the necessary military manpower in a full-scale war. They also contend that such a "mercenary" army might constitute a political danger by attempting to gain improper power. Another drawback they cite is that an all-volunteer army would probably be largely black, which they find undesirable.

Whether you are for or against it, obviously one of the relevant facts is how much an all-volunteer army would increase the defense budget. In 1964, President Johnson asked that a study be made to determine whether it would be possible to shift from reliance on the draft to a system in which defense manpower needs would be met entirely by volunteers. A team of economists attempted to learn what it would cost.[4] Essentially they applied the kind of analysis described in this chapter. The basic approach was to estimate the supply curve for labor to the Department of Defense.

Figure 26.5 shows the relationship between the proportion of the male population that enlists and

[4] See S. Altman and A. Fechter, "The Supply of Military Personnel in the Absence of a Draft," *American Economic Review,* May 1967; and literature cited there.

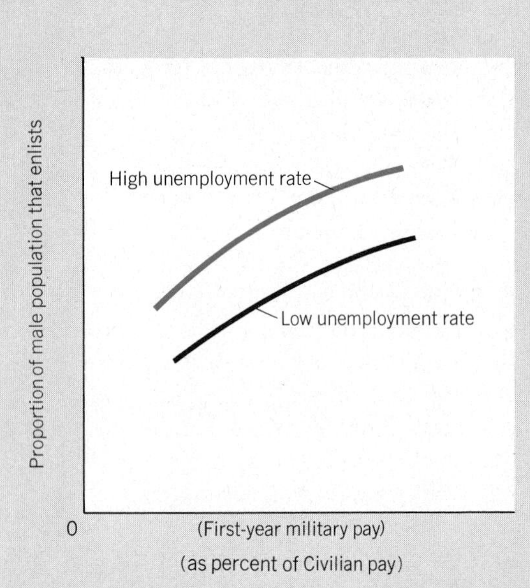

Figure 26.5
Relationship between Military Pay and Number of Enlistments

Holding the unemployment rate constant, the proportion of the male population that enlists is directly related to the level of military pay (as a percent of civilian pay). Using this supply curve, one can determine the level of military pay required to bring forth the extra enlistments needed to eliminate the draft.

the level of military pay (as a percent of civilian pay), the unemployment rate being held constant at two alternative levels. As would be expected, the number of enlistments increases with the level of military pay and the unemployment rate. Using this supply curve, which was estimated by the economists, one can determine (for given values of the unemployment rate) the level of military pay that would be required to bring forth the number of extra enlistments needed to eliminate the draft.

According to the economists, a 60 to 90 percent increase in enlistments would have been needed to eliminate the draft. To bring forth these extra enlistments, they estimated on the basis of the supply curve that first-term military pay for enlisted men would have to be increased by about 110 percent (if the unemployment rate were 5.5 percent). Using 1964 military earnings as a base, increases in first-term pay for enlisted men would have to be about $3,000 to attract enough volunteers to maintain a 2.65-million-man defense force. Multiplying 2.65 million men by the average increase in pay, the economists estimated that the increased cost to the Defense Department would be about $5 billion per year.[5] This estimate is very crude, as the economists stress, since many noneconomic factors influence the enlistment rate and the data and underlying assumptions are rough.

By 1973, the draft was no longer being used to obtain military manpower. Whether it will be reactivated in the near future is hard to say. For present purposes, the important point is that economic analysis, based on the fundamental concepts in this chapter, played a very significant role in the discussion and resolution of this major issue. And if conditions or attitudes change in such a way that this issue must be reconsidered, you can be sure that economics will continue to play a significant role in its resolution.

Monopsony

In previous sections, we have assumed that perfect competition exists in the labor market. In some cases, however, ***monopsony*** exists instead. *A monopsony is a market structure where there is a single buyer.* For example, a single firm may hire

[5] Note that the average increase in pay is less than the average increase in first-term pay. The way Altman and Fechter proceed from the latter to the former is described in their work. Also, note that the costs to the Defense Department, which are estimated here, may be quite different from the social costs of switching to an all-volunteer army.

all the labor in an isolated "company town," such as exists in the coal mining regions of West Virginia and Kentucky. What determines the price of labor under monopsony? Suppose the firm's demand curve for labor is *DD′* in Figure 26.6 and the supply curve of labor in *SS′*. Because the firm is the sole buyer of labor, it takes into account the fact that to acquire more labor it must pay a higher wage to *all* workers, not just the extra workers. The total additional cost of hiring an additional worker is shown by *AA′* in Figure 26.6. *AA′* lies above *SS′*, since *SS′* shows the cost of hiring an additional worker if workers already employed do *not* have to be paid a higher wage when the additional worker is hired.

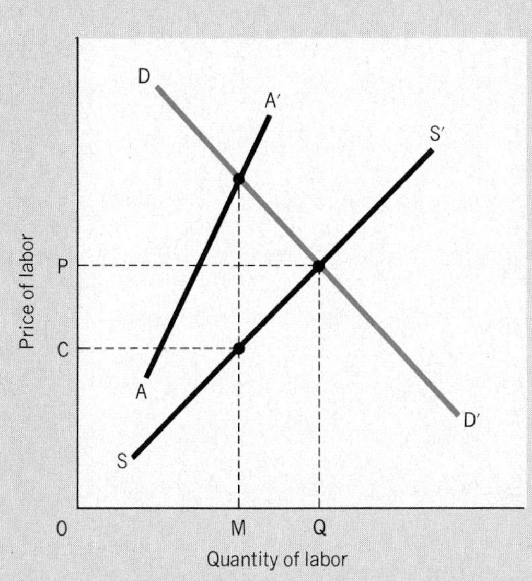

Figure 26.6
Equilibrium Wage and Quantity of Labor under Monopsony

The monopsonistic firm, if it maximizes profit, will hire laborers up to the point where the extra cost of adding an extra laborer, shown by *AA′*, equals the extra revenue from adding the extra laborer, shown by *DD′*.

If profit is maximized, the monopsonistic firm will hire labor up to the point at which the extra cost of adding an additional laborer (shown by *AA′*) equals the extra revenue from adding the additional laborer (shown by *DD′*). Thus the quantity of labor purchased will be *OM* and the price of labor will be *OC* in Figure 26.6. In contrast, under perfectly competitive conditions the equilibrium quantity and price would be at the intersection of the demand and supply curves. That is, the quantity of labor purchased would be *OQ* and the price of labor would be *OP*.

What is the effect of monopsony on the wage rate and the amount of labor hired? In general, ***the wage rate, as well as the quantity hired, is lower under monopsony than under perfect competition.*** This is the case in Figure 26.6, and it will generally hold true. Certainly this makes sense. One would expect a monopsonist, free from the pressures of competition, to pay workers less than would be required under perfect competition.

Labor Unions

About 1 in 4 nonfarm workers in the United States belong to unions, and the perfectly competitive model does not apply to these workers any more than it does to monopsonistic labor markets. Obviously, then, we must discuss labor unions in some detail. There are about 200 national unions in the United States; the biggest are the Teamsters, the United Auto Workers, and the United Steel Workers, each with over a million members. Next come the Electrical Workers, the Machinists, the Carpenters, the Mine Workers, and the Retail Clerks, each with over 500,000 members. A national union is composed of branches or chapters, each of which is a local union in a given area or plant. A worker joins his local union, which may have only a few members or as many as several thousand. The local union, with its own president and officers, often plays an important role in collective bargaining.

The national unions[6] are of great importance in the American labor movement. The supreme governing body of the national union is the convention, which is held every year or two. The delegates to the convention have the authority to set policy for the union. However, considerable power is exercised by the national union's officers. Union presidents—men like Leonard Woodcock of the Auto Workers, I. W. Abel of the Steel Workers, and Frank Fitzsimmons of the Teamsters—exercise great power. The extent to which the local unions maintain their autonomy varies from one national union to another. In industries where markets are localized (like construction and printing), the locals are more autonomous than in industries where markets are national (like steel, automobiles, and coal).

Finally, there is the AFL-CIO, a federation of national unions created by the merger of the American Federation of Labor and the Congress of Industrial Organizations in 1955. The AFL-CIO does not include all national unions. For example, the United Mine Workers refused to join the AFL-CIO, the Auto Workers recently left it, and the Teamsters were kicked out (because of corruption). The AFL-CIO is a very important spokesman for the American labor movement; but, because the national unions in the AFL-CIO have given up relatively little of their power to the federation, its authority is limited.

Early History of the American Labor Movement

To understand the nature and behavior of labor unions, it is necessary to look briefly at the history of the American labor movement. Unions arose, of course, because workers recognized that acting together gave them more bargaining power than acting separately. They frequently felt that they were at the mercy of their employers, and they formed fraternal societies and unions to promote economic and social benefits for the members. The first recorded case of collective bargaining in the United States took place in 1799, when Philadelphia shoemakers negotiated collectively with their employers. However, until the 1930s unions in the United States were not very strong, partly because of employers' efforts to break up unions, and partly because the courts held that the unions' attempts to increase wages and influence working conditions were conspiracies in restraint of trade. It is not difficult to understand the antiunion feelings of management, but it is difficult to exonerate the ruthlessness with which some managements attempted to stamp out unionism. Not only were prounion workers fired and blacklisted; they were sometimes beaten up or locked out of the plant. And when strikes occurred, strike breakers were sometimes hired to teach the striking workers a lesson.

The courts were also hostile to unions. The prevailing doctrine in much of the nineteenth century was that unions were criminal conspiracies, and even when this doctrine was abandoned the courts frequently regarded strikes, picketing, and other such union tactics as illegal. In addition, they sometimes used the Sherman Act of 1890 to stop unions, on the grounds that unions were conspiracies to restrain trade. Moreover, the courts often issued ***injunctions,*** which are cease-and-desist orders, to prevent unions from striking, boycotting, picketing, or carrying out other activities against the interests of their employers. In this way, the courts prevented unions from utilizing their potential power effectively.

In 1886, the *American Federation of Labor* came into existence. In contrast to many early unions, which were aimed at political goals, the AFL, led by Samuel Gompers, concentrated on economic issues. Basically, the AFL was an association of national craft unions, each of which was autonomous; but although it had limited power over the national unions, Gompers was a very important spokesman for the American labor movement.

[6] Sometimes they are called international unions because some locals are outside the United States—for example, in Canada.

The AFL came to be the dominant federation in American labor history, and its philosophy exerted great influence on the development of trade unionism in the United States. This philosophy was built on several tenets. First, Gompers and his associates felt that it would be a mistake to promote the development of a labor party in the United States. The AFL would try to elect its friends and defeat its enemies, but it would not form a third party and it would not align itself with either of the two major political parties. Second, the AFL would concentrate its efforts on bread-and-butter economic issues, not on attempts to alter the basic form of society. Higher wages and better working conditions, not social revolution or elimination of private property, were its aims. Third, the AFL was suspicious of government regulation. It felt that the interests of labor would be served best if the government interfered as little as possible in collective bargaining.

The AFL was relatively successful in increasing union membership; total union membership was about 2 million in 1904 and about 5 million in 1920. In part, this increase resulted from tight labor markets and the government's support of collective bargaining during World War I in return for labor's help in the war effort. After the war, union membership dropped from more than 5 million to about 2.6 million in 1933, due in part to the onset of the Great Depression. The period after World War I was marked by strong antiunion sentiments. Employers resisted unions strenuously—and successfully. For example, in 1919 the U. S. Steel Corporation—led by our old friend from Chapter 24, Elbert Gary—crushed a strike resulting from an attempt to organize its plants. Firms pushed hard for an "American Plan" under which union members would not be hired. Certainly the 1920s were a difficult period for American labor unions.

The New Deal and World War II

During the early 1930s, the tide began to turn. To a great extent, this was because of government encouragement of unions, the first important step being the *Norris-LaGuardia Act* of 1932. This act made it much more difficult for courts to issue injunctions against unions, and it made ***yellow-dog contracts***—agreements in which a worker promised his employer not to join a union—unenforceable in federal courts. The next important step occurred in 1935, when Congress passed the ***Wagner Act,*** which made it an unfair labor practice for employers to refuse to bargain collectively with unions representing a majority of their workers, or to interfere with their workers' right to organize. In addition, this act established the *National Labor Relations Board* to investigate unfair labor practices, to issue orders enforceable in federal courts, and to hold elections to determine which, if any, union would represent various groups of employees. The Wagner Act was a very important factor in encouraging the growth of labor unions in the United States—so important that it has often been called American labor's Magna Carta.

Another important factor in the growth of unions during the 1930s was the emergence of industrial unions. The more favorable atmosphere for union organization and growth led to the creation in 1935 of a new federation, the *Congress of Industrial Organizations*. The unions that created and formed the CIO rebelled against the AFL's apparent inability to take advantage of the opportunity to organize the mass production industries like autos and steel. The AFL was composed primarily of unions organized along craft lines: the carpenters had one union, the machinists had another union, and so on for other crafts. This is in contrast to industrial unions, which include all workers in a particular plant or industry.

The young CIO, led by the United Mine Workers' president, John L. Lewis, set out to establish industrial unions in the mass-production industries.[7] The CIO was very successful in its organization drives during the late 1930s. In 1937

[7] Before leaving the AFL, Lewis emphasized the strength of his convictions by knocking down and bloodying up his principal opponent, William Hutcheson, president of the Carpenters' Union, on the floor of the 1935 AFL Convention.

U. S. Steel, formerly a bulwark of antiunionism, recognized the Steel Workers as bargaining agent for its more than 200,000 workers. Using the sit-down strike—in which strikers occupy the plant—as a weapon, workers in the automobile and rubber industries organized CIO unions too. In addition, the CIO organized unions in electrical machinery, petroleum refining, textiles, meat packing, longshoring, and other industries.[8]

The 1930s were a period of spectacular union growth. Aided by the prounion attitude of the Roosevelt administration, the new legislation, and the energy of its leaders, total union membership rose from less than 3 million in 1933 to more than 10 million in 1941. World War II witnessed a further growth in total union membership. Stimulated by the increase in total employment and the government's favorable attitude toward their growth, unions increased their membership from over 10 million in 1941 to almost 15 million—or about 36 percent of all nonfarm workers—in 1945. As in World War I, the government helped unions gain recognition in exchange for union cooperation in promoting war production. By the end of World War II, labor unions were conspicuous and powerful features of the economic landscape.

The United Automobile Workers: A Case Study[9]

To illustrate the growth of the labor movement in the 1930s and early 1940s, consider the history of the United Automobile Workers, currently one of the nation's largest unions. The U.A.W. was organized in August 1935 and affiliated with the CIO in 1936, but was not recognized by either General Motors or Ford until 1937. In late 1936, a sit-down strike occurred in some of General Motors' factories, with the result that other GM factories were closed for lack of parts. GM got an injunction that ordered the men to vacate the plants, but when it was determined that the judge who issued the injunction had over $200,000 worth of GM stock, the injunction was declared invalid.

Faced with this situation, GM president Alfred P. Sloan Jr.—an acquaintance of ours from Chapter 7—said, "General Motors will never recognize any union as the sole bargaining agency for all its employees." On January 11, 1937, violence broke out between the police and the strikers, when the police tried to stop the delivery of food to the sit-down strikers occupying the plants. On the following day, the governor of Michigan sent the National Guard to maintain the peace. Finally, on February 11, 1937, General Motors agreed to recognize the union as the bargaining agency for its workers, and the union agreed to end the strike. The union leaders hailed the agreement as a tremendous victory.

However, the Ford Motor Company was still unorganized. Henry Ford was dead set against the unionization of his employees and used strong tactics to discourage it. For example, in 1937 Walter Reuther, a young union organizer who was later to become president of the U.A.W., received a savage beating from Ford's men. In 1938, the U.A.W. reported various unfair practices of the Ford Motor Company to the National Labor Relations Board. Although Ford succeeded in delaying a final decision until 1941, the company was finally ordered to rehire and pay back wages to over 2,000 employees who had been illegally fired for union membership. In 1941, Ford signed a contract with the U.A.W., thus completing the unionization of the major automobile producers.

From these violent beginnings there gradually has developed a viable system of collective bargaining in the automobile industry. During the 1940s the relationship between labor and management was sometimes closer to an armed truce than a permanent peace treaty, but time has mellowed this relationship considerably. And as the U.A.W.

[8] Confronted with the CIO's successes, the AFL also organized new industrial unions, although craft unions remained by far the most important part of the federation.
[9] This section is based in considerable part on A. Paradis, *Labor in Action,* New York: Messner, 1963.

has grown older, it also has gotten richer. By the 1960s it had over $50 million in assets. Moreover, it has become an important factor in politics, particularly in Michigan. Through the efforts of Reuther and his colleagues, the U.A.W. has become a major force in the American economy.

Creation and Structure of the AFL-CIO

In 1955, a merger occurred between the AFL and the CIO. Given the acrimony marking the relationship between these two organizations in the 1930s, the merger may seem surprising. But the differences in their attitudes toward the question of organization along industrial versus craft lines had diminished in importance over the years. And the old leaders, including those like Lewis of the Mine Workers and Hutcheson of the Carpenters who had traded blows in earlier days, had died—or, as in Lewis's case, were no longer in either federation.[10] Moreover, the merger had advantages. The labor movement, despite large-scale organization drives in the South after the war, was unable to increase union membership appreciably during the 1950s. Many unions attributed this fact to the rivalry between the AFL and the CIO and argued that a united front would result in increased membership. Also, and perhaps most important, Congress passed several pieces of legislation, including the Taft-Hartley Act of 1947, that were heartily disliked by the unions, and it was felt that the merger would increase labor's political clout.

The AFL-CIO is organized along the lines indicated in Figure 26.7. The organization closely resembles that of the AFL (the larger of the merging federations). The constitution of the AFL-CIO puts supreme governing power in the hands

[10] Lewis resigned from the presidency of the CIO because workers would not follow his lead and vote for Wendell Willkie for president of the United States in 1940. Later he took his union back into the AFL, but withdrew from the AFL in 1947 because the AFL did not boycott the National Labor Relations Board in an effort to defeat the Taft-Hartley Act.

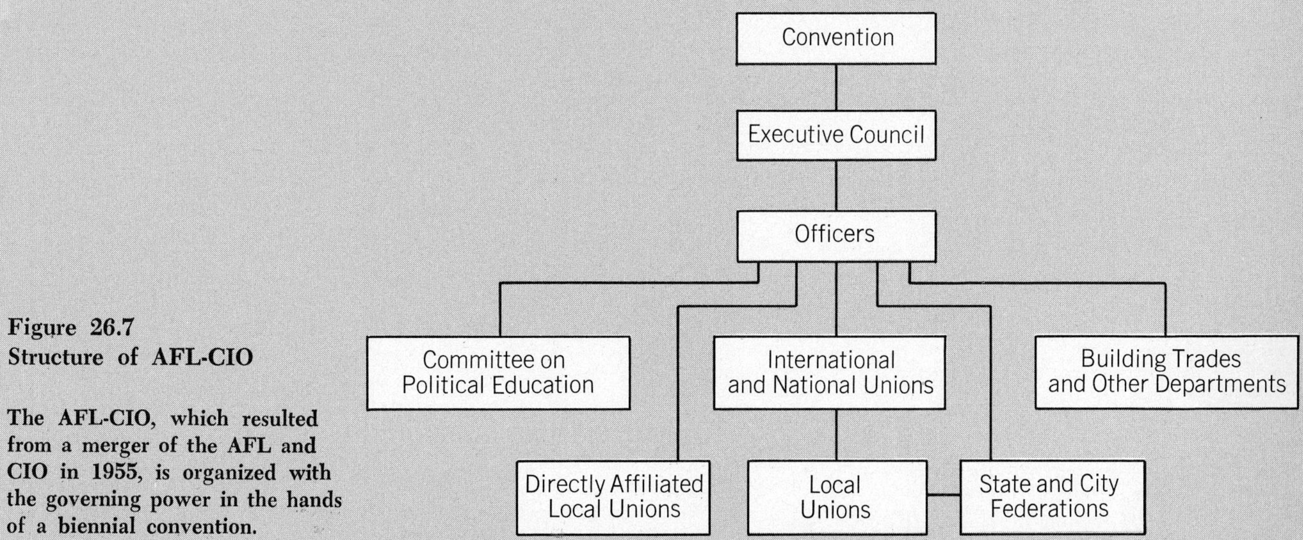

Figure 26.7
Structure of AFL-CIO

The AFL-CIO, which resulted from a merger of the AFL and CIO in 1955, is organized with the governing power in the hands of a biennial convention.

of a biennial convention. The national unions are represented at these conventions on the basis of their dues-paying membership. Between conventions, the AFL-CIO's business is directed by its president and secretary-treasurer, as well as by various committees and councils composed of representatives of various national unions or people elected at the convention. The AFL-CIO contains seven trade and industrial departments, such as building trades, food and beverage trades, maritime trades, etc. Also, as indicated by Figure 26.7, a few local unions are not affiliated with a national union, but are directly affiliated with the AFL-CIO.

Internal Problems in Labor Unions

As unions have grown older and more secure and powerful, there has been more and more concern about the nature of their internal practices and leadership. After all, they are no longer the underdogs that they were 50 years ago. They are huge organizations with immense power. Both in this country and in Europe, observers have charged that unions are often far from democratic. Members are frequently apathetic, for there is less interest in union affairs now than in the early days when unions were fighting for survival; and the leadership of some unions has become entrenched and bureaucratic. Moreover, there are frequent charges that unions engage in racial and other forms of discrimination.

The leadership of a union, like the management of a large corporation, is not easy to overturn. The leadership controls a staff, the union paper, and other levers to help maintain itself in power. These advantages, together with worker apathy, enable leaders to stay in power for many years without being very responsive to majority rule. As Clark Kerr, former president of the University of California and a distinguished labor economist, put it, "Unions have usually ended up by being a business serving the members, but sometimes with the members having little more influence over the conduct of the business than the stockholders have over a corporation. Unions have almost never ended up as a town meeting."[11]

It is important, however, that this problem not be exaggerated. Union leaders know that they must produce results that are roughly satisfactory to at least a substantial number of their membership. Although local union meetings are seldom attended by more than 10 percent of the members, the rest always *can* show up. Moreover, although there are difficulties in overturning an entrenched leadership, it is seldom impossible. Just as the management of a large corporation will be sacked if it departs sufficiently from the wishes of the stockholders, so the leaders of a union will be kicked out of office if they depart sufficiently from the wishes of the members. In recent years, the presidents of the United Steelworkers; International Union of Electrical Workers; State, County, and Municipal Workers; and United Mine Workers have been defeated in contested elections.

Another problem is corruption within labor unions. In the 1950s, a Senate committee—the so-called McClellan Committee—conducted lengthy and revealing investigations which showed, for example, that the leaders of the Teamsters Union had misused union funds, had questionable relations with the underworld, and had "shamefully betrayed their own members." Other unions were also accused of corrupt practices. It is important, however, to avoid smearing the entire labor movement. Although racketeering and fraud unquestionably are problems, they tend to be localized in a relatively few industries—particularly the building trades, trucking, longshoring, laundries, and hotels. Many responsible and honest leaders of the labor movement have tried hard to rid the labor movement of these unsavory practices.

Postwar Labor Legislation

After World War II, public sentiment turned somewhat against unions. Strikes and higher prices got

[11] Clark Kerr, *Unions and Union Leaders of Their Own Choosing*, New York: Fund for the Republic, 1957, p. 10.

James Hoffa: A Man Who Understands the Economics of Trucking

Past president of the International Union of Teamsters, Chauffeurs, and Longshoremen, James Riddle Hoffa, accused of peddling sweetheart contracts, using violence as an organizing tool, and siphoning off money from the Teamsters pension fund, was convicted of jury tampering and sent to jail (by Robert Kennedy during the latter's term as attorney general). Yet many feel that if the conditions of his parole were suspended so that he could run for union office again, the trucking industry as well as the Teamsters Union would welcome him back. Why? Because, as the president of one of the largest national trucking firms observed, "He understands the economics of the industry."

When Hoffa ascended to the general presidency of the Teamsters, the trucking industry was fairly competitive. The independent owner-operator, a man owning and driving his own truck, bidding on delivery jobs, and competing with the majors, made up about 40 percent of the industry. These free-lance competitors went after work very agressively, often offering flexibility in number of stops and pickups at a speed that the majors could not match. Moreover, because they were in business for themselves, the independents were often willing to forgo some of the benefits the drivers for the bigger companies demanded.

Hoffa appreciated the downward pressure these independents put on profit rates and, indirectly, on wages. "These little guys give me a pain," he observed. By the mid-fifties, after his elimination of opposition within the union, Hoffa was able to do something about the problem. He negotiated (and enforced) three collective bargaining clauses that squeezed the little operator—payment by the mile (rather than by the trip), a required relief time, and a mandatory fringe benefit contribution. By 1962, when Hoffa made his untimely exit, the small operators were less than 20 percent of the industry and dropping fast. The result? A less competitive, more profitable industry, and since Hoffa was there to insist on his share, a higher wage for the teamster. For it was Hoffa who had taken a fragmented industry, dominated by local barons of varying strength and competence, and made it into a national industry by negotiating a National Master Freight Agreement which brought all unionized over-the-road trucking companies into the same rate structure. He thereby dethroned nearly all the barons. Clearly, the Teamsters and the industry may have benefited—even if the public didn't. E.A.

under the skin of the consumer as well as the employer, and there began to be a lot of talk in Congress and elsewhere about the prewar Wagner Act having been too one-sided, giving the advantages to labor and the penalties to the employer. In 1947, despite bitter labor opposition, the ***Taft-Hartley Act*** was passed, with the purpose of redressing the balance between labor and employers. The act established standards of conduct for unions as well as employers, defined unfair union practices, and stated that unions can be sued for acts of their agents. Also, the act outlawed the closed shop, which requires that firms hire only workers who are already union members, and stipulated that, unless the workers agree in writing, the ***checkoff*** is illegal. (The checkoff is a system in which the employer deducts union dues from each worker's pay and hands them over to the union.)

In addition, the act tried to increase protection against strikes in which the public's safety and health are involved. If the president decides that an actual or impending strike imperils the national health or safety, he can appoint a fact-finding committee to investigate the situation. After receiving the committee's report, he can tell the Attorney General to obtain an injunction forbidding a strike for 80 days, during which the parties can continue to negotiate. A Federal Mediation Service was established to help the parties settle such negotiations. The act does not forbid a strike at the end of the 80 days, if no agreement has been reached.

In response to the evidence of union corruption presented by the McClellan Committee, Congress passed the *Landrum-Griffin Act* in 1959. This act attempts to protect the rights of individual union members from abuse by union leaders. It contains a "bill of rights" for labor guaranteeing that each member can participate in union elections, that elections be held by secret ballot, and that other steps be taken to protect the rights of the members. It also requires unions to file financial reports, forbids payments (beyond wages) by employers to union representatives, and prohibits loans exceeding $2,000 by unions to union officials.

Recent Trends in Union Membership

In recent years, union membership has increased rather modestly; indeed, during the late 1950s and early 1960s, it didn't increase at all. To some extent, this has been due to dissension within the labor movement and to a diminution of the zeal that characterized the movement in earlier years. Also, rightly or wrongly, unions have lost a certain amount of public sympathy and respect because of racial discrimination, unpopular strikes, evidence of corruption, and the belief that they are responsible in considerable part for cost-push inflation. But these factors only partly explain this lack of growth. In addition, important changes in the labor force have tended to reduce union membership.

Specifically, the increasing proportion of *white-collar workers* seems to have raised important problems for unions. To date, unions have made relatively little progress in organizing white-collar workers. For example, in the early 1960s, only about 3 percent of engineers, and about 9 percent of office workers were union members. One reason for this lack of progress is that white-collar employees tend to identify with management. Also, the increasing proportion of *women* in the labor force seems to raise important problems for unions. It is sometimes claimed that female workers are harder to organize because they do not stay in the labor force very long and because they are concentrated in jobs—clerical and sales positions—that are difficult to organize. Nonetheless, almost 1 in 5 union members in 1962 were women; and the majority of the Retail Clerks, the Clothing Workers, and the International Ladies Garment Workers were women.

However, even though union membership has not been growing in recent years, it would be a mistake to jump to the conclusion that the American labor movement is stagnant or that unions are declining in importance. For one thing, membership is not a very good measure of power. A small union can sometimes bring an enormous amount of pressure to bear if it is located strategically in the economy. Also, union membership has been growing rapidly in some areas, notably ***public employment.*** Between 1956 and 1968, union membership among public employees grew from 915,000 to 2,155,000, with the bulk of the membership in 6 unions, 3 of federal employees and 3 of state and local employees.[12] For many years, there was a tradition, as well as legal prohibitions, against strikes by public employees. But during the 1960s, when these workers seemed to be left behind economically, various executive orders and legislative enactments encouraged unionism among public employees. Needless to say, difficult problems have arisen when union members manning vital public services have chosen to strike. For example, teachers' strikes have shut down schools, often for weeks.

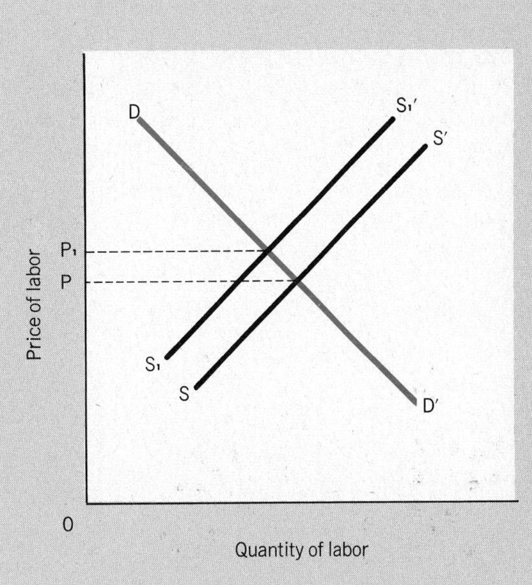

Figure 26.8
Shift of Supply Curve for Labor

A union may shift the supply curve from *SS'* to S_1S_1' by getting employers to hire only union members and then restricting union membership, or by other techniques.

How Unions Increase Wages

Clearly, unions wield considerable power, and economists must include them in their analysis if they want their models of the labor market to reflect conditions in the real world. We shall now see how this is done. Let us begin by supposing that a union wants to increase the wage rate paid its members. How can it accomplish this objective? In other words, how can it alter the market supply curve for labor, or the market demand curve for labor, so that the price of labor—its wage—will increase?

First, the union may try to shift the supply curve of labor to the left. For example, it may shift the supply curve in Figure 26.8 from *SS'* to S_1S_1', with the result that the price of labor will increase from *OP* to OP_1. (Of course, *DD'* is the demand curve for labor.) How can the union cause this shift in the supply curve? Craft unions have frequently forced employers to hire only union members, and then restricted union membership by high initiation fees, reduction in new membership, and other devices. In addition, unions have favored legislation to reduce immigration, shorten working hours, and limit the labor supply in other ways.

Second, the union may try to get the employers to pay a higher wage, while allowing some of the supply of labor forthcoming at this higher wage to find no opportunity for work. For example, in Figure 26.9, the union may exert pressure on the employers to raise the price of labor from *OP* to OP_1. At OP_1, not all of the available supply of

[12] The three unions of federal employees are the American Federation of Government Employees, the National Association of Letter Carriers, and the United Federation of Postal Clerks. The three unions of state and local employees are the American Federation of State, County, and Municipal Employees; the American Federation of Teachers; and the International Association of Firefighters.

labor can find jobs. The quantity of labor supplied is OQ_2, while the amount of labor demanded is OQ_1. The effect is the same as in Figure 26.8, but in this case the union does not limit the supply directly. It lets the higher wage reduce the opportunity for work. Strong industrial unions often behave in this fashion. Having organized practically all the relevant workers and controlling the labor supply, the union raises the wage to OP_1. This is a common and important case.

Third, the union may try to shift the demand for labor upward and to the right. For example, in Figure 26.10, it might try to shift the demand curve from DD' to D_2D_2', with the result that the price of labor will increase from OP to OP_2. To cause this shift in the demand for labor, the union may resort to "featherbedding." That is, it may try to restrict output per worker in order to increase the amount of labor required to do a certain job. For example, the railroad unions have insisted on much unnecessary labor. Unions also try to shift the demand curve by helping the employers compete against other industries, or by helping to make Congress pass legislation that protects the employers from foreign competition.

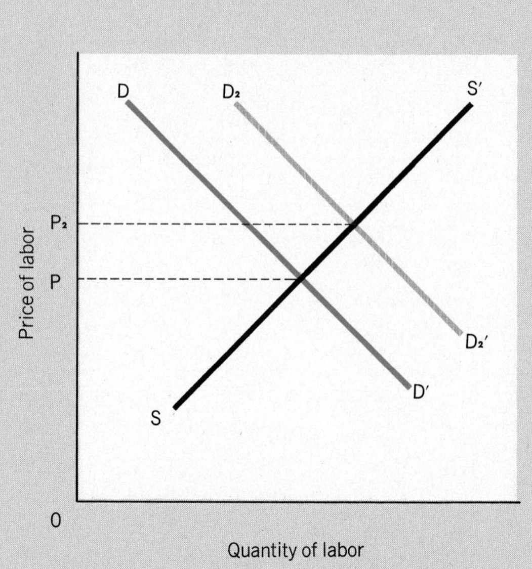

Figure 26.10
Shift in Demand Curve for Labor

A union may shift the demand curve for labor from DD' to D_2D_2' by "featherbedding" or other devices, thus increasing the wage from OP to OP_2.

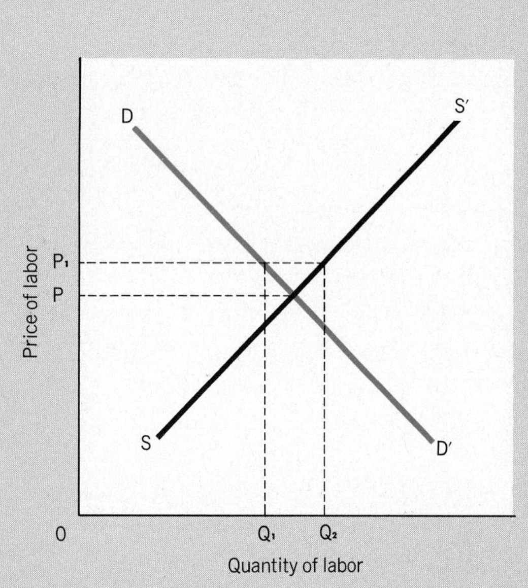

Figure 26.9
Direct Increase in Price of Labor

A union may get the employer to raise the wage from OP to OP_1, and let the higher wage reduce the opportunity for work. This is commonly done by strong industrial unions.

Collective Bargaining

Collective bargaining is the process of negotiation between the union and the management over wages and working conditions. Representatives of the union and management meet periodically to work out an agreement or contract; this process generally begins a few months before the old labor contract runs out. Typically, each side asks at first for more than it expects to get, and compromises must be made to reach an agreement. The union representatives take the agreement to their members, who must vote to accept or reject it. If they reject it, they may vote to strike or to continue to negotiate.

Collective bargaining agreements vary greatly. Some pertain to only a single plant while others apply to an entire industry. However, an agreement generally contains the following elements: it specifies the extent and kind of recognition that management gives the union, the level of wage rates for particular jobs, the length of the workweek, the rate of overtime pay, the extent to which seniority will determine which workers will be first to be laid off, the nature and extent of management's prerogatives, and how grievances between workers and the employer will be handled.

Historically, industries and firms have extended recognition to unions by accepting one of three arrangements: the closed shop, the union shop, or the open shop. In a ***closed shop,*** a worker must be a union member before he can be hired. This gives the union more power than if there is a ***union shop,*** in which the employer can hire nonunion workers who must then become union members in a certain length of time after being hired. In an ***open shop,*** the employer can hire union or nonunion labor, and nonunion workers need not, once employed, join the union. As we have seen, the closed shop was banned by the Taft-Hartley Act. The Taft-Hartley Act also says that the union shop is legal unless outlawed by state laws; and in about 20 states there are "right-to-work" laws that make the union shop illegal. Needless to say, these "right-to-work" laws are hated by organized labor, which regards them as a threat to its security and effectiveness.

Besides the kind of recognition accorded the union, collective bargaining deals with a variety of issues concerning employee compensation. Should workers be paid by the hour, or should they receive a certain amount of pay for each unit they produce? If they are paid by the hour, how much should each occupation receive per hour, and how much variation in this amount should be permitted to compensate for extra merit or skill? How much should each worker receive in the way of fringe benefits: paid holidays, medical insurance, sick leave, and so forth? What should be the standard workweek, and what should be the overtime rate paid for work exceeding the standard workweek? These and other related questions are obviously of great importance, both to the workers and to the employers.

In addition, collective bargaining agreements generally provide for some way to iron out grievances and disagreements between the workers and management during the life of the contract. It would be unrealistic to assume that such problems will not occur. Often, it is stipulated that disagreements that cannot be resolved by the parties will be settled by submitting them to an arbitrator whose decision will be final. The arbitrator, who is impartial and acceptable to both sides, will hear the case at issue and decide what, in the light of the written contract, seems to be an appropriate resolution of the problem.

Strikes and Pattern Bargaining

Most contracts are settled without resort to a discontinuance of work. But not always. If the union stops work, it is called a ***strike,*** whereas if the employer precipitates the work stoppage, it is called a ***lockout.*** Whoever is immediately responsible, the result is the same: the workers lose income and the employer loses output and profits. The threat of a work stoppage is a potent force encouraging both sides to reach agreement. Strikes occur less frequently than is generally recognized; only about 0.2 percent of all mandays is lost through strikes. (The amount of time lost through strikes is much less than the time spent on coffee breaks!) Without the right to strike, labor's bargaining powers would be greatly weakened. However, when strikes take place in strategic areas involving the nation's health and safety, the government must step in to protect the interests of the public. No government will let a crippling strike go on very long. Presidents, both Republican and Democratic, have used the provisions of the Taft-Hartley Act to stop strikes in important areas. As noted in a previous section, the increasing unionization of public employees—firemen, air controllers, teachers—makes such strikes more and more of a problem.

Collective bargaining is a power struggle. At each point in their negotiations, both the union and the employer must compare the costs (or benefits) of agreeing with the other party with the costs (or benefits) of continuing to disagree. The costs of disagreement are the costs of a strike, while the costs of agreement are the costs of settling on terms other than one's own. These costs are determined by basic market forces. For example, during periods when demand is great, employers are more likely to grant large wage increases because the costs of disagreement seem higher (a strike will prove more costly) than those of settlement. The outcome of the negotiations will depend on the relative strength of the parties. The strength of the employer depends on his ability to withstand a strike. The strength of the union depends on its ability to keep out nonunion workers and to enlist the support of other unions, as well as on the size of its financial reserves.

It is important to note that a union's wage demands are likely to be influenced by what other unions are getting for their memberships. If some unions are getting increases of one dollar an hour, another union may feel that it must do at least as well to show its membership that it can produce for them. For this reason, wage negotiations in a few important industries like steel and autos may set a pattern for other industries. Right after World War II, the pattern setters were the auto, mine, steel, electrical, and rubber unions. Within an industry, pattern bargaining often exists. Once a contract is signed with one major producer, the other firms in the industry accept—and are given—essentially identical terms.

The Pros and Cons of Big Unions

Finally, we should discuss briefly some of the criticisms that are made of the big unions. These criticisms are based largely on their monopoly power. Critics charge that by exerting such power unions push up the price of labor and reduce the level of employment in various industries. This results in badly allocated resources, since the price of labor no longer signals accurately the relative scarcity of labor of various types. Moreover, it is argued that the resulting upward pressure on wages is an important element in cost-push inflation. Opponents of big unions have proposed at least four policies designed to reduce their power: first, that the antitrust laws be applied to unions as well as firms; second, that industry-wide bargaining, which allows a union to shut down an entire industry, be banned; third, that the union shop be banned; and fourth, that big unions be broken up into a number of smaller ones.

On the other hand, many economists feel that labor unions are an important positive force in the American economy. They argue that it is foolish to believe that without unions labor markets would be perfectly competitive—and that the price of labor would be the proper one from the point of view of resource allocation. They point out that unions tend to be an antidote to the monopsonistic power held by some employers in the labor market. And they argue that unions are not really the prime movers in cost-push inflation, but rather that unions often respond to prior price increases by firms. Thus, many economists believe that public policy should encourage the growth and power of big unions.

These issues are complex and involve basic political values as well as economic analysis. They will be debated for a long time, since it seems highly unlikely that the big unions will fold their tents and disappear. Certainly the big unions, like the big corporations, must be watched carefully to try to insure that their vast power is utilized responsibly. But it is extremely difficult to define responsible or socially desirable behavior in specific instances. Just as it is hard to deal with the power of the large corporation, so it is hard to deal with the power of the big union.

Summary

Assuming perfect competition, a firm will employ each type of labor in an amount such that its marginal product times the product's price equals its wage. In other words, the firm will employ enough labor so that the value of the marginal product of labor equals labor's price. Consequently, the firm's demand curve for labor—which shows, for each price of labor, the amount of labor the firm will use—is the firm's value-of-marginal-product curve (if labor is the only variable input). The market demand curve for labor shows the relationship between its price and the total amount of labor demanded in the market.

Labor's price depends on its market supply curve as well as on its market demand curve. Labor's market supply curve is the relationship between the price of labor and the total amount of labor supplied in the market. Labor's market supply curve may be backward bending. An input's price is determined under perfect competition in essentially the same way that a product's price is determined: by supply and demand. The price of labor will tend in equilibrium to the level at which the quantity of labor demanded equals the quantity of labor supplied. By the same token, the equilibrium amount of labor utilized is also given by the intersection of the market supply and demand curves.

If there are qualitative differences among workers, the differential in their wages will correspond to the differential in their marginal products. Some of the differences in the wage rates workers receive are due to differences in ability. However, even if all workers were of equal ability, there would still be differences in wage rates to offset differences in the characteristics of various occupations and areas. For example, occupations differ in the cost of training and stability of earnings, and geographical areas differ in the cost of living.

There are about 200 national unions in the United States, the biggest being the Teamsters, the Auto Workers, and the Steel Workers. Each national union is composed of local unions, which operate within the context of the constitution of the national union. The AFL-CIO is a federation of national unions created by the merger in 1955 of the American Federation of Labor and the Congress of Industrial Organizations. The AFL-CIO is a very important spokesman for the American labor movement, but because the national unions in the AFL-CIO have given up relatively little of their power to the federation, its authority is limited.

The first national unions date back to about 1850. The American Federation of Labor was founded in 1886 and was led by Samuel Gompers. The AFL's philosophy of "bread-and-butter" unionism became the dominant philosophy of American labor. Union membership grew to 5 million by 1920, but dropped to about 2.6 million by 1933, the 1920s being marked by strong antiunion sentiments.

During the 1930s the tide began to turn with the passage of the Norris-LaGuardia Act and the Wagner Act. The late 1930s saw great increases in union membership and power. By the end of World War II, the unions were powerful and conspicuous features of the economic landscape. As unions have grown older and stronger, there has been more and more concern over the nature of their internal practices and leadership. However, many of these problems, although serious, have pertained only to certain areas and industries. After World War II, public sentiment turned somewhat against unions, and both the Taft-Hartley Act and the Landrum-Griffin Act were passed over union opposition. In recent years, union membership has increased rather modestly.

There are several ways that unions can increase wages—by shifting the supply curve of labor to the left, by shifting the demand curve for labor to the right, and by influencing the wage directly. Collective bargaining is the process of negotiation between union and management over wages and working conditions. An agreement generally specifies the extent and kind of recognition that management gives the union—such as the closed shop, union shop, or open shop. In addition, it specifies the level of wage rates for particular jobs, the length of the workweek, the rate of overtime pay, the extent to which seniority will determine which workers will be first to be laid off, the nature and extent of management's prerogatives, and how grievances between workers and the employer will be handled. The union's power is based to a considerable extent on its right to strike.

Critics of big unions charge that they possess considerable monopoly power, and that, by pushing up the price of labor and reducing the level of employment, they cause a mal-allocation of resources and contribute to cost-push inflation. Opponents of big unions often suggest that the antitrust laws be applied to them and that other measures be adopted to curb their power. Supporters of big unions reply that it is foolish to believe that the price of labor would be the proper one from the point of view of resource allocation if there were no big unions. Moreover, they argue that unions are needed to offset the monopsonistic power of employers, and they deny that unions are the prime movers in cost-push inflation.

CONCEPTS FOR REVIEW

Local union
National union
Monopsony
Derived demand
Backward-bending supply curve
American Federation of Labor
Injunction
Norris-LaGuardia Act
Yellow-dog contract
Wagner Act
National Labor Relations Board
Congress of Industrial Organizations
Craft union
Industrial union
Taft-Hartley Act
Closed shop
Landrum-Griffin Act
Strike
Lockout
Pattern bargaining
Featherbedding
Union shop
Open shop

QUESTIONS FOR DISCUSSION AND REVIEW

1. Suppose that you were the president of a small firm that hired nonunion labor. How would you go about estimating the marginal product of a certain worker, or of certain types of workers? Would it be easy? If not, does this mean that the theory of wage determination is incorrect or useless?

2. Describe the various ways that labor unions can influence the wage rate. Do you think that they attempt to maximize the wage rate? If not, what do you think their objectives are?

3. Suppose that the marginal product of skilled labor to a perfectly competitive firm is 2 units and the price of skilled labor is $4 an hour, while the marginal product of unskilled labor is 1 unit and the price of unskilled labor is $2.50 an hour. Is the firm minimizing its costs? Explain.

4. The national unions in the AFL-CIO have given up much of their power to the federation. True or False?

CHAPTER 27

Interest, Rent, and Profits

Charles Lamb, the famous English essayist, said, "The human species, according to the best theory I can form of it, is composed of two distinct races, the men who borrow and the men who lend." Whether or not such a cleavage exists, most of the human species, at one time or another, are borrowers or lenders of money. Thus practically everyone is familiar with ***interest,*** which is a payment for the use of money. More specifically, *the rate of interest is the amount of money one must pay for the use of a dollar for a year*. Thus, if the interest rate is 5 percent, you must pay 5 cents for the use of a dollar for a year. Note that you must pay the dollar back at the end of the year, for interest is the cost of using a dollar *and then paying it back*.

Everyone who borrows money pays interest. Consumers pay interest on personal loans taken out to buy appliances, mortgages taken out to buy houses, and many other types of loans. Firms pay interest on bonds issued to purchase equipment and on short-term bank loans taken out to finance inventories. And governments pay interest on bonds issued to finance schools, highways, and other public projects.

Interest rates vary, depending on the nature of the borrower and the type of loan. One of the most important determinants of the rate of interest charged a particular borrower is the *riskiness* of the loan. Naturally, if the lender has doubts about his chances of getting his money back, he will charge a higher interest rate than if he is sure of being repaid. Thus, small, financially rickety firms have to pay higher interest rates than large blue-chip firms; and the large, well-known firms have to pay higher interest rates than the federal government. Another factor that influences the interest rate is the *cost of bookkeeping and collection.* If a firm makes many small loans and must hound the borrowers to pay up, these costs are a great deal larger than if it makes one large loan. Consequently the interest rate that must be charged for such small loans is often considerably higher than for bigger loans.

Despite the diversity of interest rates encountered at any point in time in the real world, it is analytically useful to speak of the ***pure rate of interest,*** which is the interest rate on a riskless loan. The rate of interest on U.S. government bonds—which are about as safe as one can get in this world—comes close to being a pure rate of interest. Actual interest rates will, of course, vary from the pure rate, depending on the riskiness of the loan together with other factors, but the distribution of actual interest rates will tend to move up and down with the pure interest rate.

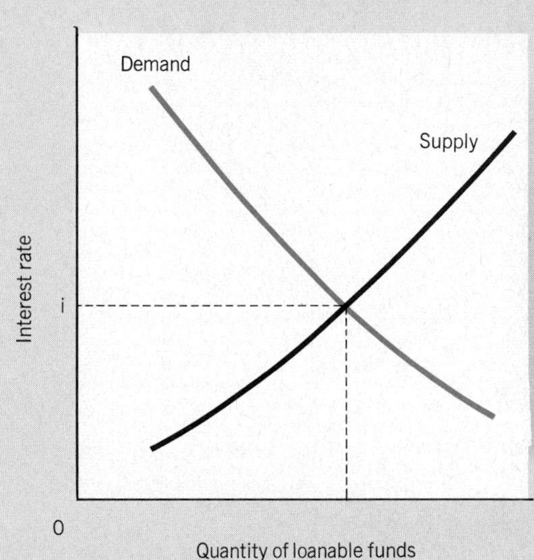

Figure 27.1
Determination of Equilibrium Rate of Interest

The interest rate is determined by the demand and supply of loanable funds, the equilibrium level of the interest rate being *Oi*.

What Determines the Interest Rate?

Since the interest rate is the price paid for the use of loanable funds, it—like any price—is determined by demand and supply. The ***demand curve for loanable funds*** shows the quantity of loanable funds demanded at each interest rate. As shown in Figure 27.1, the demand curve slopes downward to the right, indicating that more loanable funds are demanded at a lower rate of interest than at a higher rate of interest. The demand for loanable funds is a demand for what these funds will buy. Money is not wanted for its own sake, since it cannot, for example, build factories or equipment. Instead, it can provide command over resources—men and equipment and materials—to do things like build factories or equipment. Although obvious, this is an important point.

A very large demand for loanable funds stems from firms who want to borrow money to invest in capital goods like machine tools, buildings, and so forth. At a particular point in time a firm has available a variety of possible investments, each with a certain ***rate of return,*** which indicates its profitability or net productivity. *An asset's rate of return is the interest rate earned on the investment in the asset.* For example, suppose that a piece of equipment costs \$10,000 and yields a permanent return to its owner of \$1,500 per year[1] (this return having allowed for the costs of maintaining the machine). The rate of return on this piece of capital is 15 percent. Why? Because if an investment of \$10,000 yields an indefinite annual return of \$1,500, the interest rate earned on this investment is clearly 15 percent. If the firm maximizes profit, it will borrow to carry out investments in which the rate of return, adjusted for risk, exceeds the interest rate. Consequently, the higher the interest rate, the smaller the amount the firms will be willing to borrow.

Large demands for loanable funds are also made by consumers and the government. Consumers borrow money to buy houses, cars, and many other items. The government borrows money to finance the building of schools, highways, housing, and many other types of public projects. As in the case of firms, the higher the interest rate, the smaller the amount that consumers and governments will be willing to borrow. Adding the demands of firms, consumers, and government together, we find the aggregate relationship at a given point in time between the pure interest rate and the amount of funds demanded—which is the demand curve for loanable funds. For the reasons given above, this demand curve looks the way a demand curve should: it is downward-sloping to the right.

The ***supply curve for loanable funds*** is the relationship between the quantity of loanable funds supplied and the pure interest rate. The supply of loanable funds comes from households and firms that find the available rate of interest sufficiently attractive to get them to save. In addition, the banks play an extremely important role in influencing the supply of loanable funds. Indeed, banks can actually create or destroy loanable funds, but only within limits set by the Federal Reserve System, which has an important influence on the supply of loanable funds. The Federal Reserve is, of course, our central bank.

The pure interest rate is determined by the interaction of the demand and supply curves for loanable funds. The equilibrium pure interest rate is given by the intersection of the demand and supply curves. In Figure 27.1, for example, the equilibrium rate of interest is Oi. Factors that shift the demand curve or supply curve for loanable funds tend to alter the interest rate. For example, if people become more willing to postpone consumption to future time periods, the supply curve for loanable funds will shift to the right, and the interest rate will decline. Or if inventions result in very profitable new investment possibilities, the demand curve will shift to the right and the interest rate will increase.

However, this is only part of the story. Because of the government's influence on both the demand and supply sides of the market for loanable funds, the interest rate at any point in time is to a considerable extent a matter of public policy. A nation's monetary policy can have a significant effect on the level of the interest rate. More specifically, when the Federal Reserve pursues a policy of easy money, this generally means that interest rates tend to fall in the short run because the Fed is pushing the supply curve for loanable funds to the right. On the other hand, when the Federal Reserve pursues a policy of tight money, interest rates generally tend to rise in the short run because the Fed is pushing the supply curve for loanable funds to the left.

The government is also an important factor on the demand side of the market for loanable funds, because it is a big borrower, particularly during wartime. Between 1941 and 1945, it borrowed almost \$200 billion to help finance World War II. At the present time, total federal debt (excluding the debt of state and local governments) is about ¼ as big as total private debt.

Finally, note that the equilibrium level of the pure interest rate can be determined by John May-

[1] Of course, it is unrealistic to assume that the yield continues indefinitely, but it makes it easier to understand the principle involved.

nard Keynes's ***liquidity preference theory,*** as well as by the loanable funds theory described in this section. The liquidity preference theory focuses attention on all money, not just loanable funds, and says that the interest rate is determined by the demand and supply of all money in the economy. The two approaches are not contradictory; rather, they complement one another.

Functions of the Interest Rate

Interest has often been a relatively unpopular and somewhat suspect form of income. Even Aristotle, who was hardly noted for muddleheadedness, felt that money was "barren" and that it was improper to charge interest. And in the Middle Ages, church law outlawed usury, even though interest continued to be charged. In real life and in fiction, the money lender is often the villain, almost never the hero. Yet, it is perfectly clear that *interest rates serve a very important function: they allocate the supply of loanable funds.* At a given point in time, funds that can be used to construct new capital goods are scarce, and society faces the problem of allocating these scarce funds among alternative possible uses.

One way to allocate the loanable funds is through freely fluctuating interest rates. When such funds are relatively scarce, the interest rate will rise, with the result that only projects with relatively high rates of return will be carried out since the others will not be profitable. On the other hand, when such funds are relatively plentiful, the interest rate will fall, and less productive projects will be carried out because they now become profitable. The advantage of using the interest rate to allocate funds is that only the most productive projects are funded.

Although interest is sometimes represented as a product of greedy capitalists, even socialist and Communist economies must use something like an interest rate to help allocate funds. After all, the socialists and Communists face the same sort of allocation problem that capitalists do. And when they try to screen out the less productive projects and to accept only the more productive ones, they must use the equivalent of an interest rate in their calculations, whether they call it that or not. (However, they do not, of course, pay interest income.) In the Soviet Union there have been published acknowledgments that a misallocation of resources resulted from decisions made in earlier years when interest rates—or their equivalent—were ignored. At present, Soviet decision makers use what amount to interest rates in their calculations to determine which capital investments should be made and which should not.

Besides its role in allocating the supply of loanable funds, the interest rate plays another important part in our economy: *it influences the level of investment, and thus the level of net national product.* Increases in the interest rate tend to reduce aggregate investment, thereby reducing total spending, whereas decreases in the interest rate tend to increase aggregate investment, thereby increasing total spending. Through its monetary policies, the government attempts to influence the interest rate (and the quantity of money) so that total spending pushes net national product towards its full-employment level with reasonably stable prices.

Capital and Roundabout Methods of Production

Labor and land are often called the ***primary inputs*** because they are produced outside the economic system. Labor is created by familiar biological processes (which usually are not economically oriented, one would hope), and land is supplied by nature. *Capital,* on the other hand, *consists of goods that are created for the purpose of producing other goods.* Factory buildings, equipment, raw materials, inventories—all are various types of capital. In contrast to labor and land, capital is an input produced by the economic system itself.[2] A machine tool is capital; so is a boxcar or an electric power plant. These inputs are produced by firms, and they are purchased and used by firms. But they are not final consumption goods; instead, they are used to produce the final goods and services consumed by the public.

Our economy devotes a considerable amount of its productive capacity to the production of capital. The giant electrical equipment industry produces generators used by the electric power industry. The machine tool industry produces the numerically controlled tools used by the automobile, aircraft, and hundreds of other industries. The result in many sectors of the economy is a *roundabout method of production*. Consider the stages that lead to the manufacture of an automobile. Workers dig iron ore to be used to make pig iron to be used to make steel to be used to make machine tools to be used to make cylinders to be used to make a motor to be used to make the automobile.

Why does the economy bother to produce capital? After all, it may seem unnecessarily circuitous to construct capital to produce the goods and services consumers really want. Why not produce the desired goods and services—and *only* the desired goods and services—directly? For example, why produce plows to help produce agricultural crops? Why not forget about the plows and just produce the crops the consumers want? The answer is, of course, that the other inputs—labor and land—can produce more of the desired consumer goods and services when they are used in combination with capital that when they are used alone. A given amount of labor and land can produce more crops when used in combination with plows than when used alone.

The production and use of lots of capital make the other inputs—labor and land—more productive. But this does not mean that any society would be wise to increase without limit its production and use of capital. After all, the only way a society can produce more capital is to produce less goods and services of direct use to consumers. (For society as a whole, there are no free lunches, if resources are used fully and efficiently.) As the production of capital increases, consumers must cut further and further into their level of consumption at the present time in order to increase their capacity to produce in the future. Beyond a point, the advantage of having more in the future is overbalanced by the disadvantage of having less now. At this point, a society should stop increasing its production of capital goods.

The process by which people give up a claim on present consumption goods in order to receive consumption goods in the future is called ***saving***. Just as a child may (infrequently) give up a lollipop today in order to get a lollipop and a candy cane next week, so an entire society may give up the present consumption of automobiles, food, tobacco, clothing, and so forth in order to obtain more of such goods and services later on.

In a more poetic vein, this process has been described as follows by William M. Thackeray:

> Though small was your allowance,
> You saved a little store;
> And those who save a little
> Shall get a plenty more.

If it does nothing else, the foregoing helps explain why Thackeray is better known as a novelist than a poet.

[2] Obviously, this distinction requires qualification. After all, land can be improved, and the quality of labor can be enhanced (by training and other means). Thus, land and labor have some of the characteristics of capital since to some extent they can be "produced"—or at least enhanced—by the economic system. More will be said about "human capital" in a later section.

Capitalization of Assets

In a capitalist economy, each capital good has a market value. How can we determine what this value is? How much money is a capital good worth? To keep things reasonably simple, suppose that you can get 5 percent on various investments open to you; specifically, you can get 5 percent by investing your money in the stock of a local firm.

That is, for every $1,000 you invest, you will receive a permanent return of $50 a year—and this is the highest return available. Now suppose that you have an opportunity to buy a piece of equipment that will yield you a permanent return of $1,000 per year. This piece of equipment is worth $1,000 ÷ .05 = $20,000 to you. Why? Because this is the amount you would have to pay for any other investment open to you that yields an equivalent amount—$1,000—per year. (If you must invest $1,000 for every $50 of annual yield, $20,000 must be invested to obtain an annual yield of $1,000.)

In general, if a particular asset yields a permanent amount—X dollars—each year, how much is this asset worth? In other words, how much should you be willing to pay for it? If you can get a return of 100 i percent per year from alternative investments, you would have to invest $X \div i$ dollars in order to get the same return as this particular asset yields. Consequently, this asset is worth $X \div i$ dollars to you.

This process of computing an asset's worth is called ***capitalization.*** Note one important point about an asset's capitalized value. Holding constant an asset's annual returns, the asset's worth is higher, the lower the rate of return available on other investments. For example, if the rate of return on alternative investments had been 3 percent rather than 5 percent in the example above, the worth of the piece of equipment would have been $1,000 ÷ .03 = $33,333 (since $X = \$1,000$ and $i = .03$). This is the amount you would have to pay for any other investment open to you that yields an equivalent amount—$1,000—per year. To see this, note that, if you must invest $1,000 for every $30 (not $50, as before) of annual yield, $33,333 (not $20,000, as before) must be invested to obtain an annual yield of $1,000.

Capital Budgeting

At any point in time, there exists an interest rate at which firms can borrow. For simplicity, assume that all investments are riskless. *If firms can borrow all the money they want at this rate of interest, and if they maximize their profits, they obviously will buy all capital goods and accept all investment opportunities, where the rate of return on these capital goods or investment opportunities exceeds the interest rate at which they can borrow.*[3] The reason for this is clear enough. If one can borrow money at an interest cost that is less than the rate of return on the borrowed money, clearly one can make money. For example, if you borrow $1,000 at 3 percent per year interest and buy a $1,000 machine that has a rate of return of 4 percent per year, you receive a return of $40 per year and incur a cost of $30 per year. Since you make a profit of $10 per year, it obviously pays to buy this machine.

At a particular point in time, there is a variety of possible capital goods that can be produced and investment projects that can be carried out. Their rates of return vary a great deal; some goods or projects have a much higher rate of return than others. Suppose that we rank the capital goods or projects according to their rates of return, from highest to lowest. If only a few of the goods or projects can be accepted, only those at the top of the list will be chosen. But as more and more can be accepted, society and private investors must go further and further down the list, with the consequence that projects with lower and lower rates of return will be chosen. How many of these capital goods and investment projects will be carried out? As noted above, firms will continue to invest as long as the rate of return on these goods or projects exceeds the interest rate at which they can borrow. Thus it follows that all projects with rates of return exceeding this interest rate will be carried out.

These principles can be applied to the operations of individual firms. In particular, they help to indicate how a firm should make decisions on the choice of investment projects. Suppose, for exam-

[3] We assume here that the investment opportunities are independent in the sense that the rate of return from each opportunity is not influenced by whether some other opportunity is accepted.

Table 27.1

Investment Opportunities for Bugsbane Music Box Company

Rate of return (percent)	Amount of money the firm can invest at given rate of return
30	$2 million
25	4 million
20	4 million
15	6 million
10	7 million

ple, that the Bugsbane Music Box Company believes that it will have $10 million from internal sources—primarily retained earnings and depreciation allowances—to invest next year, and surveys all its investment opportunities, with the results shown in Table 27.1. That is, it finds that it can invest $2 million in projects (investments in new equipment) with rates of return of 30 percent. In addition, it finds that it can invest $4 million in projects with rates of return of 25 percent. (These projects consist of investments in real estate.) And so on, as shown in Table 27.1. Applying the principles just discussed, Bugsbane can maximize its profits by allocating the $10 million available from internal sources as follows: all projects yielding rates of return of 20 percent or more should be accepted; and all projects yielding less than 20 percent should not be undertaken.

This is a very useful step toward solving the firm's problem, but it assumes that the firm is unable or unwilling to borrow. If this is true, then nothing more needs to be said. But, as shown in Table 27.1, the firm has investment opportunities yielding 15 percent per year that it is not undertaking. It would pay the firm to undertake these projects even if it had to pay 10 or 12 percent interest—or anything less than 15 percent, for that matter. If the firm can borrow all the money it wants (within reason), but must pay 12 percent interest, what investment opportunities should it accept? Clearly, all whose rate of return exceeds 12 percent. Thus, looking at Table 27.1, we see that the firm should invest its $10 million from internal sources and borrow an additional $6 million in order to undertake projects totaling $16 million.

This is an extremely simple case, but it illustrates how the interest rate and the concept of an asset's rate of return are used in practical business situations. ***Capital budgeting***—the term applied to this area—has become an extremely important part of a firm's operations, as businessmen have relied more and more on economic concepts in allocating their firms' resources. Unaided hunch and intuition will no longer do in most major firms. Instead, most big firms insist that the prospective rate of return be estimated for each proposed investment, and that, making allowances for differences in risk, funds be allocated to the projects with the highest rates of return.[4] Of course, it is often difficult to make such estimates, but if funds are to be allocated rationally, it is essential that an analysis of this sort be carried out, formally or on the back of an envelope.

Rates of Return from Investing in Human Capital

In recent years, economists have shown a great interest in "human capital." Certainly it is true that many expenditures on education and training, as well as on other things like health, can be viewed as investments, because these expenditures, like an investment in physical capital, result in deferred increases in income. In other words, just as a firm may invest in a machine in order to increase its future earnings, so a student (or his parents) may invest in his education to increase his future earnings. Moreover, just as a firm can estimate the rate of return from its investment in the machine, so the student can estimate the rate

[4] In practice, firms often base their decisions on discounted cash flow rather than rates of return, but the two methods generally give the same result.

of return from his investment in his education. In this way the student, like the firm, can determine whether this investment is more profitable than others he might make instead.

How big an investment does a student make when he attends college? There are the costs of tuition, room, board, books, and other such cash outlays. But there is another cost that students often forget to include: the forgone earnings the student could make if he worked instead of going to college. Perhaps the simplest way to estimate the increase in earnings from a college education is to compare the average income of high school graduates with the average income of college graduates of the same age. The difference between these two averages is a rough measure of the increase in income, at each age level, from a college education.

Based on estimates of this sort, economists have calculated that the rate of return from the investment in a college education is about 10 to 12 percent. This is an interesting result, both for private decision-making and for public policy, but it is important to note its limitations. First, this is an average figure for white males only, which may differ a great deal from the figure pertaining to any particular individual. Further, some of the increase in income attributed to a college education may result from the fact that the people who graduated from college were abler, more conscientious, more highly motivated, or better prepared at home than those who did not go to college. It is very difficult to sort out the effects of the college education from the effects of other factors.

Nonetheless, the idea of viewing education as a form of investment in human capital is a fruitful one. For one thing, it permits deeper insight into the reasons why some people get paid more than others. Thus, people who invest a great deal in their education—like doctors, dentists, and lawyers—must receive higher incomes after graduation to make this investment worthwhile. Also, this concept is useful in analyzing ways in which a society can increase its level of per capita income. Clearly, one way may be to increase its investment in education and other forms of human capital. In addition, the concept of human capital tends to underline the common elements in the analysis of the pricing of labor and nonlabor inputs.

Rent: Nature and Significance

Land is defined by economists as *any input that is fixed in supply, its limits established by nature.* Thus, since certain types of minerals and natural resources are in relatively fixed supply, they are included in the economist's definition of land. Suppose that the supply of an input is completely fixed. Increases in its price will not increase its supply and decreases in its price will not decrease its supply. Following the terminology of the classical economists of the nineteenth century, *the price of such an input is* ***rent.*** Note that rent means something quite different to an economist than to the man in the street, who considers "rent" the price of using an apartment or a car or some other object owned by someone else.

If the supply of an input is fixed, its supply curve is a vertical line SS' as shown in Figure 27.2. Thus, the price of this input, its rent, is determined entirely by the demand curve for the input. For example, if the demand curve is D_0D_0', the rent is OP_0; if the demand curve is D_1D_1', the rent is OP_1. Since the supply of the input is fixed, the price of the input can be lowered without influencing the amount supplied. Thus a *rent is a payment above the minimum necessary to attract this amount of the input.*[5] Why is it important to know whether a certain payment for inputs is a rent? Because a

[5] In recent years, there has been a tendency among economists to extend the use of the word rent to encompass all payments to inputs above the minimum required to make these inputs available to the industry or to the economy. To a great extent these payments are costs to individual firms; the firms must make such payments to attract and keep these inputs, which are useful to other firms in the industry. But if the inputs have no use in other industries, these payments are not costs to the industry as a whole (or to the economy as a whole) because the inputs would be available to the industry whether or not these payments are made.

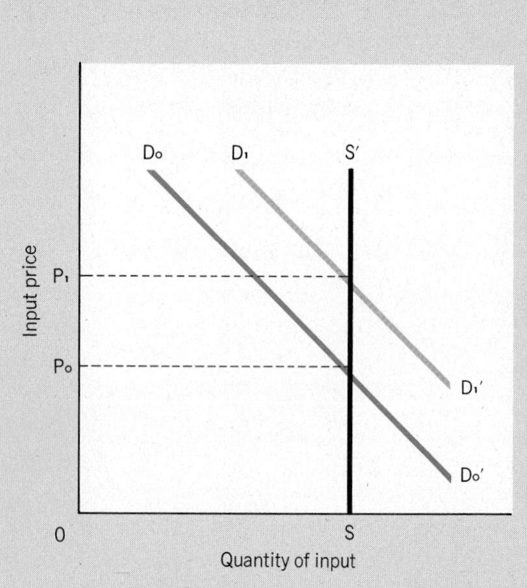

Figure 27.2
Rent

Rent is the price of an input in fixed supply. Since its supply curve is vertical, the price of such an input is determined entirely by the demand curve for the input. If the demand curve is D_0D_0', the rent is OP_0; if the demand curve is D_1D_1', the rent is OP_1.

reduction of the payment will not influence the availability and use of the inputs if the payment is a rent; whereas if it is not a rent, a reduction of the payment is likely to change the allocation of resources. For example, if the government imposes a tax on rents, there will be no effect on the supply of resources to the economy.

In 1879, Henry George (1839–1897) published a book, *Progress and Poverty,* in which he argued that rents should be taxed away by the government. In his view, owners of land were receiving substantial rents simply because their land happened to be well situated, not because they were doing anything productive. Since this rent was unearned income and since the supply of land would not be influenced by such a tax, George felt that it was justifiable to tax away such rent. Indeed, he argued that a tax of this sort should be the only tax imposed by the government. Critics of George's views pointed out that land can be improved, with the result that the supply is not completely price-inelastic. Moreover, they argued that if land rents are "unearned" so are many other kinds of income. In addition, they pointed out that it was unrealistic to expect such a tax to raise the needed revenue. George's single-tax movement gained a number of adherents in the last decades of the nineteenth century, and he even made an unsuccessful bid to become mayor of New York. Arguments in favor of a single tax continue to surface from time to time.

To make the concept of rent more concrete, consider the following example. There is a lot at the corner of Third Avenue and Winchester Street in a California suburb; this property is on the edge of the town. What will be the rent for this lot? It has various possible uses. It could be the location of a store or restaurant, a small farm, a site for an apartment building, or used for some other purpose. In each possible use, this lot has a certain value as an input. In other words, its marginal product has a certain value.

In a competitive market, this lot will tend to rent for an amount equal to its value in its most productive use. That is, if the value of its marginal product is highest when it is used as the location for a store, a store will be built on it, and the lot will command a rent equal to the value of its marginal product. In this way, the lot will be drawn into the use that seems to yield the highest returns to the renter. From society's point of view, this has much to recommend it, since the use that yields the highest returns is likely to be the one consumers value most highly.

Classical economists viewed rent as a differential that had to be paid for the utilization of better rather than poorer land. They argued as follows: if land becomes scarce, the better lands will receive a nonzero price before the poorer lands. The rent on any acre will rise to the point where it is equal to the difference in productivity between this acre and an acre of no-rent land. Why? For exactly the same reason given in Chapter 26 to explain the difference in wages between the two workers, Arnold and Leo. Of course, this line of reasoning is just another way to get the same result we stated in the previous paragraph.

Profits: Definition and Statistics

Finally, we must devote some attention to another important type of property income, profits. Profits are not new to us. In Chapter 7, we discussed at some length the economist's concept of profit and how it varies from the accountant's concept. According to the accountant, the amounts of money the owner of a firm has left after paying wages, interest, and rent—and after providing proper allowance for the depreciation of buildings and equipment—is profit. The economist dissents from this view; his position is that the alternative costs of the labor, capital, and land contributed by the owner should also be deducted.

Available statistics concerning profits are based on the accountant's concept, not the economist's. Before taxes, corporation profits average about 10 percent of gross national income. Profits—expressed as a percent of either net worth or sales—vary considerably from industry to industry and from firm to firm. (For example, the drug industry's profits in the postwar period have frequently been about 15–20 percent of net worth—considerably higher than in most other manufacturing industries.) Also, profits vary greatly from year to year, and are much more erratic than wages. They fall more heavily in recessions and rise more rapidly in recoveries than wages do. Table 27.2 shows profit as a percent of stockholders' equity in each major industry in the United States in 1971.

Table 27.2

Annual Rates of Profit (After Taxes) on Stockholders' Equity, By Industry, United States, 1971

Industry	Rate of profit (percent)
All manufacturing	9.7
Nondurable goods:	10.3
Food	11.0
Tobacco	15.7
Textiles	6.6
Apparel	11.0
Paper	4.8
Printing	10.7
Chemicals	11.8
Petroleum	10.3
Rubber	9.6
Leather	8.2
Durable goods:	9.1
Motor vehicles	13.0
Aircraft	5.8
Electrical equipment	9.4
Other machinery	8.7
Other fabricated metal products	8.3
Primary metals	4.8
Stone, clay, and glass	9.1
Furniture	9.5
Lumber	11.3
Instruments	13.5
Miscellaneous	9.0

Source: Statistical Abstract of the United States, 1972.

To some extent, the measured differences in profits among firms come about because the profit figures are not corrected for the value of the inputs contributed by the owners. Because they are smarter and more resourceful, some owners provide managerial labor of a much higher quality than other owners do. "Profits" arising from this fact are, at least in part, wages for superior management. Similarly, some owners put up a lot of the capital and work long hours. "Profits" arising from these sources are, at least in part, interest on capital and wages for time spent working in the firm.

Innovation, Uncertainty, and Monopoly Power

Why do profits—as the economist defines them—exist? Three important factors are innovation, uncertainty, and monopoly power. Suppose that an economy was composed of perfectly competitive industries, that entry was completely free, and that no changes in technology—no new processes, no new products, or other innovations—were permitted. Moreover, suppose that everyone could predict the future with perfect accuracy. Under these conditions, there would be no profits, because people would enter industries where profits exist, thus reducing these profits eventually to zero, and leave industries where losses exist, thus reducing these negative profits eventually to zero. This sort of no-profit equilibrium has already been discussed in Chapter 23.

But in the real world, innovations of various kinds are made. For example, DuPont introduces a new product like nylon, or Henry Ford introduces the assembly line, or Marconi introduces the radio. The people who carry out these bold schemes are the ***innovators,*** the men with vision and the daring to back it up. The innovators are not necessarily the inventors of new techniques or products, although in some cases the innovator and the inventor are the same. Often the innovator takes another man's invention, adapts it, and introduces it to the market. According to economists like the late Joseph Schumpeter of Harvard, profits are the rewards earned by innovators. Of course, the profits derived from any single innovation eventually erode with competition and imitation, but other innovations replace them, with the result that profits from innovation continue to be made.

In the real world, uncertainty also exists. Indeed, one of the hazards in attempting to be an innovator is the risk involved. According to a theory set forth several decades ago by Frank Knight of the University of Chicago, all economic profit is due to uncertainty. Profit is the reward for risk bearing. Assuming that people would like to avoid risk, they will prefer relatively stable, sure earnings to relatively unstable, uncertain earnings—*even if the latter are, on the average, higher.* Consequently, to induce people to take the risks involved in owning businesses in certain industries, a profit—a premium for risk—must be paid to them. This is similar to the higher wages that, according to the previous chapter, must be paid for jobs where earnings are unstable or uncertain.

Still another reason for the existence of profits is the fact that markets are not perfectly competitive. Under perfect competition, there will, of course, be a tendency in the long run for profits to disappear. But, as we have seen, this will not be the case if an industry is a monopoly or oligopoly. Instead, profits may well exist in the long run in such imperfectly competitive industries. And, as we know from Chapter 25, virtually our entire economy is composed of imperfectly competitive industries. Monopoly profits are fundamentally the result of "contrived scarcities." Since a firm's demand curve is downward-sloping if competition is imperfect, it pays the firm to take account of the fact that the more it produces, the smaller the price it will receive. In other words, the firm realizes that it will spoil the market if it produces too much. Thus it pays firms to limit their output, and this contrived scarcity is responsible for the existence of the profits they make as a consequence.

The Functions of Profits

To many people, profit seems to be "something for nothing." They do not recognize the innovative or risk-bearing functions of the owners of the firm, and consequently see no reason for the existence of profits. Other people, aware that profits arise because of imperfect competition, ignore the other functions of profit and regard it as entirely the ill-gotten gain of fat monopolists, often smoking big cigars and properly equipped with a rapacious leer. But no group is more hostile to profits than the followers and disciples of Karl Marx. According to Marx, laborers in a capitalist system receive a wage that is barely enough to cover the minimum amount of housing, food, clothing, and other commodities needed for survival. The difference between the amount the employers receive for their products and the amount they pay the laborers that produce them is "surplus value." And, according to Marx, this "surplus value," which includes what we would call profit, is a measure of, and consequence of, exploitation by owners of firms.

Marx's views and those of others who look on profits with suspicion and even distaste are rejected by most economists; to them profits play a legitimate and very important role in a capitalistic system. In a free enterprise economy, each consumer, each supplier of inputs, and each firm tries to advance his own interests. Workers try to maximize their earnings, capitalists look for the highest interest returns, landlords try to get the highest rents, and firm owners seek to maximize their profits. At first glance, this looks like a chaotic, dog-eat-dog situation; but, as we have seen, it actually turns out to be an orderly and efficient system—if competition is present. Profits and losses are mainsprings of this system. They are signals that indicate where resources are needed and where they are too abundant. When there are economic profits in an industry, this is the signal for resources to flow into it; when economic losses exist in an industry, this is the signal for resources to leave it.

Also, profits are very important incentives for innovation and for betting on the future. For an entrepreneur like Joseph Wilson of Xerox, profits are the bait society dangles before him to get him to take the risks involved in marketing a new product, like xerography. If his judgment turns out to be faulty, losses—negative profits—are the penalties society imposes on him.

In addition, profits are society's reward for efficiency. Firms that use inefficient techniques or produce an inappropriate amount or type of product are penalized by losses. Firms that are particularly alert, efficient, and adaptive receive profits. Further, profits enable firms to embark on new projects. For example, the profits that Xerox earned on xerography are currently being used to support its new ventures into other types of business machines. The importance of profits in a free enterprise economy is clear enough. However, this does not mean that all profits are socially justified or that the system as a whole cannot be improved. Clearly, monopoly profits are not socially justified. (Moreover, it is worth noting that a competitive system, despite its advantages, may produce many socially undesirable effects—for example, an undesirable income distribution. Much more will be said on this score in the next chapter.)

Summary

Interest is a payment for the use of money. Interest rates vary a great deal, depending on the nature of the borrower and the type and riskiness of the loan. The pure interest rate—the interest rate on riskless loans—is, like any price, determined by the interaction of supply and demand. However, because of the influence of the government on both the demand and supply sides of the market, it is clear that the pure interest rate is to a considerable extent a matter of public policy. One very important function of interest rates is to allocate the supply of loanable funds.

Capital is composed of inputs produced by the economic system itself. Our economy uses very roundabout methods of production and devotes a considerable amount of its productive capacity to the production of capital. If more and more capital is produced during a particular period, consumers must cut further and further into their consumption during that period. In a capitalist system, each capital good has a market value that can be determined by capitalizing its earnings. Holding constant an asset's annual return, the asset's worth is higher, the lower the rate of return available on other investments. Any piece of capital has a rate of return, which indicates its net productivity. An asset's rate of return is the interest rate earned on the investment in the asset. If firms maximize profits, they must carry out all projects where the rate of return exceeds the interest rate at which they can borrow.

Rent is the return derived by inputs that are fixed in supply. Since the supply of the input is fixed, its price can be lowered without influencing the amount supplied. It is important to know whether a certain payment is a rent because a reduction of the payment will not influence the availability and use of the inputs if the payment is a rent. If it is not a rent, however, a reduction of the payment is likely to change the allocation of resources. Thus, if the government imposes taxes on rents, there will be no effect on the supply of resources to the economy.

Another important type of property income is profits. Available statistics on profits are based on the accountant's concept, not the economist's, with the result that they include the alternative costs of the labor, capital, and land contributed by the owners of the firm. Profits play a very important and legitimate role in a free enterprise system. Two of the important factors responsible for the existence of profits are innovation and uncertainty: profits are the rewards earned by innovators and a payment for risk-bearing. Still another reason for the existence of profits is monopoly power; due to contrived scarcity, profits are made by firms in imperfectly competitive markets.

CONCEPTS FOR REVIEW

Rate of interest	Rate of return	Liquidity preference
Pure rate of interest	Risk	Saving
Primary inputs	Capital budgeting	Land
Capitalization	Rent	Innovator

QUESTIONS FOR DISCUSSION AND REVIEW

1. Do you agree with Henry George's view that rents should be taxed away by the government? Why or why not?

2. Describe the social functions of the interest rate. Do you agree with Aristotle that it is improper to charge interest?

3. Suppose that a candidate for president proposes that all profits be taxed away. Would you support his proposal?

4. Suppose that you can get 10 percent per year from alternative investments and that, if you invest in a particular business, you will get $1,000 per year indefinitely. How much is this investment worth to you?

5. If a firm can borrow money at 10 percent per year and is willing to accept only those (riskless) investments that yield 12 percent per year or more, is the firm maximizing profit?

CHAPTER 28

Income Inequality, Poverty, and Discrimination

Although the United States is the richest country on earth, it is not a land of milk and honey to all its inhabitants. Some Americans are poor—so poor that they suffer from malnutrition—and while poverty may not be a sin, it is no less an inconvenience to the poor. Given the affluence of American society, one is led to ask why poverty exists and whether it cannot be abolished by proper public policies. One purpose of this chapter is to examine these questions.

Poverty does not exist in a social vacuum; for example, it is intimately bound up with the problems of discrimination that have played an important role in American life for many years. Unquestionably, discriminatory barriers have tended to depress the incomes of females, non whites, and other minority groups. Besides looking at poverty in the United States, this chapter also discusses some relevant aspects of discrimination.

Table 28.1

Percentage Distribution of Families, by Income, 1972

Money Income	Percent of all families	Percent of total income received	Percent of families with this and lower incomes	Percent of income received by families with this and lower income
Under $2,000	4	[a]	4	[a]
2,000– 3,999	8	2	12	2
4,000– 5,999	10	4	22	6
6,000– 7,999	11	6	33	12
8,000– 9,999	11	8	44	20
10,000–14,999	26	26	70	46
15,000–24,999	23	36	93	82
25,000 and over	7	18	100	100
Total	100	100		

Source: Department of Commerce.
[a] Less than 0.5 percent.

Inequality of Income

One doesn't have to be a very perceptive social observer to recognize that there are great differences in income levels in the United States. But a person's idea of what the distribution of income looks like depends on the sort of family and community he comes from. A child brought up in Lake Forest, a wealthy suburb of Chicago, is unlikely to be as aware of the incidence of poverty as a child brought up on Chicago's poor South Side. For a preliminary glimpse of the extent of income inequality in the United States, scan Table 28.1, which shows the percentage of all families in the United States that were situated in various income classes in 1972. According to the table, 22 percent of the nation's families received an income of less than $6,000 in 1972. On the other hand, 7 percent of the nation's families received an income of more than $25,000 in 1972.

It may come as a surprise to some that so large a percentage of the nation's families made less than $6,000 and that so few families made more than $25,000. The image of the affluent society projected in the Sunday supplements and women's magazines is strangely out of tune with these facts. Yet, to put these figures in world perspective, it should be recognized that Americans are very rich relative to other peoples. This fact is shown clearly by Table 28.2, which gives for various countries the 1973 level of income per person, which is the total income of each nation divided by its population. The United States is the leader in this table. But our relative prosperity should not blind us to the substantial inequality of income in our own country.

What accounts for this inequality of income? To some extent it occurs because some people possess greater abilities than others. For example, since Wilt Chamberlain has extraordinary skill as

Table 28.2

Selected Countries Grouped by Approximate Level of Income per Capita, 1973

I. Countries with income per capita exceeding $5,000		
United States		
II. Countries with income per capita between $3,000 and $5,000		
Canada	Denmark	France
Sweden	West Germany	Norway
III. Countries with income per capita between $2,000 and $3,000		
Japan	Italy	
United Kingdom	Israel	
IV. Countries with income per capita between $1,000 and $2,000		
Soviet Union		
Czechoslovakia		
V. Countries with income per capita less than $1,000		
India	Middle East	Most of Africa
China	Latin America	Most of Asia

a basketball player, it is easy to understand why he makes a lot of money. Also, prevailing income differences reflect differences in the amount of education and training people receive. Thus, physicians or lawyers must receive a higher income than people in occupations requiring little or no training. Otherwise it would not pay people to undergo medical or legal training. Some people receive relatively high incomes because they own large amounts of property. For example, because of a shrewd choice of ancestry, the Fords, Rockefellers, and Mellons get high incomes from inherited property. Some people have high incomes because they have managed to obtain monopoly power, and others largely through luck. As in most areas of life, chance plays a role in determining income.

A Measure of Income Inequality

Some philosophers, many economists, and practically all thieves are interested in altering the extent of income inequality, each in his own way. Many distinguished social philosophers have debated the merits and demerits of making income distribution more equal. We shall take up this important issue in detail below. For the moment, however, let's ask a somewhat different, but still critical, question: to what extent has income inequality in the United States decreased in recent years? Some people say that because of the advent of the "welfare state" the nation is moving rapidly toward greater equality of income. Others say that the rich are getting richer and the poor are getting poorer. Who is right?

To answer this question, we need some way to measure the degree of income inequality. The most commonly used technique is the ***Lorenz curve,*** which plots the percentage of people, going from the poorest up, on the horizontal axis, and the percentage of total income they get on the vertical axis. For example, the Lorenz curve based on the figures in Table 28.1 is shown in Figure 28.1. To see how this diagram was constructed, note that in Table 28.1 families with incomes under $4,000 accounted for 12 percent of all families, but only 2 percent of all income. Thus, plotting 12 percent on

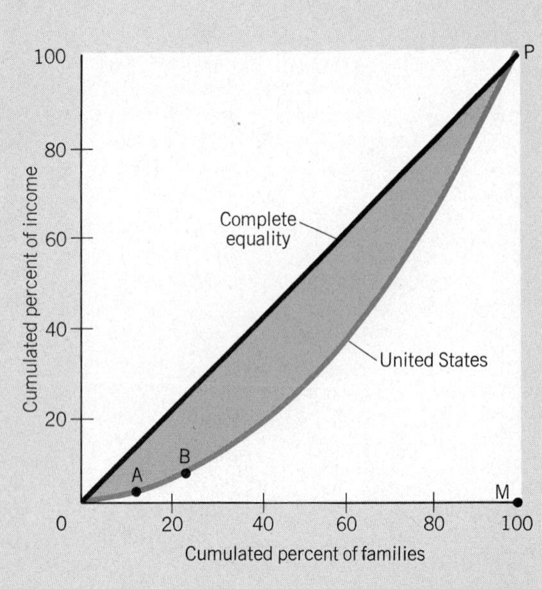

Figure 28.1
Lorenz Curve for Family Income, United States, 1970

***OP* is the Lorenz curve if income were distributed equally. The shaded area between this hypothetical Lorenz curve and the actual Lorenz curve is a measure of income inequality.**

the horizontal axis against 2 percent on the vertical axis, we get point *A*. The table also indicates that families with incomes under $6,000 accounted for 22 percent of all families, but only 6 percent of all income. Plotting these figures in the same way, we get point *B*. Connecting up all points like *A* and *B*, we obtain the Lorenz curve in Figure 28.1.

Two extreme cases must be understood to see how the Lorenz curve is used. First, if incomes were the same for all families (or whatever kinds of recipients are under consideration), the Lorenz curve would be a straight line connecting the origin of the diagram with its upper right hand corner. That is, it would be *OP* in Figure 28.1. To see this, note that if incomes are distributed equally, the lowest 10 percent of the families receive 10 percent of the total income, the lowest 20 percent of the families receive 20 percent of the total income, and so forth. Plotting 10 percent on the horizontal axis against 10 percent on the vertical axis, 20 percent on the horizontal axis against 20 percent on the vertical axis, and so forth, one gets a Lorenz curve of *OP*.

Second, if incomes were distributed completely unequally—that is, if one person had all of the income and the rest had none—the Lorenz curve would lie along the horizontal axis from *O* to *M* and along the vertical line from *M* to *P*. It would be *OMP* in Figure 28.1. You can check this by

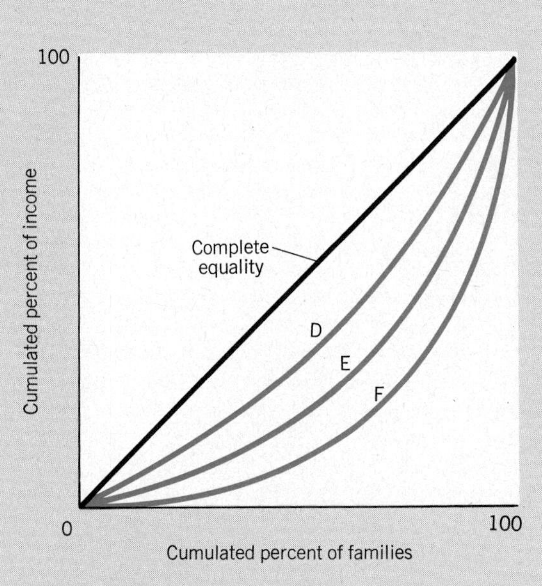

Figure 28.2
Lorenz Curves for Countries D, E, and F

Income inequality is greater in country F than in country E, and greater in country E than in country D.

noting that the lowest 10 percent of the families have zero percent of the total income, so do the lowest 20 percent of the families, and so, in fact, do the lowest 99 percent of the families. Plotting 10 percent on the horizontal axis against zero percent on the vertical axis, 20 percent on the horizontal axis against zero percent on the vertical axis, and so on, one gets a Lorenz curve that lies along the horizontal axis from O to M. But since 100 percent of the families must receive 100 percent of the income, the Lorenz curve must then jump up from M to P.

These two examples make it clear that *the shaded area in Figure 28.1—the deviation of the actual Lorenz curve from the Lorenz curve corresponding to complete equality of income—is a measure of income inequality.* The larger this shaded area, the greater the extent of income inequality. For example, Figure 28.2 shows the Lorenz curve for the income distributions in three countries: *D, E,* and *F.* As reflected in the Lorenz curves, income inequality is greater in *F* than in *E,* and greater in *E* than in *D.*

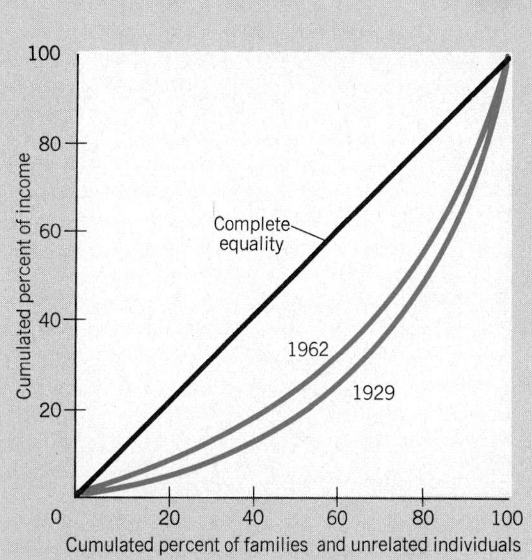

Figure 28.3
Changes over Time in Lorenz Curves for Family Income in the United States

Income inequality in the United States has decreased over time, as indicated by the Lorenz curves for 1929 and 1962.

Trends in Income Inequality

Let us now return to the question posed at the beginning of the previous section: to what extent has income inequality in the United States decreased in recent years? Figure 28.3 shows the Lorenz curves for the income distributions in 1929 and 1962. These curves make it clear that there has been a considerable reduction in income inequality. For example, the share of income going to the top 20 percent declined by ⅕ between 1929 and 1962. This change, described by some writers as an "income revolution," did not occur gradually throughout the period. Instead, essentially all the reduction in income inequality occurred before the end of World War II. Since then, there has been little change in the degree of income inequality.

One of the reasons for the reduction in income inequality between 1929 and the end of World War II was the increased importance of wages and salaries relative to other sources of income: wages and salaries are more equally distributed than income from self-employment and property. Also, many public programs were established to provide income for the poor; the details of these programs are described below. In addition, the shift from substantial prewar unemployment to the full employment of World War II narrowed wage differentials among various types of workers.[1] Fur-

[1] See Selma Goldsmith, "Changes in the Size Distribution of Income," *American Economic Review,* May 1957; and Robert Solow, "Income Inequality Since the War," in *Postwar Economic Trends in the United States,* edited by Ralph Freeman, Massachusetts Institute of Technology, 1960.

ther, the inequality in the distribution of wealth was reduced during this period.

Finally, it is interesting to compare the extent of income inequality—and the rate of change of income inequality—in the United States with that in other countries. For example, reasonably comparable data are available for the United Kingdom, Germany, Sweden, and the Netherlands. During the 1930s, the United States had a slightly more unequal distribution of pretax income than the United Kingdom, about the same as the Netherlands, and a somewhat more equal distribution than Germany or Sweden. In all these countries, there has been a movement toward equality. However, in the United Kingdom, the Netherlands, and Sweden, this movement seems to have continued during the postwar period. This has not been the case in the United States.

The United States now has a more equal distribution of income than the Netherlands and West Germany, about the same as the United Kingdom, and somewhat less equal than Sweden. Data for the less developed countries, like India or Ceylon, are sparse and not very reliable, but they seem to indicate that these countries often have greater income inequality than heavily industrialized countries like the United States or the United Kingdom. The contrast between a very rich minority and the very poor masses seems much more striking in many less developed countries than in the United States.

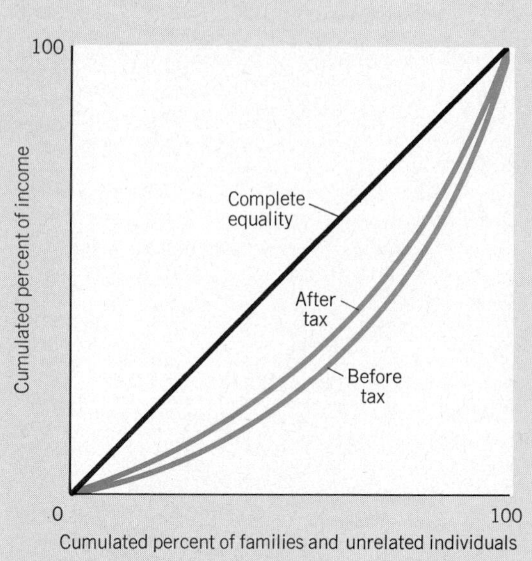

Figure 28.4
Effect of Federal Income Tax on Lorenz Curve, United States

In the United States, inequality of aftertax income is less than inequality of pretax income.

Effects of the Tax Structure on Income Inequality

So far, we have looked at the distribution of pretax income. But we must also consider the effect of the tax system on income inequality. Let's begin with the personal income tax. Figure 28.4 shows that income is more equally distributed after personal income taxes are deducted. However, the effect of the federal income tax, although noteworthy, is not as large as some people believe. For example, the top 20 percent of families received 45.5 percent of the pretax income and 43.7 percent of the aftertax income—a difference of only about 2 percentage points.[2] The federal income tax is ***progressive,*** since the rich pay a higher proportion of their income for this tax than the poor. In contrast, some other taxes, like sales taxes, are ***regressive:*** the rich pay a lower proportion of their income for these taxes than do the poor.

Needless to say, people who feel that the tax system should promote a redistribution of income from rich to poor favor progressive, not regressive taxes. Besides the personal income tax, other pro-

[2] See Edward Budd, *Inequality and Poverty,* New York: Norton, 1967, pp. xiii and xiv.

gressive taxes are inheritance or estate taxes. According to the federal estate tax, the first $60,000 of a person's estate is exempt from taxation, as is 50 percent of his estate if it goes to his spouse. Above this amount, an estate of $100,000 is subject to an estate tax of $20,140, an estate of $500,000 is subject to an estate tax of $133,300, and an estate of $1 million is subject to an estate tax of $289,140. The federal government also levies a gift tax to prevent wealthy people from circumventing the estate tax by giving thier money away before death. State governments also levy inheritance taxes (on persons who inherit money) and estate taxes (on the deceased's estate). All of this is applauded by reformers who oppose accumulation and preservation of inherited wealth. But, as in the case of the personal income tax, the portion of an estate subject to taxes can be reduced through clever use of trusts and other devices, all quite legal. Thus, the estate tax is not quite as progressive as it looks.

Not all taxes are progressive; examples of regressive taxes are not hard to find. General sales taxes of the sort used by most states and some cities are regressive, since high-income people pay a smaller percentage of their income in sales taxes than do low-income people. The Social Security and payroll tax is also regressive. So is the property tax, according to estimates by Richard Musgrave of Harvard University. In the mid-1950s, he estimated that this tax took about 5 percent of incomes under $2,000, but about 3½ percent of incomes over $10,000. It is difficult to tell whether the corporation income tax is progressive or regressive. At first glance, it seems progressive because the owners of corporations—the stockholders—tend to be wealthy people; and to the extent that the corporate income tax is paid from earnings that might otherwise be paid to the stockholders, one might conclude that it is progressive. But this ignores the possibility that the corporation may pass the tax on to the consumer by charging a higher price; in this case the tax may not be progressive.

To get a better picture of the extent to which government—in terms of both the money it spends and the taxes it levies—takes from the rich and gives to the poor, studies have been carried out to determine how much people in various income brackets pay in taxes and receive in services. The results of one important study of this sort are shown in Figure 28.5. They indicate that the percentage of income paid in federal taxes increases from the $1,000 to $5,000 income levels, then goes down between $5,000 and $8,000, and then goes up markedly beyond $8,000. At the state and local level, taxes as a percent of income go down steadily as income increases. Thus, if we add up federal, state, and local taxes and consider their sum, the entire tax structure is progressive up to about $5,000, regressive from $5,000 to about $9,000, and progressive above $9,000.

But this gives only a partial and distorted picture of the effects of government, because it only considers taxes and ignores expenditures. When government expenditures are considered too, it turns out—as shown in Figure 28.5—that people with incomes below $6,000 receive more in benefits from government expenditures than they pay in taxes. From $6,000 to $10,000, the ***net tax rate*** (taxes minus benefits as a percent of income) rises from zero to about 5 percent. Beyond $10,000, the net tax rate increases markedly. Thus, when government expenditures as well as taxes are considered, it appears that people with incomes under $6,000 gain on balance, and that people with incomes over $10,000 are in the income range where the taxes net of benefits are quite progressive.

These figures are very interesting, but it must be recognized that they are based on a number of rather arbitrary assumptions about how the benefits of government expenditures are allocated between rich and poor. Also, it is difficult to predict the ***incidence*** of some taxes—that is, it is difficult to know who *really* pays them. Of course, the incidence of certain taxes is relatively easy to determine. For example, it is generally accepted that the personal income tax is paid by the person whose income is taxed. But there are other cases—such as the corporation income taxes we just mentioned—where it is difficult to tell how much of

Figure 28.5
Burden of Taxes, by Income Level, United States

People with income below $6,000 received more in benefits from government expenditures than they paid in taxes. From $6,000 to $10,000, taxes minus benefits as a percent of income rises slowly; above $10,000, it rises much more rapidly.

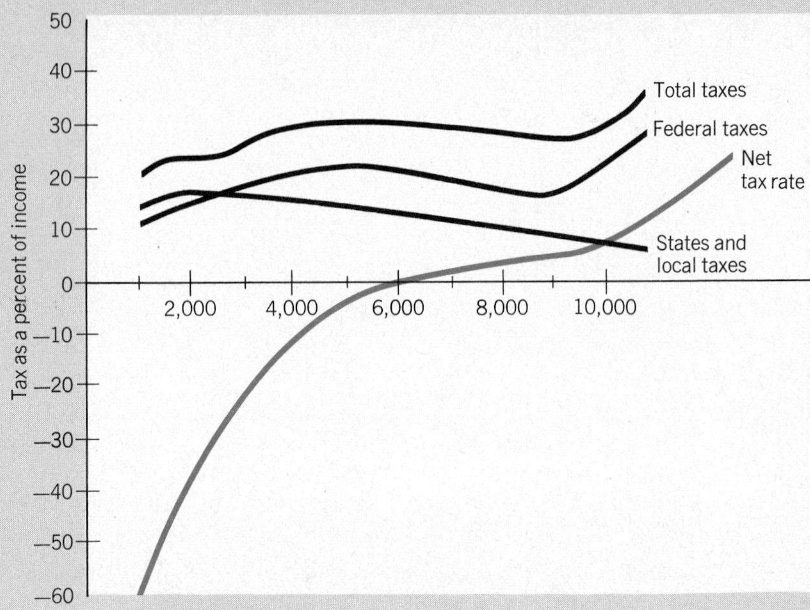

the tax burden the firm shifts to the consumer.[3] For these and other reasons, there is considerable controversy over the extent to which the spending and taxing activities of the government really are progressive or regressive.

[3] To see how the burden of a tax can be shifted, consider the case of an *excise* tax—a tax imposed on each unit sold of a particular product. The federal government imposes excise taxes on liquor and tobacco, among many other products. The immediate effect of these taxes is to raise the price of the commodity since the supply function will be shifted upward and to the left. If demand is price inelastic, most of the burden of the tax is shifted to the consumer. Under these circumstances, firms sell almost as many units of the product as before the tax was imposed, despite the higher price induced by the tax. On the other hand, if supply is relatively inelastic, the burden is borne mainly by the producer. Usually, the aim of excise taxes is to put the burden on consumers. For example, in the case of liquor and tobacco there clearly is a feeling that drinking and smoking smack of sin and sinners should pay, in this world and the next. For a discussion of excise taxes, see Joseph Pechman, *Federal Tax Policy,* revised edition, New York: Norton, 1971.

Income Inequality: The Pros and Cons

Few economists or social philosophers favor poverty (despite the teachings of St. Francis), yet their views concerning income inequality range over a broad spectrum. We cannot consider all the subtler points, but those who oppose income inequality make three main arguments. First, *they say that inequality of income lessens total consumer satisfaction because an extra dollar given to a poor man provides him with more extra satisfaction than the loss of a dollar takes away from a rich man.* For example, according to A. C. Pigou, "It is evident that any transference of income from a relatively rich man to a relatively poor man of similar temperament, since it enables more intense wants to be satisfied at the expense of less intense wants, must increase the aggregate sum of satisfactions."[4]

[4] A. C. Pigou, *Economics of Welfare,* Fourth Edition, London: Macmillan, 1948, p. 89.

The flaw in this very appealing argument is its assumption that the rich man and the poor man have the same capacities to gain enjoyment from income. Most economists believe that there is no scientific way to make such comparisons, as we shall see in the next chapter. They deny that the satisfaction one person derives from an extra dollar of income can be measured with precision against the satisfaction another person derives from an extra dollar. Although such comparisons may be drawn, they rest on ethical, not scientific, grounds.

Second, *some critics point out that income inequality is likely to result in unequal opportunities for young people to gain advanced education and training*. The children of the rich can get an education, while the children of the poor often cannot. The result is that some able and productive people may be denied an education simply because their parents happen to be poor. Clearly, this is a waste of resources. Third, *it is argued that income inequality is likely to lead to political inequality*. The rich may well influence legislation and political decisions more heavily than the poor, and there is likely to be one kind of justice for the rich and another kind for the poor.

In general, people who favor income inequality also make three arguments. First, *they argue that income inequality is needed to give people an incentive to work and create*. After all, if everyone receives the same income, why bother to increase your production, or to try to invent a new process, or to work overtime? Whatever you do, your income will be the same. This is an important point, though it overlooks the fact that nonmonetary incentives like pride in a job well done can be as important as monetary incentives. One often hears that progressive taxation is dampening incentives for effort and risk taking, but statistical studies do not seem to turn up any clear-cut evidence of the extent of this effect.

Second, *advocates of income inequality claim that it permits greater savings, and thus greater capital formation*. Although this seems reasonable, it is not hard to cite cases where countries with greater inequality of income invest less, not more, than countries with less inequality of income. For example, some Middle Eastern countries with great income inequality have not had relatively high investment rates.

Third, *advocates of income inequality say that the rich have been important patrons of new and high-quality products that benefit the entire society*. They argue that there are social advantages in the existence of certain people with the wherewithal to pioneer in consumption and to support art and culture. In their view, a completely egalitarian society would be a rather dull affair.[5]

This is an age-old argument that involves much more than economics. Whether you favor greater or less income inequality depends on your ethical and political beliefs. It is not a matter economics alone can settle. However, economists can assess the degree of income inequality in a country and suggest ways to alter the gap between the haves and havenots in accord with the dictates of the people or their leaders.

What Is Poverty?

Some people are fond of saying that everything is relative. Certainly this is true of poverty. For example, recalling our discussion in Chapter 4, relative to Aristotle Onassis, practically all of us are poor; but relative to the Rios family practically all of us are rich. Moreover, poverty is certainly subjective. For example, consider the average young executive making $20,000 a year. After a bad day at the office or a particularly expensive family shopping spree, he is likely to tell anyone who will listen that he is as poor as a church mouse.

There is no well-defined income level that can be used in all times and places as a touchstone

[5] Another point that is often made and worth noting is that, even if everyone received the same income, the poor would not be helped a great deal, because the wealthy are relatively few. If the riches of the rich were transferred to the poor, each poor person would get only a little, because there are so many poor and so few rich.

to define poverty. Poverty is partly a matter of how one person's income stacks up against that of others. What most people in America today regard as stark poverty would have seemed like luxury to many Americans of 200 years ago—and would seem like luxury in some parts of Asia and Africa today. However, one must be careful not to define poverty in such a way that it cannot be eliminated—and then try to eliminate it. If, for example, poverty is defined as the bottom 10 percent of the income distribution, how can a war against poverty ever be won?

Perhaps the most widely accepted definition of poverty in the United States today is the one developed by the Social Security Administration. It begins by determining the cost of a *minimal* nutritionally sound food plan (given by the Department of Agriculture). Then, since low-income families spend about ⅓ of their incomes on food, this food cost is multiplied by 3 to obtain an income level that is used as a criterion for poverty. Families with less income are regarded as "living below the poverty level."

Based on these computations, an urban family of four needed an income of about $4,300, while an urban couple needed about $2,700, to make it barely over the Social Security Administration's poverty line in 1972. Since farm families typically have lower food costs, the estimates for them are lower. A farm family of four required an income of only about $3,600, and a couple an income of only about $2,300 in 1972. Although one could quarrel with these figures on various counts, most people would agree that families with income below these levels are poor—as indicated by the fact that these incomes only permit a family to spend about $.35 per person on each meal. If you don't think that is poverty, try to live on those meals![6]

Particular cases of poverty are generally more illuminating and impressive than discussions in the abstract. Consider the following two actual cases in New York City (though the names, of course, are fictitious). First, there is the Smith family. In 1967, the Smiths—Christopher, 47, and Irene, 35—opened a small restaurant after years of saving. Within a month, Christopher had a severe heart attack and was laid up in the hospital. The Smiths lost the restaurant, and Irene went to work as a nurse's aide to supplement her husband's small disability benefits. After about a year of working and trying to take care of her husband and two children—John, 13, and Deborah, 12—Irene collapsed from the strain and had to enter a mental hospital. While she was away, a relative took care of Christopher and the children. After getting out of the hospital, Irene learned that her husband had cancer and required expensive surgery. She became so upset that the doctor called in one of the city's charity agencies, which tried to help this troubled and impoverished family as best it could.

Second, consider the Jones family. Jean Jones, 35, is trying to raise seven children. Her husband, an unskilled laborer, never made much money. He drank a lot, terrified Mrs. Jones and the children with his abuse, and was an unfaithful husband. Four years ago, Mrs. Jones separated from him. She gets along as best she can on public assistance, but is having a difficult time. Two of the children have been arrested for theft; two others are in trouble in school; and one daughter is pregnant out of wedlock. Mrs. Jones feels beaten. In recent months, through the help of neighbors, she has consulted a community service bureau where the social workers have given her help and encouragement. But she obviously needs a great deal of aid if she and her family are to get their heads above water.

Neither of these cases is typical. Since they were cited by the *New York Times* as being among New York's 100 neediest cases, it is fair to say that their plight is probably worse than that of the great bulk of America's poor. But they provide some idea of just how bad things can get; and one has to be hardhearted indeed not to feel compassion for people like the Smiths and Mrs. Jones.

[6] The basic figures come from the Department of Commerce's *Current Population Reports,* which explain in detail the way in which these figures are derived. The method described in the text is crude, but it provides results that are quite close to those of more complicated methods.

The Characteristics of the Poor

Because college students tend to come from relatively well-off families, they often are unaware of the number of families in the United States whose incomes fall below the Social Security Administration's poverty line. According to estimates made by the federal government in 1972, about 12 percent of the population in the United States was below this line. In absolute terms, this means that over 24 million people were poor—perhaps not as poor as the Smiths or Mrs. Jones, but poor enough to fall below the criterion described above.

Fortunately, the incidence of poverty (measured by this criterion) has been declining in the United States. In 1947, about 30 percent; in 1960, about 20 percent; and in 1972, about 12 percent of the people were poor by this definition. Of course, this is what we would expect. As the average level of income rises, the proportion of the population falling below any relatively fixed income level will tend to decrease. Nonetheless, the fact that poverty is being eliminated in the United States does not mean that this process is going on as fast as it should. No, many observers feel, as we shall see in subsequent sections, that poverty could and should be eradicated more rapidly.

Naturally, the poor are not confined to any particular demographic group, but some types of families are much more likely than others to be below the poverty line. In particular, *nonwhites are much more likely to be poor than whites.* In 1972, 20 percent of nonwhites in families headed by a male were poor, whereas 6 percent of whites in families headed by a male were poor. Also, *families headed by females are much more likely to be poor than families headed by males.* 29 percent of whites in families headed by females were poor, opposed to 6 percent of whites in families headed by males. In addition, very large families—7 persons and over —are much more likely than others to be poor.

Poverty strikes a particularly hard blow at children. Even the most hardhearted citizens are prone to agree that the young should be shielded from the crippling impact of dire poverty. According to a government survey carried out in 1968, *over 12 million children under 18 in the United States were being raised in families below the poverty line.* This is a very striking fact indeed.

To a considerable extent, the reasons why families are poor lie beyond the control of the families themselves. About ⅓ of the poor adults have suffered a disability of some sort, or the premature death of the family breadwinner, or family dissolution. Some have had to face a smaller demand for their occupation (because of technological or other change) or the decline of their industry or geographical area. Some have simply lived "too long" —their savings have given out before their minds and bodies did. Another instrumental factor in making some families poor is discrimination of various kinds. The most obvious type is racial, but others exist as well: discrimination based on sex, religion, age, residence, education, and seniority.

These barriers are important. As the University of Wisconsin's Robert Lampman points out,

> Barriers, once established, tend to be reinforced from the poverty side by the alienated themselves. The poor tend to be cut off from not only opportunity but even from information about opportunity. A poverty subculture develops which sustains attitudes and values that are hostile to escape from poverty. These barriers combine to make events nonrandom: e.g., unemployment is slanted away from those inside the feudalistic walls of collective bargaining, disability more commonly occurs in jobs reserved for those outside the barriers, the subculture of poverty invites or is prone to self-realizing forecasts of disaster.[7]

In addition, of course, some people are poor because they have very limited ability or little or no motivation. These factors should not be overlooked.

Most of the heads of poor families do not have jobs. For example, in 1966, about 40 percent did not work at all, and another 27 percent worked only part of the year. However, it is worth noting that almost ⅓ of the heads of poor families worked

[7] Robert Lampman, "Approaches to the Reduction of Poverty," *American Economic Review,* May 1965.

all year round, but simply could not make enough to get above the poverty line. Judging from the available evidence, poverty tends to be self-perpetuating. Families tend to be poor year after year, and their children tend to be poor. Because the families are poor, the children are poorly educated, poorly fed, and poorly cared for, and poverty is transmitted from one generation to the next. It is a vicious cycle.

Social Insurance

Until about 40 years ago, the federal government played little or no role in helping the poor. Private charity was available in limited amounts, and the state and local governments provided some help, but the general attitude was "sink or swim." Self-reliance and self-support were the watchwords. The Great Depression of the 1930s, which changed so many attitudes, also made a marked change in this area. In 1935, with the passage of the Social Security Act, the federal government established a social insurance system providing compulsory old-age insurance for both workers and self-employed people, as well as unemployment insurance. By 1970, about 30 million Americans were receiving benefits from the resulting system of old-age and survivors' insurance.

To finance this program of ***old-age insurance,*** payroll taxes must be paid by each worker and his employer. The tax on each party is 5.2 percent of the first $7,800 of the worker's wages per year. (The percentage will rise to 5.9 percent by 1987.) The worker receives benefits when he turns 65; and when he dies, his survivors receive benefits. The size of the individual's benefit depends on the amount he has contributed in taxes to the program. At the end of 1970, the average benefit was about $110 per month. These Social Security checks have undoubtedly made an important reduction in the extent and seriousness of poverty in the United States. Without Social Security, poverty would be much more of a problem than it is.

In 1965, the Congress extended the Social Security program to include ***Medicare,*** a compulsory hospitalization insurance plan plus a voluntary insurance plan covering doctors' fees for people over 65. The hospitalization insurance pays for practically all the hospital costs of the first 90 days of each spell of illness, as well as some additional costs. The voluntary plan covers about 80 percent of doctors' fees after the first $50. The cost of the compulsory insurance is included in the taxes described above. This program is also an important factor in preventing and alleviating poverty. The incidence of illness is relatively high among the elderly; and with the rapid rise in medical costs, it has become more and more difficult for them to afford decent care.

Besides instituting old-age, survivors, and medical insurance, the Social Security Act also encouraged the states to set up systems of ***unemployment insurance.*** Such systems now exist in all states, financed by taxes on employers. Once an insured worker is unemployed, he can obtain benefits after a short waiting period, generally a week. The weekly benefits—and the length of time they continue—vary from state to state. These state programs also help to prevent some people from falling below the poverty line. However, it is important to recognize that many workers are not covered by this insurance, and that the average benefit is only about $50 per week. Moreover, after a worker is unemployed for a certain period of time, the benefits run out.

Antipoverty Programs

According to the great English poet and essayist, Samuel Johnson, "A decent provision for the poor is the true test of civilization." There is general agreement that our social insurance programs, although useful in preventing and alleviating poverty, are not an adequate or complete antipoverty program. For one thing, they focus largely on the elderly, which means that they do not aid many poor people. Nor do they help the working poor; and even for the unemployed, they provide only limited help for a limited period of time.

Consequently, the government has started a number of additional programs specifically designed to help the poor, although many of them are aimed more at the symptoms of poverty than at its basic causes. For example, there are programs that provide goods and services to the poor. Perhaps the most important of these are the ***food programs,*** which distribute surplus food—generally from the surpluses (before 1973) due to the farm programs described in Chapter 5—to needy families. The food is supplied by the federal government, but the state governments sometimes limit the amounts that can be provided. There are also food-stamp programs, in which the federal government gives stamps that can be used to buy food to local agencies, which sell them (at less than the equivalent of market prices) or give them to needy families.

More important in quantitative terms than programs that give particular commodities to the poor are programs that provide them with cash. These are what people generally have in mind when they refer to "welfare." There are advantages, of course, to cash payments. They allow a family to adapt its purchases to its own needs and circumstances. There are obvious disadvantages too, since the money may be spent on liquor and marijuana rather than on food and milk. In recent years, about 10 million people in the United States have received about $5 billion per year in cash payments under these programs.

The most important single program of cash payments gives ***aid to families with dependent children.*** In the late 1960s, this program alone paid out more than $3 billion per year to the nation's poor. The amount paid to a family under this program varies from state to state, since each state administers its own program and sets its own schedule of payments—as well as contributes part of the cost of the program, with the federal government providing the balance. In the late 1960s the average payment was about $2,000 for a family of four, but it was higher in states like New York and Massachusetts and lower in states like Mississippi and Alabama. To determine eligibility, the family's affairs are examined; and while receiving aid the family is under the surveillance of a social worker who supervises its housekeeping and child care.

Many additional programs are aimed at alleviating poverty. For example, our vast investment in public education is certainly a very important weapon in any war on poverty. Beyond this, a number of new antipoverty programs were started in the 1960s. ***Regional development programs*** were established to improve employment opportunities in economically stagnant areas like Appalachia. ***Training programs*** were set up to increase the skills of out-of-work young people (and adults) with little education. The *Office of Economic Opportunity* was established in 1964 to coordinate the antipoverty program and to administer programs like Vista, Headstart, and others.

The Negative Income Tax

There is widespread dissatisfaction with current antipoverty—or "welfare"—programs. The cost of these programs has risen alarmingly; the programs themselves are judged by many experts to be inefficient; and, in some people's view, the welfare recipients are subjected to unnecessary meddling and spying. Moreover, there is little incentive for many people to get off welfare. Both Republicans and Democrats seem to agree that current welfare programs are a mess. What sorts of changes might be made? One suggestion that has received serious consideration is the negative income tax, an idea proposed by the University of Chicago's Milton Friedman (an adviser of presidential candidate Barry Goldwater in 1964 and of President Nixon) and Yale's James Tobin (an adviser of President Kennedy).

A ***negative income tax*** would work as follows: just as families with reasonably high incomes *pay*

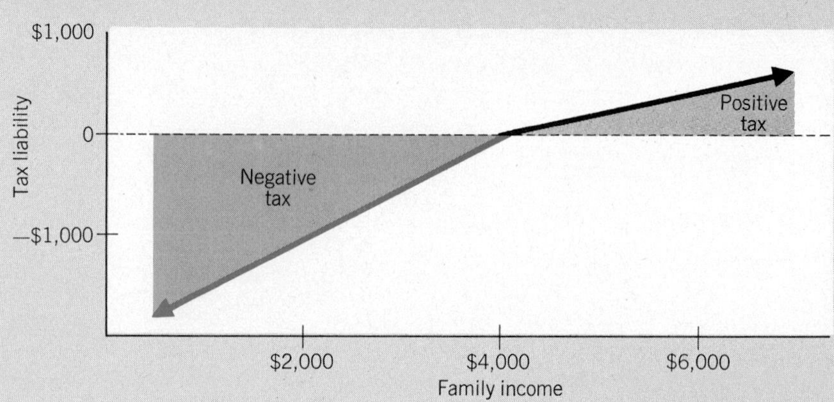

Figure 28.6
Example of Negative Income Tax

A family with more than $4,000 in income pays taxes; for example, a family with an income of $6,000 pays $500 in taxes. A family with an income less than $4,000 receives a payment; for example, a family with an income of $1,000 is paid $1,500.

taxes, families with low incomes would *receive* a payment. In other words, the poor would pay a *negative* income tax. Figure 28.6 illustrates how a negative income tax might work; it shows the amount a family of four would pay—or receive—in taxes for incomes at various levels. According to Figure 28.6, $4,000 is the ***break-even income***—the income at which a family of four neither pays nor receives income taxes. Above $4,000, a family pays taxes; for example, a family with an income of $6,000 pays $500 in taxes. Below $4,000 a family receives a payment; for example, a family with an income of $1,000 is paid $1,500.

There are several advantages of a negative income tax. First, it would give people on welfare more incentive to work. As indicated in Figure 28.6, for every extra dollar it earns, the family receives only $.50 less from the government under this kind of negative income tax. Thus, the family gets to keep half of every extra dollar (up to $4,000) it earns, which is a larger portion of this extra dollar than under the present system. Second, there would be no "means tests" and no regulations that cut off welfare payments if the husband remains with his family. In the past, the welfare system has given families an incentive to break up, and encroached on the dignity of poor people. Third, it might cost less to administer the negative income tax than the present system, and differences among states in benefits might be reduced.

Despite these advantages, many citizens remain skeptical about the negative income tax. For one thing, they are antagonistic to the idea of giving people an income without requiring any work in return. They also are unwilling to transfer large amounts from rich to poor. The amount would depend, of course, on how high the break-even income was set and on the negative tax rates. In the late 1960s, it was estimated that a negative income tax based on the sort of plan described in Figure 28.6 would have meant that those above the break-even income level would transfer about $25 billion to those below the break-even level. Despite the attractive features of a negative income tax, a transfer of this magnitude has proved unacceptable in many quarters.[8]

The Rise and Fall of "Workfare"

In 1969, President Nixon proposed a reform of the welfare system, which he termed "workfare." He called for a Family Assistance Plan that would

[8] For further discussion of the negative income tax, see James Tobin, "On Improving the Economic Status of the Negro" in E. Mansfield, *Economics: Readings, Issues, and Cases,* New York: Norton, 1974.

guarantee every family an annual income of $500 per year for each of the first two members of the family, plus an additional $300 for each extra member. He also outlined an expansion of the food stamp program so that a family of four earning no income would get about $850 in food stamps. A major feature of his proposal was its emphasis on incentives for work. Specifically, his plan allowed a family to earn $720 per year without losing any benefits; and if a family earned more than $720, it lost one dollar in benefits for every two dollars it earned in excess of $720. Consequently, a family had an incentive to increase its earnings. Moreover, everyone receiving these benefits, except women with small children, would have to sign up for employment or training at state employment offices. Day care would be provided for children beyond a certain age, enabling their mothers to work.[9]

Although critics argued that the benefits were too low to raise many of the poor population above the poverty line, the workfare proposal seemed to be an improvement over the existing system. Its adoption seemed likely to eliminate many inequities, to help the working poor, to aid in keeping families together, and to provide additional incentives for work. The House of Representatives twice approved modifications of this plan, but the Senate could not agree on a bill. By 1972, critics charged that President Nixon had lost interest in this proposal, though he affirmed his continuing support.

In 1973, President Nixon abandoned, at least for the time being, this plan for welfare reform. In his State of the Union message on human resources, he said, "The legislative outlook seems to preclude passage of an over-all structural reform bill." Instead, he said that his administration would take "vigorous administrative and legislative steps to strengthen welfare management." In particular, Caspar Weinberger, Secretary of Health, Education, and Welfare, suggested that the government might experiment with flat grants "to replace degrading investigations of family budgets" and with other new administrative techniques. At the same time, the administration set out to eliminate the Office of Economic Opportunity and to redistribute its programs to other agencies. Critics felt that the president was dismantling many programs designed primarily to benefit the poor, whereas the administration claimed that these changes would increase the effectiveness of the programs.

[9] See Richard Nixon, "Welfare Reform" in *Economics: Readings, Issues, and Cases, op. cit.*

Racial Discrimination in the United States

Poverty, discrimination, and race are closely intertwined. Despite recent improvements, the sad fact is that racial discrimination occurs in many walks of life in many areas of the United States. Table 28.3 shows certain aspects of the relative position

Table 28.3

Economic Characteristics of Whites and Nonwhites, United States, 1971

	White	Nonwhite
Median income	$10,700	$6,400
Percent of persons in poverty	10	32
Percent unemployed (men)	4	7
Percent unemployed (women)	5	9
Percent unemployed (teenagers)	15	32
Median years of school completed[a]	12	9
Percent of persons over 25 who are college graduates[b]	11	5

Source: Bureau of the Census and Bureau of Labor Statistics.
[a] Men 25 years or older, 1967.
[b] 1967.

of the white and nonwhite population in the United States. The average income of nonwhites is only about ⅔ that of whites. About ⅓ of the nonwhite population are below the poverty line, compared to only about 1/10 of the white population. On the average, whites complete about 12 years of schooling, while nonwhites complete only about 9 years. About 10 percent of the white population over 25 are college graduates, compared to only about 5 percent of the nonwhite population over 25.

There is considerable agreement that at least part of these economic differences is the result of discrimination. Blacks are often prevented from reaching certain occupational or managerial levels. For example, it is rare to find a black in the higher reaches of management in a major corporation. To a considerable extent, of course, they are cut off from job opportunities at this level by lack of education. But even at much lower levels, they are kept out of certain occupations by union policy (the building trades are a good example); and even when blacks do essentially the same kind of work as whites, there is sometimes a tendency to pay blacks less.

Some important effects of racial discrimination can be demonstrated by using the theory of wages discussed in Chapter 26. (The general point of this discussion holds true whether discrimination is on racial or other grounds.) The important thing to recognize at the outset is that black labor is not allowed to compete with white labor. This results in two different labor markets, one for whites and one for blacks. As shown in Figure 28.7, the demand curve for black labor is quite different from the demand curve for white labor, reflecting the fact that blacks are not allowed to enter many of the more productive occupations. Because of the difference in the demand (and supply) curves, the equilibrium wage for blacks (P_B) is lower than for whites (P_w).

How does this equilibrium differ from a situation of no discrimination? If blacks and whites competed in the same labor market, the total demand for labor—regardless of color—would be $D_T D_T'$, the total supply of labor—regardless of color—would be $S_T S_T'$, and the wage for all labor —regardless of color—would be P_T. A comparison of P_T with P_B shows that the wage rate of blacks would be increased considerably. A comparison of P_T with P_w shows that the wage rates of whites would be decreased slightly. The slight cut in

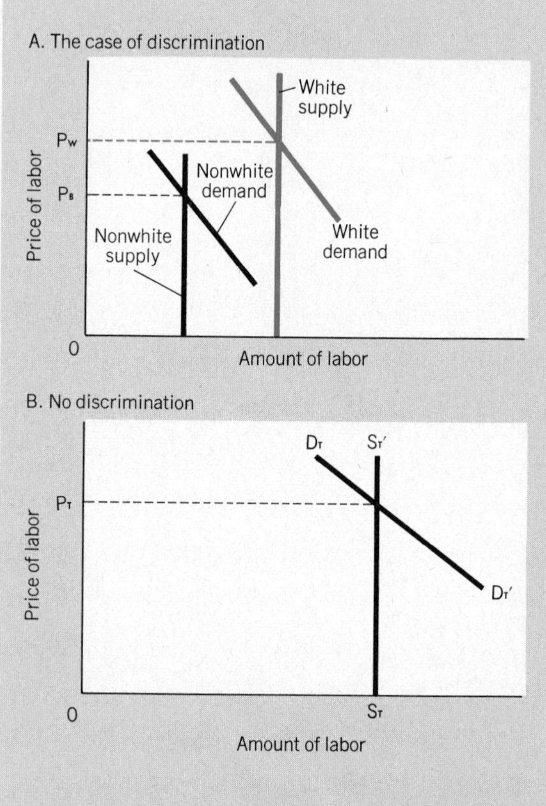

Figure 28.7
Racial Discrimination

Under discrimination, the demand curve for white labor is quite different from that for black labor, and the supply curve of white labor is quite different from that of black labor, so that the equilibrium wage for blacks (P_B) is lower than for whites (P_w). If there were no discrimination, the wage for all labor, black or white, would be P_T.

white wages would be much smaller than the considerable increase in black wages, since the nation's total production (and income) would increase because blacks could be put to more productive use.

Thus, the effect of discrimination is to exploit blacks—by reducing their wages relative to whites—and to lower the nation's total output. Fortunately, there is evidence that racial discrimination is lessening. In part because of changing attitudes among whites, the growing restiveness of the blacks, and the coming of age of new leadership, the old patterns of segregation and discrimination are breaking down. For example, blacks are now being recruited actively by many prestigious colleges, and they are being hired and promoted to responsible positions in firms where formerly they remained at a relatively menial level. The ratio of nonwhite to white average income rose from about 50 percent in the 1950s to about 60 percent in the 1970s. Progress is slow, but it unquestionably exists.

What opportunities exist for blacks to become entrepreneurs, to start and develop their own firms? Because of lack of funds and education, relatively few nonwhites own the stores and shops in the black ghetto. The white storeowners are often regarded as exploiters by the blacks, and it is sometimes suggested that the blacks displace the whites as owners of these stores and businesses. However, many influential and well-informed observers, both black and white, feel that the potential gains from such a policy are not very great. The stores and businesses that are involved are currently not very profitable, and it is doubtful that they could be made much more so by new and relatively inexperienced ownership. Also, it is argued that any such movement toward black separation will work to the disadvantage of blacks as well as whites.

Nonetheless, some steps could be taken to encourage black enterprise. Perhaps the most important is to help blacks develop basic business skills. In addition, of course, the government could insure that promising black businesses have adequate access to capital. Measures of this sort have been suggested by government officials, but thus far only limited progress seems to have been made.

Discrimination against Women

Needless to say, discrimination is not limited to blacks. Similar barriers to economic advancement confront Puerto Ricans, Mexican-Americans, and American Indians. There is also some discrimination against older workers. Even more widespread is discrimination against women. Figure 28.8 shows that, holding age and education constant, women earn much less than men. To some extent, this difference in earnings arises because women work shorter hours and often have less experience in their jobs than men. But even after adjusting for factors such as education, work experience during the year, and lifetime work experience, there remains a differential of about 20 percent between the earnings of men and women. To a considerable extent, this differential is probably the result of

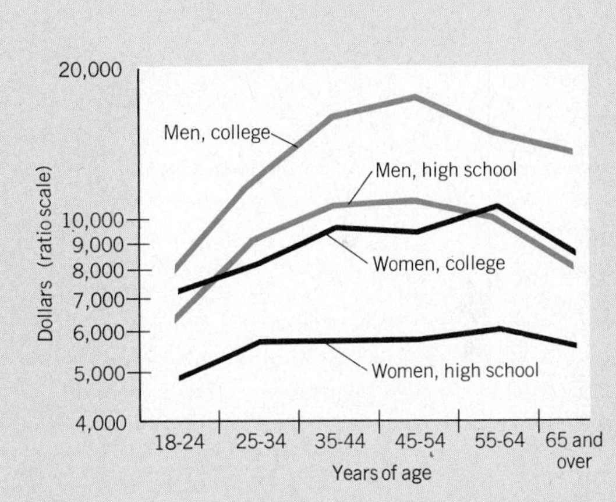

Figure 28.8
Annual Income, by Age, for Male and Female High School and College Graduates

At the same age and with the same level of education, women tend to be paid appreciably less than men.

discrimination, the nature of which is well described by the following passage from the 1973 Annual Report of the Council of Economic Advisers:

> There is clearly prejudice against women engaging in particular activities. Some patients reject women doctors, some clients reject women lawyers, some customers reject automobile saleswomen, and some workers reject women bosses. Employers also may have formulated discriminatory attitudes about women, exaggerating the risk of job instability or client acceptance and therefore excluding women from on-the-job training which would advance their careers. In fact, even if employers do estimate correctly the average job turnover of women, women who are strongly committed to their jobs may suffer from "statistical discrimination" by being treated as though their own behavior resembled the average. The extent to which this type of discrimination occurs depends on how costly it is for employers to distinguish women who will have a strong job commitment from those who will not. Finally, because some occupations restrict the number of newcomers they take in and because women move in and out of the labor force more often, more women than men tend to fall into the newcomer category and to be thus excluded. For example, restrictive entry policies may have kept women out of the skilled crafts.
>
> On the other hand, some component of the earnings differential and of the occupation differential stems from differences in role orientation which start with differences in education and continue through marriage, where women generally are expected to assume primary responsibility for the home and subordinate their own outside work to their household responsibilities. It is not now possible to distinguish in a quantitative way between the discrimination which bars women from jobs solely because of their sex, and the role differentiation whereby women, either through choice or necessity, restrict their careers because of the demands of their homes. Some may label the latter as a pervasive societal discrimination which starts in the cradle; nonetheless, it is useful to draw the distinction.[10]

[10] *The Economic Report of the President,* 1973, pp. 106–7.

In various ways, the government has set out to discourage discrimination against women. For example, the Equal Pay Act of 1963 requires employers to pay men and women equally for the same work, and Title VII of the Civil Rights Act of 1964 bars discrimination in hiring, firing, and other aspects of employment. Moreover, the Equal Rights Amendment to the Constitution, which provides that "equality of rights under the law shall not be denied or abridged by the United States or by any State on account of sex," passed the Senate in 1972 and was ratified by 22 states by the beginning of 1973. In addition, a number of women have been appointed to high-ranking government jobs, including economist Marina Whitman of the University of Pittsburgh, who has served as a member of the President's Council of Economic Advisers. An Advisory Committee on the Economic Role of Women has also been organized by the president. All these measures undoubtedly will have a beneficial effect, but it must be recognized that eliminating discrimination of this kind will require basic changes in the attitudes of both males and females. The problem of discrimination against women is likely to be with us for a long time.[11]

Summary

Americans are very rich relative to other peoples. Per capita income in this country is considerably higher than in Europe and Japan and much, much higher than in many Asian, African, and South American countries. Nonetheless, 22 percent of all American families received less than $6,000 in 1972. (At the upper end of the income distribution, 7 percent received more than $25,000 in the same year.) Lorenz curves are used to measure the

[11] See Barbara Bergmann, "The Economics of Women's Liberation," and Marilyn Power Goldberg, "The Economic Exploitation of Women," in *Economics: Readings, Issues, and Cases, op. cit.*

extent of income inequality. They make it clear that there has been a considerable reduction in income inequality in the United States since the late 1920s. Practically all this reduction occurred before the end of World War II.

Many factors are responsible for existing income differentials. Some people are abler, better educated, or luckier than others. Some people have much more property, or more monopoly power, than others. Critics of income inequality argue that it lessens total consumer satisfaction because an extra dollar given to a poor man provides him with more extra satisfaction than the loss of a dollar takes away from a rich man. Also, they argue that income inequality leads to social and political inequality. Defenders of income inequality point out that it is scientifically impossible to make interpersonal comparisons of utility, and argue that income inequality is needed to provide incentives for people to work and create, that it permits greater capital formation, and that a completely egalitarian society would be a dull affair.

There is no well-defined income level that can be used in all times and all places to determine poverty. Perhaps the most widely accepted definition of poverty in the United States today is the one developed by the Social Security Administration, according to which about 12 percent of the population in the United States—over 24 million people—fall below the poverty line. The incidence of poverty has been declining, but many observers feel that poverty could and should be eradicated more quickly. Nonwhite families, families headed by a female, and very large families are more likely than others to be poor. To a considerable extent, the reasons for their poverty lie beyond the control of the poor people. About ⅓ of poor adults have suffered a disability of some sort, or the premature death of the family breadwinner, or family dissolution. Discrimination is also an obvious factor. Most heads of poor families do not have jobs.

Because private charity is inadequate, the nation has authorized its government to carry out various public programs to aid the poor. There are programs to provide them with goods and services—for example, food stamp programs. Other programs, like aid to families with dependent children, give them cash. There is widespread dissatisfaction with existing antipoverty—or "welfare"—programs. They are judged to be inefficient; their costs are increasing at an alarming rate; and they provide little incentive for people to get off welfare. One suggestion to remedy these problems is a negative income tax. Although this scheme has attractive features, in most of the forms put forth it involves a transfer of income that may be beyond the present realm of political feasibility. In 1969, President Nixon proposed his "workfare" plan, which would have established a guaranteed annual income, together with various incentives to get people off the welfare rolls and into employment. But in 1973, this plan was abandoned as unacceptable to the Senate.

Despite recent improvements, the sad fact is that racial discrimination occurs in many walks of life in many areas of the United States. Blacks often are cut off from educational and job opportunities; and even when blacks do essentially the same kind of work as whites, there is sometimes a tendency to pay them less. The effects of discrimination are to exploit blacks by reducing their wages relative to whites and to lower the nation's total output. In recent years, the nation's colleges and universities have become much more willing to admit nonwhites. Although it is sometimes suggested that blacks attempt to displace the white storeowners in the ghetto, many observers feel that the potential gains from such a policy are not very great. There is also much discrimination against women, making them less likely than men to enter the better-paying occupations. Even after adjusting for factors such as education and work experience, women earn about 20 percent less than men.

CONCEPTS FOR REVIEW

Poverty
Negative income tax
Welfare
Aid to dependent children
Workfare
Discrimination
Lorenz curve
Progressive tax
Regressive tax
Net tax rate
Medicare
Office of Economic Opportunity

QUESTIONS FOR DISCUSSION AND REVIEW

1. According to James Tobin, "The defects of present categorical assistance programs could be . . . greatly reduced by adopting a system of basic income allowances integrated with and administered in conjunction with the federal income tax [in other words, a negative income tax]." Do you agree? Why or why not?

2. According to Marilyn Power Goldberg, capitalism "is inherently exploitative" of women, and "women cannot successfully defeat their exploitation within the context of the present economic system." Do you agree? Why or why not?

3. If incomes were the same for all families, the Lorenz curve would be U-shaped. True or False?

4. It was estimated in 1972 that about what percent of the population in the United States fell below the poverty line?
a. 1 percent b. 2 percent c. 12 percent d. 30 percent

CHAPTER 29

General Equilibrium and Welfare Economics

A few years back, a cigarette commercial proclaimed that "Kent gets it all together." Without judging the validity of this claim, we can say with considerable justification that the study of general equilibrium and welfare economics "gets together" much of what we have already discussed concerning consumers, firms, inputs, and markets. It shows how various markets for products and inputs interact. Rather than focusing on a single market, industry, firm, or consumer, it looks at the economic system as a whole. It also examines the nature of the policy recommendations economists can make. It goes beyond mere analysis and description of the workings of the economic system to indicate that certain ways of allocating society's resources are better than others. For many economists, these conclusions concerning the optimal allocation of resources are much of the real "pay dirt" from economic analysis.

Partial Equilibrium versus General Equilibrium Analysis

In previous chapters, we looked in detail at the behavior of individual decision-making units and the workings of individual markets. We looked at consumers, at firms, and at various types of product markets and input markets. We almost always viewed each single market in isolation. According to the models we have used, the price and quantity in each such market are determined by supply and demand curves, with these curves drawn on the assumption that other prices are given. Each market is regarded as independent and self-contained for all practical purposes. In particular, it is assumed that *changes in price in the market under consideration do not have serious repercussions on the prices in other markets.* This is ***partial equilibrium analysis.***

General equilibrium analysis recognizes that changes in price may affect other prices, and that the changes in other prices may have an impact on the market under consideration. No market can adjust to a change in conditions without causing some change in other markets, and in some cases this change may be substantial. For example, suppose that an upward shift occurs in the demand for barley. In previous chapters, it was generally assumed that when the price and output of barley changed in response to this change in conditions, the prices of other products would remain fixed. However, the market for barley is not sealed off from the markets for rye, corn, wheat, and other foodstuffs. (For that matter, it is not completely sealed off from the markets for nonfood products like sewing machines and autos.) Thus the market for barley cannot adjust without disturbing the equilibrium of other markets *and having these disturbances feed back on itself.*

Both partial and general equilibrium analysis are very useful, each in its own way. Partial equilibrium analysis is perfectly adequate when a change in conditions in one market has little repercussion on prices in other markets. For example, in studying the effects of a proposed excise tax on the production of a certain commodity, we often can assume that prices of other commodities are fixed and remain close to the truth. However, if a change in conditions in one market has important repercussions on other prices, a general equilibrium analysis may be required.

Suppose that the tastes of consumers shift toward barley products and away from rye products, causing an upward shift in the demand for barley and a downward shift in the demand for rye. To determine the effects on the prices of the two commodities, the economist must look simultaneously at the market for barley and the market for rye, as well as at the relationships between them. To do so, he employs general equilibrium analysis, which shows that the immediate effect is a rise in the price of barley (because of the upward shift in the demand curve for barley) and a drop in the price of rye (because of the downward shift in its demand curve).

This is the response in the market period. What happens in the short run when firms can adjust their output? Assuming that both the barley industry and the rye industry were in long-run equilibrium before the pattern of demand changed, the immediate result of the price rise in the barley industry is to increase barley production. Firms will find it profitable to produce up to the point where marginal cost equals the new, higher price level. Similarly, in the rye industry, the result of the price decrease is to cut production because firms will find it profitable to produce only up to the point where marginal cost equals the new, lower price level. If some of the inputs used in rye production can be adapted to barley production, they may be transferred directly from the rye industry to the barley industry. Otherwise, adjustments occur in various related markets, with the result that the barley industry gains resources while the rye industry loses them.

So much for the short run. In the long run, when firms can enter or leave each industry, they will enter the barley industry, since economic profits are being earned there. The increased demand for inputs will raise input prices and cost curves in barley production, and the price of barley will be depressed by the movement to the right of the supply curve because of the entry of new firms. Eventually, when economic profits are no longer earned, entry will cease. Meanwhile, in the rye industry, firms will leave rye production since economic losses are being incurred there. As they leave, the supply curve shifts to the left, causing the price to rise. The transfer of resources out of rye will stop when losses there no longer occur. (Recall our discussion of similar cases in Chapter 23.)

General equilibrium analysis is concerned with problems like this one, where more than one market is involved. Often, it is necessary to look at a fairly large number of markets simultaneously to do justice to the problem. We have simplified matters considerably by confining our attention to the markets for barley and rye, since in all likelihood the markets for other foodstuffs, as well as various input markets, would also be affected. Cases of this sort often call for the solution of a complex system of equations to estimate the equilibrium price and quality in each market.

The Nature and Existence of General Equilibrium

General equilibrium analysis, like partial equilibrium analysis, can be used to solve problems of many kinds. One of the most fundamental theoretical problems it has been used to solve is this: if we could somehow establish a perfectly competitive economy, would a set of prices exist such that all markets would be in equilibrium simultaneously? To be more specific, let us define a state of ***general equilibrium*** as a state of the economy in which the following conditions hold: (1) every consumer chooses his preferred market basket subject to his budget line, which is determined by the prices of inputs and the prices of products; (2) every consumer supplies whatever amount of inputs he chooses, given the prevailing input and product prices; (3) every firm maximizes its profits subject to the constraints imposed by the available technology, the demand for its product, and the supply of inputs, but in the long run profits are zero; and (4) the quantity demanded equals the quantity supplied at the prevailing prices in all product and input markets.

Given this definition of a state of general equilibrium, the problem is: can a state of general equilibrium be achieved? Such noted economists as Kenneth Arrow, Gerard Debreu, Lionel McKenzie, and others have established that in a perfectly competitive economy a general equilibrium can be achieved under a fairly wide set of conditions, such as each consumer's wants must not be satiable, at least one primary input must be used to produce each commodity, and so on. Economists have concluded that under certain circumstances a perfectly competitive economy has a variety of desirable characteristics; and for this reason, a perfectly competitive economy is sometimes held up as an ideal. It would be embarrassing for those who put forth this view to find that this kind of economy is based on behavioral assumptions and market mechanisms that are incompatible in the sense that general equilibrium cannot be achieved. Fortunately, no such embarrassment is necessary.

Input-Output Analysis

Input-output analysis, due largely to Harvard's Nobel Laureate, Wassily Leontief, puts general equilibrium analysis in a form that is operationally useful to governments and firms faced with a variety of important practical problems. An important feature of input-output analysis is its emphasis on the interdependence of the economy. Each industry uses the outputs of other industries as its inputs, and its own output may be used as input by the same industries whose output it uses. Recognizing this interdependence, input-output analysis attempts to determine the amount each industry must produce so that a specified amount of various final goods will be turned out by the economy. This type of analysis has been used to help predict production requirements to meet estimated demands. For example, economic planners have applied it to military mobilization and to problems of economic development in less developed countries.

To put general equilibrium analysis in a usable form, input-output analysis makes a number of simplifying assumptions. Thus it uses as variables the *total* quantity of a particular good demanded or supplied, rather than the quantity demanded by a particular consumer or supplied by a particular firm. This reduces enormously the number of variables and equations in the analysis. Also, in the simpler versions of input-output analysis, it is assumed that consumer demand for all commodities is known. Input-output analysis attempts to find out what can be produced, and the amount of each input and intermediate good that must be employed to produce a given output. It views these questions as largely a matter of technology.

Finally, input-output analysis assumes that inputs are used in fixed proportions to produce any product and that there are constant returns to scale. This is a key assumption of Leontief's input-output system. For example, in the production of steel, Leontief would assume that, for every ton of steel produced, a certain amount of iron ore, a certain amount of coke, a certain amount of fuel, and so on would be required. The amount of each input required per unit of output is assumed to be the same, whatever the level of output. For example, if a certain amount of iron ore is required to produce 1 million tons of steel, it is assumed that 10 times that amount is required to produce 10 million tons of steel.[1]

With some basic algebra, the essentials of input-output analysis are quickly grasped. Suppose that

Table 29.1

Amount of Each Input Used per Dollar of Output

Type of input	Type of output: Electric power	Coal	Chemicals
Electric power	$ .10	$ .30	$ .00
Coal	.50	.10	.00
Chemicals	.20	.00	.90
Labor	.20	.60	.10
Total	1.00	1.00	1.00

the economy consists of only three industries: coal, chemicals, and electric power. Each industry uses the products of the other industries in the proportions shown in Table 29.1. For instance, the second column of Table 29.1 states that every dollar's worth of coal requires \$.30 worth of electric power, \$.10 worth of coal, and \$.60 worth of labor. (Of course one could just as well carry out the analysis with inputs and outputs measured in physical units—manhours or tons per year—as in money.)

This economy has set consumption targets of \$100 million of electric power, \$50 million of coal, and \$50 million of chemicals. Input-output analysis takes up the question: how much will have to be produced by each industry in order to meet these targets? Let's begin with coal. If electric power output is E, chemical output is C, and coal output is X (E, C, and X are measured in millions of dollars), it follows from Table 29.1 that

$$X = .5E + .1X + 50 \tag{29.1}$$

if the target is met. Why? Because the electric power industry needs an amount of coal equal in value to .5 E, the coal industry needs an amount equal in value to .1 X, and an amount equal in value to 50 must be produced for consumption. Thus the total output of coal must be equal to the

[1] In previous chapters, we said that the proportion in which inputs are combined can generally be altered. This, of course, is a direct contradiction of the assumption of fixed proportions in input-output analysis. But it often takes a fair amount of time for changes to be made and they are often gradual, with the result that Leontief's assumption of fixed proportions may work reasonably well in the short run.

sum of these three terms, as shown in Equation (29.1).

If we construct similar equations for electric power output and chemical output, we find that

$$E = .1E + .3X + 100 \quad (29.2)$$
$$C = .2E + .9C + 50 \quad (29.3)$$

if the targets are to be met. For example, Equation (29.3) must hold because chemical output must equal the amount needed by the electric power industry ($.2E$) plus the amount needed by the chemical industry itself ($.9C$) plus 50 for consumption.

Since Equations (29.1) to (29.3) are three equations in three unknowns, X, E, and C, we can solve for the unknowns, which turn out to be $X = 144$, $E = 159$, and $C = 818$. We have answered our question: \$144 million of coal, \$159 million of electric power, and \$818 million of chemicals must be produced to meet the consumption targets. We can also find out how much labor will be required to meet these targets, since (according to Table 29.1) the total value of labor required equals

$$.2E + .6X + .1C \quad (29.4)$$

Substituting the 144, 159, and 818 for X, E, and C, respectively, in (29.4), we find that \$206 million of labor is required. If this does not exceed the available labor supply, the solution is feasible; otherwise the targets must be scaled downwards.

This simple example illustrates the fundamentals of input-output analysis. It also suggests why the assumption that inputs are used in fixed proportions is so convenient. Without this assumption, the input-output table in Table 29.1 would not hold for each output level of the industries. Instead, the numbers in the table would vary depending on how much of each commodity was produced. The added complexity that would arise (without this assumption) is obvious. Even with the assumption, the computational and estimation problems involved in solving large input-output models can be substantial. Government agencies, such as the Departments of Commerce and Labor, have constructed a model of the U.S. economy involving several hundred industries. Usually, however, far fewer industries are included in such models.

Applicability of Input-Output Analysis

Whether input-output analysis can be applied fruitfully in a particular situation depends in part on whether the ***production coefficients***—the numbers in Table 29.1—remain constant. (See footnote 1). There are at least two important factors that might cause changes over time in such coefficients. First, changes in technology may change the relative quantities of inputs used. For example, the amount of coal required to produce many goods decreased considerably in the years since World War II. Second, changes in the relative prices of inputs may result in changes in production coefficients as cheaper inputs are substituted for more expensive ones.

Since World War II, much has been done to implement and extend input-output analysis. Basic research has been conducted by academic economists interested in the quantitative significance of various types of economic interdependence. Applied research has been devoted to formulating techniques that would be useful in decision making in government and business. For example, a large government-sponsored program in the United States in the early 1950s was carried out to analyze problems of defense and mobilization. And other countries have used input-output analysis to determine the relationship of imports and exports to domestic production, as well as to analyze various problems of economic development. Also, business firms have used input-output analysis to forecast their sales.[2]

To illustrate how input-output analysis can help

[2] W. Leontief, *Input-Output Economics,* New York: Oxford University Press, 1966; and H. Chenery and P. Clark, *Interindustry Economics,* New York: Wiley, 1959.

solve important problems of public policy, consider the economic effects of disarmament. If the United States were to reduce its military budget by $1 billion, what would be the effect on sales and employment in various industries? Clearly, one can determine from the composition of the military budget the effect of such a reduction on the sales and employment of each industry. Moreover, one can determine the net effect on each industry if this reduction in the military budget is counterbalanced by a $1 billion increase in civilian demand. Based on input-output analysis, Leontief and his associates concluded that, in 1958, an $8 billion reallocation of military purchases to civilian demand would result in an 18 percent reduction in aircraft employment, a 6 percent reduction in radio employment, a 1 percent increase in automobile employment, and a 1 percent increase in textile employment, among other things.

The Nature of Welfare Economics

One of the great goals of economics is to determine how best to allocate society's scarce resources. Questions concerning the optimal allocation of inputs among industries and the optimal distribution of commodities among consumers are general equilibrium problems, since the optimal usage of any input cannot be determined by looking at the market for this input alone, and the optimal output of any commodity cannot be determined by looking at the market for this commodity alone. On the contrary, the optimal allocation of resources between two products depends on the relative strength of the demands for the products and their relative production costs.

The term ***welfare economics*** covers the branch of economics that studies policy issues concerning the allocation of resources. (Do not confuse welfare economics with the various government "welfare" programs you read about in the previous chapter.) It should be stressed from the start that welfare economics, although useful, is certainly no panacea. By itself, welfare economics can seldom provide a clear-cut solution to issues of public policy. But in combination with other disciplines, it can frequently show useful ways to structure and analyze these issues.

Perhaps the most important limitation of welfare economics stems from the fact that there is no scientific way to compare the utility level of different individuals. There is no way to show scientifically that a bottle of Château Haut-Brion will bring you more satisfaction than it will me, or that your backache is worse than mine. This is because there is no scale on which we can measure pleasure or pain so that interpersonal comparisons can be made scientifically. For this reason, the judgment of whether one distribution of income is better than another must be made on ethical, not scientific, grounds. For example, if you receive twice as much income as I do, economics cannot tell us whether this is a better distribution of income than if I receive twice as much income as you do. This is an ethical judgment.

However, most problems of public policy involve changes in the distribution of income. A decision to increase the production of jet aircraft and to reduce the production of railroad locomotives may mean that certain stockholders and workers will gain, while others will lose. Because it is so difficult to tell whether the resulting change in the distribution of income is good or bad, it is correspondingly difficult to conclude whether such a decision is good or bad.

Faced with this problem, economists have adopted a number of approaches, all of which have significant shortcomings. Some economists have simply paid no attention to the effects of proposed policies on the income distribution. Others have taken the existing income distribution as optimal, while still others have asserted that less unequal income distributions are preferable to more unequal ones. Purists have argued that we really cannot be sure a change is for the better unless it hurts no member of society, while others have suggested that we must accept the judgment of Congress (or the public as a whole) on what is an optimal distribution of income.

For now, the major thing to note is that the conditions for an optimal allocation of resources, described in the following section, are incomplete, since they say nothing about the optimal income distribution. Whatever the income distribution you or I may consider best on ethical or some other (nonscientific) grounds, the conditions below must be met if resources are to be allocated optimally. Remember, however, that there may be many allocations of resources that meet these conditions, and the choice of which is best will depend on one's feelings about the optimal income distribution.

Conditions for Optimal Resource Allocation

Fundamentally, there are three necessary conditions for optimal resource allocation. The first pertains to the optimal allocation of commodities among consumers, and states that *the ratio of the marginal utilities of any two goods must be the same for any two consumers who consume both goods.* That is, if the marginal utility of good A is twice that of good B for one consumer, it must also be twice that of good B for any other consumer who consumes both goods. The proof that this condition is necessary to maximize consumer satisfaction is quite simple. We need only note that, if this ratio were unequal for two consumers, both consumers could benefit by trading.

Thus, assume that the ratio of the marginal utility of good A to that of good B is 2 for one consumer, but 3 for another consumer. This means that the first consumer regards an additional unit of good A as having the same utility as 2 extra units of good B, whereas the second consumer regards an additional unit of good A as having the same utility as 3 extra units of good B. Then, if the first consumer trades 1 unit of good A for 2.5 units of good B from the second consumer, both are better off. (If this isn't obvious to you, pause for a moment and convince yourself that it is so!)

The second condition, which pertains to the optimal allocation of inputs among producers, states that *the ratio of the marginal products of two inputs must be the same for any pair of producers that use both inputs.* That is, if the marginal product of input 1 is twice that of input 2 in one firm, it must also be twice that of input 2 in any other firm that uses both inputs. If this condition does not hold, total production can be increased merely by reallocating inputs among firms.

To illustrate this, suppose that for the first producer the marginal product of input 1 is twice that of input 2, whereas for the second producer the marginal product of input 1 is three times that of input 2. Then, if the first producer gives 1 unit of input 1 to the second producer in exchange for 2.5 units of input 2, both firms can expand their output. To see this, suppose that the marginal product of input 1 is M_1 for the first producer M_2 for the second producer. Then the output of the first producer is reduced by M_1 units because of its loss of the unit of input 1, but it is increased by $2.5 \times M_1/2$ units because of its gain of the 2.5 units of input 2, so that on balance its output increases by $M_1/4$ units because of the trade. Similarly, the output of the second producer is increased by M_2 units because it gains the 1 unit of input 1, but it is decreased by $2.5 \times M_2/3$ units because it loses the 2.5 units of input 2, with the consequence that on balance its output increases by $M_2/6$ units because of the trade.

The third condition pertains to both the optimal allocation of inputs and the optimal allocation of consumers' goods. It states that *the slope of the product transformation curve for any two goods must equal the slope of the indifference curve of any consumer of these goods.* The ***product transformation curve*** is the curve that shows the maximum amount of good X that can be produced, given various output levels of good Y. Suppose that UU' in Figure 29.1 is the product transformation curve for good X and good Y. In addition,

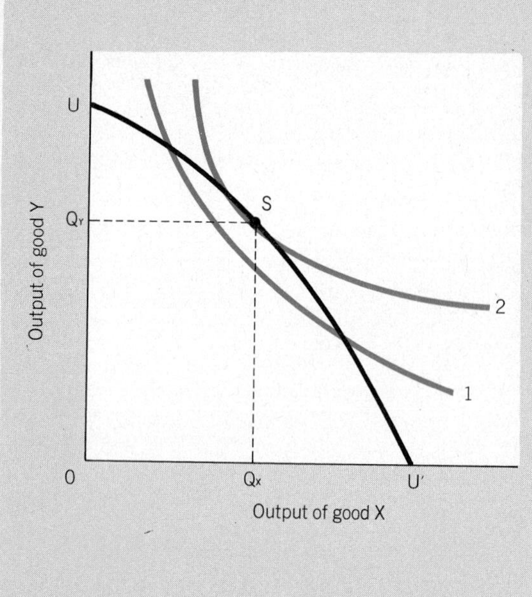

Figure 29.1
Condition for Optimal Resource Allocation

If society consisted of only one consumer, the optimal point would be *S*, where his indifference curve was tangent to the society's product transformation curve, *UU′*.

suppose that curves 1 and 2 in Figure 29.1 represent the indifference curves of a consumer who, for simplicity, is assumed to be the only consumer in the economy. To maximize the consumer's satisfaction, production must take place at point S, the output of good X being OQ_X and the output of good Y being OQ_Y. Clearly, S is the point on the product transformation curve that is on the consumer's highest indifference curve—and S is a point where the product transformation curve is tangent to the indifference curve. Thus, the third condition must hold if consumer satisfaction is to be maximized. (And this result will hold for any number of consumers, not just one.)

Let's turn now to a case study of how these conditions can be applied to one of our most important commodities—water. If the first condition is to hold, the ratio of the marginal utility of water to that of any other good must be the same for all consumers. To be specific, suppose that the other good is money. Then the ratio of the marginal utility of water to the marginal utility of money must be the same for all consumers. That is, if resources are allocated optimally, *the amount of money a consumer will give up to obtain an extra unit of water must be the same for all consumers.* This follows because the ratio of the marginal utility of good *A* to the marginal utility of good *B* equals the number of units of good *B* that the consumer will give up to get an extra unit of good *A*.

The common sense underlying this condition has been described well in a study of water resources done at the RAND Corporation:

> Suppose that my neighbor and I are both given rights (ration coupons, perhaps) to certain volumes of water, and we wish to consider whether it might be in our mutual interest to trade those water rights between us for other resources—we might as well say for dollars, which we can think of as a generalized claim on other resources like clam chowders, babysitting services, acres of land, or yachts. . . . Now suppose that the last acre-foot of my periodic entitlement is worth \$10 at most to me, but my neighbor would be willing to pay anything up to \$50 for the right. . . . Evidently, if I transfer the right to him for any compensation between \$10 and \$50, we will both be better off in terms of our own preferences. . . . But this is not yet the end. Having given up one acre-foot, I will not be inclined to give up another on such easy terms (and) my neighbor is no longer quite so anxious to buy as he was before, since his most urgent need for one more acre-foot has been satisfied. . . . Suppose he is now willing to pay up to \$45 (for another acre-foot), while I am willing to sell for anything over \$15. Evidently, we should trade again. Obviously, the stopping point is where the last (or marginal) unit of water is valued equally (in terms of the greatest amount of dollars we would be willing to pay) by the two of us. . . . At this point no more mutually advantageous

trades are available—and efficiency has been attained.[3]

If people can trade water rights freely—as in this hypothetical case—an efficient allocation of water rights will be achieved. But what if water rights cannot be traded freely, because certain kinds of water uses are given priority over other types of uses, and it is difficult, even impossible, for a low-priority user to purchase water rights from a high-priority user? Clearly, the effect is to prevent water from being allocated so as to maximize consumer satisfaction. Unfortunately, this question is not merely an academic exercise: it focuses attention on a very practical problem. In fact, there is a wide variety of limitations on the free exchange of water rights in the United States. For example, some legal codes grant certain types of users priority over other types of users, and free exchange of water is limited. Experts believe that these limitations are a serious impediment to the optimal allocation of water resources.

Perfect Competition and Welfare Maximization

One of the most fundamental findings of economic theory is that a perfectly competitive economy satisfies the three sets of conditions for welfare maximization set forth in the previous section. The argument for competition can be made in various ways. Some people favor it simply because it prevents the undue concentration of power and the exploitation of consumers. But to the economic theorist, the basic argument for a perfectly competitive economy is that such an economy satisfies these three conditions. In this section we prove that this is indeed a fact.

The first condition states that the ratio of the marginal utilities of any pair of commodities must be the same for all consumers buying both commodities. Recall that under perfect competition consumers choose their purchases so that the marginal utility of a commodity is proportional to its price. Since prices, and thus price ratios, are the same for all buyers under perfect competition, it follows that the ratio of the marginal utilities between any pair of commodities must be the same for all consumers. For example, if every consumer can buy bread at $.25 a loaf and butter at $1 a pound, each one will arrange his purchases so that the ratio of the marginal utility of butter to that of bread is 4. Thus the ratio will be the same for all consumers: 4 for everyone.

The second condition states that the ratio of the marginal products of any pair of inputs must be the same for all producers using both inputs. We have already seen in an earlier chapter that under perfect competition producers will choose the quantity of each input so that the ratio of the marginal products of any pair of inputs equals the ratio of the prices of the pair of inputs. Since input prices, and thus price ratios, are the same for all producers under perfect competition, it follows that the ratio of the marginal products must be the same for all producers. For example, if every producer can buy labor services at $4 an hour and machine tool services at $8 an hour, each one will arrange the quantity of its inputs so that the ratio of the marginal product of machine tool service to that of labor is 2. Thus the ratio will be the same for all producers: 2 for each.

The third condition states that the slope of the product transformation curve for any two goods must equal the slope of the indifference curve of any consumer of these goods. This condition will also be met under perfect competition. Producers will operate at a point on the product transformation curve where the slope of this curve equals the ratio of the prices of the goods. Why? Because the slope of the product transformation curve equals the ratio of the marginal costs of the goods, since this ratio obviously equals the amount of one good that must be given up to produce an

[3] J. Hirshleifer, J. Milliman, and J. DeHaven, *Water Supply,* Chicago: University of Chicago Press, 1960, p. 38, reprinted in E. Mansfield, *Microeconomics: Selected Readings,* New York: Norton, 1971.

additional unit of the other good. Since marginal cost equals price under perfect competition, it follows that producers will operate at a point where the slope of the product transformation curve equals the ratio of the prices of the goods. And since the slope of an indifference curve must equal the same price ratio (because this is the slope of the budget line), the product transformation curve must have the same slope as any consumer's indifference curve under perfect competition.

Thus, in summary, all three conditions for optimal resource allocation are satisfied under perfect competition. This is one of the principal reasons why economists are so enamored of perfect competition and so wary of monopoly and other market imperfections. If a formerly competitive economy is restructured so that some industries become monopolies, these conditions for optimal resource allocation are no longer met. As we know from Chapter 23, each monopolist produces less than the perfectly competitive industry that it replaces would have produced. Thus, too few resources are devoted to the industries that are monopolized, and too many resources are devoted to the industries that remain perfectly competitive. This is one of the economist's chief charges against monopoly. It wastes resources because it results in overallocation of resources to competitive industries and underallocation of resources to monopolistic industries. The result is that society is less well off. Similarly, oligopoly and monopolistic competition are charged with wasting resources, since the conditions for optimal resource allocation are not met there either.

However, in evaluating this result and judging its relevance, one must be careful to note that it stems from a very simple model that ignores such things as technological change and other dynamic considerations, risk and uncertainty, and external economies and diseconomies. Also, there is the so-called "theory of the second-best," which states that unless all of the conditions for optimal resource allocation are met, it may be a mistake to increase the number of such conditions that are fulfilled. Thus, piecemeal attempts to preserve or impose competition may do more harm than good.

Marginal Cost Pricing

The previous section showed that the three conditions for optimal resource allocation are satisfied under perfect competition. Economists interested in the functioning of planned, or socialist, economies have pointed out that a price system also could be used to increase social welfare in such economies. According to economists like Abba Lerner[4] of the City University of New York, rational economic organization could be achieved in a socialist economy that is decentralized, as well as under perfect competition. For example, the socialist government might solve the system of equations that is solved automatically in a perfectly competitive economy, and obtain the prices that would prevail under perfect competition. Then the government might publish this price list, together with instructions for consumers to maximize their satisfaction and for producers to maximize profit. (Of course, the wording of the instructions to consumers might be a bit less heavy-handed than "Maximize your satisfaction!")

Under a socialist system of this sort, the government does not have to become involved in the intricate and detailed business of setting production targets for each plant. It need only compute the proper set of prices. In following the rules to maximize "profits," plant managers will choose the proper production levels. Thus decentralized decision making, rather than detailed centralized direction, could be used, thus reducing administrative costs and bureaucratic disadvantages.

The prices the government would publish, like those prevailing in a perfectly competitive economy, would equal marginal cost. Many economists have recommended that government-owned enterprises in basically capitalist economies also adopt ***marginal cost pricing,*** i.e., that they set price equal to marginal cost. Taking the case of a bridge where the marginal cost (the extra cost involved in allowing an additional vehicle to cross) is zero, Harold Hotelling argued in a famous arti-

[4] Abba Lerner, *The Economics of Control,* New York: Macmillan, 1944.

cle that the socially optimal price for crossing the bridge is zero, and that its costs should be defrayed by general taxation. If a toll is charged, the conditions for optimal resource use are not met.[5]

Marginal cost pricing has fascinated economists during the 30 years that have elapsed since Hotelling's article,[6] but there are a number of problems in the application of this idea. One of the most important is that if the firm's average costs decrease with increases in its scale of output (as is frequently the case in public utilities), it follows from the discussion in Chapter 21 that marginal cost must be less than average cost, with the consequence that the firm will not cover its costs if price is set equal to marginal cost. This means that marginal cost pricing must be accompanied by some form of subsidy if the firm is to stay in operation. However, the collection of the funds required for the payment of the subsidy may also violate the conditions for optimal resource allocation. This subsidy also means that there is a change in the income distribution favoring users of the firm's output and penalizing nonusers. The difficulties in determining whether such a change is good or bad have already been stressed.

To illustrate the reasoning that underlies marginal cost pricing, consider once more the case of water supplies. We saw earlier that economic efficiency requires that the amount of money a consumer will give up to obtain an extra unit of water must be the same for all consumers. In other words, the price of water must be the same for all consumers. But what determines the level at which this price should be set?

> Suppose that at a certain moment in time [consumers are willing to pay] $30 per unit. Then, if the community as a whole can acquire and transport another unit of water for, say, $20, it would clearly be desirable to do so; in fact, any of the individual customers to whom the unit of water is worth $30 would be happy to pay the $20 cost, and none of the other members of the community would be made worse off thereby. We may say that, on efficiency grounds, additional units should be made available so long as any members of the community are willing to pay the additional or marginal costs incurred. . . . So the . . . rule is to make the price equal to marginal cost and equal for all customers.[7]

Unfortunately, it seems that water pricing practices do not often conform to this rule. For example, some types of water users are commonly charged lower prices than other types of water users, although the marginal cost of the water is the same. According to the study carried out at the RAND Corporation,

> In Los Angeles, for example, there is an exceptionally low rate for irrigation use. Domestic, commercial, and industrial services are not distinguished as such, but they are differentially affected by the promotional volume rates. More serious, because much more common, is the system of block rates, with reductions [in price] for larger quantities used. . . . [This system leads] to wasteful use of water by large users, since small users would value the same marginal unit of water more highly if delivered to them. . . . The customer paying the lower price will on the margin be utilizing water for less valuable purposes than it could serve if transferred to the customer paying the higher price.

External Economies and Diseconomies

Up to this point, we have assumed implicitly in this chapter that there is no difference between private and social benefits, or between private and social costs. For example, costs to producers have been assumed to be costs to society, and costs to society have been assumed to be costs to producers.

[5] Harold Hotelling, "The General Welfare in Relation to Problems of Taxation and of Railway and Utility Rates," *Econometrica,* 1938.

[6] For example, see J. Nelson, *Marginal Cost Pricing in Practice,* Englewood Cliffs, N.J.: Prentice-Hall, 1964.

[7] Hirshleifer, Milliman, and DeHaven, *Water Supply* pp. 40–41.

Benefits to producers have been assumed to be benefits to society, and benefits to society have been assumed to be benefits to producers. In many instances, however, these assumptions do not hold. Instead, producers sometimes confer benefits on other members of the economy but cannot obtain payment for these benefits, and they sometimes act in a way that harms others without having to pay the full costs. In these cases, the pursuit of private gain will not promote the social welfare.

It is convenient and customary to classify divergences between private and social returns into four types. First, there are external economies of production. As we know from Chapter 5, an external economy occurs when an action results in uncompensated benefits to others. When such benefits are the result of an increase in a firm's production, they are called ***external economies of production.*** The firm may benefit others directly. For example, it may train workers who eventually go to work for other firms, which do not have to pay the training costs. Or the firm may benefit other firms indirectly because its increased output may reduce the cost of services provided to other firms in the industry. For example, a great expansion in an aircraft firm may make it possible for aluminum producers to take advantage of economies of scale, thus enabling other metal fabricating firms to get cheaper aluminum. In either case, there is a difference between private and social returns; the gains to society are greater than the gains to the firm.

Second, there are ***external economies of consumption,*** which occur when an action taken by a consumer, rather than a producer, results in an uncompensated benefit to others. For example, if I maintain my house and lawn, this benefits my neighbors as well as myself. If I educate my children and make them more responsible citizens, this too benefits my neighbors as well as myself (and my children!) The list of external economies of consumption could easily be extended, but the idea should be clear now.

Third, there are external diseconomies of production. As we know from Chapter 5, an external diseconomy occurs when an action results in uncompensated costs to others. When such costs are due to increases in a firm's production, they are called ***external diseconomies of production.*** For example, a firm may pollute a stream by pumping out waste materials, or it may pollute the air with smoke or other emissions. Such actions result in costs to others. For instance, Chesapeake Bay's oyster beds and Long Island's clam beds are being threatened by water pollution. However, the private costs of waste disposal paid by the firms and cities responsible for the pollution are not equal to the full social costs, because they are not charged for their contribution to poorer water and their harm to industries dependent on good water. There are many examples of external diseconomies of production, such as traffic congestion and the defacement of scenery.

Fourth, there are ***external diseconomies of consumption,*** which occur when an action taken by a consumer results in an uncompensated cost to others. Some external diseconomies of consumption can be fairly subtle. For example, a family that feels that a three-year-old Chevrolet is perfectly adequate may become dissatisfied after moving to a community where everyone drives a new Pontiac.

At first glance, these instances of divergences between social and private costs and benefits may not seem very important. But when all these types of external economies and diseconomies are considered, their aggregate significance can be substantial. In the case of water pollution, the wastes discharged into a river by a single firm may not seriously harm the water quality but the combined effects of many firms' actions will. The importance of various types of external economies of production is also clear, and it is equally obvious that consumer tastes and well-being are determined by the tastes and well-being of other members of society.

How do these external economies and diseconomies alter the optimality of resource allocation under perfect competition? If a person (or firm) takes an action that contributes to society's welfare but results in no payment for him, he will probably take this action less frequently than would be socially optimal. Thus, if the production of a certain good, say beryllium, creates external economies, less than the socially optimum amount of beryllium will be produced under perfect competition. The producers are unlikely to increase output simply because the increase will reduce the costs of other companies. By the same token, if a person (or firm) takes an action resulting in costs to others that he is not forced to pay, he is likely to take this action more frequently than is socially desirable. Thus, if the production of a certain good is responsible for external diseconomies, more of this good will probably be produced under perfect competition than is socially optimal.[8]

The Planning of Urban Land Use

To illustrate the importance of external economies and diseconomies, consider urban land use in the United States. Americans have become more and more concerned about the plight of their cities in recent years. To a considerable extent, of course, urban problems are closely related to poverty and racial problems. The poor tend to huddle together in the central cities. Often these slums are inhabited largely by nonwhites, resulting in black ghettos in the heart of the city. But there are other aspects of our urban problems too. Crime and delinquency are prevalent and highly visible in the densely populated urban core, urban transportation is often criticized as being slow and inefficient, and our metropolitan areas are viewed by some as characterized by a suburban sprawl that is both inefficient and socially unhealthy.

To help solve some of the city's problems, urban planners have attempted to influence the allocation of land in the metropolitan area. There are a number of useful legal devices at their disposal. First, there is *zoning*. In most areas, local governments can deny a citizen the right to develop land as he chooses; instead, a proposed use must be in accord with the community's overall plan. Second, there is *code enforcement*, by which the government sees to it that minimum standards of maintenance and construction are met. Third, the government can *condemn private property* and use it for public purposes, including urban renewal. Fourth, the government can *invest directly* in structures (e.g., public housing). Fifth, it can influence the use of land by changing its *tax rates*.

Although these are powerful tools, it is obvious that most of the basic decisions on land use are made by families and firms. So long as we maintain anything approaching a free enterprise system, this must remain true. Thus the planner's influence on urban land use is considerably circumscribed. Moreover, the city planner typically does not control all the powers mentioned above. Instead, they reside in various parts of a local government, and there is no assurance that the planner's views will be accepted by other local officials. The planner's job is further complicated by the difficulty of defining goals and by the multitude of governments in most metropolitan areas.

During the past 20 years, the federal government has promoted and encouraged the redevelopment of the inner core of our major cities. Old tenements have been knocked down and new buildings have taken their place. Both federal loans and capital grants (covering up to two-thirds of the net cost of the project) have been provided. In all, over 100,000 housing units, most of them substandard, were demolished—and tens of thousands of new housing units were constructed—by urban renewal programs between 1950 and 1960.

Urban renewal rests on the idea that the market mechanism does not work properly for urban land

[8] It should be noted that private costs and benefits can in many instances be made to equal social costs and benefits by legal requirements that assign liabilities for damages and compensate for benefits. However, such systems often are impractical or too costly to be useful. See G. Stigler, *The Theory of Price,* New York: Macmillan, 1966, pp. 110–14; R. Coase, "The Problem of Social Cost," *Journal of Law and Economics,* 1961; and W. Baumol, *Economic Theory and Operations Analysis,* Englewood Cliffs, N.J.: Prentice-Hall, 1965, pp. 368–71 and 375–80, on which this section is partly based.

Table 29.2

Returns from Investment, Two Property Owners

		Owner *B*	
		Invest	Not invest
		Owner *A*'s rate of return	
Owner *A*	Invest	.07	.03
	Not invest	.10	.04
		Owner *B*'s rate of return	
Owner *A*	Invest	.07	.10
	Not invest	.03	.04

Source: O. Davis and A. Whinston, "The Economics of Urban Renewal," *Law and Contemporary Problems,* Winter 1961, reprinted in Mansfield, *Economics: Readings, Issues, and Cases,* New York: Norton 1974.

use. Why is this idea reasonable? Why do profit-maximizing individuals not find it worthwhile to keep up their property? The answer lies in the fact that the value of a piece of property depends on the neighborhood in which it is situated as well as on its own characteristics and state of repair. The enjoyment people get from a piece of property depends on its surroundings. In other words, in the jargon of the previous section, there are important external economies and diseconomies with regard to land use.

To see why this fact can cause urban blight, consider two adjacent properties. Suppose that the two owners, *A* and *B,* are each trying to determine whether to invest some money to redevelop their properties. The rate of return on the investment by each owner is shown in Table 29.2. This rate of return depends on whether the other owner redevelops his property as well. If both redevelop, each will make 7 percent on their investment. If neither redevelops, each can obtain 4 percent by investing the money in some other type of investment. If one redevelops but the other does not, the owner who redevelops makes only 3 percent since little is accomplished as long as the other owner does not redevelop. The owner who does not redevelop earns 10 percent on his investment because his property benefits (at no cost) from the improvements in the other property.

Under these circumstances, neither owner will redevelop his property. For example, take owner *A*. If owner *B* redevelops, owner *A* receives a higher return if he does not redevelop than if he redevelops. If owner *B* does not redevelop, owner *A* also receives a higher return if he does not redevelop than if he redevelops. In either case, owner *A* believes that he is better off not to redevelop. The situation is similar for owner *B*. Nevertheless, from society's point of view or from the point of view of the two owners' acting together as a unit, redevelopment may be desirable. Needless to say, this example is highly simplified and rather extreme, but it does illustrate the basic point that external economies and diseconomies may prevent redevelopment, even though it is socially desirable.

One need only look at portions of New Haven, Philadelphia, Atlanta, or other cities to recognize that urban renewal has been beneficial in many respects. Unfortunately, however, not all its effects have been good. For example, it has sometimes hurt the poor. When old tenements are knocked down, the people who lived in them often have a hard time finding another place to live, since the people who occupy the new buildings that displace the tenements are often middle-class. Unless proper attention is paid to rehousing those whose homes are being demolished, the dispossessed—typically poor and often nonwhite—will be victimized by what seems at first glance to be a very desirable development.

Summary

An analysis that takes account of the interrelations among various markets is called a general equilibrium analysis. Whereas partial equilibrium analysis assumes that changes in price do not have serious repercussions on other prices (which in turn affect the market under consideration), general equilibrium analysis deals explicitly with the effect of one market on another, as well as with the feedback from the second market to the first. One of the most fundamental theoretical problems to which general equilibrium analysis has been applied is whether equilibrium can occur simultaneously in all markets in a perfectly competitive economy. Modern work has established that in a perfectly competitive economy a general equilibrium can be achieved under a fairly wide set of conditions.

Input-output analysis is a technique that makes the general equilibrium model empirically useful. It assumes that inputs are used in fixed proportions in producing any product and that there are constant returns to scale. An important feature of input-output analysis is its emphasis on the interdependence of the economy. Using simultaneous linear equations, input-output analysis answers questions like: if consumption targets for each of a number of industries are given, how much will have to be produced by each industry to meet these targets; and given the available resources, can these production levels be achieved?

Welfare economics deals with the optimal allocation of resources. A major limitation of welfare economics is that there is no scientific way to compare the utility levels of different individuals, so that the question of whether one distribution of income is better than another must be settled on ethical, not scientific, grounds. Putting aside income distribution, three conditions must be met if resources are to be allocated optimally. First, the ratio of the marginal utilities of two commodities must be the same for any two consumers buying both commodities. Second, the ratio of the marginal products of two inputs must be the same for any pair of producers using both inputs. Third, the product transformation curve for any two commodities must have a slope that is equal to the slope of the indifference curve of any consumer.

A perfectly competitive economy satisfies all three of these sets of conditions for welfare maximization. This is one of the fundamental arguments for a perfectly competitive economy. In principle, a price system could be used in a similar way in planned, or socialist, economies. The prices set would equal marginal cost. Many economists have recommended that government-owned or government-regulated enterprises in basically capitalistic economies also adopt marginal cost pricing. However there are a variety of practical problems involved in applying it.

External economies occur when the actions of a firm or consumer result in uncompensated benefits to third parties. External diseconomies occur when the actions of a firm or consumer result in uncompensated costs to third parties. If external economies or diseconomies exist, a perfectly competitive economy is unlikely to result in an optimal allocation of resources. For example, urban renewal is based on the idea that the market mechanism does not work properly for urban land use, because the value of a piece of property depends on the neighborhood in which it is located, as well as on its own characteristics and state of repair.

CONCEPTS FOR REVIEW

Partial equilibrium analysis
General equilibrium analysis
Input-output analysis
Welfare economics
Marginal cost pricing
Efficient allocation of resources

QUESTIONS FOR DISCUSSION AND REVIEW

1. Suppose that you are given the job of forecasting the amount produced by each of the industries in Table 29.1 in the year 2000. Do you think that input-output analysis would be useful in this context? What would be some of the key problems in using it?

2. Should American Telephone and Telegraph use marginal cost pricing? Why or why not?

3. According to Edward Banfield, "'Doing good' is becoming—has already become—a growth industry, like other forms of mass entertainment." Do you agree? Why or why not? What has welfare economics got to do with "doing good"? How can one tell whether or not he is "doing good"?

4. Urban renewal is based on the idea that the market mechanism does not work properly with respect to urban land use. True or False?

5. Input-output analysis has been used to
a. analyze problems of defense and mobilization.
b. determine the relationship of imports and exports to domestic production.
c. analyze problems of underdeveloped countries.
d. all of the above.

PART NINE

International Economics

CHAPTER 30

International Trade

It takes the average human being little time to realize that he is not an island unto himself and that he benefits from living with, working with, and trading with other people. Exactly the same is true of nations. They too must interact with one another, and they too benefit from trade with one another. No nation can be an island unto itself—not even the United States. To understand how the world economy functions, you must grasp the basic economic principles of international trade.

This chapter discusses many of the fundamental questions about international trade. What is the nature of American foreign trade? What are the effects of international trade? What determines the sorts of goods a nation will import or export? What are the advantages of free trade and the arguments against it? What are the social costs of tariffs and quotas, and what has been their history in the United States? What are some of the major issues regarding protectionism in the United States today? Some of these questions have occupied the attention of economists for hundreds of years; some are as current as today's newspaper.

America's Foreign Trade

America's foreign trade, although small relative to our national product, plays a very important role in our economic life. Many of our industries depend on other countries for markets or for raw materials (like coffee, tea, or tin). Our ***exports***—the things we sell to other countries—amount to about 5 percent of our gross national product, which seems small relative to other countries like Germany, France, Italy, and the United Kingdom, where exports are about 15–20 percent of gross national product. But this is because our domestic market is so large. In absolute terms, and relative to those of other countries, our exports seem very large indeed. In recent years, they have represented about 15 percent of total world trade. Without question, our way of life would have to change considerably if we could not trade with other countries.

When we were a young country, we exported raw materials primarily. For example, during the 1850s about 70 percent of our exports were raw materials and foodstuffs. But the composition of our exports has changed with time. More are now finished manufactured goods and less are raw materials. In the 1960s, about 60 percent of our exports were finished manufactured goods, and only about 20 percent were raw materials and foodstuffs. Table 30.1 shows the importance of machinery and industrial supplies in our merchandise exports. Table 30.2 indicates to whom we sell: Western Europe and Canada take over ½ of our exports, and Latin America takes about 15 percent.

What sorts of goods do we buy from abroad? About ⅒ of our ***imports*** are agricultural commodities like coffee, sugar, bananas, and cocoa. About ⅕ are raw materials like bauxite, rubber, and wool. But the bulk are neither raw materials nor foodstuffs. Over ½ of our imports, as shown in Table 30.3, are manufactured goods like bicycles from England or radios from Japan. Just as we sell more to Western Europe than any other area, so we buy more from these countries too (see Table 30.4). But the pattern varies, of course, from product to product. For example, Canada is our leading foreign source for wood pulp and nonferrous metals, while Latin America is our leading source of imported coffee and sugar.

Finally, several general observations on the pattern of world trade are worth making. First, much of world trade involves the industrialized richer countries. This is no surprise, since these countries account for so large a share of the world's productivity and purchasing power. Second, the industrialized, richer countries of the world tend to trade with one another, while the nonindustrialized, poorer countries tend to trade with the industrialized countries, not with one another. The reasons for this are clear enough. The nonindustrialized countries supply the industrialized countries with raw materials and foodstuffs, and receive manufactures in return. The nonindustrialized countries have little reason to trade with one another since they cannot get from one another the manufactures they need. Third, neighboring nations tend to trade with one another. This too is predictable: lower transportation costs and greater familiarity tend to promote trade between neighbors.

Specialization and Trade

We have discussed the extent and nature of our trade with other countries, but not *why* we trade with other countries. Do we—and our trading partners—benefit from this trade? And if so, what determines the sorts of goods we should export and import? These are very important questions, among the most fundamental in economics. The answers are by no means new. They have been well understood for considerably more than a century, due to the work of such great economists as David Hume, David Ricardo, Adam Smith, and John Stuart Mill.

Table 30.1

U.S. Merchandise Exports, 1972

Product	Amount (millions of dollars)
Food, feed, and beverages	7,492
Chemicals	3,228
Industrial supplies and materials (other than chemicals)	10,754
Machinery	13,135
Automotive vehicles and parts	5,125
Consumer goods (excluding autos)	3,491
Military-type goods	1,200
Aircraft	3,217
Other	2,126
Total	49,768

Source: Survey of Current Business, March 1973.

Table 30.2

U.S. Exports of Goods and Services, 1972

Country	Amount (millions of dollars)
Japan	6,672
Australia, New Zealand, and South Africa	2,447
Latin America	11,262
Canada	16,415
Eastern Europe	929
United Kingdom	4,584
European Economic Community	11,930
Other Western Europe	5,592
Other	13,715
Total	73,546

Source: See Table 30.1.

Table 30.3

U.S. Merchandise Imports, 1972

Product	Amount (millions of dollars)
Food, feed, and beverages	7,257
Fuels and lubricants	4,882
Paper	1,756
Metals	6,738
Other industrial supplies and materials	4,947
Machinery	5,135
Automotive vehicles and parts	9,307
Consumer goods (excluding autos)	11,355
Other	4,178
Total	55,555

Source: See Table 30.1.

Table 30.4

U.S. Imports of Goods and Services, 1972

Country	Amount (millions of dollars)
Japan	11,434
Australia, New Zealand, and South Africa	1,727
Latin America	9,778
Canada	16,739
Eastern Europe	431
United Kingdom	5,511
European Economic Community	14,369
Other Western Europe	6,543
Other	11,235
Total	77,765

Source: See Table 30.1.

As a first step, it is useful to recognize that the benefits *nations* receive through trade are essentially the same as those *individuals* receive through trade. Consider the hypothetical case of John Jones, a lawyer, with a wife and two children. The Jones family, like practically all families, trades continually with other families and with business firms. Since Mr. Jones is a lawyer, he trades his legal services for money which he and his wife use to buy the food, clothing, housing, and other goods and services his family wants. Why does the Jones family do this? What advantages does it receive through trade? Why doesn't it attempt to be self-sufficient?

To see why the Jones family is sensible indeed to opt for trade rather than self-sufficiency, let's compare the current situation—where Mr. Jones specializes in the production of legal services and trades the money he receives for other goods and services—with the situation if the Jones family attempted to be self-sufficient. In the latter case, the Joneses would have to provide their own transportation, telephone service, foodstuffs, clothing, and a host of other things. Mr. Jones is a lawyer—a well-trained, valuable, productive member of the community. But if he were to try his hand at making automobiles—or even bicycles—he might be a total loss.

Clearly, *trade permits specialization, and specialization increases output:* this is the advantage of trade, both for individuals and for nations. In our hypothetical case, it is obvious that, because he can trade with other families and with firms, Mr. Jones can specialize in doing what he is good at—law. Consequently, he can be more productive than if he were forced to be a Jack-of-all-trades, as he would have to be if he could not trade with others. The same principle holds for nations. For example, because the United States can trade with other nations, it can specialize in the goods and services it produces particularly well. Then it can trade them for goods that other countries are especially good at producing. Thus both we and our trading partners benefit.

Some countries have more and better resources of certain types than others. Saudi Arabia has oil, Canada has timber, Japan has a skilled labor force, and so on. *International differences in resource endowments, and in the relative quantity of various types of human and nonhuman resources, are important bases for specialization.* For example, countries with lots of fertile soil, little capital, and much unskilled labor are likely to find it advantageous to produce agricultural goods, while countries with poor soil, much capital, and highly skilled labor will probably do better to produce capital-intensive, high-technology goods. We must recognize, however, that the bases for specialization do not remain fixed over time. Instead, as technology and the resource endowments of various countries change, the pattern of international specialization changes as well. For example, as we saw in the previous section, the United States specialized more in raw materials and foodstuffs about a century ago than it does now.

Absolute Advantage

To clarify the benefits of trade, consider the following example. Suppose that the United States can produce 2 electronic computers or 5,000 cases of wine with 1 unit of resources. Suppose that France can produce 1 electronic computer or 10,000 cases of wine with 1 unit of resources. Given the production possibilities in each country, are there any advantages in trade between the countries? And if so, what commodity should each country export, and what commodity should each country import? Should France export wine and import computers, or should it import wine and export computers?

To answer these questions, assume that the United States is producing a certain amount of computers and a certain amount of wine—and that France is producing a certain amount of computers and a certain amount of wine. If the United States shifts 1 unit of its resources from producing wine to producing computers, it will increase its production of computers by 2 computers and reduce its

Table 30.5

Case of Absolute Advantage

	Increase or decrease in output of: Computers	Wine (thousands of cases)
Effect of U.S.'s shifting 1 unit of resources from wine to computers	+2	− 5
Effect of France's shifting 1 unit of resources from computers to wine	−1	+10
Net effect	+1	+ 5

production of wine by 5,000 cases of wine. If France shifts 1 unit of resources from the production of computers to the production of wine, it will increase its production of wine by 10,000 cases and reduce its production of computers by 1 computer.

Table 30.5 shows the *net* effect of this shift in the utilization of resources on *world* output of computers and of wine. World output of computers increases (by 1 computer) and world output of wine increases (by 5,000 cases) as a result of the redeployment of resources in each country. Thus, *specialization increases world output.*

Moreover, if world output of each commodity is increased by shifting 1 unit of American resources from wine to computers and shifting 1 unit of French resources from computers to wine, it follows that world output of each commodity will be increased further if each country shifts *more* of its resources in the same direction. This is because the amount of resources required to produce each good is assumed to be constant, regardless of how much is produced.

Thus, in this situation, one country—the United States—should specialize in producing computers, and the other country—France—should specialize in producing wine. This will maximize world output of both wine and computers, resulting in a rise in both countries' standards of living. Of course, complete specialization of this sort is somewhat unrealistic, since countries often produce some of both commodities, but this simple example illustrates the basic principles involved.

Comparative Advantage

The case just described is a very special one, since one country (France) has an absolute advantage over another (the United States) in the production of one good (wine), whereas the second country (the United States) has an absolute advantage over the first (France) in the production of another good (computers). We say that Country *A* has an ***absolute advantage*** over Country *B* in the production of a good when Country *A* can produce a unit of the good with less resources than can Country *B*. Since the United States can produce a computer with fewer units of resources than France, it has an absolute advantage over France in the production of computers. Since France requires fewer resources than the United States to produce a given amount of wine, France has an absolute advantage over the United States in the production of wine.

When one country has an absolute advantage in producing one good and another country has an absolute advantage in producing another good, obviously each country will specialize in producing the good in which it has the absolute advantage, and each can benefit from trade. But what if one country is more efficient in producing both goods? If the United States is more efficient in producing both computers and wine, is there still any benefit to be derived from specialization and trade? At first glance, you are probably inclined to answer no. But if this is your inclination, you should reconsider—because you are wrong.

To see why specialization and trade have advantages even when one country is more efficient than another at producing both goods, consider the following example. Suppose the United States can produce 2 electronic computers or 5,000 cases of wine with 1 unit of resources, and France can produce 1 electronic computer or 4,000 cases of wine with 1 unit of resources. In this case, the United States is a more efficient producer of both computers and wine. Nonetheless, as we shall see, world output of both goods will increase if the United States specializes in the production of computers and France specializes in the production of wine.

Table 30.6 demonstrates this conclusion. If 2 units of American resources are shifted from wine to computer production, 4 additional computers and 10,000 fewer cases of wine are produced. If 3 units of French resources are shifted from computer to wine production, 3 fewer computers and 12,000 additional cases of wine are produced. Thus, the combined effect of this redeployment of resources in both countries is to increase world output of computers by 1 computer and to increase world output of wine by 2,000 cases. Even though the United States is more efficient than France in the production of both computers and wine, world output of both goods will be maximized if the United States specializes in computers and France specializes in wine.

Basically, this is so because, although the United States is more efficient than France in the production of both goods, it has a greater advantage in computers than in wine. It is twice as efficient as France in producing computers, but only 25 percent more efficient than France in producing wine. To derive these numbers, recall that 1 unit of resources will produce 2 computers in the United States, but only 1 computer in France. Thus, the United States is twice as efficient in computers. On the other hand, 1 unit of resources will produce 5,000 cases of wine in the United States, but only 4,000 cases in France. Thus, the United States is 25 percent more efficient in wine.

A nation has a ***comparative advantage*** in those products where its efficiency relative to other nations is highest. Thus, in this case, the United States has a comparative advantage in the production of computers and a comparative disadvantage in the production of wine. So long as a country has a comparative advantage in the production of some commodities and a comparative disadvantage in the production of others, it can benefit from specialization and trade. A country will specialize, of course, in products where it has a comparative advantage, and import those where it has a comparative disadvantage. The point is that *specialization and trade depend on comparative, not absolute advantage*. One of the first economists to understand the full significance of this fact was David Ricardo, the famous English economist of the early nineteenth century.

Table 30.6

Case of Comparative Advantage

	Increase or decrease in output of: Computers	Wine (thousands of cases)
Effect of U.S.'s shifting 2 units of resources from wine to computers	+4	−10
Effect of France's shifting 3 units of resources from computers to wine	−3	+12
Net effect	+1	+ 2

Comparative Advantage: A Geometric Representation

Some people understand things better when they are presented graphically. For them, as well as for others, it is useful to demonstrate the principle of

Figure 30.1
Benefits of Specialization and Trade

AC represents the various amounts of computers and wine that the United States can end up with, if it specializes in computers and trades them for French wine. The slope of AC equals minus 1 times the ratio of the price of a case of wine to the price of a computer, assumed to be $\frac{1}{3,333}$. BD represents the various amounts of computers and wine that France can wind up with, if it specializes in wine and trades for U.S. computers. AC lies above America's product transformation curve and BD lies above France's product transformation curve. Thus both countries can have more of both commodities by specializing and trading than by attempting to be self-sufficient.

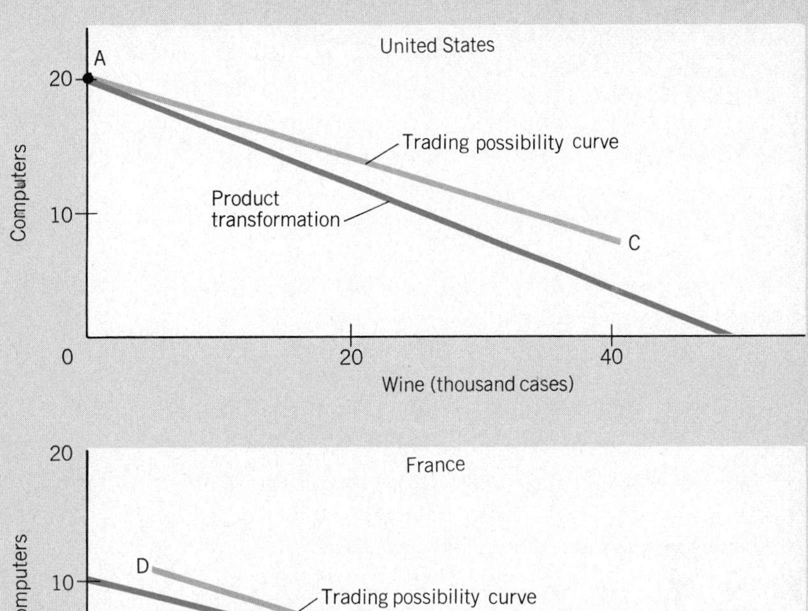

comparative advantage with a diagram. Again, we suppose that in the United States 1 unit of resources will produce 2 electronic computers or 5,000 cases of wine. Consequently, the ***product transformation curve*** in the United States—the curve that shows the maximum number of computers that can be produced, given various outputs of wine—is the one in the top panel of Figure 30.1. The United States must give up 1 computer for every additional 2,500 cases of wine that it produces; thus, the slope of the American product transformation curve is $-\frac{1}{2,500}$.[1] Also, as in the previous section, we suppose that in France 1 unit of resources will produce 1 electronic computer or 4,000 cases of wine. Thus the product transformation curve in France is as shown in the bottom panel of Figure 30.1. France must give up 1 computer for every additional 4,000 cases of wine it produces; thus, the slope of France's product transformation curve is $-\frac{1}{4,000}$.

Now suppose that the United States uses all its resources to produce computers and that France uses all its resources to produce wine. In other words, the United States operates at point A on its product transformation curve and France operates at point B on its product transformation curve. Then suppose that the United States trades its computers for France's wine. AC in the top panel of Figure 30.1 shows the various amounts of com-

[1] As we know from Chapter 3, the product transformation curve shows the maximum amount of one commodity that can be produced given various outputs of the other commodity. Since the United States must give up 1/2,500 computer for each additional case of wine that it produces, the slope must be −1/2,500.

puters and wine the United States can end up with if it specializes in computers and trades them for French wine, *AC* is the ***trading-possibility curve*** of the United States. The slope of *AC* is minus 1 times the ratio of the price of a case of wine to the price of a computer, since this ratio equals the number of computers the United States must give up to get a case of French wine. Similarly, the line *BD* in the bottom panel of Figure 30.1 shows France's trading-possibility curve. That is, *BD* represents the various amounts of computers and wine France can wind up with if it specializes in wine and trades it for U.S. computers.

The thing to note about both panels of Figure 30.1 is that each country's trading-possibility curve —*AC* in the top panel, *BD* in the bottom panel— lies above its product transformation curve. This means that both countries can have more of both commodities by specializing and trading than by trying to be self-sufficient—even though the United States is more efficient than France at producing both commodities. Thus, Figure 30.1 shows what we said in the previous section: if countries specialize in products where they have a comparative advantage and trade with one another, each country can improve its standard of living.

In addition, two other points should be noted. First, it is assumed in Figure 30.1 that the ratio of the price of a computer to the price of a case of wine is 3,333:1. We determine this ratio by starting with the fact that it must be somewhere between 2,500:1 and 4,000:1. By diverting its own resources from computer production to wine production, the United States can exchange a computer for 2,500 cases of wine. Since this is possible, it will not pay the United States to trade a computer for less than 2,500 cases of wine. Similarly, since France can exchange a case of wine for $\frac{1}{4,000}$ of a computer by diverting its own resources from wine to computers, it clearly will not be willing to trade a case of wine for less than 1/4,000 of a computer. But where will the price ratio lie between 2,500:1 and 4,000:1? The answer depends on world supply and demand for the two products. The stronger the demand for computers (relative to their supply) and the weaker the demand for wine (relative to its supply), the higher the price ratio. On the other hand, the weaker the demand for computers (relative to their supply) and the stronger the demand for wine (relative to its supply), the lower the price ratio.

Second, Figure 30.1 shows that the United States should specialize completely in computers, and that France should specialize completely in wine. This result stems from the assumption that the cost of producing a computer or a case of wine is constant. If, on the other hand, the cost of producing each good increases with the amount produced, the result is likely to be incomplete specialization. In other words, although the United States will continue to specialize in computers and France will continue to specialize in wine, each country will also produce some of the other good as well. This is a more likely outcome, since specialization generally tends to be less than complete.

Comparative Advantage and Actual Trade Patterns: A Case Study

The principle of comparative advantage is useful in explaining and predicting the pattern of world trade, as well as in showing the benefits of trade. For example, consider the exports of Great Britain and the United States. Robert Stern of the University of Michigan compared British and American exports in 39 industries in 1950.[2] In some of these industries, Britain exported much more than we did, while in others we exported more than the British. In all these industries, labor productivity—output per manhour—was higher in the United States than in Great Britain. But in some industries labor productivity in the United States was over three times as great as in Britain, whereas in other industries labor productivity was less than

[2] Robert M. Stern, "British and American Productivity and Comparative Costs in International Trade," *Oxford Economic Papers,* October 1962.

three times as great as in Britain. According to the principle of comparative advantage, the industries where the United States is most efficient relative to the British should be the ones where the United States exports more than the British.

To what extent is this hypothesis borne out by the facts? In 21 of the 24 industries where our labor productivity was more than three times that of the British, our exports exceeded British exports. In 11 of the 15 industries where our labor productivity was less than three times that of the British, our exports were less than British exports. Thus, in 32 out of 39 industries, the principle of comparative advantage, as interpreted by Stern, predicted correctly which country would export more. This is a high batting average, since labor is not the only input and labor productivity is an imperfect measure of true efficiency. Moreover, as we shall see in subsequent sections, countries raise barriers to foreign trade, preventing trade from taking place in accord with the principle of comparative advantage. Further, many factors, discussed below, besides comparative advantage play an important role in determining the pattern of world trade.

International Trade and Individual Markets

We have emphasized that nations can benefit by specializing in the production of goods for which they have a comparative advantage and trading these goods for others where they have a comparative disadvantage. But how do a nation's producers know whether they have a comparative advantage or disadvantage in the production of a given commodity? Clearly, they do not call up the local university and ask the leading professor of economics (although that might not always be such a bad idea). Instead, as we shall see in this section, the market for the good provides the required signals.

To see how this works, let's consider a new (and rather whimsical) product—bulletproof suspenders. Suppose that the Mob, having run a scientific survey of gunmen and policemen, finds that most of them wear their suspenders over their bulletproof vests. As a consequence, the Mob's gunmen are instructed to render a victim immobile by shooting holes in his suspenders (thus making his trousers fall down and trip him). Naturally, the producers of suspenders will soon find it profitable to produce a new bulletproof variety, an innovation which, it is hoped, will make a solid contribution to law and order. The new suspenders are demanded only in the United States and England, since the rest of the world wears belts. The demand curve in the United States is *DD*, as shown in the left-hand panel of Figure 30.2, and the demand curve in England is *D′D′*, as shown in the right-hand panel. Suppose further that this product can be manufactured in both the United States and England. The supply curve in the United States is *SS*, as shown in the left-hand panel, and the supply curve in England is *S′S′*, as shown in the right-hand panel.

Take a closer look at Figure 30.2. Note that prices in England are expressed in pounds (£) and prices in the United States are expressed in dollars ($). This, of course, is quite realistic. Each country has its own currency, in which prices in that country are expressed. Roughly speaking, £1 is equal to $2.50. In other words, you can exchange a pound note for two dollars and a half—or two dollars and a half for one pound note. For this reason, the two panels of Figure 30.2 are lined up so that a price of $2.50 is at the same level as a price of £1, $5 is at the same level as £2, and so on.

To begin with, suppose that bulletproof suspenders can not be exported or imported, perhaps because of a very high tariff (tax on imports) imposed on them in both the United States and England. (One can readily imagine members of both Congress and Parliament defending such a tariff on the grounds that a capacity to produce plenty of bulletproof suspenders is important for national defense.) If this happens, the price of bulletproof suspenders will, of course, be $3 in the United States and £4 in England. Why? Because, as shown in Figure

Figure 30.2
Determination of Quantity Imported and Exported under Free Trade

Under free trade, price will equal $7.50, or £3. The United States will export *XY* units, the English will import *UV* units, and *XY* = *UV*.

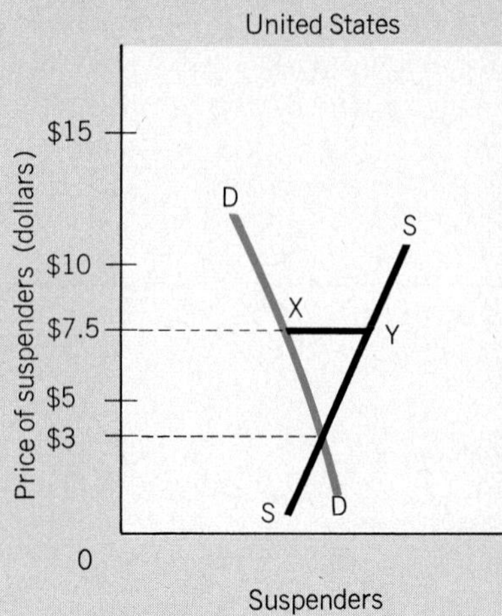

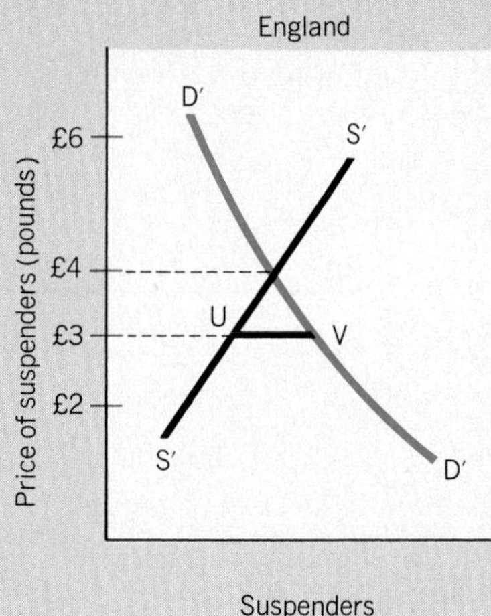

30.2, these are the prices at which each country's demand curve intersects its supply curve.

Next, suppose that international trade in this product is permitted, perhaps because both countries eliminate the tariff. Now what will happen? Since the price is lower in the United States than in England, people can make money by sending this product from the United States to England. After all, they can buy it for $3 in this country and sell it for £4 (= $10) in England. But they will not be able to do so indefinitely. As more and more suspenders are supplied by the United States for the English market, the price in the United States must go up (to induce producers to produce the additional output) and the price in England must go down (to induce consumers to buy the additional quantity).

When an equilibrium is reached, the price in the United States must equal the price in England. If this did not happen, there would be an advantage in increasing American exports (if the price in England were higher) or in decreasing American exports (if the price in the United States were higher). Thus, only if the prices are equal can an equilibrium exist. At what level will this price—which is common to both countries—tend to settle? Obviously, the price must end up at the level where the amount of the good one country exports equals the amount the other country imports. In other words, it must settle at $7.50 or £3. Otherwise, the total amount demanded in both countries would not equal the total amount supplied in both countries. And any reader who has mastered the material in Chapter 4 knows that such a situation cannot be an equilibrium.

At this point, we can see how market forces indicate whether a country has a comparative advantage or a comparative disadvantage in the production of a certain commodity. *If a country has a comparative advantage, it turns out—after the price of the good in various countries is equalized and total world output of the good equals total world demand for it—that the country exports the good under free trade and competition.* For example, in Figure 30.2, it turns out—as we've just seen—that the United States is an exporter of bulletproof suspenders under free trade, because the demand and supply curves in the United States and England take the positions they do. The basic reason why the curves take these positions is that the United States has a comparative advantage in the production of this good. Thus, to put things in a nutshell, a nation's producers can tell (under free trade) whether they have a comparative advantage in the production of a certain commodity by seeing whether it is profitable for them to export it. If they can make a profit, they have a comparative advantage.[3]

Economies of Scale, Learning, and Technological Change

International trade is beneficial if each nation specializes in the production of goods in which it has a comparative advantage. This is a very important reason for trade, but it isn't the only reason. For example, suppose that there is no difference among countries in the efficiency with which they can produce goods and services. In a case like this, although no nation has a comparative advantage, specialization and trade may still be of benefit, because there may be economies of scale in producing some commodities. Thus, if one country specializes in one good and another country specializes in another good, firms can serve the combined markets of both countries, which will make their costs lower than if they could only reach their domestic markets. This is a major argument for forming an international economic association like the European Common Market, discussed below.

Another reason for specialization is that it may result in learning. It is well known that the cost of producing many articles goes down as more and more of the articles are produced. For example, in the aircraft and machine tool industries, producers are well aware of the reduction in costs from learning. The unit costs of a new machine tool tend to be reduced by 20 percent for each doubling of cumulated output, due to improved efficiency through individual and organizational learning. Clearly, if such learning is an important factor in an industry, there are advantages in having one nation's producers specialize in a certain good. Specialization can reduce costs to a lower level than if each nation tries to be self-sufficient. Longer production runs cut costs since the more a producer makes, the lower the unit costs.[4]

International trade also arises because of technological change. Suppose, for example, that a new product is invented in the United States and an American firm begins producing and selling it in the American market. It catches on, and the American innovator decides to export the new product to Europe and other foreign markets. If the new product meets European needs and tastes, the Europeans will import it from the United States; and later, when the market in Europe gets big enough, the American firm may establish a branch plant in Europe. For a time at least, European firms do not have the technological know-how to produce the new product, which is also often protected to some extent by patents.

Trade of this sort is based on a technology gap between countries. Consider the plastics industry. After the development of a new plastic, there is a period of 15 to 25 years when the innovating country has a decisive advantage and is likely to lead in per capita production and exports. It has a head start, as well as the benefits of patents and commercial secrecy. Production may be licensed to other countries, but usually on a limited scale and only after a number of years. Soon after the patents expire, a different phase begins. Imitation is easier, technical know-how spreads more readily, direct technical factors lose importance, and such other factors as materials costs become much more important. Industry from other countries may challenge the innovator in export markets, and sometimes in the innovator's home market as well, although the innovator still benefits to some extent from his accumulated knowledge and experience

[3] In reality, of course, things are not quite so simple. For one thing, high transport costs are often involved in moving goods from one country to another. These costs can impede trade in certain commodities. Also, tariffs or quotas can be enacted by governments to interfere with free trade.

[4] Also, another reason for trade is a difference in national tastes. If Country *A* likes beef and Country *B* likes pork, it may pay both countries to produce both beef and pork, and Country *A* may find it advantageous to import beef from Country *B* and Country *B* may find it advantageous to import pork from Country *A*.

and his ongoing research and development.

The United States tends to export products with a high technological component—relatively new products based on considerable research and development. For example, if the 5 U.S. industries with the largest research programs are compared with the 14 other major industries, we see that the high-research industries export 4 times as much per dollar of sales as the others.[5] During the 1960s, Europeans expressed considerable concern over the "technological gap" between the United States and Europe. They asserted that superior know-how stemming from scientific and technical development in the United States had allowed American companies to obtain large shares of European markets in areas like aircraft, space equipment, computers, and other electronic products.

It is difficult to separate technical advantages from other competitive factors in explaining why American firms left their European rivals far behind in some fields. Differences in educational levels and managerial skills, economies of scale, and other such factors may have been very important. As we shall see in the following chapter, our technological lead seems to have narrowed in recent years, as the Japanese, Germans, and others have upgraded their technology. According to many observers, some American exports will be, and are being, hurt as a consequence.[6]

Multinational Firms

One of the most remarkable economic phenomena of the last 20 years has been the growth of multinational firms—firms that make direct investments in other countries and produce and market their products abroad. For example, Coca-Cola is produced and bottled all over the world. Most multinational firms are American, but companies like Shell in petroleum and Hoffman-LaRoche in drugs are examples of foreign-based multinational firms. The available data indicate that the multinational firms have grown by leaps and bounds, and that their shipments have become a bigger and bigger proportion of international trade. Indeed, according to economists like Lawrence Krause of the Brookings Institution, they are "now having a revolutionary effect upon the international economic system."[7]

The reasons why firms have become multinational are varied. In some cases, firms have established overseas branches to control foreign sources of raw materials. In other cases, they have invested overseas in an effort to defend their competitive position. Very frequently, firms have established foreign branches to exploit a technological lead. After exporting a new product (or a cheaper version of an existing product) to foreign markets, firms have decided to establish plants overseas to supply these markets. Once a foreign market is big enough to accommodate a plant of minimum efficient size, this decision does not conflict with economies of scale. Moreover, transport costs often hasten such a decision. Also, in some cases, the only way a firm can introduce its innovation into a foreign market is through the establishment of overseas production facilities.

By carrying its technology overseas, the multinational firm plays a very important role in the international diffusion of innovations. A firm with a technological edge over its competitors often prefers to exploit its technology in foreign markets through wholly owned subsidiaries rather than through licensing or other means. To some extent, this is because of difficulties in using ordinary market mechanisms to buy and sell information. The difficulties of transferring technology across organizational, as well as national, boundaries also con-

[5] Charles Kindleberger, *International Economics*, Homewood, Ill.: Richard D. Irwin, 1968, p. 67.

[6] See R. Vernon, "International Investment and International Trade in the Product Cycle," *Quarterly Journal of Economics*, May 1966.

[7] Lawrence Krause, "The International Economic System and the Multinational Corporation," *The Annals*, 1972. Some of this and the previous section is based on my "The Multinational Firm and Technological Change," to appear in a book published by Allen and Unwin.

Figure 30.3
Effect of a Tariff on Swiss Watches

Under free trade, price would equal $10, or 30 Swiss francs. If a tariff of $10 is imposed on each watch imported from Switzerland, there will be a complete cessation of imports. Price in the U.S. will increase to $16, and price in Switzerland will fall to 21 Swiss francs.

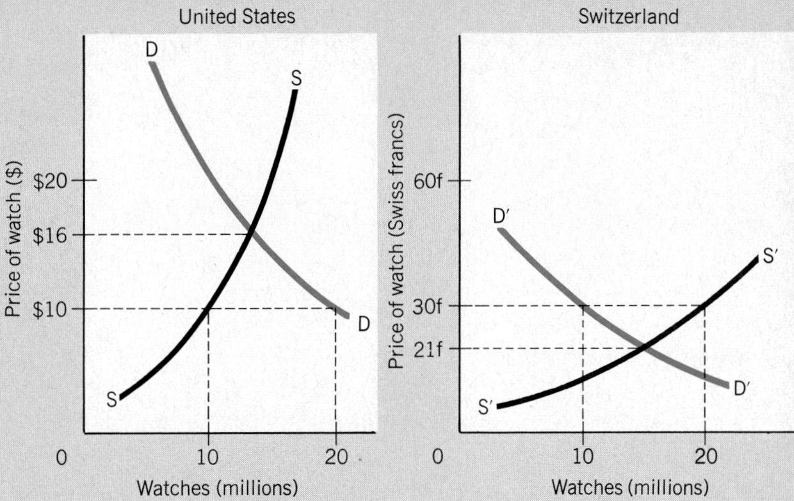

tribute to the decision. For these and other reasons, the innovating firm may find it advantageous to transfer its technology to other countries by establishing subsidiaries abroad.

One of the most important effects of the multinational firm has been to integrate the economies of the world more closely into a worldwide system. In other words, multinational firms have tended to break down some of the barriers between nations. Besides speeding the diffusion of new technology, they have linked the capital markets of many countries and promoted the international transfer of important managerial labor. However, a number of problems are also associated with multinational firms. One is the possibility that they will attain undesirable monopoly power in some industries. In addition, as we shall see in subsequent chapters, they may put undesirable stress on the international financial system and threaten the sovereignty of some nation-states.

The Social Costs of Tariffs

Despite its advantages, not everyone benefits from free trade. On the contrary, some firms and workers may feel that their well-being is threatened by foreign competition; and they may press for a ***tariff***, a tax the government imposes on imports. The purpose of a tariff is to cut down on imports in order to protect domestic industry and workers from foreign competition. A secondary reason for tariffs is to produce revenue for the government.

To see how a tariff works, consider the market for wristwatches. Suppose that the demand and supply curves for wristwatches in the United States are *DD* and *SS*, as shown in the left-hand panel of Figure 30.3, and that the demand and supply curves for wristwatches in Switzerland are *D′D′* and *S′S′*, as shown in the right-hand panel. Clearly, Switzerland has a comparative advantage in the production of wristwatches, and under free trade the price of a wristwatch would tend toward $10 in the United States and toward 30 Swiss francs in Switzerland. (Note that 3 Swiss francs are assumed to equal $1.) Under free trade, the United States would import 10 million wristwatches from Switzerland.

Now if the United States imposes a tariff of $10 on each wristwatch imported from Switzerland, the imports will completely cease. Any importer who buys watches in Switzerland at the price (when there is no foreign trade) of 21 Swiss francs—

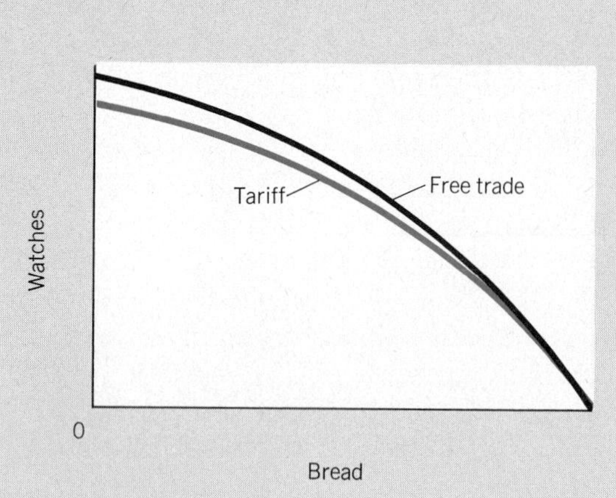

Figure 30.4
Consumption-Possibility Curves, Given Tariff and Free Trade

Under free trade, the consumption-possibility curve is farther from the origin than with the tariff. Consequently, society as a whole is better off under free trade.

which equals $7—must pay a tariff of $10; this makes his total cost $17 per watch. But this is more than the price of a watch in the United States when there is no foreign trade (which is $16). Consequently, there is no money to be made by importing watches—unless Americans can be persuaded to pay more for a Swiss watch than for an identical American watch.

What is the effect of the tariff? Clearly, the domestic watch industry receives a higher price—$16 rather than $10—than it would without a tariff, so the American watch industry (or its workers) is likely to benefit from the tariff. For example, the workers in the domestic watch industry may have more jobs and higher wages than without the tariff. The victim of the tariff is the American consumer, who pays a higher price for wristwatches.

Thus the domestic watch industry benefits at the expense of the rest of the nation. But does the general public lose more than the watch industry gains? In general, the answer is yes. The tariff reduces the consumption possibilities open to the nation. For example, suppose that wristwatches and bread were the only two commodities. A nation's ***consumption-possibility curve*** shows the various combinations of goods that can be consumed. Under free trade, the consumption-possibility curve is higher, as shown in Figure 30.4, than it is with the tariff. Clearly, the tariff reduces the consumption possibilities open to the nation.

The tariff in Figure 30.3 is a ***prohibitive tariff***—a tariff so high that it stops all imports of the good in question. Not all tariffs are prohibitive. (If they were, the government would receive no revenue at all from tariffs.) In many cases, the tariff is high enough to stop some, but not all, imports; and, as you would expect, the detrimental effect of a nonprohibitive tariff on consumption possibilities and living standards is less than that of a prohibitive tariff. But this does not mean that nonprohibitive tariffs are harmless. On the contrary, they can do lots of harm to domestic consumption and living standards.

The detrimental effects of tariffs have long been recognized, even in detective stories. For example, in the course of solving the mystery concerning the Hound of the Baskervilles, Sherlock Holmes expressed his enthusiastic approval of a newspaper editorial that read as follows:

> You may be cajoled into imagining that your own special trade or your own industry will be encouraged by a protective tariff, but it stands to reason that such legislation must in the long run keep away wealth from the country, diminish the value of our imports, and lower the general conditions of life on this island.[8]

Of course, Holmes considered this point elementary (my dear Watson) but worth hammering home.

[8] Arthur Conan Doyle, *The Hound of the Baskervilles*, in *The Complete Sherlock Holmes*, Garden City, N.Y.: Garden City Publishing Co., 1938, p. 802.

The Social Costs of Quotas

Besides tariffs, other barriers to free trade are ***quotas,*** which many countries impose on the amount of certain commodities that can be imported annually. For example, the United States sets import quotas on sugar and exerts pressure on foreigners to get them to limit the quantity of steel and textiles that they will export to us. To see how a quota affects trade, production, and prices, let's return to the market for wristwatches. Suppose the United States places a quota on the import of wristwatches: no more than 6 million wristwatches can be imported per year. Figure 30.5 shows the effect of the quota. Before it was imposed, the price of wristwatches was $10 (or 30 Swiss francs), and the United States imported 10 million wristwatches from Switzerland. The quota forces the United States to reduce its imports to 6 million.

What will be the effect on the U.S. price? The demand curve shows that, if the price is $12, American demand will exceed American supply by 6 million watches; in other words, we will import 6 million watches. Thus, once the quota is imposed, the price will rise to $12, since this is the price that will reduce our imports to the amount of the quota. Clearly, a quota—like a tariff—increases the price of the good. (Note too that the price in Switzerland will fall to 25 francs. Thus, the quota will reduce the price in Switzerland.)

Both a quota and a tariff reduce trade, raise prices, protect domestic industry from foreign competition, and reduce the standard of living of the nation as a whole. But most economists tend to regard quotas with even less enthusiasm than they do tariffs. Under many circumstances, a quota insulates local industry from foreign competition even more effectively than a tariff does. Moreover, a (nonprohibitive) tariff provides the government with some revenue, while quotas do not even do that. The windfall price increase from a quota accrues to the importer who is lucky enough or influential enough—or sufficiently generous with favors and bribes—to get an import license.

Finally, ***export subsidies,*** another means by which governments try to give their domestic industry an advantage in international competition, are also a major impediment to free trade. Export subsidies, and other such measures, frequently lead to countermeasures. For example, to counter foreign export subsidies, the U.S. government imposes duties against such subsidies on goods sold here.

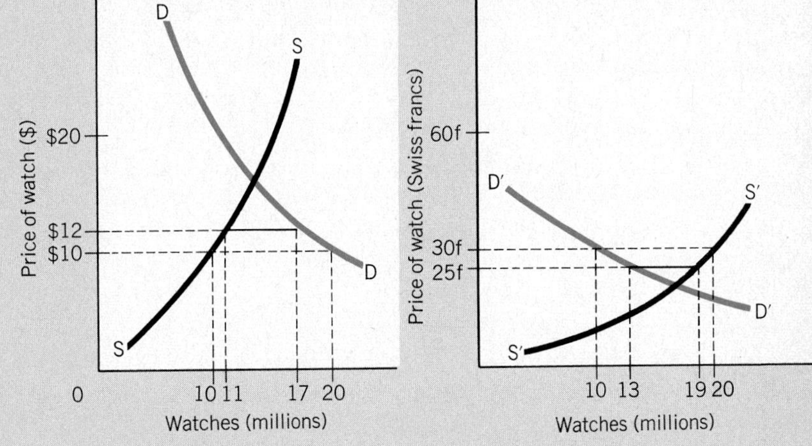

Figure 30.5
Effect of a Quota on Swiss Watches

Before the quota is imposed, the price is $10, or 30 Swiss francs. After a quota of 6 million watches is imposed, the price in the United States rises to $12, and the price in Switzerland falls to 25 Swiss francs.

Considerations of National Defense

Given the disadvantages to society at large of tariffs and other barriers to free trade, why do governments continue to impose them? There are many reasons, some sensible, some irrational. One of the most convincing is the desirability of maintaining a domestic industry for purposes of national defense. For example, even if the Swedes had a comparative advantage in producing airplanes, we would not allow free trade to put our domestic producers of aircraft out of business if we felt that a domestic aircraft industry was necessary for national defense. Although the Swedes are by no means unfriendly, we would not want to import our entire supply of such a critical commodity from a foreign country, where the supply might be shut off for reasons of international politics (like the Arab oil embargo).

This is a perfectly valid reason for protecting certain domestic industries, and many protective measures are defended on these grounds. To the extent that protective measures are in fact required for national defense, economists go along with them. Of course the restrictions entail social costs (some of which were described in the previous two sections), but these costs may well be worth paying for enhanced national security. The trouble is that many barriers to free trade are justified on grounds of national defense when in fact they protect domestic industries only tenuously connected with national defense. Moreover, even if there is a legitimate case on defense grounds for protecting a domestic industry, subsidies are likely to be a more straightforward and efficient way to do so than tariffs or quotas.

Besides national defense, there are other noneconomic reasons for protecting particular domestic industries. Some countries—Canada, for one—use a tariff to protect certain industries that they feel help them to be more independent of foreign domination and influence. Many Canadians, for understandable reasons, are intent on maintaining their traditions and values, and on resisting the penetration of American ways. Such noneconomic reasons for protection are perfectly reasonable if the nation as a whole understands the economic cost and agrees that the game is worth the candle (and if the reasons are sufficiently understood by foreigners that the measures do not provoke retaliation).

Oil Import Quotas: A Case Study

In 1973 newspaper headlines told of an "energy crisis" involving a shortage of clean fuel in the United States. To illustrate the nature and effect of barriers to free trade, as well as to shed light on this "crisis," let's consider the oil import quotas that existed until recently in the United States. These quotas were the subject of great controversy. First established by President Eisenhower in 1959, the Mandatory Oil Import Quota allowed firms to import only a certain amount of oil. Supporters of the quota argued that we could not afford to depend on foreigners for our oil because foreign sources might be cut off in war or other emergencies. Opponents argued that the costs to the consumer of these quotas were very high and that the oil requirements for national security were overstated.

Economists at Charles River Associates estimated the costs to the consumer in a study prepared for President Nixon's Office of Science and Technology.[9] Figure 30.6 shows the demand curve for petroleum in the United States, labeled DD'. The supply curve for domestically produced petroleum is SS'. The supply curve for foreign-produced petroleum is FF', a horizontal line at \$1.75. Clearly, the price of petroleum under the import quota is set at the level—\$3.00 per barrel—where the horizontal distance between the quantity demanded and the quantity supplied is equal to the import quota. If there were free trade, the price of petroleum would be at the intersection of the FF' and DD' curves—or \$1.75 per barrel.

Thus, in 1968, for example, consumers paid

[9] James Burrows and Thomas Domencich, *An Analysis of the United States Oil Import Quota,* Lexington, Mass.: D. C. Heath, 1970.

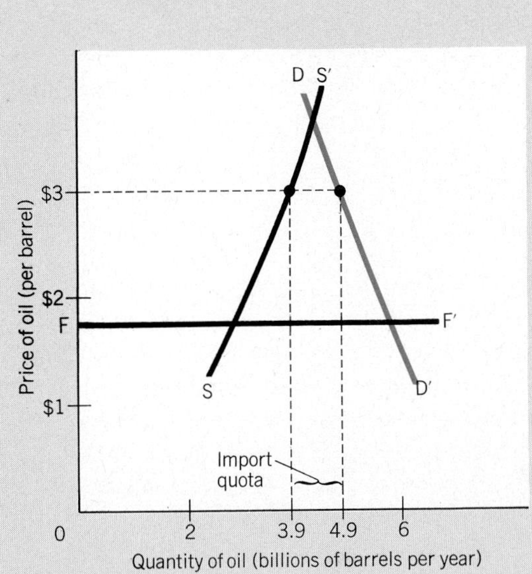

Figure 30.6
Effect of the Import Quota

***SS′* is the supply curve for domestically produced petroleum, *FF′* is the supply curve for foreign produced petroleum, and *DD′* is the demand curve for petroleum in the United States. With an import quota of 1 billion barrels, the price will be $3; the price would be $1.75 if the import quota were removed.**

about $5.6 billion more for petroleum than they would have under free trade. We arrive at this figure by noting that consumers bought about 4.9 billion barrels of oil in 1968. If they paid $1.25 extra for each barrel, they paid 4.9 billion times $1.25—or $5.6 billion—more than under free trade. Moreover, this does not include all the costs to the consumers. Additional costs arise because some consumers used less oil at the price of $3.00 than they would have if the price had been $1.75. They would have increased their satisfaction if they could have expanded their oil consumption.[10]

This was an enormous cost. Could it be justified on grounds of national security? It was difficult to tell, but many economists were doubtful. During his first term in office, President Nixon asked for a "full review of the nation's oil-import policies by the executive offices of the president." A task force—composed of the Secretaries of Labor, Defense, State, Interior, and Commerce, as well as the Director of the Office of Emergency Preparedness—was appointed to study the issue. Though many questions were raised concerning the merits of the oil import quota, it was continued nonetheless.

In 1973, when government officials became increasingly concerned about impending fuel shortages, opposition to the oil import quota mounted. Finally, in April 1973, President Nixon announced he was suspending direct control over the quantity of crude oil and refined products that could be imported. The oil import quota was dead. But in late 1973, the Arabs announced a cut in oil exports to us.[11]

Other Arguments for Tariffs

Besides national defense, several other arguments for tariffs can make economic sense. First, tariffs or other forms of protection can be justified to foster the growth and development of young industries. For example, suppose that Japan has a comparative advantage in the production of a certain semiconductor, but Japan does not presently produce this item. It may take Japanese firms several years to become proficient in the relevant technology, to engage in the learning described in a previous section and to take advantage of the relevant economies of

[10] Of course, one must distinguish between the costs to the consumer and the costs to the nation as a whole. For example, some of the costs to the consumer represented the transfer of money to the oil producers. See *ibid.*

[11] According to a report by the Federal Trade Commission, anticompetitive practices by the big oil companies were responsible in part for the "crisis." The oil companies denied this. MIT's Adelman charges that the oil companies are "tax collectors" for the oil-producing nations.

scale. While this industry is "growing up," Japan may impose a tariff on such semiconductors, thus shielding its young industry from competition it can not yet handle. This "infant industry" argument for tariffs has a long history; Alexander Hamilton was one of its early exponents. Needless to say, it is *not* an argument for *permanent* tariffs, since infant industries are supposed to grow up—and the sooner the better. (Moreover, a subsidy for the industry would probably be better and easier to remove.)

Second, tariffs sometimes may be imposed to protect domestic jobs and to reduce unemployment at home. In the short run the policy may succeed, but we must recognize that other nations are likely to retaliate by enacting or increasing their own tariffs, so that such a policy may not work very well in the long run. A more sensible way to reduce domestic unemployment is to use the tools of fiscal and monetary policy described in Chapters 10 and 14 rather than tariffs. If workers are laid off by industries that cannot compete with foreign producers, proper monetary and fiscal policy, together with retraining programs, should enable these workers to switch to other industries that can compete.

Third, tariffs sometimes may be imposed to prevent a country from being too dependent on only a few industries. For example, consider a Latin American country that is a major producer of bananas. Under free trade, this country might produce bananas and little else, putting its entire economy at the mercy of the banana market. If, for instance, the price of bananas fell, the country's national income would decrease drastically. To promote industrial diversification, this country may establish tariffs to protect other industries, for example, certain types of light manufacturing. In a case like this, the tariff protects the country from having too many eggs in a single basket.

Fourth, tariffs may sometimes improve a country's terms of trade—that is, the ratio of its export prices to its import prices. For example, the United States is a major importer of bananas. If we impose a tariff on bananas, thus cutting down on the domestic demand for them (because the tariff will increase their price), the reduction in our demand is likely to reduce the price of bananas abroad. Consequently, foreign producers of bananas will really pay part of the tariff. However, other countries may retaliate; and if all countries pursue such policies, few, if any, are likely to find themselves better off.

Frequently Encountered Fallacies

Although, as we have just seen, tariffs can be defended under certain circumstances, many of the arguments for them frequently encountered in political oratory and popular discussions are misleading. Although no field of economics is free of popular misconceptions and fallacies, this one is particularly rich in pious inanities and thunderous non sequiturs. For example, one frequently encountered fallacy is that, if foreigners want to trade with us, they must be benefiting from the trade. Consequently, according to this argument, we must be giving them more than we get—and it must be in our interest to reduce trade. This argument is, of course, entirely erroneous in its assumption that trade cannot be beneficial to *both* trading partners. On the contrary, as we have seen, the heart of the argument for trade is that it can be mutually beneficial.

Another fallacy one often encounters in polite conversation—and not-so-polite political debate—is that a tariff is required to protect our workers from low-wage labor in other countries. According to this argument, since American labor (at $4 an hour) clearly cannot compete with foreign labor (which works at "coolie" wage levels), we have no choice but to impose tariffs. If we do not, cheap foreign goods will throw our high-priced laborers out of work. This argument is wrong on two counts. First, high wages do not necessarily mean high unit costs of production. Because the productivity of American workers is high, unit labor costs in the United States are roughly in line with those in other countries. (Recall from Chapter 15 that unit labor cost equals the wage rate divided by labor productivity.

Obviously, unit labor cost may be no higher here than abroad, even though the wage rate here is much higher, if labor productivity here is also much higher than abroad.) Second, if our costs were out of line with those of other countries, there should be a change in exchange rates, which would tend to bring them back into line. As we shall see in Chapter 31, exchange rates should move to bring our exports and imports into balance.

Still another fallacy that makes the rounds is that it is better to "buy American" because then we have both the goods that are bought and the money, whereas if we buy from foreigners we have the goods but they have the money. Like some jokes, this fallacy has an ancient lineage—and one that borders on respectability, since Abraham Lincoln is supposed to have subscribed to it. Basically, the flaw is the implicit assumption that money is somehow valued for its own sake. In reality, all the foreigners can do with the money is buy some of our goods, so that really we are just swapping some of our goods for some of theirs. If such a trade is mutually advantageous, fine.

Why do politicians (both Democrats and Republicans) sometimes utter these fallacies? No doubt an important reason is simply ignorance. There is no law that prevents people with little understanding of economics from holding public office. But this may not be the only reason. Special-interest groups—particular industries, unions, and regions—have a lot to gain by getting the government to enact protective tariffs and quotas. And Congress and the executive branch of the government are often sensitive to the pressures of these groups, which wield considerable political power.

Faced with a choice between helping a few powerful, well-organized groups and helping the general public—which is poorly organized and often ignorant of its own interests—politicians frequently tend to favor the special-interest groups. After all, these groups have a lot to gain and will remember their friends, while the general public—each member of which loses only a relatively small amount—will be largely unaware of its losses anyhow. Having decided to help these groups, a congressman or senator may not exert himself unduly to search out or expose the weakness in some of the arguments used to bolster their position. For example, there is the story of a well-known southern senator who, about to deliver a certain oration, wrote in the margin of one section of his speech: "Weak point here. Holler like hell."

Tariffs in the United States

How high are American tariffs? In our early years, we were a very protectionist nation. The argument for protecting our young industry from the competition of European manufacturers was, of course, the "infant industry" argument, which, as we saw above, can be perfectly sensible. However, our own industries understandably found it advantageous to prolong their childhood for as long as possible—and to press for continuation of high tariffs. During the nineteenth century and well into the twentieth, the industrial Northeast was particularly strong in its support of tariffs. Furthermore, the Republican party, which generally held sway in American politics between the Civil War and the New Deal, favored a high tariff. Thus, as shown in Figure 30.7, the tariff remained relatively high from about 1870 until the early 1930s. With the exception of the period around World War I, average tariff rates were about 40 to 50 percent. With the enactment of the Smoot-Hawley Tariff of 1930, the tariff reached its peak—about 60 percent. Moreover, these tariff rates understate the extent to which the tariff restricted trade: some goods were completely shut out of the country by the tariff, and do not show up in the figures.

With the Democratic victory in 1932, a movement began toward freer trade. The Trade Agreements Act of 1934 allowed the president to bargain with other countries to reduce barriers to trade. He was given the power to lower U.S. tariffs by as much as 50 percent. In 1945, he was given the power to make further tariff reductions. Between 1934 and 1948, tariff rates fell substantially, as

The European Economic Community

The EEC, born in the embers of World War II, was fathered by a desire to bind Germany to the rest of Europe. The success of the European Steel and Coal Community and the Benelux union encouraged the "Europeanists," and in 1957 the Treaty of Rome formally proclaimed the birth of a six-country free trade area in which labor, capital, and goods were to move freely. None of this was to happen instantaneously, but the six countries—France, Germany, Italy, Belgium, the Netherlands, and Luxembourg—did agree on a timetable for the removal of centuries-old barriers and on a commission and council to manage the details of the process.

There are ample statistics to tell the story since 1958—growth rates of above 4 percent, increased competitiveness by European firms, increases in per capita incomes, and increased membership (including Great Britain). But the flavor of this customs union comes through best by seeing what it has meant to three prototype economic men.

Nino T. was born in southern Italy, where reported unemployment is 14 percent.* If disguised unemployment were included, the rate might run as high as double that. Wages, for those with jobs, averaged about $20 per week. In 1965, he migrated to Germany to work in an automobile plant in Frankfort, where he could make $75 a week, and send back $40 to his family. He plans to stay for another two years—perhaps until he has saved enough to buy a small business.

HEADQUARTERS OF THE EUROPEAN ECONOMIC COMMUNITY, BRUSSELS

John C. works for a leather-goods firm in London. As a new member of the Common Market, he will be able to migrate to the Continent and find a job, at considerably higher wages. He has no plans to do so, however, and what the Common Market will bring to him, at least initially, is higher food prices. When Britain enters the market, he will pay 20 percent more for his bread and butter and 40 percent more for his cheese. Why? Because the technologically inefficient but politically powerful French farmer was able to demand protection from cheap American and Canadian food. Thus, while French wheat will flow freely into Great Britain, the high external tariff will now keep out North American wheat.

Richard B., an American businessman, now lives in Paris, managing the French subsidiary of a large New-York-based corporation. He was moved to Paris about ten years ago, when company officials decided that the removal of internal barriers by the EEC would allow U.S. companies to operate on the scale to which they were accustomed. To stay competitive in the European market, they decided to build production facilities inside the EEC, rather than producing in the U.S. and shipping abroad. Richard now finds himself very much at home in France, and seriously considers living out his days in Paris.

E. A.

*George Hildebrand, *The Italian Economy*, New York: Harper and Row, 1967, p. 337.

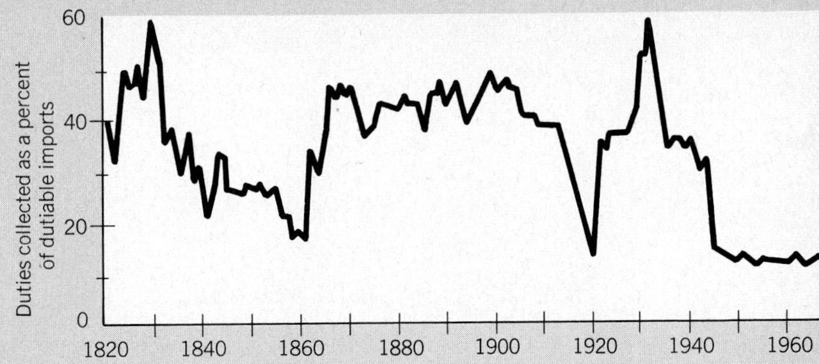

Figure 30.7
Average American Tariff Rates

The tariff generally remained high from about 1870 to the early 1930s; in recent years it has decreased very substantially.

shown by Figure 30.7. By 1948, the United States was no longer a high-tariff country; the average tariff rate was only about 10 percent. During the 1950s, there were no further decreases in the tariff —but there were no substantial increases either. The movement toward freer trade was continued by President Kennedy in 1962, and during the 1960s, the "Kennedy round" negotiations took place among about 40 nations in an attempt to reduce tariffs. In 1967, the United States agreed to cut tariffs by about one-third on a great many items.

The negotiations during the 1960s were prompted by the establishment of the European Economic Community—or "Common Market." The E.E.C. was composed originally of Belgium, France, West Germany, Holland, Italy, and Luxembourg; and since 1970, Britain, Denmark, and Ireland have joined. When the E.E.C. was formed, the member countries agreed to reduce the tariff barriers against one another's goods—but not against the goods of other nations, including the United States. The formation and success of the Common Market—and the likelihood that other European countries would join—posed a problem for the United States. The Common Market is a large and rich market, with about as many people and about half as large a combined gross national product as ours. With the reduction of tariff barriers *within* the Common Market, trade *among* the members of the Common Market increased rapidly, and prices of many items were cut. But American exporters were less than ecstatic about all of this, because the members of the Common Market still maintained their tariff barriers against American goods. While the "Kennedy round" negotiations succeeded in reducing some of the tariff barriers between the United States and the Common Market, important tariff barriers remain, particularly for agricultural products.

Recent years have seen some increase in protectionist feelings in the United States. As Western Europe and Japan have become more formidable competitors abroad and at home, many industries have begun to press for quotas and higher tariffs. The textile and steel industries have been particularly vocal and have managed to increase trade barriers. Some unions have joined the protectionist forces in an effort to hold on to jobs. The Hartke-Burke bill, which would increase trade barriers and attempt to impede the international diffusion of technology, has received considerable attention in Congress. It is to be hoped that this upsurge of protectionist spirit will be short-lived, and developments here and abroad will enable us and our trading partners to move closer to the realization of the benefits of free trade.

Summary

International trade permits specialization, and specialization increases output. This is the advantage of trade, both for individuals and for nations. Country *A* has an absolute advantage over Country *B* in the production of a good when Country *A* can produce a unit of the good with less resources than can Country *B*. Trade can be mutually beneficial even if one country has an absolute advantage in the production of all goods. Specialization and trade depend on comparative, not absolute advantage. A nation is said to have a comparative advantage in those products where its efficiency relative to other nations is highest. Trade can be mutually beneficial if a country specializes in the products where it has a comparative advantage and imports the products where it has a comparative disadvantage.

The principle of comparative advantage is of use in predicting the pattern of world trade, as well as in showing its benefits. If markets are relatively free and competitive, producers will automatically be led to produce in accord with comparative advantage. If a country has a comparative advantage in the production of a certain good, it will turn out—after the price of the good in various countries is equalized and total world output of the good equals total world demand—that this country is an exporter of the good under free trade. Specialization is not the only reason for trade: others are economies of scale, learning, and differences in national tastes. Also, some countries develop new products and processes, which they export to other countries until the technology becomes widely available.

A tariff is a tax imposed by the government on imports, the purpose being to cut down on imports in order to protect domestic industry and workers from foreign competition. Tariffs benefit the protected industry at the expense of the general public, and, in general, a tariff costs the general public more than the protected industry (and its workers and suppliers) gains. Quotas are another barrier to free trade. They too reduce trade, raise prices, protect domestic industry from foreign competition, and reduce the standard of living of the nation as a whole. Tariffs, quotas, and other barriers to free trade can sometimes be justified on the basis of national security and other noneconomic considerations. Moreover, tariffs and other forms of protection can sometimes be justified to protect infant industries, to prevent a country from being too dependent on only a few industries, and to carry out other national objectives. But many arguments for tariffs are fallacious.

Although only about 5 percent of our gross national product, foreign trade is of very considerable importance to the American economy. Many of our industries rely on foreign countries for raw materials or for markets, and our consumers buy many kinds of imported goods. In absolute terms, our exports are large and have represented about 15 percent of total world trade. Both our exports and imports are mostly finished manufactured goods. In our early years, we were a very protectionist country. Our tariff remained relatively high until the 1930s, when a movement began toward freer trade. Between 1934 and 1948, our tariff rates dropped substantially. Again during the 1960s, there was a significant reduction in our tariffs. But more recently, as some of our industries (like steel) have been hit hard by imports, there has been some tendency to push for more protectionist measures.

CONCEPTS FOR REVIEW

- Comparative advantage
- Absolute advantage
- Product transformation curve
- Trading-possibility curve
- Tariff
- Quota
- Prohibitive tariff
- Export subsidy
- Technology gap
- Multinational firm
- European Economic Community

QUESTIONS FOR DISCUSSION AND REVIEW

1. According to Hendrik Houthakker, "Our workers get high real income not because they are protected from foreign competition, but because they are highly productive, at least in certain industries." Do you agree? Why or why not?

2. According to Richard Cooper, "Technological innovation can undoubtedly strengthen the competitive position of a country in which the innovation takes place, whether it be one which enlarges exports or displaces imports." Give examples of this phenomenon, and discuss various ways that one might measure the effects of technological innovation on a country's competitive position.

3. Discuss the effects of the multinational firm on the world economy. Do you think that the activities of multinational firms should be regulated in new ways? If so, why?

4. Suppose that the United States can produce 3 electronic computers or 3,000 cases of wine with 1 unit of resources, while France can produce 1 electronic computer or 2,000 cases of wine with 1 unit of resources. Will specialization increase world output?

5. United States exports as a percentage of gross national product are quite small relative to Germany, France, and the United Kingdom. True or False?

CHAPTER 31

Exchange Rates and the Balance of Payments

In recent years, any American at all acquainted with the financial or international news has become aware that the United States has been having "balance of payments difficulties"—or, a bit more specifically, we have been experiencing deficits in our balance of payments. In response to these deficits, President Nixon devalued the dollar twice between 1971 and 1973, and then, together with the other major trading nations of the world, agreed in 1973 to allow exchange rates to "float." Even in the nation's less prestigious and more sensational newspapers, these events managed to crowd the juiciest sports and criminal news, and even Henry Kissinger, off the front pages.

To understand these developments, we must consider several questions. What are exchange rates, and how are they determined? How are international business transactions carried out? Should there be fixed or flexible exchange rates? What is the balance of payments, and what is its significance? What problems has the United States had with its balance of payments in recent years, and how can they be brought under control? These questions, which are both fundamental and timely, are taken up in this chapter.

International Transactions and Exchange Rates

Suppose you want to buy a book from a German publisher, and that the book costs 20 marks. (The German currency consists of marks, not dollars.) To buy the book, you must somehow get marks to pay the publisher, since this is the currency in which he deals. Or, if he agrees, you might pay him in dollars; but he would then have to exchange the dollars you give him for marks, since he must pay his bills in marks. Whatever happens, either you or he must somehow exchange dollars for marks, since international business transactions, unlike transactions within a country, involve two different currencies.

If you decide to exchange dollars for marks to pay the German publisher, how can you make the exchange? You can buy German marks at a bank, just as you might buy lamb chops at a butcher shop. Just as the lamb chops have a price (expressed in dollars), so the German marks have a price (expressed in dollars). The bank may tell you that each mark you buy will cost you $.40. This makes the exchange rate between dollars and marks .4 to 1, since it takes .4 dollars to purchase 1 mark (or 2½ marks to purchase 1 dollar). In general, *the exchange rate is simply the number of units of one currency that exchanges for a unit of another currency*. The obvious question is what determines the exchange rate. Why is the exchange rate between German marks and American dollars what it is? Why doesn't a dollar exchange for 10 marks, rather than 2½ marks? This basic question will occupy us in the next three sections.

Exchange Rates under the Gold Standard

Before the 1930s, many important nations were on the ***gold standard.*** *If a country was on the gold standard, a unit of its currency was convertible into a certain amount of gold.* For example, before World War I the dollar was convertible into $\frac{1}{20}$ ounce of gold, and the British pound was convertible into ¼ ounce of gold. Thus, since the pound exchanged for 5 times as much gold as the dollar, the pound exchanged for $5. The currency of any other country on the gold standard was convertible into a certain amount of gold in the same way; and *to see how much its currency was worth in dollars, you divided the amount of gold a unit of its currency was worth by the amount of gold ($\frac{1}{20}$ ounce) a dollar was worth.*

Why did the exchange rate always equal the ratio between the amount of gold a foreign currency was worth and the amount of gold a dollar was worth? For example, to see why the price of a British pound stayed at $5 before World War I, suppose that the price (in dollars) of a pound rose above this ratio—above $5. Instead of exchanging their dollars directly for pounds, Americans would have done better to exchange them for gold and then exchange the gold for pounds. By this indirect process, Americans could have exchanged $5 for a pound, so they would have refused to buy pounds at a price above $5 per pound. Similarly, if the price of a pound fell below $5, the British would have refused to sell pounds, since they could have obtained $5 by converting the pound into gold and the gold into dollars. (In practice, the pound could be a few cents above or below $5 without triggering this response because it costs money to transport gold in order to carry out the conversion.)

But what insured that this exchange rate, dictated by the gold content of currencies, would result in a rough equality of trade between countries? For example, if one pound exchanged for $5, perhaps the British might find our goods so cheap that they would import a great deal from us, while we might find their goods so expensive that we would import little from them. Under these circumstances, the British would have to ship gold to us to pay for the excess of their imports from us over their exports to us, and eventually they would run out of gold. Could this happen? If not, why not? These questions occupied the attention of many early economists. The classic answers were given by David Hume, the famous Scottish philosopher, in the eighteenth century.

Hume pointed out that under the gold standard a mechanism insured that trade would be brought into balance and that neither country would run out of gold. This mechanism was as follows: If, as we assumed, the British bought more from us than we bought from them, they would have to send us gold to pay for the excess of their imports over their exports. As their gold stock declined, their price level would fall. (Recall the quantity theory of money.) As our gold stock increased, our price level would rise. Thus, because of our rising prices, the British would tend to import less from us; and because of their falling prices, we would tend to import more from them. Consequently, the trade between the two countries would tend toward a better balance. Eventually, when enough gold had left Britain and entered the United States, prices here would have increased enough, and prices in Britain would have fallen enough, to put imports and exports in balance.

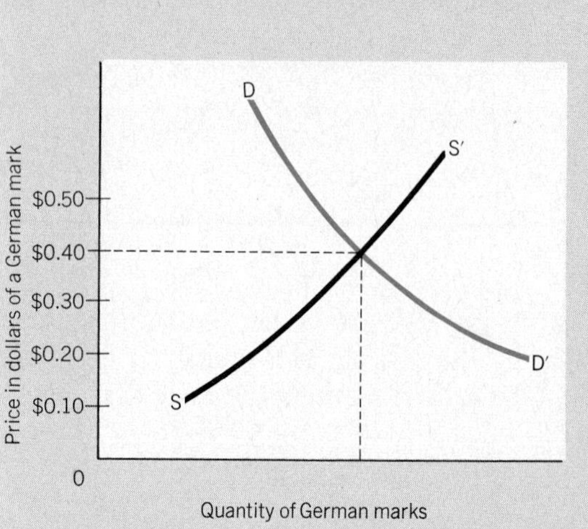

Figure 31.1
Determination of the Exchange Rate between Dollars and German Marks under Freely Fluctuating Exchange Rates

Under freely fluctuating exchange rates, the equilibrium price of a German mark would be $.40 if *DD′* is the demand curve for marks and *SS′* is the supply curve.

Flexible Exchange Rates

The gold standard is long gone; and after many decades of fixed exchange rates (discussed in the next section), the major trading nations of the world began to experiment with flexible exchange rates in early 1973. Let's consider a situation where exchange rates are allowed to fluctuate freely, like the price of any commodity in a competitive market. In a case of this sort, exchange rates—like any price—are determined by supply and demand. There is a market for various types of foreign currency—German marks, British pounds, French francs, and so on—just as there are markets for various types of meat.

In the case of the German mark, the demand and supply curves may look like those shown in Figure 31.1. The demand curve shows the amount of German marks that people with dollars will demand at various prices of a mark. The supply curve shows the amount of German marks that people with marks will supply at various prices of a mark. Since the amount of German currency supplied must equal the amount demanded in equilibrium, the equilibrium price (in dollars) of a German mark is given by the intersection of the demand and supply curves. In Figure 31.1, this intersection is at $.40.

Let's look in more detail at the demand and supply sides of this market. On the demand side are people who want to import German goods (like the book you want to buy) into the United States, people who want to travel in Germany (where they'll need German money), people who want to build factories in Germany, and others with dollars who want German currency. The people on the supply side are those who want to import American goods into Germany, Germans who want to travel in the United States (where they'll need American money), people with marks who want to build factories in the United States, and others with marks who want American currency. Thus it is obvious that when Americans demand more German cameras or Rhine wine (causing the demand curve to shift upward and to the right), the price (in dollars) of the German mark will tend to increase. Conversely, when the Germans demand more American cars or computers (resulting in a shift of the supply curve downward and to the right[1]), the price (in dollars) of the German mark will tend to decrease.

Changes in tastes affect the equilibrium level of the exchange rate, as shown by the usual sorts of supply-and-demand diagrams that we introduced in Chapter 4. For example, if Americans become fonder and fonder of German goods and less fond of their domestic goods, there will be an increase in the demand for goods imported from Germany, and an attendant increase in the demand for German marks. As shown in Figure 31.2, the demand curve for marks may shift from *DD′* to *EE′*, causing a rise in the price (in dollars) of a German mark. For example, in Figure 31.2, the price of a mark may increase from $.40 to $.44. Also, differences between the two countries in many other factors, including the rate of inflation and the rate of economic growth, will affect the exchange rate.

Note that such a change in exchange rates would not have been possible under the gold standard. Unless a country changed the amount of gold that could be exchanged for a unit of its currency, exchange rates were fixed under the gold standard. Sometimes, governments did change the amount of gold that could be exchanged for their currencies. For example, in 1933 the United States increased the price of gold from $21 an ounce to $35 an ounce. When a country increases the price of gold, this is called a ***devaluation*** of its currency.

Two other terms frequently encountered in discussions of exchange rates are ***appreciation*** and ***depreciation.*** When Country *A*'s currency becomes more valuable relative to Country *B*'s currency, Country *A*'s currency is said to appreciate relative to that of Country *B*, and Country *B*'s currency is said to depreciate relative to that of Country *A*. In Figure 31.2, the mark appreciated relative to the dollar and the dollar depreciated relative to the mark. This use of terms makes sense. Since the number of dollars commanded by a mark increased,

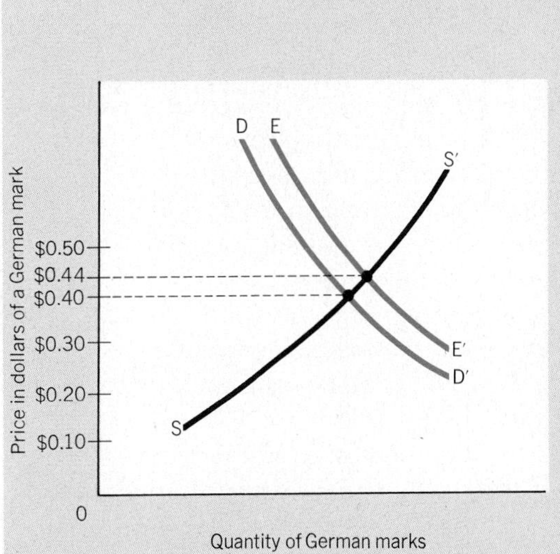

Figure 31.2
Effect of Shift in Demand Curve for German Marks

If the demand curve shifts from *DD′* to *EE′*, the equilibrium price of a German mark increases from $.40 to $.44.

[1] To see why an increase in German demand for American goods shifts the supply curve downward and to the right, recall that the supply curve shows the amount of marks that will be supplied at each price of a mark. Thus, a shift downward and to the right in the supply curve means that more marks will be supplied at a given price (in dollars) of the mark. Given the posited increase in German demand for American goods, such a shift in the supply curve would be expected.

the mark clearly became more valuable relative to the dollar and the dollar became less valuable relative to the mark.

Under flexible exchange rates, what insures a balance in the exports and imports between countries? The situation differs, of course, from that described by David Hume, since Hume assumed the existence of the gold standard. Under flexible exchange rates, the balance is achieved through changes in exchange rates. For example, suppose once again that for some reason Britain is importing far more from us than we are from Britain. This will mean that the British, needing dollars to buy our goods, will be willing to supply pounds more cheaply. In other words, the supply curve for British pounds will shift downward and to the right from S_1S_1' to S_2S_2', as shown in Figure 31.3. This will cause the price of a pound to decline from P_1 dollars to P_2 dollars. Or, from Britain's point of view, the price (in pounds) of a dollar will have been bid up by the swollen demand for imports from America.

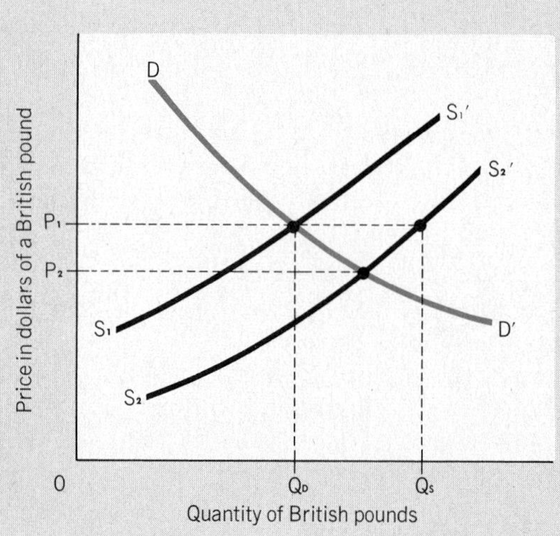

Figure 31.3
Adjustment Mechanism

If Britain imports more from us than we do from Britain, the supply curve will shift from S_1S_1' to S_2S_2', resulting in a decline of the price of the pound from P_1 to P_2 dollars. If Britain tries to maintain the price at $\$P_1$, the British government will have to exchange dollars for $(Q_S - Q_D)$ pounds.

Because of the increase in the price (in pounds) of a dollar, our goods will become more expensive in Britain. Thus, the British will tend to reduce their imports of our goods. At the same time, since the price (in dollars) of a pound has decreased, British goods will become cheaper in the United States, and this, of course, will stimulate us to import more from Britain. Consequently, as our currency appreciates in terms of theirs—or, to put it another way, as theirs depreciates in terms of ours—the British are induced to import less and export more. Thus, there is an automatic mechanism (just as there was under the gold standard) to bring trade between countries into balance.

Fixed Exchange Rates

Although many economists believed that exchange rates should be allowed to fluctuate, very few exchange rates really did so in the period from the end of World War II up to 1973. Instead, *most exchange rates were fixed by government action and international agreement.* Although they may have varied slightly about the fixed level, the extent to which they were allowed to vary was small. Every now and then, governments changed the exchange rates, for reasons discussed below; but for long periods of time, they remained fixed.

If exchange rates remain fixed, the amount demanded of a foreign currency may not equal the amount supplied. For example, consider the situation in Figure 31.4. If DD' and SS' are the demand and supply curves for German marks, the equilibrium price of a mark is \$.40. But suppose the fixed exchange rate between dollars and marks is .35 to 1: that is, each mark exchanges for \$.35.

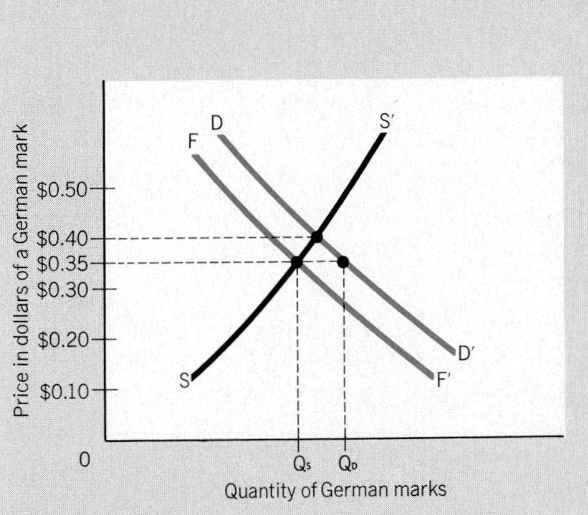

Figure 31.4
Fixed Exchange Rate

The equilibrium price of a German mark is $.40, if *DD′* is the demand curve. If $.35 is the fixed exchange rate, the U.S. government may try to shift the demand curve for marks from *DD′* to *FF′*, thus bringing the equilibrium exchange rate into equality with the fixed exchange rate.

Unless the government intervenes, more German marks will be demanded at a price of $.35 per mark than will be offered. Specifically, the difference between the quantity demanded and the quantity supplied will be $Q_D - Q_S$. Unless the government steps in, a black market for German marks may develop, and the real price may increase toward $.40 per mark.

To maintain exchange rates at their fixed levels, governments can intervene in a variety of ways. For example, they may reduce the demand for foreign currencies by reducing defense expenditures abroad, by limiting the amount that their citizens can travel abroad, and by curbing imports from other countries. Thus, in the case depicted in Figure 31.4, the American government might adopt some or all of these measures to shift the demand curve for German marks downward and to the left. When the demand curve had been pushed from *DD′* to *FF′*, the equilibrium price of a German mark would be equal to $.35, the fixed exchange rate. There would no longer be any mismatch between the quantity of marks demanded and the quantity supplied.

However, such mismatches are bound to occur, at least temporarily, when exchange rates are fixed. When they do, governments enter the market and buy and sell their currencies in order to maintain fixed exchange rates. This happened in post-World War II Britain. At times the amount of British pounds supplied exceeded the amount demanded. Then the British government bought up the excess at the fixed exchange rate. At other times, when the quantity demanded exceeded the amount supplied, the British government supplied the pounds desired at the fixed exchange rate. As long as the fixed exchange rate was close to (sometimes above and sometimes below) the equilibrium exchange rate, the amount of its currency the government sold at one time equaled, more or less, the amount it bought at another time.

However, the government might try to maintain a fixed exchange rate far from the equilibrium exchange rate. For example, the British government might have tried to maintain the price (in dollars) of the pound at P_1 in the situation in Figure 31.3, when the supply curve for British pounds was S_2S_2'. Since the quantity of British pounds supplied exceeded the quantity demanded at that exchange rate, the British government would have to buy the difference. That is, it would have to buy $(Q_S - Q_D)$ pounds with dollars. Moreover, it would have to keep on exchanging dollars for pounds in these quantities for as long as the demand and supply curves remained in these positions. Eventually, the government would run out of dollars and would have to impose restrictions to shift the supply or demand curves (as described above) or change the exchange rate. How long it could maintain the price of the pound at P_1 would depend on how big its reserves of foreign currency were.

Fixed versus Flexible Exchange Rates

Why, until 1973, did most countries fix their exchange rates, rather than allow them to fluctuate? One important reason was the feeling that flexible exchange rates might vary so erratically that it might be difficult to carry out normal trade. For example, an American exporter of machine tools to Britain might not know what British pounds would be worth 6 months from now, when he would collect a debt in pounds. According to the proponents of fixed exchange rates, fluctuating rates would increase uncertainties for people and firms engaged in international trade and thus reduce the volume of such trade. Moreover, they argued that the harmful effects of speculation over exchange rates would increase if exchange rates were flexible, and that flexible exchange rates might promote more rapid inflation.

Many economists disagreed, feeling that flexible exchange rates would work better. They asked why flexible prices are used and trusted in other areas of the economy, but not in connection with foreign exchange. They pointed out that a country would have more autonomy in formulating its fiscal and monetary policy if exchange rates were flexible, and they claimed that speculation over exchange rates would not be destabilizing. But until 1973, the advocates of flexible exchange rates persuaded few of the world's central bankers and policy makers.

However, considerable attention was devoted to a compromise between fixed and completely flexible exchange rates—the so-called *crawling peg*. According to the crawling peg (which admittedly sounds more like an insect than a system of exchange rates), the exchange rate between currencies would be allowed to change, but only up to a certain amount—perhaps 1 or 2 percent per year. Thus, if supply and demand dictated that the dollar should depreciate relative to the German mark, the price (in dollars) of the mark could increase 10 or 20 percent over a decade. Moreover, at any point in time, more variation in exchange rates about the fixed, "parity" level would be allowed.

The advantage of the crawling peg is, of course, that it allows exchange rates to move in a way that eventually results in international equilibrium. However, in contrast to flexible exchange rates, the crawling peg insures that changes in exchange rates will be gradual enough to preserve many of the benefits of fixed exchange rates. In particular, the risks and uncertainties involved in international trade might be less than under flexible rates (see Figure 31.5).

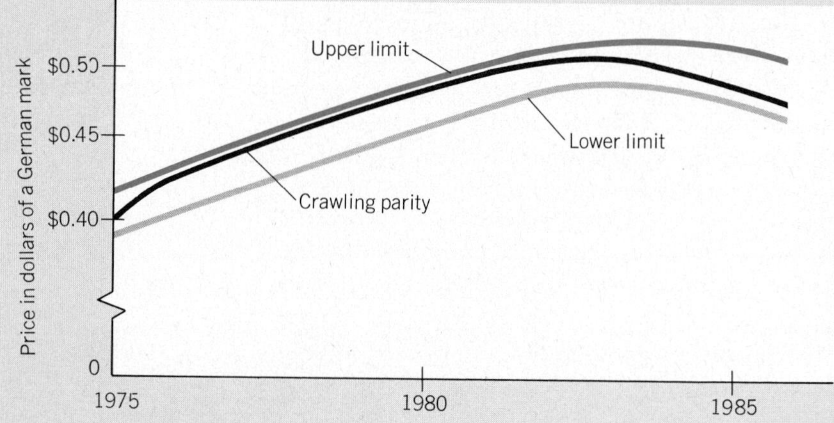

Figure 31.5
The Crawling Peg

According to the crawling peg, the exchange rate can vary by a certain amount each year. The upper and lower limits and crawling parity are shown here for a hypothetical case. Supply and demand can push the exchange rate between the upper limit and lower limit.

In early 1973, after a series of attempts to alter the system of fixed exchange rates to maintain its viability, the major trading nations of the world agreed to allow exchange rates to fluctuate—in other words, to "float." However, they did not go as far as to establish completely flexible exchange rates. Instead, the float was to be managed. Central banks would step in to buy and sell their currency. For example, the United States agreed that, "when necessary and desirable" it would support the value of the dollar. Also, some European countries decided to maintain fixed exchange rates among their own currencies, but to float jointly against other currencies. How long this new system of fluctuating exchange rates will last is an open question that even the most distinguished experts cannot answer. However, hope is widespread that the new system will be less crisis-prone than the old one.

Experience with the Gold Standard and Gold Exchange Standard

What has been our experience with various types of exchange rates? During the latter part of the nineteenth century, the gold standard seemed to work very well, but serious trouble developed after World War I. After going off the gold standard during World War I, for reasons we will discuss in the next chapter, some countries tried to reestablish the old rates of exchange in the postwar period. Because the wartime and postwar rates of inflation were greater in some countries than in others, under the old exchange rates the goods of some countries were underpriced and those of other countries were overpriced. According to the doctrines of David Hume, this imbalance should have been remedied by increases in the general price level in countries where goods were underpriced and by reductions in the general price level in countries where goods were overpriced. But wages and prices proved to be inflexible, and, as one would expect, it proved especially difficult to adjust them downward. When the adjustment mechanism failed to work quickly enough, the gold standard was abandoned.

During the 1930s, governments tried various schemes. This was, of course, the time of the Great Depression, and governments were trying frantically to reduce unemployment. Sometimes a government allowed the exchange rate to be flexible for a while, and when it found what seemed to be an equilibrium level, fixed the exchange rate there. Sometimes a government depreciated the value of its own currency relative to those of other countries in an attempt to increase employment by making its goods cheap to other countries. Of course, when one country adopted such policies, others retaliated, causing a reduction in international trade and lending, but little or no benefit for the country that started the fracas.

In 1944, the Allied governments sent representatives to Bretton Woods, New Hampshire, to work out a more effective system for the postwar era. It was generally agreed that competitive devaluations, such as occurred in the 1930s, should be avoided. Out of the Bretton Woods conference came the *International Monetary Fund* (IMF), which was set up to maintain a stable system of fixed exchange rates and to insure that when exchange rates had to be changed because of significant trade imbalances, disruption was minimized.

The system developed during the postwar period is generally labeled the *gold-exchange standard,* as opposed to the gold standard. Under this system, the dollar—which had by this time taken the place of the British pound as the world's key currency—was convertible into gold at a fixed price (not, however, for monetary purposes by private American citizens, as we saw in Chapter 12). And since other currencies could be converted into dollars at fixed exchange rates, other currencies were convertible indirectly into gold at a fixed price.

During the early postwar period, this system worked reasonably well. However, throughout the 1960s our gold stock decreased substantially, as year in, year out, we had a deficit in our balance of payments, described below. To prevent speculators and others from depleting our gold stock, the major central banks agreed in 1968 to establish a ***"two-tier" gold system***—an ***official tier*** in which gold, used solely for monetary purposes, was traded back and forth between central banks at the official exchange rates, and a ***private tier*** in which the rest of the world's gold supply was traded on a free market. The central banks agreed not to sell gold to the private tier.

But this remedy could only postpone the breakdown of the gold-exchange standard. In August 1971, President Nixon announced that the United States would no longer convert dollars into gold for foreign central banks. Thus the link between gold and exchange rates was shattered. Also, pressure was exerted on other countries, particularly Japan and Germany, to allow their currencies to appreciate in terms of our own. Since this would make their goods more expensive to us and cut down on their exports, they resisted such changes. But eventually they allowed their currencies to become more expensive in terms of ours, and (what amounts to the same thing) we allowed our currency to become cheaper in terms of theirs. A new system of fixed exchange rates was approved in 1971, when representatives of the major trading nations met at the Smithsonian Institution.

Although President Nixon hailed the Smithsonian agreement as "the greatest international monetary agreement in the history of the world," events were to prove it unequal to the tasks it faced. In February 1973, scarcely more than a year after the agreement, the United States felt obliged to devalue the dollar again, as the outflow of dollars to other countries continued. Then, in March 1973, representatives of the major trading nations met in Paris to establish a system of fluctuating exchange rates, thus abandoning the Bretton Woods system of fixed exchange rates. How long the new system will last, and what role the International Monetary Fund will play, are difficult to predict. Uncertainties abound at present in the field of international finance.

The Fight to Save the Pound: A Case Study

From this discussion it is clear that although exchange rates were generally fixed until 1973, from time to time they were altered to respond to changes in basic economic conditions. To illustrate how these alterations occurred, consider the case of Great Britain in the mid-1960s. Since 1949, the exchange rate between dollars and pounds had been 2.8 to 1, which meant that a British pound was worth $2.80. But at this exchange rate, Britain found it very difficult to export as much as she bought from foreigners. In other words, at this exchange rate the quantity of pounds supplied exceeded the quantity demanded. If the market for pounds had been free, the price of the pound would have dropped. That is, the pound would have depreciated relative to the dollar.

Britain's Labor government, elected in 1964, declared that it would not depreciate the pound. Prime Minister Harold Wilson claimed that maintaining the exchange rate at $2.80 was of primary importance and called the fight to maintain the exchange rate a "second battle of Britain." (The original battle of Britain occurred early in World War II, when Britain fought off air attacks by Nazi Germany.) In 1964, the government slapped a 15 percent tax on imports to shift the supply curve for pounds to the left. In 1965, the government restricted foreign travel and exports of capital. Finally, in 1966, the government froze wages, increased taxes, and cut government expenditures to curb inflation in an attempt to promote exports. All these measures were designed to push the equilibrium exchange rate—the rate at which the demand and supply curves for pounds intersect—up toward $2.80.

But it was to no avail. In 1967, the British were forced to devalue the pound. The exchange rate was reduced from $2.80 to $2.40, a depreciation of about 14 percent. It was hoped that this change would expand British exports, now cheaper to non-Britons, and discourage foreign imports, now more expensive to Britons. In other words, it was hoped that $2.40 was close to the equilibrium exchange rate. From 1967 to 1971, when the Smithsonian agreement took place, the exchange rate remained at this level.[2]

The Balance of Payments

We have referred repeatedly in this chapter to the importance of the balance of payments. Now we will discuss it in some detail. *Any country's* ***balance of payments*** *measures the flow of payments between it and other countries.* Consider the U.S. balance of payments in 1972, reproduced in Table 31.1. There are two types of items in the balance of payments: debit items and credit items. ***Debit items*** are items for which we must pay foreigners —items that use up the foreign currency we have. ***Credit items*** are items for which foreigners pay us—items that provide us with a stock of foreign currency. For example, if a French importer buys an American car to sell in France, this is a credit item in the U.S. balance of payments because a foreigner—the French importer—must pay us for the car. On the other hand, if an American importer buys some French wine to sell in the United States, this is a debit item in the U.S. balance of payments. We must pay the foreigner—the French winemaker—for the wine.

It is essential to understand at the outset that *the balance of payments always balances.* The total of credit items must always equal the total of debit items, because the sum of the debit items is the total value of goods, services, and assets we received from foreigners. These goods, services, and assets must be paid for with credit items, since credit items provide the foreign currency required by foreigners. Since the debit items must be paid for by foreign currency provided by the credit items, the sum of the credit items must equal the sum of the debit items. Or put differently, *debit items use up foreign currency and credit items provide foreign currency. Since the amount of foreign currency used up must equal the amount required, the sum of the credit items must equal the sum of the debit items.*

To see exactly what the balance of payments tells us, let's look at each of the entries in Table 31.1, starting with the debits column. During 1972, we imported about $56 billion worth of merchandise. This, of course, is a debit item, since it requires payments to manufacturers abroad. Also, we spent about $2 billion (net) for foreign services (including travel and transportation), about $3 billion for net military transactions, about $1 billion for remittances abroad (such as Social Security payments to Americans now living abroad), about $4 billion for net government grants and long-term capital outflows (such as our foreign aid programs and government finance for exports), and about $1 billion for net nonliquid short-term private capital outflows. These are all debit items, since they entail payments by us to foreigners.

To see how we paid for these debit items, we must look at the credits column. We exported about $49 billion worth of merchandise. This, of course, is a credit item, since it represents payments to us by foreign purchasers of American goods. Also, we received $8 billion in net income from foreign investments, and about $4 billion in net liquid private capital inflows from abroad; both of these are credit items. Thus, adding up these credit items and these debit items (and noting that we must add $4 billion to the debit items to offset errors and omissions), our payments abroad totaled about $71 billion and payments to us equaled about $61 billion. The remaining items in the balance of payments show how we paid for the difference of $10 billion. As shown in Table 31.1, foreigners accepted $10 billion in additional IOUs from us. This covered the $10 billion difference.

This is all extremely important information. It is no wonder that bankers, economists, traders, and policy makers pore over the balance of payments.

[2] For further discussion, see Richard Cooper's contribution to R. Caves, *Britain's Economic Prospects,* Washington: Brookings, 1968, and J. B. Cohen, *Balance-of-Payments Policy,* Baltimore: Penguin, 1969.

Table 31.1

United States Balance of Payments, 1972[a]

	Credit	Debit
	(billions of dollars)	
Goods and services		
Merchandise exports	49	
Merchandise imports		56
Net services (including travel and transportation)		2
Net military transactions		3
Net investment income	8	
Transfers, capital movements, and movements of reserve assets		
Remittances		1
Net U.S. government grants and capital outflows		4
Net U.S. private long-term capital flows	[b]	
Net nonliquid short-term capital flows		1
Errors and omissions		4
Net liquid private capital flows	4	
Net change in liabilities to foreign official agencies	10	
Net change in U.S. reserves	[b]	
Total	71	71

Source: Survey of Current Business, March 1973.
[a] Excludes the allocation of SDR's of less than $1 billion.
[b] Less than one-half billion dollars.

Goods and Services

Having looked briefly at the entire balance of payments, let's break the table into two parts: (1) goods and services, and (2) transfers, capital movements, and movements of reserve assets. First, consider goods and services. As you can see from Table 31.1, this part of the balance of payments shows the amount of goods and services we exported and imported. Note that exports and imports include *invisible* items, as well as *visible* items (that is, merchandise). Among the invisible items are transportation services, tourist expenditures, military sales and expenditures, and earnings on investments in other countries. They must be accounted for in the balance of payments, since they entail payments by one country to another. For example, when a British vessel carries our merchandise, we must pay for this service. Or when an American tourist stays at the George V Hotel in Paris, we must pay for this service—and judging from the George V's rates, pay dearly at that. Or when foreigners lend us capital, we must pay them interest.

You will recall from the previous section that credit items supply us with foreign currency while debit items use up our foreign currency. Thus it is clear that when foreign carriers transport our goods or people, this is a debit item, but when we carry other countries' goods or people, this is a credit item in our balance of payments. Expenditures by American tourists traveling abroad are debit items, but money spent here by foreign tourists is a credit item. Further, interest we pay to foreigners on money they lent us is a debit item, but interest foreigners pay us on money we lent them is a credit item. (Also, when immigrants to America send money back to the "old country," this is a debit item in our balance of payments. In fact, such private remittances—taken up in the next section—are responsible for debits of several hundred million dollars in recent years.)

Besides the transactions made by private citizens, the government's transactions must be included too in our balance of payments. The United States government supports a vast network of military bases around the world. Every now and then, we become involved in "police actions" and other euphemisms and circumlocutions which, to the naked eye, look very much like wars. We also engage in a host of other government activities abroad (like the work of the State Department, the Peace Corps, and so on), and all these programs affect our balance of payments. In the main, they result in debit items since they involve payments abroad. For example, money spent by U.S. military authorities stationed in Wiesbaden, Germany, to buy supplies from local German companies is a debit item.

We can tell a great deal about America's transactions with other countries by looking at the individual figures for goods and services in Table 31.1. First, it is clear that in 1972 we imported about $7 billion more merchandise than we exported. Second, we spent about $2 billion more on foreign transportation and other services and on tourism abroad than foreigners spent on our transportation and other services and on tourism here. Third, foreigners paid us far more—about $8 billion more—in interest and dividends on money we invested abroad than we paid foreigners for similar investments here. Fourth, the U.S. government spent (net) about $3 billion abroad for military transactions.

The newspapers often mention the balance of trade. The ***balance of merchandise trade*** refers only to a part of the balance of payments. A nation is said to have a favorable balance of merchandise trade if its exports of merchandise are more than its imports of merchandise, and an unfavorable balance of merchandise trade if its exports of merchandise are less than its imports of merchandise. As Table 31.1 shows, the United States had an unfavorable balance of merchandise trade of about $7 billion in 1972. But obviously the balance of merchandise trade tells only part of what we want to know about a country's transactions with other countries. As shown in Table 31.1, there is much more to the balance of payments than a comparison of merchandise exports with merchandise imports. Moreover, a "favorable" balance of trade is not necessarily a good thing, since imports, not exports, contribute to a country's standard of living.

Finally, note that the United States had a *net deficit with respect to goods and services* of about $4 billion in 1972. In other words, the credit items for goods and services added up to $57 billion, while the debit items added up to $61 billion. This means that we spent about $4 billion more on foreign goods and services than foreigners spent on our goods and services. Any deficit with respect to goods and services must be offset by a surplus in the rest of the balance of payments. This is because, as stressed in the previous section, the total of the debit items must equal the total of the credit items. Similarly, any surplus with respect to goods and services must be offset by a deficit in the rest of the balance of payments. In the following sections, we shall see exactly how the deficit with respect to goods and services was offset in 1972.

Transfers, Capital Movements, and Reserve Assets

Let's turn now to the rest of the balance of payments, which shows transfers (gifts, pensions, etc.), capital movements, and movements of reserve assets from one country to another. Take a close look at

Table 31.2

Transfers, Capital Movements, and Movements of Reserve Assets, 1972

	Credit (billions of dollars)	Debit
Remittances		1
Net U.S. government grants and long-term capital flows		4
Net U.S. private long-term capital flows	—	
Net nonliquid short-term private capital flows		1
Errors and omissions		4
Net liquid private capital flows	4	
Net change in liabilities to foreign official agencies	10	
Net change in U.S. reserves	—	

Source: Table 31.1.

the second part of our 1972 balance of payments, reproduced in Table 31.2. You will see that the entries regarding capital movements are classified as transactions by the government or by private parties. This classification seems self-explanatory; for example, when an American lends money to a German firm by buying its long-term bonds, this is clearly a private capital outflow.

Recall from previous sections that a credit item supplies us with foreign currency and a debit item uses up our foreign currency. Let's apply this rule to a case where we lend money abroad. Clearly, such a transaction requires that we use foreign currency, since we will be buying foreign bonds or other securities. Thus, lending abroad results in a debit item. On the other hand, borrowing from abroad supplies us with foreign currency, since foreigners pay us with their currency when they buy our bonds or other securities. Thus, borrowing abroad results in a credit item.

Table 31.2 shows that in 1972 the United States government granted or lent (long-term) about $4 billion abroad (net of repayments), and private citizens and firms made net nonliquid short-term capital outflows of about $1 billion. Also, we sent $1 billion abroad in remittances—for example, gifts and pensions. As we just pointed out, these are all debit items. Combined with the $4 billion net deficit for goods and services (and the debit item of $4 billion to offset errors and omissions), this meant a total of about $14 billion of debits to be financed, one way or another, by the United States. This is frequently referred to as the "deficit on a liquidity basis" in our balance of payments. The use of the term "deficit" does not mean that our entire balance of payments is in deficit. That could never be the case, since by definition the total of the debits must always equal the total of the credits. What this "deficit" really means is that we spent about $14 billion more on foreign goods, services, and long-term or nonliquid investments than foreigners spent on our goods, services, and long-term or nonliquid investments. This is shown in Table 31.2.

Another frequently used concept is the *deficit on an official-settlements basis*. The difference between this concept and the liquidity concept in the previous paragraph is that the former takes account of net liquid private capital flows, which were a credit item of about $4 billion in 1972. Thus, on an official-settlements basis, the deficit in 1972 was about $10 billion, the amount we owed other central banks and were obliged to pay in reserve assets. This is shown in Table 31.3.

Table 31.3

Deficit in U.S. Balance of Payments, 1972

	Credit (billions of dollars)	Debit
Merchandise exports	49	
Merchandise imports		56
Net services		2
Net military transactions		3
Net investment income	8	
Remittances		1
Net U.S. government grants and capital outflows		4
Net U.S. private long-term capital outflows	[a]	
Net nonliquid short-term capital flows		1
Errors and omissions		4
Total	57	71
Net liquid private capital flows	4	
Total	61	71

Deficit on liquidity basis = \$71 billion − \$57 billion = \$14 billion

Deficit on official-settlements basis = \$71 billion − \$61 billion = \$10 billion

Source: Survey of Current Business, March 1973.
[a] Less than one-half billion dollars.

Financing the Deficit

Next we must consider how this deficit (on an official-settlements basis) of about \$10 billion was financed. What credit items in other parts of the balance of payments offset this debit balance? To answer this question, we must look at the last two items in the balance of payments—net change in U.S. liabilities to foreign official agencies, and net change in U.S. reserves. First, consider the net change in U.S. liabilities to foreign central banks. As you can see from Tables 31.1 and 31.2, our debt to foreign central banks increased by about \$10 billion during 1972. In other words, foreign central banks built up their short-term investments here. They invested about \$10 billion in our short-term debt, which is how we financed the deficit.

Next, let's look at the change in the level of U.S. monetary reserves, including gold. Such changes are another way the deficit could have been financed. For example, in 1970, foreign central banks asked us for about \$3 billion in reserves. Thus, the 1970 deficit was financed partly by transferring our reserves to other countries and partly by our increased liabilities. Of course, as noted above, the situation now is somewhat different than it was in 1970. The U.S. government will no longer exchange gold for dollars held by foreign central banks. But other reserve assets, including foreign exchange, can be used to make settlements. In 1972, however, there was little or no net change in U.S. reserves.

Finally, when we get down to the bottom of the balance of payments, we achieve the balance between debit items and credit items that logic—and arithmetic—assures us will prevail, since we must pay in cash or IOUs for what we get from other nations.[3]

U.S. Balance of Payments Deficits, 1950–72

In the previous sections, we noted that the United States incurred a balance of payments deficit in 1972. Was this deficit just a temporary occurrence? After all, one would expect any country to run a deficit in some years, even if in the long run it was not in a deficit position. Deficits in one year might be canceled out by surpluses in other years. Figure 31.6 shows that this was not the case. *During the period from 1950 to 1972, the United States showed a chronic deficit.* Taking this 22-year period as a whole, deficits have far exceeded surpluses in our balance of payments.

This chronic deficit in our balance of payments has caused considerable uneasiness and concern, both here and abroad. Several factors have been responsible for it. First, the Western European and Japanese economies have recovered from the devastation of World War II, they have been alert and aggressive in adopting new technology, and they have become tough competitors. To cite but one example, the Japanese have been particularly adept at absorbing modern electronic technology and at producing electronic goods for civilian markets. In many areas of technology, the United States continues to enjoy a lead, but the gap seems to be narrowing. As productivity in Western Europe and Japan has risen more rapidly than ours, their costs have fallen relative to ours, and they have

[3] However, even this certainty is clouded a bit by the fact that there are errors and omissions in the statistics that mean that a perfect balance is never achieved. But this only reflects the limitations of the data: logic dictates that if complete data could be obtained, a perfect balance would always be achieved.

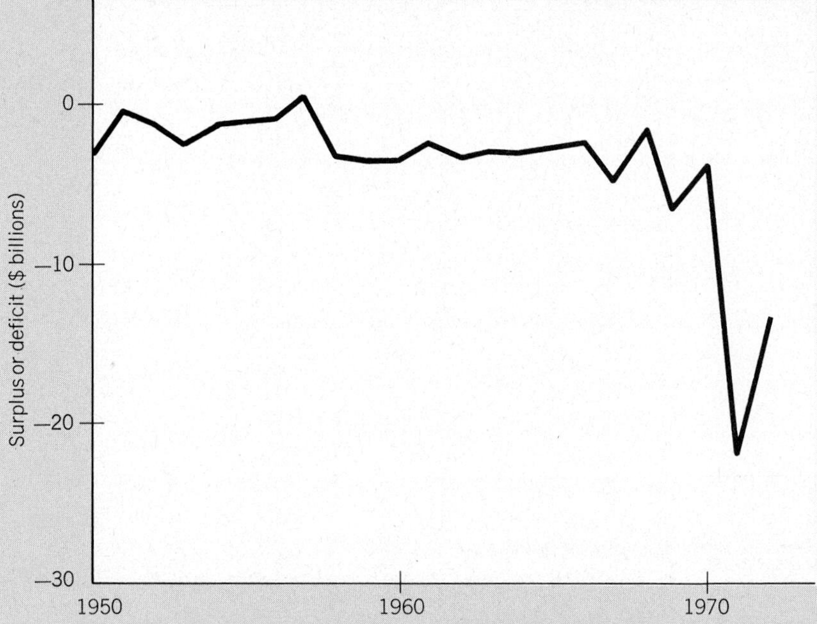

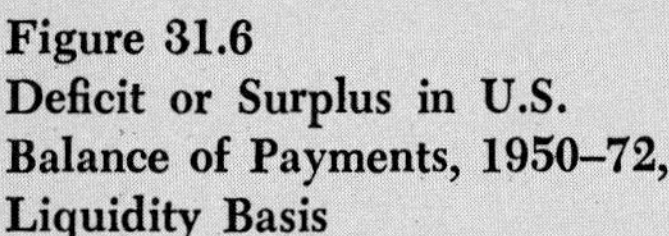

Figure 31.6
Deficit or Surplus in U.S. Balance of Payments, 1950–72, Liquidity Basis

The United States has experienced a chronic deficit, particularly large in 1971 and 1972.

been able to undersell us much more in their own markets, third markets, and sometimes even our own market. Thus, since the mid-1960s, our imports have grown more rapidly than our exports.

Second, we have spent enormous amounts abroad for military purposes and for foreign aid. Our military expenditures abroad were particularly high during the Vietnamese war. For example, they were about $4.5 billion in 1968. Not only did this war take a heavy toll in lives and in social disruption; it also helped keep our balance of payments in deficit. Note, however, that some of our government spending abroad has involved the use of "tied" funds, which can be used only to buy American goods. Since these programs result in exports that would not otherwise be made, the elimination of some of these programs would not reduce the deficit. If the government spending were cut, the exports it finances would be cut as well.

Third, American firms have invested enormous amounts of money abroad. U.S. investors have acquired oil refineries, assembly lines, and hundreds of other types of plants. The rate of private investment abroad increased spectacularly during the 1950s and 1960s. In the early 1950s, new American private investment abroad was about $2 billion per year; in the late 1950s, over $3 billion per year; in the early 1960s, over $4 billion per year; and in the late 1960s, over $8 billion per year. The reason for this growth is fairly obvious. The markets of Western Europe (and other parts of the world) were growing rapidly and the construction of plants abroad was a profitable move. To help reduce our balance of payments deficit, the government introduced a voluntary program to limit such investment abroad in 1965, and made the program compulsory in 1968.

Fourth, a number of other factors, including inflation in the United States and discrimination abroad against U.S. products, also contributed to our balance of payments deficits. Clearly, inflation in the United States—such as occurred in the late 1960s and early 1970s in particular—makes our exports more expensive abroad. It is true, of course, that inflation in the United States has not been as great as in many other countries, but in many industries, like steel, our prices have risen relative to those abroad. Also, foreigners have maintained various quotas, tariffs, and other devices to keep out American exports. Many of these discriminatory regulations were enacted during the period of the dollar shortage, when such policies were more understandable. Under present conditions, they contribute, of course, to our balance of payments deficit.

Autonomous and Accommodating Transactions

One of life's certainties is that the balance of payments of any nation will balance, but this, like many of the certainties of life, is merely a tautology. The important point is not that a balance is achieved, but *how it is achieved*. Sometimes a balance is achieved in a way that results in a stable equilibrium. In other cases, a balance is achieved in a way that results in disequilibrium, which, as we know, is a situation that cannot be maintained indefinitely. In the latter cases, something has to change; things cannot go on as they are. In the late 1960s and early 1970s, economists and bankers generally agreed that the U.S. balance of payments was in disequilibrium.

To see more clearly what disequilibrium means, it is convenient (if perhaps, somewhat oversimplified) to distinguish between autonomous transactions and accommodating transactions. *Autonomous transactions* occur for reasons quite independent of the balance of payments. Exports, imports, and net capital movements occur because of people's tastes, comparative costs, and relative rates of return in various countries. Government expenditures abroad are made for military, political, and other reasons. Thus it is customary to treat these transactions as autonomous. On the other hand, *accommodating transactions* are made to bring about the necessary balance in the balance of payments. They compensate for differences between the total credits and total debits resulting from the autonomous transactions. For example, changes in a country's gold stock and other reserve assets, as well as short-term investments in the country's currency and other assets by foreigners, may be accommodating transactions.

Accommodating transactions are evidence of disequilibrium in a country's balance of payments. The United States's autonomous transactions—exports, imports, government expenditures abroad, long-term capital movements—resulted in a debit balance during the 1960s and early 1970s. This meant that certain accommodating transactions (reductions in our gold stock and other reserve assets, and increases in foreign investments in our currency and short-term investments) had to occur. These accommodating transactions were evidence of disequilibrium. They could not go on forever.

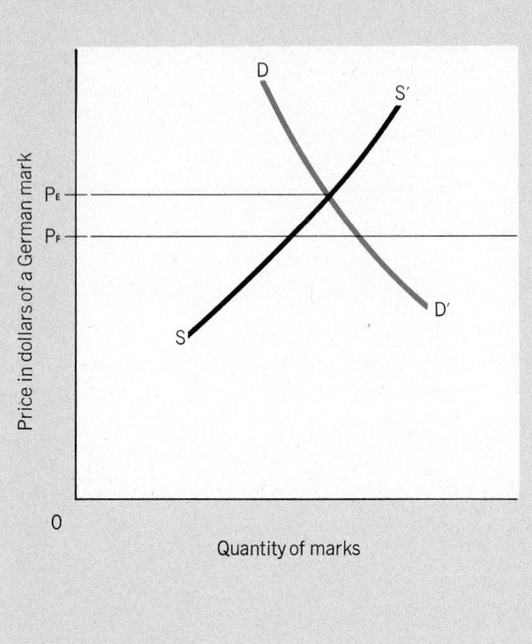

Figure 31.7
"Overvaluation" of the Dollar

Whereas the fixed exchange rate was only $\$P_F$ for a German mark, the equilibrium price was $\$P_E$.

Ways to Restore Equilibrium

When a country's balance of payments is in disequilibrium, what can it do to restore equilibrium? Consider, for example, the situation facing President Nixon in 1970 and the alternatives his advisers could have laid before him. First, recall the discussion of exchange rates earlier in this chapter. A country might adjust its exchange rates to restore equilibrium in its balance of payments. In the United States, the dollar in the 1960s was overvalued relative to other currencies, like the German mark. The situation was as shown in Figure 31.7, where *DD′* and *SS′* are the demand and supply curves for marks. In a free market for foreign exchange, the price (in dollars) of a German mark would have risen from the fixed exchange rate, P_F, to P_E. This would have discouraged American imports, encouraged American exports, and brought the U.S. balance of payments into equilibrium. In other words, it would have increased the autonomous transactions resulting in credits and decreased the autonomous transactions resulting in debits.

Thus, one step President Nixon might have taken in 1970 was to depreciate the dollar. But the United States was reluctant to depreciate its currency relative to others. Depreciation of our currency would hurt friendly nations who had been willing to hold large dollar balances. The United States wanted to discourage speculation against the dollar. And there was a chance that depreciation of the world's leading currency would seriously disrupt the entire world monetary system. Also, it must be noted that depreciation would have required the cooperation of other countries. For example, unless the Germans were prepared to let the mark rise in value relative to the dollar, they could stop it by also depreciating the mark. In presenting the alternative of depreciating the dollar to the president in 1970, his advisers undoubtedly stressed these problems.

Second, recall our discussion of the gold standard. A country might change its general price level in order to restore equilibrium in its balance of payments. This was the sort of mechanism the gold standard used to restore equilibrium. In a country with a chronic deficit, like the United States, the remedy would be a lowering of its general price level relative to that of other countries. This would reduce our imports and promote our exports. In contrast to the previous alternative, it would not have meant any alteration in exchange rates. However, it might well have led to a depression in the United States. Because wages and prices are very difficult to push downward, any serious attempt to reduce aggregate spending in an effort to reduce the price level would probably cut output and increase unemployment. For this reason, economists are not enthusiastic about this route to equilibrium. Since it is a safe bet that President Nixon, like any president, would not favor the political consequences of such action, his advisers probably skipped over this alternative. However, they may well have counseled the president to keep inflation to a minimum —for balance of payments reasons as well as others discussed in previous chapters.

Third, a country might adopt various types of controls to interfere with market forces in order to restore equilibrium in the balance of payments. For example, a country might impose controls over the exchange market. Thus, the United States government might have required all foreign exchange received by exporters (or others) to be sold to the government, and the government might have rationed this foreign exchange among importers and others who wanted it. By so doing, the government would see that equilibrium in the balance of payments was restored. However, this kind of scheme has many disadvantages. For example, it obviously limits freedom of choice and is difficult for the government to enforce.

Another type of government control is aimed at trade rather than the exchange markets. In this case, the government tries to influence imports and exports through quotas, tariffs, subsidies, and other such controls. For example, the United States might have raised tariffs and imposed quotas to cut its imports, and subsidized some of its exports to increase their volume. It might also have imposed limits on the amount American tourists could spend abroad. Of course, an important difficulty with such interference with free trade is that it reduces world efficiency, as we saw in Chapter 30.

In addition, the government might have discouraged American investment abroad—and in fact it did so in various ways, including the imposition in 1963 of an "interest equalization tax" of 15 percent (later reduced to 11½ percent) on any purchase of a foreign stock or bond by an American from a foreigner. Despite the serious problems in controls of this sort, presidential advisers certainly mentioned such alternatives in 1970.

Fourth, in the special circumstances facing the United States, one way to restore equilibrium to our balance of payments might have been to convince other countries to increase their share of the responsibilities for defense and foreign aid. For example, Western Europe might pay a larger share of the costs of maintaining a defensive shield that protects us all. The United States has been pressing for this for many years, with some success. Also, the United States might try to persuade other countries to remove discriminatory barriers to our goods.

Fifth, the United States might try to step up its rate of productivity increase and product innovation. This would make our exports more competitive. However, it is not easy for a country to influence its rate of productivity increase or its rate of innovation in the short run. Nonetheless, increased expenditure on research and development —and the rapid diffusion of existing modern technology—would be likely to help.

Having set forth some of the principal ways that a country can restore equilibrium in its balance of payments, it is interesting to look at the kind of actions President Nixon took in the early 1970s. As you might expect, he adopted many of the measures described above. In December 1971, he depreciated the dollar relative to all major foreign currencies. On the average, the dollar was depreciated by about 10 to 15 percent. Moreover, throughout the early 1970s a serious effort was made to contain inflation at home, and, for better or worse, some protectionist controls were established or continued. Also, the president's Special Assistant on International Economic Policy, Peter Peterson (later Secretary of Commerce), beat the drum for subsidies or encouragement for added research and development by American industry. In February 1973, the dollar was depreciated again, this time by about 10 percent. And when renewed speculation against the dollar caused a further crisis in March 1973, other countries decided to allow the dollar to float, and an international agreement was reached to this effect in Paris.

Britain's Balance of Payments: A Case Study

The United States is not the only country that has had trouble with its balance of payments. You will recall from a previous section that a persistent deficit in its balance of payments forced Great Britain to devalue the pound in 1967. Let's take a closer look at the nature of Britain's balance of payments problems in the mid-1960s. During that period, Britain was chronically unable to earn enough foreign exchange to finance the net outflow of private long-term capital and the government's expenditures outside Britain for military and aid purposes. One factor that hampered Britain's exports at that time was the existence of considerable cost-push inflation.

One way for a country to combat a persistent deficit in its balance of payments is to keep a close rein on inflation. By keeping its price level down, it can stimulate its exports. During the 1950s and early 1960s, the British government reacted to deficits in its balance of payments by adopting deflationary monetary and fiscal policies. This was the "stop" phase of the "stop-go" policies it adopted during this period. When the balance of payments crisis was eased, the government adopted expansionary measures which led to increases in the price level. This was the "go" phase of these policies. Then, because of the price increases (and other factors), the balance of payments deficit would crop up again and the government would go back to its "stop" phase, which generally produced considerable unemployment.

A country can also try to combat a persistent deficit in its balance of payments by interfering with free markets and trade. In 1964, Britain imposed a 15 percent tax on imports other than food, tobacco, and basic raw materials. Subsequently, travel outside Britain was reduced considerably. British citizens were allowed to spend only \$140 a year for travel outside the "sterling area," where the pound prevailed as the local currency. In 1965 the British government took steps to reduce long-term investment abroad; and in 1966 the tax system was changed to reduce the aftertax profitability of British overseas investment (relative to investment in Britain). But all these actions—plus others, like cuts in Britain's overseas military forces—were not enough to persuade traders and speculators that devaluation of the pound would not be necessary.

By late 1967, the British government was over a barrel. Its "stop-go" policies had failed to remedy the deficit. Its tax on imports, travel restrictions, and other such measures had not produced the desired results. And it could not count on continued international loans to finance the persistent deficit. When the October figures indicated the worst deficit in over a year, people, fearing imminent devaluation, rushed to exchange pounds for other currencies. The exchange rate fell to \$2.78¼ (the lowest level permitted by IMF); and Britain's central bank, the Bank of England, had to buy all the excess supply of pounds, which nearly exhausted its reserves of foreign exchange. In November 1967, the British government resorted to devaluation, thus losing the self-styled "second battle of Britain." As we saw in a previous section, the British pound was devalued by about 14 percent.

The International Money Game

Q: What contributes to, or aggravates, an international monetary crisis?

A: It's not a what, but a who. In a period of international financial stress, speculators move vast sums of money out of weak currencies into strong currencies, and force the central banks to intervene in order to maintain orderly foreign exchange markets.

Q: Why would a speculator do a thing like that?

A: Because it's very profitable.

Q: How can I get to be a speculator?

A: It depends. Right after the war (World War II, that is), the "in" speculator was a small Swiss banker (sometimes referred to as a Gnome of Zurich). More recently, much of the speculation business is rumored to be centered in the OPEC (Organization of Petroleum Exporting Countries). As long as the U.S. keeps exchanging billions of U.S. dollars for oil, the sheiks have plenty to speculate with.

INTERNATIONAL MONEY DESK AT A SWISS BANK, ZURICH.

Q: But suppose I don't speak Arabic?

A: No problem. There's another way in. Become a treasurer of a multinational corporation, preferably one with more than $100 million in annual sales.

Q: I thought companies dealt in foreign exchange only to cover costs of their imports. Aren't they the honest merchants?

A: Some still do. Most small companies deal in foreign exchange only when converting receipts from an overseas customer into dollars. But a select group of multinationals have come to be major powers in foreign exchange markets. The biggest 200 American-based MNFs (multinational firms) own about $25 billion in cash, and have another $100 billion or so in inventories and receivables. In comparison, West Germany's reserves—the largest of any Western nation—amount to about $31 billion. During the currency crises of the sixties, these MNFs learned that it was not wise to be caught in pounds sterling or dollars, and so began to move money on a large scale.

Q: By ship?

A: No, by prepayment and borrowings. For example, branches of a multinational continuously buy and sell from each other. If a treasurer sees an appreciation of the mark coming on, he urges the German subsidiaries to pay its sister subsidiaries as slowly as possible.

Q: It sounds unpatriotic.

A: Depends on whom you ask. The treasurer would claim enlightened profit-maximizing. Isn't that what you want a firm to do? E.A.

International Lending

Before concluding this chapter, we must discuss international capital movements in somewhat more detail. The factors underlying international transactions with regard to goods and services are clear enough. For example, we saw in the previous chapter why countries find it profitable to import and export goods and services. But we need to know more about the reasons why nations lend to one another. What factors are responsible for the capital movements shown in the balance of payments?

If the world were free of political problems and nationalist fervor, the answer would be easy. Because different parts of the world are endowed with different amounts and qualities of land and other resources, and have different population densities and amounts of capital, the rate of return to be derived from investments will vary from place to place. Consequently, nations where savings rates are high and investment opportunities are relatively poor will invest their capital in nations where the investment opportunities are better.

Such international lending helps both the lender and the borrower. The lender receives a higher rate of return than it would otherwise, and the borrower gains by having more capital to work with, so that the borrower's output and wages are higher than they would be otherwise. So long as the lender receives a relatively high return from the borrowing country, there is no reason why it should ask for repayment. It may continue to lend money to the borrowing country for years and years. For example, England was a net lender to the United States for about a century. To pay interest to the lender, the borrowing country must sell the lender more goods than it buys, thus building up a credit in its balance of payments that it can use to finance the interest, which is, of course, a debit item.

But the world is not free of political problems and nationalist fervor. Wars occur, governments topple, devastating inflations take place, property is confiscated. Only a fool contemplates investment in another country without taking some account of these and other risks; and because these risks are present, international lending that would otherwise be profitable and beneficial—and would take place if only economic considerations were involved—is sometimes stymied. Suppose that you had $1 million to invest, and that you could invest it at 15 percent interest in a country with an unstable government, where the chances were substantial that the property in which you invested would be confiscated and that you would get back only a fraction of the $1 million. Would you make the loan? Maybe; maybe not. Unfortunately, such risks discourage many international loans that would otherwise be advantageous to both lender and borrower.

America's Role as International Lender

As a country grows and develops, its balance of payments tends to go through four stages. First, a country, when it is relatively undeveloped, is often a net borrower with an "unfavorable" balance of trade. Its imports exceed its exports, and it borrows from other countries to finance the difference between its imports and exports. It needs the goods, supplies, and equipment it imports to put it on the road to economic development. For example, during the first century of American history we were a substantial net borrower of capital from Europe. This capital helped fuel the early economic growth of the United States, described in Chapter 17.

Second, as the country pays back more and more of its debts, it gets to the stage where debt repayment exceeds new borrowing, and its balance of trade becomes "favorable." In other words, its exports exceed its imports, with the difference being used to reduce the country's outstanding debts and to pay interest on them. The United States entered this stage in the 1870s and remained in it for about half a century.

Third, as the country becomes richer and more advanced, it becomes a net lender to other countries, and its balance of trade continues to be "favorable." This excess of exports over imports is to be expected, since other countries borrow to finance such a net flow to them of goods and services. The United States entered this stage during and after World War I, when it lent huge amounts to its wartime allies for equipment and relief. Recall from the previous chapter that the 1920s were a period when the United States erected high tariffs and barriers to imports. So long as we continued to lend abroad, foreigners could get the dollars to buy our exports. However, when we cut back our foreign lending in the 1930s, serious trouble developed.

Fourth, the country becomes a mature creditor. At this point, the interest it receives from its foreign investments is so great that it exceeds the new loans made to foreigners. Thus its balance of trade must become "unfavorable." Its imports will exceed its exports. In real terms, this difference represents payment of goods and services by foreigners for the use of capital. This "unfavorable" balance of trade is not unfavorable at all, since a country consumes imports, not exports. England reached this stage years ago; the United States is currently heading in this direction.

The United States is now the world's great creditor country—the great international lender. We continue to invest vast amounts abroad, both as private firms and individuals take advantage of profitable opportunities and as our government engages in large foreign aid and military programs. The United States is now entering the fourth stage; it is becoming a mature creditor. Our interest from foreign investments made in previous years must finance our net imports and our military and aid programs.

Summary

An important difference between international business transactions and business transactions within a country is that international business transactions involve more than one currency. The exchange rate is simply the number of units of one currency that exchanges for a unit of another currency. Before the 1930s, many major countries were on the gold standard, which meant that their currency was convertible into a certain amount of gold. The relative gold content of currencies determined exchange rates. For example, to see how much a country's currency was worth in dollars, all you had to do was to divide the amount of gold a unit of its currency was worth by the amount of gold ($1/20$ ounce) a dollar was worth.

The gold standard is long gone. Another way to determine exchange rates is to allow the market for foreign exchange to function like any other free market, the exchange rate being determined by supply and demand. Under such a system, exchange rates, which are flexible, tend to move in a way that removes imbalances among countries in exports and imports. Under the gold standard, such adjustments were supposed to occur as a consequence of changes in relative price levels in various countries.

Until the early 1970s, when exchange rates became more flexible, most exchange rates were fixed by government action and international agreement. They were allowed to vary slightly, but only slightly, about the official rate. If exchange rates are fixed, the amount of a foreign currency demanded may not equal the amount supplied. To maintain exchange rates at the official levels, governments enter the market and buy and sell their currencies as needed. They also intervene by curbing imports, limiting foreign travel, and other measures.

Although exchange rates tended to be fixed until 1973, the official fixed exchange rates had to be altered from time to time, generally when other methods would not stem the tide. For example, the British pound was devalued in 1967. In 1973, many major countries, including the United States, allowed their currencies to "float," resulting in much more flexibility of exchange rates. There has been considerable discussion over the relative advantages of fixed and flexible exchange rates.

A country's balance of payments measures the

flow of payments between it and other countries. Debit items result in a demand for foreign currency, whereas credit items supply foreign currency. The total of the debit items must equal the total of the credit items because the total of the debit items is the total amount of goods, services, and assets we received from foreigners, and these goods, services, and assets must be paid for with credit items. The balance of merchandise trade refers only to part of the balance of payments. A nation is said to have a favorable (unfavorable) balance of merchandise trade if its exports of merchandise exceed (are less than) its imports of merchandise.

If a country's balance with regard to goods and services, transfers, and long-term capital movements is negative, it is said to have a deficit in its balance of payments. The United States experienced a chronic deficit during the 1950s, 1960s, and early 1970s. This deficit—the result of the growing productivity of other economies, our large investments abroad, and our military and foreign aid expenditures abroad—was financed by reductions in our gold stock and by foreigners' acceptance of our short-term debt. Our balance of payments was in disequilibrium. To bring it into equilibrium, we could depreciate the dollar, curb inflation at home, impose controls of various kinds, or try to step up domestic productivity and innovation. Several steps along this line were attempted, including devaluations of the dollar in 1971 and 1973 and allowing the dollar to "float" in 1973.

The United States is now the world's great creditor country. As a country develops, its balance of payments tends to go through four stages. The United States is entering the fourth stage.

CONCEPTS FOR REVIEW

Exchange rate
Devaluation of currency
Appreciation
Depreciation
Crawling peg
International Monetary Fund
Gold exchange standard
Official tier
Private tier
Balance of merchandise trade
Balance of payments
Deficit on a liquidity basis
Deficit on an official settlements basis
Autonomous transactions
Accommodating transactions
Gold standard
Debit items
Credit items

QUESTIONS FOR DISCUSSION AND REVIEW

1. Do you think that we should return to the gold standard? Why or why not? Do you think that this is a live possibility?

2. What are the most important reasons for the chronic deficit in the U.S. balance of payments? Do you think that these deficits will continue? Why or why not? What further actions should the United States take in this regard?

3. The balance of merchandise trade refers only to a small part of the balance of payments. True or False?

4. To remedy a chronic deficit in its balance of payments, a country's government might
a. raise the general price level.
b. encourage investment abroad.
c. slow the rate of productivity increase.
d. remove protectionist controls.
e. devalue the currency.

CHAPTER 32

International Finance: History, Problems, and Policies

To many people, international finance is a rather esoteric subject. Nonetheless, one U.S. president after another has had to grapple with it, and many of the nation's leading private citizens have had to learn about it, as one international monetary crisis after another has occurred. No area of economics has received more attention in the press in recent years, and none seems more unsettled at present. We need to look in some detail at the evolution of international financial relationships in the recent past, since we cannot understand the present situation unless we know how we got where we are—and what was tried (and with how much success) in the past.

This chapter will describe the history of international financial relationships over the past 50 years and show how existing problems have developed. In addition, we will examine the effect of foreign trade on domestic output and employment; describe some of the organizations, such as the International Monetary Fund, that have played a major role in international finance; and discuss proposed solutions to existing problems, as well as the formation of recent American policy.

Pre-World War II Days

The late nineteenth century and the period up to World War I were the heyday of the gold standard. Several dozen countries, including practically all the economically powerful ones, were on the gold standard. This was a period of international specialization, relatively low tariffs, relatively free trade, and a large volume of international transactions. Although it—like every period—had its problems and crises, it is often regarded as a golden age of international trade and finance, a period of harmonious and closely knit international economic relations. Unfortunately, this golden age, like the peace of the world, was shattered by the events of 1914.

During World War I, practically all the warring nations went off the gold standard to keep people from hoarding gold or from sending it to neutral countries. After the war, there was serious inflation in some European countries. (For example, you will recall Germany's runaway inflation from Chapter 12.) During the 1920s many countries went back on the gold standard, but after the economic troubles of the previous decade, the old exchange rates were no longer appropriate, and when the adjustment mechanism (based on changes in domestic price levels) failed to work quickly (and painlessly) enough, the gold standard was abandoned. In September 1931, England, in response to serious gold drains, went off the gold standard.

The 1930s were the years of the Great Depression. In response to the deep drop in output and swollen unemployment rolls, governments adopted protectionist policies like higher tariffs and import quotas. At the same time, confidence in the banks and the monetary system sank. Austria's biggest bank failed in 1931, followed by bank failures and runs on the banks in Germany and England. In the United States, President Roosevelt took gold out of circulation as money in 1933. Moreover, to stimulate American exports (and thus increase jobs), Roosevelt devalued the dollar by about 40 percent in early 1934, raising the price of gold from about \$20 to \$35 an ounce.

As would be expected, other countries reacted to our devaluation by retaliatory measures. They too devalued or went off the gold standard. In addition, they increased their tariffs and erected other barriers to our exports. It was a time when governments around the world adopted "beggar-thy-neighbor" policies that aimed at the "export" of unemployment. After all, an increase in net exports—like an autonomous increase in private investment or government spending—will increase a country's net national product, and thus increase its employment. Consequently, if a country can reduce its imports or increase its exports, it can increase its employment.

But the "beggar-thy-neighbor" policies of the 1930s did not achieve this end. They brought about retaliatory measures that prevented a country from increasing its net exports, and all that resulted was a mutually disadvantageous drying up of international trade.

The Effects of Foreign Trade on Net National Product

To understand more clearly what "beggar-thy-neighbor" policies were designed to achieve, let's look more closely at the effects of foreign trade on NNP and domestic employment. Recall from Chapter 8 that net national product = consumption + investment + government spending + net exports, where net exports equal exports minus imports. In other words,

$$Y = C + I + G + X, \tag{32.1}$$

where Y is NNP, C is consumption, I is investment, G is government spending, and X is net

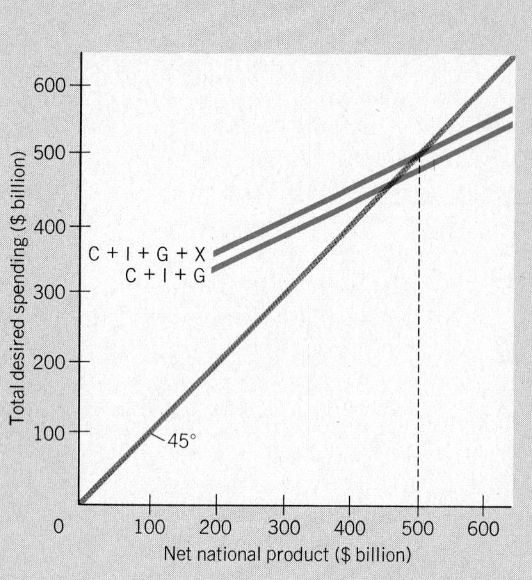

Figure 32.1
Effects of Foreign Trade on Net National Product

The equilibrium level of NNP is at the point where the $C + I + G + X$ line intersects the 45-degree line; in this case, $500 billion.

exports. Recall too that the equilibrium level of NNP will be at the point where desired spending on NNP—which equals desired consumption + desired investment + desired government spending + desired net exports—equals NNP.

Thus, in Figure 32.1, the equilibrium level of NNP must be $500 billion, since this is the level at which the $C + I + G + X$ line intersects the 45-degree line. To see this, note that we are merely carrying out a straightforward extension of the analysis in Chapter 10, where we assumed that net exports were zero. Once this assumption is relaxed, desired net exports must be added to the $C + I + G$ line to get total desired spending, and the equilibrium level of NNP is at the point where the resulting total-desired-spending line—$C + I + G + X$—intersects the 45-degree line.

Once this is understood, it is clear why governments during the 1930s wanted to increase their exports and decrease their imports. Spending on net exports results in increases in NNP. For example, if desired spending on net exports increases from X to X', as shown in Figure 32.2, the equilibrium level of NNP increases from $500 billion to $550 billion. Moreover, increases in spending on net exports have a multiplier effect, which is like the multiplier effect for investment or government spending. Thus, a $1 increase in desired spending

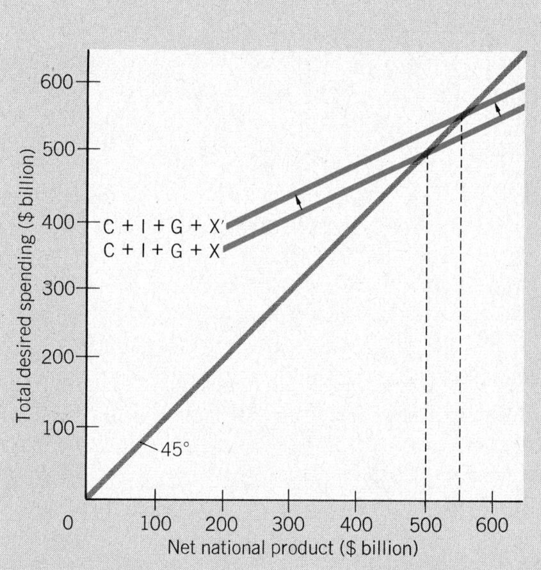

Figure 32.2
Effect of Increase in Net Exports on Net National Product

If net exports increase from X to X', the equilibrium level of *NNP* increases from $500 billion to $550 billion.

on net exports results in more than a $1 increase in NNP. Since governments during the 1930s wanted desperately to increase their NNP to reduce unemployment, it is clear why they tried to increase their net exports. However, as emphasized in the previous section, all that resulted was a reduction in international trade, because of retaliatory measures.

World War II

Major wars have a way of changing international economic relationships. Once World War II got under way, the combatants changed their trading patterns, with war materiel, not consumer goods, the paramount concern. Export industries were shifted to war production, while attempts were made to increase imports of strategic materials and equipment. The inevitable problem for the combatants was how to pay for these imports. For some time, the United States provided these items to its allies on the basis of loans and "lend-lease" programs. (In all, we contributed about $37 billion worth of goods in lend-lease.) Besides affecting trading patterns, wars also have an effect on the price levels of various countries. Some countries suffer from much greater inflation than others, with the result that countries with relatively high rates of inflation tend to incur deficits in their balance of payments unless changes occur in exchange rates.

Perhaps the most spectacular effect of World War II was on the productive capacities of most of the warring nations. Countries like Germany, France, and the United Kingdom suffered a great reduction in their capacity to produce goods and services. Their factories were bombed to the ground. Their towns and cities were shelled and sometimes overrun by enemy forces. Their farms were run down and in some cases turned into battlegrounds. Even factories that were not hit by enemy fire were old and dilapidated at the end of the war because there had been little wartime investment not related to the war.

When World War II finally ended, it was clear that international economic relationships would be subject to many strains and stresses in the postwar period, due in part to the ravages of the war. In addition, the Allies were seriously divided on ideological grounds. The Western nations distrusted the Communist nations and vice versa, and trade between the two blocs was cut substantially as the cold war proceeded. Also, there was a strong tide of nationalism among the less developed countries of the world. Many colonies became independent and tried to lessen their dependence upon the richer countries by adopting measures that reduced international trade. Further, most governments emerged from the war intent on following policies that would promote full employment at home. (Recall the Employment Act of 1946 in the United States.) Laudable as these objectives were, they were not always compatible with smooth international economic relationships.

The Dollar Shortage

Had you been studying economics right after World War II, one of the phrases you would have heard repeatedly was "the dollar shortage." Everyone—whether he knew what it meant or not—talked about the dollar shortage in the late 1940s and early 1950s. There *was* a dollar shortage in the sense that, at the official fixed exchange rate, foreigners could not get as many dollars as they wanted. The situation was like that shown in Figure 32.3. Given *DD′* and *SS′*, the existing demand and supply curves for dollars by foreigners, there was a gap between the quantity demanded and the quantity supplied at the existing price (in foreign currency) of a dollar. Had the exchange rate been allowed to fluctuate, the dollar would have been bid up considerably. That is, it would have appreciated relative to other currencies.

It is easy to see why foreigners wanted dollars so much. Other countries badly needed to rebuild

Figure 32.3
The Dollar Shortage

At the fixed exchange rate, the quantity demanded of dollars exceeded the quantity supplied. The equilibrium exchange rate exceeded the fixed exchange rate.

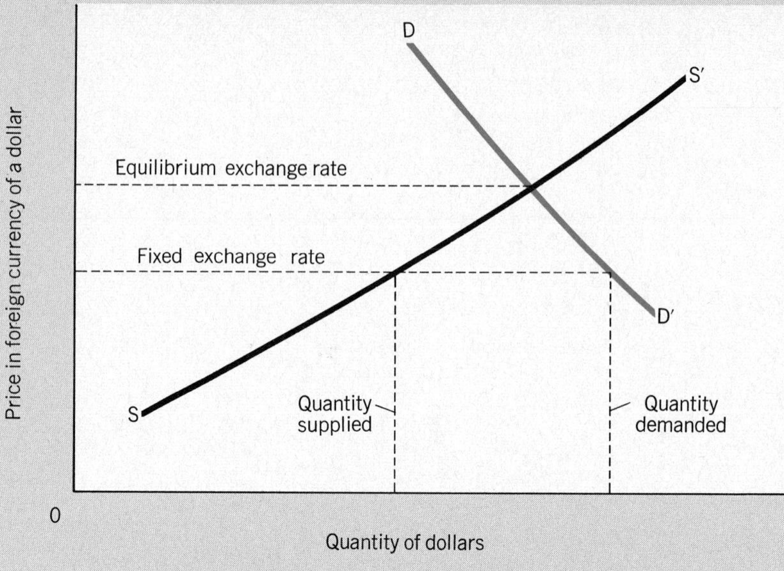

their economies, and since the United States was the one major economic power that emerged relatively unscathed from the war, foreigners needed dollars to put their own economies back into reasonable order. The United States responded to their plight, not by allowing the dollar to appreciate in terms of other currencies, but by simply giving or lending dollars to those in need. Foreign countries then used various types of controls over foreign exchange and imports—of the sort described in the previous chapter—to direct the use of this American aid.

Postwar Aid Programs

American financial assistance took several forms in the period after World War II. In the immediate postwar period, the primary objective was, of course, to help the populations of the war-ravaged countries and to get the European economies back on their feet. For example, the United Nations Relief and Rehabilitation Administration (UNRRA) provided $4 billion of food, clothing, and medical services, about three-quarters of which was financed by the United States. In addition, other forms of relief, aid, and loans were extended. In all, the United States provided about $17 billion in aid between the war's end and 1948, about half in loans and about half in grants.

By 1948, it was clear that Europe needed a more comprehensive program to stimulate its economic recovery and political stability. Secretary of State George Marshall, in a famous address at Harvard in June 1948, set forth the outlines of a plan—the "Marshall Plan"—to speed Europe's recovery. This plan established the European Recovery Program, which poured over $10 billion in aid into Europe, much in the form of grants. Most observers regarded the Marshall Plan as a success. European productive capacity grew dramatically during the late 1940s and early 1950s.

By the early 1950s, Europe's economy was in pretty good shape, but this did not spell the end of our foreign aid programs. On the contrary,

Table 32.1

Foreign Economic and Military Aid Program, 1949–71 (billions of dollars)

Year	Military	Economic Grants	Economic Loans	Total
1949	—	5.1	1.2	6.3
1950	—	3.5	0.2	3.7
1951	1.0	2.6	0.0	3.6
1952	1.5	1.8	0.2	3.5
1953	4.2	1.9	0.0	6.1
1954	3.3	2.1	0.1	5.5
1955	2.4	1.6	0.2	4.2
1956	2.9	1.3	0.2	4.4
1957	2.1	1.3	0.3	3.7
1958	2.4	1.2	0.4	4.0
1959	2.1	1.3	0.6	4.0
1960	1.7	1.3	0.6	3.6
1961	1.4	1.3	0.7	3.4
1962	1.4	1.2	1.3	4.0
1963	1.9	1.0	1.3	4.2
1964	1.5	0.8	1.3	3.6
1965	1.3	0.9	1.1	3.3
1966	1.2	1.3	1.2	3.7
1967	1.0	1.2	1.1	3.2
1968	0.9	1.0	0.9	2.7
1969	0.9	0.9	0.6	2.3
1970	0.8	1.0	0.7	2.5
1971	1.7	1.1	0.7	3.5

Source: Statistical Abstract of the U.S.

much of our aid shifted toward the less developed nations. Table 32.1 shows the total amount the United States spent on foreign aid between 1949 and 1971. During this period, we spent almost $90 billion—a huge sum by any standard. About 40 percent of these expenditures have been grants for military purposes, about 40 percent have been grants for nonmilitary purposes, and about 20 percent have been loans. No nation has ever contributed as much to the economic development of poorer countries as we have.

Why have we engaged in these foreign aid programs? In part, because we wanted to keep people in faltering economies from espousing communism. Starvation and misery are good breeding grounds for revolution. Also, we wanted to provide our friends and allies with modern and effective weapons. Thus, one need not be a cynic to attribute a good deal of this aid to our own self-interest. But it is simplistic—and overly harsh—to dismiss many of these programs in this way. The truth is that the United States was also motivated by old-fashioned humanitarianism, which, reports to the contrary notwithstanding, is still alive (although sometimes embattled) in the United States, as well as other parts of the world.

The World Bank

In 1944, late in World War II, the major economic powers agreed to establish the International Bank for Reconstruction and Development, also known as the World Bank. The World Bank was formed to make long-term loans, for its originators recognized that the less developed countries—in Latin America, Asia, Africa, and elsewhere—desperately needed capital, while the rich, economically advanced countries, like the United States, had capital to lend. The World Bank was to channel funds from rich nations to poor, thus supplementing private investment, which was often scared off by the apparent risks. More specifically, the major economic powers contributed a certain amount of money to form the Bank, with each country's share determined by its economic size. About one-third of the total was put up by the United States. The Soviet Union helped organize the World Bank, but later declined to join.

Now about 30 years old, the World Bank still makes loans to people or governments with sound investment projects who have been unable to get private financing. Moreover, by floating its own bond issues it can lend money above and beyond what was originally put up by the major powers. In other words, the World Bank sells its own IOUs, which are considered safe by investors because they are guaranteed by member countries. In addition, it helps less developed countries get loans from private lenders by insuring the loans. That is, the World Bank can tell the lender that if the loan goes sour it will see that he is paid back.

Of course, this movement of capital from the capital-rich nations to the capital-poor nations should prove beneficial for both rich and poor. The poor countries are enabled to carry out projects that will result in economic returns high enough to pay off the lender with interest and have some net benefits left over. The rich countries are enabled to invest their capital at a higher rate of return than they could obtain at home. Thus, both parties benefit, as long as the loans are economically sound.

Up to now, the World Bank's loans have been so sound—and its losses so small—that the bank has amassed an embarrassingly large amount of profits, a "problem" that can be solved, of course, by taking somewhat larger risks. The bank has established the International Development Agency to make "soft" loans, as well as the International Finance Corporation, which lends to foreign development banks. An increasing percentage of the bank's financing is being channeled through these two agencies.

The International Monetary Fund

1944 was a vintage year for international financial institutions. It saw the basic agreements underlying both the World Bank and the International Monetary Fund. Both evolved from international conferences held at Bretton Woods, New Hampshire, where representatives of 16 countries met to try to establish a new international monetary system. Out of these historic conferences came a system that survived—with some crises and changes—for almost 30 years. A cornerstone of this system was the International Monetary Fund (IMF), established by 40 nations to insure reasonable stability of exchange rates. The Fund was composed initially of about $30 billion of gold and currency, contributed by the member countries. It has been enlarged greatly since then, and membership has grown to over 100 countries.

The IMF has three purposes. First, it provides a permanent mechanism for consultation by various countries on international financial problems. Second, it tries to promote the stability of exchange rates and to avoid competitive depreciation of currencies. Third, it is empowered to make temporary loans to member countries to give them time to correct disequilibria in their balance of payments, thus promoting smoother international financial adjustments.

Note that the Fund is built on a philosophy of fixed exchange rates. The men who met at Bretton Woods were impressed with the problems of flexible exchange rates, at least as they were used in the 1930s, and agreed that exchange rates should be reasonably stable. Of course, they recognized that from time to time changes in certain exchange rates would be required. (Among the people at Bretton Woods was John Maynard Keynes, which suggests that the conferees were hardly financial babes in the woods.) But changes in exchange rates should, they felt, be made only in response to persistent disequilibria. In this respect, the spirit behind the IMF differed substantially from the old gold standard. Whereas the IMF recognized that exchange rates should sometimes change, the gold standard emphasized exchange stability under all circumstances.

To see more precisely what the IMF was designed to do, suppose that a member country is in temporary difficulties with its balance of payments, which shows a large deficit. The IMF can lend foreign currencies to the country running the deficit. In any year, a country can readily borrow in foreign currencies up to ¼ of its quota at the Fund, which is determined by its contribution to the Fund. After formal consultation with the Fund, the country can borrow even more than this amount if it is working hard to cure the basic disequilibrium in its balance of payments. This allows the country to make the necessary adjustments more gradually, and lessens the likelihood that it will be forced into a position where it must depreciate its currency or impose controls over exchange or imports. The country is expected to pay back all the foreign currency that it borrows in 3 to 5 years at most.

Suppose, however, that the basic disequilibrium in a country's balance of payments is so great that no reasonable action short of depreciating its currency will restore equilibrium. In such cases, members of the IMF are permitted to change their exchange rates after consultation with other members of the Fund. Since 1944, there have been numerous changes in exchange rates. For example, in 1949 the United Kingdom reduced the dollar value of the pound from $4.00 to $2.80. Moreover, the values of some currencies have increased, not decreased. For example, in 1973, West Germany increased the official value of its currency by about 5 percent.

How well has the IMF worked? During its early years, it did not have the resources or financial muscle to deal with the tremendous dollar shortage. From the mid-1950s to 1973, the IMF turned in a more impressive performance as a stabilizing force in international financial relationships, even though it could not cope with large disequilibria. The role of the Fund under the system of "floating" exchange rates adopted in 1973 has not yet become clear.

The IMF in Action: A Case Study

Let's consider an important case where the International Monetary Fund was involved in maintaining an exchange rate—the case of Great Britain in 1964. As we saw in the previous chapter, Great Britain ran a serious deficit in its balance of payments in the early 1960s. In 1964, amid considerable speculation that devaluation would have to come, the British government fought to maintain the existing value of the pound. It began by obtaining assistance from the central banks of Belgium, Canada, France, Italy, the Netherlands, Switzerland, Germany, and the United States. This assistance took the form of so-called "swaps agreements" and gave Britain about $200 million in aid by the end of September 1964. But this aid was not enough. In addition, Britain turned to the International Monetary Fund.

At the beginning of December 1964, Britain borrowed $1 billion from the Fund. This drawing was made in the following currencies:

Currency	*Millions of dollars worth*
Austrian schillings	38
Belgian francs	57
Canadian dollars	69
German marks	273
French francs	163
Italian lire	23
Japanese yen	54
Netherland guilders	66
Spanish pesetas	40
Swedish kronor	27
U.S. dollars	200
Total	1,000

Thanks to this assistance, as well as to subsequent international aid to the British, the battle to maintain the British pound at $2.80 was won, at least temporarily. Thus the International Monetary Fund allowed the British a breathing spell to get their balance of payments in better shape. As we have noted, providing such breathing spells is one of the important functions of the IMF.

In this case, however, the breathing spell was not very long, and the battle, although temporarily won, was to be lost soon afterward. Despite the IMF action, the British still could not make the necessary adjustments to reduce the deficit in their balance of payments and were forced to devalue the pound from $2.80 to $2.40 in 1967. Fortunately, IMF assistance was able to overcome temporary disequilibria in many other cases—for example, that of Italy in 1964. In these cases the victories were longer lasting.[1]

The Dollar Glut

The dollar shortage in the period immediately after World War II gradually disappeared. Recently, there has been a "dollar glut." The train of events that led to this change is quite clear. After World War II, American exports grew enormously and were financed only in part by our imports. Additional financing came from our foreign aid programs and private investment abroad. As the European economies got back on their feet, private investment abroad seemed more and more profitable. Moreover, our foreign aid programs—redirected toward the less developed countries and military assistance—continued.

During the 1950s, our balance of payments showed a persistent deficit, since our private investment abroad and our foreign aid more than offset the surplus of our exports over our imports. Since foreigners received more in payments from us than we did from them, they could either hold dollar balances or ask us for gold. In general, they took the dollar balances during the 1950s. Dollars were considered "as good as gold," since they could be exchanged for gold at $35 an ounce. And they had the advantage that bank balances held in the United States or short-term U.S. securities brought interest, while gold did not. However, in the late 1950s, foreigners began to take more and more gold as their dollar balances became bigger and bigger (Figure 32.4).

By the late 1950s bankers and others, both here and abroad, expressed growing concern about the large deficit in our balance of payments. Foreigners warned us that confidence in the dollar was being impaired, and some members of our own financial community cautioned us to move toward eliminating our persistent deficit. By the 1960s, there was considerable feeling that the dollar would have to be depreciated or devalued, or both. This resulted in a sharp reduction in our gold stock, as shown in Figure 32.4. If the dollar were devalued, money could be made by buying gold. So investors exchanged dollars for gold.

Foreign central banks viewed dollar balances as reserves, since these balances could be converted into gold. But by the late 1960s these central banks had all the dollars they wanted. Indeed, they had more than they wanted. But many held dollars because

[1] See Brian Tew, *International Monetary Cooperation*, London: Hutchinson University Library, 1965, pp. 197–8.

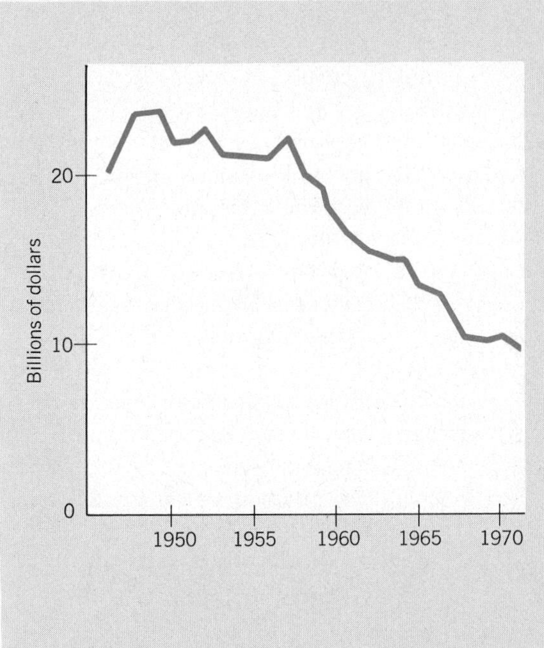

Figure 32.4
Size of U.S. Gold Reserves, 1946–71

Since the late 1950s the U.S. gold reserves have decreased considerably.

they knew that if they tried to turn them into gold, the United States would have to end the convertibility of dollars into gold since our gold stocks were much less than foreign dollar balances.

It is worth emphasizing the fact that most nations (in the West) held their basic reserves in the form of both dollars and gold. This seemed perfectly reasonable since dollars were convertible into gold at $35 an ounce. The dollar was the "reserve currency"—the "key currency"—of the world. However, as foreign dollar balances spurted upward and the U.S. gold stock fell, it became increasingly questionable whether we could continue to stand behind the convertibility of dollars into gold.

In 1968, the 10 leading Western economic powers met in Washington and Stockholm and agreed to introduce a two-tier gold system. As you will recall from the previous chapter, all the gold held by central banks at the time was included in the official tier. This gold was to be traded only for monetary purposes among central banks at the official rates. The rest of the world's gold supply was included in the private tier, where the price of gold was to be determined by supply and demand. No gold from the public tier was to be sold in the private tier.

The two-tier gold system was a step toward the reduction of gold's importance in the world's monetary system. Although there was some worry that governments might try to profit by buying gold at $35 an ounce in the official tier and selling it at a higher price in the private tier, this two-tier system seemed to work reasonably well for several years. (In 1973, it was abandoned.) But it was only an interim measure and in 1971, President Nixon announced that the United States would no longer sell gold to foreign governments. The convertibility of dollars into gold was suspended.

At a conference at the Smithsonian Institution in Washington in late 1971, the major Western nations agreed to a depreciation of the dollar against their currencies averaging about 10–15 percent. As part of the agreement, the United States agreed to devalue the dollar by about 9 percent. In 1973, the dollar was again depreciated, this time by about 10 percent.

Alchemy in the Nuclear Age

As we have stressed, the short-term dollar balances held by foreigners were an important part of the reserves of foreign governments in the 1950s and 1960s. The U.S. balance of payments deficit, by providing these dollar balances, was providing the non-Communist world with an important part of its international monetary reserves. By the late 1960s, about ⅓ of the non-Communist world's monetary reserves were in the form of U.S. short-term debt to foreign central banks and international monetary organizations. The rest was in the form of gold.

Obviously, as the volume of international trade increased, the volume of international monetary reserves had to increase as well. But the amount of gold in existence increased rather slowly.

Since the volume of international monetary reserves had to increase—and since it was obviously foolish to rely on a continuing U.S. balance of payments deficit to increase reserves—the leading Western economic powers agreed in 1968 to allow the International Monetary Fund to establish *Special Drawing Rights* (SDRs). These SDRs are a new kind of reserve asset created by the International Monetary Fund. Member countries can use them much as they used gold in the past. SDRs can be created if 85 percent of the IMF's votes favor it. Unlike garden-variety IMF loans, SDRs do not have to be repaid to the IMF. However, their allocation among countries must be in accord with their IMF quotas.

SDRs are sometimes called "paper gold." Apparently, international economists accomplished at long last what the alchemists tried so hard—and with so little luck—to achieve. They managed to create gold out of baser materials. "Paper gold" is backed by nothing other than the member countries' pledge to accept it in exchange for currencies. It is much like our domestic money—which, as we know from Chapter 12, is not convertible into gold or silver. In 1970, over $3 billion worth of "paper gold" was created by the IMF. The United States received about $900 million, the United Kingdom about $400 million, and France and Germany about $200 million each.

Problems of International Adjustment

The international financial system experienced some serious problems during the 1960s and early 1970s, with one crisis following another. Some of these crises reached the front pages of the newspapers, but many did not. One of the most serious problems was the difficulty in making international adjustments. The existing system did not provide a very effective way for countries to cure their balance of payments ills. Although in theory countries could change their exchange rates to cure chronic deficits (or surpluses), in practice exchange rates tended to be very rigid. The fact that a country could borrow from the IMF to ward off depreciation of its currency meant that the adjustment of exchange rates was postponed. Thus chronic deficits became more chronic, and the adjustments required to correct these deficits were delayed.

At the same time, governments, for understandable reasons, often refused to sacrifice major domestic objectives for international adjustment. For example, when a country with a balance of payments deficit had a soft domestic economy, it was likely to pursue a stimulative, expansionary policy even though this policy did not promote international adjustment. The United States did just this in the early 1960s. Of course, since no country can ignore its balance of payments problems, a nation's international problems will influence its domestic economic policy, but modern nations resist making great sacrifices on the domestic front for the sake of international adjustment.

However, international adjustments must ultimately be made, unless the system is to break down. A country with a chronic balance of payments deficit has only three choices: to get rid of its deficit, to persuade foreigners to hold more of its currency, or to fail to fulfill its obligations. Of course, if a country has enormous gold and currency reserves, as the United States did in the 1960s, it can avoid facing these choices for a long time. But eventually even the biggest reserves are depleted; and then, since it is foolish to expect foreigners to hold more and more of its currency, the nation must correct its deficit. This may be painful, since it may mean the sacrifice of some domestic objectives, but there is no alternative.

The Relation between International and Domestic Economic Policies

In the previous section, we pointed out that governments often have refused to sacrifice domestic objectives for international adjustment. As an illustration, consider the case of the United States during the 1960s, a period when American economists and politicians complained loud and long about the slack in our economy. Responding to our relatively high unemployment (about 6 percent) and our relatively low rate of economic growth, President John F. Kennedy, newly elected, promised "to get this country moving again."

What sorts of domestic economic policies would promote this objective? Clearly, economic policy should stimulate the economy. Fiscal policy should add to aggregate demand, and money should be easy. But what about our international financial problems? At that time, we also had serious difficulties with our balance of payments. What sorts of domestic economic policies would help reduce the chronic deficit in our balance of payments? According to our discussions in Chapter 31, the conventional answer would be that economic policy should be restrictive. Inflation should be fought hard, through a combination of tight fiscal and monetary policies.

Thus, the sort of medicine that would help the nation's domestic problems would have unwanted international side effects, and vice versa. Faced with this unhappy choice, economic policy makers during the early 1960s generally opted for stimulating the economy. (Recall, for example, the tax cut of 1964.) They tried to "get this country moving again," even if it meant further trouble with our balance of payments. And given the high social costs of unemployment, this choice was quite understandable. However, they continually had to take account of the effects of various actions on our balance of payments. For example, monetary policy during the 1960s reflected the fact that public officials felt that low interest rates would worsen our balance of payments problems.

However, it should not be assumed that a country's domestic objectives are always at odds with its international objectives. This is by no means the case. At times there may be a conflict between them; at times they may be quite compatible. For example, in the United States in the late 1960s they were quite compatible. As you will recall from earlier chapters, inflation due to inadequate fiscal policies and monetary expansion became an increasingly serious problem in the United States in the late 1960s. There was widespread agreement among economists that a restrictive fiscal and monetary policy was the proper one to achieve our domestic objectives. Such a policy was also right from the point of view of our international economic problems.

The Liquidity Shortage

Besides the difficulty in making international adjustments, another basic problem in the international financial system was the possibility that international monetary reserves could grow too slowly. Consider what has happened to the chief international reserves—gold and dollars—since World War II. The amount of gold to be used for reserves was determined in considerable measure by the amount of gold produced. But since the price of gold was maintained at $35 an ounce for many years, gold mining became less profitable as the costs of producing gold increased. The result was that the amount of gold reserves increased rather slowly. The rate of growth of dollar reserves depended on the size and growth of the U.S. balance of payments deficit. In a very real sense, our deficits provided other countries with reserves. Convenient as this may have been, however, it could not go on forever, since other countries were increasingly restless about the lack of discipline such a dollar-based reserve system implied for the United States.

Thus, since gold reserves were increasing slowly and our deficits could not be counted on to continue to provide new reserves, many economists during the 1960s feared that there would be a shortage of reserves. For example, the Council of Economic Advisers pointed out in 1968 that while world trade had increased by over 7 percent annually since 1960, international monetary reserves had increased by less than 3 percent annually.[2] Moreover, the two-tier gold system made it all the more likely that international monetary reserves would not grow fast enough.

The establishment of Special Drawing Rights—"paper gold"—certainly seemed a step toward a more sensible way to expand international reserves, although it will take much more time before the impact of SDRs can be fully assessed. There has been considerable disagreement among economists over the rate at which reserves should be increased. Some have favored the creation of lots of reserves so that countries with balance of payments deficits would not be forced to take drastic actions, while others have argued that if reserves were plentiful, countries would postpone and evade the distasteful actions needed to achieve international adjustment.

Flexible Exchange Rates: A Suggested Remedy

During the 1960s and early 1970s, it was clear that the international monetary system badly needed repair. The response was a profusion of suggestions by economists and bankers. "Everybody has a plan," as Yale's James Tobin put it, with perhaps some pardonable exaggeration. As we have seen, one of the basic problems is to reconcile national autonomy in domestic economic policy with effective and reasonably prompt international economic adjustments. This problem was made more difficult in recent years by powerful multinational firms, which transferred large amounts of short-term capital from one country to another in response to differentials in interest rates and opportunities for speculative gains.

According to some economists, the answer to this problem is flexible exchange rates, which, as we saw in Chapter 31, are determined by supply and demand in a free market. Advocates of flexible exchange rates argue that they would bring about a quick and automatic equilibrium in each nation's balance of payments. For example, if a country began with a balance of payments deficit, flexible exchange rates would cause a reduction in the price of its currency—that is, a depreciation of its currency relative to other currencies. This in turn would increase its exports and reduce its imports, thus cutting its balance of payments deficit. The depreciation would go on until the deficit was eliminated.

Note that this international adjustment will take place under flexible exchange rates regardless of the sorts of domestic policies the various countries espouse. Even if one country is inflating recklessly, while another country is deflating itself into mass unemployment, international adjustment will still occur. To many economists, this is a great advantage of flexible exchange rates. They point out that flexible exchange rates allow governments much more leeway in formulating domestic economic policy. On the other hand, some critics of flexible exchange rates feel that this freedom from balance of payments discipline may lead to an unacceptable rate of inflation.

As we noted in Chapter 31, one of the principal arguments against flexible exchange rates is that they would make foreign trade more risky because no one would be able to predict what foreign currency would be worth. The result would be to reduce international trade. Those who support flexible exchange rates reply that it would be possible to establish "futures" markets for foreign currencies, similar to the markets that exist for some commodities. In other words, one could buy or sell British pounds or German marks, to be delivered at a given date in the future.

In March 1973, the major world economic powers decided to experiment with the use of more

[2] Council of Economic Advisers, *Annual Report,* 1968, p. 179.

flexible exchange rates. The American dollar, the Japanese yen, the German mark, and other important currencies were allowed to float. The resulting exchange rates were to be determined to a considerable extent by supply and demand. But it was agreed that the float would be managed. Governments would still buy and sell their currencies to keep exchange rates within broad limits. Moreover, fixed exchange rates continue to prevail between certain currencies, such as between some neighboring countries in Europe. It is hard to say how long this situation will last and what the outcome of this experiment will be. Perhaps flexible exchange rates will be adopted permanently and completely. Perhaps the world will go back to some system of fixed exchange rates. Only time will tell.

The Formation of Recent American Policy

Let's look in more detail at the way America's balance of payments problems were handled during the 1960s and 1970s. It is clear that the Kennedy, Johnson, and Nixon administrations were all deeply concerned with these problems. At the beginning of his administration, President Kennedy set up a Cabinet Committee on Balance of Payments, consisting of the Secretaries of Treasury, State, Commerce, Defense, and Agriculture, as well as the Chairman of the Council of Economic Advisers. The Chairman of the Fed was also invited to all of the meetings. This committee met often to consider our balance of payments problems. The people at the Treasury Department—particularly Secretary Douglas Dillon and Under Secretary Robert V. Roosa—were much more concerned about the problem than the people at the Council of Economic Advisers, like Walter Heller. But the president seemed to agree with Dillon and Roosa:

> "I know that everyone thinks that I worry about this too much," [President Kennedy] said as we pored over what seemed like the millionth report on [the balance of payments problem]. "But if there's ever a run on the bank, and I have to devalue the dollar or bring home our troops, as the British did, I'm the one who will take the heat. Besides it's the club that De Gaulle and all the others hang over my head. Any time there's a crisis or a quarrel, they can cash in all their dollars, and where are we?"[3]

In the Johnson administration, the Treasury Department continued to exert leadership in this area. President Johnson, in contrast to President Kennedy, had little interest in the technical aspects of the issues concerning our balance of payments. The Cabinet Committee established by President Kennedy became less important in the Johnson administration, while an informal committee of people from the Treasury, State, and Commerce Departments, Federal Reserve, and Council of Economic Advisers became more important. When our balance of payments showed a huge deficit in late 1967, it was decided that President Johnson should make a major policy statement on our balance of payments at the beginning of 1968. The new program was devised largely by senior officials at the Departments of Treasury and State, the Federal Reserve, and the Council of Economic Advisers.

Like its predecessors, the Nixon administration has been forced to spend much time and thought on our balance of payments problems. Secretary of the Treasury George Shultz and Federal Reserve Chairman Arthur Burns, as well as Under Secretary of the Treasury Paul Volcker and the Council of Economic Advisers, have been particularly influential and have worked closely with foreign governments. For example, before the 10 percent depreciation of the dollar in February 1973, Paul Volcker traveled to Western Europe and Japan to make sure that such a move would be acceptable to various important foreign governments. The quest for a solution to the world's international financial problems consumes an appreciable portion of the time of the nation's leading economic policy

[3] Theodore Sorensen, *Kennedy*, New York: Harper & Row, 1965, p. 408, as quoted in G. L. Bach, *Making Monetary and Fiscal Policy*, Washington: Brookings, 1971, p. 133. Some of the material in this section is based on Bach's discussion.

makers. One can only hope that these problems will be resolved before too long.

Summary

The late nineteenth century and the period up to World War I were generally times of harmonious and close-knit economic relationships. The gold standard was in its heyday until World War I; and after the war many countries returned to it. But during the Great Depression of the 1930s, Britain and other countries were forced off the gold standard; and protectionist and "beggar-thy-neighbor" policies were adopted. Since changes in net exports have a multiplier effect on NNP, each country tried to increase net exports to reduce unemployment. But such policies resulted in retaliation, with the result that world trade diminished.

Once World War II got underway, the combatants changed their trading patterns, putting military, not civilian, objectives first. Loans and lend-lease programs were adopted by the United States to help finance some of our wartime exports of strategic materials and equipment. When World War II ended, some countries—like Germany, France, and the United Kingdom—had suffered a great reduction in their productive capacity. The United States embarked on a series of foreign aid programs to help the populations of the war-ravaged countries and to get the European economies back on their feet.

During the late 1940s and early 1950s, there was a severe "dollar shortage." Given the existing demand and supply curves for dollars by foreigners, there was a gap between the quantity demanded and the quantity supplied at the existing price (in foreign currency) of dollars. Gradually, however, this situation has changed, until recently there has been a "dollar glut." For reasons discussed in the previous chapter, we have experienced a chronic deficit in our balance of payments.

The International Monetary Fund was established at the end of World War II to provide a permanent mechanism for international consultation, to promote stability of exchange rates, and to make temporary loans to member countries, giving them time to correct disequilibria in their balance of payments. The IMF, built largely on a philosophy of fixed exchange rates, has been a cornerstone of the postwar international monetary system.

The international monetary system had some serious problems during the 1960s and early 1970s. One was the difficulty of making international adjustments. Although in theory countries could change their exchange rates to cure chronic deficits (or surpluses) in their balance of payments, in practice exchange rates tended to be very rigid. Moreover, governments, for understandable reasons, often refused to sacrifice major national objectives for international adjustment. For example, when a country with a balance of payments deficit had a soft domestic economy, it was likely to pursue an expansionary policy even though this did not promote international adjustment.

Another basic problem was concerned with the rate of growth of international monetary reserves. Since gold reserves increased at a relatively slow pace and since U.S. balance of payments deficits could not be counted on to continue to provide new reserves, many economists were concerned during the 1960s that there would be a shortage of reserves. Special Drawing Rights—or "paper gold"—were established in 1968 to deal with the problem of inadequate reserves. SDRs can be created by the IMF and can be used much like gold by member countries.

In 1973, the major economic powers decided to experiment with the use of more flexible exchange rates. The American dollar, the Japanese yen, the German mark, and the other important currencies were allowed to float. The resulting exchanges rates were to be determined to a considerable extent by supply and demand; but it was agreed that the float would be managed, meaning that governments would still buy and sell their currencies to keep exchange rates within broad limits. How long a float of this sort will last is very difficult to say. Also, the role of the International Monetary Fund in this new situation is hard to predict. No area of economics is more unsettled at present than this one.

CONCEPTS FOR REVIEW

Fixed exchange rates
Flexible exchange rates
Dollar shortage
Dollar glut
World Bank
International Monetary Fund
Marshall Plan
Special Drawing Rights

QUESTIONS FOR DISCUSSION AND REVIEW

1. According to Milton Friedman, "It is not the least of the virtues of floating exchange rates that we would again be master in our own house." What does he mean? Do you agree or not? What are some other virtues of flexible exchange rates?

2. According to Henry Wallich, "The reason why flexible rates are inadvisable is that their successful functioning would require more self-discipline and mutual forbearance than countries today are likely to muster." What does he mean? Do you agree or not? What are some other arguments against flexible exchange rates?

3. The United States announced that it would no longer convert dollars into gold in 1971. True or False?

4. The International Monetary Fund was set up to
a. provide a permanent mechanism for international consultation.
b. promote stability of exchange rates.
c. make temporary loans to member countries.
d. all of the above.

CHAPTER 33

The Less Developed Countries

Fresh from a raid on the well-stocked family refrigerator or comfortably placed in front of a television set, the average American finds it difficult to believe that hunger is a problem in the world. Yet it is true. The industrialized countries—like the United States, Western Europe, Japan, and the USSR—are really just rich little islands surrounded by seas of poverty in Asia, Africa, and much of Latin America. This chapter deals with the problems of these so-called "less developed countries" (LDCs)—the poor countries of the world. We take up several questions. Which countries are poor, and why? How badly do they need additional capital? How great is the danger of overpopulation? To what extent do they lack modern technology? How can they stimulate their rate of economic growth? What can the United States do to help them? These questions are crucial, both to the people in the less developed countries and to us.

What Is a "Less Developed Country"?

Economics abounds with clumsy terms. A profession responsible for "marginal rate of substitution" and "average propensity to consume" cannot claim a prize for elegant language. The term "less developed country" is not a model of clarity. For a country to be "less developed" it must be poor, but *how* poor? Any answer has to be arbitrary. Often countries with a per capita income of $500 or less are called "less developed." Although the $500 cutoff point is arbitrary, it certainly is low enough so that any country unfortunate enough to qualify is most certainly poor. Recall that per capita income in the United States is about $6,000.

Table 33.1 shows that many countries have a per capita income of $500 or less. Thus, much of the world is, by this definition, less developed. Indeed, *the staggering fact is that more people live in the less developed countries than in the developed countries (with per capita incomes of over $1,000) or the intermediate countries (with per capita incomes of $501 to $1,000)*. Specifically, about 800 million people live in the developed countries, about 500 million people live in the intermediate countries, and over 2 billion people live in the less developed countries.

Imagine what life might be like if you grew up in a country with per capita income of $500 or less

Table 33.1

Countries Classified by Level of Per Capita Income

A. Countries with per capita income exceeding $1,000			
United States	Netherlands	Finland	East Germany
Canada	Denmark	Austria	Hungary
Sweden	United Kingdom	Italy	Ireland
Switzerland	Norway	Australia	Venezuela
West Germany	USSR	New Zealand	Japan
France	Belgium	Czechoslovakia	
B. Countries with per capita income of $501 to $1,000			
Poland	South Africa	Uruguay	Mexico
Greece	Spain	Chile	
Bulgaria	Portugal	Cuba	
Rumania	Argentina	Panama	
C. Areas with per capita income of $500 or less			
Most of Middle East and Southeast Europe	All of Africa (except South Africa)	Most of Latin America All of Asia (other than countries listed above)	

Source: United Nations and E. Hagen and O. Howrylyshyn, "World Income and Growth" *Economic Development and Cultural Change,* October 1969.

per year.[1] Chances are that you would be illiterate. You would probably work on a farm with little tools and technology. You would have few possessions (and sometimes only enough food to keep body and soul together) and be likely to die young. This is life in most of Asia, Africa, and Latin America.

The unpleasant fact is that this harsh existence —not the affluent way of life portrayed in *Better Homes and Gardens* or even the *Jersey City Journal*—is the lot of most earth dwellers. Of course this does not mean that the less developed countries do not have rich citizens: indeed they do. But the rich are a tiny minority surrounded by masses of poor people. Nor does it mean that many of these people do not live in cities. Bombay, for example, is the home of over 4 million, most of them poor.

It must also be recognized that many of the less developed countries have gained their political independence in recent years. Before World War II, the major European powers had substantial empires. For example, the British had colonies all over the globe. In the postwar period, many colonies have achieved independence. These new countries are often fiercely nationalistic. They resent what they regard as exploitation at the hands of the former European colonists and demand power and status. Although weak individually, together they represent a force that must be reckoned with.

Moreover, because of better communications and altered religious and cultural beliefs, the expectations and demands of people in less developed countries have changed enormously. Years ago, they were more likely to accept a life of privation and want, since their eye was on the next world. Now the emphasis has shifted to this world, and to material comforts—and getting them quickly. People in less developed countries have become aware of the high standards of living in the industrialized societies, and they want to catch up as fast as they can.

Although the available data on the less developed countries are not as accurate as one would like, these countries seem to have increased their per capita output in recent years. As Table 33.2 shows, the average rate of growth of per capita output in 15 major less developed countries was about 2.3 percent per year from 1950 to 1967. But since the average growth rate in the major developed countries was about 4 percent per year during the same period (see Table 17.1), *the gap between income per capita in the less developed countries and in the developed countries has been increasing.* This is a disturbing fact. Apparently, the gap between

Table 33.2

Annual Rate of Growth of Per Capita National Product, 1950–67

Less developed country	Average annual growth rate
Brazil	2.1
Ceylon	0.8
Colombia	1.3
Egypt	2.7
Ghana	1.3
India	1.6
Malaya	0.8
Mexico	2.8
Pakistan	1.5
Peru	2.9
Philippines	1.8
South Korea	3.8
Taiwan	5.3
Thailand	3.2
Turkey	2.8
Average	2.3

Source: A. Maddison, *Economic Progress and Policy in Developing Countries,* New York: Norton, 1970.

[1] It must be noted that these income figures *overestimate* the gap between the rich and poor nations, since the procedure used to translate local currencies into dollars is to look at prices of internationally traded goods, which are generally more expensive than goods and services consumed locally. Thus a per capita income of $500 or less isn't as low as it seems, but is still very low.

rich and poor will not decrease, unless recent trends are altered.

A Closer Look at the LDCs

Needless to say, the less developed countries vary enormously. Some, like China, are huge; others, like Paraguay, are small. Some, like Taiwan, have lots of people jammed into every square mile of land; others, like Brazil, have relatively few people spread over lots of land. Some, like India, have had great civilizations many, many centuries old; others have had ruder histories. Nonetheless, although it is not easy to generalize about the less developed countries, most of them, besides suffering from relatively low productivity, have the following characteristics.

First, the less developed countries generally devote most of their resources to food production. Agriculture is by far their largest industry. This contrasts markedly with industrialized countries like the United States, where only a small percentage of output is food. Moreover, food makes up most of the goods consumed in less developed countries. They are so poor that the typical family has very little besides food, a crude dwelling, some simple clothing, and other such necessities.

Second, many less developed countries have two economies, existing side by side. One of these is a *market-oriented* economy much like that in developed countries. This economy is generally found in the big cities, where there may be some modern manufacturing plants, as well as government agencies, wholesale and retail outlets, and services for the small number of rich people in the country. Coexisting with this relatively modern economy is a *subsistence* economy based largely on barter, innocent of all but the crudest technology and capable of producing little more—and sometimes less—than a subsistence wage for the inhabitants. This subsistence economy often includes most of the rural areas. It has little or no capital, few decent roads, only the most rudimentary communications. Unfortunately, this is the economy in which the bulk of the population exists.

Third, some of the less developed countries have relatively weak, unstable governments. Thus, the climate for long-term investment and planning is relatively poor in such countries. Moreover, some governments are controlled by a small group of wealthy citizens or by other groups with a vested interest in resisting social change. Corruption among government officials is encountered too often, and honest officials are sometimes not very well trained or experienced in their duties. To some extent, these problems stem from the relative youth of many of these countries. But whatever the reasons, they hamper the effect of government on economic development.

Fourth, most of the less developed countries have a relatively high degree of income inequality. Indeed, there is much more income inequality than in the industrialized countries. Typically, a few landowners or industrialists in a less developed country are rich, sometimes enormously rich. But all outside this tiny group are likely to be very poor. The middle class, so important in the industrialized countries, is very small in most less developed countries.

Barriers to Development and the Need for Capital Formation

Why are the less developed economies so poor, and what can they do to raise their income levels? These are very difficult questions, both because the answers vary from country to country and because the answers for any single country are hard to determine. A variety of factors generally are responsible for a country's poverty, and these factors are so intermeshed that it is difficult to tell which is most important. Nonetheless, certain factors stand out; among these is the lack of capital in less developed countries.

Without exception, the people in the less developed countries have relatively little capital to work with. There are few factories, machine tools, roads, tractors, power plants, miles of railroad, and so on. If you visited one of these countries, you would be struck by the absence of mechanical aids to production. Workers use their hands, legs, and simple tools, often as their ancestors did long ago.

There are several reasons why the less developed countries have not accumulated much capital. First, a country must usually reduce consumption to accumulate capital, but for the less developed countries, with their very low income levels, a reduction in consumption can be painful. Equally important, much of the saving that does go on in less developed countries is not utilized very effectively. Second, there are important barriers to domestic investment, such as the smallness of local markets, the lack of skilled labor, and the lack of qualified entrepreneurs (faced with the right incentives) who are willing and able to take the risks involved in carrying out investment projects. Third, fear that property will be confiscated deters industrialized countries from investing in the less developed countries. As we pointed out above, many of the less developed countries are relatively young nations, filled with nationalistic fervor and fearful of becoming economically dependent. They are suspicious of foreign investment in their countries—and in some cases are quite capable of confiscating foreign-owned property. Needless to say, this does not make foreigners particularly anxious to invest in some of them.

Recognizing their need for additional capital, the less developed countries have used three principal methods to increase investment. First, they have taxed away part of the nation's resources and used them for investment purposes or made them available to private investors. Second, they have tried to mobilize "surplus labor" from agriculture to carry out investment projects. Third, they have increased government spending on investment projects without increasing taxes, thus producing inflation. All these methods are tried, but each has important limitations. Taxes may dull incentives and in any event are often evaded; "surplus labor" is difficult to transfer and utilize; and a little inflation may soon develop into a big inflation. As shown in Table 33.3, the rate of inflation in some less developed countries has been impressive indeed. Besides these three methods, a country can use foreign aid to increase investment. It too has its problems and limitations, but it is hard to see how many less developed countries can scrape up the capital they need without it.

Table 33.3

Annual Rate of Increase of the Domestic Price Level, 1950–65

Country	Average annual rate of increase (percent)
Brazil	31.0
Ceylon	− 0.1
Colombia	9.3
Egypt	1.6
Ghana	5.7
India	2.3
Malaya	1.4
Mexico	6.2
Pakistan	2.3
Peru	8.2
Philippines	1.8
South Korea	19.8
Taiwan	6.6
Thailand	1.6
Turkey	8.2
Average	7.1

Source: See Table 33.2.

Methods of this sort have enabled many less developed countries to increase the proportion of their national output devoted to capital formation. For example, Table 33.4 shows that in 15 major LDCs the average proportion of national output devoted to capital formation increased from about 8 percent in 1950 to about 14 percent in 1966. This proportion is still significantly less than in the developed countries, where it averaged about 17 percent in 1966, but it is increasing. Needless to say, these

Table 33.4

Nonresidential Gross Investment as a Percentage of National Product, 1950 and 1966

Less developed			Developed		
Country	1950	1966	Country	1950	1966
Brazil	11.3	10.9	France	13.6	15.5
Ceylon	7.1	11.0	Germany	14.3	19.9
Colombia	11.4	12.1	Italy	14.8	12.3
Egypt	10.2	16.3	Japan	15.7	25.2
Ghana	7.4	12.0	United Kingdom	10.3	14.3
India	7.4	13.8	United States	13.7	14.6
Malaya	5.0	15.1			
Mexico	10.8	14.8	Average	13.7	17.0
Pakistan	4.8	12.9			
Peru	11.0	13.9			
Philippines	7.4	16.5			
South Korea	5.7	18.1			
Taiwan	9.8	16.7			
Thailand	11.9	19.3			
Turkey	6.9	10.4			
Average	8.5	14.3			

Source: See Table 33.2.

figures are very rough, and not too much reliance should be placed on them. But they do indicate that the less developed countries are progressing in their attempts to increase their rate of capital formation.

The Population Explosion

Another very important reason why per capita income is so low in some (but by no means all) less developed countries is that they suffer from overpopulation. Many less developed countries have sizably increased their total output. In Latin America, Africa, and Southeast Asia, it may have grown at about 5 percent per year in recent years. If population in these areas had remained approximately constant, output per capita would also have increased at about 5 percent per year. But population has not remained constant. It has grown at almost 3 percent per year, so that output per capita has increased at only about 2 percent per year.

Table 33.5 shows the rate of population growth in a variety of less developed countries, as well as some major developed countries. Clearly the rate has been higher, without exception, in the less developed countries than in the developed ones. The most important reason is that modern methods of preventing and curing diseases have been introduced into the LDCs, thus reducing the death rate, particularly among children. It used to be that al-

Table 33.5

Annual Rates of Growth of Population, Less Developed and Developed Countries, 1950–67

Less developed		Developed	
Country	Average annual growth rate	Country	Average annual growth rate
Brazil	3.1	France	1.1
Ceylon	2.5	Germany	1.2
Colombia	3.2	Italy	0.7
Egypt	2.5	Japan	1.1
Ghana	2.7	United Kingdom	0.5
India	2.2	United States	1.6
Malaya	3.0		
Mexico	3.3	Average	1.0
Pakistan	2.4		
Peru	2.6		
Philippines	3.2		
South Korea	2.8		
Taiwan	3.1		
Thailand	3.0		
Turkey	2.7		
Average	2.8		

Source: See Table 33.2.

though the birth rate in the less developed countries was higher than in the developed countries, the death rate was also higher, so that the rate of population growth was about the same in the less developed countries as in the developed ones. But in recent years, the death rate in the LDCs has been reduced by better control of malaria and other diseases, whereas the birth rate has remained high. The result has been a population explosion. For example, in parts of Latin America the population is doubling every 20 years.

This growth of sheer numbers recalls the work of Thomas Malthus (Chapter 16); but numbers do not tell the whole story of the LDCs. Their populations are not only large and growing: they are also illiterate and ill-nourished. Thus, they do not have the skills required to absorb much modern technology. In addition, many workers have little or nothing to do. They live with their relatives and occasionally hold a job. Although they may not be included in the official unemployment figures, they represent a case of *disguised unemployment.* In sum, the population of many less developed countries is large (relative to the available capital and natural resources), fast-growing, of relatively poor economic quality, and poorly utilized.

The less developed countries have responded to the population explosion in at least two ways. Where birth control is opposed on religious or cultural grounds, the LDCs often concentrate on the widespread unemployment that results from population increase. The rapidly expanding labor force cannot be employed productively in agriculture, since there is already a surplus of farm labor in many LDCs, and the capital stock is not increasing rapidly enough to employ the growing numbers in industry. Governments faced with serious unemployment of this sort often are induced to create public works programs and other projects to make jobs, even if these projects do not really promote economic growth.

The LDCs have also responded to the population explosion by attempting to lower the birth rate through the diffusion of contraceptive devices and other birth control techniques. In many of the less developed countries, there is no religious barrier to the adoption of such techniques. For example, Hinduism does not frown on birth control. However, their adoption has been slow. One reason is the medical drawbacks of existing contraceptive devices. Also, there are obvious problems in communicating the necessary information to huge numbers of illiterate and often superstitious people. India has made considerable efforts to disseminate birth control information, but the problems are enormous. In some of the smaller LDC's, such as Singapore, South Korea, and Taiwan, birth control programs seem to have had a more definite effect on the rate of population increase.

Besides trying to cope with or influence the growth rate of their population, the LDCs have also tried to increase the economic quality of their human resources. In other words, *they have been investing in human capital.* Such an investment seems warranted; educational and skill levels in many less developed countries have been quite low. Table 33.6 shows that in 15 major less developed countries, the proportion of the population aged 5 to 19 in primary or secondary school increased, on the average, from about 30 percent in 1950 to about 50 percent in 1964. This is certainly a step in the right direction, although enrollment in school is obviously only a crude measure of the quality of the labor force. In order to absorb and utilize, and eventually develop, modern technology, the LDCs must continue to invest in a more productive labor force.

Table 33.6

Percentage of Population Aged 5 to 19 Enrolled in Primary and Secondary Education, 1950 and 1964

Country	1950	1964
	(percentage)	
Brazil	22	46
Ceylon	54	65
Colombia	22	45
Egypt	20	41
Ghana	14	57
India	19	38
Malaya	35	50
Mexico	30	52
Pakistan	16	25
Peru	34	50
Philippines	59	57
South Korea	43	53
Taiwan	38	64
Thailand	38	48
Turkey	24	40
Average	31	52
United States	80	84

Source: Statistical Yearbook, UNESCO.

Technology: A Crucial Factor

Still another very important reason why per capita income is so low in the less developed countries is that these countries use rudimentary and often backward technology. In previous chapters, we have seen that to a considerable extent the increase in per capita income in the developed countries has resulted from the development and application of new technology. Too often, the less developed countries still use the technology of their forefathers—the agricultural and manufacturing methods of long, long ago. Why is this the case? Why don't the less developed countries copy the advanced technology of the industrialized countries, following the examples of the Japanese and Russians, among others, who promoted their economic development during the twentieth century by copying Western technology?

There are several reasons, one being that some types of modern technology require considerable capital. Modern petroleum refining technology, to choose one, cannot be used without lots of capital, which the less developed countries, with their low rates of investment, find difficult to scrape up. But many technological improvements do not require substantial capital. Indeed, some technological improvements are capital-saving. That is, they reduce the amount of capital needed to produce a given amount of output.

A second reason why the less developed countries find it difficult to copy and use modern technology is that they lack both a skilled labor force and entrepreneurs. Imagine the difficulties in transplanting a complicated technology—for example, that involved in steel production—from the United States to a less developed country where there are few competent engineers, fewer experienced and resourceful managers, and practically no laborers with experience in the demanding work required to operate a modern steel plant.

Even more fundamental is the fact that much of our advanced Western technology is really not very well suited to circumstances in the less developed countries. Because the industrialized countries have relatively great amounts of capital and relatively little labor, they tend to develop and adopt technology that substitutes capital for labor. But this technology may not be appropriate for less developed countries where there is little capital and lots of labor. Thus, it is very important that the less developed countries pick and choose among the technologies available in the industrialized countries, and that they adapt these technologies to their own conditions. Mindless attempts to ape the technologies used in the industrialized countries can result in waste and failure.

In agriculture, important technological advances have taken place in the less developed countries in recent years. In particular, new types of seeds have been developed, increasing the yields of wheat, rice, and other crops. Some of this research was supported by the Rockefeller and Ford Foundations. The resulting increase in agricultural productivity has been so impressive that many observers call it a "green revolution." There is no question that wheat and rice production has increased greatly in countries like Mexico, the Philippines, Iran, Ceylon, India, and Pakistan. Plenty of opportunity remains for improvements in livestock yields as well, but religious beliefs and traditional prejudices are sometimes an important barrier to change.

In industry, most of the new technology adopted by the less developed countries is taken from the developed countries. Very little attempt is being made to devise new technologies more appropriate to conditions in the less developed countries, both because the less developed countries do not have the engineering and scientific resources to develop them, and because such attempts have not been very successful in the past. In countries where the private sector finds it unprofitable to carry out research and development, government research institutes sometimes try to fill the void, but these institutes frequently devote too much of their limited resources to projects not closely related to economic development. In addition, Productivity Centers have been created in some countries to teach managers and supervisory personnel how to make better use of new technology. Such Centers have helped promote the diffusion of new technology in Mexico and Taiwan, among other countries.

Entrepreneurship, Social Institutions, and Natural Resources

Yet another important reason why per capita income is so low in the less developed countries is that they lack entrepreneurs and favorable social institutions. This point was noted in the previous section but needs more discussion. In some LDCs there is a rigid social structure. One "knows one's place" and stays in it, people distrust and resist change, and things are done in the time-honored way they have always been done (as far as anyone can remember). No wonder these countries lack entrepreneurs. The basic social and political institutions discourage entrepreneurship. Moreover, these institutions also are at least partially responsible for the ineffective utilization of savings, relatively high birth rates, and difficulties in transferring technology noted above. As Richard Gill of Harvard University has put it, "In many underdeveloped countries, a complete social and political revolution is required while the industrial revolution is getting underway."

The governments of many less developed countries are relatively weak and unstable. It is difficult enough for any government to give these countries an effective tax system and a rational program of public expenditures, including proper provision for the highways, public utilities, communications, and other "social overhead capital" they need. But the problems are made even more difficult when the government is weak, unstable, and perhaps somewhat corrupt. Even more fundamental, the population's value systems and attitudes sometimes do little to promote economic development. Again quoting Gill, "A sharp desire for material betterment, a willingness to work hard and in a regular, punctual manner, an awareness of the future benefits of present sacrifices—these attitudes may be the prerequisites of economic growth; yet they may be largely absent in many underdeveloped countries."[2]

Finally, it should also be pointed out that some of the LDCs have little in the way of natural resources. Moreover, technological change has made some of their resources less valuable, as in the case of synthetic rubber, which affected the market for natural rubber, an important natural resource of Malaya. But this is not true of all the less developed countries: Iraq and Libya, among others, are well endowed with oil. And in any event, the skimpiness of natural resources in some less developed countries does not mean that they are condemned to poverty. Neither Denmark nor Switzerland is endowed with great natural resources, but both are prosperous.

The important thing is how a country uses what it has. International trade allows a country to compensate, at least in part, for its deficiencies in natural resources. Thus, although some of the less developed countries have been dealt a poor hand by Mother Nature, this lack alone does not explain their poverty. Of course, they might have been more prosperous with more natural resources; but even with what they have, they might have done much better.

There are several ways for them to use their resources more effectively. In many of the less developed countries, a peasant may farm several strips of land that are very small and distant from one another, working a small patch here and a small patch there. Obviously, this procedure is very inefficient. If these small plots could be put together into larger farms, output and productivity could be increased. In other LDCs, huge farms are owned by landlords and worked by tenant farmers. This system too tends to be inefficient, because the tenant farmers have little incentive to increase productivity (since the extra output will accrue to the landlord) and the landlords have little incentive to invest in new technology (since they often fear that the tenant farmers will not know how to use the new equipment).

Land reform is a very lively—indeed an explosive—issue in many less developed countries, and one of the issues the Communists try to exploit. Recall that agriculture is a very important part of the economy of most of the less developed countries. Thus the land is the major form of productive wealth. No wonder there is a bitter struggle in some countries over who is to own and work it.

[2] Richard Gill, *Economic Development: Past and Present*, Englewood Cliffs, N.J.: Prentice-Hall, 1967, p. 87.

The Role of Government

There are several opinions on the role the governments of the less developed countries should play in promoting economic growth. Some people go so far as to say that these countries would fare best if they allowed market forces to work with a minimum of government interference. But the less developed countries themselves believe a free enterprise system would produce results too slowly, if at all. Thus, the prevailing view in the less developed countries is that the government must intervene—and on a large scale.

In some less developed countries—China, for example—the government exercises almost complete control over the economy. As we shall see in Chapter 34, China's economy is planned. The government makes the basic decisions on what is produced, how it is produced, and who gets it. But even in the non-Communist LDCs, such as India, the government makes many decisions on what sorts of investment projects will be undertaken, and it controls foreign exchange. Needless to say, the government also has the responsibility for providing the important social overhead capital—roads, public utilities, schools, and so on—that is so badly needed.[3]

Most economists would agree that the government has a very important role to play in promoting economic development. But there is a tendency to put less weight on the government's role than in the past. Experience has made it clear that some of the less developed countries are plagued by incompetent and corrupt government officials and by a plethora of bureaucratic red tape. Moreover, many governments have gone on spending sprees that have resulted in serious inflation. Even those who are very mistrustful of free markets find it difficult to put their faith in such governments, well-intentioned though they may be. Recent years have seen more and more emphasis on self-interest and individual action as the mainsprings of growth. Recalling the discussion in Chapter 2, we can be reasonably sure that, if Adam Smith is peering down from the Great Beyond, he is smiling with agreement at this change in attitude.

[3] Of course, the government may also foster social and political change. The distinguished economist, Simon Kuznets, commented: "The problem of strategy is essentially the problem of how fast you can change an inadequate set of social and political institutions, without provoking a revolution internally, or losing allies and partners externally. The question is to know what institutions you want to change, and how." (Communication to the author.)

Balanced Growth

An important issue facing the governments of most less developed countries is the extent to which they want to maintain a balance between the agricultural and industrial sectors of the economy. That is, how much more rapidly should they expand industry than agriculture? According to some economists, less developed countries should invest heavily in industry, since the long-term trend of industrial prices is upward, relative to agricultural prices. In addition, advocates of unbalanced growth argue that the development of certain sectors of the economy will result in pressures for development elsewhere in the economy. Advocates of this approach point to the Soviet Union, which stressed industrialization in its growth strategy.

Other economists argue that industry and agriculture should be expanded at a more nearly equal rate. Successful industrial expansion requires agricultural expansion as well, because industry uses raw materials as inputs and because, as economic growth takes place, the people will demand more food. Balanced growth has other advantages. Various sectors of the economy are closely linked and an attempt to expand one sector in isolation is unlikely to succeed. Proponents of balanced growth deny that the long-term trend of industrial prices is upward, relative to agricultural prices. And to illustrate the wisdom of their approach, they cite as examples the United States and Britain, where industry and agriculture both expanded in the course of the development process.

In all 15 LDCs included in Table 33.7, indus-

Table 33.7

Annual Rate of Growth of Employment, by Sector, 1950–65

Country	Industry	Agriculture	Services
		Percentage	
Brazil	4.5	1.6	4.2
Ceylon	3.0	0.7	3.0
Colombia	2.6	1.2	3.6
Egypt	1.5	0.7	3.2
Ghana	n.a.	n.a.	n.a.
India	5.2	1.3	4.0
Malaya	2.2	0.0	4.7
Mexico	4.9	2.2	4.0
Pakistan	4.5	2.2	2.3
Peru	1.2	0.1	3.2
Philippines	6.0	0.7	4.5
South Korea	12.1	-0.1	4.2
Taiwan	7.3	0.2	1.8
Thailand	8.2	2.3	5.1
Turkey	2.9	1.3	3.5
Average	4.7	1.0	3.7

n.a. = not available

Source: See Table 33.2.

trial employment has increased more rapidly than agricultural employment in recent years. Without question, the less developed countries are expanding industry relative to agriculture. In some cases, such as Argentina, India, and Pakistan, it is generally agreed that more balance—less emphasis on agriculture—would have been preferable. Moreover, in many cases, the allocation of resources within industry could certainly have been improved. Countries have sometimes put too much emphasis on substituting their own production—even when it is not efficient—for imports. For example, Chile has prohibited the import of fully assembled cars to promote domestic production, but Chile's automobile plants have been uneconomic.

One reason why the less developed countries tend to push industrialization is that they see heavy industrialization in the wealthier countries. The United States, Western Europe, Japan, the USSR, all have lots of steel plants, oil refineries, chemical plants, and other kinds of heavy industry. It is easy for the less developed countries to jump to the conclusion that, if they want to become richer, they must become heavily industrialized too. It certainly seems sensible enough—until you think about the theory of comparative advantage.

Another reason why the leaders of some less developed countries are fascinated by steel plants, airlines, and other modern industries is that they think such industries confer prestige on their countries and themselves. Such prestige may be costly. Given their current situation, many of these countries might be well advised to invest much of their scarce resources in promoting higher productivity in agriculture, where they have a comparative advantage. Of course, we are not saying that many of these countries should not attempt to industrialize. We *are* saying that some of them have pushed industrialization too far—and that many have pushed it in uneconomic directions.

Development Planning in Less Developed Countries

The governments of many LDCs have established development plans to specify targets or goals for the economy. In some countries, these goals are set forth in very specific, detailed form; in others, they are more generally formulated. An important purpose of these plans is to allocate scarce resources, such as capital, in order to achieve rapid economic growth or whatever the country's social objectives may be. For example, in India, estimates are made of the amount of capital that will be generated internally, as well as the capital that can be imported from abroad. Then the plan attempts to set a system of priorities for the use of this capital.

Some plans are merely window dressing, full of bold words and little else. But others are the result of careful investigation and hard work. Clearly, to be useful, a plan must set realistic goals, ones that take proper account of the country's resources, available capital, and institutions. An unrealistically ambitious plan, if actually put in effect, is likely to lead to inflation, while a plan that is too easily satisfied is likely to mean a less than optimal rate of economic growth. A useful plan should specify the policies to be used to reach the plan's goals, as well as the goals themselves. It should also forecast carefully how the various components of gross national product will change over time, the extent to which inflationary pressures will develop, the adequacy of the supply of foreign exchange, and the effects of the development program on various regions and parts of the population.

Planning techniques have benefited from the application of many tools of modern economic analysis, among them linear programming and input-output analysis. Linear programming can be used to determine how resources should be allocated to maximize output, and input-output analysis can determine how much capacity there must be in various industries to produce a desired bill of goods (see Chapters 22 and 29). These modern tools have undoubtedly helped in formulating development plans, but their importance should not be exaggerated. It would be a great mistake to think that making a good plan is merely a job for an electronic computer.

If the plan is realistic, it can be a useful tool, but unless it is implemented properly, it will achieve very little for the economy. How well it is implemented will depend on the government's ability to marshal resources through taxation and foreign aid, to work effectively with the private sector, and to pick productive public investment projects. In some countries, like India, "the plan" has sometimes become a political symbol, but in many others, like Mexico, planning has been politically less visible. Countries where economic growth has been most rapid seem to have viewed "the plan" less as holy writ, and planning has tended to be more modest and low-key.

Planning in Action: The Case of India

Perhaps the best way to understand the operation of development plans is to look at the nature of a particular country's plans and how they have been fulfilled. For example, consider the very interesting case of India, which has had four five-year plans.[4] The First Five-Year Plan was for 1951–

[4] It is worthwhile emphasizing that the development strategies of *small* LDCs, because of their necessarily greater reliance on foreign trade, must be quite different from that of *large* LDCs, like India.

56. Its targets were to increase net investment in India from 5 to 6.75 percent of national income, to reduce income inequality, to cut the rate of population increase to 1 percent per year, and to lay the groundwork for a doubling of per capita output in a generation. To achieve these targets, the government relied heavily on capital formation. In particular, it sought to carry out many of the investment projects that had been discussed and planned under the British for as much as 50 years. The First Five-Year Plan was accompanied by moderate growth. Per capita output grew by about 1.7 percent per year, and net investment rose from 5 to 8 percent of national income.

At the beginning of 1956, the Indian Planning Commission published its Second Five-Year Plan, which called for much heavier investments—and more emphasis on investment in industry and mining, rather than agriculture and power—than the First Plan. Moreover, the Second Plan relied more heavily on deficit financing than did the First Plan, and devoted much more attention to the expansion of employment opportunities, since unemployment was a considerable problem. Unfortunately, the Second Plan ran into severe difficulties. One big problem was the loss of foreign exchange, as imports grew much more rapidly—and exports less rapidly—than expected. But perhaps more important was the fact that output did not grow as rapidly as the plan called for. By the end of the Second Five-Year Plan, all sectors of the economy, other than the service sector, were producing less than the planned targets. Nonetheless, per capita output grew by about 1.8 percent per year.

India's Third Five-Year Plan—for 1961–66—involved bigger investments and somewhat more emphasis on agriculture than the Second Plan. Responding to the fact that agricultural imports had been much higher than expected under the Second Plan, the Third Plan called for more investment in agriculture. Unfortunately, however, agricultural production during the Third Plan did not come up to expectations. Indeed, India might have experienced a serious famine in 1966 if it had not received substantial food imports from the United States. During the course of the Third Plan, India did increase the percentage of national income devoted to investment from 11 to 14 percent, but a substantial proportion of her investment was financed by foreign aid. Unfortunately, India's output grew by ⅙, instead of the planned ⅓, during the Third Plan, and there was little or no increase in per capita output.

Although the failure of the Third Plan was due in considerable measure to India's involvement in two wars and to two bad harvests, it nonetheless shook many Indians' confidence in the planning process. There was a three-year delay before the Fourth Five-Year Plan was unveiled, and its political significance was played down. The Fourth Plan shifted the emphasis to agricultural development, including irrigation and fertilizers; it stressed a large birth control program; and it called for a 5½ percent increase per year in national output, as well as further increases in investment. The Fourth Plan put somewhat more emphasis on the price system and somewhat less on detailed planning. In practice, however, according to some experts, the latter changes seemed to have been slow to occur.[5]

Choosing Investment Projects in Less Developed Countries

Clearly, one of the crucial problems any less developed country must face is how the available capital should be invested. Countless investment projects could be undertaken—roads, irrigation projects, power plants, improvements in agricultural equipment, and so on. Faced with this menu of alternatives, how should a country choose? One procedure often used is to accept projects resulting in high output per unit of capital invested.

[5] Much of the material in the section comes from Benjamin Higgins, *Economic Development*, New York: Norton, 1968, J. Bhagwati and P. Desai, *India: Planning for Industrialization*, Oxford: Oxford University Press, 1970, R. Gill, *op. cit.*, A. Maddison, *op. cit.*, and W. Malenbaum, *Modern India's Economy*, Columbus: Charles Merrill, 1971.

That is, projects are ranked by the ratio of the value of the output they produce to the capital they require. For example, if a project yields $2 million worth of output per year and requires $1 million of capital, its ratio would be 2. Projects with high values of this ratio are accepted. This procedure, which is crude but sensible, is based on the correct idea that capital is the really scarce resource in many of the less developed countries. It is aimed at maximizing the output to be derived from a certain amount of capital.

However, a better technique for choosing projects is the concept of rate of return, which is used by profit-maximizing firms to choose among alternative investment opportunities. A less developed country, like a firm, can compute the rate of return from each investment opportunity. That is, it can estimate the rate of interest that will be obtained from each investment. Then it, like a firm, should choose the *projects with the highest rates of return.*

In computing the rate of return from each investment project, it is necessary to attach values to the resources it uses and to the returns it produces. At first glance, it may seem adequate to use market prices of inputs and outputs as these values. For example, if unskilled labor's market price is $.10 an hour, this would be the value attached to unskilled labor. Unfortunately, there are some important pitfalls in using market prices in this way. In particular, market prices of inputs in the less developed countries often do not indicate social costs properly. For example, although the market price of unskilled labor may be $.10 an hour, there may be lots of unskilled labor doing essentially nothing in the countryside, with the result that the social cost—the true alternative cost—of using such labor is zero, not $.10 an hour. Moreover, the market prices of some outputs may not indicate their social worth.

Thus, when computing each project's rate of return, it is important to make proper adjustments so that inputs are valued at their social cost and outputs are valued at their social worth. This is easier said than done, but even crude adjustments in the right direction can be worthwhile.

American Foreign Aid

The plight of the less developed countries is of concern to Americans, both because it is good morality and good policy to help them. From the point of view of humanitarianism, the United States and the other rich nations have a moral responsibility to help the poor nations. From the point of view of our self-interest, the promotion of growth in the less developed countries should help to preserve and encourage political and international stability and to make them more effective trading partners.

How can the United States be of help? With regard to many of their problems, we can do relatively little. But one thing that we can do is to provide badly needed capital. Responding to that need, we have given and lent a substantial amount of capital to the less developed countries in the past 20 years.

One important type of foreign aid consists of loans and gifts made by the United States government. It has amounted to over $100 billion since World War II. At first, the emphasis was on aid to Europe (recall the Marshall Plan, discussed in Chapter 32), but since the late 1950s, the emphasis has been on the less developed countries. About ⅓ has been for military aid; about ⅔ for nonmilitary aid. As noted in Chapter 31, much of this aid is in the form of loans or grants of money that must be spent on American goods and services. Also, much of it consisted of our giving away part of what were then surplus stocks of food. (Recall the agricultural programs discussed in Chapter 5.) India has been the leading recipient of U.S. agricultural surpluses, as shown in Table 33.8.

Table 33.9 shows the amount of economic aid received by selected LDCs from the United States and other countries between 1960 and 1965. Clearly, the aid provided by the United States was concentrated in a relatively few countries, with India, Pakistan, South Korea, Brazil, and Turkey accounting for about ⅔ of the total. Looking at the total amount of aid received from all countries on a per capita basis, Table 33.10 shows that by this measurement Israel, Chile, and Egypt received the

Table 33.8

Shipments of U.S. Agricultural Surpluses to Selected Countries, 1953–66

Country	Shipments ($ millions)	Country	Shipments ($ millions)
Argentina	18	Mexico	71
Brazil	706	Pakistan	1,112
Ceylon	190	Peru	88
Chile	72	Philippines	112
Colombia	145	South Korea	753
Egypt	902	Spain	470
Ghana	14	Taiwan	341
Greece	259	Thailand	5
India	3,327	Turkey	441
Israel	346	Venezuela	20
Malaya	10	Yugoslavia	1,153

Source: Agency for International Development.
Note: Not all of these shipments were gifts.

most economic aid.

In addition, the United States has established various kinds of technical assistance programs designed to help the less developed countries borrow some of our technology, administrative techniques, medical knowledge, educational methods, and so on. The emphasis frequently is on training people from the less developed countries to the point where they can teach their fellow countrymen. Often, the costs of these programs are shared by the United States and by the recipient of the aid. Most observers seem to believe that these technical assistance programs have been worthwhile and successful.

Some other aspects of American policy are also important, although they are not aid programs. For one thing, the United States and other developed countries can help the LDCs by reducing trade barriers, thus allowing them to increase their national incomes through trade. However, it seems unlikely that trade alone can substitute for aid, and the situation is clouded by the trade barriers the LDCs themselves have been erecting to protect their own industry. Another way that the United States can help is through private investment. American corporations have invested an enormous amount in the less developed countries—about $2 billion a year during the 1960s, most of it in Latin America. To the less developed countries, this is a significant source of capital.

Besides providing capital, the multinational corporations have also been a source of needed technology. However, these firms have faced much more difficult problems in transmitting technology to less developed countries than to industrialized countries. Many of the techniques of the multinational firms are not very well suited to the less developed countries, with their plentiful unskilled labor, few skills, and little capital. Moreover, there is sometimes little incentive for multinational firms to adapt their products, production techniques, and marketing methods to the conditions present in developing countries. And when they do manage to make a technological transplant, its effects are often restricted to narrow segments of the economy. Still further, it should be noted that the multina-

Table 33.9

Economic Aid to Selected Countries, 1960–65

Country	American economic aid	Economic aid from other Western governments and international agencies	Communist economic aid	Total
Argentina	168	34	10	212
Brazil	951	201	5	1,157
Ceylon	37	52	25	114
Chile	519	160	—	679
Colombia	226	177	—	403
Egypt	851	241	450	1,542
Ghana	60	73	65	198
Greece	178	104	—	282
India	3,904	1,642	450	5,996
Israel	251	460	—	711
Malaya	26	74	—	100
Mexico	74	252	—	326
Pakistan	1,882	585	35	2,502
Peru	36	89	—	125
Philippines	157	173	—	330
South Korea	1,273	98	—	1,371
Spain	245	2	—	247
Taiwan	488	1	—	489
Thailand	177	88	—	265
Turkey	910	198	5	1,113
Venezuela	122	6	—	128
Yugoslavia	592	236	—	828
Total	13,127	4,946	1,045	19,118

Source: See Table 33.2.

tional firms are often viewed with some suspicion and fear by the host governments.

In recent years, American foreign aid has been reduced because of considerable feeling in Congress and elsewhere that our aid programs were not working very well. During the early 1960s an average of about $4 billion per year was spent on such aid programs, but by the early 1970s this figure had been cut to about $3 billion. Foreign aid has been a controversial subject in the United States for some time. Many critics argue that the money could better be spent at home to alleviate domestic poverty. They claim that other industrialized countries—like Germany and Japan—should contribute a bigger share of the aid to the less developed countries. And they assert that our aid programs have not had much impact on the less developed countries so far.

Table 33.10

Net Receipts of Economic Aid, Per Capita, 1960–65

Country	Amount of aid per person (dollars per year)	Country	Amount of aid per person (dollars per year)
Argentina	1.6	Mexico	1.3
Brazil	2.4	Pakistan	3.6
Ceylon	1.6	Peru	1.8
Chile	13.2	Philippines	1.7
Colombia	3.7	South Korea	7.7
Egypt	8.7	Spain	1.3
Ghana	4.3	Taiwan	6.3
Greece	5.5	Thailand	1.4
India	2.0	Turkey	5.9
Israel	46.2	Venezuela	2.5
Malaya	2.1	Yugoslavia	6.1

Source: OECD.

Many suggestions have been made for ways to improve the effectiveness of our foreign aid. One prominent suggestion is that we go further in concentrating the bulk of our aid on a relatively few countries—those that really want to do what is necessary to develop, that can use the money well, and that are important from the point of view of size and international politics. Obviously adopting this suggestion means reducing aid to some other countries. Another suggestion is that, rather than impose political conditions on aid, we should give money with no strings attached. This suggestion entails a great deal more than economics. To evaluate it, one must decide what the goals of foreign aid should be. To what extent should it be aimed at raising the standard of living of the world's population, whatever the effect on the United States? To what extent should it be aimed at furthering American goals and American foreign policies? In practice, foreign aid has been bound up closely with our foreign policy. Given the political facts of life, it is difficult to see how it could be otherwise.

The World Bank and Other Aid Programs

The United States has provided a large percentage of the aid that has flowed from the industrialized countries to the less developed countries, but, as shown in Table 33.9, it has by no means been the sole contributor. Other industrialized nations also have aid programs. For example, France contributed almost $1 billion a year in the late 1960s, and West Germany and the United Kingdom contributed about $500 million a year. Moreover, the Soviet Union has formulated a significant aid program. Aid from the Soviet bloc now totals about $1 billion a year. Indeed, it is often claimed that the Russian programs have had more political effect than our own because they allow the recipient countries more freedom to build "prestige" projects like steel mills and because they make their aid look somewhat less like charity.

In addition, the International Bank for Reconstruction and Development (the World Bank) has channeled large amounts of capital into the less developed countries. As you will recall from Chapter 32, the World Bank was set up to lend money to finance development projects and to insure private loans made for this purpose. In the late 1950s and early 1960s, the World Bank set up the International Finance Corporation and the International Development Association, affiliated agencies that have become increasingly important as sources of funds for the poor nations. Since its inception, the World Bank has lent over $10 billion to the less developed countries, as well as providing significant technical assistance. Nonetheless, despite its achievements, many economists believe that in the past the World Bank has sometimes been too conservative and that it should have been willing to take bigger risks. Since the late 1960s, the Bank has become less conservative in this respect.

To illustrate the size and nature of foreign aid, consider the case of India. In 1951, foreign aid equaled about 1 percent of India's national product; by 1958, it had risen to about 2.7 percent; and by 1965, it had increased to about 3.8 percent. Clearly, India receives vast amounts of foreign aid, most of it as loans, but some as grants and assistance under Public Law 480, which involves the transfer of commodities like wheat and is close to being a grant. An interesting feature of the foreign aid India receives is that it comes from so many sources. Non-Communist aid to India has been channeled in through the Aid-India Consortium, composed of Canada, Japan, the United Kingdom, the United States, West Germany, Belgium, France, Italy, Holland, the World Bank, and others. The United States has put up the bulk of the consortium's aid funds—over 70 percent in the First Plan, over 55 percent in the Second Plan, and over 58 percent in the Third Plan. India has also received some aid from the Soviet bloc countries. During the Second Plan, about 6 percent of India's aid came from the Soviet bloc, and during the Third Plan, about 12 percent came from this source. Soviet bloc aid generally has been used for heavy industrial projects.

What are the maturity of the loans and the interest rate for the loan segment of India's aid? The average maturity for loans authorized during the Third Five-Year Plan was 36 years for American loans, 25 years for British loans, 17 years for German loans, 15 years for Japanese loans, and 12 years for Russian loans. The average interest rate was 1.9 percent for American loans, 4.4 percent for British loans, 4.8 percent for German loans, 5.8 percent for Japanese loans, and 2.5 percent for Russian loans. Thus American lenders set the easiest terms. Aside from commodity assistance, the bulk of the aid received by India has been used for power projects, harbor development, railroads, and industrial projects such as iron and steel plants. This reflects India's emphasis on industrialization. This emphasis also has meant that India has had to rely on substantial technical assistance programs to provide the necessary skills and training. The United States has provided much of this assistance, and the United Nations has sponsored trips to India by foreign experts, as well as fellowships enabling Indians to study and gain experience abroad.[6]

Summary

A country is defined as a "less developed country" if its per capita income is $500 or less. Over 2 billion people live in the less developed countries, which include most of the countries in Asia, Africa, and Latin America. In recent years, there has been a great increase in the expectations and material demands of the people in these countries. The less developed countries vary greatly, but they generally devote most of their resources to the production of food, are composed of two economies (one market-oriented, the other subsistence), often have relatively weak, unstable governments and a relatively high degree of income inequality.

One obvious reason why income per capita is so low is that the people in the less developed coun-

[6] For further discussion, see Bhagwati and Desai, *op. cit.*

tries have so little capital to work with. The less developed countries, with their low incomes, do not save much, they lack entrepreneurs, and the climate for investment (domestic or foreign) often is not good. Also, some less developed countries suffer from overpopulation; and as total output has increased, these gains have been offset by population increases. Modern medical techniques have reduced the death rate, while the birth rate has remained high. The result is a "population explosion." Another very important reason why per capita income is so low in these countries is that they often use backward technology. The transfer of technology from one country to another is not as easy as it sounds, particularly when the recipient country has an uneducated population and little capital. Also, these countries lack favorable social institutions and sometimes have few natural resources.

To promote development, most of the less developed countries seem to believe that the government must intervene on a large scale. An important issue facing the governments of most less developed countries is the extent to which they want to maintain a "balance" between the agricultural and industrial sectors of the economy. Without question, the LDCs are expanding industry relative to agriculture. In some cases, such as Argentina, India, and Pakistan, more balance—less emphasis on industry, more on agriculture—would have been preferable. Moreover, some countries have put too much emphasis on substituting their own production for imports, even when their own production is uneconomic.

Many of the less developed countries have established development plans that specify targets or goals for the economy and policies designed to attain them. One criterion often used to determine whether a given investment project should be accepted or rejected is the ratio of the value of the output produced to the capital used. Only projects with high values of this ratio are accepted. A more sophisticated criterion is the rate of return from the project, the method used by firms in capital budgeting. However, when computing each project's rate of return, it is important that inputs be valued at their social cost and that outputs be valued at their social worth. Modern tools of economic analysis—like linear programming and input-output analysis—are used in formulating some plans.

The United States has been involved in a number of major aid programs to help the less developed countries. During the early 1960s, our government gave or lent about $4 billion per year to the LDCs and carried out a variety of technical assistance programs. In recent years, these aid programs have come under increasing attack, and expenditures have been reduced. One suggestion frequently made is that we go further in concentrating our aid on a relatively few countries that really want to do what is necessary to develop, can use the money well, and are important in terms of size and politics. Besides the United States, other countries—including the Soviet Union—have carried out significant aid programs. Moreover, the World Bank has channeled large amounts of capital into the less developed countries.

CONCEPTS FOR REVIEW

Less developed country	**Birth control**	**Population explosion**
Balanced growth	**Development plan**	**International Finance Corporation**
Green revolution	**Foreign aid**	**International Development Association**
Comparative advantage	**World Bank**	
Multinational corporation		

QUESTIONS FOR DISCUSSION AND REVIEW

1. According to Simon Kuznets, "A substantial economic advance in the less developed countries may require modification in the available stock of material technology, and probably even greater innovations in political and social structure." What does he mean? If he is correct, what are the implications for the less developed countries? For the developed countries?

2. According to Hans Morgenthau, "Foreign aid for economic development has a chance to be successful only within relatively narrow limits which are raised by cultural and political conditions impervious to direct outside influence." Do you agree? If he is correct, what are the implications for the less developed countries? For the developed countries?

3. In recent years, industrialized countries have grown more rapidly than less developed countries. True or False?

4. The increase in agricultural productivity in the LDCs due to technological advances in seeds is known as
a. balanced growth. b. green revolution. c. Seward's Folly. d. Philippine ecstasy.

CHAPTER 34

The Communist Countries, Marxism, and Radical Economics

Everybody talks and reads about communism. You hear the word frequently on television and see it frequently in the newspapers, but if you really know what it means, you are in the minority. It is a safe bet that most people have only a vague and distorted idea of what communism is, partly because the relationship in recent years between the Communist and non-Communist countries has been marked by suspicion, dissension, and sometimes war. Yet about ⅓ of the world's population lives under Communist rule. The Soviet Union, China, Yugoslavia, Cuba, and many other countries are Communist. Clearly, you should know something about the nature of communism to understand what is going on in a large part of the world.

In this chapter, we describe and analyze the nature and workings of the economic system in various Communist countries, with our major emphasis on the Soviet Union, China, and Yugoslavia. After a brief discussion of the doctrines of Karl Marx, the intellectual father of communism, we describe how the Soviet economy works. Since economic planning plays a major role in its functioning, the USSR's planning system is described in some detail. Next, we turn to the economies of China and Yugoslavia, and to some of the major differences between communism and democratic socialism. Finally, we describe briefly the nature of radical economics, a new, and still very small, movement in the United States that draws heavily on Marx's views.

Karl Marx and the Class Struggle

The name Karl Marx probably makes you think of revolutionaries meeting by candlelight in damp cellars to plot the overthrow of nineteenth-century European governments. If this is the picture you associate with the name, you are quite right! Karl Marx was a revolutionary who wanted the masses to revolt against the existing social order. In 1848, he and Friedrich Engels published the famous *Communist Manifesto*, the spirit of which is given by its closing lines:

> Communists . . . openly declare that their ends can be attained only by the forcible overthrow of all existing social conditions. Let the ruling classes tremble at a Communist revolution. The proletarians have nothing to lose but their chains. They have a world to win. Workers of the world, unite!

This is stirring language, no doubt about it. But why did Marx preach revolution, and what goals do the Communists want to achieve? To understand their objectives, it is helpful to look at Marx's famous treatise, *Das Kapital* (the first part of which was published in 1867), which states much of his economic and political thought. According to Marx, the fundamental causes of political and social change are socioeconomic factors. Changes in the ways goods and services are produced and distributed—and in the ways in which men enter into "productive relations" with one another (for example, the feudal lord with the serf under feudalism, or the capitalist with the worker under capitalism)—are responsible for the great political and social movements of history. History can be viewed as a series of class struggles. In ancient times, the struggle was between masters and slaves. In feudal times, it was between lords and serfs. And in modern times, it is between the ***capitalists,*** who own the means of production, and the workers, or ***proletariat.***

According to Marx, every economic system—ancient, feudal, or modern—develops certain defects or internal contradictions, which eventually cause it to give way to a new system. As the old system begins to weaken, the new system gains strength. Thus, the feudal system grew out of the ancient system, and the modern system grew out of the feudal system. In Marx's view, *the struggle between the capitalists and the proletariat will eventually result in the defeat of the capitalists. This will set the stage for a new economic system—**socialism,** a transitional phase toward communism.* Communism, according to Marx, is the ultimate, perfect form of economic system.

The reasons for Marx's belief that in modern times there must be a struggle between capitalists and workers lie in his theory of value and wages. *According to Marx, the **value** of any commodity—that is, its price relative to other commodities—is determined by the amount of labor time used in its manufacture.* In other words, if a shirt requires twice as much labor time to produce as a tie, its price is twice that of a tie. By labor time, Marx meant both the amount of labor used in making a commodity and the amount of labor time "congealed" in the machinery used to make the commodity. According to Marx, wages tend to equal the lowest level consistent with the subsistence of the workers, because capitalists, driven by the profit motive, pay the lowest wage they can.

Combining his theory of value and his theory of wages, Marx concluded that workers produce a ***surplus value***—a value above and beyond the subsistence wage they receive—which is taken by the capitalists. This surplus value arises because the capitalists make the workers labor for longer hours

Karl Marx
on Capitalism

As soon as the laborers are turned into proletarians, their means of labor into capital, as soon as the capitalist mode of production stands on its own feet, then the further socialization of labor and further transformation of the land and other means of production into socially exploited and, therefore, common means of production, as well as the further expropriation of private proprietors, takes a new form. That which is now to be expropriated is no longer the laborer working for himself, but the capitalist exploiting many laborers. This expropriation is accomplished by the action of the immanent laws of capitalistic production itself, by the centralization of capital. One capitalist always kills many. Hand in hand with this centralization, or this expropriation of many capitalists by few, develop, on an ever extending scale, the co-operative form of the labor-process, the conscious technical application of science, the methodical cultivation of the soil, the transformation of the instruments of labor into instruments of labor only usable in common, the economizing of all means of production by their use as the means of production of combined, socialized labor, the entanglement of all peoples in the net of the work-market, and this, the international character of the capitalistic regime.

Along with the constantly diminishing number of the magnates of capital, who usurp and monopolize all advantages of this process of transformation, grows the mass of misery, oppression, slavery, degradation, exploitation; but with this too grows the revolt of the working-class, a class always increasing in numbers, and disciplined, united, organized by the very mechanism of the process of capitalist production itself. The monopoly of capital becomes a fetter upon the mode of production, which has sprung up and flourished along with, and under it. Centralization of the means of production and socialization of labor at last reach a point where they become incompatible with their capitalist integument. This integument is burst asunder. The knell of capitalist private property sounds. The expropriators are expropriated.

Karl Marx, *Capital*, Modern Library, 1906, pp. 836-37. Originally published in 1867.

than are required to produce an amount of output equal to their wage. For example, a worker may be made to work 10 hours a day, even though his output in 6 hours equals the value of his wage. The output produced in the remaining 4 hours is surplus value.

According to Marx, surplus value is what makes the capitalist world tick. Indeed, the reason why capitalists engage in production is to make this surplus value, which they steal from the workers. Capitalists also use some of it to purchase new capital. Thus, capital formation, in Marx's view, comes about as a consequence of surplus value. If the capitalist class is exploiting the workers in the way Marx visualized, it is not difficult to see why he felt that a class struggle between capitalists and workers was inevitable, and even easier to see why he was on the workers' side.

Marx's Vision of the Future

In Marx's view, capitalism would eventually reveal certain fundamental weaknesses that would hasten its demise. As more and more capital is accumulated, Marx felt that the profit rate would be driven down, that unemployment would increase (because of a rise in technological unemployment), that business cycles would become more severe (depressions becoming more devastating), and that monopoly would grow more widespread. As these developments imposed greater and greater hardships on the working class, the chance of revolution would increase. Eventually the workers, recognizing that they "have nothing to lose but their chains," would throw off the yoke of capitalism.

However, Marx did not visualize an immediate progression to communism. Instead, he saw socialism as a waystation on the road to communism. *Socialism would be a "dictatorship of the proletariat."* The workers would rule. Specifically, they would control the government, which, according to Marx, is merely a tool of the propertied class under capitalism. Moreover, the socialist government would own the means of production—the factories, mines, and equipment. Under socialism each person would receive an amount of income related to the amount he produced.

Finally, after an unspecified length of time, Marx felt that socialism would give way to communism, his ideal system. Communism would be a classless society, with all men as brothers, everyone working, and no one owning capital or exploiting his fellow man. Under communism, the state would become obsolete and wither away. The principle of income distribution would be: "From each according to his ability, to each according to his needs." Marx was a visionary and a social prophet, and communism was his promised land, the ultimate goal for which he prodded the workers to revolt—and the land into which the forces of history would ultimately propel them.

Since Marx's doctrines have captured the imagination of huge numbers of people, and hundreds of millions now march under his banners, it is clear that Marx was a remarkable success as a social philosopher and political activist. But what about Marx the economist? Most economists feel that his economic theories have basic flaws, and that many of his economic predictions have gone badly astray. Although there is almost universal admiration for the power and originality of his mind, few economists in the non-Communist world buy his economic doctrines.

Specifically, there are at least five problems with his theories. First, his labor theory of value simply will not hold water. As we have seen in previous chapters, the price of a commodity depends on nonlabor costs as well as labor costs. In particular, other factors of production—including entrepreneurship—contribute to production. Moreover, the price of a commodity depends on the demand for it as well as on its costs. (You will recall that price is determined by the intersection of the demand curve and the supply curve.) Second, Marx's subsistence theory of wages has long been discredited. It simply isn't true that wages are set at the subsistence level. If you have any doubts on this score, look around you and see. Third, Marx's prediction that the working class would experience greater and greater misery has not been fulfilled. On the contrary, the standard of living of workers in the West has increased at a remarkable rate in the century since Marx wrote *Das Kapital*. Fourth, his prediction that the rate of profit would fall has been wrong. Instead, the rate of profit has moved up and down, with no clear trend in either direction. Fifth, his prediction of greater warfare between capitalists and workers has not materialized. On the contrary, workers have tended to buy shares in corporations, thus joining the capitalist class. And the lines of demarcation between the working class and the capitalist class have been blurred, not accentuated, by time.

Nonetheless, despite these and other flaws in his theories, Marx was a very important figure in economics. He recognized some of the most important problems of capitalism—in particular the problems of unemployment, income inequality, and monopoly power—and analyzed these problems forcefully and originally. One need not agree with his ideas, or sympathize with some of his followers, to recognize his remarkable talents.

Communism in the USSR

The economy of the Soviet Union provides an important example of the application of Marxian theories. By the beginning of the twentieth century, Marxism was an international political force of some significance. In 1917, a Marxist-oriented party established itself in Russia. This was the first time any major country went communist. With V. I. Lenin at its helm, the Communist party overthrew the Russian government in November 1917, and set up the Union of Soviet Socialist Republics several years later. The stated goal of the party was to establish Marxian socialism—and eventually communism—in the USSR. When Lenin died in 1924, his place was taken by Josef Stalin, who ruled until his death in 1953. Then Nikita Khrushchev, and more recently, Leonid Brezhnev, have become the Soviet leaders. Since the USSR is now by far the most economically advanced and militarily strongest Communist country, we need to understand how its economy works.

Two characteristics of the Soviet economy should be stressed at the outset. First, although Marx seemed to want the state eventually to wither away, the Soviet government is a remarkably hardy perennial. The USSR is a political and economic dictatorship, with power centralized in the hands of a relatively few Communist officials who make the big decisions about what is to be produced, how it is to be produced, and who is to receive how much. This contrasts with capitalist economies like ours, where these decisions are made largely in the marketplace.

Second, in accord with Marx's views, most productive resources in the Soviet Union are publicly owned. The government owns the factories, mines, equipment, and so on. This too is quite different from the situation in the United States, where most productive resources are privately owned. Specifically, the Soviet government owns practically all industry, most retail and wholesale stores, and most urban housing. Some farms are government-owned, but most are collective farms. The principal case of private ownership in the Soviet Union is the small strip of land each family on a collective farm is allowed to work for itself. In addition, people are allowed to own furniture, clothing, utensils, and sometimes houses.

The Soviet Union's central planners decide what the country will produce. How do they go about making these decisions, what steps do they follow, and who is involved in this process? Before trying to answer these questions, it is important to recognize that the procedures followed by the central planners change from time to time as they recognize their mistakes and try to rectify them. Planning and controlling a vast economy like the Soviet Union's is enormously complicated. In the period immediately after the Russian revolution of 1917, the Communists made some whopping mistakes, but as time went on, the planners became better able to carry out their jobs.

Table 34.1

The Ninth Five-Year Plan for the Soviet Union, 1971–75

Item	Actual output in 1970	Planned output for 1975
Electric power (billions of kilowatt hours)	740	1,030–1,070
Oil (million tons)	349	480–500
Natural gas (billion M^3)	198	300–320
Coal (million tons)	624	685–695
Steel (million tons)	116	142–150
Chemicals (billion rubles)	21	36
Plastics and synthetic resins (thousand tons)	1,672	3,457
Chemical fibers (thousand tons)	623	1,050–1,100
Pulp (thousand tons)	5,110	8,490
Paper (thousand tons)	4,185	5,560
Cement (million tons)	95	122–127
Motor vehicles (thousands)	916	2,000–2,100
Instruments (million rubles)	3,102	6,155
Farm machinery (million rubles)	2,115	3,500
Tractors (thousands)	458	575
Grain harvester combines (thousands)	99	138

Source: Directives of the 24th Congress of the Communist Party of the Soviet Union for the Five-Year Economic Development Plan of the U.S.S.R. for 1971–75, Moscow, 1971.

This is the general procedure that evolved: First, the principal officials of the Communist party made the fundamental decisions as to how much output would be allocated for consumption and how much for investment, which industries would be expanded and which would be cut back. Once these decisions were made, people at a lower level decided the details concerning how various plants should be operated. Then these decisions were transmitted to and carried out by managers, engineers, and workers. This decision-making process is clearly very centralized. During the 1960s, the Russians began to experiment with greater decentralization, delegating more of the planning to the individual plants and industries, and doing less of it centrally. It is still too early to tell exactly how far this decentralization will go or how much it will change the planning process.

Several groups are involved in planning. The top officials of the Communist party establish the overall goals for the economy. These goals are generally enunciated in a ***five-year plan,*** which shows where the economy should be in five years. Table 34.1 shows part of the Soviet Union's Ninth Five-Year Plan, for 1971–75. For example, one goal was to increase electric power production by about 42 percent (about 8 percent per year). When the broad goals are decided, the detailed production plans are drawn up by *Gosplan,* the State Planning Commission. Gosplan obtains enormous amounts of data from the ministries responsible for the performance of particular industries. These data describe production capacities of various productive units and available productive resources. On this basis, Gosplan formulates a tentative production plan.

Once Gosplan's tentative plan is formulated, a host of other groups enter the picture. A number of ministries, each concerned with a particular industry, report to Gosplan in the Soviet administrative hierarchy. These ministries review Gosplan's tentative plan, as do individual plant managers. The purpose of this evaluation is to make sure that the plan is realistic and feasible. Some plant managers will argue that the amount they are asked to produce is too high or that the amount of labor and materials they are allocated is too low. Negotiations take place, and suggestions for revision are sent back to Gosplan. Eventually Gosplan produces the final five-year plan.

Soviet Economic Planning: Problems and Controls

The job faced by the Soviet planners is difficult and complex. Unless you have some appreciation of how tough it is, you cannot understand the difficulties any planned economy must face. Suppose you are handed the job of planning the performance of a small economy consisting of a chemical industry, a coal industry, and an electric power industry. To produce electric power, coal, chemicals, electric power, and labor are required as inputs. To produce coal, electric power, coal, and labor are required as inputs. To produce chemicals, chemicals and labor are required as inputs. In addition, suppose that the country's political rulers have said that in five years they want the country to consume $100 million of electric power, $50 million of coal, and $50 million of chemicals.

Clearly, it is not easy to decide what production targets to establish for each industry. For one thing, the output set for one industry must depend on the output set for another industry because each industry uses another's output. Thus, if you are not careful, one industry will be unable to achieve its target because another industry has produced too little. Suppose that each industry uses the products of the other industries in the proportions shown in Table 34.2. The second column of figures, for example, states that every dollar's worth of coal requires $.30 worth of electric power, $.10 worth of coal, and $.60 worth of labor. Under these circumstances, what should the production targets be? The answer certainly isn't obvious. Try it and see. However, it can be shown that the production targets must be as follows: in five years, $144 million of coal, $159 million of electric power, and $818 million of chemicals must be produced. For a proof, see pages 598–99.

This simple illustration gives you some inkling of the problems faced by the Soviet planners—but

Table 34.2

Amount of Each Input Used per Dollar of Output

	Type of output		
Type of input	Electric power	Coal	Chemicals
Electric	$0.1	$0.3	$0.0
Coal	0.5	0.1	0.0
Chemicals	0.2	0.0	0.9
Labor	0.2	0.6	0.1
Total	1.0	1.0	1.0

only an inkling. Our illustration has only three industries, while in fact the Russians have to deal with thousands. In the illustration, the input-output coefficients (in Table 34.2) were assumed known. In fact, these coefficients change over time and are not very accurately known. In this simple illustration, we can work out the production target for each industry, using straightforward mathematical techniques. In fact, the Soviet planning problem is so much bigger and more complicated that it is impossible, even with the most sophisticated mathematical techniques and the biggest computers, to solve their planning problem the way we could solve it for the three-industry economy.

To make the planning problem more tractable, the Soviets set higher priorities for certain production goals than for others. For example, they may set a goal for the production of houses and a goal for the production of missiles, but the production of missiles may be given higher priority. Thus, if trouble arises in meeting this production goal, the planners may take resources away from the housing industry to make sure the higher-priority goal is achieved. This makes the planner's job a little easier, but does not guarantee that the economy will be very efficient.

The best-laid plans can go awry. To make sure theirs do not, the Russians have a number of important organizations to check on the performances of plants and managers. First, there is the *Gosbank,* the state-run banking system. When the plan is published, the Gosbank gives each manager enough money to buy the resources—labor, materials, and so on—allocated to him. If the manager runs out of money, clearly he is using more resources than the plan called for. Also, when the manager sells his plant's output, he must deposit the receipts in the Gosbank. If he deposits less than the value of output specified in the plan, it is clear that he has produced less than the plan called for. Thus, the Gosbank keeps close tabs on the performance of various plants. Second, the *State Control Commission* has inspectors who visit plants and go over the records of the Gosbank. Third, officials of the Communist party are expected to report poor performance to the party bosses.

The Soviet economy is a ***command economy:*** people are told what to do. The manager of an industrial plant is told that to fulfill the plan, he must produce a certain amount, his ***quota.*** Moreover, he is authorized to spend a specific amount on wages (he is free to hire labor in the labor market), and to purchase a specified amount of raw materials and equipment. His job is to carry out these orders, but he is not told *how* to run his plant: that is up to him. The Soviets have introduced managerial incentives not too different from those in the West. If a manager is resourceful and diligent, he may be able to exceed his quota. In this case the Soviets—like good capitalists—reward him with extra pay, honors, and perhaps a promotion. If he is lazy, foolish, or unlucky, he may fall short of his quota, which may lead to a pay cut or disgrace.

However, because managers have generally been judged on whether they have met their quotas, certain problems have arisen. Managers have tried to underestimate what their plants could produce in order to get easy quotas. They have tried to hoard and conceal materials and labor so that they would appear to use less resources than they did. And they have sometimes allowed the quality of their product to decline in order to meet their quota. Moreover, managers have been loath to introduce new methods or other innovations because of the risks involved. If a new method did not pan out, it could mean Siberia for the manager. Better play it safe, even though this hurts productivity over the long run.

Soviet workers have considerable freedom to determine where they work. However, farm workers are not allowed to leave the farms, and personnel are not allowed to leave certain projects of great importance to the government. To get work of the right kind done to fulfill the plan, the planners set up wage differentials to induce people to do the needed work. This, of course, is quite similar to the sorts of incentives that prevail under capitalism. In addition, however, other pressures are used to get people to work hard and in accord with the plan. The government provides medals and awards to workers who do very well. The labor unions, which are really part of the state, push for higher productivity. And people who perform poorly may be fined (or even sent to Siberia). Nonetheless, labor problems of various kinds exist. For example, there are many complaints that Soviet workers are unnecessarily late and absent from their jobs, and that labor turnover is far higher than it should be.

Prices in the USSR

As we have seen in earlier chapters, prices in a market economy allocate resources in a way that promotes the goals and satisfactions of the consumers. Obviously, prices in the Soviet Union do not function like this. On the contrary, they are set by the government to promote the goals of the state. Note that there are two fundamental differences here between the United States and the Soviet Union. Prices are set largely by the market in the United States; they are set by the government in the USSR. And prices should promote the goals of consumers in the United States, but promote the goals of the government in the USSR.

More specifically, how are prices set—and how are they used—in the Soviet Union? The answer varies depending on whether one adopts the point of view of a producer or a consumer. First, consider a producer: a plant producing shoes, say. The government sets the price of the shoes, as well as the prices of the labor, materials, and other inputs the producer uses. The government tries to set these prices so that a firm of average efficiency will run neither a profit nor a loss. Thus, the system of prices is used to determine whether a producer is relatively efficient or relatively inefficient. If he makes a profit, this is evidence that he is efficient; a loss is evidence that he is inefficient.

This is no different from capitalism. But in the USSR, prices of inputs do not reflect the relative scarcity of inputs, as they do in capitalistic economies. Moreover, the price system in the USSR does not determine the output of each commodity, as it does under capitalism. Instead, as we saw in the previous section, government planning determines target output levels.

Next, let's consider the prices consumers must pay for goods and services. The function performed by these prices is quite different from that performed by the prices that producers must pay. While the prices facing producers are used to gauge the producers' efficiency (and how well they perform according to the plan), the prices facing consumers are used to ration the consumer goods that are produced. Thus, the price of a commodity to the producer is likely to be quite different from its price to the consumer. For example, the price of a pair of shoes may be 10 rubles to the producer and 20 rubles to a consumer. Why 20 rubles to the consumer? Because 20 rubles is the price the government feels will equate the amount demanded with the amount being produced. Consumer prices are set with an eye toward raising the planned revenue needed for investment.

The gap between the price to the consumer and the price to the producer is the ***turnover tax.*** The turnover tax rate—100 percent in the case of the shoes, since the difference between the two prices, 10 rubles, is the same as the price to the producer—varies considerably from commodity to commodity. It provides a good deal of the Soviet government's revenue, and is a way to reduce inflationary pressures and make consumer spending fit in with the government's economic plan.

The Distribution of Income

At this point, recall that one of the fundamental tasks of any economic system is to distribute the society's output among the people. Does each citizen in the Soviet Union receive income in accord with his need, as Marx envisioned? The answer clearly is no. The Soviet planners set incomes in accord with the type of work a person does, how hard he works, and how productive he is. The result is a great deal of income inequality in the Soviet Union. If we look only at income from labor, the extent of income inequality is about as great there as in the United States. However, for all types of income (including interest, dividends, and capital gains, none of which exist in the Soviet Union), there is more income inequality in the United States.

It is important to recognize that about ¾ of all Soviet industrial workers are paid according to ***piece rates.*** The amount each of these workers receives is determined by how much output he or she turns out. Thus, to a much greater extent than in the United States, income is tied directly to a person's production. This, of course, is an important reason for the considerable income inequality in the USSR. Moreover, the Soviet labor unions do not play the same role American unions do. Thus, whereas wage differentials in the United States have often been narrowed by union pressures, such pressures have not been exerted by unions in the USSR. It is very interesting, and understandable, that the Communists have emphasized monetary incentives to coax people to produce more.

In the Soviet Union, as in the United States, occupations differ greatly in pay and status. Distinguished Soviet scientists and professors, leading ballet and opera stars, and important government officials and industrial managers are at the top of the heap. Their incomes are perhaps 20 times as high as that of an unskilled laborer, and they have the good housing, the plush vacations, the cars, and other luxuries that are scarce in the Soviet Union. The unskilled and semiskilled workers get the lowest incomes in the Soviet Union, as they do elsewhere. This doesn't mean, however, that various occupations cannot change their position in the salary scale. On the contrary, the Soviet planners push wages for various types of work up or down in order to get the labor required to help fulfill the plan.

To put a floor under the living standards of the poor, the Soviet government provides many free services, including education and health care. Also, the government provides other services at a very low price. For example, very low-rent housing—most of which is government-owned—is available. These programs help reduce income inequality by supplementing the incomes of the poor. The turnover tax, discussed above, is used to finance these programs.

Economic Growth

A nation's rate of economic growth is often used as an indicator of its performance. Has the Soviet economy been growing more rapidly than the economies of the United States and other non-Communist countries? Before trying to answer this question, it is essential to recognize that the United States is far in front of the Soviet Union economically. *Our gross national product (in real terms) is about double that of the Soviet Union. Consequently, since our population is smaller than theirs, per capita gross national product in the United States is more than twice that in the Soviet Union.* When comparing the growth rates of the two countries, keep these facts in mind.

In the 1950s, the Soviet Union achieved a very rapid rate of economic growth. American observers watched with some uneasiness as the Soviet gross national product increased at about 7 percent per year, while our own increased much more slowly. This remarkable Soviet performance was partly responsible for President Kennedy's decision in the early 1960s to attempt to increase our own growth rate. One important reason for the rapid Soviet growth was the heavy investment by the Russians in plant and equipment. Investment constituted about 30 percent of gross national product, in contrast to about 15 percent in the United States. Soviet planners kept a tight lid on consumption. Indeed, consumption per capita grew little, if at all, from the late 1920s to the late 1950s. The Soviet consumer was not allowed to increase his standard of living. The increases in production went primarily to build factories and equipment and to build military power. Other reasons for the high Soviet growth rate were the fact that the Soviets could—and did—borrow Western technology, and that the Soviet system does not tolerate unemployment.

In the 1960s and early 1970s, the Soviet growth rate seemed to slump, while ours increased. This, together with the fact that people began to place somewhat less emphasis on the growth rate as a measure of economic performance, resulted in less concern in the United States over the Soviet growth rate, less pressure for government measures to increase our growth rate, and less talk about "growthmanship." According to leading Kremlin watchers, an important reason for the decline in the Soviet growth rate was the greater emphasis on consumption in the post-Stalin Soviet Union. The Communist leaders began to allocate more to the consumer, and this increase in consumption goods meant a decrease in the production of investment goods, which in turn lowered the growth rate.

It should now be clear that the social mechanisms determining the rate of economic growth in the Soviet Union are entirely different from those that determine the rate of economic growth in the United States. In the Soviet Union, the central planners attempt to determine the growth rate by their decisions on the rate of investment in various industries, the amount spent on research and development, and the rate of expansion of the educational system. In the United States, on the other hand, decision making is decentralized. The American growth rate is determined largely by countless decisions by consumers and producers, each attempting to reach his own goals.

Since per capita gross national product is so much lower in the Soviet Union than in the United States, it seems extremely doubtful that the Soviet Union will catch up with us for a long time. Even if the Soviet growth rate exceeds ours by a full percentage point, it will be sometime in the twenty-first century before their GNP catches up with ours, and since their population exceeds ours, it will be even further in the future before their per capita GNP equals ours. Moreover, as their economy grows, maintaining a high growth rate may become more difficult. In addition, an even more fundamental question is whether any real tragedy would ensue if the Russians did narrow the income gap considerably. Since gross national product is a poor measure of military power, an increase in Soviet GNP by itself certainly would not imperil American security.

The Performance of the Soviet Economy

In previous sections, we've described the salient features of the Soviet economy. Now let's try to evaluate its performance. Needless to say, any such evaluation must be incomplete. And since we look at the Soviet economy through American eyes, it is sure to be biased—at least in the eyes of the Soviets and other Communists. But we cannot avoid trying to make such an evaluation, despite the many formidable problems involved.

One's evaluation of the Soviet economy must depend fundamentally on the value one places on freedom. The USSR is a totalitarian state, and its economy is not free. The planners decide what is produced, how it is produced, and who is to get what. A centrally planned economy of this sort may be able to push industrialization and economic growth at a rapid rate, but at a great cost in economic freedom and in living standards. The Soviet planners have decided to build tractors, not cars; dams, not housing; and blast furnaces, not refrigerators. Of course, this emphasis on investment has increased future living standards, but that may be small comfort to those called on to make these sacrifices—people who, it should be recalled, have had a much lower standard of living than their counterparts in the industrialized Western countries.

It is difficult to say much about the equity of the income distribution, since there is no scientifically valid way to say that one income distribution is better than another. This is an ethical question, which each person must answer for himself. Perhaps the most interesting aspect of the income distribution in the Soviet Union is that it contains so much inequality. There is less difference between the Soviet Union and the Western industrialized countries in the extent of income inequality than one might expect. Thus, those who favor more income equality may find less to say for the Soviet economy than they expected.

As for efficiency, it is clear that the Russian economy works—and that in many respects it works very well indeed. However, it is plagued by problems. First, as noted above, incentives for innovation have been weak. Managers, fearful of not meeting their quotas, often resist new techniques. Second, since the planners, not the market, dictate what will be produced, goods consumers do not want are sometimes produced. The link between consumers and producers is not as firm as in the Western economies. Third, the use of production quotas and targets has led to inefficiency. For example, if the quota for a pencil factory is expressed in terms of number of pencils, the manager of the factory may reduce the quality or size of the pencils in order to meet his quota. Fourth, since input prices do not reflect relative scarcities, they may give improper signals to producers.

Changes in the Soviet Economy

The Soviet economy experienced a substantial decrease in its growth rate in the early 1960s. This led to a considerable amount of self-criticism by Soviet economists. Many of the problems just cited —resistance to innovation, mismatches between what is produced and what consumers want, inefficiency due to the stress on production quotas—were admitted by some Soviet economists, and there was much discussion of possible solutions. Among the most influential economists arguing for economic reforms was Professor Y. Liberman of Kharkov University, who proposed several kinds of changes. First, he favored more decentralized decision making. Plant managers should be allowed to decide on their work force, the wages they want to pay, the supplies they want to use, and the improvements they want to make in their equipment. Second, a plant's efficiency should be gauged by the ratio of its profit to its capital investment—a dangerously capitalistic concept. To prod managers and workers to increase efficiency, the bonuses received by managers and the benefits received by workers should vary with the plant's profits. Third, to promote a better match between the goods produced and what consumers want, the profits of a plant should be linked to the amount of goods sold rather than the amount of goods produced. Fourth, interest—long banished from the Communist world—should be resurrected. Recognizing that the interest rate is a device to ration scarce capital, Liberman proposed that interest charges, imposed as a tax, be made for the use of capital by plants.

During the early 1960s, the Communists began to experiment with changes of this sort. As favorable results were achieved by the decentralization, freer prices, and emphasis on "profits" that Liberman proposed, these innovations spread throughout the economy. By 1968, perhaps ¼ of the Soviet economy was characterized by this "new look"—a remarkable shift toward decentralization and Western economic concepts. But the Soviets have had difficulties in operating an economy that is part planned and part market-oriented, and many of the Soviet central planners distrust the "new look." When the Soviet economy fell short of its production goals in the late 1960s, there was a shift back toward centralization. The future direction of the Soviet economy remains uncertain. It may move further toward greater decentralization and Western economic concepts, or it may revert to its older style of operation.

Communism in China

In 1949, another of the world's major powers—China—joined the Communist ranks. With Mao Tse-tung at its head, the Communist army entered Peking, the capital of a nation containing ¼ of the world's population. China was a poor country, with little capital, little technology, and little education—a less developed country par excellence, despite its ancient civilization. Further, the Communists inherited an economy marred by many years of war with the Japanese. Clearly, the country needed as much economic growth as possible, and quickly.

The Chinese Communists responded with a ruthless drive toward industrialization. China's five-year plan of 1952–57 emphasized investment in heavy industry like steel and machinery and some expansion of light industry. It also called for a massive reorganization of agriculture, involving collective ownership of some farms and transfer of land from the rich to the poor. To permit the high rate of investment called for by the plan, the Chinese government pared consumption to the bone. The Chinese people were asked to work long and hard—for little return in goods and services.

Most observers agree that the plan achieved its goal of rapid economic growth. Even though China's population increased considerably, output per capita increased by about 4 or 5 percent per year during the 1950s. This was an enormous achievement for a country whose economy had been stagnant for centuries. To accomplish these objectives, China adopted measures that seem stern even when compared with the Soviet Union. China, like the USSR, is a totalitarian country, but far to the left of the Soviet Union—and there is considerable tension between them. (To buttress its own position, each nation claims that the other has abandoned the true faith of Marxism.)

Having succeeded in pushing the economy ahead in the five-year plan of 1952–57, in 1958 China's leaders launched a more ambitious plan, called the Great Leap Forward. Its aim was to increase per capita output by 25 percent. The large number of underemployed workers in China were to be swept into the employed labor force, and there was to be a great increase in investment. It all sounded very impressive on paper, but it turned out to be a disaster. Despite all the slogans and propaganda, the Great Leap Forward proved to be a Great Leap Backward, because the plan was foolish and unrealistic. For example, literally millions of people were asked to produce steel in primitive furnaces in their backyards. The result, of course, was a lot of unusable scrap metal. Also, poor planning directed millions of workers to produce other goods of little or no value. And too many people were ordered to leave agriculture and enter factories, with the result that far too little food was produced.

By 1960, the Great Leap Forward was obviously a failure of catastrophic proportions, and China's leaders had little choice but to alter their policies. In 1961, they published their new economic plan, which called for more emphasis on agriculture and less on industry. For example, industries that contributed to agricultural productivity—like the tractor industry—would receive more capital, while less would be devoted to industries that did not affect agriculture. Also, higher priority was given to the production of consumer goods for the peasants. Despite the new emphasis, the gains in agricultural production and efficiency seem to have been modest during the 1960s. Apparently, the Great Leap Forward had wreaked so much havoc that it was difficult to get agriculture moving ahead. By 1968, both food and industrial output seemed to be below the levels achieved 10 years earlier.

The so-called Cultural Revolution that began in 1968 saw large-scale political disorders in Communist China. Because the data on Chinese economic performance are meager and unreliable, even the experts find it difficult to estimate the effects of this social turmoil on the economy. But by 1971, it seemed likely that the economy had recovered in large part from the economic disorders arising from the Cultural Revolution.

Economic Life in China

Despite the economic gains it has achieved, China is still a less developed country. In 1970, the average wage in industry was about $270 per year, and the average wage in agriculture was about $200 per year. Over 50 percent of the typical wage earner's income goes for food, and many consumer goods, like rice and cloth, are rationed, so that a family can buy only a certain amount per month. Automobiles are uncommon in China; the bicycle is the usual means of private transportation in cities. Workers are divided into a number of strata, and wages are uniform within each strata. The government plays an important role in determining where and in what position a particular person works. Labor markets are not nearly as free as in the United States.

To step up its rate of economic growth, China devotes about 20 percent of its national output to capital formation. This is a high rate of investment, relative to developed countries as well as to other less developed countries. However, it must be recognized that this does not come from voluntary saving. Instead, it is due to government action. Because the educational and skill level of the population is low, it is difficult to invest this forced saving as productively as would otherwise be the case. The Russians, when they were on better terms with the Chinese, provided some technical assistance, but those days are long gone. At present, China finds it difficult to absorb the technology it so badly needs.

About 4/5 of China's population is engaged in agriculture, which contributes about 40 percent of GNP. Industrial production, which constitutes about 1/3 of GNP, has been growing more rapidly than agricultural output. Indeed, industrial output grew at about 10 percent per year in 1971, and at a somewhat lesser rate in 1972. But agriculture experienced a setback in 1972, when grain output was hard hit by drought in western and northern China, resulting in a 4 percent decrease in grain production from 1971 to 1972. Consequently, China increased her wheat imports from Canada, Australia, and the United States from 3.2 million tons in 1971 to 4.5 million tons in 1972.

The distribution of income in China is much less unequal than it was 30 years ago. Some economists, like John Gurley of Stanford University, believe that China has been able to eradicate abject poverty despite her economic adversities. According to Gurley, "The basic, overriding economic fact about China is that for twenty years she has fed, clothed, and housed everyone. . . Millions have not starved; sidewalks and streets have not been covered with multitudes of sleeping, begging, hungry, and illiterate human beings; millions are not disease-ridden."[1] It is difficult, however, to obtain reliable information about living conditions in so huge and diverse a country, particularly when very few Americans were allowed in China before President Nixon's visit in 1972. Many economists are less enthusiastic than Gurley about China's economic performance.[2]

For many years, economists and politicians around the world have watched the relative economic performance of China and India. Both are huge countries with enormous populations and ancient civilizations, and both are poor. But China is Communist and centrally planned, while India is democratic and much freer economically. Thus, in a field where controlled experiments are impractical, the relative performance of India and China gives some idea of whether a Communist or a democratic system results in faster economic development. In the late 1950s, it looked as if China was forging ahead more rapidly than India. This was not very good news in the Western democracies, but many people felt that, even if the Chinese did achieve a higher rate of economic growth, it was not worth the price they paid in regimentation and lack of political and social freedom. In the late 1960s, as we have seen, the Chi-

[1] John Gurley, "Maoist Economic Development," in E. Mansfield, *Economics: Readings, Issues, and Cases*, New York: Norton, 1974.

[2] For example, see James Tobin, "The Economy of China: A Tourist's View," in E. Mansfield, *Economics: Readings, Issues, and Cases, op. cit.*

nese suffered major setbacks, with the result that the issue now is in more doubt. It will be interesting in the years ahead to see whether China or India will achieve the more rapid and sustained rate of economic development.

Communism in Yugoslavia

After World War II, Yugoslavia, like China, entered the Communist ranks, led by Tito, the leader of its wartime resistance to the Nazis. The Yugoslavs, like the Chinese, have developed their own brand of economic system under communism. But whereas the Chinese are considerably to the left of the Soviet Union, the Yugoslavs are considerably to its right. During the late 1940s, the Yugoslavs tried to use Soviet-style central planning, but after deciding that it would not work well for them, they proceeded to develop an economic system that is much more decentralized and much closer to the market-directed economies than the Soviet Union's. However, it is important to recognize that Yugoslavia remains a one-party Communist country, dedicated to Communist goals.

The Yugoslav economy is a mixture of planning and decentralized decision making. Most of the productive resources are collectively owned, and much investment has been centrally planned. In other words, the central planners have decided where much of the investment funds, obtained by taxation, were to be spent. (For example, they have figured out whether the textile industry should be expanded or whether some other industry—perhaps machinery—should be expanded instead.) But since 1965, most of the country's investment has been allocated through firms, not central planning.

In agriculture, the Yugoslavs began by trying to collectivize the farms, but gave up this idea in the early 1950s. Most land was returned to private ownership, and the rest was made into cooperative farms. Since the Yugoslavs seem to have achieved a higher rate of growth of farm output than the Soviets, this policy seems to have been justified.

Yugoslavia's rate of economic growth has been among the highest in the world. Between 1950 and 1967, output per capita grew at an average rate of 5.6 percent per year, which is very high indeed. One important reason for this high rate of growth was that Yugoslavia devoted a relatively large proportion—about 20 percent—of its output to capital formation. Also, the Yugoslavs have channeled much surplus rural labor to the cities, where its productivity is higher. Foreign aid also contributed to Yugoslavia's economic growth. The United States, for example, gave Yugoslavia $2¼ billion up to 1964. Also, Yugoslavia has not experienced particularly rapid population growth. Its population increased by about 1.2 percent per year between 1950 and 1967, a lower rate of increase than that of the United States.

Despite its very significant economic advances, Yugoslavia is still a fairly poor and predominantly rural country. Income per capita was about $800 in 1965, and the Communist government has stressed the importance of continued economic growth. One consequence of Yugoslavia's rapid economic growth has been considerable inflationary pressure. In the period from 1950 to 1965, the domestic price level increased at an average rate of about 4.9 percent per year. In an attempt to reduce these pressures, the government has often imposed price controls. There has been substantial unemployment in Yugoslavia, much of it because of the difficulty of finding work for people with very low technical skills.

A distinctive feature of the Yugoslav economy is its system of *workers' management*. Most firms in Yugoslavia are worker-managed, at least in theory. The workers own the firm where they work and choose the people who run it. Firms attempt to maximize profits, just as in the United States, and whatever profits remain after taxes may be distributed to the workers or plowed back into the firm. Each worker is guaranteed a certain minimum income. How much he receives above the minimum depends on the firm's profits. Thus, there are monetary incentives for managers and workers to increase a firm's efficiency, cut its costs, increase its sales, and raise its profits.

Most observers seem to agree that the Yugoslav economic system has worked quite well, although its performance has been uneven. In particular, it seems to have achieved greater industrial democracy and to have relied less on administrative pressure than the Soviet Union, while at the same time doing a better job of catering to consumer tastes and tapping individual initiative. Although there is some skepticism concerning the amount of power actually exercised by the workers, many observers, both Communist and non-Communist, view the Yugoslav economy as an interesting alternative to the Russian or Chinese versions of communism.

Democratic Socialism

We have described three brands of communism—Russian, Chinese, and Yugoslav. And in previous chapters, we have described capitalism. But we must stress that there are other types of economic systems besides capitalism and communism. One of the most important of these is ***democratic socialism,*** which includes Sweden's socialist government and Britain's Labor government, among others. In many ways, the democratic socialist economies occupy a middle ground between our more capitalist system and the Communist systems. They generally favor government ownership of heavy industry like coal and steel (although the fervor for nationalization of such industries has died down in recent years); heavy taxation of the rich; and extensive welfare programs (social security, medical care, and so on); as well as a certain amount of economic planning, rather than the unfettered play of market forces.

But in contrast to the Communists, the democratic socialists generally do not favor violent revolution. Instead, they believe that democratic means should be used to obtain power. A good example is the British Labor government, which came into office after World War II. During the 1920s and 1930s, the Labor party had worked within the existing political system and gained strength. Finally, after the war it got its hands on the reins. Since then the Labor party has remained a major influence in British politics (although it has been in and out of office). As it has gathered further experience, its goals have changed somewhat. For example, because government ownership of industry seems to have been inefficient, the socialists are much more tolerant of private property, and less interested in nationalizing industry, than they were 25 years ago.

To a considerable extent, the more capitalist countries—like the United States—have taken over many of the socialist programs. For example, the United States has moved a long way toward heavy taxation of the rich and toward extensive welfare programs. If Calvin Coolidge could be retrieved from the Great Beyond—and if Silent Cal could be induced to comment—he surely would be impressed (and perhaps dismayed) by how far the United States has traveled toward socialism since his presidency in the 1920s. Even though "planning" remains a dirty word in the United States, the government has become more and more involved in various aspects of our economic life, as we have seen in earlier chapters. The adoption by essentially capitalistic countries of many of their programs has taken some of the appeal—and some of the vitality and direction—from the socialists.

Radical Economics and the New Left

In the United States in recent years, a new force in economics has appeared—radical economics. The radical economists, mainly young and still in the process of shaping their own contributions to the field, draw heavily on the views of Karl Marx. Looking at the urban, racial, environmental, and poverty problems of today, they argue that the conventional tools of economics are too biased toward maintaining the status quo to analyze many of these problems properly. They challenge the methods and assumptions of conventional economics, criticize conventional economists for neglecting many important social problems, and question the reasonableness of many of our society's economic goals.

The analytical framework underlying radical economics consists largely of the following hypotheses. First, following Marx, the radical economists argue that the structure of any society is determined principally by the society's dominant mode of production, and that the most distinctive features of the mode of production under capitalism is the use of the wage-contract, the dominance of impersonal markets, and the private ownership of capital. Second, according to the radical economists, the pressure under capitalism for capital accumulation and riches tends to create a momentum in and of itself, which creates important contradictions and social problems. Third, according to the radical economists, the United States has reached a state of economic development where class struggles are not necessary or rational, since there is enough productive capacity so that all citizens can share adequately in wealth and leisure. To solve existing social problems, the radicals argue that the basic institutions of our society must change. In their eyes, nothing less will suffice.

The flavor of the radical position is well conveyed by this quotation from David Gordon:

> Radicals criticize capitalist society essentially because it evolves irrationally. Its basic mode of production and the structures of its institutions create conflicts which do not need to exist. In the language of economics, it forces "trade-offs" that are not necessary. Fundamentally, radicals argue, capitalism forces a conflict between the aggregate wealth of society (and obviously the enormous wealth of some individuals) and the freedom of most individuals. In another, truly democratic, humanist and socialist society, radicals argue, conditions could be forged in which increases in aggregate social wealth complemented the personal freedom of all individuals. Edwards and MacEwan mention some of the other unnecessary conflicts created (or sustained) by capitalist societies: "income growth versus a meaningful work environment, employment versus stable prices, private versus social costs, public versus private consumption, and income versus leisure." Other conflicts can be specified, but the criticisms gain force in the context of the radical vision of a "better" society. It should be emphasized in discussing the radical vision that many modern radicals, though socialist, do not view most modern socialist countries with great approval. To many Western radicals, the purposes and the realities of the socialist revolution in Cuba provide the closest manifest approximation to their ideals. Che Guevara, in many ways a more important ideologue of that revolution than Fidel Castro, has often expressed those ideals most eloquently.[3]

Response to Radical Economics

As you would expect, the economics profession has responded in a variety of ways to the emergence of radical economics, with its relatively small number of followers. Some economists have chosen to ignore them, while others, like Robert Solow of M.I.T., have responded sharply. In Solow's view,

> Radical economics may conceivably be the wave of the future, but I do not think that it is the wave of the present. In fact, to face the issue head on, I think that radical economics as it is practiced contains more cant, not less cant; more role-playing, not less role-playing; less facing of the facts, not more facing of the facts, than conventional economics. In short, we neglected radical economics because it is negligible. There is little evidence that radical political economics is capable of generating a line of normal science, or even that it wants to.[4]

Since radical economists are still engaged in the work that will tell whether theirs is really a contribution to science, it is premature to attempt to evaluate the accuracy or importance of their efforts.

[3] D. Gordon, *Problems in Political Economy: An Urban Perspective,* Boston: Heath, 1971, p. 7.
[4] R. Solow, "The State of Economics," *American Economic Review,* May 1971.

Admittedly, they have attracted considerable attention, despite the smallness of their numbers, but attention and agreement are two different things. The vast majority of the economics profession unquestionably would disagree with their conclusions. Most economists do not believe that capitalism should be replaced. Nor do they agree with the radicals' view of how our society works, or with their indictment of conventional economics.

Most economists today do not seem to believe that our modern version of capitalism is about to wither on the vine. This is particularly noteworthy, since at the end of World War II, many distinguished non-Marxist economists and social seers, as well as the Marxists, were predicting the demise of capitalism and the rise of socialism. One of the most significant developments of the past 30 years has been the extent to which these prophecies have fallen flat on their faces. The essentially capitalistic economies of the West have shown a tremendous vitality, have grown at a relatively rapid rate, and have avoided any deep depressions. This is a tremendous achievement, and one that should be recognized and appreciated. Of course it does not mean that we do not have many problems. On the contrary, much of this book has been devoted to the discussion of our important social problems. But it does mean that our modern version of capitalism seems to be more than holding its own in today's world.

Summary

Karl Marx was the intellectual father of communism. According to him, the fundamental causes of political and social change are socioeconomic factors. He viewed history as a series of class struggles, the present class struggle being between the capitalists, who own the means of production, and the workers. In Marx's view, the struggle will eventually result in the defeat of capitalism, which will be replaced by socialism, a transitional stage toward communism. To Marx, communism is the ultimate, perfect form of economic system. Capitalists and workers struggle because the workers are exploited. Marx, who subscribed to a labor theory of value, believed that the workers create a surplus value, the difference between the value of what they produce and the subsistence wage they receive. Capital formation, in Marx's view, comes about as a consequence of this surplus value.

According to Marx, the lot of the workers would inevitably get worse. Consequently, capitalism would eventually be overthrown and succeeded by socialism, then by communism. Socialism would be a "dictatorship of the proletariat." The workers would control the government, the government would own the means of production, and each person would receive an amount of income related to the amount he produced. After an unspecified period of time, Marx felt that socialism would give way to communism, which would be characterized by a classless society, the withering away of the state, and the distribution of income according to the principle "From each according to his ability, to each according to his needs." Marx's economic theories have many flaws. For example, his labor theory of value and his subsistence theory of wages are discredited, and many of his predictions have been quite wrong. Nonetheless, Marx was an extremely important figure in economics, and his political and social theories have had an enormous impact on the world.

The Soviet Union, the first country to embrace Marxian socialism, is a political and economic dictatorship—a command economy where power is concentrated in the hands of a relatively few Communist officials who make the big decisions on what is to be produced, how it is to be produced, and who is to receive how much. The government owns the factories, mines, equipment, and other means of production—and gives no evidence of withering away. The problem of planning and controlling a vast economy like the Soviet Union's is enormously complicated, and many mistakes have been made. The top officials of the Communist party establish the overall goals for the economy. The detailed production plans to realize these broad goals are drawn up by Gosplan, the State Planning Commission. These plans are reviewed by individual industries and plants, and after negotiations and revision, Gosplan issues the final plan. To see to it that the plan is carried out, each plant manager is judged by how well he meets his production quota and whether he uses more or less resources than the plan calls for.

In the Soviet Union the government, not the market, sets prices. Prices facing producers are set in such a way that a firm of average efficiency will make neither a profit nor a loss. Prices facing consumers are set to ration the consumer goods produced and to raise the planned revenue needed for investment. The difference between the price to the consumer and the price to the producer is the turnover tax. There is a great deal of income inequality in the Soviet Union. Monetary incentives are widely used to increase production, and about ¾ of all industrial workers are paid by piece rates.

In the 1950s, the Soviet Union achieved a very rapid rate of economic growth, largely because of a high rate of investment and the borrowing of Western technology. But in the 1960s and 1970s, the Soviet growth rate seemed to slump, due in part to a greater emphasis on consumption. Since per capita income in the Soviet Union is less than half of ours, it seems extremely doubtful that the Soviet Union will match our per capita income level in the near future. To increase the efficiency of the Russian economy, there was some movement toward decentralized (and more market-oriented) decision making in the 1960s.

Two other types of Communist systems are found in China and Yugoslavia. China, politically to the left of the Soviet Union, is a very poor country despite its ancient civilization. China's first five-year plan was an ambitious and ruthless drive toward industrialization that seemed to achieve its objectives, but Mao's Great Leap Forward was a disaster that set back the country's economic development. Between 1958 and 1968, there was little or no economic growth. Yugoslavia, to the right of the Soviet Union, has developed an economic system that is much more decentralized and closer to the market-oriented economies than the USSR's. Most firms in Yugoslavia are worker-managed and profit-oriented. Yugoslavia's rate of economic growth has been among the highest in the world. Both China and Yugoslavia have devoted a relatively large percentage of national output to capital formation.

Marxian socialism—or communism—is not the only brand of socialism. There are many democratic socialist parties and governments in the world today. They occupy a middle ground between our more capitalistic system and the Communist systems. In the United States, a new force in recent years has been radical economics, which is based largely on Marxism. The radical economists challenge the methods and assumptions of conventional economics, and advocate basic institutional change. Many economists question whether radical economics is a contribution to science at all. At present, it is difficult to say, since radical economics is so new.

The essentially capitalist economies of the West have shown great vitality in the postwar period. They have grown at a relatively rapid rate, and have managed to avoid any deep depressions. Contrary to many predictions of 30 years ago by some distinguished social seers, our modern version of capitalism seems to be more than holding its own in the world of today.

CONCEPTS FOR REVIEW

Communism
Marxism
Socialism
Capitalism
Proletariat
Surplus value
Capital
Command economy
Gosplan
Gosbank
Turnover tax
Democratic socialism
Radical economics

QUESTIONS FOR DISCUSSION AND REVIEW

1. Compare the economic systems of the Soviet Union, China, and Yugoslavia. To what extent have they departed from Marx's teachings? To what extent are their economic institutions much the same? What are the major differences in the way economic decisions are made? Which of them seems to be performing best economically? Which of them seems to be performing worst?

2. Are the radical economists right in their indictments of conventional economics? What are the most important problems that the American economy will experience in the next 40 years? Can existing economic knowledge solve these problems? What kinds of research are most badly needed?

3. The value of any commodity, according to Marx, is determined by the amount of labor time used in its manufacture. True or False?

4. In regard to the Soviet economy
a. managers tend to resist the introduction of new techniques.
b. the goods that are produced are always the ones that consumers want.
c. the use of production quotas and targets has led to increased efficiency.
d. input prices reflect relative scarcities.

INDEX

Definitions of terms appear on pages set in **boldface** type.

Absolute advantage, 616–18, **617**
Acceleration principle, 211–15, **213**
Accommodating transactions, **651**, 651–52
Accountants, profits as defined by, 127–28
Accounting, *see* Balance sheet; Profit and loss statement
Accounts payable, **124**
Activity level of a process, **463**
Actual price, equilibrium price versus, 56–57
Adams, Henry, 390
Adams, Walter, 510
Addition to surplus, **127**
Adelman, Morris, 494, 523, 629
Advertising, 525
  by automobile industry, 503–4, 512
  consumer behavior and, 422–23
  Galbraith on, 72, 95, 119, 422–23
  in nonprice competition, 511–12
  by oligopoly, 511–12, 514
  by retailers, 502–3
Advisory Committee on the Economic Role of Women, 592
AFL (American Federation of Labor), 548–49, 551
AFL-CIO (American Federation of Labor–Congress of Industrial Organizations), 548, 551–52
Africa, population growth in, 334, 681
Aged, the, *see* Old people; Older workers
Aggregate production function, **329**
Agricultural Adjustment Act (1933), 84
Agriculture, agricultural products
  causes of problems in, 82–84
  in China, 709, 710
  demand curves for, 82–84, 86, 87
  equilibrium price for, 83
  government role in American, 81–90
  in less developed countries, 679, 684, 685–88
  number and receipts of firms in (1971, U.S.), 114
  supply curves for, 82–84
  technological changes and, 82, 83
  in Yugoslavia, 711
Agriculture, Department of, 406
Aid to families with dependent children, 587
Aid-India Consortium, 694
Air pollution, 6, 75, 367-71, 378, 379, 381
Aircraft industry, 4
Alcoa, 50, 484, 490, 526
All-volunteer army, 545–46
Allis-Chalmers, 509
Allocation of resources
  economic growth and, 329
  monopolistic competition and, 520
  monopoly and, 491–92, 518–19
  optimal, conditions for, 601–6
  perfect competition and, 482–83, 491–92, 603–4, 606–7
  United States economic growth and, 353
  wage and price controls and, 314
  welfare economics and, *see* Welfare economics
  See also under Price system
Alternative cost, **435**
Aluminum Company of America, 50, 484, 490, 526
Aluminum industry, 4
Amacher, Peter, 49–50
Amalgamated Clothing Workers Union, 554
American Cyanamid, 512
American economic growth, 347–65
  capital formation and, 337–39, 352
  case for and against, 354–56
  education and, 349–50
  1870–1964 average rates of, 348–49
  future prospects for, 362, 364
  gross national product gap and, 353
  human capital investment and, 339
  natural resources and, 352
  population and human resources and, 349–50
  social and entrepreneurial environment and, 352–53
  technological change and, 350–52
  unemployment and, 358–62
American economy, overview of, 31–47; *see also specific topics*
American Federation of Labor (AFL), 548–49, 551
American Federation of Labor–Congress of Industrial Organizations (AFL-CIO), 548, 551–52
American Meat Institute, 457
American Motors, 503
"American Plan," 549
American Revolution, *see* Revolutionary War, American
American Stock Exchange, 117
American Telephone and Telegraph Company (A.T.&T.), 118
American Tobacco Company, 525, 526
Antipoverty programs, 586–87
Antitrust cases, prosecution of, 525–27
Antitrust Division, Justice Department, 525, 526, 529
Antitrust laws, 4, 9, 73, **524**, 524–25
  collusion by oligopolies and, 508, 509
  effectiveness of, 528–29
  Justice Department, the Courts, and, 525–26
  See also specific antitrust laws
Antitrust policy, 527–31
Appreciation of currency, **639**
Appropriations Committees of U.S. Congress, budget and, 93, 104, 206
Arc elasticity of demand, **410**
Argentina, 87
Aristotle, 565
Armco, 167, 318
Army, all-volunteer, 545–46
Arnold, Thurman, 526

Arrow, Kenneth, 19, 597
Asia, population growth in, 334
Asset holdings, money supply and public's, 304
Assets
capitalization of, 566–67, **567**
current, **124**
fixed, **124**
reserve, in balance of payments, 647–48
Atkinson, L. J., 419, 421
Atomic Energy Commission, 97
Australia, 87
Austria, 52, 53, 313, 661
Automatic stabilizers, 196, 216
Automation, **359**
unemployment due to, 358–59
Automobile industry, 4, 215
advertising by, 503–4, 512
as oligopoly, 503–4, 512–13
pollution and, 10
pricing system of, 513
See also specific automobile manufacturers
Automobiles
demand curve for, case study, 418–19, 421
as pollution source, 368, 373, 374, 378
Autonomous transactions, **651**, 652
Average costs, *see under* Cost functions; Costs
Average product of an input, **426,** 426–27
Average product of labor, **330,** 426–27
Average propensity to consume, 165, **166**

B. F. Goodrich, 351
Babbage, Charles, 340
Bach, G. L., 194, 293*n*, 673*n*
Backward bending supply curve, **541**
Bain, Joe, 503, 514
Balance of merchandise trade, 640, **647**
Balance of payments, 636, **645**
autonomous and accommodating transactions and, 651–52
deficits in, *see* Deficits–balance of payments
domestic economic policies and, 670, 671
goods and services in, 646–47
international adjustment problems and, 670
International Monetary Fund, and, 667, 670
monetary policy and, 288*n*, 671
restoring equilibrium to, 652–55, 670
transfers, capital movements, and reserve assets in, 647–49
United States, 645–55, 668–69; *see also under* Deficits–balance of payments
Balance sheet, **123,** 123–24
of commercial banks, 257–59
profit and loss statement and, 126–27
Balanced budget, 194, 200–2
Banfield, Edward, 610
Bank deposits, *see* Demand deposits; Savings deposits; Time deposits
Bank examiners, 261
Bank of America, 256–58, 260
Bank of England, 655
Bank of Italy, 256
Bankers, investment, 243
Banks
central, 242; *see also* Federal Reserve Board
commercial, *see* Commercial banks
failures, 243, 261, 661
Federal Reserve, *see* Federal Reserve Banks
Federal Reserve System and, *see* Federal Reserve System
loanable funds supply and, 564
monopoly, 265, 270–71
mutual savings, 243
national, 241
runs on, 261, 661
safety of, 261
savings, *see* Mutual savings banks; Savings and loan associations
state, 241
Baran, Paul, 423
Barometric-firm price leadership, **510**
Barter, 46, 234
Base year, 143
Becker, Gary, 339
Beer containers, 371, 372
Belgium, 313
Bell Telephone System, 351
Benefit-cost analysis, 93–95
Benson, Ezra Taft, 88, 414
Berle, A. A., 522
Bethlehem Steel Corporation, 510–11
Beverage containers, 371–72
Beveridge, Lord William, 20
Big business
economic power and, 522–23
See also Corporations–giant
Birth control programs, 683
Bituminous Coal Act (1937), 532
Bituminous coal industry, 483, 532
Black workers
discrimination against, 311–12, 589–91
displacement of, 362
Blatz Brewing Company, 529–30
Blough, Roger M., 318
Boards of directors of corporations, **116,** 119
Bonds
corporate, **117,** 118
federal government, 105, 107–8
state and local government, 103, 257
See also Government bonds
Bonds payable, **124**
Bonneville Dam, 76
Booms, business, *see* Peaks of business cycles
Boston and Maine Railroad, 22–24, 407–8
Bottles, beverage, 371–72
Brannan, Charles F., 88, 414
Brannan Plan, 414
Break-even charts, **449,** 449–50
Break-even income, **588**
Break-even point, **450**
Bretton Woods conference (1944), 643, 666, 667
Broadway theater, price system in, 64–65
Brookings Quarterly Econometric Model of the United States, 224–25
Broun, Heywood, 200
Brown, E. Cary, 200
Brown Shoe case, **527**

Budget, government, **93**
alternative policies on, 201–2
balanced, 194, 200–2
consumer behavior model and allocation of, 399–401
deficit in, **194**, 199–203, 302
federal, 93–95
full-employment, **202**, 202–3
functional finance policy of, **202**
priorities approach to, **399–400**
program, *see* PPB system
surplus in, 200–3
See also Fiscal policy
Budget line, consumer's, **394**, 394–96
Budgeting, capital, 567–68, **568**
Buick division of General Motors, 119
Buick Motor Company, 112
Building construction, business cycles and, 210*n*
Burke, Edmund, 100, 400
Burns, Arthur F., 194*n*, 226, 279, 287, 673
Business cycles (business fluctuations), 208–18, **209**
avoidance of, possibilities, 216–17
budget balancing over course of each, 201
consumption and, 210
Federal Reserve policies and, 293, 294
forecasting, 217–18
inflation and, 210, 211, 216–17
investment and, 210–16
monetary factors in, 216
multiplier and, 213–15
net national product and, 216
phases of, 209–10
See also Depression; Inventory cycles; Prosperity; Recessions
Business failures as leading series, 218
Business firms, *see* Firms, business
Business fluctuations, *see* Business cycles
Business Week (magazine), 226, 458
Businessmen's expectations, 167–68, 211

C + *I* + *G* line (consumption + investment + government expenditures), 186–88, 190–93, 219, 343–44, 359–60; *see also* Net national product
C + *I* + *G* + *X* line (consumption + investment + government expenditures + net exports), 661–62; *see also* Net national product
Cabinet Committee on Balance of Payments, U.S., 673
Canada, 77, 348, 349, 614, 615, 628
Cans, 372
Capacity, excess in monopolistic competition, 501, 502, 520
Capital, **34, 565–66**
accumulation of, **44**
government ownership of, 41
human, *see* Human capital
marginal product of, **336**, 336–37
per worker, in American economy, 45, 352
private ownership of, **40**
production of, 565–66
Capital budgeting, 567–68, **568**
Capital formation
in China, 710
economic growth and, 335–39, 352
less developed countries' need for, 679–81
Ricardo's views on, 335–37
See also Plant and equipment, expenditure (investment) on
Capital gains, 104, **116**
Capital goods, **39**
investment determined by, 167
product transformation curve and, 39–41
Capital movements
in balance of payments, 647–48
in international lending, 656–57
Capital-output ratio, 336–38, **338**
in less developed countries, 690
See also Marginal product of capital
Capitalism, 40–47
basic economic tasks and, 43–44
characteristics of, 40–42

Communist economies compared to, 7, 41–43
consumers' rule under, 42–44, 59–60
government role in, 41–42, 44–45
Marx on collapse of, 160, 354, 700–1
price system in, *see* Price system
radical economists' view of, 713–14
Capitalists, in Marx's theory, 698, 700
Capitalization of assets, 566–67, **567**
Carlson, Chester, 351
Carlyle, Thomas, 333
Carpenters Union, 547
Cartels, **508**, 508–9
Cash, 258; *see also* Coins; Currency
Castro, Fidel, 712
Caves, Richard, 513
Celler-Kefauver Anti-Merger Act (1950), 525, 527
Central banks, 242; *see also* Federal Reserve Board
Chamberlin, Edward, 501, 503*n*
Chance, business fluctuations and, 215
Charles River Associates, 628
Chase Econometrics, 227
Checking accounts, *see* Demand deposits
Checkoff, **554**
Checks, collection of, 242
Chevrolet, 113
Chile, 687
China
capitalism compared to economy of, 41, 42
economic system of, 686, 709–11
Choice
in economic problems, 8
freedom of, in capitalism, **42**
Chow, Gregory, 419, 421
Chrysler Corporation, 503
Cigarette industry, 4
CIO (Congress of Industrial Organizations), 549–51
Circular flows of money and products, 65–66
Cities, *see* Urban areas

Civil Rights Act (1964), 592
Civil War, American, 237–39, 308
Civilian Industrial Technology program, 357–58
Clark, Sir Kenneth, 325
Class struggle
  Marx's theory of, 698, 700, 701
  Ricardo's views on, 335
Classical economists
  determination of national output in view of, 159–62
  rent as viewed by, 570–71
Classical range, **306,** 306–7
Clayton Act (1914), 525
Clean Air Act (1967), 378
Cleveland (Ohio), 367
Cleveland, Grover, 526
Clorox, 527
Closed shop, **557**
Club of Rome, 352
Coal
  energy crisis and, 98–99
  perfect competition in bituminous, 483
Coal miners, 361
COED pilot plant, 98
Cohen, Morris, 227
Coincident series, **218**
Coins, 235, 240–41
Collective bargaining, 548, 549, **556–57,** 556–58
Collusion by oligopolies, 507–10
Command economy, Soviet Union as, **704**
Commerce, Department of, GNP estimates by, 142, 219
Commercial banks, 255–75
  balance sheets of, 257–59
  checking accounts in, *see* Demand deposits
  creation of money by, 262–73
    how money can be created, 265–66
    how money cannot be created, 262–65
    impact on other banks, 266–69
    monopoly banks, 265, 270–71
    total effect, 270–72
  currency withdrawals from, 274
  demand deposits in, *see* Demand deposits
  Federal Reserve System and, *see under* Federal Reserve System
  functions and activities of, 243, 257
  interest rate ceilings on time or savings deposits in, 284
  investments by, 243, 257, 259, 261, 263–72, 274–75
  loans by, *see* Loans—by commercial banks
  reserves of, *see* Reserves, commercial bank
  ten largest, 256
Common Market, 485, 529, 623, 632–33
Common stock, **116**
  capital gains from sale of, 104, **116**
  dividends from, **116,** 117
  Great Crash and (1929), 117–18
  1960s–1970s popularity of, 117, 118
Commoner, Barry, 355
Communism, Marx's views on, 160–61, 698, 700
Communist economies
  capitalism compared to, 7, 41–43
  economic growth policy and, 327
  interest rate in, 565
  See also Socialist economies; *and specific Communist countries*
Comparative advantage, 617–23, **618**
Competition
  capitalism and, 42
  classical economists' view of, 159–60
  flexibility of prices and wages and, 162
  government role in maintaining reasonable, 72–73
  imperfect, *see* Monopolistic competition; Monopoly; Oligopoly
  inflation and, 308–9
  monopolistic, *see* Monopolistic competition
  nonprice, 511–12
  perfect, *see* Perfect competition
  restriction of, government policies, 530–32
  Smith's ideas on, 18, 491–92, 517, 519
  social benefits of, 4
  unfair, prohibition of, 525
  wage increases and, 309
Complements, **422**
Computers, 33, 462
  economic growth and, case study, 340–41
Concentration ratios, market, **523,** 523–24, 528, 529
Conglomerate mergers, **504,** 527, 528
Congress of Industrial Organizations (CIO), 549–51
Congress of the United States
  budgetary role of, 93, 206
  economics and, 10
  Federal Reserve System and, 242, 279
  fiscal policy and, 205–6
  taxation and, 99, 198, 205
  See also specific committees
Conlan, Donald R., 227
Connor, John, 119
Conservative view of government's role, 70, 71
Consolidation Coal Company, 98
Constant cost industry, **480**
Constant dollars, gross national product and, **143,** 143–45
Constraints in linear programming, **463,** 463–68
Construction, *see* Building construction; Residential construction
Consumer behavior, 387–403
  budget lines and, **394,** 394–96
  equilibrium market basket and, **395,** 395–96
  indifference curves and, **391,** 391–96, 416
  model of, 390–401, 418, 422–23, 435
  optimal budget allocation and, 398–401
  purchasing a sprinkler system as case study of, 397–98
  utility and, **392,** 392–96
  See also Demand; Demand curves
Consumer finance companies, 243
Consumer loans, 257
Consumer Reports, 401–2
Consumer sovereignty, principle of, **43,** 44

Consumer's demand curve, individual, 415–18
Consumers, **49**
  behavior of, *see* Consumer behavior
  capitalism and role of, 42–44, 59–60
  expenditures by, 388–90; *see also* Consumption expenditures
  optimal allocation of resources and, 601–3, 606
  protection of, 401–2
  as rational decision makers, 393–97
  satisfaction of, *see* Utility, consumer's
  See also Demand curves
Consumers' goods, **39–40**
Consumption expenditures, **151**
  business cycles and, 210
  disposable income in relation to, 152, 153, 162, 163; *see also* Consumption function
  economic growth and, 328
  external diseconomies of, **606**
  external economies of, **606**
  forecasting gross national product and, 219–24
  net national product equilibrium level and, 168–82, 186–92
  1964 tax cut and, 198
  See also Average propensity to consume; Marginal propensity to consume
Consumption function, 163–65, **164**
  money supply and, 246*n*
  multiplier and, 175–77
  multiplier effects of shifts in, 179–81, 188
  net national product equilibrium level and, 175–77, 179–81, 186–88
Consumption-possibility curve, **626**
Continental Air Lines, 457–58
Cookenboo, Leslie, 123
Coolidge, Calvin, 425, 712
Cooper, Richard, 635
Copernicus, 15
Corn Laws, 335
Corporate income tax, *see* Income taxes—corporate
Corporate securities, *see* Bonds—corporate; Stocks
Corporations, 115–16, **116**
  board of directors of, **116,** 119
  giant (large), 118–20, 308, 309, 529; *see also* Big business
  monopolistic, *see* Monopolistic competition; Monopoly
  profit maximization and, 120
Cost functions (cost curves), **436,** 436–50
  average total, short-run, 443–46, **444,** 448
  break-even charts and, 449–50
  long-run average, **444,** 444–49, 478–79
  marginal, *see* Marginal cost function
  measurement of, 447–50
  in perfect competition, 478–82
  short-run, 443–46, 448, 455–56
  total, **443–44,** 443–45, 447–49, 453–54
Cost of Living Council, 315, 316
Cost per manhour, and Phillips curve, 309, 311
Cost-plus pricing, **511**
Cost-push inflation, **308,** 309, 314–16, 520, 558
Costs, **435**
  alternative, **435**
  average fixed, **438–39,** 438–42, 456
  average total, 438–43, **439,** 456
  average variable, **439,** 439–42, 449, 456–57, 459
  fully allocated, **458**
  historical, of company's assets, **492**
  implicit, **436**
  manufacturing, in profit and loss statement, 125–26
  marginal, *see* Marginal cost
  opportunity, **435**
  optimal input decisions and, 431–50
  optimal output decisions and, 453–59
  out-of-pocket, **458**
  per manhour, Phillips curve and relation between inflation and total, 309, 311
  per unit of output, Phillips curve and determination of, 309, 311
  private, *see* Private costs
  reproduction, of company's assets, **492**
  social, *see* Social costs
  total fixed, **436,** 436–38, 453, 456–57
  total short-run, 436–38, 441, 453–57
  total variable, **436,** 436–38, 453, 457
Cotton-Wheat Act (1964), 88
Council of Economic Advisers, 194–95, 197
  on economic growth (1962), 327
  forecasting of gross national product by, 219, 220, 225
  monetary policy and, 293, 294
  on wage and price guidelines (1968), 315
  wage-price guidelines and, 317, 318
Council on Environmental Quality, 378
Countervailing power, **514**
Crawling peg, **642**
Credit
  money supply and availability of, 245, 246*n*
  1950s–1960s monetary policies and, 286, 288
  1966 "crunch" on, 286, 288, 291
  selective control of, **284**
  See also Interest rate
Credit items in balance of payments, **645,** 645–48
Creeping inflation, **238,** 239–40
"Creeping socialism," 76
Cross elasticity of demand, **421,** 421–22
Crossman, R. H. S., 358–59
Crude quantity theory of money and prices, 249–50, **250,** 300
Cuba, 713
Cultural Revolution, Chinese, 709
Currency, 235
  appreciation of, **639**
  depreciation of, **639,** 670
  devaluation of, **639**

exchange rates for, *see* Exchange rates
quantity in circulation of, determinants of, 240–41
withdrawals from banks of, effects, 274
See also Balance of payments
Current assets, **124**
Current dollars, gross national product and, **143,** 143–45
Current liabilities, **124**
Cuyahoga River, 6, 367
Cycles, business, *see* Business cycles
Cyclical unemployment, **134**

Daniel, Eleanor, 227
Data Resources econometric model, 227
Dean, Joel, 448
Debit items in balance of payments, **645,** 645–48
Debreu, Gerard, 597
Debt, national, *see* National debt
Decision making
by business firms, 7–8, 11
by consumers, rational, 393–97, 433–35
private, 11–12, 295, 327, 328
Decreasing cost industry, **481**
Deductions, tax, 104–5
Defense, Department of, benefit-cost analysis used by, 94–95
Defense, national, 74–75
government spending on, 78, 97–98, 198–99, 211
international trade and, 628
Defense industry, 76, 97–98
Deficits
balance of payments
financing of, 649–50
flexible exchange rates, 672–73
of Great Britain, 655
international adjustments problems, 670
on a liquidity basis, 648
liquidity shortage, 671–72
on an official-settlement basis, 648
United States (1950–1972), 650–53, 668–73
government budget, **194,** 199–203, 302
Deflating, price index and, **144**
Deflation, *see* Monetary policy
De Gaulle, Charles, 673
Demand
elasticity of, *see* Arc elasticity of demand; Cross elasticity of demand; Income elasticity of demand; Price elasticity of demand; Unitary elasticity of demand
market, *see* Market demand
markets and, 50–52
for money, 244–45
supply and, classical view, 159
Demand curves, **22,** 22–23
for loanable funds, **563,** 563–64
for money, 244–45; *see also* Liquidity preference function
of monopolistic competition, 499, 501, 502
of monopoly, 486–87, 490–91
of oligopoly, kinked, 505
See also Firms, business—demand curves of; Individual demand curve; Industry demand curve; Market demand curves
Demand deposits (checking accounts), **235,** 243, 257
converted into time deposits, 274*n*
creation of money by banks and, 262–72
currency withdrawals from banks and, 274
decrease in bank reserves and, 272–73
excess reserves and, 274–75
Federal Reserve System and amount of, 241
fractional-reserve banking and, 258, 259
interest not permitted on, 283
legal reserve requirements for, 260, 282
money supply and, 241
Demand-pull inflation, **308,** 309, 319
Democratic socialism, 712
Demonstration effects, 423
Denison, Edward, 350
Depletion allowance, **104**
Deposits, bank, *see* Demand deposits; Savings deposits; Time deposits
Depreciation, **126,** 357, 358, 448*n*
of currency, **639**
in gross national income, 148, 149
net national product and, 146
straight-line, **126**
Depression, **210**
monetary policy and, 240, 300, 301
money supply and, 240
1930s, *see* Great Depression
prevention of, 216, 294
Dernburg, Thomas, 104, 205*n*
Desmond, Ralph, 261–62
Devaluation of currency, **639**
Developed countries, **677;** *see also* Industrialized nations
Development planning in less developed countries, 688
Dictatorship of the proletariat, **700**
Diffusion process, technological, **340,** 521
multinational firms and, 624–25
Dillon, Douglas, 198, 673
Diminishing marginal returns, law of, **329, 427**
economic growth and, 329–31, 333
optimal input combinations and, 427–29, 441, 442
Diminishing marginal utility, law of, **399,** 418
Direct market experiment, **406,** 408
Discount rate, **283,** 286
Federal Reserve and changes in, 282–83
Discrimination against minorities, 589–92
Phillips curve shifts and, 311–12, 314
Diseconomies, external, **70–71,** 75, **606**
of consumption, **606**
environmental pollution and, 370–71
of production, **606,** 607
Disinvestment, 173
Displacement of labor, 361–62

Disposable income, 150–53, **151**
consumption in relation to, 152, 153, 162, 163; *see also* Consumption function
gross national product and, 152, 153
money supply increase and, 304
net national product equilibrium level and, 168, 189–91
saving and, *see* Marginal propensity to save; Saving function
Disraeli, Benjamin, 347
Distribution of goods and services, 35, 39
Distribution of income
capitalism and, 43–44
Marx on, 700
monopoly and, 519
by percentage of families (1972), 5
poverty and, 5
price system and, 61, 70
product transformation curve and, 39–40
in Soviet Union, 705–6, 708
welfare economics and, 600–1
See also Redistribution of income
Dividends
as automatic stabilizer, 196
common stock, **116,** 117
preferred stock, 117
Dollar
constant, **143,** 143–45
current, **143,** 143–45
devaluation or depreciation of, 668
1934, 661
1971–1973, 87, 636, 652–53, 655
exchange rates and, 636–37, 642–44
floating of (1973), 655
"glut" of, 668–69
shortage of, post–World War II, 663–64
value of, 237
Dominant-firm price leadership, **510**
Doolittle, Eliza, 37
Dorfman, Robert, 468–69
Double taxation of income, 102, 116
Dow-Jones average, 118
Draft, military, 545–46
Dropout rate in high school, program to reduce, 94–95
Duesenberry, James, 225, 240
Dun and Bradstreet, 219
Dunlop, John, 316
Du Pont Corporation, 167, 215, 351
Du Pont family, 113
Durant, William C., 50, 112–13

East India Company, 331
Eastman Kodak, 351, 526
Eckert, J. Presper, 340
Ecology, *see* Environmental pollution
Econometric models, **220,** 220–26, 248
Economic growth, 325–65, **326**
advantages and disadvantages of, 354–56
aggregate production function and, 329
American, *see* American economic growth
capital formation and, 335–39
in China, 709–11
diminishing marginal returns and, law of, 329–31
displacement of labor and, 361–62
education and, 339, 349–50, 357, 358, 362
electronic computer development as case study in, 340–41
environmental pollution and, 355, 373–74
gap between actual and potential output and, 343–44, 353, 357, 358
as government policy objective, 326–28, 356–58
in India, 710, 711
investment in plant and equipment and, 336–39, 357
in Japan, 326, 338, 344–45, 348, 349
Kennedy administration and, 24, 327, 347, 354, 357–58, 706
in less developed countries, 327, 685–88
Malthus's population growth theory and, 331–37, 353, 354
manpower and training policies and, 362
measures of, 326
past and present views on, 353–54
population growth and, 331–34
product transformation curve and, 328–29
public policies to stimulate, 356–57
Ricardo's theory of, 335–37, 353, 354
social environment and, 343
in Soviet Union, 706–8
technological change and, 329, 334, 336–37, 339–42, 354, 356–57
unemployment and, 358–62
in Yugoslavia, 711
Zero, 373
Economic Report of the President, 194
Economic resources, **34**
allocation of, *see* Allocation of resources
of less developed countries, 685
See also Capital; Inputs; Labor; Land; Product transformation curve
Economic stabilization, *see* Stabilization, economic
Economic Stabilization Agency, 315
Economic systems, tasks (functions) of, 34–40
Economics, **1–2, 12**
common characteristics of problems in, 8–9
methodology of, 19–27
normative, **26**
positive, **24,** 26
private decision making and, 11–12
public policy and, 9–11
radical, 712–14
rational decision making and, 7–8
as science, 18–19, 26
as social science, 12–13
typical problems faced by, 2–8
welfare, **600,** 600–8

Economies of scale
 in international trade, 623
 oligopoly and, 503
Economists
 classical, *see* Classical economists
 normative economics and, 26
 salaries of, 19
Edison, Thomas Alva, 351, 504
Edison General Electric, 505
Education, 75
 economic growth and, 339, 349–50, 357, 358, 362
 income inequality and, 583
 Kennedy policy on (1962), 358
 in less developed countries, 683
 rate of return from investment in, 568–69
 technological change influenced by, 341
 of workers, *see* Training or education of workers
E.E.C., *see* Common Market
Efficiency
 monopoly and, 519, 527
 price system and, 44
 See also Inefficiency
Effluent fees, **374**, 374–77
Eisenhower, Dwight D. (Eisenhower administration), 98, 202, 226, 317, 628
Elasticity of demand, *see* Arc elasticity of demand; Cross elasticity of demand; Income elasticity of demand; Price elasticity of demand; Unitary elasticity of demand
Elections, presidential, 10–11, 300
Electric energy, 33
Electric power industry, regulation of, 492–93
Electrical equipment industry, collusion in, 508–10, 526–27
Electrical Workers Union, 547
Employment
 full, *see* Full employment
 Keynes's view on, 161
 public, 555
 See also Unemployment
Employment Act (1946), 74, 134–35, 194, 663
Energy Advisory Panel, 99
Energy crisis, 8, 65–66, 98, 366, 494, 628–29
 Arab oil embargo, 65–66, 629
 coal gasification and liquefaction, 98–99
 fuel shortages, 8
 natural gas regulation and, 494
 nuclear power, 368
 oligopolistic and monopolistic considerations, 629*n*
 pollution control, effect on, 366
 rationing proposals, 65–66
 shale and tar sands as eventual sources of oil, 352
 termination of oil import quotas, 629
Engels, Friedrich, 698
England, *see* Great Britain
ENIAC computer, 340
Entrepreneurship
 economic growth and, 343, 352–53
 in less developed countries, 685
Environmental pollution, 5–7, 9, 366–84
 air pollution, 6, 75, 367–71, 378, 379, 381
 costs of cleaning up, 379–82
 direct regulation as solution to, 374–75
 economic growth and, 355, 373–74
 effluent fees to control, **374,** 374–77
 external diseconomies and, 370–71
 government policy toward, 6, 75, 374–76, 378–79
 gross or net national product does not reflect, 147
 nature and extent of, 367–70
 noise pollution, 370
 private costs of, 370–71
 Ruhr valley as case study of, 376–77
 social costs of, 370–71, 379
 tax credits as means of combating, 374, 377
 thermal pollution, 370
 United States programs to combat, 377–79
 waste disposal and, 368, 370–71, 374–76, 382
 water pollution, 6, 75, 367, 368, 370–71, 374–79, 381
Environmental Protection Agency, 10, 378
Equal Pay Act (1963), 592
Equal Rights Amendment, 592
Equation of exchange, **249,** 250, 300–1, 344
Equilibrium, **55**
 of economy, *see* Stabilization, economic
 general, **597**
 market basket, **395,** 395–96
 of net national product, 168–82, 186–91, 245–47, 305–8
Equilibrium price, **55,** 55–59, 61, 542–44
Equipment, *see* Plant and equipment
Estate taxes, 100
Europe
 United States aid to, 664–65, 668, 690
 United States trade with, 614, 615
European Economic Community, *see* Common Market
European Recovery Program, 664
Evans, Michael, 224
Excess reserves of commercial banks, **268,** 268–71, 274–75, 294; *see also* Free reserves
Exchange, equation of, **249,** 250, 300–1, 344
Exchange rates, 636–46, **637,** 661
 balance of payments equilibrium and, 652, 672
 fixed, 640–43, 667, 673
 flexible, 638–40, 642–43, 672–73
 "floating," 655, 667, 673
 International Monetary Fund and, 666–68
Excise taxes, 81, 582*n*
Executive branch of government, *see* President of the United States *and specific departments and agencies*
Expansion in business cycle, **209,** 210, 213
Expectations
 businessmen's, 167–68, 211
 people's, 284, 312, 314

Expenditures, *see* Consumption expenditures; Government expenditures; Investment; National expenditure; Net exports of goods and services
Experimentation, economics and, 20–21
Exploitation of labor, 27
Export subsidies, **627**
Exports
  American, 614, 615
  net, of goods and services, **152**
  net national product and, 661–63
External diseconomies, **70–71**, 75, **606**
  of consumption, **606**
  environmental pollution and, 370–71
  of production, **606,** 607
External economies, **70,** 71*n*, 75, 481*n*, **606**
  of consumption, **606**
  of production, **606,** 607

"Factors," 243
Failures
  bank, 243, 261, 661
  business, as leading series, 218
Fallacies, economic, 27
Family Assistance Plan, 588–89
Farm products
  price elasticity of demand for, 413–15
  price supports for, 85–90, 196, 406, 414, 532
Farmers, farm workers
  decrease in number of, 84, 361
  incomes of, 82
Featherbedding, 556
Fed, the, *see* Federal Reserve System
Federal Advisory Council, 242
Federal Communications Commission (FCC), 4, 406
Federal Deposit Insurance Corporation, 80, 243, 261
Federal government
  expenditures of, 78, 152; *see also* Government expenditures
  grants to local and state governments by, 104–5
  revenue sharing by, **105**
  tax legislative process of, 99
  tax receipts of, by tax (1973), 80
  See also specific departments and agencies of federal government
Federal Mediation Service, 554
Federal Open Market Committee (FOMC)
  organization and functions of, 242, 279
  sale and purchase of government securities and, 281, 291
Federal Power Commission (FPC), 9, 406, 493, 494
Federal Reserve Bank of New York, 281
Federal Reserve Bank of Philadelphia, 225
Federal Reserve Bank of Saint Louis, 294
  econometric model of, 225*n*, 248
Federal Reserve Banks
  organization of, 241–43
  reserve requirements and, 260
Federal Reserve Board, 220
  Chairman of, 279
  changes in legal reserve requirements of, 282
  decision making by, case study, 285–86
  monetary policy indicators (variables) used by, 284–85, 290
  monetary policy role of, 279, 284
  1950s–1960s policies of, 286, 288
  Nixon's monetary policy and, 289
  organization of, 242
Federal Reserve Notes, 235, 241–42
Federal Reserve System, 80, 235
  Board of Governors of, *see* Federal Reserve Board
  Congress and, 242, 279
  discount rate and, *see* Discount rate
  evaluation of performance of, 291–93
  independence of, 292
  interest rate ceilings set by, 283–84
  "lean against the wind" policy of, criticized, 286, 293–94
  legal reserve requirements of, *see* Legal reserve requirements
  loanable funds supply and, 564
  loans to member banks by, 283
  margin requirements of, **284**
  monetarists' criticism of, 293–94, 302
  monetary policy tools of, 279–84
  moral suasion by, **283**
  national debt and, 108, 290
  organization of, 241–42
  Regulation Q of, 283–84
  Regulation W of, 284
  responsibilities and functions of, 242–43, 279
  rule to govern policy of, proposed, 293–94, 302, 304
  sale and purchase of government securities and, *see* Federal Open Market Committee; Open market operations
  Treasury and, 290–91, 293
  See also Monetary policy
Federal Trade Commission (FTC), 401, 402, 525, 629*n*
Federal Trade Commission Act (1914), 525
Feudal system, 698
Final goods and services, **142**
  expenditures on, *see* Consumption expenditures; Government expenditures; Investment; National expenditure; Net exports of goods and services
Finance Committee, United States Senate, 99
Financial statements, *see* Balance sheet; Profit and loss statement
Firms, business, **49–50,** 111–30
  balance sheets of, **123**, 123–24, 126–27
  characteristics of, 113–14
  cost-push inflation and reduction of market power of, 315
  demand curves of, **419–20**
    for labor, 539–41, **540**
  multinational, 624–25

number and receipts of, by industry, 114
output determination by, 453–58
perfectly competitive, **453**, 538–39
price system and, 49–50, 65–66
production function and, 122–23
profit and loss statements of, **125**, 125–27
profit maximization as motive of, 120–21
supply curves for, 458–60, **459**
technology and inputs and, 121–22
types of, 114–16
First Pennsylvania Bank and Trust Company, 243
Fiscal drag, **203**
Fiscal policy, 18–19, 185–207
contractionary, 193
economic stabilization and, 298–300, 302
expansionary, 192, 203, 306, 307
inflation and, 192–93, 197–98, 203, 319
Keynesian views on, 193, 300
makers of, 194
monetary policy and, 278, 286, 293–95, 298–300
nature and objectives of, 192–94
Nixon's, 204–5, 289
proposals to improve working of, 205–6
recent American experience with, 203–5, 671
tools of discretionary, 197–98
unemployment and, 192, 193, 197–98, 313
Vietnam war and, 198–99, 201*n*, 203
wage-price guidelines and, 319
See also Budget, government; Government expenditures; Taxation
Fischer, Bobby, 45
Fisher, Frank, 512
Five-year plans
Chinese, 709
Indian, 688–89, 694
Soviet Union, 702–3
Fixed assets, **124**
Fixed costs, *see under* Costs
Fixed exchange rates, 640–43, 667, 673
Fixed incomes, creeping inflation and people with, 239
Fixed input, **121**
Flexible exchange rates, 638–40, 642–43, 672–73
Floating of currencies, 655, 667, 673
FMC Corporation, 98
Food programs, 587
Food stamp program, 80, 86, 587, 589
Ford, Henry, 412, 512–13, 550
Ford Foundation, 684
Ford Motor Company, 503, 513, 550
Forecasting, economic, 9, 218–28
business fluctuations (cycles), 217–18
by Federal Reserve System, 289, 291
gross national product, 218–20
leading indicators in, 218
models and, 19–20, 22, 217
net national product, 217–18, 247, 248, 252
short-range, 18, 289
Foreign aid programs
Soviet Union, 693, 694
United States, 86, 664–66, 668, 690–94, 711
World Bank, 666, 693–94
Foreign trade, *see* International trade
Forrester, Jay, 352
Fortune (magazine), 157, 219, 528, 534
Fox, Karl, 51, 409
Fractional-reserve banking, **258**, 258–60
creation of money and, 262–72
France, 77, 670, 693
economic growth in, 326, 338, 348, 349
Free reserves, **285**, 293
Free resources, **34**
Freedom in American economy, 32, 72
Freedom of choice, capitalism and, **42**
Freeman, Orville, 88
Freund, William, 227
Frictional unemployment, **134**
Friedland, Claire, 493
Friedman, Milton, 71, 163, 196, 288, 303, 321, 587, 675
Federal Reserve policy rule proposed by, 293–94, 302
monetary theory of, 247–48, 254
on Phillips curve, 313
Friend, Irwin, 222
Friend-Taubman model, 222–25
Frisch, Ragnar, 19, 215
Full employment (4% unemployment), 3*n*
budget, **202**, 202–3
budget balancing policies and, 201, 202
business cycles and, 209–11, 216, 217
economic growth and, 343, 344, 357
government role in bringing about, 3, 74, 104
monetary policy and, 278, 290
money supply and, 278
potential and actual gross national product and, 154–55
stable prices with, achievement of, *see* Stabilization, economic
without inflation, *see* Stabilization, economic
Full-employment budget, **202**, 202–3
Fulton, Robert, 351
Functional finance, **202**

Gaines, Tilford C., 227
Gainsbrugh, Martin, 227
Galbraith, John Kenneth, 206, 327, 534
on advertising and consumer behavior, 72, 95, 119, 422–23
countervailing-power concept of, **514**
on government spending, 95–96
Hayek on, 422–24
on large corporations and "technostructure," 119–20
on technological change, 520–22
on wage and price controls, 314
Games, theory of, **506**, 506–7
Gary, Elbert, 510, 549
Gas, energy crisis and, 98–99

General Electric, 351, 491
antitrust action against (1961), 526–27
econometric model of, 227
as oligopoly, 504–5, 509–11
value-added and claims against output of, 148–49
General equilibrium, **597**
General equilibrium analysis, **596,** 596–97; *see also* Input-output analysis
General Motors, 50, 419, 503
bonds of, 117
financial statements of, 128–29
history of, 112–13
organizational chart of, 112, 113
pricing system of, 511, 513
United Automobile Workers and, 550
George, Henry, 570
Germany, 529
inflation after World War I in, 238–39, 250, 661
See also West Germany
Giannini, Amadeo Peter, 256
Gift taxes, 581
Gill, Richard, 685
GNP, *see* Gross national product
Gold
fractional-reserve banking and, 259–60
money not backed by, 235, 237
Gold-exchange standard, "two-tier," **643,** 643–44, 668–70, 672
Special Drawing Rights and, 670
Gold reserves
decrease in United States of, 643–44, 668–69
international adjustments and, 670
liquidity shortage and, 671–72
Gold standard, **637,** 653
exchange rates under, 637–39, 643, 661
money supply and, 241
Goldberg, Arthur, 318
Goldberg, Marilyn Power, 594
Goldman, M., 371
Gompers, Samuel, 548–49
Goods and services
in balance of payments, 646–47
capital goods, **39,** 39–41, 167
final, *see* Final goods and services
government purchases of, **152,** 152–54; *see* also Government expenditures
intermediate goods, **142,** 145
net exports of, **152**
public goods, **70,** 74–75, 96–97
Goodyear, Charles, 351
Gordon, David, 713
Gordon, Robert, 313, 316*n*
Gosbank, 704
Gosplan, 702–3
Government, 69–91
agriculture and role of, 81–90
capitalism and role of, 41–42, 44–45
changes in views of responsibilities of, 79–80
economic growth as policy of, 326–28
expenditures by, *see* Government expenditures
federal, *see* Federal government
full employment and role of, 3, 74, 104
legal, social, and competitive framework as responsibility of, 72–73
local, *see* Local government
mixed capitalist system and, 44–45
price system and, 44–45, 70–71
production of goods and services by, 75–76
purchases of goods and services by, **152,** 152–54; *see also* Government expenditures
redistribution of income by, **44,** 70, 71, 73
regulatory functions of, 3–4, 45, 73, 79–80
Smith's views on role of, 18
stabilization of economy and, 74
state, *see* State government
unemployment and, 3, 74, 134–35, 140–41
what functions should be performed by, 71–72
Government bonds, 236–37, 257; *see also* Bonds—federal government; Bonds—state and local government; Government securities
Government expenditures
business cycles (fluctuations) and, 211
consumer behavior model and allocation of, 399–401
on defense, 78, 97–98, 198–99, 211
deficit spending, **194,** 199–203, 302
as destabilizing force, 211
forecasting gross national product and, 219, 222–24
Galbraith on, 95–96
gross private domestic investment and, 152–54
inflation and, 192–93
in less developed countries, 680, 685
money supply and, 246*n*
net national product equilibrium and, 186–89
Nixon's policy on, 10
as percentage of total output (1929–1970), 76–77
on research and development (1945–1970), 351
size of, 76–78
social balance and, 95–97
surplus, 200–3
unemployment and, 192, 193
Vietnam war and, 199
wars and, 153, 154
See also Budget, government; Fiscal policy
Government securities
short-term, 261
Treasury–Federal Reserve relations and sale of, 290–91
Government transfer payments, **77,** **143,** 150; *see also* Social Security; Unemployment compensation; Welfare programs
Great Britain (England; United Kingdom), 77, 580, 693, 694
balance of payments problem of, 655
banks in, 242, 243
democratic socialism in, 712
economic growth in, 335, 338, 348, 349
International Monetary Fund and, 667–68, 670

Ricardo's views on economy of, 335
in Smith's time, 16
United States trade with, 614, 615, 620–22
See also Pound, British
Great Crash (1929), 117–18, 285, 294
Great Depression of 1930s, 39, 73, 74, 82, 113, 178
classical economics and, 162
deficit spending by government and, 200
exchange rates and, 643
gross national product gap and, 353
Keynesian views and, 161, 300, 353
monetary policy and, 294, 300
unemployment in, 2, 134, 135, 162, 200
Great Leap Forward, Chinese, 709
Griliches, Zvi, 512
Gross national expenditure, **151,** 151–53
Gross national income, **148,** 148–50
Gross national product (GNP), **141,** 141–44
business cycles and, 209, 210
consumption and, relationship between (1950–1970), 221
disposable income and, 152, 153
economic growth and percentage of invested, by country, 338
economic growth measured by rate of growth of, 326, 354
estimates of, 142
forecasting, 218–28
gross national expenditure and, 151
gross national income and, 148
growth of, *see* Economic growth
limitations of, 146–47
measurement of, 142–43
net national product and, 146
per capita real, as economic growth measure, 326, 354, 355
potential, **154**
potential versus actual, 154–55, 353
price changes and adjustment of, 143–44
value-added and, 145
Gross private domestic investment, **152,** 152–54
Growth, economic, *see* Economic growth
Guevara, Ernesto Che, 713
Gurley, John, 710

Hamilton, Alexander, 630
Hammerstein, Oscar, 64
Hargreaves, James, 358
Harrod, Sir Roy, 338*n*
Harrod-Domar growth model, 338*n*
Hartke-Burke bill, 633
Hayek, Friedrich von, 422–24
Heady, Earl, 434, 435
Heilbroner, Robert, 14, 331*n*
Heller, Walter W., 24, 105, 194*n*, 198, 227, 293*n*, 303, 673
on zero economic growth, 373
Hemingway, Ernest, 240
Heraclitus, 57
Hercules, 6
Hicks, Sir John, 19, 213, 307, 519
High school dropouts, program to reduce, 94–95
Highway user taxes, 81
Hinduism, 683
Historical cost, **492**
Hitch, Charles, 400
Hitler, Adolf, 16
Hoffa, James, 553
Holmes, Sherlock, 626
Home construction industry, 295
Hoover Dam, 76
Horizontal mergers, **504,** 527, 528*n*
Hotelling, Harold, 604–5
House of Representatives, United States, taxation and, 99
Houthakker, Hendrik, 635
Hudson River, 371
Human capital
economic growth and, 339
less developed countries' investment in, 683
rate of return from investing in, 568–69
Hume, David, 638, 640, 643
Hunt Commission report, 244*n*
Hutcheson, William, 549*n*, 551
Huxley, Thomas, 228
HYGAS pilot plant, 98

IBM (International Business Machines), 11, 340
"Ice," 64, 65
Implicit costs, **436**
Import quotas, **627,** 627–29
American, 614, 615
net exports and, 152
Incidence of taxes, **581**
Income
break-even, **588**
demand for commodities and, *see* Income elasticity of demand
distribution of, *see* Distribution of income
fixed, creeping inflation and people with, 239
gross national, **148,** 148–50
inequality of, 576–83, 679, 706
national, **150,** 150–51, 350
per capita, *see* Per capita income
personal, *see* Personal income
redistribution of, *see* Redistribution of income
savings and, classical view, 159
See also Wages
Income effect, **418**
Income elasticity of demand, 420, 420–21
Income taxes
as automatic stabilizer, 196
corporate
double taxation, 102, 116
general principles and structure, 101–2
income inequality, 581
1968 surcharge, 199, 208
1970–1973 revenues, 80, 81
personal
evasion, 101
general principles and structure, 100–1
income inequality, 580
legal avoidance by the rich, 100, 101
negative, 587–88
1970–1973 revenues, 80, 81
state and local finance and, 104
tax reform, 103
Income velocity of money, 249*n*
Incomes policy, 316–17, 320; *see also* Wage and price guidelines

Increasing cost industry, **481**
India, 77, 678, 680–83, 686–94
  Five-Year Plans of, 688–89, 694
Indifference curves, consumers', **391,** 391–96, 416, 601–4
Indirect business taxes, 148, 149
Individual demand curve, 415–18
Industrial concentration, **523,** 523–24, 529
Industrial extension service, 357–58
Industrial management, technological change and, 341–42
Industrialization
  in China, 709
  of less developed countries, 686–88
Industrialized nations, economic growth in, 334, 338, 354
Industry demand curve, 419–20
Inefficiency, product transformation curve and, 38
"Infant industry" argument, 630, 631
Infinitely elastic demand curve, price elasticity of, 411, **420**
Inflation, 104, 133, **137,** 137–41
  automatic stabilizers and, 196
  balance of payments deficit and, 651, 671, 672
  budget balancing policies and, 201–2
  business cycles and, 210, 211, 216, 217
  in Civil War, 237, 239, 308
  common stocks and, 117
  cost-push, **308,** 309, 314–16, 520, 558
  creeping, **238,** 239–40
  demand-pull, **308,** 309, 319
  fiscal policy and, 192–93, 197–98, 203, 319
  full employment without, *see* Stabilization, economic
  functional finance policy and, 202
  in Germany after World War I, 238–39, 250, 661
  Kennedy-Johnson wage-price guidelines and, 317–19
  late 1960s, 319; *see also* Nixon's policy on (*below*)
  in less developed countries, 680
  monetary policy and, 278, 279, 285–91, 293, 294, 300, 319
  money supply and, 250, 278, 285–89
  money's value and, 238–40
  1954–1955, 288
  1956–1958, 309
  1965–1966, 286
  Nixon's policy on, 3, 19, 197, 204–5, 288–89, 315
  Phillips curve and relationship of output per manhour to, 309, 311
  policy choices on, 140–41
  in Revolutionary War, 239, 308
  runaway, **238,** 238–39
  unemployment and, 2–3, 138–41, 309–13
  Vietnam war and, 199, 203, 211, 286, 308, 319
  wage and price controls to reduce, *see* Wage and price controls
  during World War II, 237–38, 294
  after World War II, 137–38
Inheritance taxes, 41, 100, 581
Injunctions against labor unions, **548,** 549
Inland Steel Corporation, 318
Innovations, technological, *see* Technological innovations
Innovators
  profits and, **572**
  technological, **340**
Input-output analysis, **597–98,** 597–600, 688
Inputs, **121**
  average product of an, **426,** 426–27
  fixed, **121**
  in linear programming, 463
  marginal product of, **426,** 426–27, 431–33, 601, 603
  optimal combinations of, 428–35
  primary, **565**
  production function of, *see* Production function
  in short run and long run, 121–22
  variable, **121**
  See also specific inputs
Installment contracts, 284
Institute of Gas Technology, 98
Insurance companies, 243
Interest, **562**
Interest rate, **563**
  capital budgeting and, 567–68
  classical economists' view of, 159
  determinants of, 563–65
  equilibrium net national product and, IS and LM curves, 305–8
  on federal funds, 286*n*
  on Federal Reserve loans to banks, *see* Discount rate
  functions of the, 565
  investment function and, 245–47
  monetary policy and, 278, 284–85, 293, 295
  money demand and, 244–45
  money supply and, 245–47, 278, 299, 302
  on mortgages, 295
  1958–1959 rise in, 288
  1966 increase in, 286
  Nixon's monetary policy and, 289
  pure, **563,** 563–65
  on savings and time deposits, Regulation Q ceilings, 283–84
Intermediate goods, **142,** 145
Internal Revenue Service, 99
International adjustments, 670, 672
International Bank for Reconstruction and Development, 666, 693–94
International Business Machines (IBM), 11, 340
International Development Agency, 666, 694
International finance, 660–75
International Finance Corporation, 666, 694
International Harvester, 526
International Ladies Garment Workers Union, 554
International lending, 656–57
International Monetary Fund (IMF), 643, 666–68, 670
International monetary reserves, 669–72
International Nickel Company, 484
International trade, 613–35
  America's, 614, 615, 620–21, 624, 631–33

economies of scale and, 623
fallacies in, 630–31
individual markets and, 621–23
national defense and, 628
net national product as affected by, 661–63
specialization and, 614, 616–21
tariffs in, **625**, 625–33
technological change and, 623–25
See also Balance of merchandise trade; Balance of payments; Exchange rates
Interstate Commerce Commission, 79
Inventions, 215; *see also* Technological innovations
Inventories
acceleration principle and, 213, 214
investment in
business cycles, 211, 213, 214
forecasting GNP, 219, 222–24
Inventory cycles, **214**
Investment, **151–52, 159**
business cycles and, 210–16
classical economists' views on, 159, 161
and commercial banks, 243, 257, 259, 261, 263–72, 274–75
determinants of net, 167–68
economic growth and, 336–39, 357
in education, *see under* Education
expectations of businessmen and, 167–68, 211
and financial institutions, 243–44
forecasting gross national product and, 219–20
gross private domestic, **152**, 152–54
in human capital, *see under* Human capital
induced, 181–82
interest rates and, 245–47
inventory
business cycles, 211, 213, 214
forecasting GNP, 219, 222–24
in less developed countries, 680–81, 689–90
money supply and, 245–47
net, 152, 167
net national product equilibrium level and, 168–82, 186–88, 305, 306
on plant and equipment, *see* Plant and equipment, expenditure on
sales as determinant of, 167–68; *see also* Acceleration principle
savings and, 159, 161–62, 172–73
technological change and, 167
See also Capital formation
Investment bankers, 243
Investment function, 245–47, 278
IS curve, 305–8
Isocost curves, **432**, 432–34, 466–68
Isoquants, 429–35, **430**, 466–68
Italy, 313, 326, 338, 348, 349, 668

Jackson, Henry, 99
Jallow, Raymond, 227
Japan, 77, 529, 694
economic growth in, 326, 338, 344–45, 348, 349
United States balance of payments deficit and, 650–51
United States trade with, 614, 615
Johnson, Lyndon B., 19, 80, 94, 226
balance of payments problem and, 673
discount rate increase opposed by, 286
Vietnam war and, 198, 199, 286
wage-price guidelines of, 317–19
Johnson, Robert, 227
Johnson, Samuel, 120, 586
Joint Economic Committee of Congress, 194, 294
Justice, Department of, antitrust laws and, 525–28

Kahn, Herman, 364
Kaiser Steel Corporation, 318
Kaysen, Carl, 512, 527
Kekish, Bohdan, 227
Kennedy, John F. (Kennedy administration), 16, 80, 88, 226, 671
balance of payments problem and, 673
economic growth policy of, 24, 327, 347, 354, 357–58, 706
economic models used by, 24
on education (1962), 358
incomes policy (wage-price guidelines) of, 317–19
monetary policy of, 288
steel price increase and (1962), 317–18, 510
tax cut urged by (1962–1963), 24, 198, 288
trade policy of, 633
unemployment and, 24
Kennedy, Mrs. John F., *see* Onassis, Mrs. Aristotle
Kennedy-Johnson guidelines, 317–19
"Kennedy round" negotiations, 633
Kerr, Clark, 552
Keynes, John Maynard, 74, 118, 161–64, 178, 353, 354, 667
biography of, 161
on economic future, 363–64
fiscal policy and, 193, 300
The General Theory of Employment, Interest, and Money, 161–63
liquidity preference theory of, 564–65
Marx and, 161
Keynesian economics (New Economists), 163
fiscal policy and, 193, 300
Great Depression and, 161, 300, 353
monetarists and, 247, 252
money supply–NNP relationship in view of, 245–47, 278, 299
Keynesian models
for determination of national output, 161–63, 247, 252
for forecasting gross national product, 218–20
money's role in, 245–47
Khrushchev, Nikita S., 355
Killian, James, 119
Kinney, R. G., 527
Klaman, Saul, 227

Klein, Lawrence, 178*n*, 224, 225
Kneese, Allen, 374–75, 376*n*
Knight, Frank, 572
Korean war, 211, 286, 315
Krause, Lawrence, 624
Kreps, Juanita, 321
Kuznets, Simon, 19, 142, 210*n*, 686*n*, 696
Kuznets cycles, 210*n*

Labor (labor force) (workers), **34, 538**
  average product of, **330,** 426–27
  capital available to Americans, 45
  displacement of, 361–62
  equilibrium price and quantity of, 542–44
  exploitation of, 27
  firm's demand curve for, 539–41, **540**
  in less developed countries, 680, 683, 684
  marginal product of, **330,** 334, 426–27
  market demand curve for, **540–41,** 540–43, 556
  market supply curve for, **541,** 541–43, 555–56
  mobility of, 311, 314
  monopsony and quantity of, 547
  1920–1970 size of, 349
  occupational composition of, 538
  perfectly competitive firm's utilization of, 538–39
  productivity of, *see* Productivity of labor
  training or education of, *see* Training or education of workers
  See also Black workers; Class struggle; Employment; Labor unions; Older workers; Unemployment; Wages; White-collar workers; Women workers; Young workers
Labor legislation
  1930s–1940s, 549–50
  post–World War II, 552, 554
Labor party, British, 712
Labor unions, 547–59
  big, pros and cons of, 558–59
  collective bargaining by, 548, 549, **556–57,** 556–58
  cost-push inflation and, 308, 315, 558
  history of, 548–51
  incomes policy and, 316–17
  internal problems of, 552
  Kennedy-Johnson guidelines and, 317–19
  market power of, inflation and reduction of, 315
  membership of, recent trends, 554–55
  national, 547–48; *see also* AFL-CIO
  in Soviet Union, 706
  strikes by, 550, 552, 554, 555, **557,** 557–58
  technological change and, 353
  wage flexibility and, 162
  wage increases and, 555–58
  wage increases' relationship to unemployment and, 309
Lagging series, **218**
Lamb, Charles, 541, 562
Lampman, Robert, 585
Land, **34, 569**
  planning of use of urban, 607–8
Land-diversion program, 88–89
Land reform, 685
Landrum-Griffin Act (1959), 554
Latin America
  population growth in, 334, 681–83
  United States trade with, 614, 615
Leading indicators, **218**
Leading series, **218**
Legal reserve requirements, 260–61, 274*n*, 283
Legal system, 72
Leisure, 147, 326
Lend-lease program, 663
Lenin, V. I., 701
Leo XIII, Pope, 134
Leontief, Wassily, 19, 597, 598, 600
Lerner, Abba, 604
Less developed countries, 5, 676–96, **677**
  capital formation in, 679–81
  economic growth in, 327, 685–88
  entrepreneurship, social institutions, and natural resources in, 684–85
  government role in, 686
  population growth in, 333–34, 681–83
  Public Law 480 and, 86
  technology in, 682–85
  United States aid to, 86, 665, 690–93
  World Bank and, 666
Lewis, John L., 549, 551
Liabilities
  current, **124**
  long-term, **124**
Liberals, government's economic role in view of, 70–72
Liberman, Y., 708
Lincoln, Abraham, 115, 631
Linear programming, **462,** 462–69, 688
Liquidity preference function, **244,** 244–45
  interest rate and, 565
Liquidity shortage, 671–72
Liquidity-trap range, **307**
LM curve, 305–6
Loans
  by commercial banks, 243
    lending decision, case study, 261–62
    consumer loans, 257
    creation of money by banks, 263–72
    excess reserves, 268–69, 274–75
    fractional reserve banking, 259
    monetary policy and private decisions, 295
    safety of the banks, 261
  by Federal Reserve to member banks, 284
  international, 656–57, 666
Local government
  bonds issued by, 103, 257
  expenditures of, 78–79, 152
  federal grants to, 104–5
  property tax administration by, 102–3
  revenue sharing and, 105
  tax revenues of (1970), 81
Lockheed Aircraft Corporation, 76
Lockheed C5A transport plane, 98
Lockout, **557**

Lone Star National Bank of Houston, 261–62
Long run, **121**, 121–22
Long-term liabilities, 124
Lorenz curve, **577**, 577–79

McClellan Committee, 552, 554
McCormick, Cyrus, 351
McDougall, Duncan, 104, 205*n*
McGovern, George, 16, 103
Machinists Union, 547
McKean, Roland, 400, 403
McKenzie, Lionel, 597
McKinney, George W., Jr., 227
Magnavox, 11
Maisel, Sherman, 281, 286, 297
Malthus, Thomas, 331–37, 353, 354, 364, 682
  on population, 332
Management, 343
  industrial, 341–42
  in Soviet Union, 704
Management science, 469
Manager of the Open Market Account, 281
Mandatory Oil Import Quota, 628
Manpower, *see* Labor
Mansfield, Edwin, 340, 521, 540, 624
Manufacturing costs, in profit and loss statement, 125–26
Mao Tse-tung, 709
MAPCAST, 227
Margin requirements for stock purchases, **284**
Marginal cost, short-run, **441**
  input decisions and, 441–44, 449
  in monopolistic competition, 499–501, 520
  of monopoly, 487–91, 518, 519
  output determination and, 454–59
Marginal cost function (curve), **444**
  input decisions and, 443, 444, 448
  for oligopoly, 505
  output determination and, 455–56, 459, 460
Marginal cost pricing, **604**, 604–5
Marginal product of capital, **336**, 336–37
Marginal product of inputs, **426**, 426–27, 431–33; *see also* Diminishing marginal returns, law of
  optimal allocation of inputs and, 601, 603
Marginal product of labor, **330**, 426–27
  technological change and, 334
Marginal propensity to consume, 164–66, **165**
  multiplier and, 176–77
Marginal propensity to save (MPS), **166**, 166–67
  multiplier and, 174–75, 177
Marginal returns, law of diminishing, *see* Diminishing marginal returns, law of
Marginal revenue, **486**
  in monopolistic competition, 499–501
  in monopoly, 486–91
  in oligopoly, 505
Marginal tax rate, **101**
Marginal utility, **398**, 398–400, 433–34, 442–43
  diminishing, law of, **399**, 418
  optimal resource allocation and, 601, 603
Market concentration ratio, **523**, 523–24, 528, 529
Market demand, 404–24
Market demand curves, **50**, 50–52, 57–60, 405–6
  individual demand curve and, 417–18
  for labor, **540–41**, 540–43, 556
  measurement of, 406–8
  monopoly and, 485–86
  in perfect competition, 477, 478, 480, 481
  shifts in, 51–52
Market period, **477**
Market structure or organization
  antitrust policy and, 527–28
  See also Monopolistic competition; Monopoly; Monopsony; Oligopoly; Perfect competition
Market supply curves, **52**, 54–55, 57–59
  firm's supply curves and, 458–60
  for labor, **541**, 541–43, 555–56
  measurement of, 460–62
  in perfect competition, 477–78, 480–82
  price elasticity of supply and, 461–62
Marketing, research and development and, 341–42
Marketing research, 406
Markets, **50**
  capitalism and, 42
  demand side of, 50–52; *see also* Market demand curves
  product, **65**, 65–66
  resource, **65**, 66
  supply side of, 52, 54–55; *see also* Market supply curves
Markups, in cost-plus pricing, 511
Marshall, Alfred, 159, 384
Marshall, George, 664
Marshall Plan, 664
Martin, William McChesney, 198, 279, 286, 287, 297
Marx, Karl, 353, 364, 697–701, 712, 713
  on capitalism, 699
  capitalism's collapse predicted by, 160, 354, 700–1
  class struggle theory of, 698, 700, 701
  Das Kapital, 160, 698
  future as viewed by, 700–1
  Keynes and, 161
  on profits, 573
  technology in view of, 160, 358
  unemployment in view of, 160–61, 358
Marxism, 27
Mason, Edward, 528
Mass Transportation Commission of Massachusetts, 22–24, 407
Mauchly, John, 340
Maximization of profits, 120–21
  input decisions and, 431–32
  output determination and, 453–58, 489–90
Meany, George, 10
Measurement, economic, 20–22
Medicare, 586
Mergers, **504**
  antitrust laws and, 525, 527–29
  oligopoly and, 504–5
Mexico, 77

Michigan econometric model, 225
Military-industrial complex, 97–98
Mill, John Stuart, 159
Miller-Tydings Act (1937), 532
Mills, Edwin, 382
Mishan, E. J., 327, 355, 365
Mitchell, Wesley C., 218
Mixed capitalist system, 44–45
Models, economic, **19,** 19–26
- econometric, **220,** 220–26, 248
- economic stabilization policies and, 299
- forecasting based on, 19–20, 22, 217
- Keynesian, *see* Keynesian models
- measurement and, 20–22
- monetarist, 252
- profit maximization as basis of, 120–21
- quantification of, **22**

Monetarists, 254, 285
- Keynesians and, 247, 252, 298–300, 302–4, 307–8
- money supply–net national product relationship in view of, 247, 252, 301, 302
- money's role in view of, 300–1
- reasons for growing acceptance of views of, 247–48, 300
- rule to govern monetary policy advocated by, 293–94, 302
- *See also* Friedman, Milton; Monetary theory

Monetary base, **285,** 293
Monetary policy, 18–19, 277–97, **278**
- advantages and disadvantages of, 294–95
- aims and role of, 278–79
- balance of payments and, 288*n*, 671
- business fluctuations and, 216
- easy, 284–85, 290, 293
- economic stabilization and, 298–300, 302–4
- expansionary, IS and LM curves, 307–8
- fiscal policy and, 278, 286, 293–95, 298–300
- inflation and, 278, 279, 285–91, 293, 294, 300, 319
- lag between changes in policy and effects on economy, 290, 291, 293, 300
- makers of, 279
- 1950s–1960s, 286, 288
- of Nixon administration, 288–89
- private decision making and, 295
- problems in formulating, 289–90
- rule proposed to govern, 293–94, 302, 304
- tight, 284–85, 290, 293
- tools of, 279–84
- unemployment and, 313
- wage-price guidelines and, 319
- *See also under* Federal Reserve Board; Federal Reserve System

Monetary reserves, international, 669–72
Monetary theory, 252
- Friedman and, 247–48, 254
- *See also* Monetarists

Money, 46
- circular flows of products and, 65–66
- creation by banks of, 262–73
- demand for, 244–45
- demand curve for, 244–45; *see also* Liquidity preference function
- easy, 278, 286; *see also* Monetary policy—easy
- gold not a backing for, 235, 237
- income velocity of, 249*n*
- inflation and depreciation of, 137
- as medium of exchange, 234
- monetarist view of role of, 300–1; *see also under* Monetarists; Monetary theory
- near-, 236–37, **237**
- paper, *see* Currency
- quantity of, *see* Money supply
- quantity theory of, 247–52, 299
- as standard of value, 234
- as store of value, 234
- supply of, *see* Money supply
- tight, 278, 286; *see also* Monetary policy—tight
- transactions velocity of, 249*n*
- value of, 237–40
- velocity of circulation of, **248,** 248–52, 300–2, 304
- *See also* Coins; Currency; Demand deposits; Monetary policy; *and specific currencies*

Money supply (quantity of money), **236**
- asset holdings and increase in, 304
- banking system and, 255–76
- central banks and, 242
- creation of money by banks and, 266–68, 270–72
- crude quantity theory of prices and, 249–50, **250**
- determinants of, 240–41
- Friedman's views on, 247–48, 293–94
- full employment and, 278
- growth at fixed rate proposed for, 294, 302
- inflation and, 239, 250, 278, 285, 286, 289
- interest rate and, 245–47, 278, 299, 302
- Keynesian view of relationship of net national product and, 245–47, 278, 299, 300, 302
- monetary base and, 285
- as monetary policy indicator, 285, 293
- narrow versus broad definitions of, **236**
- net national product and, 245–52, 278, 299–302
- 1947–1972 behavior of, 235–36
- 1950s–1960s monetary policies and, 288
- Nixon's monetary policies and, 289
- quantity theory of, 247–52, 299
- reserves of banking system and, 260, 268–73, 278–81, 283
- runaway inflation and, 239
- unemployment and, 240
- velocity of circulation of, **248,** 248–52
- *See also* Monetary policy

Monopolistic competition, 497–503, **498,** 519, 520
Monopoly, **483,** 483–94
- causes of, 484–85
- defense of, 520–22
- demand curve under, 485–86
- economic power and, 522–23

income distribution and, 519
marginal revenue under, 486–89
misallocation of resources by, 518–19
monopolistic competition compared to, 498, 501–2
natural, **484,** 484–85
oligopoly compared to, 498
patent system and, 530–31
perfect competition compared to, 490–92
price and output under, 486–92
public regulation of, 492–94
technological change and, 519–22, 527
Monopoly banks, creation of money by, 265, 270–71
Monopsony, **546,** 546–47
Moral suasion, **283**
Morgan, J. P., 504
Morgenthau, Hans, 696
Morse, Samuel, 351
Mortgages, 285, 295
Mueller, Willard, 522
Multinational firms, 624–25, 654
Multiplier, the, 174–81, 175, 304
acceleration principle and, 213–15
algebraic interpretation of, 175–77
application of, after World War II, 178–81
consumption function shifts and, 179–81, 188
geometric formulation of, 174–75
government expenditure and, 188
marginal propensity to save and, 174–75
spending process and, 177–78
Musgrave, Peggy, 93*n*, 107
Musgrave, Richard, 93*n*, 107, 581
Mutual savings banks, 243
My Fair Lady, 64–65

Nader, Ralph, 401–3
National Advisory Commission on Rural Poverty, 82
National Aeronautics and Space Administration, 97
National banks, 241; *see also* Commercial banks
National Bureau of Economic Research, 218
National debt, 105–8, 200
National defense, *see* Defense, national
National expenditure, **151**
gross, **151,** 151–53
National income, **150,** 150–51, 350
National income accounts, 142
National Labor Relations Board, 549
National output
determination of, 158–84
classical view, 159–62
consumption function, 163–65
equilibrium level, *see* Net national product—equilibrium level of
investment determinants, 167–68
Keynes's views, 161–63
marginal propensity to consume, 164–66
product transformation curve, *see* Product transformation curve
saving function and marginal propensity to save, 166–67
efficient combinations of, *see* Product transformation curve
fluctuations in, *see* Business cycles
gap between actual and potential, economic growth and, 343–44, 357, 358
inflation and, 137
inputs' relationship to potential, *see* Aggregate production function
See also Gross national product; Net national product
National product, *see* Gross national product; Net national product
National Steel Corporation, 509
Natural gas industry, 494
Natural monopoly, **484,** 484–85
Nazism, 16
Near-money, 236–37, **237**
Negative income tax, 587–88
Nerlove, Marc, 462
Net exports of goods and services, **152**
Net investment, 152, 167
Net national product (NNP), **146**
business fluctuations and, 211, 213, 214, 216–18
businessmen's expectations and, 211
capital-output ratio and increase in full-employment, 338
determination of, 158–84
as economic growth measure, 326
equilibrium level of, determination of, 168–82, 186–92, 245–47, 305–8
forecasting, 217–18, 247, 248, 252
foreign trade and, 661–63
inventory investment and, 214
limitations of, 146–47
monetary policy and, 278, 299
money supply and, 245–52, 278, 299–302
velocity of circulation of money and, 248–52
See also Gross national product
Net tax rate, **581**
Net worth, **124**
Netherlands, the, 327, 580
Neumann, John von, 340, 506*n*
Neutral nations, 327
New Deal, 549–50
New Economic Policy, Nixon's, 204, 289
New Economists, *see* Keynesian economics
New York City, 81, 94
New York Stock Exchange, 117
New York Times, 11
Newton, Sir Isaac, 15
Nigeria, 77, 78
Nixon, Richard M. (Nixon administration), 16, 163, 226, 710
balance of payments problem and, 652, 653, 655, 673
banking policy of, 244*n*
energy program of, 98–99
exchange rate policy of, 644, 652, 653, 655, 669
fiscal policy of, 204–5
foreign trade policy of, 10
full-employment budget adopted by, 202, 203
government-spending policy of, 10, 204

inflation and, 3, 19, 197, 204–5, 288–89, 315
monetary policy of, 288–89
New Economic Policy of, 204, 289
oil-import policy of, 628, 629
revenue sharing and, 105
tax policy of, 204
unemployment and, 141, 204
wage and price controls of, 3, 204, 205, 289, 315–16
"workfare" program of, 588–89
NNP, *see* Net national product
Nobel Prize in economics, 19
Noise pollution, 370
Noncompeting groups, **544**
Nonprice competition, 511–12
Nonwhites, racial discrimination against, 589–91
Nordhaus, William, 147
Normative economics, **26**
Norris-LaGuardia Act (1932), 549
Norway, 327
Notes payable, **124**
Noyes, Guy E., 227
Nylon, 167, 215

Office of Coal Research, 97–99
Office of Economic Opportunity, 587, 589
Office of Management and Budget, 93, 194, 201*n*
Office of Science and Technology, 99
Office of Tax Analysis, 99
Office of the Tax Legislative Counsel, 99
Official tier for gold, **644,** 669
Oil-import quotas, 628–29
Oil industry, 103–4, 352, 367
Okun, Arthur, 19, 25, 137, 154, 155, 194*n*, 198
Old-age insurance, 586
Old people, creeping inflation and, 239
Older workers, displacement of, 361–62
O'Leary, James, 227
Oligopoly, 497–98, **498,** 503–14, 519–20
differentiated, **498**
pure, **498**
Onassis, Aristotle, 49
Onassis, Mrs. Aristotle, 49
Open Market Account, Manager of the, 281
Open market operations, 279–81, 285
Open shop, **557**
Operations research, 469
Opportunity cost, **435**
Optimal input decisions, 425–51
Optimal output decisions, 452–75
Organization for Economic Cooperation and Development, 343
Organization of Petroleum Exporting Countries (OPEC), 654
Ortner, Robert, 227
Output
determination of
by cartels, 508–9
by economic system, 34, 37–38
by firms, 453–60
linear programming, **462,** 462–69
by monopolistic competition, 499–503
by monopoly, 486–92, 518–19
national, 158–84
by oligopoly, 514
by perfect competition, 477–80
government spending as percentage of total (1929–1970), 76–77
gross national income and claims on, 148, 149
national, *see* National output
optimal decisions on, 452–75
per capita, 353–54, 356
per man, growth of, 338
per manhour, 309, 311, 342; *see also* Productivity of labor
production function and rate of, 122–23
restriction of agricultural, 85–89
taxes as percentage of total, for various countries, 77
total cost per unit of, Phillips curve, 309, 311

Pabst Brewing Company, 529–30
Packard automobile plant, 361, 362
"Paper gold," 670
Parity, **84,** 84–85
Parker Pen Company, 406
Parks, Robert, 227
Partial equilibrium analysis, **596**
Partners, "silent," 115
Partnerships, **115**
Passell, Peter, 352, 355
Patent system, 530–31
Pay Board, 315, 316
Payoff, **506**
Payoff matrix, **506,** 506–7
Peaks of business cycles, **209,** 210, 218
Pechman, Joseph, 99*n*, 105, 207
Peck, Merton J., 98
Per capita gross national product, as economic growth measure, 326, 354, 355
Per capita income
demand curves and, 52, 53
distribution of, *see* Distribution of income
growth of, 24, 35–36, 39–40, 44, 61–62
of less developed countries, 677, 678, 683
of selected countries, 33
Per capita output, 353–54, 356
Perfect competition, **50,** 308–9, 475–83, **476**
allocation of resources under, 482–83, 491–92, 603–4, 606–7
constant, increasing, and decreasing cost industries in, 480–81
monopolistic competition compared to, 498, 501–2
monopoly compared to, 490–92, 520
oligopoly compared to, 498, 511–14, 520
price and output under, 477–80
welfare maximization and, 603–4
See also Firms—perfectly competitive
Personal income, **150,** 150–51
allocation of, aggregate data for United States, 389–90
disposable, *see* Disposable income
Personal income tax, *see* Income taxes—personal
Peterson, Peter, 655
Phase IV program, 316

Phelps, Edmund, 313
Phillips, A. W., 309
Phillips curve, **309,** 309–14
Piece rates in Soviet Union, 706
Pigou, A. C., 159, 582
Planned economies, 7; *see also* Communist economies; Socialist economies
Planning, economic
in less developed countries, 688–89
in Soviet Union, 701–5, 707
Planning horizon, 444
Planning-Programming-Budgeting System (PPB System), 94
Plant and equipment, expenditure (investment) on
economic growth and, 336–39, 357, 358
forecasting gross national product and, 219, 222–24
Kennedy policy on, 358
Ricardo's capital-formation theory on, 336, 337
tax credits for, 357
See also Capital formation
Platt, Robert, 11
Player, **506**
Politics
economic stabilization and, 299–300
taxation and, 198
Pollution, *see* Environmental pollution
Poor, the
antipoverty programs and, 586–87
characteristics of, 585–86
national debt and, 108
sales taxes and, 103
urban land use and, 607
See also Poverty
Poor countries, *see* Less developed countries
Poor Laws, 325
Population growth, 18
economic growth and, 331–37, 349, 354
in less developed countries, 333–34, 681–83
Malthus's theory of, 331–37
Zero, 373–74
Positive economics, **24,** 26
Pound, British, exchange rate for, 637, 644–45, 667–68
Poverty, 575, **583–84,** 583–87
economic growth and, 325, 354–56
elimination of, 4–5
racial discrimination and, 589–91
rural, 82, 89
social insurance and, 586
See also Poor, the
PPB system, 94
Precautionary demand for money, **244**
Predictions, economic, *see* Forecasting, economic
Preferred stock, **117,** 118
President of the United States
budgetary role of, 93
discretionary taxation powers proposed for, 205
Economic Report of the, 194
Federal Reserve System and, 242, 279
fiscal policy and, 194
tax legislative process and, 99
Presidential elections, 10–11, 300
Presidents of corporations, 119
Price, Don, 76
Price and wage controls, *see* Wage and price controls
Price Commission, 315, 316
Price controls, *see* Wage and price controls
Price discrimination, **525**
Price elasticity of demand, 408–15, **409,** 419, 503
Price elasticity of supply, **461,** 461–62
Price fixing, 4, 508, 509
Price freeze (1973), 205, 289, 316; *see also* Wage and price freeze (1971)
Price index, **144,** 145
Price inelastic, **411,** 413
Price leadership, **510,** 510–11
Price stability or stabilization
incomes policy and, 316
monetary policy and, 290
oligopoly and, 505–6
wage and price controls and, 314, 315
See also Stabilization, economic
Price supports
for farm products, 85–90, 196, 406, 414, 532
for government securities, 291
Price system, **43,** 48–68
in agriculture, 84
basic economic tasks and, 43–44
in Broadway theater, 64–65
circular flows of money and products and, 65–66
coercion in, 72, 91
consumers and, 49
distribution of income and, 61, 70
economic growth and, 352, 353
equilibrium price and, 55–59; *see also under* Equilibrium price
firms and, 49–50, 65–66
government role and, 44–45
growth of per capita income and, 61–62
how goods are produced and, 60
liberals' criticism of, 71–72
limitations of, 70–72
markets and, 50–54
monopoly and, 518
overview of, 48–68
in socialist economies, 604–5
in Soviet Union, 705
technological changes and, 60–62
what gets produced and, 59–60
who gets what and, 61
in World War II prisoner of war camp, case study, 62–63
Prices
"area," 494
classical economists' view of, 159–60, 162
controls on, *see* Wage and price controls
equilibrium, *see* Equilibrium price
flexibility of, 159–60, 162
in general equilibrium analysis, 596–97
incomes policy and, 316–17
increase in, *see* Inflation
monopolistic competition and, 499–503, 520
monopoly and, 486–94, 518–19
oligopoly and, 505–6, 508–14, 519–20

output determination and, 454–57
perfect competition and, 477–80
in Soviet Union, 705
stability of, *see* Price stability
supply curves and, 54, 55, 459–60
wars and, 237–38
wholesale, 237–38
Primary inputs, **565**
Primary treatment, 367
Pricing
cost-plus, **511**
marginal cost, **604,** 604–5
Priorities approach to budget, **399–400**
Private costs
environmental pollution and, 370–71, 436
See also External diseconomies; External economies
Private tier for gold, **644,** 669
Processes, in linear programming, 463–68
Procter and Gamble, 527
Product differentiation, 498, **499,** 502, 511, 512, 514, 527
Product group, **499,** 503*n*
Product transformation curve, **37,** 37–40, **601**
economic growth and, 328–29
how goods are produced and, 38–39
income distribution and growth and, 39–40
international trade and, 619
optimal allocation of resources and, 601–4
for public and private goods, 96–97
what is produced and, 36–38
Production
discontinuation of, by firms, 456–58, 489
economic system's determination of, 34–35, 36–39, 59–60
external diseconomies of, **606,** 607
external economies of, **606,** 607
government, 75–76
linear programming approach to, **462,** 462–69
roundabout methods of, 45, 566
See also Output
Production coefficients, 599
Production function, **122,** 122–23, 426, 462
aggregate, **329**
Productivity Centers, 684
Productivity of labor, 317, 339, 342, 544–45
Profit and loss statement, **125,** 125–27
Profit motive, price system and, 59–60
Profits, **120, 436, 571**
economic versus accounting, 127–28
functions of, 572–73
gross national income and, 148, 149
innovation and, 572
maximization of, *see* Maximization of profits
of monopolies, 487–90, 492, 493, 518, 527, 572
in monopolistic competition, 499–502
of oligopolies, 511, 514
in retail trade, 503
in Soviet Union, 708
uncertainty and, 572
See also Cost-plus pricing; Target rate of return
Proletariat, 698
dictatorship of the, 700
Propensity to consume, *see* Average propensity to consume; Marginal propensity to consume
Property taxes, 81, 103–4, 581
Proprietorships, **114,** 114–15
Prosperity, **210**
Protestant ethic, 343
Proxies, 119
Public employees, 555
Public goods, **70,** 74–75, 96–97
Public Law 480, 86, 694
Public ownership, 75–76
in Soviet Union, 701
Public services, 44
Public utilities, regulation of, 492–94
Public works programs, 197
Pure Food and Drug Act (1906), 72, 80, 402
Quality of life, 326, 355
Quantity theory of money and prices, 247–52, 299
crude, 249–50, **250,** 300
Quotas
import, **627,** 627–29
in Soviet Union, 704

R and D, *see* Research and development
Racial discrimination, poverty and, 589–91
Radical economists, 712–14
RAND Corporation, 605
Rate of return, **564**
capital budgeting and, 567–68
from investing in human capital, 568–69
target, **511**
See also Profits
Rationing, 65
fuel shortage and, 65–66
Ray, 465
Recessions, **209,** 210
monetary policy and, 278, 288, 290, 291, 293
money supply and, 240
multiplier-acceleration principle interaction and, 214
1953–1954, 211, 288
1957–1958, 202, 211, 288, 309
1960, 288
prevention of, possibility of, 216
Red Cross, 62
Redistribution of income
government role in, 44, 70, 71, 73, 89
pollution control and, 381–82
taxation and, 100, 580–81
Regional development programs, 587
Regulation Q, 284–85
Regulation W, 285
Regulatory commissions, 4, 73, 492, 493; *see also specific commissions*
Reierson, Roy L., 227
Remington Rand, 340
Rent, **569,** 569–71
Reproduction cost, **492**
Republican party, 631
Resale price maintenance, **532**

Research and development (R and D)
for coal, 98–99
economic growth and, 341–42, 356–57
for electronic computer, 340–41
government support of, 75
Kennedy administration and, 357–58
marketing and, 341–42
military, 97
by oligopolies, 512
product transformation curve and, 39–40
space, 97
technological change and, 341–42
United States expenditures on, 351–52
Research Seminar in Quantitative Economics, 225, 227
Reserves, commercial bank, 242
creation of money by banks and, 262–72
currency withdrawals and, 274
decrease in, 272–73
discount rate changes and, 284
excess, **268,** 268–71, 274–75, 294
free, **286,** 293
legal requirements for, 260–61, 274*n,* 283
monetary policy and, 278–79
money supply and, 260, 268–73, 278–81, 283
open market operations and, 279–81
Residential construction
Federal regulation of mortgage terms and, 285
forecasting gross national product and, 219, 222–24
monetary policy and, 295
Resource markets, **65,** 66
Resources, **34**
allocation of, *see* Allocation of resources
of less developed countries, 685
product transformation curve and utilization of, *see* Product transformation curve
See also Capital; Inputs; Labor; Land
Retail Clerks Union, 547, 554
Retail trade, 114
monopolistic competition in, 502–3
resale price maintenance and, 532
restriction of competition in, 531–32
Returns to scale, **446,** 446–47
Reuther, Walter, 550, 551
Revenue, *see* Marginal revenue; Taxes; Total revenue
Revenue sharing, **105**
Revolutionary War, American, 16, 239, 308
Ricardo, David, 335–37, 353, 354, 364, 618
Rich, the
income inequality and, 580–83
legal avoidance of taxes by, 100, 101
national debt and, 108
sales taxes and, 103, 581
"Right-to-work" laws, 557
Rinfret, Pierre, 19
Risser, Hubert, 478
Robinson-Patman Act (1936), 531–32
Rockefeller, John D., 501, 504
Rockefeller Brothers Fund, 327
Rockefeller Foundation, 684
Rodgers, Richard, 64
Ronk, Sally, 227
Roos, C. F., 419, 421
Roosa, Robert V., 673
Roosevelt, Franklin D., 76, 80, 162, 200, 550, 661
Roosevelt, Theodore, 80, 526
Ross, Leonard, 352, 355
Ruff, L., 371
Ruhr valley, 376–77
Rule of reason, **525,** 525–26
Rules of the game, **506**
Runaway inflation, **238,** 238–39
Runs on banks, 261
Ruskin, John, 1, 12–13
Russia, *see* Soviet Union

Sabinus, 425
Sackrin, S. M., 424
Saint Francis, 325
Salaries, *see* Wages
Sales
acceleration of, **213**
acceleration principle and, 211–14
inventory investment and, 213, 214
investment and, 167–68
Sales taxes, 81, 102, 103, 580, 581
Samuelson, Paul, 19, 72*n,* 91, 213, 217, 219
Santa Barbara channel, 367
Santow, Leonard, 227
Saulnier, Raymond J., 194*n,* 227
Saving function, **166,** 166–67
multiplier and, 174–75
Savings, **566**
as automatic stabilizer, 196
classical economists' view of, 159, 161
income and, *see* Saving function
income inequality and, 583
inflation and, 239
investment and, 159, 161–62, 172–73
Keynes's views on, 161–62
net equilibrium level and level of desired and actual, 168, 169, 172–73
See also Marginal propensity to save
Savings accounts, *see* Savings deposits
Savings and loan associations, 243, 284–85
Savings deposits, 243, 244*n*
and broad definitions of money, 236–37
Regulation Q ceilings on interest on, 284–85
Say, J. B., 159
Say's Law, **159**
Scherer, F. M., 98, 509
Schott, Francis, 227
Schultz, Theodore, 339
Schultze, Charles, 13–14, 94*n*
Schumpeter, Joseph, 340, 520
Science
economics as, 18–19
pure, **34**
SDRs (Special Drawing Rights), 670, 672
Secondary treatment, 367
Securities and Exchange Commission, 80, 119, 219

Selective credit control, **285**
Senate, United States, taxation and, 99
Service industries, 114, 146
Services, 142; *see also* Goods and services
Sewage treatment, 367, 371, 375
Shares of stock, **116**
Sherman Antitrust Act (1890), 79–80, 508, 524–26, 548
Shilling, A. Gary, 227
Short run, **121,** 121–22
Shultz, George P., 10, 25, 673
Silver, 235
Sloan, Alfred P., Jr., 113, 550
Smith, Adam, 15–18, 44, 45, 159*n*, 335, 353, 509, 686
  on competition, 18, 491–92, 517, 519
  on the "invisible hand," 17
Smithsonian agreement (1971), 644, 669
Smoot-Hawley Tariff (1930), 631
Soap industry, 4
Social costs
  environmental pollution and, 370–71, 379, 436
  of quotas, 627
  of tariffs, 625–26
  See also External diseconomies; External economies
Social environment, economic growth and, 343, 352–53
Social insurance, 586
Social science, 12–13, 16
Social Security, 150, 197, 586
Social Security Act (1935), 586
Social Security Administration, 584
Social Security tax, 581
Socialism
  creeping, 76
  democratic, 712
  in Marx's theory, 160, 698, 700
  radical economists and, 713
  in United States, 712
Socialist economies, 41, 76
  interest rate in, 565
  price system in, 604–5
  See also Communist economies
Solow, Robert, 120, 320, 365, 371*n*, 713
Sommers, Albert T., 227
Soviet Union, 327, 355, 374*n*, 686, 710
  capitalism compared to, 7, 41, 42
  economic system of, 701–8
  foreign aid programs of, 693, 694
  United States agriculture and, 87
  World Bank and, 666
  World War II's effects on civilian goods production in, 38–39
Space program, 97
Spain, 77, 250
Special Drawing Rights, 670, 672
Specialization
  in American economy, 45–46
  international trade and, 614, 616–23
Speculative demand for money, **244**
Sprinkel, Beryl, 227
Stability, price, *see* Price stability
Stabilization, economic, 298–321
  cost-push inflation and, 308, 309, 314–16
  fiscal policy and, 298–300, 302
  full-employment budget and, 202–3
  government role in, 74, 197–98
  incomes policy and, 316–17, 320
  Keynesian-monetarist disagreement on, 298–300, 302–4, 307–8
  monetary policy and, 298–300, 302–4
  Phillips curve and, *see* Phillips curve
  wage and price controls and, *see* Wage and price controls
Stabilizers, automatic, 196, 216
Stalin, Josef, 701
Standard Oil Company, 525, 526
Stans, Maurice, 207
State banks, 241; *see also* Commercial banks
State Control Commission, Soviet Union, 704
State government
  bonds issued by, 103, 257
  expenditures of, 78–79, 152; *see also* Government expenditures
  federal grants to, 104–5
  tax revenues of, 81
State Technical Services Act (1965), 357*n*
Steel industry, 4, 167
  1962 price increase by, 317–18, 510
  price leadership in, 510–11
  production of, by country, 33
  See also specific steel companies
Stein, Herbert, 194*n*, 206, 346
Stern, Robert, 620
Stigler, George, 71, 91, 493, 527
Stock market, 117–18
  1929 crash of, *see* Great Crash
Stockholders, 118–19
Stocks, **116**
  margin requirements for purchase of, **285**
  See also Capital gains; Dividends
Straight-line depreciation, **126**
Strategy in game theory, **506,** 506–7
Strikes, labor, 550, 552, 554, 555, **557,** 557–58
Structural unemployment, **134, 360,** 360–61
Studebaker-Packard, 503
Subsidiaries, wholly owned, 624–25
Substitutes, 410–11, **422**
Substitution effect, **418**
Suits, Daniel B., 227, 419, 421
Sullivan, Leon, 119
Supply and demand, classical view of, 159
Supply curves
  for firms, 458–60, **459**
  for loanable funds, **564**
  market, *see* Market supply curves
  for monopoly, 491
Supreme Court, United States, antitrust laws and, 524–26
Surplus, **127**
  addition to, **127**
  government budget, 200–3
Surplus controls for farm products, 85–86
Surplus value, **573,** 698, 700
Surtax (1968), 199, 288, 300
Survey of Current Business, 219
Survey Research Center, 220
Sweden, 77, 327, 580
Sweezy, Paul, 505, 506
Swift, Robert, 261–62
Szeliski, V. von, 419, 421

Tacitus, 425
Taft-Hartley Act (1947), 551, 554, 557, 558
Target rate of return, **511**
Tariffs, **625,** 625–33
  American, 631–33
  prohibitive, **626**
Taubman, Paul, 222
Tax base, 103
Tax credits, 357, 374, 377
Tax cuts (reductions)
  1964, 24, 96*n*, 198, 203, 358, 671
  1972, 204
  Nixon proposal for (1971), 204
  tax reform and, 104
Tax rates
  automatic changes in, proposal, 205
  marginal, **101**
  net, **581**
Tax reform, 10, 103–4
Taxation, 75
  Congress and, 99, 198, 205
  as fiscal policy tool, 197–98
  income inequality and, 580–82
  net national product equilibrium value and, 189–92
  politics and, 198
  president and, 99, 205
  principles of, 100
  redistribution of income and, 100, 580–81
  reform of, *see* Tax reform
  unemployment and, 197, 198, 204, 205
  See also Fiscal policy
Taxes
  cuts in, *see* Tax cuts
  estate, 100, 581
  excise, 81, 582*n*
  gift, 581
  highway user, 81
  incidence of, **581**
  income, *see* Income taxes
  indirect business, 148, 149
  inheritance, 41, 100, 581
  loopholes in, 10
  national debt and, 108
  payroll, 581
  as percentage of total output, by country, 77
  progressive, **580**
  property, 81, 102–3, 581
  regressive, **580**
  sales, 81, 102, 103, 580, 581
  Social Security, 581, 586
  turnover, **705**
  See also Revenue sharing; Surtax
Teamsters Union, 547, 548, 552
Technological change
  determinants and measurement of, 341–42
  diminishing marginal returns and, law of, 428
  economic growth and, 329, 334, 336–37, 339–42, 350–52, 354, 356–57
  environmental pollution and, 373
  international trade and, 623–24
  investment and rate of, 167
  labor unions and, 353
  marginal product of capital and, 337
  marginal product of labor and, 334
  monopoly and, 519–22, 527
  price system and, 60–62
  product transformation curve and, 39, 40
  supply curves and, 54, 55
  unemployment and, *see* Unemployment—technological
Technological gap between countries, 623–24
Technological innovations, 35, **340,** 493
  business cycles and, 215
  diffusion process for, **340,** 521, 624–25
  monopoly and, 519–21
Technological innovator, **340**
Technological unemployment, 358
Technology, **34,** 120–23
  in agriculture, 82, 83
  in less developed countries, 682–85
  research and development of, *see* Research and development
  See also Processes
Technostructure, **119**
Tennessee Valley Authority, 41, 76
Thackeray, William Makepeace, 566
Theater, pricing system for, 64–65
Thermal pollution, 370
Third World, *see* Less developed countries
Thomson-Houston, 505
Time (magazine), 11
Time deposits, 243, 244*n*, 257
  and broad definitions of money, 236–37
  legal reserve requirements for, 260, 274*n*, 282
  Regulation Q ceilings on interest on, 284–85
Tinbergen, Jan, 19
Tire industry, 4
Tito, 711
Tobin, James, 147, 313, 587, 594
Torrio, Joseph, 136
Total costs, *see under* Cost functions; Costs
Total revenue
  of monopoly, 485–86, 488
  output determination and, 453–57
Townsend-Greenspan econometric model, 227
Trade, *see* International trade
Trade Agreements Act (1934), 631
Trade unions, *see* Labor unions
Trading-possibility curve, **620**
Training or education of workers
  economic growth and, 362
  Phillips curve shifts and, 311, 313, 314
  wage differentials and, 545
Training programs, 587
Transactions demand for money, 244
Transactions velocity of money, 249*n*
Transfer payments
  business, 150*n*
  government, **77, 143,** 150; *see also* Social Security; Unemployment compensation; Welfare programs
  private, **143**
Transfers in balance of payments, 647–48
Treasury Department, United States, 99, 104, 106, 194, 220, 243, 279, 290–91, 293
  and the national debt, 106
Troughs of business cycles, **209,** 210, 218

Truman, Harry S, 88, 291, 317
Trusts, 243
Truth in Lending Act (1969), 402
Turner, Donald, 527
Turnover tax, **705**
Two-person games, **506**
"Two-tier" gold system, **644**, 669, 672
Tying contract, **525**

Uncertainty, profits and, 572
Underdeveloped countries, *see* Less developed countries
Underemployment, 135–36
Unemployment, 133–37, **134**
  American economic growth and, 358–62
  automatic stabilizers and, 196
  budget balancing policies and, 201–2
  classical economists' view of, 159–60
  cyclical, **134**
  displacement of labor and, 361–62
  economic growth and, 329
  Federal Reserve policy and, 293
  fiscal policy and, 192, 193, 197–98, 313
  frictional, **134**
  functional finance policy and, 202
  government's role in curbing, 3, 74, 134–35, 140–41
  in Great Depression, 2, 134, 135, 162, 200
  inflation and, 2–3, 138–41, 309–13
  Kennedy and, 24
  Keynes and, 161
  in less developed countries, 682–83
  Marx's view of, 160–61, 358
  measurement of, 135–36
  monetary policy and, 313
  money supply and, 240
  1929–1972 rates of, 135
  1962–1965 rates of, 198
  1972 forecast of, 227
  Nixon and, 141, 204
  of older workers, 361–62
  potential gross national product and, 154–55
  public policy and, 9
  in recessions, 214
  structural, **134, 360**, 360–61
  taxation and, 197, 198, 204, 205
  technological, 358–59
  wage increases' relationship to, *see* Phillips curve
  See also Full employment (4% unemployment)
Unemployment compensation, 196, 197
Unemployment insurance, 586
Union shop, **557**
Unions, *see* Labor unions
Unitary elasticity of demand, **413**
United Automobile Workers, 547, 548, 550–51
United Kingdom, *see* Great Britain
United Mine Workers, 547, 548
United Nations, 694
United Nations Relief and Rehabilitation Administration (UNRRA), 664
United Shoe Machinery Company, 484
United States Steel Corporation, 318, 504, 510–11, 550
  antitrust laws and, 525, 526
United Steel Workers, 547, 550
Univac I computer, 340
University of California, 227
University of Michigan, 220, 225, 227
Urban areas (cities)
  decay of, 5
  migration of farmers and farm workers to, 84, 361
  planning land use in, 607–8
Urban renewal programs, 607–8
U.S.S.R., *see* Soviet Union
Utilities, public, 492–94
Utility, consumer's, **392**, 392–96, 600; *see also* Marginal Utility

Value-added, **145**, 145–46, 148, 149
Value of commodities, Marx on, **698**
Values, economics and, 24, 26
Variable costs, *see under* Costs
Variable input, **121**
Velocity of circulation of money, **248**, 248–52, 300–2, 304
Vertical mergers, **504**, 528
Vietnam war
  fiscal policy and, 198–99, 201*n*, 203
  inflation and, 199, 203, 211, 285, 308, 319
  monetary policy and, 286
Volcker, Paul, 673
Von Neumann, John, 340, 506*n*
Von Szeliski, V., 419, 421
Von's Grocery case (1965), 527

Wage and price controls
  disadvantages of, 314–15
  Nixon administration's, 3, 204, 205, 289, 315–16
Wage and price freeze (1971), 315
Wage and price guidelines, 315
  Kennedy-Johnson, 317–19
  See also Incomes policy
Wage differentials, 544–45
Wage-price spiral, **308**, 309, 314
Wage taxes, *see* Income taxes
Wages
  in China, 710
  classical economists' views on, 160, 162
  in cost-push inflation, 308, 309
  determinants of, 537–47
  differentials in, 544–45
  flexibility of, 160, 162
  gross national income and, 148–50
  incomes policy and, 316–17
  inflation and, 137, 138, 312, 313
  labor unions and increases in, 555–58
  Marx on, 698, 700–1
  monopsony and, 546–47
  racial discrimination and, 590–91
  sex discrimination and, 591–92
  in Soviet Union, 706, 708
  supply curves and, 54, 55
  unemployment's relationship to increases in, *see* Phillips curve
Wagner Act (1935), 549
Wall Street Journal, The, 11, 510
Wallich, Henry, 297, 675

Wallis, W. Allen, 68, 327
War of 1812, 237
Warren, Earl, 527
Wars, prices and, 237–38, 663
Waste material, pollution and, 368, 370–71, 374–76, 382
Water pollution, 6, 75, 367, 368, 370–71, 374–79, 381
Water Quality Improvement Act (1970), 378
Water resources, optimal allocation of, 602–3, 605
Ways and Means Committee, House of Representatives, 10, 99, 194
Wealthy, the, *see* Rich, the
Webb-Pomerene Act (1918), 532
Weinberger, Caspar, 589
Weisbrod, Burton, 94–95
Weiss, Leonard, 502, 503
Welfare economics, **600**, 600–8
Welfare programs, 44, 73
  as automatic stabilizer, 196
  as fiscal policy tool, 197
  negative income tax and, 587, 588
  Nixon program to reform, 588–89
West Germany, 77, 326, 338, 670, 693, 694
Westinghouse Corporation, 526
Wharton econometric model, 224–27
Wheat, 59
  government program on, 88–89
  market demand curves for, 50–53, 405
  supply curve for, 52, 54
White-collar workers, 554
Whitman, Marina, 592
Whitney, Eli, 343, 351
Wicksteed, Philip, 4–5
Wiener, Anthony J., 364
Willkie, Wendell, 551*n*
Wilson, Harold, 644
Wisconsin, PPB system in, 94
Wold, Herman, 421, 422
Women workers, 311–12, 314, 554, 591–92
Workers, *see* Labor
Workers' management in Yugoslavia, 711–12
"Workfare," 588–89
World Bank, 666, 693–94
World War I, 661
World War II, 76, 82
  business fluctuations and, 211
  financing of, 290–91
  increased production of war goods at beginning of, 38–39
  inflation after, 137–38
  inflation during, 237–38, 294
  international finance and, 663
  inventory investment after, 214
  multiplier as applied at end of, 178–81
  national debt and, 105–8
  price system in prisoner-of-war camp in, 62–63
Wright, Kenneth, 227

Xerox Corporation, 573

Yellow-dog contracts, **549**
Young workers, 314
Yugoslavia, 711–12

Zero Economic Growth, 373
Zero Population Growth, 373–74
Zero-sum games, **506**